Short Story Criticism

Guide to Gale Literary Criticism Series

For criticism on	Consult these Gale series
Authors now living or who died after December 31, 1999	*CONTEMPORARY LITERARY CRITICISM (CLC)*
Authors who died between 1900 and 1999	*TWENTIETH-CENTURY LITERARY CRITICISM (TCLC)*
Authors who died between 1800 and 1899	*NINETEENTH-CENTURY LITERATURE CRITICISM (NCLC)*
Authors who died between 1400 and 1799	*LITERATURE CRITICISM FROM 1400 TO 1800 (LC)* *SHAKESPEAREAN CRITICISM (SC)*
Authors who died before 1400	*CLASSICAL AND MEDIEVAL LITERATURE CRITICISM (CMLC)*
Authors of books for children and young adults	*CHILDREN'S LITERATURE REVIEW (CLR)*
Dramatists	*DRAMA CRITICISM (DC)*
Poets	*POETRY CRITICISM (PC)*
Short story writers	*SHORT STORY CRITICISM (SSC)*
Literary topics and movements	*HARLEM RENAISSANCE: A GALE CRITICAL COMPANION (HR)* *THE BEAT GENERATION: A GALE CRITICAL COMPANION (BG)* *FEMINISM IN LITERATURE: A GALE CRITICAL COMPANION (FL)* *GOTHIC LITERATURE: A GALE CRITICAL COMPANION (GL)*
Asian American writers of the last two hundred years	*ASIAN AMERICAN LITERATURE (AAL)*
Black writers of the past two hundred years	*BLACK LITERATURE CRITICISM (BLC-1)* *BLACK LITERATURE CRITICISM SUPPLEMENT (BLCS)* *BLACK LITERATURE CRITICISM: CLASSIC AND EMERGING AUTHORS SINCE 1950 (BLC-2)*
Hispanic writers of the late nineteenth and twentieth centuries	*HISPANIC LITERATURE CRITICISM (HLC)* *HISPANIC LITERATURE CRITICISM SUPPLEMENT (HLCS)*
Native North American writers and orators of the eighteenth, nineteenth, and twentieth centuries	*NATIVE NORTH AMERICAN LITERATURE (NNAL)*
Major authors from the Renaissance to the present	*WORLD LITERATURE CRITICISM, 1500 TO THE PRESENT (WLC)* *WORLD LITERATURE CRITICISM SUPPLEMENT (WLCS)*

AUG 1 9 2008   6105969850

S.O. Gale

181.00

Ref.
808.31
S

ISSN 0895-9439

Volume 113

Short Story Criticism

Criticism of the
Works of Short Fiction Writers

Jelena Krstović
Project Editor

GALE
CENGAGE Learning

Detroit • New York • San Francisco • New Haven, Conn • Waterville, Maine • London

GALE
CENGAGE Learning™

Short Story Criticism, Vol. 113

Project Editor: Jelena O. Krstović

Editorial: Dana Ramel Barnes, Tom Burns, Elizabeth A. Cranston, Kathy D. Darrow, Kristen A. Dorsch, Jeffrey W. Hunter, Jelena O. Krstović, Michelle Lee, Thomas J. Schoenberg, Lawrence J. Trudeau, and Russel Whitaker

Data Capture: Frances Monroe, Gwen Tucker

Indexing Services: Factiva®, a Dow Jones and Reuters Company

Rights and Acquisitions: Katherine Alverson, Beth Beaufore

Composition and Electronic Capture: Gary Leach

Manufacturing: Cynde Bishop

Associate Product Manager: Marc Cormier

For product information and technology assistance, contact us at **Gale Customer Support, 1-800-877-4253.**
For permission to use material from this text or product, submit all requests online at **www.cengage.com/permissions.**
Further permissions questions can be emailed to **permissionrequest@cengage.com**

While every effort has been made to ensure the reliability of the information presented in this publication, Gale, a part of Cengage Learning, does not guarantee the accuracy of the data contained herein. Gale accepts no payment for listing; and inclusion in the publication of any organization, agency, institution, publication, service, or individual does not imply endorsement of the editors or publisher. Errors brought to the attention of the publisher and verified to the satisfaction of the publisher will be corrected in future editions.

Gale
27500 Drake Rd.
Farmington Hills, MI, 48331-3535

LIBRARY OF CONGRESS CATALOG CARD NUMBER 88-641014

ISBN-13: 978-1-4144-2183-4
ISBN-10: 1-4144-2183-4

ISSN 0895-9439

Printed in the United States of America
1 2 3 4 5 6 7 12 11 10 09 08

Contents

Preface vii

Acknowledgments xi

Literary Criticism Series Advisory Board xiii

Preface

*S*hort Story Criticism (SSC) presents significant criticism of the world's greatest short-story writers and provides supplementary biographical and bibliographical materials to guide the interested reader to a greater understanding of the authors of short fiction. This series was developed in response to suggestions from librarians serving high school, college, and public library patrons, who had noted a considerable number of requests for critical material on short-story writers. Although major short-story writers are covered in such Gale series as *Contemporary Literary Criticism (CLC)*, *Twentieth-Century Literary Criticism (TCLC)*, *Nineteenth-Century Literature Criticism (NCLC)*, and *Literature Criticism from 1400 to 1800 (LC)*, librarians perceived the need for a series devoted solely to writers of the short-story genre.

Scope of the Series

SSC is designed to serve as an introduction to major short-story writers of all eras and nationalities. Since these authors have inspired a great deal of relevant critical material, *SSC* is necessarily selective, and the editors have chosen the most important published criticism to aid readers and students in their research.

Approximately three to six authors, works, or topics are included in each volume, and each entry presents a historical survey of the critical response to the work. The length of an entry is intended to reflect the amount of critical attention the author has received from critics writing in English and from foreign critics in translation. Every attempt has been made to identify and include the most significant essays on each author's work. In order to provide these important critical pieces, the editors sometimes reprint essays that have appeared elsewhere in Gale's Literary Criticism Series. Such duplication, however, never exceeds twenty percent of an *SSC* volume.

Organization of the Book

An *SSC* entry consists of the following elements:

- The **Author Heading** cites the name under which the author most commonly wrote, followed by birth and death dates. Also located here are any name variations under which an author wrote, including transliterated forms for authors whose native languages use nonroman alphabets. If the author wrote consistently under a pseudonym, the pseudonym will be listed in the author heading and the author's actual name given in parentheses on the first line of the biographical and critical introduction. Uncertain birth or death dates are indicated by question marks. Single-work entries are preceded by the title of the work and its date of publication.

- The **Introduction** contains background information that introduces the reader to the author and the critical debates surrounding his or her work.

- The list of **Principal Works** is ordered chronologically by date of first publication and lists the most important works by the author. The first section comprises short-story collections, novellas, and novella collections. The second section gives information on other major works by the author. For foreign authors, the editors have provided original foreign-language publication information and have selected what are considered the best and most complete English-language editions of their works.

- Reprinted **Criticism** is arranged chronologically in each entry to provide a useful perspective on changes in critical evaluation over time. All short-story, novella, and collection titles by the author featured in the entry are printed in boldface type. The critic's name and the date of composition or publication of the critical work are given at the beginning of each piece of criticism. Unsigned criticism is preceded by the title of the source in which it appeared. Footnotes are reprinted at the end of each essay or excerpt. In the case of excerpted criticism, only those footnotes that pertain to the excerpted texts are included.

- Critical essays are prefaced by brief **Annotations** explicating each piece.

- A complete **Bibliographical Citation** of the original essay or book precedes each piece of criticism. Source citations in the Literary Criticism Series follow University of Chicago Press style, as outlined in *The Chicago Manual of Style,* 15th ed. (Chicago: The University of Chicago Press, 2006).

- An annotated bibliography of **Further Reading** appears at the end of each entry and suggests resources for additional study. In some cases, significant essays for which the editors could not obtain reprint rights are included here. Boxed material following the further reading list provides references to other biographical and critical sources on the author in series published by Gale.

Indexes

A **Cumulative Author Index** lists all of the authors that appear in a wide variety of reference sources published by Gale, including *SSC*. A complete list of these sources is found facing the first page of the Author Index. The index also includes birth and death dates and cross references between pseudonyms and actual names.

A **Cumulative Nationality Index** lists all authors featured in *SSC* by nationality, followed by the number of the *SSC* volume in which their entry appears.

An alphabetical **Title Index** lists all short-story, novella, and collection titles contained in the *SSC* series. Titles of short-story collections, separately published novellas, and novella collections are printed in italics, while titles of individual short stories are printed in roman type with quotation marks. Each title is followed by the author's last name and corresponding volume and page numbers where commentary on the work is located. English-language translations of original foreign-language titles are cross-referenced to the foreign titles so that all references to discussion of a work are combined in one listing.

In response to numerous suggestions from librarians, Gale also produces an annual paperbound edition of the SSC cumulative title index. This annual cumulation, which alphabetically lists all titles reviewed in the series, is available to all customers. Additional copies of this index are available upon request. Librarians and patrons will welcome this separate index; it saves shelf space, is easy to use, and is recyclable upon receipt of the next edition.

Citing *Short Story Criticism*

When citing criticism reprinted in the Literary Criticism Series, students should provide complete bibliographic information so that the cited essay can be located in the original print or electronic source. Students who quote directly from reprinted criticism may use any accepted bibliographic format, such as University of Chicago Press style or Modern Language Association (MLA) style. Both the MLA and the University of Chicago formats are acceptable and recognized as being the current standards for citations. It is important, however, to choose one format for all citations; do not mix the two formats within a list of citations.

The examples below follow recommendations for preparing a bibliography set forth in *The Chicago Manual of Style,* 15th ed. (Chicago: The University of Chicago Press, 2006); the first example pertains to material drawn from periodicals, the second to material reprinted from books:

Morrison, Jago. "Narration and Unease in Ian McEwan's Later Fiction." *Critique* 42, no. 3 (spring 2001): 253-68. Reprinted in *Short Story Criticism.* Vol. 57, edited by Jelena Krstovic, 212-20. Detroit: Gale, 2003.

Brossard, Nicole. "Poetic Politics." In *The Politics of Poetic Form: Poetry and Public Policy,* edited by Charles Bernstein, 73-82. New York: Roof Books, 1990. Reprinted in *Short Story Criticism.* Vol. 57, edited by Jelena Krstovic, 3-8. Detroit: Gale, 2003.

The examples below follow recommendations for preparing a works cited list set forth in the *MLA Handbook for Writers of Research Papers,* 6th ed. (New York: The Modern Language Association of America, 2003); the first example pertains to material drawn from periodicals, the second to material reprinted from books:

Morrison, Jago. "Narration and Unease in Ian McEwan's Later Fiction." *Critique* 42.3 (spring 2001): 253-68. Reprinted in *Short Story Criticism.* Ed. Jelena Krstovic. Vol. 57. Detroit: Gale, 2003. 212-20.

Brossard, Nicole. "Poetic Politics." *The Politics of Poetic Form: Poetry and Public Policy.* Ed. Charles Bernstein. New York: Roof Books, 1990. 73-82. Reprinted in *Short Story Criticism.* Ed. Jelena Krstovic. Vol. 57. Detroit: Gale, 2003. 3-8.

Suggestions are Welcome

Readers who wish to suggest new features, topics, or authors to appear in future volumes, or who have other suggestions or comments are cordially invited to call, write, or fax the Associate Product Manager:

Associate Product Manager, Literary Criticism Series

Gale

27500 Drake Road

Farmington Hills, MI 48331-3535

1-800-347-4253 (GALE)

Fax: 248-699-8054

Acknowledgments

The editors wish to thank the copyright holders of the excerpted criticism included in this volume and the permissions managers of many book and magazine publishing companies for assisting us in securing reproduction rights. Following is a list of the copyright holders who have granted us permission to reproduce material in this volume of *SSC*. Every effort has been made to trace copyright, but if omissions have been made, please let us know.

COPYRIGHTED MATERIAL IN *SSC*, VOLUME 113, WAS REPRODUCED FROM THE FOLLOWING PERIODICALS:

*American Literary Realism,*v. 30, spring, 1998. Copyright © 1998 by the Department of English, The University of New Mexico. Reproduced by permission of the publisher.—*American Literary Realism 1870-1910,* v. 22, winter, 1990. Copyright © 1990 by the Department of English, The University of New Mexico. Reproduced by permission of the publisher.—*American Review of Canadian Studies,* v. 29, summer, 1999. Reproduced by permission.—*American Transcendental Quarterly,* v. n.s. 13, September, 1999. Copyright © 1999 by The University of Rhode Island. Reproduced by permission.—*ANQ: A Quarterly Journal of Short Articles, Notes, and Reviews,* v. 19, fall, 2006. Copyright © 2006 by Helen Dwight Reid Educational Foundation. Reproduced with permission of the Helen Dwight Reid Educational Foundation, published by Heldref Publications, 1319 18th Street, NW, Washington, DC 20036-1802.—*Arbeiten aus Anglistik und Amerikanistik,* v. 28, 2003. Copyright © 2003 Gunter Narr Verlag Tubingen. Reproduced by permission.—*Colby Quarterly,* v. 34, March, 1998. Reproduced by permission.—*English Literature in Transition, 1880-1920,* v. 24, 1981; v. 33, 1990. Copyright © 1981, 1990 *English Literature in Transition: 1880-1920.* Both reproduced by permission.—*English Studies in Canada,* v. 5, spring, 1979. Copyright © 1979 by Association of Canadian University Teachers of English. Reproduced by permission.—*Essays in Literature,* v. 20, fall, 1993. Copyright © 1993 by Western Illinois University. Reproduced by permission.—*The Explicator,* v. 62, summer, 2004. Copyright © 2004 by Helen Dwight Reid Educational Foundation. Reproduced with permission of the Helen Dwight Reid Educational Foundation, published by Heldref Publications, 1319 18th Street, NW, Washington, DC 20036-1802.—*The Gissing Journal,* v. 39, October, 2003 for "From 'Phoebe's Fortune' to 'Phoebe' by Courtesy of George Bentley, Temple Bar's Hatchet Man" by Barbara Rawlinson; v. 42, January, 2006 for "Gissing's Literal Revenge and Jordan's Collected Silences in 'The Prize Lodger'" by Markus Neacey. Both reproduced by permission of the publisher and the respective authors.—*Journal of the Short Story in English,* autumn, 2000. Copyright © 2000 by Presses de l'Université d'Angers. Reproduced by permission.—*Legacy,* v. 19, 2002. Copyright © 2003 by the University of Nebraska Press. All rights reserved. Reproduced by permission of the University of Nebraska Press.—*Marvels & Tales,* v. 20, 2006. Copyright © 2006 by Wayne State University Press. Reproduced with permission of the Wayne State University Press.—*MELUS,* v. 14, summer, 1987. Copyright © 1987 by *MELUS: The Society for the Study of Multi-Ethnic Literature of the United States.* Reproduced by permission.—*Modern Fiction Studies,* v. 28, spring, 1982. Copyright © 1982 by Purdue Research Foundation, West Lafayette, IN 47907. All rights reserved. Reproduced by permission of The Johns Hopkins University.—*Modern Language Studies,* v. 19, spring, 1989 for "'Julia' and Julia's Son" by Edward Gillin. Copyright © 1989 by Northeast Modern Language Association. Reproduced by permission of the publisher and the author.—*North Dakota Quarterly,* v. 60, fall, 1992. Copyright © 1993 by The University of North Dakota. Reproduced by permission.—*Papers of the Bibliographical Society of America,* v. 68, 1974; v. 83, December, 1989. Copyright © 1974, 1989 by the Bibliographical Society of America. Both reproduced by permission.—*South Carolina Review,* v. 36, spring, 2004. Copyright © 2004 by Clemson University. Reproduced by permission.—*Southern Literary Journal,* v. 33, fall, 2000. Copyright © 2000 by the University of North Carolina Press. Used by permission. *Studies in American Humor,* v. n.s. 3, 2002. Copyright © 2002 American Humor Studies Association. Reproduced by permission.—*Studies in Bibliography,* v. 36, 1983. Copyright © 1983 by the Rector and Visitors of the University of Virginia. Reproduced by permission.—*Studies in Short Fiction,* v. 3, summer, 1966; v. 19, fall, 1982; v. 35, spring, 1998; v. 35, fall, 1998. Copyright © 1966, 1982, 1998, by *Studies in Short Fiction.* All reproduced by permission.—*Thomas Hardy Journal,* v. 16, February, 2000; v. 22, autumn, 2006. Both reproduced by permission.—*Thomas Wolfe Review,* v. 27, 2003; v. 28, 2004. Both reproduced by permission.—*Victorian Poetry,* v. 31, spring, 1993 for "The Poetics of Interruption in Hardy's Poetry and Short Stories" by Norman D. Prentiss. Copyright © 1993 by West Virginia University. Reproduced by permission of the author.

COPYRIGHTED MATERIAL IN *SSC*, VOLUME 113, WAS REPRODUCED FROM THE FOLLOWING BOOKS:

Bernardi, Debra. From "'The Right to Be Let Alone': Mary Wilkins Freeman and the Right to a 'Private Share,'" in *Our Sisters' Keepers: Nineteenth-Century Benevolence Literature by American Women.* Edited by Jill Bergman and Debra

Gale Literature Product Advisory Board

The members of the Gale Literature Product Advisory Board—reference librarians from public and academic library systems—represent a cross-section of our customer base and offer a variety of informed perspectives on both the presentation and content of our literature products. Advisory board members assess and define such quality issues as the relevance, currency, and usefulness of the author coverage, critical content, and literary topics included in our series; evaluate the layout, presentation, and general quality of our printed volumes; provide feedback on the criteria used for selecting authors and topics covered in our series; provide suggestions for potential enhancements to our series; identify any gaps in our coverage of authors or literary topics, recommending authors or topics for inclusion; analyze the appropriateness of our content and presentation for various user audiences, such as high school students, undergraduates, graduate students, librarians, and educators; and offer feedback on any proposed changes/enhancements to our series. We wish to thank the following advisors for their advice throughout the year.

Mary E. Wilkins Freeman
1852-1930

(Full name Mary Eleanor Wilkins Freeman) American short story writer, novelist, and playwright.

The following entry provides an overview of Freeman's short fiction. For additional information on her short fiction career, see *SSC,* Volumes 1 and 47.

INTRODUCTION

Freeman is recognized as a preeminent chronicler of late nineteenth-century New England life. During her lifetime, her short stories were often viewed merely as examples of local color writing, yet subsequent criticism has emphasized the psychological acuity, dialogic accuracy, and class sensitivity of her fiction. In this sense, she has been cited as a precursor to such authors as Katherine Anne Porter and Katherine Mansfield, while her regional focus has prompted comparisons to contemporaries like Sarah Orne Jewett. Freeman's stories often deal with strong female characters who are forced to cope in a man's world—a fact that has attracted the attention of feminist critics and contributed to her rehabilitation as an important American author.

BIOGRAPHICAL INFORMATION

Freeman was born in Randolph, Massachusetts, to carpenter Warren Wilkins and his wife, Eleanor Lothrop Wilkins, both from old New England families. When Mary was fifteen her family moved to Brattleboro, Vermont, where her father had bought a partnership in a dry goods shop. After attending high school, she left for Mt. Holyoke Female Seminary in 1870, returning home after one year to take classes at Glenwood Seminary. In an effort to supplement the family's dwindling income, she tried teaching at a girl's school, but she soon turned to writing instead. The deaths of her immediate family members (her sister Anna in 1876, her mother in 1880, and her father in 1883) left Freeman on her own. She returned to Randolph, where she continued writing, and lived in the house of her close childhood friend Mary Wales. Her first published story, "Two Old Lovers," appeared in *Harper's Bazaar* in 1883. Freeman's reputation as a successful American writer was established with the short-fiction collec-

tions *A Humble Romance* (1887) and *A New England Nun* (1891). In 1892 she met Dr. Charles Manning Freeman, whom she married in 1902 after a long engagement. Although the relationship apparently began happily, by 1909 her husband entered a sanatorium because of his alcoholism, and in 1920 Freeman committed him to the New Jersey State Hospital for treatment. She obtained a legal separation from him in 1922, and he died the next year. Their relationship likely had an impact on Freeman's diminishing creative output, as did changing American literary tastes. After 1918 Freeman published no more books and only a few essays. Although her greatest literary successes were behind her, she was such a respected national figure that in 1925 she was awarded the first William Dean Howells Medal from the American Academy of Arts and Letters, and the next year she was one of the first four women to be elected to the National Institute of Arts and Letters (now the American Academy of Arts and Letters), sharing that honor with Agnes Repplier, Margaret Deland, and Edith Wharton.

MAJOR WORKS OF SHORT FICTION

Written with a female readership in mind, Freeman's stories generally portray the lives of women set against the backdrop of New England's economic decline in the years following the Civil War. Two of Freeman's most popular and highly regarded works of short fiction are "A New England Nun" and "The Revolt of 'Mother.'" In "A New England Nun" the unmarried Louisa Ellis takes great delight in her housekeeping duties (which, most prominently, include caring for her dog, Caesar), enjoying self-sufficiency and calm that is disrupted by the intrusion of Joe Dagget, a suitor who, after fourteen years, returns from wealth-seeking travels to make good on an earlier offer of marriage. Ultimately Louisa releases Joe from his commitment, allowing him to marry someone else and preserving the integrity of her meticulously kept home. Although she briefly mourns for the future that she may have had with Joe, Louisa wakes the next day feeling "like a queen" and thankfully embraces the "serenity and placid narrowness" of her life. "The Revolt of 'Mother'" revolves around an aging couple, Adoniram and Sarah Penn, who are in conflict over the husband's desire to build another barn on their farmland. Adoniram has gone back on his promise to replace the inadequate house he and his wife have lived in for years. Despite his wife's protests, Adoniram is determined to improve the condition of the farm at the expense of the homestead. Once the barn is completed, the husband goes away for a few days to buy livestock, and "Mother" demonstrates the strength of her revolt by moving both the furniture and family out of the home and into the new barn. Expecting anger and resistance from Adoniram, the family is surprised at his reaction of acceptance and remorse. Domestic strife also provides the focus of "Gentian," in which a woman married to a domineering man—who has become seriously ill and who distrusts doctors and medicines—doses his food with gentian, an herbal tonic. The remedy works, but the stubborn husband thereafter refuses to eat or drink anything that his wife has prepared. The plight of the helpless and underprivileged is examined in "Sister Liddy," a plotless sketch evoking the grim atmosphere of a New England poorhouse. The story records the dreary existence of a group of paupers, many of whom are mentally ill. Presented to the reader are a tall, demented elderly woman who predicts the end of the world; an obese old woman who amuses herself with vicious gossip; Polly Moss, homely and pathetic, who regales the others with stories about a lovely and glamorous sister named Liddy (on her deathbed Polly admits that Liddy never existed); an insane old woman named Sally whose pastime is tearing apart her bed; and a sickly and depressed young woman whose lover has abandoned her. "A Mistaken Charity" features Harriet and Charlotte Shattuck, two sisters who take pleasure in their decrepit home and wild, overgrown property. Although they receive gifts of apples, butter, and milk from neighbors, they insist that their own wild varieties of food are better. After a woman named Mrs. Simonds persuades them to move into an "Old Ladies' Home," Charlotte and Harriet become so disheartened that they run away from the institution, returning to their ramshackle house to revel in its cracked walls, which they experience as wellsprings of beautiful light.

Freeman highlighted the interconnectedness and divinity of the natural world with the story collections *Understudies* (1901) and *Six Trees* (1903). Similar thematically to Ovid's *Metamorphoses*, *Understudies* contains sketches based on the transcendental quality of animals and flowers. "The Parrot," for instance, tells of a young woman whose repressed despair over losing the man whom she expected to marry is voiced by her pet parrot. The stories in *Six Trees* each take an arboreal name that also serves as an allegorical centerpiece for spiritual transformation. For example, in "The Lombardy Poplar," the eponymous tree typifies

to an elderly single woman the self-sufficiency that she needs to break out of a lifelong subservience to the opinion of others. Similarly, in "The Elm-Tree" an insane old man's bitterness is transformed into tranquil acceptance when he climbs a great elm, while the protagonist of "The White Birch" is brought by contemplation of a birch tree to a realization of nature's bounty. "The Apple-Tree" contrasts the fulfilling life of the slovenly, poor Maddox family with the empty, neurotic existence of their neighbors, the Blakes. The joyfulness of the Maddox clan is symbolized by the apple tree that grows in their disheveled front yard. The sailor in "The Great Pine" is returning home after many years at sea to the wife and child he had deserted. To his increasing frustration, he continues to get lost in the wild terrain through which he is walking. Time and again he circles back to a certain lofty pine. In a fit of anger he sets fire to the tree, but extinguishes it after a change of heart. Feeling spiritually renewed, he makes his way to his old home, and though he finds that his wife has died, he commits himself to caring for his child and the ailing man that his wife had married in his absence. The theme of "The Great Pine" is later echoed in "The Slip of the Leash," which tells of Adam Andersen, a man whose communion with nature compels him to rejoin the family that he had previously abandoned. The perils of class consciousness exhibited by "The Apple-Tree" recur in "Old Woman Magoun," which tells of a proud countrywoman who lets her deceased daughter's illegitimate fourteen-year-old daughter eat the berries of deadly nightshade rather than permit her to be taken by her father, the degenerate son of a once-respected family. Mrs. Jameson, the main character of Freeman's novella of class conflict *The Jamesons* (1899), provokes the ire of the citizens of rural Linnville when she moves in and tries to elevate the community's cultural tastes. Her farming ineptitude and her predilection for health fads further perplexes her neighbors, but when her daughter, Harriet, marries the son of a prominent village couple, Mrs. Jameson learns to live in harmony with her surroundings. Another look at village life, *The People of Our Neighborhood* (1898) consists of a series of humorous sketches of stock village characters originally published in *The Ladies' Home Journal*.

The strong-willed female protagonist is a hallmark of Freeman's stories. The title character of "Louisa" refuses to marry a rich suitor, insisting instead on wresting a living from the single acre of farmland owned by her family, while Hetty Fifield, the protagonist of "A Church Mouse," is a belligerent church boarder who barricades herself in the church after overstaying her welcome, vociferously addressing the unfair treatment of women in her community. In "The Secret," Catherine Gould leaves her fiancé when he insists on knowing her reason for returning home late. "One Good Time" is the story of Narcissa Stone and her mother, who happily squander the life-insurance money left to them upon the death of the family patriarch. On the other hand, many of Freeman's short stories detail the bitter disappointments of her female characters. The eponymous character of "Juliza" thwarts social convention by proposing to her male friend only to discover that he loves another woman. The beleaguered housewife in "A Tragedy from the Trivial," Charlotte May, gives up her extravagant clothes and jewelry (as well as her job at a department store) to please her frugal husband. Based on the Deerfield Massacre of 1704, "Silence" depicts the hardships of frontier life in a small Puritan community that is violently attacked by a joint French and Native American battalion during Queen Anne's War by focusing on the broken heart of the titular heroine. Freeman also composed a number of ghost stories during her lifetime. One of her earliest stories, "A Symphony in Lavender," concerns a woman who rejects a proposal of marriage because her suitor resembles a figure from one of her nightmares.

The otherworldly tone of "A Symphony in Lavender" reverberates throughout her later collection, *The Wind in the Rose-Bush* (1903). In "Luella Miller," a ruthless invalid depletes the energy of all those who attend to her needs. Great-Aunt Harriet in "The Southwest Chamber" is such a strong and malignant figure that her mere presence changes the reflections cast by others in her mirror. In "The Wind in the Rose-Bush" little Agnes, who died of neglect, is glimpsed by the child protagonist at play in her garden, and her phantom presence is signaled by the stirring of roses on the bough. Equally sentimental in tone, "The Lost Ghost" features a similarly neglected ghost-child whose bewilderment and loneliness are finally set aside when she is taken in hand by the spirit of a kind old lady. In addition to her work in other genres, Freeman composed stories designed for the edification of children, such as "The Dickey Boy," in which a boy from a disreputable family earns the trust and sympathy of the women who have taken him into their home.

CRITICAL RECEPTION

At the time of their original publication, Freeman's stories earned the respect of realist writers like William Dean Howells and Hamlin Garland, but fell into relative obscurity following her death. However, the modern feminist movement sparked a renewed critical interest in her work, and her short fiction has subse-

quently been lauded for its humor, psychological insights, and treatment of women's issues. For instance, reviewers have traced the comedic tone of *The Jamesons* back to the underlying emotional tension in the novella, and have highlighted the playful reassessment of gender-oriented courtship traditions in "Juliza" and "One Good Time." Conversely, they have considered the appropriation of conventional male behavior exhibited by the title character of "Louisa" somewhat humorous, but ultimately disastrous in that it causes her community to perceive her as being mentally unstable. Scholars have likewise mined the psychological implications of Louisa Ellis's social detachment in "A New England Nun." Furthermore, they have read that story as an allegory of the limited choices available to female artists in nineteenth-century society, and have interpreted Louisa Ellis's private sexual proclivities on a subtextual level. The subtle sexuality identified in many of Freeman's stories has been interpreted as part of a larger commentary on the growth of consumerism in her day. According to commentator Monika M. Elbert, Freeman "probes deeply into the economic realities of her time and their means of stymying women's development. She then critiques women's spending habits, which were draining the source of women's creativity, sexuality, and spirituality. . . . Noteworthy in the context of the psychology of Freeman's consuming women is this 'sexualization' of the material world." Elbert also cited the male-oriented advertisements in many of the periodicals that published Freeman's work as examples of the problematic portrayal of gender differences that likely influenced her short fiction. Although Freeman is recognized for her sensitivity to female empowerment, critics have stressed the frequently contentious relationship between women in her stories, and have contrasted her depiction of the comforting aspects of domesticity with the more cynical opinion of domestic duties displayed in the works of Kate Chopin and Charlotte Perkins Gilman. Scholars also have extolled Freeman's trenchant exploration of the social dynamics of poverty. Reviewer Debra Bernardi, in her analysis of the lack of social space allotted to Freeman's impoverished characters, asserted that "Freeman needs to be understood as a writer involved with a central political question of the late nineteenth and early twentieth centuries: what rights of privacy does the poor individual have if she or he requires aid?" In addition, critics have described the nature mysticism evinced in works like *Six Trees* as an infusion of the philosophy of Ralph Waldo Emerson into socially relevant issues. Moreover, commentators have praised Freeman's commingling of traditional genre motifs, such as those found in fairy tales and supernatural stories, with elements that speak to the fears and concerns of a modern audience.

PRINCIPAL WORKS

Short Fiction

The Cow with Golden Horns, and Other Stories 1884

The Adventures of Ann: Stories of Colonial Times 1886

A Humble Romance, and Other Stories 1887; republished in two volumes as *A Humble Romance and A far-away Melody, and Other Stories,* 1890

A New England Nun, and Other Stories 1891

The Pot of Gold, and Other Stories 1892

Young Lucretia, and Other Stories 1892

The People of Our Neighborhood 1898; republished as *Some of Our Neighbors,* 1898

Silence, and Other Stories 1898

The Jamesons 1899

The Love of Parson Lord, and Other Stories 1900

Understudies: Short Stories 1901

Six Trees: Short Stories 1903

The Wind in the Rose-Bush, and Other Stories of the Supernatural 1903

The Givers: Short Stories 1904

The Fair Lavinia, and Others 1907

The Winning Lady, and Others 1909

The Copy-Cat, and Other Stories 1914

Edgewater People 1918

Short Fiction of Sarah Orne Jewett and Mary Wilkins Freeman 1979

Selected Stories of Mary E. Wilkins Freeman 1983

The Uncollected Stories of Mary Wilkins Freeman 1992

A Mary Wilkins Freeman Reader 1997

Other Major Works

Jane Field: A Novel (novel) 1892

Giles Corey, Yeoman: A Play (play) 1893

Pembroke: A Novel (novel) 1894

Madelon: A Novel (novel) 1896

Jerome, a Poor Man: A Novel (novel) 1897

The Heart's Highway: A Romance of Virginia in the Seventeenth Century (novel) 1900

The Portion of Labor (novel) 1901

The Debtor: A Novel (novel) 1905

By the Light of the Soul (novel) 1906

"Doc." Gordon (novel) 1906

The Shoulders of Atlas: A Novel (novel) 1908

The Butterfly House (novel) 1912

The Yates Pride: A Romance (novel) 1912

An Alabaster Box [with Florence Morse Kingsley] (novel) 1917

The Infant Sphinx: Collected Letters of Mary E. Wilkins Freeman (letters) 1985

CRITICISM

Mary R. Reichardt (essay date winter 1990)

SOURCE: Reichardt, Mary R. "'Friend of My Heart': Women as Friends and Rivals in the Short Stories of Mary Wilkins Freeman." *American Literary Realism* 22, no. 2 (winter 1990): 54-68.

[*In the following essay, Reichardt suggests that relationships between women in Freeman's stories are contentious as often as they are amicable and nurturing.*]

> What particularly distinguishes the women of Wilkins . . . is that theirs is a world in which women's primary relationships are to each other rather than to men. Wilkins's women . . . are dependent on each other economically as well as emotionally. This dependence, of course, leads to hostility as well as affection. These women fight, envy, disagree, compete, bicker, and manipulate.
>
> But underlying the hostility are loyalty and intense involvement with each other, phenomena unique in fiction. For fiction has tended to ignore these aspects of a woman's life which are not affected by men.[1]

Although many of Mary Wilkins Freeman's nearly 220 short stories concern women's experiences with men and marriage, women's relationships to other women also figure prominently in her themes and constitute, in fact, one of the more interesting elements of her fiction. Men are important to Freeman's women: women strive to understand and accept them, and they may choose to compromise their hopes and desires in order to marry. Yet Freeman consistently shows us that in her world women's relationships with other women are at once more fundamental, substantial and tenacious than women's relationships with men.

In and of itself, perhaps, this statement is not surprising. Recent sociologists of women's history have made us aware of the importance and necessity of women's mutual bonds, especially in an earlier era. Lillian Faderman's study of women's relationships throughout history *Surpassing the Love of Men,* for example, explains that previous generations were far more content than our own to regard males and females as largely inexplicable to one another, as "virtually separate species." Moreover, the nineteenth-century concept of separate spheres, Faderman continues, dictated such disparate work and leisure activities for men and women that "outside of the practical necessities of raising a family there was little that tied the sexes together. But with other females a woman . . . could be entirely trusting and unrestrained."[2] Carroll Smith-Rosenberg's influential *Disorderly Conduct* likewise speaks of nineteenth-century women forming "supportive networks" full of "emotional richness and complexity" in the face of "severe social restrictions on intimacy between young men and women."[3] And Nancy Chodorow's equally influential *The Reproduction of Mothering* has argued that because women have not traditionally been "cared for" by men in the way they themselves extend care to men and children, they have learned to "support themselves emotionally by supporting and reconstituting *one another*."[4]

A study of Freeman's stories, however, only partially corroborates these findings. Often estranged emotionally or physically from fathers, husbands, or lovers, Freeman's women form an intricate social network with each other on which they depend for emotional interaction. These female-female relationships are fundamental and enduring: women strive to initiate, develop, and maintain contact with each other on a daily basis. Moreover, a Freeman woman understands her women friends' needs and concerns in a way she can never hope to understand those of men.

Because of these positive aspects reflected in the close women's relationships in Freeman's works, some recent critics have considered Freeman to be a type of proto-feminist writer: such intimate and fulfilling bonds, they maintain, indicate Freeman's women characters—as well as the author herself—were triumphantly independent of men. Marjorie Pryse, for example, speaks of a "sisterhood" of common "vision" among Freeman's female protagonists, concluding that "women in Freeman's fiction have available to them . . . a community [of other women] that sustains their spirit and validates their vision."[5] Josephine Donovan likewise considers Freeman's women as forming intense and intimate bonds with each other in order to ensure the preservation of a "woman-centered matriarchal world," thereby "keep[ing] relationships between women from being destroyed by the male intruder."[6]

However, much as we would perhaps like to see her stories comply with this kind of model for women's relationships, evidence for such a conclusion is lacking from Freeman's canon. Only a few of her tales, in fact, depict women who, on equal status in class, wealth, or intellect, can truly qualify as friends. No Freeman story, therefore, illustrates the celebrated nineteenth-century relationship called a "Boston marriage" which typically involved cultural and intellectual exchange between "new women," that is, those financially or emotionally independent of men. Indeed, women's friendships in Freeman's stories rarely approach the level of mutual exploration of ideas or sympathetic sharing of feelings and concerns.

Rather, the emotional and mutually dependent bonds women form with other women in Freeman's New England stories more often than not take on a disturb-

ingly threatening or ominous tone. Freeman consistently portrays relationships between women as inequitable, often to an extreme. Many of her stories are based on a rivalry or power struggle—over a man, a possession, a reputation—between a dominant or strong woman and a much weaker one. Although intimate to a degree, these unequal relationships usually require both women involved to protect themselves from their "friend's" emotional abuse or scorn. Thus these relationships are in no way honest or open, but rather cautious and restrained. Many of these stories therefore turn on themes of cheating, theft, or false identity, all "sins" committed by a woman to raise or protect her acceptance and esteem in her rival's eyes. Moreover, Freeman's frequent depiction of the sister-sister bond, an especially close and tenacious one, often carries with it a similarly threatening note: one sister's tyranny or jealous control over the other lurks just beneath the surface, if not overtly forming the events, of the plot.

In portraying these types of female-female relationships, Freeman generally writes from the viewpoint of the weaker or more childlike woman. Interestingly, facts from Freeman's biography indicate a woman who, after both her mother and her only sister Anna died, depended on "managing" women all her life to care for her daily needs as well as to provide critical advice for her writing. Her relationship with Mary John Wales, the childhood friend with whom she lived nearly twenty years of her adult life, was apparently both a close and yet unequal one, much the same as those portrayed in her stories. "As children it had always been 'strong, vital [and] maternal' Mary Wales who stepped in to protect her 'timid . . . clinging [and] sensitive' friend whenever she was frightened by other youngsters," Brent Kendrick tells us in his recent collection of Freeman letters *The Infant Sphinx*, quoting Edward Foster's unpublished dissertation.[7]

Foster's 1956 biography, *Mary E. Wilkins Freeman*, moreover, indicates Wales played much the same role in their adult years together: "In Mary Wales [Freeman] had a mother and a sister, who misunderstood her at times but always accepted her moods of petulance and rebellion."[8] Yet Foster also suggests that Freeman at times rebelled against such domination. He writes of at least one period in her life when, "feeling the need to think her own thoughts free from the pressure of Miss Wales' strong personality [she] devised a scheme for having a few days alone."[9] Freeman mentions Wales briefly but affectionately in several letters to others; if she wrote to Mary John after her wedding (at the age of forty-nine), however, none of these letters survive.

Later, as a woman of letters, Freeman formed a number of epistolary relationships with other women writers or editors such as Kate Upson Clark, Mary Louise Booth, and Eliza Farman Pratt. Her letters, often signed with a nickname such as "Pussy Willow" or "Dolly," indicate these were close and affectionate friendships. Effusive in greetings, apologies for wrongs done, excuses for work she considered inadequate, or requests for advice, however, these letters further suggest that despite her steadily increasing popularity and success over the years, Freeman never completely felt these women's equal. Rather, in many ways these women too apparently played a more maternal than friendly role in Freeman's adult life.

Freeman, then, turned to other women to provide her with emotional, practical, and artistic support, yet at the same time she perhaps feared and resented such stronger women for their control of or domination over her life. This conclusion can be drawn primarily from her many tales involving women friends who, unequal in social status, talent, or wealth, assume a relationship in which one woman, stronger and more maternal, controls or otherwise dominates a more dependent or childlike woman. Eventually the weaker woman rebels, and the stronger woman, made to "see" her error, is humbled and (usually) relents. In many ways, this theme emerges as a pattern in Freeman's depiction of women and their relationships: in some way and with many variations, a domineering or proud woman is rejected or humbled, and a meeker and more dependent woman quietly triumphs. This paper, then, explores this female-female dynamic in Freeman's stories by considering the relationships Freeman portrays between women friends and adult sisters.

I

"The tenderness of one woman for another is farther reaching in detail than that of a man, because it is given with a fuller understanding of needs." So Freeman's narrator comments on the relationship between two women in her story **"The Tree of Knowledge"** (1900). Women in Freeman's stories understand each other's needs well; they may respond kindly and generously, but are also quite capable of using those needs in jealousy or envy to harm or hurt a rival. In other words, women's intimate knowledge of each other allows them a great amount of both power and vulnerability in the relationship, far more, Freeman indicates, than that in the relationship between a woman and man.

As mentioned, very few of Freeman's women can be said to be "friends" in the sense that they relate to each other on an equal basis, mutually sharing concern or sympathy. One of the stories in which women appear to have an affectionate bond is **"Criss-Cross"** (1914), a delightful tale in which two elderly neigh-

borhood women, cheated out of their vacation by an unscrupulous third woman, agree to switch households merely to alter their usual routine. For a week they wear each other's clothes, care for each other's houses, and assume each other's habits, returning home refreshed from the very act of sympathetic identification with each other. But their friendship is far from one based on an exchange of intimacies, feelings, or ideas.

Much more commonly, Freeman portrays the relationship between women friends as unequal and thus competitive. One of the women is the other's superior in strength, beauty, wealth, or even morality; the other woman, often envious, strives to imitate her. Although they may continue for years as "best" friends, these women keep their inner lives secret: they know little about each other's true thoughts or feelings. Three stories will illustrate this. In **"Sweet-Flowering Perennial"** (1915), an odd story with a "fountain of youth" theme, middle-aged Clara, poor and ill, envies yet is mystified by her school friend Selma's continuing youthfulness and energy. Though Selma has taken Clara into her wealthy home to nurse her, Clara spies on her friend in an attempt to learn her "secret."[10]

In **"The Amethyst Comb"** (1914), Jane Carew believes that her best friend Viola Longstreet has stolen jewelry from her; nevertheless, though suspicious, she remains silent about the matter for years, even inviting Viola to live with her when that friend falls upon hard times. And finally in **"Friend of My Heart"** (1913), two maiden ladies, both in their youth courted by the same man, find their lives disturbed when he returns, unmarried, to town. Though Catherine, the stronger and more secure woman, knows in her heart he has come back for her and not Elvira, she "gives up" Lucius in a self-renunciatory gesture to her weaker, unstable, and unhappy friend. "The women who need men to take care of them are the women who make men able to take care of them," she concludes.[11] Elvira never realizes the truth.

Freeman's women compete over other matters as well, including money, clothing, and children. All do so primarily to gain esteem in their rivals' eyes, yet Freeman consistently shows us how paltry and, in the long run, ridiculous their efforts are. In **"The Winning Lady"** (1909) fashionable Mrs. Adeline Wyatt is proud of her "superior" and righteous appearance: she "regarded many of the other ladies [at her card party] with a somewhat pharisaical feeling."[12] However, to her own horror, she cheats at the game and for a cheap prize at that. "When she had entered Mrs. Lennox's house that afternoon," she later despairs, "she had been a good, handsome, happy, self-satisfied, within-the-limits-of-virtue woman. She would leave it a fool and a sinner; that she was becomingly clad in prune-color would make not a whit of difference."

Selma Woodsum in **"The Liar"** (1918), one of Freeman's several patriotic war stories, is embarrassed because her son is one of the few young men in the neighborhood who has not enlisted. She therefore steals an ink-stained uniform; hanging it on her line, she allows her neighbors to think her son has not only fought but has even earned a "red badge." Selma's evasive answer to friends' queries are so convincing that soon the entire neighborhood is "under the firm impression that poor, gallant Leon Woodsum had returned wounded from the front, and had lost the sight of one eye, if not both."[13]

As will be noted from the brief summaries above, many of Freeman's plots involving women rivals turn on themes of cheating, lying, or theft as a woman, generally without forethought, breaks all her tightly held moral convictions (and thereby faces the threat of eternal damnation, a very real concern in Freeman's world) in order to gain her women friends' admiration. Much as she cannot condone the action, however, Freeman's disapprobation for these women is never sharp. Rather, she seems to understand the powerful inner need they have for security or approval from their peers. They seek above all and at all costs to maintain the appearance of a "good" (or smart, or fashionable) woman, and often thereby succeed in deceiving their friends. However, Freeman shows us that these women's overweening pride or vanity merely masks the fearful and guilty goadings of their own consciences.

Finally, in one of Freeman's more well-known stories, **"A Village Singer"** (1891), elderly Candace Whitcomb finds she must compete with another woman in order to preserve nothing less than her own identity and integrity. After forty years of faithful service, Candace is suddenly displaced, by her minister's decree, from her position as lead singer at Sunday meeting. She revenges herself—though guiltily—by singing as loudly as possible from her home across the way each Sunday, thereby drowning out the new female singer. Her eventual victory in the situation, while a Pyrrhic one, is nevertheless a triumph of her own defiant courage and spirit: on her deathbed, she delivers what Marjorie Pryse considers no less than a "warning" to her rival Alma. In criticizing the younger woman's rendition of "Jesus, Lover of My Soul," Candace tells Alma that "You flatted a little on—soul." The dying woman thus, according to Pryse, reminds Alma "not only of the inevitable decline of her voice, and therefore the congregation's potential dissatisfaction, but also of her own mortality."[14]

Freeman's women compete intensely with each other; their daily lives are often consumed with worry over others' opinions of them, and with attempts to "save face" in the absence of material or emotional security. But perhaps most disturbing in Freeman's stories of women's relationships with each other are those in which a domineering woman keeps a weaker woman, with whom she often lives, in fear of either her physical power or emotional scorn. Most often in these stories the weaker or more childlike woman has received a marriage proposal; in intense jealousy, the stronger woman forbids her to marry. Eventually, however, the dominating woman relents or is humbled. For example, in the murder mystery **"The Long Arm"** (1895), written in conjunction with Joseph Edgar Chamberlin, Phoebe Dole's jealousy leads her to murder her friend Maria Woods because she suspects Maria has become romantically involved with a man. Ostensibly based on the Lizzie Borden slayings of 1892, more evidence suggests Freeman took her subject from the equally sensational Alice Mitchell case of the same year in which a mentally disturbed Tennessee woman murdered her lesbian lover to "make it sure that no one else could get her."[15]

Similarly, in **"Julia—Her Thanksgiving"** (1909), Elsie, a clinging and dependent woman, imitates stronger Julia in all ways, even to dressing like her. "I don't believe Elsie White ever set her feet outside Julia Benham's tracks in her life," the garrulous first person narrator informs her audience. Elsie unhesitatingly lends Julia all her money at her request; Julia, however, through imprudent investments, loses the majority of it. Only when the two are reduced to poverty does Julia allow Elsie to marry the beau she has been forced, by Julia's envy, to refuse years before.

It is, of course, impossible to know whether or not Mary Freeman herself experienced discord with Mary John Wales over the possibility of Freeman's marrying. As mentioned, Freeman's letters tell us little about her relationship with Wales; we do know, however, that after 1897 when Mary Wales' father died, Freeman, as Elsie does in the story above, supported her friend financially, even lending her at one point all of the royalties from one of her novels.[16] That same year Mary Wilkins became engaged to Charles Freeman but continued to delay her wedding four and one half more years. Mary Wales, who never married, was witness to the Freemans' wedding. After moving with her husband to New Jersey, Freeman continued to help Mary Wales financially; once a year, Foster tells us, she returned to Randolph to visit. However, when Wales died in 1914, Mary Freeman did not return to Randolph for the funeral.[17]

These, then, are the few facts we know about Freeman's friendship with Mary John Wales. While we can glean little from them, Freeman's tales concerning the rivalry between adult women friends (and, as we shall see, between sisters as well) indicate Freeman knew her subject first hand. Mary Freeman may well have delayed her marriage because of some emotional pressure in the Wales' household—Mary Wales' jealousy, perhaps, or Freeman's own guilt at leaving the Wales family when they apparently badly needed her financial help. Whatever the source of these stories' themes, they expose a dark side of women's relationships with each other which, far from the "sisterhood" or "community" of shared values seen by some critics in her works, rather indicate Freeman's life-long dependence on, yet fear of, strong, maternal—and perhaps, to her, ultimately vindictive—women.

II

As friends and rivals, then, women in Freeman's stories form close emotional ties with one another. But the strongest and most tenacious bond in Freeman's New England stories, indeed the most intimate relationship this author portrays, is that between adult sisters. Historically, this relationship has been little studied. Smith-Rosenberg's research on nineteenth-century women notes the extreme centrality of close-kin relationships, especially sister relationships, in women's lives during that century. Unlike most other female-female friendships, as she concludes, "sisterly bonds continued across a lifetime."[18] Toni McNaron's recent *The Sister Bond: A Feminist View of a Timeless Connection* is a compilation of essays exploring some of the intricacies of famous sister dyads over time, such as that of Christina and Maria Rossetti and that of Emily and Lavinia Dickinson. In her introduction McNaron speaks of the ambiguous nature of her relationship with her own sibling, one which is common to many sisters. "I feel closer to her on some psychic level than to any friends or lovers," she writes; "I yearn for a kind of exchange that is not possible without our becoming the same person."[19] Yet despite such a desire for intimacy, she writes further, adult sisters are often acting out a pattern of competitive behavior ingrained from earliest childhood:

> Either one sister encourages the other to play out some complementary self that she does not or cannot become, or forces around them are such that complementarity becomes the pattern within which both act out their adult lives. It is as though unconsciously the pairs . . . evolve a system in which they develop only certain parts of themselves in order to cut down on or avoid altogether the powerful pulls toward competition found within virtually any family.[20]

Many of the sister pairs that McNaron's work examines created and evolved such role patterns for each other in order to establish separate identities within the family, often as a preventive measure for dealing with jealousy over or competition for parental atten-

tion. Each sister may thus come to define the other as her opposite or as a version of her expanded self. Moreover, twin sisters "must work unusually hard to learn to take individual responsibility for their own personalities."[21]

Freeman's many stories involving sisters point to personal experience with the kind of ambiguity and intricacy McNaron's research has uncovered in these relationships. Foster tells us that in their youth Mary's only sister Anna was considered more talented, witty, and likeable than Mary, especially among the young men of Brattleboro.[22] At the time of her death at age seventeen, Anna was not only engaged to be married, but had already won considerable public acclaim in town for her musical ability: she was organist at the Congregational Church and pianist for the Brattleboro Choral Union. Her obituary in the *Vermont Phoenix* sadly stated, "With this talent so brilliantly manifesting itself, coupled as it was with a worthy ambition and an untiring energy, to no young person in Brattleboro did the future open with brighter promise."[23]

Although Freeman's letters reveal little about her relationship with her sister, one can surmise her feelings at Anna's death. Born in 1859 soon after the death of the Wilkins' infant son, Anna was the beloved baby of the family, seven years younger and of a markedly different personality than Mary. Whereas Mary was quiet, shy, and retiring, Anna was outgoing, lively, and cheerful. Both young women were musically inclined; but although Anna continued her early training in music, Mary turned first to painting and then later to writing.[24] To some extent then, Mary and Anna seem to have unconsciously evolved for each other the kind of "complementarity" McNaron speaks about in sister relationships; each developed a part of herself different from that of her sister in order perhaps to avoid the potential threat of competition in the family.

Several of Freeman's stories concerning sister pairs, moreover, indicate that Freeman may have in Anna's lifetime felt some jealousy of her "baby" sister's talents, popularity, and in particular, her forthcoming marriage. Evidence from her stories further suggests that at Anna's death, Freeman experienced the grief of losing an intimate friend, the fear of evolving a separate identity away from that of her sister, and the guilty apprehension at being the remaining child in the family, the one who must now "make up" to her parents all they had lost. In various ways, each of the following stories reveals Freeman's inner turmoil over her complex relationship to her sister, turmoil which apparently lasted throughout her entire adult life.

Freeman's most poignant statement about the closeness and even necessity of the sister bond is expressed in a skillfully executed story in which, ironically, the presence of a sister is merely illusory. **"Sister Liddy"** (1891) is set in the village poorhouse.[25] With disconcerting realism, Freeman sketches for us portraits of its poverty-stricken or mentally imbalanced inhabitants. One woman has "overworked" on her farm: she "sat in a rocking-chair and leaned her head back . . . she kept her mouth parted miserably, and there were ghastly white streaks around it and her nostrils." Another woman violently pulls her bed to pieces the moment the matron has made it up. Still others crouch silently in corners as children play ball across the floor of the barren room. The more vociferous of the older women spend their days bickering about who has once possessed the finest clothing, household goods, or other such evidence of wealth. Only Polly Moss who "had been always deformed and poor and friendless" is unable to join in the rivalry. Searching for some memory to make her these women's equal yet finding none, she "invents" the best possession of all: a sister. "You'd orter have seen my sister Liddy," she blurts out to the stunned group:

> My sister Liddy was jest as handsome as a pictur' . . . she could sing the best of anybody anywheres around. . . . She used to sing in the meetin'-house, she did, an' all the folks used to sit up an' look at her when she begun. She used to wear a black silk dress to meetin', an' a white cashmire shawl, an' a bunnit with a pink wreath around the face, an' she had white kid gloves . . . she married a real rich fellar from Bostown . . . an' she had a great big house with a parlor an' settin'-room, an' a room to eat in besides the kitchen. . . . An' her furnitur' was all stuffed, an' kivered with red velvet, an' she had a pianner. She was allers dretful lovin', an' had a good disposition.

Polly's story develops over time: "[she] was questioned and cross-examined concerning her sister Liddy . . . and the glories of her sister were increased daily." Only on her deathbed does a conscience-stricken Polly confess her deception. "'I s'pose I've been dretful wicked,' she mourns, 'but I ain't never had nothin' in my whole life. I—s'pose the Lord orter have been enough, but it's dretful hard sometimes to keep holt of him, an' not look anywheres else, when you see other folks a-clawin' an' gettin' other things, an' actin' as if they was wuth havin'. . . . I s'pose I—was dretful wicked . . . but—I never had any sister Liddy.'"

"Sister Liddy" is a telling story for a woman to write whose sister had died fifteen years earlier. Polly's beautiful and talented but imaginary sister represents for her all she is not, the fulfillment of her frustrated, limited self. Polly develops her story through the process of storytelling and embellishment: she has found that merely by postulating herself as sister to a woman who is charming, talented, and wealthy, she is able to gain the admiration and respect of her women friends and to rest secure in a new-found identity. In using

Polly's point of view, and having Polly create a literary persona Liddy, Freeman may have been essentially repeating her own position here *vis-à-vis* her relationship with Anna: like Polly, Freeman has created through her art an ideal "other," a substitution for the role she ultimately could *not* play in real life—that of her sister.

The extreme, even cloying closeness of the sister bond, and often the inner chaos that results when one sister is left alone, is expressed in other Freeman tales. Several of these show two adult women who, having lived together for years, are nearly merged into one identity: each sister has become for the other a type of expanded self. In **"A Gala Dress"** (1891), for example, sisters Elizabeth and Emily Babcock, poor yet proud elderly women of a once genteel family, own between them only one good black silk dress, that staple of a nineteenth-century woman's wardrobe. Over the years, therefore, as they "starved daintily," they have carefully evolved a plan of sharing the dress while assiduously avoiding the suspicions of their nosy friend Matilda Jennings: each sister retrims the dress, one with lace and one with velvet, when it is her turn to appear at a social function.

In **"A far-away Melody"** (1887), an early story revealing perhaps Freeman's lingering emotional distress over Anna's death, an extremely close relationship between elderly twins is wrenched apart by one of the sister's dying. The remaining woman's grief at being left behind is coupled with guilt that she may have spoken sharply to her sister hours before she died. "'I was cross with her this afternoon,' [she sobs:] 'I loved her, but I don't think she knew.'" "This sister-love was all she had ever felt, besides her love of God, in any strong degree," the narrator explains. "All the passion of devotion of which this homely, commonplace woman was capable was centered in that, and the unsatisfied strength of it was killing her."[26]

Finally, in a very short, odd tale **"The Three Old Sisters and the Old Beau"** (1900), three elderly maiden sisters, who have virtually no separate identities, are even courted for years by the same man. When two of the sisters die, Camilla, the remaining sister, finally assents to marrying the "old beau." But her life-long identification with her sisters has been so complete that "no one ever knew, whether she wore her own or her sisters' wedding-gown, or had wedded her own or her sisters' old Beau."[27]

Close friendships between sisters also involve outbreaks of jealous anger over the most petty or trivial of concerns as each sister strives to establish some small token of an individual identity away from that of her sibling. In **"Billy and Susy"** (1909), for example, two elderly sisters given similar kittens quarrel bitterly over which kitten is theirs. In **"Life Everlastin'"** (1891), Mrs. Ansel rails angrily against her sister's "improper" habits: "'It seems to me sometimes if Luella would jest have a pretty new bonnet, an' go to meetin' Sabbath-days like other folks, I wouldn't ask for anything else,'" she confides to a friend. And in a humorous scene from **"Something on Her Mind"** (1912), three sisters, attempting to discover the reason behind their young niece's depression, become miffed when each contends *she*—and not her sister—has experienced the greatest trials in life:

> "We must talk to [our niece] each by herself," [Amelia suggests]. "We must tell her, if necessary, things about our own lives which we have survived. . . ."
>
> "If you think it will do her good, I have lived through troubles like most people, and I can tell her about them, although I have never spoken of them to any living soul and never expected to," said [Julia].
>
> She spoke with an air of delicate importance. Amelia eyed her sharply. "I would like to know, Julia Spencer, what dreadful troubles you have lived through that we don't know about," she said, "when you've been right here with us in this house all your life and had everything you wanted."

But rivalry among sisters has a sharper edge also. In at least seven of her short stories, Freeman portrays a situation in which a woman, in one manner or another, deprives her sister of a lover. These include **"The Scent of the Roses"** (1891); **"A Pot of Gold"** (1891); **"The Gift of Love"** (1906); **"Dear Annie"** (1914); **"Sarah Edgewater"** (1918); **"The Tree of Knowledge"** (1900); and **"Amanda and Love"** (1891). Several of these concern an "older but wiser" sister who, injured herself, seeks to "save" her younger sibling from the perils of falling in love. In **"The Tree of Knowledge,"** for example, middle-aged Cornelia finally confesses that it is she who has been sending "uplifting" letters to her much younger sister Annie and signing them with a man's name. Cornelia explains

> I had in my youth a bitter experience. I discovered the treachery and wickedness of man. I threw my heart away upon one who was unworthy, and I wanted to save my sister from a like fate. I wanted to fill her mind with such a pure ideal that there could be no danger.

In **"Amanda and Love,"** a story filled with suppressed tension and violence, an older sister's jealousy erupts when her younger sister is courted by a man. Old enough to be her mother, Amanda is fiercely protective of her younger sister Love. She scorns Love's suitor Willis, considering him unworthy of her sister's

affections. Love resents Amanda's chastisement: she once even turns on her "with a look as if she were feeling the claws which nature had denied her." A clinging and weak woman, however, Love suppresses her resentment yet manages meanwhile to continue her affair with young Willis. Love's courtship eventually forces Amanda to confront her own deepest fears. Less attractive and accomplished than Love, Amanda has long lived vicariously through Love's beauty and talents, depending on her sister as a source for her own pride and identity. When that identity is threatened by the intrusion of a rival, Amanda at first assumes a "subtle psychological warfare"[28] to drive Willis away and retain Love's affection: she consistently embarrasses the young man when he visits and afterward pampers Love with affection. However, when Willis deserts Love and the young girl falls gravely ill, Amanda, out of fear for her sister's life, chooses to overcome her selfish envy: she humiliates herself by going to the young man and pleading that he renew his courtship. Willis visits Love that evening; leaving the two alone in the sitting room and retiring to the kitchen, Amanda sat by the window and "wept patiently."

Unlike her stories of women friends who are rivals, Freeman in these tales of one sister's jealous emotional control of another seems to sympathize with the dominant and more powerful woman. As in the two stories described above, this older sister slowly comes to realize her selfish manipulation is driving her younger sibling's affection further and further from her, the very opposite of the effect she has wished her caretaking efforts to have. Her final, self-abasing surrender of power, however, comes only after much inner conflict: indeed, Freeman portrays such a woman as valiant in her struggle to release the pride, fear, and guilt which have long bound her in an unhealthy relationship to her sister.

What we know of Freeman's own friendships with other women as well as with her sister Anna is sketchy at best. However, from her many tales exploring the dynamic of intimacy and envy in women's relationships with other women, it is probable that Freeman experienced these relationships as both close and problematic. Needing other women's affection and approval, she nevertheless appears to have been painfully cognizant of the damage one woman could inflict upon another through emotional cruelty. Both Freeman's women friends and sister pairs play out roles involving highly intricate patterns of dependence and domination, of power and weakness. In her careful probing of these tacit and complex elements in female-female relationships, Freeman shows herself above all an extremely perceptive analyst of women's psychology.

Notes

1. Michele Clark, ed. *"The Revolt of 'Mother'" and Other Stories* (New York: Feminist Press, 1974), p. 195.

2. Lillian Faderman, *Surpassing the Love of Men: Romantic Friendship and Love Between Women from the Renaissance to the Present* (New York: William Morrow, 1981), p. 159.

3. Carroll Smith-Rosenberg, *Disorderly Conduct: Visions of Gender in Victorian America* (New York: Knopf, 1985), p. 60.

4. Nancy Chodorow, *The Reproduction of Mothering: Psychoanalysis and the Sociology of Gender* (Berkeley: Univ. of California Press, 1978), p. 36.

5. Marjorie Pryse, "Afterword" to *Selected Stories of Mary E. Wilkins Freeman* (New York: Norton, 1983), p. 335.

6. Josephine Donovan, *New England Local Color Literature: A Women's Tradition* (New York: Frederick Ungar, 1983), p. 129.

7. Brent L. Kendrick, ed. *The Infant Sphinx: Collected Letters of Mary E. Wilkins Freeman* (Metuchen, NJ: Scarecrow Press, 1985), p. 51.

8. Edward Foster, *Mary E. Wilkins Freeman* (New York: Hendricks House, 1956), p. 133.

9. Foster, p. 141.

10. Freeman was obviously disturbed at the prospect of aging: several other stories such as "The Travelling Sister" (1909), "A Patient Waiter" (1891), and "The Three Old Sisters and the Old Beau" (1900) involve women protagonists who seek, even desperately, to retain the beauty and vitality of youth. Yet Freeman was fully aware of the folly of such enterprise. "When a man or woman holds fast to youth, even if successfully," her narrator states in "The Amethyst Comb," "there is something of the pitiful and the tragic involved."

11. Freeman has many self-renunciatory women in her works. As in this story, she usually applauds the stronger woman's act of "giving" a weak or unstable man to her weaker or dependent friend. The stronger woman is, the narrator implies, ultimately better off without him. See also the stories "A Moral Exigency" (1887) and "Emmy" (1891), and the novels *Pembroke* (1894), *By the Light of the Soul* (1906) and *The Shoulders of Atlas* (1908).

12. Freeman's "society novel" *The Butterfly House* (1912) satirizes such "ladies' clubs," presenting women's relationships to each other in the worst possible light: grasping, petty, and envious, these women compete intensely for social adulation from their peers. Foster tells us that Freeman used Metuchen, New Jersey, the town where she moved after her marriage, as the model for "Fairbridge" (182).

13. Other war stories include "The Prop" (1918), "The Return" (1921), and "Both Cheeks" (1918). Freeman was an ardent patriot and wrote several non-fiction articles as well about the American role in World War I.

14. Marjorie Pryse, "The Humanity of Women in Freeman's 'A Village Singer,'" *Colby Library Quarterly,* 19 (1983), 74.

15. See Faderman's *Surpassing the Love of Men* for an account of the origin of this story, which won Freeman and Chamberlin a substantial monetary prize as the 1895 winner of the Bacheller Syndicate short story contest. A number of other Freeman characters evince signs of lesbianism, although the author never develops the subject enough to make this relationship clear. Donovan's *New England Local Color Literature* briefly discusses such ambiguous female liaisons in *The Portion of Labor* (1901) and *The Shoulders of Atlas* (1908). The latter is especially interesting in the several oddly intense female-female relationships it presents, including a particularly volatile "quasi-lesbian, quasi-mother-daughter relationship" between an older woman and her much younger ward (128).

16. Foster, p. 141.

17. Foster, p. 183.

18. Smith-Rosenberg, p. 62.

19. McNaron, *The Sister Bond* (New York: Pergamon Press, 1985), p. 3.

20. McNaron, p. 4.

21. McNaron, p. 7.

22. Foster, p. 32.

23. Kendrick, p. 43.

24. The 1880 Brattleboro census lists Mary Wilkins' occupation as "music teacher." Mary evidently taught piano for a year or more. Moreover, she confessed years later, "I did not want to write at all. I wanted to be an artist. But for lack of paint, etc., and sufficiency of pens, ink, and paper, I wrote" (Kendrick, p. 410).

25. In Brattleboro, the Wilkins family lived less than one block from the village poorhouse. Several of Freeman's stories, including "Sister Liddy" and "A Gentle Ghost" (1891), are set in or near the poorhouse.

26. Of interest too in considering the effect of Anna Wilkins' death on Freeman's family is the story "A Gentle Ghost" (1891) where a mother and her surviving daughter are haunted by a dead daughter's spirit.

27. See Susan Toth's "Mary Wilkins Freeman's Parable of Wasted Life" (*American Literature*, 42 [January 1971], 564-67) for an interesting analysis of the ominous "death-in-life" theme of this strange story.

28. John W. Crowley, "Freeman's Yankee Tragedy: 'Amanda and Love,'" *Markham Review*, 5 (Spring 1976), 59.

Shirley Marchalonis (essay date 1991)

SOURCE: Marchalonis, Shirley. "The Sharp-Edged Humor of Mary Wilkins Freeman: *The Jamesons*—and Other Stories." In *Critical Essays on Mary Wilkins Freeman,* edited by Shirley Marchalonis, pp. 222-34. Boston: G. K. Hall & Co., 1991.

[*In the following essay, Marchalonis underscores the emotional basis for the dry, often dark, humor in* The Jamesons *and in several of Freeman's stories.*]

To propose a humorous reading of Mary Wilkins Freeman's work certainly contradicts most published criticism. Yet her earliest important critic, William Dean Howells, and most contemporary reviewers, even as they gave her the "local color realist" label that has so limited reading of her work, saw a mixture of "humor and tenderness" or "humor and pathos," particularly in her stories.[1]

It was scholars like Fred Lewis Pattee and Perry D. Westbrook who established Freeman as the "grim recorder of the last act of the Puritan drama in America," or, to quote a Pattee title, the "Terminal Moraine of New England Puritanism"—with *Puritanism* defined as a dark and bitter creed having no redeeming virtues.[2] Sadly, much of the criticism that followed built on these established perceptions. According to Perry D. Westbrook, "one need read very few pages of Mary Wilkins to realize that to her . . . life is moral struggle within the soul of two wills opposing each other, one driving the individual on to destruction, the other to salvation."[3]

But there is more to Freeman than the Howells label and the limited vision and direction of Pattee, Westbrook, and others perceived, and to read her work without these preconceptions, as her contemporaries did and now as more recent critics with wider viewpoints are beginning to do, brings unexpected discoveries and pleasures. Newer scholarship is in fact reaching out in a variety of ways and finding that Freeman's work is neither so restricted nor so repetitive as earlier scholars believed—finding that she is concerned with individualism, with integrity, autonomy, and self-definition, and that her "puritanism" is laced with wry humor.

In 1899 Freeman published a short novel called *The Jamesons.*[4] Since very little attention is paid to her novels, it is not surprising that little notice has been taken of this one, although it was a popular work. *The Jamesons* is a village novel, as her stories are village stories, and it is part of a tradition that includes not only the works of Sarah Orne Jewett and other American local-color writers but Elizabeth Gaskell's *Cranford* and Mary Russell Mitford's *Our Village*—two English works widely read in the United States; like these, *The Jamesons* fits into the group Sandra Zagarell has recently identified as the narrative of community.[5]

In 1891, several years before *The Jamesons,* Mary E. Wilkins had written to thank Joseph Knight for the copy of *Cranford* he had sent her.[6] "Yes, I already knew 'Cranford,'" she wrote, "but not in any such beautiful guise as this, and indeed I did not own it in any guise." Elizabeth Gaskell's *Cranford* was published in 1853 and had already won critical and popular approval. Sarah Orne Jewett's *Country of the Pointed Firs* appeared in 1896 and was followed three years later by Wilkins's *The Jamesons.*[7] All three novels, besides being village stories, are lighthearted, humorous, and written in a tone of affectionate goodwill. They present the mores of a closed village society in which small events are vitally large, and they focus on a group of people, chiefly women, within a nearly manless village. Gaskell makes this point in the opening lines of her text: "In the first place, Cranford is in possession of the Amazons; all the holders of houses, above a certain rent, are women. If a married couple come to settle in the town, somehow the gentleman disappears; he is either fairly frightened to death of being the only man in the Cranford evening parties, or he is accounted for by being with his regiment, his ship, or closely engaged in business all the week in the great neighboring town of Drumble. . . . In short, whatever does become of the gentlemen, they are not at Cranford" (1).

Gaskell and Jewett structured their stories in the same way. *Cranford*'s narrator is a perceptive young woman with connections in the village, who visits at varying periods and chronicles the oddities and activities of her friends there. That plan makes the story somewhat episodic, but Gaskell uses the structure advantageously; there are ongoing subplots, and what happened between the narrator's visits can be summarized, usually by Miss Matty as she recounts news of the village and her own reactions, a process that allows Gaskell to advance the action and show Miss Matty's character at the same time. Other subplots can begin and end within the space of one visit. This description of narrator and structure also fits *Country of the Pointed Firs*. In that novel the relationship between the narrator and the village is similar; the narrator is the objective but affectionate chronicler of the village life and people, while Mrs. Todd reveals herself in her actions and in her tales of others.

Cranford may have directly influenced Jewett and Freeman, or both writers may simply have been working within a familiar genre; perhaps the directness of the influence is not important. Critics certainly compared both Jewett and Freeman with Gaskell, and both American writers had done something of the kind before: sketches of people and life held together by their village location, as in Jewett's *Deephaven* (1877) and Freeman's **People of Our Neighborhood** (1898). A search for sources and influences would push back even farther, to Mary Russell Mitford's *Our Village* (1824), enormously popular in both England and America.[8] There are differences; Mitford's book is a kind of anatomy of a farming village, with much emphasis on nature and the changing seasons, and the village she portrays is not manless. But her introductory paragraph could apply to any of these works: "[A] little village far in the country . . . a little world of our own, close-packed and insulated like ants in an ant-hill, or bees in a hive, or sheep in a fold, or nuns in a convent, or sailors in a ship; where we know everyone, are known to everyone, interested in everyone, and authorized to hope that everyone feels an interest in us" (3). Mitford, in her turn, cites Jane Austen's novels and Gilbert White's *History of Selbourne* as her models of good reading.[9]

The similarities among *Our Village, Cranford, Country of the Pointed Firs,* and **The Jamesons** make it worthwhile to examine at least the last three, however briefly, as examples of the same kind of work. Such an examination discovers in Mary Wilkins Freeman's writing a side of her talent that is frequently, if not consistently, overlooked.

What is common to this kind of story is, first, the village setting, realistically portrayed. These small worlds are governed by codes—mores, customs, usage: patterns of behavior, not consciously learned but known to all, that regulate attitudes and actions. If the worlds are small, they are nevertheless full of variety and are vital to the people who live in them, and the writers present the details of daily life in the microcosm pleasantly but unromantically.

The second likeness is the tone: affection, warmth, humor—qualities attributed to Gaskell and Jewett but not often associated with Freeman. Much of the humor lies in the importance of seemingly small events within the depicted world. The social hierarchy the ladies of Cranford uphold, for example, presents them with earthshaking questions: when widowed Lady Glenmire marries the doctor, several social levels beneath her, what is her place in society? It is a situation that brings disorder into an orderly microcosm.

Like the others, **The Jamesons** tells the story of the interaction of an outsider with a country village. Its tone, too, is affectionate and gently humorous, and it is a tale of small events that loom large within a small world. But if **The Jamesons,** like *Country of the Pointed Firs,* may be an American *Cranford,* Freeman is neither Jewett nor Gaskell, and she gives the theme her own characteristic knife-edge.

One difference is that the first-person narrator is part of the village. Mrs. Sophia Lane is a widow, not rich but financially comfortable, living in her own house, which she shares with her sister-in-law and her niece. The outsider is Mrs. Jameson, who brings her city sophistication to "widen the spheres" of the country people among whom she will spend the summer.

In *Cranford* the top of the social hierarchy is the Honorable Mrs. Jameson, who occupies that position because her husband was the younger son of a baron, and whose pronouncements on matters social are the last word. She is not like her American namesake, since Gaskell describes her as being "fat and inert," or "apathetic," but she can be roused on matters of precedence, and she remains the village arbiter. When the ladies want to defy her—specifically, to call on the former Lady Glenmire, who has become Mrs. Hoggins—they wonder, "Would they [the Hogginses] be visited? Would Mrs. Jameson let us?" (208). Unalike as the two ladies are in character (the American is explosively and aggressively energetic), the similarity of names and the position of arbiter, or would-be arbiter, suggest that the *Cranford* lady may have been a model in reverse for Freeman's character.

Mrs. Jameson, her three children, and her mother board for the summer in Linnville, a village whose inhabitants, in the words of the narrator and in contrast to the people of neighboring towns, "plumed ourselves upon our reputation of not taking boarders for love or money" (2). Why Caroline Liscom, with plenty of money, is opening her home to strangers is the subject of speculation as the story begins. The narrator and the reader first meet the incomer when a false alarm summons firemen and watchers to the Liscom house.

Though the false alarm was accidentally caused by her son, Mrs. Jameson does not apologize, and ignores the cold fury with which her landlady surveys the water-soaked ruin of her once-immaculate kitchen. As Mrs. Lane is leaving the house, she hears a voice call, "My good woman," an address she cannot think is meant for her. When her attention is finally caught she goes to Mrs. Jameson, who commands her to find them another place to board. Mrs. Lane, astonished, says she knows of none:

> "My good woman," said [Mrs. Jameson], "you look very neat and tidy yourself, and I don't doubt are a good plain cook; I am willing to try your house if it is not surrounded by trees and there is no standing water near; I do not object to running water."
>
> In the midst of this speech the elder daughter had said in a frightened way, "Oh, mamma!" but her mother had paid no attention. As for myself, I was angry. The memory of my two years at Wardville Young Ladies Seminary in my youth and my frugally independent life as wife and widow was strong upon me. I had read and improved my mind. I was a prominent member of the Ladies Sewing Society of our village; I wrote papers which were read at the meetings; I felt, in reality, not one whit below Mrs. H. Boardman Jameson, and moreover, large sleeves were the fashion, and my sleeves were every bit as large as hers, though she had just come from the city. That added to my conviction of my own importance. "Madam," said I, "I do not take boarders. I have never taken boarders, and I never shall take boarders." Then I turned and went out of the room, and downstairs, with, it seemed to me, much dignity.

(22-23)

So it goes on. At the village picnic, traditionally an event that allows the women to display their finest cooking skills, Mrs. Jameson arrives and, with "a brisk air which rather took our breaths away, it was so indicative of urgent and very pressing business" (38), pulls other women's offerings out of their boxes, destroying some delicious cookies in the process; comments, "These are enough to poison the whole village" (39); sets out her own health food, "thick, hard-looking biscuits" (41); and calls, "Ladies, attention!" before she delivers a lecture on her own version of nutrition.

She reads Browning to the Ladies Sewing Circle, whose members do not want to hear him, preferring to exchange news, gossip, and opinions, and she continues to read while the supper spoils in the kitchen. In short, as the village women realize, Mrs. Jameson is determined to improve them, and there is no polite way of penetrating her armor of complacency and her complete belief in her own infallibility.

The stage is set at this point for what could be an ugly tale of anger, hatred, and all the supposed dark New England suppressed passions or the neurotic behavior some of Freeman's critics have expected from her characters. In fact, it does not take long for the villagers to find Mrs. Jameson absurd. In the beginning they tolerated her actions out of shock: "We were all quiet, peaceful people who dreaded altercation; it made our hearts beat too fast. Taking it all together, we felt very much as if some great, overgrown bird of another species had gotten into our village nest, and we were in the midst of an awful commotion of wings and beak. Still we agreed that Mrs. Jameson had probably meant well" (43-44).

Gradually, as she reveals herself, their attitude changes. When a farmer complains that her children have picked his squash and potato blossoms, everyone hears her grandly assure him that "if, when you come to dig your squashes, you find less than usual, and when you come to pick your potatoes the bushes are not in as good condition as they usually are, you may come to me and I will make it right with you" (46). Realizing that she is completely out of her depth in his world, the farmer is no longer angry and laughs, and the villagers discover that Mrs. Jameson's overbearing ways, her complacency, and her complete absence of sensitivity toward others do not have to change their lives. She becomes a source of fascination: she is the most interesting and amusing thing that has happened to the village in years. By the time she moves to a farm where she can plant her crops in August and make shoes of thick cloth for her hens to keep them from scratching, the townspeople wait delightedly to see whether this imposing woman will really get the better of nature.

She returns to the village for a second summer: "'I consider that my own sphere has been considerably widened this winter,' said Mrs. Jameson, and Louisa and I regarded her with something like terror. Flora Clark said, when she heard that remark of Mrs. Jameson's, that she felt, for her part, as if a kicking horse had got out of the pasture, and there was no knowing where he would stop" (116). This summer Mrs. Jameson has determined to reform dress, advocating a bicycling costume for daily wear; a few other women follow her lead. The always-suitably-dressed narrator notes that "Mrs. Jameson was very stout, and the short skirt was not, to our way of thinking, becoming" (117); she and her sister-in-law imagine other women in the same dress: "Some of our good, motherly, village faces, with their expressions of homely dignity and Christian decorousness, looking at us from under that jaunty English walking-hat, in lieu of their sober bonnets, presented themselves to our imaginations, and filled us with amusement and consternation" (118-19).

More important, Mrs. Jameson plans to beautify the village. Jonas Martin, hired by Mrs. Jameson as her gardener, probably best represents the attitude all the villagers eventually share. He quickly learns not to reason with her but to let her go and enjoy the results. Instructed by Mrs. Jameson, who ignores the village wisdom that vines bring spiders and are bad for expensive paint, he digs up vines from the woods and plants them wherever she thinks they are needed: "The calm insolence of benevolence with which Mrs. Jameson did this was inimitable. People actually did not know whether to be furious or amused by this liberty taken with their property. . . . If they did expostulate, Mrs. Jameson only directed Jonas where to put the next vine, and assured the bewildered owner of the premises that he would in time thank her" (122-23). She extends her efforts beyond individual houses to the countryside:

> When, thinking that corn-cockles and ox-eyed daisies would be a charming combination at the sides of the country road, she caused them to be sowed, and thereby introduced them into Jonas Green's wheatfield, he expostulated in forcible terms, and threatened a suit for damages; and when she caused a small grove of promising young hemlocks to be removed from Eben Betts' woodland and set out on the sandy lot in which the schoolhouse stands, without leave or license, it was generally conceded that she had exceeded her privileges as a public benefactress. . . . Mr. H. Boardman Jameson had to pay a goodly sum to Eben Betts to hush the matter up; and the trees soon withered, and were cut up for firewood for the schoolhouse.
>
> (124-25)

Through all this, Jonas the gardener is enjoying everything. A man who had had a "steady, hard grind of existence," he now has "a quizzical cock to his right eyebrow, and a comically confidential quirk to his mouth, which were in themselves enough to provoke a laugh" (123). Mrs. Jameson has revitalized him. And Jonas represents the village in his way as the narrator does in hers.

For it is not so much Mrs. Jameson's activities that create the comedy as it is the village attitude. Though they watch warily, the villagers do not really feel threatened, and they have no intention of changing their lives, but they give Mrs. Jameson her head and watch with incredulity, steadily growing amusement, kindness, and tolerance this new source of interest and humor. Part of the fun is ironic: the difference between the way the village perceives her and the way she perceives herself in relation to them. That the villagers watch her with amusement and grow to anticipate her next performance never occurs to her, and she misinterprets the good manners with which she and her acts are received. In fact, her city sophistication is far surpassed by the village people in their politeness, their kindness, and their willingness to accept this "overgrown bird" who has taken up residence in their orderly nest. But in one way she is right; she has indeed "widened the sphere," although not in the way she planned or recognizes.

Individuals get angry, but generally their anger is overcome by laughter. And Mrs. Jameson's commanding self-image is undercut by her wisp of a husband; by her unpretentious and somewhat vulgar mother, who visits all over the village and talks incessantly and honestly; and by the affection the village people quickly learn to feel for her children. The only person who can neither tolerate nor forgive is Mrs. Liscom, her first landlady. The romance between the Jameson daughter and the Liscom son provides a subplot, since the watching villagers know that both mothers will be violently opposed to a marriage: Mrs. Jameson because she considers a country boy, no matter how handsome, good, and prosperous, as beneath her family, and Mrs. Liscom because Harriet Jameson has been so inadequately brought up that she cannot create a comfortable home for Mrs. Liscom's cherished son. Mrs. Jameson, guided by her interpretation of a Browning poem, gives in, but Mrs. Liscom remains adamant. By the time the situation is resolved, Mrs. Jameson has been, certainly not reformed, but accepted as she is, with all her foibles, into village life, thus providing the classic ending for comedy.

The Jamesons dismayed some critics and delighted others but was immediately popular with the public. According to Brent L. Kendrick,

> The first large edition published in May 1899 was exhausted by advance orders, and by June eight thousand copies had been printed. Most of the reviewers agreed with the public. They delighted in the humorous, tender, and shrewd sayings: "The note throughout is a joyous one, a welcome change from some of her recent books." They also praised the descriptive powers and vivid character portrayal; "Mrs. Jameson is not a caricature: such reformers exist on this side as well as on the other side of the Atlantic, and on the whole in real life they afford quite as much amusement and exasperation."[10]

That Freeman could write a novel that must be classified as comedy suggests critics should look for this quality in other places. Her letters, for example, reveal a gentle, straight-faced humor that is often ironic and frequently rests on the perception of absurdities. And the brisk, no-nonsense, attractive unmarried aunt who upset the other contributors to the multiauthored novel *The Whole Family,* and especially Howells, because she at age 40 is not the stereotypical "old maid," is the strongest and most amusing character in the novel.[11] Throughout Freeman's work, including those early stories described by Pattee and others as grim, there is often a core of humor—perhaps irony, perhaps the absurd, but humor nonetheless. Characters are placed, or, rather, have placed themselves, in situations that are, quite simply, funny. Or, to put it another way, the opposing forces ("wills") have created a conflict that is both trivial and vital. The result is neither simple nor single.

The core situations, or the conflicts, of most of Freeman's short stories and a few of her novels depend on this mixture of comedy with grimness, perversity, or near tragedy.[12] In **"A Conflict Ended"** Marcus Woodman sits on the church steps every Sunday morning because 10 years earlier he objected to a ministerial candidate and swore he would never step inside the meetinghouse if the man were called to the pastorate. His grudge against the minister has long since faded, but he has made his vow; he suffers silently as his amused neighbors go into church. His face shows the inner self; he has "a mild forehead, a gently curving mouth, and a terrible chin, with a look of strength in it that might have abashed mountains" (338). Esther, the woman he was to marry, describes the problem to her apprentice and admits the situation is ridiculous: "That makes it the hardest of anything, according to my mind—when you know that everybody's laughing, and you could hardly help laughing yourself, though you feel 'most ready to die" (341). When, strengthened by Esther's decision to marry him—and, if necessary, share the steps—he at last enters the church, the watching neighbors do not laugh: "They had felt the pathos in the comedy" (348).

The two old women in **"A Mistaken Charity"** who are taken from their subsistence living and put into a comparatively luxurious home by the kindness of their neighbors are anything but grateful: "nothing could transform these two unpolished old women into two nice old ladies" (308). They are both angry and unhappy, for in spite of their infirmities they had controlled their limited world, where "all that they cared for they had in tolerable abundance" (303). With daring that intoxicates them, they escape from the home and "as jubilant as two children" (309) come back to their beloved status of poverty with autonomy.

Sarah Dunn, the protagonist of **"The Lombardy Poplar,"** lived most of her life as a twin until her sister died. A cousin who has the same name, looks like Sarah, and has inherited the dead sister's clothes is now her closest relative and companion: "Name, appearance, dress, all were identical" (451). Near Sarah's house is a single Lombardy poplar, strikingly different from nearby trees. Sarah's admiration for the tree leads to a disagreement with her cousin, who calls it an "eyesore":

> Then [Sarah] gazed at the tree again and her whole face changed indescribably. She seemed like another person. The tree seemed to cast a shadow of likeness

over her. She appeared straighter, taller; all her lines of meek yielding, or scarcely even anything so strong as yielding, of utter passiveness, vanished. She looked stiff and uncompromising. Her mouth was firm, her chin high, her eyes steady, and more than all, there was over her an expression of individuality which had not been there before. "That's why I like the popple," said she, in an incisive voice. "That's just why. I'm sick of things and folks that are just like everything and everybody else. I'm sick of trees that are just trees. I like one that ain't."

> (455)

The disagreement becomes a quarrel, but Sarah Dunn does not care. The separation from the voice that criticized her "small assertion of her own individuality" (458) and the kinship but difference she sees between her own Lombardy and a nearby silver poplar are steps to self-realization. She does something; the next Sunday,

> a shimmer of red silk and a toss of pink flowers were seen at the Dunn gate, and Sarah Dunn, clad in a gown of dark-red silk and a bonnet tufted with pink roses, holding aloft a red parasol, passed down the street to meeting. No Dunn had ever worn, within the memory of man, any colors save purple and black and faded green or drab, never any but purple or green or black flowers in her bonnet. . . . Even the old minister hesitated a second in his discourse, and recovered himself with a hem of embarrassment when Sarah entered the meeting-house.

> (460)

Absurd though she may look to the congregation and to the reader, Sarah is totally confident. As she walks out of meeting with her amazed and black-clad cousin, "[t]here seemed no likeness whatever between the two women. . . . Sarah was a Dunn apart" (461). Her cousin accepts a cheerful invitation to dinner, and Sarah goes home in deep satisfaction, with a friendly nod to the poplar tree as she enters her house.

"The Givers," one of Freeman's lesser-known stories but one of her most characteristic, further illustrates her ability to balance humor with other elements.[13] Aunt Sophia and her niece, Flora, are preparing for the young girl's wedding. They are financially secure, with their own house and enough to live on, but by no means rich; Herbert, the young man Flora loves, is hardworking and ambitious, but he must support his widowed mother, whose illness caused them to lose their farm. In spite of obstacles, the young couple decides, with Aunt Sophia's help, to marry anyway. As the story opens, cousins arrive with wedding gifts: a silver afternoon teakettle, cut-glass finger bowls, and embroidered doilies on which the bowls can sit—all expensive gifts, and all useless. Flora manages to sound grateful, but her aunt is tight-lipped. When the girl leaves, Aunt Sophia, questioned by her cousin, tells what she has done about gifts and givers.

She begins her narrative with the preceding Christmas, when kind relatives had sent Flora a "sort of a dewdab to wear in her hair! Pretty enough, looked as if it cost considerable—a pink rose with spangles, and a feather shootin' out of it; but Lord! if Flora had come out in that thing anywhere she'd go in Brookville she'd scared the natives" (25). Other presents were an embroidered silk shawl and, the target of Aunt Sophia's incredulous scorn, red and white carved ivory chessmen and a table chessboard. Her demand to know "what's them little dolls and horses for?" is followed by a swift interchange:

> 'Chess?' says I.
>
> 'A game,' says Flora.
>
> 'A game?' says I.
>
> 'To play,' says Flora.
>
> 'Do you know how to play it, Flora?' says I.
>
> 'No,' says she.
>
> 'Does Herbert?'
>
> 'No.'
>
> 'Well,' says I, and I spoke right out, 'of all the things to give anybody that needs things!'
>
> (26-27)

To make matters worse, the price tag is still on the chess set, and Sophia discovers in utter disbelief that it cost forty dollars. Furthermore, she learns from Herbert that his rich Uncle Hiram sent him a silver ashtray and, for another Christmas, a silver cigarette case; his mother received a silver card case and a cut-glass wine set. Herbert does not smoke, and his mother has neither calling cards nor wine.

Telling no one, Sophia bundles the gifts and herself into a neighbor's sleigh and sets off to return them, keeping only what she defines as "presents, because the folks that give 'em had studied up what Flora wanted, and give to her instead of themselves" (34). She flatly tells each giver why she is returning the gifts. Most of them see her logic and eventually replace the extravagant and showy presents with useful articles. Her final call is to rich Uncle Hiram, who laughs at her but also sees her point and instead of silver cigarette cases gives his nephew enough money to buy land and start a small business.

Originally published in *Harper's* as **"The Revolt of Sophia Lane,"** the story has an obvious affinity with Freeman's famous **"The Revolt of 'Mother'"** and with the lesser-known **"Gentian."**[14] Here and in other stories the protagonists violate the codes of their world, motivated by love for someone else, by personal need, or by conviction; because the world, the codes, and the people are not in themselves of conventional heroic stature, readers often miss the back-to-the-wall courage in the action, just as they miss the comedy.

Freeman's humor is Yankee: subtle, straight-faced, tongue-in-cheek, dry. Her comedy is certainly not hilarity, farce, wit, or any of the other obvious subdefinitions, nor is it the formal structure of comedy. Though it does expose human folly, the exposure is not for purposes of satire; satirists need a commitment, and Freeman remains detached. Rather, it is a wry comic perception of humanity, an ungenial Chaucerian vision of human beings in all their many-sided reality: tragic, funny, irritating, silly, generous, loving, hating, pitiful, strong, weak, but always unpredictable. It says "Lord, what fools these mortals be" in amused compassion, not contempt. Perhaps this long-ignored ability to present many-sided human beings and to bring about a resolution that is not particularly tidy contributes to what Elizabeth Meese calls "undecidability," so that the reader is left with a complex response that the author has caused to happen.[15]

Most definitions of comedy agree that its appeal is to the intellect, and that perception of incongruity, the forced joining of things that do not belong together, is the trigger that creates the shock of the unexpected. Above all, the comic writer is detached, keeping an emotional distance between herself and her characters. In Freeman's work there is the obvious incongruity between individual behavior and the conventions of the protagonist's society; there is the more subtle discordance within the mind of the character who is so often hoist with his own petard; there is the smallness of the scale contrasted with the internal importance of the protagonist's act. Many Freeman characters balance on a thin line of their own rationality, ready at any moment to fall to either side.

These stories present a meeting point of responses—a sharp edge from which the characters could drop into tragedy or comedy, or, better, into a kaleidoscope of reactions as they are saved from silliness by their integrity. The absurdities are complicated by the fact that it takes courage for the protagonist to assume and maintain an incongruous position. Marcus Woodman trapped by his will is tragic, but Marcus Woodman sitting outside the church every Sunday morning is the stuff of comedy. If Marcus Woodman is silly, he is also courageous in maintaining his position as his friends enter the church Sunday after Sunday, with amused glances in his direction; he is even braver when he breaks his vow after all those years and walks into church with his wife. If Sarah Dunn's defining herself by a tree and presenting herself in garishly unsuitable clothing is laughable, both the joy the act gives her and the need of a human being to claim her own identity are not.

Aunt Sophia's outspoken direction of gift-givers is delightful, and so are the startled responses of her neighbors, who have followed a convention without thinking about it. But while Aunt Sophia may be unconsciously humorous when she speaks out to her neighbors, the courage it takes to break through her social codes almost breaks her. At the end of **"The Givers,"** the guests rewrap their gifts, asking questions about what Flora needs as they depart:

> Sophia untied the horse, which had been fastened to a ring beside the door; still the guests did not move to get into the sleigh. A curious air of constraint was over them. Sophia also looked constrained and troubled. Her poor faithful face peering from the folds of her gray wool hood was defiant and firm, but still anxious. She looked at Mrs. Cutting, and the two women's eyes met; there was a certain wistfulness in Sophia's.
>
> "I think a good deal of Flora," said she, and there was a hint of apology in her tone.

(49)

Her guests understand—or her world understands. Sophia has taken a risk, challenging the codes and endangering her relationships with the people with whom she must live, but her mixture of common sense, honesty, courage, and love succeeds.

Not every Freeman story works this way, and not every story has the same kind of humor; Freeman ranges widely within her little worlds—one could almost say she has traveled much in Concord. If there is humor, for example, in **"Old Woman Magoun,"** whose protagonist allows her dearly loved granddaughter to die rather than be degraded, it is very dark humor indeed. Generally her tales have to do with characters who live in a small, organized world with its own rules and who, driven by legitimate (at least to them) motives, oppose or challenge the codes. The local-color label, with its implication of truth limited by geography, has hidden the fact that not only small New England villages have codes and conventions: all groups do.[16] All individuals within groups must determine how they will deal with the codes; Susan Allen Toth points to "the constant mutual adjustment necessary between individual and community."[17] To those outside, the problem, lacking immediacy and direct connection, may seem small. The conflicts for Freeman's people are both trivial and vital; the world is small, but the emotion is not.

Like **The Jamesons,** Freeman's short stories create a variety of awarenesses. Mrs. Jameson is silly, overbearing, and obnoxious, but there are things in her to admire. When she organizes the village centennial, the villagers are exasperated, amused, aware of her mistakes, but, in the end, proud. The flawed, human result of her work is something they would not have had without her. With both intellect and emotions involved, sensitive readers do not go away from this story with a single response. The story will not let them.

Despite neglect, Freeman's work has never been entirely lost, and her reputation and appeal continue to grow. She is too vital to remain in the neat category in which earlier critics placed her, and her vitality comes from her wide, detached perception of humanity in all its colors. From portrayals of self-realization or of individuals dealing with their world's codes to wry humor to sensitive perceptions of human relationships to nature (as in **Six Trees** and **Understudies**), Freeman offers a variety of readings—the mark of a fine artist.

Notes

1. In "Puritanism in American Fiction" (in *Literature and Life* [New York: Harper's, 1902], 279), William Dean Howells mentions the difficulty outsiders have in seeing Freeman's (and New England's) humor. His young visitor to the area "had been too little sensible of the humor which forms the relief of these stories, as it forms the relief of these bare, duteous, conscientious, deeply individualized lives portrayed in them." Nearly all the contemporary critics included humor as an element of Freeman's work.

2. Fred Lewis Pattee, introduction to the 1920 edition of *A New England Nun, and Other Stories* (New York: Harper's, 1920), vii; "On the Terminal Moraine of New England Puritanism," in *Side-Lights on American Literature* (New York: Century, 1922), 175-209. Early in his career Pattee praised Freeman for her contributions to the short story form; his later criticism seems to condemn her content. Since Pattee had much influence on the shaping of the American literature canon, his attitude toward Freeman may be a factor in her virtual disappearance from the literary scene.

3. Perry D. Westbrook, *Mary Wilkins Freeman* (New York: Twayne, 1967), 116-17.

4. *The Jamesons* (New York: Doubleday and McClure, 1899; Philadelphia: Curtis, 1899). Originally serialized in the *Ladies' Home Journal,* this was one of the few Freeman novels not published by Harper's.

5. Sandra Zagarell, "Narrative of Community: The Identification of a Genre," *Signs* 13 (Spring 1988): 498-527.

6. Letter to Joseph Knight (28 December 1891), in *The Infant Sphinx: Collected Letters of Mary E. Wilkins Freeman,* Ed. Brent L. Kendrick (Metuchen, N.J.: Scarecrow Press, 1985), 133;

Elizabeth Gaskell, *Cranford* (London: Oxford University Press, 1965). *Cranford* was originally published as a serial in *Household Words,* 1851-53, and in book form in 1853. All citations are to the Oxford edition.

7. Sarah Orne Jewett, *Country of the Pointed Firs* (Boston: Houghton Mifflin, 1896).

8. Mary Russell Mitford, *Our Village* (London: G. and W. B. Whittaker, 1824-32). At least six different editions of her work were published in the United States between 1830 and 1898.

9. Mitford goes on, "Nothing is so tiresome as to be whirled half over Europe at the chariot wheels of a hero, to go to sleep at Vienna, and awaken at Madrid; it produces a real fatigue, a weariness of spirit." Critics compared Jewett with Gaskell and Mitford, and Freeman with Gaskell and Jewett, although the latter comparison was usually based on their "local color writers" status. Freeman insisted she did not read any writers who might influence her.

10. *The Infant Sphinx,* 200-201. Kendrick quotes reviews from *Literary News* 20 (June 1899): 168 and *Spectator* 83 (14 October 1899): 536.

11. See the introduction by Alfred Bendixen to *The Whole Family* (New York: Ungar, 1986), xi-li, and see "*The Whole Family* and Its Troubles," *New York Times,* 24 October 1908, 590.

12. Unless otherwise noted, the stories discussed here are collected in *Short Fiction of Sarah Orne Jewett and Mary Wilkins Freeman,* ed. Barbara H. Solomon (New York: New American Library, 1979). All citations are to this text.

13. In *The Givers* (New York: Harper's, 1904), 3-50. All citations are to this text.

14. "The Revolt of Sophia Lane," *Harper's Monthly* 108 (December 1903): 20-34.

15. Elizabeth Meese, *Crossing the Double-Cross: The Practice of Feminist Criticism* (Chapel Hill: University of North Carolina Press, 1986), chap. 2, "Signs of Undecidability," 19-38.

16. There is a useful analogy here: folklorists define "group" as more than one person with at least one thing in common; as soon as a group exists, it begins to generate its own folklore, which, in the broadest sense, includes or generates mores and customs.

17. Susan Allen Toth, "Defiant Light: A Positive View of Mary Wilkins Freeman," *New England Quarterly* 46 (March 1973): 83.

Thomas A. Maik (essay date fall 1992)

SOURCE: Maik, Thomas A. "Mary Wilkins Freeman's 'Louisa': Liberation, Independence, or Madness?" *North Dakota Quarterly* 60, no. 4 (fall 1992): 137-48.

[*In the following essay, Maik notes that the title character's appropriation of a typically masculine social role in "Louisa" is viewed by her peers as evidence of mental instability.*]

For various reasons, **"Louisa"** (1891),[1] the story by the New England feminist Mary Wilkins Freeman (1852-1930), has been a long-time favorite among her readers. In a tightly constructed plot, Freeman skillfully weaves such compelling ideas as female independence, mother-daughter conflict, family economic hardship, and romance. The romance or courtship serves as the catalyst for all the other elements of the story, for by rejecting Jonathan Nye, virtually the only eligible male suitor in Louisa's immediate New England area and one favored by her mother for her daughter, the mother-daughter conflict erupts and hopes of economic salvation for the family quickly fade.

From a twentieth-century perspective, Louisa is an example of the liberated woman.[2] In **"Louisa,"** as well as many other of her stories according to Victoria Aarons, Freeman "views marriage as a social institution that restricts women's mobility and freedom to find a comfortable position within male-dominated traditions" (147).[3] By rejecting Jonathan Nye, Louisa illustrates the conflict regarding marriage which Lee Edwards and Arlyn Diamond describe as the "tension between social duty and psychological integrity" (13).

Besides these modern qualities, Louisa exemplifies quintessential New England characteristics: courage in the face of overwhelming opposition, determination, strength of conviction, and independence, among others. Despite her family's poverty, her grandfather's emerging senility and her mother's fragile health, Louisa—against her mother's wishes—is determined not to pursue a courtship with Jonathan Nye even though an eventual marriage would bring significant economic relief to the family's plight. Louisa asserts her individuality and independence by rejecting outright Jonathan's overtures. Although she avoids opportunities to get to know Jonathan better, she stands by her initial convictions regarding this suitor: she simply doesn't like him and nothing—not even the dire economic straits of her family—will change her mind. And she argues her case convincingly with her mother:

"I'd like to know what you've got against him," she [Louisa's mother] said often to Louisa.

"I ain't got anything against him."

"Why don't you treat him different, then, I want to know?"

"I don't like him." Louisa said "like" shamefacedly, for she meant love, and dared not say it.

"*Like!* Well, I don't know nothin' about such likin's as some pretend to, an' I don't want to. If I see anybody is good an' worthy, I like 'em, an' that's all there is about it."

"I don't—believe that's the way you felt about—father," said Louisa, softly, her young face flushed red.

(395)

Freeman's portrayal of Louisa as a strong, independent, and proud individual is one which modern readers readily identify with and admire. Furthermore, her actions reflect what Emily Dickinson would have referred to as living "New Englandly": strong-willed, independent, and proud—manifestations, according to Perry Westbrook, of "the Puritan will at its best" (68). Certainly, the evocativeness of Freeman's gifts as story teller permit the traditional interpretation of Louisa as the New England pillar of strength as well as the contemporary view of liberation; however, the richness of Freeman's creative abilities cannot be limited simply to these, albeit important, interpretations. On another level, the story poses the problem of madness.[4] Good as the recent criticism has been, none has examined this aspect of Freeman's fiction.[5] Freeman herself validates such an interpretation through statements she made about her novel *Pembroke* (1894), statements that pertain as well to her fiction in general. In the "Introductory Sketch" to the Biographical Edition (1899), she noted that "*Pembroke* was originally intended as a study of the human will in several New England characters, in *different phases of disease and abnormal development*" (iii, italics mine). To her, "abnormal" means characters with wills developed past the reasonable limits of nature. Clearly, "abnormal" appropriately describes many characters in Freeman's fiction world.

For example, who can forget Sarah Penn? As the defiant woman in **"The Revolt of Mother"** (1891) who has waited patiently through forty years of marriage for a new home which her husband had long ago promised, Sarah finally revolts and moves her family and household possessions into the new barn which her husband has built to house livestock he neither needs nor owns on the site designated for Mother's future home. Another of Freeman's memorable but also eccentric characters surely is Louisa Ellis in **"The New England Nun"** (1891). Having been faithful to a promise of marriage made to Joe Daggett fourteen years earlier when he left to seek his fortune in Australia, Louisa discovers on his return that the quiet life of spinsterhood, daily use of her fine china that even her rural neighbors whisper about, and her obsession for a spotless house and neatly folded clothes is preferable to marriage with an adventurer and rugged male who leaves dust tracks where he walks in her immaculate house. Similar abnormal behavior appropriately describes Marcus Woodman in **"A Conflict Ended"** (1887) who sits in protest on the church steps during Sunday services for ten long years, having vowed never to enter the church if the prospective minister whom Marcus rejected as not being "doctrinal" were selected by the church elders.

On the surface, the actions of the characters in these stories can be explained, rationalized, and justified. To a distant observer, in fact, the behavior may even be considered amusing and comic, yet upon reflection something has snapped within these characters; their eccentric behavior is extreme to say the least. Shouldn't they be considered mad, using that term, for purposes of discussion, loosely and as a reference to what Philip Martin depicts in *Mad Women in Romantic Writing* as "the range of mental conditions in which what is accepted as normal behaviour is suspended or disrupted" (1)? Lillian Feder's and Otto Friedrich's observations of madness also seem applicable to character actions in Freeman's fiction. According to Feder in *Madness in Literature,* madness is that "state . . . in which unconscious processes predominate over conscious ones to the extent that they control them and determine perceptions of and responses to experience that, judged by prevailing standards of logical thought and relevant emotion, are confused and inappropriate" (5). In an amplification, Otto Friedrich in his *Going Crazy: An Inquiry into Madness in Our Time,* cites the following criteria for insanity: ". . . a breakdown in the machinery of perception, or a breakdown in the rational mind's ability to receive and combine perceptions and to make judgments from them. And a sense of helplessness. And panic" (16). More than just defiance, stubbornness, and fierce New England independence and individuality are exemplified through the actions of these Freeman characters.

Despite our ability to justify and perhaps even explain the actions of Sara Penn, Louisa Ellis, and Marcus Woodman, their behavior is certainly unusual and eccentric for their time. Judged by prevailing community standards, to use Feder's definition, their actions unquestionably are confused and inappropriate. Because of the subtle and evolutionary change of these characters from the world of predictable and normal behavior, Freeman may delude her readers into perceiving such actions and characters as merely eccentric. Upon closer examination, however, we perceive the suspension or disruption of normal behavior. In the case of **"Louisa,"** is that story only about an independent and liberated New England woman, or does it, too, involve the study of disintegration of personality?[6]

At the outset of the story, Louisa's actions—as in Freeman's previously discussed stories—seem on the one hand extreme yet on the other hand possibly credible. As is typical of Freeman's other stories, the move from credibility to disintegration is as in real life: gradual and slow. Perhaps because of the gradualness of the characters' descent into madness, readers are left with the sense of merely eccentric behavior. Since the characters are unusual to begin with, on the surface they seem only more so at the end. Nonetheless, on closer examination, what has been accepted normal behavior is clearly *disrupted and abnormal*. Similar to her other stories, Freeman's **"Louisa"** serves effectively to illustrate the ever-so-gradual disruption or breakdown of the once normal behavior.

The story opens with an obvious on-going mother-daughter argument as Louisa's mother presses her case for Jonathan Nye as marriage material while Louisa rests briefly from her nearly-finished task of planting potatoes. She is understandably upset with her grandfather when he enters their modest New England home and proudly presents the pail of seed potatoes he has just uprooted. Frustrated as she is, Louisa knows, however, that her grandfather's behavior is only symptomatic of his senility. He means no ill will. The potatoes simply have to be replanted, and because of the frailty of her mother's health, the task is Louisa's. Obviously, Louisa is frustrated with her grandfather's behavior; however, she is just as proud of her accomplishment of having planted two-thirds of their acre potato field as her grandfather was in uprooting it. Furthermore, now that Louisa has lost her teaching job of eight years, the economic burden of providing for her mother and grandfather from this one acre of poor New England soil is even greater. In any event, we understand Louisa's emotions and are sympathetic with her determination to replant the entire large potato field that same spring day. Similarly, we understand why she ignores her mother's call for supper at 6:00 P.M.: her day has been frustrating and she needs to finish her planting. In addition, she senses rain on the wind and recognizes that no planting can be done the next day.

Even Louisa's actions later that summer seem credible. As determined as she had been about replanting the large potato field earlier in the spring, she is equally determined regarding her family's independence, even if that means doing tasks not usually associated with a New England woman. For example, Louisa prepares for the winter by chopping wood on a neighbor's woodlot and then repaying that neighbor by working for his wife:

The Brittons had been and were in sore straits. All they had in the world was this little house with the acre of land. Louisa's meagre school money had bought their food and clothing since her father died. Now it was almost starvation for them. Louisa was struggling to wrest a little sustenance from their stony acre of land, toiling like a European peasant woman, sacrificing her New England dignity. Lately she had herself split up a cord of wood which she had bought of a neighbor, paying for it in installments with work for his wife.

(394)

In almost imperceptible stages, however, Louisa's behavior changes. From a combination of circumstances—the death of her father, the senility of her grandfather, the frail health of her mother, the loss of her teaching position and the rapidly deteriorating financial situation—Louisa is *forced* to assume caretaker and provider roles—or both the traditional female and male roles. Early in the story it's apparent that Louisa's independence, strong will and determination make her unfit for the standard female role of domesticity. Furthermore, that same opening—Louisa's pride in having nearly completed the outdoor physical work of planting potatoes—confirms Louisa's own rejection of the conventional female role. And her deepening tan as the weeks pass lends additional credence to her unconventional side.

In almost infinitesimal degrees, then, her quest for independence combined with her own strong will and determination leads her (at least to her immediate family) to unorthodox and masculine behavior. The wood-chopping episode provides a good example of what must be established and rather well-defined New England sex roles. On the one hand, chopping wood is clearly a man's job, a job that Louisa demonstrates she can do; on the other hand, working for a neighbor's wife to pay for the wood she cut clearly exemplifies the traditional female role. At this point, the roles are rather sharply delineated, and Louisa successfully plays both. Moreover, her dual roles appear to be tolerated. Later in the story, however, as Louisa increasingly assumes a more masculine role, her mother becomes increasingly intolerant of such behavior.

Late in the summer and much to the chagrin of her mother, Louisa does haying for a neighbor. Her mother's outrage is apparent when Louisa returns from the field, face burning and her wet dress clinging to her arms and shoulders: "'Rakin' hay with the men?' . . . Mrs. Britton had turned white. She sank into a chair. 'I can't stan' it nohow,' she moaned. 'All the *daughter* I've got'" (398, italics mine). In response, Louisa acknowledges her behavior change: "Why can't I rake hay as well as a man? Lots of women do such things, *if nobody round here does*" (398, italics mine). At this point, Louisa acknowledges her changed gender role and admits as well that by community standards her behavior is even unconventional. Her defensive response for this behavior only seems rational and, as Otto Friedrich explains in *Going Crazy: An Inquiry into Madness in Our Time,* a breakdown in the machinery of perception or the ability to combine perceptions and to make rational judgments based on them has occurred (16). Clearly in rejecting her mother's ideal of domesticity and marriage—the conventional female roles[7]—and opting instead for the unconventional role of rugged physical labor usually associated with men, Louisa's perceptions of gender roles and acceptable behavior are awry.

Her increasingly eccentric behavior leads to her own isolation and contributes to the widening chasm within her own family. In her determination to go her own way, Louisa does things on her own terms. If planting potatoes, chopping wood, raking hay, and doing other rugged outdoor labor mean sweat and grime at the close of day, Louisa doesn't care. If such work means a tanline on Sundays when she changes from her grubby work clothes to Sunday finery which fails to cover the tanline, so be it. Nonetheless the "farmerlike" (masculine?) appearance of her only daughter does matter to her mother who, in seeking to keep a "daughter" and to camouflage the unconventional behavior, takes some old, wide lace from the bureau drawer and proudly announces: "'There, I'm goin' to sew this in your neck an' sleeves before you put your dress on. It'll cover up a little; it's wider than the ruffle'" (397).

Despite her personal determination and her masculine behavior, Louisa's physical efforts nonetheless are obviously inadequate. Just when the potato crop shows promise of providing a good harvest and adequate food for the months ahead, her grandfather once again destroys that potential, this time by mischievously plucking all the blossoms. Later, he does the same with the blossoming squash plants. Indeed, now their plight is desperate:

> There was nothing for dinner but the hot biscuits and tea. The fare was daily becoming more meagre. All Louisa's little hoard of school money was gone, and her earnings were very uncertain and slender. Their chief dependence for food through the summer was their garden, but that had failed them . . .

(398)

By August, financial disaster for the family seems apparent and starvation imminent when even porridge isn't available for Louisa's grandfather:

> One morning in August he [Louisa's grandfather] cried at the breakfast-table like a baby, because he wanted

his porridge, and Mrs. Britton pushed away her own plate with a despairing gesture.

(399)

How does Louisa respond at this point to the family's desperation? Certainly her judgment is seriously flawed, for her suggested resolution to her family's desperate dilemma is to place a mortgage on the house—the *final* and *only* security now remaining for her mother and grandfather. At this point, then, Louisa has arrived at Friedrich's next stage of madness: a feeling of general helplessness along with a sense of her own helplessness (16). Even her mother's angry reaction to the suggestion along with the raised specter of madness doesn't faze Louisa:

> Put a mortgage on this house an' by-an'-by not have a roof to cover us! *Are you crazy?* I tell you what 'tis, Louisa Britton, we may starve, your grandfather an' me, an' you can follow us to the graveyard over there . . .

(400, italics mine)

With the family on the brink of imminent starvation and economic collapse, Louisa confirms that she has lost touch with reality when, on one of the hottest days of the summer, she decides to seek help from her mother's brother who lives seven miles away. If the seven-mile trip on foot to her uncle's on one of summer's hottest days isn't itself adequate evidence of her impaired mental state, surely ignoring the reality that the families are not on speaking terms is. Clearly, Louisa exemplifies the final stage of Friedrich's definition: panic! Her lengthy trip on foot to a relative not on speaking terms with her family is sheer desperation.

Louisa's distorted perceptions and questionable judgment are further reinforced by additional quixotic behavior on this hot day when she refuses the opportunity to ride to her uncle's because the person offering the ride is one Jonathan Nye, her rejected suitor. Louisa has made her disinterest in Jonathan most obvious long before this hot August day. At this point, then, her acceptance of a ride from the previous would-be suitor could not possibly be misinterpreted. To accept a ride would only demonstrate civility and courtesy. Clearly, Louisa's eccentric behavior has removed her even from the realm of social conventions and decent human behavior. To cite Feder's observations in *Madness and Literature,* Louisa's behavior in this and other instances as judged by "prevailing standards . . . and relevant emotions is confused and inappropriate" (5). Moreover, her actions demonstrate how the once virtuous New England characteristics of independence, strong will and determination have been perverted and become instead obsessions in and for themselves.

And the twisted nature of Louisa's thinking continues as she walks home from her uncle's in the blistering heat with the food he has grudgingly offered her. Because she cannot carry all of the food at the same time, the trip back to her home takes twice as long and is easily double the actual seven-mile one-way distance since she must carry as much food as she can as far as she can, then return to get the rest, carry it and continue her trip in this alternate backtracking and leapfrogging fashion. Even Freeman's narration of this episode conveys comparable skepticism of Louisa's condition:

> Her head was swimming, but she kept on. Her resolution was as immovable under the power of the sun as a rock. Once in a while she rested for a moment under a tree, but she soon arose and went on. It was like a pilgrimage, and the Mecca at the end of the burning, desert-like road was her own maiden independence.
>
> (404-05)

Louisa's ideals of determination, perseverance, and independence have become obsessions in and for themselves. Seemingly, her quest for independence has turned fanatical. Surely the quest for independence exemplifies what for her becomes a culminating but futile gesture of masculine strength, independence, and superiority. Instead of a religion of caring and giving as her mother and community standards would dictate, Louisa's Mecca is a self-serving shrine of her own strong will and independence.

Louisa's quest not just for independence but "maiden independence" has driven her from a sense of community with her family and those around her to isolation from them. In the process of the story, as she becomes increasingly determined in her independence, her behavior becomes more eccentric. Clearly, her final actions demonstrate her desperation. However, in looking back to the beginning, it seems rather easy to trace the path of Louisa's actions from apparently normal behavior to aberration. As her family's desperation becomes greater, she loses sight of her mother and grandfather and their condition to focus fanatically and obsessively on maintaining her own independence and maidenhood.

And the independence that Louisa pursues fanatically for herself cannot be a result of the mother-daughter conflict and Louisa's stubborn determination in reaction to her mother's rather obstinate pressing of the Louisa-Jonathan Nye courtship. If Louisa were sixteen years old, her conflict and rebellion with her mother might be explicable in terms of the universal parent-child conflict in coming of age; however, at twenty-four years of age, Louisa's behavior can only be considered less than realistic. Furthermore, her rejection of Jonathan Nye on the basis of not "liking" him scarcely seems reasoned, as the narrator implies:

> Louisa had never seen anybody whom she would have preferred to Jonathan Nye. There was no other marriageable young man in the place. She had only her dreams which she had in common with other girls.
>
> (396)

Apart from rejecting her mother's opinion concerning Jonathan Nye, Louisa rejects as well even the peer assessment of Nye. In her conversation with a friend early on the day of the seven-mile, one-way walk to her uncle's, Louisa again rejects evaluation:

> The other girl, who was larger and stouter than Louisa, [with] a sallow, unhealthy face, looked at her curiously. "I don't see why you wouldn't have him," said she. "I should have thought you'd jump at the chance."
>
> "Should you if you didn't like him, I'd like to know?"
>
> "I'd like him if he had such a nice house and as much money as Jonathan Nye," returned the other girl.
>
> (402)

From beginning to end, aren't Louisa's actions suspect of someone not facing reality? Doesn't Louisa act in a rather adolescent manner? Doesn't she retreat from the real world to the security of childish dreams? And isn't fantasy confirmed by the ending? Now, as Louisa relaxes and recovers from her exhausting trip of more than twenty miles from her uncle's, she ponders her environment and her self:

> A dewy coolness was spreading over everything. The air was full of bird calls and children's voices. Now and then there was a shout of laughter. Louisa leaned her head against the door-post. The house was quite near the road. Some one passed—a man carrying a basket. Louisa glanced at him, and recognized Jonathan Nye by his gait. He kept on down the road toward the Moselys', and Louisa turned again from him to her sweet, mysterious, girlish dreams.
>
> (403)

In girlish dreams, then, Louisa discovers a safe, non-threatening "reality."

In many respects, isn't Louisa's madness a classic example of the dilemma faced by the nineteenth-century female?[8] Louisa as madwoman becomes a possible footnote in the thorough study of this topic by Gilbert and Gubar in *The Madwoman in the Attic*. According to them, even "the most apparently conservative and decorous women writers obsessively create fiercely independent characters who seek to destroy all the patriarchal structures which both their authors and their authors' submissive heroines seem to accept as inevitable. Of course, by projecting their rebellious impulses not into their heroines but into mad or monstrous women (who are suitably punished in the course of the novel or poem), female authors dramatize their own self-division, their desire both to accept the strictures of patriarchal society and to reject them" (77-78). In rejecting the traditional and conventional role of the female that her mother and community would prefer for her, Louisa embraces the masculine role, a role, however, that her society rejects as unacceptable for her. In short, Louisa, in rejecting one role and being rejected by the other role, is left with no role—or rather the synonymous roles of the retreat to childish dreams and madness.

Notes

1. Mary Wilkins Freeman, "Louisa," in Mary E. Wilkins' *A New England Nun and Other Stories,* 384-406. All further references to Freeman's fiction are to this edition.

2. Alice Glarden Brand in "Mary Wilkins Freeman: Misanthropy as Propaganda" is correct in observing that nineteenth-century society "placed a premium on marriage, self-control, and impassiveness" (84)—ideas Louisa rejects. Brand also points out that as Freeman herself becomes angrier and bolder, so did her female characters. Such is the case with Louisa.

3. Victoria Aarons' essay deals with the role of women and the treatment of marriage in selected fiction of Freeman and Susan Glaspell; however, she also includes in her discussion general observations regarding themes by female writers in late nineteenth-century and early twentieth-century American fiction.

4. Although Freeman was born and raised in Randolph, Massachusetts, a typical manufacturing community, successful in the 1850s for producing shoes for export to Australia, the town fell on hard times in the 1860s, prompting the family's move to Brattleboro, Vermont, in 1867, where her father opened a mercantile store. In Brattleboro, the family settled near the Vermont Insane Asylum, a place undoubtedly influential in her later life as she created characters for her fiction. For a discussion of her years in Randolph and Brattleboro, see Westbrook, revised edition, 5-13, and Foster, 24-40. Although both writers indicate the close proximity of the Wilkins' Brattleboro home—just forty yards north—to the Vermont Insane Asylum, neither makes the association or connection I make concerning the recurrent theme of madness in her early fiction. Interesting, in fact, is Foster's note that although Freeman talked in later life about the various houses where she had lived, she *never* mentioned the family home in Brattleboro. His closing observation regarding that failure to talk about the Brattleboro home is also revealing: "conceivedly it was associated with her first glimpses of *psychic terror*" (26, italics mine).

5. The idea of madness as it pertains to Freeman's writing has been neglected in critical scholarship of her work and at best only touched upon peripherally. In an unpublished doctoral dissertation, for example, Leah Blatt Glasser uses Freeman's fiction as an illumination of her life, exploring themes of repression and rebellion, central to her fiction, and connecting them with Freeman's own ambivalence of adhering to existing Puritan customs and codes she grew up with and yet personally rebelling against their restrictiveness and repressiveness. Glasser notes the characters' safety of self-imprisonment at the same time of their rebellion and desire for release. Perry Westbrook in his revised edition of *Mary Wilkins Freeman* notes disturbances Freeman experienced in 1897 and after, during her engagement and later marriage to Dr. Charles Freeman. "During this period her sleep was disturbed by nightmares, and she had to resort to sedatives in such quantities that she became partly addicted to them. She needed now to sleep near someone who would hear her during dreams and arouse her from them. In her waking reveries she seems somehow to have pictured herself as a renegade from God's ordering of things—a rebel and an outcast" (107). My focus is upon Freeman's fiction written earlier than the documented period when she personally experienced emotional disturbances, a period that needs critical examination as it relates to her literature.

6. Examining "Louisa" according to concepts of madness as defined by Martin, Feder, and Friedrich above, the central character's growing madness becomes apparent in Freeman's short story.

7. In what he labels the mentality of submission, John Stuart Mill in *The Subjection of Women* comments as follows regarding the expected role of women in the nineteenth century: "All women are brought up from their earliest years in the belief that their ideal of character is the very opposite of that of men: not self-will, and government by self-control, but submission and yielding to the control of others" (16).

8. A story with some parallels to this one is "The Yellow Wallpaper" by Charlotte Perkins Gilman; "Louisa" and "The Yellow Wallpaper" both deal with madness. In Gilman's story, the central character begins in a state of postpartum depression and never recovers. Confinement to and isolation in an upstairs bedroom, a room previously used as a nursery, as treatment prescribed by her doctor-husband actually drive the central character mad. By the end of the story, when total madness is apparent, she too reverts to the world of a girl—more specifically in this case, a child—and becomes the child-woman previously perceived as

trapped within the yellow wallpaper but free when the central character peels off the wallpaper. In assuming the identity of the woman freed from the wallpaper but still confined to the upstairs bedroom and former nursery, the central character, now completely mad, reverts to the role of the child—a harmless being, much like the girl Louisa at the end of Freeman's story—by monotonously creeping along the four walls on the floor.

Works Cited

Aarons, Victoria. "A Community of Women: Surviving Marriage in the Wilderness." *Portraits of Marriage in Literature*. Eds. Anne C. Hargrove and Maurine Magliocco. Macomb: Western Illinois UP, 1984. 141-49.

Brand, Alice Glarden. "Mary Wilkins Freeman: Misanthropy as Propaganda." *New England Quarterly* 50 (1977): 83-100.

Edwards, Lee and Arlyn Diamond, eds. *American Voices, American Women*. New York: Bard Books, 1973.

Feder, Lillian. *Madness in Literature*. Princeton: Princeton UP, 1980.

Foster, Edward. *Mary E. Wilkins Freeman*. New York: Hendricks House, 1956.

Freeman, Mary Wilkins. *Pembroke*. Biographical Edition. New York: Harper, 1899.

Friedrich, Otto. *Going Crazy: An Inquiry into Madness in Our Time*. New York: Simon and Schuster, 1976.

Gilbert, Sandra M. and Susan Gubar. *The Madwoman in the Attic*. New Haven: Yale UP, 1979.

Gilman, Charlotte Perkins. "The Yellow Wallpaper." *Harper American Literature*. Ed. Donald McQuade, et al. Vol. 2. New York: Harper and Row, 1987. 2 vols. 757-68.

Glasser, Leah Blatt. "'In a Closet Hidden': The Life and Works of Mary Wilkins Freeman." *DAI* 43 (1983): 3595A. Brown University.

Martin, Philip W. *Mad Women in Romantic Writing*. New York: St. Martin's, 1987.

Mill, John Stuart. *The Subjection of Women*. Cambridge: Harvard UP, 1970.

Westbrook, Perry D. *Mary Wilkins Freeman*. New York: Twayne, 1967.

———. *Mary Wilkins Freeman*. Rev. ed. New York: Twayne, 1988.

Wilkins, Mary E. *A New England Nun and Other Stories*. New York: Harper, 1919.

Wood, Ann Douglas. "The Literature of Impoverishment: The Women Local Colorists in America." *Women's Studies* 1 (1972): 3-40.

Monika M. Elbert (essay date fall 1993)

SOURCE: Elbert, Monika M. "Mary Wilkins Freeman's Devious Women, *Harper's Bazar,* and the Rhetoric of Advertising." *Essays in Literature* 20, no. 2 (fall 1993): 251-72.

[*In the following essay, Elbert centers on Freeman's response to the male-oriented tone of advertising in her stories, citing specific ads that ran in* Harper's Bazar *(now* Harper's Bazaar*) during her career.*]

> Harriet had never told a deliberate falsehood before in her life, but this seemed to her one of the tremendous exigencies of life which justify a lie. She felt desperate. If she could not contrive to deceive him in some way, the man might turn directly around and carry Charlotte and her back to the "Home."
>
> —Freeman's **"A Mistaken Charity"**[1]

This short epigraph from one of Mary Wilkins Freeman's stories establishes a paradigm for much of her fiction: woman needs to deceive man because she herself has been deceived by man, and if she does not succeed in a truthful-sounding lie, she will be returned to the "Home." In the case of **"A Mistaken Charity,"** the threat to woman is a return to the almshouse, but in most other cases, it is imprisonment in the domestic sphere; in either case, woman is sabotaged because of her economic dependence on man.

In her sociological study *Women and Economics,* Charlotte Perkins Gilman aptly describes the condition of women in the late nineteenth century as consumers; indeed, she discusses at great length the process by which man has controlled woman—trapped her into the image of "the priestess of the temple of consumption . . . the limitless demander of things to use up" (120). Gilman argues:

> the consuming female, debarred from any free production, unable to estimate the labor involved in the making of what she so lightly destroys, and her consumption limited mainly to those things which minister to physical pleasure, *creates a market* for sensuous decoration and personal ornament, for all that is luxurious and enervating, and for a false and capricious variety in such supplies, which operates as a most deadly check to true industry and true art.
>
> (120, emphasis mine)

As the idle buyer of man's marketplace baubles, woman herself becomes an extension of those baubles: nice to look at, but superfluous. Or, as Gilman describes the skewed relationship between the sexes: woman's "false economic position" "sexualizes our industrial relation and commercializes our sex-relation" (121).

It is not coincidental that advertisers had become a powerful force in the shaping of the "ideal" woman, the "types" of beauty adorning the covers of *Harper's Bazar,* by the time Gilman was writing her treatise in 1898.[2] In fact, if one looks at the history of advertising in America, one sees rather alarming ways that the mass market was shaping ideals of womanhood and creating consumer-women. As Jennifer A. Wicke states in her analysis of the influence of advertising on Henry James's fiction, "not only is the American woman marketed globally in order to sell the products of capitalism, but she is also marketed to" (117). From its inception, American advertising was an attempt to render woman a consumer, one whose powerlessness as an active participant in the marketplace was offset by her buying power within the family itself. For example, J. Walter Thompson, an early promoter of magazine advertising (for such magazines as *Godey's* and *Peterson's*), was amazed that women's journals proved a favorable medium even for products bought by men; yet, it was precisely because the idle women would be perusing these journals repeatedly (since the journals would be lying around the coffee tables, at least for a month) and it was "often the lady of the house who made the household purchases" (Fox 30) that Thompson enjoyed advertising success in the 1870s.

By the 1880s, the period in which Mary Wilkins Freeman's career was launched, journals were able to reduce the price while increasing the number of subscriptions because of the increased sales of advertisements; the *Ladies' Home Journal,* for example, which "displayed more than twice as much advertising than any other woman's magazine," could cut its annual subscription, so that by 1900, its founder Cyrus Curtis could boast "that it reached a million subscribers" (Strasser 91).[3] Indeed, as economists have noted, "the role of the publisher changed from being a seller of a product to consumers to being a gatherer of consumers for the advertisers" (Goodrum 31).

Nathaniel Fowler, who wrote one of the first books of "advertising counsel" (Presbrey 310), reiterated this stance when he advised that "advertisements should have the appearance of that generous, openhearted truthfulness which carries with it conviction and which makes a friend of the reader" (Presbrey 311); like the narrator who tried to make his fictions appear real, the advertiser had to give a semblance of truth. Fowler was also convinced that women were more gullible, that they could be implicated in the lie more easily than men, but that ironically, they were better purchasers. The question remains, of course, whether they were purchasing of necessity or out of values assigned to them by men. Indeed, for Fowler it was nearly a woman's moral duty to be a wise consumer for her husband:

> The better the woman, the more directly she is interested in her husband's stockings, his hats and other things. . . .
>
> The woman can buy better articles, from spool cotton to ulster overcoats, for less money than the average man can buy with more money.
>
> The average man doesn't know about those things that he thinks he knows about.
>
> (Presbrey 317)

Was a man really duped then because he was an illiterate reader of advertisements? Fowler counters: "Although substantially all men are readers of advertisements, and are directed by advertising argument, an advertisement has not one twentieth the weight with a man that it has with a woman of equal intelligence and the same social status" (Presbrey 317). Because he could not be moved by the advertisements, in the end a man came out the emotional victor. Fowler concludes with a definition of true womanhood in terms of her obsession with advertisements: "A woman who would not read advertisements would *not* be a woman, consequently all women read advertisements" (Presbrey 318).[4]

Though Freeman wrote only a few stories for *Ladies' Home Journal,* the journal with the most ads for women, she did find in *Harper's* a lucrative market, first (from 1880-1892) in *Harper's Bazar* and later in *Harper's Monthly,* a genteel literary monthly magazine which did not resort to advertising. While showing a less ostensible interest in advertising than *Ladies Home Journal* (the ads were found at the back and were fewer than the many ads scattered through *LHJ*), *Harper's Bazar* nonetheless was targeted to women obsessed with fashion, beauty, and flirtation. One might ask how Freeman's simple stories of New England slices of life—the drab New England local color settings which critics love to discuss in dismissing her—would be of interest to the fashionable, worldly, and idle salon lady reading *Harper's Bazar.* Certainly, the idleness is juxtaposed with the diligent nature and industrious ways of Freeman's positive characters, but certainly, too, the domestic prop or fashionable dress item becomes the icon for both the Freeman heroine and the *Harper's Bazar* peruser of ads.

Laurence Hutton, an early critic of Freeman's work, wrote that "Miss Wilkins in simple, every-day Yankee tells the story of simple, every-day Yankee life at Cross Roads and Flats in rural New England and at the present time" (71).[5] Moreover, he praised the characters as "common folk": "tin peddlers, deacons, traders, tall, bony, shambling men, thin, brokenspirited women, with scant skirts and slipshod heels; milkers of cows and hewers of wood; with hardly enough education among them all to make one orthodox minister or one district school-marm" (71). This gallery of rustics, this motley crew—though motivated by economic enterprises—is unlikely material for the fashion-plates of *Harper's Bazar.* So what is Wilkins Freeman's appeal to the genteel reader?

One Freeman critic, Leah Blatt Glasser, has pointed out that Freeman was "influenced at times by her editors' demands of 'gentility' in accordance with their sense of the codes of female behavior at the turn of the century. . . . Consequently Freeman's endings often couch rebellious content in acceptable, domestic scenes of female submission" (Heath 302). Yet Freeman is even more subversive than Glasser suggests, for at issue is not so much woman's domestic role as is woman's productive, economic role. Ostensibly, Freeman's heroines, though they might be unglamorous country women, are as enamored of the newest styles as the fashionable counterparts in the essays on high fashion in *Harper's.* Thus, models, female audience, fashion reporters, and Freeman's heroines all have this in common—the love affair with a commodity. However, by the end of Freeman's tales, the enlightened heroine learns to despise the commodity and to find pleasure or solace in something beyond consumer culture—whether that be through sisterhood (e.g., **"A Mistaken Charity"**), economic self-reliance (e.g., **"A New England Nun"**), or triumph over the man who would deceive her (e.g., **"Old Woman Magoun"**). The unenlightened heroine falls prey to sentimental ideas of patriarchal religion and duty or succumbs to a sentimentalized death (e.g., **"A Village Singer," "A Poetess," "Sister Liddy"**). In many ways, the male mastermind who creates the need for a woman's market is debunked and outwitted by the positive heroine's actions, and so Freeman quite subversively undermines the objective of *Harper's Bazar* and certainly of the ads which support it. So, the *Harper's* critic who smilingly discusses Freeman's "simplicity, purity, and quaintness" is missing Freeman's argument with consumerism.

Freeman herself was very much a product of her economic situation. Her family was forced to move from Randolph, Massachusetts to Brattleboro, Vermont, in 1867, when Mary was fifteen, because of her father's failing business. Significantly, because Brattleboro had been a fashionable health resort (the water cure) for many years prior to the Wilkins' arrival in 1867, it was a bustling city that "boasted seven hotels and more than thirteen boarding houses. It also had more than its share of dry good merchants, grocers, tailors, jewelers, opticians, attorneys, surgeons, physicians, druggists, and apothecaries as well as bookbinders, booksellers, and stationers" (Kendrick 46). Though she later returned to Randolph (1883-1902), Mary

Wilkins seems to have been scarred by this combination of economic hardship and economic plenty. In a letter of 1885, when she had returned to Randolph, she describes a "boiler accident in a manufacturing shop" realistically but sympathetically, as she also adds that she has been nursing a sick woman:

> It is so sad; there are seven children and not much money. She has heart disease, and is suffering terribly.
>
> The poor thing has probably overworked, and overworked, when she was far from well. No body knows how some of these country women, with large families, and small purses do work. O they are the ones I would help, if I were rich. Nothing, hardly, touches me so much.

> (Kendrick 62)

The basic contradiction in Wilkins's own attitude towards commodities is expressed in an interview for *Ladies' Home Journal* (Sept. 1903); curiously, she says that if she were wealthy, she would not give "to the tenement-house poor" but rather "to the unacknowledged poor," whom she describes as "those . . . who are not actually suffering physically for what money can do, but who have much mental distress over the prospect of an unprovided-for-old-age, and who lack the little amenities which redeem life from a sordid grind" (10).

Her interview ends with an affirmation of material goods, even of luxuries: "I should even like to buy some pretty things for young girls who would have to do without them and hunger for them. I should give to old people those pleasures of which they have dreamed all their lives, and of which they have been deprived because all their money had to go for the stern necessities" (10). Certainly, Freeman's ambivalence towards amenities and necessities could account for the mixed messages of her stories. And that ambivalence was shared by other female writers of this time period, most notably by Sarah Orne Jewett. In "The Flight of Betsey Lane" Jewett depicts a woman, enamored of commodity culture, who escapes from the poorhouse (very much like Freeman's poorhouses in **"Sister Liddy"** or **"A Mistaken Charity"**) to explore the world of the Philadelphia Centennial, where she sees "di'monds . . . as big as pigeon's eggs" and where she purchases souvenirs for the other aging women at the poorhouse. The split between wealth and poverty, between man's Centennial Exposition and woman's poorhouse, is extreme and reflects the different spheres of man's/woman's work and tastes. Yet, the Philadelphia Centennial Exposition (1876), with its myriad display of products—an advertiser's dream of 30,000 exhibits—for the gawking visitor to admire and crave, might well be the emblem of the late nineteenth-century American obsession with material goods.

Addressing an audience preoccupied with material goods did not at all please Freeman, but her own financial needs compelled her. In a letter to her editor Mary Louise Booth, she complained, "To day I have written a little tale, concluding with a neat allusion to church for *The Congregationalist.* I wouldn't write these if I did not like the money. However it only takes a very little while. But it does not seem to me just right, to write things of that sort on purpose to get money, and please an editor" (Kendrick 66).

This ambivalence toward sentimentalized popular writing became the subject for a story Freeman wrote for *Harper's Monthly,* **"A Poetess"** (July 1890). In the story Mrs. Caxton, who has lost her little boy, asks Betsey to write an obituary poem for him, feeling that this favor will help her economically: "You folks that write poetry wouldn't have a single thing to eat growin' if they were left alone" (376). Betsey is a more than willing poetess for this occasion, and, looking like "the very genius of gentle, old-fashioned, sentimental poetry" (378), she withdraws into her room to write. The narrator is rather suspicious of her writing, implying that there were lines "wherein flowers rhymed sweetly with vernal bowers, home with beyond the tomb, and heaven with even" (378). Her work niche is adorned with the typical accoutrements of *Harper's,* among them "a framed sampler," "a steel engraving of a female head taken from some old magazine," and "vases and tumblers of flowers" (378). Though we do not hear the words of her poem, we can imagine that it is sentimental tripe, and as "heavy and sweet" as the air in her room. Meanwhile, the bereaved mother has Betsey's poems printed up, and Betsey imagines future financial success as a writer. She has been frugal in the past, writing her first draft on "backs of old letters and odd scraps of paper" (379). When she hears Mrs. Caxton's praise, which to Betsey sounds as good as the acceptance "by one of the great magazines" (381), she imagines a time when she will even be able to afford a frame for her first successful poem. Still fantasizing about the cost of a frame, she is interrupted by Mrs. Caxton, who has now changed her tune: she has heard the rumor that the minister, who himself has published in a magazine, has called all of Betsey's poetry "a dreadful waste of time" (383).

Totally disheartened, Betsey burns all her poetry and begins to will her own death. Meanwhile, the community of gossiping women try to cheer her up by bringing her "little delicacies." Indeed, this is a story weighed down by economy and commodity: Betsey Dole is living off a meager inheritance from her father, and Mrs. Caxton has nervous fits about the dusty weather spoiling her good "black dress" and "black bonnet" and announces at one point that she really needs a raincoat to save her clothes. And ironically,

but perhaps fittingly, in a most pathetic way, Betsey keeps the ashes of her poetry in a "blue sugarbowl." In her deathbed confession to the minister, she stuns the bewildered poet, by saying "I found out it wa'nt worth nothin'" (386). To Betsey the hallmark of a good poem would have been its publication in one of the "great magazines" (like *Harper's Bazar*), but she does not realize that for the most part, they publish the same type of sentimental sappy poetry. Because the minister has published some of his poems "in a magazine," Betsey deems them good, successful ones, and her deathbed wish is for him to pen off some lines about her; failing to gain immortality as a poetess, she hopes to gain some stature as the object of a death poem, however sentimental that poem may be. Betsey has the last macabre laugh as the reader realizes that both she and the minister have written the same type of sentimental verse; indeed, Mrs. Caxton's earlier well meant suggestion to Betsey about the good minister's poems probably are similar to Freeman's attitude toward the "great" women's magazines: "Maybe them magazine folks jest took his for lack of something better. I'd like to have you sent that poetry there" (383).[6]

As one critic points out, Freeman "wrote to earn her living and as she understood her market, she made compromises at times" (Glasser, *Legacy* 41). This could explain why some of her stories—the sentimental, melodramatic ones—were not as successful in the way she wished them to be. When asked to give advice to aspiring female writers, Freeman recommended that they be true to themselves:

> She must not write to please an editor or a public incapable of being pleased with the best, because in that very long run of the world she will by so doing defeat her own ends. She will end by not pleasing, although she be hailed with acclamations at first. The applause will die and her audience be gone.
>
> (272)

If Freeman felt that the woman writer should be self-motivated and oblivious to public taste, she also attempted to demystify the reasons for writing. In fact, like heroines who are obsessed with the latest fashions, Freeman explained the motivation for writing rather materialistically: "a woman may write something for money with which *to buy a French hat*" (272, my emphasis).

Significant, too, in a discussion of Freeman's ambivalence to the publication market is that she had an affectionate, even intimate relationship with the editor of *Harper's Bazar,* Mary Louise Booth, going so far as to call her "Pussy Willow" and declaring her love for her (Kendrick 66), and that this camaraderie often centered on a discussion of woman's commodities, e.g., a new dress or needlework. Wilkins writes Booth, "I have a new blue dress, and I am going to send you a bib. Isn't it a pretty color? I want to embroider it, but I don't know" (Kendrick 66), and a few weeks later, "I am glad you like my dress" (Kendrick 68). Although creating a feeling of female bonding, this superficial banter in the shop talk between writer and editor is peculiar. But Booth was also a bundle of contradictions: she was one of the "fashionable feminists" of the 1850s who enjoyed the life of the salon—"the vehicle for the very best fashionable activity—good dinners, good wine" and good conversation initiated by the most "urbane and informed women" (Leach 239). In this way, Booth attempted to "establish standards of behavior for feminists and fashionables alike" (Leach 252).

With Booth as editor, *Harper's Bazar* was inevitably also a journal of mixed messages. For example, interspersed between the stories by such contemporary writers as Freeman, Hardy, and James were articles on charity work (e.g., "A Novel Way of Observing Easter" 11 April 1891, written by one Frances J. Dyer), on the one hand, and the latest spring fashions from Paris, illustrated with glamorous corseted and bustled women, on the other ("Paris Fashions," 30 March 1886), or the newest fads in "Tennis Parties" (7 August 1886). And if Freeman seems peculiar company for Parisian fashion plates, certainly so does the urbane James.[7] Indeed, his articles on American women's speech and manners in *Harper's Bazar* (in a series between 1906-1907) were anything but approving of the fashionable cover girl of *Harper's*. Yet even more bizarre than the discrepancy between the flirtatious woman whom *Harper's* extolled and whom James despised was the extreme distance between Freeman's indigent heroines (who nonetheless had exorbitant tastes) and *Harper's* idle and complacent ladies of leisure. One of the most striking examples of this pathetic juxtaposition of wealth and poverty can be found in the 18 February 1887 issue, where the top column was "Corsages and Flowers for Evening Dresses" and the bottom column, "The Kitchen Girl's Wages" (136), written by an author with genteel sympathies who complains that house masters and mistresses have had to pay too much for their servants as of late (since the Civil War). This stunning—almost obscene—juxtaposition between real need and imagined need characterizes *Harper's Bazar*—its articles, illustrations, cartoons, and, ultimately, its advertisements. Ironies abound: *Harper's Bazar's* subtitle is *A Repository of Fashion, Pleasure, and Instruction,* but in one of the personal columns, we hear instruction to avoid the material realm of fashion:

> President Timothy Dwight, of Yale College, laments that the temptation to get money and spend it, to view it as the means of all good and the end of all desire, is continually becoming stronger and seemingly more irresistible. He assures his students that if they are to be a force in the world for the higher things as against the lower, they must show that material prosperity or wealth is not essential to happiness.
>
> (23 July 1887, 515)

Surely these words fell on the deaf ears of *Harper's* unheeding women readers.

And, finally, the ideal woman of *Harper's Bazar* appears to be both reactionary and moral—a throwback to a docile image of womanhood, certainly not the "new woman" of the late nineteenth century. In one unsigned article entitle "Pushing Women," the *Harper's* author critiques the materialistic, ambitious woman:

> The world is full of pushing women, who, not satisfied with the goods the gods have provided, are still reaching after something else. It does not follow that they are poor or obscure; they may drive in their carriages, have their names bruited about in every daily fashion report, live in ease and luxury, but still, if their nature is pushing, push they will, and will not be happy in any condition, even upon a throne. . . . However we may appreciate the pushing woman, her anxieties and patience, we do not care to know her. . . . And although she resembles a heroine of a novel, and we are amused by her difficulties, and her manoeuvres interest and instruct us, still we sympathize with her failure if we do not approve of her success.
>
> (17 Dec. 1887, 874)

The editor/author apparently does not see that her magazine is catering to this type of materialistic "pushing woman" who wants it all; indeed, the journal provides the wherewithal on how to achieve the golden looks and the model home.

Harper's Bazar was also intent upon making deception palatable, so that even the editorials seem to extol the virtues of untruth. In a short unsigned article entitled "Some People," for example, the author asserts that it is preferable to utter "pleasant" truths than unpleasant ones, "As if truths must be unpleasant to be true!" (*Harper's Bazar,* 7 February 1891). Keeping "unpleasant truths" concealed or disguised in the pleasantries of fashionable sentiment seemed to be the way.

If one were to look at a sampling of the ads in the back of *Harper's Bazar,* one could easily see the tension that such magazines created for woman: she was made to feel incomplete, unsatisfactory, and even neurotic. The images appeal to her vulnerabilities in matters of grooming, fashion, and beauty, and to her resignation of power to a limited role as buyer of cereals, patent medicines, and soaps for the household. A random sampling of ads gives a good sense of the pressures thrust upon women: "Lablache" face powder "for the fair sex" will remove and prevent "tan, freckles, pimples, irritation, and all blemishes of the skin"; moreover, it is designed for the woman who has aspirations to high society: "It supplies a want most sensibly felt by ladies of society"; and it promises to prolong the "bloom of youth," a necessary commodity for the sexualized market. "Mrs. Julian's Specific" guarantees the end of superfluous hair, without harm, without "tortorous electricity" or "any of the advertised poisonous stuffs." In addition, successful women often gave testimonials; cosmetics, like "Champlin's Liquid Pearl" used literary allusions, Keats's "A thing of Beauty is a joy forever," as well as testimonials from literary women to support their products; indeed, even Sarah Orne Jewett, in one "Champlin's Liquid Pearl" ad, testifies to the "excellency" of the cosmetic. For the domestic woman, ads promote "Granula" and "Anglo-Swiss Milk Food," made expressly for the infants and invalids of the family; "Roche's" herbal remedies for "hooping-cough croup"; "Cerealine Flakes," a most economical breakfast food for the family; the "Richmond Range" for comfort and convenience; the "Keystone Washer," which promises "less injury to clothes than any other in the world"; "Haviland & Co.'s China," a necessity for those women who would set "a handsome table"; the "Wilmot steam cooker," "used in the best hotels and now made simple for family use"; and for the woman who would enjoy a modicum of independence in her dress-making, the "Hall's Bazar Form," "a household necessity," "indispensable to ladies who do their own dressmaking," most especially for the woman who "knows how she wants a dress made, but sometimes the dressmaker will not understand and must be shown what is wanted." In the way of health potions and elixirs, "Cuticura," a family panacea, promises "a positive cure for every form of skin and blood disease from pimples to scrofula"; "Soden mineral pastilles" are advertised, with testimonials, to cure "diseases of the throat, chest, and lungs, and also . . . consumption"; "Tamar Indien Grillon" lozenges are meant for "constipation, loss of appetite, bile, headache, hemorrhoids, and cerebral congestion[!]"; and "Digestylin" offers a cure for everything from indigestion to vomiting in pregnancy to cholera! There are instruments with which to "curl or frizz" one's hair and bleaches to lighten one's hair. There are tonics for sleeplessness, powders for whiter teeth (which will make the difference between "pretty girls and plain girls"), "imperial hair regenerators," camouflaging creams for "ill-shaped or large Noses," "Mme. Velaro's" and "Palm Kosmeo" creams for unsightly wrinkles, Seeley's elastic abdominal belts for corpulency, and "Garfield's" teas for headaches, complexion, and constipation. If one did not feel neurotic, sick, inadequate, or downright ugly before opening the ad pages, one certainly did after a short perusal.

Fashionable gloves from Paris are also advertised, as are bridal outfits, tailor-made gowns from Paris and London, fur capes, "Regatta silks," undergarments, "Miller's parasols," designer fashions from Messrs. "Redfern" (ladies' tailors), and all varieties of corsets with which to distort women's bodies—from "Dr. Scott's Electric Corset" (which guarantees the "true French shape"), "Dr. Schelling's Health Preserving Corset," and "Madame Foy's Skirt Supporting Corset" to the "Judic Corset" (available in five styles and "suitable for all figures"), the "Yatisi Corset" (yielding to every movement of the wearer!), and the "patented improved Lotta Bustle" ("warranted to always regain its shape after pressure, no matter in what position the wearer may sit or recline"). Women literally felt pushed, prodded, and squeezed into the right form.

Moreover, *Harper's Bazar* itself was great for the fashion industry, filled as it was with articles and pictures of "New York Society Women," spring bonnets, Worth evening gowns, Paris fashions, fall spectaculars, and Christmas gowns, lace items, and frills. And to whet the consumer-woman's appetite, the magazine generally included a large center-fold portrait of women adorned with the seasonal fashions. The basic ingredient of the advertiser's success was the concoction of a lie—whether it was to deceive woman into thinking she needed cosmetics or new fashions to beautify herself, or to present a product as an elixir for the entire family's ills—from acne to blood diseases, from deafness to kidney disease. As one social critic says about the early years of advertising, "If the medicine ads were lies, how true were the clothing and real estate ads?" (Goodrum 29). What is more, the ads in *Harper's Bazar* fueled the competition that fashion created among women: as Frances E. Willard suggested in her book of advice for young women, *How to Win: A Book for Girls* (1887), women dressed for the sake of other women, or as she quotes from a Boston lawyer, "women do not dress so much to please men, but to escape the criticism or excite the envy of each other" (qtd. in Habegger 121).

In her stories, Freeman often emphasizes deception as the basis of the narrative (or male plot): the unraveling of the heroine's conflict occurs only when her lie has succeeded, and the catharsis occurs when she reveals the lie to her closest female friend or relative. It is useful at this point to outline a few of the cultural "plots" to make women consumers, and Freeman's feisty way of responding to these male plots through a female counterplot.

In the early stories which she wrote for *Harper's Bazar*, Freeman often portrayed women competing with each other: each wanted to be the proud possessor of the most beautiful object with which to adorn herself or her home. On the surface, these plots would correspond to the advertisers' wishes to manipulate women's taste for nice clothes and furnishings. In the most insidious way, though, women seem their own worst enemies, but one must recall the motivation behind their wanting these items. In **"A Gala Dress"** (*Harper's Bazar*, 14 July 1888), for example, we hear the story of two sisters who take turns wearing their Sunday best on public occasions: "They mended their old muslins and Thibets, and wore one dress between them for best, taking turns in going out" (152). They feel compelled to do so because of a prying, gossiping, fashion-conscious neighbor, who competes with them for center stage by wearing the nicest outfits. At a Fourth of July Celebration, the Sunday dress gets burned when one sister steps upon a smoldering firecracker, but to save the day, the sisters inherit a closet of silken dresses from an aunt; thus, they can both go visiting on the same day. This incident prompts, however, a confession on the part of the older sister, Elizabeth, who explains to her pesty neighbor that there was a reason for their never having appeared in public at the same time before: "You've been trying to find out things every way you could, and now I'll tell you. You've drove me to it. We had just one decent dress between us, an' Emily used to wear lace on it, an' I used to rip off the lace an' sew on black velvet when I wore it, so folks shouldn't know the difference" (159). This confession of deception prompts the friend to reveal her own lie: she would have been able to warn Emily of the accident to her dress, but she avoided telling her out of malicious pride; the final words of the story read: "I want to tell you—I see them firecrackers a-sizzlin' before Em'ly stepped in 'em" (161). This sort of deception among women is the basic pattern of Freeman's early stories. Critics often talk about female community in Freeman, but more often there is a tension about who has the best dresses, the nicest flowers, the most beautiful home.[8]

In **"Sister Liddy"** (*Harper's Bazar*, 9 March 1889), for example, a group of aging women in an almshouse are driven together by economic circumstances, but their bonding is a rather grotesque version of community. What is so striking is their rancor and boastfulness when it comes time to describe their accumulation of earthly wealth—a "Kaffeeklatsch" of the worst kind, but a daily habit they indulge themselves in. This gallery of grotesques brags in a similar fashion: one says, "I had a handsome blue silk when I was married" (171) and another, "I had a white one, drawn silk, an' white feathers on't, when I was married, and

they all said it was real becomin'n" (172). The bragging gradually intensifies: "I had a fitch tippet an' muff that cost twenty-five dollars an' a cashmere shawl" (172); another, "I had two cashmere shawls, an' my tippet cost fifty dollars"; and finally, another, as if to say babies also meant a lot in the intersecting boundaries between domestic life and marketplace, "My fust baby had an elegant blue cashmire cloak, all worked with silk as deep as that" (172). Polly Moss, the most dejected of the group, can finally no longer take the bragging, so she makes up her own story: "My sister Liddy was jest as handsome as a pictur'. . . . She was jest as fair as a lily—a good deal fairer than you ever was, Mis' Handy, an' she had long yaller curls a-hangin' clean down to her waist, an' her cheeks were jest as pink, an' she had the biggest blue eyes I ever see, an' the beautifulest leetle red mouth" (175). This language of diminutives is the artificially sweet stuff of *Harper's* articles, especially when it comes to a discussion of baby's wardrobe.

After Polly describes the physique of the perfect woman, a "type" of *Harper's* beauty embellishing covers and inserts of the journal, she goes through a catalogue of fashionable clothing: a black silk dress, a white cashmire shawl, white kid gloves, and a feather fan (175). Moreover, she describes her sister Liddy as a bride "in a blue silk dress, an' a black lace mantilly, an' a white bunnit trimmed with lutestring ribbon." This sister then moved into "a great big house with a parlor an' settin'-room, an' a room to eat in besides the kitchen"; the house was adorned with "real velvet carpets," "great pictur's in gilt frames," red velvet furniture, and large marble statues (176). Additionally, Liddy had a "hired girl" and a doting husband to cater to her. And, following the lead of the *Harper's* heroine, Liddy "had the beautifulest baby you ever see, an' she had a cradle with blue silk to rock him an, an' he had a white silk cloak, an' a lettle lace cap" (176). Of course, the story is a lie, as much as the advertiser's notion of the perfect beauty, as represented in *Harper's* cover girl. However, poor Polly needs to live with the subsequent feeling of guilt and inadequacy, and it is only on her deathbed that she confesses to the other women, "I ain't never had nothin'" (179). As we know from Gilman's treatise on the economic condition of women, such women as Polly—without the ornamentation of their sex and the commodities of reproduction, babies—were tantamount to nothing in this society, and it is no wonder that Polly expires with the thought that she "ain't never had nothin'." What makes this deathbed scene ever more pathetic is that an impoverished young girl who begrudgingly had spent some time at the almshouse rushes in to tell of her rescue at the exact moment of Polly's death. She exuberantly announces also that a husband has appeared who will buy her a house: "Charley has come. He's got a house already. He's going to marry me, an' take me home, an' take care of me" (178). Such had been the early dreams of the matrons and spinsters who now inhabit the almshouse—salvation in the form of domestic space (with home and husband commodified). The same folly is perpetuated by the young woman in the name of man, and the matrons of society are left out for good. So much for female bonding. And so much for continuity between generations of women; there are no daughter figures here to assuage the mothers' babbling about their children's baby clothes. The only daughter figure runs off with a man who will encourage her to be a consumer.

Sometimes the commodity as icon is seen more positively, as it becomes first a stepping stone and then a stumbling block on the woman's way to personal development.⁹ However, in this type of story, too, the action hinges around self-deception and finally, self-enlightenment. In **"One Good Time"** (*Harper's Monthly*, Jan. 1897), for example, Freeman portrays a young woman, aptly named Narcissa, who, after her father's death, decides to have at least one good fashionable time with her mother in New York—squandering, of course, her father's legacy, fifteen hundred dollars, all within six days! This consumerism is initially what prompts her to leave her New England town and her fiancé in search of the life style of the rich and the famous, but she is forced finally to explore herself without the embellishments. Indeed, this is the quest of the consumer-woman. This story hinges upon woman's insatiable desire for fashion: in the town dressmaker's home, one finds the weapons of the image-maker: "A number of fashion papers were neatly piled on a bureau in the corner, and some nicely folded breadths of silk lay beside them" (434). Narcissa, with her "blue eyes," "thin nose," and "a frown like a crying repetition of some old anxiety and indecision . . . on her forehead," wants to be pretty and have fun once and for all; "neither she nor her mother had any clothes which were not deemed shabby, even by the humbly attired women in the little mountain village" (433). However, the town consensus was that Narcissa "would be quite good-looking now if she had a decent dress and bonnet" (433). Unfortunately, Narcissa reads her consumerism as her desire to be independent, and so, tentatively, she leaves her fiancé shortly after her father's funeral. She and her mother buy all sorts of new clothes and jewelry in the city, they attend the opera and dine on truffles, and Narcissa enjoys a flirtation; nonetheless, within a week the funds are exhausted.

Narcissa returns home to her fiancé, but she does not feel defeated; she is described as "regal" in appearance: "soft lengths of blue silk and lace trailed about her, blue ribbons fluttered" (445); her hair is in an ornate twist and she "wore a high shell comb," and the diamonds at her throat dazzle her fiancé William. This story, like a modern allegory, shows Narcissa a triumphant but wiser woman at the end of her experience as a consumer: she admits that she's been "wasteful an' extravagant" but that she is not sorry for having had one good time. Indeed, she is no longer hysterical and emotional concerning the state of her wardrobe as she was at the outset of the story. Pale and sedate, she responds to her fiancé's question whether she will be content to "stay on [his] side of the wall now" that she wouldn't go out again "if the bars were down" (449); i.e., she will accept the matrimonial prison he has to offer her as she forfeits the illusory gains of material culture for domestic imprisonment.¹⁰

While Narcissa is submissive in the end, other Freeman stories center on women who dupe the male of the household. In **"Gentian"** (*Harper's Bazar*, 23 January 1886), Hannah Orton advises her sister Lucy Tollet to trick her ailing husband into taking gentian, a type of bitters for indigestion (in the vein of *Harper's* "Digestylin" advertisement); her rationale is that some people need to be deceived for their own good: "Ef folks don't know enough to take what's good fo 'em, they'd orter be made to by hook or crook. I don't believe in deceivin' generally, but I don't believe the Lord would have let folks hed the faculty for deceivin' em if it wa'nt to be used for good sometimes" (313). This leads the wife Lucy into a web of deception: she goes to the apothecary to get some gentian and tries to cover every track. To the store proprietor she says she is buying the bitters for herself; to the "autocrat" husband, who wants to know her every move, she says she had gone out shopping for a bar of soap. She reveals, however, the lie to her sister, that she has been slipping gentian into her crotchety husband's tea on a daily basis: "I—deceived him, an' it's been most killin' me to think on't ever since" (317). Thus, the women become accomplices in their deceptive attitude towards men. When Lucy breaks down and tells her husband the truth about gentian, he sends her off packing to her sister's, and after spending an entire season with Hannah, Lucy devises a plan whereby she can leave the sister and return to her husband (based on another deception, as she pleads sick, misses church, and thus escapes her sister's tyranny). Finally, however, Lucy wins, at least in the domestic realm, although there is some ambiguity as to who is in control. Lucy returns to her husband's home, and he orders her back to his sister's, so that he can come over in courtly fashion to make up for his stubbornness. Thus, on the one hand, the husband wins because he can order Lucy around; on the other hand, he loses the domestic strife because he is the one to apologize for his behavior and announces that Lucy may have been right about her herbal treatment: "I'm a-feelin' kinder poorly this spring—an'—I want you ter stew me up a little gentian" (232). Like a good advertiser for the all-around panacea, Lucy gets her husband to take the bitters, and even has him asking for it.

In her later stories, Freeman gives a solution to woman's dilemma as an obsessed consumer with few property or labor rights. In fact, she suggests that a new type of female economy be exchanged for a male economy; nonetheless, the narrator is sufficiently pessimistic that the reader feels this solution is hardly likely. In **"The Revolt of Mother"** (*Harper's Monthly*, September 1890), for example, the mother, Sarah Penn, devises a scheme to remove her husband from town for a brief period, so that she can transform the barn he had been building for himself (his second one) into a house for their fragile daughter, who is soon to be married. Conspiring with her daughter Nanny, Mrs. Penn essentially hushes the father and the son, who from the beginning have been able to hush the mother; in fact, the story starts with the word "Father," and ends with a stunned father looking at the triumphant mother and saying, "Why, mother . . . I hadn't no idee you was so set on't as all this comes to" (432).[11] Whereas Mrs. Penn is depicted as childlike in appearance at the start of the story, Mr. Penn is infantilized by the end.

Mrs. Penn succeeds by wit and deception. When Mr. Penn is called out of town to buy a horse from her brother, she seizes her opportunity: "Unsolicited opportunities are the guide-posts of the Lord to the new roads of life" (427). When father returns he finds his barn turned into a cozy home—symbolic of the male economic realm being feminized or domesticated—and is left speechless but transfixed by his wife's power. In Mr. Penn's absence, Mrs. Penn has rationalized like a true materialist to the scolding minister, who tries to maintain the patriarchal status quo; she defends her domestic interests: "I think it's right jest as much as I think it was right for our forefathers to come over from the old country 'cause they didn't have what belonged to 'em" (430). Thus, she alludes to the basis of the American dream—consumerism—in her defense; the narrator, too, compares the barn threshold to Plymouth Rock, the site where the forefathers came to assert their property rights.

Though **"The Revolt of Mother"** was not Freeman's favorite story, contemporary readers enjoyed it most (Welch 69). Indeed, there is a problematic element about this work and also about how Freeman perceived it. First of all, Mrs. Penn is still cooking dinner for her husband in the end; she is still stuck in her domestic identity, although her role has been strengthened. Moreover, her domestic tastes are really as extravagant as her husband's earlier dreams of barns, cattle, and tools; whereas he had imagined an extension of his marketplace world (the barn), she imagines the growth of her domestic economy. In fact, before her eyes, she sees man's economy transformed into feminine economy:

> Sarah Penn saw at a glance its possibilities. Those great box-stalls, with quilts hung before them, would make better bedrooms than the one she had occupied for forty years, and there was a tight carriage-room. The harness-room, with its chimney and shelves, would make a kitchen of her dreams. The great middle space would make a parlor, by-and-by, fit for a palace.
>
> (429)

This wish for a "kitchen of her dreams" or "a palace" is as materialistic as any of her husband's desires for a barn. One critic has concluded that in several Freeman stories, "female characters emerge from their homes to test the value of their entrepreneurship and their goods publicly in the marketplace, but in each case they return to the domestic sphere to enact personal economies" (Fienberg 504). The underlying motives of woman's "personal economies," however, are the same as those underlying man's public economy: capitalistic competition and the inordinate desire for luxury items. The public sphere of the marketplace and the private sphere of domesticity are not so far removed, as they have the same underlying roots. Women do not enjoy the triumph of "personal economies" at the end of the story.

Another critic makes the same error Lorne Fienberg has. Martha J. Cutter sees Freeman's world as bifurcated when she asserts that "To Father, value resides in money, commerce, and getting ahead" (and these endeavors are embodied in the barn), whereas "To Mother . . . value resides in people, family, generativity" (or all the values associated with "Home") (287). Since Mrs. Penn, however, has just exchanged one mode of production for another—simply by reversing the husband's economic structure and exchanging feminine capitalistic values for masculine ones—she is still working within the same system; thus, she cannot be "a speaking subject" of her own discourse (Cutter 288). Mr. Penn is silent in the end not "because he finally understands what it is that Sarah now wants" (Cutter 290); instead, Sarah has beat him at his own game, and since they're still competing for the economic power rather than sharing it, no one has really won.

Freeman herself felt that **"The Revolt of Mother"** was based (ironically enough) upon an untruth, that such an economic/gender upheaval would never have occurred in real life. In fact, later, she retracts the premise of the story, saying that a woman like Mother would never have existed in New England, that she simply would have "lacked the nerve . . . and the imagination"; moreover, she shows that both men and women are equally slaves to the market society: "New England women of the period coincided with their husbands in thinking that the sources of wealth should be better housed than the consumers" (qtd. in Foster 92).[12] Ironically, Freeman is actually in league with her devious female protagonists when she submits that she wrote the story for purely economic reasons and that she forfeited truth in the process: "I sacrificed truth when I wrote that story, and at this day I do not know exactly what my price was. I am inclined to think coin of the realm" (qtd. in Foster 92).

Freeman's most pessimistic story is a rather late one, written for *Harper's Monthly,* **"Old Woman Magoun"** (Oct. 1905). Its implications are terrifying: if woman is to establish her own economic system, she must choose separatism and literally sever the bridge between the sexes. The initial bridge motif offers a clue to the story: Old Woman Magoun, a remnant of matriarchy, feels that a bridge should be constructed to make the town "Barry's Ford" more civilized, less masculine. In the process of trying to bridge the gap between the sexes, Old Woman Magoun loses her daughter and granddaughter to the male world of trade. Indeed, she forsakes the sentimentalized notion of domesticity with which she has instructed her granddaughter Lily, but if by the end she becomes economically self-sufficient (a male virtue), she has gone mad in the process. Freeman shows man's predatory consumer nature at its worst in this story. Lily, the grandchild, is a potential victim of her father's debauchery. Though she is barely fourteen, the father, who has been absent from her life, tries to reclaim her and to peddle her off as a sexual bargain to a businessman friend to whom he owes money. Before he can accomplish this, though, the sibyllike Old Woman Magoun takes the power into her own hands: she deceives both Jim Willis, the would-be buyer of her granddaughter, and the scheming father by killing Lily off. Because she knows that men "ain't [nice], take them all together" (496), she allows her granddaughter to pick the berries from deadly nightshade.

Old Woman Magoun's triumph has a deadly price: the loss of life (her own life blood) and the loss of her mind. She continued to

> . . . support herself by the *produce* of her tiny farm; she was very *industrious,* but people said that she was a trifle touched, since every time she went over the log bridge with her eggs or her garden vegetables to *sell* in Greenham, she carried with her, as one might have carried an infant, Lily's old rag *doll.*
>
> (502, emphasis mine)

Though Magoun is economically self-supporting by peddling off her produce, she also hangs on to a vestige of matriarchy—Lily's doll, a mummified version of the child she killed. Freeman clearly shows that crossing economic or emotional gender boundaries is dangerous; in fact, this story, more than others, self-destructs, as no viable mythology exists for either sex, not economic autonomy or domestic bliss.

"Old Woman Magoun" offers a scathing statement about the relationship between the sexes, especially since the sexual act itself is perceived as an exchange of goods, or a bargain. Moreover, the buying and selling of man's marketplace world, when carried over to woman's domestic world (of ostensibly moral and social values), means death. It is more than coincidental that when Old Woman Magoun sacrifices Lily, the latter is dressed in the most provocative manner, worthy of the young adolescent flirts of *Harper's Bazar.* Lily is permitted to wear her new dress, her new hat, and her grandmother expressly curls her hair for the special day.

> The little face peeped like a rose out of two rows of golden spirals. Lily wore her new muslin dress with a pink sash, and her best hat of a fine white straw trimmed with a wreath of rosebuds; also the neatest black open-work stockings and pretty shoes. She even had white cotton gloves.
>
> (496)

Wearing a "black gown and cape and bonnet" in stark and grotesque contrast to Lily, Old Woman Magoun looks at her granddaughter lovingly and admiringly; yet, this is the same little girl who has evoked a sexual-economic response in Jim Willis and in her father. Woman is depicted finally as the victim and the victimizer of man's economic system, as Old Woman Magoun is driven to kill her next of kin. Motherhood and sexuality become commodities, as Gilman had predicted, and yet these are the most valuable assets or weapons for women in men's economic arena.

Late nineteenth-century American culture may be perceived as a period when the colonization of women in the domestic sphere occurred through advertisement, a male-dominated business which was coming into its own. Mary Wilkins Freeman, pejoratively labeled a local colorist by contemporary male realists, wrote stories which ostensibly focused on women's domestic props—furniture, household goods, and homemade panaceas—and fashion. This is the realm of housewifely and matronly duties assigned to woman by advertising. However, even though the rhetoric of advertising which catered to a female audience, as in those magazines where Freeman first published her stories (most notably *Harper's Bazar*), sought to make woman a consumer and motherhood a commodity, Freeman is able to subvert the meanings which the male business of advertising has assigned to woman.

The psychology and slogans of early advertising tried to undermine woman's authority by limiting her role in the world and by showing her ignorance of that realm to which she was relegated. The imperialization over the kitchen culture hinged upon deception, but Freeman's plots and conversations revolve around a deception, a counter-deception of sorts, to undermine the male plot to dictate woman's life style. So, what seems innocuously domestic, an example of woman's local color, is quite insidiously anti-capitalistic and anti-competitive. In order to outwit their men and to critique the male mode of productivity, Freeman's women use the same type of deception that advertisers have enforced upon them: the women bestow upon the male ruler of the household an illusion of power, while they themselves deviously remain in control. In the end, Freeman is much more than a retiring local colorist. She responds to and undermines the capitalist jargon of the ad-man. Indeed, her stories are not simply about how to run a household but how to counter men's deceptions, how to compete in the male business world, and, finally, how to beat men at their own game.

Notes

1. "A Mistaken Charity" is collected in Solomon (310). In my discussion of "A Gala Dress" and "Sister Liddy," I cite parenthetically from Pryse's edition. My citations from "Gentian," "A Poetess," "The Revolt of 'Mother'," "One Good Time," "The Lombardy Poplar," and "Old Woman Magoun" are to Solomon. I give the dates and places of original publication in parentheses. I quote directly from the two *Harper's Bazar* stories which I did not find in any collection: "The Proud Lucinda" and "An Unwilling Guest." Because I cite so many unsigned articles in *Harper's Bazar*, I note articles besides Freeman's parenthetically.

2. This phenomenon of "types" of women and beauty in the late nineteenth century is best described by Banta: "The figure of the Girl was projected as a variety of types. Types, in turn, were made to bear the weight of significant cultural meaning" (144). She discusses types from the "American Girl" to "La Femme Inconnue," from the Jamesian Daisy Miller type, the "beautiful charmer" to the "bitch goddess," from the "spinster" to the "fatal woman," from the "sibyl" to the "mother."

   Harper's Bazar in a portrait interview of Mary W. Freeman inadvertently makes her out to be a kind of "masculine" New England type of woman (as

Banta describes this type 56). Margaret Welch, who interviewed Freeman, describes her as belonging "physically, to that class of blond women whose *type* is represented wholly in the coloring of hair and eyes and complexion . . . In conversation she has a straightforward simple manner that has a touch of *mannishness* in its directness, while at the same time her femininity is one of her most prominent characteristics" (69, my emphasis). It is significant that both writers and illustrators cannot avoid this rhetoric of typology.

Significant, too, that early critics tended to read Freeman's fiction in terms of "types." Welsh, for example, reads in her characters "types rather than individuals" (70). Hutton, on the other hand, concludes that her characters are "more than types" but are apt depictions of human nature (Eichelberger 258).

3. Although Cyrus H. Curtis built his publishing empire on advertising, he owed his wife a great deal for the success of his enterprise: she poked fun at his selections for his journal, until he exclaimed, "If you can do it better, do it!" (Presbrey 479). She did—by writing and by soliciting articles that were "fresh and up to date" and "which women found a real service" (Presbrey 480).

4. Female commentators tried to de-emphasize this role of woman as spender. Besides Gilman, there were critics such as Ellen Richards (author of the popular *The Cost of Living as Modified by Sanitary Science*), who condemned women's extravagance and idleness, and advocated "the virtues of parsimony, respectability, and self-control" (Horowitz 79).

5. Even in the ads which *Harper's Bazar* ran for Freeman's collections of short stories, this quaint New England quality was emphasized. In the 10 May 1891 edition, *A New England Nun and other Stories* is advertised as "full of graphic touches, and earnest, strenuous character"; moreover, the stories are described as "clear, simple, natural, moving to a beautiful or pathetic, but always strong, finale."

6. The minister figure seems to be at once a conspirator and a competitor with women in Freeman's stories (most notably in "A Poetess" and "The Revolt of Mother"). This might have something to do with the decreasing power ministers felt in their "cultural isolation" with women (Douglas 91). Douglas posits that this odd alliance of clergy and women promoted a sentimentalized culture and the start of modern popular culture. Moreover, her reading that "the new advertising agencies . . . knew that . . . women would operate as the subconscious of capitalist culture which they must tap" (79) accords with mine.

7. Hardy's *The Woodlanders* was serialized in *Harper's Bazar* between 1886-1887, interesting considering Hardy's propensity for describing women's beauty and fashions, especially his fetish for the shoe.

I would like to thank Leland S. Person, Jr. for telling me of James's publications in *Harper's Bazar.* James's critiques of American womanhood are consistent with his portrait of Daisy Miller: to his dismay, American women are brash, outspoken, superficial, and too free. Though he would wish the "romping maidens" of America to display more decorum, more "sweet shyness" (*Harper's Bazar,* April 1907, 358), and though he would have them speak more eloquently and submissively—"We might accept this labial and lingual and vocal independence as a high sign of the glorious courage of our women if it contained but a spark of the guiding reason that separates audacity from madness" (Nov. 1906, 982)—he inadvertently sympathizes with the plight of the idle American middle-class social woman by suggesting "the huge hard business-world which had found no direct use for her has, by leaving her so cruelly to herself, given her away" (July 1907, 650).

8. See, for example, Donovan, who argues that the New England local colorists, Jewett and Freeman among them, "created a counter world of their own, a rural realm that existed on the margins of patriarchal society, a world that nourished strong, free women" (3). My reading insists that there is no world elsewhere—that male and female economies are inextricably linked, and always have been, and unlike Donovan, I don't feel that the women in Freeman's community are "in alliance with other women" or find their subjective identity (3). I think Donovan is more accurate in her last chapter on Freeman when she states that "Mother and a woman-centered world" are dying (119).

Bader lumps Jewett, Freeman, and Gilman together by stating that they share an "understanding of the bonds that unite communities of women amidst solid landscapes, as well as a portrayal of the plight of the helpless, overworked, isolated women who are driven to misunderstand and misperceive their settings" (196-97). I disagree with Bader's optimistic conclusion that the Freeman's protagonists "go through processes of change, learn from experience, and are rescued from or imprisoned in their distorted visions according to the more or less optimistic visions of female possibility held by their authors" (197).

The supportive networking system ("the long-lived, intimate, loving friendship") between women in Victorian America, as described by Smith-Rosenberg (53), is not viable in Freeman's world.

9. Even in Freeman's later stories, the garment becomes a central icon, one that proves at times beneficial. In "The Lombardy Poplar," for example, clothes are used in a positive way, to show how two cousins grow in autonomy. Sarah Dunn can break away from the memory of her dead sister, from her living cousin, and from the curse of the Dunn past through a simple declaration of independence in her wardrobe: after having worn drab clothing all her life, Sarah, "clad in a gown of dark-red silk, and a bonnet tufted with pink roses, holding aloft a red parasol" (460), enters the meeting-house. A real fashion statement!

10. A variation of this is "The Proud Lucinda," an allegory of a woman who uses clothes and sexuality to seduce a younger lover; in the end, though, she is outdone by a younger woman, Esther, who is sexually innocent but who also resorts to clothes to catch the same man, George. Esther's future mother-in-law actually conspires with Esther with the advice that she should wear her best "gray silk dress" upon her son's return (103). Some odd and grotesque poetic justice finds Lucinda disfigured and crippled.

The odd juxtaposition of fashion and paralysis is common to Freeman and creates the grotesque atmosphere. In "An Unwilling Guest," Susan Lawson, paralyzed and houseridden for a decade, has an opportunity to stay with her friend and hesitates because she has no new clothes. But her "feminine pride" triumphs as she "tied on nervously the flat Neapolitan bonnet, with its little tuft of feathery green grass, which had flourished bravely in some old millinery spring" (194), and this newborn feeling allows her to escape her husband's home, at least tentatively.

11. Much of Cutter's argument deals with the function of silence and speech in "The Revolt of Mother" and communication patterns between the sexes: I'm not as optimistic as she, though, that Mother has finally "wrested control of language from her husband and placed it in her own hands" (290).

12. For an interpretation of a feminist subcoding to Freeman's retraction of this story, see Meese (21-38); Meese feels that Freeman "authorizes" the conflicting gender codes in her story, but that in her renunciation, "she constructs a duplicitous story concerning her view of Mother's action and herself as a writer" (34).

Works Cited

Bader, Julia. "The Dissolving Vision: Realism in Jewett, Freeman, and Gilman." *American Realism: New Es-*

says. Ed. Eric J. Sundquist. Baltimore: Johns Hopkins UP, 1982. 176-98.

Banta, Martha. *Imaging American Women: Idea and Ideals in Cultural History.* New York: Columbia UP, 1987.

Cutter, Martha J. "Frontiers of Language: Engendering Discourse in 'The Revolt of Mother.'" *American Literature* 63 (1991): 279-91.

Donovan, Josephine. *New England Local Color Literature: A Women's Tradition.* New York: Continuum, 1983.

Douglas, Ann. *The Feminization of American Culture.* New York: Knopf, 1978.

Eichelberger, Clayton L., ed. *Harper's Lost Reviews: The Literary Notes by Laurence Hutton, John Kendrick Bangs and Others.* Milwood, NY: KTO Press, 1976.

Fienberg, Lorne. "Mary E. Wilkins Freeman's 'Soft Diurnal Commotion': Women's Work and Strategies for Containment." *New England Quarterly* 62 (1989): 483-504.

Foster, Edward. *Mary E. Wilkins Freeman.* New York: Hendricks House, 1956.

Fox, Stephen. *The Mirror Makers: A History of American Advertising and Its Creators.* New York: Morrow, 1984.

Freeman, Mary E. Wilkins. *Selected Short Stories of Mary E. Wilkins Freeman.* Ed. Marjorie Pryse. New York: Norton, 1983.

———. *Short Fiction of Sarah Orne Jewett and Mary Wilkins Freeman.* Ed. Barbara H. Solomon. New York: Signet, 1979.

———. "The Girl Who Wants to Write: Things to Do and to Avoid." *Harper's Bazar* 47 (June 1913): 272.

———. "The Proud Lucinda." *Harper's Bazar,* 7 Feb. 1891: 101-03.

———. "An Unwilling Guest." *Harper's Bazar,* 20 March 1886: 194-95.

Gilman, Charlotte Perkins. *Women and Economics.* Ed. Carl Degler. New York: Harper, 1966.

Glasser, Leah Blatt. "Mary E. Wilkins Freeman: Profile." *Legacy: A Journal of Nineteenth-Century American Women Writers* 4 (1987): 37-46.

———. "Mary E. Wilkins Freeman." *The Instructor's Guide for The Heath Anthology of American Literature.* Ed. Judith A. Stanford. Lexington: Heath, 1990. 299-304.

Goodrum, Charles, and Helen Dalrymple. *Advertising in America: The First Two Hundred Years.* New York: Abrams, 1990.

Habegger, Alfred. *Gender, Fantasy, and Realism in American Literature.* New York: Columbia UP, 1982.

Horowitz, Daniel. *The Morality of Spending: Attitudes toward the Consumer Society in America, 1875-1940.* Baltimore: Johns Hopkins UP, 1985.

Kendrick, Brent L., ed. *The Infant Sphinx: Collected Letters of Mary E. Wilkins Freeman.* Metuchen: Scarecrow, 1985.

Leach, William. *True Love and Perfect Union: The Feminist Reform of Sex and Society.* New York: Basic, 1980.

Meese, Elizabeth A. *Crossing the Double-Cross: The Practice of Feminist Criticism.* Chapel Hill: U of North Carolina P, 1986.

Presbrey, Frank. *The History and Development of Advertising.* New York: Greenwood, 1968.

Smith-Rosenberg, Carroll. "The Female World of Love and Ritual: Relations Between Women in Nineteenth-Century America." *Disorderly Conduct: Visions of Gender in Victorian America.* New York: Oxford UP, 1985.

Strasser, Susan. *Satisfaction Guaranteed: The Making of the American Mass Market.* New York: Pantheon, 1989.

Stuart, Ruth McEnery. "If They Had a Million Dollars; What Nine Famous Women Would Do if a Fortune Were Theirs." *Ladies Home Journal,* Sept, 1903: 10.

Welch, Margaret Hamilton. "American Authoresses of the Hour: Mary E. Wilkins." *Harper's Bazar,* 27 Jan 1900: 69-70.

Wicke, Jennifer A. *Advertising Fictions: Literature, Advertisement, and Social Reading.* New York: Columbia UP, 1988.

Mary R. Reichardt (essay date 1997)

SOURCE: Reichardt, Mary R. "Later Stories, 1904-1928: Continuing Interests, New Moods and Subjects, Interrelated and Child-Protagonist Stories." In *Mary Wilkins Freeman: A Study of the Short Fiction,* pp. 87-114. New York: Twayne Publishers, 1997.

[*In the following excerpt, Reichardt outlines themes of family strife, rebellion against society, impoverishment, and romantic relationships in Freeman's last major phase of short fiction.*]

Though Freeman focused on short fiction in various subgenres throughout the middle portion of her career, she continued to pen her signature New England village tales as well. Such stories as **"A Stress of Conscience"** (1892), **"Juliza"** (1892), **"One Good Time"**

(1897), and **"Hyacinthus"** (1904) involve subject matter and situations characteristic of her earliest efforts. Moreover, during this time she continued to produce at least two commissioned holiday tales per year: **"An Unlucky Christmas"** (1896), **"The Pumpkin"** (1900), **"Susan Jane's Valentine"** (1900), and **"An Easter-Card"** (1901) are some examples. In the last phase of Freeman's writing, from 1904 to 1928, she therefore did not so much return to her typical village stories as cease experimenting with the subgenres that mark the middle period.

There may be several reasons for that decision. Although *The Wind in the Rose-Bush, Understudies,* and *Six Trees* received favorable reviews and sold well, Freeman's publishers and the several literary agents she employed after 1905 evidently did not encourage the author to continue in these directions; they dissuaded her from composing, for example, the series of insect pieces to complement the animal stories of *Understudies* and, later, a series of jewel tales designed to follow **"The Jade Bracelet."** Though it remained steady, Freeman's popularity around the turn of the century partly resulted from the afterglow of the widespread acclaim her earliest volumes had received. Critically and artistically, however, her reputation had been increasingly jeopardized by her novels. Though each had its loyal following, the 12 novels that appeared after 1894, some running to hundreds of thousands of words, received at best mixed reviews and at worst outright condemnation by critics who lamented that the author persisted in writing ill-wrought, even preposterous novels at the expense of her established forte, the short story. Of the six novels she produced during the last phase of her career, only *The Shoulders of Atlas,* ironically written in just two months for a newspaper contest, is significant in its realistic plot involving a favorite Freeman theme, that of hidden crime and the agonizing deliberations of the morbidly sensitive, guilty conscience. *Shoulders* is also notable in Freeman's oeuvre as the author's most candid exploration of the sexual basis of the New England character's neuroses or obsessions.

Without abandoning her steady stream of short stories and against the advice of her critics, Freeman continued to concentrate her primary energies in the last phase of her career on writing novels. The novel was to her a greater achievement, a "grand opera" as opposed to a "simple little melody," and she ambitiously strove to reach such a lofty artistic goal (Kendrick, 382). In addition, some of her impetus for pursuing other genres besides the short story most likely derived from her desire to ward off the early typecasting that, to her dismay, hounded her throughout her career. Her public not only demanded more of the usual "Mary Wilkins" tales of spinsters in many-turned

gowns, poor but proud old folk, and quiet rural villages but even expected the author herself to step out of their pages: as late as 1916, Freeman recorded with thinly veiled scorn how a visiting publisher "seemed really a bit indignant because he did not find me attired in my best black silk and living in New Jersey in these latter days in a little white New England cottage" (Kendrick, 349). But although one can sympathize with Freeman's artistic goals, one can also understand her publishers' wincing each time a new Freeman novel arrived on their desks. Constructive criticism was not welcomed; increasingly peevish as she grew older, Freeman would impetuously "delete whole paragraphs, undoubtedly to the further detriment of the manuscript" if even the slightest suggestion for revision was offered (Kendrick, 280). Yet Freeman persisted in her goal to write longer fiction: at the time of her death from heart failure in 1930, she was considering both an autobiography and a sequel to *Pembroke.*

Freeman's continued focus on novels throughout the last decades of her career no doubt contributed to the marked unevenness of the short stories she also wrote during this time. There are several personal reasons for this unevenness as well. Her worry over not having enough time for her career once married was apparently not borne out in the first few years she lived with Charles; he was sympathetic to his famous wife's endeavors, and he arranged for domestic help so that she could write as much as she pleased. As time went on, however, Freeman became preoccupied with the numerous details involved in the couple's building of an elaborate new home in Metuchen, a showpiece financed with the $20,000 contest money she won for *The Shoulders of Atlas.* The house was completed in 1907, the same year Charles ran for mayor of Metuchen, an election he lost largely because of his growing reputation as an alcoholic; over the next 10 years, his mental and physical health steadily deteriorated. Around the time the couple moved into their new home, Mary Freeman's letters begin to indicate that she was suffering the effects of severe fatigue generated by a long habit of overwork. "I am straining every nerve to write. . . . even my faithful typewriter shows signs of fatigue," she confided to a fellow author (Kendrick, 308). Increasingly, that exhaustion was accompanied by numerous other ailments, including insomnia, headaches, severe bronchial colds, and deafness. Still, though their combined assets rendered the couple quite wealthy, Mary Freeman showed no signs of slackening her strenuous writing pace.

Freeman published 89 short stories for adults between 1904 and 1928 and left at least four others in manuscript form at her death. Approximately half of these were not collected in her lifetime; the other half were reissued by Harper's in five final collections, *The Givers* (1904), *The Fair Lavinia and Others* (1907), *The Winning Lady and Others* (1909), *The Copy-Cat and Other Stories* (1914), and *Edgewater People* (1918). Many of these later stories are holiday tales; both *The Givers* and *The Fair Lavinia* contain a number of them. Others, as Kendrick has noted, are likely re-worked versions of earlier manuscripts Freeman had not published but had kept on file (Kendrick, 375). But also among this body of work are a number of pieces that attain the superb depth of theme and quality of execution Freeman achieved more consistently earlier in her career. Most of these pieces reiterate Freeman's primary themes of rebellion against social codes, the quest for authentic spirituality, the mending of family feuds, issues of poverty and pride, and relationships in courtship and marriage.

"The Revolt of Sophia Lane" (1903; later renamed **"The Givers"**) is a first-person narrative told by the title character to well-meaning but thoughtless relatives as an object lesson on the necessity of giving appropriate gifts, a recurrent concern of Freeman's. Motivated by love for her niece Flora, who is about to wed a poor farmer, Sophia relates to the visitors, who have come to congratulate Flora on her engagement, how she mustered the courage the previous Christmas to return every one of the elegant but useless gifts Flora received. Among them were a fancy hair ornament, a precious silk shawl, and a chess set that no one knew how to use ("For the land sake! what's them little dolls and horses for? It looks like Noah's ark without the ark," Sophia exclaimed when she saw it; *MWFR* [*A Mary Wilkins Freeman Reader*], 306). The visiting relatives grasp the meaning of Sophia's parable and tactfully take their impractical engagement gifts—finger bowls and doilies, an "afternoon" tea kettle—back home with them; presumably, more appropriate items will soon follow. Sophia's is the classic Freeman revolt: the sudden eruption of a long-suffering sensibility. This time, however, the situation is as humorous for the reader as it is serious for the protagonist. Like Sarah Penn in **"The Revolt of 'Mother'"** and numerous other Freeman heroines, Sophia breaks a tacit and seemingly impenetrable social code, in this case the ritual of gracious gift giving and receiving. Also like Sarah Penn, she does so with trepidation and is surprised when she succeeds as well as she does. The comic ending here, in fact, makes for a delightful tale. The humor is Freeman's best: the image of lanky old Sophia trundling fiercely through the snow as she returns the inappropriate presents to their astonished givers evokes a wry irony, at once hilarious and poignant:

> Then I took [back to her] Lizzie Starkwether's bed-shoes, [Sophia relates].

"Don't they fit?" says she.

"Fit well 'nough," says I. "We don't want 'em. . . . Because you've given us a pair every Christmas for three years," says I, "and I've told you we never wear bed-shoes; and even if we did wear 'em," says I, "we couldn't have worn out the others to save our lives. When we go to bed, we go to sleep," says I. "We don't travel round to wear out shoes. We've got two pairs apiece laid away," says I, "and I think you'd better give these to somebody that wants 'em—mebbe somebody that you've been givin' mittens to for three years, that don't wear mittens."

(311-12)

Another late story of rebellion is also one of Freeman's finest. **"The Balking of Christopher"** (1912) presents a new rendition of Freeman's frequent theme of an individual's search for spiritual fulfillment in a harsh, demoralizing environment. The story is unique in part because its protagonist is one of Freeman's few believable and well-rounded male characters. An intelligent and sensitive man, Christopher Dodd suddenly "balks" one day at the monotonous, unrelenting labor he has had to perform on the farm every day of his life to eke out a meager living. Without explaining the reason to his wife, Myrtle, he seeks out the town minister and there recites a litany of the hardships that have dogged him throughout his 50 years. "Why did I have to come into the world without any choice?" he demands. "I came into the world whether I would or not; I was forced, and then I was told I was a free agent. I am no free agent. . . . I am a slave—a slave of life" (*MWFR*, 403-4). Wisely, the Reverend Stephen Wheaton listens to the torrent of words without interrupting. When he learns that the revolt Christopher is planning is not as extreme as his bitter words might imply, Stephen agrees to support him in it. Christopher's scheme is to "do just once in my life what I want to do," to abandon the usual spring plowing and planting and, instead, live apart for a while in a cabin on the mountainside so as to "have the spring and the summer, and the fall, too, if I want it . . . to get once, on this earth, my fill of the bread of life" (406-7). He carries out his purpose and, in only a few months, is thoroughly rejuvenated by his rest. Returning down the mountain, he resumes his chores with renewed courage. He has, in addition, gained a new appreciation for the tolerant Myrtle, a woman he wed more out of compassion than out of love but whom he now realizes is exactly the partner most suitable to him.

In **"The Balking of Christopher,"** Freeman combines the Emersonian mysticism that informs some of her mid-career stories with her typical study of rebellion. From the heights of the mountaintop, Christopher gains a spiritual perspective on nature's seasons, as he has the leisure to observe, for the first time in his life, the glory of the trees and flowers in their spring bloom and later in their summer fullness. He now comprehends that, like the ebb and flow of the seasons, his existence is composed of a necessary blending of suffering and pleasure and that both work together for his welfare. His question of "why" to life has been answered through his new perception of the incarnation of spirit: "I have found out that the only way to heaven for the children of men is through the earth," he states finally, a conclusion remarkably similar to that of Robert Frost's birch swinger, who also finds new perspective as a result of his lofty assent (413).[1] As Beth Wynne Fisken has demonstrated in "'Unusual' People in a 'Usual Place,'" this story likewise involves the more subtle but equally complex rebellions and transformations of the three principal characters besides Christopher.[2] Freeman's usual disdain in her fiction for ineffective or impotent ministers gives way in this story to sympathy in her portrayal of the Reverend Wheaton, who is able to empathize with Christopher's plight because he too "sometimes chafed under the dull necessity of his life" (409). For the first (and only) time in Freeman's world, a clergyman condescends to listen to and learn from one of his flock. Through his vicarious participation in Christopher's quest, Stephen is similarly rejuvenated in spirit; Stephen and Christopher are, in fact, alter egos who achieve a common transformation though they have started from different paths in life. Although she is anxious about her husband, Myrtle, "in her quiet dignity, refuses to condemn what she does not understand; she will not be the nagging wife urged by Christopher's mother and sister" (Fisken 1985, 100). Finally, Christopher's niece Ellen, who takes over the farm during his absence and who eventually marries Stephen Wheaton, is an unusual young woman: she is fearless, strong, and emotionally balanced. It is Ellen, in fact, who comes to represent in the tale the promise of renewal that each succeeding generation—like each cycle of the seasons—carries with it.

Other tales of revolt from Freeman's later group of stories include the skillful **"One Good Time"** (1897), a story that, like **"The Balking of Christopher,"** concerns a character's onetime rebellion against life's harsh restrictions staged, in this case, by the lavish spending of money; **"The Slip of the Leash"** (1904), in which a man who abruptly "went wild" deserts his family, only to remain in the vicinity, secretly observing them; **"The Strike of Hannah"** (1906), a Thanksgiving tale in which an impoverished woman steals a holiday dinner from her wealthy employer "to set the law of equals right"; and the inferior **"The Willow-Ware"** (1907) and **"Dear Annie"** (1910), both of which are weakly plotted studies of young women who attempt to resist repressive family circumstances.

In her late fiction, Freeman also pursued her repeated theme of the difficulty of maintaining harmonious relationships and resolving family feuds. In **"The Reign of the Doll"** (1904), elderly sisters Fidelia and Diantha harbor ill will toward each other that stems from the division of their dead mother's property years before. Though they live in adjacent houses and spy on each other through the curtains, they do not speak or exchange visits and treat each other with the "dignified hostility" that Freeman's obstinate, proud villagers tend to assume (*MWFR,* 319). The mysterious delivery of a doll to one of the sisters begins to act as a balm to their injured sensibilities. Spurred on by memories of their girlhood, the two lonely, childless women are gradually reunited by their care for the doll as they come together to stitch little garments to clothe it:

> As the two women worked, their faces seemed to change. They were tall and bent, with a rigorous bend of muscles not apparently so much from the feebleness and relaxing of age as from defiance to the stresses of life; both sisters' backs had the effect of stern walkers before fierce winds; their hair was sparse and faded, brushed back from thin temples, with nothing of the grace of childhood, and yet there was something of the immortal child in each as she bent over her doll-clothes. The contour of childhood was evident in their gaunt faces, which suddenly appeared like transparent masks of age; the light of childhood sparkled in their eyes; when they chattered and laughed one would have sworn there were children in the room. And, strangest of all, their rancor and difference seemed to have vanished; they were in the most perfect accord.
>
> (325)

This unexpected softening of stubborn spirits through an object as ludicrous and unlikely as a doll is pure Freeman. So is the telling of the story partly through neighborhood gossip, which hints that the doll may have been sent to the sisters as either a mockery of their old-lady, maiden ways or as a well-calculated means to their reconciliation. As in much of her best fiction, Freeman makes fine use here of multiple points of view, indicating both the persistent quality of small-town gossip and the many sides to human relationships. Oblivious to their neighbors' prying eyes and wagging tongues, Fidelia and Diantha sew on in quiet harmony, the enigmatic doll between them "smiling with inscrutable inanity" (332). The final incongruous but winsome image is one of Freeman's most memorable.

Finally, **"The Selfishness of Amelia Lamkin"** (1908) is also representative of Freeman's most accomplished later short fiction. A hardworking wife and mother in a large household, Amelia Lamkin collapses one day from sheer exhaustion. Near death, she lies prone in bed under doctor's orders for several weeks while her husband, children, and visiting sister try to undertake the numerous chores that Amelia had customarily performed alone. As they struggle to cope, their emotions range from grief and love to "monstrous self-pity" and "unreasoning anger" at Amelia's inability to serve them as she always has (*MWFR,* 389). As time passes, however, each begins to realize the extent of his or her selfishness, which has led to Amelia's illness. Remorse even provokes her daughter Addie to reject her sweetheart and vow to devote the rest of her life to helping her mother.

But the story's examination of selfishness runs deeper than is apparent from this brief sketch of the plot. The doctor, a voice of reason and objectivity amid the clamor and chaos that results from the family's distress, points out to them that the ailing Amelia is equally guilty of selfishness, for "she has worked too hard for everybody else, and not hard enough for herself" (388). Indeed, Amelia epitomizes the domestic ideal, or "true," woman: meek and self-sacrificing, she has even come close to starving herself by eating only the leftover scraps from the others' plates. As the narrator explains, "she had always waited upon [her family] and obliterated herself to that extent that she seemed scarcely to have a foothold at all upon the earth, but to balance timidly upon the extreme edge of existence" (379). Amelia's spinster sister, Jane Strong, has long tried to convince Amelia that her catering to others was not only harming her own health but turning her family members into persons incapable of existing independent of her solicitous care. As Amelia lies exhausted in bed, Jane is now apparently vindicated in her belief. But though professing to be as self-sufficient and hardy as her name implies, Jane Strong collapses into an emotional wreck when confronted with the possibility of her sister's death. When she trips down the cellar steps and lies helpless and alone on the floor with a broken foot, she is able to perceive for the first time that her life has become a sham:

> Jane Strong had kept all the commandments from her youth up. She had always been considered a most exemplary woman by other people, and she had acquiesced in their opinion. Now suddenly she differed with other people and with her own previous estimation of herself. She had blamed her sister Amelia Lamkin for her sweet, subtle selfishness, which possibly loved the happiness of other people rather than their own spiritual gain; she had blamed all the Lamkin family for allowing a martyr to live among them, with no effort to save her from the flame of her own self-sacrifice. Now suddenly she blamed herself. She pictured to herself her easy, unhampered life in her nice little apartment, and was convicted of enormous selfishness in her own righteous person. "Lord!" she said, "what on earth have I been thinking about? I knew Amelia was overworked. What was to hinder my coming here at least half the

> year and taking some of the burden off her? . . . You've made a nice mess of it, Jane Strong! Instead of snooping around to find the sins of other folks, you'd better have looked at home. Good land!"

(392-93)

The haughty self-complacency of the single woman who revels in freedom from all obligations and judges others who don't have that luxury is thus revealed as destructive. The result is that both Jane and Amelia, doubles and mirrors of each other, are indicted for their selfishness. As Martha Cutter explains, "a radical critique of the two most prevalent images [of nineteenth-century women]—the 'Domestic Saint' and the 'New Woman'—exists in **'The Selfishness of Amelia Lamkin,'** reflecting Freeman's understanding of the debilitating nature of *all* patriarchal images of femininity. . . . For Freeman, the image of the New Woman is not different from the True Woman; it is just another stereotype."[3] Freeman dissects those two stereotypes and also provides her tale with an "undecidable" open ending. Readers are left to speculate about how both Amelia (who recovers) and Jane will change their behavior given their newfound understanding of themselves. Is a third alternative available for these women—for all women? Freeman, who spent a lifetime exploring the effects of ingrained patterns of behavior, doesn't seem to provide much room for optimism here. Rather, Doctor Emerson's words to the family seem to ring prophetic as, at the story's conclusion, Amelia rises from her bed: "I realize," he has warned them, "how almost impossible it is to prevent self-sacrificing women like your mother from offering themselves up" (388). "Almost impossible," perhaps, but not completely hopeless. Freeman allows her readers the privilege of the final judgment, not only about Amelia and Jane but about the future of women's roles in general as they evolve into a new century.

NEW MOODS AND SUBJECTS

As we have seen, many of Freeman's most effective later stories echo the themes and situations of her earliest efforts; the continuity between them is clear. In terms of style, these well-crafted works also retain an emphasis on dialogue in developing plot, although the tightly compressed prose and heavy use of regional dialect from the earlier period is generally absent. Weaker stories from Freeman's late career exhibit the same faults as others scattered throughout her short fiction: contrived or improbable plotting; overly sentimental or conventional endings; and from mid-career on, a tendency toward a verbose, overwritten style. Though Freeman experimented ambitiously, one cannot claim that she developed significantly as a writer over the course of her long career: her best stories from each period resemble each other, as do her poorest.

Some shift in tone from the early to the late stories is apparent, however. The understated yet devastating irony of the early tales gives way in several of Freeman's last pieces to a strident, caustic tone and a frankness of subject matter heretofore unexhibited in the bulk of her short fiction. Alice Glarden Brand recognizes this change in temper, correctly noting that "in [Freeman's] early stories, women, particularly the young, sense the inevitability of their existences as vulnerable to the social order. Society placed a premium on marriage, self-control, and impassiveness. . . . As Freeman becomes angrier and bolder, her women become angrier and bolder. . . . As masculine offenses become more odious, the female defenses become similarly outrageous" (Brand, 84, 96). Thus these seemingly atypical pieces in the author's canon—including **"Old Woman Magoun"** (1905), **"The Secret"** (1907), **"The Old-Maid Aunt"** (1908), **"Noblesse"** (1913), **"The Jester"** (1928), and the fragment referred to as **"Jane Lennox"** (undated)—can be viewed as culminations of issues that Freeman explored time and again, particularly the plight of society's vulnerable or outcast and the social restrictions placed on women, whether married or single.

Both **"Noblesse"** and **"Old Woman Magoun"** are tragic tales of women's relative defenselessness in the face of unchecked male power and greed. In each story, a man decides to "sell" a woman to pay a gambling debt. **"Noblesse,"** though not a successful story due to its melodramatic ending, is appalling in its premise. Margaret Lee, an enormously overweight woman, finds herself in late middle age alone in the world and dependent on distant relatives. Sensitive and genteel, she can hardly bear the vulgar young couple with whom she lives, and they in turn are capable of little but crude pity for her. When the husband, Jack, loses on his investments and then gambles away the remainder of his fortune, he forces Margaret to exhibit herself as a circus sideshow freak in order to earn money. Margaret faints when she learns of the plan, but "there was no course open but submission. She knew that from the first."[4] Though Margaret is a religious woman, even her faith in the existence of a better life to come wavers as the horrifying situation is perpetuated: "Daily her absurd unwieldiness was exhibited to crowds screaming with laughter. . . . It seemed to her that there was nothing for evermore beyond those staring, jeering faces of silly mirth and delight at sight of her. . . . [She] became a horror to herself" (*CC* [*The Copy-Cat*], 173). Margaret is eventually saved by a noble man, equally overweight, who sacrifices himself by taking her place in the freak show. The narrator's comments on the man's decision summarize Freeman's dark mood in this and other late

stories: "There was no romance about it. These were hard, sordid, tragic, ludicrous facts with which he had to deal" (178).

"Old Woman Magoun" is perhaps the most pessimistic of all of Freeman's stories. In this case, the female in peril is a mere child, a naive young girl named Lily, and the degenerate male is her father. The majority of the inhabitants of Barry's Ford are sloven drunkards and half-wits, remnants of the vitiated Barry lineage, of which Lily's father is among the worst. Sheltered after her mother's death by her maternal grandmother, Old Woman Magoun, Lily is kept from contact with her father until she meets him by chance when she is 14 years old. Though Lily is still childlike and clutches a rag doll, Nelson Barry immediately targets her as potential payment to another man for his gambling debt. When Old Woman Magoun becomes aware of Nelson's purpose, her worst fears are realized, for she has long suspected the extent of his depravity. She has no choice, nevertheless, but to turn Lily over to her father. Before doing so, she makes a desperate effort to convince a lawyer from a neighboring town to adopt the girl. When this move fails, she resorts in sheer panic to the only available alternative to Lily's impending rape and exploitation. On the return trip from the lawyer's, Old Woman Magoun allows the unsuspecting Lily to eat poisonous berries. Lily dies in great agony that evening, just before her father arrives to claim her. From that time on, the formerly strong and defiant Old Woman Magoun is considered a "trifle touched"; she is seen walking the village streets, cradling Lily's doll in her arms.

Besides its deeply cynical tone, **"Old Woman Magoun"** is outstanding among Freeman's short stories for its frankly sexual content. In keeping with her generation, Freeman was fairly reticent about sex, but she was not prudish. The early novel *Pembroke* describes an illegitimate pregnancy and a shotgun wedding, and as noted, thinly veiled references to same-sex relationships can be found in several of her novels and stories. Nevertheless, although the majority of Freeman's tales involve courtship situations, frank discussion of sexuality is largely absent from her short fiction, in part, no doubt, because of the stipulations of the various popular magazines that bought her stories. It is worth noting that when Freeman does dwell on sexuality, it is usually in the context of a threatening or otherwise ominous relationship: for example, Joe Dagget's disturbing presence is symbolized by the chained Caesar in **"A New England Nun,"** and Phoebe Dole jealously murders Maria Wood's male lover in **"The Long Arm."** In its darkly foreboding subject matter and tone, **"Old Woman Magoun"** epitomizes Freeman's few but significant stories of sexual strife and plunder.

"The Secret" and **"The Old-Maid Aunt"** exhibit a fresh boldness about issues of marriage and single life. In the former piece, Catherine Gould becomes incensed when her fiancé, John Gleason, demands that she tell him where she has been when she returns home later than expected one evening. After John angrily stomps out of the house, Catherine's mother and aunt chastise her for not submitting to him, but Catherine insists that she will never marry a man who exerts such jealous control. "John suspected me of going somewhere or doing something I should not," she retorts. "He questioned me like a slave-owner. If he does so before I am married, what will he do after? My life would be a hell. If I see that a door leads into hell, I don't propose to enter it if I can keep out. That's all I have to say."[5] Later, Catherine discusses her now-dwindled prospects for marriage with her worried mother; in the course of their conversation, the generational difference between the two women comes to the forefront:

> "What do I care if I never get married?" [Catherine stated]. "Most of the married women I know would say they wished they were out of it, if they told the truth. . . . Mother," said she—she hesitated a moment, then she continued—"did you never regret that you got married?"
>
> The mother blushed. She regarded her daughter with a curious, dignified, yet shamed expression. "Marriage is a divine institution," said she, and closed her lips tightly.
>
> "Oh, nonsense!" cried Catherine. "Tell the truth, mother, and let the divine institution go. I know father was a fretful invalid two-thirds of the time. . . . [He] never was much of a success as a doctor; he had such a temper and was so miserable himself. And I know you had five children as fast as you could, and they all died except me. Now tell me the truth—if you had it all to live over again, would you marry father?"
>
> The flush faded from Mrs. Gould's face. She was quite pale. "Yes, I would, and thank the Lord for His unspeakable mercy," she said, in a low, oratorical voice, almost as if she were in a pulpit.
>
> (*FL* [*The Fair Lavinia*], 200-201)

"The Secret" thus pairs mother and daughter to contrast the attitudes of an older and younger generation of women on the issue of marriage: the theme is one Freeman has examined before, but its handling through the outspoken, liberated Catherine is unique. In addition, the story presents a variation on the author's characteristic study of petty quarrels perpetuated by proud, headstrong individuals. Catherine and John are doubles in this matter, sharing a "terrible similarity of unyielding spirit" (192). After they argue and part ways, Catherine holds out easily enough; she loves John, but she does not need him. In fact, unlike in some Freeman tales, such as **"A Patient Waiter"**

(1886) or **"The Witch's Daughter"** (1910), here it is not the woman who becomes "love-cracked" over a broken engagement but the man. During the several years they are separated, John grows increasingly ill and morose, whereas Catherine waxes in health, vitality, and beauty. Eventually, John capitulates and returns to Catherine; even then, Freeman has Catherine deliberate at length, like Esther in **"A Conflict Ended,"** over whether she'd be better off marrying him or remaining single. She finally opts to wed him, but not without regret at forgoing the "peaceful and beautiful and good" aspects of her single life. Ultimately, however, she determines that by never marrying she might "miss the best and sweetest of food for her heart. There was nothing of the nun about her. She was religious, but she was not ascetic" (225).

Catherine Gould is yet another in Freeman's long line of female protagonists who challenge social and familial prohibitions in asserting their freedom in marriage issues. When compared to earlier characters in similar struggles (for instance, Louisa Britton in **"Louisa,"** Louisa Ellis in **"A New England Nun,"** and Lucy Greenleaf in **"Arethusa"**), it is apparent that Catherine is bolder and more strident. However, although the entrance of an independently minded, fearless young woman like Catherine—truly a "new" woman—is welcome in Freeman's canon, one also recalls that it is precisely the conflict between assertion and repression, between resistance and conformity, that lends Freeman's best short fiction its sharp-edged power and keen psychological insight. Since Catherine experiences little tension of this kind, she remains a relatively flat character and **"The Secret"** an interesting but not superior story.

"The Old-Maid Aunt" is technically not a short story. Nevertheless, it can be read as one and as such adds considerably to our understanding of the forceful tone detectable in Freeman's later work. Freeman composed the piece as the second chapter for *The Whole Family* (1908), a novel Harper's promoted as a "round-robin" literary gimmick with contributions by 12 popular authors of the day, including Freeman, William Dean Howells, Henry James, Alice Brown, and Elizabeth Stuart Phelps. Each author was to write the first-person narrative of a particular family member; as patriarch of the group, Howells led with the first installment, "The Father," and then forwarded the project to Freeman to continue. Freeman's chapter presents a lively, ironic look at turn-of-the-century expectations for unmarried women past age 30. The "old maid aunt," Lily Talbot, is considered "unfortunate" by family members who patronize her and assume that, because she is a spinster, she cannot possibly be interested in anything but her knitting. Scorning her "brainless" family's lack of sophistication, Lily delights in antagonizing them by, among other things, wearing scandalous pink dresses instead of the drab black more appropriate to her age. She likewise holds in contempt the dowdy, predictable housewives among her circle of acquaintances, especially the dull Mrs. Temple, who even positions the books on her parlor table, as Lily disdainfully relates, "with the large ones under the small ones in perfectly even piles!" "Anything is better," Lily determines, "than the dead level of small books on large ones, and meals on time" (*MWFR*, 347, 358). The sardonic jab is, of course, aimed at Freeman's own famous **"A New England Nun,"** in which the methodical Louisa Ellis hastens to rearrange her books back into their customary order after Joe Dagget has displaced them.

Lily is educated, well traveled, beautiful, and wealthy. Nevertheless, she is reminded daily that she is confined to the limited role of a spinster in others' estimation. To the extent that it is possible, therefore, she uses that role to her advantage. "But I am willing, even anxious, to be quite frank with myself," she states. "Since—well, never mind since what time—I have not cared an iota whether I was considered an old maid or not. The situation has seemed to me rather amusing, inasmuch as it has involved a secret willingness to be what everybody has considered me as very unwilling to be. I have regarded it as a sort of joke upon other people" (345). When the narrative reveals that the young man engaged to Lily's teenaged niece Peggy is actually in love with Lily, Freeman sets up a tantalizing turn of events that purposely distorts Howells's conception of *The Whole Family*'s plot as a homey, nostalgic, and low-keyed one. Howells was dismayed by Freeman's decision and tried to bar her installment. Freeman, however, remained unrepentant (one recalls that she herself married a man seven years her junior), and the chapter stayed. She explained her reasoning at the time to Elizabeth Jordan, editor of *Harper's Bazar* and the project's convener:

> Mr. Howells evidently clings to the old conception of [the spinster]. You and I know that in these days of voluntary celibacy on the part of women an old maid only fifteen years older than a young girl is a sheer impossibility, if she is an educated woman with a fair amount of brains. Moreover, a young man is really more apt to fall in love with her. Why, the whole plot of the novel must be relegated back to Miss Austin [*sic*], and *Godey's Lady's Book* and all that sort of thing, if the old conception holds. . . . I don't think Mr. Howells realizes this. He is thinking of the time when women of thirty put on caps, and renounced the world. That was because they married at fifteen and sixteen, and at thirty had about a dozen children. Now they simply do not do it.

> (Kendrick, 313)

Freeman's deliberate twist of plot upset the authors of the subsequent chapters as well as Howells. Though

divided on the chapter's merit, the 10 writers followed Freeman's lead in focusing the novel increasingly on family tensions, divisions, and jealousy. Moreover, the story line also came to reflect some of these writers' personal dissensions and artistic rivalries.[6] Though *The Whole Family* intrigued the public because each chapter was issued anonymously in the *Bazar* before being released together as a book, at its conclusion Elizabeth Jordan deemed the entire frustrating project a "mess."

Several of Freeman's later stories concern characters who, like Lily Talbert, chafe at the roles others have assigned them yet use them to their advantage. Her last published story, **"The Jester,"** for example, is a deeply cynical study of a young man who employs his skill at amusing others to mask his lonely soul; tragically, his constant role-playing eventually makes him incapable of authentic human love. The undated fragment **"Jane Lennox"** may have been written as a type of preliminary sketch for **"The Old-Maid Aunt"**; the first-person narrative voice is similar, although the mood of **"Jane Lennox"** is far more bitter. "I am a rebel and what is worse a rebel against the Overgovernment of all creation," states the unmarried protagonist, evidently speaking or writing to herself in a moment of intense self-reflection. "I often wonder," she continues, "if I might not have been very decent, very decent indeed, if I had laid hold on the life so many of my friends lead. If I had only had a real home of my own with a husband and children in it. . . . I am a graft on the tree of human womanhood. I am a hybrid. Sometimes I think I am a monster, and the worst of it is, I certainly take pleasure in it" (Foster, 142-43). The protagonist delights in outwitting those around her in small things, such as lending her unsuspecting neighbor diluted rather than pure vanilla. Thus, although she rages within at the injustice of her single state, the outward manifestation of her rebellion is carefully contained; that she alone knows she is fooling others is part of her secret triumph. She revels in her potential for and not her actual enacting of wholesale revolt: "Here I am, a woman, rather delicately built, of rather delicate tastes, perfectly able to break those commandments, to convert into dust every one of those Divine laws. I shudder before my own power, yet I glory because of it" (Foster, 143). Unfortunately, Freeman broke off this provocative piece at this juncture and never returned to complete it.

Freeman's characteristic theme, that of revolt against stifling social restrictions and the divided self that results from the fray, finds its boldest rendition in these late pieces. As both a single and a married woman, Freeman seems to have experienced such self-division during at least some periods in her life. Her letters testify to the fact that she sometimes felt she possessed two very different sides to her personality; she was also aware of dissonance between how she appeared to others and how she regarded herself. For example, after posing for a photograph in 1892, she remarked to a friend, "I have tried very hard to look cheerful, but I should have enjoyed 'making a face' much more. You think I am modest, but I am not. I am vicious" (Kendrick, 141). Some 20 years later, in 1915, she echoed her character Jane Lennox in telling *Woman's Home Companion* editor Hayden Carruth, "I have a frightful conviction that I look capable of nothing except afternoon teas or breaking all the Commandments and sulking because there are no more" (Kendrick, 347). But the most convincing evidence that the author knew her subject firsthand is her abiding interest in issues of rebellion and self-division throughout her entire career. Some of her final explorations of these issues, in such works as **"The Old-Maid Aunt," "The Jester,"** and **"Jane Lennox"** indicate Freeman's increasing desire to speak frankly about the ramifications of such inner tension, however dark or disturbing they may be.

When Freeman relocated to New Jersey after her marriage, she assumed she would discover there ample material for her writing. After all, "people are all alike, especially if they happen to be women, whether they live in Massachusetts or Metuchen," she stated optimistically to a newspaper reporter at the time of the move.[7] To her dismay, she proved herself wrong. The upper middle class, staid Metuchen lifestyle bored her and yielded little fruit for her imagination. Consequently, although she continued to write prolifically after her marriage, she rarely employed New Jersey settings or characters. Her few efforts to do so resulted in some of her weakest novels, *The Debtor* (1905), *"Doc" Gordon* (1906), and *The Butterfly House* (1912), works that rankled Metuchenites because of their unflattering portraits of the locale and its inhabitants. Only a handful of the post-1902 stories have New Jersey-like settings. During her years in Metuchen, Freeman relied on her frequent trips back to Randolph and, less occasionally, to Brattleboro for fresh material.

Though her New England settings remain a constant, a number of Freeman's later stories incorporate modern subject matter and reflect the author's new pastimes and concerns. Both Mary and Charles Freeman were avid bridge players in several Metuchen circles, and **"The Winning Lady"** (1909) satirizes the petty ambitions of card-playing society women. **"A Guest in Sodom"** (1912), about a man who is driven to distraction by an automobile that perpetually breaks down, is a lighthearted poke at both Freemans, who enjoyed motoring, employed a chauffeur, and owned six automobiles by 1912, one of which, a Studebaker E. M. F., Mary Freeman dubbed "Every Mechanical Fault"

(Kendrick, 339). A handful of stories expresses Freeman's anxiety over the prospect of aging, a fear she mentions several times in her letters. These include **"The Travelling Sister"** (1908), about a woman who "vacations" by retreating into past memories, and **"The Amethyst Comb"** (1914) and **"Sweet-Flowering Perennial"** (1915), both of which concern aging women who, because they are in love with much younger men, desperately attempt to hold on to their youth. Finally, the advent of World War I brought out an ardent patriotic spirit in Freeman, resulting in **"The Liar"** (1917), **"Both Cheeks"** (1917), **"The Return"** (1921), and several nationalistic poems.

Interrelated and Child-Protagonist Stories

Two final categories of Freeman's stories deserve brief mention. Since her tales of village life and characters often seem closely connected (the name she originally proposed for her first collection was *Among New England Neighbors*), it is not surprising that Freeman tried her hand at composing several series of interrelated pieces over the course of her career. She had precedent in doing so: village sketches united by a first-person narrator who relates her tale with indulgent goodwill and a nostalgic tone were popular throughout the nineteenth century both in Britain and in the United States. These included Mary Russell Mitford's *Our Village* (1824-1832), Elizabeth Gaskell's *Cranford* (1853), and Sarah Orne Jewett's *Country of the Pointed Firs* (1896). Freeman read Gaskell and Jewett and no doubt knew Mitford's work as well. She published her own slender volume of interrelated village sketches, ***The People of Our Neighborhood,*** in 1898, and the following year produced the short novel ***The Jamesons,*** which is based on a similar premise. Thereafter, Freeman penned two further series of interrelated pieces: 6 stories about children written between 1911 and 1914, which subsequently formed the first half of ***The Copy-Cat,*** and 12 stories written between 1914 and 1918 that, together with a brief preface, make up ***Edgewater People,*** Freeman's final short-story collection.

Of these interrelated works, only the stories in ***People of Our Neighborhood*** and two or three in the other two collections are significant. The tales in ***People of Our Neighborhood*** are connected by a garrulous female narrator. As is true with other of Freeman's first-person narratives, such as **"Luella Miller,"** we soon find ourselves less interested in the story being told than in the character of the storyteller. A village insider, the narrator is adept at summarizing the gist of local gossip even as she unapologetically, perhaps even unwittingly, shares in its prejudices. Her first six observations are about various local folk who have been so severely typecast by the community that each has been reduced to little more than an epithet: the unlucky man, the neat woman, the friend of cats, and the like. In her last three tales, the narrator describes the courting activities of some young people at several village events. Although all of her sketches seem innocent on the surface, the fact that the narrator has not only imbibed but thoroughly accepts village biases is disconcerting given Freeman's lifelong empathy for those who vehemently resist such stereotyping. Yet we are provided with little room for further speculation about the speaker: she never fully identifies herself, her position in the village, or her intent in relating her observations. We are, moreover, never made privy to others' conversations with or about her. Consequently, although pleasant reading, the sketches in *People of Our Neighborhood* remain flat and undeveloped. In addition, the volume's organization is loose at best. Freeman wrote the nine sketches for *Ladies' Home Journal* over a two-year period, from December 1895 to December 1897; six were published under the heading "Neighborhood Types" and the remaining three under "Pleasures of Our Neighborhood." Although she evidently strove for some consistency in the tales in narrative voice and in certain individuals who reappear, she made no further revisions to unify the pieces when they were finally collected into one volume. Despite *People* [*The People of Our Neighborhood*]'s flaws, however, it is interesting to note that the book's caricatures were lifelike enough to offend Randolph residents, who murmured that the author "was going too far in writing about her own neighbors, who were just as good as she was" (Foster, 136).

Freeman revisited the genre of interrelated village tales a year later with the novel *The Jamesons.* Here, unlike in *People,* she creates tension and intrigue by establishing a foil to the gossiping insider narrator, Mrs. Sophia Lane, with the arrival of the outsider Mrs. Jameson, a sophisticated city woman bent on improving her "backward" country neighbors. Mrs. Jameson's reforms are, of course, met with skepticism by the villagers, who soon come to tolerate the busybody as just one more type of village eccentric. A broad farce on the "country mouse/city mouse" theme, *The Jamesons* was a popular success, selling more than 8,000 copies in its first month of publication.

Freeman continued writing interrelated works later in her career, although with little distinction. The six stories that feature the same set of children in *The Copy-Cat* ("The Copy-Cat," "The Cock of the Walk," "Johnny-in-the-Woods," "Daniel and Little Dan'l," "Big Sister Solly," "Little Lucy Rose") and two others collected in *The Winning Lady* ("Little-Girl-Afraid-of-a-Dog," "The Joy of Youth") hold little appeal today for most readers, although they were evidently welcomed by their original *Harper's Monthly* audience. As do the other tales with child protagonists scattered throughout Freeman's adult fiction, these concern youthful capers, puppy-love romances, and sentimentalized parent and child relationships. "Little-Girl-Afraid-of-a-Dog" (1906) is the best of this group of stories. Forced to deliver baskets of eggs to a family with a fierce dog, little Emmeline daily undergoes mental and physical anguish over the prospect, yet both embarrassed by her fear and too young to verbalize it, she is unable to convey her terror to her mother. Freeman succeeds in capturing the full extent of Emmeline's inner agony. Always sympathetic to children, Freeman never lost her ability to comprehend the magnified fears and distorted perceptions of a child's world.

Edgewater People was both Freeman's last collection and her final attempt to compose a series of related stories. A brief introduction was inserted in the volume to explain the stories' relationship: purportedly, they demonstrate how the old coastal town of Barr expanded and divided over time into smaller villages, each of which still bears the stamp of its strongly rooted original settlers, especially the Edgewater, Leicester, and Sylvester families. The idea of a fictional study of how certain villages derive their unique characters from their inhabitants is an intriguing one. Unfortunately, this promise is not at all fulfilled in the loosely connected stories that follow. In fact one suspects that Freeman, probably at Harper's bidding, merely tacked on the preface in order to provide some plausible context for uniting the 12 stories, which were originally published in three very different magazines (*Harper's Monthly, Woman's Home Companion, Saturday Evening Post*) over a four-year period. Several of the tales involve Sarah Edgewater, a middle-aged, unmarried, well-off New England woman who acts as a type of family retainer for her various relations. Two of the stories in which she appears present late variations on quintessential Freeman themes. "Sarah Edgewater" (1916) illustrates the ongoing feud between the two Edgewater sisters that originated when, in their youth, Laura "stole" and subsequently married Sarah's beau. The story is convincing in its description of the intense hatred the sisters feel toward each other—Sarah loathes Laura for obvious reasons; Laura's feelings for Sarah are "subtler and more deadly, the hatred of the wrong-doer for the victim of the wrong"—but it falls short in the contrived reconciliation that forms its conclusion.[8] "Value Received" (1916) recalls such early tales as "A Gala Dress" and "Old Lady Pingree" in its portrayal of two impoverished but proud elderly sisters who disdain, but must accept, Sarah Edgewater's charity. To reciprocate, one of the women sews a bonnet for Sarah to wear at her niece's wedding. Though the hat is ridiculously out-moded, Sarah swallows her pride and wears it to the occasion, wisely perceiving "that the one who gives has a duty aside from giving—a sacred duty to the receiver of the gift." "[Sarah] knew that the old sisters had quailed in spirit before her benefits," the narrator explains. "Now it was her turn. She owed it to them to endure the humiliation which she included—whether she would or not—in her weekly gift to the sisters" (*EP* [*Edgewater People*], 98). Indeed, Sarah's wisdom, stability, and serenity make her one of Freeman's strongest female protagonists. Unfortunately, none of the other stories in *Edgewater People* features her in a prominent manner. Moreover, by the middle of this volume, any attempt to unify the stories in any manner has been completely abandoned.

Because of its novel situation, **"The Outside of the House"** (1914) is the most interesting story among the uneven works in *Edgewater People*; its intimate mixture of pathos and humor also mark it as typical in the author's canon. Retired ship captain Joe Dickson and his taciturn wife, Martha, live quietly in a humble dwelling by the sea. The couple have a clandestine pleasure, however: every year, they eagerly await their wealthy neighbors' departure to Europe so they can dress in their Sunday best and take up daily residence on the gracious home's huge front porch. Freeman reveals the couple's guilty delight gradually, and its utter unexpectedness for two such aged, unassuming people lends the story great charm. As we have seen elsewhere, one of Freeman's unique strengths is her ability to crystallize a story around one sharply drawn picture, to distill, as it were, events and characters into a single, striking image. Candace Whitcomb's screeching out a hymn over her parlor organ in **"A Village Singer"**; Ann Millet angrily tossing squash out her back door in **"An Object of Love"**; a parrot pecking a bride's bonnet into shreds in **"The Parrot"**; Evelina Leonard's midnight pouring of boiling water on a splendid garden in **"Evelina's Garden"**; two old sisters bent over an inanely smiling doll in **"The Reign of a Doll"**—these are but a few examples. In **"The Outside of the House,"** the image of Joe, Martha, and the absent neighbors' serving man (who cares for the mansion during the summer and who is in on Joe and Martha's scheme) rocking contentedly in the summer breeze on the well-appointed porch—almost as if they owned the place!—is wonderfully memorable.

As is also characteristic of her most skillful short fiction, Freeman uses nature symbolically in **"The Outside of the House."** In this story, it serves to complicate the plot as well. The omnipresent sea forever pounding in the background of the tale becomes a type of metaphoric leveling device. Though the home owners possess money and influence, they do not rec-ognize the ocean's power and fail to properly maintain the seawall before they leave for their vacation abroad. Joe and Martha, on the other hand, close to nature and attentive to its rhythms, easily interpret the weather's signs and manage to save the neighbors' property from disaster during a furious nor'easter. Far more important to them than the financial reward they receive for their vigilance is the fact that, because the owners decide to remain overseas for a longer period, they will be able to inhabit the mansion's grand porch undetected for an entire year.

* * *

On a recent trip to New York, I made a pilgrimage to the American Academy of Arts and Letters on West 155th Street to view the ornamental doors that in 1938 were dedicated posthumously to Freeman. Inscribed "To the memory of Mary E. Wilkins Freeman and the Women Writers of America," the solid bronze doors stand as a fitting tribute to a writer whose work has ridden the vicissitudes of literary fashion—high popularity in the latter part of the nineteenth century, near obscurity throughout much of the twentieth—and yet has withstood the test of time, having been discovered anew and with delight a century after it first began to appear. Freeman's permanent position in American letters is assured. Grounded in a time and place that have disappeared—late-nineteenth-century rural New England—her short stories exhibit a universality of character that makes them as fully readable and enjoyable today as they were in her own time. The human heart struggling against odds to obtain inner fulfillment, love, and a sense of belonging is the underlying theme of all her fiction. But Freeman's best stories achieve their value through the author's deft and unique handling of this universal theme. With clear and direct vision, Freeman records the myriad, often conflicting forces of personality and society, of individual temperament and cultural norms, that converge to produce the circumstances in which her protagonists find themselves enmeshed. With a carefully balanced tone of empathy and judgment, she quickly cuts through peripheral matters to focus on the characters' secret inner lives as they weigh possibilities and act according to their available options. That their choices are often severely circumscribed is an essential part of Freeman's vision, one that borders on tragicomedy in its understanding of the deep ironies inherent in the human condition.

Moreover, as the inscription on the academy's doors attests, Freeman was at the vanguard of modern professional American women writers in her lifetime. Unapologetically, she made her writing the central fact of her life and forged a career by combining native talent with acquired business acumen. She wrote to express her creative sensibility, and she wrote to sell; she experimented with genre and technique to satisfy her artistic ambition, and she penned hack pieces to maintain the increasingly comfortable lifestyle she craved. That she failed nearly as often as she succeeded—that is, failed by modern critical standards, since nearly all of her work sold well in her lifetime—is not surprising, nor should it be considered a mark against her given the large quantity and variety of her literary output. Finally it is perhaps most important to stress that, though many have attempted it over the years, Freeman's writing simply resists easy categorization. Though the arena in which her characters' struggles are played out is small and largely unchanging, Freeman succeeds in creating a gallery of people in her fiction whose responses to life are as varied as would be those of any sampling of human beings. Freeman's great power comes from her ability to see—really *see*—individual persons and not groups, causes, or agendas. Her stories, therefore, can disturb us with their unshrinking view of reality and entertain us with their poignant humor, but above all, they leave us with sharply etched portraits of memorable characters—Sarah Penn of **"The Revolt of 'Mother,'"** Martha Elder of **"A Balsam Fir,"** Christopher Dodd of **"The Balking of Christopher,"** Sophia Lane of **"The Revolt of Sophia Lane"**—characters that, after we are made privy to their tales of rebellion and quiet triumph, we are not soon likely to forget.

Notes

1. like to get away from earth awhile hen come back to it
   and begin over.
   May no fate willfully misunderstand me
   And half grant what I wish and snatch me away
   Not to return. Earth's the right place for love:
   I don't know where it's likely to go better.

   Robert Frost, "Birches," in *Robert Frost's Poems*,
   ed. Louis Untermeyer (New York: Simon
   and Schuster, 1971), 90

2. Beth Wynne Fisken, "'Unusual' People in a 'Usual Place': 'The Balking of Christopher' by Mary Wilkins Freeman," *Colby Library Quarterly* 21 (June 1985): 100; hereafter cited in the text.

3. Martha J. Cutter, "Beyond Stereotypes: Mary Wilkins Freeman's Radical Critique of Nineteenth-Century Cults of Femininity," *Women's Studies* 21 (1992): 383-84.

4. Freeman, *The Copy-Cat and Other Stories* (New York: Harper and Brothers, 1914), 172; hereafter cited in the text as *CC*.

5. Freeman, *The Fair Lavinia and Others* (New York: Harper and Brothers, 1907), 195; hereafter cited in the text as *FL*.

6. For a discussion of the writing of this "corporate" novel, see Alfred Bendixen's introduction to Mary

Wilkins Freeman et al., *The Whole Family: A Novel By Twelve Authors* (New York: Frederick Ungar, 1987), xi-li.

7. "Mary E. Wilkins Freeman at Home at Metuchen, N.J.," *New York Herald*, literary section (31 May 1903): 2.

8. Freeman, *Edgewater People* (New York: Harper and Brothers, 1918), 13; hereafter cited in the text as *EP*.

Selected Bibliography

Primary Works

Adult Short Story Collections

The Best Stories of Mary E. Wilkins. Ed. and intro. Henry Wysham Lanier. New York: Harper and Brothers, 1927. "A Humble Romance," "The Revolt of 'Mother,'" "Little-Girl-Afraid-of-a-Dog," "A New England Nun," "One Good Time," "The Last Gift," "A New England Prophet," "A Village Singer," "Old Woman Magoun," "The Joy of Youth," "Billy and Susy," "The Butterfly," "Both Cheeks," "A Solitary," "Two Old Lovers," "Gentian," "The Wind in the Rose-Bush," "A Conflict Ended," "A Conquest of Humility," "The Apple-Tree," "Noblesse," "The Outside of the House," "Coronation," "The Gold," "The Gospel According to Joan."

The Copy-Cat and Other Stories. New York: Harper and Brothers, 1914. "The Copy-Cat," "The Cock of the Walk," "Johnny-in-the-Woods," "Daniel and Little Dan'l," "Big Sister Solly," "Little Lucy Rose," "Noblesse," "Coronation," "The Amethyst Comb," "The Umbrella Man," "The Balking of Christopher," "Dear Annie."

Edgewater People. New York: Harper and Brothers, 1918. "Sarah Edgewater," "The Old Man of the Field," "The Voice of the Clock," "Value Received," "The Flowering Bush," "The Outside of the House," "The Liar," "Sour Sweetings," "Both Cheeks," "The Soldier Man," "The Ring with the Green Stone," "'A Retreat to the Goal.'"

The Fair Lavinia and Others. New York: Harper and Brothers, 1907. "The Fair Lavinia," "Amarina's Roses," "Eglantina," "The Pink Shawls," "The Willow-Ware," "The Secret," "The Gold," "The Underling."

The Givers. New York: Harper and Brothers, 1904. "The Givers," "Lucy," "Eglantina," "Joy," "The Reign of the Doll," "The Chance of Araminta," "The Butterfly," "The Last Gift."

A Humble Romance and Other Stories. New York: Harper and Brothers, 1887. "A Humble Romance," "Two Old Lovers," "A Symphony in Lavender," "A

Tardy Thanksgiving," "A Modern Dragon," "An Honest Soul," "A Taste of Honey," "Brakes and White Vi'lets," "Robins and Hammers," "On the Walpole Road," "Old Lady Pingree," "Cinnamon Roses," "The Bar Light-House," "A Lover of Flowers," "A Far-Away Melody," "A Moral Exigency," "A Mistaken Charity," "Gentian," "An Object of Love," "A Gatherer of Simples," "An Independent Thinker," "In Butterfly Time," "An Unwilling Guest," "A Souvenir," "An Old Arithmetician," "A Conflict Ended," "A Patient Waiter," "A Conquest of Humility."

The Love of Parson Lord and Other Stories. New York: Harper and Brothers, 1900. "The Love of Parson Lord," "The Tree of Knowledge," "Catherine Carr," "The Three Old Sisters and the Old Beau," "One Good Time."

A Mary Wilkins Freeman Reader. Ed. and intro. Mary R. Reichardt. Lincoln: University of Nebraska Press, 1997. "An Honest Soul," "A Conflict Ended," "An Independent Thinker," "A New England Nun," "Christmas Jenny," "Life-Everlastin'," "A Village Singer," "A Church Mouse," "A Poetess," "The Revolt of 'Mother,'" "Louisa," "Evelina's Garden," "One Good Time," "The Parrot," "Arethusa," "The Balsam Fir," "The Great Pine," "Luella Miller," "The Lost Ghost," "Eglantina," "The Revolt of Sophia Lane," "The Reign of the Doll," "The Gold," "The Old-Maid Aunt," "Old Woman Magoun," "The Selfishness of Amelia Lamkin," "The Balking of Christopher," "The Outside of the House."

A New England Nun and Other Stories. New York: Harper and Brothers, 1891. "A New England Nun," "A Village Singer," "A Gala Dress," "The Twelfth Guest," "Sister Liddy," "Calla-Lilies and Hannah," "A Wayfaring Couple," "A Poetess," "Christmas Jenny," "A Pot of Gold," "The Scent of the Roses," "A Solitary," "A Gentle Ghost," "A Discovered Pearl," "A Village Lear," "Amanda and Love," "Up Primrose Hill," "A Stolen Christmas," "Life-Everlastin'," "An Innocent Gamester," "Louisa," "A Church Mouse," "A Kitchen Colonel," "The Revolt of 'Mother.'"

The People of Our Neighborhood. Philadelphia: Curtis Publishing Company, 1898. "Timothy Sampson: The Wise Man," "Little Margaret Snell: The Village Runaway," "Cyrus Emmett: The Unlucky Man," "Phebe Ann Little: The Neat Woman," "Amanda Todd: The Friend of Cats," "Lydia Wheelock: The Good Woman," "A Quilting Bee in Our Village," "The Stockwells' Apple-Paring Bee," "The Christmas Sing in Our Village."

The Revolt of Mother and Other Stories. Ed. and afterword Michele Clark. New York: Feminist Press, 1974. "A Mistaken Charity," "A Moral Exigency," "A Taste of Honey," "Louisa," "A New England Nun," "A Gala Dress," "The Revolt of 'Mother,'" "A Church Mouse."

Selected Stories of Mary E. Wilkins Freeman. Ed. and intro. Marjorie Pryse. New York: W. W. Norton, 1983. "Two Old Lovers," "An Honest Soul," "On the Walpole

Road," "A Mistaken Charity," "A Gatherer of Simples," "A Conflict Ended," "A Patient Waiter," "A New England Nun," "A Village Singer," "A Gala Dress," "Sister Liddy," "A Poetess," "Christmas Jenny," "A Solitary," "A Village Lear," "Up Primrose Hill," "A Church Mouse," "The Revolt of 'Mother.'"

Short Fiction of Sarah Orne Jewett and Mary Wilkins Freeman. Ed. and intro. Barbara H. Solomon. New York: New American Library, 1979. "A Mistaken Charity," "Gentian," "An Independent Thinker," "A Conflict Ended," "A New England Nun," "A Village Singer," "A Poetess," "Louisa," "A Church Mouse," "The Revolt of 'Mother,'" "One Good Time," "The Lombardy Poplar," "The Selfishness of Amelia Lamkin," "Old Woman Magoun."

Silence and Other Stories. New York: Harper and Brothers, 1898. "Silence," "The Buckley Lady," "Evelina's Garden," "A New England Prophet," "The Little Maid at the Door," "Lydia Hersey, of East Bridgewater."

Six Trees. New York: Harper and Brothers, 1903. "The Elm-Tree," "The White Birch," "The Great Pine," "The Balsam Fir," "The Lombardy Poplar," "The Apple-Tree."

The Uncollected Stories of Mary Wilkins Freeman. Ed. and intro. Mary R. Reichardt. Jackson: University Press of Mississippi, 1992. "Emmy," "Juliza," "A Tragedy from the Trivial," "The Prism," "The Hall Bedroom," "Humble Pie," "The Slip of the Leash," "For the Love of One's Self," "The Witch's Daughter," "The Horn of Plenty," "A Guest in Sodom," "The Doll Lady," "The Blue Butterfly," "Friend of My Heart," "Criss-Cross," "Sweet-Flowering Perennial," "The Cloak Also," "Mother-Wings," "The Jester," "The White Shawl."

Understudies. New York: Harper and Brothers, 1901. "The Cat," "The Monkey," "The Squirrel," "The Lost Dog," "The Parrot," "The Doctor's Horse," "Bouncing Bet," "Prince's-Feather," "Arethusa," "Mountain-Laurel," "Peony," "Morning-Glory."

The Wind in the Rose-Bush and Other Stories of the Supernatural. New York: Doubleday, Page and Company, 1903. Reprinted with an afterword by Alfred Bendixen. Chicago: Academy Chicago, 1986. "The Wind in the Rose-Bush," "The Shadows on the Wall," "Luella Miller," "The Southwest Chamber," "The Vacant Lot," "The Lost Ghost."

The Winning Lady and Others. New York: Harper and Brothers, 1909. "The Winning Lady," "Little-Girl-Afraid-of-a-Dog," "The Joy of Youth," "Billy and Susy," "The Selfishness of Amelia Lamkin," "The Travelling Sister," "Her Christmas," "Old Woman Magoun," "Eliza Sam," "Flora and Hannah," "A New-Year's Resolution."

UNCOLLECTED ADULT SHORT STORIES

"About Hannah Stone." *Everybody's* 4 (January 1901): 25-33.

"The Auction." *Woman's Home Companion* 36 (October 1909): 7-8, 93.

"Away from the Sunflower Ranch." *Boston Evening Transcript: The Holiday Transcript* (December 1890): 4.

"Betsey Somerset." *Harper's Bazar* 26 (18 March 1893): 205-7.

"The Boomerang." *Pictorial Review* 18 (March 1917): 22-24, 44.

"The Bright Side." *Harper's Monthly* 146 (April 1923): 630-44.

"The Brother." MS. (c. 1927). Reference from Foster, 213.

"A Brotherhood of Three." *Harper's Weekly* 41 (18 December 1897): 1248-50. Also in *Illustrated London News* 111 (18 December 1897): 879-81.

"The Cautious King, and the All-Round Wise Woman." *Harper's Weekly* 53 (26 June 1909): 22-24.

"The Christmas Ghost." *Everybody's* 3 (December 1900): 512-20.

"A Christmas Lady." *Ladies' Home Journal* 27 (December 1909): 17-18.

"D.J.: A Christmas Story." *Mail and Express Illustrated Saturday Magazine* (New York; 5 December 1903): 14-15, 22, 30. Also in *Advance* 46 (17 December 1903): 766-69.

"A Devotee of Art." *Harper's Bazar* 27 (27 January 1894): 69-71.

"Down the Road to the Emersons." *Romance* 12 (November 1893): 3-24.

"An Easter-Card." *Everybody's* 4 (April 1901): 372-77.

"Emancipation." *Harper's Monthly* 132 (December 1915): 27-35.

"Eunice and the Doll." *Boston Evening Transcript* (13 December 1897): 8; (14 December 1897): 10. Also in *Pocket Magazine* 5 (March 1898): 1-41 and in *Best Things from American Literature,* ed. Irving Bacheller. New York: The Christian Herald, 1899, 369-82.

"Far Away Job." *Woman's Home Companion* 36 (December 1909): 6-7, 72-75.

"The Fighting McLeans." *The Delineator* 75 (February 1910): 113-14, 150-52.

"General: A Christmas Story." *10 Story Book* 1 (January 1902): 10-15.

"The Gift of Love." *Woman's Home Companion* 33 (December 1906): 21-22, 73.

"The Happy Day." *McClure's* 21 (May 1903): 89-94.

"The Home-Coming of Jessica." *Woman's Home Companion* 28 (3 November 1901): n.p. Also in *The Home-Coming of Jessica* [by Mary E. Wilkins]; *An Idyl of Central Park* [by Brander Matthews]; *The Romance of a Soul* [by Robert Grant]. New York: Crowell and Kirkpatrick, 1901, 3-17.

"Honorable Tommy." *Woman's Home Companion* 43 (December 1916): 15-16, 68.

"How Charlotte Ellen Went Visiting." *Boston Evening Transcript* 1 (November 1897): 10; (2 November 1897): 8. Also in *New York Ledger* 54 (14 May and 21 May 1898): 17-18 each issue.

"Hyacinthus." *Harper's Monthly* 109 (August 1904): 447-58. Also in *Quaint Courtships,* ed. William Dean Howells and Henry Mills Alden. London: Harper and Brothers, 1906, 75-107.

"The Jade Bracelet." *Forum* 59 (April 1918): 429-40.

[Jane Lennox.] Undated MS., privately owned. Reference from Foster, 142-43.

"Josiah's First Christmas." *Collier's* 44 (11 December 1909): 9-10.

"Julia—Her Thanksgiving." *Harper's Bazar* 43 (November 1909): 1079-82.

"The Little Green Door." *New York Times* (13-15 April 1896): 9 each issue. Also in *Pocket Magazine* 3 (July 1896): 56-90 and in *New York Ledger* 52 (25 April 1898): 16-17.

"The Long Arm." By Mary E. Wilkins and J. Edgar Chamberlin. *Pocket Magazine* 1 (December 1895): 1-76. Also in Mary E. Wilkins et al. *The Long Arm and Other Detective Stories.* London: Chapman and Hall, 1895, 1-66.

"A Meeting Half-Way." *Harper's Bazar* 24 (11 April 1891): 273-75.

"Mrs. Sackett's Easter Bonnet." *Woman's Home Companion* 34 (April 1907): 5-7.

"The Mystery of Miss Amidon." *Boston Evening Transcript* (22 December 1900): 18.

"Nanny and Martha Pepperill." *Harper's Bazar* 28 (14 December 1895): 1021-23.

"A Narrow Escape/How Santa Claus Baffled the Mounted Police." *Detroit Sunday News* (25 December 1892): 12.

"An Old Valentine." *Home-Maker* 8 (February 1890): 367-74. Also in *Romance* 9 (February 1893): 50-64.

"One." MS. (c. 1928). Reference from Foster, 213.

"Other People's Cake." *Collier's* 42 (21 November 1908): 14-15, 32, 34, 36-37.

"The Other Side." *Harper's Bazar* 24 (26 December 1891): 993-95.

"The Price She Paid." *Harper's Bazar* 21 (10 March 1888): 158-59.

"The Prop." *Saturday Evening Post* 190 (5 January 1918): 12-13, 109-10.

"A Protracted Meeting." *Housewife* 6 (February 1891): 6; 6 (March 1891): 6.

"The Proud Lucinda." *Harper's Bazar* 24 (7 February 1891): 101-3.

"The Pumpkin." *Harper's Bazar* 33 (24 November 1900): 1863-71.

"The Return." *Woman's Home Companion* 48 (August 1921): 21-22, 83.

"The Rocket." Undated MS, also entitled "One Old Lady." Manuscript and Archives Division, New York Public Library.

"Rosemary Marsh." *Harper's Bazar* 30 (11 December 1897): 1026.

"A Rustic Comedy." *Ladies' Home Journal* 8 (March 1891): 7-8.

"Santa Claus: Two Jack-Knives." *Springfield* [Mass.] *Sunday Republican* (15 December 1901): 24.

"The Saving of Hiram Sessions." *Pictorial Review* 16 (May 1915): 20-21, 70-72.

"The School-Teacher." *Harper's Bazar* 28 (6 April 1895): 262.

"The School-Teacher's Story." *Romance* 13 (February 1894): 5-18.

"Serena Ann's First Valentine." *Boston Evening Transcript* (5 February 1897): 9. Also in *New York Ledger* 53 (13 February 1897): 6-7 and in *English Illustrated* 17 (June 1897): 235-42.

"Serena Ann: Her First Christmas Keeping." *Hartford Daily Courant* (15 December 1894): 10.

"The Shadow Family." *Boston Sunday Budget* (1 January 1882): n.p. . . .

"She Who Adorns Her Sister Adorns Herself." *Harper's Bazar* 38 (May 1904): 456-60.

"A Slayer of Serpents." *Collier's* 44 (19 March 1910): 16-17, 19, 36, 38.

"Something on Her Mind." *Harper's Bazar* 46 (December 1912): 607-8.

"Sonny." *Lippincott's* 47 (June 1891): 776-85. Also in *Romance* 8 (November 1892): 13-27.

"Starlight." *Woman's Home Companion* 35 (December 1908): 19-20, 74.

"The Steeple." *Hampton-Columbian* 27 (October 1911): 412-20.

"The Story of Little Mary Whitlow." *Lippincott's* 21 (May 1883): 500-504.

"A Stress of Conscience." *Harper's Bazar* 25 (25 June 1892): 518-19. Also in *Illustrated London News* 100 (25 June 1892): 785-87.

"The Strike of Hannah." *Woman's Home Companion* 33 (November 1906): 9-10, 50-52.

"A Study in China." *Harper's Bazar* 20 (5 November 1887): 766-67.

"Susan: Her Neighbor's Story." *Harper's Bazar* 32 (23 September 1899): 801, 804.

"Susan Jane's Valentine." *Harper's Bazar* 33 (17 February 1900): 132-33.

"Sweet-Williams." *Harper's Bazar* 28 (25 May 1895): 418.

"Tall Jane." *St. Louis Republic* (25 October 1891): 5. Also in *Detroit Sunday News* (25 October 1891): 12.

"Thanksgiving Crossroads." *Woman's Home Companion* 44 (November 1917): 13, 58, 60.

"A Thanksgiving Thief." *Ladies' Home Journal* 9 (November 1892): 1-2.

"Two for Peace." *Lippincott's* 68 (July 1901): 51-70.

"Two Friends." *Harper's Bazar* 20 (25 June 1887): 450-51.

"Uncle Davy." *Detroit Sunday News* (10 January 1892): 10.

"An Unlucky Christmas." *Harper's Bazar* 29 (12 December 1896): 1037-39.

"A Wandering Samaritan." *Cosmopolitan* 2 (September 1886): 28-33.

"A War-Time Dress." *Cosmopolitan* 25 (August 1898): 403-16.

"Wrong Side Out." *10 Story Book* 1 (July 1901): 10-16.

WORKS IN OTHER GENRES

The Butterfly House. New York: Dodd, Mead and Company, 1912. Novel.

The Debtor. New York: Harper and Brothers, 1905. Novel.

"Doc" Gordon. New York: Authors and Newspapers Association, 1906. Novel.

The Jamesons. New York: Doubleday and McClure Company, 1899. Novel.

Pembroke. New York: Harper and Brothers, 1894. Novel.

The Shoulders of Atlas. New York: Harper and Brothers, 1908. Novel.

The Whole Family: A Novel by Twelve Authors. Mary Wilkins Freeman, William D. Howells, Henry James, et al. New York: Harper and Brothers, 1908. Chapter in novel.

Secondary Works

Books

Foster, Edward. *Mary E. Wilkins Freeman.* New York: Hendricks House, 1956.

Kendrick, Brent L., ed. *The Infant Sphinx: Collected Letters of Mary E. Wilkins Freeman.* Metuchen, N.J.: Scarecrow Press, 1985.

Critical Articles and Chapters in Books

Brand, Alice Glarden. "Mary Wilkins Freeman: Misanthropy as Propaganda." *New England Quarterly* 50 (March 1977): 83-100.

Cutter, Martha J. "Beyond Stereotypes: Mary Wilkins Freeman's Radical Critique of Nineteenth-Century Cults of Femininity." *Women's Studies* 21 (1992): 383-95.

Fisken, Beth Wynne. "'Unusual' People in a 'Usual Place': 'The Balking of Christopher' by Mary Wilkins Freeman." *Colby Library Quarterly* 21 (June 1985): 99-103.

Susan Garland Mann (essay date March 1998)

SOURCE: Mann, Susan Garland. "A House of One's Own: The Subversion of 'True Womanhood' in Mary E. Wilkins Freeman's Short Fiction." *Colby Quarterly* 34, no. 1 (March 1998): 39-54.

[*In the following essay, Mann contends that the female characters in Freeman's stories have a largely positive relationship with their domestic surroundings and she contrasts this characteristic with the stifling domesticity portrayed in the stories of Charlotte Perkins Gilman and Kate Chopin.*]

Mary E. Wilkins Freeman's short fiction is grounded in the common lives of rural New England women.[1] Freeman pays attention to the "woman's sphere," chronicling in detail the houses in which her charac-ters live and the domestic work that gives their lives significance. There are reasons—both historic and personal—why this was the case. In the nineteenth century, the status of American women changed as the country began to industrialize, home production shifting gradually to the factory. Nancy Woloch describes this "unspoken bargain between middle-class women and men" that changed women's roles:

> While men were still heads of families, their real domain was now in the world—a world of business . . . and money making. Family status depended on their earned income and public roles. Women were expected to devote themselves entirely to private life, to the 'chaste circle of the fireside.' . . . Woman's sphere was in fact a new social space, one that had not been recognized before. On the one hand, it was an enclosed, limited, private space. On the other, it was an improvement over having no space at all.

(114-17)

During the nineteenth century, women were conditioned by ladies' magazines such as *Godey's Lady's Book,* by books on domesticity such as Catharine E. Beecher's *Treatise on Domestic Economy for the Use of Young Ladies at Home and at School* (1841; reprinted annually until 1856; expanded in 1869), and by the pulpit to accept that "a true woman's place was unquestionably by her own fireside—as daughter, sister, but most of all as wife and mother" (Welter 162). There were additional social and economic pressures during the last quarter of the nineteenth century that further validated the significance of home life for the middle class. As Page Smith emphasizes when discussing Sarah Orne Jewett, the writer who exercised the greatest influence on Freeman, "the tidy, carefully cared-for female household . . . became, in the work of all the New England women writers, a symbol of their determination to create and preserve a simple domestic order in the face of the chaotic and disintegrating larger society" (761). Not only did the Civil War continue to take its toll for the remainder of the century, but the unparalleled growth in industry brought with it economic uncertainty and upheaval.

As examples, consider Randolph, Massachusetts, the town where Freeman was born and to which she returned after the death of her parents, and Brattleboro, Vermont, where she lived between the ages of fifteen and thirty-one. Crippled in the 1860s when larger mills took over much of their shoe manufacturing and other domestic industries, Randolph was a typical New England factory town in economic decline (Foster 16; Westbrook 5-8). Two years after the end of the Civil War, Warren Wilkins (Freeman's father) chose to leave Randolph to set up a dry goods business in Brattleboro, Vermont, even though he had been trained as a builder and an architect (Kendrick 41). In the decade just before Freeman began publishing, Brattleboro—which must have appeared prosperous compared to Randolph—absorbed a series of financial shocks. Black Friday, 24 September 1869, ruined some local businesses (Foster 28), and in the 1870s, other financial tremors were felt. Bank failures and financial panic in 1873 initiated a four-year depression, and farm prices fell in the United States almost continuously from 1870 to the end of the century (Smith 361).

The Wilkins household in Brattleboro was affected by this debilitating economic climate, and from adolescent years into her adulthood, Mary Wilkins witnessed her family's status in the community steadily decline. This was most clearly reflected by the places where they lived. Although he had purchased a lot in a fashionable residential section of Brattleboro, Warren Wilkins could never afford to build a house there. Instead, the family lived in a small cottage near the Common until desperation forced them in 1875 to move into an apartment in the building Wilkins had recently constructed for a friend (Foster 25, 38). Only two years later, the family suffered the humiliation of moving into the home of the Reverend Thomas Pickman Tyler, where Eleanor Lothrop Wilkins (Mary's mother) functioned as housekeeper. It must have been painful for a man described by Brent L. Kendrick as "an architect and builder of some note" (41) to be unable to provide a house for his own family. Similarly, it must have been difficult for Mrs. Wilkins—whose ancestors included prominent landowners and notable professionals (Kendrick 41) and who was, one assumes, a skillful housekeeper—to have to keep house for another family.

If Mary E. Wilkins Freeman was preoccupied with the spaces in which her characters lived, part of her interest must reflect her own anxiety about housing. When Mrs. Wilkins died suddenly in 1880, Mary and her father had to leave the Tylers' house. Mary Wilkins must have been concerned about the prospect of no permanent residence, and, because she was beginning to publish her poetry and short fiction to help earn a living, about a suitable place in which to write. After all, as Virginia Woolf emphasized almost fifty years later, "it is necessary to have five hundred a year and a room with a lock on the door if you are to write . . ." (109). Mary lived with her father until he left for Florida to regain his strength and to work on a construction job. When he died in Florida in 1883, Mary stayed with a series of relatives and acquaintances until she took permanent residence in the family home of one of her closest friends from childhood, Mary John Wales, in Randolph, Massachusetts.

Life with the Wales family provided Wilkins with comfortable and private rooms, apparently the "whole north side of the house," containing both a study on the first floor and a secluded room on the second used for writing (Foster 60, 87). Furthermore, Mary Wales attended to household matters, encouraging the author to focus on her writing. From all accounts, the young women were extremely close and supported each other, emotionally, intellectually, and financially. As Leah Blatt Glasser suggests in her recent biography of Freeman, *In a Closet Hidden,* their relationship was "intense and primary, and most likely engendered the intimacy she channeled into her description of women's friendships in her fiction" (156). Mary Wilkins stayed with the Waleses for seventeen years.[2] Only after 1897, when Mr. Wales was dying, does Foster note that the domestic situation became "difficult," for the tension apparently escalated between Mary Wales and her brother, characterized as "lazy, sullen, dissolute" (140). In any case, Mary Wilkins met and agreed to marry Charles Freeman in 1897.

Although postponed for five years, the marriage of Mary Wilkins to Charles Freeman took place in 1902. Just before the wedding, Mary Wilkins expressed excitement to her old friend Evie Sawyer Severance about having a place of her own: "I [shall] have a house in Metuchen with twenty-eight doors, and five pairs of stairs . . ." (Kendrick 257). While the Freemans' first house was rented, it was entirely restored just before the wedding, and within four years they built an impressive Colonial Revival residence in Metuchen, financed primarily by her novel *The Shoulders of Atlas.* Foster's biography describes the pleasure that Mary E. Wilkins Freeman took in the house—called Freewarren—that she and her husband designed, had built, and decorated with care. A groundbreaking ceremony took place, marked by a commemorative poem written by Freeman. Kendrick describes the "grand fashion" in which the house was furnished: "mahogany furniture, Oriental rugs (thirty-eight in all, many of them antique), fine silver and antique Chinese pewter . . . and many objects of art from all over the world" (265).

It is difficult to determine the extent to which Freewarren satisfied the writer's longing for a house of her own. Although she separated from her husband in 1921—when he refused treatment for alcoholism from the New Jersey State Hospital for the Insane—the author remained in Freewarren until her death in 1930.

* * *

In her own fiction, Mary E. Wilkins Freeman seldom features residences as refined as Freewarren; instead, they generally resemble more modest places, apparently based on houses in which Wilkins lived before she was married and other typical New England structures that she would have observed in Randolph and Brattleboro. But regardless of whether they are cottages built for factory workers (**"Two Old Lovers"** or **"A Wayfaring Couple"**) or an old "mansion-house" with Corinthian pillars (**"Evelina's Garden"** 113)— all of the houses that she creates are psychologically important for her women protagonists both as projections of themselves and as a means of achieving freedom and self-dignity.

Moreover, examination of her domestic settings helps demonstrate how Freeman, the writer, both conformed to and subverted the stereotypical definition of womanhood that extended through the last decades of the nineteenth century. In her highly influential article, Barbara Welter identifies specific expectations that society held for middle-class women in antebellum America. The character traits that Welter describes were still highly regarded after the War, despite the fact that more and more women must have resisted this "ideal":[3]

> The attributes of True Womanhood, by which a woman judged herself and was judged by her husband, her neighbors, and society could be divided into four cardinal virtues—piety, purity, submissiveness and domesticity.

> (152)

Welter's definition of True Womanhood helps establish what expectations Freeman probably inherited from her parents' generation and from the institutions around her, and helps determine the extent to which her own characters—many of whom would have been born before 1850—resist these expectations.

At first glance, Freeman's protagonists may seem to possess some of the qualities that Welter cites, especially given their preoccupation with domesticity, but they deviate from the prescribed norm in significant ways. An examination of these four cardinal "virtues" in her short fiction shows how Freeman's women subvert the concept of domesticity to achieve freedom and independence. While another critic, Martha J. Cutter, has already argued that Freeman critiques stereotypes of nineteenth-century femininity, including both the True Woman and the New Woman, her statements are based on only one story, **"The Selfishness of Amelia Lamkin."** I find Cutter's analysis insightful and my article follows her lead, but it attempts a more detailed examination of the concept of True Womanhood and the women's sphere, as it applies to Freeman, and takes into consideration the entire canon of Freeman's short fiction.

So far as the first characteristic is concerned, Freeman's protagonists are not especially interested in religion or piety or are even necessarily churchgoers.

While Freeman's parents were faithful Congregationalists and she herself attended Mount Holyoke Female Seminary,[4] many of the writer's characters are less committed to religious institutions or, if church members, experience difficulties within these institutions. For example, in **"The Balsam Fir"** Martha Elder baffles the community because, in spite of "all Martha's sweetness and serenity, she had not professed religion and united with the church" (111). Both **"A Village Singer"** and **"A Church Mouse"** provide criticisms of the way older women in the church are treated by officials as well as by church members. After forty years of service, Candace Whitcomb is dismissed from the church choir to make way for a younger lead soprano. Left homeless, Hetty in **"Church Mouse"** becomes a squatter in the local meeting house after she is told by the chair of the selectmen that, as a woman, she cannot be church sexton. In many stories women follow their own consciences, as might be expected since the author was the descendant of Calvinists, but the issue of religion or piety is not generally important, except where the author compares favorably the moral behavior of the outcast or nonchurchgoer with the actions of the clergy or church member in good standing. While Freeman becomes more interested in the relationship between nature and the human spirit in her later fiction, as illustrated by the stories in *Six Trees* (1903), this interest is not connected to any particular religion.

There is also relatively little attention paid in Freeman's fiction to the dangers of sexual impurity or to fallen women—except, perhaps, in **"Old Woman Magoun,"** where a grandmother kills her thirteen-year-old granddaughter rather than allow her to be marketed for sexual exploitation, and here the real horror is the father's eagerness to sell his daughter's sexuality as if it were a commodity. Yet, the second quality of True Womanhood—sexual purity—does receive attention in her stories, although Freeman's treatment of virginity is much different than that envisioned in the doctrine of True Womanhood: "Woman must preserve her virtue until marriage and marriage was necessary for her happiness" (Welter 158). Most of Freeman's woman characters are presumably virginal or celibate, but they rarely appear to be saving themselves for marriage. For a variety of reasons, they do not marry and in some stories their motivation is not explained to the reader. Nevertheless, a number of her protagonists resist or reject marriage offers primarily because they wish to preserve their independence. They resemble, to some extent, the members of the "Cult of Single Blessedness," described by Lee Chambers-Schiller in *Liberty, A Better Husband*:

> . . . [as] the select women in postrevolutionary America who suggested new, more modern reasons for rejecting marriage. For these, the decision not to marry

followed from a rigorous assessment of the marital institution that found it wanting and in conflict with female autonomy, self-development, and achievement.

(2)[5]

The issue of a woman's sexual purity (or lack thereof) is only important in Freeman's short fiction in one other way. A delicate nature—that is, a lack or avoidance of sexual feeling—was often assumed to be characteristic of women in nineteenth-century America, an idea about women that no doubt contributed to their chastity. When sexual undercurrents do appear in her stories, they generally involve a character's unconscious fear of sexuality, which is introduced as one of a number of reasons why a woman such as Caroline Munson in **"A Symphony in Lavender"** is reluctant to marry. As Munson explains, her decision to refuse a young suitor years ago was a response to her nightmare where he appeared "at once beautiful and repulsive." Associated in the story with the scent and bloom of flowers, Munson carries in her dream a basket of flowers: "I wanted at once to give him the lily and would have died rather than give it to him, and I turned and fled . . ." (45). In this same story, the first-person narrator acknowledges an attraction to Caroline, "an exceeding, even a loving interest in her," which the narrator has difficulty understanding or articulating as she resorts to metaphors (42). Thus, on the one hand, several of Freeman's characters conform to the social expectation that sexual feelings should be denied or repressed; on the other, the author or narrator in these same stories questions the norm, encouraging the externalization of such emotions and indicating that denials may be self-limiting.

The third attribute—submissiveness—best demonstrates how Freeman's characters deviate from True Womanhood. A husband's dominance over his wife is thematically less important in Freeman than it is in some other women writers of the period, such as Kate Chopin or Charlotte Perkins Gilman, because Freeman's protagonists are generally either single women or widows and, therefore, exempt from the control of a husband. In part, the large number of single women in Freeman's fiction is a reflection of the period and geography, the "quasimatriarchy" cited by Marjorie Pryse resulting from Civil War casualties and the departure of young men to seek employment elsewhere (viii). Still, many of Freeman's women have (or had) matrimonial opportunities, but choose (or chose) to remain single. Some women, such as Louisa in **"A New England Nun,"** reject their suitors, largely because they do not want to be answerable to a husband (in some cases, a husband *and* mother-in-law); others, like Catherine in **"The Secret,"** do not allow themselves to be controlled by their fiancés. When Catherine refuses to answer her fiancé's question about why she returns home a half-hour late, the engagement is broken off until he learns to trust her and be less overbearing. Although self-assertion is more difficult for Freeman's relatively few married protagonists, they are capable of asserting their wills. Despite her husband's refusal to see a doctor or to take medicine, the otherwise obedient Lucy Tollet secretly doses his food with gentian (**"Gentian"**) until he becomes well again.

Freeman's women repeatedly refuse to acknowledge the masculine authority of suitor, husband, minister, deacon, or selectman; and this is especially true when men represent a threat to women's self-sufficiency or their ability to stay in their own homes. When Jenny's (**"Christmas Jenny"**) help is enlisted to assist a stubborn man who has taken a fall and refuses to get up despite his wife's pleas, Jenny uses the ploy of food to circumvent the husband's self-destructive exercise in masculine pride and power. Likewise, the wife, Mrs. Carey, takes the local minister and deacon to task when they enter Jenny's house to investigate the rumor that she starves small animals and abuses an orphan boy in her care. A much younger woman, Louisa (**"Louisa"**) refuses to acknowledge her suitor, the most eligible bachelor in town, despite the fact that her family is barely able to survive; instead, she labors in the field and cleans for a neighbor until she is able to support the family by returning to teaching. Inez Morse (**"A Taste of Honey"**), who does wish to marry, refuses to do so until she pays off the mortgage remaining on the family farm, even though she loses her suitor by making him wait. Inez assumes that these financial responsibilities are entirely her own, her father having died several years before; she does not think her fiancé is capable of helping: "Willy ain't got anything laid up, and he ain't very strong. Besides, he's got his mother and sister to do for" (102).

Freeman's characters may appear to satisfy fully the fourth characteristic of True Womanhood: domesticity. The woman characters frequently take pleasure in domestic tasks and a number are skilled enough at such work that they are described as artists. The narrator in **"A Symphony in Lavender"** insists that she has never enjoyed a tea as much as the one served by Caroline Munson (42); Hetty's "fancy-work" in **"A Church Mouse"** is "quite celebrated" (416) when she decorates the church with her art; Hannah in **"Calla-Lilies and Hannah"** boasts of her luck growing flowers and the protagonist in **"Evelina's Garden"** is compared to Flora herself because of her "grace and her constancy" (121) in her garden. Freeman's women clearly value homelife or a home of their own. They would, one suspects, thoroughly endorse the sentiment incorporated into Catharine Beecher and Harriet Beecher Stowe's *The American Woman's Home* (1869): "It is the aim of this volume . . . to render each department of woman's [domestic] profession as much desired and respected as are the most honored professions of men" (17).[6] Where Freeman's women characters would be most likely to disagree with Beecher and Stowe is their presumption that domestic life must necessarily include a husband and/or children and that domestic work is necessarily performed for the good of God and one's family. Freeman's women may be domestic artists or deeply satisfied by domestic pleasures—the household representing the only arena in which they would as lower-middle or middle-class women have been allowed to excel—but they seek to satisfy themselves as much as anyone else.

The subversiveness of Freeman's handling of domesticity and the image of the home may be as difficult for late twentieth-century readers to perceive as it was for editors at the turn of the century.[7] Freeman's women are typically ordinary, lower-middle- or middle-class[8] rural New Englanders. Relatively few of her characters have attended high school,[9] they have not travelled to Europe (or, most of them, even to Boston), they do not work in factories or department stores, they are not immigrants, they do not attend women's clubs, they do not discuss "the vote"—nonetheless, they would never be mistaken for the Victorian "angel in the house." They are women who have learned to esteem homelife from the institutions around them; but they have actively redefined the value of domestic life.

Since many nineteenth-century women had little control over the world beyond their houses and yards, the control they retained over private living spaces was vitally important. Most of all, Freeman's protagonists understand that a house of one's own is a prerequisite for personal freedom. Whether or not characters have paid off their mortgages—have a clear title—is crucial, and it reminds one of Freeman's own anxiety about housing as an adolescent and adult. In a number of stories, the plot revolves around the fear of not paying off the mortgage, of not having a place to live, or of being forced away from one's home. If they lose their houses, characters increasingly lose control over their own lives, forced to behave as others dictate while living in the home of a relative or a neighbor or while renting a room from someone who takes in boarders.[10] Most degrading, of course, are the institutions of charity, the poorhouse or almshouse or even the Ladies' Home, which Freeman's characters naturally avoid at all costs. Two elderly sisters in **"A Mistaken Charity"** run away from the Old Ladies' Home, where they feel like prisoners, in order to return to their own home, a dilapidated structure with a roof that doesn't even protect them from rain and snow. In **"An Independent Thinker,"** Esther Gay takes in a neighbor, Lavinia, who is afraid of dying in the poor-

house. Freeman even wrote one story, **"Sister Liddy,"** which takes place in an almshouse, focusing on the fictional accounts of their previous domestic lives that old women share with one another in order to give their present life meaning.

In those stories where the major plot does not feature a struggle to acquire or retain housing, significance is almost always given to the owning of a house. Most important, the freedom *not* to marry, or not to marry and live with one's in-laws, is often the result of home ownership. Although marriage was not considered the social and economic obligation it had been during the colonial period (Mintz and Kellogg 56), most women in late nineteenth-century America felt enormous pressure to marry, and marriage was often the result of financial necessity. This point is driven home frequently in Freeman's fiction. In **"Louisa,"** for example, the protagonist's mother thinks of her daughter's marriage to the town's largest landowner as "a royal alliance for the good of the state" (395), and a friend of Louisa's indicates that she would be interested in any man—regardless of whether or not she liked him—if he had enough money and an attractive house. Because they own their families' homes, women such as Aurelia Flower in **"Gatherer of Simples"** or Evelina in **"Evelina's Garden"** would find it easier not to marry.[11]

Owning a house also makes it easier for women—such as Aurelia Flower and the protagonist in **"Christmas Jenny"**—to live as they wish and pursue unorthodox lives. Both women are perceived as living outside the community, primarily because the things they do to earn a living are considered singular and unfeminine. Aurelia makes her living selling medicinal herbs, and every room in her house was "festooned" with them, the walls of her kitchen being "as green as a lady's bower" (281). Living in isolation on a mountain, Jenny goes to the village to sell evergreens in winter and vegetables in the summer. The interior of her house "has a curious sylvan air; there were heaps of evergreens here and there, and some small green trees leaned in one corner" (170). Other protagonists may appear more conventional, but even a woman like Louisa in **"New England Nun"** recognizes that many of the activities that she most enjoys and that best define her, such as distilling essences, would no longer be practiced if she married. Louisa knows that she will be expected by others to assume her marital role selflessly and to deny those aspects of herself that are not essential to the success of the new household. Therefore, she preserves her sense of self by encouraging the dissolution of her long engagement and by remaining in her own house. Although not one of the character traits cited by Welter, selflessness would be a necessary adjunct to submissiveness and the other three virtues required for True Womanhood.[12]

While there are many ways in which a woman's domestic world is linked to her identity or her attempt to establish an identity, the most frequent and obvious example is a woman's identification with flowers or other materials (gardens, shrubs, and trees) in the home landscape. In some cases, plants are merely used as a vehicle for communicating essential qualities of the characters. For example, the narrator in **"A Symphony in Lavender"** explains that the protagonist Caroline Munson "did make me think of a flower . . . a lilac: there was that same dull bloom about her, and a shy, antiquated grace" (41). The first paragraph of the story describes huge lilac trees in bloom on either side of the front steps to Munson's house and a hedge of well-trimmed lilacs bordering the front yard. In **"Gatherer of Simples,"** Aurelia's last name is Flower and "the sweetness of thyme and lavender seemed to have entered into her nature" (288). And Arabella in **"Peony"** is said to be as "prodigal of her belongings as the peony out in the yard of its bloom" (196).

In a number of stories, the correspondence between horticulture and characters is more complex than the previous examples demonstrate. In **"Brakes and White Vi'lets,"** for instance, plants in the landscape are used to represent the entire home and the protagonist's attitude toward it. Although her son wishes her to sell her house, arguing that the damp environment is unhealthy, Marm Lawson refuses to part with the house even though her attachment to it separates her from the granddaughter Lavinia, whom she loves. The strongest emblems of the house, giving the story its title, are the white violets that cover the meadow next to the house and the brakes (probably ferns) growing under the windows, both plants attracted to moist areas. In **"The Lombardy Poplar,"** the protagonist, the last surviving member of her family, thinks that the tree "seems like my own folks" (145). After the death of her twin, Sarah Dunn understands how to live alone and independently through the example of the sole surviving poplar standing in front of her house. Like other protagonists in *Six Trees,* Sarah learns from and receives solace as a result of her strong connection with nature or landscape gardening. Gardening was promoted as legitimate work for middle-class women of this period; according to *The Lady's Token,* an antebellum gift book, "A Woman never appears more truly in her sphere, than when she divides her time between her domestic avocations and the culture of flowers" (cited by Welter 165). And in *American Woman's Home,* there are how-to chapters on "Care of Yards and Gardens," "Propagation," and "Cultivation of Fruit." Nevertheless, Freeman endows flowers and landscape gardening with a significance much different than the utilitarian and decorative functions that Catharine Beecher underscores.[13]

In Mary E. Wilkins Freeman's short fiction, then, women characters tend to identify with domestic surroundings instead of seeing themselves in conflict with their environment. In this respect, her short stories often contrast with other well known and frequently anthologized fiction written by women during this period. Kate Chopin's *The Awakening* and Charlotte Perkins Gilman's "The Yellow Wallpaper" provide useful comparisons. In these works, domestic settings emphasize the extent to which middle-class women are confined to the home—or even to their rooms in the case of "The Yellow Wallpaper"—or the extent to which they find their homes suffocating, yet they are unable to create new spaces in which they can achieve greater freedom or define new roles for themselves. In "The Yellow Wallpaper," the first-person narrator is confined to a bedroom with bars on the window as a rest therapy, while her sister-in-law ("a perfect and enthusiastic housekeeper" 36) assumes her position within the household. In *The Awakening,* Edna Pontellier moves out of her husband's house because she says "it never seemed like mine, anyway—like home" (76), and she succeeds in creating her own space. But while she moves out of the family house on Esplanade Street and begins to live in her own "Pigeon" house, freed from the domestic trappings of her marriage, Edna seems unable to create another world that can sustain her. Unable to reinvent herself—no doubt an almost insurmountable task for a woman of her period—and still influenced by the social conventions that she rejects, she commits suicide in what must seem to her the infinite space of the sea.

Contrasted to the woman's sphere described in the Gilman and Chopin narratives, Freeman's handling of domestic spaces appears positive—if necessarily limited or restricted. Her rural women did not have the option of living in other worlds outside their houses, of moving between public and private spaces, of retreating from "the public place of performance to a private space where the imagination feels at home" (Fryer 9). Furthermore, unlike their author, or the nameless first-person narrator in "Yellow Wallpaper," they do not use their privacy to establish a connection to a larger world through writing or the written word. That her characters' lives are in some ways narrow, Freeman acknowledges, but this admission is always subordinated to her admiration for their achievements. Freeman's protagonists represent a transitional generation of late nineteenth-century women who are not generally recognized in literary history. They are not single-issue reformers, not "New Women," not even "Independent Women" who preserved traditional class and gender distinctions but worked outside of the house. Instead, Freeman's women characters remain within the house, focused on the home and domesticity. What makes them remarkable is their mutual support of one another and their rejection of the submissiveness and selflessness inculcated in middle-class women even late in the century.

As others have discussed at greater length, Freeman's work is connected to other American women regionalists in the late nineteenth century, especially as her fiction reveals a search for the lost mother, or the lost mother's world, and focuses on a community of women whose sense of identity is "collective, connected, and collaborative" (Fetterley and Pryse xvi). Freeman, in her twenties, mourned not only the deaths of her younger sister and her mother but also what they represented in her life: as Josephine Donovan describes matriarchal New England after the War, "a world controlled by the mothers and their values" (9). The homes and the communities of women that Freeman creates in her fiction are reenactments of her early life with her grandmother,[14] mother, and sister. Moreover, they record and pay tribute to her domestic life and the sense of adult womanhood that she achieved with Mary Wales during the most artistically productive period of her life, sustained by a relationship that encouraged her independence as well as her best fiction.[15] Domestic life, delineated from this perspective, must have provided the most durable and dependable forms of satisfaction in Mary E. Wilkins Freeman's life. Despite her flawed marriage, her devotion to Freewarren—described in her correspondence as "a sort of Eden" (Glasser 175)—might have been her attempt to reestablish herself within a female sanctuary.

With the exception of her mentor Sarah Orne Jewett, and Rose Terry Cooke, Freeman remains distinct among most women regionalists; the women's spheres that she creates are largely unsponsored by men, despite the historical reality that women could only gain independence within the home by their husbands' or fathers' economic achievement elsewhere.[16] In Freeman's fiction, these men—husbands prospering by work outside of the home, fathers supporting unmarried daughters, brothers providing for unmarried sisters—have generally been removed from the social and economic arrangement defined by the doctrine of spheres. The roles that men are given in her fiction make them appear diminished or they tend to be absent altogether.[17] Her distinctive, subtly subversive handling of the women's sphere reflects the circumstances of her personal life. Freeman not only experienced a sense of "homelessness" in her adolescence as her family's social status deteriorated; more traumatic was her subsequent loss of the three surviving members of her family in rapid succession. In response to

her financial situation,[18] Freeman effected her own financial solvency, supporting herself for the remainder of her life by her writing, and offering much needed financial assistance to the Wales family whose farm was no longer prosperous.

In her stories, Freeman repeatedly focuses on an ordinary woman, or two or more women living together, generally no longer young and often in financially constrained circumstances. Her protagonist's rebellious nature is demonstrated more frequently by her motivation and choices than by her defiance, by her avoidance of marriage instead of by her rebellion against a domineering husband. Although she did create women who could act boldly, especially if their domestic worlds were threatened, most of Freeman's women characters do not define themselves primarily in resistance to oppressive forces. They prefer to live quietly in their own homes, reveling in their independence from husband or father, their often meager solvency, and their talent and artistry, however impractical or unrecognized by the outside world. Their sense of self depends on an identification with domestic spaces. This is why an aura of dignity and contentment often accompanies Freeman's domestic scenes, despite the unexceptional nature of the tasks and objects being discussed. As the narrator in **"An Independent Thinker"** describes Esther Gay's square, unpainted cottage, "a poor little structure" (299):

> That little house, which, with its precipitous stair and festoons of morning-glories, had something of a foreign picturesqueness, looked to [Esther] like a real palace. . . . There was a certain beauty in it, although it was hardly the one which she recognized. It was full of a lovely, wavering, gold-green light, and there was a fine order and cleanness which gave a sense of peace.
>
> (300)

Bestowed at times with a secular religious significance, houses and domesticity in Freeman's short fiction are significant because they represent a woman's ability to achieve by herself or with other women—within their own space—beauty and coherence and independence.

Notes

1. I benefitted from comments from Leah Blatt Glasser (Mount Holyoke), Patricia A. Onion (Colby), and David D. Mann (Miami University), who generously responded to earlier drafts.

2. The chronology that I construct in this section of the paper is based on Foster, Glasser, Kendrick, Pryse ("Mary E. Wilkins Freeman"), and Westbrook. Although these accounts differ slightly, it seems clear that Freeman lived with Wales from 1884, after her father's will had been executed (Foster 59), until the end of 1901.

3. As Mary P. Ryan emphasizes, "many women passed the last half of the nineteenth century secluded in middle- and upper-class American homes, oblivious to the advances and the hazards of industrialization" (224).

4. Wilkins attended Mt. Holyoke for only a year. Like Emily Dickinson, Freeman found the school too intensely religious, and she went home after the first year "a nervous wreck" (Freeman in a letter to a classmate, Foster 31). The college catalogue for Mt. Holyoke endorsed female education as "'a handmaid to the Gospel and an efficient auxiliary in the great task of renovating the world'" (Welter 153).

5. Freeman's characters differ from the members of the "Cult of Single Blessedness," as defined by Chambers-Schiller, in several ways. Unlike the author's characters, most women identified with "Single Blessedness" are highly educated, religious, and devoted to self-abnegation. Nevertheless, Chambers-Schiller helps define the cultural context that produced the women in Freeman's stories, especially their solidarity with one another and their New England belief in the autonomy of the individual soul or conscience.

According to Chambers-Schiller, "the percent of native-born unwed women in Massachusetts was virtually double that of American spinsters in general: 14.6 in Massachusetts as compared to 7.3 percent nationally in the 1830s, 16.9 to 7.7 percent in 1850, 22.6 to 10.9 in 1870" (5).

6. *The American Woman's Home* (1869) is an expansion of Catharine Beecher's *Treatise on Domestic Economy* (1841). In their introduction to *American Woman's Home,* Beecher and Stowe claim that "during the upward progress of the age, and the advance of more enlightened Christianity, the writers of this volume have gained more elevated views of the true mission of woman—of the dignity and importance of her distinctive duties" (15-16). Nancy F. Cott, in *The Bonds of Womanhood,* emphasizes the role that domestic manuals played in encouraging higher standards: "The canon of domesticity created great expectations in and of women to excel in their vocation" (74).

7. Monika M. Elbert has already described how Freeman's fiction questions the materialism and capitalism that were promoted by many of the same consumer-oriented magazines (e.g., *Ladies' Home Journal, Harper's Bazaar*) that published her stories: "even though the rhetoric of advertising which catered to a female audience . . . sought to make woman a consumer and motherhood a commodity, Freeman is able to subvert the meanings which the male business of advertising has assigned to woman" (268).

8. While most of Freeman's characters are middle-class or have middle-class origins, there are exceptions such as the Shattuck sisters in "A Mistaken Charity" or Hetty in "A Church Mouse." While the working-class women are characterized by their language and more extreme financial difficulties, they do not seem very different from their middle-class sisters so far as their attitudes toward domesticity are concerned. The domestic ideal in the nineteenth century was, at least theoretically, supposed to apply to women of all classes: "the canon of domesticity enshrined the unifying, leveling, common identity of the domestic 'American lady' . . . for all" (Cott 99).

9. By the end of the nineteenth century, only seven percent of Americans went to high school, but the majority of these students were women (Woloch 276).

10. In some stories, free housing is offered to the unfortunate. When the cottage her family has lived in for years is sold, Elsie goes to live with her half-brother and his wife ("Cinnamon Roses"). Both Aurelia ("A Gatherer of Simples") and Jenny ("Christmas Jenny") take in orphaned children. Sydney Lord and his sister ("Noblesse") take in a woman who would otherwise have to continue performing as a freak in a circus.

There are numerous examples of housing offered in exchange for money or domestic labor. Although homeless, Hetty ("A Church Mouse") rejects a woman's offer for board in exchange for domestic work: "[Miss Radway]'s used to havin' her own way, and I've been livin' all my life with them that was" (424). Ann Lyman ("Bouncing Bet") hides in her feather bed, trying to escape the selectmen, rather than be forced out of her family's house to go live with Mrs. Jackson Smith, "with whom the town occasionally boarded people whose former estate . . . seemed to prohibit from the town farm" (103-04). The landlady and her boarders are the major characters in "The Hall Bedroom."

11. There are numerous examples of women in Freeman's short fiction who are single and own their own homes, often but not always the result of inheriting the family home; for example, Candace in "A Village Singer," Caroline in "A Symphony in Lavender," Sophia and Amanda in "The Southwest Chamber," Arabella and her niece Sarah in "Peony," Martha in "The Balsam Fir," Sarah in "The Lombardy Poplar," Amanda in "Amanda and Love," and Luella in "Life-Everlastin'."

12. As Cutter emphasizes in her discussion of Amelia Lamkin ("The Selfishness of Amelia Lamkin"), Freeman rejected the ideal of selflessness as a ste-

reotype that damaged not only women but also the husbands and children who depended on their selflessness.

13. The significance of horticulture in Freeman's short fiction is discussed at length in my "Gardening as 'Women's Culture' in Mary E. Wilkins Freeman's Short Fictions," *The New England Quarterly* 71 (March 1998): 33-53.

14. Freeman's maternal grandmother, Clara Holbrook Lothrop, lived next door to the Wilkins family in Randolph and was very much involved in their lives (Foster 6-7).

15. Both Mary Wales and Charles Freeman encouraged Freeman to write fiction and ensured that she was not burdened by domestic chores, but the husband was more controlling, even directing her reading ("only the frothiest books"). Charles Freeman seems to have encouraged his wife's writing primarily because it was financially lucrative (see Foster 161-62).

16. "[The middle-class woman's] authority expanded only as the family productive functions contracted, and those functions contracted only when family income went up. Rising income was at the center of woman's sphere" (Woloch 116).

17. One important exception should be noted. Much like Jewett, Freeman is interested in male characters whose lives endorse women's values. Although she features relatively few male protagonists in her short fiction, Freeman endows many of them with the same domestic qualities that her women possess. For examples, see Silas in "A Lover of Flowers," William in "Joy," Dick in "The Great Pine," and Abel in "A Kitchen Colonel."

18. Her inheritance could not have supported her for long. When her father died, she inherited $969 in cash and half-interest in a small business property (Foster 59).

Works Cited

Beecher, Catharine E., and Harriet Beecher Stowe. *The American Woman's Home.* 1869. Hartford, Conn.: The Stowe-Day Foundation, 1994.

Chambers-Schiller, Lee Virginia. *Liberty, A Better Husband: Single Women in America: The Generations of 1780-1840.* New Haven: Yale UP, 1984.

Chopin, Kate. *The Awakening: An Authoritative Text, Biographical and Historical Contexts, Criticism.* Ed. Margo Culley. 2nd ed. New York: Norton, 1994.

Cott, Nancy F. *The Bonds of Womanhood: "Woman's Sphere" in New England, 1780-1835.* New Haven: Yale UP, 1977.

Cutter, Martha J. "Beyond Stereotypes: Mary Wilkins Freeman's Radical Critique of Nineteenth-Century Cults of Femininity." *Women's Studies* 21.4 (1992): 383-95.

Donovan, Josephine. *New England Local Color Literature: A Woman's Tradition.* New York: Ungar, 1983.

Elbert, Monika M. "Mary Wilkins Freeman's Devious Women, *Harper's Bazaar,* and the Rhetoric of Advertising." *Essays in Literature* 20 (Fall 1993): 251-72.

Fetterley, Judith, and Marjorie Pryse, eds. *American Women Regionalists: 1850-1910.* New York: Norton, 1992.

Foster, Edward. *Mary E. Wilkins Freeman.* New York: Hendricks, 1956.

Fryer, Judith. *Felicitous Space: The Imaginative Structures of Edith Wharton and Willa Cather.* Chapel Hill: U of North Carolina P, 1986.

Gilman, Charlotte Perkins. *The Yellow Wallpaper.* Ed. Thomas L. Erskine and Connie L. Richards. New Brunswick: Rutgers UP, 1993.

Glasser, Leah Blatt. *In a Closet Hidden: The Life and Work of Mary E. Wilkins Freeman.* Amherst: U of Massachusetts P, 1996.

Kendrick, Brent L. *The Infant Sphinx: Collected Letters of Mary E. Wilkins Freeman.* Metuchen. N.J.: Scarecrow, 1985.

Mintz, Steven, and Susan Kellogg. *Domestic Revolutions: A Social History of American Family Life.* New York: Free, 1988.

Pryse, Marjorie. Introduction. *Selected Stories of Mary E. Wilkins Freeman.* New York: Norton, 1983.

———. "Mary E. Wilkins Freeman." *Modern American Women Writers.* Ed. Elaine Showalter, Lea Baechler, and A. Walton Litz. New York: Scribner's, 1990. 141-53.

Ryan, Mary P. *Womanhood in America: From Colonial Times to the Present.* New York: New Viewpoints, 1975.

Smith, Page. *The Rise of Industrial America: A People's History of the Post-Reconstruction Era.* Vol. 6 of *A People's History of the United States.* 1984, New York: Penguin, 1990.

Welter, Barbara. "The Cult of True Womanhood, 1820-1860." *American Quarterly* 18 (1966): 151-74.

Westbrook, Perry D. *Mary Wilkins Freeman.* Rev. ed. Boston: Twayne, 1988.

Woloch, Nancy. *Women and the American Experience.* 2nd ed. New York: McGraw, 1994.

Woolf, Virginia. *A Room of One's Own.* 1929. New York: Harbinger-Harcourt, 1957.

Freeman Short Stories Cited

"Amanda and Love." *A New England Nun and Other Stories*. New York: Harper, 1891.

"The Balsam Fir." *Six Trees*. New York: Harper, 1903.

"Bouncing Bet." *Understudies*. New York: Harper, 1901.

"Brakes and White Vi'lets." *A Humble Romance and Other Stories*. New York: Harper, 1887.

"Calla-Lilies and Hannah." *A New England Nun and Other Stories*. New York: Harper, 1891.

"Christmas Jenny." *A New England Nun and Other Stories*. New York: Harper, 1891.

"A Church Mouse." *A New England Nun and Other Stories*. New York: Harper, 1891.

"Cinnamon Roses." *A Humble Romance and Other Stories*. New York: Harper, 1887.

"Evelina's Garden." *Silence and Other Stories*. New York: Harper, 1898.

"A Gatherer of Simples." *A Humble Romance and Other Stories*. New York: Harper, 1887.

"Gentian." *A Humble Romance and Other Stories*. New York: Harper, 1887.

"The Great Pine." *Six Trees*. New York: Harper, 1903.

"The Hall Bedroom." *The Uncollected Stories of Mary Wilkins Freeman*. Ed. Mary R. Reichardt. Jackson: UP of Mississippi, 1992.

"An Independent Thinker." *A Humble Romance and Other Stories*. New York: Harper, 1887.

"Joy." *The Givers*. New York: Harper, 1904.

"A Kitchen Colonel." *A New England Nun and Other Stories*. New York: Harper, 1891.

"Life-Everlastin'." *A New England Nun and Other Stories*. New York: Harper, 1891.

"The Lombardy Poplar." *Six Trees*. New York: Harper, 1903.

"Louisa." *A New England Nun and Other Stories*. New York: Harper, 1891.

"A Lover of Flowers." *A Humble Romance and Other Stories*. New York: Harper, 1887.

"A Mistaken Charity." *A Humble Romance and Other Stories*. New York: Harper, 1887.

"A New England Nun." *A New England Nun and Other Stories*. New York: Harper, 1891.

"Noblesse." *The Copy-cat and Other Stories*. New York: Harper, 1914.

"Old Woman Magoun." *The Winning Lady and Others*. New York: Harper, 1909.

"Peony." *Understudies*. New York: Harper, 1901.

"The Revolt of 'Mother.'" *A New England Nun and Other Stories*. New York: Harper, 1891.

"The Secret." *The Fair Lavinia and Others*. New York: Harper, 1907.

"The Selfishness of Amelia Lamkin." *The Winning Lady and Others*. New York: Harper, 1909.

"Sister Liddy." *A New England Nun and Other Stories*. New York: Harper, 1891.

"The Southwest Chamber." *The Wind in the Rose-Bush and Other Stories of the Supernatural*. New York: Doubleday, 1903.

"A Symphony in Lavender." *A Humble Romance and Other Stories*. New York: Harper, 1887.

"A Taste of Honey." *A Humble Romance and Other Stories*. New York: Harper, 1887.

"Two Old Lovers." *A Humble Romance and Other Stories*. New York: Harper, 1887.

"A Village Singer." *A New England Nun and Other Stories*. New York: Harper, 1891.

"A Wayfaring Couple." *A New England Nun and Other Stories*. New York: Harper, 1891.

Joseph Csicsila (essay date spring 1998)

SOURCE: Csicsila, Joseph. "Louisa Ellis and the Unpardonable Sin: Alienation from the Community of Human Experience as Theme in Mary Wilkins Freeman's 'A New England Nun.'" *American Literary Realism* 30, no. 3 (spring 1998): 1-13.

[*In the following essay, Csicsila explores the psychological and spiritual malaise that prevents Louisa Ellis from enjoying a fulfilling life within her community in Freeman's "A New England Nun."*]

Although scholars generally disagree about the thematic implication of Louisa Ellis' decision to remain unmarried at the end of Mary Wilkins Freeman's **"A New England Nun"** (1891), few commentators have viewed this pivotal act outside the all too literal and constricted contexts of marriage and spinsterhood. Indeed, critical debate over this story (especially in the last twenty-five years) seems to have limited itself basically to a discussion of whether or not Louisa's rejection of marriage represents a heroic disavowal of cultural norms or a tragic submission to historical circumstance. In the process of evaluating this and other of her works, then, commentators have more or less branded Freeman a perceptive social critic of small-town New England life. This very narrow assessment of Freeman's art is unfortunate, for it has prevented a proper appreciation of the broader thematic concepts central to **"A New England Nun."**

Numerous scholars from Fred Lewis Pattee to Mary Reichardt have rightly recognized the aesthetic imprint of Nathaniel Hawthorne in Freeman's fiction. But Hawthorne's work ultimately furnished Freeman with more than the oft-discussed and relatively minor precedents of a small New England village setting and the short story form. Arguably, Hawthorne's most profound and enduring legacy to Freeman is the theme of radical individualism and its resulting spiritual isolation, what Perry Westbrook describes as "the dehumanization of the heart that afflicts so many of Hawthorne's characters [which] is the result of a wrongly directed but virtually irresistible will."[1] The narrator of Hawthorne's "Ethan Brand" (1851), for example, observes near the story's conclusion that its protagonist, as a result of his fanatical mission, "had ceased to partake of the universal throb," therein committing the most abominable crime against the human spirit. Although neither as ostensibly dark nor grim as "Ethan Brand," or for that matter, "Young Goodman Brown" (1835), "Wakefield" (1835), "The Minister's Black Veil" (1836), "Rappaccini's Daughter" (1844), or *The Scarlet Letter* (1850), to name only a few of Hawthorne's works which also consider this theme, **"A New England Nun"** rightly belongs within this literary tradition of exploring the spiritual consequences of self-imposed alienation from the community of human experience. With her portrayal of Louisa Ellis, Freeman depicts not merely one woman's dilemma over whether to marry, but more profoundly the human condition as it recedes into social and spiritual isolation. And despite its considerable air of ambiguity, abundant evidence within **"A New England Nun,"** specifically the use of nature imagery and the employment of several highly significant symbols, suggests that Freeman in fact expected her readers to draw certain unequivocal conclusions about Louisa Ellis and her actions.

Biographers of Mary Wilkins Freeman also agree that Freeman was affected and inspired by the essays and poetry of Ralph Waldo Emerson. Edward Foster, for example, asserts that Emerson "had been one of her spiritual fathers,"[2] a conclusion with which Westbrook concurs and which many others echo. Foster elaborates further, pointing out that in her formative years, having read "Nature" (1836) and "Self-Reliance" (1841), Freeman "found the romantics intensely stimulating; Goethe's deity or Emerson's was crowding out the Jehovah" of her New England Calvinist upbringing, and consequently she began "feeling herself part of a great breathing oneness."[3] Although the depth to which Freeman cared to penetrate Emerson's transcendental philosophy remains speculative, it is obvious that Freeman profoundly shared Emerson's fundamental appreciation of Nature, particularly the belief (which Emerson explores perhaps most extensively in "Nature") that an individual's sympathy with the natural universe is a supreme expression of, and absolutely necessary for, one's spiritual well-being. Allusions to and expressions of the organic world abound in Freeman's work and unquestionably carry a notable degree of significance. Freeman's application of this very sort of Emersonian appreciation of Nature is perhaps among the most intriguingly consequential elements within **"A New England Nun."**

Literally framing **"A New England Nun"** and recurring variously throughout the story is the juxtaposition of the outside natural world against the aseptic interior of Louisa's home. With the opening passage Freeman sketches a richly vital scene:

> It was late in the afternoon, and the light was waning. There was a difference in the look of the tree shadows out in the yard. Somewhere in the distance cows were lowing and a little bell was tinkling; now and then a farm-wagon tilted by, and the dust flew; some blue shirted laborers with shovels plodded past; little swarms of flies were dancing up and down before the peoples' faces in the soft air. There seemed to be a gentle air arising over everything for the mere sake of subsidence—a very premonition of rest and hush and night.
>
> (349)[4]

The lowing cows and blue-shirted laborers amid the dust and flies, all against the larger implied backdrop of farmland and pasture, establishes immediately an organic, thriving natural setting for the story's action. Directly following this initial scene, however, Freeman introduces Louisa Ellis in marked contrast to the outside world. First, Louisa is introduced *indoors,* inside her meticulously kept home, where she remains for most of the story. But what is most striking about this setting is that Louisa's home is uncommonly pristine and orderly. We are told, for instance, that the dining table rests "exactly in the centre of the kitchen" (356), and that Louisa is relentless in her pursuit to keep the windows "polished until they shone like jewels" (355), her household decorations and knicknacks in precise locations, and her entire home absolutely dust-free. The meticulous condition of the interior of Louisa's home moves far beyond simple neatness, and as it represents a converse to the scene sketched in the opening passage, the static unnatural order of Louisa's home seems to symbolize her attempt to purge from her existence all traces of life's inherent organic complexity. And with these images of aseptic rigidness

Freeman deftly begins to suggest Louisa's spiritual disconnection from the natural world.

Continuing the peculiar tenor of the narrative, Freeman provides a subtle but direct comparison between the protagonist and the outside world:

> Louisa used china everyday—something which none of her neighbors did. They whispered about it among themselves. Their daily tables were laid with common crockery, their sets of best china stayed in the parlor closet, and Louisa Ellis was no richer nor better bred than they. Still she would use the china.
>
> (350)

That Louisa's neighbors use "common crockery" is significant, for it connotes in general a sense of simplicity, earthiness, and warmth that echoes the rustic vitality of the story's opening passage. On the other hand, Louisa's everyday use of china, which of course is normally reserved for domestic ceremony, suggests at once an affected and unemotional air of artificiality. Although Marjorie Pryse argues that Louisa's daily use of china is to be viewed positively as an expression or achievement of her "artistic perfection,"[5] when the china use is placed among the various descriptions of Louisa and her home, there can be little doubt the china is, more critically, one of the many manifestations of the fundamental dichotomy in this story between the organic vitality of the outside world and the relative sterility of Louisa's surroundings.

When introducing Joe Dagget, Louisa's betrothed of fourteen years, into the plot, Freeman underscores the story's fundamental dichotomy. Joe is the very embodiment of life and natural vigor. He is by trade a farmer, a thoroughly active participant in Nature, whose character throughout the narrative exudes vitality and figuratively represents the antithesis to Louisa's artificial existence. As Joe enters Louisa's home, for instance, Freeman reports that

> [h]e seemed to fill up the whole room. A little canary that had been asleep in his green cage at the south window woke up and fluttered wildly, beating his little yellow wings against the wires. He always did so when Joe Dagget came into the room.
>
> (350)

Here Joe's virile presence seems to invigorate the life-deprived interior of Louisa's residence. As Westbrook and other critics have pointed out, Freeman obviously intends the reader to recognize the canary's frenzied reaction as symbolic of Louisa's slightly masked, panicked response to Joe's arrival. For aside from the larger parallel of the caged bird and Louisa's caged existence in her home (which in the context of the organic versus the inorganic underscores the notion that

just as the bird has been removed from its natural habitat in the outside world of Nature, so Louisa has removed herself from the natural world), the green interior of the bird's cage recalls Louisa's green apron, mentioned two paragraphs previous, and just before that the reader is told that Louisa eats bird-like, "in a delicate, pecking way" (350). Joe's mere presence in Louisa's immaculately kept parlor is enough to distress Louisa, who views Joe's every movement as a potential threat to the pristine order of her home. Other elements of Joe's visit stress the development of this important motif.

As Louisa and Joe strain to converse during their painfully tense (and probably typical) visit, Joe breaks the silence with what appears to be small-talk. But again the juxtaposition of the outside world and the interior of Louisa's home becomes the narrative focus. After Louisa inquires whether Joe has been working out in the fields all day, Joe responds that he has and adds that it is "pretty hot work," to which Louisa returns: "It must be" (351). Louisa's remark is notable as it delicately re-emphasizes the story's basic thematic contrast and indicates that she has little if any substantive experience in the outside natural world. The narrator then begins to propose the effects of Louisa's rejection of Nature with a telling description of the narrative principals:

> He [Joe] was not very young, but there was a boyish look about his large face. Louisa was not quite as old as he, her face was fairer and smoother, but she gave people the impression of being older.
>
> (351)

Joe, the story's representative embodiment of vitality, appears boyish and youthful. In contrast, Louisa, physically and spiritually withdrawn from Nature, seems to be aging more quickly than normal, an ominous suggestion of lifelessness and an unmistakable diametric opposite to Joe. Finally, Freeman concludes the scene of Joe's visit to Louisa's home in nearly the same fashion as it began—as Joe steps through Louisa's door into the night Freeman's narrator notes: "When Joe Dagget was outside he drew in the sweet evening air with a sigh" (352). While intimating a distinction between the air inside the house and the air outside, Freeman reminds the reader of not only Joe's fundamental appreciation of Nature, but also the state of utter lifelessness inside Louisa's home.

Van Wyck Brooks perceptively observes that Freeman characteristically depicts "people who were filled with a passion for life."[6] That Louisa Ellis seems to be an exception to Brooks' conclusion should be of at least some significance. In **"A New England Nun"** as well as in dozens of other stories Freeman routinely portrays a character's spiritual fitness as a healthy and proper appreciation of Nature. **"A Mistaken Charity"** (1887), for example, is a story of two impoverished elderly sisters whom Freeman depicts not only as living comfortably in their decrepit, rural shell of a home, but also as individuals who are absolutely teeming with life. From their lush, wild garden with its pumpkins, apples, and currants, to their home, which "nature had almost completely overrun" with moss, vines, and birds' nests (315)[7], everything associated with Harriet and Charlotte suggests animation and organic vitality.

Contrasted against this portrait of vitality are the villagers of the story—particularly the widow—who arrange for the sisters' somewhat involuntary re-location to a retirement home. By describing the widow as "childless" and "elderly" (319), Freeman associates this woman with images of sterility and death. When these details are coupled with the fact that she is also "rich" (319), the widow embodies a complete antithesis to the two sisters. Together with the aseptic and sterile atmosphere of the "Old Ladies' Home," everything about the village's suspect act of charity seems to exemplify opposition to Harriet's and Charlotte's ability to experience the richness and fullness of life. In the end, Freeman roundly condemns the villagers for violating the sanctity of Nature by removing the sisters from their thoroughly organic existence and placing them in the retirement home, as she concludes her story with Harriet and Charlotte's escape from the Old Ladies' Home and return to their rural shack, thereby restoring their natural and vital way of life.

In like manner, Freeman introduces additional indications of Louisa's rejection of an organic, natural existence as the plot of **"New England Nun"** moves forward. As a central image in **"A New England Nun,"** Louisa's dog, Caesar, is unquestionably key to understanding the story as a whole. While several critics have tended to view Caesar in terms of "dog-as-phallus,"[8] symbolizing variously Louisa's sexual repression or her "control over masculine forces which threaten her autonomy,"[9] a more plausible and perhaps more easily understood explanation of the dog is suggested within the story. Significantly, Caesar has been chained up and lived as a hermit "for fourteen years" (361), which corresponds to the fourteen years that Louisa has lived as an "uncloistered nun" (365) apart from Joe and the community of human experience. This conspicuous parallel between Caesar and Louisa suggests that the reader might apply Freeman's sentiments regarding the dog's unusual living conditions to Louisa's overall situation. Indeed, just as with Louisa and her caged bird, there are a number of intriguing similarities between Louisa and Caesar.

Briefly near the beginning of the story after Louisa has eaten her curiously delicate dinner consisting of "sugared currants," "little cakes," "light white biscuits," and "a leaf or two of lettuce" (350), the narrator reports that Louisa takes a plate of "nicely baked thin corn-cakes" (350) out into her backyard to feed Caesar, described as a "large" dog (350). A diet of thin corn-cakes certainly seems strange fare for a sizable dog, and with the description Freeman seems to be drawing the reader's attention to the fact that Louisa's and Caesar's eating habits are equally peculiar. Further, Caesar's living accommodations, "a tiny hut, which was half hidden among the tall grasses and flowers" (350), appears to echo in small the description of Louisa's residence, which is of course also an island of seclusion surrounded by a richly organic and vital outside world. Thus, subtly, almost imperceptibly laying the groundwork for subsequent development of the crucial parallel between Louisa and Caesar, this early scene proves to have enormous implication later in the story.

During the fourteen years of Joe's absence, Louisa gradually descended into a solitary and isolated existence, withdrawing herself effectually from any sort of meaningful participation in life:

> In that length of time much had happened. Louisa's mother and brother had died, and she was all alone in the world. But greatest happening of all—a subtle happening which both [Joe and Louisa] were too simple to understand—Louisa's feet had turned into a path, smooth maybe under a calm, serene sky, but so straight and unswerving that it could only meet a check at her grave, and so narrow that there was no room for any one at her side.
>
> (353)

While slightly ambiguous on the surface, Freeman's synopsis of Louisa's spiritual retreat over the last fourteen years has a decided undercurrent of negative connotation: two references to death frame the passage and Louisa's life is characterized as an unswerving, narrow, and solitary path—hardly a list of resplendent traits. Other less overtly bleak descriptions of Louisa's path, "smooth, maybe under a calm, serene sky," suggest resignation to a "half-wistful" (354), uneventful state of being. Indeed, during the interim between Joe's departure and return, the reader is told that Louisa has devoted herself to several household hobbies, among them sewing, distilling aromatic essences, and maintaining a rigid order and cleanliness within her home. These pastimes, which Edward Foster describes as mere "time-killing activities,"[10] have long outlived any sense of purposefulness and have actually become, sadly, poor substitutes for human interaction in Louisa's detached life, as the reader is told Louisa looks upon these hobbies as "dear friends" (354). The narrator also points out that Louisa continues to distill despite the fact that "her store was already considerable" (354) and that "more than once she had ripped a seam for the mere delight of sewing it together again" (354). Freeman's point with respect to Louisa's hobbies is clear: though at one time these activities may have been productive, benign endeavors, they have become useless and completely devoid of purpose and are now spiritually debilitating to Louisa. That she continues to enjoy sewing, distilling, and cleaning cannot justify nor excuse her continued indulgence in them. For tragically, Louisa's hobbies have facilitated and maintained her withdrawal from the community of human experience.

It is precisely the inevitability that she will be pulled from this realm of spiritual oblivion which underlies Louisa's fears about her new life as Joe's wife. "Sterner tasks than these graceful but half-needless ones," Freeman ironically observes, "would probably devolve upon her" (354). The narrator explains specifically that these "sterner tasks" would include maintaining a larger house, caring for Joe and his elderly mother, and entertaining company. Not surprisingly, the horrors of Louisa's new life involve and demand the very fundamentals of human interaction: a domestic family, an extended family, and communal social relationships. Louisa's fears seem slightly justified as the story's narrator reports that Joe's mother is "rigorous and feeble" (354) and "a domineering, shrewd old matron" (355); however, as with other situations throughout **"A New England Nun,"** Louisa's anxiety about Joe's mother is presumably greatly exaggerated. After all, Lily Dyer manages to perform all of the duties that terrify Louisa, including looking after Joe's mother, quite cheerfully and without appearing to be inhumanely overworked. Again, Louisa's fears are grounded fundamentally in the reality that she will soon be forced to confront the community of human experience.

Once Louisa's character is fully delineated, Freeman returns the narrative focus to a substantial account of Caesar. She writes:

> Caesar was a veritable hermit of a dog. For the greater part of his life he had dwelt in his secluded hut, shut out from the society of his kind and all innocent canine joys. . . . he had lived at the end of a chain, all alone in a little hut, for fourteen years.
>
> (355)

This passage, absolutely pregnant with Freeman's masked commentary, refers not only to Caesar but also to Louisa. Just as Caesar, for the better part of fourteen years, had been "shut out from the society of his kind" and been deprived of all the "innocent ca-

nine joys," so too has Louisa, for the better part of fourteen years, shut herself out from the society of mankind and deprived herself of all the innocent joys of life. Recalling the story's broader motif of the natural versus the unnatural, one may reasonably conclude that Caesar's extremely secluded existence (which unquestionably approaches cruelty,[11]) like Louisa's life, is not at all typical and is, in fact, symbolically a violation of Nature.

Freeman also symbolically revisits Louisa's fears about joining the community of human experience during these descriptions of Caesar. The narrator reveals that Louisa keeps the dog chained to its hut because she fears it poses a potential threat to the village: "She pictured to herself Caesar on the rampage through the quiet and unguarded village. She saw innocent children bleeding in its path" (356). But like her anxiety about Joe's mother, Louisa's visions of Caesar's bloody rampage through the village are ultimately unfounded and absurd, for the reader is told that Joe "with his good-humored sense and shrewdness saw him [Caesar] as he was": "'There ain't a better natured dog in town,' he would say, 'and it's downright cruel to keep him tied up there. Someday I'm going to take him out'" (356). Joe's promise to unchain Caesar, which thoroughly unnerves Louisa, at a deeper level represents Joe's promise to unchain Louisa from her solitary life and bring her into the human community. "Louisa," reports the narrator in the very next line, "had very little hope that he would not, one of these days, when their interests and possessions should be more completely fused into one" (356). A few lines further in this paragraph, near the end of the scene, Freeman skillfully unifies the parallel between Louisa and Caesar: "Louisa looked at the old dog munching his simple fare, and thought of her approaching marriage and trembled" (356). Therefore, considering the myriad analogues within the story between Louisa and Caesar, the candid commentary concerning Caesar suggests that Freeman is far less ambiguous about her attitude toward Louisa than most critics have recognized.

In the last major movement of **"A New England Nun"** Freeman brings to the fore once again the juxtaposition of the natural world and the sterility of Louisa's existence. On a night a week before her marriage to Joe, Louisa ventures out of her solitude for a very peculiar evening walk:

> About nine o'clock Louisa strolled down the road a little way. There were harvest-fields on either hand, bordered by low stone walls. Luxuriant clumps of bushes grew beside the wall and trees—wild cherry and old apple-trees—at intervals. Presently Louisa sat down on the wall and looked about her with mildly sorrowful reflectiveness. Tall shrubs of blueberry and

meadow-sweet, all woven together and tangled with blackberry vines and horsebriars, shut her in on either side.

(357)

The extraordinary profusion of Nature in this passage can hardly be overlooked. As Louisa wanders away from the rigid order of her home she is met and "shut in" by harvest-fields, wild cherry and old apple trees, and various tangles of shrubbery and berry bushes (not only literally but figuratively as reference to her in the passage is surrounded by descriptions of Nature), to which she reacts and observes "with a mild sorrowful reflectiveness." Louisa's evening walk among the abundance of organic vitality represents a consideration of her life after marriage and puts her into a state of melancholy, reaffirming for the reader her symbolic spiritual state of inorganicity. She is not invigorated by the lush scene as one might expect, but on the contrary is depressed. Ironically, during this immersion into Nature Louisa overhears a conversation between Joe and Lily Dyer that allows her to call off the wedding and maintain her alienation from the community of human experience.

This interpretation of the scene involving Louisa's evening stroll can be corroborated through comparison with a curiously similar situation in Freeman's **"The Slip of the Leash"** (1904). In this later story Freeman presents Adam Andersen, a character reminiscent of the protagonist of Hawthorne's "Wakefield," who deserts his family and over the course of several years observes them from afar. Unlike Louisa, however, Adam resolves to take up once again his communal responsibilities directly after immersing himself in the natural world:

> It was a beautiful day in spring, and a sudden warm spell had brought out the leaves on the trees. *His feet were sunken in a bed of wild flowers* [my emphasis]. He heard running water and pipes of birds, and it seemed to him that he also heard something else—the trumpet of freedom of life and earth which calls a man to the battlefield of God. But he knew that the time was come when he must return to the trammels of love and happiness and anxiety, which his day and generation had made incumbent upon him, and which, although his soul after a manner delighted in them, were not yet the best for a man of his kind who had in him the memory of the old which is the new.[12]

Adam ultimately comes to the understanding that he must embrace again his myriad responsibilities as a husband, father, and human being, adversities and all, referred to here as returning "to the trammels of love and happiness and anxiety." That is to say he accepts his onus, the "leash" of responsibility placed on him by family and society at large, and recognizes it as a necessary part of the human condition. More than in-cidental is the fact that Adam, who throughout **"The Slip of the Leash"** revels in his various wilderness surroundings, eventually assumes his familial and social obligations after his communion with the natural world and that Louisa, who continually rejects Nature, withdraws into solitude after her brief experience outdoors. And in addition to confirming the thematic role of Louisa's excursion to the outside world in **"A New England Nun," "The Slip of the Leash"** is significant as it completes, so to speak, a circuit of influence with Hawthorne. That **"The Slip of the Leash"** is clearly indebted to Hawthorne's "Wakefield" for certain elements of plot and theme, as Mary Reichardt and others have pointed out, suggests not only the probability that Freeman read and appreciated "Wakefield," but also the much more portentous possibility that she esteemed Hawthorne's fiction in general and likely modeled the thematic design of other stories, namely **"A New England Nun,"** after his work. At the very least, regardless of the actual source of the motif, the similarities between **"A New England Nun"** and **"The Slip of the Leash"** indicate a persistent and recurring concern in Freeman's canon with exploring the spiritual consequences of isolation from the community of humankind.

Freeman employs the character of Lily Dyer in large part to bolster the story's fundamental dichotomy in its final scenes. As the woman with whom Joe has recently fallen in love, Lily functions literally as a benign sort of adversary to Louisa. But this opposition clearly extends much deeper as she comes to represent, like Joe, the very essence of life and vitality. Aside from the obvious symbolic implications of her name, Lily is described in one instance as "a girl full of a calm rustic strength and bloom" (357) and later as "tall and erect and blooming" (360). Together with the fact that she demonstrates full human interaction in her love for Joe and in the care of his mother, Lily represents a complete opposite to Louisa.

When Louisa overhears Joe and Lily's conversation the night of her evening stroll she feels confident that she has found a way to preserve her solitary way of life and in fact takes advantage of this unforeseen opportunity the very next night to call off the wedding. After she and Joe "came to an understanding" (359) and he departs for the last time, something unexpected and quite out of Louisa's character occurs: "Louisa, all alone by herself that night, wept a little, she hardly knew why" (359). Brought to the threshold of the human community only to turn away from it for good, Louisa weeps intuitively because of the innate spiritual loss she experiences after breaking off her relationship with Joe. She is unable to understand the loss or its full consequence because she does not comprehend the necessity of community, but she feels the sorrow nevertheless because she is human after all.

Within the final paragraph of **"A New England Nun"** Freeman revisits all of the story's primary motifs and delivers irrefutable condemnation of Louisa. First, the reader is assured that Caesar will remain chained in his hut surrounded by the "tall weeds and grasses" (359), the canary "will turn itself into a peaceful yellow ball night after night, and have no need to wake and flutter with wild terror against its bar" (359), and Louisa will continue to practice her household hobbies, thereby confirming once again the symbolic parallels between the story's protagonist and her pets. Next, Freeman juxtaposes Lily, described as "tall and erect and blooming" (360), and Louisa, characterized by her "serenity and placid narrowness" (360). To highlight the contrast and provide further commentary Freeman inserts an allusion to the Biblical story of Jacob and Esau. Referring to Louisa's decision to break her engagement, the narrator notes: "If Louisa Ellis had sold her birthright she did not know it, the taste of the pottage was so delicious, and had been her sole satisfaction for so long" (360). Seemingly ambiguous, this passage unequivocally denounces Louisa's decision to remain alienated from the universal throb. Although the conditional "if" appears to elicit an air of ambiguity in the first half of the statement, the second half is conspicuously clear. Louisa has indeed metaphorically subsisted on menial pottage by indulging her fear of partaking fully in life, and therefore implied is her relinquishment of the profound and spiritually affirming birthright that is Joe and Lily's gain.

Last, bringing the story to a close, Freeman contrasts the sterile interior of Louisa's home with the organic vitality of the outside world:

> That afternoon she sat with her needle-work at the window, and fairly steeped in peace. . . . Outside was the fervid summer afternoon; the air was filled with the sounds of the busy harvest of men and birds and bees; there were halloos, metallic clatterings, sweet calls, and long hummings. Louisa sat, prayerfully numbering her days, like an uncloistered nun.
>
> (360)

Freeman brings **"A New England Nun"** full circle with this final passage, leaving the reader with a deceptively bleak and disturbingly hollow portrait of Louisa. Surrounded by the burgeoning throngs of Nature, Louisa succumbs to a lifeless state of being in exile from the community of human experience, uncloistered not because she has managed to break free from the oppressive societal norms of her culture, as some critics have suggested, but uncloistered because

she has broken all bonds with her fellow humankind. In his analysis of these last few lines, David Hirsch argues that Louisa's submission is to her a future of "prayerfully numbered days . . ."; "[i]n their inert monotonous, endless, sameness, they suggest death itself."[13] Similarly, Reichardt asserts that "the 'peace' Louisa seeks at all costs is hardly peace at all, but merely the facade of it."[14] Indeed, Freeman creates a deceptively tranquil ending ready to snare unsuspecting readers oblivious to Louisa's final act of regression.

Throughout her fiction Freeman is ultimately critical of individuals who, like Louisa Ellis, tragically sell their birthright of a full life, and celebrates those who, like Joe Dagget, Lily Dyer, and Adam Andersen, are able to embrace living with all of its richness as well as its adversities. Louisa's spiritually inert existence results not from her inability to marry Joe Dagget but from the reason *why* she will not marry him, namely her refusal to participate within the community of human experience. Indeed, Freeman clearly goes to great pains to indicate that Louisa's solitary existence is firmly rooted in a deep spiritual and psychological malady. In the end, Freeman's ability to distinguish herself as a complex writer of fiction is due mainly to her portrayal of the responsible celebration of life as guide to individual morality. With **"A New England Nun,"** she places herself beside writers such as Hawthorne within the literary tradition exploring the spiritual consequences of living apart from the universal throb. As such, Mary Wilkins Freeman rightly deserves consideration as a writer of deeply profound themes and relevance.

Notes

1. Perry Westbrook, *Mary Wilkins Freeman* (Boston: Twayne, 1988), p. 64.

2. Edward Foster, *Mary E. Wilkins Freeman* (New York: Hendricks House, 1956), p. 52.

3. Foster, p. 34.

4. This quotation and all subsequent quotations from "A New England Nun" are taken from *Short Fiction of Sarah Orne Jewett and Mary Wilkins Freeman,* ed. Barbara Solomon (New York: Signet, 1979).

5. Marjorie Pryse, "An Uncloistered 'New England Nun,'" *Critical Essays on Mary Wilkins Freeman,* ed. Shirley Marchalonis (Boston: G. K. Hall, 1991), p. 141.

6. Van Wyck Brooks, *New England: Indian Summer* (New York: E. P. Dutton, 1940), p. 472.

7. This quotation and all subsequent quotations from "A Mistaken Charity" are taken from *Short Fic-*

tion of Sarah Orne Jewett and Mary Wilkins Freeman, ed. Barbara Solomon (New York: Signet, 1979).

8. David Hirsch, "Subdued Meaning in 'A New England Nun,'" *Critical Essays on Mary Wilkins Freeman,* ed. Shirley Marchalonis (Boston: G. K. Hall, 1991), p. 132.

9. Pryse, p. 142.

10. Foster, p. 108.

11. In a letter written to Mary Louise Booth on 28 April 1886, Freeman mentions a similarly treated dog: "Monday afternoon, I went a-hunting material too: We went to an old lady's birthday party. But all I saw worth writing about there was a poor old dog, who had been chained thirteen years, because he bit a man once, in his puppy-hood. I have felt like crying every time I have thought of him. He wagged his tail, and looked so pitiful, he is half-blind too" (*The Infant Sphinx: Collected Letters of Mary E. Wilkins Freeman,* ed. Brent Kendrick [Metuchen, NJ: Scarecrow Press, 1985], p. 69). Many biographers point to this passage as the germ for "A New England Nun," and clearly Freeman was outraged by the inhumane treatment of this precursor to Caesar.

12. Mary Wilkins Freeman, "The Slip of the Leash," *Harper's,* 109 (October 1904), p. 675.

13. Hirsch, p. 169.

14. Mary Reichardt, *A Web of Relationship: Women in the Short Stories of Mary Wilkins Freeman* (Jackson: Univ. Press of Mississippi, 1992), p. 93.

Ben Couch (essay date spring 1998)

SOURCE: Couch, Ben. "The No-Man's-Land of 'A New England Nun.'" *Studies in Short Fiction* 35, no. 2 (spring 1998): 187-98.

[*In the following essay, Couch focuses on the sexuality of Louisa Ellis in "A New England Nun," arguing that the story subtly alludes to her masturbatory habits, symbolically encoding her sexual appetite via the figure of her dog, Caesar.*]

Critics have held widely varying opinions on the quality of Mary E. Wilkins Freeman's **"A New England Nun,"** the quality of the characters, and even whether or not Freeman liked the spinster Louisa Ellis who is, ironically, the protagonist in this sexually dynamic short story. As Mary R. Reichardt says, "It is a tribute to the artistry of **'A New England Nun'** that various interpretations of the work have evolved over the

years. The story, quite simply, is a masterpiece of ambiguity." By way of illustration, Reichardt then contrasts Marjorie Pryse's analysis of Louisa as "an 'artist' and a 'visionary,' 'heroic, active, wise, ambitious, and even transcendent'" with David Hirsch's view that the story is "a study in obsession and sexual repression, a 'rejection of life'" (91). Glasser poses the question, "Is Louisa, the heroine . . . who has rejected the possibility of sexual fulfillment, as Hirsch suggests? Or is she the victorious, autonomous woman described by so many recent feminist critics . . . , a brave woman who has in fact chosen her singular definition of self-fulfillment through defiant spinsterhood?" (33).

It is certainly tempting to see the story as one detailing the sexual frustrations and struggles with marriage in Freeman's life. The time in her own life most closely paralleling **"A New England Nun"** is that part including Hanson Tyler, a naval ensign upon whom Freeman apparently had a crush. He would be gone for long intervals of time, returning only when on leave (Reichardt 12). The long periods of absence and an assumed frustration at her apparently unrequited love may encourage biographically informed readers to read the story of Louisa and Joe as the story of Freeman and Tyler. Edward Foster says of this,

> Hamlin Garland and Willis Boyd Allen, who knew the writer, have at least inferentially suggested the identification of Miss Wilkins and her Louisa Ellis. Knowing that her parents had died while she was relatively young and perhaps guessing at the Tyler episode, they found the speculation difficult to resist.
>
> (108)

It is, indeed, "difficult to resist" because, as readers, we want to know what prompted the writer to write. "In my opinion, they were mostly mistaken," says Foster (108).

Even if Garland and Allen were not mistaken in their inferences, I think that it would certainly be a mistake to look for nothing other than biographical significance in this short story. Perhaps Freeman did draw from this relationship. Reichardt says, "Though little evidence exists that Hanson Tyler returned Freeman's affection, he evidently occupied a place in Freeman's romantic imagination for the rest of her life. In her last years, she wore his naval uniform buttons on her own clothing and once remarked to a friend, '[I]f there is an afterlife, he [Tyler] is the one person I should like to see' (Foster 194)" (Reichardt 76). She may have had this episode in her life partially in mind when writing the story. Additionally, Reichardt quotes a journal entry wherein Freeman recounts her discovery of an old dog that had been chained for 13 years because he bit someone when he was a puppy (93). This is, of course, the dog that would become Caesar in **"A New England Nun."** However, this dog was brought to a much different level by Freeman. In her hands, he was transformed from a simple chained dog into a powerful image of sexuality. The story may function, at some level, as biographical, but if it is a recounting of her relationship with Tyler, it has been transformed: as a subtle tale of sexual tension and ambiguity, it has taken on a life of its own.

The heart of the debate revolves around Louisa, her role in the story, and her role in New England life. We are struck immediately by the title of the piece, a powerful indicator of Louisa's unconventionality as well as her distinguishing qualities. A nun must give up sexuality and society in order to pursue a higher purpose, the service of God. Louisa gives up society in order to serve her own higher purpose, her autonomy. David Hirsch examines the story from a psychological standpoint, looking at a scene easily misconstrued as "'dull,' . . . embarrassed and awkward," and seeing instead a scene pulsating "with tightly controlled dramatic tension" (125). He says,

> Mrs. Freeman does not seem to deviate greatly from the subject matter and methods of her sister writers in the New England local-color tradition. . . . But what distinguishes the scene I have singled out, and, indeed, the entire story . . . is the undercurrent I have already referred to.
>
> (127)

This undercurrent Hirsch considers points out many passages in the text as indicating "an obsessive neurosis" (125) in Louisa. Hirsch points out the following passage as one of the more blatant examples of what he refers to as compulsive and unreasonable activity (125):

> Presently Dagget began fingering the books on the table. There was a square red autograph album, and a Young Lady's Gift-Book which had belonged to Louisa's mother. He took them up one after the other and opened them; then laid them down again, the album on the Gift-Book.
>
> Louisa kept eyeing them with mild uneasiness. Finally she rose and changed the position of the books, putting the album underneath. That was the way they had been arranged in the first place.
>
> Dagget gave an awkward little laugh. "Now what difference did it make which book was on top?" said he.
>
> Louisa looked at him with a deprecating smile. "I always keep them that way," murmured she.
>
> "You do beat everything," said Dagget, trying to laugh again. His large face was flushed.
>
> (4-5)

Here is an attempt on Freeman's part to establish Louisa as a compulsive character and that personality trait as a motivating factor in her reluctance to marry Joe. Thus, it is essential that we see to what lengths Louisa will go to preserve order in her house. However, we are left wondering how we are supposed to feel about Louisa. Compulsivity is certainly not a trait to be admired in a person. It can be a debilitating force, keeping people from walking outside their houses without counting their steps, from going to bed at night without checking the stove five times, and, ultimately, from living. This may be a detraction from Louisa as a person, but not as a character. It enriches her since we now see her as a more multi-dimensional force. She is truly undergoing a desperate struggle to retain the essential Louisa. Her identity requires her to be a very neat and orderly person surrounded by her own idiosyncrasies. Thus, we are forced to ask ourselves, when does perfectionism go too far? Is Louisa compulsive or precise? Does her compulsiveness simply prevent her from wanting to marry Joe, or from living? And finally, if she is happy, does it matter what we think of her compulsiveness?

Louisa is a character far from living within the bounds of societal opinion. Her decision to remain a "spinster" indicates that fact clearly enough. If we criticize her for her way of life, it could be argued that we are no better than her gossipy neighbors who whisper about her daily use of china. While Louisa's compulsiveness is important in understanding her motivations, Freeman is challenging us to rise above the role of the small-town busybody. Therefore, I cannot view her "neurosis" as being quite as essential to the understanding and interpretation of this story as Hirsch does.

Louisa is precise and enjoys what she does. As Glasser says,

> Freeman's story actually captures the isolation and quiet that attention to one's craft requires. Every gesture of Louisa's work is described lovingly and quietly, as though her work is an extension of the landscape described in the first paragraph in its "premonition of rest and hush and night."
>
> (34)

While Hirsch makes an interesting study of her character, he accepts the idea of the spinster, an idea bred by a male-dominated society, and is perfectly happy in joining the townspeople in putting Louisa's defining characteristics in a negative light. Glasser may present a more plausible interpretation when she asserts that "the major function of her [Louisa's] work . . . is to offer her time for self-reflection, time for self-love. Her work . . . is not done out of necessity or to achieve any specific purpose" (35). It is, however, a kind of work that cannot be allowed within the bounds of marriage, an example of "the self-love that attention to a husband might destroy" (Glasser 34). Glasser reads the story as a celebration of "the unrecognized joy and worth of Louisa's autonomy" (35) and an examination and celebration of the character of Louisa herself. Louisa is a woman who is content and happy, but still willing to sacrifice her very self for the sake of honoring a 14-year-old pledge. She is a quietly noble character.

I would, however, take issue with calling Louisa a "victorious, autonomous woman" (Glasser 33). While Louisa loves her autonomous life and is pleased, self-confident, and happy in being her own woman, she is willing to give all of this up for a man, Joe Dagget, with full understanding that she is giving up herself. One of the most striking passages describes her morning rituals as she prepares for the wedding:

> Every morning, rising and going about among her neat maidenly possessions, she felt as one looking her last upon the faces of dear friends. It was true that in a measure she could take them with her, but, robbed of their old environments, they would appear in such new guises that they would almost cease to be themselves.
>
> (8)

She knows that "There would be a large house to care for," "company to entertain," and "Joe's rigorous and feeble old mother to wait upon" (9). Perhaps the worst blow comes to those things that define her identity. She will no longer have ample time to distill fragrances or sew linen, essential actions if Louisa is to enjoy her life. The order valued so highly by Louisa will be continually disrupted. Realizing all of this, she accepts her suitor and continues work on her wedding dress. She does not break free in the name of her female individuality, asserting herself as a woman who loves who she is and who will not compromise herself for any man. Her "maidenly possessions" are a thinly disguised metaphor for herself. Louisa realizes that she will be losing her identity by marrying Joe. She is determined, however, to go through with the marriage in order to prevent breaking her promise and, as far as she knows, Joe's heart.

Despite Louisa's hesitations, despite her tendency to place the marriage "so far in the future that it was almost equal to placing it over the boundaries of another life" (7-8), there are indications that she is upset at Joe's "betrayal." After overhearing Joe's conversation with Lily, Louisa "slunk softly home" (15) and seems more hurt than relieved by the initial impact of the blow. She has a hard time believing and accepting "that she had heard aright, and that she would not do Joe a terrible injury should she break her troth-plight"

(15). We can see the disappointment over this sexual rejection when we are told that "all alone by herself that night, [she] wept a little" (16). Though she overcomes her grief with joy, it would not do justice to the complexity of the story were we to ignore the fact that Louisa is a bit disappointed when the barbarian at her gate gives up without a struggle.

Glasser sets forth the apparent polarity of Louisa's options: "[L]iving alone meant burying the sexual self; marrying meant burying the creative, independent self" (32). Two very separate worlds have been established: one that is portrayed as being full of life and vitality as well as control, and one filled with the intolerable small talk that takes place between Louisa and Joe, talk so unimportant that Freeman brushes over the vast majority of their time together with "He remained about an hour longer" (5). Hirsch discusses the apparent opposition of Louisa and Joe in terms of an order-disorder pattern:

> To Louisa . . . , Joe represents a constant threat of potential chaos. He does not, indeed, cannot, belong in the established order of Louisa's home life and his intrusion into that life brings inevitable discord. . . . After the impoverished small talk between Joe and Louisa has run its course, Joe literally upsets the established order of album and gift-book. Not only that—when Louisa attempts to restore order, Joe challenges her purpose in doing so.
>
> (127)

I would add that Louisa does not, indeed, cannot, belong in the established disorder of Joe's home life, and her intrusion into that life would bring inevitable discord as well. Thus, we are left with two characters in two separate worlds. How do they manage a resolution of this relationship and find peace with each other and, more importantly, themselves? Caesar, Louisa's dog and perhaps the most compelling symbol of the story, bridges the gap between these two opposing worlds, enabling each character, especially Louisa, to find contentment.

Joe is a sensual creature with stereotypical male sexual urges. In much the same way that Caesar is chained to the doghouse, Joe is chained to Louisa, a woman who, though "not quite as old as he," "gave people the impression of being older" (4). A reasonably well-off man, Joe is bound to Louisa by a promise made in his youth, although he is now in love with the beautiful and socially accepted and admired Lily Dyer. Like Louisa, Joe is compromising his own character in his stubborn commitment to the fiancée of his youth. He never makes any sexual advances toward Louisa; it may be assumed that this is because of the fear and self-consciousness Louisa arouses in him. They would be incompatible sexually for the same reason that they are incompatible as partners in life: Joe would always be afraid of putting "a clumsy foot or hand through the fairy web, and he had always the consciousness that Louisa was watching fearfully lest he should" (6). Both would always be sexually frustrated and neither would ever be relaxed. It certainly seems likely that Joe would always walk out of the bedroom feeling like that "innocent and perfectly well-intentioned bear . . . after his exit from a china shop," and Louisa would always feel like "the kind-hearted, long-suffering owner of the china shop . . . after the exit of the bear" (5).

Whereas Joe is a gentleman in the presence of Louisa, we are given a hint toward the ending of the story that he is suppressing his sexuality while near her. After Lily's passionate speech to Joe ("No, Joe Dagget, . . . I'll never marry any other man. . . . I ain't that sort of a girl to feel this way twice" [15]), we are told that "Louisa heard an exclamation and a soft commotion behind the bushes; then Lily spoke again. . . . 'This must be put a stop to'" (15). From what we are told, we can only assume that they have engaged in a passionate embrace, a burst of physical activity brought on by emotions that are a far cry from those found in the tense and strained conversation of Louisa and Joe (3-5).

Although Hirsch suggests that the 14 years of Caesar's imprisonment link him to Joe Dagget due to Joe's 14 years away from home (129), and Reichardt says "her [Freeman's] sympathy for the chained dog and her desire to release it were eventually worked into the character of Joe Dagget" (94), I would argue that the story shows Caesar to be a personification of *Louisa's* sexuality.

> Caesar was a veritable hermit of a dog. For the greater part of his life he had dwelt in his secluded hut, shut out from the society of his kind and all innocent canine joys. Never had Caesar since his early youth watched at a woodchuck's hole; never had he known the delights of a stray bone at a neighbor's kitchen door. And it was all on account of a sin committed when hardly out of his puppyhood. No one knew the possible depth of remorse of which this mild-visaged, altogether innocent looking old dog might be capable; but whether or not he had encountered remorse, he had encountered a full measure of righteous retribution. Old Caesar seldom lifted up his voice in a growl or a bark; he was fat and sleepy; there were yellow rings which looked like spectacles around his dim old eyes; but there was a neighbor who bore on his hand the imprint of several of Caesar's sharp white youthful teeth, and for that he had lived at the end of a chain, all alone in a little hut, for fourteen years.
>
> (Freeman 10)

Caesar's life as a hermit closely parallels Louisa's life as a spinster. Caesar is "shut out from the society of his kind and all innocent canine joys." By remaining unmarried, Louisa, in effect, removes herself from society. She does not have many, if any, friends. Caesar has been kept from all of the things that a dog is supposed to enjoy, cut off from the world in his youth. Louisa is cut off in her youth by Joe. He proposes to her and then leaves her, presumably expecting her to keep her pledge to him. Thus, this "sin" she has committed by keeping her engagement to a man who runs away has kept her from watching at woodchuck holes or begging for a stray bone "at a neighbor's kitchen door," very sexual images both. Joe has kept her from having a normal life, from experiencing the joy of having boyfriends, getting married in her earlier youth, and exploring her sexuality with a man who was willing to settle down with her. The narrator tells us that "No one knew the possible depth of remorse of which this mild-visaged . . . old dog might be capable; but whether or not he encountered remorse, he had encountered a full measure of righteous retribution."

I argue that it is truly Louisa's sexual self that suffers the remorse of having given her pledge too soon, thus leaving her sexual self chained, and scarring Joe with this pledge, leaving her indelible mark on him and preventing him from marrying the girl of his choice, Lily. This provides us with a sort of vicious undercurrent between the two in that Louisa has scarred Joe, implying that Joe may sub-consciously feel that Louisa has left a violent mark on him all these years, preventing him from exploring his own sexuality. The "bite," though, is returned by what may be seen as Joe's demand that she preserve herself for him. We are told that "for that [bite] he had lived at the end of a chain, all alone in a little hut, for fourteen years." In a very real way, when the "neighbor" (Joe), demands "either Caesar's death or complete ostracism" (10), he is demanding that Louisa either kill her sexuality or keep it on such a tight leash that "Caesar's" spirit will be broken, thus assuring that she will remain true to him. When Joe returns, he finds that she has done exactly that. Though she has remained true to him, she no longer feels sexually attracted to Joe. This scene brings out the dynamic sexual tension between the two, as well as a bitterness and sense of loss felt on Louisa's part, and a violent, albeit subconscious, undercurrent in the attitudes held by Joe and Louisa toward each other.

Hirsch points to the relationship between the myth of St. George's dragon and the character of Caesar (129):

> One need not . . . try to push Mrs. Freeman beyond her natural depth by insisting that she was consciously manipulating . . . Jungian archetypes. . . . Neither will it do to insist that Joe is actually St. George. . . . Still, even a casual consideration of the comic association between Joe and St. George-Perseus may be illuminating.
>
> (130)

And: "Joe—without being St. George or a sun god—stands as a sexual threat to Louisa; and it is quite fitting that she should associate him in her fantasies with fertility figures and fertility-sterility myths" (131). As Northrop Frye has it in *Anatomy of Criticism,* "In the dragon-killing legend of the St. George and Perseus family . . . a country under an old feeble king is terrorized by a dragon who eventually demands the king's daughter, but is slain by the hero. This seems to be a romantic analogy . . . of a myth of a waste land restored to life by a fertility god" (Frye 137, qtd. in Hirsch 130). In the two myths mentioned, the sea-monster and dragon are instruments in keeping the "wasteland" barren. They are oppressing the people and are demanding what is presumably the most fertile, beautiful, eligible woman in the kingdom, the king's daughter. Were she to die, the best chance for the renewal of life would be destroyed with her, thus plunging the wasteland into a darker time than ever. The hero is a figure of fertility, one who will bring life to the barren land. By killing the beast, he is killing a sort of famine in the land.

New England is not suffering from famine. While Louisa may subconsciously fantasize about being the beautiful princess who can bring fertility to the land (as can be seen in her disappointment over Joe's love for Lily Dyer), she knows that, in reality, she is not. She is the one who restrains Caesar in a dramatic role-reversal. In wishing, underneath that suppressed exterior, to be the princess about to be swallowed by the sea-monster, she has actually become the monster and Caesar has become her image of fertility that is to be rescued by the hero—in this case, Joe. Because she needs someone to restrain her sexuality for the fantasy to be fulfilled, she must do it herself and pretend that Caesar is the one holding her back. As opposed to the Perseus and St. George myths, the beast is contained and takes on a radically different role. Hirsch hints in this direction when he writes:

> Louisa views her own "salvation" from spinsterhood as a prelude to the destruction of society. Joe intends not to kill the dragon but to release him. And it is this possibility, precisely, that terrifies Louisa, though, apparently, she does not apply the consequences of Joe's projected deed to herself alone, but to the town and the townspeople, that is, to society at large. Andromeda's salvation goes hand in hand with the slaying of the monster, Louisa's with the freeing of him.
>
> (130)

When Joe says, "Some day I'm going to take him out" (11), he is threatening the reign of the monster (Louisa) over the sexual icon (Caesar). Louisa represses her sexual urges creating the monster of barrenness inside herself. Her fear is that sexuality (specifically her world of sexual fantasy) is the real monster, that Andromeda is more dangerous than Poseidon's serpent. Were she to give in to her sexual urges (personified, I would argue, in Caesar), it would endanger a society in which sexuality is kept behind closed doors. We see, therefore, Louisa's fear about "innocent children bleeding in his path" (12), a fear of her society gone wrong because Joe Dagget has let out the sexual beast within her. This is what leads me to disagree with Pryse's assertion that "Louisa's real fear is Joe's dominance rather than her own sexuality" (293). Rather, Louisa is afraid of and enchanted by her own sexuality, even to the point of constructing a Perseus fantasy around her life, and, ultimately, projecting these fantasy roles onto the characters around her.

Pryse also discusses the role of Louisa's aprons as they are presented in the following scene:

> Louisa took off her green gingham apron, disclosing a shorter one of pink and white print. She lighted her lamp, and sat down again with her sewing.
>
> In about half an hour Joe Dagget came. She heard his heavy step on the walk, and rose and took off her pink-and-white apron. Under that was still another—white linen with a little cambric edging on the bottom. . . .
>
> (3)

I agree with Pryse when she says "She wears not one but three aprons, each one suggesting symbolic if not actual defense of her own virginity" (293). I cannot, however, agree with her when she submits that "In Joe's absence she [Louisa] replaces the additional two aprons, as if to protect herself from his disturbing presence" (293). It seems odd to me that, if this were the case, Louisa would not put on additional aprons as company *arrives*. The text supports a reading that allows us to see Louisa letting down the guard on her virginity with the man she is about to marry. I believe that she is, in a subtle way, offering herself to Joe Dagget, wanting him to make a "soft commotion" (15) with her as he does with Lily Dyer.

We see only one adventure into the wildness of the world on Louisa's part. When she goes out for a walk one night, the scene is described as follows:

> There was a full moon that night. About nine o'clock Louisa strolled down the road a little way. There were harvest-fields on either hand, bordered by low stone walls. Luxuriant clumps of bushes grew beside the wall, and trees—wild cherry and old apple-trees—at intervals. Presently Louisa sat down on the wall and looked about her with mildly sorrowful reflectiveness. Tall shrubs of blueberry and meadow-sweet, all woven together and tangled with blackberry vines and horse-briers, shut her in on either side. She had a little clear space between them. Opposite her, on the other side of the road, was a spreading tree; the moon shone between its boughs, and the leaves twinkled like silver.

> The road was bespread with a beautiful shifting dapple
> of silver and shadow; the air was full of a mysterious
> sweetness.
>
>   (12-13)

This is the most sexually charged setting of the story.
Outside her house Louisa cannot control what happens. It is in this seductive setting that she is hurt because she is not in control of any leash, including Joe
Dagget's or Lily Dyer's. She realizes that her own
sexual energy, Caesar, is the only thing she can control, and this is the task she takes on for the rest of her
life. She permits herself the fantasy that her sexual
drive could go so far as to destroy the society in which
she lives. However, Caesar's chain is never released:
the leash is never dropped. She elects to retain her
sexual self as it now stands, having become too afraid
of her sexuality to ever let it out in the sensual setting
where Joe and Lily passionately embrace. Louisa does
not, however, choose a life of devotion to her work
that will exclude the possibility of any sexual contact.

Given Louisa's tendency toward compulsive neatness,
it strikes the reader as odd that Caesar's doghouse
would be "half hidden among the tall grasses and flowers" (2). The "tall grasses and flowers" may be taken
as metaphors for male and female genitalia. She has
preserved a semblance of her sexuality, a very private
and "chained up" sexual self at the door of Caesar's
hut. She has not unleashed her sexuality upon the
town, or upon any men, but has, rather, kept her own
private patch of it.

I would suggest that by portraying Caesar as a male,
Freeman implies that behind the spinster image, Louisa has a very powerful sexual drive. Perhaps our own
prejudices about the spinster character make it hard
for us to see Louisa as a sexual being, thus limiting
our perception of the story. Louisa is not giving up her
sexuality. She retains her reign over Caesar and preserves her sexual fantasy, her idealistic vision of her
overpowering sexuality, which must be contained lest
it destroy mankind. If anything, Louisa has an overde-
veloped perception and awareness of her own sexuality. As we realize that she does not give up her sexuality and her fantasies, and as we begin to investigate
the story for clues as to how Louisa releases this
built-up sexual energy, we are led toward one of the
most startling discoveries about Louisa's character:
that Louisa lives out her sexual fantasies by masturbating. This shocks our sensibilities for several reasons. Masturbation is still a tender topic over one hundred years after the publication of this story. Traditional
notions of propriety about spinsters and about women
in general make it difficult for us to accept that Louisa, an unmarried spinster, could seek sexual satisfaction by masturbating. It is difficult enough to accept

Louisa as a sexual entity, let alone as a woman who
explores her own sexuality as intimately as I believe
she does. Yet Freeman gives us this picture of Louisa:

> Louisa dearly loved to sew a linen seam, not always
> for use, but for the simple, mild pleasure which she
> took in it. She would have been loath to confess how
> more than once she had ripped a seam for the mere de-
> light of sewing it together again. Sitting at her window
> during long sweet afternoons, drawing her needle gen-
> tly through the dainty fabric, she was peace itself.
>
>   (9)

Just as Louisa is "loath to confess" her masturbation,
Freeman hides this facet of her character deeply within
the text. The passage is, however, a powerful representation of this sexual act.[1] The significance of the
marriage is then brought to a new level in the following sentence: "But there was small chance of such
foolish comfort in the future" (9). While Joe would release Louisa's sexuality, freeing her to experience this
part of herself with another human being, he would, at
the same time, be taking away her personal fantasy.
Were she to discover that "Caesar" would not tear
apart children and destroy the village, she could no
longer masturbate. Thus, the preservation of her distorted Perseus-St. George fantasy is vital for Louisa to
continue with her personal sexual pleasure. We can
see her awareness of this when we are told that "Louisa had very little hope that he [Joe] would not [let
Caesar out], one of these days, when their interests
and possessions should be more completely fused in
one" (11). We see here that marriage is not necessarily
linked to sex for Louisa, and that she is not relying on
Joe Dagget to fulfill her fantasies. Rather, she is worried that once they are married, Joe will make a much
more forward request to let Caesar off the chain. As
we are told, Joe is "afraid to stir lest he should put a
clumsy foot or hand through the fairy web, and he had
always the consciousness that Louisa was watching
fearfully lest he should" (6). This "fairy web," Louisa's hymen, is the supreme indicator of her virginity,
and will be the "maidenly possession" most obviously
out of place within the bounds of marriage. An added
pressure is placed upon Louisa in needing to work out
a way to preserve her "fairy web" within an institution
that expects Joe to break it.

Despite critics' claims that Louisa must choose between sexual pleasure (marriage to Joe) and autonomy,
we see that marriage to Joe actually involves giving
up both sexual pleasure and autonomy. Therefore, Louisa's choice is not between one thing or the other; it is
between all or nothing. Consequently, her resolution to
keep her word and marry Joe is even more noble, the
breaking of this engagement even more of a relief.
She retains her autonomy and individuality, everything

that is precious to her, while achieving a personal sexual pleasure without relying on a man to fulfill that sexual need.

Louisa feels safe because she controls her sexuality by permitting it to live in this wild zone around the hut while keeping it firmly chained lest it venture out into the wildness of the world. Glasser says that "For many women of her time, denying one's sexuality was the price of autonomy" (37). While this may be true for the women in general of Louisa's time, it is not true for Louisa. She is empowered by her masturbation because it allows her to find happiness in a role that lies outside social expectations; it allows her to find happiness without the help of a man: a bold social statement in Freeman's day and not yet a commonplace in ours.

Note

1. I am indebted to Frank Bergmann for this suggestion.

Works Cited

Foster, Edward. *Mary E. Wilkins Freeman.* New York: Hendricks, 1956.

Freeman, Mary E. Wilkins. *A New England Nun and Other Stories.* New York: Harper, 1891.

Frye, Northrop. *Anatomy of Criticism: Four Essays.* Princeton: Princeton UP, 1957.

Glasser, Leah Blatt. *In a Closet Hidden: The Life and Work of Mary E. Wilkins Freeman.* Amherst: U of Massachusetts P, 1996.

Hirsch, David H. "Subdued Meaning in 'A New England Nun.'" *Studies in Short Fiction* 2 (1965): 124-36.

Pryse, Marjorie. "An Uncloistered 'New England Nun.'" *Studies in Short Fiction* 20 (1983): 289-95.

Reichardt, Mary R. *A Web of Relationship: Women in the Short Stories of Mary Wilkins Freeman.* Jackson: UP of Mississippi, 1992.

William J. Scheick (essay date September 1999)

SOURCE: Scheick, William J. "The Shadow Narrative in Mary Wilkins Freeman's 'Silence.'" *American Transcendental Quarterly* n.s. 13, no. 3 (September 1999): 233-45.

[*In the following essay, Scheick observes a feminist subtext in "Silence," stating that the story "implies the future emergence of female potentiality from the shadows of convention."*]

There are several puzzling features in Mary Wilkins Freeman's **"Silence,"** which first appeared in an 1893 issue of *Harper's Magazine*. Why, for example, does the scene with Silence Hoit calling for her lost fiancé in a shrieking north-wind apparently recall a famous episode in *Wuthering Heights* (1847) when Catherine Earnshaw calls for Heathcliff in the stormy moors? Why is Goody Crane, who is associated with witchcraft, critical to the realization of Silence's desire to be with David Walcott, her fiancé? Why does Goody Crane, in perhaps the most mysterious scene in the narrative, specifically employ a sheep skin to effect the reunion of Silence and David? Such unexplained elements, in a story bearing a title suggestive of more than the name of its protagonist, seem to cut across the grain of the conventional fictional formulae otherwise evident in **"Silence."**

This short story presents a typical chronicle of separated lovers finally reunited. Embedded in this plot, however, is a triad of provocative narrative properties that contribute structurally to another story suggested in the shadows of the conventional romance. In contrast to the focus on the relationship between Silence and David in the domestic romance, the relationship between Silence and Goody Crane is emphasized in the shadow tale. Goody Crane is the enabling agent in this phantom tale. She can in effect be read as a shadow figure, a type (as defined by Maxine Harris 43-55) whose rebellious behavior represents an archetype of the hidden or as yet unrealized part of a collective female identity presently delimited by social decorum. The shadow tale of **"Silence"** recounts Goody Crane's role in authorizing the autonomous expression of the witch-like power of female desire.

My mission in this discussion is to disclose this shadow plot. The presence of this plot in **"Silence"** can be interpreted as symptomatic of the warring sentiments, the authorial self-division, that various critics have generally detected in Freeman's work. Just as, for example, Freeman's compelling psychological portraits of strong women are often framed "with safe, sentimental beginnings and endings," the two storylines of **"Silence"** may be construed as further evidence of her ambivalent performance as an author: "Freeman wanted to rebel openly, but at the same time she sought shelter and acceptability, even at the price of enslavement to standards that she knew to be oppressive and unjust" (Glasser xv).

That Freeman nonetheless manifested a feminist sensibility—whether adequately or inadequately—is currently also a critical consensus, and this view is likewise supported by the phantom tale in **"Silence."** So whereas, on the one hand, this submerged plot may be read in terms of Freeman's ambivalence, it may, on the other hand, also be contextualized in terms of a characteristic of resistance literature. The shadow tale in **"Silence,"** in other words, exemplifies the way resistance in fiction is frequently embedded in the tropes and figures of conventional narrative forms (Slemon 31). While my emphasis necessarily falls on such resistance elements because of the very nature of the shadow tale, I do not deny the possibility that in another sense such an embedding of the phantom narrative reflects Freeman's personal ambivalence concerning its feminist implications. My primary aim is to disclose a heretofore unrecognized facet of Freeman's artistry in a neglected story that provides further and different evidence of her skill with narrative technique (McElrath 255) and her revision of fictional conventions (Gardner 451).

At the level of historical or domestic romance, **"Silence"** is uncomplicated and unexceptional. It opens on the night of 28 February 1704, when the Abenaki warriors and French soldiers would destroy the western frontier settlement of Deerfield, Massachusetts. Silence Hoit has several premonitions of, and Goody Crane predicts, the massacre of that night. The actual devastation is daunting, with many captives, including Silence's fiancé, taken to Canada. During the attack Silence exhibits fortitude, but afterwards she seems to suffer from a post-traumatic disorder. The people around her worry about her mental state, especially whenever Silence ritualistically looks northward over a meadow and calls for David Walcott. Eighteen months later David returns from captivity, but despite his efforts Silence does not recognize him. Eventually Goody Crane directs David to wear a white sheep's fleece over his shoulders in the meadow under a full moon. Prompted by Goody Crane, Silence goes to her familiar haunt and calls for David, who appears in the sheep skin. Silence recovers her vision and now recognizes him. The story closes with the lovers embracing each other.

As this synopsis suggests, the main plot in **"Silence"** conforms to the formula for domestic fiction. The conventionality of **"Silence"** is not redeemed by its historical setting, and so it is not surprising that this work has been ignored by critics and excluded from collections of Freeman's best fiction. On casual encounter, this short story seems to offer little of special interest. It is, however, precisely against the textual fabric of such conventionality that three peculiar features in the work are accentuated. Insofar as these provocative narrative elements counter the sense of the ordinary conveyed by the main plot, they draw attention to themselves. They appear to intimate some obscure meaning within the shadows of the seemingly obvious.

All of these unusual narrative properties are related to Goody Crane. On first encounter, Goody Crane seems to contribute only to the historical matrix of the story:

> She was a lonely and wretched old creature whom people sheltered from pity, although she was somewhat feared and held in ill repute. There were rumors that she was well versed in all the dark lore of witchcraft, and held commerce with unlawful beings. The children of Deerfield village looked askance at her, and clung to their mothers if they met her on the street, for they whispered among themselves that old Goody Crane rode through the air on a broom in the night-time.

(9)

Goody Crane is "held to have occult knowledge" by adult figures, some of whom are "fain to believe that the old woman had been in league with the powers of darkness . . . and had so escaped harm" on the night of the raid on Deerfield (42-43). At one point, Silence's Aunt Eunice Bishop warns Goody Crane, "You'll be burned for a witch yet, Goody Crane, an you be not careful" (31).

Goody Crane is also associated with witchcraft, albeit not conclusively identified as a witch, by the narrative voice. On the day following the massacre, for instance, we are told that "Goody Crane slid in[to a room] like a swift black shadow out of the daylight" (30).[1] The narrative also indicates that Goody Crane's predictions do indeed come to pass, especially the bleak forecast of the destruction of Deerfield (4) and the heartening forecast of the return of David (36). At one point she reads Silence's palm (50), another indication of her occult knowledge. Pertinent, too, is an emphasis throughout the account on Goody Crane's unruly speech, a lingual trait considered in colonial America to be a characteristic of a witch (Kamensky 158-89). "Mutterings" (44) are typical of Goody Crane, who is manifestly insubordinate and defiant in her verbal responses to people. This is why Eunice Bishop warns her about the consequences of sounding like a witch.

Goody Crane, moreover, is well aware of her image in the community. On the day following the massacre she brazenly remarks to people, already inclined to believe that she has survived the night through occult powers, that "the living echo the dead, and that is enough wisdom for a witch" (31). Later, in the course of disclosing her scheme for David's moonlight deception, she assures him, "I'll try no witch-work but mine own wits. . . . If they would hang me for a witch for that, then they may. None but I can cure her" (50). Whether or not Goody Crane is truly a witch is less important to the shadow tale in **"Silence"** than is the fact of her management of the town's identification of her as a witch. She derives power from this perception, so much so that at one point even the upbraiding, narrow-minded Eunice is "tempt[ed] to consult old Goody Crane" (43). In fact, as her successful plan to unite David and Silence demonstrates, Goody Crane uses the power that proceeds from the communal perception of her as a witch for her own and others' advantage. Goody Crane seems to practice a medicinal form of witchery that was customary in early New England (Weisman 41-42), in this instance beneficent conjuring to further romance.[2]

At the level of the romance formula of the story, Goody Crane simply brings the lovers together. As a medicinal witch, she cures Silence of her post-traumatic mental condition. In the shadow tale, however, the connection between these two women is more complex. That they are more deeply associated in some way is hinted at in a fleeting, albeit revealing, reference to a similitude between them: "Silence looked at her. There was a strange likeness between the glitter in her blue eyes and that in Goody Crane's black ones" (31-32). This scene, curiously set off as a discrete paragraph, intimates some meaning never explicit in the short story. The word "strange" is particularly provocative in the passage because it very briefly insists on some indistinct implication in this mysterious similarity between the two women. Ideally a thought emerges in the reader's mind: What has this seemingly fugitive passage to do with an account about lovers separated and reunited? The historical romance, however, proceeds towards its formulaic resolution as if this "strange" moment had never occurred.

The unexplained silent exchange, with its stress on a "likeness" between the two women, has no function in the main story. Omit this moment and nothing is lost from the domestic plot of the reunion of David and Silence. The association of the two women is a shard from another narrative barely glimpsed in the shadows of the conventional story. This shadow narrative is not about the relationship between David and Silence; it is about the relationship between Goody Crane and Silence. The account of their relationship is presented in a way that narratively imitates Goody Crane's entrance on the day after the massacre. That is to say, the phantom tale of the bond between Goody Crane and Silence "slid[es] in[to the text] like a swift black shadow out of the daylight" of a conventional romance (30).

Goody Crane is cowed by neither public expectation nor individual censure. In fact, she derives personal sovereignty and power from the communal impression of her as a witch. She is outspoken, as if the conventions governing female decorum simply do not apply to her. Yet, for all her fierce independence, Goody Crane is not an isolate. She is one of those Freeman women who assert their autonomy yet also maintain relationships with other women (Reichardt xiv). Goody Crane allows other women in the community to pity and shelter her. She seeks their company. Still more indicative, she looks after Silence as if she were the mother of this orphaned young woman. In fact, she saves Silence at the cost of possibly being burned as a witch. Goody Crane's relationship with her surrogate daughter is troped as an act of restorative curing effected through the application of female "wit," intelligence and cunning. "I'll try no witch-work but mine own wits," Goody Crane promises David, and she indeed succeeds in "sav[ing the] poor maid's wits" (46, 50). As the enabling agent in the shadow tale, Goody Crane exhibits wit not only in her dramatic rescue of Silence; she also displays wit in her everyday behavior and speech, designed to exploit her communal image as a witch.

In the domestic romance Silence needs awakening from a trance-like mental state induced by David's absence; in the shadow tale she needs deliverance from the trance-like mental state of her subjection to authority figures such as her aunt. Eunice Bishop, Silence's custodial aunt, is the antithesis of Goody Crane. Eunice is vain, as is indicated by her preoccupation with a "gilt-framed looking-glass" (19-20). She can be insensitive, as is suggested by her annoyance with the men who save captives rather than secure her requested items (46). Her primary attribute, however, is a strict conformity to social expectations. As an authority figure, she insists on proper female behavior. She berates Silence for "unmaidenly" conduct, including her alleged inattention to chores and her courtship with David (11-13). Eunice stresses female submission to old-fashioned standards of normative behavior as a guarantee of a "good name" (53). "I stayed at home, and your uncle did the courting," she tells Silence; "I never went after nightfall to his house that he might see me home . . . I trow my mother would have locked me up in the garret, and kept me on meal and water, had I done aught so bold" (13). For Eunice, the ideal female is submissive and silent.

Eunice points to the example of her own mother to authorize her surrogate maternal role in reproving Silence. But this traditional claim is contested in the shadow narrative by a competing maternal figure, namely the very woman whose reputation as a witch makes children cling to their mothers (9). Goody Crane lurks in the shadows of the domestic romance where she dimly emerges as a more suitable mother-figure for Silence.

Although as her name suggests, Silence has yet much to learn from her outspoken mentor in the shadows, she and Goody Crane share personal traits, not just a "likeness" in their eyes. Like Goody Crane, Silence possesses a "steady heart that be not so easy turned as some" (41). Also pertinent is Silence's demonstration of autonomous power, especially in her speech, during the crisis of the French and Indian attack. On that occasion she speaks with a "firm voice," at one point even curtly telling her aunt to "stand off" and "be quiet" (16). Silence has a will, a sense of autonomy, but it tends to exert itself only in extraordinary circumstances. Such is the case of the sudden kiss she gives David "of her own accord, as if she had been his wife" (10), a spontaneous act inspired by her premonition of an attack on Deerfield. Normally Silence "wishe[s] him good-night . . . without a kiss," for she is "chary of caresses" (10). In ordinary circumstances, in other words, Silence usually subordinates her wishes and defers to the social norms defended by her aunt.

When her aunt orders her to bind her hair, she does so. The symbolism of female constraint is evident in this gesture and in her subsequent behavior: "Silence bound up her hair, and sat down by her wheel meekly, and yet with a certain dignity" (40). This incident occurs after the onset of Silence's post-traumatic disorder. It is crucial to observe, however, that this occasion is a replay of an earlier scene before the attack, when her aunt berates Silence for talking to David rather than attending to domestic chores. Then, too, without argument Silence obediently "pulled a spinning-wheel before the fire and fell to work" (13).

On both occasions Silence conforms to expectations, although her potential for a different response is also suggested in the two spinning wheel scenes. Silence holds "up her head like a queen" (12) and works "with a certain dignity" (40). Such hints of resistance suggest that Silence possesses a latent capacity for the same personal sovereignty evident in Goody Crane's attitude toward social expectations based on past patterns of female behavior. Goody Crane "leer[s] up . . . undauntedly" (30) to criticism, an action more resistant than but also certainly akin to rebuked Silence's holding her head like a queen. A shared sensibility of independence—one manifest, the other latent—accounts for the "strange likeness between" Goody Crane and Silence.

The diptych of the spinning wheel scenes also provides insight into the meaning of Silence's trance-like condition. It is significant that both before and after her affliction, little has changed in Silence's experience at home. This detail suggests, in the shadow narrative, that the time after the impairment of her wits is like the time before. In the domestic romance David's return should heal Silence. That it does not, that Goody Crane rather than David effects the cure, intimates that something more than David's absence accounts for Silence's temporary loss of her wits. In the shadow tale

Silence suffers a temporary attenuation of her wits not because of the captivity of David but because of the captivity of her autonomy. Her vocalization of desire in calling for her fiancé represents a potential power as yet spellbound in her. That the efficacy of this power is as arrested before the trauma as it is afterward is a deeper implication of the dual spinning wheel scenes where Silence conforms to her aunt's demands as if hypnotized.

The shadow tale implicitly critiques the communal (domestic romance) perception of Silence's loss of wits as an illness. Is not her traumatic condition in effect an extreme version of Eunice Bishop's communal ideal of "witless," trance-like female submission? A clue to such an interrogation emerges in the fact that the community is disturbed less by Silence's hypnotic behavior than by her compulsive vocalization: "people heard her and sighed and shuddered" (47). The witch-like aberrant expression of Silence's voice, recalling Goody Crane's equally undisciplinable speech, is the chief cause of the community's concern over Silence's condition.

In **"Silence"** resistant female vocalization represents the autonomous expression of the witch-like power of female desire. Goody Crane enables Silence to find her voice, to break free of a trance-like existence. The process commences when Goody Crane tells Silence that David is alive in Canada (32) and "will come back over the north meadow" (35). As a result of Goody Crane's counsel, "there was never a day nor a night that Silence called not over the north meadow" (47). Silence's determined vocalization expresses her personal desire, as yet spellbound. After Goody Crane's prediction Silence becomes a divided woman. She physically complies with the demands of her social milieu, but she mentally attends to the claims of her own desire: "She paid no heed, for she was not there" (36). From within her trance-like state, representing women's social situation, emerges Silence's socially disturbing voice. Silence's insistent/resistant voice allies her to Goody Crane, her surrogate mother, even more than does the mere likeness between their eyes. All that is needed is a further "maternal" intervention by Goody Crane. Goody Crane's midwifery (as it were) in the moonlight facilitates the birth of Silence's desire from a spellbound potentiality to a liberated actuality.

The presentation of Silence calling over the meadow is reproduced in the frontispiece of *Silence and Other Stories,* which reprints the original magazine illustration. It is a particularly dramatic moment:

> "David!" she called. "David! David! David!" The north
> wind bore down upon her, shrieking with a wild fury
> like a savage of the air; the dry branches of a small

tree near her struck her in the face. "David!" she called again. "David! David!" She swelled out her white throat like a bird, and her voice was shrill and sweet and far-reaching.

(38)

This scene dominates the remainder of the story. In fact, the story concludes with the reunion of the lovers at this very site of Silence's vocalized yearning.

This scene recalls a powerful episode in *Wuthering Heights,* in which Catherine Earnshaw calls in vain for Heathcliff in the windy moors. In Brontë's novel Catherine confesses to her housemaid, Ellen Dean, that she loves Heathcliff but will not marry him because he is an uncouth, penniless orphan. Heathcliff, who feels as passionately about Catherine as she does about him, overhears this conversation and furiously runs off into the stormy moors, where he disappears. Catherine, "in a state of agitation" and heedless of "the growling thunder, and the great drops," calls at intervals, "crying outright" into the night (76). Cold and wet, Catherine falls into a feverish delirium, from which she recovers physically but not emotionally. From this point onward, disaster awaits the separated lovers. Even after their death, villagers claim to hear their restless spirits roaming the moors.

It is unlikely that the meadow scene in **"Silence"** is an accidental or casual allusion to this famous passage in *Wuthering Heights.* Within three years after the periodical version of **"Silence,"** Freeman published a novel evidently influenced by Emily Brontë's book (Glasser 129-31), and within three years after the collection version of **"Silence,"** Freeman explicitly lavished extraordinary praise on *Wuthering Heights* as "an unflinching masterpiece" (67). One of Freeman's attractions to *Wuthering Heights,* it has been suggested (Westbrook 89), is Brontë's fearlessness in presenting her story, in contrast to Freeman's personal sense of the inhibiting restraints imposed on her by the expectations of her audience. In this sense, the allusion to *Wuthering Heights* may be read as a homage to Brontë. However, since the appropriated scene dominates the second half of Freeman's story, something more than a mere testament seems to be implied.

Read in light of the domestic romance formula in **"Silence,"** the allusion to *Wuthering Heights* possibly suggests that the story of Silence Hoit revises the story of Catherine Earnshaw. In contrast to Catherine, Silence succeeds in uniting with her lover, an orphan (like Heathcliff). Happiness, not misery, is the destiny of Silence and David Walcott. This reading is not very satisfying, however, because Freeman's account of Silence's experience pales considerably in comparison to Brontë's impassioned account of Catherine's expe-

rience. Instead of pointing to **"Silence"** as a revision of *Wuthering Heights,* the echo of the famous scene of Catherine calling for Heathcliff more likely draws attention to itself. It is just too powerful, too "stormy" an allusion to function well at the level of the domestic romance narrative in **"Silence."** This allusion potentially causes the reader to hesitate or sense some disjunctiveness at this point in the story. The allusion to *Wuthering Heights,* like the earlier mention of a strange likeness between Silence and Goody Crane, is a shard from some other narrative barely glimpsed in the shadows of the conventional story.

Read in terms of this phantom narrative, the reference to *Wuthering Heights* suggests another revision in Freeman's short story. The shadow tale suggests that Silence is joined to her lover in the domestic romance specifically because she does not betray her desire. In contrast to Catherine's decision not to marry Heathcliff despite being in love with him, Silence gives full expression to her desire regardless of social consequences. Silence's heedless determination is like Goody Crane's resolution to risk her life in order to save her surrogate daughter. Silence, who pays "no heed" and is "not there," also revises wild and undisciplined Catherine, who (in Freeman's phrasing) is caught "in a whirlpool of emotion" (69). Silence, as mentored by Goody Crane, fulfills Catherine's thwarted desire.

Wuthering Heights struck its Victorian reviewers as coarse, vulgar, even repulsive in its indecorous account of tempestuous passions apparently presented without a moral. Freeman likewise acknowledges that Brontë's "great work" indeed "offends and repels" (69). It is precisely this received history of Brontë's novel that would have prevented the allusion to *Wuthering Heights* from functioning comfortably in **"Silence"** as a mere tribute. Freeman's contemporaries who recognized the allusion would potentially have been arrested by it, their attention at least momentarily diverted from the domestic romance plot. There was even some risk on Freeman's part of being charged of plagiarism by readers disturbed by the allusion.

As a feature of the shadow tale, however, the allusive scene of Silence calling for David in a meadow potentially functions like Goody Crane. It, too, is a sudden "shadow" cloaking some secret (occult-like) meaning in the "daylight" of what appears to be a conventional historical or domestic romance.

The same secret about female desire informs another allusion in **"Silence."** Appearing at the end of the short story, this peculiar episode completes a structural triad of pieces from the shadow narrative that includes, first, the similarity between Goody Crane and Silence, and then the allusion to *Wuthering Heights*. The third incident occurs when Goody Crane facilitates Silence's recognition of David by having him appear in the moonlight while wearing a sheep skin over his shoulders. Goody Crane's reasons for this strategy are not revealed, nor is the tactic prepared for by any preceding feature in the domestic romance. Why this arrangement should succeed is never indicated. At best, when the "white fleece of a sheep thrown over [David's] back [catches] the moonlight" (53), we may suspect that somehow the visual effect attracts Silence's eye. But, even so, why would Silence's attention be distracted by a sheep? And why would this attention make any difference? Nothing in the domestic romance explains why Goody Crane's ruse works. Accordingly, it would not be surprising if a reader finally suspected that the detail is meant merely as an indication of witchcraft and finally is unimportant in itself, perhaps only introduced to conclude the story.

Nevertheless, the particulars of the scene seem significant, as if elements of some ritual beyond witchery are involved. This final episode involving the sheep skin is affiliated with the other two odd narrative features in the short story. Silence's likeness to Goody Crane and Freeman's revision of Catherine Earnshaw lead to this occasion when an alleged medicinal witch cures Silence of a malaise—a condition akin to blindness—associated with the suppression of female desire.

This concluding incident seems to re-present an Old Testament event recorded in Chapter 27 of Genesis. This may at first seem an odd proposition. It is well known that Freeman, who rarely quotes Scripture in her work, was generally skeptical about religion. Her fiction nonetheless reflects the influence of the Bible on New England culture. Freeman's writings, it has been argued, include a new sort of Calvinism in which women assert an independent authority based on an inward revelation (Razzari 227). Her work has also been said to feature undeclared biblical themes, especially concerning judgment, that inform Freeman's recovery of female history (Morey 759). **"Silence"** provides an instance of a specific and clever revision of Scripture.

In Genesis aged Isaac, who is virtually blind, wishes to bless his son Esau. His wife Rebekah prefers Jacob, and she conspires with him to trick her husband into giving her younger son the blessing intended for the older twin brother. As the primary means of deception devised by his mother, Jacob dons goat skins on his hands, neck, and shoulders to simulate Esau's hairiness. Touching these skins convinces Isaac that Jacob is Esau, and he gives Jacob the irrevocable blessing

that positions him at the head of the family. The brothers are now divided, and Jacob flees for his life. A reconciliation between the brothers will occur many years later.

Goody Crane, like Rebekah, conspires with David to secure Silence's favor. In her virtual blindness, Silence, like Isaac, is deceived by donned animal skins. The ruse succeeds, albeit with a significant difference from the Old Testament version. David receives Silence's blessing, as it were, but a union rather than a division results with the restoration of Silence's vision. The union of the lovers is the point of the domestic romance, whereas the realization of Silence's voice (desire) after the restoration of Silence's vision (health) is the point of the shadow tale. Like Rebekah in the scriptural account, Goody Crane exerts a powerful female agency in the shadow tale. From the likeness of her eyes to Silence's, through her initiation of Silence's watch over the meadow, to her attainment of Silence's restoration with the sheep skin, Goody Crane wields a witch-like power on behalf of Silence, her surrogate daughter.

Freeman's story revises the Old Testament story not only by emphasizing a union but also by reading a shadow tale in the biblical story. In the shadows of the official story about patriarchal succession is an indirect account of Rebekah's power. Expressing her desire, Rebekah resists her patriarchal husband's will, persuades her reluctant son to deceive his father, and tears a family asunder. So, finally, if the sheepskin allusion to Esau and Jacob provides a structural feature of the shadow tale in **"Silence,"** this phantom narrative in turn provides a hermeneutic, a newer testament, for rereading that biblical story in terms of the might of expressed (vocalized) female desire. In this suggestion Freeman anticipates a late twentieth-century feminist understanding of Rebekah (Exum 65-66). It would seem, moreover, that Goody Crane, as a revised version of Rebekah, is as good at applying scriptural learning as she is thought to be in applying occult knowledge.

Goody Crane and her protégé are gifted with precognition, and this trait is mirrored in Freeman's own narrative. The story ends with an intimated prediction: David and Silence hold each other "as if they . . . might reappear hundreds of spring-times hence" (54). At this point the domestic romance and the shadow tale meet. Here the reunion of the lovers and the actualization of female desire share the same narrative space. This narrative juncture implies more than the mysterious endurance of love; it also implies the future emergence of female potentiality from the shadows of convention. As represented by reactions to Silence's voice in the short story, the prospect of such an actualization of female power makes adults sigh and shudder. The children, however, "had no fear of her": "They [the children] eyed with a mixture of wonder and admiration Silence's beautiful bewildered face. . . . Many a time when Silence called to David from the terrace of the north meadow, some of the little village maids in their homespun pinafores would join her and call with her" (42). These young women are the future, Freeman predicts. They, like Silence, will enjoy "far-reaching" voices (38) in "hundreds of spring-times hence," when being as outspoken as a witch will be normal rather than aberrant for women. At its conclusion **"Silence"** forecasts the eventual realization, the triumph, of the autonomous expression of the witch-like power of female desire. This prediction is the message of the shadow tale in **"Silence,"** a narrative that imitates Goody Crane—Silence's enabling surrogate mother of "strange likeness"—by "slid[ing] in[to the text] like a swift black shadow out of the daylight" of a conventional romance (30).

Notes

1. In "The Witch's Daughter" (1910) Freeman relies on similar phrasing to represent a witch, who "pass[es] like a shadow" (128).

2. "White witchery" is specifically differentiated from the black arts in "The Witch's Daughter" (128), which is also about conjuring in the moonlight to further romance.

Works Cited

Brontë, Emily. *Wuthering Heights.* Ed. William M. Sale, Jr. New York: W. W. Norton, 1972.

Elrod, Eileen Razzari. "Rebellion, Restraint, and New England Religion: The Ambivalent Feminism of Mary Wilkins Freeman." *Studies in Puritan American Spirituality* 6 (1997): 225-63.

Exum, J. Cheryl. "The Mothers of Israel: The Patriarchal Narratives from a Feminist Perspective." *Bible Review* 2, i (1986): 60-67.

Freeman, Mary Wilkins. "Emily Bronte and Wuthering Heights." In *The World's Great Women Novelists.* Philadelphia: Book Lover's Library, 1901; rpt. in *Critical Essays on Mary Wilkins Freeman.* Ed. Shirley Marchalonis. Boston: G. K. Hall, 1991. 67-69.

———. *Silence and Other Stories.* New York: Harper and Brothers, 1898.

———. "The Witch's Daughter." In *The Uncollected Stories of Mary Wilkins Freeman.* Ed. Mary R. Reichardt. Jackson: UP of Mississippi, 1992. 125-30.

Gardner, Kate. "The Subversion of Genre in the Short Stories of Mary Wilkins Freeman." *New England Quarterly* 65 (1992): 447-68.

Glasser, Leah Blatt. *In a Closet Hidden: The Life and Work of Mary E. Wilkins Freeman.* Amherst: U of Massachusetts P, 1996.

Harris, Maxine. *Sisters of the Shadow.* Norman: U of Oklahoma P, 1991.

Kamensky, Jane. *Governing the Tongue: The Politics of Speech in Early New England.* New York: Oxford UP, 1997.

McElrath, Joseph R. "The Artistry of Mary E. Wilkins Freeman's 'The Revolt.'" *Studies in Short Fiction* 17 (1980): 255-61.

Morey, Ann-Janine. "American Myth and Biblical Interpretation in the Fiction of Harriet Beecher Stowe and Mary E. Wilkins Freeman." *Journal of the American Academy of Religion* 55 (1987): 741-63.

Reichardt, Mary R. *A Web of Relationship: Women in the Short Stories of Mary Wilkins Freeman.* Jackson: UP of Mississippi, 1992.

Slemon, Stephen. "Unsettling the Empire: Resistance. Theory for the Second World." *World Literature Written in English* 28 (1990): 30-41.

Weisman, Richard. *Witchcraft, Magic, and Religion in Seventeenth-Century Massachusetts.* Amherst: U of Massachusetts P, 1984.

Lucia Cherciu (essay date autumn 2000)

SOURCE: Cherciu, Lucia. "'A Veritable Guest to Her Own Self': Mary Wilkins Freeman's Humorous Short Stories." *Journal of the Short Story in English,* no. 35 (autumn 2000): 21-41.

[*In the following essay, Cherciu evaluates Freeman's humorous critique of traditional courtship rituals in "Juliza" and "One Good Time," and comments on Narcissa Stone's obsession with clothing.*]

In a letter sent in 1886 to her friend Mary Louise-Booth, the editor of *Harper's Bazar,* Mary E. Wilkins expresses succinctly the apparent paradox of her short stories, according to which laughter and tears are often interchangeable:

> I have just finished a story, which I do not dare send as yet. It is so very tragic. Mary Wales who always giggles at my pathetic points, has just burst into a flood of tears much to my alarm. I thought she was laughing, and there she was crying. I may change it, and marry the man instead of killing him, but I fear it won't be as artistic.
>
> (68)

Most of Freeman's stories of ludicrous courtship combine strategies of revolt disguised in the apparently innocuous mask of humor with often improbable eva-sions out of the constricting limits of reality. Interpreting the humor and pathos in Freeman's stories of courtship, I will try to bypass the popular **"A New England Nun,"** a story that has become an icon within the increasing body of criticism on Freeman's work. Instead, I will analyze two less known stories, **"Juliza"** and **"One Good Time."**

In an attempt to enlarge the scope of her reception, Freeman took pains to disengage herself from the radical message in her enormously successful story **"The Revolt of 'Mother.'"** Sarah Penn, or the "Mother" in the title, decides to move her family into the barn her husband has stubbornly built instead of their long promised new house. Her brave decision scandalizes her community but convinces her husband about the power of her determination. Discussing this model of a woman's revolt in an article somewhat misleadingly called "An Autobiography," Freeman claims that the story is not true: "When I wrote that little tale I threw my New England traditions to the winds and trampled on my New England conscience" (134). By the same token, one could argue that the conflicts in **"Juliza"** and **"One Good Time"** might be improbable. Definitely, they do not correspond to a traditional definition of what women should be. However, the delicate balance of humor manages to recuperate the truth in what might appear as an irreverent revolt against tradition.

The mixture of pathos and humor in Freeman's stories became apparent quite early. Although most early reviews signaled the presence of humor, Shirley Marchalonis and Gregg Camfield have published the only studies dedicated exclusively to Freeman's humor. Specifically, Marchalonis develops a theory of humor starting from the limitations and the benefits of the local color label. In her view, the function of humor is relevant in its connection with other modes: "Throughout Freeman's work, including those early stories described by Pattee and others as grim, there is often a core of humor—perhaps irony, perhaps the absurd, but humor nonetheless. Characters are placed, or, rather, have placed themselves, in situations that are, quite simply, funny" (229). Constructing "a conflict that is both trivial and vital," Freeman's work combines humor with other genres. Marchalonis gives priority to the value of humor that triggers "the shock of the unexpected" as a development of incongruity theory and the perception of logical distortion. The identification of incongruity as a conflict between "individual behavior and the conventions of the protagonist's society" defines, in Marchalonis's terms, the specifics of revolt in Freeman's work (232).

Freeman's own life offers examples of ludicrous courtship. Under the public surveillance imposed by the attention of the press that came with the increase of popularity, Wilkins' protracted engagement became a subject of ridicule. She had shared a house with her childhood friend, Mary Wales, from 1883 till 1902, when she was almost forty years of age. Around 1893, she met Charles Freeman. Their courtship lasted about five years, mainly because the writer had strong hesitations. Seizing the news of her engagement, the papers announced their marriage several times. *The New York Telegraph,* for example, declared, "the public is really tired of the love affairs of the literary old maid, and the sooner she marries the doctor and takes him out of the public view the more highly will the action be appreciated." Similarly, another paper worded its headline, "Please, Miss Wilkins, Marry Dr. Freeman" (qtd. in Kendrick 207). For the private Mary Wilkins, the bitter humor of this public bantering must have been painful. Indeed, the marriage was reported several times in the papers before it actually took place, and when it finally happened, it was done in secret.[1]

Ludicrous courtship is a common theme in Freeman's stories, whose goal, as she expressed it, was to expose the "exaggerations and deformities" in the New England character (qtd. in Martin 148). Freeman captures the main aspects of distorted courtship in **"Two Old Lovers,"** her first story published in *Harper's Bazar* in 1883. Describing the situation of two lovers who spent all of their lives deferring reciprocal confessions, the narrator comments, "There was something laughable, and at the same time rather pathetic, about Maria's and David's courting" (279). After they have been closely observed by the community all their lives and indulgently laughed about, the two finally get to communicate openly. David's speech is precipitated only by his deathbed farewell to his lifetime friend to whom he never got the courage to propose. The other quintessential courtship story which has long been embraced by criticism is **"A New England Nun,"** in which Louisa prefers the suspension of an indeterminate courtship of fourteen years to the actual presence of her fiancé, and ultimately to the realization of their marriage.[2]

Carrying over the main theme in **"Two Old Lovers,"** the two stories **"Juliza"** and **"One Good Time,"** are both laughable developments of passion. Juliza and Narcissa, the heroine of **"One Good Time,"** spend vast amounts of energy in a distorted spectacle of the self. They become actors on a public stage dominated by the close surveillance of their community. Charles Miner Thompson, an early enthusiastic reviewer of Freeman's work, identified "a monstrous example of stubbornness" in most of Freeman's characters (665). Indeed, the two heroines excel in the adamant pursuit of their dreams to the point of exaggeration and ridicule. Thompson's interpretation of Freeman as "an idealist in masquerade" works well for both stories.

The two heroines' efforts toward independence and self-determination are often distorted through an absurd evasion of reality, combined with complicated strategies of deception.[3] On the whole, the treatment of ludicrous courtship in Freeman's stories foregrounds the feelings of inadequacy characters experience when they leave behind the conventions of their communities.

"Juliza" (1892) is one of the emblematic cases of revolt against courtship in its rigid rituals of action and passivity, subject and object. Juliza is a talented young woman who excels as a performer of public recitations. Misunderstanding the meaning of her long friendship with Frank Williams, Juliza proceeds to propose marriage to him. Completely ignorant of her breech of gender roles, she further discovers that Frank is in love with another person, Lily Emmons. Juliza facilitates the relationship between the two and finally even offers to perform a moving recitation at Frank and Lily's wedding. However, her apparent selflessness is only a public spectacle, meant to disguise her own suffering and to protect her from the community's opprobrium. Powerful in its affirmation of women's rights and especially of women's ability to take their destiny into their own hands, **"Juliza"** has only recently started to receive critical attention.[4] The title character has been predestined through her quaint name to trace a double path and follow a double destiny. As a form of paying homage to her aunts, "Juliza had been named for both of them by a judicious combination of Julia and Eliza, and had inherited their money" (23).

The heroine's stark unconventionality results from her unusual upbringing and from her artistic talents. An only child, Juliza has been home schooled, and has not had direct contact with the other girls of her age.[5] Consequently, she remains ignorant of common societal norms. Her isolation makes her feel more mature, giving her "a demeanor like that of a woman of fifty" (22). Juliza's own family provided her with models likely to predestine her for a unique trajectory. Her mother, Mrs. Peck, is first described as covered in a "curious majesty," sitting "in her rocking-chair as if it were a throne" (26). It is from her mother that Juliza inherits her gift for public speaking and her special voice, "deep, with solemn inflections" (26). The arrangement of her parents' marital relations is peculiar too, in the sense that Mrs. Peck's domination is openly acknowledged, while Juliza's father "never dreamed of disobeying his impetuous wife, but covered his docility with taciturnity, which gave him a show of masculine dignity" (28). Both parents are inclined towards posing, and from them Juliza inherits her talent for theater and for controlling herself in public. Apt to imitate the spectacular voice of her mother, who also

trains her to deliver speeches, and equally to withdraw into taciturnity and repress her feelings, as her father does, Juliza is presented from the outset as a masterful candidate for public simulation.

Completely in control of her qualities as a public speaker, Juliza is active as an entertainer in her community, reputed for her talent and invited to perform at sociables. Her performances are patronized by the church. Her mother denies her the right to perform for the sake of art for two reasons: first, because it is not appropriate for a woman to display herself in public, and, paradoxically, because she has sufficient resources and thus lacks the excuse of needing art for survival:

> I'm willin' she should speak to accommodate as she does here in town, but I ain't willin' to have her go round speakin' in public. It ain't a woman's place. And Juliza's got enough; she don't need to.
>
> (23)

The creative impulses behind her art are demystified, suggesting a controversy between genteel values and artistic performance. Juliza's recitations offer an outlet for her singular personality and repressed passion.

Juliza's performance in public at "a sewing-circle and sociable" is marked by her peculiar ignorance of public rituals. Described as "a heavily-built girl with a back as broad as a matron's," her physical appearance sets her apart from the other young women of her age (21). Since Juliza is the center of attention during the evening entertainment, her relationship with Frank Williams is singled out as well. The narrator describes the reactions of the two friends as they see each other, emphasizing their awkward behavior: Frank blushes, avoids her eyes, and does not initiate conversation. The condoned ritual of courtship at the end of the sociable, when young men are waiting to walk home with their girlfriends, provides an occasion for the public embarrassment of the two:

> When Juliza Peck appeared, Frank Williams shrank back; several of the young men tried to push him forward, laughing, but he stood his ground. Juliza paused in the doorway, and stood looking back at him calmly, as if waiting.
>
> (23)

Although the tension is obvious for the ones present, Juliza is herself ignorant of the power structure of the scene, and thus breaks the rules of the courting ritual. She initiates conversation on the long way back, overturning the most rigid of social codes and actually proceeding to propose to Frank.

Proposing, Juliza fails to act according to expectations about feminine weakness and compulsory demure behavior. When Frank complains that his mother is sick,

Juliza volunteers to help, in a manner unencumbered by any restraints, business-fashion: "'There ain't but one thing to do,' said she, 'I'll come over there whenever you want me'" (25). The details she adds to her matter-of-fact proposal demystify the ritual, hitting into the core of convention: "I can come any time next week, if you say so. I haven't much to do to get ready. I've got clothes enough. I never thought I'd want to lay in a great stock when I was married. Anyway, I always thought it was foolish." Her quick dismissal of traditional romance is quite baffling for Frank, who needs time to process her information, unable to conceive of her meaning. Defying propriety, Juliza enumerates her own qualities of housewife: "I mean I'll get married to you right away, and come over to your house. That'll settle it. I'm a good cook and a good housekeeper" (25).

The painful comedy of the scene derives from the confusion of gender roles. Through her nonconformity, Juliza castigates the hypocrisy of gender distribution, questioning an oppressive power structure. Ignorant of the prescriptive ideology of romance, Juliza "steals the language" of men, trying to perform roles typically ascribed to them.[6] In addition to her peculiar upbringing, through which she managed to elude convention, it is her training in manipulating language that makes her take for granted her right to speak her mind. Martha J. Cutter discusses the "frontiers of language" in **"The Revolt of 'Mother,'"** noting that the distribution of power among gender categories is negotiated in Freeman's most famous story through a similar disputation of language. Cutter interprets Mother's attributes as a "speaking subject" who strives "to redefine a linguistic frontier" (280). Acting as a speaking subject, Juliza's peremptory attitude masquerades as masculine, signaling the inherently ridiculous aspect of rigid romantic codes. However, once she has broken the code, Juliza has given Frank power over herself, a fact that he points out to her unflinchingly: "You mustn't think I shall say anything about this to-night, . . . I shan't ever speak of it" (26).

Comedy is a contingent category, dependent on conventions that are assumed, commonly shared by a given community and familiar to the reader, but never explicitly stated. The humor of Juliza's interference with prescribed gender roles offers a productive chance for the writer to assert one of the absurd limits dictated by patriarchy. Later that night, when Juliza tells her mother about Frank's refusal, Juliza's ignorance provides an opportunity for explaining the premise that "There's something to be considered besides common-sense" (26). The repartee between mother and daughter is exemplary of their theatrical talents. Innocently, Juliza ask her mother: "[W]hat do you suppose the reason is that Frank don't want me to marry him?", and the dialogue continues in a punctuated exchange:

> Juliza Peck, you didn't ask Frank Williams to marry you?
>
> No, I didn't ask him; I told him I would.
>
> Do you know what you've done?
>
> What?
>
> What? You've made yourself a laughin' stock all over Stony Brook.
>
> I don't see why I have, I'm sure.
>
> Don't you know girls don't tell young men they'll marry'em unless they're asked.
>
> I don't see why they don't.
>
> (27)

The dialogue between the two includes references to a social code Juliza does not perceive. Instead, she confesses her blindness—which emphasizes the ludicrous in the scene, quite disconcerting for her mother—by admitting, "I don't see what I've done to be laughed at" (27).

Playing the role of the fool, Juliza is apt to speak her mind and endanger her image in the community through an innocent lack of "modesty" and of conventional femininity. In training her for recitations, her mother once accuses her of not being sufficiently fragile and sophisticated for a woman, lacking intuition and insight into what goes beyond common-sense. In her mother's view, Juliza's physical appearance precludes her from playing the part of a feminine, gracious woman. Her mother claims that Juliza is too strong to play a feminine woman convincingly: "You plank your arm up an' down like a pump-handle . . . your arm ain't put in with a hinge, it's put in with your feelin's, when you're speakin . . . I s'pose it's because you're built so solid" (28). Juliza would not masquerade femininity, and in so doing, she acts out her own vision of herself truthfully. The dark humor of the training scene emphasizes the mother's violence towards her daughter: although she trains her to speak in public, the mother does not comprehend that the success as a speaking subject will trigger Juliza's failure.

Juliza once more overrules her mother's code of demure behavior by challenging Frank to talk over his refusal. The scene in which Juliza invites him in is striking in its distribution of gender roles. Embarrassed when dared to explain his feelings, Frank finds refuge in the trivial, noticing details and using them as a source of violence:

Frank was blushing; he looked down at his snowy boots, saw the snow melting on the carpet, and thought fiercely to himself that he did not care if it was spoiled.

(29)

Asked why he doesn't want to marry her, he responds,

[Y]ou may not know it, but you're doing a dreadful thing. How do you suppose I can answer you a question like that if I'm a man.

(31)

Social limits are thus working on both sides, restricting the possibilities of their behavior. Caught in the routine, Frank is incapable of dealing with new situations, unable to respond to Juliza's alternative solutions.

Given the courage of her invention of new roles, Juliza could be considered an exponent of the New Woman, whose most important features are creativity in devising new images for the self and especially outstanding linguistic endowment. Articulate, Juliza acts through language. Analyzing the negotiation of stereotypes between the cult of the True Woman and the development of the New Woman, Martha Cutter concludes, "Much of what characterized the independence of the New Woman was linguistic" (389). In this respect, Juliza excels in a skillful manipulation of language, convincing Frank to confess his infatuation with another young woman, and proceeding to help him.

Juliza's apparent altruism may be meant to prevent the development of a possible blackmail on Frank's part. Divining the object behind Frank's obsession, Juliza acts as an intermediary, providing him with a much-needed language. His confusion and lack of decision are solved through Juliza's intrepid linguistic resourcefulness aided by a beneficial literal-mindedness. When Frank hesitates, admitting, "I have written fifty letters, an' torn 'em up. I don't even know how to begin 'em," Juliza responds with a placid, "I should say, 'Dear Friend'" (32-33). Her aggressive, adept language and her ability to take quick decisions help her secure another bride for Frank.

Contributing to a complicated act of deception, Juliza's violent manipulation of denotative language becomes a source of irony.[7] Granted her talent for terse expressions, Juliza devises a ploy to restore her reputation. As she explains to her mother, "If—I go over there to stay while he's gone, he won't think, an' nobody else will think, I want him" (33). Simulating impenetrability and heroic indifference to public scrutiny, Juliza engages in a painful performance, worthy of her theatrical talent. Repressing her feelings, she pretends

to be motivated by a concern for others, thus winning Frank's gratitude: "Oh, Juliza! you've been the best friend to me I ever had in my life, comin' over here. I'll never forget it" (35). Juliza performs a false script in front of her mother, her friend, and her community, simultaneously affecting concern for public opinion.

In the last pseudo-celebratory scene, comedy masks violence. Juliza's mother dares her to give a recitation at Frank's wedding to the other woman, making a public display of herself, and thereby acting out her indifference. Her appearance is appropriately staged by her mother, who buys her "a garnet breastpin," with the ambiguous remark, "You might just as well have things" (36). Public display is crucial for the constricting stage of a close community, in which the limits of intimacy are renegotiated. Juliza's breach of rituals is threatened to be punished by public opprobrium and violent laughter.

Juliza's recitation at the wedding is a manifestation of her power of self-control. Since everyone present is aware of the play of tension, her artistic recitation becomes both a form of self-expression and defiance of public opinion:

She began to speak, and she spoke as she had never done before. Her gestures were full of fire; every line of her form and face seemed to conform to the exigencies of the situation; her voice rang out with a truth that was deeper than her own personality.

(36)

In this comedic celebration, the presence of the crowd has the power to confirm Juliza's perception of her own identity as a speaking voice. Furthermore, her spectacle makes her a successful director, able to control others. While reciting her piece, Juliza also engages in an affirmation of the self in her successful disguise of her feelings. Frank's final response translates as recognition of her power, where his wedding becomes one of her scripts. Acknowledging that he feels "as if it's all due to" Juliza, he ends by restating the existence of the threat of the secret, and the bondage of a possible disclosure that cannot be erased: "I want you to forgive me for—that night. I haven't told a soul, not even Lily, an' I never shall. I know you just meant to be kind, that was all" (36). His reminder has a paradoxical effect in that it reinforces the promise, in its suspension, since it can always be broken through the suggested interdiction.

This final scene is a complicated performance in which Juliza plays her role as if she were someone else, in complete alienation. The masquerade of the self guarantees her temporary success on the public stage. Mary R. Reichardt interprets the last scene as "a strong statement about artistic sublimation." Discussing Juliza's form of art, Reichardt comments on the symbolic meaning of the recitation: "[H]er art is of necessity compensatory, as well as being a means of channeling her feelings into acceptable forms. Juliza's art consists of repeating what others have written, just as her life is bound by what others decide. She does resist, however, and does so successfully, within the limits of her options" (*A Web of Relationships* 82). In her more recent book, *Mary Wilkins Freeman*, Reichardt resumes her work on **"Juliza."** Here, she elaborates on her previous interpretation of Juliza's recitations. Reichardt demonstrates that, in addition to simply rendering a preexisting text, Juliza also mimics her mother in the process, since "she has evolved her skill by copying her mother's voice and gestures" and thus she ends by "fully aping Mrs. Peck" (30).

Juliza simultaneously performs a text, imitates her mother, and deceives Frank and her community about her feelings. Juliza manages to steal the show, turning people's attention from the wedding itself: "Everybody listened. The bridal couple were forgotten." While talking to Frank, Juliza is still performing, as the narrator's precise stage directions clearly indicate: "She had the same proud lift to her head, that she had when reciting" (36). Instead of reducing her performance to mere repetition of texts, I would argue that through recitation, Juliza experiments with various voices. Representing herself as someone else, Juliza becomes a comedian, playing the wise fool at the same time as she stages the mimicry of feminine stereotypes, and trying to invent alternative images for the self. In the limelight of an invisible stage, Juliza performs in front of her community, improvising as she goes along, and striving to manipulate her image. Her training in public speaking provided her with a form of survival. Ultimately, notwithstanding her audience, Juliza performs her recitation for herself.

In addition to the script and the difficult art of speaking, costumes and props are elements necessary in directing the spectacle of the self whereby women behave as actors on a stage, controlled by public surveillance as a structural mechanism of patriarchy and reinforced by the self-inflicted control of women's gossip. In this respect, **"One Good Time"** (1900) is a paradigmatic example of an exacerbated interest in costume and props as a means of liberation of the self and open revolt against public opinion. One of Freeman's less-known stories, it deserves attention given the multiple levels with which it operates, molded together by humor. Upon Richard Stone's death, Narcissa and her mother, Jane, refuse to dress in mourning as a form of protest. Despite the fact that they expect to receive fifteen hundred dollars in insurance money, they decide to wear their everyday shabby

clothes. Moreover, once they do receive this money, they plan a one-year trip to New York. To the general astonishment of their community, they return from New York only one week later. Although they have spent all the insurance money, Narcissa is satisfied that she had a break from her life of privation and hard work. After years of waiting, she finally accepts William Crane's proposal, a marriage that her father had strongly opposed.

"One Good Time" has much in common with **"Juliza"**: they both share the presence of a heroine articulated as a speaking subject, able to express herself and moreover engage in direct revolt against norms. Structurally another twisted story of courtship centered on an unpredictably stated proposal, **"One Good Time"** is also a poignant account of escape, staged as a temporary release from the constraints of community and of a tyrannical home in its domestic corollary, and a story of mourning turned into celebration.

Unlike Juliza, however, who is characterized by restraint and the capacity to plan out her actions, Narcissa, the protagonist of **"One Good Time"** lacks the ability to draw up her plans convincingly, and that is why her escape is excessive. The unexpected turn of events creates a fantasy of consumerism common to many of Freeman's female characters. Planning an escape of excessive proportions, Narcissa combines her craving for money with a denouncement of its worthlessness. The courtship structure serves here as a means to measure the distance between William Crane's expectations and his complete lack of knowledge about his long-awaited lover.

The story's inception is defined in terms of control, where gossip is a form of surveillance within the community, dictating the "common-sense" of external behavior. Narcissa Stone and her mother, Jane, show their contempt for public opinion by refusing to dress up in mourning for the death of Richard Stone, a tyrannical husband and father. Granted, in the words of a gossip, "They ain't got a thing that's fit to wear" (82), public opprobrium decides that "They'd ought to be ashamed of themselves" (83). While the same raconteur agrees that the women's behavior "ain't showing proper respect to the poor man" (83), Narcissa and Jane defy their community by refusing to express their feelings in public. From the outset, the two women contradict everyone's expectations in terms of physical appearance, where clothes as a form of display become an overdetermined signifier. Wearing their shabby clothes at the funeral, they engage in an active process of revolt, carefully planned out by the daughter. The narrator describes the general reaction: "In truth, all the village was scandalized at the strange attire of the widow and daughter of Richard Stone, at his funeral, except William Crane" (84). Narcissa's lover is the only one not taken by external appearance, completely ignorant of the show she is planning: "[H]e could not see her robes at all in such a dazzlement of vision" (84). It is in fact his acceptance all through Narcissa's detailed adventure that makes the escape more excessive, verging on the absurd.

The heroine's carefully mapped-out strategy of escape could be taken as a feminist statement of individualism, except that her obsession with luxurious clothes renders her a gullible victim of consumerism, thereby making her escape questionable. Narcissa explains the complicated reasons of her yearning for escape in an elaborate discourse, the obvious result of extensive rehearsal. After the funeral, the Stones' house still bears the traces of a tyrannical father, in a gloomy atmosphere that even the thought of an impending insurance payment cannot enlighten. Narcissa explains her decision to spend the insurance money in New York as a form of revolt and escape: "I ain't never done anything my whole life that I thought I ought not to do, but now I'm going to. I'm going to if it's wicked. I've made up my mind. I ain't never had one good time in my whole life, and now I'm going to even if I have to suffer for it afterward" (88). Undeterred by the consequences of her decision, Narcissa withstands the pressure of common-sense and thus formulates an explicit statement of internalized oppression.

Narcissa's denunciation of her life in the house of a tyrannical father gives meaning to her gesture of escape, despite the absurdity of its means. She sees the pressure of domestic labor as a form of alienation, deadening in its confinement:

> I ain't never had anything like other women. I've never had any clothes nor gone anywhere. I've just stayed at home here and drudged.

After an inventory of her daily routine of work, she exposes the limitations of her experience:

> I've just drudged, drudged, ever since I can remember. I don't know anything about the world nor life. I don't know anything but my old tracks.
>
> (88)

Breaking the rules about expressing affection, Narcissa gets to explain her feelings to Richard without falling into a conventional pattern of sentimentalism. Freeman constructs here an unglamorous portrait of marriage, in which romantic passion is replaced by the stark realism of domestic work, and love is stripped of its idealism. Narcissa's response to her lover could be read as a manifesto against the cult of domesticity: "If . . . I had to settle down in your house, as I have done in father's, and see the years stretching ahead

like a long road without any turn, and nothing but the same old dog trot of washing and ironing and scrubbing and cooking and sewing and washing dishes till I drop into my grave, I should hate you, William Crane" (90). In the articulation of her feminist discourse, Narcissa develops one of the most explicit statements of the New Woman. Claiming her right to escape, she admits, "I've got to have a break; I've got to have one good time. I—like you, and—I like father; but love ain't enough sometimes when it ties anybody" (90). At last, Narcissa unleashes her fantasies about her pressing need for change, the more effective if improbable.

In spite of Narcissa's liberating discourse of escape from the domestic world, her fantasy of consumerism changes the focus of the story. Gregg Camfield has defined humor as a combination of "extravagant fantasy, caricature, exaggeration, and absurd implausibilities" (137). In terms of his definition, Freeman's story departs from realism, embracing the improbable realm of fantasy, turning into a consumer's fairy-tale. The incongruence between the clarity of Narcissa's political discourse, her well-planned escape, and its outcome, is a source of scathing irony. Intending to stay in New York for a whole year in order to spend all the insurance money of fifteen hundred dollars, Narcissa and her mother prepare themselves for a long journey, letting the community enjoy the spectacle of their unexpected trip. Ultimately, humor derives from the clash between Narcissa's logical language, which makes her a candidate for feminist activism in Freeman's work, and the absurdity of her form of revolt, given her fixation on consumerism.

Narcissa has a clothes fetish. To her, luxurious clothes become signifiers of power and independence in the constricting spectacle of the self within an inquisitive community. Her gratuitous and indecent craving for ornaments equates hollow glamour with a form of revolt against the utilitarianism and functionalism of everyday life: "I'm going to buy us some jewelry, too; I ain't never had a good breastpin even; and as for mother, father never even bought her a ring when they were married." The inventory of items Narcissa confesses to have been craving—"I've got a list of things written down on paper"—reflects a long deliberation, in which her lifelong deprivation projected an equally exaggerated release (91). In this respect, Narcissa's strategy of revolt is unique in its absurd proportions.[8]

Many fantasies of courtship, escape, and revolt in Freeman's stories take the form of consumerism. Monika M. Elbert reveals the apparently paradoxical fact that, although most of Freeman's characters are "unglamorous country women" (254), they are all influenced by consumerism, to the extent that "the domestic prop of fashionable dress item becomes the icon for both the Freeman heroine and the *Harper's Bazar* peruser of ads" (253). Elbert analyzes the types of advertisement found in the periodicals where Freeman published her work most often, noticing that the poverty in most of Freeman's stories contrasts with the lavish descriptions of the most recent trends of fashion described in the same pages of the magazine. Elbert's concept of a "love affair with a commodity" (254) could be identified in a paroxysmal form in **"One Good Time,"** with the difference that the passion for objects resulting from deprivation is here carried to an extreme. The humor in Narcissa's excess is the result of the peculiar juxtaposition of poverty and luxury. Although Narcissa is not directly influenced by advertising, she explains the various sources of her craving for objects which are completely unnecessary.

The two women's momentous departure to New York is witnessed by a community avid for entertainment, amazed by their unheard of extravagance. While "all the windows were set with furtively peering faces," most members of the community are denied direct access to Narcissa's story, with the exception of her lover. After general anticipation and rumors, prepared for an absence of at least a year, the community is shocked when the two women return six days later. William Crane listens with consternation to Narcissa's account of her adventures in New York. Freeman's opulescent description of the journey lavishes Narcissa and Jane in absurd attire, as impressive and expensive as it is unnecessary. The gratuitous aspect of Narcissa's purchases is rendered through the inventory that contradicts their low social origin. Wrapped in silk and fur, the two women buy themselves gold watches and diamonds, go to the theater and the opera. Narcissa's story sounds like an excessive fantasy, as exaggerated as the economic scarcity that triggers it.

Their ludicrous situation is enhanced by the two women's lack of knowledge about the value of things, so that they manage to spend in six days the amount of money they had estimated to suffice for a whole year. Moreover, they are ignorant of the moment when they run out of money, incurring further debts. In a succinct analysis of **"One Good Time,"** Perry Westbrook argues that the account of their mishaps weakens the general message: "[T]he story itself is seriously blemished by Miss Wilkins' descent into slapstick as she describes the adventures of the two countrywomen in the big city" (146). The painful humor of their adventures seems, I suggest, to reveal more convincingly the confinement of their world, making the escape more effective. The gap between the two women's real status and their exorbitant posing and spending is made clear in the scene of their break-down when they discover that they have spent all the money. In an indecent public scene, Narcissa remembers, "Folks came crowding around." The two women turn into fools, sharing their predicament:

> Mother, she broke right down an' cried, an' said it was all we had in the world besides the farm, an' it was poor father's insurance money, an' we couldn't get home, an' we'd have to go to prison.
>
> (100)

Narcissa's dream of a rich life, as a "quest of the consumer-woman," to use Elbert's phrase (263), takes the form of a satisfying break with norms and an excessive release from everyday routine. The inventory of Narcissa's trespassing has carnivalesque features, resplendent in abundance and deceiving glamour. Cyclical-end-of-the-season release, Narcissa's escape from her dull life involves both exorbitant shopping and possible romance. She prides herself on the scale of her adventure:

> I've been wasteful an' extravagant an'—There was a gentleman beautifully dressed who sat at our table, an' he talked real pleasant about weather, an'—I got to thinking about him a little.
>
> (101)

The proportions of her flashy spending create a seasonal dream, according to which deprivation is counterpoised in the absurdity of a temporary release. Laughter itself in this context becomes a form of liberation, allowing Freeman to express a woman's anger at the restraints of her limited experiences. Narcissa's denunciation of women's hardships and her demystification of domesticity is counterbalanced by her gratuitous and ludicrous form of release, whereby humor offsets anger and pain.

The final scene between Narcissa and her lover falls back into the convention of ludicrous courtship, when the heroine rehearses her proposal, recounting with delight, "I've been and wasted fifteen hundred dollars; I've let my thoughts wonder from you . . . I've had one good time, an'—I ain't sorry." She dares him to make his decision, "You—can just do what you think best, William, an'—I won't blame you" (101). Breaking with convention, Narcissa manipulates language, boasting her new experience. William Crane's response reaffirms the boundaries of the old order, making her choose between her domestic role and her recent glimpse of liberty: "Do you think you can be contented to—stay on my side of the wall now, Narcissa?" (101). An initiator of action, like most comedic figures in women's humorous work, Narcissa defies the norms of her New England code of restraint through her escape. However, in a truly comedic pose, she reinforces the existence of an imaginary cage of convention at the very moment she breaks it, stating, "I wouldn't go out again if the bars were down" (101).

The double message of **"One Good Time"** is power-ful in its incongruity. A rebellious figure throughout the story, Narcissa returns to William Crane. She is willing to marry him while at the same time affirming her loss of independence. Leah Blatt Glasser has read the conclusion of **"One Good Time"** as a case of "un-decidability." To her, the appeal of Freeman's story stands in its doubleness: "Freeman manages to express both the voice that longs for sheer self-indulgent and excessive pleasure and the voice that accepts the ex-pectations of conventional womanly submission and self-denial" (80-81). Humor allows for these appar-ently incongruous messages to abide in the same space without destroying the unity and the credibility of the story.

The manipulation of humor in **"Juliza"** and **"One Good Time"** provides a complex language for ex-pressing the contradictions in women's lives. Although both heroines are powerful, they use their extraordi-nary linguistic endowment to fight false wars. While Juliza exhausts her artistic energy in disguising a will-ful mistake in the courtship game, Narcissa projects her frustrations, both sexual and economic, in an over-indulgent shopping spree, thus fulfilling a consumer's dream of escape. As Shirley Marchalonis has observed, in Freeman's stories, "The absurdities are complicated by the fact that it takes courage for the protagonist to assume and maintain an incongruous position" (232). It could be stated that Juliza and Narcissa are heroic actors in scripts of courtship to be sanctioned by an inquisitive community.[9] Both act as comedians, at-tempting to manipulate their public image and estab-lish some control on the formation of their identity. The language of humor allows them to temporarily evade the prescribed codes of behavior and experi-ment with alternative forms of revolt.

The two stories appear to be written in the same vein as **"The Revolt of 'Mother.'"** Analyzing this story, Perry D. Westbrook posits a dichotomy in its mes-sages: "The greatest disservice done to this story was President Theodore Roosevelt's comment in a speech that American women would do well to emulate the independence of Sarah Penn. From then on, the story was removed from the category of comic fantasy where it belongs and placed before the public as a se-rious tract on women's rights, which it surely is not" (65-66). Westbrook tends to suggest here an exclusive distinction between serious and humorous fiction. In her own efforts to distance herself from the story which she was "lamentably best known for" (134), Freeman resists the process of assessing her work only in terms of revolt. In the light of this dichotomy, **"Juliza"** and **"One Good Time"** are intriguing in their combination of a feminist statement on women's rights and an imaginary, often improbable, flight into humorous

resolution. Finally, Freeman's work that endures best in time includes stories that combine feminist revolt with humorous fantasy, inviting readers to pendulate between laughter of joy and pain.

The heroines in Freeman's stories attempt to reinvent courtship in order to empower themselves. Juliza and Narcissa are both inclined to introspection. In an un-published story, Freeman's heroine Jane Lennox ex-presses the result of her self-analysis, "Sometimes I think I am a monster and the worst of it is, I certainly take pleasure in it" (qtd. in Glasser 55). Reading this statement of self-celebration, Glasser lauds Freeman's "vision of spinsterhood as both exhilarating and terri-fying" (55). By critiquing conventional courtship sce-narios, Freeman liberates women from a compulsory obsession with marriage. Like Louisa, her heroines work diligently at breaking the advice in manuals of behavior, each learning to accept herself in her own terms, as "a veritable guest to her own self" (38).

Notes

1. The total absence of letters from Freeman to Mary Wales makes it hard to decide whether theirs was a Boston marriage or the type of relationship that Carroll Smith-Rosenberg reveals in her essay "The Female World of Love and Ritual." In his intro-duction to the carefully edited volume of Free-man's letters, *The Infant Sphinx*, Brent L. Ken-drick explains, "[N]o letters survive to Mary Elizabeth Wales, her earliest Randolph friend and her constant companion and confidante between 1883 and 1902 . . . However, when Wales died on August 4, 1916, she bequeathed to Charles M. Freeman all of her books and manuscripts. The fate of that collection, which might have included letters, is unknown" (17)

2. There are many similarities between "A New En-gland Nun" and "Juliza." Involved in parallel courtship scenarios, Louisa and Juliza both find out about the existence of another woman. In a true system of relationship with other women, they choose to help them. Instead of feeling jilted, Lou-isa steps back. Similarly, Juliza offers to facilitate the courtship between Frank and Lily Emmons.

3. Charles Miner Thompson concludes his essay with a general statement, revealing the basic contradic-tion in Freeman's work. For him, Freeman is "an idealist masquerading in the soiled and ragged cloak of realism" (675). Thompson notices that some of the most memorable of Freeman's char-acters are "nonconformists to their backbones. They are fanatics or martyrs according to the point of view" (671). The characters' spiritual dimen-sion develops a conflict of conscience that appears to go beyond realism, suggesting an analogy with Hawthorne's work.

4. Mary R. Reichardt briefly analyzes the story "Juliza" in *A Web of Relationships*. In her more recent book, *Mary Wilkins Freeman* (1997), Reichardt offers an extensive, thorough interpretation of this story in an attempt to draw attention to neglected work in Freeman's corpus of texts (26-31). Reichardt makes clear that although less known, "Juliza" is "highly characteristic" of Freeman's style (21).

5. Freeman's own childhood could be the model for Juliza's education. Because two of her brothers had died in their infancy, Mary became the center of her parents' attention. Leah Blatt Glasser discusses the "particularly protective and almost fearful approach to her upbringing," whereby "Mary was frequently made aware of her fragility rather than her strength" (*In a Closet Hidden* 6).

6. I am using here Alicia Suskin Ostriker's insightful development of the concept "stealing the language."

7. Monika M. Elbert identifies the theme of "deception as the basis of narrative" (261), indicating that many of Freeman's successful stories are based on a common conflict in which women are involved in a complex process of deception as a means of masquerade and finally empowerment.

8. Freeman often refers to the deprivations that drove her to writing. As late as 1921, in "My Maiden Effort," she remembers the excitement about the things she bought with some of her first earned money for a story published in *Harper's Magazine*: "I gave away a tenth . . . but I was wearing a shabby black. I bought at once a fine gown, trimmed with black fur, and a fur-trimmed silk cloak, and sailed down Main Street in a certain village, disgracefully more elated over my appearance than possible literary success" (138).

9. Discussing the concept of heroes in relation to Freeman's characters, Jay Martin contends, "Lacking a heroic society, Mary Wilkins' heroes are debased; noble in being, they are foolish in actions" (151).

Works Cited

Camfield, Gregg. *Necessary Madness: The Humor of Domesticity in Nineteenth-Century American Literature.* New York: Oxford UP, 1997.

Cutter, Martha J. "Beyond Stereotypes: Mary Wilkins Freeman's Radical Critique of Nineteenth-Century Cults of Femininity." *Women's Studies* 21 (1992): 383-95.

———. "Frontiers of Language: Engendering Discourse in 'The Revolt of "Mother."'" *American Literature* 63 (1991): 279-91.

Elbert, Monika M. "Mary Wilkins Freeman's Devious Women, *Harper's Bazar,* and the Rhetoric of Advertising." *Essays in Literature* 20 (1993): 251-72.

Freeman, Mary E. Wilkins. "An Autobiography." Reichardt. *Mary Wilkins Freeman: A Study of the Short Fiction.* 134-36.

———. *Best Stories of Mary Wilkins Freeman.* Ed. Henry Wysham Lanier. New York: Harper, 1927.

———. "The Girl Who Wants to Write: Things to Do and to Avoid." Reichardt. *Mary Wilkins Freeman: A Study of the Short Fiction.* 128-33.

———. *The Infant Sphinx: Collected Letters of Mary E. Wilkins Freeman.* Ed. Brent L. Kendrick. Metuchen: Scarecrow, 1985.

———. "My Maiden Effort." Reichardt. *Mary Wilkins Freeman: A Study of the Short Fiction.* 137-38.

———. *A Mary Wilkins Freeman Reader.* Ed. Mary R. Reichardt. Lincoln: U of Nebraska P, 1997.

———. *The Uncollected Stories of Mary Wilkins Freeman.* Ed. Mary R. Reichardt. Jackson: UP of Mississippi, 1992.

Glasser, Leah Blatt. *In a Closet Hidden: The Life and Work of Mary E. Wilkins Freeman.* Amherst: U of Massachusetts P, 1996.

———. "*Legacy* Profile: Mary E. Wilkins Freeman." *Legacy* 4 (1987): 37-45.

Marchalonis, Shirley. "The Sharp-Edged Humor of Mary Wilkins Freeman: *The Jamesons*—and Other Stories." *Critical Essays on Mary Wilkins Freeman.* Ed. Shirley Marchalonis. Boston: Hall, 1991. 222-34.

Martin, Jay. *Harvests of Change: American Literature 1865-1914.* Englewood Cliffs: Prentice, 1967.

Pattee, Fred Lewis. *The Development of the American Short Story: An Historical Survey.* New York: Harper, 1923.

Reichardt, Mary R. *Mary Wilkins Freeman: A Study of the Short Fiction.* London: Twayne, 1997.

———. *A Web of Relationships: Women in the Short Fiction of Mary Wilkins Freeman.* Jackson: UP of Mississippi, 1992.

Smith-Rosenberg, Carroll. *Disorderly Conduct: Visions of Gender in Victorian America.* New York: Oxford UP, 1985.

Thompson, Charles Miner. "Miss Wilkins: An Idealist in Masquerade." *Atlantic Monthly* 82 (1899): 665-75.

Welter, Barbara. "The Cult of True Womanhood." *American Quarterly* 8 (1966): 151-74.

Westbrook, Perry D. *Acres of Flint: Writers of Rural New England 1870-1900.* Washington, D.C.: Scarecrow, 1951.

———. *Mary Wilkins Freeman.* New York: Twayne, 1967.

Monika M. Elbert (essay date 2002)

SOURCE: Elbert, Monika M. "The Displacement of Desire: Consumerism and Fetishism in Mary Wilkins Freeman's Fiction." *Legacy* 19, no. 2 (2002): 192-215.

[*In the following essay, Elbert explores the sexualization of the material world in several of Freeman's stories, comparing this aspect of her fiction with themes of capitalism and commodification in Frank Norris's novel* McTeague.]

> It is not improbable that every fetishist is a lost poet.
>
> Wilhelm Stekel

In the face of an impending marriage with a man who has absented himself for many years, Louisa in Mary Wilkins Freeman's **"A New England Nun"** (1887) prefers her domestic collectibles—the little "female appurtenances" which have made her solitary life bearable, if not fulfilling. Similarly, the narcissistic Narcissa in **"One Good Time"** (1897) decides to postpone her marriage so she can indulge in one good shopping spree in New York, and Charlotte in **"A Tragedy from the Trivial"** (1900) literally dies from tubercular consumption in a repressive marriage to a greedy husband after having lived a life of economic consumption prior to marriage. What these women share in common is a sense of frustration, whether that be sexual or creative, which leads to an excess of senseless and compulsive behavior reflected in frenzied and repeated activities, such as spending money, sewing incessantly, or collecting useless knick-knacks.

These women fetishize in an effort to compensate for their thwarted creativity or stunted sexuality; from an inability to acknowledge their anger, arising from repressed sexual desires; or to express this rage to the men who marry or propose marriage to them.[1] The Freeman protagonists project their displaced desires or aborted dreams onto household objects and/or the newest fashions, and these fetishes then begin to assume more prominence than the men in their lives. But these objects also begin, most insidiously, to eradicate the identities of the women themselves—so that in the end, the women face martyrdom, death, or domestic imprisonment as a grim alternative to the annihilating frenzy of shopping or collecting "female appurtenances." In each case, in trying to resist objectification as wife or ownership by males, the women, feeling powerless and inadequate, identify with and fixate on material possessions with which the men have come

to identify them; ironically, they turn themselves unwittingly into objects and choose a death-in-life situation or death itself.

Freeman, far from being an innocuous local colorist who writes of women's pastoral landscapes,[2] probes deeply into the economic realities of her time and their means of stymying women's development.[3] She then critiques women's spending habits, which were draining the source of women's creativity, sexuality, and spirituality. Charlotte Perkins Gilman was also warning about the deleterious effect of consumerism on women, especially when women's identities through relationships with men became confused with marketplace transactions: women's "false economic position" essentially "sexualizes" their "industrial relation" and "commercializes" their "sex-relation" (121). Though Gilman does not specifically discuss the rage and futility of such consuming women, she describes in *Women and Economics* (1898) the "spending" process whereby women's energies are frittered away and their creativity or vitality diminished:

> [T]he consuming female, debarred from any free production . . . and her consumption limited mainly to those things which minister to physical pleasure, creates a market for sensuous decoration and personal ornament, for all that is luxurious and enervating, and for a false and capricious variety in such supplies, which operates as a most deadly check to true industry and true art.
>
> (120-21)

Woman becomes the "priestess of the temple of consumption . . . the limitless demander of things to use up" and lives in a perverse "sexuo-economic" relationship with man (120). Gilman critiques the "over-sexed woman" who, "in her unintelligent and ceaseless demands, hinders and perverts the economic development of the world" (121).

Noteworthy in the context of the psychology of Freeman's consuming women is this "sexualization" of the material world. It is a vicious cycle as women are taught, on a subliminal level, to desire the material goods which the marketplace has deemed necessities and not just luxuries. Gilman attacks the "useless production" wrought by "the creation and careful maintenance of this false market" (121). Even if many of Freeman's women are poor, or living on the edge of poverty, they participate in the fantasies and desires of the middle class. As Thorstein Veblen observed, even the classes below the leisure class tried to emulate the upper class by participating in the display of their worldly goods. Veblen asserts that this idea of "conspicuous consumption" is more prevalent in the urban, middle classes than in the rural, agrarian population (87-89), but certainly, this is not true of Freeman's rural women, who take great delight in displaying their possessions and spend much energy contemplating what they have. This "false market," as Gilman expresses it, infiltrates and distorts relationships between and among various class populations.

Certainly, Freeman is never so simplistic or predictable as to portray a single type of consuming women; there is often a higher-level productive woman who stands in superior contrast to the insatiable woman consumer, but both types are caught up in a cycle which finally destroys or demoralizes them. Thus, in **"The Cloak Also"** (1917), Freeman pits the wise wife who financially supports her naive husband in a failed dry-goods business against the harpy women who descend upon his store, usurping his good nature and his wares, by constantly charging and never paying for the clothes they purchase. The husband/merchant is deceived by the advice of a traveling salesman to allow women with their voracious appetites to purchase on credit: "He said a woman with cash would squeeze a dollar until the eagle squealed, but a woman with a charge account never knew where she was. She'd go right ahead and buy everything in sight and never know she'd bought anything" (254). Shopping, in this case, like collecting or amassing curios in other Freeman stories, is a frenetic, intoxicating, and benumbing activity. Though there is no spend-thrift wife to cause her husband's demise, there is an entire town of mindless women who cause the husband's eventual nervous prostration and suicide, but not before he delivers a biblical parable, much in the vein of Twain's "The Man that Corrupted Hadleyburg," about the "meanness" and materialism of the appropriately named town of Racebridge. Freeman very adeptly shows that the victim of this feminine longing and consumerism is not just the frivolous spendthrift women but the men who are the middle-men of capitalistic desire (like the husband Joel) as well as the well-intentioned women who do work honestly for a day's wages and know the value of a day's labor (like the wife Susan). Buying on "credit," or not paying for what one owns, appears as the evil outgrowth of consumer desire.

The promise of some intangible fulfillment or illusory transcendence through possession of a purchasable object prevents many of Freeman's women, trapped in the capitalistic dream of accumulation, from ever realizing themselves in any relationship—with other women, with men, with children, nor certainly with themselves. Indeed, their emptiness is shown in their fixation upon material goods; their desires become frenzied, inordinate, and insatiable. As consumers, these women are motivated by an overwhelming need to fulfill themselves—not in relationship to women, as early feminist critics such as Josephine Donovan and Carroll Smith-Rosenberg have asserted, but rather

through a burning desire to purchase, possess, or collect products with which the marketplace tantalizes them and which replace the urge to consummate relationships with others. Though I focus on Freeman stories which deal with heterosexual displacement, one can also examine other stories in which women deny sisterly bonds, lesbian longings, maternal urges, and creative inclinations by obsessing about their worldly goods or by fetishizing one sole object. One is struck by the surreal sense of compulsive repetition in many of these stories; whether the protagonist is on the producing or consuming end, she is caught in the vicious cycle of commodity culture. Louisa in **"A New England Nun"** is involved in repetitive housework and saving; Narcissa in **"One Good Time"** participates in repetitive spending; and Charlotte in **"A Tragedy from the Trivial"** uses her time first spending and then producing and saving repetitively.

Whether or not characters "buy into" the frenzied consumer activity of producing or consuming, they are alienated from their true feelings. Women seem to be rivals or competitors in the so-called sisterhood stories (e.g., **"Sister Liddy"** and **"A Gala Dress"**), as the main covetous character often vies for possession of something superior to what the neighbor owns in order to charm a potential suitor or to impress other townswomen. When there is an attempt at sisterly bonding or homoerotic desire, one is left with a fragmentary impression or a fleeting image of a dress, a ribbon, or a bauble as a sad testament of these objects' inability to actually sustain emotional connection or for the onlookers' lack of imagination to invest the objects with meaning. Thus, even for Freeman's women characters who do not give in to the possibilities of the fetish, even in the stories of self-renunciation and martyrdom, the women must "pay." Action revolves around an object which fails to unite but whose presence makes the absent or missing lover, mother, or child more poignant. In **"A Taste of Honey"** (1887), for example, the main character, practical Inez, initially experiments with her burgeoning sexuality by uncharacteristically giving in to the temptation of buying an unnecessary frill, "a bright red ribbon bow to wear at her throat" (39). Though the ornament wins over a suitor, she extends her courtship period so she can pay off her mother's mortgage; the wait is too long for her suitor, who deserts her for another woman. In the end, she consoles herself and her mother with an image that had tantalized them during their years of saving: they finally indulge themselves with the warm honey biscuits they had been denying themselves, a rather sad substitute for the possibilities of the red ribbon necklace. Moreover, her final attempt to appease her mother, indeed to bond with her mother, is to focus on a potential shopping spree and the possibility of another fetish: "To-morrow . . . we'll drive to Bolton, and get you a new dress, mother" (52). Her consuming desires have been displaced to the imaginary needs of her mother. Finally, in **"A Moral Exigency"** (1887), the main character, Eunice, steals the local belle's boyfriend, but only momentarily, as her world becomes topsy-turvy and disheveled. The disorder of her room becomes a mirror of her guilty conscience. In a surreal way, the many objects and collectibles which she loved in their familiarity now haunt her: with a look of "horror" on her face, Eunice "stared . . . at all the familiar objects in the room, but the most common and insignificant of them had a strange and awful look to her" (34). In a world where objects give meaning, this grotesque array of things disorients her and finally causes her to forsake her one chance at love, and she displaces her love onto her young rival, Ada Harris. Indeed, it is the potential maternal bond which finally convinces Eunice that she must relinquish her love of the man for her love of Ada, for Eunice recalls that at school recess, Ada "had played she was her little girl, and held her in her lap, and that golden head had nestled on her bosom" (33). This maternal feeling is imbued with eroticism in the last scene, in which Eunice relinquishes the only possibility she would have had for marriage. Focusing on the fetishized baby of her imagination, Eunice "drew the golden head on her bosom, just as she had on that school-day" (35). Her last words say all as she is desperately trying to find something, someone to connect with: "Love me all you can, Ada . . . I want—something" (35). This longing "for something" intangible characterizes most of Freeman's women.

Many times, the contending impulses of maternal desire, heterosexual love, homosocial bonding, or creative/artistic instincts converge in the fetishized object. This convergence becomes most clear in a story such as Freeman's **"The Blue Butterfly"** (1913), in which Marcia Keyes, a dressmaker, is immediately described as leading "a double life"—one of austerity (like one of many of Freeman's New England nuns, she "lived a life as austere as a nun's, eating meat seldom") and one of passionate creativity ("a life which would if known, have made her a stranger beyond ken to those who thought they knew her best" [180]). Marcia puts her "whole heart" into her work, and the narrator insists that she "would have been an artist under different environments" had she possessed "canvas and paints" rather than "needles and thread" (180). Marcia initially cares "very little for herself," but her natural desire is stimulated when she is commissioned to sew a "coming-out" gown for the local beauty, Alice Streeter (181); in many ways, this is the story of Alice's as well as Marcia's "coming-out." Like a feminized version of Pygmalion, she invests

her Galatea with all those qualities that a lover would. She fantasizes about dressing this perfect body: "She had never really made one gown for a woman with a perfectly good figure who was well corseted" (184). Alice, a "superb young thing" (184), elicits a lover's response from Marcia: "She had caught a look in those blue eyes of the dressmaker which would have befitted a lover" (185). The making of the gown becomes like the writing of a "great poem" or composition of a "sonata" (188); the final product is seen as "a poem, a symphony of white lace, white chiffon, silver, gold, and touches of blue" (188). The erotic element infused with the creative process is undeniable. Finally, the women are bonded together by the image of "a great blue butterfly" which Marcia generously purchases and affixes to a lovely silvery hairband for Alice. Initially, the fetishized blue butterfly becomes a sign of maternal connection; it causes the dressmaker to see her handiwork as her child, as well it may be: "The girl with the blue butterfly atilt in her fair hair . . . was to her more than any daughter could ever have been" (193). But the butterfly makes Marcia more poignantly aware of the absence of her maternity: "This woman without the usual life of a woman, who had never been wedded, nor borne children, knew in one instant all the joy and sorrow she had missed" (193). In addition to eliciting maternal pride from Marcia, the fetishized ornament/girl also evokes an erotic joy the dressmaker has never felt. She lives vicariously through the girl's pleasures on the night of the ball: "She watched every moment of the lovely young thing. . . . Every dance of the girl whom she had adorned she danced, every smile of joy she smiled" (194). Marcia is strategically positioned as voyeur outside the window of Alice's house, as Alice had suggested to Marcia, her social inferior, for the purpose of gazing at her. Indeed, Marcia's gaze turns from that of proud mother to lover; the gaze is that of a male voyeur or that of the lesbian fetishist (see Grosz 113). Moreover, by admiring and identifying with Alice's beau, she experiences heterosexual and lesbian longing at the same moment. To Marcia, the young man appears as "handsome as a prince," but in the next moment, she experiences the conquest of the love object, the woman, through her vicarious association with the male suitor. The entire scene hovers about the ethereal butterfly that she has created: "A queer vicarious love for him leapt into her heart as she saw the face over which the blue butterfly fluttered, upturned to his in the dance" (195). Thus, the fetish allows her to entertain maternal possibilities, heterosexual longing from the male and female points of view, and lesbian desires. Marcia narcissistically, in the vein of the fetishist, feels that her art has caused the consummation of the young couple's love and thus enjoys the imaginative possibilities of eros: "They are in love, and they will be married, and it is because of my dress" (195). Both Marcia and Alice become obsessed with the miniature butterfly in the last scene: Alice feels that her boyfriend only notices the intensity of her blue eyes for the first time because of Marcia's butterfly ornament. Marcia is terrified when she imagines the actual erotic potential between the couple; watching them embrace, Marcia "shuddered lest the blue butterfly be crushed" (195). Thus, though the fetishized butterfly has sexual connotations, Marcia has a horrible fear of allowing the butterfly free flight, and finally, the butterfly becomes a sign of her continual repression.

In the sentimental Freeman stories revolving around children, such as **"A Poetess"** (1891) or **"The Reign of the Doll"** (1904), there is a false sense of longing for "missing" or "absent" or non-existent children in a sentimental and mawkish description of childhood bric-a-brac and bibelots.[4] One striking example of women's displaced maternal urges can be found in **"The Reign of the Doll."** Two feuding women, who have fought about the inheritance left by their mother, find themselves reunited by a prank present someone sends them for Christmas, a naked baby doll. They project all their anger and all their lost maternal instincts onto this doll, as they focus their energy in making baby clothes from old scraps of their own clothing, and thereby become reconciled for the first time since the mother's death; one comes full cycle from deceased mother to hollow baby. The baby doll becomes so fetishized that they bicker about who should own it and have a problem giving it back to the child to whom it really was sent. The doll brings them back to their own childhood, and thus "they could not spare her to another child" (331). Both feel guilty and greedy about stealing another child's baby, but they rationalize that the child would simply have destroyed it (nuances of the wild dog in **"A New England Nun"**). Interestingly, there is no fond sentiment for the actual child but an outpouring of love for the fetishized baby doll who "smiles with inscrutable inanity" (332), a grotesque imitation of a real baby. If the two feuding sisters do finally achieve sisterhood through the collaborative efforts of dressing their new baby doll, it is a regressive, childlike picture of sisterhood, one which does not admit of the possibilities of adult maternity. As in many Freeman stories, there is a real animus or at least ambivalence toward motherhood and babies, and maternity, a creative endeavor, is as thwarted as sexuality. Freeman's is an inversion of the kind of maternal fetishism—or "mother's memorabilia"—"a lock of hair" or "a tooth"—which allows the mother to stay connected to the child (Kelley and Apter 353).

Another variant of maternal displacement takes place in **"For the Love of One's Self"** (1905). Here, the protagonist, Amanda Dearborn, suffers emotionally—and financially—after her mother's death. She gives up the joint boarding-house business she shared with her mother to work in a shoe factory. A generous soul who does not spend much on herself, Amanda is eventually weaned off the kind of charitable giving that her mother taught her. Instead of sending her relatives expensive gifts one Christmas, she splurges and buys herself "a lace collar" to adorn her simple black dress. Her spending is prompted by a sexual attraction to an admirer at work (Frank Ayres) that is beginning to make her forget her mother's absence. Spending, maternal displacement, and sexuality all converge in the image of the Christmas present Frank sends Amanda: an ornate box of "dainty bonbons and fruits glacés" wrapped in "lace paper" (117-18). This experience of possessing a useless bauble is new for Amanda. She does not enjoy sweets, but "there was something about the very uselessness of the thing which gave it a charm to her" (118). In the end, Frank and Amanda are united through maternal longing that is transferred to romantic desire. Initially, when Amanda feels sexualized by Frank, her reactions are maternal; he inspires her dormant "maternal instinct" (111), and she views him with "the feeling that she had sometimes experienced at seeing a beautiful change" (111). The last tableauesque scene has Arabella and Frank both declaring their grief about their mothers' deaths and contemplating a future together as a married couple living in one house. Amanda enters the house and retreats to her room, where "she took the pretty box out of the drawer and sat with it in her lap, thinking about Frank Ayres and her mother, and kept Christmas holy" (124). As is typical of Freeman, consumerism, sanctity, sexuality, and motherhood all merge for the obsessive/alienated protagonist through this fetishistic image which provokes some sensual response, whether it is a gift, a bauble, an article of clothing, a collectible, or a household object.

COMMODITY FETISHISM AND GILDED-AGE DESIRE

The collecting, spending, and greedily acquisitive woman is the prototypical Freeman protagonist, whether the incessant activity substitutes for heterosexual, homosexual, or maternal desires. There are no maternal women, no sexual women, no sisterly women—only women who desire something intangible, projected onto the collectible, article of clothing, or household object.[5] The language of desire was ubiquitous during the Gilded Age and thereafter. As William Leach has shown, the concept of desire haunted Americans from the 1880s onward: "The upsurge in longing would trouble Americans for many decades, especially middle-class Americans, who would struggle to subdue and rationalize it and to understand its meaning and significance" ("Strategists" 102). Among the historical-linguistic developments Leach notes is the definition of consumption as the "satisfaction of desire" by Lester Ward, father of American sociology, and the description of America as the "Land of Desire" in a 1906 advertising editorial by John Wanamaker ("Strategists" 102). Simon Patten, an influential capitalist economist who advocated consumption, felt that consumers' desires would be numbed and diminished if they were allowed to keep spending. In a mad flurry of shopping and spending, they would eventually, according to Patten, burn out their desirous nature: "Quickly satiated with the next incoming commodity, consumers pursue the next good, and then the next. . . . The desire level is kept low, because it is always quickly satisfied. As consumers get more and more . . . they become less desiring" (Leach, *Land of Desire* 238). This type of tranquility is certainly not true of Freeman's protagonists, who thrive on the energies of never having enough; certainly, their incomes would never allow them to be satiated. One of Patten's economic treatises, *Product and Climax* (1909), aptly reflects the Freudian influence upon him, as he shows how sexual desire and the hunger for commodities are intertwined (Leach, *Land of Desire* 241). In terms of the longing evoked by commodities, "excessive consumption of food and objects . . . reflects a search for what has been lost in consumer culture—meaning and value" (Gamman and Makinen 219).

The attempt to invest a physical object with subjective, transcendent meaning is not uncommon to the protagonists of Naturalist writings. The attempts end in failure as the protagonist is cut off from the real source of his or her desire to merge with another person. Finally, it is the disembodied object which has most significance; the person initially connected to the object in the protagonist's mind becomes insignificant. A narcissistic, masturbatory vision of the self in relationship to the object becomes the disturbing end of the Freeman protagonist; indeed, in the end, self and object are indistinguishable. Moreover, mediating relationships through the commodity was an easy way to avoid emotions: "The easy offering of emotions through consumer goods allowed for a growing restraint in human relations" (Bronner, "Reading" 52).

The consumer good as fetish or the locus of displaced desire becomes a hallmark of Naturalist fiction; indeed, the commodity takes on greater stature than the characters themselves. In some ways, this is also true of Realist fiction, as object becomes inseparable from person. Or, as Jay Mechling notes, "The problematic relationship between outward signs and inward reali-

ties was the subject of much public fiction, from the popular novels for youngsters to the realist and naturalist fiction of such authors as Twain, William Dean Howells, Edith Wharton, Henry James, and Frank Norris" (283). Mechling goes on to discuss the addictive behavior common to a materialistic society and suggests that the "symptoms of materialism" as represented in literary texts would later be perceived by social psychiatrists as "symptoms of narcissism" (283). Indeed, the moral fabric of Freeman's universe, a romanticized pristine vision of New England local color landscape, is simply missing. She shares with Naturalist writers the bleak vision of a life without any intrinsic or spiritual meaning. What Leach asserts about our turn-of-the-century culture at large can be applied to the Naturalist school of writers: "[T]his commodity aesthetic expressed the direction of a new commodity culture that challenged at its core the moral heritage of the nineteenth century" ("Strategists" 132).

It is time that Freeman be seen as a sexual writer, as sexual and sexy as any Naturalist writer of her age. The old conception of Freeman as prim and provincial New England regionalist or bastion of Puritan traditions and values must be obliterated if we are to give her the credit due her and place her among the ranks of the most noteworthy Naturalist male writers. As I have suggested above, the fetish becomes the overriding symbol of the Naturalist text, and thus, Freeman's work belongs to the Naturalist school of writing. I am using the term "fetish" loosely here, as a conflation of the Freudian definition and the Marxist definition; the common denominator is the longing for what is missing—whether that be the absent genitalia/phallic mother or the absence of human relationship. Alienation occurs as a result of this deep sense of loss—of forgetfulness of the bonds of humanity which create the object or the connectedness and feelings of belonging attached to childhood. Many recent critics have also noted the connection between the Marxist commodity fetish and the Freudian fetish; both schools of thought, Marxist or psychological, explore the semiotic meaning of the fetishized object as a marker of the individual's alienation and subsequent displacement of feeling.[6]

What is most unusual, from a psychological perspective, is how long women have been kept out of the fetishist's clubhouse or closet. Freud said there were no female fetishists, but then ironically, he suggests that all women are clothes fetishists; moreover, according to Freud, the fetish had its source in sexual repression: "[R]epressing their desire to be looked at naked, they idealize the clothes that prevent this" (Gammon and Makinen 41). The story of psychology follows Freud's paradigm—officially keeping the "fetish" as a male possession, and then showing individual cases where women were indeed fetishists. For example, Wilhelm Stekel, a disciple of Freud, asserts that "a creative spirit is necessary even in the construction of a fetishism" and hypothesizes that there are so few women fetishists because "women lack the rich creative capacity of men" (341).

Only recently have women been given the notorious honor of being fetishists, and not just hysterics; just as men have now been granted the labels of hysterics, and not just fetishists. In the literary context, Emily Apter has broadened the definition of fetishism to include the possibility that there are feminist fetishist writers. Though she focuses on the French naturalist writers and shows how the fetish is distinctly feminine in the male realm, she entertains the liberating possibility in her final chapter that there be "a separate study concentrating . . . on the role of the female authorial voice in turn-of-the-century representations of sexual obsession and perversion" (244). I attempt here to take up her challenge through the example of Mary Wilkins Freeman.

FREEMAN AMONG THE NATURALISTS

One reason not to have let Freeman into the ranks of Naturalist writers would have been that fetishism was not the female's province or prerogative, and in denying Freeman entry into the Naturalist ranks, the reading public or canon-makers tried to ignore or deny the sexual impulses of her characters.[7] If women could not be fetishists, then Freeman could not be a naturalist writer.

However, if we compare Frank Norris's fiction with Freeman's, we encounter astounding similarities in their use of the fetish. At least, early on, before the full gentrification of Freeman took place,[8] Norris's genius was equated with that of Freeman: "The *Literary World* announced that *McTeague* would place Norris 'in the first rank among our writers, beside Mary Wilkins [Freeman], and Howells, and Stephen Crane'" (Shi 235). What Norris, Freeman, and Crane share is the love affair with the consumer good and the sexualization of that object, or rendering that object the locus of displaced desire. And in a world altered by Darwin's beliefs about instincts, love becomes insignificant, and sexuality is the only motivating factor; love becomes a mere euphemism for sex. Moreover, commodity fetishism, which can have meaning only in a capitalist society that values the acquisition, accumulation, and adoration of material goods, becomes a substitute for missing feeling. As Laura Mulvey has pointed out, there is nothing "intrinsically fetishistic" about Marx's concept of the commodity: "Fetishism of the commodity . . . is a political symptom particular to capitalism and those societies that come under

its sway" (5). The locus of empowerment for the individual resides in his imaginative reconstruction of the meaning of the commodity.

A close reading of the two protagonists in *McTeague* shows that this love of the fetish is not gender-based but universal.[9] Various recent critics have tried to come to terms with the compulsive activity exemplified in Naturalist fiction. Jennifer Fleissner attributes the "repetitive compulsion" to the changing nature of women's work in and outside the house and a renegotiation of women's public/private spaces because of woman's new role as a worker. For Fleissner, feminized "naturalist characters . . . are shown stuck in small rooms, engaged in the most feminine of acts; putting a house in order over and over, obsessed with the details of an entrapping interiority" (61). I would suggest that men are also encumbered by an oppressive "interiority" of their minds; a careful reading of the two protagonists in Norris's *McTeague* shows that this love of the fetish is not gender-based but universal—and based on an alienating economy. Barbara Hochman adeptly shows how the characters in *McTeague* are terrified by an imminent sense of loss (of self-control) and thus become obsessed with the need to control through ritualistic habits and stabilizing redundant activities. Loss of daily routine (to McTeague) and loss of self through sexual surrender (to Trina) inspire "passion, rage, and obsession," as the characters cannot deal with their potential annihilation. Unlike Darwinian survivors, these characters suffer "a crippling incapacity to adapt to change" (189); obsessive behavior cannot replace the sense of loss.

McTeague's fetishistic attitude toward Trina is most prominent when she is actually passive or missing from the scene altogether; e.g., when he gazes at her (while she is unconscious in his dentist's chair) or when he fantasizes about Trina while he surveys the objects in her room at her father's house. He picks up her hairbrush, which evokes in him an impassioned and sensual response to her hair. The hairbrush becomes a fetishized "pars pro toto": "That heavy, enervating odor of her hair—her wonderful, royal hair! The smell of that little hair-brush was talismanic" (64). He opens the closet door and experiences an orgasmic merging with a woman of his imagination, the woman he does not "know" in his courtship phase:

> Trina's clothes were hanging there—skirts and waists, jackets, and stiff white petticoats. What a vision! For an instant McTeague caught his breath, spellbound. . . . He went further into the closet, touching the clothes gingerly, stroking them softly with his huge leathern palms. As he stirred them a delicate perfume disengaged itself from the folds. Ah, that exquisite feminine odor! . . . All at once, seized with an unreasoned impulse, McTeague opened his huge arms and

gathered the little garments close to him, plunging his face deep amongst them, savoring their delicious odor with long breaths of luxury and supreme content.

(64-65)

McTeague becomes a narcissistic type of voyeur at this point, and Trina, as an individualized woman, becomes insignificant. She is no more than the sum of the parts of her body, the clothes she wears, the smells she exudes. A true fetishist, McTeague has made love to the objects which represent her. Later, it is easy for him to murder his wife, as she is merely an object, and he can readily substitute his love for another object for his love for his wife. Shortly before he kills her, he finds that she has pawned his "beloved concertina," and that is partly how he can rationalize killing her: "Trina had sold his concertina—had stolen it and sold it—his concertina, his beloved concertina, that he had had all his life. Why, barring the canary, there was not one of all his belongings that McTeague had cherished more dearly" (281). As he traipses through Death Valley, he never relinquishes his love for the canary in the gilt cage. His love for a dumb beast becomes far more significant than his love for his wife. This kind of fetishization of one's pet is also true for Freeman characters, as we shall see shortly. Fetishistic behavior is just one step away from mechanized behavior: McTeague is easily reduced to a cog in the wheel as he returns to mining. In fact, mining, dentistry, love, and murder are all rather interchangeable in the mindless way in which McTeague performs tasks: "In the Burly drill, he saw a queer counterpart of his old-time dental engine" (295). This perception resonates with the Marxist fear of the alienation in an industrialized society of the worker from the product he helps produce and of the blindness of the consumer who is removed from the source of productivity.

But Norris does not suggest that fetishization is simply a "male perversion." Trina, on her part, also indulges in such fetishistic behavior, as she prefers the eroticism of her gold coins to her husband. When McTeague is away from home, she secretly opens her trunk and counts her money. But the behavior is characterized as obsessive, as she incessantly polishes the gold pieces "until they shone" and buries her face in the pile of gold, "delighted at the smell of it and the feel of the smooth, cool metal on her cheeks" (235, 236). In the climactic part of the scene, she actually does merge, lovingly, with the gold pieces: "She even put the smaller gold pieces in her mouth, and jingled them there. She loved her money with an intensity that she could hardly express. She would plunge her small fingers into the pile with little murmurs of affection, her long, narrow eyes half closed and shining, her breath coming in long sighs" (236). Never do the Norris characters make love as convincingly or as

well with other human beings as they do with the objects they own. Finally, like McTeague, who finds love in his concertina and his canary, Trina, when abandoned, sleeps with "the gold pieces between the sheets" and takes "a strange and ecstatic pleasure in the touch of the smooth flat pieces the length of her entire body" (274). As Marx knew, money becomes the commodity fetish which most distorts relationships.

Though Freeman's protagonists are not so overtly sexual, their fetishization of the objects which make them feel fulfilled and self-contained is just as intense. No one but David Hirsch, in his controversial essay that so enraged feminist critics, has observed the sexual repression and frustration of Louisa Ellis in Freeman's **"A New England Nun."** After the publication of Hirsch's essay in 1965, it was more politically acceptable to view Louisa as a fully realized woman, celebrating her self-reliance.[10] But after a careful analysis of the language of the story and an examination of a parallel text, **"The Parrot,"** I would like to suggest that Hirsch's initial pronouncement is right. Like Prufrock measuring the meaninglessness of his days in coffee spoons, the New England nun is involved in obsessive, incessant, and fetishistic behavior. Waiting for fourteen years for her fiancé, Joe Dagget, to return, she has grown ornery and asocial. As one psychologist has expressed it, the fetishist "struggles against his own sexuality" and, like Louisa, "becomes progressively asocial," since the fetishist's tendency is "an autoerotic one" (Stekel 343). There is something unsettling in Louisa's obsessively orderly existence and simultaneously onanistic behavior, which prevents union with another: "Now she quilted her needle carefully into her work, which she folded precisely, and laid in a basket with her thimble and thread and scissors. Louisa Ellis could not remember that ever in her life she had mislaid one of these little feminine appurtenances, which had become, from long use and constant association, a very part of her personality" (39).

The fact, too, that her household goods become "a very part of her personality" suggests that object and self have become indistinguishable. This is a woman without society of any kind, as "maidenly possessions" have become her "dear friends" (44). Not only has she been weighed down by consumer culture's incessant definition of a woman as a good housewife, she has also given in to the desires of the consumer woman. Though she is an energetic producer of household goods, she is also a voracious collector of things—china, linens, aprons, herbs, and essences—and thus seems to get caught in the compulsive and draining activity of the consumer woman. She is the type of bourgeois housewife whom Leora Auslander would describe as bridging the gap between "public and private" (103). She, like the New Woman, represents what Auslander describes as a contradictory stance toward production and consumption: "Capitalism encouraged women's individuation through goods; the state needed women to subordinate those needs to the needs of the nation" (104). Thus, on the one hand, Louisa is the housewife who represents the Protestant work ethic of the nation, but on the other, she is the avid collector who fuels the nation's economy. Though not a factory worker, her activity is that of an automaton: she never stops collecting or sorting, even when involved with the minutest activity; she picks currants and then "collect[s] the stems carefully in her apron" (38). Then she worries about whether something is out of place or untidy, "look[ing] sharply at the grass beside the step to see if any [stem] had fallen there" (39). Fastidious as a gardener, she is equally fastidious as a housekeeper, whether she carefully polishes china, dusts, or sews, and hence is deeply and excessively disturbed at the returned Joe Dagget's accidental overturning of her work-basket. She feels compelled to put back into its original place anything that he moves on the living-room table because, as she tells him, "I always keep them that way" (41). In fact, in his presence, she becomes withholding of affection, conversation, and the food that she so seems to relish. If she feels constrained out of a fear of damage to her possessions, he feels in her presence equally repressed, as if "surrounded by a hedge of lace" (42).

As a consumer woman who likes luxuries and ornamentation, Louisa has a fine linen tablecloth with a "border pattern of flowers" and enjoys using "china every day—something which none of the neighbors did" and which they "whispered about among themselves" (40). She sets the table in a compulsive, maddening way: "Louisa has a damask napkin on her tea-tray, where were arranged a cut-glass tumbler full of teaspoons, a silver cream-pitcher, a china sugar-bowl, and one pink china cup and saucer" (40). It is as if she dissociates in a rather schizophrenic manner, as if she "had been a veritable guest to her own self" (39). The narrator enumerates the types of food she eats, the listing sounding as anal-retentive as Louisa is in her collecting: "She had for her supper a glass dish full of sugared currants, a plate of little cakes, and one of light white biscuits" (40). She also has a vast array of aprons—a green gingham one for gardening, a pink-and-white one for sewing, and a "white linen" apron "with a little cambric edging on the border" for company—and is known to wear layers of aprons depending on what activity she is involved with (40). Modern psychologists would look askance at such compulsive, fetishistic behavior, especially as it deteriorates into meaningless (almost masturbatory) repetition without any obvious purpose: "Louisa dearly loved to sew a

linen seam, not always for use, but for the simple, mild pleasure which she took in it. She would have been loath to confess how more than once she had ripped a seam for the mere delight of sewing it again" (44). Freeman's Louisa could easily find herself in the company of those on McTeague's "Polk Street"; she is not particularly a New Englander, but rather a Naturalist type of woman, like the gold-plate-reminiscing Maria or hoarding Trina in *McTeague*.

Like McTeague himself, Louisa has the superficial signs of culture enshrined upon her sitting-room table. The "square red autograph album" represents her propensity for collecting and holding on to the past. "The Young Lady's Gift-Book," which would have been a collection of cheap sentiment, was passed down from her mother and, as such, represents her ties to the past but also her love of ornamentation and superfluity. She is very disturbed when Joe handles these frill objects. Similarly, McTeague is drawn to his own enshrinement to culture—the "ornaments" on his "small marble-topped centre table," including back issues of dentistry magazines and "a stone pug dog" (7). Hanging on his wall are "a rifle manufacturer's advertisement calendar which he never used" and "a steel engraving of the court of Lorenzo de' Medici, which he had bought because there were a great many figures in it for the money" (7). This is cheap culture, bought at a bargain price, but it fulfills some type of longing on his part. He also owns an encyclopedia of dentistry and a concertina, which are meant more for show than for use. This kitsch and clutter in Freeman's and Norris's works is a testament to bourgeois taste and striving, but it is much more than the desire to attain some respectability; it represents the tantalizing possibility of emotional sustenance. Certainly, the rage for kitsch and clutter was inspired by modern capitalism, which generated, according to Celeste Olalquiaga, the consumer's taste for such objects: "Mechanical reproduction not only altered the proliferation and affordability of images, but also enabled a particular modern sensibility based on the preeminence of looking and collecting." Mass production, she suggests, allowed for "the democratization of the practice of looking and collecting" (13).

As Emily Apter points out in her study of the fetish in turn-of-the-century France, collecting was becoming a mania that was perceived essentially as a feminine activity and as a sickness; it was "becoming a virulent petty-bourgeois sickness in the eyes of Maupassant and . . . his contemporaries" (58). In his psychological reading of collecting, Werner Muensterberger has noted the pleasure aspect attached to the collectible: "Collecting, then, emerges as an instrument designed not only . . . as an escape hatch for feelings of danger and the reexperience of loss. However, because it is an effective device for relief from these pressures, it is felt as a source of pleasure and wish fulfillment" (47). It is understandable then that Louisa's universe is disturbed by a man who upsets her collections and that McTeague reacts violently when Trina starts to sell his beloved possessions. When they experience loss, they are even more concerned with arranging what they have in the most fastidious and painstaking fashion. When McTeague loses his job and thereby his identity, he polishes his dental drill and arranges all his dental equipment ("excavators, pluggers, forceps, pliers, corundum disks and burrs") "with the greatest neatness and regularity" (206). And when everything in the world seems lost, he still absurdly carries his canary and gilt cage around with him in the desert! Similarly, Freeman's Louisa, upon giving up Joe Dagget to the woman vying for his affection, revels in the days ahead, which she counts away like rosary beads. Moreover, she imagines a life where she "could sew linen seams, and distill roses, and dust and polish and fold away in lavender, as long as she listed" (49). Like McTeague, she also looks forward to the sole companionship of her canary.

Louisa's displaced desires are reflected in the animals she keeps as pets. A parallel figure to Louisa is her pet dog, Caesar, "a veritable hermit of a dog" (45). Hirsch has aptly recognized that the encaged bird and leashed dog represent Louisa's pent-up sexuality.[11] But the dog also represents her denial of maternal urges, obviously allied to her negative attitude toward sexuality. When she imagines getting married, she also has a vision of the dog being unleashed and biting the neighborhood children in a most brutal and relentless fashion; this fantasy of the ferocious destruction of children is a bit exaggerated, too gloating, and a valid projection of her animus toward children. Although the rumor has spread in the village that the dog is "a very monster of ferocity" to the point that the animal has been demonized (45), there is no real evidence that this dog who feeds on Louisa's left-over corn-cakes is anything but old and docile. In fact, Joe has the key to freeing the dog and Louisa's sexuality, but she is terrified at the prospect of either liberation. Because Joe sees the dog "as he was," he ventures to pet him and even "to set him loose" (46). Like her canary, Louisa flutters at this move by Joe; she "grew so alarmed that he desisted" (46). But Joe recognizes the dog as "good-natured" and frowns upon the cruelty in tying him up, and his assertion that "[s]ome day I'm going to take him out" distresses Louisa with the frightening prospect of what married life with Joe would be like "when their interests and possessions should be more completely fused in one" (46). Again, her fear of sexual intimacy is expressed in her inability to share her worldly goods. Her final renunciation of connection

and sexuality should not be construed as positive; she is no Emersonian self-reliant woman, not even a good Protestant New England woman.[12] When we hear the narrator liken her to a nun "prayerfully numbering her days" like "pearls in a rosary, every one like the others" (49), we realize that she is not a nun in the strictest sense of the term. She is not attaining fulfillment through spirituality; indeed, the rosary beads become a meaningless religious icon and yet another fetish in the story. Louisa, sequestered with her dog and canary, will continue counting off her days in a fetishistic, ritualistic way without meaning.

In "The Parrot" (1900), an obvious companion piece to "A New England Nun" because of its fetishization of the pet bird, the sense of regret at losing a potential husband is even more intense. The plot and resolution are similar. Martha lives all alone in a New England town except for a parrot, whom she loves inordinately and shamefully: "Often she said to herself that some judgment would come upon her for so loving a bird" (212). She is also an avid collector: her house is crammed with old tables and desks, and a set of "works on divinity" adorn her bookcase. Martha reads these books, inherited from her Congregationalist minister father, "over and over with a painful concentration" and refuses to read any secular, immoral novel (211). On summer evenings, she fantasizes about lovers meeting covertly in the country lanes, and finally, a real man pays attention to her. She believes the minister is courting her and begins paying attention to the superficial accoutrements of a woman in love. She starts wearing her "best black silk," but when, to her surprise, he marries someone else, all her attention becomes refocused on the parrot: "[I]f it had not been for her parrot, she would have gone mad" (218; this resonates with McTeague's obsessive love for his canary). The connection between Martha's and the parrot's imprisonment is made explicit: "[T]hat undiminished fire of the spirit which dwelt within her . . . [was] securely caged by her training and narrowness of life as was the parrot by the strong wires of his house" (212). The parrot, like the many commodities in the Freeman landscape, becomes the mediating symbol between Martha's inner and outer worlds, helping her to retain a semblance of sanity: "[H]e was the link with that which was outside her, and yet with that which was of her truest inwardness of self" (212). Moreover, he is the emblem of a freedom she can imagine but not exercise. Her daily life is repressive and filled with deadening activities: daily or weekly visits "to church, to prayer meeting, to the village store" and monthly visits to "the missionary sewing-circle, and to the supper and sociable in the evening" (212). The parrot relieves her of this spiritual barrenness and sensory deprivation: "The tropical thing, screaming and laughing, and shrieking out dissonant words, and oftentimes speeches . . . was the one note of freedom and irresponsibility in her life" (212).

Like Louisa's canary in **"A New England Nun,"** Martha's parrot becomes her alter ego, the medium whereby she projects her dislike onto the intrusive male but also the vehicle whereby she can express and displace a feeling as taboo for women as sexuality, namely anger: "He swore such oaths that his mistress would fairly fly out of the door with hands to her ears" (212). Still, Martha cannot resist listening to his angry oaths, as if he were filling a void within her. Indeed, she fantasizes, as unreasonably as Louisa Ellis does with the vicious dog, that the brute parrot will eventually become so uncivil that she "might be driven by her sense of duty to have the bird put to death" (212). At first Martha appears to be rejecting the clamoring bird in favor of the fickle minister, but when it becomes obvious that the minister/suitor has rejected her, the bird, almost preternaturally, becomes ever more loyal to his mistress. When the minister and his new wife, her rival, pay her a visit, her anger, embodied in the parrot, is unleashed, as the parrot literally attacks the bride: the parrot, more like Poe's "Raven" than Louisa's feminine and fainting canary, hovers ominously "like a very whirlwind of feathered rage, and, with a wild shriek, he dashed upon the bridal bonnet, plucking furiously at roses and plumes" (218). Martha's anger, vented through the parrot, is directed not at the minister but at the fetishized image of the bride, her bridal bonnet, which the parrot demolishes with gusto. The marital yearning embodied in her rival's bridal bonnet recalls Martha's earlier "[v]isions of a new silk for a wedding-dress, brown instead of black" (216), when she had entertained notions of marrying the minister. But the parrot finally does offer her a vision of all-consuming love. In a passage exquisitely sensual and spiritual, Freeman shows a strange consummation of love in the union of parrot and mistress: "Martha looked at her parrot, and his golden eyes met hers, and she recognized in the fierce bird a comradeship and equality, for he had given vent to an emotion of her own nature" (218). She now feels that the bird, who, like a lover, takes "morsels of food from between her thin lips" (212), is her soulmate, as indicated in Freeman's rewriting of Poe's "Nevermore": "[S]he knew forevermore that the parrot had a soul" (218). Like the bridal bonnet, the parrot seems to embody mystical power and transcendent meaning for the lovelorn Martha. But Freeman, as a Naturalist, cannot believe in this otherworldly dimension; the bird, no ominous portent, but an apt reflection of Martha's befuddled mind, represents self-expression as well as self-annihilation.

Indefatigable Shopping and Consumption in Freeman

"One Good Time" offers an alternative approach to this vague longing and desire, but it ends on a note of resignation and desperation similar to that found in **"The Parrot"** and **"A New England Nun."** In this story Narcissa Stone, aptly named because of her narcissistic and cold nature, initially foregoes marriage to her suitor, William Crane, in order to go on a shopping spree with her mother in New York. With the inheritance that her father has left her, she plans to entertain the extravagant passion of her life—to take the fifteen hundred dollars of the inheritance and spend it on "one good time" before she settles into marriage. The story begins with the funeral of the father and the town astir with gossip about whether Narcissa and her mother will be wearing new clothes to the funeral. Veblen's description of the rural population's predilection to "neighborhood gossip" as an attempt to size up their assets ("conspicuous consumption") certainly applies to Narcissa's neighbors. The village is "scandalized" at the shabby appearance and inappropriate colors of the women's dresses, but this would be the last moment of shame for Narcissa. She leaves the town with the desire to go shopping for jewelry and clothes and to visit the theatre, museums, and concerts in New York. Always compulsive in her ways (even her frown is described as "a crying repetition of some old anxiety and indecision"), she goes into a shopping frenzy in the city. She had come up with a list of desired objects: a breast pin and a gold watch for herself, a ring and a cashmere shawl for her mother. The more she sees in New York, the longer her list gets, until a litany of objects is purchased: a hat, a bonnet, black silk dresses, a black satin dress for her mother, a green satin dress for herself, a fur cape, "a silk bed-quilt," "some handsome vases," "some green an' gilt teacups" with a matching tray, "some silk stockings," "some shoes," and "some gold-bowed spectacles" for her mother. She is also mesmerized by the interior of her sumptuous hotel room, which had a "parlor with a velvet carpet an' stuffed furniture and a gilt clock" and by the endless "kinds of things to eat" at restaurants (207, 208). This endless vision and cataloguing of commodities is intoxicating and enervating at the same time.

Narcissa's only emotional response to anything she experiences is anxiety. (Early on, we see lines in her face, expressing "discontent and worry" [194].) When her father dies, she does not mourn for him but rather dreams about how to spend his small fortune. Arriving in New York in time for Christmas, Narcissa and her mother spend much of their time and money Christmas shopping. This is in keeping with the historical reality of Christmas becoming an increasingly consumerist holiday at the end of the nineteenth century. Gift-giving, especially at Christmas, became popular and an example of "emerging expressions of obligatory kindness mediated by goods"; but it was also a way of protecting the self and withholding emotions (Bronner, "Reading" 52). Thus, Narcissa and her mother are very excited about these Christmas presents: "Mother an'me never had any Christmas presents, an' I told her we'd begin, an' buy 'em for each other" (208). Though gifts are exchanged, not much love seems to be part of the bargain. Indeed, when Narcissa and her mother go to Christmas services, they do not seem aware of the spiritual side of the event or of the ritual. It is almost as if they were visiting the opera again, as they wear their "new black silks" and admire the splendor of the church. Their fancy clothing and their performing the rituals of a Catholic mass (whose rites they do not understand) are for appearance's sake only—the utter manifestation of "conspicuous consumption." Ritual and religion become as meaningless as the shopping frenzy. In fact, the department store emerging at the end of the nineteenth century seems to become the sacred cathedral of consumerist culture. Narcissa feels caught up by the spirit of buying and also by the ornate Christmas decorations: "Everybody was buying Christmas presents, an' the stores were all trimmed with evergreen—you never see anything like it" (208).

The profane merges with the spiritual in the realm of the department store or emporium, as Elaine S. Abelson suggests:

> Women were invited to participate in a sexually stimulating environment that often elicited behavior they felt unable to control. The department store had become a social location in which the manipulation of various stimuli created an unreal world and led to behavior patterns that deviated from the range of either the desirable or the acceptable.
>
> (46)

The momentary thrill of transgressing and giving in to fantasy was overwhelming; the pleasure of satisfying the desire was linked to sexual desire, where one would enjoy for the moment and pay later. In her study of the rise of the shoplifter/kleptomaniac at the end of the nineteenth century, Abelson shows the relationship between shoplifting, shopping, and sexual desire; kleptomania and "oniomania" ("the inability to stop shopping") were perceived as types of sexual mania and female hysteria. Commodities had "overpowering effects" upon women customers, and instead of feeling deprived, women gave in to temptation, and "shoplifting and related forms of theft became common occurrences"; even honest women might "lose their heads" (Abelson 55). This is not to say that Freeman's Nar-

cissa is a shop-lifter, but her exaggerated, unthinking, repetitive behavior is very much like that of the kleptomaniac, in the extreme form, or of compulsive modern women who exceed the limits on their credit cards for momentary gratification, sexual or otherwise, if only on a subliminal level. Her binge-shopping is much like that of the destructive women in Freeman's **"The Cloak Also."** In fact, the contradictions of consumer culture emerge in this image of Narcissa as spender in a cityscape: "Bourgeois women were supposed to desire objects; department stores were explicitly designed to create desire, yet women were not to desire too much" (Auslander 103). Desire which was out of control was deemed dangerous and deviant, and kleptomaniacs were perceived as "mad" (Auslander 103). Contradictorily, though consumption was necessary for the smooth operation of the economy, unhealthy consumption "was understood as potentially profoundly disruptive of the libidinal economy, capable of deregulating and destabilizing the family and the society" (103). Thus, Narcissa can be seen as subversive as well as dangerous (from the economic and sexual point of view) because of her "one good time" which will alter her life forever. Narcissa buys on impulse, without any care for the future, and seemingly without any recognition of the actual extent of her spending: "When the money I'd taken with us was gone, I sent things to the hotel for the gentleman at the counter to pay, the way he'd told me to" (108).

Narcissa and her mother shop until they drop, literally. They go shopping for six days, until all their money runs out and the hotel informs them of their debts. Narcissa's mother cries and Narcissa faints, as they fear the possibilities of debtors' prison. Then Narcissa feels compelled to return home, to the patient and steady suitor, William, even though her intention had been to stay in New York for a year. She does not feel much remorse, or if she does, she covers it up with a Christmas present she has purchased for him, a gold watch. When she explains the shopping flurry, she says to William, "I got one for you too, William. Don't you say anything—it's your Christmas present" (208). She tries to ward off any negative reaction or withhold any real declaration of love with this gift. Like a good consumer woman, Narcissa tells William unabashedly that she is not sorry that she "wasted" fifteen hundred dollars in six days because she had finally had "one good time" (210). Though William will now be the provider for her, one wonders whether her taste for the good life has become numbed, or whether she will become even more desirous. Narcissa, lovely and coquettish in her blue robes, seductively puts her arm "around his faithful neck"—"for the first time of her own accord" (210). It is not so clear whether these amorous moves are sincere or are a sign of desperation: has her body become the final commodity of exchange? What does not bode well for the future of the couple is Narcissa's unfulfilled longing for the man she met during her stay in New York. She describes the flirtation, as she does her spending, in a bantering way to William, but one can't help noticing a sense of regret and desperation in her confession:

> There was a gentleman beautifully dressed who sat at our table, an' he talked real pleasant about the weather, an'—I got to thinking about him a little. Of course I didn't like him as well as you, William, for what comes first comes last with our folks, but somehow he seemed to be kind of a part of the good time. I sh'n't never see him again. . . .
>
> (209)

This is clearly the city gentleman who got away, the man representing money and class, the perfect emblem of "conspicuous consumption." Narcissa has come home to William not for love but for a scant survival, on his money. She gleefully tells him that she has "wasted fifteen hundred dollars," and in her mind, she connects this to cheating, in a sexual or emotional way: "I've let my thoughts wander fro you; an' that ain't all" (209). What is also disturbing about the story's ending is Narcissa's inadvertently comparing herself to the "black heifer," which, she tells William early on, her family had to sell because he "would jump all the walls" (202). In the middle of the story, Narcissa confesses that she is like that heifer in her desire to "jump the wall" and have one good time in New York. First, it is strange that a woman, even a rural woman, should talk about herself as an uncontrollable animal (Like Louisa's dog, Caesar), and finally, it is equally inexplicable that her desires would die so fast after this one visit to New York. Her last words, "I wouldn't go out again if the bars were down," ring of the same sexual and creative resignation and imprisonment which Louisa showed in her relinquishment of Joe.

Narcissa's affliction, her passion for luxuries and uncontrollable spending, would have been perceived as a type of madness having its source in "excessive vanity," according to nineteenth-century psychologists (Matlock 55); certainly Narcissa, with her lovely fetishized thick red hair, would seem to suffer from narcissism. In Freudian terms, the narcissist adorns herself for the gaze of the male other; she "strives to make her body into the phallus" and "devotes loving time and energy to the image she has for others" (Grosz 111). However, like the Freudian hysteric, Narcissa becomes female-centered, in her devotion to her mother: "The hysteric eschews masculine desire, preferring instead the now lost pre-oedipal attachment to her mother" (Grosz 111). Thus, she spends her "one

good time" in an infantile way and out of control with her mother, as a way to compensate for her father's frugal ways and withholding. Basically, she has a date with her mother, as she takes the paternal money, locus of phallic power, and runs off with mother for their "good time." Before her regressive journey to New York, she explains to William her basic neutrality toward men, as expressed in her feelings toward him and her deceased father: "I—like you, and—I liked father; but love ain't enough sometimes when it ties anybody" (201). Thus, her willingness to be tied down to William, like a tamed heifer, does not show much promise for the future.

In the "shop-'til-you-dro(o)p" Freeman story, **"A Tragedy from the Trivial"** (1900), the protagonist Charlotte May finds herself in an apt setting for the frivolous consumer woman. She is a sales-clerk at the ribbon counter of the "H. F. Crosby's Dry Goods Emporium" (37). She looks like a fashion plate from a magazine, and, like Narcissa, she takes delight in the admiring glances of others:

> Her hair was very fair, almost white, and she wore it in a quaint extreme of fashion which often caused people to turn and look after her. Her blue gingham short waist fitted her nicely, and her blue ribbon tie was wound tightly around her throat, and fastened with a cheap brooch with a stone of turquoise blue china.
>
> (37)

Charlotte seems to be no more than a cataloguing of body parts and ornaments. She works with Maud Lockwood, who is a step above her in social class and hence in value. More conspicuously attractive than Charlotte, partly because she wears a real "turquoise brooch" (38), to Charlotte's chagrin and resentment, Maud is confident about her marketplace value: sure of her "fine trimly girded figure," she "seemed to fairly thrust it upon one's attention" (37). Moreover, Charlotte envies Maud because she works not of necessity, but "by the desire of certain extras in the way of dress somewhat beyond the reach of her father's purse" (37). In addition to these two types of consumer women, Eliza Green, a thrifty, stoical woman who scorns ornamentation, works at the emporium; she had contempt "for the wearer of real turquoise and the wearer of the sham" (38). And her motto is that "only use redeemed the existence of ornament" (38). But Eliza is a woman who lacks imagination, desire, and compassion; Freeman is not sympathetic in the rendering of her character.

It is Charlotte's great misfortune to marry the frugal John Woodsum, a factory-worker, who, like Charlotte's colleague Eliza, is obsessed with living simply and not beyond his means. Charlotte's tastes seem extravagant to him, and he tries to purge her of her consumerist desires and rid her of her individuality; he makes her pack away all "her girlhood fripperies" and even makes her wear a simple, unflattering hair style that requires no ornamentation (44). Indeed, the litany of commodities that so excites Narcissa in the previous story is now denied Charlotte: "There were no more wide collars of crumpled ribbons; no jaunty puffings of blouses, no garniture of cheap flowers, and, above all, no cheap jewelry—no jewelry of any kind except her wedding ring" (43-44). Charlotte begins to weaken as her spirit is dampened; she becomes her husband's domestic servant, even though "she was devoid of domestic instincts" and fails at every attempt to keep order (44). Her experience as a sales clerk has not prepared her for this life of drudgery: "The measuring and selling of ribbon, and furbishing up of her own pretty person, had no relation to the financial diplomacy required in the simplest housekeeping" (44).

Charlotte inadvertently becomes a wastrel in her attempts to cook and to keep house. But one day she tries to surprise her husband, by baking a "frill" food, a birthday cake for him. Freeman describes her "reckless spirit" in undertaking the project, but unfortunately, as in her prior cooking attempts, Charlotte fails. The cake "falls," and she removes from the oven "a soggy, heavy mess" (46). Instinctively Charlotte knows that her husband will punish her for wasting the butter, flour, and sugar, so she takes a hint from Eliza, the next-door neighbor, and "makes it over" by adding "a little more of everything" (47). However, because she is such a poor baker, she botches the job even further: "The mixture filled two cake-tins instead of one, and the two went into the oven, and the two fell lamentably and utterly, as the first one had done" (47). Charlotte continues this onanistic, repetitive behavior of "making the cake over" until there are an "infinity" of cakes, and the batter spills over from baking tins to her best china bowls and teacups. It is a maddening process which really has Charlotte becoming ill, mentally and physically. However, in the process of reproducing the commodity that won't rise, she becomes "utterly desperate and reckless" and "freed from all restraint by the courage of utter despair"; ironically, this seemingly trivial experience allows her to retrieve "all her individuality, which had been overawed, but not obliterated, by those years of wedlock" (47). Soon the kitchen is "laden with that nightmare of utterly fallen and uneatable cake" (47).

This scene of the ever-propagating uneatable cakes is perhaps the most surreal in Freeman's fiction, and it becomes a metaphor of the enervated and enervating consumer-woman. Totally numbed by the experience of the aborted cakes, Charlotte literally walks out of her husband's kitchen and liberates herself by wearing

the clothes, hat, and "sham turquoise brooch" that she wore before her marriage and which her husband had forbidden her afterward. She returns to the emporium, receives her job back, and begins to save the fifteen dollars that she had wasted in the baking enterprise for her husband. However, when he comes to town to fetch her, he finds her indulging in eating ice cream with Maud Lockwood, and so returns home to pack away and send her all her "little foolish flipperies and trinkets which he had held in such contempt" (49).

The ending is rather tragic but fitting: Charlotte comes down with a cough, which turns out to be a symptom of consumption, a disease which had been passed down, ironically enough, from her mother's side. Her employer, Mr. Crosby, has become attentive to her from a sense of attraction as well as compassion. Charlotte does not shun his show of kindness because she needs his financial support to survive and to pay medical bills; at the same time, she keeps trying to save the fifteen dollars to pay back her husband. This saving has become just as obsessive for her as her initial spending. When Crosby buys her a real "turquoise brooch," Charlotte is overjoyed, but she sells the brooch to pay off her debt to her husband. When she returns to her husband, John, Charlotte does not have long to live. John's manly pride forces him to purchase the turquoise brooch and return it to his rival, Crosby; like the brooch, Charlotte is bartered like a commodity. In this text, the fetishes, whether they be hair ribbons, fallen cakes, or brooches, all seem to multiply at the moment of the woman's most frenzied attempt at individuation. Befitting the consumer woman, Charlotte dies of consumption, but her parting words to her husband are practical: he ought to marry the next-door neighbor, Eliza, who is so orderly and thrifty. It is almost a reversal of the plot in **"A New England Nun,"** where Louisa forfeits her fiancé to preserve her maidenly order. But Eliza's and Louisa's coldness are similar. Though the narrator's indictment of Charlotte is rather harsh, the reader does not trust the moralizing tone: "At the last she had learned her little lesson of obedience and thrift against all her instincts, and all her waste of a life was over" (54). Charlotte's repressed "instincts" seem far more healthy than her docile behavior (at one point, she is described as a "spaniel" to her husband) or the pragmatic and fastidious behavior of Eliza. Immediately prior to this moralistic conclusion, John realizes how much he has erred in his behavior toward his wife and agonizes over his mistake; his emotional reaction belies the practical tone of the narrator's words and exposes the horror that John feels toward his erstwhile practical outlook on life. His attitude has caused Charlotte to trivialize her own life, to think that fifteen dollars have more value than her health and well-being.

In **"A Tragedy from the Trivial,"** as in the previous stories, Freeman is questioning if and how the fetishistic woman "wastes" her life. In the fetishistic maternal or sexual stories, the women seem to lose their desires, their individuality, and their will to live when they are forbidden to express themselves through their fetishes. Without the fetish as the "Ersatz" object for the love they cannot receive or the creative destiny they cannot fulfill, they seem to fall apart. Not given an outlet for the desires projected onto the fetish, the women seem fragmentary and incomplete. Though I disagree with Wilhelm Stekel's sexist outlook in his assessment of women as non-creative and hence non-fetishistic (recent psychologies prove otherwise), I would endorse his view that "every fetishist is a lost poet" and apply this assessment to the Freeman women (341). It could, of course, also apply to Norris's McTeague, for after all, doesn't he have aspirations to play music on his concertina? According to Stekel, the fetishist "makes use of every external impression to increase the extent or scope of his psychic structure," whereas the poet or creative writer "rids himself" of complexes and conflicts with every "creative effort" (342). At one point, the narrator in **"A New England Nun"** states that Louisa has artistic inclinations: she "had almost the enthusiasm of an artist over the mere order and cleanliness of her solitary home" (45).[13] All the repetitive and monotonous activities of Freeman's fetishistic women—the incessant sewing and cleaning, the frenzied shopping and collecting, and the obsessive baking and inordinate saving—can be seen as symptoms of their thwarted creativity. Reduced to inchoate desires and inarticulate longings, the women latch onto the commodity fetish, which becomes an emblem of their wasted and paralyzed lives, as evidenced in their failed maternity, failed artistry, and failed sexuality.

Notes

1. Alice Glarden Brand asserts that the outbursts of rage among Freeman's women represent a venting of misplaced sexual energies. However, as I will show, the Freeman heroine finds no outlet through which to express her anger, sexuality, or creativity; instead, she obsesses about a fetish.

2. See, for example, Josephine Donovan's assessment of women's community in Freeman's New England villages; her study has influenced two generations of feminist Freeman critics. More recent, neutral analyses which show the tensions and contradictions of Freeman's works and of Freeman's conception of the domestic sphere include Leah Blatt Glasser's and Mary R. Reichardt's book-length studies as well as Susan Garland Mann's essay. Reichardt, for example, notes that Freeman writes "of women in relationships;

paradoxically, her women remain fundamentally alone" (153). Moreover, she views the Freeman protagonist as analogous to her characters: "torn between submission and rebellion, between duty and freedom, between dependence and independence" (154).

3. See my earlier essay on Freeman and advertising, in which I examine how Freeman is influenced by the market for which she writes, *Harper's Bazar,* and thus how she delineates characters who are manipulated by the deceptive advertising market, but how the women ultimately subvert the ad man's deceptions. I also show Freeman's ambivalent attitude toward fashions and commodities through an analysis of her letters to Mary Louise Booth, her editor, to whom she writes lovingly about new dresses and bonnets she has purchased. For more on the connection between Freeman's hungry, needy women and Freeman as an artist trying to make ends meet, see Virginia Blum's essay.

   For a general overview of how the capitalistic marketplace was transmitting its consumerist message through advertising to women, see the recent works by Ellen Gruber Garvey, Jackson Lears, and Jennifer Scanlon. The latter analyzes ads in the *Ladies' Home Journal* and merges women's longings for commodities with women's longing for a public and economic voice as well as sexual self. I would argue that Freeman's women stay at the first level of longing and inchoate desire.

4. Interestingly, the good/bad mother dichotomy seems to find resolution in Freeman's otherwordly Gothic stories. In "The Wind in the Rose-bush" and "The Lost Ghost," positive nurturing female characters own up to their maternal urges, even if these desires are connected to a now-dead child. Ghostly women take possession of ghostly surrogate daughters after biological or surrogate mothers have abandoned these young girls. The animus toward children is corrected in the ghoulish encounters between dead children and dead or aging women who have been bereft of the maternal experience. In some ways, the ghost becomes a fetishized version of the child they never had.

5. See Glasser's analysis of Eunice in "A Moral Exigency," and her emphasis on Eunice's final words, "I want—something" (73). As I show, this inarticulate longing resounds with meaning in most of Freeman's stories.

6. See Lorraine Gamman and Merja Makinen for extensive definitions of both Freudian fetishism and commodity fetishism from a feminist perspective. Both definitions include a portrait of a dysfunctional human being, cut off from true feelings.

Freud described fetishism as pathological when "longing for the fetish passes beyond the point of being merely a necessary condition attached to the sexual object and *actually takes the place of the* [normal] aim . . . when the fetish becomes . . . the sole object" (Gamman and Makinen 52).

The Marxist idea of commodity fetishism suggests that the commodity "produced fetishized relations between men and women" (Gamman and Makinen 174). Commodity fetishism entails "more than an attribution of magical powers to an inanimate object"; it involves "a disavowal of human labor, a displacement of value from the people who produce things onto the things themselves" (Gamman and Makinen 28). This is a vicious cycle which "hides the reality of human labor" and distorts "real social relations" (Gamman and Makinen 28). Disavowal ensues, as the commodity is seen as separate from the power of production, and the separation is intensified by advertising, which promises more than the commodity can actually be; in this way, disavowal and loss of meaning become tied up with both the concept of commodity fetishism and sexual fetishism (Gamman and Makinen 214).

More recently, Laura Mulvey has painstakingly shown the connection between Freudian fetishism and commodity fetishism: "The process of disavowal [Freud] and estrangement [Marx] produces an overvaluation of things, and the over-valuation flows onto and affects an aesthetic and semiotic of things" (3). She notes how psychoanalytic and economic fetishism overlap in their emphasis on disavowal and displacement—or the projection of desirability onto an object. Both modes of perception hold out the tantalizing fetish as a way to recover lost feeling or to cover up absence. Thus, for the Freudian, the "fetish object acts as a 'sign' in that it substitutes for the thing thought to be missing" (5). Commodity fetishism also relies upon the evocation of fantasy: "Commodity fetishism also bears witness to the persistent allure that images and things have for the human imagination and the pleasure to be gained from belief in phantasmagorias and imaginary systems of representation" (5).

For more on the relationship between commodity fetishism and sensuous desire, see William Pietz's essay.

7. Most Freeman critics overlook or neglect Freeman's sexual themes or interests as a writer. However, Deborah Lambert does an excellent analysis of sexual feeling in Freeman's novel *Pembroke*; though she does not look at clothing in the text as fetishes per se, she does reveal them as symbols, "couching sexual feeling" (200). Though Freeman

was never admitted into the Hall of Fame of Naturalist writers, there is a sense that her induction is imminent, with the new definitions of Naturalism and Realism merging. See, for example, the reformulation of definitions in Donald Pizer's collection. It has always been customary because of her local color writing to allow Freeman to creep into the camp of Realist writers, but the latter pejorative seems to belittle her greater connection to larger cultural, economic concerns. Even Michael Davitt Bell's recent reevaluation of female local color artists does not do them justice. For a spark of hope, see Susan Ward's short essay on naturalism, which, though it glosses over Freeman as a writer interested in "self-sufficient spinsterhood" (622), at least includes her among female Naturalist writers. And Julia Bader's reevaluation of Freeman has her questioning the apparent placid superficial reality of the text and looking for a more psychological reality; though she does not come out and say so, her approach to Freeman seems to equate her twofold reality with James's.

8. Wharton, for example, accused the local color writers, Jewett and Freeman, of seeing life through "rose-coloured spectacles" (293). She preferred Hawthorne's understanding of man's baser instincts; obviously, she did not look deeply enough into the psyches of the local colorist protagonists.

9. For further connections between commodity fetishism and sexual desire in *McTeague,* see the readings, compatible with mine, by William Cain and by Walter Benn Michaels. For a view which diverges from mine, see Lori Merish's "Engendering Naturalism," where she contends, in her examination of Dreiser's *Sister Carrie* and Wharton's *The House of Mirth,* that naturalism is a gender-biased movement, which seeks to undermine women's emergence as consumers. To Merish, naturalist texts sought to "contain the potential of feminine consumer desire, and to redefine the female consumer subject as commodity object" (323). Such an evaluation seems to make women's obsessive consumerism and disconnectedness positive virtues, and it also negates the imprisonment of male naturalist characters, like McTeague.

10. For vehement attacks on Hirsch's assessment and/or for an analysis of the triumph of the New England nun as single and autonomous, see essays by Martha Cutter, Lorne Fienberg, Kate Gardner, Marjorie Pryse, and Ann Romines.

11. Hirsch discusses the "dynamic tension between conscious desire and unconscious, repressed fears" (109). Louisa suppresses her sexuality and denies

the life present in "dog-as-phallus, bird-as-soul" (113). He concludes that she is finally committed not to "any human or divine values but to possession" (115).

12. Though I agree with Glasser's assessment of the contradictory voices of Freeman, I disagree with her reading of "A New England Nun." It is true that, like other solitary Freeman heroines, Louisa buries her "sexual self" (32), but I do not see that Freeman offers in this story "a brilliant analysis of the autonomy the single woman can achieve through her work . . . the self-fulfillment it brings" (36). Also, I do not perceive the married or single Freeman heroine as finding either her sexual self or her creative self, as Glasser implies (32). Alternatively, Reichardt accurately concludes that "the 'peace' Louisa seeks at all costs is hardly peace at all, but a mere facade of it" (93).

13. As one theorist on Kitsch has recently remarked, "No matter how common, an object can always be rescued from its apparent banality by the investment in it of personal meaning" (Olalquiaga 17). In a most distorted and grotesque way, then, Freeman's women do become artists, not Hawthorne's artists of the beautiful with transcendent visions, but mundane artists who sublimate feelings in order to create minuscule interior landscapes of their own neuroses or compulsions. One might, of course, render Hawthorne's Romantic artist with his trivialized mechanical butterfly as much a fetishist as Freeman's naturalistic women with their collectibles.

Works Cited

Abelson, Elaine S. *When Ladies Go A-Thieving: Middle-Class Shoplifters in the Victorian Department Store.* New York: Oxford UP, 1989.

Apter, Emily. *Feminizing the Fetish: Psychoanalysis and Narrative Obsession in Turn-of-the-Century France.* Ithaca: Cornell UP, 1991.

Apter, Emily, and William Pietz, eds. *Fetishism as Cultural Discourse.* Ithaca: Cornell UP, 1993.

Auslander, Leora. "The Gendering of Consumer Practices in Nineteenth-Century France." *The Sex of Things: Gender and Consumption in Historical Perspective.* Ed. Victoria deGrazia and Ellen Furlough. Berkeley: U of California P, 1996. 79-112.

Bader, Julia. "The Dissolving Vision: Realism in Jewett, Freeman, and Gilman." Sundquist 176-98.

Bell, Michael Davitt. *The Problems of American Realism: Studies in the Cultural History of a Literary Idea.* Chicago: U of Chicago P, 1993.

Blum, Virginia. "Mary Wilkins Freeman and the Taste of Necessity." *American Literature* 65 (1993): 69-94.

Brand, Alice Glarden. "Mary Wilkins Freeman: Misanthropy as Propaganda." *New England Quarterly* 50 (1977): 83-100.

Bronner, Simon J. "Reading Consumer Culture." Bronner, *Consuming Visions* 13-54.

———, ed. *Consuming Visions: Accumulation and Display of Goods in America.* New York: Norton, 1989.

Cain, William E. "Presence and Power in *McTeague.*" Sundquist 176-98.

Cutter, Martha. "Mary Wilkins Freeman's Two New England Nuns." *Colby Library Quarterly* 26 (1990): 213-25.

Donovan, Josephine. *New England Local Color Literature: A Woman's Tradition.* New York: Ungar, 1983.

Elbert, Monika M. "Mary Wilkins Freeman's Devious Women, *Harper's Bazar,* and the Rhetoric of Advertising." *Essays in Literature* 20 (1993): 251-72.

Fienberg, Lorne. "Mary E. Wilkins Freeman's 'Soft Diurnal Commotion': Women's Work and Strategies of Containment." *New England Quarterly* 62 (1989): 483-504.

Fleissner, Jennifer L. "The Work of Womanhood in American Naturalism." *Differences* 8.1 (1996): 57-93.

Freeman, Mary Wilkins. "The Blue Butterfly." *The Uncollected Stories of Mary Wilkins Freeman* 180-96.

———. "The Cloak Also." *The Uncollected Stories of Mary Wilkins Freeman* 248-67.

———. "For the Love of One's Self." *The Uncollected Stories of Mary Wilkins Freeman* 106-24.

———. "A Gala Dress." *A New England Nun and Other Stories* 37-53.

———. *The Infant Sphinx: Collected Letters of Mary E. Wilkins Freeman.* Ed. Brent L. Kendrick. Metuchen: Scarecrow, 1985.

———. *A Mary Wilkins Freeman Reader.* Ed. Mary R. Reichardt. Lincoln: U of Nebraska P, 1997.

———. "A Moral Exigency." *The Revolt of Mother and Other Stories* 19-35.

———. *A New England Nun and Other Stories.* New York: Harper, 1891.

———. "A New England Nun." *A Mary Wilkins Freeman Reader* 39-49.

———. "One Good Time." *A Mary Wilkins Freeman Reader* 194-210.

———. "The Parrot." *A Mary Wilkins Freeman Reader* 211-18.

———. "The Reign of the Doll." *A Mary Wilkins Freeman Reader* 317-32.

————. *The Revolt of Mother and Other Stories.* Afterword Michele Clark. New York: Feminist, 1974.

————. "Sister Liddy." *A New England Nun and Other Stories* 81-98.

————. "A Taste of Honey." *The Revolt of Mother and Other Stories* 36-52.

————. "A Tragedy from the Trivial." *The Uncollected Stories of Mary Wilkins Freeman* 37-54.

————. *The Uncollected Stories of Mary Wilkins Freeman.* Ed. Mary R. Reichardt. Jackson: UP of Mississippi, 1992.

Gamman, Lorraine, and Merja Makinen. *Female Fetishism.* New York: New York UP, 1994.

Gardner, Kate. "The Subversion of Genre in the Short Stories of Mary Wilkins Freeman." *New England Quarterly* 65 (1992): 447-68.

Garvey, Ellen Gruber. *The Adman in the Parlor: Magazines and the Gendering of Consumer Culture, 1880's to 1910's.* New York: Oxford UP, 1996.

Gilman, Charlotte Perkins. *Women and Economics.* 1898. Ed. Carl N. Degler. New York: Harper & Row, 1966.

Glasser, Leah Blatt. *In a Closet Hidden: The Life and Works of Mary E. Wilkins Freeman.* Amherst: U of Massachusetts P, 1996.

Grosz, Elizabeth. "Lesbian Fetishism." Apter and Pietz 101-18.

Hirsch, David. "Subdued Meaning in 'A New England Nun.'" Marchalonis 106-17.

Hochman, Barbara. "Loss, Habit, Obsession: The Governing Dynamic of *McTeague.*" *Studies in American Fiction* 14 (1986): 179-90.

Kelley, Mary, and Emily Apter. "The Smell of Money: Mary Kelley in Conversation with Emily Apter." Apter and Pietz 352-62.

Lambert, Deborah G. "Reading Mary Wilkins Freeman: Autonomy and Sexuality in *Pembroke.*" Marchalonis 197-206.

Leach, William. *Land of Desire: Merchants, Power, and the Rise of a New American Culture.* New York: Pantheon, 1993.

————. "Strategists of Display and the Production of Desire." Bronner, *Consuming* 99-132.

Lears, Jackson. *Fables of Abundance: A Cultural History of Advertising in America.* New York: Basic, 1994.

Mann, Susan Garland. "A House of One's Own: The Subversion of 'True Womanhood' in Mary E. Wilkins Freeman's Short Fiction." *Colby Quarterly* (1997): 39-54.

Marchalonis, Shirley, ed. *Critical Essays on Mary Wilkins Freeman.* Boston: Hall, 1991.

Matlock, Jann. "Masquerading Women, Pathologized Men: Cross-Dressing, Fetishism, and the Theory of Perversion, 1882-1935." Apter and Pietz 31-61.

Mechling, Jay. "The Collecting Self and American Youth Movements." Bronner, *Consuming* 255-86.

Merish, Lori. "Engendering Naturalism: Narrative Form and Commodity Spectacle in U.S. Naturalist Fiction." *Novel: A Forum on Fiction* 19.3 (1996): 319-45.

Michaels, Walter Benn. *The Gold Standard and the Logic of Naturalism: American Literature at the Turn of the Century.* Berkeley: U of California P, 1987. 115-36.

Muensterberger, Werner. *Collecting: An Unruly Passion: Psychological Perspective.* Princeton: Princeton UP, 1994.

Mulvey, Laura. *Fetishism and Curiosity.* Bloomington: Indiana UP, 1996.

Norris, Frank. *McTeague: A Story of San Francisco.* 1899. New York: Oxford UP, 1995.

Olalquiaga, Celeste. *The Artificial Kingdom: A Treasury of Kitsch Experience.* New York: Pantheon, 1998.

Pietz, William. "Fetishism and Materialism: The Limits of Theory in Marx." Apter and Pietz 119-51.

Pizer, Donald, ed. *The Cambridge Companion to American Realism and Naturalism.* New York: Cambridge UP, 1995.

Pryse, Marjorie. "An Uncloistered 'New England Nun.'" Marchalonis 139-45.

Reichardt, Mary R. *A Web of Relationship: Women in the Short Stories of Mary Wilkins Freeman.* Jackson: U of Mississippi P, 1992.

Romines, Ann. *The Home Plot: Women, Writing, and Domestic Ritual.* Amherst: U of Massachusetts P, 1992. 91-127.

Scanlon, Jennifer. *Inarticulate Longings: The* Ladies' Home Journal, *Gender, and the Promises of Consumer Culture.* New York: Routledge, 1995.

Shi, David E. *Facing Facts: Realism in American Thought and Culture, 1850-1920.* New York: Oxford UP, 1995.

Smith-Rosenberg, Carroll. *Disorderly Conduct: Visions of Gender in Victorian America.* New York: Knopf, 1986.

Stekel, Wilhelm. *Sexual Aberrations: The Phenomena of Fetishism in Relation to Sex.* Trans. Samuel Parker. New York: Liverwright, 1930.

Sundquist, Eric, ed. *American Realism: New Essays.* Baltimore: Johns Hopkins UP, 1982.

Veblen, Thorstein. *The Theory of the Leisure Class: An Economic Study of Institutions.* New York: MacMillan, 1899.

Ward, Susan. "Naturalism." *The Oxford Companion to Women's Writing in the United States.* Ed. Cathy N. Davidson, et al. New York: Oxford UP, 1995. 622.

Wharton, Edith. *A Backward Glance.* New York: Scribner's, 1964.

Susan K. Harris (essay date 2002)

SOURCE: Harris, Susan K. "Mary E. Wilkins Freeman's 'A New England Nun' and the Dilemma of the Woman Artist." *Studies in American Humor* n.s. 3, no. 9 (2002): 27-38.

[*In the following essay, Harris affirms Freeman's critique in her "A New England Nun" of the limited social choices available to female artists, comparing the story to the works of notable nineteenth-century authors William Wordsworth, Nathaniel Hawthorne, and Elizabeth Stuart Phelps.*]

In Mary E. Wilkins Freeman's widely anthologized story **"A New England Nun,"** Louisa Ellis comes to realize that she much prefers the life she has made for herself—a solitary life obsessively devoted to domestic routine—to the one she would have if she married Joe Dagget, to whom she has been engaged for fifteen years. At first committed to the marriage because, as a New Englander, she equates breaking a vow to committing a major sin, Louisa is delighted to discover that Joe loves another woman and that he is only marrying Louisa from his own sense of obligation. With great relief, she breaks the engagement and embraces her beloved solitude. The narrator tells us,

> She gazed ahead through a long reach of future days strung together like pearls in a rosary, every one like the others, and all smooth and flawless and innocent. [. . .] Outside was the fervid summer afternoon; the air was filled with the sounds of the busy harvest of men and birds and bees; there were halloos, metallic clatterings, sweet calls, and long hummings. Louisa sat, prayerfully numbering her days, like an uncloistered nun.[1]

I have not yet succeeded in convincing a class that this story is funny. There are no belly laughs in **"A New England Nun,"** and my students dismiss Louisa for being an annoying, neurotic old maid. What they cannot perceive is the diffuse humor that underlies this story, in part because they cannot hear the delight, embedded in the very language that describes her, with which Freeman presents her New England eccentric. This is where Nancy Walker's distinctions in *A Very*

Serious Thing: Women's Humor and American Culture become crucial: first, in her observation that women's humor is characterized by indirection rather than direction, and second, in her reminder that female humorists are storytellers rather than joketellers (xii). It is also useful to remember Walker's claim that even though American women's humor employs the same unflattering female stereotypes that male humor employs, nevertheless, "beneath the surface runs a text that directly counters these images and seeks to deny them. By presenting the *results* of women's cultural conditioning and subordination, America's female humorists implicitly address the *sources* of women's self-doubt, dependence, and isolation from the mainstream of American life" (30).

Finally, Walker notes that women's humor is premised on a different sense of power in the world than men's humor:

> Traditional male American humor rests on the premise that human events—including human failures—are somehow within our control; there is in it a consciousness that the promises that get broken were made by the same sort of people who now seek, through humor, to do the mending. In contrast, women's humor develops from a different premise: the world they inhabit is not of their making, and often not much to their liking, so their tactics must be those of survivors rather than those of saviors.
>
> (36)

Walker's observations facilitate a reading of **"A New England Nun"** that sees Louisa's willed isolation as Freeman's darkly humorous comment on the dilemma of the woman artist. Many readers have seen Louisa's retreat from heterosexual normativity as a response to cultural demands that married women relinquish their own pleasures in order to serve others. But Freeman treats Louisa's retreat as a special form of artistry—a choice not just for self but for a certain heightened appreciation of self that expresses itself in artistic terms. As Leah Glasser cogently argues in her literary biography of Freeman, **"A New England Nun"** celebrates not only Louisa's autonomy but also "the isolation and quiet that attention to one's craft requires" (35).[2] Louisa's artistry is manifested in her extraordinary attention to domestic detail, her love of domestic order and her devotion to the delicate beauties she can create and maintain in solitude. But in having to reject the world in order to practice her craft, Louisa also exposes the limitations of nineteenth-century women's lives, an exhibition that Freeman highlights through parodies, paradoxes, and inversions. On the one hand, in a classic scene of artistic solitude, Louisa's artistic expression is only possible if she gives up the world. On the other hand, the state of being isolated (which we can also read as a state of valuing the self over others) is the only distinction between what Louisa embraces and what she relinquishes. Paradoxically, Louisa's talents can be manifested only in an exaggerated form of the very domesticity she appears to have rejected.

I want to read **"A New England Nun"** against E. D. E. N. Southworth's and Elizabeth Stuart Phelps's novels *The Deserted Wife* and *The Story of Avis,* William Wordsworth's sonnet "Nuns Fret Not," Nathaniel Hawthorne's stories "The Birthmark" and "The Artist of the Beautiful," and the ongoing nineteenth-century debate over whether women artists should marry. My contention is that in exposing the contradictions inherent in a woman's choice to devote herself to art—and herself—rather than to marry, Freeman was not only critiquing the choices her contemporaries offered for women's lives, as Glasser and others have noted, but also challenging the very ideal of domesticity. The paradox arises from the observation that Louisa Ellis's culture sees women's nature fulfilled through exceptional housewifery at the same time that it insists that female fulfillment be manifested by a continuous sacrifice of self. The perfect female, in other words, cares everything about domestic concerns and nothing for herself. In **"A New England Nun,"** the protagonist epitomizes the perfect woman in that she not only accepts domesticity, she embraces it, making each element of housewifery an artistic moment. The contradiction arises from her valuing the practice of her craft over other people. While New England celebrated good housekeepers, it assumed, as Harriet Beecher Stowe's famous sketches of heroic domesticity illustrate, that they were married. Louisa's problem is that she prefers to be the sole consumer of her own labors.

In Louisa, then, Freeman creates a site for contradictory values, where the Romantic idea of the artist is juxtaposed to a cultural ideal of domestic womanhood. Southworth's and Phelps's novels, Wordsworth's sonnet, and Hawthorne's stories all contextualize the contradictions that Freeman sees in Louisa's position. Like the exemplary New England woman, Louisa lives by and through the domestic ideal. Like Southworth's protagonist, her self-possession precludes the active presence of men. Like the figures in Wordsworth's sonnet, she finds fulfillment through voluntary confinement. Like Hawthorne's artist of the beautiful, she rejects the human community in order to perfect her art. Unlike Hawthorne, however, Freeman does not censor her protagonist's choices; rather, like Phelps's narrator, she suggests that solitude is the only way a woman can practice her art. As Glasser notes, Freeman positions her "artist" within the most confined of domestic spaces—a small house shared only by a canary, with a large passive dog consigned to a doghouse at the edge of the property—and suggests that

Louisa's artistic flowering can only be nurtured within that tiny sphere and for herself alone. Feminist critics have long recognized this emphasis as a critique of a culture that insists that women marry and bear children but also so arranges the business of marriage and family as to squash women's selfhood. Freeman's variation on this theme parodies both the domestic ideal and the notion of womanhood that it implies.

WOMEN ARTISTS AND THE ROMANTIC IDEAL

Women in the later nineteenth century were just emerging from the social ethos that valued the individual only in relation to family and community to an ethos that valued the isolated individual. The Romantics had celebrated the individual, especially as symbolized in the solitary artist, since the early years of the century, but the model was almost exclusively male. Throughout the nineteenth century and well into the twentieth, women artists fought for recognition as individuated agents; as Hagar, the protagonist of E. D. E. N. Southworth's *The Deserted Wife* (1850), cries out, "*I* have a will! and tastes, and habits, and propensities! and loves and hates! yes, and conscience! that all go to make up the sum total of a separate individuality—a distinct life! for which *I alone* am accountable, and *only* to God!" (299). A singer, Hagar begins to cultivate her voice when her husband deserts her. Finding in solitude the motivation for artistic accomplishment, "she cultivated the art—*her* art by vocation and adoption—with all the passionate enthusiasm of her ardent nature; it became her solace [. . .] at length her soul began to struggle for freer, fuller utterance—for the revelation of its *own* individual life and love—and Hagar became a poet and a musician [. . .] at last she attained the power of revealing her *own* poetry—breathing her *own* music" (374-5). In tracing Hagar's evolution into a successful artist, Southworth suggests that the only way a woman could become a Romantic individual was to separate (or be separated) from the womanly roles that simultaneously "protected" her and prevented her from achieving selfhood.

The Deserted Wife was only one intervention into the debate about the woman artist. American women had fought against the social ethos that frowned on female artists ever since the seventeenth-century poet Anne Bradstreet bitterly recorded—in print—

> I am obnoxious to each carping tongue,
> Who says my hand a needle better fits;
> A poet's pen all scorn I should thus wrong;
> For such despite they cast on female wits;
> If what I do prove well, it won't advance,
> They'll say it's stol'n, or else it was by chance.
>
> (415)

Two hundred years did little to change public perceptions: among Freeman's contemporaries, women painters and sculptors were still fighting for recognition and autonomy. As Erica E. Hirshler notes in her study of late-nineteenth-century Boston women artists, female painters and sculptors suffered from a double bind: if they projected confidence and direction in their work they were faulted as being "unwomanly"; if they projected sensitivity and delicacy, they were applauded for not betraying their true nature but then promptly dismissed as unimportant (36). For many women of the late nineteenth century, especially in New England, the Arts and Crafts movement provided an avenue into the artistic life because its focus on domestic objects provided a way for women artists to be productive without leaving the sphere of acceptable femininity, which was always defined through the domestic. Sarah Wyman Whitman, for instance, went from easel painting to interior decoration, and became best known as the designer of book covers, including covers for the works of Sarah Orne Jewett, one of the members of Freeman's crowd (Hirshler 43-45). Despite such artists' success at combining the domestic and the artistic, most people still saw a radical contradiction between the demands of the artistic life and those of married life. This perception eventuated in a cultural onus against married women artists.

Elizabeth Stuart Phelps's 1877 novel *The Story of Avis* illustrates this dilemma most poignantly in its narrative of a brilliant young painter who manages to reach the threshold of artistic success—she studies in Florence and is acclaimed by her teachers—only to make the colossal mistake of marrying. The "disciplined imagination" that had propelled her as she spent six years in "patient service of her possibility," and which the narrator openly observes stems from the same source as what is more commonly understood as "feminine self-abnegation," becomes Avis's destruction, as she bitterly turns her talents to the care of her children, her household, and her selfish, unfaithful husband (37, 38). "Exiled" from her studio, Avis "was stunned to find how her aspiration had emaciated during her married life. Household care had fed upon it like a disease." Even though "she wished she were like other women—content to stitch and sing, to sweep and smile," she realizes that, for her, the self-sacrifice demanded by housewifery is devastating. In the end, she "counted the cost of her marriage in the blood of her soul" (206). Although the novel's conclusion looks forward to a time when it will be possible to combine family life with artistic endeavor, Phelps's final judgment is encapsulated in the name Avis gives her precocious daughter—"Wait." Closing the novel on the story of Sir Galahad's quest for the Holy Grail, the author makes it clear that the day when women could find both professional and familial fulfillment remains in the misty, mythical, future.

Avis's dilemma is echoed in the nonliterary writings of Annie Adams Fields, a central figure in Boston's literary and philanthropic scene in the second half of the century. An aspiring poet, Fields was conflicted by what she saw as the irreconcilable differences between the solitude she needed to compose and the demands on her time imposed by her duties to her husband and the literary circle in which she played a central role. In her diary, Fields synopsized the problem in an entry about her sister Lissie Adams, an artist who, like Avis, was studying in Italy and considering marriage:

> Nov. 24. Letters from our sister in Florence. Between the offer of marriage from England, her studies, and her desire of coming home the poor child is perplexed. How hard it is for women to work in this world, they are made to love, to sympathize, to console, & labor for others, but only when their lives are cast on desert sands do they attain pre-eminence in art. With all her talent, with her [. . .] hours of exile which have brought their fruit and given her a certain pre-eminence in Art, now comes this man who wishes her for himself—well, we shall see.

Like many of her contemporaries, Fields essentializes women's nature as "made" for selflessness and sees the dedication called for by art as antithetical to the multiple demands of family life. For her, women only choose the artistic life when they cannot realize their "natural" talents through giving to others. For many women, the choice was a painful one; as *Avis* dramatically demonstrated, either choice entailed giving up something equally precious.

Mary E. Wilkins Freeman also saw art and marriage as antithetical. But in making her protagonist a New England spinster, Freeman used the conversation about the woman artist to point out the paradoxes inherent in celebrating women who manifest their "selves" through the domestic arts at the same time that they empty themselves of all personal desire. Unlike Southworth's Hagar, Phelps's Avis, or Fields's Lissie, Louisa Ellis is an artist of the intensely private, whose greatest happiness consists of aestheticizing the domestic and performing it within the confines of her own home. Seen from the perspective of nineteenth-century gender essentialism, Louisa's feminine virtues are so exaggerated as to be parodic—the domestic tasks that Southworth's and Phelps's protagonists run from screaming become the vehicle for Freeman to demonstrate the paradox of *her* character's position. For instance, while Phelps's Avis hysterically protests that sewing "makes a crawling down my back" (27), Freeman's Louisa dearly loved to sew a linen seam, not always for use, but for the simple, mild pleasure which she took in it. She would have been loath to confess how more than once she had ripped a seam for the mere delight of sewing it together again. Sitting at her window during long sweet afternoons, drawing her needle gently through the dainty fabric, she was peace itself.

(27)

By the same logic, Louisa marks her various domestic routines by uncovering different-colored aprons: a green one for gardening, a pink and white one (worn under the green) for sewing, a white one (worn under the pink and white) for receiving company. As she moves from task to task she layers and unlayers aprons, calibrating her dress to the situation at hand. She also produces surplus domestic goods—a form of self-indulgent capital accumulation of a very feminine nature:

> Louisa had a little still, and she used to occupy herself pleasantly in summer weather with distilling the sweet and aromatic essences from roses and peppermint and spearmint. [After marriage] her still must be laid away. Her store of essences was already considerable, and there would be no time for her to distil for the mere pleasure of it.

(27)

Louisa's solitary female pleasures do not go unmarked, however. Even though they do not know the extent to which Louisa indulges her passions, Louisa's neighbors know—as village gossips always do—that her behavior is aberrant. For them, her exemplary domesticity (theoretically a good) is undermined by the fact that she devotes her time to pleasing herself rather than serving others. For the town, Louisa's oddity is manifest by the fact that she "used china every day—something which none of her neighbors did. They whispered about it among themselves. Their daily tables were laid with common crockery, their sets of best china stayed in the parlor closet, and Louisa Ellis was no richer nor better bred than they. Still, she would use the china" (22-23). Clearly Louisa's predilections, private as they are, have not escaped her neighbors' censure. Gossip, as Karen Kilcup notes in *Robert Frost and Feminine Literary Tradition,* creates communities in regionalist literature, especially communities between narrators and readers (109-11). Here, the neighbors' gossip signals both their opinion of Louisa's anomalous lifestyle *and* Freeman's own distance from the community's narrow values. Through the absurdity of Louisa's situational paradox—the fact that she is criticized even when she brilliantly performs her domestic role because she implicitly shuns the community in order to do so—Freeman foregrounds not only the female artist's dilemma but by implication, the difficulty all women faced in nurturing a conscious and

viable selfhood in a society that posits "selflessness" and community as the epitome of moral probity for the female sex. If women are censured for voluntarily forsaking the community in order to perfect their craft, how can a woman ever succeed?

WORDSWORTH AND THE IDEAL OF VOLUNTARY RESTRICTION

The benefit of voluntary restriction was certainly not an idea unique to Freeman's circle; rather, it had been celebrated by many artists, especially among the Romantics. One of Wordsworth's sonnets so perfectly anticipates the imagery and theme of **"A New England Nun"** that it is difficult to imagine that Freeman did not have it in mind when she wrote her story.[3] Published in 1807, this poem generally takes its title from the first line:

> Nuns fret not at their convent's narrow room;
> And hermits are contented with their cells;
> And students with their pensive citadels;
> Maids at the wheel, the weaver at his loom,
> Sit blithe and happy; bees that soar for bloom,
> High as the highest Peak of Furness-fells,
> Will murmur by the hour in foxglove bells:
> In truth the prison, into which we doom
> Ourselves, no prison is: and hence for me,
> In sundry moods, 'twas pastime to be bound
> Within the Sonnet's scanty plot of ground;
> Pleased if some Souls (for such there needs must be)
> Who have felt the weight of too much liberty,
> Should find brief solace there, as I have found.

(190)

In this poem about writing poetry, Wordsworth's first seven lines list the kinds of creatures for whom solitude and confinement are voluntary means to transcendent ends. Here nuns, hermits, spinners, students, weavers, and bees all savor their voluntary imprisonment, knowing that beauty—spiritual, material, intellectual—will be the fruit of their isolation. Lines eight and nine give Wordsworth's thesis: "In truth the prison, into which we doom / Ourselves, no prison is"; that is, voluntary confinement is not imprisoning, rather, it is a site for production, whether of honey, a fine piece of cloth, or spiritual enlightenment. The final quartet brings the issue to the poet himself: for Wordsworth, especially mindful of his reputation as a celebrant of free verse, voluntary confinement within the set forms of the sonnet is "pastime," play—an escape from the choices of free verse and a challenge to produce beauty within clear, formal, restrictions. For him, and for his ideal reader, the "brief" escape from "too much liberty" provides solace, a momentary resting place, where beauty manifests itself as the transcendence of confinement.

Nineteenth-century women rarely experienced "the weight of too much liberty." Rather, most women were limited to one of two choices—to marry, with all the responsibilities that entailed, or to remain single, which meant to be immediately stamped as an old maid whose value was subject to continuous social critique. As Emily Dickinson noted in one of her most socially pointed poems, for a woman to marry meant to "drop" "the Playthings of her Life" in order to assume "the honorable Work / Of Woman and of Wife." Whether married women miss the freedom—material or spiritual—of spinsterhood becomes their secret, "unmentioned—as the Sea / Develop Pearl, and Weed, / But only to Himself—be Known / The Fathoms they abide" (J732). For Dickinson, as for Phelps's Avis and Southworth's Hagar, the public status accorded married women does not compensate for the loss of self that marriage entails.

The debate about women artists takes place within this larger context, and Freeman's story takes up the issue in miniature. However, the signal (and in the end, tragicomic) difference between Wordsworth's nuns, hermits, and poets—the Romantic sensibility in general—and Louisa Ellis is that Freeman's protagonist has not *set out* to limit herself. That is, unlike Southworth's Hagar, this is not a woman who fancies herself a Romantic artist. On the contrary, Louisa is conservative, unimaginative, and timid. She does not perceive herself as extra-ordinary, and she does not long for Romantic selfhood, at least not in any form that she would recognize. Unlike all the other protagonists I have mentioned, she is not reflective, and she would be surprised to be told that she was experiencing a crisis of selfhood. Far from being a rebel, Louisa epitomizes the stolid New Englander who discovers what she likes and determines to preserve it. And even this discovery has come slowly. Fifteen years before we meet her, she had pledged herself to Joe Dagget, fully expecting her life to proceed along conventional lines: husband, children, community, responsibility. When Joe takes off for Australia to make his fortune, she loyally waits for his return. Her reversal of expectations comes not, as in Southworth's novel, as a grand revelation of self but as a hardening of quotidian patterns: during the fourteen years of Joe's absence, all unconscious that this was happening to her, "Louisa's feet had turned into a path, smooth maybe under a calm, serene sky, but so straight and unswerving that it could only meet a check at her grave, and so narrow that there was no room for any one at her side" (26). Although Joe returns still hearing "the winds of romance" whistling "as loud and sweet as ever," "for Louisa the wind had never more than murmured; now it had gone down, and everything was still" (26-27). Unlike Wordsworth's characters, Louisa does not *self-consciously* give up the world, but she reaps the identical benefits. Like them, the choice that the outside world regards as a cruel relinquishment is to her the

discovery of her true home—a narrow sphere in which she can not only blossom artistically but do so precisely as she pleases.

Critics have a tendency to read Louisa's choice as a rejection of sexuality, citing not only her reluctance to marry but also her treatment of her dog, Caesar, which she keeps chained and feeds on an "ascetic" diet of corn-mush and cakes in order to diminish his capacity (exhibited exactly once, years earlier) for breaking loose and wreaking havoc. For Louisa's fiancé, Joe Dagget, who has threatened to release Caesar after he and Louisa are married, the sleepy old dog stands for Louisa's baseless fears. For Glasser, Caesar epitomizes women's conflict between sexuality and autonomy, a conflict she sees as framing the entire tale. Even Gregg Camfield, one of the few critics to have treated this story as comedy, insists that "the image of constrained animality maintaining a reputation for ferocity regardless of the truth is obviously a *comic* metaphor for repressed sexuality" (148). I suspect that these post-Freudian critics have treated Louisa's rejection of sexuality far more weightily than Freeman herself intended. The origin of the fictional dog was an animal that Freeman herself saw chained, a lifelong punishment that she, like her character Joe Daggett, considered cruel.[4] It is more likely that Freeman intended the dog as a means of showing how much Louisa dreaded losing control over her own life than as a sign of her repressed sexuality. Louisa's expectation that Caesar, if unchained, would "rampage through the quiet and unguarded village. She saw innocent children bleeding in his path" (29), is clearly exaggerated, but Joe's threat to free the dog precipitates her recognition that marriage would radically change her ability to rule over her own possessions. Poor fat old Caesar then functions as a site for contested authorities, a marker in Louisa's realization that she desperately does not want to lose her autonomy.

We can better appreciate Louisa's forebodings if we remember the consequences of marriage for a woman in the nineteenth century. Louisa was one of the fortunate few whose circumstances gave her an independence. Presumably she had inherited her parents' modest house and income on their deaths and as a consequence controlled her own money and domicile. As a single woman, she could do as she pleased, depending on her ability to withstand her neighbors' sniping. As Shirley Marchalonis points out, Freeman, like Elizabeth Gaskell and Mary Russell Mitford, sets her stories within closed village societies and creates situations whose humor rests on the ironies of small events (222-34).[5] One of those ironies was the degree of personal freedom accorded women who defied the standard patterning for women's lives. For the women in Freeman's short stories, freedom defines selfhood.

From **"A Mistaken Charity"** through **"A Church Mouse"** to **"A New England Nun,"** her protagonists fight to maintain their independence. As "old maids," living alone or with a companion, they can arrange their lives as they see fit. Within the constraints of income, class, and location, their daily routines can be dictated by their individual whim. Although the social environment ensured that they were not burdened with "too much liberty," unmarried white women in nineteenth-century America were as close to "free" as any women during their period could be.

Conversely, both in Freeman's fiction and in the lives of her contemporaries, marriage destroyed that freedom. As the protagonist of Rose Terry Cooke's "How Celia Changed Her Mind" discovers when she trades her independence for a husband, most nineteenth-century marriages functioned as legal means for enslaving women. Nineteenth-century husbands, legally dominant, controlled their wives' property. Children demanded constant attention. Other family members—aging parents, for instance—needed time and care. Domestic concerns, even for women so fortunate as not to have to perform them personally, needed constant watchfulness. For American women, as Alexis de Tocqueville had noted a half century earlier, marriage imposed tremendous responsibilities, virtually imprisoning them in their homes for decades. Or, in columnist Fanny Fern's words, "Love is a farce; matrimony is a humbug; husbands are domestic Napoleons," and matrimony is "the hardest way on earth of getting a living—you never know when your work is done" (220, 221).

This is the future Louisa sees as she contemplates marrying Joe. Her "birthright," the cultural expectation that she will marry and reproduce, suddenly overwhelms her, not from fear of sexuality but from fear of losing the freedom that celibacy permits. For all its absurdity—manifest in the hyperbolic words that Freeman chooses to illustrate her protagonist's sensibility—Louisa's resistance to being dominated is real.

> Louisa had almost the enthusiasm of an artist over the mere order and cleanliness of her solitary home. She had *throbs* of genuine *triumph* at the sight of the window-panes which she had polished until they shone like jewels. She *gloated* gently over her orderly bureau-drawers, with their *exquisitely* folded contents redolent with lavender and sweet clover and *very purity.* Could she be sure *of the endurance of even this*? She had visions, so *startling* that she half repudiated them as indelicate, of *coarse masculine belongings* strewn about in *endless* litter; of dust and disorder arising necessarily from a *coarse masculine presence* in the midst of all this *delicate harmony.*
>
> (27-28; emphasis added)

Of course it is tempting for post-Freudians to read these passages as a repudiation of sexuality, but I would suggest that the fact that Freeman foregrounds them so explicitly indicates that she wants us to move beyond them to the *real* problem Louisa has with the idea of marriage—its disorderliness and the lack of autonomy it would entail for her. If we dismiss the importance of housewifery for Louisa—if we read it as a metaphor for fear of men—we miss the whole point—and comedy—of the story. Louisa's routines are obsessive, but they provide control over her environment, and as Nancy Walker notes, one of the sources of women's humor is women's recognition that they rarely possess such control. For Louisa, all that is imaged in the prospect of living with a man, a "coarse masculine presence," whose clumsiness and disregard for domestic order are signs of his utter devaluing of everything she loves. She has her first premonition of married life when Joe comes to visit: despite his efforts to be polite, this bumbling masculine presence disarranges her books, stumbles over her rug, knocks her work basket on the floor, and so disturbs the canary that it "flutter[s] wildly" in its cage (23-24). When he leaves, Louisa restacks the books, rearranges the workbasket, and sweeps up the dirt he has tracked in. Order—*her* order—is restored. However, she realizes that once married to Joe she will lose the ability to impose her order. Not even her time will be her own. As her own mistress she is free to spend her time sewing or distilling simply for the love of creating something beautiful. When she changes houses she will have to relinquish many of these cherished routines: "Sterner tasks than these graceful but halfneedless ones would probably devolve upon her. There would be a large house to care for; there would be company to entertain; there would be Joe's rigorous and feeble old mother to wait upon [. . .]" (27).

In fact, Louisa is even more daunted by the prospect of catering to Joe's mother than by Joe, because her mother-in-law will be the reigning domestic female, and that will *a priori* deprive Louisa of authority in her marital household. Mrs. Dagget will reign, and Louisa will not only have to serve her but endure her contempt as well. Louisa recognizes, even now, that Joe and his mother will team up against her: "Joe's mother, domineering, shrewd old matron that she was even in her old age, and very likely Joe himself, with his honest masculine rudeness, would laugh and frown down all [Louisa's] pretty but senseless old maiden ways" (27). Far more frightening than the prospect of initiating a sexual life when her own weak hormonal demands had already passed is the prospect of submitting to other people's control, at a time when she has not only established her own life patterns, but refined them so that they become, in their enactment, vehicles for exquisite pleasure. In solitude, Louisa finds fulfillment; in the community, especially as represented in conventional marriage, she would experience the obliteration of self and the denigration of all that she values.

FREEMAN AND THE AMERICAN
ROMANTIC—NATHANIEL HAWTHORNE

The tension between self and community was not only a Romantic obsession, it was also a New England one, as the descendents of Puritans worked out their latter-day variations on the Calvinist insistence that community life and community authority take precedence over private beliefs. Freeman's contemporaries often compared her stories to Nathaniel Hawthorne's, even when she disavowed the connection. "You are in soul more akin to Hawthorne than to anyone else," Fred Lewis Pattee insisted in 1919 (25 September; qtd. in Kendrick 383-86). Whether or not she admitted the connection, as a New England writer it would be difficult for her to escape Hawthorne's shadow. But influence does not mandate concurrence, and Mary Wilkins Freeman's stories take up Hawthorne's basic premises only to challenge them. For Hawthorne, for instance, it was wrong to attempt perfection, because the search inevitably subordinates human needs to the end pursued. In "The Birthmark" (1843), Aylmer, a scientist, attempts to extirpate the last vestige of imperfection—a birthmark shaped like a small hand—from his otherwise perfect wife, and kills her in the attempt. The moral he learns, as the narrator tells us, is that this mark of earthly imperfection "was the bond by which an angelic spirit kept itself in union with a mortal frame" (281). In "The Artist of the Beautiful" (1844), Hawthorne's protagonist spends five years perfecting a mechanical butterfly for his beloved, who has, in the interim, married a blacksmith and produced a sturdy young son. For Owen Warland, the artist, the butterfly symbolizes "a lofty moral [. . .]—converting what was earthly to spiritual gold" (325), but it also represents the artistic spirit, and "in an atmosphere of doubt and mockery its exquisite susceptibility suffers torture" (326). When Warland brings the butterfly to Annie Danforth's home, her toddler unwittingly crushes it in his grubby young fist. Warland, "placid" at the sight of his life's labor ruined, basks in his conviction that The Beautiful exists beyond the material artifact and that his discovery means he will possess the Knowledge of Beauty for the rest of his life. What he does not recognize is that in his single-minded pursuit, he has removed himself from his own kind. In Hawthorne's moral universe, it is far more admirable to marry and produce children than to pursue, no matter how brilliantly, the Ideal. For this father of American literature, the only path to beauty was through the human community.

But Hawthorne peered through the prism of white male privilege. From a nineteenth-century woman's point of view, "the human community" constituted as much an obliteration of possibility as an avenue to full existence. "Beauty," in most married women's lives, was so far removed from everyday reality as to be expressible only in the most abstract terms. Hence we have many "sentimental" depictions of maternal beauty and domestic bliss that overlook crabby children, colic, smoking furnaces, menstruation, demanding in-laws, lost sleep, cold, and the myriad of other frustrations on which writers like Fanny Fern commented but that abstract depictions managed to avoid.

For Freeman, the gender and moral ethos that Hawthorne established constituted an environment with which she had to contend. In her depiction of Louisa, Freeman challenges Hawthorne's contention that the only path to full human existence is through marriage and family. For Louisa Ellis, solitude and celibacy, not marriage and community, are the pathway to happiness. Like Owen Warland, she anticipates the torture her prospective in-laws would inflict on her artistic sensibility. Unlike Owen Warland, however, she is content to keep that sensibility entirely to herself. Louisa does not pursue Beauty as a means of proving something to her peers, but rather as an end in itself and for herself alone—in her contemporaries' view, the ultimate act of female selfishness. As Glasser notes, Louisa happily serves as a "veritable guest to her own self," not only eating from her best china, but doing so "quite heartily" (22, 23). Like Wordsworth's nuns, she willingly forsakes the world for a narrow existence in which the objects that she values are sanctified by her loving care, and her acts of devotion—cleaning, polishing, sewing—create the environment in which she chooses to dwell. Never an Ideal—Louisa Ellis is probably incapable of conceiving of such an idea—the beauty that Louisa pursues rests on its qualities of both tangibility and ephemerality, the fact that to exist it must always be in a continual process of recreation. Housework, as "everyone" knows, is endlessly, maddeningly, repetitive—which is precisely the reason the culture so reifies the idea of female "selflessness," especially as applied to women who are content to "lose" their sense of self in creating an environment that serves only as a springboard for other people's activities *beyond* the home. In Louisa Ellis, however, Freeman has inverted those values, presenting us with a character whose very claim to self rests in her embrace of the domestic extreme—the endless creation and recreation of beauty that only she will consume, all while secluded from the community's eyes.

In these ways Freeman parodies the domestic ideal, first, to highlight the paucity of women's choices and second, to show what kinds of strategies are necessary for a woman to truly control her own life. If, as Walker claims, "women's humor is an index to women's roles and values, and particularly to their relationship with American cultural realities" (7), then Louisa Ellis's story shows us, through inversion and paradox, just how contradictory Freeman found her contemporaries' gender values. In narrowing her character's life to a series of domestic routines, and in suggesting that Louisa lavishes on the routines themselves not only all her love but also all her talents, Freeman's protagonist becomes, in her quiet way, an exemplar of the woman artist's dilemma as well as her village's solitary artist of the beautiful.

Notes

1. Freeman 32-33. "A New England Nun" was first published on May 7, 1887, in *Harper's Bazar*. All second and subsequent quotations from this and other texts will be documented internally.

2. Glasser's reading of "A New England Nun" is certainly the basis for all subsequent readings of the story. My contribution concerns the relatively weighting of sexuality and celibacy and the humor with which Freeman approaches her subject.

3. We have little information about Freeman's literary background. Brent L. Kendrick's collection of Freeman's letters contains surprisingly few references to Freeman's reading, and Leah Glasser's literary biography also indicates how little we know about her engagement with her literary predecessors. We do know, however, that multiple American editions of Wordsworth's poems were published in the late nineteenth century, and that many featured "Nuns Fret Not." For instance, an 1873 edition of Wordsworth's poetry published both in Boston and New York used it as the lead or "Prefatory" sonnet in the section subtitled "Miscellaneous Sonnets."

4. "Monday afternoon, I went a-hunting material too: We went to an old lady's birthday-party," Freeman wrote Mary Louise Booth sometime in 1886. "But all I saw worth writing about there was a poor old dog, who had been chained thirteen years, because he bit a man once, in his puppy-hood. I have felt like crying every time I have thought of him. He wagged his tail, and looked so pitiful, he is half blind, too" (qtd. in Kendrick 69).

5. Two other essays treating Freeman's humor are by Camfield and Cherciu (although neither includes discussions of "A New England Nun").

Works Cited

Bradstreet, Anne. "The Prologue." In *The Norton Anthology of Poetry*. 4th ed. Ed. Margaret Ferguson, Mary Jo Salter, and Jon Stallworthy. New York: Norton, 1970.

Camfield, Gregg. "'I never saw anything at once so pathetic and funny': Humor in the Stories of Mary Wilkins Freeman." *ATQ*. Special Issue on Mary Wilkins Freeman. ns 13 (1999): 215-31.

———. *Necessary Madness: The Humor of Domesticity in Nineteenth-Century America*. New York: Oxford UP, 1997.

Cherciu, Lucia. "'A Veritable Guest to Her Own Self': Mary Wilkins Freeman's Humorous Short Stories." *Journal of the Short Story in English* [*Les Cahiers de la Nouvelle*] 35 (2000): 21-41.

Dickinson, Emily. *The Complete Poems of Emily Dickinson*. Ed. Thomas H. Johnson. Boston: Little, Brown, 1960.

Fern, Fanny. *Ruth Hall and Other Writings*. Ed. Joyce W. Warren. New Brunswick: Rutgers UP, 1986.

Fields, Annie Adams. Diary entry, 24 November 1865. Diary vol. 13. Annie Fields Papers, Massachusetts Historical Society, Boston, Massachusetts.

Freeman, Mary E. Wilkins. *Mary E. Wilkins Freeman: A New England Nun and Other Stories*. Ed. Sandra A. Zagarell. New York: Penguin/Putnam, 2000.

Glasser, Leah Blatt. *In a Closet Hidden: The Life and Work of Mary E. Wilkins Freeman*. Amherst: U of Massachusetts P, 1996.

Hawthorne, Nathaniel. *Nathaniel Hawthorne: Selected Tales and Sketches*. 3rd ed. San Francisco: Rinehart, 1970.

Hirshler, Erica E. *A Studio of Her Own: Women Artists in Boston 1870-1940*. Boston: MFA Publications, Museum of Fine Arts, 2001.

Kendrick, Brent L., ed. *The Infant Sphinx: Collected Letters of Mary E. Wilkins Freeman*. Metuchen: Scarecrow P, 1985.

Kilcup, Karen L. *Robert Frost and Feminine Literary Tradition*. Ann Arbor: U of Michigan P, 1998.

Marchalonis, Shirley. "The Sharp-Edged Humor of Mary Wilkins Freeman: *The Jamesons*—and Other Stories." In *Critical Essays on Mary Wilkins Freeman*. Ed. Shirley Marchalonis. Boston: G. K. Hall, 1991.

Phelps, Elizabeth Stuart. *The Story of Avis*. Ed. Carol Farley Kessler. New Brunswick: Rutgers UP, 1985.

Southworth, E. D. E. N. *The Deserted Wife*. Philadelphia: T. B. Peterson, 1855.

Walker, Nancy A. *A Very Serious Thing: Women's Humor and American Culture*. Minneapolis: U of Minnesota P, 1988.

Wordsworth, William. *The Poetical Works of William Wordsworth*. New ed. Boston: Lee and Shepard; New York: Lee, Shepard and Dillingham, 1873.

Michael Tritt (essay date summer 2004)

SOURCE: Tritt, Michael. "Freeman's 'The Revolt of "Mother."'" *Explicator* 62, no. 4 (summer 2004): 209-12.

[*In the following essay, Tritt assesses the meaning of the biblical allusions related to Sarah and Adoniram in* "The Revolt of 'Mother.'"]

In the March 1969 issue of *The Explicator,* Edward J. Gallagher deftly outlines ways in which several of the biblical names in Mary E. Wilkins Freeman's **"The Revolt of Mother"** contribute to the local color of the tale's setting and complement the dominant domestic values of the times.[1] Yet, although Gallagher's discussion certainly adds to our appreciation and understanding of the tale, further consideration, particularly of Freeman's choice of the names Sarah and Adoniram, indicates a subtle subversion of the presumed gender stereotypes prevalent in the New England of the day. In Genesis, as in Freeman's tale, Sarah is portrayed as a figure of considerable force, someone who has a dramatic influence upon her husband and the generations to follow. Similarly, Adoniram, against whom Sarah "revolts," is, like his biblical namesake, a taskmaster who himself must contend with an unexpected insurrection.

Freeman portrays Sarah Penn, a long-suffering wife and mother, as having led a life of deprivation and as sacrificing her material wants to support her husband,[2] her family, and their farm. As the story develops, however, we see her taking charge, initiating changes that will dramatically alter her relationship with her husband and the attitudes of her children. The author, herself, protested that Sarah's revolt against her husband was not true to the New England farmwife personality.[3] If such strong-mindedness is difficult to conceive in a nineteenth-century woman, however, it is certainly not so in the matriarch after whom she was named.

The biblical Sarah is a person of impressive strength. She is memorable not only for the "great action" (Gallagher 48) of her giving birth at an old age, but also for her strong-willed interactions with her husband and her self-sacrifice for the purpose of perpetuating her own and her people's lineage. In Genesis 16, for example, Sarah insists that her husband "consort" with her maid Hagar to conceive a child. The text describes how Abraham "heeded" (16.2) his wife, although Abraham seems to have reservations about Sarah's treatment of Hagar after she becomes pregnant: "Your maid is in your hands. Deal with her as you think right" (16.6).

Still, Sarah's relationship with her husband is anything but subservient, and she takes a proactive role, much as Sarah Penn does, in securing the future of her family.

In chapter 21 of Genesis, when Sarah wants to make sure that Isaac, although not the first-born of his father, receives the patriarchal inheritance, she tells (not asks) Abraham, "Cast out that slave-woman and her son [. . .]." Her husband is distressed by the idea but, significantly, God says to him, "whatever Sarah tells you, do as she says, for it is through Isaac that offspring shall be continued for you" (21.12). Through Sarah, then, the patriarchal line is guided and effectively transmitted. Writing about the forceful personalities of the matriarchs in the Bible, Norman Gottwald suggests:

> One particularly intriguing aspect of the ancestor traditions is the prominence of women within them. Sarah is a strong-willed equal of Abraham [. . .] the groups preserving the ancestor traditions were headed by males but possessed of very strong women who were regarded as forceful actors in the domestic sphere. Since the horizons of the sagas [. . .] were largely domestic, the women had significant parts to play. [. . .] These women are as sharply etched characters as the men.
>
> (Gottwald 175-76)[4]

Similarly, in Freeman's story, Sarah Penn's character is more sharply etched than her husband's. For, despite Adoniram Penn's sense of his dominant role on the farm and in his family, his wife's revolt results in his becoming, at least for a time, bereft of power and influence.

A widely used metaphor in the Bible establishes God and Israel as husband and wife. "Within the spousal relationships in Genesis," Eleanor Prosser writes, "it is the responsibility of the wife to ensure the continuation of the covenant into the next generation. The women had to act strongly and decisively. [. . . I]t was their responsibility to ensure their future. They needed to protect the covenant actively and not simply wait for God, the 'husband,' to act" (3). The way in which Sarah Penn takes it upon herself to ensure her family's welfare is thus fully consistent with biblical traditions. This tradition refutes the minister, who, in effect, acting as spokesperson for a New England theocracy, feels obliged to speak to Mrs. Penn about what he and the community conceive to be her unnatural and unprecedented behavior.

Sarah's revolt changes the destiny of her family. The move to the barn will have dramatic consequences, for Nanny who is to be married to George Eastman and for Sammy, who, until that point in the story, has been depicted as his father in miniature. Toward the end of the tale, the boy is seen moving protectively in front of his mother and telling his father that, "We've come here to live" (467). Nanny's marriage to George Eastman, as Gallagher suggests, signals a socioeconomic and even cultural change in the American fabric. Yet, the actions of both children are crucial in this regard. Sammy represents the next generation of males whose view of women is changing. No doubt his relationship to his own wife and to women in general will be affected by the events on the farm. The actions of Mother, then, even in a sphere of influence limited by comparison with her biblical counterpart, will nonetheless dramatically shape the future of her family and the generation to follow.

Adoniram Penn plays a smaller role than Sarah in **"The Revolt of Mother."** Nonetheless, the allusion to the biblical Adoniram presents a number of intriguing and significant interpretive nuances. The name itself carries ironic implications: In Hebrew, it means "The Lord is exalted."[5] Although Mr. Penn conceives of himself as exalted through much of the story, by the tale's end, the tables are turned on him, and it is Sarah (Hebrew for "princess") who is in an exalted position.

The biblical Adoniram was a taskmaster. This role fits with his early portrayal in the story. But the Israelite population grew resentful of such exactions and revolted against him. There is precedent, then, in the allusion to the biblical figure, for Sarah's revolt against her husband. Mr. Penn's image as overseer is crucial, argues Joseph R. McElrath, to the creation of the tale's suspense. McElrath isolates the passage in the text where Sarah Penn's defiance is compared with Wolfe's storming the heights of Abraham, suggesting that the reader "recall that general Wolfe was mortally wounded during that conflict" (260). Thus, he continues, there is great concern with the ominous repercussions of Sarah's actions. McElrath suggests that much of the force of the story derives from what he terms "the complicated trick ending of the tale," wherein Mr. Penn, in his sensitivity, is "totally unseated by Sarah." Yet, a further irony arises: the biblical Adoniram was stoned to death by the people when they rose up against him. The fate of the ancient taskmaster adds to the suspenseful mix: Expectation builds as the New England community (and reader) await the arrival of Mr. Penn. Biblical and more modern precedents masterfully coalesce to intensify the anticipation of a stormy meeting of husband and wife.

"The Revolt of Mother," Marjorie Pryse writes, "establishes domestic power and vision as a countervailing force to the theme of domesticity that appears throughout nineteenth-century fiction [. . .]" (xiii). What is remarkable about the way in which Freeman effects her portrayal is that, at least in part, she estab-

lishes that power through reference not exclusively to contemporary personages, but to individuals in the distant past—the matriarch Sarah and the taskmaster Adoniram.

Notes

1. Gallagher's commentary is only partially and more superficially focused upon the significance of the biblical names. More in-depth consideration is given to George Eastman's namesake, the founder of Eastman Kodak, who represents, according to the critic, "the urban, business and materialistic society towards which America was turning."

2. Adoniram Penn and the biblical Abraham both prosper as a result of their wives' sacrifices. Mrs. Penn's "sedulous attention to [her husband's] wants" (453), contributes substantially to her husband's prosperity. Abraham, as well, benefits from Sarah's, self-sacrifice: "[. . .] because of her, it went well with Abram; he had acquired sheep, oxen, asses, [. . .] and camels" (Gen. 12.16).

3. Freeman writes: "There never was in New England a woman like Mother. If there had been, she most certainly would not have moved into the palatial barn. [. . .] She would have lacked the nerve" (qtd. in Clark 191).

4. Freeman might well have had access to characterizations of Sarah and, more generally, the matriarchs in general, in *The Women's Bible* (1892), the first part of which (including Genesis), was being written at the turn of the century. Several of the editors lived in close proximity to Freeman in New England. One commentator, Clara Bewick Colby, writes: "Even as mere history the life and character of Sarah certainly does not intimate that it was the Divine plan that woman was to be a subordinate, either in person or in her home. [. . .] After long ages of freedom shall have eradicated from woman's mind and heart the thought habits of the slave, then will she be a true daughter of Sarah, the Princess" (qtd. in Stanton, commentary on Gen. 23).

5. This is the most common translation of the name. See, for example, *Encyclopedia Judaica, The Jewish Encyclopedia,* and *The Interpreter's Dictionary of the Bible. The International Standard Bible Encyclopedia* gives a slight variation: "My lord is exalted." *Smith's Bible Dictionary* and *The Family Bible Dictionary* give the meaning as "Lord of Heights." This adds an intriguing resonance to Freeman's comparison of Sarah's actions and "Wolfe's storming of the Heights of Abraham" (463).

Works Cited

Clark, Michele. "Afterward." *The Revolt of the Mother and Other Stories*. New York: Feminist Press, 1974. 191.

Freeman, Mary E. Wilkins. "The Revolt of the Mother." *A New England Nun and Other Stories*. New York: Harper and Brothers, 1891. 448-68.

Gallagher, Edward J. "Freeman's 'The Revolt of Mother.'" *The Explicator* 27 (1969).

Gottwald, Norman K. *The Hebrew Bible: A Socio-Literary Approach*. Philadelphia: Fortress Press, 1985.

McElrath, Joseph R. "The Artistry of Mary E. Wilkins Freeman's 'The Revolt of Mother.'" *Studies in Short Fiction* 17 (1980): 255-61.

Prosser, Eleanor. "Genesis: Woman's Issues." Jewish Theological Seminary of America. 5 February 2002. <http://courses.jtsa.edu/bible/intro/genesis/women.html.

Pryse, Marjorie. "Introduction." *Selected Stories of Mary E. Wilkins Freeman*. New York: Norton, 1983.

Stanton, Elizabeth Cady, et al., ed. *The Woman's Bible: The Complete Text in Two Volumes*. 1893 and 1895. <http://www.undelete.org/library/library0041.html.

Debra Bernardi (essay date 2005)

SOURCE: Bernardi, Debra. "'The Right to Be Let Alone': Mary Wilkins Freeman and the Right to a 'Private Share.'" In *Our Sisters' Keepers: Nineteenth-Century Benevolence Literature by American Women*, edited by Jill Bergman and Debra Bernardi, pp. 135-56. Tuscaloosa: The University of Alabama Press, 2005.

[*In the following essay, Bernardi discusses the significance of poverty and charity in Freeman's stories, stressing the lack of privacy endured by many of her female characters as they strive to claim a personal space for themselves.*]

"Nobody knew how frugal Betsey Dole's suppers and breakfasts were. . . . She scarcely ate more than her canary bird. . . . Her income was almost infinitesimal" (191). This description of the main character in Mary Wilkins Freeman's story **"A Poetess"** (1891) is only one of many in Freeman's work that highlight her interest in the poor at the end of the nineteenth century. Freeman herself had experienced economic reversals as a young woman, and as Mary Reichardt has pointed out, "the poor house was never far from [her] imagination" (Introduction ix).

Early responses to Freeman's stories of poor women commend the writer for her "accurate portrayal of New England life, especially in its physical and spiri-

tual decline" (Reichardt, "Mary Wilkins Freeman" 77). Later critics have focused on the gendered aspects of Freeman's work. For example, in her well-known study of "local color writers," Josephine Donovan understands Freeman's stories of unmarried, impoverished women to be about the decay of a "woman-centered matriarchal world" (119). In her literary biography, Leah Blatt Glasser argues that Freeman asserts a radical critique of the domestic lives of these women (215). Glasser writes, "At best Freeman's fiction explores and indirectly bemoans the experiences of those [Charlotte Perkins] Gilman described as 'house slaves' in *Women and Economics*" (217). While such contemporary critics understand women's struggles in Freeman's narratives in various ways,[1] most apprehend her as a writer who chronicled the harsh difficulties of women's private lives in New England.

This is not to belittle such private concerns or to suggest that they are in any way "narrow." As Judith Fetterley and Marjorie Pryse have shown in their study of regionalism, writers such as Mary Wilkins Freeman, while focusing on the insignificant, the marginalized, the "tiny" (167; 259), challenge assumptions of dominant discourses, including assumptions about masculinity and femininity and "the projects of nation and empire" (222). Sandra Zagarell also has argued that Freeman's work challenges cultural assumptions about rural life in the nation. I, too, situate Freeman's local concerns within national discourses. Specifically, I read her work as addressing the pressing public issues of poverty and poverty relief at the turn of the century. In this way, Freeman's work moves beyond its undeniable interest in women's personal lives and enters into national debates as to how a growing industrial society should help the poor. I hope such readings will continue to widen our understandings of the significance of Freeman's work. Maybe they would have even helped Sylvia Townsend Warner, who wanted to be more outspoken about Freeman's importance. In a 1966 essay originally published in *The New Yorker*, Warner writes, "If I had had the courage of my convictions downstairs, when everyone was talking about Joyce and Pound and melting pots, I would have said, 'Why don't you think more of Mary Wilkins?'" (120).

Freeman wrote much of her work during the last few decades of the nineteenth century, when poverty was becoming an increasingly visible problem in the United States. The depression of 1873 was the worst in American history. Class segregation became more apparent as factories and businesses grew larger in Northern cities and capitalist agriculture spread in the South. And the new workforce was subject to irregular, seasonal, and often badly paid work. As Michael Katz has noted, the word "tramp" is a good example of the disturbing evidence of poverty; the term entered into widespread use in the 1870s as a label with which to denigrate the soaring numbers of young men roaming the nation in search of jobs (95).

As has been noted elsewhere in this volume, in the face of such obvious economic need, civic leaders turned to the principles of scientific charity to help the poor. Central to the concept of charity organization societies was the need to study the poor within their own homes in order to extend aid. By entering the households of the poor, society agents, it was hoped, would rid the streets of beggars and eliminate indiscriminate aid to people who didn't really need it. For their part, the poor were obliged to welcome agents into their homes if they wanted to eat or keep warm (Katz 70). For poor people in want of the aid of charity organization societies, there was no fundamental right to domestic privacy.

It is within the theories of scientific charity that I situate much of the work of Mary Wilkins Freeman. Freeman needs to be understood as a writer involved with a central political question of the late nineteenth and early twentieth centuries: what rights of privacy does the poor individual have if she or he requires aid? In her major story collections, *A Humble Romance and Other Stories* (1887), *A New England Nun* (1901), and *The Best Stories of Mary E. Wilkins* (1927), and her novel *Pembroke* (1894), frequently considered her finest book-length work, Freeman asserts a fundamental right for her characters: the right for everyone—even those who need charity—to have a private space in which to live the way they choose. But, significantly, Freeman does not call for the right to private property; rather, Freeman's stories acknowledge that in the face of growing poverty, private ownership actually contradicts the right of every individual to her or his "private share." For her, the right to privacy can only be realized if all individuals share what they own.

Many of Freeman's stories of poverty were published contemporaneously with the theories of charity organization societies, which argued against simply giving the poor financial assistance. Josephine Shaw Lowell was one such major theorist of poverty relief, writing *Public Relief and Private Charity* in 1884. Reminiscent of the ideas of American romantic writers, here she asserts the threats of public relief to individual integrity: "people very soon after commencing to receive public aid lose their energy and self-respect" (55). Further, for Lowell there is also the danger that public charity will give the "idle, improvident, and even vicious man . . . the right to live in idleness and vice upon the proceeds of the labor of his industrious and virtuous fellow-citizen" (67).

Rather than this sort of public aid for the poor who want to remain in their own homes (Lowell supported institutionalizing those who couldn't stay at home), Lowell advocates a "Friendly Society," which would regain the intimacy of small-town benevolence. In small towns, people could just "step into the house of a poor friend and give him the help he requires" (97). Lowell writes,

> The only way [to help the poor] is to regain by some means the advantage that the small community had without effort. The same intimate knowledge of those who have to be helped must be got in some way.

> A small association of men and women should be formed and a special territory assigned to each so that he may become thoroughly acquainted with all who live within its limits.

> (98)

By employing this small-town model, a Friendly Society would improve the morals and lifestyles of those they visit; they would, in Lowell's words "raise the standard of decency, cleanliness, providence, and morality" among the poor through "personal influence" (111). That is, the member of the Friendly Society must keep a "constant continued intercourse" among the poor—to show their "high standard" of living to "those who have it not" (111). This would be a relief system that insures moral guidance, discipline, and education for the poor—"a distinct moral and physical improvement on the part of all those who are forced to have recourse to it" (67).

Central to this "improvement" was instruction in creating a proper middle-class home—one that was carefully managed and cleaned. Humphreys Gurteen, in his *Handbook of Charity Organizations,* 1882, asserted his concerns for the private homes of the poor. "It is a fact, a terrible fact," he writes, "that among the poor, in our large cities especially, the idea of 'home' is all but unknown. . . . The effect of pauperism, wherever it exists, is to disintegrate the family, to destroy the home, to sever the social tie, to demoralize the parents, and to send the children forth ignorant of the full meaning of the sacred name of home, ignorant of its sweet memories" (37-38).

In order to help this domestic education, Gurteen, like Lowell, recommended that relief workers become friends to those in need. He writes, "Success in dealing with pauperism can be had through the personal intercourse of the wealthier citizens with the poor at their homes, in other words, the bringing together the extremes of society in a spirit of honest friendship" (113). Gurteen stresses that these "Friendly Visitors" must enter the homes of the poor. "Each cluster of families is committed to the care of an intelligent visitor, who spends a part of his or her leisure time in going in and out among them as a friend. . . . Once let the visitor become the acknowledged friend of a poor family (not the doler out of charity), she would be a power in the home. In a very short time the house would be clean and kept clean for her reception. Her advice would be sought voluntarily on matters of household economy. . . . All avoidable pauperism would soon be a thing of the past" (113; 117). Gurteen approvingly quotes Octavia Hill, an English philanthropic worker, who gave these suggestions to American charity volunteers: "You want to know them—to enter into their lives, their thoughts; to let them enter into some of your brightness, so as to make their lives a littler fuller, a little gladder" (114). The poor were to be permanently uplifted, then, by personal relationships with relief workers who came into their private lives.

Mary Richmond's 1899 handbook for charity workers details how Friendly Visitors should effect change in all matters of private behavior. On one level, she urges that benevolence workers should take some things slowly. For example, "In urging changes in diet upon poor families, it is first necessary to become well acquainted with the families and, even then, to introduce any innovations slowly, one thing at a time" (67). Regarding taste, Richmond writes, "We may find a preference for cheap finery very exasperating, but our own example is far more likely to be followed in the long run if we do not insist on it too much at first" (68). As for addressing the notorious problem of cleanliness, Richmond recommends visitors use "great tact" (69).

Richmond's manual shows the tension between the desire to help the poor, to enter into their homes and literally change their lives, and a regard for their privacy. She cautions against "meddlesomeness" (181), but then details all the aspects of life into which Friendly Visitors should inquire. She writes that if there is a baby in the house, visitors should observe "whether the child is nursed too many months and too often" (78). Visitors should talk to doctors, employers, friends, pastors, former employers; they should investigate the poor's social history (e.g., birthplaces; marriage information; names, addresses, and condition of relatives and friends), medical history, and work history; they should also know the "hopes and plans" of the family (186-88). Richmond explains that the "seemingly inquisitorial features are justified by the fact that it is not made with any purpose of finding people out, but with the sole purpose of finding out how to help them" (189).

Richmond further recommends that visitors take action when the poor are not behaving in appropriate ways. For example, she writes approvingly of a Balti-more visitor who "cured one tired woman of scolding her husband in season and out of season by diverting her attention to other things and by seeking her cooperation in plans for improving the man's habits" (72). Even more aggressively, Richmond suggests that if the husband of a household does not support his family (or moves out), the visitor should have him punished by the courts (52).

Cautioning against "meddlesomeness" while promoting active disruptions of homes, Richmond's work reveals the problems with Friendly Visiting. While visitors were told to get close to the poor, to become their friends, this closeness came at a price: the price of privacy. Linda Gordon notes how child protective workers in the late nineteenth century visited homes of the poor late at night or early in the morning. If they were unable to gain entry, they actually climbed in windows (48).

Such strategies of philanthropic aid became increasingly problematic as the century drew closer to its end and American culture engaged in debates over rights of privacy. As Robert E. Mensel has noted in his essay on photography and privacy rights, up until the last decades of the nineteenth century, the protection of privacy had been a social propriety, a matter of etiquette, rather than law. In an 1890 essay in *Scribner's Magazine,* E. L. Godkin, editor of the *Nation,* writes that privacy was still not yet fully a matter of legal protection: "There still lingers in the minds of the public, even in this country and in England, where the duel has died out, the notion that, though one ought to rely exclusively on the police and the courts for the protection of one's goods and chattels, yet there is certain peculiar fitness in protecting reputation or privacy against libel or intrusion by the cudgel or the horsewhip" (61).

The legal system, however, was beginning to get involved. The earliest case in the United States to claim a "right to privacy," was the case of *DeMay v. Roberts,* heard by the Michigan Supreme Court in 1881. In it, the court found in favor of Alvira Roberts, a poor white woman living in rural Michigan: Roberts sued a doctor who had brought a friend along to watch while she was giving birth (Danielson 1). The court found that the "plaintiff had a legal right to the privacy of her apartment at such a time" (*DeMay v. Roberts* qtd. in Danielson 1). *DeMay* serves as evidence that "the legal maxim and popular proverb that 'a man's house is his castle' had wide application in the nineteenth century" ("Right to Privacy in Nineteenth-Century America" 1894). Other cases addressed sanctions against eavesdroppers and "peeping Toms." As stated in a contemporary *Harvard Law Review* note, "By the late nineteenth-century, the law had erected high walls around the family home by extending criminal penalties for and civil remedies against intrusion by strangers" ("Right to Privacy in Nineteenth-Century America" 1896).

Several prominent court cases in the early 1890s expanded the discussion of privacy beyond the home to other areas of personal rights. A number of cases addressed an individual's right to keep her physical image from being reproduced in media such as photographs and statues. For example, in *Schuyler v. Custis* (1891), the family of deceased philanthropist Mrs. Hamilton Schuyler sought to prevent a statue of their relative from being exhibited. The plaintiffs asserted that exhibition of the statue was an invasion of privacy. The Judge granted the injunction on the grounds that Schuyler was a private character and had a right to privacy that was entitled to protection ("Right," *Green Bag* 1894, 498). Similarly, in the case of *Marion Manola v. Stevens and Myers* (1890), given extensive coverage in the *New York Times,* the complainant alleged that while she was playing in a Broadway theater she was photographed without consent and therefore sought an injunction against use of the photo. The judge issued a preliminary injunction (Warren and Brandeis 195). Further, letters began to be understood as private documents, which retained certain rights for the sender. Public opinion began to regard the "'sanctity of the mails' in the same way it esteemed the inviolability of the home" (Right to Privacy in Nineteenth-Century America 1899).

While the courts were beginning to act on an expanded right of privacy, most historians assert that the modern concept of a legal right to privacy first came into popular thought with an 1890 article by Samuel Warren and Louis Brandeis, which claims that privacy rights have moved beyond material issues. While they note that the "common law has always recognized a man's house as his castle, impregnable" (220), they argue that these rights should be extended into intangible realms such as "the right to enjoy life;—the right to be let alone" (193). Legal protection of property for them includes "every form of possession—intangible as well as tangible" (193), including the "right to an inviolate personality" (211). They continue: "The design of the law must be . . . to protect all persons, whatsoever; their position or station, from having matters they may properly prefer to keep private, made public against their will" (214-15). Spurring their concerns were the threats to privacy brought about through "recent inventions and business methods" (Warren and Brandeis 195): these included sensational journalism and, as Mensel has detailed, the easy-to-use Kodak cameras.[2]

The Warren and Brandeis article and the court cases surrounding it inspired a series of debates in the popular press, which rehearsed before the American public the expanding privileges of Americans in this arena. For example, in 1891, the journal the *Green Bag* reprints the judicial opinion of the *Schuyler* case and parts of the Warren and Brandeis article. Again in 1894 the *Green Bag* notes that rights to privacy were being extended "beyond the body of the individual to his reputation. Thoughts, emotions, and sensations have acquired legal recognition in certain respects" ("The Right to Privacy" 498). The *Atlantic Monthly* questions this expansion of rights, bringing up issues of freedom of the press, asking if the press should not have the right "to describe the peculiarities, depravities, and deformities of [an individual] and of his household" ("The Right to Be Let Alone" 429). An 1896 article in the *North American Review* affirms the newly established rights: "I believe that the definite establishment of this right of privacy is at this time of the greatest possible moment; for, without such a right and easy enforcement of it, civilization must deteriorate" (Speed 64). The essay quotes Judge Cooley, who asserted, like Warren and Brandeis, that the right of privacy is the "right to be let alone" (64). The *North American Review* continues, "As man comes into the world alone, goes out of it alone, and is alone accountable for his life, so may he be presumed to have by the law of his nature full right to live alone when, to what extent, and as long as he pleases. . . . The modesty of good and common nature sets between him and the modern inquisition the protecting shield of that knightly order whose motto has been aptly termed the eleventh commandment—'Mind your own business'" (65).[3]

With Friendly Visitors inserting themselves into the lives of the poor, these expanding rights to privacy could not help but affect perceptions of charity relief. By 1896, even Josephine Shaw Lowell came to understand that relief work infringed on personal lives. She argues that there is no "excuse for trespassing upon the privacy of other human beings, for trying to learn facts in their lives which they prefer should not be known" (qtd. in Bremner 82). In his early-twentieth-century novel, *Crimes of Charity* (1917), Konrad Bercovici tells the tale of a relief worker horrified by his inability to help the poor within the structure of a charity organization. Among the many troubling aspects of charity that the narrator details is the violation of privacy. The narrator states, "One of the greatest injustices to the poor is the right that the charities arrogate to themselves to visit them whenever they choose. Once you depend upon charity all privacy is gone. The sanctity of the home is destroyed. It is as though the family were living in some one else's—in the charity's—home. The investigator comes into the house unannounced any time of the day or night, questions anybody she finds in the house, criticises the meals, the curtains" (101). In his introduction to Bercovici's book, John Reed echoes a similar sentiment: "[Charity] is made the excuse for lowering the recipients' standard of living, of depriving them of privacy and independence" (n.p.).

Similarly, while the motivations behind the photography of Jacob Riis may have been charitable, the poor also understood his efforts as intrusions into their private lives. A supporter of Josephine Shaw Lowell, Riis went to Boston to "see the humane way in which [she] was dealing with their homeless there" (252). He took his well-known photographs of the urban poor for his exposé *How the Other Half Lives* in 1890, just as the court cases about an individual's control over his or her image were garnering public interest. When Riis photographed his subjects, with the intent to expose the horrors of poverty and generate social action on behalf of the indigent, he rarely asked permission to enter the homes he was photographing. He notes in his 1901 memoir *The Making of an American,* "Our party carried terror wherever it went. The spectacle of strange men invading a house in the midnight hours armed with [flash] pistols which they shot off recklessly was hardly reassuring, however sugary our speech, and it was not to be wondered at if the tenants bolted through windows and down fire-escapes wherever we went. . . . Months after I found our visits hanging over a Stanton Street block like a nightmare" (268-69). At times the intended subjects of the photos pelted Riis and his associates with rocks. In an analysis of one of the Riis' photos, "A Black and Tan Dive on Broome Street," historian David Shi has noted how one of the women in the photo turns her back to the camera and drapes a shawl over her head in order to protect her privacy (192). Inherent, then, in Riis's philanthropic work was an invasive action that engendered resistance in those it was attempting to aid.

A *Harper's* story by George Madden Martin at the turn of the century, titled, significantly, "Rights of Man," takes up the issue of charitable invasions of privacy and efforts of the poor to resist these invasions. In Martin's story, Old Jim avoids the middle-class female charity worker who is "upliftin' us by idols [ideals]" (415). Miss Sidney brings in a woman to clean Jim's cabin, along with pictures for his walls and flowers for his table, violating both his space and his taste—his basic "right to be let alone." Jim complains, "Now she keeps comin' over all times I ain't lookin' for her, to see if I'm keepin' things straight. An' I ask you if that sort of uneasiness ain't upsettin' to any man?" (416). Disturbed by Miss Sidney's attempts to change him, Jim prefers the handouts of Mrs. Carter because "she don't have no strings tied to what she gives" (420). Finally, Miss Sidney goes too

far when she tries to force Jim to take a bath. He escapes the disruption of his life in the isolated comfort of a root cellar, asserting that "Ev'ey man's jestified to his quiet place" (421).

Within these discussions of charity and privacy, Freeman's stories become more than tales about individual women in New England. Even two of her best-known stories take on particular political significance when read as part of the debates surrounding privacy. For example, when Mrs. Penn demands her own house in **"The Revolt of 'Mother'"** (1891), eventually commandeering her husband's barn, the act can be apprehended as a woman's right to her "own castle, impregnable" (to reiterate Warren and Brandeis's words). In **"A New England Nun"** (1891), Louisa is so reluctant to share her fastidious home with her long-time suitor that she eventually refuses to marry, again underscoring a woman's right to a space of her own.

While these two stories do not specifically address the poor, the same interest in privacy pervades Freeman's stories about the impoverished. However, Freeman is not just interested in the privacy of material space. She also reveals the needs for the more intangible rights of private life that Warren and Brandeis talked about—for example, in their words, the rights of all people "whatsoever; their position or station, from having matters which they may properly prefer to keep private, made public against their will" (214-15). Freeman's tales specifically address an individual's need to keep her financial situation from public comment. In the 1894 novel *Pembroke,* Sylvia Crane makes every effort to keep her poverty a secret. When she must ask for help from the town selectmen, "she stole around to the back door of Squire Payne's house by night, she conducted herself as if it were a guilty intrigue, all to keep her poverty hid as long as may be" (207). Similarly in **"A Gala Dress"** (1891), the elderly Babcock sisters go to extraordinary lengths to hide their penury: They "guarded nothing more jealously than the privacy of their meals. . . . It was certain that the old women regarded intrusion at their meals as an insult, but it was doubtful if they would not have done so had their table been set out with all the luxuries of the season instead of scanty bread and butter and no sauce" (148-49). The entire story revolves around the efforts the two women make to avoid letting others in town know they only have one good dress between them.

Melissa McFarland Pennell argues that Freeman's stories about the poor show the shame of poverty that is derived from a Calvinist tradition, which considers indigence as divine judgment ("Liberating Will" 207-8). But Freeman's stories are not just about the cultural shame of poverty; they are also about the legal rights of the poor. While her stories argue for the right of each man *and* woman to have her or his own "quiet place"—going beyond Old Jim's assertion of man's rights in the *Harper's* story—she also asserts an inextricable connection between the private space of the home and the "intangible" rights of privacy—including, in Warren and Brandeis's words, "the right to enjoy life;—the right to be let alone." And while her stories represent the invasive problems of charity relief, they also picture the possibility that the poor might demand their rights and resist such invasions.

Freeman's 1903 story **"The Last Gift"** (originally appearing in the same issue of *Harper's* as Martin's "Rights of Man") traces the problems with benevolence from the perspective of the charity giver. It tells the story of the minister Robinson Carnes, whose "unselfish love for his kind . . . laudable in itself, had become in time like a flower run wild until it was a weed. His love of giving amounted to a pure and innocent but unruly passion. It had at one time assumed such proportions that it barely escaped being recognized as actual mania. As it was, people, even those who had benefited by his reckless generosity, spoke of him as a mild idiot" (103). His congregation, uncomfortable with his outlandish generosity, eventually asks him to leave their church.

However, while Carnes's obsessions create problems for himself, Freeman is actually tracing the distinction between his honest (if obsessive) generosity and the charity of typical relief workers. Carnes is contrasted with another minister who says "that one's first duty was to oneself, and unjustified giving was pauperizing to the giver and the recipient" (106). Echoing the concerns of Josephine Shaw Lowell, who feared aid could be detrimental to the poor, this other minister is cold and unkind to those who need assistance.

When he meets a destitute family on the road, Carnes knows that he, himself, has nothing to share with the family (he's given away everything he owns). As he considers how to best extend aid, Carnes considers the typical methods of philanthropy: "It became evident to him in a flash what the outside view of the situation would be: that the only course for a man of ordinary sense and reason was to . . . notify the authorities . . . that it was his duty for the sake of the helpless children [in the poor family] to have them cared for by force, if there was no other way" (112). But he realizes immediately the problems that would arise if he were to extend this kind of benevolence: "It seemed an infringement upon all the poor souls had left in the world—their individual freedom" (113). Eventually Carnes finds some money and aids the family financially while leaving their privacy intact.

In **"Cinnamon Roses"** (1887), Freeman looks at tangible privacy rights from the perspective of the indigent. Elsie's brother and sister-in-law take her in when poverty forces her to leave her home. The result is the discomfort of losing her own space, even though her brother "gave her a front chamber in his large, square white house, and furnished it with her own things to make it seem like home" (171). He can't imagine why she "shouldn't be as happy as a queen" (171). But Elsie sits "forlornly at her chamber window, her elbows on the still, her sharp chin in her hands, for many an hour" staring at her old house (172). The narrator continues, "It is sad work looking at things that were once one's own, when they have not been given away for love, and one still wants them" (172).

In her story **"A Mistaken Charity"** (1887), Freeman continues her commentary on the needs of the poor for their "castle, impregnable," but goes further, showing how the poor can resist efforts to deprive them of their rights, both the tangible rights of the private home and the more intangible rights of taste, personality, and private happiness. The story opens with two old, poor sisters living on the edges of material ruin. Their home is so rickety that "rain and snow had filtered through its roof, mosses had grown over it, worms had eaten it, and birds built their nests under its eaves" (43). Harriet and Charlotte rely on the kindness of neighbors for survival. The story reveals that such generosity—like that of Miss Sidney in George Martin's story "Rights of Man"—often ignores the personality and tastes of the recipients: the sisters' neighbor Mrs. Simonds "was a smart, energetic person, bent on doing good, and she did a great deal. To be sure, she always did it in her own way. If she chose to give hot doughnuts, she gave hot doughnuts; it made not the slightest difference to her if the recipients of her charity would infinitely have preferred ginger cookies" (49). As such, Mrs. Simonds's efforts affect the intangible privacy rights—"the right to enjoy life"—that Warren and Brandeis articulate.

Eventually Mrs. Simonds's charitable efforts impinge on the tangible space of the home. She arranges for the sisters to live in the "Old Ladies' Home" in a neighboring city. Freeman emphasizes the fact that this home is "not an almshouse under another name . . . it was comfortable, and in some respects luxurious. . . . The fare was of a finer, more delicate variety than [the sisters] had been accustomed to" (50-51). However, the widow who runs the home encourages a particular style of dress—white lace caps and delicate neckerchiefs—further invading the corporeal lives of the sisters, as well as their rights to their own tastes, their own "inviolable personalit[ies]." The sisters are miserable. "O Lord, Harriet," Charlotte exclaims, "let us go home. I can't stay here no ways in this world. I don't like their vittles, an' I don't like to wear a cap; I want to go home and do different" (52).

Similar to Riis's photographic subjects, the sisters resist these charitable efforts. They decide to leave the Old Ladies' Home: "And they went. With a grim humor Harriet hung the new white lace caps with which she and Charlotte had been so pestered, one on each post at the head of the bedstead, so they would meet the eyes of the first person who opened the door" (53). Their act is a bold move to regain "their private share of the great wealth of nature" (45). Once again in their own rickety home they are happy, finally allowed their own home, their own tastes, their own personality, their "right to be let alone."[4]

While frequently understood as a challenge to ideas of gendered separate spheres (Glasser 49; Fetterley and Pryse 14), Freeman's tale **"A Church Mouse"** (1891) also argues for a right to private space and private life. Hetty finds herself homeless after the people she's lived with move away. She curtains off a small living space for herself within the local church, where she assumes the duties of the sexton. This move disquiets the congregation, who are uncomfortable with the idea of a woman sexton, not to mention the idea of a woman "pitching her tent in the Lord's house" (282). Thus the community finds a home for her with a neighbor.

But, despite her neediness, Hetty, like Charlotte and Harriet, resists charity that impinges on her personal rights of space, taste, and happiness. "I don't like Susan Radway," she says about the woman with whom she is expected to live, "hain't never liked her, and I ain't goin' to live with her" (285). When the congregation attempts to force her to leave, she locks herself in the church and asserts her rights to live alone and maintain her own "inviolate personality": Hetty says, "[Mis Radway's] used to havin' her own way, and I've been livin' all my life with them that was, an' I've had to fight to keep a footin' on the earth, an' now I'm gittin' too old for't" (290). For Hetty, keeping a "footin' on the earth" means being able to have her own way in her own private space. "I'd 'nough sight rather be alone than have comp'ny, any day" (285), she says. In the end, the townspeople allow her to remain in her little space in the church, and she is fully satisfied when left "with no one to molest or disturb her" (291).

For Freeman, then, every individual—poor as well as moneyed—has a right to her private space and happiness. But, significantly Freeman's stories do not assert the rights of privately owned property. Instead, Freeman's stories assert that each person can only have her "private share" if people share their property, allowing the poor and propertyless the chance to have a space of their own. For Freeman, space needs to be understood as communal; paradoxically, it is the communal nature of space that allows for the privacy that is a fundamental right of the American citizen.

This aspect of Freeman's work can be understood within other theories of poverty relief circulating during the period. For example, as mentioned elsewhere in this book, in 1877 Henry George began his study *Progress and Poverty*, which argued that the unequal distribution of wealth could only be solved by making land common property. As George puts it, "The widespreading social evils which everywhere oppress men amid an advancing civilization spring from a great primary wrong—the appropriation, as the exclusive property of some men, of the land on which and from which all must live" (340). For George, "Wherever there is light to guide us, we may everywhere see that in their first perceptions all peoples have recognized the common ownership in land, and that private property in land is an usurpation, a creation of force and fraud. . . . The equal right of all men to the use of land is as clear as their equal right to breathe the air" (338). While there is no certainty that Freeman read George, her stories show a remarkable parallel to his ideas. For her, this "right of all men" is a right of all men *and* women to claim their private share of communal property. In this reading, Freeman fits a characteristic of regionalism noted by Fetterley and Pryse. They contend that regionalism disrupts the connection between place and property and can be seen to represent a world prior to capitalism (277). Or, as I would put it, Freeman attempts to reimagine property ownership in a noncapitalist way in order to locate private space for all.

Private ownership is often the root of the problem for Freeman's characters. In **"Cinnamon Roses,"** Elsie must leave her beloved home because a new owner forecloses on it. While Nancy is allowed to remain in her family home in **"Old Lady Pingree"** (1887), "down in the depths of her proud old heart rankled the knowledge that an outsider owned the home of her fathers" (153).

In the face of problems of private ownership, Freeman's stories assert a vision of communal property as a way to help the poor and maintain their legal rights of privacy. In **"A Mistaken Charity,"** the sisters return to a home that they do not actually own. A wealthy man "held a mortgage on the little house in which they had been born and lived all their lives." But he gave them "the use of it, rent and interest free" (42). Freeman asserts that private ownership of the house is ludicrous; it is a part of nature and should be open to the sisters as a tree would be to the insects and birds that inhabit it. The actual owner, the story states, "might as well have taken credit to himself for not charging a squirrel for his tenement in some old decaying tree in the woods. . . . There was as much fitness in a mortgage on the little house . . . as there would have been on a rotten old apple-tree" (42; 44). The propertied in the community, then, by renouncing their rights to personal ownership allow the sisters their "private share" (45). When the sisters return to their own space from the Old Ladies' Home, they are joyous. Harriet draws her key "triumphantly from her pocket" (56), and "everything [in the house] was just as they had left it" (56).

Similarly, in **"A Church Mouse,"** Hetty struggles with her community to be allowed to stay in the meeting house. In an act that Fetterley and Pryse understand as female resistance to male authority (250-51), two women "defiantly" allow her to stay (**"Church Mouse"** 290) and even provide her with a little room in the church rather than the curtained-off area she had arranged for herself. The end of the story underscores the privacy that this sharing of community space can provide: "Established in that small, lofty room, with her bed and her stove, with gifts of a rocking-chair and a table, and goodly store of food, with no one to molest or disturb her, she had nothing to wish for on earth" (291).

In **"Old Lady Pingree,"** Nancy Pingree may not own her home, but when a widow and her daughter need a place to stay she gives them their own room upstairs and refuses any money for it. Here, in another example of how communal property might work, Jenny and her mother get material aid and are able to have private space for themselves.

These stories set out Freeman's ideals for poverty relief: shared space can mean private space. However, this is not to say that she has no other visions of aid to the poor. In several of her stories, poor women gain economic relief through marriage. For example, in *Pembroke,* Sylvia's long-recalcitrant suitor, Richard, witnesses her trip to the poorhouse. He is moved to save her by finally marrying her. In **"Cinnamon Roses,"** Elsie is rescued from her unhappy life in her brother's house when the man who owns her old home declares he has long loved her. He marries her and consequently she returns to her home, which her new husband shares with her.

But while marriage may alleviate poverty, will it allow a woman the privacy that is her right? Marriage in Freeman's stories is often a troubling institution that negates privacy. Remember, for example, that Louisa

in **"A New England Nun"** releases her suitor in order to retain her home. The result is that she feels "like a queen who, after fearing lest her domain be wrested away from her, sees it firmly insured in her possession" (124). In a similar manner, Mrs. Penn must rebel against her husband in **"The Revolt of 'Mother'"** in order to get her own house.

So it would seem that marriage may not be a satisfactory solution to the problems of female poverty and privacy. While Glasser reads the marriages in *Pembroke* as a celebration and acknowledgment of feminine values (124), I agree with Deborah Lambert that the marriages in *Pembroke* happen only when women are at their weakest. "In *Pembroke,*" Lambert asserts, "men choose to marry when their women have suffered a significant loss of power or status" (204). Unlike the resisting poor in **"A Church Mouse"** and **"A Mistaken Charity,"** who find happiness in resisting benevolence, Sylvia succumbs to Richard's aid when she is at her weakest—on her way to the poorhouse. Marriage (and the resulting relief from poverty) is not a triumph here; rather, it is a sign of defeat.

Elsie does marry William Havers at the end of **"Cinnamon Roses,"** but here, too, there is something unsettling about this method of benevolence. Near the end of the story, Havers, the owner of Elsie's house, proclaims that he has been in love with her his entire life, and will happily give her old home back to her. But Elsie says she is uncomfortable with this act of charity. Then in the very next sentence, she offers to marry William. While her poverty and the lack of privacy she experienced living in her brother's home are alleviated by marriage, the union seems only a way to hold on to the house she loves—perhaps more than she loves the man who comes with it. In fact, Elsie shows more emotion over the house than she ever does over William. When forced to leave her home at the opening of the story, she is "disfigured by grief" (168); by contrast the only words she says to William before their wedding are, "Well, it don't seem as if thar would be much sense in my gittin' married now, anyway" (179). He talks her into it, but as a method of benevolence, marriage again seems unsatisfactory.

Certainly Freeman longed for privacy in her own married life. Living with her family until the age of thirty, she found that being single "granted her the liberty of solitude" (Glasser 10). Later supervising the construction of a new house during her marriage, she writes in a 1907 letter, "Sometimes I wish I could have a little toy house, in which I could do just as I please, cook a meal if I wanted to, and fuss around generally. . . . If I had my little toy house nobody could say anything" (qtd. in Meese 165). Here Freeman again shows the relationship between private space (the "toy house") and the "right to be let alone" ("I could do just as I please").

I need to note that two stories of Freeman's appear as jarring contradictions to her interest in privacy for the poor. In **"A Solitary"** (1891), Stephen is a complete misanthrope until the poor, ill Nicholas turns up on his doorstep, determined to avoid the poorhouse to which his sister intends to send him. Nicholas finds paradise on a cot in Stephen's home: the "poor cot in the warm room seemed to him like a couch under the balsam-dropping cedars of Lebanon, and all at once he felt that divine rest which comes from leaning upon the will of another" (233). In **"An Independent Thinker"** (1897), Esther wants Lavinia Dodge to come live with her. At first Lavinia resists (because Esther works on the Sabbath—an activity of which Lavinia heartily disapproves). But finally Lavinia agrees to the move when, after three months in the almshouse, her rheumatism intensifies so that she becomes nearly helpless. In both cases, then, privacy does not seem an issue in benevolence. But the difference here, perhaps, is that these poor are ill. Freeman makes this point in **"An Independent Thinker."** Esther realizes that Lavinia's illness means she needs constant aid. When she hears about how debilitating the rheumatism has become, Esther "dropped her knitting and stared radiantly" (310). Her neighbor even comments, "Why Esther Gay, you look real tickled cause she's sick" (310). Freeman asserts strongly the need for the poor to have their own spaces and their own lives; only when stricken by illness does the undeniable need for help supersede the need for a private home.

In most of Freeman's work, then, private space and the intangible rights to one's own tastes and pleasure—that is, the "right to be let alone"—are not just luxuries property owners can afford; they are necessary to survival—in Hetty's words, necessary to "keep a footin' on this earth." In this way Freeman's stories are remarkably current. In the face of twenty-first-century technology, the likes of which Warren and Brandeis never imagined, the rights of privacy have become all the more endangered for everyone, poor or not. As John Gilliom notes in his book on the poor and privacy rights,

> Over the past few decades, there have been dramatic expansions in the quality, the breadth, and the intensity of programs that use new generations of technology for gathering, storing, sharing, and using information. Indeed, if we add up the frequently overlapping profiles encompassing medical records, academic and professional performance, credit ratings, consumer behavior, insurance records, driving records, law enforcement data, welfare agency information, child support en-

forcement programs, Internet communications, and other information systems, it is safe to say that much of the significant activity of our lives is now subject to systematic observation and analysis.

(2)

Gilliom reminds us that this observation and analysis—through technology today as through Friendly Visiting in the nineteenth century—is an expression and an instrument of power. Echoing Michel Foucault's analysis of the Panopticon, he writes, "Surveillance of human behavior is in place to control human behavior" (3).

The poor have long borne an especially heavy burden of surveillance and lost privacy. Gilliom's work notes that "from the sixteenth-century surveys of the poor to the comprehensive computer-based Client Information Systems that most states now use, welfare administration has been inextricably a process of struggling to 'know' the poor; to measure, depict, and examine them. . . . Scientific charity . . . gradually produce[d] . . . the contemporary regimes of welfare surveillance" (22-24). But Gilliom, like Freeman, also notes that there are ways to resist this power. In his study of welfare mothers in Appalachian Ohio in the 1990s, he finds that these women are engaged in "practices of every resistance and evasion to beat, as best they could the powers of surveillance" (6).

Mary Wilkins Freeman's stories reveal underpinnings of current fears about privacy—especially the vulnerability of the poor to those who would help them at the expense of their fundamental rights of happiness. Rather than scientific charity and Friendly Visiting, Freeman's preferred method of benevolence employs a vision of communal property, which allows the poor to maintain privacy in all its diverse nineteenth-century forms. Through her focus on New England women's private lives, Freeman examines the local repercussions of major issues of her day. In these early-twenty-first-century days of John Ashcroft, the Patriot Act, and Homeland Security, the significance of her work remains.

Notes

1. For example, in her introduction to *The Selected Stories of Mary E. Wilkins Freeman,* Marjorie Pryse argues that Freeman emphasizes stigmatized women who often find strength and power in their social exclusion (x-xi). In one essay, Melissa McFarland Pennell traces Freeman's relationship to Nathaniel Hawthorne, arguing that Freeman depicts women "who choose to stand on their own, who accept their marginal lives and meager finances as a means of preserving an uncompromised self" ("Unfortunate Fall" 196). Elsewhere,

Pennell reads Freeman's work as an examination of female choices; she asserts that Freeman's characters, with all their difficulties, gain a "degree of freedom to reject social codes and expectations" ("Liberating Will" 208). Susan Allen Toth similarly sees Freeman's characters as struggling "with courageous spirit towards self-expression and independence" (123).

2. Mary Wilkins Freeman, too, had her personal suspicions about public use of images of herself. Sandra Zagarell claims that Freeman resisted editors' and publishers' requests for recent photographs. However, like many authors, she found she could "neither prevent the reuse of images already circulating nor the creation of new ones" (xiv).

3. These weren't the only popular writings on such issues. For instance, the *New York Times* also entered the debates surrounding the right of privacy in 1902, discussing a New York State case and the "amazing opinion" of Judge Parker of the Court of Appeals that the "right to privacy is not a right which in the state of New York anybody is bound to respect" ("The Right of Privacy," August 23, 1902, 8). The *Times* argues that if such a law does not exist, "then the decent people will say that it is high time that there is such a law" ("The Right of Privacy" 8).

4. Glasser argues that this story reflects the fear that aging can undermine female autonomy (209-10). I can't disagree with her point, though all these stories when apprehended together suggest that Freeman was as interested in the autonomy of the poor as she was in the independence of elders.

Works Cited

Bercovici, Konrad. *Crimes of Charity*. New York: Knopf, 1917.

Bremner, Robert. *American Philanthropy*. Chicago: U of Chicago P, 1960.

Danielson, Caroline. "The Gender of Privacy and the Embodied Self: Examining the Origins of the Right of Privacy in U.S. Law." *Feminist Studies* 25.2 (Summer 1999): 311-44.

Donovan, Josephine. *New England Local Color Literature: A Woman's Tradition*. New York: Frederick Ungar, 1983.

Fetterley, Judith, and Marjorie Pryse. *Writing out of Place: Regionalism, Women, and American Literary Culture*. Urbana: U of Illinois P, 2003.

Freeman, Mary E. Wilkins. "A Church Mouse." 1891. Pryse 273-92.

———. "Cinnamon Roses." *A Humble Romance and Other Stories*. New York: Harper, 1887. 164-79.

———. "A Gala Dress." 1891. Pryse 145-61.

———. "An Independent Thinker." *A Humble Romance and Other Stories*. New York: Harper, 1887. 296-314.

———. "The Last Gift." 1903. *The Best Stories of Mary E. Wilkins*. Ed. Henry Wysham Lanier. New York: Harper, 1927. 102-19.

———. "A Mistaken Charity." 1887. Pryse 41-56.

———. "A New England Nun." 1891. Pryse 109-25.

———. "Old Lady Pingree." *A Humble Romance and Other Stories*. New York: Harper, 1887. 148-63.

———. *Pembroke*. 1894. New Haven: College and University P, 1971.

———. "A Poetess." 1891. Pryse 180-99.

———. "The Revolt of 'Mother.'" 1891. Pryse 293-313.

———. "A Solitary." 1891. Pryse 218-36.

George, Henry. *Progress and Poverty*. 1879. New York: Robert Schalkenbach Foundation, 1955.

Gilliom, John. *Overseers of the Poor: Surveillance, Resistance, and the Limits of Privacy*. Chicago: U of Chicago P, 2001.

Glasser, Leah Blatt. *In a Closet Hidden: The Life and Work of Mary E. Wilkins Freeman*. Amherst: U of Massachusetts P, 1996.

Godkin, E. L. "The Rights of the Citizen to His Own Reputation." *Scribner's Magazine* (July 1890): 58-67.

Gordon, Linda. *Heroes of Their Own Lives: The Politics and History of Family Violence, Boston 1800-1960*. New York: Penguin, 1989.

Gurteen, Humphreys. *A Handbook of Charity Organizations*. Buffalo: Published by the author, 1882.

Katz, Michael B. *In the Shadow of the Poorhouse: A Social History of Welfare in America*. New York: Basic Books, 1986.

Lambert, Deborah G. "Rereading Mary Wilkins Freeman: Autonomy and Sexuality in *Pembroke*." Marchalonis 197-206.

Lowell, Josephine Shaw. *Public Relief and Private Charity*. 1884. New York: Arno Press, 1971.

Marchalonis, Shirley, ed. *Critical Essays on Mary Wilkins Freeman*. Boston: G. K. Hall, 1991.

Martin, George Madden. "Rights of Man." *Harper's Monthly Magazine* 106.633 (February 1903): 416-33.

Meese, Elizabeth. "Signs of Undecidability: Reconsidering the Stories of Mary Wilkins Freeman." Marchalonis 157-76.

Mensel, Robert E. "'Kodakers Lying in Wait': Amateur Photography and the Right of Privacy in New York, 1855-1915." *American Quarterly* 43.1 (March 1991): 24-45.

Pennell, Melissa McFarland. "The Liberating Will: Freedom of Choice in the Fiction of Mary Wilkins Freeman." Marchalonis 207-21.

———. "The Unfortunate Fall." In *Hawthorne and Women: Engendering and Expanding the Hawthorne Tradition.* Ed. John L. Idol, Jr., and Melinda M. Ponder. Amherst: U of Massachusetts P, 1999. 191-203.

Pryse, Marjorie. Introduction. Pryse vii-xix.

———, ed. *Selected Stories of Mary E. Wilkins Freeman.* New York: Norton, 1983.

Reed, John. Introduction. *Crimes of Charity.* By Konrad Bercovici. New York: Knopf, 1917.

Reichardt, Mary R. Introduction. *A Mary Wilkins Freeman Reader.* Ed. Mary R. Reichardt. Lincoln: U of Nebraska P, 1997.

———. "Mary Wilkins Freeman: One Hundred Years of Criticism." 1987. Marchalonis 73-89.

Richmond, Mary E. *Friendly Visiting among the Poor: A Handbook for Charity Workers.* 1899. Montclair: Patterson Smith, 1969.

"The Right of Privacy." *New York Times,* August 3, 1902, 8.

"The Right to Be Let Alone." *Atlantic Monthly* 67.401 (March 1891): 428-29.

"The Right to Privacy." *Green Bag* 3 (1891): 524-26.

"The Right to Privacy." *Green Bag* 6 (1894): 498-501.

"The Right to Privacy in Nineteenth Century America." *Harvard Law Review* 94 (June 1981): 1892-910.

Riis, Jacob. A. *The Making of an American.* New York: Macmillan, 1901.

Shi, David E. *Facing Facts: Realism in American Thought and Culture, 1850-1920.* New York: Oxford UP, 1995.

Speed, John Gilmer. "The Right of Privacy." *North American Review* 163 (1896): 64-74.

Toth, Susan Allen. "Defiant Light: A Positive View of Mary Wilkins Freeman." 1973. Marchalonis 123-31.

Warner, Sylvia Townsend. "Item, One Empty House." 1966. Marchalonis 118-31.

Warren, Samuel D., and Louis D. Brandeis. "The Right to Privacy." *Harvard Law Review* 4.5 (December 15, 1890): 193-220.

Zagarell, Sandra. Introduction. *Mary E. Wilkins Freeman: A New England Nun and Other Stories.* Ed. Sandra Zagarell. New York: Penguin, 2000.

Michael Tritt (essay date fall 2006)

SOURCE: Tritt, Michael. "Selling a Birthright for Pottage: Mary Freeman's Allusion to Genesis in 'A New England Nun.'" *ANQ* 19, no. 4 (fall 2006): 34-41.

[*In the following essay, Tritt investigates the reference to the biblical Esau at the conclusion of "A New England Nun," emphasizing the dissonance that results from juxtaposing this figure with Louisa.*]

Mary Wilkins Freeman's **"A New England Nun"** is the most widely analyzed—and controversial—of her tales. Indeed, even a cursory review of the criticism devoted to it will turn up a daunting number and diversity of interpretations.[1] Despite the long-standing and extensive discussion of the story, basic questions remain: Is Louisa a model of independence, strength, and will—a woman who manages, in a repressive nineteenth-century patriarchal society, to preserve autonomy and happiness for herself? Or is she, quite simply, neurotic, fearful, and weak? Many facets of the story resonate in confusing directions, stimulating—and complicating—interpretation. One such dimension of the tale, only narrowly discussed by critics to date, is the allusion in the final paragraph of the story to Esau's selling of his birthright to Jacob for some pottage. Criticism has neglected, in particular, a most intriguing—and pervasive—ironic dissonance in the association of Louisa and Esau. Such incongruity complements—and builds on—patterns established earlier in the story, contributing to the humor of Louisa's portrayal. The allusion also serves to contrast, pointedly, inequitable conceptions of male and female birthright. Like the story itself, however, the allusion ultimately resists closure.

The concluding paragraph of the tale portrays Louisa at peace. Apparently, she feels not the slightest sense of regret in anticipation of the solitary and insular lifestyle that she has chosen to follow, despite rejecting the conventional nineteenth-century role of wife and mother. In the process of describing Louisa's situation and feelings, the narrator alludes to an incident in the Old Testament: "If Louisa Ellis had sold her birthright she did not know it, the taste of the pottage was so delicious, and had been her sole satisfaction for so long" (Freeman 17).[2] This passage invokes the specific event in which Esau, the eldest son of Isaac, relinquishes his birthright to Jacob in exchange for some stew, in Genesis 25.29-33. By alluding to the scene, Freeman activates (particularly, but not exclusively) dissonant associations between the characters and their immediate and more general situations and contexts.

There is, of course, an obvious difference in the sex of the characters, heightened by the extent to which each is characterized by exaggerated and stereotypical gender traits. Esau is described as "a cunning hunter, a man of the field" (Gen. 25.29). He is seen to represent the active, physical side of man (*Etz Hayim* 146; Sarna, *JPS Commentary* 89), and as "an outdoorsman [. . .] rough but virile." He is a man of action, "turned to, if there was anything that [. . .] wanted do[ing]" (*Interpreter's Bible,* hereafter *IB* 666). Furthermore, because of his ruddy appearance, his hairiness, and his boorish behavior—illustrated, for example, in the way he "gulps" down Jacob's pottage, indifferently leaving the scene once satiated—Esau is often conceived as a primitive throwback. One biblical commentator even associates Esau with "a certain degree of danger" (Berlin and Brettler 53).[3]

Louisa, by contrast, offers a portrait of stereotypical, even extreme domesticity.[4] She lives a reclusive life limited to her house and its immediate environs. She spends much of her time indoors in domestic pursuits: sewing, preparing and eating her meals, and maintaining the pristine order and cleanliness of her abode. At times, she strays to her garden, in which she distills essences and raises vegetables. Louisa's activity is singularly circumscribed, whereas Esau is conceived to be a "man of the field" and "of open spaces" (Speiser 196). She does little that requires physical strength and vigor. Far from being engaged in—or having any connection to—active hunting, Louisa is a vegetarian, eating a fare of "little cakes," "light white biscuits," "sugared currants," a "leaf or two of lettuce" (Freeman 2). She eats "daintily," "in a delicate pecking way" (Freeman 2). Indeed, she is exceedingly reserved and fastidious about her person, her house, and her behavior.

The association of Louisa with Esau in the last paragraph of the story is one of a series of associations; the allusion aptly follows the narrator's description of Louisa's dog, Caesar, as well as her canary. As with Esau, the dog and the canary are male. Furthermore, the name "Caesar" connotes a male figure radically incongruous (much in the manner of the allusion to Esau) with the lifestyle and temperament of the dog and especially its owner. The repeated association of Louisa, whose activities and lifestyle are domestic in the extreme, to males[5] (particularly to Caesar and Esau) adds to the irony and humor of Louisa's portrait.[6] Here is an example of the way in which Freeman "manages to blend images and ideas, in ways that not only make the ideas for which the images stand concrete, but also make the formulations seem less serious and more playful" (Camfield 8).

Such humorous dissonance artfully echoes similar contrasts in the characterization of Joe and Louisa. Like Esau, Joe is a man associated with the outdoors. When we are introduced to him, he has just come inside

from a day spent haying in the hot sun. Indeed, he has lived for years in the wilds of Australia making his fortune, while Louisa's purview has become more and more limited to her home and garden. The author's portrayal of the couple plays humorously with gender stereotypes: Joe is the proverbial bear in Louisa's china shop. Joe Dagget's "coarse masculine presence," his "bolt upright" carriage, his "large face," "heavy" feet and step, "loud voice," and "awkward movements" are skillfully contrasted with Louisa's "gently erect" carriage, her "smoother and fairer face," her "slender hands," her "pretty manner" and "soft grace" (Freeman 3-5). Thus the reference to Esau builds on, complements, and intensifies comical stereotyping in the tale.[7]

Not only does the allusion contribute to the humor of the tale, but it underscores, in several significant ways, gender inequality as well. "Birthright," which is defined as "the rights, privileges or possessions to which one is entitled by birth" (*OED* 876), is conceived as gender-specific in a patriarchal society, whether the biblical one of Esau, or of nineteenth-century New England.

As a male living during the biblical era, Esau, is, for example, entitled to wed multiple times. In fact, he ends up marrying three local Hittite women, then later, recognizing that his parents are upset by the marriages,[8] betroths Ishmael's daughter Mahalath. As a man living during this period, his decision to marry repeatedly is his male prerogative. Louisa, on the other hand, as a woman living in nineteenth-century New England, is duty-bound to one man, as she would have been even in biblical times. She needs to fulfill her youthful pledge of marriage, "patiently and unquestionably," no matter how many years should intervene between the engagement and the actual event (Freeman 6). Even though she and Joe "had not seen each other and had seldom exchanged letters" in fourteen years, she would "never dream [. . .] of the possibility of marrying someone else," even if Joe "stayed fifty years [. . .] or *had never come home at all*" (6; emphasis added).

Louisa's fiancé, as a man of the nineteenth century, is bound to monogamy in a way that Esau is not. Yet Joe is privileged with a type of unilateral control over their relationship. There is, for instance, no sense in which Louisa and her fiancé decide their future together. Joe simply "announced" his "determination" to head off to Australia, assuring her that "[i]t won't be for long" (Freeman 7). Louisa simply "listened and assented with sweet serenity" (6-7). Joe manifests a cavalier attitude about her having to wait for him. For, when he decides to return, he feels no need to tell her of his intentions and cannot even imagine that her feelings might have changed since his departure. Furthermore, even though as a result of the drawn-out engagement and the death of her relatives in the interim, "there was no room for anyone" (7) in Louisa's life, Joe's adventurous lifestyle in Australia has had no such parallel effect. He seems to have little trouble making room for Lily Dyer when the opportunity presents itself.

As the first-born male in his family, Esau was entitled to a special birthright. In the biblical world, the elder son was privileged to a double portion of the patrimony, as well as "a seat of honor among his brothers" as next in line to assume the role of paterfamilias, a position of ultimate familial influence (Plaut 175). The position implied spiritual blessings as well. The expectation was that such an individual would become the family's "priestly representative to guide it in the ways of God" (*IB* 667). For Esau, then, birthright had much to do with the assumption of preeminent familial status and its accompanying authority and power. This dramatically (and ironically) differs from the secondary status allotted to women in Louisa's New England setting.

Louisa's birthright, culturally conceived, is her privilege/duty/right to devote herself to her husband, children, and family. Popular women's magazines of the day commonly expressed this idea: "Wife is said to be the most agreeable name in nature. It is the glory of woman that she was sent into the world to live for others rather than for herself, to live, yes and to die for them" (Juster 130). Louisa forgoes her culturally conceived birthright and the way of life it offers, replacing it (over time) with a "straight and unswerving" solitary existence (Freeman 7). This lifestyle is Louisa's "delicious" pottage, which has become "to her as the birthright itself" (17). It may well be that Louisa's solitary existence is so "delicious" to her, precisely because her actual New England birthright, (as a woman), requires that she "live [. . .] and die for others."

Esau's life is intimately connected to the lineage of the patriarchs, whose history is seminally important to the Bible story, and to the nation of Israel. His choices (with regard to his birthright, his marriages, and the like) result in the end of his participation in the lineage of the patriarchs; none of the tribes of Israel issue from him. But he still leaves a legacy through the generations. Singularly unlike Louisa, Esau has a number of children, and they in turn have children of their own. Genesis 36 is devoted to detailing the "generations of Esau" and describes him as the father of a people, the Edomites. By contrast, Louisa, a "simple" New England spinster, living a narrowly circumscribed home life in the countryside, appears to occupy no distinctive role in her community, or in history; her choices are lived out on a much less significant and smaller scale. Opportunities to play a particularly dramatic part in history, or to be acknowledged as having played such a role, were few for women like Louisa, whose birthright limited them by and large to the domestic sphere.

One might consider other, more dissonant associations and patterns activated by the allusion, though it is difficult to pursue them to a definitive conclusion. Some critics, for example, view Louisa as "heroic" (Pryse 159), and as "exercis[ing] her will in finding the life that is right for her, even if it means following an unconventional path" (Pennell 212). Yet such a perspective simply does not resonate with the experience of—and commonly accepted attitude toward—Esau. Neither does the opposed view of her withdrawal from the world and rejection of life, her fear of sexuality, of mortality and change, or her allowing "the needs of others to dictate to her fate" (Cutter 185). Bible commentators typically chastise Esau (who, as a male and seminal figure in the development of a people, appears to have so much to lose) for relinquishing his birthright indifferently for a bowl of pottage. J. H. Hertz, for example, writes,

> The spiritual inheritance of Abraham, which would normally have passed into the hands of Esau, was not worth to him as much as a dish of pottage. Like the true sensualist, this fickle and impulsive hunter readily sacrifices to the gratification of the moment that which to a man of nobler build could be of transcendent worth.
>
> (94)

Louisa cannot be similarly conceived as "fickle" or "impulsive." On the contrary, she demonstrates an incredible constancy, waiting for Joe for fifteen years. And far from impulsive, she appears to do nothing rash, living according to a rigid sense of order ("carefully" is used three times in the text to describe her actions) developed over the years of her solitude. Furthermore, Esau is commonly characterized as a man who yielded to his "primitive instincts" (Sarna, *JPS* 182), whereas Louisa is frequently conceived as repressing such instincts.

In the New Testament, in Romans 6.14, Esau figures centrally in debates concerning the "right of Christians to the blessings promised by God to the descendants of Isaac" (Metzger and Coogan 192). How might this be applied to Louisa and her situation? Is there an implication that the protagonist, whatever her choice of lifestyle, has a similar right to whatever blessings were accorded to a more conventional personality, lifestyle, and beliefs? Esau has a counterpart, his brother Jacob, in the biblical tale. Frequently, the personalities of the two brothers are contrasted; some commentators even see them as representative halves of the self as well as representing different (rival) nations (*Etz Hayim* 146). Does Louisa, as Esau, have a counterpart "sister"? Perhaps it is Lily Dyer, to whom Louisa has sold her birthright. But can we go further with the pattern of the personalities and their representativeness? In later biblical books, there are contiguous allusions to the story of Esau. Malachi 1.1-2.7 recalls the rivalry between Jacob and Esau to relate the strife between their descendants. Furthermore, Esau's spurning of his birthright for food is given a counterpart in the descendants of Jacob who scorn God through impious treatment of food for sacrifice (*Etz Hayim* 162). Can—or should—we attempt to link any of this to Louisa and **"A New England Nun"**? How can we delimit (and so control) the resonance of the allusion?

Bringing closure to such associations and intertextual patterns is exceedingly problematic. "In the labyrinth of writing," writes Laszlo Gefin, "literary allusions point to a possible exit from the maze; but the exit, when opened, turns out to be just another corridor winding endlessly on and on" (448). Yet even if there is no exit from the winding and endless corridors of associations, even if allusions link texts together in "unfixed, unpredictable intertextual patterns" (Ben-Porat 127), such allusions do enrich the work under consideration. In the instance of **"A New England Nun,"** the relation of Louisa to Esau activates a spectrum of (especially) dissonant association, in the process complementing and deepening the humor of the tale, sharpening the humorous portrait of Louisa's extreme domesticity, highlighting inequitable gender-specific conceptions of birthright and consequent lifestyle decisions.

Notes

1. For a succinct summary of some of the issues of the debate, see Glasser, particularly 33 and 238-39.

2. The conditional sense of the sentence that activates Freeman's allusion has drawn widely divergent readings. Joseph Csicsila suggests that the "if" is only "seemingly ambiguous" (11), whereas Meese (165) and Cutter (185), by contrast, argue that the passage is decidedly unclear. There is certainly nothing conditional, however, about Louisa's choice to forgo marriage to Joe. The effect of the conditional article may well be to cast doubt on whether such a marriage is in fact, despite the era's culturally defined roles for women, to be regarded as Louisa's true birthright.

3. Although Esau is commonly viewed as a most unsympathetic individual, some commentators feel that "there was a plus side to his ledger" (*IB* 666;

Spero 246). Esau has been described as a "warm-hearted man" (*IB* 666), a trait that is especially manifest in his relationship to his father and in later dealings with his brother in Genesis 33. Furthermore, some commentators see him as a type of "natural man," "open and straightforward [. . .] without a trace of guile, with emotions [. . .] strong and spontaneous" (Comay 102), someone who lives "in the realm of the senses, a man of the natural flux with all of its diversity, mutability, temporality, finitude, contingency, and relativity" (Inbinder 90). The portraits of Esau in the Bible, and Louisa in "A New England Nun," lend themselves similarly to richly complex, multifaceted interpretation.

4. Susan K. Harris suggests that "Louisa's feminine virtues are so exaggerated as to be parodic," creating a "situational paradox—the fact that she is criticized even when she brilliantly performs her domestic role because she implicitly shuns the community in order to do so" (31).

5. This association is complemented at the end of the paragraph by the reference to the "busy harvest of men" (Freeman 17).

6. Although early critics such as W. Dean Howells noted humor as a significant feature of Freeman's work, discussion of such humor has only recently gained impetus. See, for example, essays by Camfield, Cherciu, and Harris. According to Plaut, some interpreters of the scene in Genesis similarly view the tale, and more particularly the actions of Esau, with humor (175).

7. Shirley Marchalonis has isolated incongruity as a particularly significant source of humor in Freeman's tales: "perception of incongruity, the forced joining of things that do not belong together, is the trigger that creates the shock of the unexpected" (Marchalonis, "Sharp-Edged Humor" 231). Such incongruity is manifestly present in the series of juxtapositions cleverly invoked in the tale.

8. An intriguing, though tenuous, resonance may be noted here. Esau, to please his parents, marries Megalith; Louisa's original engagement to Joe seems, at least in part, influenced by the wishes of her mother.

Works Cited

Ben-Porat, Ziva. "The Poetics of Literary Allusion." *PTL* 1 (1976): 105-28.

Berlin, Adele, and Marc Zvi Brettler, eds. *The Jewish Study Bible.* New York: Oxford UP, 2004.

Camfield, Gregg. "'I never saw anything at once so pathetic and funny': Humor in the Stories of Mary Wilkins

Freeman." *American Transcendental Quarterly* 14.2 (2000): 215-32.

Cherciu, Lucia. "'A Veritable Guest to Her Own Self': Mary Wilkins Freeman's Humorous Short Stories." *Journal of the Short Story in English* 35 (2000): 21-41.

Comay, Joan. *Who's Who in the Old Testament.* New York: Oxford, 1993.

Csicsila, Joseph. "Louisa Ellis and the Unpardonable Sin: Alienation from the Community of Human Experience as Theme in Mary Wilkins Freeman's 'A New England Nun.'" *American Literary Realism* 30.3 (1998): 1-13.

Cutter, Martha J. "Mary E. Wilkins Freeman's Two New England Nuns." *Colby Quarterly* 26.4 (1990): 213-25. Rpt. in Reichardt 179-95.

Etz Hayim. Philadelphia: Jewish Publication Society, 2001.

Fienberg, Lorne. "Mary E. Wilkins Freeman's 'Soft Diurnal Commotion': Women's Work and Strategies of Containment." *New England Quarterly* 62.4 (1989): 483-504.

Freeman, Mary E. Wilkins. "A New England Nun." *A New England Nun and Other Stories.* 1891. Ridgewood: Gregg, 1967. 1-17.

Gefin, Laszlo. "False Exits: The Literary Allusion in Modern Fiction." *Papers in Language and Literature* 20.4 (1984): 431-52.

Glasser, Leah Blatt. *In a Closet Hidden: The Life and Work of Mary E. Wilkins Freeman.* Amherst: U of Massachusetts P, 1996.

Harris, Susan K. "Mary E. Wilkins Freeman's 'A New England Nun' and the Dilemma of the Woman Artist." *Studies in American Humor* 3.9 (2002): 27-38.

Hertz, J. H., ed. *The Pentateuch and Haftorahs.* London: Soncino, 1968.

Inbinder, Gary. "Jacob and Esau." *Humanitas* 16 (2003): 90-96.

The Interpreter's Bible. Vol. 1. New York: Abington, 1952.

Juster, Norman. *So Sweet to Labor: Rural Women in America 1865-1895.* New York: Viking, 1979.

Marchalonis, Shirley, ed. *Critical Essays on Mary Wilkins Freeman.* Boston: Hall, 1991.

———. "The Sharp-edged Humor of Mary Wilkins Freeman: *The Jamesons* and Other Stories." Marchalonis, *Critical Essays.* Boston: Hall, 1991. 222-34.

Meese, Elizabeth. "Signs of Undecideability: Reconsidering the Stories of Mary Wilkins Freeman." Marchalonis, *Critical Essays.* Boston: Hall, 1991. 157-76.

Metzger, Bruce M., and Michael D. Coogan, eds. *The Oxford Companion to the Bible.* New York: Oxford UP, 1973.

Pennell, Melissa McFarland. "The Liberating Will: Freedom of Choice in the Fiction of Mary Wilkins Freeman." Marchalonis, *Critical Essays.* Boston: Hall, 1991. 207-21.

Plaut, W. Gunther. *Bereshit=Genesis: Commentary.* New York: Union of American Hebrew Congregations, 1974.

Pryse, Marjorie. "An Uncloistered 'New England Nun.'" *Studies in Short Fiction* 20.4 (1983): 289-95.

Reichardt, Mary R. *Mary Wilkins Freeman: A Study of the Short Fiction.* New York: Twayne, 1997.

Sarna, Nahum M. *The JPS Torah Commentary: Genesis.* Philadelphia: Jewish Publication Society, 2003.

———. *Understanding Genesis.* New York: Schocken, 1970.

Speiser, E. A., ed. *The Anchor Bible: Genesis.* New York: Doubleday, 1964.

Spero, Shubert. "Jacob and Esau: The Relationship Reconsidered." *Jewish Bible Quarterly* 32.4 (2004): 245-50.

James Bucky Carter (essay date 2006)

SOURCE: Carter, James Bucky. "Princes, Beasts, or Royal Pains: Men and Masculinity in the Revisionist Fairy Tales of Mary E. Wilkins Freeman." *Marvels & Tales* 20, no. 1 (2006): 30-46.

[*In the following essay, Carter analyzes the subversion of traditional fairy-tale motifs in Freeman's short fiction by concentrating on her male characters and the complicated notions of masculinity that they embody.*]

Most scholars of American literature consider the works of Mary E. Wilkins Freeman (1852-1930) as falling in either or both of the two following literary traditions: regional local color realism and proto-feminist writings. Among her most noteworthy middle-twentieth-century critics are Edward Foster and Perry Westbrook, who situate her solidly in the local color regionalist convention. Freeman's many later-twentieth-century scholars, such as Marjorie Pryse, Mary R. Reichardt, and Leah Blatt Glasser, spurred by the growing feminist movement in literature and theory, later recontextualized Freeman in the proto-feminist camp of nineteenth-century women writers while otherwise staying the course that Foster and Westbrook set forth.

If Freeman could see how her legacy has unfolded, surely she would be disappointed not to be considered among the great American writers. She was an immensely popular and prolific author in the United States and the United Kingdom, publishing in the many *Harper* magazines and penning twenty-two volumes of short stories and fourteen novels, among other writings (Kendrick 4). On more than one occasion she has been considered on a par with the likes of Hawthorne and Twain.

However, it appears that if Freeman is to gain more repute in literary studies, scholars must continue to find new niches for her work. Again she must be recontextualized. Fortunately for her enduring legacy, her work is prevalent with fairy and folk themes that, to date, scholars have largely failed to recognize, lending yet another venue from which her vast literary talent and merit may be examined and revealing new and important insights into her opus.

Freeman has left clues to her fairy and folk influence for those with a quick eye. Accounts from friends and family say she was quick to read fairy stories throughout her life (Foster 15, 43n195). Her late short story **"The Prism"** (1901) is particularly telling: Diantha Fielding, a girl of twelve, lies in an open field looking at "dancing colors" through a teardrop prism from a period lamp. In the prism, Diantha sees dancing fairies. Years later, Robert Black takes Diantha into the woods and asks her to marry him. She accepts and shares the secret of her prism: "What do you see, Robert," she asks (63), but he sees only myriad colors and responds, "what else should I see?" She continues, "You have read—about fairies—and such things. . . . Ever since I was a child, I have seen, or thought so . . . beautiful little people moving and dancing in the broken light across the fields" (64). Robert is appalled, and Diantha, rejected, buries the prism. "It's all right, little girl . . . but don't let such fancies dwell in your brain. This is a plain, common world, and it won't do," Robert consoles (65). Diantha never speaks of fairies again and serves faithfully as Robert's wife from then on.

Like Diantha, Freeman too seems stuck in the authoritative whims of scholars who have appropriated her for their own limited interpretations, but the fairy-tale discourse in her work is one of Freeman's own making, and it ought to be recognized as one that helps her step out of her critics' staid preconceptions of her work. An unearthing of Freeman's prism visions reveals more than colors plain and common.

Freeman's use of fantastical imagery and fairy-tale elements in her children's poetry and prose illustrates that early in her career she certainly did not always seek realism as a hallmark of her work. Karl J. Terryberry says that many of Freeman's children's stories "resemble the folk or fairy tales that were written by the Brothers Grimm or Perrault. . . . Usually, these stories of fantasy are set in fictional lands that are ruled by good kings and queens who help young girls find husbands who are of royal descent" (21). Although they have failed to garner the same scrutiny in terms of folk and fairy genres, Freeman's adult works continue to draw from the copious fairy-tale themes that she so often employed in her children's canon. If scholars are to consider her a realist, they must also recognize the streaks of fairyland that run deep within her adult stories, even within those considered exemplary realist or local color texts. Freeman is often not working with a stoic realism but within the boundaries of magical realism, even in stories that Foster and Westbrook consider paragons of stoic New Englander realism.

Further, Freeman has been overlooked as an important revisionist of fairy tales. She revises and revamps classic fairy-tale tropes in her adult works, as have such twentieth-century women writers as Tanith Lee, Angela Carter, Olga Broumas, and Jane Yolen. Whereas Freeman may only draw from fairy tales rather than always directly rewrite them, she still joins a strong cast of women writers whose work shows clear evidence of fairy tales as influence. Jeannette Evelyn Green, for example, in her dissertation on women authors working from 1940 to 1980, notes that "Elizabeth Bowen, Angela Carter, Maxine Hong Kingston, Toni Morrison, Joyce Carol Oates, Anne Sexton, and Eudora Welty have revised traditional folktales, aware of how they could be updated, told from different perspectives, or illustrate different morals." The works of these writers, Green argues, "demonstrate how these folktale and literary fairy tale revisions subtly critique traditional notions" (1). Freeman's absent revisions do the same, though, commenting on gender roles and sexual politics. Sarah Orne Jewett, Freeman's contemporary and friend, has had her story "A White Heron" hailed by scholar Josephine Donovan as "a kind of reverse fairy tale in which 'Cinderella' rejects the handsome prince in order to preserve her woodland sanctuary" (152). Freeman wrote to Jewett in August 1889, "I never wrote any story equal to your 'White Heron.' I dont [*sic*] think I ever read a short story . . . that so appealed to me" (Kendrick 97). Although Freeman has stated in many other instances that she does "not approve of this mystical vein that I am apt to slide into" (Kendrick 96), her admiration of "A White Heron" and the considerable connections among her adult and children's works belie such commentary. She also notes in a December 1889 letter to Jewett, in reference to their inspiration for writing, that "I suppose it seems to you as it does to me that everything you have heard, seen, or done, since you opened your eyes to the world, is coming back to you sooner or later, to go into stories" (Kendrick 99). For Freeman, this "everything" includes fairy tales, which she read often as a girl and continued to read as an adult.

This essay seeks to place Freeman within the tradition of women fairy-tale revisionists. However, rather than focus on the multitudes of female characters within her works and how she revises their roles, I will enlarge the scholarly debate concerning her place as a fairy-tale revisionist by examining her male characters and the specific tropes they often replicate. These figures have received very little critical attention throughout the history of Freeman studies. Whereas her women characters do revise fairy-tale tropes, many times suggesting that women are not helpless princesses in need of saving but are more than capable of taking care of themselves, as is the case with Louisa Ellis in **"A New England Nun"** (1891) or Sarah Penn in **"The Revolt of 'Mother'"** (1891), Freeman's male characters also help the author revise fairy-tale motifs, so they deserve special attention.

Further, this examination illustrates Freeman's familiarity with the complex range of notions of masculinity during her time, an aspect of her work that has also gone largely unexplored. In terms of masculinity, Glassar comments that Freeman "does not avoid the reality of male power" (214). Indeed, masculinity *and* femininity were in flux throughout Freeman's career. Women were either accepting or railing against "the cult of domesticity." Scholars often consider masculinity during this time to be simply the opposite of cult femininity—a lack of being submissive, chaste, and domesticated—yet recent work has explored maleness in more depth. Kenneth B. Kidd, for example, in *Making American Boys: Boyology and the Feral Tale,* explores a more diverse range of concepts of masculinity emerging in the early twentieth century. Among the tropes of maleness identified in his work are the bad boy (Kidd goes so far as to consider bad boy literature a subgenre of realism and another instance of masculinity defined as that which rails against the above notion of femininity [51]), the farmer boy/avuncular boy worker, and the wolf-boy, all of whom may, upon adulthood, transform into self-reliant men, moral men, or wolf-men. In terms of Kidd's work, a thorough survey of Freeman's writings illustrates an awareness of her era's complex notions of masculinity, notions that scholars have taken almost a hundred years to recognize and study seriously. That Freeman explores various masculinities with fairy-tale nuance is striking but not surprising. Kidd makes it clear that fairy tales and boyology are inextricably combined as mythos

(especially within the wolf-boy trope). This essay will demonstrate that Freeman has an acute awareness of this as well.

In *Gender Instruction in the Tales for Children by Mary E. Wilkins Freeman,* Terryberry discusses how males are treated in Freeman's adolescent stories. He states that "the men of Freeman's fiction are heavily influenced by the exertion of feminine power demonstrated by the women that dominate this rural landscape" (93). Indeed, in Freeman's New England, males were a depleted resource thanks to the Civil War and industrialization, and they had to reassert their identity in a society that had become, population-wise, overly feminine. "Young men, in Freeman's fiction, search for strong women to operate the household and raise the children. . . . Middle-aged men are overwhelmed by the influence of femininity on their culture and begin to show signs of becoming more effeminate," Terryberry continues (93). He also asserts that women in Freeman's fiction force men out of patriarchy and into matriarchy (94). This may generally hold true in the children's literature, but in the adult literature there are *some* characters that put up more resistance, thereby disavowing Terryberry's statement as a universal claim.

Most often in Freeman's revised fairy tales or in those stories that clearly draw upon folk or fairy elements, men fall into three categories. They are princes, beasts, or royal pains. If they are princes, which I define as goodly, nice, or simply worth the while of the women with whom they associate (what Kidd might consider the good boy, or the avuncular boy worker grown-up), they usually must experience some sort of transformation of attitude, appearance, or reputation. These men do indeed, at times, find themselves willing to come into the matriarchy. In essence, these men may appear to be beasts before showing their true colors. If they are truly beasts, on the other hand, they tend to stay beasts (this too is in step with Kidd's work, which illustrates how rare it is for wolf-boys to escape becoming wolf-men). In Terryberry's terms, these are men who do not or *will not* fit the mold desired by the women characters. They are dangerous, deadly, and destructive. If they are royal pains, weak-willed, or a general nuisance, Freeman often finds ways to disregard them or to have her female figures overpower them. These men experience a "hostile takeover" from the powerful, feminine locus of power. As Westbrook states, "In Miss Wilkins' stories, New England villages were the habitat of termagants whose ferocious wills reduced their luck-less men folk to a state of whimpering subserviency" (60). Of the three categories, royal pains receive the brunt of the willpower from Freeman's reborn Cinderellas, Rapunzels, and Little Red Riding Hoods.

Royal pains, though perhaps never before named as such, are the one category of male characters that critics have given some attention to in their analyses. For example, Glasser deals effectively with these men in her book *In a Closet Hidden,* in which she explores "the intense level of protest evident in Freeman's descriptions of conflict between men and women" (214). Doris J. Turkes has also recently discussed these types of characters in a sociological interpretation of Freeman's elder women in her "Must Age Equal Failure? Sociology Looks at Mary Wilkins Freeman's Old Women." Turkes argues that the success Freeman's elderly women have in fending off assertions of masculine power relates directly to how they handle eight psychological life crises. Among those older women who, she argues, have chosen vigor over defeat through their dealing with those crises, in effect allowing them to cast off their royal pains, are Esther Gray of **"An Independent Thinker"** (1887), Hetty Fifield of **"A Church Mouse"** (1891), and Christmas Jenny the story that bears her name (1891).

Other stories in which royal pains assert their authority over women include **"A Poetess"** (1891) and **"A Village Singer"** (1891). Stories in which men do not directly oppose women but take actions that nonetheless interfere with women's desired lifestyles include **"A New England Nun"** (1891), wherein Joe Daggett is intent on keeping his promise to marry his betrothed, Louisa Ellis, who, in turn, is intent on living her own life. Since other scholars have adequately traced the paths of these assorted royal pains, this study will focus on the male characters in the other two, less-studied categories: princes and beasts.

Many of Freeman's men are honorable, charitable, loving human beings who sometimes play the role of the quintessential fairy-tale prince. Even when these men do not become princely saviors, they are rarely treated with the scrutiny that many of Freeman's lesser men receive. Or, at least the scrutiny ends once they are seen for who they truly are. Like the prince in Jeanne-Marie Leprince de Beaumont's "Beauty and the Beast," Freeman's best men, her Prince Charmings, at first seem beastly and gain little respect among the powerful, queenly women of her fiction. Ultimately, however, they experience a change that shows their true nature; they become good boys and subsequently good men.

This theme of positive transformation is evident in Freeman's children's fiction, as is readily seen in **"The Dickey Boy."** First published in *St. Nicholas* children's magazine in 1891 and later collected in *Young Lucretia and Other Stories* (1892), this tale sees Dickey, recently orphaned, change from suspicious outsider to accepted son. The boy experiences a trans-formation of reputation that, along with the changing views of the womenfolk who take him in, eventually gains him new status as one of Freeman's princes. At first Dickey appears to be one of Kidd's bad boys, but as the story progresses he grows out of it.

The story begins with Mrs. Rose and Mrs. Elvira Grayson worrying about Mrs. Rose's son Willy, who has been away digging up sassafras roots for longer than they would have liked. The boy finally appears and is followed by Mrs. Rose's brother, Hiram, who arrives in an open buggy pulled by a white horse. With him is a small, white-haired boy (195). Hiram asks if the two women need the boy to help them with chores, but once they learn he is a Dickey, they are immediately suspicious: "'One of those Dickeys?' Mrs. Rose said 'Dickeys,' as if it were a synonym for 'outcasts' or 'rascals'" (196). Hiram has the boy run off to play with Willy as he tries to convince the ladies that the boy is better than his reputation, but they are not easily convinced. Mrs. Rose believes "his folks are nothin' but a pack of thieves" (197), but Hiram finally persuades her to give the boy a trial run.

Hiram's method of persuasion is essential to the story's overall theme of transformation. Hiram uses feminine authority to help place the boy in his sister's home. Even when men or boy characters are truly good, Freeman judges them in the context of feminine approval before they can be recognized as such. Three times Hiram explains to the women that the boy's former neighbor, Mis' Ruggles, has utmost faith in the boy. He states, "Mis' Ruggles . . . says he's a real nice little fellow" (198), and he elaborates that she "says she'd trust him with anything" (198) and "he was perfectly safe" (199). This feminine approval finally wins the boy entrance into the new home, and Hiram leaves him there with a few clothes and a small box, which is nailed shut. Although Dickey, as he comes to be called, is accepted into the home, he is far from trusted. Mrs. Rose is convinced that he has a pistol in his nailed box, and the women immediately hide their valuables, such as silver spoons and assorted jewelry.

Dickey, however, has already proved them wrong. While Mrs. Rose and Elvira were examining his mysterious box, he had joined Willy in cleaning sassafras roots, proving himself to be a good helper. As time passes, "finally suspicion was allayed if not destroyed" (203), but there is still a rift among the household. Dickey sees Mrs. Rose as "almost impressive as a queen," and her son "seemed to him like a small prince" (204). Likewise, Dickey seemed to them "like an animal of another species" (205). Further, they still will not leave the boy by himself and continue to guard their valuables, even though the boy has earned some acceptance in the family. This is most notably seen when Hiram gives Dickey a sweet-apple tree from his nearby orchard, a gift the boy cares for religiously.

Finally, the women have what they believe to be a reason for all their suspicions. One morning a silver spoon comes up missing, and they immediately suspect Dickey, who denies all charges to no avail. The women simply will not trust him: "It won't make it any easier for you, holding out this way," states the adamant Mrs. Rose (209). Deeply hurt by the allegations, Dickey runs away, and the two are sure he does so "to escape a whipping" (210). Mrs. Rose then decides the spoon must be in the boy's nailed box, but when it is pried open, the impetus for transformation in the story begins. Inside, the women find the boy's mother's calico apron and his father's pipe. Sentiment overwhelms the women, who see in these items the true soul of the odd lad. The moment of truth is played out for greater drama when Willy enters with a muddy silver spoon, which he explains he used for digging in his garden days ago but forgot to return. At this moment the women are transformed. They no longer see Dickey as a "rascal" but as a caring, loving boy. They immediately search for him but do not find him until the next morning, by which time a May storm has blown through. Hiram finally finds the boy, "like a little drenched, storm-beaten bird," clinging to some branches of his sweet-apple tree; "he had flown to his one solitary possession for a refuge" (214). He is then nursed back to health, and *his* transformation is completed when he becomes as much a son to Mrs. Rose as her own Willy. She "kissed him just as she kissed Willy"; Elvira lets him hold her golden watch, and Hiram even gives the boy a silver dollar (214). Freeman drives the theme of transformation home in the last line: "She [Rose] had made room for him in her staunch, narrow New England heart" (215).

Despite its artistry and the important themes that carry over into Freeman's adult canon, **"The Dickey Boy"** has received little critical attention. Henry Steele Commager of *St. Nicholas* deemed it so exemplary that he placed it in *The St. Nicholas Anthology* (c. 1948), a book that May Lamberton Becker, in her introduction, calls "a living memory" (xvii), but few (including Terryberry), if any, have touched on it since. Freeman wrote the story when she was already established as an adult writer, and it actually postdated her short-story collection *A Humble Romance and Other Stories* (1887) by four years, illustrating that Freeman was exploring themes of transformation in her children's work alongside her adult fiction. In terms of fairy tales, the story shows a rascal or beastly young man transformed into a perfect son. He, too, has become a prince to the queen in the end of the story, his transformation at the hands of her feminine authority

yielding total acceptance into a new family. As Jack Zipes says in his preface to *Don't Bet on the Prince,* a collection of feminist fairy-tale retellings, women fairy-tale revisionists "challenge conventional views of gender, socialization, and sex roles, but they also map out an alternative aesthetic terrain for the fairy tale as genre to open up new horizons for readers and writers alike" (xi). By obviously situating Dickey's transformation of reputation within a feminine discourse and beholden to feminine approval, Freeman challenges cultural notions of what makes a good man (or boy) good and reminds her reading audience of the palpable—if not many times downplayed—power of women in terms of the development of such good men. Dickey, though obviously a good child from the beginning, is recognized as such only when the women in his life accept his goodness as fact. Essentially, the women have symbolically *made* Dickey a good boy through their recognition, just as women have always had a large part in "making men" through their roles as mothers.

Dickey is not alone in his transformation. Many other male characters in Freeman's fiction experience similar changes from that which is, or appears to be, foreign, frightening, or ill-spirited to that which, in fairy-tale terms, makes them seem more princely. Sometimes the "prince" imagery is subtly present within these tales of transformation, as it is in **"The Dickey Boy"**; in others it is more obvious.

For example, Adoniram Penn is a man who also undergoes a transformation after feminine authority asserts itself. At first glance, many might see Adoniram, who has put off fulfilling a promise to his wife to build a new house for forty years, and who has recently begun to build a new barn instead, as a candidate for being a royal pain. However, his wife's strong assertions of her own will and desires for her family, which are manifested when she moves her family into the new barn, reveal to readers another side of Sarah Penn's husband, one that causes readers to see him in a new, transformed light. Freeman says of him, once he realizes the magnitude of his ignorance, "Adoniram was like a fortress whose walls had no active resistance, and went down the instant the right besieging tools were used. 'Why, mother,' he said, hoarsely, 'I had no idee you was so set on't as all this comes to'" (**"The Revolt of 'Mother'"** 468). The war imagery established through such words as "fortress," "besieging tools," and "triumph" evokes scenes of medieval conquests, or fairy or folk tales dealing with knights, castles, dragons, and conquests. Elizabeth Meese informs us that early Freeman scholar Edward Foster called the story a "comic folktale" (172). Further, it is not too much of a stretch to suggest that Sarah is like one of the women in a nursery rhyme with which Freeman undoubtedly would have been familiar, given her inclination to the genre throughout her life. Sarah Penn, in her cluttered, small home that has rapidly outgrown her family's need, is very much like the old woman who lives in a shoe; in Freeman's revised tale, however, she knows exactly *what* to do, and Adoniram transforms once he moves out of masculine stubbornness (or downright obliviousness) and into a more feminine mode of awareness and sensitivity to others' feelings.

Further credence to seeing this otherwise seemingly realist story as fantastical or uncanny comes from Freeman herself, who later in her life, in an article in the *Saturday Evening Post* (8 Dec. 1917), said it is "the story by which I consider myself lamentably best known" (Marchalonis 65). Freeman's "discomfort" about the story may have something to do with the claim that "all fiction ought to be true"; she says of Sarah's story, it "is not in the least" (65). Freeman continues, "There never was in New England a woman like Mother. . . . New England women of that period coincided with their husbands in thinking" (65-66). Freeman clearly sees the story as something other than base realism. It is also a distinct possibility, though, that she is doing what many authors have done in similar situations: toying with her reading audience. After all, Freeman had published hundreds of poems and short stories saturated in the fantastical in children's magazines for more than thirty years when she wrote the above retraction, and she had only fourteen years before published a collection of uncanny tales in **The Wind in the Rose-Bush, and Other Stories of the Supernatural** (1903). Having experienced a decline in her popularity as early as 1900, Freeman's retraction could be a subtle criticism of those who in 1917 were already espousing reductive readings of her astoundingly diverse body of work.

The transformation motif so dominant in many fairy tales is undeniably present in this controversial work. Joseph R. McElrath Jr. has stated of Sarah that she is "the real thing, a female who successfully revolts against and liberates herself from a familial situation of pernicious male dominance" (132), but by the story's end, Adoniram has transformed into a warm, loving, even sentimental figure whom we are led to believe will no longer thwart Sarah's attempts to make a new home for her family. "Pernicious" seems a strong choice of words considering Adoniram's transformation in the face of his wife's assertion of feminine authority. Adoniram appears to be truly touched by his wife's actions. Hence, Adoniram, on the surface a royal pain, has, at the end, the possibility of becoming one of Freeman's prince figures.

Freeman introduces more definite prince figures in other stories. George Arnold in **"Calla-Lilies and Hannah"** (1891), for example, is the quintessential "hero to the rescue," saving his lover even as he transforms both their reputations and their social status. However, George is unique among Freeman's men in that he defines his own terms for his transformation and is actually the driving force behind Hannah's as well. Having been accused of stealing money from local religious leader John Arnold years ago, Hannah Redman is the town outcast. She has been dismissed from her church congregation and is the subject of much gossip. As with Dickey, no one trusts her. However, when her betrothed, George, returns to town after an extended absence, he is shocked to learn of Hannah's circumstances and reputation. George informs her that he took the money from his father (John Arnold), and, further, that it was his own money to begin with. He then selflessly proves himself an honest man and a sincere suitor: "I'll clear you, dear. Every soul in town shall know just what you are" (116). At the next church service, directly after the two are wed, he makes good on his promise. As "his yellow, curled head towered up bravely," George states to the congregation, including his father, "This lady beside me, who is now my wife, has been accused of theft from my father. She had born [*sic*] what she has had to bear from you all to shield me" (119). Then, the two leave for her house to gather her things. George has also promised to "take [her] away from the lot of them, out of the reach of their tongues" (116). His confession transforms Hannah's reputation, and his, too, is changed now that he no longer has a secret to hide.

George thus reveals himself to be a perfect prince figure in this story, which does not so much revise folk and fairy tropes as it embraces them in a modern incarnation. Unlike the case with many of Freeman's other princes, George does not have his transformation come about through feminine authority, as Terryberry speaks of it, but from his own strong sense of morality. To be sure, his masculine authority with Hannah and the congregation is what leads to Hannah's transformation. Faye Wright Hardiman, in her dissertation "Mary Wilkins Freeman's Men: Finding Masculinity in a Women's World," asserts that Freeman's work often "reflects the literary images of masculinity that emerged over the century, supporting and challenging the historical models that shaped masculinity" (1). **"Calla-Lilies and Hannah"** shows that whereas Freeman is adroit at revising those folk notions of damsels in distress and their dashing young saviors, she is indeed just as comfortable embracing them if this means revising masculine models as well.

In contrast, **"Louisa"** (1891) presents a suitor who is even better established as a prince than is George Arnold, but disagreements among feminine authorities lead to a fairy-tale revision in which the perceived princess, Louisa Britton, would rather do without this prince. According to Bruno Bettelheim, "Every child at some time wishes that he were a prince or princess—and at times, in his unconscious, the child believes he is one, only temporarily degraded by circumstances. There are so many kings and queens in fairy tales because their rank signifies absolute power, such as the parent seems to hold over the child. So the fairy tale royalty represents projections of the child's imagination" (205). Freeman revises this notion in **"Louisa"** by making Louisa Britton's mother the one whose imagination is being projected. Mrs. Britton, a born aristocrat who has recently fallen "in sore straights" (**"Louisa"** 394), sees Jonathan Nye as the young hero who will save her daughter from a life of hard work and servitude to the more wealthy Mitchells, for whom Louisa works to help make ends meet. Freeman informs her readers that Mrs. Britton "had a feeling of a queen for a princess of the blood about her schoolteacher daughter [Louisa]. . . . The projected marriage to Jonathan Nye was like a royal alliance for the good of the state" (394-95). However, although Louisa has never met a man she favored more than Nye, she does not love him, of which fact she informs her mother. For Mrs. Britton, however, "there was not more sense, to her mind, in Louisa's refusing him than there would have been in a princess refusing the fairy prince and spoiling the story" (395). But that is exactly what happens. Freeman revises those norms to her own end. In fact, at the next church meeting Louisa and Nye attend together, Louisa makes sure to thrust her dirty hands as far out from her sleeves as she can, profoundly disturbing Nye's sensibilities when he sees the brown stains on her worker's hands: "She had never heard of a princess who destroyed her beauty that she might not be forced to wed the man whom she did not love, but she had something of the same feeling, although she did not have it for the sake of any tangible lover. Louisa had never seen anybody whom she preferred to Jonathan Nye. There was no other marriageable young man in the place. She had only her dreams, which she had in common with other girls" (396). Freeman is determined that this will not be one of the multitudes of fairy tales in which the young girl finds herself forced to marry. Instead, Louisa rejects her prince, her feminine inclinations clashing with those of her mother. In the conclusion, her overpowering feminine authority again forces transformation of the prince figure. This time, however, the transformation is a change in affection and direction as Nye takes Louisa's hint and finds a new girl to court. When she later sees him walk by her window, "Louisa turned again from him to her sweet, mysterious, girlish dreams" (406). Just as **"Calla-Lilies and Hannah"** embraces fairy-tale modes, revising them by placing them in a more contemporary setting in which

their representations of male and female behavioral patterns are still widely accepted cultural norms, **"Louisa"** turns those norms on their head as Freeman portrays a worthy prince whose princess would rather be left alone with her own notions of happily ever after.

Hardiman says of Freeman's men that they are "often depicted as weak or despicable" (1). This is true to the extent that in many of Freeman's stories, men do their best to thwart the harmless desires of women simply because those desires do not mesh with social standards. These men are royal pains and are despicable mostly because they are to readers—in Freeman's age and today—annoying, closed-minded chauvinists. However, one man within Freeman's canon is despicable for more dubious reasons, and this beast appears, appropriately, in one of Freeman's most haunting fairy-tale revisions.

Structurally and thematically, it is hard not to see **"Old Woman Magoun"** (1905) as a revision of "Little Red Riding Hood." Both tales have at their center young girls who take dangerous journeys into the unknown for their grandmothers. Both also incorporate "the traditional depiction of the young girl encountering a wolf in the woods" (Zipes, *Don't Bet* 226), though Lily, the young girl in Freeman's version, enters symbolic woods on her first lone walk to the local general store. Jack Zipes, who has worked extensively with this particular fairy tale, says of the two most popular versions of "Little Red Riding Hood" that both "Charles Perrault and the Grimm Brothers [who collected versions of the story] transformed an oral folk tale about the social initiation of a young woman into a narrative about rape in which the heroine is obliged to bear the responsibility for sexual violation" (*Don't Bet* 227). Zipes has also said of the Grimms' version that it is one of the tales the brothers edited to remove most of the "erotic and sexual elements"; he further states of the tale that it "underline[s] morals in keeping with . . . patriarchal notions of sex roles" (*When Dreams* 74-75). Freeman discounts those patriarchal notions in her version by having a strong grandmother figure save her granddaughter from the wolves, though at great cost. Further, Magoun makes it her mission, once Lily is placed in a situation similar to Perrault's and the Grimms' Little Red, to see to it that Lily does not "bear the responsibility of sexual violation" through rape as, it is very possible, did her own daughter, Lily's mother.

Margaret Hunt's 1884 translation of the Grimms' "Little Red-Cap" offers the story in the form with which Freeman appears most familiar, perhaps even from Hunt's translation directly or from earlier editions or oral tellings. Both stories begin similarly with the charge to the young girl to embark on a journey.

The tale's mother demands, "Come, Little Red-Cap, here is a piece of cake and a bottle of wine; take them to your grandmother, she is ill and weak, and they will do her good. Set out before it gets hot, and when you are going, walk nicely and quietly and do not run off the path, or you may fall and break the bottle, and then your grandmother will get nothing; and when you go into her room, don't forget to say, 'Good-morning,' and don't peep into every corner before you do it." Similarly, Old Woman Magoun, Lily's grandmother, sets her granddaughter on her path. Lily's mother is dead, and within Magoun's appropriation of motherly authority we see the first trace of Freeman's revision. Magoun, who is out of salt but is too busy to go to the store herself, tells Lily, "Don't stop to talk with anybody, for I am in a hurry for that salt. Of course, if anybody speaks to you answer them polite, and then come right along" (363). The orders are strikingly similar, too similar to be disregarded. Further, Freeman sneaks in a subtle signifier when Magoun tells Lily to put on her hat, making sure her granddaughter, too, is bedecked with a riding hood of sorts. Freeman also makes sure to focus on the hat once Lily comes into contact with her first beast-figure, informing readers that the hat "form[ed] an oval frame for her innocent face" (364), just as a hood would.

Shortly after venturing into their respective new territories, both girls encounter sexual forces for the first time: "just as Little Red-Cap entered the wood, a wolf met her. Red-Cap did not know what a wicked creature he was, and was not at all afraid of him." Likewise, Jim Willis, who Lily notes "was very handsome indeed" (364), appears along Lily's way, and he begins to warm up to her upon "start[ing] at the revelation of her innocent beauty" (364). Willis eventually takes her hand and walks with her. However, Lily, who, like Little Red-Cap, at first "felt complete trust in him" and who feels an initial attraction towards Willis, soon grows uncomfortable. He asks her age, to which she replies, "Fourteen." His response is, "As old as that?" and Lily shrinks from the man: "She could not have told why. She pulled her little hand from his, and he let it go with no remonstrance. She clasped both her arms around her rag doll, in order that her hand should not be free for him to grasp again" (364). Lily's awakened sexual adult self, that which felt a strong pull to the man, appears to understand innately the sexual undertones of his surprise. From that moment on, Willis wants Lily. He does not talk with her much while they walk except to ask her age, but later, when her father tries to give her to Willis in order to settle a gambling debt, it becomes clear that Willis is of the same mind-set as Little Red-Cap's wolf, who thinks to himself, "What a tender young creature! What a nice plump mouthful."

Little Red-Cap's wolf eventually does get the better of her, tricking her into moving ever closer to her grandmother's bed, which he now inhabits, having eaten the grandmother. The girl pays for her curiosity and is also eaten by the wolf. Since, as Zipes says of the tale, "Only a strong male figure can rescue a girl from herself and her lustful desires" (*Don't Bet* 230), a nearby hunter resolves the story by splitting open the wolf and freeing the two entombed but whole and still alive bodies. Zipes points out that many scholars see this eating as a "sexual motif" (230). He continues, "As every reader/viewer subconsciously knows, Little Red Riding Hood is not sent into the woods to visit grandma but to meet the wolf and to explore her own sexual cravings and social rules of conduct" (239). Little Red-Cap escapes when the male-figure arrives, but Freeman gives Lily no such prince. Instead, Magoun saves her from the belly of the wolf, as Freeman's revision features rather an authoritative female who sets things right as best she can.

At the store, Lily meets her father, the deadbeat scoundrel Nelson Barry, whom Magoun despises for how he treated Lily's now-deceased mother. In Kidd's lexicon, he represents a wolf-boy who became a wolf-man, someone who was unable to shed his childly and adolescent animalistic urges once reaching adulthood. Lily's mother, Freeman says, "was married at sixteen. There had been rumors, but no one dare openly gainsay the old woman. She said that her daughter had married Nelson Barry, and he had deserted her" (362). It is little wonder that Magoun sees Barry as a "fairly dangerous degenerate" (362). It is also possible that Barry did not marry Lily's mother, or, even more odious, that he raped her. He is indeed the most beastly of Freeman's few beast figures in her fairy-tale revisions, Willis a close second. Upon talking with his daughter, Barry kisses her. The kiss cannot be passed off as a fatherly peck, though. Lily again "shrank away" and immediately "rubbed her mouth violently," to which action Barry replies, "Damn it all! I believe she is afraid of me" (365). Although his breath does reek of whisky, that Lily rubs her mouth proves that the kiss was more intrusive, more intimate, than she cared for. An open mouth is also a clear signifier of consumption. Barry too may be thinking, "What a tender young creature! What a nice plump mouthful." Lily, however, cannot escape all his advances. When he offers her candy, she gladly accepts, stepping ever closer to the bed of his personal designs for her.

In the 1884 version of the Grimms' tale, Little Red-Cap meets another wolf in a later journey as well. Further, his plans are thwarted by the grandmother. When Magoun learns of Lily's visit with her father, she, too, seems to know that Barry is up to no good. "You go right up-stairs to your own chamber now," she says, already knowing she needs to protect her granddaughter (367). Sure enough, Barry soon visits Magoun, and in their exchange he proves himself to be a most beastly character.

Barry is direct in his intentions: "I want her," he says (369), the sexual overtones obvious. He is direct with his desires to Magoun, and he has already physically embraced Lily in an inappropriate manner. In fact, by this time readers are aware that he and Willis have a mysterious deal in the works—he tells Willis, "Jim you got to stick to your promise" (371)—which might suggest that Lily will be swapped between the two of them, that Barry has his mind set on doing to Lily what he possibly did to her mother. Magoun appears cognizant of it all, though, and does her best to thwart Barry's ghastly scheme.

It is no easy task, however. Freeman instills Barry with an almost supernatural will of iron to rival that of any of her women characters'. He tells Magoun, "Well, there is no use talking. I have made up my mind . . . and you know what that means. I am going to have the girl" (370). Magoun, strong-willed herself, crumbles in apparent defeat, acquiescing to his demands and agreeing to have Lily ready for him within a week. Once he leaves, though, her role as Lily's savior, her prince figure in a skirt, comes into play. She will not have Lily suffer the same fate at the hands of those wolves as did her mother. She attempts to get a prominent couple from a nearby town to adopt Lily, but that fails when the couple learns that Lily is of Barry blood. At her wit's end, Magoun turns to drastic measures on their walk back home. She allows Lily to eat berries from a bed of nightshade. Here, too, sexual undercurrents become overt. Nightshade has a root system that some suggest appears to be in the form of a human body. As long as Lily lives, she is in danger of sexual predators, the beasts, in her small town. If the old woman can no longer keep the girl from the temptations of man, she chooses to let ruin happen through indulgence of a literal forbidden fruit rather than at the hands of savage men.

Lily dies of the plant's poison, which Magoun blames on the sour apples and milk Lily ate while in town. In her delirium, Lily tells her grandmother, "it is dark" (376), perhaps an echo of the exclamation made by Grimms' Little Red-Cap upon emerging from the wolf's belly, "How dark it was inside the wolf." There is no hunter, no prince to save Lily. Freeman leaves it up to a capable, desperate woman who will see her granddaughter escape the domineering men of her village, no matter what the cost. After Red-Cap's first encounter with a wolf, she reflects, "As long as I live, I will never by myself leave the path, to run into the wood, when my mother has forbidden me to do so."

Magoun makes sure Lily never drifts from a path of chaste innocence as well, leaving Barry to wonder why his daughter and his "wife" both died of sour apples and milk.

Nelson Barry shows that within her fairy-tale revisions, Freeman many times turns to women characters to play traditionally male roles, but that within those roles, women still have to work against a male-dominated social order. Women may be in control, but they are in control subversively and, at times, tentatively. Within the authority that women do maintain, however, is the power to influence that order. Indeed, feminine influence is such that Freeman's men can be divided into three categories based on how they interact with her women characters and how those willful females view them: as princes, beasts, or royal pains. These groupings are apparent in stories that show little trace of fairy-tale influence but are especially strong in those stories in which Freeman explores and adapts obvious fairy-tale themes. Therefore, Freeman's men deserve more study not only in relation to the already established approaches to her work but also, as Dickey, George Arnold, Nelson Barry, Jim Willis, and others perfectly illustrate, in attempts finally to recognize the fairy-tale influence in Freeman's complete canon and her place within the tradition of feminist fairy-tale revisionists. As well, stories such as **"Old Woman Magoun"** illustrate not only a revision of multiple fairy-tale elements but also revisions of gender roles that are indicative of an author with a deeper awareness of multifaceted sex roles—and perhaps how they interacted in conflict during her era—than has been attributed to Freeman to date.

Works Cited

Bettelheim, Bruno. *The Uses of Enchantment: The Meaning and Importance behind Fairy Tales.* New York: Vintage Books, 1976.

Commager, Henry Steele. *The St. Nicholas Anthology.* New York: Random House, 1948.

Donovan, Josephine. "Silence or Capitulation: Prepatriarchal 'Mother's Gardens' in Jewett and Freeman." *Critical Essays on Mary Wilkins Freeman.* Ed. Shirley Marchalonis. Boston: G. K. Hall and Co., 1991. 151-56.

Foster, Edward. *Mary E. Wilkins Freeman.* New York: Hendricks House, 1956.

Freeman, Mary Wilkins. "Calla-Lilies and Hannah." *A New England Nun and Other Stories.* New York: Harper, 1891. 99-121.

———. "A Church Mouse." *A New England Nun and Other Stories.* New York: Harper, 1891. 407-28.

————. "The Dickey Boy." *Young Lucretia and Other Stories.* New York: Harper, 1892. 193-216.

————. *A Humble Romance and Other Stories.* New York: Harper, 1887.

————. "An Independent Thinker." *A Humble Romance and Other Stories.* New York: Harper, 1887. 296-314.

————. "Louisa." *A New England Nun and Other Stories.* New York: Harper, 1891. 384-407.

————. "A New England Nun." *A New England Nun and Other Stories.* New York: Harper, 1891. 1-18.

————. "Old Woman Magoun." *A Mary Wilkins Freeman Reader.* Ed. Mary Reichardt. Lincoln: U of Nebraska P, 1997. 361-78.

————. "A Poetess." *A New England Nun and Other Stories.* New York: Harper, 1891. 140-60.

————. "The Prism." *The Uncollected Short Stories of Mary Wilkins Freeman.* Ed. Mary R. Reichardt. Jackson: UP of Mississippi, 1992. 55-66.

————. "The Revolt of 'Mother.'" *A New England Nun and Other Stories.* New York: Harper, 1891. 448-68.

————. "A Village Singer." *A New England Nun and Other Stories.* New York: Harper, 1891. 18-37.

————. *The Wind in the Rose-Bush and Other Stories of the Supernatural.* New York: Doubleday, Page and Company, 1903.

————. *Young Lucretia and Other Stories.* New York: Harper, 1892.

Glasser, Leah Blatt. *In a Closet Hidden: The Life and Works of Mary E. Wilkins Freeman.* Amherst: U of Massachusetts P, 1996.

Green, Jeanette Evelyn. "Literary Revisions of Traditional Folktales: Bowen, Carter, Hong Kingston, Morrison, Oates, Sexton, Welty, and Capote." Diss. U of Texas-Austin, 1989. *DAI* 51 (1989): 0511A.

Grimm, Jacob and Wilhelm Grimm. "Little Red-Cap." *Household Tales.* Trans. Margaret Hunt. London: George Bell, 1884, 1:110-114. 10 Jan. 2005 <http://www.ucs.mun.ca/~wbarker/fairies/grimm/026.html.

Hardiman, Faye Wright. "Mary Wilkins Freeman's Men: Finding Masculinity in a Women's World." Georgia State U, 1996. *DAI* 57 (1996): 3494A.

Kendrick, Brent, ed. *The Infant Sphinx: Collected Letters of Mary E. Wilkins Freeman.* Metuchen, NJ: Scarecrow P, 1985.

Kidd, Kenneth B. *Making American Boys: Boyology and the Feral Tale.* Minneapolis: U of Minnesota P, 2004.

Marchalonis, Shirley, ed. *Critical Essays on Mary Wilkins Freeman.* Boston: G. K. Hall, 1991.

McElrath, Joseph R., Jr. "The Artistry of Mary E. Wilkins Freeman's 'The Revolt of Mother.'" *Critical Essays on Mary Wilkins Freeman.* Ed. Shirley Marchalonis. Boston: G. K. Hall, 1991. 132-38.

Meese, Elizabeth. "Signs of Undecidability: Reconstructing the Stories of Mary Wilkins Freeman." *Critical Essays on Mary Wilkins Freeman.* Ed. Shirley Marchalonis. Boston: G. K. Hall, 1991. 157-76.

Pryse, Marjorie, ed. "Afterword." *Selected Stories of Mary E. Wilkins Freeman.* New York: Norton, 1983. 315-41.

————. "Introduction." *Selected Stories of Mary E. Wilkins Freeman.* New York: Norton, 1983. vii-xix.

Reichardt, Mary R. "Introduction." *The Uncollected Short Stories of Mary Wilkins Freeman.* Jackson: UP of Mississippi, 1992. xii-xiv.

————. "Mary Wilkins Freeman: One Hundred Years of Criticism." *Critical Essays on Mary Wilkins Freeman.* Ed. Shirley Marchalonis. Boston: G. K. Hall, 1991. 73-89.

Terryberry, Karl J. *Gender Instruction in the Tales for Children by Mary E. Wilkins Freeman.* Lewiston, NY: Edwin Mellen P, 2002.

Turkes, Doris J. "Must Age Equal Failure? Sociology Looks at Mary Wilkins Freeman's Old Women." *American Transcendental Quarterly* 13.3 (1999): 197-214.

Westbrook, Perry D. *Mary Wilkins Freeman.* New York: Twayne, 1967.

Wilson, James D. "The 'Fairy Web' and the Raft: Domesticity and Nature in 'A New England Nun' and 'Huckleberry Finn.'" *Xavier Review* 14.2 (1994): 42-51.

Zipes, Jack. *Don't Bet on the Prince.* New York: Routledge, 1986.

————. *When Dreams Came True.* New York: Routledge, 1991.

FURTHER READING

Criticism

Blum, Virginia L. "Mary Wilkins Freeman and the Taste of Necessity." *American Literature* 65, no. 1 (March 1993): 69-94.

Probes the tension between commercialism and aesthetics in Freeman's short fiction.

Eppard, Philip, and Mary Reichardt. "A Checklist of Uncollected Short Fiction by Mary Wilkins Freeman." *American Literary Realism* 23, no. 1 (fall 1990): 70-4.

Provides an exhaustive list of Freeman's uncollected tales.

Fisher, Benjamin F. "Transitions from Victorian to Modern: The Supernatural Stories of Mary Wilkins Freeman and Edith Wharton." In *American Supernatural Fiction: From Edith Wharton to the* Weird Tales *Writers,* edited by Douglas Robillard, pp. 3-42. New York: Garland Publishing, Inc., 1996.

Traces the transformation of Freeman's supernatural tales from traditional Gothic narratives to modern structures based upon primitive psychological motivations.

Luscher, Robert M. "Seeing the Forest for the Trees: The 'Intimate Connection' of Mary Wilkins Freeman's *Six Trees.*" *American Transcendental Quarterly* n.s. 3, no. 4 (December 1989): 363-81.

Examines Freeman's use of symbolism and her indebtedness to the work of Ralph Waldo Emerson in *Six Trees* and *Understudies,* stressing the nature-based mysticism in these collections.

Reichardt, Mary R. *A Web of Relationship: Women in the Short Fiction of Mary Wilkins Freeman.* Jackson: University Press of Mississippi, 1992, 186 p.

Study of the role of women in Freeman's stories.

Additional coverage of Freeman's life and career is contained in the following sources published by Gale: *Contemporary Authors,* **Vols. 106, 177;** *Dictionary of Literary Biography,* **Vols. 12, 78, 221;** *Exploring Short Stories;* *Feminist Writers;* *Literature Resource Center;* *Modern American Women Writers;* *Reference Guide to American Literature,* **Ed. 4;** *Reference Guide to Short Fiction,* **Ed. 2;** *St. James Guide to Horror, Ghost & Gothic Writers;* *Short Stories for Students,* **Vols. 4, 8;** *Short Story Criticism,* **Vol. 1, 47;** *Supernatural Fiction Writers,* **Vol. 1;** *Twayne's United States Authors;* **and** *Twentieth-Century Literary Criticism,* **Vol. 9.**

George Gissing
1857-1903

(Full name George Robert Gissing) English short story writer, novelist, and nonfiction writer.

The following entry provides an overview of Gissing's short fiction. For additional information on his short fiction career, see *SSC,* Volume 37.

INTRODUCTION

A leading voice of late-nineteenth-century British fiction, Gissing composed well over one hundred short stories, the best of which demonstrate a shift from Victorian to modern literature. While his early tales feature a concern for the poor and an optimistic belief in social reform, his later stories combine this Dickensian sensibility with a distinctly modern air of pessimism, moral uncertainty, and psychological intricacy. Generally devoid of sentimentality and melodrama, Gissing's short works expose the environmental basis for human perception and behavior, and reveal the fears and fantasies that account for the shortcomings of the common individual. In this sense, his depiction of the harshness of the world is balanced in his stories by a pervasive sympathy for the human condition.

BIOGRAPHICAL INFORMATION

Born in the town of Wakefield in Yorkshire, England, Gissing was the eldest child of Thomas Waller Gissing, a successful pharmacist, and Margaret Bedford Gissing. In 1870 his father died of lung disease, leaving the family destitute. Concerned friends and neighbors established a fund that enabled Gissing to attend boarding school at Alderly Edge, where his academic prowess earned him a scholarship to Owens College in Manchester. Before he could graduate, Gissing was arrested for stealing from his classmates to financially support an alcoholic prostitute, Marianne Helen "Nell" Harrison, with whom he had fallen in love. He was sentenced to thirty days of hard labor at the Manchester jail. Upon his release, his family sent him to America where he could start anew with an unblemished reputation. Settling in Chicago, Gissing began writing short stories for the local newspaper, and he returned to London in 1877 to pursue a career as a writer. Featured in 1877 in the *Chicago Tribune,* "The Sins of the Fathers" was his first published work of fiction. His debut novel, *Workers in the Dawn,* appeared in 1880. By this time Gissing had resumed his relationship with Harrison, whose alcoholism and erratic behavior put an emotional strain on the young writer. They were married in 1879, but separated in 1883. His 1886 novel *Demos* became his first popular success, but it was with *New Grub Street* (1891) that Gissing gained recognition as a respected author. Harrison died in 1888 and in 1891 he married Edith Underwood. Soon after their wedding, Underwood began manifesting signs of a severe emotional disorder that included outbursts of extreme violence, but Gissing remained with her until 1897, when the couple separated. His first collection of short fiction, *Human Odds and Ends,* was published in 1898. Stricken with emphysema, Gissing moved to the south of France in 1902. He continued to work strenuously until his death the following year.

MAJOR WORKS OF SHORT FICTION

Gissing's short stories reveal many of the concerns, anxieties, and social realities of the late Victorian era while reflecting the author's own inner tensions. "The Sins of the Fathers" draws on his troubled experiences with Nell Harrison. In the story, Leonard Vincent, a young student, meets Laura, a poor woman from an abusive family. Leonard befriends Laura just before she is driven to prostitution, helps her find a job, and then falls in love with her. His father, however, is opposed to their relationship, and sends him to America in an effort to break it off. Once there, Leonard meets and marries a more economically and intellectually suitable woman, but his life is disrupted when he attends a play in which Laura appears as a chorus girl. He finds that he still desires her, and arranges to meet her one night. The story ends on a tragic note as Laura, driven mad by passion, grabs Leonard by the neck and throws them both into an icy river in which they drown. Motifs of social transgression and quotidian life are evident in "A Freak of Nature," in which a man is seized by a "devil" that causes him to behave inappropriately, and in "The Foolish Virgin," the realistic portrayal of a young woman who realizes that she is destined to live a life of menial labor. Often cited as one of his finest tales, "The House of Cobwebs" concerns an aspiring writer, Goldthorpe, who moves into a dilapidated house owned by a timid man named Spicer. As Goldthorpe works on his manuscript, the two men develop a peaceful and satisfying domestic relationship. Their serenity comes to an end when Goldthorpe falls ill following the completion of his novel and a doctor advises him to move out of his "unhealthy" home environment. His eventual recovery is followed by the acceptance of his book by a publisher. Goldthorpe's joy is tempered by the discovery that Spicer has been hospitalized after his house caved in on him. Another writer serves as the protagonist of "The Poet's Portmanteau," in which the eponymous poet's manuscript is stolen by a young woman only to be returned years later by a mysterious female admirer. "The Prize Lodger," like "The House of Cobwebs," takes domesticity as its theme. Archibald Jordan, a successful businessman famous for his frugality and domineering nature, marries his landlady, Mrs. Elderfield. Much to his chagrin, he finds her to be a willful, yet dutiful, spouse. Her demanding behavior prompts him to spend a night in a rented room similar to those he occupied during his long bachelorhood. Expecting his wife to be vexed by his absence, he is surprised that she makes no mention of it upon his return home, and he hopes that such a domestic agreement can be carried on indefinitely.

Another story that deals with the problems of a lodger, "The Last Half-Crown" concerns a poor writer who must contend with his overbearing landlord. In "The Salt of the Earth," an unassuming clerk named Thomas Bird lives a life filled with service to others, often acquiescing to overt manipulation of his charitable nature. His most self-effacing act, however, comes in the form of his agreement to stay away from the unrequited love of his life so that her upstanding fiancé will not be offended. "An Inspiration" revolves around an act of charity extended to a stranger. On an impulse (or "inspiration"), Harvey Munden invites a poor chimney cleaner, Laurence Nangle, to dinner, and urges the downtrodden man to visit the home of his childhood love despite the wishes of her upper-class family. The theme of class tension recurs in "A Daughter of the Lodge," in which May Rockett, the free-thinking daughter of a family of lodge-keepers, insults an upper-class neighbor, Hilda Shale, by refusing to be treated as an inferior. The Shales have a claim on the Rocketts' property, and threaten to evict the entire family unless May moves away to London. "Fleet-Footed Hester" centers on another free-spirited female

protagonist. Hester is known around town for beating all of the local boys in foot races, but the man that she loves, John Rayner, finds running in public unladylike. John prepares to leave town, but Hester is able to change his mind after using her sprinting skills to arrive at the train station before his departure. Jim Mutimer, the title character of "Mutimer's Choice," is crippled in an accident but refuses the surgery necessary to save his life. Instead, he leaves his wife in the care of her ex-lover, Bill Snowdon, resulting in another of Gissing's atypical domestic relationships.

Many of Gissing's early stories were published while he was living in America. A number of these tales were signed "G. R. Gresham" (a pseudonym to which he has subsequently been linked) while others were simply published anonymously. Among the unsigned stories putatively attributed to Gissing are "Too Wretched to Live," "One Farthing Damages," "The Portrait," "The Mysterious Portrait," and "The Picture," although some scholars continue to debate their attribution.

CRITICAL RECEPTION

Scholarly assessment of Gissing's short fiction, though slim, has remained positive throughout much of the twentieth century. Critics have especially lauded the commonplace heroism of his protagonists. For instance, they have interpreted the unflappable altruism of Thomas Bird in "The Salt of the Earth" and his desperate, though courageous, effort to resist change, as a journey of salvation. Other commentators have focused attention on a number of anonymously published stories that date from Gissing's residence in Chicago and may be "lost" entries to his oeuvre. In addition, critics have noted his subtle endorsement of women's rights in such stories as "A Daughter of the Lodge" and have detected autobiographical elements in "The Prize Lodger," among other short works. In fact, the short story genre has been cited as an ideal vehicle for the author's specific style of realism. As reviewer Ralph Pordzik stated, "[M]ore than other literary genres, the short story seems to be beneficial to the writer's interest in evoking an intuitive or instantaneously embodied 'real-life' schema within a spatially restricted frame of narration. . . . Gissing realised the potentialities inherent in the genre's structure and tried to employ them for his own purpose." Moreover, his short fiction has been discussed within the historical framework of literary realism. According to commentator Barbara Rawlinson, "Gissing's major contribution to the 'new realism' was his ability to 'freeze the moment'; to place emphasis on a single moment of intense or significant experience, and thus create an epiphany that reveals a character's inner state of mind."

PRINCIPAL WORKS

Short Fiction

Human Odds and Ends: Stories and Sketches 1898
The House of Cobwebs, and Other Stories 1906
An Heiress on Condition 1923
The Sins of the Fathers, and Other Tales 1924
A Victim of Circumstances, and Other Stories 1927
Brownie 1931
Stories & Sketches 1938
*Essays and Fiction (short stories and essays) 1970
My First Rehearsal and My Clerical Rival 1970
"A Freak of Nature; or, Mr. Brogden, City Clerk": An Uncollected Short Story 1990
George Gissing: Lost Stories from America; Five Signed Stories Never before Reprinted, a Sixth Signed Story, and Seven Recent Attributions 1992
The Day of Silence, and Other Stories 1993

Other Major Works

Workers in the Dawn: A Novel. 3 vols. (novel) 1880
The Unclassed: A Novel. 3 vols. (novel) 1884
Demos: A Story of English Socialism. 3 vols. (novel) 1886
Isabel Clarendon: A Novel. 2 vols. (novel) 1886
Thyrza: A Tale. 3 vols. (novel) 1887
A Life's Morning. 3 vols. (novel) 1888
The Nether World: A Novel. 3 vols. (novel) 1889
The Emancipated: A Novel. 3 vols. (novel) 1890
New Grub Street: A Novel. 3 vols. (novel) 1891
Born in Exile: A Novel. 3 vols. (novel) 1892
Denzil Quarrier: A Novel (novel) 1892
The Odd Women: A Novel. 3 vols. (novel) 1893
In the Year of Jubilee: A Novel. 3 vols. (novel) 1894
The Whirlpool: A Novel (novel) 1897
The Town Traveller: A Tale (novel) 1898
Our Friend the Charlatan (novel) 1901
The Private Papers of Henry Ryecroft (novel) 1903
Will Warburton: A Romance of Real Life (novel) 1905
George Gissing's Commonplace Book (nonfiction) 1962
The Collected Letters of George Gissing. 9 vols. (letters) 1990-96

*Includes the stories "The Hope of Pessimism," "Along Shore," "All for Love," "The Last Half-Crown," "Cain and Abel," "The Quarry on the Heath," "The Lady of the Dedication," "Multimer's Choice," and "Their Pretty Way."

CRITICISM

Robert L. Selig (essay date 1983)

SOURCE: Selig, Robert L. "An Unknown Gissing Story from the *Chicago Daily News*." *Studies in Bibliography* 36 (1983): 205-12.

[*In the following excerpt, Selig explores similar themes and motifs in the anonymously published "Too Wretched to Live" and in several of Gissing's other short stories.*]

I recently discovered an unknown Gissing story in the *Chicago Daily News* of 1877, a story dating from his year of American exile. The search for Gissing's youthful lost fiction has lasted now some two-thirds of a century. His best-known novel, *New Grub Street* (1891), provided the earliest clue: the minor character Whelpdale, a resilient London hack, tells of first getting published during an ill-considered trip to America's Middle West. With almost no money remaining in his pockets, he wrote a short story and had it accepted by Chicago's largest newspaper. "For some months," Whelpdale adds, "I supported myself in Chicago, writing for that same paper, and for others."[1] In 1912 a thinly disguised Gissing biography by his friend Morley Roberts, *The Private Life of Henry Maitland*, asserted that Whelpdale's transatlantic adventures came from Gissing's own life—specifically from his year in the United States after his college thefts for his prostitute love, his expulsion from Owens, and his imprisonment in Manchester. Roberts challenged American scholars to look for Gissing's fiction in the *Chicago Tribune*, that city's largest newspaper in the late 1870s.

Shortly after the First World War, a group of researchers including George Everett Hastings, Vincent Starrett, Thomas Ollive Mabbott, and Christopher Hagerup found eight Gissing stories in the *Tribune* just as Roberts had foretold: three signed "G. R. G." and five without signature. The publication dates ranged from March 10 to July 29, 1877. Both manner and theme identified even the unsigned pieces as Gissing's. Next, Whelpdale's last words caught the eyes of the researchers—"for that same paper, and for others"—and they shifted their investigation to the rest of Chicago's press. Sure enough, they found three more stories in Chicago dailies other than the *Tribune*—all unsigned but clearly by Gissing. The publication of these extended from April 28 to June 2, 1877.[2]

In the late 1920s and the early 1930s, three further stories cropped up from Gissing's American stay: **"An English Coast-Picture"** in *Appletons' Journal* (New

York) (July 1877); **"The Artist's Child"** in the *Alliance* (Chicago) (30 June 1877), an obscure religious paper; and **"A Terrible Mistake"** in the *National Weekly* (Chicago) (5 May 1877), an even more obscure and ephemeral publication. All three of these pieces appeared under the pseudonym "G. R. Gresham"—the name of a villainous character in *Workers in the Dawn* (1880), Gissing's first novel. Then, after a lapse of almost fifty years, Pierre Coustillas and I found two more Gissing stories in Chicago's *Alliance*: **"A Mother's Hope"** (12 May 1877) and **"A Test of Honor"** (2 June 1877). Like the previously uncovered story in the *Alliance* and also like those in *Appletons'* and in the *National Weekly,* these two newest finds bore the pen name "G. R. Gresham."[3]

My latest discovery of an unknown Gissing story comes from a paper ignored till now in the search for Gissing's fiction—the *Chicago Daily News.* I found my clue in Professor Mabbott's description of where he and others had looked: the *Tribune,* the *Journal,* the *Post,* the *Times,* the *Inter-Ocean,* but, curiously enough, not the *News*—Chicago's largest evening paper in 1877.[4] When I read through the *News* of Gissing's American year, I found an unsigned story that I thought undoubtedly his—**"Too Wretched to Live"** (24 April 1877, p. 2). The gloomy theme and the journeyman prose have the unmistakable ring of Gissing's early work. And in the *News* of May 18, 1877, I found an important piece of corroborating evidence: **"The Warder's Daughter"**—a virtually unchanged version of Gissing's **"The Warden's Daughter,"** which had first appeared in Chicago's *Journal* of April 28, 1877, and was identified as his by both Starrett and Mabbott.

Struggling to earn his keep from one week to the next, Gissing apparently gained a second payment for a story already published by a rival Chicago daily. The *News* piece remains essentially the same as that appearing in the *Journal.* The few alterations in scattered words and in a single phrase could easily have occurred during simple recopying. For many years later, Gissing retained the habit of submitting his work in longhand. Obviously, he could not have sent the *News* the clipped-out published version, for that would have exposed it as an already-used story. He could have recopied either the *Journal*'s printed version or his own hand-written draft. One other possibility remains: simultaneous submissions of slightly different manuscripts, followed first by publication in the *Journal* and then by Gissing's failure to withdraw his story from that paper's local rival. In any case, the title change from the Americanized "Warden" to the British form "Warder" argues against a mere case of literary piracy by the *News*'s American staff—a piracy without the awareness of the young man from England. Most importantly, the appearance in the *News*

of this known Gissing piece establishes that the editors had a taste for his fiction—circumstantial evidence that tends to support his authorship, as well, of **"Too Wretched to Live."**

The publication date of **"Too Wretched to Live"**—April 24, 1877—falls well within the period of Gissing's other known stories from Chicago: March 10 to July 29, 1877. More specifically, Mabbott and Starrett established that Gissing's fiction had appeared in dailies other than the *Tribune* from April 28th through June 2nd. Indeed, **"Too Wretched to Live"** came out in the *News* four days before his first other extant non-*Tribune* story—**"The Warden's Daughter"** (the *Journal,* 28 April 1877). In view of the *News*'s prominence and its extensive use of fiction, Gissing's turning to that paper soon after the *Tribune* seems just what one would expect from a struggling young writer in Chicago of the late 1870s.

"Too Wretched to Live" contains marks of Gissing's handiwork at least as compelling as the external evidence. Consider, for example, the jilted Lilian Frasier's suicide by drowning. In Gissing's early fiction and even in works from the '90s, the plot device of drowning recurs like an obsession. In his very first story, **"The Sins of the Fathers"** (1877), the heroine commits both suicide and murder by drowning herself and her former fiancé. The heroine in **"Brownie"** (1877) avenges the murder of her poor drowned sister by driving the villain into drowning himself too. Watery suicide also turns up in the novelette *All for Love* (written 1880; pub. 1970) and in two short stories from about this same period: **"The Last Half Crown"** (written 1879-1880; pub. 1970) and **"Cain and Abel"** (written 1880; pub. 1970). Accidental drowning occurs in **"The Quarry on the Heath"** (written 1881; pub. 1970) and, most memorably, in a piece from Gissing's maturity—**"The Day of Silence"** (1893). In this late working-class story, the death of father and son during a pleasure trip on the Thames evokes an almost tragic intensity. Death by water also appears in Gissing's full-length novels. In *Workers in the Dawn* (1880), the hero chooses its most spectacular form: he throws himself into Niagara Falls. In *Denzil Quarrier* (1892) suicide by drowning ends the life of sensitive Lilian, who has the same first name as the "crushed and broken lily" in **"Too Wretched to Live."** Even *The Odd Women* (1893), one of the novelist's best known works, contains two random drownings: the first by a boating accident and the second by suicide in a mental ward's bathtub. Given this frequent pattern in much of Gissing's fiction, one can recognize the drowning in **"Too Wretched to Live"** as an identifying sign—a virtual Gissing watermark.

The broad narrative subject of **"Too Wretched to Live"**—the hero's abandonment of one woman for another—also serves to mark the story as Gissing's. He uses this theme in his early, middle, and even late fiction. At times he provides mitigating details to help excuse man's fickleness, but at others he presents the most extreme cases: males who engage themselves to an alternative woman while still engaged to a first. His earliest story, **"The Sins of the Fathers"** (10 March 1877), has the hero discard his old love for a new one, but with many extenuating circumstances. A variant of this theme appears in *Workers in the Dawn* (1880), when the hero tries to abandon his false love for his true one but is blocked by the inconvenience of having unwisely bound himself as husband of the rival female. Interestingly enough, the protagonist in *Workers* has the same first name, Arthur, as the inconstant young man in **"Too Wretched to Live."** A rather sympathetic treatment of the fast sexual shuffle occurs in both *The Unclassed* (1884) and in *A Life's Morning* (1888). By the time of *New Grub Street* (1891), however, Gissing depicts male fickleness with rueful comedy and by *Our Friend the Charlatan* (1901) with broadly satiric ridicule. In embryonic form, then, **"Too Wretched to Live"** contains a persistent and basic Gissing theme: off with the old love and on with the new.

With its stiff formal prose interspersed with attempted lyricism, the style of **"Too Wretched to Live"** provides a further mark of the youthful Gissing's authorship. Like many others of his early short stories, this one sets the scene with a flowery description of landscape, sky, and sun: "The sun was just setting as he turned the corner of the house and both sea and sky were bathed in a crimson splendor. . . ." This purple patch bears a strong resemblance to an opening passage from **"A Mother's Hope"**: ". . . The long track of sunlight, which gleamed from the horizon to the limits of the wet sands, kept ever spreading as the sun rose higher, . . . till the whole sea and shore exulted in the splendors of the new day."[5] Similar effusions about splendid suns or overarching skies open other stories from the writer's early period: **"An English Coast-Picture," "A Test of Honor," "The Death-Clock,"** and **"R. I. P."**—all from 1877. But as his art matured, Gissing outgrew this neo-romantic habit of beginning his short stories with lyrical weather reports.

Another of Gissing's stylistic quirks—the pedantic term imported from Latin or Greek—appears near the climax of **"Too Wretched to Live"**: "As he glanced at the handwriting, a woman's delicate chirography. . . ." From the Greek root *kheirographon,* that bookish final word intrudes upon a scene of supposedly high emotion. The former classics student from Owens College, Manchester, never lost his taste for ink-horn phrases. To the end of his writing career, he

retained a preference for erudite words over plain ones—for *visage* or *physiognomy* over simply *face.* Even in *Born in Exile* (1892), one of his finest novels, we find a broad sprinkling of learned expressions: "susurration," "sequaciousness," "intenerates."[6] Thus the fancy word *chirography* in the *Daily News* story provides further evidence of George Gissing's authorship.

From a biographical viewpoint, **"Too Wretched to Live"** has a special connection with **"The Sins of the Fathers,"** Gissing's first story. Both pieces construct troubled fantasies out of his guilty feelings at having left Nell Harrison on the other side of the ocean—his prostitute love for whom he had besmirched himself back at Owens College. In Gissing's later life, his romantic guilt undid him: he returned to Nell after one year abroad and eventually married this unreformed and alcoholic streetwalker. They lived together unhappily, though not quite ever after, for they separated at last in 1883.

In **"The Sins of the Fathers,"** Nell Harrison's fictional counterpart walks the streets of an English city very like Manchester. Though the hero saves her from becoming a prostitute, his father falsely tells him that she has suddenly died, and the hero marries instead a pretty American schoolgirl. At the end the Nell-like figure becomes an avenging "Medusa"—a word used to describe her in the very first paragraph. In effect, the protagonist has much justification for feeling relieved when he thinks her dead—good riddance of a wild female. Yet in **"Too Wretched to Live,"** the egoistic hero has no excuse at all but snobbery. He abandons a sweet and respectable young farm girl for a fashionable beauty who sings drawing-room opera—a beauty whose last name even suggests nobility: *Earle.* Then he discovers, too late, that he really preferred his dead former love to her more elegant rival. In a final touch of Gissing lugubriousness, the protagonist marries the rival woman anyway but lives unhappily ever after.

The contrast between the "Medusa" avenger in Gissing's first story and the tender-hearted suicide in the newly discovered piece illustrates a weakness running through his early work. The youthful writer tended to depict all women as one of two extremes: idealized angel or deplorable man-trap. His early novels usually contain both a female saint and a slut: seraphic Helen Norman versus drunken Carrie Mitchell (*Workers in the Dawn*—1880), good-hearted Ida Starr versus hateful Harriet Smales (*The Unclassed*—1884), sweet Jane Snowden versus murderous Clem Peckover (*The Nether World*—1889). Not until Gissing could achieve such complex female characters as Cecily Doran in *The Emancipated* (1890) or Marian Yule and Amy Reardon in *New Grub Street* (1891) would he attain full development in his fictional art. **"Too Wretched to Live"** records a faltering early step on his way to becoming one of late-Victorian fiction's most skillful portrayers of women.

Notes

1. George Gissing, *New Grub Street,* 3 vols. (1891), III, 110.

2. For the text of these eleven stories and an account of their discovery, see George Gissing, *Sins of the Fathers and Other Tales,* with introduction by Vincent Starrett (1924); George Gissing, *Brownie: Now First Reprinted from The Chicago Tribune Together with Six Other Stories Attributed to Him,* with introductions by George Everett Hastings, Vincent Starrett, Thomas Ollive Mabbott (1931).

3. Pierre Coustillas and Robert L. Selig, "Unknown Gissing Stories from Chicago," *Times Literary Supplement,* 12 December 1980, pp. 1417-1418. The article reprints "A Test of Honor" in its entirety.

4. Thomas Ollive Mabbott, "Introductions," "Part Three," *Brownie,* pp. 16-21.

5. G. R. Gresham [George Gissing], "A Mother's Hope," *The Alliance,* 12 May 1877, p. 364.

6. George Gissing, *Born in Exile,* 3 vols. (1892), vol. I, pt. I, 28; vol. I, pt. I, 58; vol. I, pt. II, 257.

Robert L. Selig (essay date 1990)

SOURCE: Selig, Robert L. "Three Stories by George Gissing: Lost Tales from Chicago." *English Literature in Transition, 1880-1920* 33, no. 3 (1990): 277-96.

[*In the following excerpt, Selig attempts to place the unsigned stories "The Portrait," "The Mysterious Portrait," and "The Picture" within Gissing's body of short fiction.*]

The search for lost fiction from Gissing's youthful exile in the United States has lasted now two thirds of a century—a work of intermittent bibliographic excavation. He himself planted a clue about his forgotten American pieces in a passage of almost straight autobiography from *New Grub Street*'s chapter 28 (1891): Whelpdale's account of publishing short stories in Chicago's leading newspaper. The first exploration of this hinted-at quarry appeared with the publication by a group of American scholars of *Sins of the Fathers and Other Tales* (1924) and *Brownie* (1931)—volumes containing four proven stories by Gissing and seven attributed to him on the basis of thematic evidence. Shortly afterwards, scholars learned of three

more stories from America certainly by Gissing,[1] and there matters rested for nearly half a century until Pierre Coustillas and I found two more Gissing stories in the *Alliance*—an obscure Chicago weekly—signed with his early pen name, G. R. Gresham.[2] For the past few years, I have continued this search and have discovered two more unsigned pieces from Chicago most probably by Gissing—from the *Daily News* and the *Post*.[3] Now I wish to claim as his three more unsigned stories from the *Daily News,* all on the subject of painting and all with strong resemblances to known works by him.

"The Portrait" (*Chicago Daily News,* 18 June 1877) stands as the first of the three anonymous *News* stories on the Gissing-like theme of painting. Gissing himself had a gift for drawing, and his very first publication was an art review for Boston's *Commonwealth*.[4] Throughout his career he filled his fiction with many painter-characters. In view of this throng of fictional Gissing artists, three consecutive *Daily News* stories about the theme of painting would hardly seem surprising from him.[5]

"The Portrait" shares a distinctive plot device with a proven Gissing story, **"Gretchen"** (*Chicago Tribune,* 12 May 1877): an aesthete's discovery of his ideal woman after first having glimpsed just her painted likeness. In the *News* variation, the portrait shows the heroine as a seven-year-old child with a sweet "dream-face," but when he discovers the model herself, she has become a beautiful and full-grown woman. In **"Gretchen"** the hero rhapsodizes in a quite similar way over the sweetness of the unknown heroine's portrait: "All that is sweetest in womanly beauty, all that is tenderest in womanly love, all the holiness of innocence, and the pathos of humility shone in that perfect face. . . ."[6] Both stories idealize their painted and actual heroines—a tendency persisting in Gissing's fiction until at least 1890.

In addition, a scene in **"The Portrait"** provides a very striking analogue to one from *The Unclassed* (1884), Gissing's second novel: the passage where Ida Starr asks Osmond Waymark to guard her from sexual harassment from a cad in the street.[7] In the *News* story Annie Bartlet asks Robert Southey's "protection" from a skulking man who "has followed" her down the street. Both bystanders save their damsels in distress by walking arm-in-arm with them to scare away the attacker. And each hero ultimately marries the woman whom he has protected from sexual harm.

One other plot device occurring in **"The Portrait"** seems extremely Gissing-like: at the very moment when the hero happens to meet the painting's lovely model, her mother happens to find a long-lost will. Throughout his entire career, Gissing kept returning to this well-worn convention of sudden inheritances and handouts from the dead. Legacies and wills play a central role in ten of his twenty-two novels and each of his first four. And only five Gissing novels completely avoid all complications of inheritance. Thus **"The Portrait"** juxtaposes within a very short span a number of Gissing-like characteristics along with his frequent theme of painting and idealization.

The second anonymous story dealing with paintings— **"The Mysterious Portrait"** (*Chicago Daily News,* 6 July 1877)—has a heroine called Helen, a name closely linked with Gissing as well as with his fiction. The prostitute for whom he besmirched himself in 1876 at Owens College, Marianne Helen Harrison (later Gissing's wife), was known as Nell—a shortened form of Helen. And he gave the name of Helen to the ideal heroine of his first published novel, *Workers in the Dawn* (1880), though he also included a brutal portrayal of the unideal Nell as an alcoholic prostitute named Carrie Mitchell. **"The Mysterious Portrait"** itself depicts a pure Helen Marston without any contrasting prostitute, and the heroine's mother is also a Helen, as though ideal loveliness runs in the family.

This story partly reverses the plot of **"Gretchen"** and also of **"The Portrait"**: a painting that leads the hero to his ideal mate. The artist-hero of **"The Mysterious Portrait"** has already married an ideal and lovely Helen when a strange old man commissions a portrait from only a spoken description—one of the stranger's long-dead daughter. The hero at last approximates the dead woman's face by using his wife as a model, and the stranger identifies young Helen as his own vanished granddaughter, heir to all his wealth. Instead of the picture leading to the woman, the flesh-and-blood Helen inspires its creation, which in turn leads the stranger back to Helen again.

"The Mysterious Portrait" ends with a melodramatic repentance strikingly similar to one in *The Unclassed* (1884): a father's need to atone to a long-dead daughter by kindness to that daughter's child. In that novel Woodstock pleads with Ida Starr to accept his belated repentance: "I can't do anything for *her*. . . . But you are her child, and I want to do now what I ought to have done long ago."[8] In **"The Mysterious Portrait"** Treherne announces his repentance, not once, but twice:

> ". . . For the last six months I have been vainly trying to find the child of my lost daughter, so that by kindness and devotion to my grandchild I might, in part at least, atone for my harshness toward her mother."

"But, thank heaven!" said he . . . , "I can atone in some measure for my harshness toward my Helen by taking her Helen to my heart and making her my daughter."

The mechanical repetition of these speeches suggests the author's inexperience, and we know that Gissing at this time had been writing prose fiction for only a few months.

As in much of Gissing's early fiction, this tale's high-society background is not very convincing. Until the end of the 1880s, his novels show an obsession with aristocrats, gentility, large country estates, and huge unearned incomes—a privileged world in which he remained an ill-at-ease outsider. In 1885 Chapman and Hall's editor-reader, the novelist George Meredith, specifically advised Gissing to cease his attempts to portray upper-class life.[9] Within **"The Mysterious Portrait"** an "aristocratic-looking" baronet's son considers Helen Marston "worth fifty estates." His father's estate earns "fifteen thousand a year," and fifty times this is £750,00—the apparent cash equivalent of Helen herself. At the close of this wish-fulfilling story, the baronet's son has gained not only his ideal woman—a human equivalent of fifty whole estates— but also two actual estates, hers and his. He ends up with the best of both matter and spirit: silver-fork riches and ideal love. In fact, **"The Mysterious Portrait"** seems the first published instance of Gissing's silver-fork daydreams—wishful fantasies that he had to leave behind before he could create his very best fiction, novels of shabby-genteel existence.

The opening scene of **"The Picture"** (*Chicago Daily News,* 4 August 1877)—the third anonymous story dealing with painting—resembles the beginning of Gissing's **"An Heiress on Condition"** (written between December 1879 and February 1881), a piece never published in his lifetime. In both a young artist at work outdoors on a picture sees a beautiful young woman alongside her mother. In the *Daily News* piece, the artist sketches them together: "a perfect harmony of light and shade—an exact subject for a masterpiece." In **"An Heiress on Condition,"** the hero paints a landscape until the two distract him. In **"The Picture"** he wonders "who were they, or rather who was she?"[10] After these parallel openings, both stories achieve romantic happy endings through somewhat different means. The hero of **"The Picture"** gains artistic renown for his painting of the two unknown women, and he tracks them down at last and marries the daughter. In **"An Heiress on Condition,"** he quickly learns the identity of the women and soon wins the daughter for himself, along with her inheritance. Gissing appears to have reworked materials from **"The Portrait"** into his later story—a process rather like his thoroughgoing revision of **"The Artist's Child"** from the *Alliance* (30 June 1877) into **"The Artist's Child"** in *Tinsleys' Magazine* (January 1878), a piece with all-new prose and even new names.

In a broader sense, all three unsigned stories of painting and idealism seem links in a Gissing chain, a repeated reworking of a single basic fantasy persisting in his fiction until the end of the 1880s. The ability to respond to a portrait of a beautiful woman or to paint a beautiful woman results in a double reward: the woman herself and aristocratic wealth. Art leads both to sexual bliss and material contentment. The Pygmalion myth blends with a somewhat cruder fantasy of wealth and high position for a true aesthetic soul. This mixture of aesthetic idealism and status-conscious crassness has the special flavor of Gissing's early period—strong evidence for his authorship of all three stories. Later in his fiction he would view with bitter irony these self-deceiving dreams of artists and also writers about erotic, creative, and high social rapture. The attribution to Gissing of **"The Portrait," "The Mysterious Portrait,"** and **"The Picture"** helps to fill in a stage of his earliest development.

Have we now almost reached the end of a seven-decade search for Gissing's lost stories? It would help if we had an estimate of how many he actually published in 1877. In an 1880 letter to his brother, Gissing, in fact, boasted of having produced "a story every week" during his time in Chicago.[11] The letter falsely suggests, however, that, except for his *Appletons' Journal* piece, these once-a-week stories all were written for the prestigious *Tribune,* but we now know that Gissing wrote them as well for other Chicago papers, some very small and ephemeral. Yet evidence does exist that even his story for the New York magazine, *Appletons',* was written, submitted, and accepted during his Chicago stay. On 18 June 1877 a *Tribune* advertisement for the *Appletons' Journal* announced, among its other upcoming items, **"An English Coast-Picture"** by G. R. Gresham, and Gissing remained in Chicago until sometime in July.[12] As a result, it seems reasonable to take Gissing's boast of a once-a-week story as a rough approximation of his actual output in Chicago.

A calendar shows that he stayed there for at least seventeen weeks and at most twenty-one. We have nine certain stories from this period, and we know that at least two more appeared in unlocatable issues of the humorous little paper the *National Weekly*—eleven certain stories that he wrote in Chicago.[13] Likely attributions based on theme and style come to nine. But as I have argued elsewhere, three other attributions— **"The Death-Clock," "The Serpent-Charm,"** and **"Dead and Alive"**—seem highly improbable at best.[14]

Without these, the total is an even twenty or, in fact, just about "a story every week," as Gissing himself claimed. In effect, we have at last approached, it seems, a reasonably full account of the intensity and extent of Gissing's literary apprenticeship during his time of exile. . . .

Notes

1. M. C. Richter, "Memorabilia," *Notes and Queries,* 165 (7 October 1933), 236.

2. Pierre Coustillas and Robert L. Selig, "Unknown Gissing Stories from Chicago," *TLS,* 12 December 1980, 1417-18.

3. See Robert L. Selig, "An Unknown Gissing Story from the *Chicago Daily News,*" *Studies in Bibliography: Papers of the Bibliographical Society of the University of Virginia,* 36 (1983), 205-12. Robert L. Selig, "A Further Gissing Attribution from the *Chicago Post,*" *Papers of the Bibliographical Society of America,* 80 (1986), 100-104.

4. John Spiers and Pierre Coustillas, *The Rediscovery of George Gissing: A Reader's Guide* (London: National Book League, 1971), 18-19. George Gissing's "Art Notes: 'Elaine'—Rosenthal and Tojetti" appeared in the *Commonwealth* (Boston), 28 October 1876, 3.

5. In "Gretchen" (*Chicago Tribune,* 12 May 1877), Paul Mansfield studies art in Paris. Julius Trent in "The Artist's Child" (*Alliance,* 30 June 1877) struggles to support himself by painting. *Workers in the Dawn* (1880) has a painter-hero named Arthur Golding and a painter-villain named Gilbert Gresham—an echo of Gissing's own early pseudonym. Philip Farnsworth in "An Heiress on Condition" (written between November 1879 and July 1880; published 1923) works as a professional artist. In *Isabel Clarendon* (1886) the hero envies Clement Gabriel's devotion to painting. In *Demos* (1886) Hubert Eldon displays a great aesthetic soul by taking up art criticism. Sidney Kirkwood in *The Nether World* (1889) yearns to become a painter but lacks the strong talent needed to transcend his working-class background. Ross Mallard in *The Emancipated* (1890) gains a high reputation as a gifted landscape painter. The villainous Eustace Glazzard of *Denzil Quarrier* (1892) dabbles at art. In one of Gissing's finest short stories—"A Victim of Circumstances" (written 1891; published 1893)—an inept artist-husband, Horace Castledine, passes off his wife's fine water-color landscapes as his own inspired creations. *The Crown of Life* (1899) depicts, not one, but three painters: Miss Bonnicastle, a successful commercial artist; Mr. Kite, a creator of strangely symbolic nudes; and Olga Hannaford, a

not-very-good beginner. Even Gissing's last published novel, *Will Warburton* (1905), has an artist
character, Norbert Franks, who ends up painting
fashionable portraits.

6. G[eorge]. R[obert]. G[issing]., "Gretchen," in *Sins
   of the Fathers and Other Tales,* by George Gissing (Chicago: Pascal Covici, 1924), 35-36.

7. George Gissing, *The Unclassed* (London: Chapman & Hall, 1884), I, 244-49.

8. Ibid., III, 105.

9. Letter of George Gissing to Algernon Gissing, 22
   October 1885, in *Letters of George Gissing to
   Members of His Family,* Algernon and Ellen Gissing, eds. (London: Constable and Company, 1927),
   172.

10. George Gissing, *An Heiress on Condition*
    (Philadelphia: privately printed for the Pennell
    Club, 1923), 4.

11. Letter of George Gissing to Algernon Gissing, 7
    February 1880, in *Letters of George Gissing to
    Members of His Family,* 57-58.

12. [Advertisement,] "*Appletons' Journal* for July,"
    Chicago Tribune, 18 June 1877, 7. George Giss-
    ing's American notebook from 1877, in the Bei-
    necke Rare Book and Manuscript Library of Yale
    University, gives a month-by-month itinerary:
    March to July in Chicago, July in New York City.

13. See Robert L. Selig, "The *National Weekly*: A
    Lost Source of Unknown Gissing Fiction," *Giss-
    ing Newsletter,* 18 (January 1982), 2-9.

14. Robert L. Selig, "Unconvincing Gissing Attribu-
    tions: 'The Death-Clock,' 'The Serpent-Charm,'
    'Dead and Alive,'" *The Library,* 6th ser., 9 (June
    1987), 169-72.

Barbara Rawlinson (essay date 2001)

SOURCE: Rawlinson, Barbara. "Buried Treasure:
George Gissing's Short Fiction." In *A Garland for Gis-
sing,* edited by Bouwe Postmus, pp. 33-9. Amsterdam:
Rodopi, 2001.

[*In the following essay, Rawlinson discusses the experimental aspects of Gissing's stories, most notably the
commonplace yet noble nature of his characters and the
muted tone of his melodramatic plots.*]

In his lifetime, Gissing wrote over one hundred short
stories, most of which achieved publication,[1] yet to
date this important area of the author's work has received scant critical attention. Although his output in

this field was prolific, Gissing's literary interest lay almost exclusively in novels, consequently his short fiction tended to be produced at times when his serious
writing was going badly, or when he needed a means
of supplementing his wildly fluctuating income.
Broadly, Gissing's short story production falls into
three separate phases. The first of these covers a six-
month period during 1877 whilst the author was living
in America. From 1878 to 1884, following his return
to England, Gissing produced eleven short stories, but
apart from **"The Artist's Child"**, written and published in America, and revised for *Tinsleys' Magazine*
in January 1878, only one of these achieved publication during that time, this being **"Phoebe"**, which appeared in *Temple Bar* in March 1884. The third, most
prolific and extended phase, began in 1890 and continued until shortly before his death in 1903. By this
time Gissing was an established and critically acclaimed novelist, and his short fiction was sought after
by leading magazine editors of the day.

Clearly, the short stories form an integral part of the
Gissing canon and any assessment of his work is therefore incomplete without them. It is in his short fiction
that the writer reveals his gift for experimentation; a
continuing process of adaptation, excision and refinement which ultimately led to his achieving a distinctly
singular form of realism in this field. Furthermore,
many of these tales, particularly the early ones, contain the nucleus of concepts which were substantially
revised and developed in terms of style, structure, and
psychological insight, to become major themes in his
later work. For instance, there are recognizable links
between Tim Ridley's struggles with temptation in
"Too Dearly Bought"[2] and those of James Hood in *A
Life's Morning,* but whereas the short story is a simple
melodrama about crime and remorse, the novel explores the psychological impact of the theft, not only
on Hood, but also on all the major characters in the
book. Theft is but one of a number of recurring themes
in Gissing's fiction. Others, such as poverty, abandonment, mendacity, suicide by drowning, the impoverished artist or writer, are also manifest in his early
work. The American stories were a melting pot of
ideas in embryo, to be given flesh, radically reformed,
and regenerated as major themes in his mature novels
and short fiction.

A worthy example of Gissing's experimental flair is
demonstrated by the links between three stories from
his American period and one from his third phase,
which reveal the author's innate gift for purposeful intertextuality. In **"Too Dearly Bought"**, Tim Ridley
steals ten gold sovereigns from his benefactor in order
to take his frail granddaughter to the country, in the
belief that the goodness of his motive mitigates the
crime. When the girl dies, Ridley is convinced that her

death is a punishment for his sin, and he knows not a moment's peace until he is able to repay the money, whereupon he collapses and dies. The theft theme is reversed in **"Joseph Yates' Temptation"**,[3] in that the crime is stillborn owing to the moral example of a starving waif. Joseph's request for an advance on his wages is refused, so when he finds himself in possession of a large cheque he is tempted to steal it. It takes the courage in adversity of a destitute mother and child to make him realize the superficiality of his desire to provide a little temporary Christmas cheer.

In **"Twenty Pounds"**,[4] Gissing again combines the theft motif with that of the stony-hearted employer, but here, by toning down the melodrama, he creates an entirely plausible tale of human fallibility. The story is about a man who had in the past embezzled twenty pounds, but had been saved from disgrace by the generosity of an anonymous donor. The donor, a compulsive gambler, has since fallen on hard times and has himself stolen twenty pounds from his employer, none other than the man he had once helped. The narrator, acting on behalf of his friend, tries in vain to reason with the employer, but only the threat of exposure will induce him to withdraw the charge. Earlier in the story, as he is about to hand over the money that will save the young thief, the narrator hints at an ironical outcome:

> That is the man . . . whose proceedings have been dubious, and who will, I trust, be rescued by Staining's £20. Well, if the wheel should turn, and this poor man should ever be in a position to deliver a fellow creature from such trouble as he himself is now in, by the surrender of £20, I wonder whether he'll do it? Smith, you surely know human nature well enough to answer your own question. Not he—not a bit of it.
>
> (48-49)

"The Poet's Portmanteau",[5] from Gissing's third phase of short fiction, maintains the theft motif, but takes as its focal point the cyclical theme of an object circulating back to its starting point, an idea present— the gold coins, the cheque, the twenty pounds—but not stressed in the three earlier tales. Through an error of judgment, the struggling poet foolishly leaves his portmanteau in the care of a desperate young girl, who pawns it in order to buy a railway ticket. However, the manuscript within, having no monetary value, remains in her possession. Many years later, a mysterious friend of the now dead girl returns the document to its owner, who, ironically, has achieved fame despite his terrible misfortune. As an example of the author's developing low-key approach to realistic fiction, **"The Poet's Portmanteau"** demonstrates an ongoing process of modification, refinement and elimination, which culminated in the creation of a new breed of commonplace heroes, whose successes or failures cause barely a ripple in their uneventful lives. Paradoxically, these characters are in no sense pathetic victims of life's struggle for survival, rather they are resolute individuals, ready to meet misfortune with patience, courage and occasionally even humour. Henry James wrote of Gissing: "He has the strongest, deepest sense of common humanity, of the general struggle, and the general grey, grim comedy."

By pursuing a strategy of thematic refinement, and gradually eliminating all artifice from his texts, Gissing ultimately developed an economy of style uniquely his own, one which derives its interest and veracity solely from the resilience of ordinary characters to extraordinary circumstances. **"Humplebee"**,[6] one of the finest stories in *The House of Cobwebs,* a posthumous collection from the author's third phase, cogently demonstrates the singularity of Gissing's realism in short fiction. Through a reckless act of heroism, Humplebee earns the gratitude of Mr Chadwick, the father of a boy he saves from drowning, whereupon he becomes a hostage to good fortune. Prior to the accident, the boy had attracted little attention:

> . . . a short, thin, red-headed boy of sixteen, whose plain, freckled face denoted good-humour and a certain intelligence, but would never have drawn attention amongst the livelier and comelier physiognomies grouped about him. This was Humplebee. Hitherto he had been an insignificant member of the school, one of those boys who excel neither at games nor at lessons, of whom nothing is expected, and rarely, if ever, get into trouble, and who are liked in a rather contemptuous way.
>
> (69)

Unlike the sketchy descriptions of character in earlier stories, these few lines conjure a vivid picture of the boy's nondescript appearance and retiring personality, indicative of his extreme vulnerability to the influences that are shortly to determine his future.

"Humplebee" centres on its namesake's steadfast refusal to be daunted by ill fortune. Even though Chadwick's patronage deprives him of a fulfilling career in natural history, drives his father into bankruptcy and an early grave, and, when his cause is taken up by Chadwick's son, he narrowly escapes arrest, at the end of the story Humplebee remains philosophical, calmly accepting that "he had to begin life over again—that was all".

Little trace remains of the dramatic, mid-Victorian style typical of the early Gissing, rather **"Humplebee"** is notable for its acutely perceptive characterization and benign irony, which bring out the pathos inherent in the natural dignity with which ordinary human beings meet the constant frustrations of everyday existence, finding reward enough in the simple pleasures of life.

The years 1878 to 1884, following his return to England, were very desperate times for Gissing. With the exception of **"The Artist's Child"**, he had no short fiction published until **"Phoebe"** in 1884. Despite their apparent lack of appeal to magazine editors however, a number of the tales show enormous strides in composition and characterization, revealing a progressive re-evaluation of technique and style. In contrast to the wide diversity of genres covered in his American period, the majority of stories spanning his second phase were melodramatic in tone, which is not to say that his short fiction had become less imaginative, but rather that he had hit upon a form which offered considerable potential for development. A major innovation at this time was that Gissing now tended to focus more on characters than plot, and, within an uncomplicated and plausible narrative, to observe impartially their reaction to good or ill fortune.

In **"The Last Half-Crown"**,[7] Gissing's new, low-key approach is very effective. For this toned-down melodrama he produced a narrative in which a seemingly ordinary occurrence triggers off a series of events which culminate in tragedy. Throughout, the interest rests with the protagonist and his dilemma, rather than intricacy of plot. At the heart of the tale lurks the spectre of poverty; a persistent theme in Gissing's work; like Edwin Reardon in *New Grub Street,* Harold Sansom is an impoverished writer, whose spirit has been crushed in the brutalizing struggle for survival in the competitive literary world, to whom one half-crown means the difference between life and death.

In the event, literary failure is not the principal cause of Harold's despair, rather it is Mrs Higgs, his grasping landlady, whose persistent demand for rent in advance has a dire effect on his pitifully meagre income. The consequences resonating from Mrs Higgs' greed demonstrate the laws of cause and effect with graphic realism. She holds the power of life or death over her impoverished tenant, as does he, in deciding whether or not to reclaim the coin, over his even poorer neighbours, Lizzie and Mrs Wilson. The landlady's demand sets in motion a chain reaction, that begins with the loss of the young man's last half-crown, and ends, ironically, in temporary relief from starvation for a destitute family, and death for the coin's owner. The laws of cause and effect are key to maintaining credulity in situations that might otherwise be deemed highly improbable. Gissing focusses on a single act, sometimes accidental, often not, and allows the consequences to develop naturally through a sequence of plausible events.

"Mutimer's Choice", Gissing's last story of the early Eighties, testifies to the development that has taken place in the four years since **"The Last Half-Crown"** was written. The innovations noted earlier have reached a point where melodrama is reduced to a minimum, the story is feasible and concise, and practically all trace of omniscience has disappeared.

"Mutimer's Choice"[8] is a sombre tale about a man who makes a calculated choice between two wretched alternatives. Jim Mutimer has the two-fold misfortune to marry a vain and bad-tempered woman, and suffer an industrial accident, which offers no alternative but the amputation of his legs. Faced with a choice between death and a future of bitter conflict, he refuses the operation that would save his life. The story opens to the clamour of church bells, their penetrating jangle shattering the unnatural silence pervading the Mutimer household, and prefiguring the violent quarrel about to erupt over Bella's extravagance and deceit. Wilfully, she accuses her husband of meanness, insinuating that Bill Snowdon, her ex-suitor and Jim's friend, thinks the same. Keenly aware of the attraction between Snowdon and his wife, Mutimer forbids any further contact.

After the accident, Mutimer's weighty words virtually force Snowdon into a commitment to take care of Bella: "A dying man's words stick in the mind, and they have the power either to bless or to curse" (253). (There is a hint of sadism in Mutimer's concern for his wife's future, in the certainty that Snowdon will soon be enduring the misery he is about to escape. The ironic outcome is foreshadowed in Bella's dream, in which she sees her husband "roll a great piece of stone upon Snowdon and crush him beneath it" (249).

By the 1890s, Gissing had acquired a literary agent, and was therefore in a far better position to negotiate terms. He was by now a critically acclaimed novelist, and his short stories were in popular demand. Jerome K. Jerome commissioned him to write six sketches for *To-Day* magazine, under the heading **"Nobodies at Home"**, and Clement Shorter, editor of the *Illustrated London News,* the *English Illustrated Magazine* and the *Sketch,* published two series of Gissing's stories entitled **"Human Odds and Ends"** and **"Great Men in Little Worlds"**, as well as numerous individual tales. In all, Gissing produced some seventy short stories during this latter period of his life, and the titles of the three series give a good indication of the direction his work had taken. In his preface to the posthumous collection *Stories and Sketches,*[9] Alfred Gissing recalls that his father always maintained that plot without character in a story was like a vehicle without passengers—a mere wooden show, and that it is as sketches of character and temperament that the stories should be regarded. By the mid-1890s Gissing had mastered the art of realistic representation, producing a seemingly inexhaustible array of distinctive human figures, with but one characteristic in common—the capacity to come to terms with misfortune and to rise above it.

In **"The House of Cobwebs"**,[10] one of the author's finest short stories, Mr Spicer is the owner, for one year only, of a row of derelict houses. He is content to occupy just one room in these miserable dwellings, because of the sense of pride he feels in ownership, and the sheer pleasure he gets from being able to cultivate a crop of vegetables in his weed-infested garden. When his home is destroyed in a storm, the old man puts the disaster down to "chastisement for overweening desires" (27) and considers it great good fortune that he still has his garden. Uncommonly sensitive characterization, coupled with good-natured irony, brings out both the pathos and the courage inherent in the old man's capacity to remain optimistic in adversity, and content with the simple things of life.

Undeniably, the short stories are intrinsic to the Gissing canon, yet to date they have not received the critical attention they so richly deserve. Despite the frenetic search for material from the American period which continued for more than sixty years, most of the author's later output has been neglected. Pierre Coustillas, whose work on reviving interest in Gissing's novels is renowned, has also paid considerable attention to his short fiction, having produced an invaluable bibliography in 1964, and in addition edited **George Gissing: Essays & Fiction** in 1970 and **The Day of Silence and Other Stories** in 1993, as well as being responsible for the publication of several individual tales. Nevertheless, the majority of stories, including some of the finest, remain buried in library basements.

Notes

1. The major collections of Gissing's short stories are:

   George Gissing, *Human Odds and Ends* (London: Lawrence and Bullen, 1898); *The House of Cobwebs* (London: Archibald Constable, 1906); *Sins of the Fathers* (Chicago: Pascal Covici, 1924); *A Victim of Circumstances* (London: Constable, 1927); *Brownie* (New York: Columbia University Press, 1931); *Stories and Sketches* (London: Michael Joseph, 1938); Robert L. Selig, ed., *George Gissing: Lost Stories from America* (Lewiston/Queenston/Lampeter: Edwin Mellen Press, 1992); George Gissing, *The Day of Silence and Other Stories,* ed., Pierre Coustillas (Everyman edn, 1993).

2. "Too Dearly Bought", *The Sins of the Fathers*, 91-124.

3. "Joseph Yates' Temptation", *Brownie*, 55-71.

4. "Twenty Pounds", *Brownie*, 54.

5. "The Poet's Portmanteau", *Human Odds and Ends*, 74-91.

6. "Humplebee", *The House of Cobwebs*, 68-87.

7. Pierre Coustillas, ed., *George Gissing: Essays & Fiction* (Baltimore and London: Johns Hopkins Press, 1970), 180-85.

8. "Mutimer's Choice", *George Gissing: Essays & Fiction,* 241-53.

9. George Gissing, *Stories and Sketches* (London: Michael Joseph, 1938).

10. "The House of Cobwebs", *The House of Cobwebs* (London: Archibald Constable, 1906, 1-27.

Russell Price and Francesco Badolato (essay date 2001)

SOURCE: Price, Russell, and Francesco Badolato. "Social Subordination and Superiority in Gissing's 'A Daughter of the Lodge.'" In *A Garland for Gissing,* edited by Bouwe Postmus, pp. 235-47. Amsterdam: Rodopi, 2001.

[*In the following essay, Price and Badolato probe themes of social class and women's liberation in "A Daughter of the Lodge," underscoring the relationships between the female characters.*]

Gissing wrote numerous short stories during his later career, after passing his mid-thirties. **"A Daughter of the Lodge"**[1] is one of his later stories, written in 1900, first published in 1901, and posthumously published in book form in *The House of Cobwebs and Other Stories* (1906).

It may be said that there are two main themes in this fine story, which has received almost no critical attention. As in *The Odd Women* and some other works published by Gissing in the 1890s, "the woman question" is conspicuous. The main character, May Rockett, is one of the "new women"; she is not content to remain in the station of life in which she was born, but has wanted to better herself. After early studies at the village school, she attended "the High School in the neighbouring town". At the age of seventeen, she "went in pursuit of the higher learning", which should be interpreted as meaning study at some college or university. Afterwards, she worked briefly as a governess, then as secretary to "a lady with a mission—concerning the rights of womanhood" (167-68). However, her present salary is "very modest", and she cannot afford a bicycle (a bicycle, and the lack of one, is a crucial factor in the first two encounters with Hilda Shale). May Rockett is in her mid-twenties; she decides, after a "couple of years" without having visited "the old home", to spend a few days with her family, who keep the lodge at Brent Hall, in order to rest after a period of intense work.

The second main theme is social class or, more exactly, class positions of social subordination and superiority; this theme was seldom treated so explicitly and forcefully by Gissing in a short story, though the theme of social class and its intricacies is present in many of his works, for example, *Demos, Born in Exile, A Life's Morning,* and *Our Friend the Charlatan.*

The subject of "social class" and "class distinction" is large and complicated,[2] mainly because the principal "indicators" of social class are various, and sometimes inconsistent. They may be said to be: wealth or income, occupation, education, and (these terms are vague) "way of life" or "life-style". Since space does not permit elucidation of this topic, we can only say that the named characters in **"A Daughter of the Lodge"** belong to the rural aristocracy and (probably) to the upper-middle class and to the lower-middle class. Housekeepers, lodge-keepers and head gardeners were regarded as lower-middle class.[3]

We are told that "[i]n the beginning Rockett was head gardener" (later his "health broke down, and at length he could work hardly at all"); and "his wife, the daughter of a shopkeeper, had never known domestic service [that is, she never had to earn her living as a servant, and was the wife of an upper servant] and performed her duties at the Hall gates with a certain modest dignity" (167). Their daughter, May, is clearly an "upwardly mobile" lower-middle-class woman. To say, as one critic has done, that this is "a tale of the victimization of a working-class family by a wealthy one",[4] reveals a misunderstanding of the class position of the Rocketts.

Sir Henry Shale was the baronet who engaged Rockett as head gardener; after his health had failed, the Rockett family began to look after the lodge (where they have been for about twenty years). Their duties seem to consist largely of keeping a watchful eye on persons entering and leaving Brent Hall, and of opening and closing the gates. All the duties appear to be performed by Mrs Rockett and her daughter, Betsy, and apparently it was Mrs Rockett who was engaged to keep the lodge.[5]

After Sir Henry's death, the relationship between the Hall and the lodge was not quite as satisfactory as it had been. We are told that Sir Edwin Shale, the nephew who had succeeded Sir Henry, "had in his youth made a foolish marriage". This is significant, for his wife dominates him, and their daughter, Hilda (an "only child"), rather resembles her mother in character (167).

We find, then, at the Hall, two somewhat difficult, domineering women (and a submissive baronet, who plays a very minor part in the story). In the lodge there is a man who is an "invalid" (169), together with his wife and younger daughter (there was also a Rockett son, who got into trouble, and "was by the [previous] baronet's advice sent to sea" [167]—another insignificant male, not mentioned again). The remaining member of the Rockett family is the elder daughter, May, who has lived away from home for some years; she is the "daughter of the lodge".

This story, then, is primarily concerned with the relationships, often difficult, between the women already mentioned, and with a Mrs Lindley, "who in social position [stands] on an equality" with the Shales, whom she often visits (171). (May Rockett travels to meet her, and at her house a significant incident occurs.) The only males in the story (the nominal heads of the Rockett and Shale families) play unimportant parts. At its centre are the ideas, words, and characters of the women.

With regard to social status, two of the women (Lady Shale and Hilda Shale) belong to the upper class, one (Mrs Lindley) probably belongs to the upper-middle class, and three (the Rockett sisters and their mother) belong to the lower-middle class. Two of the latter (Mrs Rockett and Betsy) are contented with their social position; they know and accept their "place" in the social "hierarchy", their condition of "subordination" (168). "The second daughter, Betsy, grew up to be her mother's help" (167). And it is suggested that it was "a reasonable hope that Betsy, good steady girl, should some day marry the promising young gardener whom Sir Edwin [Shale] had recently taken into his service, and so re-establish the old order of things at the lodge". As for Mr and Mrs Rockett, both "felt gratitude for their retention at the lodge", and "dreaded the thought" of leaving Brent Hall. Mr Rockett "often consoled himself with the thought that here he should die, here amid the fine old trees that he loved, in the ivy-covered house which was his only idea of home". In short, as the author says, "a spirit of loyal subordination ruled their blood" (168-69).

May Rockett does not share her family's attitude. Although brought up in the lodge, she has lived away for some years. She is now an "outsider" physically (a very rare visitor), and, more important, an outsider in spirit, a semi-detached member of the Rockett family.

Since her outlook is well known to her parents, they are troubled and anxious about her coming visit. She says in the letter announcing it, "Of course . . . it's unnecessary to say anything about me to the Shale people. They and I have nothing in common, and it will be better for us to ignore each other's existence". The phrase "the Shale people" is offhand, lacking in respect. And her attitude strikes her parents as "inappropriate":

> That the family at the Hall should, if it seemed good to them, ignore the existence of May was, in the Rocketts' view, reasonable enough; but for May to ignore Sir Edwin and Lady Shale . . . struck them as a very grave impropriety. Natural respect[6] demanded that, at some fitting moment, and in a suitable manner, their daughter should present herself to her feudal[7] superiors, to whom she was assuredly indebted, though indirectly, for "the blessings she enjoyed".

Personal affection for the Shales is irrelevant: in fact, the Rocketts have "no affection" for "Sir Edwin or his lady" and "decidedly" [dislike] Hilda Shale; their attitude depends upon the relative positions of the two families in the social hierarchy and, of course, upon the fact that the Rocketts are, in a sense, employees of the Shale family. This dependence, and threats to their position, give rise to feelings of unease and tensions.

It is not surprising, then, that Mrs Rockett says anxiously, "I half wish May wasn't coming . . . Last time she was here she quite upset me with her strange talk". Her domestic habits, too, are unusual: thus, whereas "the nice little sitting-room" was "of course, only used on Sunday" by them, May used it every day. The author comments, "It was one of the habits which emphasised most strongly the moral distance between her and her parents".

So the scene is set for the half-dreaded visit; trouble is looming. May Rockett arrives in a cab, with her "dress-basket . . . travelling-bag and . . . hold-all". To the cab-driver, she says, "You will bring these things inside, please," in an "agreeable" voice, but "with the tone and gesture of one who habitually gives orders". She greets her mother and sister, who come out to welcome her, "with no excess of feeling" and the rather condescending "exclamation", "Well, good people!" (168-69). Indeed, condescension marks what she says and does. She speaks disparagingly about the "country medico" who treats her father; she invites *him* to "Sit down, sit down, and make yourself comfortable". She orders tea (with "a slice of lemon . . . if you have such a thing") and toast. She is the opposite of "homely" and puts her family in "a state of nervous agitation".

Then occurs the first appearance of Miss Shale, who raps on a lodge window. Betsy "[runs] to the door"; returning, she says that "she never heard the bell" (the Rocketts are obviously expected to be alert for the sound of a bicycle-bell) and that "Miss Shale had to get off her bicycle" to open the gate, and was very "annoyed". May Rockett's reaction is a contemptuous smile, and the remark that her annoyance "will do her good. A little anger now and then is excellent for the health".

Early next morning May gives "precise directions about her breakfast", and the "tone of her instructions vexed and perturbed Mrs Rockett" very much (170); obviously, she is "vexed" because unused to such behaviour within her family, and "perturbed" because of the likelihood of trouble arising from contacts between her daughter and the Shale *women*. Indeed, we are told that soon

> The Rocketts . . . put aside all thoughts of what they esteemed May's duty towards the Hall; they earnestly hoped that her stay with them might pass unobserved by Lady and Miss Shale, whom, they felt sure, it would be positively dangerous for the girl to meet.

Nevertheless, Mr Rockett, although "a good deal troubled", shares with Betsy "a secret admiration" for May's "brilliant qualities".

On the next afternoon, May Rockett travels by train to the nearby town, and goes to Mrs Lindley's home, being "[a]t once admitted to the drawing-room". Her hostess is "a good-humoured chatty woman, [with] a lively interest in everything 'progressive'". We are told that "Miss Rockett's talk was exactly what she liked, for it glanced at innumerable topics of the 'advanced' sort, was much concerned with personalities, and avoided all tiresome precision of argument" (171).[8] Later, more callers enter the room, but May Rockett continues to take a very prominent part in the conversation. Eventually, a servant announces: "Miss Shale". (This is the first direct contact between the two young women of different social classes.) The baronet's daughter is, naturally, surprised to find the lodge-keeper's daughter in the drawing-room. It is clear from Hilda Shale's clothes ("short skirt, easy jacket, and brown shoes") that she "had come into town on her bicycle". The conversation soon turns to this subject, unsurprisingly, since cycling had recently become such a common pastime. When Mrs Lindley asks May Rockett whether she cycles, she replies, "No, I don't. The fact is, I have never found time to learn". After another lady remarks that "nowadays there [is] a certain distinction in not cycling", Miss Shale intervenes:

> It's a pity the machines can't be sold cheaper. A great many people who would like to cycle don't feel able to afford it, you know. One often hears of such cases out in the country, and it seems awfully hard times, doesn't it?

(172)

This is a critical point in Gissing's story. What is intended as a wounding personal comment (though couched in general terms) is thus interpreted by May Rockett. And it is hard to bear, because she "would have long ago bought a bicycle had she been able to afford it" (173). Mrs Lindley, however, "who made no personal application of Miss Shale's remark, [begins] to discuss the prices of bicycles" (172), and this becomes the topic of conversation.

Two years before he wrote this story, Gissing stayed with H. G. Wells and his wife, who were keen cyclists. Wells began to teach Gissing to ride, which he did within a week, and he ordered a bicycle for himself.[9] He, too, became an enthusiastic cyclist, revelling in this healthy and speedy means of transport, and in the freedom it conferred. Bicycles enabled women as well as men to move about the country quickly, and (if they wished) unaccompanied. In *Our Friend the Charlatan* (1901), Constance Bride, Lady Ogram's secretary, likes cycling and teaches Lashmar to ride (like Gissing, he needs only a week); May Tomalin, Lady Ogram's niece, also likes "physical exercise", which she regards as "a part of rational education"; she says that two days earlier she "rode thirty miles".[10] In the short story, **"The Schoolmaster's Vision"** (1896),[11] the head of a boarding school is distracted from his duties (and bewitched) by a young widow who arrives on a bicycle (alone) to visit her son. In 1898 Gissing paid £14 for his bicycle (the equivalent today of about £650); obviously, many people could not afford such a machine.

May Rockett leaves Mrs Lindley's house as soon as possible. She is angry, and is sure that Hilda Shale will "make known her circumstances" to those present (173); and the home of her "people in the country" (172) will be revealed for what it is. She wanders about the main streets of the town in a "wrathful" state, "and [can] think of nothing but her humiliation". Her state of mind is such that she loses "count of time", finds that the only train home has already gone, cannot afford a cab, and must walk three miles on a warm evening. She reaches the gates of Brent Hall "tired, perspiring [and] irritated"). Then her second encounter of the day with Hilda Shale occurs.

Miss Shale is riding her bicycle and, twenty yards from the gates, rings her bicycle-bell, and cries "imperatively, 'Open the gate, please!'" May Rockett, after looking round, ignores her, passes "through the side entrance, and let[s] the little gate fall to". Consequently, Miss Shale has to dismount and open the gate herself. When she says angrily to May Rockett, who is about to enter the lodge door,

> "Didn't you hear me ask you to open?", May makes a dignified but imprudent reply: "I couldn't imagine you

were speaking to *me* . . . I supposed some servant of yours was in sight".

(173)

This second, very brief, encounter, and May Rockett's explicit rejection of any kind of servile status for herself (as distinct, doubtless, from for her family) have serious consequences for her family, and lead to further (and very much worse) humiliation for herself.

Mrs Rockett, running out to open the gate herself, is horrified, and says, "How *could* you forget yourself, to behave and speak like that! Why, you must be crazy, my girl!" May replies that she does not "seem to get on very well here", and that she is "in a false position". She will leave in the morning, "and there won't be any more trouble".

Mrs Rockett then goes up to the Hall, to "humbly apologiz[e] for her daughter's impertinence", but the housekeeper tells her that the family must leave the lodge within two months. She is shattered and, naturally, she soon angrily reproaches her daughter for having lost them their home, because of her "conceited, overbearing mind", and says that her sister "[w]ill have to go into service",[12] that is, domestic service, which would involve her doing work appropriate for someone of a lower class. Mrs Rockett cries, "We're below you, we are; we're like dirt under your feet!" (174)

Her father is more understanding: "You can't help yourself . . . It's your nature," adding that he will see Sir Edwin, who would perhaps listen to him, and that "It's the women who make all the mischief". But when Rockett sees Sir Edwin in the morning, the baronet "said he was sorry, but could not interfere; the matter lay in Lady Shale's hands", and she refuses to accept "any excuses or apologies for the insult . . . offered [to] her daughter".

May Rockett, until now "inclined to despise her family for their pusillanimous attitude" (175), becomes frightened, and decides to act: to try to save her innocent family from eviction, by humiliating herself and apologizing for her behaviour.

She goes to the Hall, to "the servants' entrance", where "she [begs] to be allowed to see the housekeeper". While waiting, she has to endure the "stares" and "malicious smiles" of several servants. Then the housekeeper listens "[w]ith a cold air of superiority and . . . disapproval" to the apology for her "rudeness" (which her family "utterly deplore[s]"). Seeking the housekeeper's help in arranging for her to see Lady Shale, she feels constrained to address her as "ma'am" (an acknowledgement of that upper servant's superior status, which "cost[s] her a terrible effort" [176]). She is told to wait in the "servants' hall" (a further confirmation, after using "the servants' entrance", of her social status). After a very long wait, a footman shows her into a large room, where the two Shale ladies "for some moments" continue to converse "placidly", before Lady Shale designs to show awareness of her presence. When May apologizes, in broken phrases, for her behaviour of the previous evening, Lady Shale interrupts her "contemptuously", saying, "I am glad you have come to your senses;" but she remarks that the apology "must be offered to Miss Shale—if my daughter cares to listen to it". May's apology (the third she has felt constrained to make) for her "rudeness", her "impertinence", is received coolly and offhandedly. Her apology made (and "listened to", but not "accepted"), May is told by Lady Shale (and the words are those of a superior to an inferior), "You may go".

Then "the terrible thought" occurs to her that "perhaps she [has] humiliated herself for nothing" (177), and she entreats Lady Shale not to send her parents away. But *she* is sent away without an answer, and advised to leave the lodge very soon, and never to return. Leaving the room, without knowing whether her self-abasement will have a positive result, May sees the footman, who grins at her, and asks, "Any good?" To be patronized by a liveried servant is "the last blow" to her pride. She returns to London that evening, without telling "her family what she [has] done". In a day or two she learns from Betsy that "the sentence of expulsion" has been "withdrawn" (178). Lady Shale was, after all, resolved to punish only the "impertinent" member of the Rockett family, the one who did not "know her place", not the innocent members.

This story is primarily about the behaviour and relationships of women, especially the three encounters between May Rockett and Hilda Shale, and (to a lesser extent) the encounter between May Rockett and Lady Shale, that is, between a lower-middle-class woman and two upper-class women; and the differences between their respective social positions and perspectives lie at the heart of the story. The other significant relationship is that between May Rockett and her family; and what is most prominent is her behaviour towards *them,* and her scant awareness of their feelings and situation. The two men who are more than merely mentioned, Sir Edwin Shale and Rockett (nominal "heads" of their respective families) are weak and ineffectual; they "do" and say little, though Rockett shows some understanding of his elder daughter.

Two comments are made that strike us as particularly significant. After the Rocketts are given notice to leave the lodge, Mr Rockett tells May that "perhaps [Sir Ed-

win] will listen to me. It's the women who make all the mischief" (175). This doubtless reflects Gissing's view that women tend to be "difficult", that they tend to talk too much and sometimes create difficult situations or foment quarrels, either intentionally (through malice, or vengeful spirit) or unintentionally.[13] However, in the context the remark is clearly intended to apply to the Shale women, especially, doubtless, to the malicious comment of Hilda Shale (it is called by the author "her hint" (173)—but it seems much more than that, and "meant for gentle irony" (172), though the adjective seems inappropriate) about the "prohibitive cost of bicycles" (173) for many people. Yet, ironically, the remark seems equally applicable to Rockett's daughter, May. For her tactless remarks and behaviour in the lodge certainly upset and irritate her family, and what she does and says outside undoubtedly provides opportunities for mischief-making by Hilda Shale.

In the other significant comment, Mr Rockett and Betsy are said to have admired "the brilliant qualities" of May Rockett, and to be "privately agreed that May was more of a real lady" than either of the Shale women (171). This comment cannot refer to her "origins": she was not of "gentle" birth. It must refer to her "ladylike attitudes and behaviour"; but it is not at all obvious that it is true. A careful reading of the story reveals that the personal characteristics, attitudes, and behaviour of all three women (though Lady Shale is portrayed in less detail) are remarkably similar.

Cardinal Newman, in a famous passage, said that it is "almost a definition of a gentleman to say that he is one who never inflicts pain". This description is both refined and, as far as it goes, accurate.[14] This characterization, which is obviously concerned with conduct (not "birth"), seems reasonably satisfactory (though "pain" needs to be qualified by a word such as "unnecessary"). And a "lady" may appropriately be defined in similar terms.

Let us consider, then, what is said about these three women. Lady Shale is said to have "ruled" her husband, "not with the gentlest of tongues, nor always to the kindest purpose" (167). Clearly, she is a domineering woman, whose language is sometimes offensive. She is called "hard-tongued" (171), she has a "metallic voice", and she displays "cold-blooded complacency" (177).

Hilda Shale is portrayed as a rather "masculine" type of woman:

> All her movements suggested vigour; she shook hands with a downward jerk, moved about [Mrs Lindley's] room with something of a stride and, in sitting down, crossed her legs abruptly.

Her "person" is "athletic", she is "tall, strongly built", she has "a face of hard comeliness", an "abrupt and rather metallic voice" (172) and, like her mother, she displays "cold-blooded complacency" (177). She "assert[s] her rights as only child with . . . force of character" (167), she speaks "imperatively" (173); she is "disdainful" (171), and, in her final encounter with May Rockett, refers to her contemptuously as "this person" (177), speaking to her mother, and not deigning to address May, who has just offered her an apology.

May Rockett, too, is a somewhat masculine type: "nothing unduly feminine marked her appearance, and in the matter of collar and necktie she inclined to the example of the other sex"; moreover, she "manifest[s] no excess of feeling" when her mother and sister greet her. Her "tone" and "gesture[s]" are those of a person "who habitually gives orders", she gives "precise directions" or "instructions" to her mother about her breakfast (169), and "sen[ds] her sister out to post nine letters" that she has written (170). Indeed, she is a rather "bossy" woman (like Miss Rodney, in the short story, **"Miss Rodney's Leisure"** [1903]).[15] She is "proud" (176, 177) and condescending (she wonders, aloud, how her family manage to live without a London newspaper [170-71], and she doubts whether they would have lemons for a slice in her tea, instead of the usual milk [170]), and she is "inclined to despise her family for their pusillanimous attitude" towards the Shales. She is very tactless, indeed almost completely insensitive towards the feelings of others, treating her own family as if they were *her* servants, but resenting (and rejecting) any idea that *she* is, in any sense, a servant of the Shale family. Her father thinks that her conduct springs from the natural bent of her character, that she is naturally unservile: "'You can't help yourself, May,' he said . . . 'It's your nature, my girl'" (175).

It may be concluded that none of these three female characters behaves in a "ladylike" way, with kindness and consideration for the feelings of others.

Gissing wrote **"A Daughter of the Lodge"** in two or three days, between 10 and 12 May 1900. It was originally entitled **"The Rash Miss Tomalin"**.[16] The main character's name was later changed to "Rockett", because Gissing used "Tomalin" for a character in *Our Friend the Charlatan* (1901). It was published as **"A Daughter of the Lodge"** in the *Illustrated London News*. The final title is neutral, but it is certainly not inappropriate, for it implies (like, say, **"A Son of the Manse"**) the social origins of the main character (without excluding present attachments to, or presence in, the lodge). The original title indicates an unfavourable judgement on her. That May Rockett is "rash"

can hardly be doubted: she displays little or no concern for the consequences of her words and actions, and the outcome is anxiety and trouble for her family, and very painful humiliation for herself.

She may be regarded, perhaps, as a fairly typical "new woman" of the 1890s, "educated" and intelligent (even if not a close reasoner), very interested in the rights and welfare of women, not attached to a man (or even, apparently, attracted to men).

May Rockett is also of lower-middle-class origin. And her present "position" in society requires some clarification. "When will you come to understand what my position is?", she rhetorically asks her mother, when the latter expresses surprise at her proposed visit to Mrs Lindley (171). Here her "position" is that which she occupies in the wider society, her work and social contacts in London. After the second encounter with Hilda Shale, Mrs Rockett says to her daughter, "How *could* you forget yourself, to behave and speak like that!" Here "forget yourself" means "forget your social 'position' or 'status'" in relation to the Shales. After the eviction of her family is announced, she wants to leave very soon, and says, "The fact is, I'm in a false position" (174), meaning, "here, in the lodge, and in local, rural society", where, she at last realizes, she cannot behave as she does in London. Lady Shale interprets her apology as her finally "com[ing] to [her] senses", as a belated recognition of her "proper", subordinate position in the local society. However, this apology is not genuine; it has an ulterior motive, being uttered in order to "gain her end" (177) and have the expulsion notice revoked. Once returned to London, May Rockett soon recovers her "self-respect" (178); for in the large city the social distinctions so important in rural society no longer matter very much, nor do her origins and upbringing in the lodge. Gissing's story provides a fine study of subordination and superiority in English rural society at the turn of the century.

Notes

1. George Gissing, "A Daughter of the Lodge", in *The Day of Silence and Other Stories,* ed. Pierre Coustillas (Everyman edn, 1993), 167-78.

2. Nicholas Abercrombie and Alan Warde, *Contemporary British Society: A New Introduction to Sociology* (Oxford: Polity Press, 1988) begin their chapter on "Class" by saying, "Social class must be the most debated concept in sociology" (110). Like most sociologists (especially Marxists), they place most emphasis on "occupation".

3. For the various types and grades of servant, see Pamela Horn, *The Rise and Fall of the Victorian Servant* (Dublin: Gill & Macmillan, 1975), chs 4,

5; Frank Dawes, *Not in Front of the Servants: Domestic Service in England 1850-1939* (London: Wayland Publishers, 1973), ch. 5.

4. John Halperin, *Gissing: A Life in Books* (Oxford: Oxford University Press, 1982), 304.

5. Towards the end of the story, the housekeeper says: "Mrs Rockett, I'm sorry to tell you that you will have to leave the lodge. My lady allows you two months, though, as your wages have always been paid monthly, only a month's notice is really called for" (174). Since modern English has no second-person singular personal pronoun, "you" and "your" are ambiguous. But it seems likely that Mrs Rockett is formally employed to look after the lodge (for her husband is an invalid and, in effect, retired), and the monthly wages would be paid to her, to use and distribute as she thinks fit.

6. That is, the respect required from social inferiors towards "natural" social superiors.

7. The word "feudal" is apparently used loosely or metaphorically. For the Rocketts' position results from a contract, and only one month's notice of dismissal or resignation is required (174). See above, note 5.

8. Disparaging comment of this kind is sometimes found in Gissing's writings. For example, in *Our Friend the Charlatan*, ed. Pierre Coustillas (Hassocks: The Harvester Press, 1976), 40, there is the authorial comment that Dyce Lashmar has personal qualities that "drew attention, especially the attention of women, in circles of the liberal-minded, that is to say, among people fond of talking more or less vaguely about very large subjects".

9. Gissing's diary entry for 3 July 1898 records that Wells had begun to teach him (*London and the Life of Literature in Late Victorian England: The Diary of George Gissing, Novelist* [hereafter cited as *Diary*] ed. Pierre Coustillas [Hassocks: The Harvester Press, 1978]), 496. He ordered his bicycle on 8 July, and received it on 2 August 1898.

10. *Our Friend the Charlatan* (see above, note 8), 71, 141-42, 148, 153, 233, 240, 432.

11. In George Gissing, *A Victim of Circumstances and Other Stories* (Boston & New York: Houghton Mifflin, 1927), 127-44.

12. These words imply that Betsy will need to find paid employment, and that "domestic service" would be the obvious work for her to undertake (even though it would involve some loss of status). At present she is not formally a domestic servant (even if she has occasional services—such as gate-opening—to perform); she is certainly not personally at the beck and call of a master or mistress.

13. The following passage in *Our Friend the Charlatan* (240) appears to be authorial comment, though it might be authorial exposition of Lashmar's ideas: ". . . were not man and woman, disguise the fact as one might, condemned by nature to mutual hostility? Useless to attempt rational methods with beings to whom reason was fundamentally repugnant". A sentence on page 238 is probably an instance of authorial exposition: "Women think queerly, and are no less unaccountable in their procedure."

The Paying Guest, ed. Ian Fletcher (Brighton: The Harvester Press, 1982 [reprint of the first edition, 1895]) contains numerous authorial comments of a similar kind. Mrs Mumford is portrayed as being, by nature, an exceptionally calm and reasonable woman. Before being greatly upset by the troubles resulting from Louise Derrick's presence in her home, "she could discuss difference of opinion" (139) without heat, as men often do (Cobb and Mumford "converse . . . with masculine calm" (136) after the fire in Mumford's drawing-room, for which Cobb is partly responsible). However, "now a hint of diversity [of opinion] drove her at once to the female weapon—angry and iterative assertion" (139). And after Mrs Higgins criticizes her, she struggles to overcome "the feminine rage which impelled her to undignified altercation" (149). Again, Mrs Mumford, though "not one of the most foolish of her sex" (41), is slightly jealous. Jealousy is dangerous; there is the authorial comment: "When there enters the slightest possibility of jealousy, a man can never be sure that his wife will act as a rational being". (86). And there is also an authorial comment on the natural force of female jealousy: "Emmeline [Mumford], though not sufficiently enlightened to be above small jealousies, would have been ashamed to declare her [jealous] feeling with the energy of unsophisticated female nature" (113).

14. J. H. Newman, *The Idea of a University Defined and Illustrated* [1852] (Oxford: Clarendon Press, 1976), 179. The words quoted begin section 10 (the last section) of Discourse VIII, and this section is almost entirely devoted to characterizing "gentlemanly" conduct (see 179-80).

15. In George Gissing, *The Day of Silence and Other Stories,* ed. Pierre Coustillas (Everyman edn, 1993), 194-210.

16. *Ibid.,* xxiv; Gissing, *Diary,* 524.

Ralph Pordzik (essay date 2003)

SOURCE: Pordzik, Ralph. "Narrating the Ecstatic Moment: George Gissing and the Beginnings of the Modern Short Story." *Arbeiten aus Anglistik und Amerikanistik* 28, no. 2 (2003): 349-62.

[In the following essay, Pordzik contends that Gissing's stories are more faithful than his novels to his realistic aesthetic, and he points out that the limitations inherent in the short-story form enhance Gissing's prose style.]

> Perhaps more nonsense has been written about the short story than any other literary form.

James T. Farrell

1.

In his study *The Hero in Eclipse in Victorian Fiction* (1956), Mario Praz described the widespread movement towards the "democratic art" of the late-nineteenth century in the following words:

> Lacking heroes and heroines, attention becomes concentrated on the details of common life, and these aspects of life are closely studied; the most ordinary things, by dint of being looked at with intensity, acquire an important significance, and intimate beauty of their own, more profound for the very reason that it is muted.

(375)

This tendency to transform minute realistic observation into representations that enliven the ordinary and irradiate the commonplace worlds with "intimate beauty" Praz adequately termed "Intimism" (374). To him, the novel or short narrative which employed this method to intensify the reader's gaze or to produce a rare brand of intimacy between reader and text presented the most suitable approach to the modern age and the new perspectives and literary techniques it required.

In addition to that, Praz's description answers to George Gissing's (1857-1903) representation of the metropolis and its people in his short stories and narrative sketches. The late-Victorian writer's rendering of social reality is frequently more sympathetic and aesthetically convincing when it comes to employing shorter forms. Forced to keep himself to the limitations of a restricted number of words, Gissing refrains from expanding his minimalist plots and thus succeeds in portraying his characters and their motives with a pointed sharpness and vitality his novels often seem to lack. It is interesting to note that this formal dimension of Gissing's shorter work has received very little attention from readers and critics. In this essay I seek to analyse some of Gissing's shorter narratives with regard to their special way of bringing to life late Victorian London and the London poor, its frustrated drop-outs and writers, workers, businessmen and 'new women'. I shall focus especially on the narrative and descriptive techniques Gissing employs to render his characters credible and their actions plausible. My questions are: why is it that the short story—a still relatively new and emerging form in the nineteenth century—seems so much more conducive to Gissing's particular art of literary realism? Is there a connection between the genre's focus on shortness and intimacy and Gissing's 'new' fluency and elegance in composing anecdotal scenes of striking insight and intense emotional and experiential fullness?[1]

Many readers are familiar with Brander Matthews's views on the aesthetic 'superiority' of the genre as outlined in his essay "The Philosophy of the Short-Story". Let me quote the passage for the sake of completeness:

> A Short-story deals with a single character, a single event, a single emotion, or the series of emotions called forth by a single situation. [. . .] The Short-story is the single effect, complete and self-contained, while the Novel is of necessity broken into a series of episodes. Thus the Short-story has [. . .] the effect of "totality," as Poe called it, the unity of impression.

(73)

Taking their cue from Poe's and Matthews's argument, critics today agree that the most essential trait of the genre is the "presentational immediacy" (Curnutt 1997: 10) of its descriptive technique and the brevity of the narrated sequence. To a considerable degree, short prose narratives depend for their functioning on the creative role of these components (cf. Friedman 1989: 30f., Curnutt 1997: 1). But who can really define the effect they may produce in the reader? How can the impact of immediacy and qualitative unity in the actual process of reading be explained? I suggest to approach this problem through narrative theory. In her ground-breaking study *Towards a 'Natural' Narratology* (1996), Monika Fludernik redefines narrativity on the basis not of plot and character but of experientiality, a term she derives from the linguist Labov (1972) and one which has become prominent in a whole array of 'post-linguistic-turn' theories of literature (cf. Leypoldt 2000: 57). Thus, e.g., the issue of integrative experiences in art features prominently in John Dewey's philosophy (cf. Dewey 1987). The American pragmatist and his followers[2] investigated those situations in the perceptual process in which the qualities of a certain transitive or climactic experience impinge on readers' behaviour and persistently direct or orient their thinking.

A similarly pragmatist viewpoint lies at the heart of recent narratology. According to Fludernik, narrativity must be identified first and foremost with conversational parameters in a 'natural' storytelling situation.

"Narrativity is a function of narrative texts and centres on experientiality of an anthropomorphic nature." (Fludernik 1996: 26) She argues, persuasively, that storytelling correlates with perceptual parameters of human experience depending on a specific historical and socio-cultural context. Fictional situations within storytelling seek to evoke or embody the parameters of a 'real-life' pattern of existence in a specific time and space frame. Thus, a literary text may visualise the inner life and emotions of a character in a way that answers to the problems of subjectivity and identity as they are seen to exist at a certain time. It may, for instance, restrict itself mainly to dialogue or to a covert narrator as a means to question the value of traditional authorial comment (as in numerous modern novels or short stories); it may also penetrate the consciousness of a character through the medium of an external 'focalizer' structuring thoughts and incidents in a causally and logically related manner (as in most nineteenth-century novels).

On the reader's side, the emotional involvement with an experience as described in a literary text provides crucial reference points for the constitution of narrativity: naturally, readers tend to explain difficult or awkward moments in a text by taking recourse to available interpretive patterns (cf. Fludernik 1996: 13). They tend to construct a system of frames or hypotheses that create "maximal relevancy" (Perry 1979: 43) among the various data of the text, thus ensuring their co-presence in the text according to models derived from physical reality. These patterns or parameters of "real-world knowledge" (38), Fludernik argues further, are still at work in experimental texts of the twentieth century, in which the 'objective' events essential to narrative art in traditional poetics are often presented selectively and obliquely. For instance, the formal difficulties and inconsistencies of a modern(ist) novel cease to be problematic when the reader views them as a series of inherently related events telescoped through the registering mind of a teller concerned with the unconscious or subconscious workings of the human mind. Texts written after this fashion tend to plunge us into a flowing stream of experience with which we gradually familiarise ourselves by a process of inference and association relying on generally acceptable real-world patterns of knowledge and understanding.

In my view, this narratological concept can be applied to short stories as well. In a short story, real-life patterns and the experience of events as they impinge on the narrating mind are often related in terms of a situation of presentational immediacy and compressed meaning. It is the internally experienced 'fullness' of a concrete and revealing situation which makes the reader 'understand' life in its embodiedness, its actuality and experiential vibrancy. This is important insofar as the notion of expanded plot is only of secondary importance in the modern short story (cf. Pattee 1923; Curnutt 1997: 10 ff). As Fludernik puts it, events or "actantial parameters" (Fludernik 1996: 146) in themselves constitute only a minimal frame for the production of narrativity. In other words, it is not the actual sequence of events that matters in this revised narratological model ('the king died and then the queen died of grief . . .') but the 'embodiedness' of patterns of experienced reality and their centrality to the narrated sequence. And in short stories, these patterns are often presented as embodiments of knowledge or intuition generated through some striking minimal incident or situation. They appear to be closer to the fleeting impressions and transient emotions of everyday life than the patterns of experience and cognition deployed in the full panorama of long fiction. In addition, they are produced through the mediating function of a minutely registering consciousness. Consciousness, as Fludernik puts it, is the actual site of experientiality in a literary text; it emerges on various levels and in different forms—and one of the most important levels in a short story is that of immediately experienced meaning and mediation of ecstatic 'intuition'.

2.

In 1983, Robert Selig wrote that Gissing's shorter narratives "deserve to rank among the best of the late Victorian era." (Selig 1983: 112) It was as a writer of short stories that Gissing made his literary debut, several years before he turned to the novels on which his reputation now rests. Whereas Gissing the novelist was often frowned on for his late-Victorian volubility and "saturation" (James 1897: 754), his stories show how admirably he could work on a smaller scale, minimizing extensive dialogue and psychological case studies in favour of stylistic simplicity and emotional intensity. They also show him as a writer with an intuitive grasp of reality often verging on the epiphanic. Conrad Aiken praised his stories for their "new tone and manner" and compared them to the "sort of thing which, in the hands of such a writer as Katherine Mansfield, critics hailed as revolutionary." (Aiken 1927: 514)[3] While to many early reviewers Gissing's stories read like unfinished "notes and jottings to be further amplified" (Anonymous 1897: 9), from a modern point of view they seem to offer a unique literary vision answering to the disruptive forces shaping British society in the late nineteenth century. Seeing how traditional society was transformed by the rise of modern consumer culture and the slow decline of the concept of progressive history, Gissing looked for a suitable literary mode to describe the lives of those drawn into the whirl of economic life, those trying to escape from the dislocating influences, both scientific and social, working upon them. His interest in literary form as a powerful instrument reflecting these changes is documented in a letter he wrote to his brother as early as in 1885:

> Thackeray and Dickens wrote at enormous length, and with profusion of detail; their plan is to tell everything and leave nothing to be divined. Far more artistic, I think, is the later method of merely suggesting; of dealing with episodes instead of writing biographies. The old novelist is omniscient; I think it is better to tell a story precisely as one does in real life, hinting, surmising, telling in detail what can be told and no more. In fact, it approximates to the dramatic mode of presentment.

(Gissing 1970: 166)

Gissing's point of view as articulated in this letter is even more revealing as it entails a deliberate change in his overall strategy of representation. Although he remained a writer of novels for the rest of his life, Gissing seems to have conceived of the short narrative as a medium more suited to his specific needs at that time. Employing a literary mode known for its vivid and almost lyric intensity, the master of "saturation" developed a new taste for the marvellous, the single, permeative effect and the dramatic potential of unforeseen encounters. Removing metaphor and psychological depth, especially from his later novels (cf. Collie 1979: 154 f., 171 f.), Gissing reintroduced both in his shorter prose narratives. It is curious to note that in many of his tales, story in the sense of a linear succession of incidents amounts to little or nothing. Straightforward action is eliminated in favour of literary technique and the creation of concentrated scenes of embodied experience. This is not to say that the familiar world of actions and characters is dispensed with, but attention to it ceases to be paramount. Buried under the unexciting flow of surface description, a second narrative gravitates towards the permeative event or striking insight and its meaning in the larger 'scheme of things'.

This is already vividly explored in **"Fleet-Footed Hester,"** one of Gissing's best-known stories of the 1890s.[4] In this remarkable tale about a gifted young girl from Hackney, Gissing draws on the classical model of Ovid's *Metamorphoses* (cf. Tintner 1981) to make a point about the fugitive moments of life in the modern metropolis. Hester is a young woman who "running races with the lads in London fields" could beat all but the "champion runner of that locality." (25) She attracts John Rayner, the foreman of the gasworks where both are employed, but the couple separates because John regards running in public as not proper for his fiancée. Before a reunion becomes possible, Hester has to undertake her last great race and run against time for her life's happiness. Making a trip of three

miles in "five and twenty minutes," she arrives on time at the railway station, with "her eyes dazzled, and her limbs fail[ing]." (36) That is the moment when John Rayner speaks to her and the couple finally becomes reconciled. They decide to take the next train to Portsmouth in order to go on board a ship heading for South Africa.

In **"Fleet-Footed Hester,"** Gissing transforms Ovid's poetry into the language and contemporary figures of his day. He creates his own version of a metamorphosis from passivity and subordination to female power and self-assertion. The urgency of the heroine's moral dilemma is fully matched by the incidental situation deployed in the tale. It deals with an experience which declares its own paradigmatic quality; in essence, Hester's dramatic race to Waterloo station must be seen as an intrusion into human ordinariness, a crucial moment in time framed to epitomize *and* undo a life of humdrum dailiness. As in a classical modern short story, Hester's transformation is 'shown' rather than 'told', marked as incidental where Gissing the novelist would have provided lengthy description and narrative explanation. His narrator knows exactly what the reader knows at a given moment, and does not pretend to know more. Thus, we are left without information as to Hester's sudden change of mind with respect to her former boyfriend. What precisely is her motive for still loving him after all that happened? When Mrs Heffron, Hester's young widow friend, tells her that John is going to leave with the first train in the morning and mournfully exclaims "'My God!' [. . .] 'If it was me, Hetty, he wouldn't go,'" Hester only flashes a look at her face, and says nothing. Her eyes fall "in abashment." (32) In the next paragraph, however, Hester is described walking to the nearest railway-station and talking to a clerk. She seems to have made a decision but returns to Mrs Heffron's lodging without any further details about her future plans given; neither is her emotional conflict explained. Every narrative detail is recorded in a kind of flash that suddenly illumines and then passes, revealing a single moment or isolated object—such as, e.g., the silhouette of St. Paul's Cathedral at the break of dawn, "black against a red rift in the sky." (36) Symbolically, this image interconnects with the "red rift of the eastern sky broadened into day" (37) that emerges when the couple finally leaves Waterloo station to turn a new page of life. In this manner, one moment leads over to the next, sudden decisions are made which halt the flow of time and leave everything permanently altered once they have occurred: "She tried to speak, but had no voice. [. . .] Hester did not know what she had started until they were rushing past Vauxhall." (37)

Connotations of suddenness are not the only features that strike the reader's eye. The embodiedness of the heroine's experience is also shown in her emotional complexity which does not accumulate gradually through an extended time-structure as it does in the traditional novel. Because Gissing cannot reproduce extended periods or lapses of time within the bounds of a short narrative, what is shown is always a representative, single phase of an emotionally important moment. Nineteenth-century notions of time and continuity are thus effectively subverted. Linear time, for Hester, is transformed into an infinity of instantaneous experience and emotional involvement. Incidents occur as they enter the heroine's mind, isolated and unconnected, detaching themselves from established patterns of temporal and causal succession: "There was a sudden revelation of busy life." (35) Marginal objects enter her field of vision and then dissolve again, "packages of newspapers, piles of them thrown back to await the slow train," "porters unload[ing] vehicles" or "the sound of a jangling bell." (36) All these components are embodiments of the compact, industrious world of late-Victorian capitalism, but what they amount to here is a cluster of discrete objects without cogent relation to the heroine's inner experience. Hester herself, in a magical moment of collapsing time, has temporarily entered a kind of 'beyond', and the reader is left with an enlivening sense of transience and climactically fulfilled experience.

Many of Gissing's tales are marked by this sense of surprise and incidental novelty. **"An Inspiration,"** first published in the *English Illustrated Magazine* in 1895, contains moments of heightened awareness in which the qualities of the marvellous, usually hidden within the mundane or obscured by habit and dullness of perception, suddenly enter the life of an average individual. In the tale, protagonist Harvey Munden asks an unexpected and late visitor to dine with him at a London restaurant. The host's "shabby companion" (70) is Laurence Nangle, a typical Gissing character and reject of Victorian society. He gives a simple and "very lamentable" (69) account of his life which entertains Munden the Samaritan to a considerable degree and leads him to the following observation: "he had given a good dinner to a poor devil oppressed with ills; he desired to warm the man's chilly blood and to improve its quality; he wished to study the effects of such stirring influence in this particular case." (77) However, what reveals itself to be Munden's detached and coldly analytical stance is undermined by the fortuity of the human encounter itself. The reader quickly becomes aware that the dinner does more than just make a point in terms of the prejudices and class-based orientations of the Victorian gentleman; it also profoundly changes the course of two separate lives. Munden's unforeseen invitation to dinner sparks off a series of incidents which remain basically untold but

eventually lead to the poor man's relief from poverty and destitution. Disguised as the "finger of providence" (79), the randomness of real-life experience breaks into the dreary routine and ordinariness of Victorian business life and reconnects the lives and experiences of individuals formerly separated by class, wealth and prejudice. An intrinsically tense situation, one charged with implicit allusions to the squalor and injustice of nineteenth-century life, challenges the individual's desire to control others and questions the 'power of will' and active idealism so highly estimated in the Victorian age.

The actual success of this strategy lies in Gissing's ability to picture his characters in a way that reveals the adjustments and alterations in their relationship without explaining them to us. Thus, it remains unclear whether Munden's *ad hoc* invitation springs from subliminal forces or from the dictates of divine inspiration. He fails to explain himself to his visitor who provides a (rather tenuous) motive for his host's generosity: "You thought I looked hungry. Yes, so I was; and the dinner has done me good." (72) This remark certainly suffices to give the reader a logical explanation for the speaker's "meagre form" (69), but as Munden doesn't bother to assent we cannot know whether this *really* was his intention. Is Munden supposed to be an emissary of God? This seems hardly possible in view of Gissing's agnosticism and sense of religious disillusionment.[5] Or is the tale supposed to be a general critique of the shallowness and superficiality of Victorian social life and manners? Some readers may remember that Gissing, in *Born in Exile,* assaulted those who "desire to be convinced that agnosticism is respectable," who "take their rationalism as they do a fashion in dress, anxiously only that it shall be 'good form.'" (94) Looked at from this angle, Munden's act of charity appears like a concession to late-Victorian *zeitgeist* indeed, a "good-humoured jest" (77) to appease his own sense of guilt. There is even a third alternative: the tentative manifestation of the divine as expressed in **"An Inspiration"** may be interpreted as a first sign of Gissing's disenchantment with the social realism of the 'French school' he adhered to for so long. In *The Private Papers of Henry Ryecroft* (1903), his most successful book in economic terms, we are offered a revised picture of Gissing the realist: less occupied with his own predicament or that of others and indulging in the happiness and *joie de vivre* that some of his contemporaries associated with him as a student. Written without the sense of grudge and agitated depression that mark his realistic novels, *Henry Ryecroft* presents Gissing's *alter ego* as a man sufficient unto himself, a loner and enthusiastic reader content with spending his remaining days in the countryside, musing, taking long walks and interrogating the role of literature in an age of war-mongering and "fluent irresponsibility [. . .] But I will read no more such writing." (Gissing 1982: 96)

All in all, it must be seen that the short story's interest in capturing a supreme moment of perception, its preference for the ineffable and unexplained, is particularly amenable to this kind of speculation. Like so many other short narratives, **"An Inspiration"** registers a fleeting moment of revelation which ends, for the readers, with an implied 'over-to-you'. They are asked to provide what the text leaves unanswered; they are the ones who are pulled along towards a climactic moment when they find impressed on their minds an effect very similar to what Joyce in *Stephen Hero* referred to as the "epiphanic"—a single, transitive moment of experience framing itself by virtue of its revelatory nature (cf. Joyce 1991: 161-200). As I see it, this understanding of the epiphanic answers to what Monika Fludernik describes as our modern sense of "embodiedness in the world." (Alber 2002: 54) It is an apprehension of a thing's or person's unique particularity in time and space, and not a symbol of something else; it represents the 'givenness' of the real, in time and place, rendered through the mediating function of narrative consciousness and revealing itself along with the cultural and moral truths we connect to it. In other words, chance is shown to be more powerful than development or human resolution, a melancholy perception of the random quality of life which suits the brevity and presentational immediacy of short stories and undermines the realist novel's claim to representational completeness.

This is not to suggest that the surface of Gissing's tales, with their realistic detail and subtleties of dialogue, should be disregarded in pursuit of some definitive interpretation rooted in modernist theophany. It is not that Gissing's largely functional concept of literature has undergone a decisive change: it still stands in the service of showing its readers 'the world as it really is'. However, the means to achieve this end have changed: now it is the focus on the single and sharp incident, the realizing of the embodied experience of 'being-in-the-world', undimmed by lengthy description or elaboration, which serves the aim of instruction and correction. At times, this has the—possibly intended—effect of making the stories appear complete yet unfinished, revelatory yet only partially so; they create sensations which put the reader in a receptive frame of mind and demand he actively participate in the aesthetic interchange between the writer and his subject. Singly and cumulatively, they achieve what William James saw his brother Henry consciously aiming to do in his early stories, namely "to suggest a mysterious fullness which you do not lead your reader through." (quoted in Gard 1968: 26) In my opinion,

this sense of abruptness and discontinuity is a largely neglected quality, which points to the essentially modern and innovatory dimension of Gissing's work.

3.

The said qualities of the short story as a genre still in its formative stages are conducive to Gissing's approach in another respect. Many of his tales address the spiritual and emotional conflicts of individuals caught in the maelstrom of modern urban life. **"The Foolish Virgin,"** printed first in the *Yellow Book* in January 1896, depicts its central character as a woman "wrought by fears and vanities, urgencies and desires, to a strange point of exaltation." (90) By presenting these traits as a motivation for all her actions, Gissing achieves the curious effect of structural and emotional unity. An entire life is dramatized in a rhythm which alternates between descriptions of habitual actions and vividly realized scenes of emotional confusion. Although the protagonist is rendered as a victim of social circumstances, her actual life reveals a dimension setting her apart from her fellow *odd women* who struggle to make a living in the metropolis. As a modern character, she succeeds by *not* marrying the only male who would have been able to provide the means for an agreeable life. Rejected but "mute in thankfulness" (100), she returns to her former employer, accepting the duties allotted to her by an unmerciful destiny. As this suggests, a life of self-determined work and sacrifice seems to be the only alternative open to the growing number of females 'produced' by the uneven social development of late nineteenth-century society. It remains for the reader to decide whether Gissing actually supported this view or not (cf. Enzer 1978). The narrative itself consists of a series of realistic episodes in which, once again, traditional plot is subordinate to 'as-if-real' character. Action is telescoped through a succession of scenes that depend for their consistency more on tone and embodied mood than on plot, scenes in which the main character's movement is repeatedly frozen at the peak of expressiveness: "The whole hateful world had conspired against her. [. . .] And her poor life was wasted, oh! oh! She would soon be thirty—thirty! The glass mocked her with savage truth. And she had not even a decent dress to put on." (97) This scenic method of narration points to the development of the modern short story as initiated by Mansfield, Chekhov and Joyce. In their tales, there always comes a moment when realization breaks over the readers, when they become aware of the narrative's final point. Similarly, in **"The Foolish Virgin,"** it takes the readers several moments to fully grasp the strangely ambiguous note on which the tale ends: "'For goodness' sake,' urged the practical woman, 'don't let her think she's a martyr. [. . .] Work she must, and there's only one kind of work she's fit for. It's no small thing to find your vocation—is it?'" (100-1) This finale suggests the opportunities of working life but also points to the humiliations to which it exposes the individual person. Again, the focus is on a visual moment of human experience framing as well as epitomizing the continuing dreariness of life which for the individual to escape seems to be impossible. A humiliating situation is evoked and exploited for utmost effect, then unexpectedly modified, in a brief sentence or two, to communicate an entirely different response or complex state of feeling.

Another instance of embodied experientiality in the short story is **"A Freak of Nature"** (*Harmsworth Magazine*, 1899), which anticipates the split of self so often engaged in modern literature. In this tale, a "devil" seems to have "taken possession" (118) of Mr Brogden, the central character, a "voice that [. . .] did not seem his own" (119), and which makes him say and do things he does not want to say or do. The flawless respectability of Victorian society is effectively confronted in this tale of suppressed anger and frustration. In addition, the story's theme is mediated by Gissing's rather unusual choice of 'free indirect discourse' as a narrative mode.[6] Brogden frequently contemplates his faulty actions and the problems they occasion: "Better to end by suicide, and so get the benefit of the assumption that he was a victim of lunacy. Yes. He would drown himself in a river or pond." (123) What we perceive is a shift of focus from the writer's preoccupation with plot and character to his renewed interest in the unexplored possibilities of consciousness and literary form. Again, recent narrative theory may help to explain this modification with reference to the role experientiality and 'real-life experience' play in the tale. As Monika Fludernik writes (1996: 30), narrativity can also consist in the "experiential depiction of human consciousness *tout court*," that is, the unspoken thoughts and feelings of a character may be rendered in a flow of images and associations without resorting to conventional patterns of action. Gissing's tentative choice of mode in **"A Freak of Nature"** shows that he tried to adapt his narrative voice to the new experiential patterns it sought to represent. Loss of individual identity, anonymity in urban societies and the return of the repressed are the major themes of **"A Freak of Nature"** and call for a new treatment in aesthetic terms. Gissing therefore shifts the locus of experientiality from the authorial narrator to the narrated subject and thus enhances the short story's most prominent feature: its aiming at a discrete moment of truth or revelation through which the monotony of everyday reality is broken up and presented in a fresh and uncommon light. Human experience is still given in a largely realistic fashion;

however, the sense data belonging to the individual's movements and actions are rendered in a way that shows how they may arrange themselves into unique and often impalpable forms and patterns. As thus envisaged, the 'single striking effect' of the modern short story is only another method of representing experiential embodiment. The older notion of experience as subsumed under temporality and incident gives way to one which pays tribute to other parameters involved, such as the individual's sense of instantaneity, his or her emotional involvement, and the representation of mental states and habits or situations of crisis in narrative. Looked at from this angle, unquestioned elementary distinctions begin to dissolve: both Victorian and modern short fictions, then, are 'realistic' in that they formally presuppose their respective readers' attempt to interpret them 'mimetically', namely as articulations of historically divergent 'real-world' experiences one needs to make conform to one's own interpretive and cultural pattern. They are made intelligible by their readers who bring them into relation with a type of discourse or mode which is always already, in some sense, natural and legible in the eyes of those who accept it.

To conclude: more than other literary genres, the short story seems to be beneficial to the writer's interest in evoking an intuitive or instantaneously embodied 'real-life' schema within a spatially restricted frame of narration. The supreme moment in a tale is always the supreme pattern of embodiment framing a crucial, ineffable or even 'unsayable' moment in life. Unacknowledged by many, Gissing realised the potentialities inherent in the genre's structure and tried to employ them for his own purpose, namely to respond in a unique and adequate fashion to the new forces challenging Victorian beliefs and attitudes at the end of the century. In his stories, the representation of the dynamics of modern experience no longer depends on the changes brought about by plot or the development of a central character. Rather, it is related to the vivid effect of experiential embodiedness to which all the details gravitate, the need for a striking image or figure through which the tale's objective is actualised. Real-life patterns as experienced by his characters and mediated through the narrating consciousness are presented in an intrinsic fashion, producing a rare effect of human credibility and an often unexpected density of meaning. On the whole, it is thus the situational coherence of a revealing and textually embodied moment of insight which makes readers feel they can participate in the lives and sufferings of Gissing's characters in a way that matches their own experiences—physically grasping the changes modernity brings about as well as finding a tentative mode to articulate and explain them.

Notes

1. This essay should be seen as a contribution to narratology as well as to the study of Gissing's fiction in its historical, cultural and material context.

2. See in particular Shusterman 1992 and 1997.

3. Given this early and deserved praise, it is curious to note that neither Orel (1986) nor Hanson (1985), who both agree that the "short story matured as a genre during the Victorian age" (Orel), mention Gissing at all in their studies of the English short story.

4. Collected in the volume *The Day of Silence and Other Stories* (Gissing 1993). All references in the text refer to this edition.

5. See, e.g., his novel *Born in Exile* (1892), in which Gissing concerns himself with biblical criticism and evolutionary theory and attacks the Victorian Church on the grounds of its incompatibility with the modern world.

6. A narrative mode in which the language is read as that of a "focalising character". In effect, what the character would be thinking in the first person present tense is expressed in third person past tense. (cf. Richter 1996: 326)

Works Cited

Aiken, Conrad (1927). "George Gissing". *The Dial* (December 1927) 512-14.

Alber, Jan (2002). "The 'Moreness' or 'Lessness' of 'Natural' Narratology: Samuel Beckett's 'Lessness' Reconsidered". *Style* 36.1: 54-75.

Anonymous (1897). "Mr George Gissing's Last". *Daily News* (26th November 1897) 9.

Collie, Michael (1979). *The Alien Art: A Critical Study of George Gissing's Novels*. Folkestone, Dawson: Archon Books.

Curnutt, Kirk (1997). *Wise Economies: Brevity and Storytelling in American Short Stories*. Moscow, Idaho: U of Idaho P.

Dewey, John (1987). *Art as Experience*. Carbondale: Southern Illinois UP.

Enzer, Sandra S. (1978). *Maidens and Matrons: Gissing's Stories of Women*. Unpublished Ph.D. dissertation. State University of New York at Stony Brook.

Farrell, James T. (1945). "Nonsense and the Short Story." *The League of Frightened Philistines and Other Papers*. New York: Vanguard, 65-78.

Fludernik, Monika (1996). *Towards a 'Natural' Narratology*. London and New York: Routledge.

Friedman, Norman (1989). "Recent Short Story Theories: Problems in Definition." *Short Story Theory at a Crossroads*. Ed. Susan Lohafer and Jo Ellyn Clarey. Baton Rouge: Louisiana State UP.

Gard, Roger (ed.) (1968). *Henry James: The Critical Heritage*. London: Routledge & Paul, and New York: Barnes & Noble.

Gissing, George (1982). *The Private Papers of Henry Ryecroft*. Introduction by John Stewart Collis. Brighton, Sussex: Harvester Press.

Gissing, George (1993). *The Day of Silence and Other Stories*. Ed. Pierre Coustillas. Everyman Series. London: J. M. Dent.

———. (1993). *Born in Exile*. Edited by David Grylis. Everyman Series. London: J. M. Dent.

Gissing, Algernon and Ellen Gissing (eds.) (1970). *George Gissing: Letters of George Gissing to his Family*. With a Preface by His Son. [1927]. New York: Kraus repr.

Hansen, Clare (1985). *Short Stories and Short Fictions, 1880-1980*. New York: St. Martin's Press.

James, Henry (1897). "London July 1, 1897". [Review of Gissing's *The Whirlpool*.] *Harper's Weekly* (31st July 1897) 754.

Joyce, James (1991). *Poems and Shorter Writings*. Ed Richard Ellmann, A. Walton Litz and John Whittier-Ferguson. London: Faber & Faber.

Labov, William (1972). *Language in the Inner City: Studies in the Black English Vernacular*. Philadelphia: U of Pennsylvania P.

Leypoldt, Günter (2000). "The Pragmatist Aesthetics of Richard Shusterman: A Conversation". *Zeitschrift für Anglistik und Amerikanistik* 48.1, 57-71.

Matthews, Brander (1885). "The Philosophy of the Short-Story". *Lippincott's* 36: 366-74. Reprinted in: *The New Short Story Theories*. Ed. Charles E. May. Athens, GΛ: Ohio UP, 1994. 73-80.

Orel, Harold (1986). *The Victorian Short Story: Development and Triumph of a Literary Genre*. Cambridge: Cambridge UP.

Pattee, Fred Lewis (1923). *The Development of the American Short Story: An Historical Sketch*. New York: Harper & Brothers.

Perry, Menakhem (1979). "Literary Dynamics: How the Order of a Text Creates its Meanings." *Poetics Today* 1.1, 35-64, 311-61.

Praz, Mario (1956). *La crisi dell'eroe nel romanzo vittoriano* [1953]. Firenze: Sansoni, 1981. *The Hero in Eclipse in Victorian Fiction*. Translated from the Italian by Angus Davidson. London et al.: Oxford UP.

Richter, David H. (ed.) (1996). *Narrative/Theory*. London et al.: Longman.

Selig, Robert L. (1983). *George Gissing*. Boston: Twayne.

Shusterman, Richard (1992). *Pragmatist Aesthetics: Living Beauty, Rethinking Art*. Oxford: Blackwell.

———. (1997). *Practicing Philosophy: Pragmatism and the Philosophical Life*. London and New York: Routledge.

Tintner, Adeline R. (1981). "Gissing's 'Fleet-footed Hester': The Atalanta of Hackney Downs". *Etudes Anglaises* 4, 443-47.

Barbara Rawlinson (essay date October 2003)

SOURCE: Rawlinson, Barbara. "From 'Phoebe's Fortune' to 'Phoebe' by Courtesy of George Bentley, *Temple Bar*'s Hatchet Man." *Gissing Journal* 39, no. 4 (October 2003): 15-33.

[*In the following excerpt, Rawlinson chronicles the severe alterations made to Gissing's story "Phoebe" (originally titled "Phoebe's Fortune") by the editors of* Temple Bar *magazine.*]

Having endured three barren years since the publication of his novel, *Workers in the Dawn*, George Gissing was delighted to write to his brother Algernon, on 30 October 1883, that a piece of his work had been published in *Temple Bar*'s November issue, and then added that he would try to get the magazine "to take a short tale."[1] In a letter to his sister Margaret three days later, he mentioned that he was writing a short New Year's tale, and by 24 November the story was in Bentley's hands. On 31 December he wrote to his sister Ellen that he expected **"Phoebe's Fortune"** would appear in the February issue of *Temple Bar,* and suggested that she should read it, as "it deals with a phase of life quite new to you."[2]

Gissing received the proofs of **"Phoebe's Fortune,"** on 9 January 1884, and clearly at this stage no excisions had been made, since the author's only comment to his brother on 11 January was that his signature had been omitted from the end; this clearly annoyed him, so he had added it to the proofs.[3] In the event the story, entitled **"Phoebe,"** was not published until March 1884. Gissing sent a copy of the magazine to Algernon, and although he complained that he had been deceived over his fee—eight guineas instead of the fifteen he had anticipated—he made no mention that Bentley had tampered with the text.[4] Curiously, he later wrote of the story: "In many ways I think it the best piece of writing I have done yet."[5] In view of this, one can only assume that he never read the final version of the story. Either that or, he was so desperately in need of the money that he decided to accept the matter as a *fait accompli*.[6] It should also be remembered that Gissing was still awaiting Bentley's decision on **"Mrs. Grundy's Enemies,"** with a problem looming large regarding Chapman & Hall's imminent publication of *The Unclassed,* so perhaps he was reluctant to aggravate the situation.[7]

Pierre Coustillas' article "Aspects of the Late Victorian Publishing Scene: George Gissing and his Publishers," briefly noted that the published **"Phoebe"** was a severely edited version of Gissing's original work.[8] A recent study of the manuscript at the Lilly Library, Indiana University, has revealed the extent to which Bentley bowdlerised the story. Coming near the end of the piece, the excisions and substitutions relate almost exclusively to the calculated way in which Jenny Evans robbed Phoebe of her fortune by introducing her to the demon drink.

In view of Bentley's nervousness regarding the publication of **"Mrs. Grundy's Enemies,"** it is not surprising that he balked at the idea of publishing, unabridged, a story that featured two young women engaged in a drinking bout, but unfortunately the excisions merely rendered the piece colourless. The censor altered the whole tenor of the tale by erroneously casting Phoebe as a gullible fool rather than an innocent abroad, as Gissing intended her to be.

Algernon sold the manuscript to Frank Redway, a Wimbledon book dealer, on 17 March 1915. Consequently, when the collection *Stories and Sketches* was published in 1938, **"Phoebe"** was reprinted in its bowdlerised form.[9]

Notes

1. *The Collected Letters of George Gissing, Volume Two 1881-1885,* ed. P. F. Mattheisen, A. C. Young and P. Coustillas (Athens, Ohio: Ohio University Press, 1991), p. 173.

2. *Ibid.,* p. 187.

3. *Ibid.,* p. 191. Editorial note 1 confirms that the story was printed with Gissing's signature.

4. *Ibid.,* pp. 199-200. Letter to Algernon dated 27 February 1884.

5. *Ibid.,* p. 200. Letter to Algernon dated 4 March 1884.

6. *Ibid.,* p. 195. In a letter to Algernon dated 30 January 1884, regarding the expected publication of "Phoebe" in the February issue of *Temple Bar,*

Gissing wrote: "The story is not in Temple Bar. If Bentley had busied himself in devising disappointments for me he could not well do more than he is doing. The present one is rather serious, as I needed the cash. [. . .] as likely as not, it will follow the fate of 'Mrs. Grundy.'"

7. *Ibid.,* p. 198. Letter to Algernon dated 20 February 1884: "What will Bentley say, I wonder? And how about 'Mrs. Grundy' now? If she comes out close on the heels of 'The Unclassed' there will have to be a complication of explanations."

8. *The Journal of the Eighteen-Nineties Society,* No. 23 (1996), p. 9.

9. London: Michael Joseph Ltd., 1938, pp. 15-44.

Markus Neacey (essay date January 2006)

SOURCE: Neacey, Markus. "Gissing's Literal Revenge and Jordan's Collected Silences in 'The Prize Lodger.'" *Gissing Journal* 42, no. 1 (January 2006): 19-28.

[*In the following essay, Neacey maintains that "The Prize Lodger" was written, in part, in response to Gissing's negative personal experiences with boarding houses, but he extols the story as a satisfying work of fiction regardless of its autobiographical subtext.*]

In recent times several Gissing scholars[1] have lamented "the general disinterest of critics in his short fiction."[2] A survey of articles and biographies about Gissing, which have appeared since 1950, reveals that the short stories do not have the same weighty place in his complete *œuvre* as, say, the short stories of Joseph Conrad or Thomas Hardy in their respective works. Emanuela Ettorre suggests "that many critics have considered his short stories to be the inferior product of an otherwise talented author"[3] because the need of money drove him to write them. This combined with Gissing's own unfortunate dismissal of a few stories as mere potboilers largely accounts for their poor reputation, as critics have seized upon this to prove that they are unworthy of him. Yet Balzac wrote so-called pot-boilers too—in this case to pay off debts; many of these are nonetheless considered to be great novels. Robert L. Selig[4] also suspects that the biographical approach of some critics, which treats Gissing's stories as disguised autobiography rather than as the works of imagination they actually are, has contributed to their literary devaluation.

Another reason for their almost complete neglect is their unavailability. The only English publications of the stories to appear since 1950, none of which remain in print, are *A Freak of Nature or Mr. Brogden, City*

Clerk,[5] Coustillas's *Essays and Fiction*[6] and *My First Rehearsal and My Clerical Rival,*[7] Selig's *Lost Stories from America,*[8] and *The Day of Silence and Other Stories.*[9] In all 36 stories have seen the light of day in this time, only sixteen of them in a mainstream edition. If we compare this with the number of mainstream editions of Conrad's, Kipling's, and Hardy's stories, which are currently in print, then we have to concede that this is a sad state of affairs. Furthermore, there has been just one full-length study of the stories, this appearing in German in 1973.[10] Rather surprisingly Gissing's stories have had far more success in Japan, where there have been a staggering number of editions.[11]

Gissing wrote 115 short stories,[12] the great majority of which are a delight to read. Of these 62 were written between April 1893 and June 1896. This intense preoccupation with the short story form accounts for a tremendous improvement in the quality of his productions. There is maturity in the handling of the narrative, depth in his characterizations, and more skilful use of description. Moreover, he shows himself a master of irony and of satire. In these stories Gissing plunges us into a unique world in which he describes the daily conflicts of lower middle-class and working-class characters. It has often be said that these stories are generally undramatic, but that is their virtue and their gain. These stories are above all realistic and charming representations of a particular milieu and a particular type of character, be it of a clerk like Mr. Brogden, of a down-at-heel writer like Goldthorpe, or of a book collector like Christopherson.

As closer acquaintance with the stories will show, there is a whole new Gissing world to be discovered in them. Not only do they complement the novels, they also throw a new light on his complete works. Here and there we find a sunnier contrast to the darker novels and not a few delightful sketches of London and country life. To open his first volume of short stories, *Human Odds and Ends,*[13] is to encounter a refreshing breeziness of style seldom found in the longer works of fiction. This volume contains 29 stories, originally published in magazines and journals between 1893 and 1896. Among them we find such pearls as **"The Poet's Portmanteau,"** about a lost manuscript; **"The Day of Silence,"** about an afternoon boat trip which turns into a tragedy; and **"In Honour Bound,"** in which a poor scholar lends his charwoman ten pounds to enable her to open a chandler's shop in exchange for ten weeks' lodgings.

I shall now focus on another story from this collection, **"The Prize Lodger."**[14] I aim to show through the study of this story that Gissing was a conscientious, ambitious writer who was able to produce entertaining and competent, if not excellent, works of imaginative fiction even under the most trying of circumstances. Gissing wrote **"The Prize Lodger"** between 15 and 18 November 1895 at a time when his second wife, Edith, was heavily pregnant, and servant trouble and illness were affecting his domestic life. The story, one of six commissioned by Clement Shorter, first appeared in the *English Illustrated Magazine*[15] in August 1896.

As in most of Gissing's short stories, there is little plot in **"The Prize Lodger."** The story is about a nomadic lodger, Archibald Jordan, who for many years has "flitted from house to house" (p. 142), "distressing the souls" (p. 142) of various landladies within the borough of Islington. When the arrangement proves no longer to his liking or "he felt that, in the eyes of a landlady, he was becoming a mere everyday person" (p. 139), he would give notice and remove to different lodgings. Eventually he arrives at what he believes to be the ideal lodgings in Mrs. Elderfield's house, only to have a rude awakening.

One can imagine with what relish Gissing wrote this story. For it is both a bitter attack upon the evils of lodging houses and a vehicle of revenge for what he himself had to endure as a lodger. That said, **"The Prize Lodger"** is a piece of fiction. Even though he could at one time be called a nomadic lodger, Gissing's experience in lodging houses differs vastly from Jordan's. In contrast he suffered torments in the twelve or more lodging houses he dwelt in between returning from America in October 1877 and moving into 7.K. Cornwall Residences in December 1884. Furthermore, he neither wielded power over his landladies, nor did he marry one, and he only lived in one Islington lodging-house.[16] Significantly, as late as 15 August 1891 Gissing records in his diary how the mental anguish due to "vile squabbles"[17] with his Exeter landlord has given him "an idea for a vol. of short stories, to illustrate the wretchedness of life in lodgings."[18] This volume was never written, but several stories which appeared in the early to mid-1890s take up this theme, including **"The Prize Lodger."**

The title sets the tone for the story. Referring to Jordan, the narrator explains, "To speak of lodgers as of cattle, he was a prize creature" (p. 136). From the start the narrator relates the story with a refreshing undercurrent of irony and satire. Of course Gissing was always a master of irony and satire as the "Io Saturnalia" chapter in *The Nether World*[19] proves. But the story is in addition highly amusing. Yes indeed, and contrary to the "doom and gloom" view of Gissing's works which has predominated up to very recently, **"The Prize Lodger"** makes one laugh out loud. That Gissing had a strong, native capacity for humour has

in recent decades been highlighted in several new readings of works such as *The Town Traveller,*[20] **"A Daughter of the Lodge,"**[21] and **"Comrades in Arms."**[22]

Gissing's descriptive powers are seen at their best in his careful portrayal of the two principal characters. The main character, Jordan, is a middle-aged, fussy type, who esteems domestic comfort above wealth, and is conservative in his tastes. For twenty-five years he has been willing to pay over the odds in order to obtain the standard of living he desires:

> 'Twenty-five shillings a week, you say? I shall give you twenty-eight. *But*—' and with raised forefinger he went through the catalogue of his demands.
>
> (p. 136)

Most at home in a small world of local "bar-parlours" and "billiard-rooms" (p. 134) and "familiar thoroughfares" (p. 135), Jordan regards any sign of change "with a look of thoughtful criticism" (p. 135). More than anything, as the narrator explains in an amusing aside, he is a master of silent reproach.

> . . . it was his conviction that no man's eye had a greater power of solemn and overwhelming rebuke, and this gift he took a pleasure in exercising, however trivial the occasion.
>
> (p. 135)

He also derives cruel satisfaction in giving notice:

> It gave him the keenest pleasure of which he was capable when, on abruptly announcing his immediate departure, he perceived the landlady's profound mortification. To make the blow heavier he had even resorted to artifice, seeming to express a most lively contentment during the very days when he had decided to leave and was asking himself where he should next abide. One of his delights was to return to a house which he had quitted years ago, to behold the excitement and bustle occasioned by his appearance, and play the good-natured autocrat over grovelling dependents.
>
> (pp. 139-40)

Doubtless this is a passage Gissing thoroughly enjoyed writing. It is wish-fulfilment on a grand scale, a vicarious form of literal revenge. Jordan the rigorous bachelor, the bane of landladies, and an eccentric *par excellence,* is one of Gissing's most delightful creations, comparable with the likes of Biffen and Christopherson.

On moving into Mrs. Elderfield's house, Jordan is pleasantly surprised by her "zeal and efficiency" (p. 139). A "neatly dressed" (p. 137) widow of thirty-three, she behaves with "studious civility" (p. 137), like himself is "plain" (p. 138), and has "resolute lips" (p. 138). Telling details like the last combined with her lack of "subservience" (p. 137) to Jordan, give ample hint as to the direction his fortunes will eventually take. After a few days in her house, in a wry comment on lodging-house conditions, the narrator has Jordan comparing Mrs. Elderfield's home with those of former landladies:

> . . . he knew for the first time in his life the comfort of absolutely clean rooms. The best of his landladies hitherto had not risen above that conception of cleanliness which is relative to London soot and fog. His palate, too, was receiving an education. Probably he had never eaten of a joint rightly cooked, or tasted a potato boiled as it should be; more often than not, the food set before him had undergone a process which left it masticable indeed, but void of savour and nourishment.
>
> (p. 139)

In another story from this collection, **"The Tout of Yarmouth Bridge,"** which also deals satirically with lodging-house life, a similar passage of biting humour describes how the eponymous "tout" "assisted her aunt in keeping the house dirty, in pilfering the lodger's groceries, and spoiling food given to be cooked."[23] In Gissing's fictional world, it would seem that landladies and their underlings are a subversive force, conspiring to exploit and harass their lodgers, just like the Thénardiers in Victor Hugo's *Les Misérables*. Doubtless this was Gissing's own experience. But Jordan finding himself better off at Mrs. Elderfield's house declares "Here I shall stay" (p. 139).

It is not Jordan's "habit to chat with landladies" (p. 141) except to dictate to them or silently reprimand them. However, he so warms to Mrs. Elderfield that he goes so far as to exchange "personal confidences" (p. 141) with her. As a result he learns to his dismay of her intention to move away from Islington. In another comical passage, we find Jordan, a city man through and through, considering the prospect of going with her and quite unable to see any appeal in the name of her intended destination:

> It was open to him to accompany Mrs. Elderfield, but he shrank from the thought of living in so remote a district. Wood Green! The very name appalled him, for he had never been able to endure the country.
>
> (p. 142)

Nevertheless he takes a look at Wood Green and begins to talk to Mrs. Elderfield more intimately. Jordan, whose strongest trait was his cultivation of silence, makes the mistake of imparting "a complete knowledge" (p. 142) of his most private concerns to his landlady. Suddenly there is a change in him and he becomes vulnerable: he loses his "self-confident and superior tone" (p. 142) and "the foundations of habit crumble[d] beneath his feet" (p. 142).

Although "resident in Islington" (p. 137) Mrs. Elderfield, coming from the Midlands, is regarded as an outsider, "an alien!" (p. 143). Jordan's former landladies by contrast belong to a fiercely tribal community. As soon as they learn that she is going to marry Jordan, they are infuriated. After all, their former "lodger" may have been seen as a "prize" catch, but not as a potential husband. As a result of Mrs. Elderfield breaking the rules of the game, they ask themselves, "What base arts had she practised?" (p. 143). And verily she has spun a spell on Jordan. For the last the reader had heard of him "he seemed to have lost his pleasure in the streets of Islington, and spent all his spare time by the fireside, perpetually musing" (p. 143). This doesn't sound like someone intent upon marrying.

Marry her he does, although he keeps the time and place of the wedding a secret. And by now powerless to assert himself, Jordan is left running after his ex-landlady and "signing cheques" (p. 145), while she conducts all the business concerning the new house. To his "consternation" (p. 145), having previously "lived with such excessive economy" (p. 145), he finds himself occupying "a ten-roomed 'villa,' with appointments which seemed to him luxurious" (p. 145). Within the space of a month Jordan has become, as the narrator writes, "quite a different kind of man from his former self" (p. 144). No longer the complacent autocrat, he has lost his silent powers. Jordan's and his wife's roles have reversed completely and now Mrs. Jordan is the dominating force. At the start of **"The Justice and the Vagabond"** Mr. Rutland finds himself in a similar predicament for his strong-willed wife "ruled him in every detail of his life."[24] Gissing accomplishes this plot reversal in **"The Prize Lodger"** with marvellous skill. Meanwhile we learn belatedly that Mrs. Jordan's "first marriage had been a sad mistake; it had brought her down in the world. Now she felt restored to her natural position" (p. 145). Clearly she has used Jordan to hoist herself up the class ladder.

There soon follows a delicious scene in which Jordan's wife rebukes him for returning home late from work and then rudely chastises him for "coming into the room with muddy boots!" (p. 147). In an amusing line Jordan replies "It was my hurry to speak to you" (p. 147). This phrase which literally ought to bespeak his passion for his wife, but is merely "murmured" (p. 147) dispassionately, speaks volumes about his present mood and reveals to what extent he has been dethroned. If before he was uncomfortably aware that "he had lost something" (p. 146) in marrying his landlady, Jordan now realises where he really stands in relation to his wife. From this point on, as the story moves towards its dénouement, their marriage becomes a battle of wills.

From day to day things go from bad to worse for Jordan. Much troubled by his wife's behaviour he recalls how:

> He himself, in the old days, had plagued his landladies by insisting upon method and routine, by his faddish attention to domestic minutiæ; he now learnt what it was to be subjected to the same kind of despotism, exercised with much more exasperating persistence.
>
> (p. 147)

It seems to him as if he is paying the price for his own despotism. In an epoch in which men considered themselves superior to women in every respect, Jordan's subjection to his wife is "galling" (p. 147). At length, when he is severely admonished for reading his newspaper at the breakfast table, things come to a head. It dawns upon him that he is faced with the terrible prospect of "downright slavery! He had married a woman so horribly like himself in several points that his only hope lay in overcoming her by sheer violence" (p. 149). This is a wonderful piece of self-revelation and irony. For Jordan, like the dog biting its own tail, is just as much a despot, just as much a stickler for details, and just as fastidious in his tastes, as his wife. All at once, feeling displaced and lost in Wood Green, he yearns for his native Islington: "The thought of Wood Green revolted him; live there as long as he might, he would never be at home" (p. 149). **"Transplanted,"**[25] a story written two months earlier, is completely devoted to the theme of displaced persons. In this story the tramp, Long Bill, experiences a similar longing for London after removing to a country house to work as a gardener.

Returning from "a lamentable day" (p. 149) at work, Jordan determines to have it out with Mrs. Jordan in a scene which vibrates with humour:

> He thought of his wife (now waiting for him) with fear, and then with a reaction of rage. Let her wait! He—Archibald Jordan—before whom women had bowed and trembled for five-and-twenty years—was *he* to come and go at a wife's bidding? And at length the thought seemed so utterly preposterous that he sped northward as fast as possible, determined to right himself this very evening.
>
> Mrs. Jordan sat alone. He marched into the room with muddy boots, flung his hat and overcoat into a chair, and poked the fire violently. His wife's eye was fixed on him, and she spoke first—in the quiet voice that he dreaded.
>
> 'What do you mean by carrying on like this, Archibald?'
>
> 'I shall carry on as I like in my own house—hear that?'
>
> 'I do hear it, and I'm very sorry to. It gives me a very bad opinion of you. You will *not* do as you like in your own house. Rage as you please. You will *not* do as you like in your own house.'

> There was a contemptuous anger in her eye which the man could not face. He lost all control of himself, uttered coarse oaths, and stood quivering.
>
> (pp. 149-50)

This scene sparkles with all that is best in Gissing's short fiction. Jordan's internal deliberations are hilarious. Moreover, Gissing makes very effective use of the verbs "sped," "marched," "flung," and "poked" to convey Jordan's pent-up anger. And his war-like entrance "with muddy boots" is another telling detail which brilliantly demonstrates his mood of defiance. All at once their marital home has literally become a battlefield. Yet Jordan's main weapon, his silent reproof—he is after all a connoisseur of silence—proves marvellously ineffectual up against Mrs. Jordan's "quiet" (p. 151) restraint. In the end he loses "all control of himself" (p. 150) and is left "quivering" (p. 150) impotently. Ironically, in the man's world they inhabit, his wife's quiet authority has not only unmanned him, but also neutralized his manliness.

Lectured into submission "until night was at odds with morning" (p. 151), Jordan is to all appearances a "defeated" (p. 151) man. He seems unable to combat his wife's tyranny. A lull descends upon the battlefield as he retreats into silence. In the meantime she, who spends the day ordering her troops about, so to speak, and devoting herself to domestic duties, rules absolutely in their marital home. When, after a few days, Jordan breaks his silence and again offers "combat" (p. 152), his ultimatum—"Look here . . . either you or I are going to leave this house" (p. 152)—is yet again scornfully repulsed. As his wife makes clear, any "recourse to personal violence" (p. 152) on his part would only lead to a pyrrhic victory, in short, to "shame and ridicule" (p. 152). Even the last resort of outraged masculinity, the use of physical violence against the so-called weaker sex, is denied Jordan. So, unlike Long Bill in **"Transplanted"** who avenges himself on his hated benefactress by destroying her plants, Jordan is powerless against the enemy at home.

The end of the story is surprising and effective. Jordan, taking refuge in absolute silence for a few days, stays away from Wood Green to haunt his former abodes in Islington. When he returns home, he remains doggedly monosyllabic or silent, and even though his wife still reprimands him for "stepping on the paint when he went up and down stairs" (p. 153), she makes no comment upon his absence. On going to bed, he is kept awake, this time not by his wife's "admonitions" (p. 152), but by the thought: "What! Was he, after all, to be allowed his liberty *out* of doors, provided he relinquished it within?" (p. 153). The battle of wills ends then in a kind of truce or silent agreement as Jordan regains his liberty outside the home.

We see then that it is possible, as Robert L. Selig[26] has previously shown, to approach Gissing's stories purely as works of fiction. And there is plenty in these stories, as we have seen in **"The Prize Lodger,"** to hearten the Gissing admirer. The relentless realism of *The Nether World* is rarely discoverable in them. In these stories Gissing focuses on the everyday life, the quiet comings and goings of his characters. We, the readers, are made privileged spectators of domestic scenes or bohemian aspirations, of petty concerns or fluttering hearts, of the search for quiet contentment or, as in **"The Prize Lodger,"** of the escape from human bondage. The world of Gissing's stories is charming and entertaining. Scenes follow upon one another with the revealing detail and moral colourfulness of a Hogarth canvass. Taken as a whole they represent a human comedy in miniature and a sociological document of their time. For it is here in the short story, in his concentration upon character and milieu that Gissing's achievement most closely compares with Balzac's. In my view then, it is time that the short stories be made more widely available so as to enable new readings of them in relation to Gissing's other works.

Notes

1. See Emanuela Ettorre, "'The Salt of the Earth' and the Ethics of Denial," *Gissing Journal*, July 1995, p. 19; Robert L. Selig, "The Biographical-Critical Circle: 'A Lodger in Maze Pond,'" *Gissing Journal*, January 2002, pp. 25-30; Pierre Coustillas, ed., *The Day of Silence and Other Stories* (London and Vermont: J. M. Dent, 1993), pp. xiv-xx.

2. Ettorre, p. 19.

3. *Ibid.*

4. See Robert L. Selig's article, note 1.

5. Pierre Coustillas, ed., *A Freak of Nature or Mr. Brogden, City Clerk* (Edinburgh: Tragara Press, 1990).

6. Pierre Coustillas, ed., *Essays and Fiction* (Baltimore and London: The Johns Hopkins Press, 1970).

7. Pierre Coustillas, ed., *My First Rehearsal and My Clerical Rival* (London: Enitharmon Press, 1970).

8. Robert L. Selig, ed., *George Gissing: Lost Stories from America* (Lewiston, Queenston, and Lampeter: The Edwin Mellen Press, 1992).

9. Pierre Coustillas, ed., *The Day of Silence and Other Stories* (London and Vermont: J. M. Dent, 1993).

10. Ulrich Annen, *George Gissing und die Kurzgeschichte* (Bern: A. Francke AG Verlag, 1973).

11. See Pierre Coustillas, "The Romance of Japanese Editions: The 'Selected Works of George Gissing' in their Bibliographical Context," *Gissing Newsletter*, July 1988, pp. 35-43.

12. Several other stories including "At Eventide," "How a Misfortune Made a Philosopher," "A Minstrel of the Byways," "A Merry Wooing," and a children's story are known to have been written. There may also be some lost stories from America.

13. London: Lawrence and Bullen, 1898.

14. *Human Odds and Ends* (London: Sidgwick and Jackson, 1911), pp. 133-154. Hereafter references given in the text are to this edition.

15. Pp. 386-93.

16. He lived at 5 Hanover Street, Islington, from early December 1879 until late February 1881.

17. Pierre Coustillas, ed., *London and the Life of Literature in Late Victorian London. The Diary of George Gissing, Novelist* (Hassocks: Harvester Press, 1978), p. 253.

18. *Ibid.*, pp. 253-54.

19. Smith & Elder, 1889. Rptd 1974 (Brighton: Harvester Press), pp. 104-13.

20. See Judith Brigley, "*The Town Traveller*: a Comic Novel," *Gissing Newsletter*, July 1990, pp. 15-25.

21. Robert L. Selig, "An Upstart Odd Woman: 'A Daughter of the Lodge,'" *Gissing Journal*, April 2001, pp. 19-23.

22. Robert L. Selig, *George Gissing*, Revised Edition (New York: Twayne Publishers, 1995), pp. 98-100.

23. *Human Odds and Ends* (London: Sidgwick and Jackson, 1911), p. 210.

24. *Ibid.*, p. 21.

25. *Ibid.*, pp. 244-50.

26. See note 4.

Barbara Rawlinson (essay date 2006)

SOURCE: Rawlinson, Barbara. "The Place of Realism in Gissing's Short Fiction." In *A Man of Many Parts: Gissing's Short Stories, Essays, and Other Works*, pp. 149-70. Amsterdam: Rodopi, 2006.

[*In the following excerpt, Rawlinson places Gissing's short stories within the context of literary realism as a historical movement, highlighting his attention to detail and his ability to call attention to epiphanies in everyday life.*]

Lilian Furst's Introduction to *Realism* argues that, as an artistic movement, Realism is the product and expression of the dominant mood of its time that eschews the fantasies of Romanticism in favour of the political, social, scientific and industrial advances of its day.[1] In similar vein, David Lodge suggests that a working definition of Realism in literature might be:

> the representation of experience in a manner which approximates closely to descriptions of similar experience in nonliterary texts of the same culture. Realistic fiction, being concerned with the actions of individuals in time, approximates to history . . .[2]

Of course, not all literary critics share this point of view. In *Concepts of Criticism* (1965) René Wellek argues that even in modern English literary criticism the use of "realism" as a period concept is rare, rather:

> Reality is conceived as . . . a world of cause and effect, a world without miracle, without transcendence. . . . The term "reality" is a term of inclusion; the ugly, the revolting, the low are legitimate subjects of art.[3]

Despite Thackeray having been referred to as "chief of the Realist school" in 1851, Wellek believes there was no realist movement of note in England before George Moore and George Gissing, the latter writer's realism being rooted in the European school, having grown out of the influence of Zola.[4] Against such an argument, Ian Watt's discussion of the realistic novel in *The Rise of the Novel* (1957), posits the view that time is an essential category in defining individuality: "the characters of the novel can only be individualised if they are set in a background of particularised time and place."[5] Watt's argument is reinforced by that of Wallace Martin in *Recent Theories of Narrative* (1986), which states that modern critics see realism both "as a period concept, best exemplified in the art and literature of the nineteenth century" and more generally, as "designating a true reflection of the world, regardless of when the work was created".[6] Martin claims that the plots and characters in realistic fiction reveal what actually took place in history. Undoubtedly the pro-particularists' argument is sound, and certainly in the case of Gissing's short fiction, its vivid snapshots of late Victorian working and middle-class life, provide the reader with potted histories of a diverse section of the lower reaches of society—the schoolteacher, the clerk, the clergyman, the pharmacist, the writer, the commercial traveller—at a specific point in time.

By the late nineteenth century a significant number of English writers held the firm conviction that literature should reject Romanticism, and deal directly with contemporary life and observed phenomenon. Continental Europeans however, were far more aware of the inadequacy, in terms of sincerity and plausibility, of romantic literature than their British counterparts, and as early as 1856, Edmond Duranty proclaimed in the first issue of his journal *Réalisme*: "The litterateurs and versifiers have spoiled artists and the calling of art by their insistence on upholding the noble genre, on acclaiming the noble genre, on shouting that we must poetize and idealize."[7]

Up to the 1880s English writers had made little more than a token gesture towards the new movement, focusing mainly on "realistic criteria such as truth of observation and a depiction of commonplace events".[8] From the mid-Eighties, however, there was an upsurge of interest in the more outspoken techniques of their Continental counterparts. As previously mentioned, the rejection of George Moore's *A Modern Lover* by Mudie's Circulating Library on account of its offensive content, prompted an incensed response from the author in the form of a satiric polemic entitled *Literature at Nurse, or Circulating Morals*. The pamphlet launched a bitter attack on the immutability of English social and literary conventions. Gissing was equally inflamed by such Draconian censorship: in his article "Morrison, Gissing and the Stark Reality", Roger Henkle points out that particularly in *The Nether World*, Gissing directly confronts "the insidious integration of the London poor into the social discourses of popular culture" by resisting the "easy representation of slum life that facilitates such an appropriation".[9]

In Lilian Furst's view, the nineteenth-century realists "placed truth-telling at the core of their beliefs", thereby suggesting directness, simplicity and artlessness.[10] However, despite George Eliot's and other serious writers' earlier attempts to represent the life of the working man realistically and truthfully, it was still common practice, even late in the century, for the "cultural establishment to assume that all depiction and expression of lower-class life will be kept within the power of the middle class to assimilate it and represent it".[11] Such practice was utterly discredited by Henry James, who, in his essay "The Art of Fiction", asserted:

> Art is essentially selection, but it is a selection whose main care is to be typical, to be inclusive. For many people art means rose-coloured windows and selection means picking a bouquet for Mrs Grundy.[12]

Guy de Maupassant, in his Preface to *Pierre et Jean* (1888), sets out the realist's criteria:

> By dint of seeing and meditating he has come to regard the world, facts, men, and things in a way peculiar to himself, which is the outcome of the sum total of his studious observation. . . . To make the spectacle of

life as moving to us as it has been to him, he must bring it before our eyes with scrupulous exactitude.[13]

Further, Maupassant points out that contrary to yesterday's novelist, who "preferred to relate the crises of life, the acute phases of the mind and heart", his counterpart of today

> writes the history of the heart, the soul, and intellect in their normal condition. To achieve the effects he aims at—that is to say, the sense of simple reality, and to point the artistic lesson he endeavours to draw from it—that is to say, a revelation of what his contemporary man is before his very eyes, he must bring forward no facts that are not irrefragable and invariable.[14]

Similarly, in his article "Realism in Art" George Lewes insists that "Art always aims at the representation of Reality, i.e., of Truth; and no departure from truth is permissible, except such as inevitably lies in the nature of the medium itself". Lewes claims that "Realism is thus the basis of all Art, and its antithesis is not idealism but *Falsism*", consequently he deplored the tendency among artists to represent "peasants with regular features and irreproachable linen" and novelists to allow their characters to "speak refined sentiments in unexceptionable English".[15] For Lewes and like-minded intellectuals, "truth to life" indicated a commitment by the artist to incorporate within his vision, the essentially everyday, commonplace aspects of human existence. The truth to life portrayal must avoid the exceptional, its primary aim being to induce in the reader the desire to think, and, through the author's subtle emphasis on significant everyday incidents, to appreciate the hidden depth of the story. In his discussion of Henry James' views on realism in *The Rhetoric of Fiction* (1983), Wayne Booth fully concurs with the writer's belief that the "moral sense of a work of art" depends completely "on the amount of felt life concerned in producing it".[16]

In an article published in November 1896 in two consecutive Saturday issues of the *Labour Leader*, Alfred R. Orage, editor of the *New Age*, ranks Gissing's contribution to the school of realism alongside such as Zola, Ibsen, Hardy and Crane.[17] He argues that through the voice of Harold Biffen in *New Grub Street*, the author iterates his artistic intention to reproduce life verbatim from no other point of view than that of honest reporting. Such an enterprise, confesses Biffen, would inevitably produce a work of unutterable tedium, because "if it were anything *but* tedious, it would be untrue".[18] Biffen's or, as Orage suggests, Gissing's view is very much in line with that expressed by Flaubert in his correspondence with Louise Colet regarding the composition of *Madame Bovary*:

> I am in a completely different world now, that of attentive observation of the dullest details. My eyes are

fixed on the spores of mildew growing on the soul. . . . In my book, I do not want there to be a *single* movement, or a *single* reflection of the author.[19]

Undoubtedly Gissing was influenced by the European Realists, a debt he acknowledged in a letter to sister Margaret: "the writers who help me most are the French & Russian; I have not much sympathy with English points of view."[20] Echoes of Maupassant and other European Realists are much in evidence in Gissing's short works. His posthumously published *The House of Cobwebs* (1906) was greeted with almost unanimous acclaim, the *Glasgow Herald*'s anonymous review, which extols the "very rare and special excellencies" of Gissing as a storywriter, being a typical laudatory example:

> The more than Maupassant-like disdain of mere plot of the conventional "story" is here unfettered. . . . A terse, mature, yet exquisitely unusual style, a descriptive accuracy which might be called photographic if it could be attained by any but a very great artist, and a psychological insight which . . . is so admirably apportioned as to endow every one of his personages with an absolutely self-consistent individuality—such are the distinguishing features of this, as of all the best work, of a writer who hewing at the sodden dough of London proletarian existence with the chisel of a great craftsman, raised English fiction higher into the region of pure literature than any writer since Thackeray.[21]

Gissing's major triumph in short story construction was his creation of fully rounded figures drawn from everyday life. First encountered in the shape of Slythorpe in **"One Farthing Damages"**, by the time the author reached his third phase, three-dimensional characterisation of the commonplace individual had become a defining feature of Gissing's short fiction. In a letter suggesting that the vital incident in a short story that Algernon sent to him for his critical opinion, is too slight, he advises that in cases where there is "good as no incident at all . . . there must be one of two things: either a peculiar strangeness of situation, or an exceptional vividness in the picturing of individuals".[22] Furthermore, an earlier letter proposing certain measures intended to enliven his brother's narrative technique, outlines the very principles to which the author himself strenuously adhered:

> the secret of art in fiction is the *indirect*. Nothing must be told too plumply. Play about your facts & intersperse them with humour or satire.

> —

> Think out the *characters* till you get them very distinct. Here is a rule. Try to let no one say a word that could have been said by anyone else but themselves. That avoids triviality of talk, & keeps the character well to the front.[23]

It is just such painstaking attention to detail that gives the impression of fidelity to life, which Ian Watt argues, stems above all from the amount of attention given in the story both to "the individualisation of its characters and to the detailed presentation of their environment".[24]

In her critical study *The Short Story,* Valerie Shaw quotes Mario Praz' definition of "democratic art" in the short story:

> lacking heroes and heroines, attention becomes concentrated on the details of common life, and these aspects of life are closely studied; the most ordinary things, by dint of being looked at with intensity, acquire an important significance, and intimate beauty of their own, more profound for the very reason that it is muted.[25]

In Shaw's view the two-fold sense of seeking out and revealing the hidden beauty of obscure lives is a recurring feature of short fiction, as is the use of its brevity to intensify the reader's gaze and thus create a degree of intimacy between reader and story.[26] In other words, the reader embarks on a voyage of discovery with the author, a search that reveals the unique embodied within the mundane.

The need to stimulate interest in the commonplace necessarily demanded the development of new techniques that conveyed a sense of sustained quietism in the face of adversity rather than the traditional dramatic peaks and troughs of romantic fiction, and furnished ordinary events with thematic overtones, such as, in the case of Gissing, obsession, class transgression and abandonment. As Wallace Martin points out, "Realism involves a doctrine of natural causality, as opposed to the chance, fate and providence of romantic fiction", a principle strictly observed by Gissing in his mature short fiction.[27] In addition it was important that events taking place in, and at the conclusion to, a realistic story should replicate everyday life, and since much of everyday life is anticlimactic and inconclusive, it became necessary to abandon both the overtly improbable incident and the dramatic ending. In W. V. Harris' opinion, the best of Gissing's stories "seem finished without being final, significant without being striking".[28]

Since the 1890s, a significant shift in the development of the short story has been made by a group of writers generally regarded as the new realists. New realism, argues Hèctor Agosti in "A Defense of Realism" espouses the notion that "artistic creation appears as judge of the interplay between the action of reality and the reaction of consciousness".[29] He claims:

> The difference between the new realism and any other theory of art consists in the fact that it hopes to make conscious that consciousness at times unconscious with which the artist approaches objects. This, far from impelling him to an art of frozen rational projections, on the contrary hurls him into the boiling whirlpool of living ideas. Art is able to seize "directly" in things themselves, conceptions which in the present state of society and of consciousness are apprehended apart from things, outside of them.[30]

Grounded midway between the polar opposites of objectivism and subjectivism (what Agosti calls *supersubjective*), new realism sought to express reality through the artist's temperament, "a temperament which is determined and conditioned by the conflicts of his time, modified in his innermost thoughts by his social relations, and constrained to mould his individual consciousness in conjunction with or in opposition to the prevailing order".[31] In Agosti's view, the incessant movement between the action of things and his consciousness places the artist in a position where the merging of the objective and the subjective enables him to recreate essential reality. Gissing articulated very similar ideas in his essay "The Place of Realism in Fiction" when referring to literature as "all but dead material until breathed upon by 'the shaping spirit of imagination,' which is the soul of the individual artist".[32] He was unequivocal in his belief that the novelist must work subjectively. "The Place of Realism in Fiction" was written in 1895 at a time when subjectivity was anathema to the general run of realists, thus distinguishing Gissing's realism, and by definition his short fiction, from that of his contemporaries by its modernity and innovativeness of style.

Gissing's major contribution to the "new realism" was his ability to "freeze the moment"; to place emphasis on a single moment of intense or significant experience, and thus create an epiphany that reveals a character's inner state of mind. In a sense this particular aspect of realism has much in common with the short fiction of James Joyce. The epiphanic moment, defined by Stephen Hero in Joyce's novel of the same name, as a "sudden spiritual manifestation, whether in the vulgarity of speech or of gesture or in a memorable phase of the mind itself", takes the form of a manifestation out of proportion to the significance of whatever produces it.[33] In John Bayley's view the short story affords the epiphany, or spot of time, "complete and conscious existence".[34] Interestingly, although Joyce's attitude towards Gissing's work was scornfully dismissive—"His books remind me of what Effore calls *Pastefazoi*"—there are strong affinities between **"The Prize Lodger"** from Gissing's *Human Odds and Ends* and "A Painful Case" in Joyce's *Dubliners* (1914).[35] Like Mr Duffy, Jordan, the prize lodger, values an orderly lifestyle; both men live in lodging houses, both become attracted to women who seem to offer an escape from their lonely, humdrum existences. Duffy's epiphany occurs when he learns that his ideal has been killed in a train accident while wandering around in a drunken stupor: Jordan's significant moment comes in the form of a sudden revelation that he has been hoist with his own petard—the wife he thought perfect was in reality a tyrant, just as he had been when seeking to reinforce his reputation as "the prize lodger".

Many of Gissing's stories of the Nineties have as their central character a sociological misfit, whose epiphanic experience opens the floodgates to self-knowledge. **"The Foolish Virgin"** is a story about an impoverished spinster, whose desperate search for a husband at any price brings her near the brink of disaster, when a timely moment of truth informs her that her survival depends on her willingness to accept menial work, rather than her ability to snare a husband.[36] **"Christopherson"** is a tale about a bibliophile who cherishes his books at the expense of his wife's health. The threat of her imminent death reveals to Christopherson the awful truth that his excessive love of books is no more than a selfish obsession.[37] In **"The Fate of Humphrey Snell"**, Humphrey is a free spirit who finds his vocation as a gatherer and vendor of wild herbs.[38] In the course of time he falls in love and willingly sacrifices his freedom to return to the "mind-forg'd manacles" of city life. Snell's rude awakening occurs when, after hearing nothing from his beloved since they parted, the news of his having found a job brings an enthusiastic response by return of post. Ironically, he recognises, but chooses to ignore, the significance of the row of crosses at the foot of the letter, that a "cross is frequently set upon a grave . . . .".[39] Numerous other stories from Gissing's third phase reach their climax by way of a frozen moment in time, when a character undergoes a life changing experience.

From a stylistic viewpoint, Gissing's stories differ greatly from those contained in *Dubliners*. There is an overarching unity in Joyce's work, as the author himself reveals in his letter to Constantine Curran: "I am writing . . . a series of epicleti—ten—for a paper . . . I shall call the series *Dubliners* to betray the soul of that hemiplegia or paralysis which many consider a city."[40] *Dubliners* is not about individuals, but rather it consists of a continuous theme that encompasses the condition of Dubliners as a whole—society stagnating in the stultifying atmosphere of a demoralised and decaying city. Conversely, Gissing's stories are specifically about individuals who, in their stubborn refusal to be daunted by adversity, bring a degree of vitality, as well as a moral challenge, to the prevailing social order.

One of the most notable exponents of the new realism of the 1890s was Arthur Morrison, whose *A Child of the Jago,* which depicted life in the East End slums as

the author himself had experienced it, engendered critical outrage on its publication in 1896. Morrison's style of realism stood in stark contrast to the more sanitised versions of urban working-class life portrayed in contemporary literature, which provided "a means of appropriating the lower classes into formulas recognizable to the upper strata" by the creation of an "individual subject that could be brought within the hegemonizing of middle-class English culture".[41] As P. J. Keating points out, through his assimilation into the popular culture, the lower class individual becomes:

> of inestimable use to a democratic society. So long as his wit, drunkenness, violence, sentimentality and love of freedom are expressed in individual terms, he is socially harmless; so long as these qualities are viewed from a distance he is even attractive and picturesque.[42]

In presenting the urban poor as an essentially alienated sub-stratum of society, Morrison was accused in H D Traill's article "The New Realism", of fallaciously depicting deprivation and gratuitous violence in his novel of the slums, *A Child of the Jago.* Morrison's article "What Is a Realist?" sought to disabuse Traill and equally ill-informed critics of the notion that "the function of the imagination is the distortion of fact", claiming that when squalor and poverty are allowed by society to exist, it is the duty of the artist to reveal the unembellished truth.[43] In his Introduction to *Working-class Short Stories of the 1890s* (1971), Keating is of the view that it was Arthur Morrison's interpretation of working-class life in *Tales of Mean Streets* (1894) that "established the predominant tone of slum fiction in the nineties". Morrison wrote "A Street", the Introduction to the novel, in order to correct hitherto unrealistic representations of working-class life, and while acknowledging the poverty and deprivation of the East End, he regarded "its most characteristic quality as being oppressive, all-pervading monotony":

> By means of graphic vignettes, all conveyed in a flat, terse style expressive of the monotony he is describing, Morrison succeeded in creating an interpretation of a working-class environment unlike anything earlier in Victorian fiction. . . . In this sketch ["A Street"] he dispensed with the Victorian tradition of hysterically described slum environments peopled by the suffering poor, the debased and the jolly, and offered instead the ordinariness of working-class life.[44]

As Clare Hanson points out in *Short Stories and Short Fictions, 1890-1980,* Morrison "used factual, non-emotional language in order to throw into greater relief the misery and pain he depicted". She also maintains that the move to bring the "freshness of colloquial speech" into the short story was a further innovative development of the "'new realists' of the 1890s".[45] The vernacular reveals something of "the social status and personal characteristics" of a speaker and is essentially "unpoetic".[46] Although Gissing tended not to focus specifically on misery and squalor in his later short fiction, it is evident from many of his stories, such as **"Mutimer's Choice"**, **"Phoebe"**, **"Letty Coe"**, **"The Day of Silence"** and **"Fleet-Footed Hester"**, that he held an equally strong belief that the use of accurate colloquial dialogue gave increased authenticity to working class narratives. Hester's language in **"Fleet-Footed Hester"** is precisely that of "a noble savage", her speech is the speech of Hackney, and a "fit expression of an elementary, not a degraded mind".[47] Ironically, critics frequently dismissed such strict adherence to the vernacular as ungrammatical. On the occasion of a review in the *National Observer* of Elsa d'Esterre-Keeling's *Appassionata: A Musician's Story* (1893), a critic's careless misreading of the text prompted an angry response from Gissing in the novelist's defence:

> surely it is obvious that the dialogue of a novel should imitate as closely as possible the speech of life. . . . Reviewers frequently quote from an author's dialogue to support a charge of weakness in grammar. Worse than that, the novelist is often represented as holding an opinion which he has simply attributed to one of his characters. There *are* people who read, or glance over, notices of novels, and in these cases are misled by a carelessness which has all the effect of deliberate misrepresentation. The author of *Appassionata*, for instance, had taken pains with her work; as a reward, her reviewer informs the public that she does not know the difference between "as" and "like".[48]

Not only is Gissing attacking critics' inability to appreciate colloquial language as a defining characteristic of the lower classes, but he is also touching on an issue that continued to irk him throughout his literary career; that of reviewers' and readers' inability to distinguish between the voices of the characters and that of the author. In his discussion in *Mimesis* of the works of Flaubert, Erich Auerbach refers to the author's realism as impartial, impersonal and objective, consequently when his characters express themselves they reveal no trace of their creator. Flaubert worked, writes Auerbach, in the conviction that every event, if expressed purely and simply, "interprets itself and the persons involved in it far better and more completely than any opinion or judgment appended to it could do".[49] As seen from his response to Algernon's misreading of *The Unclassed*, these were clearly the principles Gissing sought to embody in his art:

> You evidently take Waymark's decl[n] of faith as my own. Now this is by no means the case. Waymark is a *study of character*, & he alone is responsible for his sentiments. . . . If my own ideas are to be found anywhere, it is in the practical course of events in the story; my characters must speak as they would actually, & I cannot be responsible for what they say.[50]

There were those however, who could appreciate the important difference between omnipresence and autho-

rial distance. Frederic Harrison for instance, though he found much of *The Unclassed* unpalatable, nevertheless assured the author that he made "the clearest distinction between the Unclassed & George Gissing".[51]

From the mid-1890s Gissing narrowed his scope in the field of short fiction, concentrating almost exclusively on the shabby genteel, a vast alienated class of society that had hitherto eluded literary attention. In his article "Not Enough Money", which referred to Gissing as "the best novelist we have produced", George Orwell designated the author "the chronicler of poverty, not working class poverty . . . but the cruel, grinding, 'respectable' poverty of underfed clerks, downtrodden governesses and bankrupt tradesmen".[52] This narrowing of focus entailed a shift of emphasis from tragedy to pathos, for instance from the horrific experiences of Bertha and Harold in **"The Quarry on the Heath"** to the moral courage displayed by Mr Tymperley in **"A Poor Gentleman"**.[53] Once a gentleman of substance, Mr Tymperley has been brought to financial ruin as a result of improvident speculation in a friend's dubious business ventures. Although now living at the edge of poverty, he has never lost hope of a return to his former life, consequently he has stubbornly clung on to his evening suit, his last vestige of respectability. After a chance meeting with his former colleague's widow, Tymperley is invited to dinner, which he feels able to accept in the knowledge that his evening attire ensures social acceptance. Pride forces him to lie to his hostess, maintaining that he has chosen to live in a run-down neighbourhood in order to devote himself to social work. On receiving a cheque to aid his charitable work from one of the guests, Tymperley is sorely tempted to keep it for himself, and on impulse buys a pair of new boots, which he subsequently discovers pinch and creak. After a night of self-recrimination, the poor man, having handed the cheque to a clergyman, writes to the donor, confessing that he was living in poverty out of necessity not choice, and that his desire for material comfort had almost added a criminal act to his catalogue of woes. The pinching and creaking boots are a symbol of Tymperley's struggle to retain his moral integrity in the face of adversity. In *The Private Papers of Henry Ryecroft* Gissing expresses very strong views about the debilitating effect of poverty:

> What kindly joys have I lost, those simple forms of happiness to which every heart has claim, because of poverty! Meetings with those I loved made impossible year after year; sadness, misunderstanding, nay, cruel alienation, arising from inability to do things I wished, and which I might have done had a little money helped me; endless instances of homely pleasure and contentment curtailed or forbidden by narrow means.[54]

As Orwell points out in *The Road to Wigan Pier* (1937):

In the kind of shabby-genteel family that I am talking about there is far more *consciousness* of poverty than in any working-class family above the level of the dole. . . . Practically the whole family income goes on keeping up appearances. It is obvious that people of this kind are in an anomalous position, and one might be tempted to write them off as mere exceptions and therefore unimportant. Actually, however, they are or were fairly numerous. Most clergymen and schoolmasters . . . a sprinkling of soldiers and sailors and a fair number of professional men and artists, fall into this category.[55]

Such were the characters that informed Gissing's short fiction some fifty years earlier.

Simultaneously, as he excluded extremes from his narratives, Gissing necessarily excluded them from character, paring his figures down until they were outwardly indistinguishable from the ordinary man in the street, but whose unique quality lay in an inner core of resistance to an indifferent world, a capacity to withstand "the slings and arrows of outrageous fortune". The ability of an individual to recognise his own weaknesses, and accept his alienation from the external world, frees him from the desire for self-assertion and rebellion. Georg Lukács maintains that resignation plays an integral part in the bourgeois literature of the nineteenth century.[56] The short story of the 1890s created a special niche for itself by becoming the vehicle for discontinuity and alienation, where the individual is portrayed in isolation, "detached from the great social and historical continuum".[57] At their most characteristic, Gissing's later short stories reveal an intense awareness of human isolation, of alienated individuals who have learned that they "must make peace with what they have daily to bear".[58] *Human Odds and Ends,* the author's first collection of stories and sketches, examines the lives of those who exist at the edge of society, individuals whose centrality to that society has hitherto been neither acknowledged nor understood. The powerful sub-text of **"An Inspiration"**, a story from the collection, stresses the need for social responsibility towards the hapless by demonstrating how a morally upright individual is able to revitalise the life of one less fortunate than himself.[59] On a whim, Harvey Munden invites a poor, demoralised salesman to dine with him. As a result of this act of kindness, the salesman regains a sense of self-worth, which gives him the courage to confront and outmanœuvre the unscrupulous brother-in-law of the woman he loves.

Harvey Munden appears in two other Gissing stories; as a minor character in **"A Capitalist"**, where he acts as an intermediary between the alienated protagonist and the narrator and, as in **"An Inspiration"**, a *raisonneur* in **"A Lodger in Maze Pond"**, each story re-

vealing a psychological shortcoming in the major character's nature.[60] The two latter tales focus on Munden's efforts to subvert the consequences of human fallibility: in **"A Lodger in Maze Pond"** he tries unsuccessfully to dissuade his friend from repeating a mindless folly; conversely, in **"An Inspiration"**, his timely intervention brings out an unsuspected spark of rebellion in his demoralised guest. Munden is the Good Samaritan in a largely indifferent world. **"Lodger"** [**"A Lodger in Maze Pond"**] and **"Inspiration"** highlight the plight of the alienated individual, and the fact that mankind rarely perceives the sociological problems at the root of that plight.

In his discussion of the theme of revolt versus resignation in "Gissing as a Romantic Realist", Coustillas claims that at heart Gissing was a Romantic, pointing out that the dichotomy of revolt versus resignation that often informs his work has romantic overtones:

> The revolt is born of poverty and suffering in the working-class novels, which have affinities with Dickens's and Dostoievsky's as Gissing implicitly admitted in his critical study of Dickens, but the romanticism of his social rebels usually finds an outlet in behaviour which is less grotesque than that of his predecessors'; humorous eccentricity was not consonant with his temper, human or artistic. With his characters, revolt is largely an affair of the mind, and if it assumes a social dimension, violence is usually absent from it; revolt only seeks to come through in nonconformity of social behaviour.[61]

Coustillas suggests that Gissing's choice of subjects was influenced by his temperament, and sees this as the author's personal view of realism, as Realism grafted on to Romanticism, and "often enough realism and romanticism combined harmoniously and the result was a series of satirical stories of which he delivered himself in the mid-nineties". However, in Coustillas' view "one feels the romanticism of youth quivering under the stern self-imposed discipline of a realistic approach".[62]

In *Short Stories and Short Fiction,* Clare Hanson argues that from the 1880s it is possible to distinguish two separate strands of development in the short story, the chief distinction being that one strand places its major emphasis on plot, the other insists that plot should be subordinate to psychology and mood. In her view the plotless story is the more closely related to realism, "but it is usually a realism which is subjectively conceived".[63] As Hanson points out, a distinctive feature of the "plotless" story, particularly associated with writers of *The Yellow Book,* an *avant-garde* periodical launched in 1894, is the psychological sketch.[64] A "sensation in its day", the *Yellow Book* published some of the best short fiction of the late nineteenth century, containing within its covers stories by Henry James, H. G. Wells, Kenneth Grahame, and of course, George Gissing, whose **"The Foolish Virgin"** was published in January 1896.[65] The psychological sketch tends to deal with "an apparently trivial incident which has significance for what it reveals of a character's inner mood or state of mind".[66] Much of Gissing's mature fiction delves into the consciousness of alienated, disillusioned figures: **"A Victim of Circumstances"** for example, explores the minds of both Hilda and Horace Castledine, the former a gifted artist whose talents are sacrificed to her husband's ego and pride.[67] By entering into the consciousnesses of both husband and wife, the reader is able to understand the plight of Hilda as a frustrated woman artist, and the patriarchal mindset of Horace.

Focusing on the Russian realists, Andrew Wachtel's "Psychology and society" argues that nineteenth-century Eastern European novelists differed from their Western counterparts in that they were largely concerned with individual psychology because it provided a window into social psychology, whereas English and Continental realists, such as George Eliot, Hardy and Flaubert, tended to be more interested in portraying individuals as individuals.[68] Nonetheless, the psychological problems addressed appear to be very similar to those articulated by the Eastern Europeans, namely doubt, pride, spite, envy, those mental conditions that were very much the province of Gissing's second and third phases of short fiction, **"The Last Half-Crown"**, **"A Poor Gentleman"**, **"The Tout of Yarmouth Bridge"** and **"Their Pretty Way"**, being but a few examples.

When the subject is of a more psychological nature, the author excises his own personality and allows the characters to express their inner feelings indirectly. There was a growing tendency among realists, particularly Gissing, to view the process of thinking as more important than the unfolding of dramatic physical events, in that it provided the opportunity to replace overt action with the activity of the mind. In his critical study of the author, Swinnerton maintains:

> Even in **The House of Cobwebs,** we become aware that Gissing had his own conception of the short story. Most of the stories in **The House of Cobwebs** are little narratives. . . . They are in short, undramatic. . . . When we find the incidents in Gissing's short stories humdrum, or mild, we recognise that we had expected to be stirred in some way, or to be given some precisely poignant moment, whether of suspense or sympathy. The lack of this emotional heightening in the whole of Gissing's work is notable; in his short stories it becomes, according to the dramatic test, a positive defect.[69]

Undeniably, Gissing's stories are undramatic, that is what he intended them to be. Swinnerton is wrong however, in claiming that they lack emotional heightening; it is his instinctive insight into the human condition that enables the author to understand the psychology of the mind. Almost every story in **The House of Cobwebs,** the collection on which Swinnerton bases his case, concerns a character who experiences what can be likened to an instant feeling of strong emotion, a significant moment of intense awareness totally unlike anything previously known, such experience being expressly designed to elicit the sympathy or otherwise of the assiduous reader.[70]

In *The Modes of Modern Writing* (1977), David Lodge's chapter on "Two Kinds of Modern Fiction" argues that in view of its experimental nature:

> Modernist fiction is concerned with consciousness, and also with the subconscious and unconscious workings of the mind. Hence, the structure of external 'objective' events essential to traditional narrative is diminished in scope and scale, or presented very selectively and obliquely, or is almost completely dissolved, in order to make room for introspection, analysis, reflection and reverie.

In Lodge's view modernist fiction "has no real 'beginning', since it thrusts the reader into a flowing stream of experience . . . and its ending is usually 'open' or ambiguous, leaving the reader in doubt as to the final destiny of the characters", a view which Gissing clearly supported, seeing that many of his short stories follow a similar pattern of construction.[71] **"Comrades in Arms"**, **"The Salt of the Earth"**, **"The Poet's Portmanteau"**, **"A Drug in the Market"**, **"Spellbound"**, **"The Foolish Virgin"**, **"The Prize Lodger"** and many others, all begin on the brink of a personal crisis and proceed towards an indeterminate ending. In *Concepts of Criticism,* René Wellek addresses the German approach to Realism. He discusses the conclusion reached by Richard Brinkmann in *Wirklichkeit und Illusion,* that "Realism . . . is found ultimately in the stream of consciousness technique, in the attempt to dramatise the mind", pointing out that Brinkmann's theory that the subjective experience . . . is the only objective experience, "identifies impressionism, the exact notation of mental states of mind, with realism and proclaims it the only true realism".[72] In the field of short fiction, Gissing too can claim to have made an important contribution to the development of psychological realism.

Contiguous with the plotless story is the inconclusive ending. George Levine argues that the refusal of satisfaction to the reader is in effect a refusal of plot, a refusal to permit the conventions of romanticism to distort the conventions of realism. Furthermore, Levine points out that ironically "the refusal of satisfaction is a way of sustaining both desire and narrative because it keeps the quest alive and denies any ending".[73] **"The Sins of the Fathers"**, the first of many of Gissing's stories in which psychological insight is the key to unravelling the complexities of unfulfilled desire, reveals the author's fascination with the destructive power of desire when it flouts rigid social codes.

Gissing's mature stories frequently feature a character whose persona constitutes a blend of the psychological, environmental and sociological influences that together determine that character's behaviour. Thus, by revealing the fears and fantasies that are rooted within the human psyche, Gissing allows a degree of sympathy even to the seemingly most self-indulgent and undeserving of his protagonists, the artist in **"A Victim of Circumstances"** being a case in point. Equally, the sub-text of **"The Tout of Yarmouth Bridge"** suggests that the fact that Serena was abandoned and forced to live on her wits from the age of nine provides a measure of justification for her becoming an artful procurer of lodgers for her aunt's dingy boarding house, and ultimately the revengeful betrayer of her aunt's trust.[74] Conversely in **"The Peace Bringer"**, the implication is that it is the influence of privileged environmental and sociological forces that have moulded Jaffrey into the self-centred malcontent he has latterly become.[75] Jaffrey has throughout his life enjoyed a comfortable, self-indulgent lifestyle, but since contracting a terminal illness, he has fallen into a state of inertia and total disenchantment both with his wife and his life. As he lies dying, Jaffrey cruelly arranges for a former lover to visit him almost daily, ostensibly to play soothing music. Out of pity his wife accepts her husband's disloyalty without recrimination. It is only when his paramour reveals that she visits him only for the money he provides, and then deserts him as he nears his end, that he realises the pain he has caused his wife and at what cost his selfishness has been gratified. Approaching death opens Jaffrey's mind to the realisation that desire had been futile; the secret of true peace and happiness lay in reality and the here and now.

In her essay "Time and the Short Story", Jean Pickering points out that the short story "tends to deal with the unchanging elements of character and emphasises the stability of the essential self".[76] Many of the protagonists in Gissing's psychological studies have one distinctive characteristic in common, that of single-mindedness, each following an unchanging pattern of existence. A typical feature of the short story is that it focuses on "people whose identity is determined by their circumstances", which again suited Gissing's short story technique.[77] According to Coustillas, "Gissing found keen intellectual satisfaction—perverse pleasure if you like—in collecting evidence that man is a prisoner of his own condition, for instance that an in-dividual's character never changes, that the metaphysical urge in average humanity will not yield to reason."[78]

To summarise: the place of realism in Gissing's short fiction is firmly grounded in his rejection of society's demand for an idealised representation of the under classes and his use of colloquial language to give fidelity to the lives of the poor. Furthermore, his three-dimensional characterisations, which unveil the pathos of society's misfits, are designed to reveal the psychological, environmental and sociological influences that determine human behaviour. In addition, his stories are generally plotless, and the events in and endings to the tales are in the main anticlimactic and inconclusive, as Harris puts it, "finished without being final, significant without being striking". Even more significantly, Gissing was a pioneer of the notion of expressing reality through the artist's temperament, by inscribing his material with "the shaping spirit of imagination". In line with Clare Hanson's view that the plotless story is often subjectively conceived, and what Hèctor Agosti terms the "super-subjective", Gissing's realism is rooted midway between objectivism and subjectivism. More importantly, however, the author made a major contribution to the "new realism" of the 1890s through his emphasis on the epiphany, the single moment of intense awareness.

Notes

1. *Realism*, 1.

2. David Lodge, *The Modes of Modern Writing* (London: Edward Arnold, 1989), 25.

3. René Wellek, *Concepts of Criticism* (New Haven: Yale University Press, 1965), 234, 241.

4. *Ibid.*, 229, 234. Quotation from "William Makepeace Thackeray and Arthur Pendennis, Esquires", *Fraser's Magazine,* 43 (January 1851), 86.

5. Ian Watt, *The Rise of the Novel* (London: The Hogarth Press, 1987), 21.

6. Wallace Martin, *Recent Theories of Narrative* (Ithaca, New York: Cornell University Press, 1986), 57.

7. Quoted in *Documents of Modern Literary Realism,* ed. George J. Becker (Princeton: Princeton University Press, 1967), 24.

8. *Concepts of Criticism,* 229.

9. Roger Henkle, "Morrison, Gissing and the Stark Reality", *The Novel* (Spring 1992), 312-13.

10. *Realism*, 2-3.

11. "Morrison, Gissing and the Stark Reality", 308.

12. Henry James, "The Art of Fiction", *Longman's Magazine* (September 1884), 515.

13. Guy de Maupassant, *The Works of Guy de Maupassant, Vol VIII: Pierre et Jean and Other Stories* (London: Harper and Brothers, 1909), Preface, 6.

14. *Ibid.,* 7.

15. *Realism,* 34. Quotation from George Lewes, "Realism in Art", *The Westminster Review,* 70 (1958), 492-93.

16. Wayne C. Booth, *The Rhetoric of Fiction* (London: Penguin, 1987), 45. Quotation from *The Art of the Novel: Critical Prefaces of Henry James,* ed. R. P. Blackmur (New York: 1947), 45.

17. [A. R. O.], "George Gissing", *The Labour Leader,* III, 137 and 138 (14 and 21 November 1896), 392 and 400.

18. *New Grub Street,* 174.

19. *Documents of Modern Literary Realism,* 91. Quotation from Gustave Flaubert, *Oeuvres Complètes Correspondance,* Vols I-V (Paris: Louis Conrad, 1926-1933), II, 365. To Louise Colet, 8 February 1852.

20. *Collected Letters,* III, 47.

21. *The Critical Heritage,* 503-504.

22. *Collected Letters,* IV, 58.

23. *Ibid.,* II, 178-79.

24. *The Rise of the Novel,* 18.

25. Valerie Shaw, *The Short Story: A Critical Introduction* (London: Longman, 1998), 60-61. Quotation from Mario Praz, *The Hero in Eclipse in Victorian Fiction,* trans. Angus Davidson (Oxford: Oxford Paperback Edition, 1969), 375.

26. *Ibid.,* 133, 61.

27. *Recent Theories of Narrative,* 60.

28. Wendell V. Harris, *British Short Fiction in the Nineteenth Century* (Detroit: Wayne State University Press, 1979), 122.

29. *Documents of Modern Literary Realism,* 493. Quotation from Héctor P. Agosti, *Defensa del realismo* (Montivideo: Editorial Pueblos Unidos, 1945), 9-25.

30. *Ibid.,* 495.

31. *Ibid.,* 497.

32. *Gissing on Fiction,* 85.

33. James Joyce, *Stephen Hero* (London: Paladin, 1991), 216.

34. John Bayley, *The Short Story: Henry James to Elizabeth Bowen* (Brighton: The Harvester Press), 9.

35. *Critical Heritage,* 518. "*Pastefazoi*" is a monotonous Tuscan dish of noodles and beans; *Human Odds and Ends,* "The Prize Lodger", 133-54; James Joyce, *Dubliners* (London: Penguin, 1992), "A Painful Case", 103-14.

36. *A Victim of Circumstances,* "The Foolish Virgin", 187-216.

37. *The House of Cobwebs,* "Christopherson", 47-67.

38. *A Victim of Circumstances,* "The Fate of Humphrey Snell", 53-71.

39. *Ibid.,* 71.

40. *Dubliners,* xxxiii-iv.

41. "Morrison, Gissing and the Stark Reality", 312.

42. P. J. Keating, *The Working Classes in Victorian Fiction* (London: Routledge and Kegan Paul, 1971), 221.

43. Arthur Morrison, "What Is a Realist?", *The New Review,* XVI/94 (March 1897), 327.

44. P. J. Keating, *Working-class Stories of the 1890s* (London: Routledge and Kegan Paul, 1971), xiii.

45. *Short Stories and Short Fiction,* 18.

46. J. P. Stern, *On Realism* (London: Routledge and Kegan Paul, 1973), 10.

47. *A Victim of Circumstances,* "Fleet-footed Hester", 292.

48. *Gissing on Fiction,* 75; *Collected Letters,* V, 176.

49. *Realism,* 81. Quotation from "In the Hôtel de la Mole" in *Mimesis,* trans. Willard R. Trask (Princeton: Princeton University Press, 1953), 400-34.

50. *Collected Letters,* II, 228.

51. *Ibid.,* II, 232.

52. George Orwell, "Not Enough Money: A Sketch of George Gissing", *The Gissing Newsletter,* V/3 (July 1969), 2.

53. *The House of Cobwebs,* "A Poor Gentleman", 106-23.

54. *The Private Papers of Henry Ryecroft,* 15.

55. George Orwell, *The Road to Wigan Pier* (London: Penguin, 1989), 115-16.

56. *Realism,* 102, from George Lukács, "Balzac: Lost Illusions", in *Studies in European Realism,* trans. Edith Bone (London: Hillway, 1950).

57. *British Short Fiction in the Nineteenth Century,* 109.

58. George Levine, *The Realistic Imagination: English Fiction from Frankenstein to Lady Chatterley* (Chicago: University of Chicago Press, 1981), 160.

59. *Human Odds and Ends,* "An Inspiration", 56-73.

60. *The House of Cobwebs,* "A Capitalist" 28-46; "A Lodger in Maze Pond", 241-64.

61. Pierre Coustillas, "Gissing as a Romantic Realist", *The Gissing Newsletter,* XVII/1 (January 1981), 19.

62. "Gissing as a Romantic Realist", 18, 25.

63. *Short Stories and Short Fictions,* 7.

64. *Ibid.,* 14-15.

65. Walter Graham, *English Literary Periodicals* (New York: Octagon Books, 1966), 268, 265-66.

66. *Short Stories and Short Fictions,* 15.

67. *A Victim of Circumstances,* "A Victim of Circumstances", 3-36.

68. *The Cambridge Companion to the Classic Russian Novel,* eds Malcolm V. Jones and Robin Feuer Miller (Cambridge: Cambridge University Press, 1998), 130.

69. *George Gissing: A Critical Study,* 129.

70. Typical examples are Spicer in "The House of Cobwebs", Christopherson in "Christopherson", Tymperley in "A Poor Gentleman", Whiston in "The Scrupulous Father" and May Rocket in "A Daughter of the Lodge."

71. *The Modes of Modern Writing,* 45-46.

72. *Concepts of Criticism,* 237. Quotation from Richard Brinkmann, *Wirklichkeit und Illusion* (Tübingen: (1957), 298.

73. *The Realistic Imagination,* 139.

74. *Human Odds and Ends,* "The Tout of Yarmouth Bridge", 210-17.

75. *Stories and Sketches,* "The Peace Bringer", 225-41.

76. *Re-reading the Short Story,* ed. Clare Hanson (London: Macmillan, 1989), 48.

77. *The Lonely Voice,* 126.

78. "Gissing as a Romantic Realist", 24-25.

Bibliography

PRIMARY SOURCES

WORKS BY GEORGE GISSING

NOVELS

The Unclassed (London: Chapman and Hall, three volumes, 1884; Lawrence and Bullen, revised edition, one volume, 1895; Brighton: The Harvester Press, reprint of revised edition, 1976).

The Nether World (London: Smith Elder, 1889; Brighton: The Harvester Press, 1982).

New Grub Street (London: Smith Elder, 1891; Penguin Classics, 1985).

SHORT STORY COLLECTIONS

Human Odds and Ends (London: Lawrence and Bullen, 1897; Sidgwick and Jackson, 1911).

The House of Cobwebs (London: Constable and Co., 1906; reprinted June 1906, December 1906 and 1914).

A Victim of Circumstances and Other Stories, with Preface by Alfred C. Gissing (London: Constable and Co., 1927).

Stories and Sketches (London: Michael Joseph, 1938).

NOTEBOOKS, DIARY, LETTERS

The Collected Letters of George Gissing, 9 vols, eds Paul F. Mattheisen, Arthur C. Young and Pierre Coustillas (Athens, Ohio: Ohio University Press, 1990-1997).

MISCELLANEOUS

The Private Papers of Henry Ryecroft (London: Constable and Co., 1903; Brighton: The Harvester Press, 1982; reprinted 1983).

SECONDARY SOURCES

Bayley, John, *The Short Story: Henry James to Elizabeth Bowen* (Brighton: The Harvester Press, 1988).

Becker, George E., ed., *Documents of Modern Literary Realism* (Princeton, New Jersey: Princeton University Press, 1963).

Booth, Wayne C., *The Rhetoric of Fiction* (Chicago: University of Chicago Press, 1983; London: Peregrine Books, 1987).

Furst, Lilian F., ed., *Realism* (London: Longman, 1992).

Graham, Walter, *English Literary Periodicals* (New York: Octagon Books, 1966).

Hanson, Clare, *Short Stories and Short Fictions, 1880-1980* (London: Macmillan, 1985).

———, ed., *Re-reading the Short Story* (London: Macmillan, 1989).

Jones, Malcolm V. and Robin Feuer Miller, eds., *The Cambridge Companion to the Classic Russian Novel* (Cambridge: Cambridge University Press, 1998).

Keating, P. J., *The Working Classes in Victorian Fiction* (London: Routledge and Kegan Paul, 1971).

————, *Working-Class Stories of the 1890s* (London: Routledge and Kegan Paul, 1971).

Levine, George, *The Realistic Imagination: English Fiction from Frankenstein to Lady Chatterley* (Chicago: Chicago University Press, 1981).

Lodge, David, *The Modes of Modern Writing* (London: Edward Arnold, 1977; paperback reprint, 1989).

Martin, Wallace, *Recent Theories of Narrative* (Ithaca, New York: Cornell University Press, 1986).

Shaw, Valerie, *The Short Story: A Critical Introduction* (Harlow: Addison Wesley Longman, 1983; Longman, 8th Impression, 1998).

Stern, J. P., *On Realism* (London: Routledge and Kegan Paul, 1973).

Swinnerton, Frank, *George Gissing: A Critical Study* (London: Martin Secker, 1912; New Edition, 1924).

Watt, Ian, *The Rise of the Novel* (London: Chatto and Windus, 1957; London: The Hogarth Press, 1987).

Wellek, René, *Concepts of Criticism,* ed. Stephen G. Nichols, Jr. (New Haven: Yale University Press, 1965).

ARTICLES

Coustillas, Pierre, "Gissing as a Romantic Realist", *The Gissing Newsletter,* XVII/1 (January 1981), 14-16.

Henkle, Roger, "Morrison, Gissing, and the Stark Reality", *Novel* (Spring 1992), 302-20.

James, Henry, "The Art of Fiction", *Longman's Magazine* (September 1884), 130-41.

Morrison, Arthur, "What Is a Realist?" *The New Review,* XVI/94 (March 1897), 326-36.

O[rage], A[lfred] R., "George Gissing", *The Labour Leader,* III, 137 and 138 (November 14 and 21, 1896), 392 and 400.

Orwell, George, "Not Enough Money: A Sketch of George Gissing", *The Gissing Newsletter,* V/3 (July 1969), 1-4.

FURTHER READING

Criticism

Coustillas, Pierre. "'Joseph': A Forgotten Gissing Story of the Mid-Nineties." *Gissing Newsletter* 24, no. 1 (January 1988): 1-14.
  Discusses a lesser-known Gissing story.

Ettorre, Emanuela. "'The Salt of the Earth' and the Ethics of Self-Denial." *Gissing Journal* 31, no. 3 (July 1995): 19-31.
  Analyzes the "paradigm of negation" in "The Salt of the Earth," suggesting that the protagonist's resistance to change is fundamental to his journey toward salvation and redemption.

Mizokawa, Kazuo. "A Japanese View of 'The House of Cobwebs.'" *Gissing Newsletter* 24, no. 1 (January 1988): 27-30.
  Investigation of "The House of Cobwebs" from a Japanese cultural perspective.

Selig, Robert L. "A Further Gissing Attribution from the *Chicago Post.*" *Papers of the Bibliographical Society of America* 80 (1986): 100-04.
  Provides contextual evidence that establishes the anonymously-published "One Farthing Damages" as a Gissing story.

————. "Gissing's 'Spellbound' and *New Grub Street.*" *Gissing Journal* 35, no. 2 (spring 1999): 27-31.
  Brief analysis of the story "Spellbound."

Thomas Hardy
1840-1928

English short story writer, novelist, poet, playwright, essayist, author of nonfiction, and autobiographer.

The following entry provides an overview of Hardy's short fiction. For additional information on his short fiction career, see *SSC,* Volumes 2 and 60.

INTRODUCTION

Widely regarded as one of England's major novelists and poets, Hardy was also an influential author of short fiction. His stories, like his novels, reflect the influence of Charles Darwin and other nineteenth-century scientists and philosophers in their portrayal of a mechanistic universe in which existence is a constant struggle for survival and human character is a matter of one's fate, heredity, or environment. This literary philosophy, known as naturalism, colors his depictions of the cruel ironies that beleaguer his characters. Unlike his novels, his short fiction often features an element of the supernatural, related to his interest in folklore and local legend. While Hardy's reputation as a novelist and poet generally overshadows his other literary accomplishments, his short stories are nevertheless acknowledged as noteworthy examples of Victorian fiction.

BIOGRAPHICAL INFORMATION

Born in the village of Higher Bockhampton in the rural county of Dorset, England, Hardy was the eldest of four children. His father, Thomas Hardy II, was a builder and stonemason, and his mother, Jemima Hand Hardy, imparted her love of reading to her son. A precocious child, Hardy could read by age three. He was educated at home by his mother until age eight, and then attended the village school of Lower Bockhampton before transferring to a private school in Dorchester. Though he left school at age sixteen, Hardy continued to educate himself throughout his life. Following in his father's profession, Hardy was apprenticed to Dorchester architect John Hicks. By the time he was twenty years of age, Hardy had abandoned the religion in which he had been raised, convinced of the intellectual validity of a godless universe. He also formed, during these same years, a friendship with schoolmaster and dialect poet William Barnes, and ultimately saw himself as a successor to Barnes, who brought the rich vernacular of Dorset to life in his verse. After spending six years in Dorchester, and having fulfilled his apprenticeship to Hicks, Hardy moved to London, where he lived and worked from 1862 to 1867. Pursuing more advanced architectural work, he took a position with Arthur Blomfield, a distinguished architect, while continuing to pursue his interest in the arts. During this time he also began writing poetry, but failed to publish anything before leaving London due to poor health. Back in Dorset, where he worked with Hicks on church restoration projects, he also set about writing a novel, realizing that poetry could not advance his literary career. His first attempt at a novel, *The Poor Man and the Lady,* failed to find a publisher, and he later destroyed the manuscript. However, it did attract the attention of editor and novelist George Meredith, who rejected the book but ultimately contacted Hardy and encouraged him to continue writing.

In 1870 Hardy was commissioned to restore a local parish church in Cornwall. While there he made the acquaintance of the rector's sister-in-law, Emma Lavinia Gifford, who supported Hardy's literary efforts. His next endeavor, the anonymously published and self-financed *Desperate Remedies* (1871) was moderately successful, but it wasn't until the publication of *Far from the Madding Crowd* (1874), his first work set in the fictional county of Wessex, that Hardy finally earned enough income to give up architecture and marry Emma. The couple lived both in London and Dorset for their first years together, but they settled permanently in Dorset in 1885 at Max Gate, a home designed and built by Hardy. During the 1880s Hardy turned his hand to short stories. *Wessex Tales,* his first collection, appeared in 1888. After publishing his final novel, *Jude the Obscure* (1895), which was publicly decried for its frank depiction of sexuality, Hardy devoted himself to poetry. In 1910 Hardy was named to the Order of Merit by the British crown; two years later his wife died. In 1914 Hardy married again, this time to teacher and author Florence Emily Dugdale, a woman forty years his junior. He continued to live at Max Gate and spend time in London each year. From 1920 to 1927 Hardy worked on his autobiography, which, upon its release, was disguised as being the work of his wife. Following his death from pleurisy, his body was interred in Poet's Corner at London's Westminster Abbey, while his heart was buried in his first wife's grave.

MAJOR WORKS OF SHORT FICTION

Distinguished by their prevailing concern with ironic circumstance and human destiny, Hardy's stories, like his novels, frequently incorporate pastoral settings and the rural vernacular. On a deeper level, his tales apply a traditional, oral method of storytelling in conjunction with techniques and themes that are recognizably modern, literary, and adverse to familiar conventions or readers' expectations. Ranging in length from the vignette to the novella, the stories collected in *Wessex Tales* deal with both the mundane and the imaginative aspects of rural life. "The Three Strangers" takes place on a stormy night in the home of Shepherd Fennel during a party in honor of his daughter's christening. One by one, three strangers arrive—the first is an escaped convict, Timothy Summers, who conceals his identity; the second is the hangman sent from another town to execute Timothy; and the third is Timothy's brother. When news reaches the home that the convict is on the loose, the shepherd's family mistakenly apprehends Timothy's brother while the criminal makes his escape. Hardy later turned the story into a one-act play entitled *The Three Wayfarers* (1893). One of Hardy's most notable supernatural works is "The Withered Arm." In this story, Rhoda Brook bitterly resents Farmer Lodge's pretty new bride, Gertrude. Rhoda dreams one night that Gertrude is sitting on her chest, as an evil, old hag, mocking her; she consequently seizes the apparition by the left arm and hurls the ghost off of her. At the same time, miles away, Gertrude is awakened by a sharp pain in her arm, only to discover the next morning that it is marked by bruises consistent with a forceful grip. As time passes, the arm grows progressively worse, and does not respond to treatment. Gertrude pays a visit to Conjurer Trendle, who tells her that the cure is to lay the arm against the neck of a recently hanged man. After much scheming, she manages to get to the jail to accomplish her objective. The dead man, however, turns out to be Rhoda's illegitimate son, and Gertrude dies of shock. "The Distracted Preacher" concerns Mr. Stockdale, the new minister in Nether-Moynton, and his love for the local smuggler, Lizzy Newberry. Her life of crime makes him uneasy, but he begins to understand that her participation in this illegal enterprise, which provides a livelihood for virtually the whole community, intensifies his attraction to her. Employing military history as a backdrop, "A Tradition of Eighteen Hundred and Four" recounts a fictional "legend" about Napoleon's visit to the Dorset coast to plan an invasion, while

"The Melancholy Hussar of the German Legion" focuses on a woman's love for a German soldier who is employed by the King of England and later shot for desertion.

The tales in *A Group of Noble Dames* (1891) are unified by a frame narrative about storytellers, members of the South-Wessex Field and Antiquarian Club who are trapped in a museum by a rainstorm and thus pass the time by relating the histories of "gentle and noble dames, renowned in times past in that part of England." Set in the seventeenth and eighteenth centuries, many of these stories focus on sexual alliances across class boundaries and the plight of children. Emmeline, the eponymous character of "The Duchess of Hamptonshire," attempts to escape her husband's cruelty by asking her former lover, Alwyn, a young curate, if she can run away with him. Alwyn loves her but is nonetheless appalled by her suggestion and sets off from England without her. Years later, having heard of the death of the Duke, he smugly returns to marry her, only to find that another woman has replaced her as Duchess of Hamptonshire. After making some inquiries, Alwyn learns that Emmeline followed him on the night of his departure from England and subsequently died aboard the ship. The protagonist of "Barbara of the House of Grebe" has married handsome young Edmond Willowes, whom she loves mostly because of his good looks. When she begins to grow distant following his disfigurement in a fire, Edmond disappears from her life. Eventually, Barbara marries Lord Uplandtowers; without her new husband's knowledge, she keeps a statue of Edmond in a secret alcove, visiting it at night and caressing it. When her husband discovers this, he has workmen alter the statue's face to replicate Edmond's burn wounds. Barbara, coming upon this horror during one of her nightly visits, veers toward insanity. Lord Uplandtowers, however, makes her gaze at it every night until she turns to him to escape her terror. The plot of "Squire Petrick's Lady" takes several ironic turns. On her deathbed, Petrick's wife confesses that their son is not theirs, and Petrick therefore persuades his grandfather to cut the child out of his will. Later, after talking to his wife's doctor, Petrick learns that his wife's dying words were merely hysterical and untrue. "Lady Mottisfont" features an illegitimate child over whom two mothers fight but ultimately reject, while "The Lady Icenway" tells of a man named Anderling who is separated from his son because he married the child's mother bigamously.

Life's Little Ironies (1894) presents stories in a contemporary setting that illustrate the tragic component of social conventions. In "To Please His Wife," Joanna Phippard marries Captain Jolliffe, but convinces him to retire from the sea and open a grocery store. His ineptitude as a shopkeeper causes them to slide into poverty, forcing him to go back to sea with their two sons, never to return. Ella Marchmill, in "An Imaginative Woman," falls in love with a poet whom she has never met. After she dies in childbirth, her husband finds a picture of the poet with a lock of his wife's hair, and, wrongly assuming that the pregnancy was the result of adultery, disowns his child. "The Son's Veto" exposes the cruel effects of the class system in a narrative about a widow whose snobbish son forbids his mother to accept the proposal of a working-class man with whom she has fallen in love. In "The Fiddler of the Reels," Mop Ollamoor casts a mysterious spell over Car'line Aspent with his fiddle playing. At first he uses this as a way to seduce her; then after several years of absence he returns to make Aspent (now a married woman, but with a daughter that presumably resulted from her affair with the fiddler) dance a jig until she falls in a fit. Ollamoor then disappears forever with the child. In the same year that *Life's Little Ironies* was published, Hardy collaborated with novelist Florence Henniker on the short story "The Spectre of the Real." Featuring a characteristic twist of fate, "The Spectre of the Real" centers on the secret marriage of Rosalys Ambrose—the niece of a wealthy woman—and Jim Durrant, a poor soldier. Immediately following their wedding, the couple begin to grow weary of one another, and decide to part ways. They agree that if they hear nothing of each other for seven years, they may assume that the other has died and move on with their lives. Seven years pass and Rosalys is set to marry a nobleman, Lord Parkhurst, when Jim unexpectedly returns. Rosalys is prepared to tell her fiancé of her previous marriage, but the discovery of Jim's drowned body the following day allows her to proceed with her plans to become Lady Parkhurst. The story concludes with a telegram reporting the suicide of Lord Parkhurst during their honeymoon. The bleak conclusion goes unexplained, with the narrator stating: "No reason can be assigned for the rash act."

Hardy's final volume of short fiction, *A Changed Man* (1913), brings together previously uncollected stories. His most frankly supernatural tale, "The Romantic Adventures of a Milkmaid" utilizes archetypal fairy-tale motifs. Margery Tucker, the titular milkmaid, saves the dark and mysterious Baron von Xanten from committing suicide. In gratitude he grants her any one wish, and she decides that what she wants most of all is to go to a ball. While at the ball, Margery falls in love with a young man, Jim, whom she later marries. One day, the Baron returns and tries to coax Margery to come away with him on his yacht. Though tempted, she refuses to go, and returns to Jim. The Baron is never seen again. "The Grave by the Handpost" begins with the suicide of Sergeant Holloway and ends with the self-inflicted death of his son, Luke, after he

fails to secure a proper burial for his father. In "A Committee-Man of 'The Terror,'" a young Frenchwoman has a chance encounter with the man who beheaded her entire family years earlier. The volume also contains tales of class conflict, such as "The Waiting Supper," which revolves around a wealthy woman who must decide between her love for a neighboring farmer and her admiration for a man of high social standing. Uncollected until 1977, "The Doctor's Legend" concerns a crass nobleman whose misdeeds cast a curse-like pall over his suicidal heir. Despite his reputation for creating somber fictions, Hardy also wrote some stories for children, most notably "The Thieves Who Couldn't Help Sneezing," in which a boy outwits a gang of robbers, and "Our Exploits at West Poley," which introduces a group of friends that discovers the secret source of a river.

CRITICAL RECEPTION

While evaluations of Hardy's work continue to focus primarily upon his novels and poetry, scholarly interest in his short fiction has steadily increased over the years. Critics have studied the composition and revisions of "The Spectre of the Real" as an example of the collaborative process between a major and a minor writer, and have noted echoes of the story in Hardy's "The Waiting Supper." Likewise, they have traced alterations made in subsequent publications of "The Duchess of Hamptonshire" and have analyzed the concurrent publication of many of his stories and novels as an indicator of thematic unity between the two genres. Additionally, reviewers have underlined Gothic motifs and Christian symbols in Hardy's short fiction, linking the Gothic elements back to his work as an architect, and interpreting Timothy Summers in "The Three Strangers" as a Christ-like figure. They have also examined the transformation of "The Three Strangers" from story to play, and have detected dramatic staging effects throughout Hardy's short-fiction oeuvre. Furthermore, commentators have illustrated a unique aspect of Hardy's narrative construction by studying his stories alongside his poetry. Scholar Norman D. Prentiss, in his evaluation of Hardy's prose and verse, stresses "a structural awkwardness that, far from being the result of carelessness, is essential to Hardy's artistic achievement. Hardy's most characteristic effect depends on abrupt juxtaposition, most easily seen at the level of plot: gaps in a narrative's chronology, for example, bring conflicting situations into awkward proximity." Similarly, critics have cited the significant influence of oral tradition on his poems as well as on his tales, most notably "The Withered Arm," which is highlighted as an example of Hardy's reliance on local legend and folklore. Scholars have affirmed the author's evocation of the fairy-tale genre in "The Romantic Adventures of a Milkmaid" and have centered on the link between clothing, body, and mind in the story. Moreover, they have extolled *A Group of Noble Dames* for outlining the aesthetic ramifications of the interplay between interpersonal connections and individual will, while treating "Barbara of the House of Grebe" as an example of the negative effects of Victorian aestheticism. Overall, reviewers have concurred with Desmond Hawkins that Hardy's works of short fiction, though less renowned than his writings in other genres, "extended his talents in new ways and enriched his resourcefulness as a writer of prose fiction."

PRINCIPAL WORKS

Short Fiction

Wessex Tales: Strange, Lively, and Commonplace. 2 vols. 1888
A Group of Noble Dames 1891
Life's Little Ironies: A Set of Tales 1894
A Changed Man, The Waiting Supper, and Other Tales 1913
The Short Stories of Thomas Hardy 1928
*The Stories of Thomas Hardy. 3 vols. 1977
The Distracted Preacher, and Other Tales 1979
Collected Short Stories 1988
The Complete Stories 1996

Other Major Works

Desperate Remedies: A Novel. 3 vols. (novel) 1871
Under the Greenwood Tree: A Rural Painting of the Dutch School. 2 vols. (novel) 1872
A Pair of Blue Eyes: A Novel. 3 vols. (novel) 1873
Far from the Madding Crowd. 2 vols. (novel) 1874
The Hand of Ethelberta: A Comedy in Chapters. 2 vols. (novel) 1876
The Return of the Native. 3 vols. (novel) 1878
A Laodicean; or, The Castle of the De Stancys. 3 vols. (novel) 1881
Two on a Tower: A Romance. 3 vols. (novel) 1882
The Mayor of Casterbridge: The Life and Death of a Man of Character. 2 vols. (novel) 1886
The Woodlanders. 3 vols. (novel) 1887
Tess of the d'Urbervilles. 3 vols. (novel) 1891
The Three Wayfarers (play) 1893
Jude the Obscure (novel) 1895
Wessex Poems, and Other Verses (poetry) 1898
Poems of the Past and the Present (poetry) 1902

The Dynasts: A Drama of the Napoleonic Wars. 3 vols. (drama) 1904-08
Time's Laughingstocks, and Other Verses (poetry) 1909
Moments of Vision, and Miscellaneous Verses (poetry) 1917
Life and Art (essays and letters) 1925
†The Early Life of Thomas Hardy, 1840-1891 (autobiography) 1928
†The Later Years of Thomas Hardy, 1892-1928 (autobiography) 1930
The Letters of Thomas Hardy (letters) 1954
Personal Writings (nonfiction) 1966
The Complete Poems of Thomas Hardy (poetry) 1976
The Collected Letters of Thomas Hardy. 7 vols. (letters) 1978-88
The Works of Thomas Hardy in Prose and Verse. 18 vols. (novels, short stories, and poetry) 1984

*Includes *Old Mrs. Chundle, and Other Stories*; *Wessex Tales*; *A Group of Noble Dames*; *Life's Little Ironies*; *A Changed Man*; and *The Waiting Supper, and Other Tales*.

†Ghostwritten by Hardy and published under the name of his wife, Florence E. Hardy.

CRITICISM

James L. Roberts (essay date September 1962)

SOURCE: Roberts, James L. "Legend and Symbol in Hardy's 'The Three Strangers.'" *Nineteenth-Century Fiction* 17, no. 2 (September 1962): 191-94.

[*In the following essay, Roberts comments on the sympathy shown by the townspeople toward Timothy Summers's plight in "The Three Strangers" and notes the Christian symbolism in the story.*]

In a recent article, William Van O'Connor maintained that "Writers tend to have a persistent view of things throughout their poetry or fiction, and knowing their work as a whole one can often get a clue to the meaning of any individual part of their work."[1] Using this approach, O'Connor forced Hardy's **"The Three Strangers"** into the established pattern of cosmic irony—"seeing human affairs not as they appear to human participants but from great distances of time and space. A human struggle viewed close up has intensity; viewed from a great distance the struggle will seem rather pointless, for time and space cause any human concern to dwindle into insignificance."[2] Several aspects of the story, however, do not easily fit this pattern; Albert Guerard's belief that "Hardy's novels, read in sequence, are by no means uniformly gloomy"[3] may be a more accurate approach to **"The Three Strangers."**

The story of the condemned man, Timothy Summers, is widespread "in the country about Higher Crowstairs." In fact, Hardy presents the story as a well-known legend, an integral part of the lives of the people. Though the cosmic irony theory suggests that men's actions will seem pointless when viewed from a great distance, Hardy indicates the condemned man's struggle has an intensity and meaning that have not "dwindled into insignificance," even after fifty years. If the story had been forgotten or if the legend had involved a pessimistic view of life, then one could interpret the entire narrative in terms of cosmic irony. However, neither of these were the case. The simple story evolved into a legend and then, due to Hardy's craft, into art.

To understand the meaning of the legend, it is necessary to understand the values of the people among whom it grew. Throughout the story, Hardy emphasized that the lives and values of the people are dependent upon the country and climate around Higher Crowstairs. Since the time of "Senlac and Crecy," these people have been involved in an eternal struggle with the country and its long inimical seasons. This struggle with the elements has affected their lives which, in turn, have been imbued with an elemental quality—a quality of stubborn endurance that relies upon a firm grasp of the fundamentals of life. The values the people look for are courage, resourcefulness, shrewdness, and composure. Timothy Summers possessed these qualities, and his every act became meaningful to the people.

His original act—taking a sheep to feed his family—captured their sympathy. To hang such a man is perversion of justice; to escape from such a punishment is a sign of courage and resourcefulness. His subsequent encounter with the hangman showed his shrewdness and composure, and his ultimate escape indicates the victory of the simple man over the injustice of the law. Therefore, through his adventures, the condemned man became a representative of the simple man's triumph over injustice and a legendary symbol of those values or qualities necessary for preservation in the country around Higher Crowstairs. That these meanings are inherent in the condemned man's actions is immediately demonstrable through the manner in which the shepherds protected him from the law, and ultimately, through their retelling of his story until it became legend. .

These values account for the story of the condemned man being made into legend. In transposing the legend into art, Hardy universalizes its meaning by the use of symbols. In his imaginative recreation of the legend, Hardy used Christian symbols so as to correlate the legend of the condemned man with the Christian leg-

end. This correlation thereby emphasizes the inherent values in the condemned man's story, and by the use of this analogy, a further level of significance is added to the latter legend.

The symbols are well integrated into the story and do not demand attention for a full appreciation of the story. However, the frequent use of symbol and the repeated use of the mystical number "three" can hardly be viewed as accidental. There are three strangers, three stanzas of the hangman's song, and three knocks upon the door which is opened to the third stranger during the third stanza of the song. The action takes place at the PASTORAL dwelling of some SHEPHERDS who are celebrating a CHRISTENING. Their house, in which a fire of thorns burns brightly, is located at the CROSS of the roads. A condemned man, victim of an injustice, appears at the cross of the roads, approaches the house, kneels and drinks a "copious draugh" of water, and knocks. (In the dramatized version, *The Three Wayfarers,* the man is thirty years old.) The door is readily opened, and he is offered all the comforts of home—a pipe, the choice seat by the fire, and the family's communal cup with the engraving:

> There is no fun
> Untill I cum.

The second stranger arrives—a man in cinder grey—but his presence is resented. He is described in terms befitting the Devil (Guerard believes that "Hardy introduced an at least metaphorical Devil into three of his stories,"[4]) and the hangman's profession makes him a foil to the condemned man. When the hangman arrives at the christening, it is the condemned man who offers the communal cup to the hangman, who, in turn, quaffs it down and blatantly calls for more. After he reveals his profession in the third verse, the simple shepherds formed a circle around the hangman whom they "seemed to take for the Prince of Darkness himself." Such an open conflict enhances the values already inherent in the legend, especially when the conflict is seen as one between these two opposing forces and the persecuted innocent comes out the victor.

There seems, therefore, to be a rather clear analogy to the Christian myth, but we should in no way view the condemned man as a Christ figure. Rather, by using this analogy to an established legend, Hardy was able to emphasize the legendary characteristics of his story and the basic values inherent in his legend. Furthermore, by making the comparison to an already established legend, Hardy establishes the condemned man's encounter with the hangman as a struggle of great import.

In conclusion, Hardy was concerned with the creation of a legend, the values of that legend and its continuation, and the meaning of the legend viewed from a distance of fifty years. Rather than being a story about cosmic irony, **"The Three Strangers"** illustrates by the use of legend and symbol that the endeavors of certain human beings have an innate importance—an importance that increases rather than diminishes with time.

Notes

1. O'Connor, "Cosmic Irony in Hardy's 'The Three Strangers,'" *The English Journal,* XLVII (May, 1958), 249.

2. O'Connor, p. 250.

3. Guerard, *Thomas Hardy,* p. 2.

4. Guerard, p. 3.

James F. Scott (essay date March 1963)

SOURCE: Scott, James F. "Thomas Hardy's Use of the Gothic: An Examination of Five Representative Works." *Nineteenth-Century Fiction* 17, no. 4 (March 1963): 363-80.

[*In the following essay, Scott studies the influence of Hardy's architectural background—as well as of his admiration for the works of Edmund Burke and Walter Scott—on the Gothic elements found in his short fiction.*]

Waning esteem for literary naturalism has substantially altered the view that scholars and critics take of Thomas Hardy's fiction. Time-honored statements deprecating the sensational and melodramatic elements in his works have come to seem stale and shopworn, lacking penetration. Once dismissed as eccentricity, Hardy's perduring interest in the irrational and the occult now receives serious study. As a corrective to earlier scholarship, so often preoccupied with Hardy's realism, this marked turn of critical inquiry towards other facets of his art has already justified itself by recalling attention to the variety and complexity of his imagination.[1] But in seeking new perspectives critics have sometimes blurred the focus of old ones. Even today this focus still lacks sharpness.

Fascinated by the protean shifts of fortune, Hardy was temperamentally inclined to relish mystery and incongruity. Only during the last two decades, however, have critics begun to discuss the impress this disposition left upon his fiction. Exploring this question, Albert Guerard has related Hardy to a class of "deliberate anti-realists,"[2] and Morton Zabel has called him a "realist tending towards allegory."[3] Either approach seems more satisfactory than the pat realist label. But a third possibility is offered by Lord David Cecil who refers to the "Gothic" quality of Hardy's sensibility.[4] This last term recommends itself strongly as a piece of critical nomenclature and deserves wider application to Hardy's works. Its specific advantages to Hardy criticism are several: 1) a neutral word, Gothic is not burdened with the unfavorable connotations inevitably attached to words like sensationalism or melodrama; 2) the term Gothic does not necessarily imply, as the terminology of Guerard and Zabel seems to, that Hardy regularly departed from the prescripts of realism in a conscious effort to achieve symbolic effects; 3) the epithet Gothic suggests, as an analogue of Hardy's fiction, a particular literary tradition which flourished early in the nineteenth century and fragments of which survived into Hardy's own time. The use of the term, then, promises greater objectivity in the analysis of Hardy's fiction as well as greater insight into the historical forces which shaped it. And this paper proposes to demonstrate the relevance of the term by identifying the Gothic elements in Hardy's minor fiction.[5]

I

Although Hardy curtly dismissed the fare of the Victorian lending library as a "literature of quackery"[6] and fully endorsed the growing candor of late nineteenth-century realism, there lingers in his novels and tales a pervasive element of inspiration drawn from folklore, balladry, and the tale of terror. Of course, the presence of this influence does not make Hardy a conscious imitator of Gothic fiction. It means only that both he and the Gothic writers drank of the same waters, from streams which retained the tincture of their original spring though they followed separate courses. Hardy never borrowed subject matter directly from Gothic fiction, but the similarities of theme and tone surely are not accidental. Hardy gleaned from the Gothic tradition, as well as from the allied arts which influenced this tradition, certain devices conducive to spectacular terror. Inclined to vivid description, he discovered in art, poetry, and romance effective means to arrange intensely sensuous details of sight and sound. From contact with the Gothic, he also acquired the ability to clothe the macabre folk tales of Dorset in appealing literary garb. Furthermore, the brooding insistence of Gothic fiction upon the mischances and caprices of destiny consorts well with Hardy's painful sensitivity to the fits and turns of nature's purblind doomsters. Like the figures of Gothic romance, Hardy's protagonists are baffled and mocked by forces beyond their comprehension or control. These common elements are not mere surface phenomena. How close Hardy's conception of the novel is to that of the Gothic romancers can be inferred from one of his early journal entries: "The real, if unavowed, purpose of fiction is to give pleasure by gratifying the love of the uncommon in human experience, mental or corporeal."[7] The duty of the novelist is to play the role of the Ancient Mariner, to transfix the audience with a daemonic leer and arrest attention with a rollicking tale.[8]

Hardy's literary apprenticeship compares closely with the experience of those writers who created the Gothic novel. Schooled in the doctrine of the sublime style, both Hardy and the Gothic romancers strove to project into their scenes a feeling of awe and terror. To accomplish these sublime effects both turned to the example of art and architecture. Hardy speaks on a subject very close to him when he commends impressionistic painting for its value to the student of literature.[9] Much of the inspiration for his own fiction derives from pictorial and plastic art. Should it surprise us then that his scenes are often similar to the vivid, eye-catching spectacles of Harrison Ainsworth or Ann Radcliffe? The landscape art of Turner supplied Hardy with much the same imaginative stimulus that Salvator Rosa's wild and terrible mountain scenes gave to Mrs. Radcliffe. Each artist taught his respective literary disciple the relationship of scene to mood and the specific pictorial effects obtained from blending or contrasting color and drab, light and shade.[10] Although Turner is more sophisticated than Rosa and Hardy more subtle than Radcliffe, the substance of the lesson remains much the same.

Hardy's youthful apprenticeship to John Hicks aroused his interest in architecture and made him especially sensitive to the "cunning irregularity" of Gothic lines.[11] This preference for asymmetrical shapes and forms was soon converted into a love of old ruins, a fact which figures importantly in his fiction. Like the Gothic writers before him, Hardy was much impressed by the remains of antiquity, and these dreary relics often find their way into his works. Few serious students of Hardy have failed to notice how frequently he associates the personal mood of a character with some massive, ominous ruin, like Stonehenge, thus creating a physical image which organizes and conditions the reader's response. The scene itself makes us feel whatever anxiety or dread is experienced by the protagonist. This technique is common to nearly all the Gothic writers. In their works, as in Hardy's, the sublime ruin adds a spatial dimension to the mood of melancholy or terror evoked by a particular complex of events.

In all probability, Hardy strove quite consciously for these sublime effects, as did the Gothic romancers. For Hardy, too, was conversant with Burke's *Enquiry into the Sublime and the Beautiful,* a work which since its first publication in 1759 had influenced most writers who were interested in the aesthetics of terror.[12] Burke's book is crucial to the Gothic movement in literature because it draws attention to all the technical devices suggestive of terror. Burke explains the attrac-

tion of the Augustans to mouldering Gothic piles and Rosa's fretful scenes in terms of associational psychology. And in the process of the discussion he lists nearly all the machinery which later became the property of Gothic romancers: the stark cliffs, the fierce tempests, the swift and startling changes from light to darkness or darkness to light, the shades and shadows, the eerie, half-seen forms. Of course, no one ever mastered the craft of fiction by consulting a philosophy textbook. But Burke's ideas were in the air when the Gothic romance began to flourish, and they provided a theory which justified and encouraged the practice of the Gothic writers. Much the same can be said of Burke's influence upon Hardy. A self-educated man, Hardy was always a little embarrassed by his lack of literary sophistication and continually sought out the works of those whom he thought acquainted with the refinements of art. Anxious to have his own feelings confirmed by authority, Hardy found in Burke's aesthetics of the sublime an endorsement of the techniques that came naturally to him. Perhaps J. T. Boulton has this in mind when he says, "Burke's *Enquiry* made its finest contribution to imaginative literature through the stimulus it gave Thomas Hardy."[13] For sublimity is one of the most striking features of Hardy's work.

The similarity of Hardy's fiction to the Gothic romance is not exclusively a matter of technique. Both Hardy and the Gothic romancers drew their subject matter from similar sources, among the most important of which are legend and folklore. Hardy delighted in the ballads of the Wessex country and throughout his life diligently collected popular tales of a lurid hue. This material is often directly comparable to the weird stories of crime and disaster which writers like Monk Lewis and Robert Maturin culled from the diverse resources of English and Continental folklore and then incorporated into their own novels. Consider, for example, this jotting about peasant superstitions found among Hardy's papers:

> Among the many stories of spell-working that I have been told, the following is one of how it was done by two girls about 1830. They killed a pigeon, stuck its heart full of pins, made a tripod of three knitting needles, and suspended the heart on them over a lamp, murmuring an incantation while it roasted, and using the name of the young man in whom one or both were interested. The said young man [*sic*] felt racking pains about the region of the heart. . . .[14]

In Hardy we are confronted by the paradox of a man who often spoke out against credulity, yet remained eternally fascinated by the strange and the marvelous. Nor was he sparing in the use of popular superstitions to heighten the pitch of his own stories.[15]

Finally, there is in Hardy's fiction the inspiration of a strictly literary tradition. Hardy was drawn to the same poetic and dramatic literature that excited the Gothic romancers. As a child he devoured Macpherson's *Ossian* and often underscored vivid descriptive passages,[16] a practice which reminds us of the delight the Gothic novelists took in Augustan "recovery" poems. Like the Gothic writers, Hardy also dearly loved the Elizabethan and Jacobean drama, particularly Shakespeare and Webster, with all their sublimity and horror.[17] What Hardy knew of the Gothic novel itself he learned from his reading of Harrison Ainsworth and Walter Scott. This influence should not be taken lightly. To demonstrate Hardy's indebtedness to Ainsworth, Carl Weber has collected a convincing number of peculiar rhetorical mannerisms common both to Hardy and to this nearly forgotten Gothic novelist.[18] The bulk of evidence seems to preclude accidental correspondence. Even whole scenes from Hardy's major novels, particularly tempests or other striking natural phenomena, often compare very closely in arrangement and design to similar episodes in Ainsworth's fiction.[19] We also know that Hardy retained into his mature years considerable respect for some of Scott's fiction. Significantly, he disparages Scott's realistic novels and lauds those written in the Gothic manner. *The Bride of Lammermoor,* which Ernest Baker calls the "masterpiece of Gothic fiction,"[20] Hardy recommended as a model work, "an almost perfect specimen of form."[21] Such enthusiasm betokens more than casual interest. Nor is the appeal of Scott and Ainsworth difficult to understand. Hardy could find in Ainsworth all the dreadful details of the charnel house and in Scott the full wonder of Gothic spells and enchantments. But while each preserved according to his respective talents the essence of the Gothic spirit, both Ainsworth and Scott undertook to adapt the most extravagant Gothic devices to a realistic context.[22] To accomplish the same kind of adaptation became one of Hardy's controlling literary ambitions.

To this whole complex of interests and influences must be added the example of Collins and Reade, from whom Hardy probably learned a few of the refinements of melodrama while he scanned their pages for the formula needed to create a marketable literary product. Though his attraction to their work was fleeting and insubstantial, this study apparently did convince Hardy that the "sensation novel" was a respectable literary form, honored by novelists of repute. Later in his career, Hardy constructed a rather impressive defense of sensation fiction:

> A "sensation-novel" is possible in which the sensationalism is . . . not physical but psychical. . . . The difference between the latter kind of novel and the novel of physical sensationalism—i.e., personal adventure, etc.,—is this: that whereas in the physical the adventure itself is the subject of interest, the psychical results being passed over as commonplace, in the psychical

the casualty or adventure is held to be of no intrinsic interest, but the effect upon the faculties is the important matter to be depicted.[23]

Well before he had formulated this aesthetic, however, Hardy had already ceased to feel any qualms about writing according to his own instincts, which continually tugged him towards exorbitant spectacle and dreadful terror. The example of Collins and Reade merely freed him of any lingering inhibitions. Hence, after his early fiasco, *The Poor Man and the Lady,* Hardy habitually worked with the sensation novel. But he wrote in a manner not typical of his Victorian contemporaries, for his inspiration welled up from sources which lay deeper in the recesses of his mind than the influence of Collins and Reade had ever penetrated.

II

Quite often in his minor fiction, Hardy actually restores the mood of Gothic romance and recreates the disquieting, crepuscular Gothic world. In this world the atmosphere of ordinary experience vanishes: the scene glows with an eerie light that surrounds the familiar furniture of life with strange shadows and brings the startling and unexpected into sharp relief; events succeed each other not according to any discernible cause and effect pattern but through the frightening, incongruous logic of a nightmare. Both the setting and the action are contrived to horrify, usually through the introduction of the preternatural and through an absorption in the terrible and the grotesque. These three elements—the preternatural, the terrible, and the grotesque—are abundantly distributed through the fiction of Hardy. They occur more frequently, however, in the minor novels and tales, where the absence of assimilation makes them easily recognizable.

The preternaturalism of Gothic fiction ranges from forthright diabolism and witchcraft to a subtle manipulation of legends and tales which merely hint at the sorcery of the dark powers. Generally, incursions of the occult are the more effective as they are the less overt, and only the more skillful devices for handling such material persisted in English fiction after a momentary craze for Germanic horror had subsided. Launching his literary career a half century after the Gothic bloom had withered, Hardy was compelled to exercise the utmost sophistication in his treatment of the marvelous. Like Scott, who often achieves very graceful adaptations of Gothic convention, Hardy appreciates the necessity of modifying the preternatural to fit a realistic situation. In his fiction, the spectres and fiends of Gothic romance lose their odor of infernal brimstone and acquire the manners and gestures of the Wessex peasantry. Artfully, Hardy provides the groundless fancies of Gothic romance with a credible basis in regional custom and belief. Rarely does the preternatural enter directly, and sometimes a quasi-rational explanation is appended to account for unlikely events. More frequently, Hardy resorts to the use of a persona, when he wishes to imply that a particular story is more well-found than well-founded. Having placed this modest disclaimer, he is then free to recount the tale with relish and verve. Personal skepticism never reduces Hardy's enthusiasm for the mysterious dreams, strange portents, or dark curses and spells of Gothic fiction, all of which he parades in copious array.

Hardy's ability to domesticate the occult by giving it a realistic backdrop is effectively illustrated in **"The Withered Arm."** Conceived ingeniously and written with great force, this tale is one of the most Gothic in the whole corpus of Hardy's works. The tale attains a horrific pitch in the early moments of the action as Rhoda Brook grapples with a spectral assailant, finally overthrowing the shadowy visitant: "Gasping for breath, Rhoda, in a last desperate effort, swung out her right hand, seized the confronting spectre by its obtrusive left arm, and whirled it backward to the floor. . . ."[24] Still sensing the terror of having clutched a ghostly arm, Rhoda pursues her attacker in vain: "She could feel her antagonist's arm within her grasp even now—the very flesh and bone of it, as it seemed. She looked on the floor whither she had whirled the spectre, but there was nothing to be seen."[25] This incident is replete with Gothic mystery. The sudden appearance of a phantom shape in the ill-lighted chamber and Rhoda's fitful ordeal with her otherworldly antagonist are details reminiscent of scenes from Lewis and Maturin. But Hardy heightens the effect of the episode by shrouding it in enough obscurity to blur the distinction between illusion and reality.

A note of pathos gives added substance to the tale, as Rhoda becomes hysterical with grief upon discovering that in their somnambulistic combat she has inadvertently placed a curse upon Gertrude Lodge. Hardy's humane touch, however, does not diminish the Gothic terror of the discovery itself. Rhoda loses all composure as she beholds the withered arm:

> There was nothing of the nature of a wound, but the arm . . . had a shrivelled look, and the outline of the four fingers appeared. . . . Moreover, she [Rhoda], fancied that they were imprinted in precisely the relative position of her clutch upon the arm in the trance. . . .[26]

Hardy makes no effort either to disguise or to rationally explain the heroine's unwitting sortilege. From the moment Rhoda seizes Mrs. Lodge in the bedchamber until she dies as a result of the conjurer's eccentric therapy, this unfortunate woman bears upon her arm

the scar of an unearthly curse. A sense of the diabolic permeates the entire tale. But the horror of Gothic preternaturalism is adeptly balanced by a realistic treatment of character which evokes sympathy for both the protagonists. In Hardy's hands, the waxworks' mannikins of romance are transformed into flesh and blood creatures capable of genuine human emotions. This counterpoise saves Hardy from artificial pastiche yet enables him to exploit the histrionic possibilities of Gothic thaumaturgy.

Scenes of ghostly visitation occur infrequently in Hardy, but another memorable apparition enlivens **"The Committee-Man of 'the Terror.'"** Here, Hardy introduces the preternatural in a rather oblique manner. We look upon the scene with the eyes of the heroine, emotionally distraught though she is. Her nervousness and insecurity accentuate the impact of the apparition. Hardy dims the lights, muffles the incidental sound effects, and scrupulously arranges all the other details of the scene to prepare for the entrance of those frightful shades who march through the bedchamber. Caught between sleep and consciousness, the astonished girl stares fretfully at the solemn procession:

> That night she saw . . . a divinely sent vision. A procession of her lost relatives—father, brother, uncle, cousin—seemed to cross her chamber between her bed and the window, and when she endeavoured to trace their features she perceived them to be headless, and that she had recognized them by their familiar clothes only. . . .[27]

As in **"The Withered Arm,"** the subject matter here derives mostly from folklore. Legends of fearful curses and midnight apparitions had circulated in the Wessex country centuries before Hardy was born. Such material is also familiar to students of popular balladry. But Hardy has revised the raw substance to suit his own needs. Instead of the austere realism of the ballad, we find a conscious effort to whet the imagination and stimulate the emotions. And instead of a rambling, disjointed folk narrative, we see the material selected and arranged so as to effect a dramatic climax. To be sure, these headless revenants still bear striking family resemblances to their ancestors in English folklore, and the belief that the dead return to proffer mute counsel to the living is a motif hoary with age. Hardy, however, has adapted the material in the manner of his Gothic forebears. Sifting out the dramatic qualities of the folk tale and transforming ballad conventions to intensify the effect of terror, Hardy proves his ability to exercise his ledger-demain within the framework of Gothic artifice.

Even when they contain nothing explicitly preternatural, Hardy's tales often sustain a pitch of terror comparable to that of Gothic fiction. These accents of terror are more than merely sensational. Gothic terror is always sensational, but the sensational is not necessarily Gothic. Of course, the sensational and the terrible are integrally related because each assumes the interruption of a natural narrative order. Once the interior logic of cause and effect is violated, the plot develops haphazardly, by chance and coincidence rather than according to a calculable pattern. Incidents may then be introduced without consideration of their organic relationship to the total context. But an appreciable qualitative difference still remains between events contrived to frighten or shock and those intended only to surprise or excite. The difference, in fact, is evident in Hardy's own fiction. Events such as the introduction of long-lost heirs or the entanglements of misremembered instructions are merely sensational. On the other hand, Hardy's preoccupation with graves and corpses, an interest augmented by his unfailing attention to all the emotionally disturbing particulars of these scenes, often begets a sense of terror which shades easily into the macabre. This latter quality, especially, relates Hardy to the Gothic tradition.

Hardy's taste for graveyard lore contributes an inordinate number of funerals, burials or exhumations, and other assortments of cemetery rendezvous to nearly all the novels and tales. Even when the setting is other than sepulchral, the figure of the corpse generally is not far from Hardy's mind. Often, details of the charnel house operate in conjunction with other elements naturally provocative of terror. Hardy thus masters the ecology of terror: the whole environment surrounding an event elaborates the original shock of intrigue or violence.

Scenes of discovery effectively challenge Hardy's ability to awaken a sense of terror. Again, this Gothic terror goes beyond mere sensationalism, for surprise alone is often foreign to Hardy's purposes. Notice, for example, the exhumation of Mrs. Manston in *Desperate Remedies*. The full impact of this episode depends not upon the reader's complete ignorance of what is to come but upon half-certain expectation. The details of the discovery are more frightful because we suspect from the outset that Manston, undertaking his gruesome burial mission, carries the partially decomposed corpse of his murdered wife carefully bundled upon his shoulders. The human body, mutilated or decayed, is one of the standard stage properties of Gothic terror. Fully aware of its potential, Hardy employs this piece of machinery to the best advantage. The success of the scene lies in its balance of suspense and surprise. Having implied the nature of Manston's crime, Hardy conceals as much detail as possible and withholds the complete revelation until the subordinate effects of

suspense are achieved. At every turn we expect to confront the figure of a woman long dead, but this dire prospect is not soon fulfilled.

The darkness which pervades the scene adds much to its effect. Once Manston has extinguished his lantern, the action reveals itself primarily through sound—the rhythm of footsteps, the rustle of leaves, the crunch of a spade breaking turf. No light is admitted until the suspense builds to a crisis; then Hardy allows the gleam of a newly kindled lantern to play over the scene. The chosen moment is apt, for the corn sack containing the remains of Mrs. Manston has just experienced a hasty resurrection at the hands of a local law officer. The revelation comes suddenly: "He [the officer] raised his hand to the glass, and . . . peered at an almost intangible filament he held between his finger and thumb. It was a long hair; the hair of a woman."[28] The inspector, of course, has fastened upon the exact detail necessary to sustain the effect of Gothic terror. As the reader shares the experience of discovery, he needs little imagination to associate this wisp of loose hair caught by the light with the horrifying death's-head still concealed beneath the tarpaulin. Once this association is made, further amplification becomes superfluous. And in spite of the profusion of startling incidents, Hardy here uses the technical apparatus of sensationalism to provoke horror, not surprise. The focus shifts from the unexpected to the terrible, thus giving the scene its intensity and power.

This distinction between astonishment and terror becomes more sharply pronounced when we consider the third element of the Gothic in Hardy's fiction—the grotesque. Gothic grotesquerie deforms the texture of human experience and distorts the natural character of human responses. A highly specialized variety of sensationalism, the grotesque is distinguished by its morbid absorption in the abnormal and the perverse. To the dislocation of logical order which characterizes all forms of sensationalism the grotesque adds an interest in certain kinds of incongruity, remarkable for their capacity to provoke horror. Hardy uses such material sparingly, but often enough to leave a recognizable imprint upon his fiction. Although his robust spirit and healthy imagination preserve him from the vulgar excesses of Lewis or Maturin, Hardy occasionally introduces the grotesque to achieve an immediate and overwhelming effect of horror. The infrequency with which he employs the material really accentuates rather than diminishes its force. A scene of comic relief or a piece of incidental stage business quickly returns attention to some more pleasant subject, but the primal impact of the grotesque remains.

Hardy's taste for the grotesque reveals itself clearly in two tales which are particularly Gothic in their inspiration, **"Barbara of the House of Grebe"** and **"The**

Doctor's Legend." To give these stories their horrific turn, Hardy assembles nearly all the standard equipment of Gothic grotesquerie: mental imbalance, sexual abnormality, mutilation and disfiguration, sadistic brutality. These two works define the furthest limits of Gothic incursions into Hardy's fiction.

A romance convention stereotyped by centuries of use, the theme of human attraction to a statue is not inherently grotesque, but becomes so in **"Barbara of the House of Grebe"** because of Hardy's concentration upon the physical details of the relationship. Furthermore, the circumstances under which we learn the extent of Barbara's infatuation with the image of her former husband are arranged to generate horror and revulsion. Although many earlier details hint at the unnatural ardor of Barbara's interest in the icon, we still feel the full shock of Lord Uplandtowers' discovery: "Arrived at the door of the boudoir, he [Lord Uplandtowers] beheld the door of the private recess open, and Barbara within it, standing with her arms clasped tightly round the neck of her Edmond, and her mouth on his."[29] Barbara's fondling gestures and apostrophes of endearment themselves approach the grotesque, but the lord's ghoulish exploitation of his wife's illness soon gives the tale a greater horrific effect.

After a dextrous sculptor has desecrated the image of Willowes according to prescription, Lord Uplandtowers ceremoniously reveals the disfigured statue to his wife:

> He [Lord Uplandtowers] pulled a cord which hung covered by the bedcurtains, and the doors of the wardrobe slowly opened, disclosing that the shelves within had been removed throughout, and the interior adapted to receive the ghastly figure, which stood there as it had stood in the boudoir, but with a wax candle burning on each side of it to throw the cropped and distorted features into relief.[30]

Every particular of this description supports the total impression. A gradual and deliberate preparation, interspersed with fragments of casual stage business, establishes a mood of uneasy anticipation. The opening of the cabinet doors then focuses absolute attention upon the grotesque object while the unpredictable glare and shadow of candlelight accents the hideousness and deformity of the image. Finally, Barbara's baleful shrieks of hysterical terror add a dimension of sound to the already dreadful spectacle. Rarely does the idiom of horror attain so intense a pitch in Hardy's fiction.

Motifs of disfigurement and deformity also operate in **"The Doctor's Legend."** As in **"Barbara of the House of Grebe,"** the horror of this tale results from a well-planned revelation scene. Here, the horrific object is a young girl whose features have been so distorted by chronic attacks of epilepsy that playmates have cruelly nicknamed her "Death's-Head." Ironically, the child's distraught mother uses this affliction as an instrument of vengeance upon the Squire whom she holds responsible for her daughter's condition. Concealing herself behind a cemetery wall, the aggrieved peasant woman intercepts the Squire's wife and stuns her with the grotesque image of the deformed girl. Looking towards the top of the wall, Lady Cicely is suddenly confronted by a grinning death's-head:

> The moonlight fell upon the sepulchral face and head, intensifying the child's daytime aspect till it was only too much like that which had suggested the nickname. The unsuspecting and timid lady—a perfect necrophobist by reason of the care with which everything unpleasant had been kept out of her dainty life—saw the deathlike shape, and, shrieking with sudden terror, fell to the ground.[31]

Several aspects of technique relate this description to the Gothic tradition. The death's-head itself is horrible, and its presence alone immediately suggests the grotesque. But the lighting arrangement, typical of the Gothic, corroborates this effect in other ways: the dimness of the light obliterates background objects which might distract one's vision from the central figure; the light's paleness removes all color from the scene and, consequently, all emotions naturally associated with color (warmth, energy, vitality); the position of the light source creates shadows and shades, thus serving to further transmogrify the deformity of the object itself. Moreover, the timing of the episode is calculated to emphasize the suddenness of the revelation. The image is thrust above the wall at precisely the instant Lady Cicely's glance is lifted in the appropriate direction. And, of course, the grotesque sepulchral association is supplied by the cemetery and its environs. In this tale Hardy bedevils his readers with the most subtle refinements of Gothic horror.

Within the confines of Gothic convention, Hardy maneuvers with exceptional skill. He controls the standard devices of terror with a poise that suggests these arts came effortlessly and instinctively to him. Admittedly, the effects gained are cheap ones, because the thrill and the shock necessarily remain dramatically shallow. In even the best Gothic fiction, elaborate contrivance and fitful activity disguise but thinly a want of insight into the human character and a reluctance to confront the serious issues of life. When Hardy too sedulously adheres to the precedent of the Gothic romancers, his perception is dulled and his imagination revels in a superfluity of incidents, which remain trivial even though they are exciting and captivating. Whatever the inherent limitations of the genre, however, we must admire the dexterity with which Hardy arranged and adapted the conventions of the Gothic tale and the inspiration with which he refurbished and revitalized its mood. Nor should we forget that in his great works of fiction Hardy is quite capable of transforming and revaluing these Gothic conventions, even while he continues to use many of the techniques associated with them.

III

On the strength of this analysis, the relevance of the term Gothic to Hardy criticism seems assured. One value which accrues from its application is that the historical point of view uncovers certain techniques all but obscured by the blanket word "sensationalism." Reference to the Gothic immediately puts us in touch with a whole complex of artistic strategems which evolved under both literary and extra-literary pressure. Studying Hardy's work in the light of this tradition enables us to identify those elements his fiction shares in common with the Gothic romance. Then we may go on to show how the excitement and intrigue of conventional melodrama fuse and comingle in Hardy with the occult and macabre spirit of the Gothic. This classification of material is more than an academic exercise because it helps define the unique, poetic quality of Hardy's sensationalism. And as critics now generally recognize, sensationalism is integral to Hardy's art.

The use of the term Gothic, then, may be expected not only to afford insight into Hardy's minor fiction but also to illumine the idiom and design of his great novels. Perhaps it may even clarify the relationship between Hardy's major and minor works. At least it should increase our understanding of Hardy's symbolism, a topic upon which many recent critics have spoken.[32] For the effectiveness of Hardy's symbols is often contingent upon the energy with which he absorbs and assimilates Gothic motifs. Hardy's imagination functions at two levels of seriousness. Writing casually, he concocts engaging trivia. Writing from the fullness of his vision, he creates profound meditations upon life and man. The difference here is one of intent, not merely a matter of success or failure. Hardy's lesser works are not noble experiments that went awry, only clever bread-and-butter performances which earned their author an agreeable number of shillings. Hence we must exercise caution in using the terms symbolic and allegorical to discuss Hardy's work, lest we impute symbolic intent where none exists. The advantage of the term Gothic is that it applies to either of Hardy's creative moods and even suggests how the one shades into the other. In works of negligible thematic import Gothic conventions merely help Hardy devise stirring adventures. On the other hand, when he chooses to write as a serious artist, his subordination of Gothic motifs to the demands of theme enables him to create meaningful symbols and to project into the literal action a dimension of myth or allegory.

When these Gothic motifs become organically coherent with the form and theme of his novels, Hardy's art is remarkably expanded and enriched. At such moments, elements of the preternatural, the legends and portents we have explored, lose much of their superficial Gothic flavor and come to betoken a fate beyond man's ken encircling him and frustrating his desires. Then sensationalism may unite with the occult in suggesting the terrifying effect of chance in a world ruled by irrational doomsters. Sometimes the grotesque adds a further ingredient of horror to man's titanic struggle against depraved institutions and cosmic blindness. Over all these scenes is cast the awe and splendor of Gothic sublimity, whose technical effects universalize the action by giving it mythic overtones and bestow upon the characters a tragic grandeur not reducible to the literal gestures of their behavior. Collectively, this material furnishes a counterpoise to Hardy's realism and fuses with the complex pattern of image and allusion which distinguishes his best fiction.

Hardy now appears both more and less modern than was once assumed. The compression of his vision into symbols puts us in mind of twentieth-century novelists, even though his attraction to the tale of terror connects him with a tradition already passé in his own time. The definitive feature of Hardy's genius is his ability to play the dual role of symbolist and yarn spinner, while preserving the illusion that he is writing realistically. Recognizing this, we may still criticize his occasionally pretentious rhetoric and deride his clumsy, ramshackle plots. But we must acknowledge that not all Hardy's melodramatic impulses are awkward and that the eccentricities of his rhetoric arise from an attempt to develop a new prose idiom. The motifs of Gothic romance contribute appreciably to these ends. Inconsequential in themselves, Hardy's stories and tales gave him facility in the handling of Gothic material and his minor novels allowed him to elaborate Gothic choreography in a more ample literary form. Without consciously experimenting, Hardy perfected in these undistinguished works the arts that were to grace his mature fiction. He gained the ability to crystallize a scene in a single sublime image, the power to intensify visual effects through the contrast of light and shadow, and the subtlety to probe abnormal states of consciousness in a manner foreign to most Victorian fiction. The development of Hardy's serious art describes an increasingly more resourceful and more imaginative adaptation of Gothic convention. From the stagy Gothic contrivance of *Far from the Madding Crowd* evolves the mature power of *The*

Return of the Native and finally the tragic horror of *Jude the Obscure*. The Gothic tradition, transmitted to him from both oral and literary sources, gave Hardy not only a set of stock techniques which enlivened his popular entertainments but also a quality of vision which liberated him from the fetters of documentary realism and allowed full play to his romantic genius. We shall read all of Hardy's fiction more perceptively if we remain sensitive to this tradition.

Notes

1. The tendency to overemphasize Hardy's realism was most pronounced in the 1910's and 1920's, when even highly capable scholars were prone to think of his art in these terms. See, for example, Mary Ellen Chase, *Thomas Hardy from Serial to Novel* (Minneapolis, 1927). Miss Chase often leaves the impression that most of Hardy's departures from realism were concessions to the poor taste of his reading public.

2. *Thomas Hardy: The Novels and Stories* (Cambridge, Mass., 1949), p. ix.

3. "Hardy in Defense of his Art: The Aesthetic of Incongruity," *Southern Review,* VI (Summer, 1940), 148.

4. *Hardy the Novelist: An Essay in Criticism* (London, 1943), p. 81. Earlier, this term had been employed in a very specialized context by Samuel C. Chew, *Thomas Hardy: Poet and Novelist* (New York, 1921), p. 60.

5. The distinction between "major" and "minor" in Hardy's fiction is less difficult to draw than in most other cases. It is generally agreed that Hardy intended his "novels of character and environment" to be taken as his contribution to serious fiction. The novels which succeeding generations have called "great" all belong to this series: *Far from the Madding Crowd, The Return of the Native, The Mayor of Casterbridge, The Woodlanders, Tess of the D'Urbervilles,* and *Jude the Obscure*. The majority of Hardy's other prose works are classified either as "romances and fantasies" or "novels of ingenuity," categories which suggest levity or contrivance.

6. "Candour in English Fiction," *Thomas Hardy: Life and Art,* ed. Ernest Brennecke (New York, 1925), p. 76.

7. Florence E. Hardy, *The Early Life of Thomas Hardy* (New York, 1928), p. 193.

8. Hardy himself coined this metaphor. See Florence E. Hardy, *The Later Years of Thomas Hardy* (New York, 1930), pp. 15-16.

9. *The Early Life,* p. 241.

10. The influence of painting upon the technique of Hardy's fiction has been explored with customary Germanic thoroughness in Gunther Wilmsen, *Thomas Hardy als Impressionisticher Landschaftsmaler* (Marburg, 1934).

11. See *The Later Years,* p. 78.

12. The nature and extent of Burke's influence upon Hardy has been considered at length by S. F. Johnson, "Hardy and Burke's 'Sublime,'" *Style in Prose Fiction,* ed. Harold C. Martin (New York, 1959), pp. 55-86. That Hardy did study Burke's aesthetics with some care is corroborated by the testimony of Carl J. Weber, *Hardy and the Lady from Madison Square* (Waterville, Maine, 1952), p. 89.

13. Burke's *Enquiry into the Sublime and the Beautiful* (New York, 1958), p. cxx.

14. *The Later Years,* p. 11.

15. Hardy's use of folklore is given detailed attention in Ruth A. Firor, *Folkways in Thomas Hardy* (Philadelphia, 1931). See also Donald Davidson, "The Traditional Basis of Thomas Hardy's Fiction," *Southern Review,* VI (Summer, 1940), 162-178.

16. Evelyn Hardy, *Thomas Hardy: A Critical Biography* (New York, 1954), p. 39.

17. Hardy's interest in Webster is treated in Marcia L. Anderson, "Hardy's Debt to Webster in *The Return of the Native,*" *Modern Language Notes,* LIV (1939), 497-501. Hardy's personal copies of Webster's works contain underscorings and annotations in Hardy's hand.

18. "Ainsworth and Thomas Hardy," *Review of English Studies,* XVII (1941), 193-200.

19. Weber traces in great detail the similarities between the storm scene in Ainsworth's *Rookwood* and Hardy's *Far from the Madding Crowd*. See pp. 195-196.

20. *History of the English Novel,* VI (London, 1935), 168.

21. "The Profitable Reading of Fiction," *Life and Art,* p. 69.

22. Ainsworth makes this the avowed purpose of his fiction, pledging himself in the preface of *Rookwood* to "write in the bygone style of Mrs. Radcliffe." Scott's connection with Gothic fiction is less close, but he too remained under the spell of the tale of terror. The transformation Scott worked upon Gothic conventions can be observed by comparing *The Bride of Lammermoor* to Maturin's *The Milesian Chief*. See Miilo Idman, *Charles Robert Maturin: His Life and Works* (London, 1923), esp. pp. 97-98.

23. *The Early Life,* p. 268.

24. *The Writings of Thomas Hardy in Prose and Verse,* IX (New York, 1920), 77-78. All references are to the Harper Anniversary Edition of Hardy's works. The problem of editions is a crucial one in Hardy's case because his works have so often been adapted and revised from serial versions bowdlerized by the pressure of censorship. Based upon the "Autograph Edition" of 1912 which received Hardy's personal approval, the Anniversary Edition provides the student with a correct and relatively complete text of Hardy's works. See Carl J. Weber, *Hardy in America* (Waterville, Maine, 1946), esp. pp. 101-103.

25. *Ibid.,* p. 78.

26. *Ibid.,* pp. 82-83.

27. *Ibid.,* XVII, 227.

28. *Ibid.,* XIV, 417-418.

29. *Ibid.,* XIII, 83.

30. *Ibid.,* p. 88.

31. *Revenge is Sweet: Two Short Stories,* uncollected tales ed. Carl J. Weber (Waterville, Maine, 1940), pp. 51-52.

32. See, for example, Arthur Mizener, *"Jude the Obscure* as a Tragedy," *Southern Review,* VI (Summer, 1940), 193-213, and John Paterson, *"The Return of the Native* as Antichristian Document," *Nineteenth-Century Fiction,* XIV (1959), 111-127. For the discussion of Hardy's symbolism in a more general context, see Richard C. Carpenter, "Hardy's 'Gargoyles,'" *Modern Fiction Studies,* VI (1960), 223-232.

Alexander Fischler (essay date summer 1966)

SOURCE: Fischler, Alexander. "Theatrical Techniques in Thomas Hardy's Short Stories." *Studies in Short Fiction* 3, no. 4 (summer 1966): 435-45.

[*In the following essay, Fischler examines the dramatic staging effects in many of Hardy's stories, highlighting the balance of the common and the uncommon in these works.*]

It is difficult to read Hardy's short stories without being aware of an element of theatricality in the setting, in the positioning of characters, and in the use of "things" almost as stage properties to further plot development. To a large extent this may be due to convention, to the period style; but with Hardy the use of stage device goes also beyond mere convention: it becomes an important technique for the realization of his basic theories about fiction.

On the rare occasions when he indulged in formulating theories, Hardy was likely to apply them equally to the novel, the short story, and the drama. The writer, he says, must not only be able to respond "to everything within the circle of the sun that has to do with life," but he must also possess the kind of intuition that allows him to see a total picture suggested by a fragment of a situation,[1] so that he can transform even the smallest hint of a story, perhaps only the coincidence of marriage and death dates in an old family record into "palpitating drama" (p. 489).[2] This drama, however, will be successful only if it strikes the proper balance between the two elements Hardy considers essentials—the ordinary and the uncommon. A work must be sufficiently rooted in the ordinary to give the sense of reality, yet incorporate enough of the unusual to attract the interest of the reader and imply unique significance for unexceptional details. Hardy considered maintenance of the proper tension between these two elements the basic problem the writer must face, regardless of the genre in which he was working: "The whole secret of fiction and the drama—in the constructional part—lies in the adjustment of things unusual to things eternal and universal. The writer who knows exactly how exceptional and how unexceptional his events should be made, possesses the key to the art."[3]

He was ever prone to use the word *drama* when speaking of his fiction, and, indeed, the General Preface to the Wessex Edition has among its primary concerns the establishment of "Wessex" as a stage suitable for the enactment of the novels and tales which follow as dramas "of grandeur truly Sophoclean." He was eager apparently not only to enlarge the scope of the works, but also to justify his attitude towards the characters and his rather obvious desire to retain a share in their drama. Long before *The Dynasts,* apparently even from the time of the never-published first novel *The Poor Man and the Lady* on, Hardy staged his works and assumed the role of director in addition to that of author. In the novels the effects of this double role tend to be lost in a complex of stylizations; but they remain very obvious in the short stories, usually painfully obvious, and they suggest some interesting things not only about Hardy's views on fiction, but also about the dissatisfaction that ultimately led him to abandon writing it.

Like the director, Hardy knew the importance of composing the stage and getting his characters "on" at the appropriate moment. He opened a number of stories with the presentation of a prepared and waiting stage, or with what in effect is a theatrical tableau used for establishing mood or atmosphere. In **"The Three Strangers"** (*Wessex Tales*), in **"What the Shepherd Saw"** (*A Changed Man*), and to an extent in **"The Honourable Laura"** (*A Group of Noble Dames*), Hardy foreshadows the action by carefully setting a grandiose stage, very much as he does in *The Return of the Native* through the introductory description of Egdon Heath.[4] Elsewhere he uses a more modest setting—a house, a village square, and the like—arranging it with a care that the subsequent action seldom justifies. In any case, the setting described becomes a stage, and Hardy asks the reader to be an audience to whom he can present characters and backgrounds with the formality of a program, prologue, or first act. Thus, in the introduction to **"A Few Crusted Characters"** (*Wessex Tales*), where he will place a second audience on stage, Hardy addresses his reading audience with the following program notes: "It is a Saturday afternoon of a blue and yellow autumn time, and the scene is the High Street of a well-known market-town. A large carrier's van stands in the quadrangular forecourt of the White-Hart Inn, upon the sides of its spacious tilt being painted in weatherbeaten letters: 'Burthen, Carrier to Longpuddle'" (p. 423). The characters arrive one by one and enter the van. When they are finally all inside, Hardy shifts the scene from High Street to the inner carriage, and the now travelling occupants build a play within a play, using characters from their own narratives.

The "unseen observer" device, a favorite of Hardy's from the first short story, the uncollected **"Destiny in a Blue Coat"** (1874), to the very last, **"A Changed Man"** (1900), frequently involved a tour de force of stage setting, blocking, and character placement. Hardy's attraction to this and related devices is usually dismissed as a carry-over from the gothic novel; only Albert Guerard, in his *Thomas Hardy,* allows it serious consideration and suggests that it reflects a tendency to voyeurism in Hardy.[5] No doubt, however, even more than it catered to his urge to see, the unseen observer device catered to Hardy's urge to arrange and shape scene and event so that he could imply that a character's fate or action is part of a recurrent universal pattern. If the author enjoys a partnership with the unseen observer, it is because he cannot only see with him, but also see far beyond him. Thus, in the short story entitled **"The Waiting Supper"** (*A Changed Man*), it takes almost the entire two opening pages to locate the yeoman Nicholas in relation to the house through whose window he is observing his beloved and her father, and in relation to the road from which he cannot be seen. But these pages are not wasted, for in the process, Hardy establishes for his reader not only the physical, but also the social distance that separates his lovers. In **"Barbara of the House of Grebe"** (*A Group of Noble Dames*), the sadism of Uplandtowers is underlined by his role of silent, unseen observer as his wife goes to be "cured" by meeting with a statue of her lover which he had ordered disfigured the day before. The most interesting application of the device occurs in **"What the Shepherd Saw"** (*A Changed Man*). The story, ostensibly about the changes in one man's life that result from his being witness to a murder, is extended in scope by means of the addition of another, inanimate, witness, a "Druidical Trilithon" known locally as the Devil's Door; it dominates the landscape, witnessing both witness and crime. Finally, the opening of **"The Son's Veto"** (*Life's Little Ironies*) may illustrate fusion between the unseen observer device and the opening tableau considered earlier. "To the eyes of a man viewing it from behind, the nut-brown hair was a wonder and a mystery" (p. 283). The reader must assume the eyes of this observer, focus his attention on the elaborate hairdo, main adornment of an invalid lady at a garden concert, come to see it as the melancholy fruit of hours of idleness, and finally join the narrator in his exploration of the tragedy behind the idleness, the tragedy of deracination.

Staging considerations were among Hardy's initial thoughts when preparing to write a short story, or so one would conclude from the evidence of "Plots for Five Unpublished Short Stories," edited by Evelyn Hardy.[6] These "Plots," as the editor points out, are but "bare bones of fact and character," some suggesting a standard theme, some a favorite subject or variations on a subject, and some establishing different steps in the outline of a plot. There is no great promise in them, but there is the remarkable similarity between the bare bones and the finished stories pointed out by Miss Hardy and the almost obsessive concern for setting stages. The use of "things" in the manner of stage properties essential to plot development is also evident in these earliest forms of Hardy stories. The characters are barely outlined (*e.g.,* the shyness of the lovers in "Plot Five" is the only definite trait noted); the role of a given character is likely to change from one alternative to another; the degree of plot complication is unsettled (*e.g.,* will the violinist of "Plot One" be guilty of adultery only or bigamy as well?); however, through the vagaries of the plots and their alternatives, settings and "things" remain constant, and it appears that as early as 1874, the date he gave to "Plot One," Hardy saw that such details held the key to the development of his stories.[7]

Details in setting and "things" are much more reliable messengers than characters and are more easily made the bearers of fate in the notorious Hardy coincidences. This too is already evident in the plot outlines. Consider, for example, "Plot Four," the project for a story about the musician Barthélémon, who after a depressing night spent playing the violin for dancers at Vauxhall, sees the rising sun from Westminster Bridge and is inspired to compose the well-known music for Bishop Ken's "Morning Hymn."[8] The significant fact is that a man's entire reputation was to rest on a few scraps of paper, one morning's inspiration, forgotten in a drawer for many years and rediscovered by coincidence. It would be hard to estimate how many similar scraps of paper determine the course of events throughout Hardy's fiction. More than just properties, they are inanimate actors, and they are partly responsible for Hardy's insistence upon elaborate stage settings; for even if he does not feel called upon to apologize for strange coincidences, he invariably tries to account for them by means of structural detail. This is the adjustment of the uncommon and the ordinary; messages must slip out of view in a likely spot, and messengers must be detained by probable distractions along their path. Hardy's indulgence in what his critics have long condemned as "architectonics" is usually a result of over-preparation for coincidences. But the particular drama-like fiction that fascinated him demanded the coincidences: they were the *coups de théâtre* which precipitated a dramatic action either into a dénouement dictated by the way of the world (*e.g.,* happiness cannot last; whatever goes up must come down), or into a surprise dénouement, usually one whose effect was to assert an element of the wayward and the supernatural, upsetting the norm and the routine which one had been prepared to anticipate. The well-prepared sequence with an unforeseen climax served Hardy best in the short stories. In dealing with the well-known, he could most easily wrest control from his characters or, rather, relinquish control to some cosmic force or fatal law. Thus, throughout the drafts of the fragmentary story of Barthélémon, the agents of fate, that is the scraps of paper, are subordinated to the message of fate, the well-worn truth that Fame and the artist may meet beyond frustration and suffering only by chance. In contrast, however, in a story like **"Netty Sargent's Copyhold"** (from **"A Few Crusted Characters"** in *Life's Little Ironies*), where the pattern is not ready-made, the maneuvering of characters rather than fate or chance determines the outcome of the plot.

The comparison is worth making in detail. Netty's fate, like Barthélémon's, depends on a piece of paper, the copyhold, though unlike Barthélémon, she is very active in turning it out favorably. The cause-and-effect sequence in "Plot Four" is only loosely established: the inspiration for composing the hymn is the radiance of the world, contrasting with the grimness of Vauxhall; the song is apparently stashed away because Barthélémon's enthusiasm is gone, and there is even a

hint from his wife (in version B) that this is routine procedure. In **"Netty Sargent's Copyhold,"** on the other hand, the sequence is carefully set up: Netty's fate depends upon her inheriting an uncle's house, for it will make her an attractive prospect to Jasper Cliff, the man she is set on marrying; but the fate of the house depends upon renewal of the copyhold, and this can be done only upon request by the uncle. The uncle procrastinates because he would like to see Netty marry someone else; and though he finally gives in, makes the preliminary arrangements and is ready to sign, he dies a couple of hours before the arrival of the clerk to witness his signature. Elsewhere, in a similar situation in *Woodlanders,* for instance, Hardy sets his climax at this point, with the ironic triumph of death; the copyhold is a symbolic lease on life that the young are seeking and that the old, and fate, conspire to deny them. Here, however, he allows the pattern to extend to a second climax beyond the timeless irony, and he places in Netty's own hands the task of reconciling her anticipation with the circumstances. It involves her ability to make the uncle look as though he were still alive; to convince the clerk that the sight of an official might frighten the old man; to justify the necessity of guiding his hand; and to arrange the scene in such a manner that the clerk will witness the signature without actually seeing too much of the signer. The scene is ideal for Hardy the amateur director: blocking of the action is necessary for verisimilitude, but the plot has allowed the character to take over the process. The narrator may remain in the background and enjoy the oddity of the circumstances. The tale hangs on a house, a piece of paper, and a girl's ability to purse her lips in a charming manner; and these are all details of the kind Hardy is seeking to dramatize as the creator breathing life into dry bones. Furthermore, the odd circumstances in Netty's story, made acceptable to the reader by the author's excellent alignment of stage device with plot, are precisely the kind of ground that Hardy required in fiction and drama. The reader, if inclined, should be able to join the narrator as he himself joins the clerk in observing how Netty guides her dead uncle's hand and, together with it, the hand of fate. Hardy thrives on the strange circumstance, for it allows him to lift the curtain on a stage reflecting the everyday world but extending beyond it into infinity.

In some instances Hardy tried to borrow from the theatre far more than staging devices. In **"The Grave by the Handpost"** (*A Changed Man*), for example, he borrowed or tried to adapt the stylized presentation and rhetoric of Greek tragedy. The story is notable chiefly for its failure to reconcile form and content, but as such it is also an interesting example of Hardy's experiments with form. The stage presented in the opening is stark: only a handpost at a crossroad that, we are told, is located exactly halfway between two villages. The inhabitants of one village are here to bury a suicide. No sound is heard until another group appears, the choir from the other village on a Christmas carol singing tour. Now the strange ceremony is explained, the occupant of the grave is identified, and the cause of his suicide (a reproachful letter from his son) is revealed. Exit the grave diggers, and the choir decides to offer the dead man a carol—a token of good will to make up for the ignoble burial. No sooner are they done, than the son of the buried man enters from the direction taken by the grave diggers. Should the reader have missed the implication that the carol is a modern equivalent for a choric ode, Hardy now presents a scene which takes its form so obviously from a Greek tragedy that the Wessex dialect required by the setting is painfully incongruous. Chorus-like, the village choir speaks through an unidentified leader in the first person: "What—do my eyes see before me Young Luke Holway, that went wi' his regiment to the East Indies . . .?" (p. 833). It is Luke, of course, and he makes a formal statement of grief and remorse which is met by a no less formal moral: "Don't ye be rash, Luke Holway, I say again; but try to make amends by your future life. . . . Try and be worthy of your father at his best. 'Tis not too late" (p. 833). The wisdom is wasted. Luke, in the role of tragic hero, is as grotesque as the choir in the role of chorus; several complications later, he commits suicide, having been unable to bear his remorse. Long before this unheroic death, from his first appearance, in fact, he had merely served to underline the futility of trying to build Wessex dramas on an Athenian scale with the stuff of the village gossip or, at best, of the popular ballad.

Hardy's reliance on the theatrical is a mixed blessing. He is not a displaced playwright: his weak and fortunately rare attempts at playwrighting combined with his heavy reliance on stagecraft in fiction merely point to a much greater problem he faces in writing. On the one hand, in fiction, he demands externalized action and relies upon the restless protagonists and the relentless chain of events; on the other hand, however, he trusts neither the action nor the actors to convey his view of the world. The elaborate stage directions, manipulations of setting, prologues, epilogues, and omnicient asides, for which he is generally blamed, are the result of attempts to retain control over what the characters and events communicate. The incongruous mixture of drama and contrivance evident in the novel is even more obvious in the short stories, where, however, it also lends itself more easily to explanation: Hardy seems to feel that the inherently limited framework that he was ever expanding) must prevent his ideas from being conveyed and his characters from

transcending their humble origin in record or imagination, and so he tries to insure the leap from the realm of commonplace to that of "things eternal and universal." When the characters make this leap by ignoring or transcending routine, the story is not weakened—as Netty and many others prove. What counts is the distance he can set between himself and the manipulated cast operating on a prepared stage. Also, and this may involve distance as well, a degree of taste or discretion is required to prevent tragedy from seeming like farce, as it does in the case of "The Grave by the Handpost." However, inasmuch as the stage device replaces a more obvious kind of author involvement, its effect is usually preferable. Indeed, when Hardy uses a form like the diary that will not accommodate outside intervention, the result is the insipid "Alidia's Diary" in *A Changed Man*. Sound instinct causes him likewise to avoid the first person in his prose.

Apparently, total reliance on action and the dramatic form did not suggest itself to Hardy. He had been made aware very early of his particular talent for describing country scenes and for creating characters who are inevitably rooted in their circumstances, physical or moral. The expansive Victorian prose fiction was ideally suited to such a talent; the barren Victorian theatre was not. As was already suggested, Hardy's rare attempts at conventional dramatization are disasters. Most notable is the adaptation of his very successful short story "The Three Strangers" into a play, *The Three Wayfarers*. The story relies on the theatrical devices discussed earlier: a well-defined stage (the shepherd's cottage), details about the position and movement of the characters, and highly theatrical handling of the successive entrances of the three strangers. With the exception of the opening view and a brief chase outside the cottage, unity of place is strictly maintained; dialogue and events move rapidly to climax and dénouement; and indeed the story seems ideally suited to transformation into a one-act play. But Hardy's dramatization fails: he is unable to transpose to an actual stage what he had conceived on a cosmic scale, and he cannot adjust to the need for dispensing with or absorbing the descriptive detail. Consequently, the position of the shepherd's house, a crossroads in the midst of an otherwise uninhabited tract, does not come into the play at all. Not only is this location necessary to establish some sense of probability for the coincidence of all three men calling at the same house, but also it supplies a unifying symbol that raises details above the level of circumstantial ironies. At the crossroads, contraries intersect: birth and death, freedom and captivity, boldness and timidity, natural violence and rural domesticity, justice and law. To assimilate the entire long descriptive passages which precede the entrance of the first stranger is, of course, out of the question; but altogether to eliminate location seriously curtails the scope of the story. The play sacrifices also the other real merit of the short story—the suspension of the identification of the strangers. Timothy Sommers, who in the short story is less of a simpering flatterer than in the play, indeed does fool with his boldness and confidence not only the shepherd and the hangman, but the reader as well. Although even in the story the hangman is quite readily unmasked, his identity is ambiguous until he sings his song. Apparently Hardy felt that the dramatic form could not bear this suspense, or that the audience would enjoy the scene only by knowing more than any of the characters except Timothy. Hence, he gave little identifying asides to Timothy Sommers and to "Jack Ketch," strongly reminiscent of the standard "little do they know" speech of the villain in melodrama, and he converted the story from a model of restrained and disciplined telling to a rather ordinary rural narrative in play form.[9]

Hardy writing for the theatre is the devoted fan who one day stumbles across the footlights. Not so the Hardy writing fiction and poetry; he is seeking a long term lease on a congenial environment, and he has some definite notions about what it ought to include. They are not very revolutionary, and indeed, looking back it is hard to comprehend how they could have caused such a stir. Had it rested on the new note or new ideas that he is supposed to have brought to fiction, Hardy's reputation would indeed be a thing of the past by now. Fortunately for him, his critics in the last two decades decided to take a closer look at his works, including some of the manuscripts, and to reexamine the supposedly crude or heavy-handed in them. As a result, Hardy's experiments with form now seem far more significant than his experiments with ideas. Little has yet been said about the short stories, where the experiments often began, probably because on the whole the short stories never became much more than experiments. Yet what they reveal about Hardy's techniques of presentation is considerable.

Throughout his career, Hardy remained fascinated by the manner in which the narrator may alternately assume roles as incongruous as those of the fair-barker, the sophisticated commentator, and the uncouth, but nonetheless awe-inspiring, magician. For in such roles creator and actor tended to fuse, at times even sweeping the audience along into the creation. Obviously, Hardy sought in his presentations something akin to county-fair magic; his discovery of "the whole secret of fiction and the drama" in an adjustment of the uncommon and the ordinary or in the resuscitation of dry bones of fact must indeed seem naive until it becomes apparent how consistently and how systematically he attempted the juggler's precarious balance and the ma-

gician's sleight of hand. Hardy was cramped by the traditional boundaries set on an author's domain within prose fiction, and there is no reason to doubt his repeated assertions that this is why he abandoned fiction and turned to the lyric. He was miscast in the role of a fighter of tradition and convention; he was more prone to renew the old or to combine the traditional genres in a search for the single point of origin and the universal law ("the whole secret"). The resuscitated, pastoral "Wessex" was therefore an ideal stage: old, varied, changing, yet illustrating the operation of timeless forces. By going to the theatre for some of his fiction techniques, Hardy was going to a source that most readily afforded the point of view he required: that of a spectator, sometimes amused, sometimes bewildered, sometimes indignant, sometimes even aloof—a spectator who is a composite of the various spirits in *The Dynasts,* dominated, of course, by the Spirit of the Years. Neither the traditional fiction that Hardy wrote, nor the traditional drama that he could have written, would accommodate such a point of view—so he abandoned fiction and embraced the lyric. And not until the writing of *The Dynasts* did he find the long-sought technical emancipation, the opportunity to play freely, at last, with all the devices without the limitations imposed by genre. Here, indeed, the alternation between genres, the consequently changing manner of presentation, and the manipulation of protagonists with more-or-less obvious ropes were to become the very characteristics of a world presented as a huge stage, a stage on which direction as well as action seems magnificent because of its futility.

Notes

1. Thomas Hardy, *Life and Art,* Ernest Brennecke, Jr., ed. (New York, 1925), p. 90.

2. All page references in this text are to the Macmillan Collected Edition: *The Short Stories of Thomas Hardy* (London, 1928).

3. Florence Emily Hardy, *The Later Years of Thomas Hardy: 1892-1928* (New York, 1930), p. 16.

4. Similar stages are actually set in the novels from *Under the Greenwood Tree* on; the landscapes of the early novels develop into the complex microcosms of Egdon, Stonehenge, and Christminster, which evoke historical and prehistorical associations to dissolve time and space and to provide a commentary, usually ironic, about the protagonists and dramas on hand. Richard C. Carpenter, in "Thomas Hardy and the Old Masters," *Boston University Studies in English,* v (Spring 1961), 18-28, has demonstrated Hardy's indebtedness to the painter in constructing these tableau-like scenes; they have also, however, all the markings of the theatrical tableau, down to the suggestion

of a message on the moral plane, of the kind the late eighteenth century passed on to the authors of melodrama in the nineteenth.

5. *Thomas Hardy, The Novels and Stories* (Cambridge, Mass., 1949), pp. 115-117. Guerard is taken to task for this by a reviewer who points out that peeking is the artist's job (*The Times Literary Supplement,* July 14, 1950, p. 436); but this is obviously unfair, for Guerard is the first to stress the artistic effects and the metaphysical perspective Hardy achieved by means of his "peeping" protagonists.

6. Evelyn Hardy, ed., "Plots for Five Unpublished Short Stories," *The London Magazine,* v (November 1958), 34-45.

7. Thus, Hardy plans to use his favorite stage for melodrama, the church or cathedral, in "Plot One" and in "Plot Five" (the latter is a series of "glimpses" by an unseen observer in the shape of a peeping sparrow); "Plot One" also goes into details about properties and their suitability to the décor (*e.g.,* furniture in the love nest above the school must be "of the lighter kind, because of getting it there").

8. The episode, suggested to Hardy by a note in Grove's *Dictionary of Music,* culminated not in a short story, but in a mediocre sonnet, "Barthélémon at Vauxhall," that did not allow Hardy to develop the ironies which had attracted him to the subject.

9. The extent to which Hardy's success in this story depends on omniscience and on the vague identification of "strangers" is discussed in Alan Ryan's analysis of the story in *Insight II,* John V. Hagopian and Martin Dolch, eds. (Frankfurt a/M, 1965), pp. 173-174.

Michael Benazon (essay date spring 1979)

SOURCE: Benazon, Michael. "'The Romantic Adventures of a Milkmaid': Hardy's Modern Romance." *English Studies in Canada* 5, no. 1 (spring 1979): 56-65.

[*In the following essay, Benazon analyzes the psychological and fairy-tale aspects of "The Romantic Adventures of a Milkmaid," claiming that the end of the story resembles a Shakespearean romance.*]

"The Romantic Adventures of a Milkmaid" (1883) is an amusing tale of novella length, a characteristic outgrowth of Hardy's predilection for romance. It has suffered, unfortunately, from adverse criticism, including some deprecation from Hardy himself. Hardy's

bibliographer, Richard Purdy, quotes the author's remark that "this story was written only with a view to a fleeting life in a periodical, and having, moreover, been altered from its original shape, was not deemed worth reprinting."[1] It seems likely that Hardy was swayed by the adverse opinions of his reviewers. *Lippincott's Magazine* had commented, for example, that "'**The Romantic Adventures of a Milkmaid**' will be widely read . . . half with amusement and half with vexation at being so tricked and befooled by a clever writer who ought to do better for his admirers."[2]

The early critics were embarrassed or disdainful. Joseph Warren Beach calls the story "the most arrant pot-boiler that was ever turned out by [a] tired and harassed writer of novels."[3] Evidently Beach disapproved of writers "who maintained throughout the nineteenth century the sentimental and Gothic traditions of the eighteenth!"[4] Rutland dismisses it with the summary remark that it is "wholly impossible, but entertaining."[5] Weber, writing some years later, thought it to be a "worthless trifle."[6] But despite the scorn of these critics **"The Romantic Adventures"** [**"The Romantic Adventures of a Milkmaid"**] was at first eagerly read by the public. Purdy remarks that it "was widely pirated . . . and more frequently and cheaply reprinted in America through many years than perhaps any other work of Hardy's."[7] Clearly **"The Romantic Adventures"** had a certain appeal that was overlooked or discounted by the reviewers and early critics. No doubt the provocative title contributed to its popularity.[8] But *caveat emptor*! Those expecting to witness the ruin of yet another passionate milkmaid were in for a disappointment. Hardy's use of the word "Romantic" was somewhat different from the expectations of his readers.

Since that time, interest in **"The Romantic Adventures"** has flagged. It has been neither anthologized nor, until recently, awarded separate publication. For years it remained relatively inaccessible to the public, buried in that volume of the Macmillan Wessex Edition known as *A Changed Man.* A summary of its contents is therefore desirable. In the opening episode of the novella the dairymaid, Margery Tucker, inadvertently interrupts the melancholy Baron Von Xanten in an attempt at suicide. Repenting of his rash gesture the Baron asks her to name her reward; after some thought Margery asks him to take her to a ball. Though the Baron is somewhat apprehensive of the consequences, he feels obliged to keep his word.

Margery is ecstatic at the ball, but, as the Baron feared, she finds it difficult afterwards to adjust to the realities of her life as a humble dairymaid. In particular, she no longer wishes to become the wife of plain Jim Hayward, the lime-burner. Feeling responsible for Margery's sudden discontent with her lot, the Baron tries to assist Jim—first by giving him handsome furniture to impress the by now snobbish and materialistic Margery, and later, when he is gravely ill, by coercing her into a sudden marriage with Jim. Margery agrees to the wedding ceremony only on the condition that she and Jim live apart until she is ready to consummate the union. The Baron then leaves the country, supposedly to recuperate in a more salubrious climate. However, rumors later reach Margery that he has died abroad.

Jim, finding that he is no closer to Margery than before, now decides to bring matters to a climax. He joins the local regiment and, resplendent in his new red uniform, pays public court to the lusty widow, Mrs. Peach. Jim's ruse does indeed awaken Margery's possessive instincts, but to everyone's surprise the mysterious Baron makes a sudden reappearance, and for a moment it seems likely that he will succumb to temptation and carry Margery away with him to become his mistress. However, honor prevails. The Baron masters his feelings, restores Margery to Jim, and disappears forever. Jim and Margery settle down into a passionless, but reasonably happy marriage.

It is not true, as some critics have alleged,[9] that **"The Romantic Adventures"** lacks a theme. Hardy is concerned with the effects of sexual desire, with courtship and marriage, and with the analysis of character. He recognizes that what is called love is basically sexual attraction, and that marriage, if it is to have any chance at all of succeeding, must have the more important ingredient of compatibility. The Baron himself states the novella's theme. In recommending Jim to the reluctant Margery the Baron observes: "He is an honourable man, and will make you a good husband. You must remember that marriage is a life contract, in which general compatibility of temper and worldly position is of more importance than fleeting passion, which never long survives."[10]

Margery, however, is very little attracted to Jim. Hardy stresses this point in an addition he made to the ending. In the original version, published in *The Graphic* in the summer of 1883, when Jim asks her whether she would now go with the Baron should he so request her, Margery replies: "'Yet no,' she added, hearing the baby cry, 'he would not move me now.'" To this Hardy added in revision: "It would be so unfair to baby" (399). Margery is not unhappy with Jim; on the other hand, she is obviously not deeply in love with him. It is the Baron who appeals to her strongest and deepest feelings: "Indeed, the Baron's power over this innocent girl was curiously like enchantment, or mesmeric influence" (349). Her submissive reaction is like Cytherea's to Manston (*Desperate Remedies*), Elf-

ride's to Knight (*A Pair of Blue Eyes*), or Bathsheba's to Troy (*Far from the Madding Crowd*). It is a sexual power almost always in Hardy preceded by a symbolic or physical action—passionate music, rescue from danger, or a display of swordsmanship.

In another interesting addition to the ending, Hardy makes Margery's passion for the Baron explicit: "After a moment she added: 'Now that he's dead I'll make a confession, Jim, that I have never made to a soul. If he had pressed me—which he did not—to go with him when I was in the carriage that night beside his yacht, I would have gone. And I was disappointed that he did not press me'" (399). The effect of the revision is to change Margery's character. In the original text she had been able to refuse the Baron's proposal to elope, but in the later version it is he who saves her honor (and perhaps her soul) by rejecting the temptation to exploit her weakness.

The narrator observes that "The Baron's power . . . was so masterful that the sexual element was almost eliminated" (349). Margery is of course awed by the Baron's rank, wealth, and stature, but Hardy makes it plain that the "sexual element" is not the least of his charms. Her ambition to become the Baron's wife is, however, totally unrealistic. No matter how we regard his offer to take her with him, it is certainly not a marriage proposal. Though Margery has the power to raise him from his fits of melancholy, there is never the slightest suggestion that they are in any other way compatible. Fortunately for her, the Baron's sense of responsibility saves her from what sooner or later would have been a "fate worse than death." In Hardy's view, sexual passion is a most unreliable foundation for happiness in marriage.

Despite his restraint there are many hints that the Baron is a demonic figure possessed of supernatural powers, and certainly the villagers view him in this light. To country people familiar only with their own parish, any stranger may become an object of suspicion. If, in addition, such a person were foreign,[11] and alone, or simply unfamiliar with local customs, a superstitious peasantry might suppose him to be an emissary of evil. In folk literature the devil is often presented as one who dresses differently from others. Mysterious strangers are common enough in the Romantic and post-Romantic literature that Hardy grew up on. The Baron is one of a series of outsiders, usually malevolent, who come to disrupt the peace and order of the agricultural communities Hardy describes.

The Baron is also a skilful *mélange* of the Gothic villain-hero, the Byronic fatal man, and the conventional devil of folklore. Where previously Hardy had drawn on Childe Harold for his portrait of Captain de Stancy (*A Laodicean*), and Don Juan for Swithin St. Cleeve (*Two on a Tower*), the appearance and behavior of Baron Von Xanten owe something to the heroes of Byron's romantic verse narratives and possibly to *Manfred*. To begin with, he is a wealthy, leisured nobleman. Since little is known about him for certain, his mysteriousness inevitably inspires conjecture among the villagers: "That he had committed some folly or hasty act, that he had been wrongfully accused of some crime, thus rendering his seclusion from the world desirable for a while, squared very well with his frequent melancholy" (356). The Byronism of this passage is obvious. The Baron's characteristic philosophical pessimism and pronounced death-wish may also derive from *Manfred*.

Hardy particularly emphasizes the Baron's Satanic quality. He is "an unknown and handsome stranger" (308), tall and dark (304). It is perhaps significant that Margery first encounters him in the garden as she is committing a small act of trespass.[12] The postman remarks that the Baron has "lived in England so long as to be without any true country . . . so that 'a must be born to something that can't be earned by elbow-grease and Christian conduct."[13] To Margery he is a "demi-god" (354); the narrator compares him to Rhadamanthus (327). He smokes; his eyes appear to burn with an unearthly light (395); his horses and carriage seem "black and daemonic" (393). Jim unwittingly brings all these allusions together when he remarks: "Anybody would think the devil had showed you all the kingdoms of the world since I saw you last!" (334) The Baron occasionally signs himself "X" (328), traditional symbol of a person or object unknown or unrevealed.[14] Perhaps in revising the locale of the romance from the Valley of the Swenn to the Valley of the Exe Hardy sought to imply a link between the Baron's signature and the name of the river. It is presumably not merely a coincidence that he arranges to meet Margery at Three-Walks-End in Chillington Wood (317).

Margery and the Baron are dramatic opposites. In a sense she is a persecuted maiden, he the oppressive villain-hero. Her sanguine temperament and pink complexion contrast with his sickliness and unhealthy pallor. She is a country girl, "nature's own image" (305), he a product of aristocratic decadence. She is the "orange-flower" to his "sad cypress" (361). He leans towards death; she has the power to revive him. Hardy is clearly working in a traditional mythic context.

Margery's weaknesses make it relatively easy for Jim and the Baron to manipulate her. In the wedding scene Margery is a "lamb" being led to the sacrifice (363). Her bitter complaint that "'tis a footy plot between you men to—snare me!" (371) expresses her view that she has been victimized by the men. But Margery is not simply a persecuted maiden. Hardy finds pathos in a young woman's loss of freedom and independence when she is compelled to accept male domination. He touches on this motif in several of the novels and tales. In **"The Romantic Adventures,"** however, Hardy does not mean us to feel pity for Margery; her plight is largely the result of her ludicrous social ambitions and desire for material goods; hence the overthrow of her independence, pathetic and tragic elsewhere in Hardy, is here merely a comic rendering of justice in keeping with the light-hearted tone of the romance. In this fiction, Hardy's attitude to social climbing is one of disapproval. If the Baron had not impinged on Margery's life she would probably have quietly settled down with Jim. But by allowing her a taste of high society the Baron stimulates her latent ambition for luxury. The Baron, aware of the dangers, plays the role of Margery's tempter unwillingly, but feels obliged by his promise to take her to the ball.

The story is open to an intriguing psychological interpretation: it can be understood as an attempt on the part of Margery to work out in real life the dreams, fantasies, and desires of her unconscious mind. Hardy suggests that her character is basically childish (306, 328, 395). She seems to feel, for example, that she is not properly appreciated, either by her father or by Jim. Whenever she has trouble at home she flees to her grandmother's: "She had a place of refuge in these cases of necessity, and her father knew it, and was less alarmed at seeing her depart than he might otherwise have been. This place was Rook's Gate, the house of her grandmother, who always took Margery's part when that young woman was particularly in the wrong" (353). She is unable either to reject or accept Jim decisively. In order to put off the marriage, Margery complains of his lack of material goods. When these make a miraculous appearance she reluctantly agrees to the marriage. Still unwilling to face her problem directly, she uses the Baron's summons as a reason to disrupt the wedding. Her reaction when she supposes that Jim has deserted her for Mrs. Peach is typical of her childishness: "a' seemed very low. Then she said to me, 'I don't like standing here in this slummocky crowd. I shall feel more at home among the gentlepeople.' And then she went to where the carriages were drawn up" (389). At the precise moment when Margery is running away from her problem with Jim, the Baron makes another miraculous appearance. The Baron may therefore be regarded as an expression of her escapist tendencies and even of her unconscious sexual fantasies—the desire to be swept off her feet by a powerful, handsome Prince Charming. She sets the stage for this by making the unusual request that the

Baron reward her by taking her to a ball, and by failing to tell him that she is engaged to Jim. But Margery does not simply want to go to a ball; she wants to be taken there by the Baron.

In his presence her normal traits of determination and independence fade. As noted previously, Hardy revised the ending to show that Margery is incapable of resisting him. Her loss of will, the conscious side of her psyche, is striking; as the Baron warns her, she is risking her salvation (350). In psychological terms the Baron is the animus in his negative aspect, that side of her psyche that seeks to lure her away from the difficult task of creating a mature relationship with a real man. The least of her dangers is a prolonged childishness. She is in fact risking her very existence, for there is more than one hint that the Baron is a demon of death. He is obviously suicidal. The narrator remarks on the "deadly" whiteness of his skin (303). In the course of the tale he falls sick and supposedly dies, only to make a sudden reappearance at the end. He offers to carry her away in his black coach and yacht to a distant region which we must assume to be infernal, and to which he eventually returns. Hardy blends his intuitive understanding of human psychology with his conscious knowledge of myth to create a fascinating presentation of the critical period in the psychic development of an immature woman—the moment when she must choose either to accept reality and full womanhood or to languish, perhaps forever, in a childish realm of daydream and fantasy.

While **"The Romantic Adventures"** has a sufficient theme, it is undoubtedly the non-realistic technique which creates the special atmosphere needed to enable Hardy to blend the disparate elements into a satisfactory whole. Albert J. Guerard and Douglas Brown have noted the similarity of **"The Romantic Adventures"** to ballad; Evelyn Hardy, Richard Carpenter and Guerard see the likeness to fairy tale, and Millgate argues that it is another of Hardy's modern or contemporary romances.[15] All these aspects are present, and others as well.

"The Romantic Adventures" bears some resemblance to "The Demon Lover," a ballad that recounts the fate of an unfaithful, avaricious woman who deserts house, husband, and baby to sail away with her former lover, now mysteriously wealthy. In the course of his research in the Dorset County Museum, Michael Millgate discovered a note in Hardy's copy of *A Changed Man* which suggests that there may originally have been a connection between the ballad and Hardy's romance:

> The foregoing finish of the Milkmaid's adventures by a re-union with her husband was adopted to suit the requirements of the summer number of a periodical in which the story was first printed. But it is well to inform readers that the ending originally sketched was a different one, Margery, instead of returning to Jim, disappearing with the Baron in his yacht at Idmouth after his final proposal to her, & being no more heard of in England.[16]

At least two references in the revised text apparently prepare the reader for a calamitous conclusion (315, 350). In most versions of the ballad the demon lover is a revenant, returned from the dead to test and finally punish the faithless wife. In Hardy's story the Baron returns unexpectedly at the end like a ghost, it being supposed by the villagers that he had died abroad.

Like the fickle lady in "The Demon Lover," Margery is egotistic, materialistic, and socially ambitious. As we read the story we wonder if she will suffer the same fate. But Hardy is careful not to blacken Margery's character unduly: she never in fact behaves immorally with the Baron. Perhaps Hardy's decision to dispense with the expected ending was guided in part by a reluctance to allow the tale to become too obviously similar to the ballad. At any rate, his disapproval of Margery's frivolity is expressed mildly through his ironic and sometimes comic treatment of her.

Several incidents in the story have a fairy-tale quality to them. Margery, tripping through the fields on her way to her grandmother's with a basket on her arm, does remind us of Little Red Riding Hood. Margery's almost miraculous transformation in the hollow tree from milkmaid to lady, the journey to the ball in the Baron's carriage, her dancing with him, and the subsequent reversion to her former state—are similar to the Cinderella story. Even the moral, the danger of aspiring above one's social level, is characteristic of the fairy tale and, needless to say, of Hardy's other fictions.

Presumably the purpose of the non-realistic elements in **"The Romantic Adventures"** is to create a world in which the reader will be content to suspend his disbelief and give credence while the story lasts to the extraordinary situations that abound therein. Far more conducive to the creation of that world than even the allusions to ballad and fairy tale is the use Hardy makes of Shakespearian romantic comedy.[17] There is first of all an allusion to *As You Like It*. The melancholy Baron is said to be "the Jaques of this forest and stream" (344). A few pages further on, the narrator compares the Baron's enchantment of Margery to the power of "Prospero over the gentle Ariel" (349). But these allusions are less important than the subtler feeling that Hardy is once again leading us into a delightful dream-world that never was.

This feeling is largely conveyed through Hardy's treatment of setting. In the original version Hardy did not attempt to date the story,[18] but in revising it for publication in *A Changed Man* Hardy chose to set the action in the 1840s (299), the period of Hardy's childhood when the full impact of the industrial revolution had not yet reached Dorset. For Hardy, and possibly for his readers, it was a period both remote and dimly remembered, conducive to the mood of romance. At any rate, **"The Romantic Adventures"** has something of the same carefree pastoral quality as *Under the Greenwood Tree*. It contains too, a similar cyclic alternation of the seasons: the Baron appears to Margery on a May morning (299). He "dies" in October (360), only to reappear once more at the time of the Yeomanry Review in May (378, 389).

The action takes place at Silverthorn:

> It was half-past four o'clock (by the testimony of the land-surveyor, my authority for the particulars of this story, a gentleman with the faintest curve of humour on his lips); it was half-past four o'clock on a May morning in the eighteen forties. A dense white fog hung over the Valley of the Exe, ending against the hills on either side.

> But though nothing in the vale could be seen from higher ground, notes of differing kinds gave pretty clear indications that bustling life was going on there. This audible presence and visual absence of an active scene had a peculiar effect above the fog level. Nature had laid a white hand over the creatures ensconced within the vale, as a hand might be laid over a nest of chirping birds.

(299)

In the scene that follows, Margery emerges out of the foggy valley bottom and ascends into the light of an early May morning (a time of year associated with fertility and other folk rituals). It is on Mount Lodge that she has her initial encounter with the Baron. All the marvellous, glamorous experiences she has with him stand in sharp contrast to her life as a milkmaid in her father's dairy and to the humdrum, passionless life that awaits her as Jim's wife and to which she returns at the end. Throughout the tale, the scenes alternate between the real world of Silverthorn below and the enchanted dream-like realm above, which is similar in atmosphere to the "green world" of Shakespeare's romantic comedies. In retrospect, the name Silverthorn[19] carries with it a sense of the doubleness that pervades Hardy's romance—the silvery elegance of the Baron's social sphere pitted against the thorniness of the everyday world.

The last two chapters resemble the final act of a Shakespearian romance: the characters, hopelessly confused, rush madly off in various directions in a comic attempt to find each other. Finally, however, a general reconciliation takes place. Husband and wife are reunited, the father makes peace with the young couple, and the melancholy Jaques departs, never again to trouble the peace. As in Shakespearian comedy, the characters enter the realm of romance tainted by the vices and folly of society. Inside they are somehow purged, purified, or at least chastened. This is roughly the experience of Hardy's major characters. He may have regretted that he was unable to give the story the traditional calamitous ballad ending, but the present conclusion is quite consistent with the prevailing ironic tone, the logic of fairy tales, and, moreover, is thoroughly characteristic of the author of *Desperate Remedies, Under the Greenwood Tree,* and *Far from the Madding Crowd*.

The early critics disapproved of **"The Romantic Adventures"** largely because of what they considered to be its gross improbability. But this cannot be a legitimate objection. In the first place, beneath the façade of magic, mystery, and romance a keen psychological analysis of female behavior is taking place. Secondly, Hardy is successful in creating a neo-Shakespearian world of fantasy and romance within which the weird Baron and the improbable events have their being. We are charmed and amused, never outraged as we sometimes are when Hardy tacks on an arbitrary ending to a basically realistic story. In **"The Romantic Adventures"** the elements of fairy tale, ballad, and myth are ironically and skillfully played off against the rationalistic presuppositions of the reader. As earlier noted, several aspects of the story promote the assumption that the ruin of the milkmaid is well nigh inevitable. However, Hardy surprises the reader with an unexpected ending, at the same time satisfying him with the feeling that it is true to the nature of the characters and the atmosphere he has created. The main characters and events are memorable because Hardy allows full scope to his flair for fantasy and romance. **"The Romantic Adventures of a Milkmaid"** is not a major work, yet it accomplishes admirably what it sets out to do, and is closely related in theme to the novels; it deserves recognition as one of the more successful of his short fictions.

Notes

1. Quoted in Richard L. Purdy, *Thomas Hardy: A Bibliographical Study* (1954; rpt. Oxford: Clarendon Press, 1968), p. 49.

2. Rev. of Hardy's "The Romantic Adventures of a Milkmaid," *Lippincott's Magazine,* 32 (September 1883), 336.

3. Joseph Warren Beach, *The Technique of Thomas Hardy* (1922; rpt. New York: Russell & Russell, 1962), p. 125.

4. Ibid., p. 127.

5. William R. Rutland, *Thomas Hardy: A Study of His Writings and Their Background* (Oxford: Blackwell, 1938), p. 219.

6. Carl J. Weber, *Hardy of Wessex: His Life and Literary Career,* rev. ed. (1940; rpt. New York: Columbia Univ. Press, 1965), p. 301.

7. Purdy, pp. 48-49.

8. See Joseph Warren Beach, "News for Bibliophiles," *The Nation,* 94 (25 January 1912), 82, for evidence that the piratical publishers exploited the title to attract the prurient.

9. See, for example, Beach, *The Technique,* p. 124.

10. Thomas Hardy, "The Romantic Adventures of a Milkmaid" in the Macmillan Wessex Edition (1912-1931) of *A Changed Man,* pp. 365-66. Subsequent references to this edition will appear in parentheses following the quotation.

11. While Purdy took the trouble to check over Hardy's manuscript and compare it with the initial publication of the romance in *The Graphic,* he evidently neglected to compare the magazine publication with the revised version published thirty years later in *A Changed Man.* Purdy reports only that "a few slight verbal changes were made in it at that time, and the scene shifted to Lower Wessex, more to the west, Casterbridge and the Valley of the Swenn giving place to Exonbury and the Valley of the Exe, possibly to remove the story from the scene of *Tess*" (p. 49). In fact, Hardy's revisions were considerable. The effect of one such revision is to stress the Baron's foreign qualities: Hardy changed his exclamation "My God" to "My Gott" (304), and the narrator remarks on the uncommonness of his mustachios (303).

12. Margery's dance with the Baron in the "moonlight at the top of her father's garden" subtly recalls the witches' sabbaths in which initiates were popularly supposed to dance with the devil, or with the fairies, by the light of the moon.

13. See p. 309. This was another addition to the 1913 publication. It is interesting that Hardy heightened the Baron's demonic qualities in a series of such revisions.

14. In Hebrew cabalist lore "X" can signify discord or fugitive.

15. See Douglas Brown, *Thomas Hardy* (London: Longman's 1954), p. 116; Albert J. Guerard, *Thomas Hardy,* rev. ed. (1949; rpt. Norfolk, Conn.: New Directions, 1964), pp. 93-96; Evelyn Hardy, *Thomas Hardy: A Critical Biography* (London: Hogarth, 1954), p. 185; Richard C. Carpenter, *Thomas Hardy* (New York: Twayne, 1964), p. 77; Michael Millgate, *Thomas Hardy* (New York: Random House, 1971), p. 198.

16. Millgate, p. 283. The note is dated 1927.

17. Borrowings from Shakespearian romantic comedy are scattered throughout Hardy's fiction, but they are most obvious in *Under the Greenwood Tree.*

18. In *The Graphic* publication, however, Hardy's reference to the Baron's "steam yacht" (subsequently deleted) implies a contemporary setting. It would be characteristic of Hardy to associate machinery with the demonic: cf. the farm machinery in *An Indiscretion in the Life of an Heiress, The Mayor of Casterbridge,* and *Tess of the d'Urbervilles.*

19. The Tucker dairy was originally placed at Stickleford in the Valley of the Swenn. Hardy may have wanted to differentiate "The Romantic Adventures" from *Tess* and from "The Fiddler of the Reels" which he published some years after the first appearance of "The Romantic Adventures" in *The Graphic.* It is also possible that he sought to make his place names more suggestive.

Keith Wilson (essay date 1981)

SOURCE: Wilson, Keith. "Hardy and the Hangman: The Dramatic Appeal of 'The Three Strangers.'" *English Literature in Transition, 1880-1920* 24, no. 3 (1981): 155-60.

[*In the following essay, Wilson chronicles the various versions and revisions of the stage adaptation of "The Three Strangers," deeming the play "a small triumph of atmosphere and stagecraft."*]

The recent publication by Macmillan's education division of what is described as an "adaptation" of Hardy's one-act play, *The Three Wayfarers,*[1] which was itself an adaptation of his short story **"The Three Strangers"** from *Wessex Tales,* invites speculation about the dramatic appeal this story had, both for Hardy himself and for many of his contemporary readers. His own interest in adapting **"The Three Strangers"** for the theatre is well documented. His first version of the drama opened in London at Terry's Theatre on 3 June 1893. It shared the bill with four other one-acters and, not altogether surprisingly, was deemed the best.[2] Hardy and Emma themselves attended the first performance, accompanied by the enthusiastic Mrs. Jeune, who complimented him the next day on the play's success:

> Dear Mr. Hardy,
>
> You behaved very badly last night in running away as you did and leaving us, because everybody was most anxious to see you and they all called for you. Your

play was simply delightful, full of life and very dramatic. Nobody but you would ever have thought of the hangman showing his victim how the rope was to be put round his neck. Anyway, I congratulate you and think you ought to dramatise something else only I'm not sure which story you ought to dramatise. I am thinking it over deeply.[3]

The play ran for only a week, but a revised version was presented by the Stage Society (4 Nov 1900), and the Dorchester Debating and Dramatic Society performed a version in Dorchester (15, 16 Nov 1911), in London (27 Nov) and in Weymouth (15 Dec). Still another performance was given at the Little Theatre in London (21 Nov 1913). The sporadic correspondence between Hardy and the theatrical agent R. Golding Bright indicates that productions were considered, and in at least one instance given, on other occasions between 1907 and 1913. Hardy's end of this correspondence, published by Carl Weber in his edition of the letters in the Colby College Hardy collection,[4] shows him, in September 1907, willing to hunt up a manuscript for Bright who is enquiring, on behalf of the American agent Elisabeth Marbury, about the possibility of a New York production.[5] Though these negotiations seem to have come to nothing, a brief note from Hardy to Bright in January 1910 wishes him success in a production of *The Three Wayfarers,* and a letter to Barrie in December 1911 mentions, with typically Hardyesque precision about things financial, that "a Mr. Golding Bright got me nine guineas for some performances of it some time ago."[6] The letter is written to Barrie after Hardy has received requests from commercial theatre companies to stage *The Three Wayfarers,* requests that were a direct result of the success of the Dorchester Dramatic Society production. He asks Barrie's advice about agents and is reintroduced to Golding Bright, an acquaintanceship that culminates in the Little Theatre production of 1913. Both in the letter to Barrie and the letter to Bright that follows from it, Hardy mentions "requests from music-halls" to stage the play and, somewhat surprisingly, seems willing for musical hall sketches to be made from it as long as money is forthcoming: "I am willing to let anybody play it for a guinea a night, but I cannot possibly attend to the matter myself."[7]

Purdy suggests that Hardy did make further revisions to the text of *The Three Wayfarers* and that these were incorporated into a production at Keble, Oxford (1926), but it seems likely that this was simply the same long-since revised version. Four typescripts, three with manuscript changes, survive in the Dorset County Museum, along with one copy in the hand of Emma Hardy. The manuscript in Emma's hand differs in no significant respect from the version that Florence Hardy had published by Henry Ling (1935), which was claimed as the first English edition (not entirely

accurately, since the limited edition printed at the Merrymount Press, Boston [Feb 1930] was published under the imprint of both the Fountain Press, New York, and the Cayme Press, London, which might be said to give it a prior claim, even given the country of origin). That gives a terminal date of November 1912 for a final revision, and, given the relationship between Hardy and Emma in her final years, the Emma manuscript would probably have been done considerably earlier. An extant letter from Arthur S. Owen, a tutor at Keble who had enlisted the support of the warden, Walter Lock, in approaching Hardy for permission to stage *The Three Wayfarers,* thanks Hardy "for sending me, through Dr. Lock, your copy of *The Three Wayfarers,* and for giving permission to us to act it, if circumstances enable us to do so" (30 Oct 1925). Since one of the four surviving typescripts, with manuscript corrections in Hardy's hand, has a return address pencilled on its frontpage, with the memorandum "To be returned," we might even reasonably theorize that this was the actual copy sent to Owen for the use of the Keble players. Whatever the case, the play was duly performed in Oxford in June of 1926, as a postcard from Warden Lock, dated June 22nd, confirms:

> Dear Mr. Hardy,
>
> My sister and I have today been to see **"The Three Strangers"** acted at Keble College and we think that you will like to know how well it went. It lends itself excellently to dramatisation and (though my sister says it was not done so well as at Dorchester) yet it went with a great swing and the Dorset Dialect was very fairly given. We are all very grateful to you for lending your copy and giving leave for it to be acted.

The help which Hardy gave to the Keble players, indicative perhaps of his customary regard for the older universities, was relatively unusual, as correspondence surviving from others responsive to either the play or the dramatic potential of the short story shows. For Hardy was not alone in sensing the inherent theatricality of **"The Three Strangers."** Significantly, the two correspondents who, next to Arthur Owen, were most successful were both British schoolmasters. On April 19, 1921, James B. Ritchie, a master at Kelvinside Academy, Glasgow, writes to ask permission for some of his boys to adapt **"The Three Strangers"** for a school performance. A few months later, on October 21, 1921, another schoolteacher, Clifford Druse, the English master at Marling School, Stroud in Gloucestershire, writes to ask whether he may be allowed to dramatise the story for the school stage. Both would-be adaptors emphasize that the resulting works will receive *only* amateur performance within school boundaries and before the school community and parents, and both, judging from pencilled comments in Hardy's hand, were given permission under those provisos.

Less successful are the professionals and semi-professionals. A Mrs. Macardle wants to dramatise the story, which would be "very suitable for performance by the Abbey Theatre Dublin" who have three of her plays in repertory. She receives a brusque reply that pointedly indicates the existence already of a dramatisation which has received a number of performances over the years. More ambitious still is Hubert Bath of the Royal Carl Rosa Opera Company, who wants to produce an operatic version. This is of some passing interest in that the letter is written in February of 1924, at a time when the composer Rutland Boughton is already at work on the operatic version of *The Famous Tragedy of the Queen of Cornwall,* which was to receive its first performance at Glastonbury in August of that year. The two works, one a stylised version of one of the great tales of medieval myth, the other a jeu d'esprit of Casterbridge folk-life, the one close to high tragedy, the other close to low comedy, could not be more different from each other. Yet two different composers respond to the operatic possibilities of both. This perhaps suggests the kind of economy and discipline of story-line, and the ritualistic element in the presentation, that Hardy's dramatic instincts lead him to create. It also points the irony that the writer who, of all others, had been so often taken to task for convolutedness and manipulativeness in plot, can produce works so incisive and direct in plot that they can seem eminently suitable for adaptation to the rituals of opera. However, suitable or not, Mr. Bath's ideas seem to have been no better received than Mrs. Macardle's.

Requests for permission to adapt and perform came also from America. Conrad Seiler of Hollywood writes in July 1926 for permission to adapt **"The Three Strangers"** for inclusion in a volume "of dramatizations of short stories by eminent writers." The letter is marked "unansd." in pencil in Hardy's hand. Similarly marked is a request from an American student, a request couched in terms so inevitably productive of the reverse of the desired end as to be touching in its naivety, if at the same time irritating in its self-regard:

> My dear Sir:
>
> I trust you will excuse the liberty which I am taking in writing to you, but I am doing so at the suggestion of the Professor of our Dramatic Class at Columbia University, where I am a student.
>
> We, as members, were asked to dramatize a short story, and I chose **"The Three Strangers,"** hoping that a little of the light of your genius might be reflected in my poor endeavor. As it turned out my selection was a happy thought, because the one-act play which I wrote has been adjudged as very creditable, and they are now desirous of acting it at the University.
>
> Had I dreamed of such good fortune, I would have written to you beforehand, as naturally I realize that this cannot be done without your permission. If it were

> one of your more important stories (although all of them are gems) I could easily realize that you might hesitate some time knowing nothing of my qualifications, but under the circumstances above stated, I am hoping that you may be willing to allow me this privilege.
>
> As I am forced to speak of the business end of it, of course, any profits that may accrue from either the acting or its publication, I shall be only too happy to divide with you on any terms which you may stipulate. I hesitate to speak of this, as it seems hardly worthy of your consideration.
>
> If it is not too much to ask, I should very much appreciate an answer as soon as convenient, owing to the fact that the plays are to be put on before long.
>
> In anxious anticipation of a favourable reply, I am, one of your many sincere admirers, and
>
> Respectfully yours
>
> Eleanor Frances Young.

The mixture of tactlessness in phrasing—"if it were one of your more important stories"—"we authors" geniality, and impatience must have done much to ensure the silence that they produced.

Other correspondents are in pursuit of the elusive Hardy version of the play. On August 31, 1912, B. F. Stevens and Brown, American Library and Literary Agents, write for a copy of the play, and a year and a half later want permission to print "15 copies of a special first edition in book form" (24 Jan 1914). Permission refused. On July 13, 1922, Elisabeth Marbury writes on behalf of the American Play Company; a New York manager who is planning a season of one-act plays would like a copy of *The Three Wayfarers.* In November 1924, Margaret Drew, play-reader to the Arts League Service of London, writes for permission to include "The Three Wayfarers," "of which we have a typescript copy," in the League's play lending library. This *does* receive a rapid reply, since Hardy wants to know how the League came into possession of a work that is unpublished and in copyright; Margaret Drew covers her tracks by telling him that the League was given a typescript "a long while ago by one of our supporters whose name we cannot now trace" and by assuring him that they will *not* lend out this copy but hold on to it as "a treasured private possession." Clearly Lieutenant Colonel Harry E. King, writing to Hardy in December 1926, had the acquisition of something similar in mind. Regretful that he cannot pick up Bournemouth on his radio, and will therefore miss a forthcoming broadcast of the play by the Hardy players, he writes to know whether it has been published and where he can obtain a copy. For him too, the rest is silence.

The interest in this story as a drama is not hard to understand, even if the survival of this group of letters in the Dorset County Museum—possibly a purely fortuitous one that reflects an accident of fate rather than exceptional interest in this minor work among Hardy's public—gives an artificial impression of the public attention it received. The story itself has a combination of ironic humour, circumscription of event and suspense that make it easily adaptable to the demands of dramatic irony and dramatic unity, especially of the type required in the limited scope of a one-act play. It has the flavour of some of Lady Gregory's one-act comedies—in that at least Mrs. Macardle's comments about suitability for production at the Abbey theatre were perceptive ones. It shows well Hardy's feel for the stage moment—the build-up of the public identification of the hangman, the entry of the convict's brother Joseph and the shift of focus it occasions, the final exchange between the unwitting hangman and the escaped convict—and the "swing" that Walter Lock felt it went with was undoubtedly a function of Hardy's familiarity with the elements of stage illusion within a limited compass. Dramatist he wasn't, but competent, indeed sometimes inspired, creator of the dramatic moment he undoubtedly was—as certain key scenes in *The Dynasts* so graphically attest. The one-act play is ideally suited to the fleeting intensity of moments of stage vision. While *The Dynasts* will always have to remain unactable in toto (even the cinema, though constantly implicitly invited to do so by criticism, has not yet seen fit to wrestle with it), and while *The Queen of Cornwall* comes uncomfortably close to the static tableau of poetic drama for modern theatre tastes, *The Three Wayfarers* is a small triumph of atmosphere and stagecraft. The new Macmillan "Dramascripts" edition will be valuable indeed if it causes wider recognition, in the form of frequency of performance, to be given to the fact.

Notes

1. Thomas Hardy, *The Three Wayfarers,* adapted by Guy Williams (London: Macmillan Education, 1979). Strictly speaking, this edition is not an "adaptation" of Hardy's play but the play itself. The only changes are a slight modifying and modernising of the stage directions—"thereon" becomes "on it," "damsel" becomes "village-girl," etc. The dialogue is entirely Hardy's. Macmillan's statement on the reverse of the title page that it was first published in New York in 1893 is incorrect. An earlier and substantially different version was published then, by Harper in a printing of only six copies, to secure copyright before the play was performed in London. Carl Weber prepared a facsimile edition of this rare original in 1943 (NY: Scholar's Facsimile and Reprints). Macmillan also lists the Cayme Press edition of 1930 as the first published in Great Britain, but do not indicate that they seem to have based their text on the edition published for Florence Emily Hardy by Henry

Ling in April 1935. This edition is slightly different from the Cayme Press one in minor wording.

2. See Purdy, p. 79. The four other plays were *Foreign Policy* by Conan Doyle, *Bud and Blossom* by Lady Colin Campbell, *An Interlude* by Mrs. W. K. Clifford and W. H. Pollock, and *Becky Sharp,* a scene from Thackeray, by J. M. Barrie.

3. MS., Dorset County Museum, Thomas Hardy Memorial Collection. All mss letters cited are in this repository and are printed with the kind permission of The Trustees of the Thomas Hardy Memorial Collection in the Dorset County Museum, Dorchester.

4. Carl J. Weber (ed). *The Letters of Thomas Hardy, Transcribed from the Original Autographs Now in the Colby College Library* (Waterville: Colby College P, 1954).

5. Weber, pp. 70-71.

6. Ibid, p. 91.

7. Ibid, p. 91.

Suzanne Hunter Brown (essay date spring 1982)

SOURCE: Brown, Suzanne Hunter. "'Tess' and *Tess*: An Experiment in Genre." *Modern Fiction Studies* 28, no. 1 (spring 1982): 25-44.

[*In the following essay, Brown evaluates a section of Hardy's novel* Tess of the d'Urbervilles *as if it were a short story in order to show how the reader's preconceived notions of genre and historical context affect the literary experience as a whole.*]

A good Short-story is no more the synopsis of a Novel than it is an episode from a Novel.

—Brander Matthews

The very same verbal segment, without changing a single word, may construct a totally different reality in different genres.

—Menakhem Perry

I

In "Pierre Menard, Author of *Don Quixote,*" Jorge Louis Borges plays on the fact that a literary work's meaning is in part determined by its historical context. His narrator's scholarly commentary on a twentieth-century *Don Quixote* demonstrates that the second *Quixote,* though verbally identical to the original, is not only different from the previous text but "almost infinitely richer."[1] Although the story is a parody of intellectual language and procedure, it is also a serious refutation of any narrowly New-Critical belief in the text itself as sole and sufficient source of literary meaning.

Borges' game reveals the influence of our knowledge of external context on our reading of a work. By reading a section of *Tess of the D'Urbervilles* as if it were a short story rather than an episode from that novel, I mean to suggest how our knowledge of generic, as well as historical, contexts governs our experience of literature. Regarding a text as a short story affects the way in which a reader will relate the words of that text to one another; thus the activation of a generic frame is part of a text's meaning. Comparing the readings of a section of *Tess* as a short story and as an episode in a novel should reveal those aspects of meaning created by our assumptions concerning genre and so should tell us something about how we respond to all works that we regard as short stories.

In presuming to "read" as a short story a text that was composed as part of a novel, I am, or course, suggesting that a reader may recreate the work as a short story by interpreting it as such. I use "genre" to refer to the interpretive conventions and psychological tendencies which the reader brings to the text. For the purposes of this experiment, genre is not a function of properties but rather of the expectations and assumptions that organize perception.[2]

A novel is longer than a short story, and the *dimension* of a work affects our perception of that work and hence the meaning it has for us. That readers are likely to establish different kinds of relationships among the elements of short and long works accounts for many of the differences between **"Tess"** and *Tess*. Recent work in psycholinguistics suggests that the number of words in a text, the quantity of verbal material, influences (1) the degree of attention readers bestow on each word; (2) the aspects of the text to which readers will direct their attention; (3) which elements they will remember; and (4) the kinds of connections they will make among elements.[3] The amount of verbal material obviously affects our memory for individual items in the text, and theorists concerned with reader response have noted the relation between memory and the connections a reader makes. Wolfgang Iser, for example, writes, "The fact of recall marks the limit to which the linguistic sign can be effective, for the words in the text can only denote a reference, and not its context; the connection with context is established by the retentive mind of the reader."[4] Because reading is a temporal activity, memory limits our ability to organize a text as a system of coexistent data. Obviously, in some sense we remember both the eight volumes of the un-

abridged *Clarissa* and Robert Frost's lyric "Nothing Gold Can Stay," but it is also true that we remember these works in terms of different kinds of units and of different sorts of relationships among units. Criticism, and the meaning a text has for a reader, are more a product of this representation in memory than of the text itself.[5]

I will digress here to consider the obvious question: if length is so important, why have so many generic theories ignored it? Traditional generic theories *invite* neglect of brevity's impact on the short story. The division between poetry and prose is assumed by many critics to be the most basic distinction in generic criticism. Stanley Fish complains that this assumption has fostered disinterest in all prose.[6] If criticism of the novel has suffered, theoretical investigation of the short story has suffered far more. "Prose" is often a shorthand for "novel." Thomas Gullason notes that the division between poetry and prose is institutionalized in textbooks and in the frameworks of university courses, commenting, "Rarely are the short-story writers asked what they think of this, for if they were, critics, anthologists, and others would be shocked to learn that most modern short-story writers are agreed that their medium is closer to poetry than to the novel."[7] Not only the customary division between poetry and prose but also the traditional classifications of drama, epic, and lyric have tended to subsume the short story in discussions of the novel. According to the criterion of "form," as a prose narrative the short story belongs with the novel to the epic category.[8]

Gullason is correct that short-story writers have generally been the ones to remind us of the obvious importance of brevity. It takes a certain crudeness, as well as a certain insight, to state, as does William Carlos Williams, "The principle feature re the short story is that it is short. . . ."[9] Though theorists have been less interested in generic dimension than writers, the Russian Formalists have emphasized the brevity of the short story. Boris Eichenbaum focused on the genre's form of closure and suggested that the short story culminates at a high point of intensity whereas the novel continues after the climax and concludes with some sense of epilogue. This difference he attributed to the opposition of big and small form.[10] This work by Russian Formalists should be seen in light of the theoretical tradition that relates the size or "magnitude" of an artwork to our perception of it. Aristotle was the first theorist I know of to suggest that magnitude influences our memory for the features of an artwork and the way in which we assemble the parts of an artwork into a whole. In the famous passage from the *Poetics,* he insisted that a huge animal could not be beautiful, "for as the eye cannot take it all in at once, the unity and sense of the whole is lost for the spectator." Likewise, readers require in a plot "a length which can be easily embraced by the memory."[11] Elder Olson's more recent formulation of Aristotle's speculations is refined; Olson believes that some kinds of relations between parts are more burdensome to the memory than others. Hence he connects memory limitations with generic characteristics and contends that "burdens" on the memory are "relative to the species": "a given lyric might be too long to be remembered, while a given tragedy might not."[12] Studies by psycholinguists have now demonstrated which aspects of a text *are* more burdensome to the memory and so indicated the sort of "processing" that will be more possible—and more satisfying—in brief works.

In emphasizing readers' expectations and psychological characteristics and factors, such as length, that affect perceptual tendencies, I am not claiming that genre has no relation to the text. A work may or may not reward reading according to a particular set of expectations, and some texts might, for a given set of readers, absolutely defeat the attempt to process them in a particular way. Because this is so, I would not claim that a random segment of a novel could be profitably treated as a short story. Writers themselves find that some texts called "short stories" are more pleasing when regarded in this way than others. Since we approach novels and short stories with differing sets of expectations and allocate our resources of attention differently in processing them, a "good" section of a novel might be a "bad" short story. Interestingly, Elizabeth Janeway candidly told John Cheever that she found the sections of Cheever's *The Wapshot Scandal* published piecemeal in *The New Yorker* less satisfying "as stories" than read as episodes in the context of the novel. Indeed Cheever agreed with her criticism and declared, "I would much sooner not do it that way; but that's the only way I've been able to do it," citing the economic advantages of such multiple publication.[13]

Some texts will be more satisfying than others when viewed as short stories because brevity alone cannot sustain the sort of attention I shall attribute to it in this article; it merely inclines us to bestow it. Samuel Taylor Coleridge made a similar point in discussing the poetic "properties" of verse; once poetic "devices" have inclined readers to bestow a special sort of attention, the linguistic structure must further reward this concentration: "If meter be superadded, all other parts must be made consonant with it. They must be such as to justify the perpetual and distinct attention to each part which an exact correspondent recurrence of accent and sound are calculated to excite."[14] In the same way, "good" short stories reward the expectations "excited" by brevity. Because the text of a novel may not otherwise fulfill the expectations created in the reader

by meter, Coleridge concluded that "the mere superaddition of meter" would not "entitle" novels "to the name of poems." For the same reason, I had to choose the section of *Tess* that I read as a short story with care; not all sections of the novel would "reward" the attention "excited" by brevity.

The segment of the novel that I have chosen to regard as a short story, entitled **"Tess,"** narrates the journey by Tess and her brother Abraham to Casterbridge market, a journey which ends when the family horse, Prince, is accidentally killed, pierced through the chest by the shaft of an on-coming mailcart. This slice of text does not coincide with a chapter of the novel. I omit the description of the Durbeyfields at Rolliver's tavern from **"Tess"**; it seems more suited to the pace of a novel than that of a short story. That scene makes the same points about the family fortunes and about Tess's relationship to her parents as does the section I have retained. The description fills out Hardy's chapter nicely, but it seems "too long" in the short story. When readers apply the close attention to detail that I believe they are likely to bestow on brief texts, they may well find this repetition "redundant"; it is perhaps to this generic convention that writers refer when they speak of the short story's "economy."[15] Furthermore, with this scene deleted, the action becomes continuous in time; there is no episodic gap in the "short story" like that indicated by the white space in Hardy's text.

I have decided to terminate the short story at the point where Abraham cries, "'Tis because we live on a blighted star, isn't it, Tess?" This decision is more problematic. To continue my short story through the description of Prince's burial at the end of the chapter would be possible—it is worth noting that the chapter ends with the same patterning as does the section I have chosen; both conclude with Abe's appeal to the supernatural and with Tess's acceptance of total responsibility for the death of Prince. Yet the slackening from the death of the horse—the crisis of the event—is, for reasons that I shall explain later, more typical of a novel chapter than of a story. One could of course regard the entire chapter as a short story, but it seems to me to work less well as a short fiction than the section I have chosen.

My model of a short story determines the slice of text I have chosen to treat as such. But if my **"Tess"** seems a successful short fiction, whereas Hardy's chapter regarded as a short story seems repetitive, rambling, or anticlimactic, such responses reveal much about the differing psychological tendencies and conventions upon which each genre draws. The reading in the second part of this article is mine. But the "I" who reads this short story is in part a product of a literary community and so to some degree representative of a "we," all those with experience of short stories extensive enough to command, if not to articulate, those conventions by which texts called "short stories" are interpreted as meaningful structures. Conventional reactions to "short stories" are of course shared by readers with a similar cultural experience of them; reactions limited by psychological constants are even more deeply shared by human beings.

II

My short story, **"Tess,"** begins as follows:

> It was eleven o'clock before the family were all in bed, and two o'clock next morning was the latest hour for starting with the beehives if they were to be delivered to the retailers in Casterbridge before the Saturday market began, the way thither lying by bad roads over a distance of between twenty and thirty miles, and the horse and waggon being of the slowest.[16]

The first sentence establishes that the Durbeyfield family is very poor and must endure hardship. Someone must perform a difficult journey if the family is not to squander an important source of income.

The second sentence, in which Mrs. Durbeyfield enters "the large bedroom where Tess and all her little brothers and sisters slept," initiates a verbal pattern which dominates the story: a series of words designating sleep or some state opposed to everyday waking consciousness. When her mother wakens her with the news that her father cannot go to market because he is *drunk,* Tess is "lost in a vague interspace between a dream and this information"; Abraham, too, is roused from a "deep sleep" and dresses "while still mentally in the other world." He continues to move "in a sort of trance." The significance of this pattern emerges when Abe prattles throughout the ride of what impresses "his imagination." The connection between sleep, dreaming, and imagination is reinforced later in the story by Tess's deep "reverie" about "fantastic scenes outside reality." From this state Tess again falls asleep and is awakened for the second time in the story when the mailcart drives into the horse.

The other-worldly atmosphere of the story contributes to the effect of the verbal associations. Darkness and eerie shapes seen in the half-light blend with the strange imaginings of Tess and her brother. Abe talks about "the strange shapes assumed by the various dark objects against the sky; of this tree that looked like a raging tiger springing from a lair; of that which resembled a giant's head." The narrator's descriptions also animate the surroundings: "the elevation called Bulbarrow, or Bealbarrow, well nigh the highest in South Wessex, swelled into the sky, engirdled by its earthen trenches." Tess's dreams are less childish than her brother's, but her projection of her speculations onto the dim landscape resembles his: "The mute procession past her shoulders of trees and hedges became attached to fantastic scenes outside reality."

This atmosphere overwhelms the family's efforts to cope with a demanding situation—we see them stumbling about in a foglike sleep. The strangeness of the world at night becomes emblematic of the Durbeyfields substitution of dreams for the harsh reality that is their daily situation. Each member of the family has a favorite scheme that will magically alter his or her life. Joan Durbeyfield wishes to avoid the difficulty of the journey to market by exploiting her daughter's beauty ("Some young feller, perhaps, would go?"). Abe reveals later in the text that the mother plans to raise the family fortunes by marrying Tess to a rich gentleman. The name of the rickety horse—Prince—is ironic in light of Mrs. Durbeyfield's project, and when Tess conjures up "the gentlemanly suitor awaiting herself in her mother's fancy," he is "grimacing" like a spectre. The woman's dreams thus have sinister connotations of deterioration and death.

Jack Durbeyfield concentrates his hopes for better times on his knightly ancestry, and he fails to drive the wagon to market because he is "too tipsy." His fancies, too, are destructive. Abraham, affected by the atmosphere of schemes and escapism, wonders if Tess will have enough money when she marries a rich gentleman to purchase "a spy-glass so large that it would draw the stars as near to her as Nettlecombe-Tout."

Tess at first seems a contrast to the rest of the family. She is the most responsible of the Durbeyfields and offers to drive the cart herself rather than casting about for ways to avoid the unpleasant task. While the others are heavy with sleep, we are told that Tess wakes as soon as her mother touches the door. She is ashamed of her mother's suggestion that she ask one of her suitors to take the beehives, and she is impatient with Abe for repeating Mrs. Durbeyfield's talk of a rich marriage, a project which Tess knows is unrealistic. But Tess has her own fantasy, which she reveals to her small brother. She tells him that the family's poor situation and the present hard trip result from life on "a blighted star." Tess, too, imagines a better life on a "sound" planet where "Father wouldn't have coughed and creeped about as he does and wouldn't have got too tipsy to go this journey; and Mother wouldn't have been always washing and never getting finished." According to Tess, the stars are "most of them splendid and sound" with "only a few blighted." Abraham reveals that his sister, too, views matters in terms of luck rather than of human responsibility, remarking, "'Tis very unlucky that we didn't pitch on a sound one, when there were so many more of 'em!" The little boy relates Tess's theory to the other family fantasies, asking whether on a sound star Tess "would have been a rich lady ready-made and not have had to be made rich by marrying a gentleman." After telling her imaginative story, Tess falls into reverie, and then into sleep. The description stresses the connection between sleep and a realm beyond reality: "Everything grew more and more extravagant, and she no longer knew how time passed. A sudden jerk shook her in her sleep, and Tess awoke from the sleep into which she, too, had fallen."

Tess discovers that she has allowed the horse to drift to the wrong side of the road and that Prince has been killed. She assumes total responsibility for the event: "'Tis all my doing—all mine." Overwhelmed, she exclaims, "Why I danced and laughed only yesterday! To think that I was such a fool!" Tess blames herself for the accident; the catastrophe convinces her that her lapse is responsible for the general suffering which it seems must follow. The short story ends with Abe's murmur, "'Tis because we be on a blighted star, and not on a sound one, isn't it, Tess?" We are reminded of the earlier allusion to Tess's observation that humans are *not* in fact responsible for the evil that befalls them, that somehow human effort is annulled by a "blight," some force beyond individual control. The girl's almost oracular pronouncement about life's limitations stems from knowledge which she shares with the rest of her family. A deep, inarticulate fatalism underlies the Durbeyfields' escapism, though their fantasies at first seem merely shiftless and foolish. At the end of the story, Tess rejects the star where human effort is necessarily blighted for a universe that rewards and punishes her own activity. The misfortune suggests an opposite insight to the reader, however. Tess's attempt to hold back the horse's blood with her hand makes her seem as helpless as the animal which can only stand until it collapses. Like her father's drinking and her mother's suitor who changes to a grimacing spectre in the girl's mind, Tess's own dreams end in destruction. The girl sees that, though the Durbeyfields cannot win, they can lose, and that fantasy and fatalism, though born of a kind of peasant wisdom, ultimately hasten deterioration. Her perception of "blight" cannot help her disentangle the mesh of circumstance in which she and her family are caught; a sense of futility would only make her less able to cope with her immediate problem and any future misfortunes. Tess sees her sleep as the fault that caused the accident. Her shame at her earlier dreams suggests that she will suppress any future fantasies—her "sleep" and lapse into her own version of the family dreams have been destructive, and she now says she *is* responsible for

her plight. One imagines that Tess brushes aside Abe's reminder of the unfortunate star in her efforts to understand the accident and to deal with Prince's corpse.

The reader, however, must contemplate the child's echo of his sister. For the reader, the death of the horse confirms the girl's statement that responsible efforts such as this morning journey are subject to "blight." The narrator's voice, his description of the stars "whose cold pulses were beating amid the black hollows above, in serene dissociation from these two wisps of human life," suggests that we must go beyond Tess's response to the accident. Although she has no leisure to dwell on her fatalistic intuitions if the situation is not to deteriorate further, the reader perceives that constant human effort is necessary to slow collapse, but is too circumscribed to stave it off forever.

III

> The novel and the short story are forms not only different in kind but also inherently at odds. . . .
>
> —Boris Eichenbaum

How does such a reading of the text as a short story differ from one's response to it as an episode from *Tess of the D'Urbervilles*? Perhaps more important, does regarding the segment as a short story make a difference in one's way of creating meaning from the text? Both **"Tess"** and the section of *Tess* relate the start and finish of a coherent event, a journey which ends with the death of a horse. But in another sense, the two have different beginnings and endings. **"Tess"** is complete as a literary event, but the segment of *Tess* has its literary opening when Jack Durbeyfield learns of his aristocratic heritage from the parson and concludes with Hardy's famous indictment of the President of the Immortals.[17] Literariness implies wholeness; we assume a work's artistic structure, and thus the claim to relate its parts in a meaningful way, on the basis of this sort of integrity. Our "sense of an ending" and of a beginning retrospectively governs interpretation. Thus, in verbally identical texts, the "meaning" of a detail may change according to the whole of which it is seen as a part; an element in our text may function quite differently in **"Tess"** and in *Tess*.

This is not to say merely that **"Tess"** is concluded whereas the section of *Tess* is not. The details of **"Tess"** are not just parts of a different whole; they are parts of a brief whole—a short story rather than a novel. We know in advance that we must form a tight network of connections among the elements of a short story like **"Tess"**; within a few pages we must arrive at the stasis of ending. The sorts of connections we expect determine those we perceive; as Mari Riess Jones puts it, "Expectancy and remembering . . . are opposite sides of the same coin."[18] Our knowledge of the size of a work governs our expectations and so affects our interpretation of particular details. As television viewers, we often answer the question "What will happen next?" by asking how much time is left in the show. The most primitive experience of narrative teaches us that "What will happen" is related to length and thus to genre. In **"Tess,"** for example, Mrs. Durbeyfield's plan to find a rich husband for the girl serves mainly to characterize the mother, whereas in the novel it also generates on-going narrative "suspense." Hardy's novel in fact rewards this expectation; looking back, one relates the scheme to Tess's later trip to Trantridge. In a secondary way, of course, her scheme also characterizes Mrs. Durbeyfield in the novel, but this effect is less important than in the short story; the difference is one of stress. As Gary Saul Morson observes, "to identify the structure of a work is to construct a *hierarchy* of relevance that makes some of its details central and others peripheral." Furthermore, he notes that such ordering may be a product of genre: "Different genres, for instance, imply different rules for ordering. . . ."[19] In reading the novel, readers may be inclined to label Mrs. Durbeyfield a dreamer and wonder what will happen as a result of her ambition; both contexts for meaning exist in the novel, but the work's genre might cause us to foreground the second. The reverse, however, is not true; in **"Tess,"** the potential suspense value of the mother's plan is never activated, not even in a minor way. We "know" that a short story is too brief for the detail to be developed in this way; therefore, we assign it another value, that of characterization.

In my reading of **"Tess,"** I emphasized verbal echoes. The repetition of the word "sleep" and its variants forms a pattern that may direct interpretation, whereas the repetition is less crucial when the text is read as an episode from *Tess*. The pattern is, of course, objectively present in both novel and short story—the difference lies in the weight given the pattern in the overall structure of meaning the reader supplies. Let us examine how the same detail—Tess's falling "asleep" on the journey—might be treated by someone responding to the text as an episode of *Tess*. Rather than seeing it as the culmination of a verbal pattern, the reader of the novel would be likely to see it as part of a pattern of cause-and-effect: because the ride takes place in the early morning, Tess is sleepy, and because she goes to sleep, the horse drifts to the wrong side of the road and is killed. The reader of *Tess* is likely to perceive this design because it corresponds to a larger cause-and-effect pattern: because Prince is killed in this way, Tess is more tractable under her mother's

pressure and agrees to seek out the D'Urbervilles. Menakhem Perry suggests why we are likely to subordinate the cause-and-effect pattern to the verbal design in our reading of a short story, though such a pattern is also present in that text:

> The reader prefers those frames that link the highest number of disparate items. Items which go to support any particular frame are not only verbal items appearing in the text, but also other frames constructed from the text. Thus, for instance, a decision on the genre-frame of a text enters as an important factor into the determination of other, different frames.[20]

Psycholinguistic research indicates further reasons why readers are more likely to process in terms of gross narrative "chunks" rather than verbatim detail when confronted with a lengthy text and why we prefer relationships based on verbatim recall when we read short works. Our representation of a text in memory is the result of our "packaging" material in short-term memory for storage in long-term memory. Hence, as Teun A. Van Dijk writes, "The representation of stories in episodic memory will be a function of the structures assigned during comprehension." The verbatim structure of a text—the pattern of phonemes and morphemes—is generally quickly converted in short-term memory into a series of "propositions" that will be stored. Our reading of a text is—and to some degree, because of processing limitations, must be—reductive. We do not remember the text; we mostly remember the propositions we form as we read. Criticism and the meaning a text has for a reader are more a product of this reductive version than of the text itself. Though experienced readers expect to focus special attention on the verbatim structure of a text which they regard as literature, Van Dijk explains why cognitive facts must hold to some degree for literary texts as well as for others: although directing attention to exact words can increase our memory for them, our ability to recall a text verbatim can only be stretched so far by this adjustment in the cognitive set.[21]

Processing literary discourse, then, involves a fundamental tension between the psychological necessity to repackage words or chunk material according to some schema and the convention of artistic discourse which disposes experienced readers to remember verbatim structures of a text which they regard as literature. The length of a work obviously affects this tension; the shorter a literary text, the better able an experienced reader of literature will be to fulfill the literary convention of focusing on the verbatim structure of the text. Van Dijk links the way in which we process texts to the quantity of verbal material. Because we need extra memory resources to store verbatim detail, we can explain "why most poems are relatively short" and why "literary conventions require that poems are read more attentively, more repeatedly (learned by heart), than, for instance, novels."[22] Though Van Dijk lays the groundwork for supposing that the brevity of the short story would allow the sort of "local" processing he associates with poetry, he reverts to the prose/poetry distinction when discussing genre and does not mention the short story. Short stories are actually curious hybrids. Like novels, they exhibit narrative features which would allow a reader to process them "globally," according to plot, but like lyric poems they are brief and so enable local processing, close attention to verbatim text structure, and need not rely on overarching narrative schemas to be retained at all. Close verbal connections are made possible by brevity; thus short stories with intricate, tight verbal structures are likely to please us because they reward the tendency to process brief works locally. Verbal echoes are much easier to perceive if they occur close together; a short story, like a lyric poem, can exploit this effect and generate a corresponding verbal density.

In *Tess,* a reader is likely to foreground the unfolding of events; in **"Tess,"** he or she is more likely to categorize details according to similarity and difference. The resemblance among the family fantasies, the repetition of words which cluster around "sleep"—these patterns, unlike the cause-and-effect sequence which dominates the episode of *Tess,* depend on a "contemporaneous" likeness, not on an order that is temporal. That Abraham voices his wish for a spy-glass after Jack Durbeyfield gets "tipsy" *obscures* the resemblance between the two rejections of reality. We could reverse the sequence of the two details without affecting our synchronic memory of the story. In **"Tess,"** the protagonist jumbles her ordinary perceptions of time and space through sleepiness and imagination just as the reader must rearrange the sequential events of the story to construct its meaning. Thus when a reader regards this text as a short story, he tends to prefer repetitive to temporal links in creating it as a meaningful structure, organizing its elements in a way some theorists contend characterizes our perception of lyric poetry.

We have seen that a reader is likely to order the minimal units of **"Tess"** synchronically, whereas he will probably order textual elements from *Tess* in a diachronic fashion.[23] For my own purposes, I prefer the informal terms "configuration" and "succession" that Paul Ricoeur uses to distinguish these two basic modes of perceptual patterning:

> . . . every narrative combines two dimensions in various proportions, one chronological and the other non-chronological. The first may be called the episodic dimension, which characterizes the story as made out of events. The second is the configurational dimension,

according to which the plot construes significant wholes out of scattered events. . . . the humblest narrative is always more than a chronological series of events and . . . in turn the configurational dimension cannot overcome the episodic dimension without suppressing the narrative structure itself.: . . . The temporal dialectic, then, is implied in the basic operation of eliciting a configuration from a succession.[24]

Brevity affects the perceptual tension that Ricoeur describes. Because the perception of an artwork's "parts" is a temporal process, our ability to repattern them as a "simultaneous" whole is dependent on our memory for those individual elements. Ricoeur maintains that configuration emphasizes the *wholeness* of an artwork and is essentially a reflective act dependent on memory. Any work can be organized as a configuration or as a successive structure, and both possibilities are probably utilized to some degree in the perception of any artform. However, there are two reasons to believe that brevity inclines readers to foreground an achronological model or at least makes it easier for them to do so. First, it is obviously easier to "grasp together" minimal semantic units in a synchronic "reflective act" when there is less material for our memories to deal with. Configurational interpretation clearly makes special demands on memory that can be offset by brevity. Second, we can process the parts of a short text more rapidly, and, as Gothold Lessing pointed out in regard to a perceiver's processing of the parts of a painting, "this rapidity is indispensable, if we are to form an idea of the whole, which is nothing more than the resultant of the ideas of the parts and of their combination." Lessing had little faith in human memory and felt that verbal art labored under a considerable disadvantage in creating an impression of a simultaneous whole. For we lose, he wrote, a sense of the parts "if they are not retained in the memory," and even if we do remember such individual parts, "what trouble and effort it costs us . . . to pass them at one time under review with but moderate rapidity, in order to attain any possible idea of the whole!" According to Lessing, visual and verbal art can be considered neighbors with shared territory only when "in the poet the several features, representing the various parts and properties in space, follow one another with such speed and condensed brevity that we fancy that we hear all at once."[25] Because a sense of the whole is more vital to configurational than to successive patterning, the length of a text will influence this organizational choice. The faster we are able to apprehend the separate parts of a work and "grasp them together" into a whole, the freer a work is to reinforce nonsequential structures, even when a narrative order is present.

In contrasting **"Tess"** and *Tess,* we can see that the varying kinds of associations we make among the details of novels and short stories affect our perception of the plots of each. Metaphoric connections lead naturally to a more precise understanding of a state of affairs through perception of its likeness to and difference from others. Our understanding of Tess's situation is heightened in reading the short story, but her condition does not change. On the other hand, a sequence governed by the logic of cause-and-effect will lead to a stasis of action in which conflict is resolved; the final situation is not the cause of any future result in which we have interest. The episode of *Tess* finds this kind of resolution. The conflict between Tess's desire to help her shiftless family and her dislike of her mother's marriage scheme is resolved only when Tess returns to Alec because her family is homeless, kills him in resentment when Clare returns, and is herself executed as a result. In my reading of the short story, this conflict does not find resolution in action. Rather, it underlines a difference of character.

In Roland Barthes's theoretical terms, we structure **"Tess"** as a plot of revelation whereas we are more inclined to perceive the plot of *Tess* as one of resolution. Tzvetan Todorov's similar division of plot types makes it clear that different ways of establishing relationship can lead to these different types of interest and plot. In defining two types of organization and two types of narrative according to time, he suggests that sequential ordering reinforces the plot of resolution, whereas the plot of revelation is based on configurational perception: "One unfolds on a horizontal line: we want to know what each event provokes, what it *does*. The other represents a series of variations which stack up along a vertical line: what we look for in each event is what it *is*."[26] Seymour Chatman, too, finds that "a strong sense of temporal order is more significant in resolved than in revealed plots."[27] Brevity inclines readers to make close verbal connections and to perceive relationships of resemblance. Such reading can lead to a heightened perception of a static situation, yet no theorist except Eichenbaum sees length of narrative as an important factor in discussions of plot.

When we do consider the relation between length and plot type, we can also explain the fact which Eichenbaum noted about the short story, namely that short fictions tend to culminate at a high point of intensity, whereas novels slacken after the crisis and conclude with some sense of "epilogue." If the short story finds its ending at a moment of insight while the novel concludes when the conflict producing a chain of action reaches its stasis, it is easy to see why this it true. Moreover, since the plot of revelation does rely on a heightening of response in the reader, it is reinforced by the short story's *duration*; readers can maintain mounting aesthetic involvement for the entire experience of a short work. Because local processing makes special demands on a reader's attention, we might ex-

pect also that reading a short story would be a particularly absorbing experience. Poe's linking of brevity and intensity is the most familiar, if the most primitive, formulation of this perceptual theory; he postulated that emotional or aesthetic "arousal" can be sustained only for brief periods.[28] Poe's recommendation of "a single sitting" is his attempt to indicate in a flexible way the period during which we can sustain a mounting level of aesthetic interest. The frequent reference to "a single sitting" suggests its basic function. Aristotle, too, referred to "the group of tragedies that could be presented at a single sitting" and shared Poe's preference for artistic experiences of limited duration.[29] The prevalence of the one-to-three-hour format for artistic events—concerts, plays, films—would suggest that this range is relevant to aesthetic attention.

The above point about dimension and genre helps explain the frequent association of the short story with the "epiphany." "Epiphanies" are grounded in *reader* response. The heightened insight reinforced by the short story's brevity *may* occur for a character or *only* for the reader. I suggest in my reading of **"Tess,"** for example, that its effect derives from the gap between the heroine's awareness and the reader's. Although Tess's sensitivity to her condition is increased in the story, only the audience has the detachment necessary to articulate the implications of her plight.

An important difference between **"Tess"** and the episode from *Tess* is that the first locates meaning in the moment, whereas the second concerns itself with the pattern of a life. The story culminates in a moment of psychological reaction for the character and of insight for the reader. The novelistic episode, on the other hand, records an incident that assumes its full significance in the literary work only as part of the history of a woman's life. Thus if the death of the horse is in both cases a form of learning for Tess, the importance of the education in the novel lies in how it governs Tess's behavior under future circumstances, whereas in the short story her change of attitude has intrinsic value. In **"Tess,"** the girl's attempt to assert responsibility in a circumscribed life has meaning by its very isolation from her unique past and future—our understanding of her reaction is more important than anything else this Tess has done or will do. The feeling of responsibility that Tess voices in the novel chapter, however, develops its full significance over the course of the work and of her life. Her claim that the accident is her fault leads her to regard herself "in the light of a murderess," a phrase which resonates ironically when Tess kills Alec. That the girl who feels "like a murderess" for the chance stabbing of an animal should become a woman who deliberately stabs a man and that her action is the result of a chain of circumstances over which her control is perhaps as nebulous as over that leading to Prince's death are ironies of *time*. Again, the difference is not just that the episode is unfinished; the kind of effect it achieves is a function of time and is foreign to the way in which short stories often work.

Differences between my reading of **"Tess"** and accepted generalizations about the setting of *Tess of the D'Urbervilles* suggest a tendency to universalize geographical details in brief works. The same text, when read as a short story rather than as a segment of the novel, seems to become less "mimetic"; perceiving the work as a short story creates a strong drive to render all details "symbolic," that is, to interpret them metaphorically. Physical geography is not "withheld" in **"Tess"**; the short story is not so extreme in this respect as the lyric, but setting is both more limited and more universal than in the section of *Tess*.[30] This difference resides in the generic context, not in the words of the text. In both story and episode of novel we are told that the events take place in Dorsetshire. But the mimetic particularity of this setting can only be developed through the length of the novel with its loving recreation of Dorsetshire speech, customs, and way of life. The following sentence, for example, yields to quite different associations in the short story and in the novel: "Still higher, on their left, the elevation called Bulbarrow, or Bealbarrow, well nigh the highest in South Wessex, swelled into the sky, engirdled by its earthen trenches." In *Tess* we probably stress the first part of the sentence, connecting its specific place names with other lengthy descriptions of Hardy's county in the novel. When reading **"Tess,"** I linked the *second* half of the sentence with other instances of imaginative, disoriented perception in the story. Readers of the novel are likely to prefer the first emphasis because the concrete bit of "local color" forms part of the larger picture of the countryside established throughout *Tess of the D'Urbervilles*. Although both **"Tess"** and *Tess* are set in Dorsetshire, a reader's sense of "setting" in the short story is thus more highly metaphorical and symbolic—one stresses the eerie, dreamy atmosphere of the cart ride. In the novel, however, readers note Hardy's accurate and detailed rendering of life in the English farm village of the later nineteenth century. Although there may be in *Tess of the D'Urbervilles* some slight overtone connecting the strangeness of the morning objects with the Durbeyfields' misty perception of reality, readers would probably lean less on this suggestion in creating the work as a meaningful structure, if, indeed, they become aware of it at all. Asked the setting of the short story, a reader of **"Tess"** might well reply, "on a wagon" or "in the early morning"; asked the same question about the novel, he would probably state "Dorsetshire" or "rural England of the 1880s."

Not only is the recreation of a milieu in all its historical particularity more easily achieved in a genre with the compass of a novel, but readers are more likely to be satisfied with a historical interpretation of or a sense of a verisimilar representation of life in longer works. Whereas the settings of novels *can* be given a generalized metaphorical interpretation, it is more *necessary* for readers to view the situational details of brief works metaphorically if the latter are not to be seen as "slight." The broader historical context is certainly existent and even important in short stories—Hemingway's old man at the bridge is clearly backgrounded by Spain of the 1930s, but still one is likely to give the answer, "at a bridge," as the setting of the work. The historical setting, although still important to the meaning of the short story, is outside and beyond and must be brought to the work, whereas a historical context often informs and infuses the novel. Because the historical situation tends to be more nebulous in very short works, it can be more easily universalized. For example, we speak of "all war" as the subject of Hemingway's story, not the Spanish Civil War of 1936, though that is the specific war in question. In treating history and time as important forces, the novel suggests that given conditions are the product of a particular society at a given point in time and space. Thus they can be changed. And hence the fondness most Marxist critics express for the longer form. In **"Tess,"** however, I am more likely to ascribe the girl's plight to "the human condition." When I regard the text as an episode from *Tess,* however, I tend to indict nineteenth-century industrialism for her hardships.

That geographical details function in a metaphorical, nonmimetic way is an interpretive tendency facilitated by the small dimension of the genre. If the length of a novel makes it easier to create a historical milieu, it makes it harder to create an abstract setting with fewer situational details. H. E. Bates connects a reader's willingness to tolerate such a metaphorical setting to a work's size:

> A novel whose characters were never named, whose location and time were never stated, might well impose on its readers a strain that they would justifiably refuse to bear. Yet many a short story has characters which bear no more marks of identification than the anonymous and universal label of "boy" or "girl" . . . and no more topographical exactitude than "the street," "the field," "the room," or any seashore between Brighton and Botany Bay.[31]

An interesting example of the novel's resistance to symbolic treatment of its setting, characters, and situation occurs in Hardy's handling of the execution which concludes *Tess*. When the heroine dies, Hardy attempts a symbolic substitution—Clare goes off arm-in-arm with Liza-Lu, Tess's sister, and, we are told, a more "spiritualized" version of her. We are to understand that Tess lives on in Liza-Lu and that Angel has a new Tess, embodying the same qualities of womanly purity and peasant vitality. However, a survey of the criticism on *Tess of the D'Urbervilles* or a visit to any classroom where the book is taught shows that if readers even remember this "ending," they do so with indignation. Bates is correct about the way in which generic dimension affects reader tolerance. Tess is Tess, and no mere embodiment of her qualities. We have lived with a particular character over time, and our sense of her is so mimetic that we will allow no substitution of her qualities in another guise to compensate us for the absence of the actual character. Hardy tries, but he is pulling against the interpretive tendencies elicited by characterization in the novel, which we tend to interpret less metaphorically than the short story.

IV

The size of a thing, the quantity of verbal material, is not an indifferent feature; we cannot, however, define the genre of a work if it is isolated from the system. . . . The study of isolated genres outside the features characteristic of the genre system with which they are related is impossible.

—Jurij Tynjanov

Dimension is theoretically most useful when viewed as one variable among many in our response to literature. Though I have not been able to consider the many other factors which may influence the sort of attention we focus on a piece of literary discourse, I would like to mention a few that should be considered.

Brevity inclines us to process material locally, but so does printing discourse as verse and "adding" such features as rhyme and meter. Line breaks, particularly short ones, force readers to pause on more individual words, probably slowing reading rate and focusing attention on the verbatim aspect of a text. When poetic line breaks counter syntactic stops, our inclination to abstract the "gist" and relinquish verbatim content is probably lessened. For this reason, local processing would be more intense in short poems than in short prose works, and long poems, such as *Paradise Lost,* might be processed more locally than novels.

We also need to consider the interaction of brevity with historical and cultural factors. New Critical analysis and the tendency to "spatial" organization in modern literature have probably influenced the ways in which we process texts, possibly encouraging us to read novels more like short stories.³² Yet psychological constants remain important factors; if we do experience a sudden sense of configurational patterning at the end of some modern novels, it is unlikely that this sense of "simultaneous" design will involve recall of any great percentage of words or smaller verbal units, because the very process of "reading" the novel necessitates relinquishing most words in favor of larger, more abstract narrative "chunks." Not only particular critical approaches but also certain literary styles may interact more effectively with the psychological tendencies engendered by short or long works; naturalism, for example, has generally been more successfully employed in long works. A complete account of dimension and genre would have to consider all the hybrids, the possible combinations of "short" and "long." What about volumes of stories? Story cycles? Picaresque narratives with interpolated tales? Novels with long chapters, short chapters, or, as in *Gravity's Rainbow,* film sprockets creating segments rather than traditional chapters? And what about "soliloquies" or other isolated set pieces in longer works that signal us to pay close attention? Size and genre interact in ways as variable and dynamic as our human experience of literature.

Notes

1. Jorge Luis Borges, "Pierre Menard, Author of *Don Quixote,*" in *Ficciones,* ed. Anthony Kerrigan, trans. Emecé Editores (New York: Grove Press, 1962), p. 52.

2. As Gary Saul Morson points out, to the extent that "interpretive conventions rather than formal features determine a work's genre, genre is not manifest in the work itself." *The Boundaries of Genre* (Austin: University of Texas Press, 1981), p. viii.

3. For some recent studies of discourse processing, see Jean M. Mandler, "A Code in the Node: The Use of a Story Schema in Retrieval," *Discourse Processes,* 1 (1978), 14-35; Perry W. Thorndyke, "Cognitive Structures in Comprehension and Memory of Narrative Discourse," *Cognitive Psychology,* 9 (1977), 77-100; Michael Townsend, "Schema Activation in Memory for Prose," *Journal of Reading Behavior,* 12 (1980), 49-53.

4. Wolfgang Iser, *The Act of Reading: A Theory of Aesthetic Response* (Baltimore, MD: The Johns Hopkins University Press, 1978), p. 116.

5. Allen Tate was well aware of this fact. He wrote, "Who can remember, well enough to pronounce upon it critically, all of *War and Peace,* or *The Wings of the Dove,* or even *Death in Venice,* the small enclosed world of which ought at least to do something to aid our memories? I have re-read all three of these books in the past year; yet for the life of me I could not pretend to know them as wholes, and without that knowledge I lack the materials of criticism." *The Man of Letters in the*

Modern World (New York: The Noonday Press, 1955), p. 79.

6. Fish writes, "In the area of specifically literary studies, the effects of a naive theory of utterance meaning and of its attendant assumption of ordinary language can be seen in what is acknowledged to be the sorry state of the criticism of the novel and of prose in general. This is usually explained with reference to a distinction between prose and poetry, which is actually a distinction between ordinary language and poetic language." "Literature in the Reader: Affective Stylistics," *New Literary History*, 2 (Autumn 1970), 129.

7. Thomas A. Gullason, "The Short Story: An Underrated Art," *Studies in Short Fiction*, 2 (Fall 1964). Reprinted in *Short Story Theories*, ed. Charles E. May (Athens: Ohio University Press, 1976), p. 19.

8. Paul Hernadi, surveying past generic systems, observes that dimension is indeed an aspect of genre which this often-evoked triad system has slighted. See *Beyond Genre: New Directions in Literary Classification* (Ithaca, NY: Cornell University Press, 1972), *passim*; see especially p. 101.

9. William Carlos Williams, *A Beginning on the Short Story* (Yonkers, NY: The Alicat Bookshop Press, 1950), p. 5. See also Frank O'Connor, *The Lonely Voice* (Cleveland, OH: World Publishing, 1962) and Sean O'Faolain, *The Short Story* (Cork: The Mercier Press, 1948).

10. Boris Eichenbaum, *O. Henry and the Theory of the Short Story*, trans. I. R. Titunik (Ann Arbor: Michigan Slavic Contributions, 1968), p. 4.

11. Aristotle, *Poetics*, trans. S. H. Butcher, in *Aristotle's Theory of Poetry and Fine Art*, 4th ed. (London: Macmillan, 1911), pp. 31-32.

12. Elder Olson, "An Outline of Poetic Theory," in *Critics and Criticism*, ed. R. S. Crane (Chicago, IL: The University of Chicago Press, 1952), p. 559.

13. "Is the Short Story Necessary?" from *The Writer's World*, ed. Elizabeth Janeway (New York: McGraw-Hill, 1969). See *Short Story Theories*, p. 103.

14. Samuel Taylor Coleridge, *Biographia Literaria*, ed. J. Shawcross (1817; rpt. London: Oxford University Press, 1954), II, 9-10.

15. Susan Rubin Suleiman considers redundancy a generic issue; she writes, "Since in reading a text of any length one of the most obvious kinds of 'noise' is the reader's forgetfulness, we can predict that the longer the text the more it will need to multiply its redundancies," adding that "the degree and the type of redundancy in a given text are a manifestation of its genre. . . ." "Redundancy and the 'Readable' Text," *Poetics Today*, 1 (1980), 122.

16. All quotations are from Thomas Hardy, *Tess of the D'Urbervilles* (1891; rpt. New York: Signet, 1964).

17. Mikhail Bakhtin identified these two types of unity: "every work has a beginning and an end, the event represented in it likewise has a beginning and an end, but these beginnings and endings lie in different worlds. . . ." *The Dialogic Imagination*, ed. Michael Holquist, trans. Caryl Emerson and Michael Holquist (Austin: The University of Texas Press, 1981), p. 255.

18. Mari Riess Jones, "Only Time Can Tell: On the Topology of Mental Space and Time," *Critical Inquiry*, 7 (1981), 575.

19. Morson, p. 42.

20. Menakhem Perry, "Literary Dynamics: How the Order of a Text Creates its Meanings," *Poetics Today*, No. 1 (1979), p. 45.

21. Teun A. Van Dijk, "Story Comprehension: An Introduction," *Poetics*, 9 (1980), *passim*; see especially p. 18.

22. Teun A. Van Dijk, "Cognitive Processing of Literary Discourse," *Poetics Today*, No. 1 (1979), p. 154. Interestingly, Frank Kermode also makes attention to verbatim detail a generic issue and wonders why readers are so likely to ignore it in favor of plot when reading novels. He writes that it "is not uncommon for large parts of a novel to go virtually unread; the less manifest portions of its text (its secrets) remain secret, resisting all but abnormally attentive scrutiny, reading so minute, intense, and slow that it seems to run counter to one's 'natural' sense of what a novel is, a sense which one feels to have behind it the history and sociology of the genre." "Secrets and Narrative Sequence," *Critical Inquiry*, 7 (Autumn 1980), 88. Kermode attributes the disinclination to process novels according to verbal repetitions not to their length and to the allocation of resources this makes necessary, but to a cultural convention, a "collusion" between author and public. Novel readers may have such conventional expectations, of course, but the convention is probably reinforced by the psychological factors I have described.

23. Many other terms exist for the same opposition. Some theorists refer to "paradigmatic" and "syntagmatic" structures. "Temporal" is often equated

with "succession" and is then opposed to "spatial." The question of "spatial" form and "simultaneous" perception has vexed literary criticism since Joseph Franks' 1945 essay on the subject. See his *The Widening Gyre* (New Brunswick, NJ: Rutgers University Press, 1963).

24. Paul Ricoeur, "Narrative Time," *Critical Inquiry,* 7 (1980), 178.

25. Gothold Lessing, *Laökoon,* trans. E. C. Beasley, in *Selected Prose Works of G. E. Lessing,* ed. Edward Bell (London: George Bell, 1879), pp. 98-99, 105-106.

26. Tzvetan Todorov, *The Poetics of Prose,* trans. Richard Howard (Ithaca, NY: Cornell University Press, 1977), p. 135.

27. Seymour Chatman, *Story and Discourse* (Ithaca, NY: Cornell University Press, 1978), p. 48.

28. Edgar Allan Poe, "The Philosophy of Composition" and "Nathaniel Hawthorne," in *Poe's Poems and Essays,* Everyman's Library (London, 1927; rpt. New York: E. P. Dutton, 1958).

29. Aristotle, pp. 91, 111.

30. The many discussions of abstract, metaphorical settings in lyric poems suggest some similarity in the treatment of setting in brief literary texts. Hernadi, for example, writes, "It is characteristic of shorter lyric poems to go without much background. . . . Our attention is directed to the metaphoric depth rather than the communicatory width of verbal meaning" (pp. 172-173). Asked by an interviewer why he chose the short story as his medium, O'Connor replied, "Because it's the nearest thing I know to lyric poetry. . . . A novel actually requires far more logic and far more knowledge of circumstances, whereas a short story can have the sort of detachment from circumstances that lyric poetry has." "Interview," *Writers at Work: The Paris Review Interviews,* ed. Malcolm Cowley (New York: The Viking Press, 1958), p. 165.

31. H. E. Bates, *The Modern Short Story* (1941; rpt. Boston: The Writer, 1972), pp. 19-20.

32. Interestingly, Fredric Jameson finds Formalism and other modes of criticism which isolate synchronic verbal patterns more appropriate to brief forms than to novels. See "Metacommentary," *PMLA,* 86 (January 1971), 12. Though no New Critic ever suggested that his tools were more appropriate for one genre than another, in practice New Critics gravitated toward poems and short stories.

George Wing (essay date 1987)

SOURCE: Wing, George. "*A Group of Noble Dames*: 'Statuesque Dynasties of Delightful Wessex.'" In *Thomas Hardy Annual No. 5,* edited by Norman Page, pp. 75-101. Basingstoke, U.K.: Macmillan, 1987.

[*In the following essay, Wing uses Hardy's youthful "[d]iagrams showing human passion, mind and character" (a set of drawings depicting the vagaries of will, intellect, and emotional connection) to delineate the aesthetic and thematic contours of the stories in* A Group of Noble Dames.]

In 1863 Hardy 'designed' some 'Diagrams showing human passion, mind and character' and later stuck them on the inside of the fly leaf of his 'Literary Notes I' which contains entries, mainly quotations from other writers, from 1875-88.[1] Of the four diagrams, one shows a 'Line of energy' in which energy peaks at about age nineteen and then after a series of ups and downs to age forty steadily declines until 'Life ends'. The two major drawings are of a tree, with trunks, roots, creepers possibly and branches. At the base, in the soil perhaps, are 'intellect', 'passions' and 'will'. At the lower end of the trunk three excrescences are separately named 'Impossible monster of Intellect . . . Passions . . . and Will.' Higher up the trunk these fuse into either fungi or fruit called 'Moral Harmony'. A main stem from the trunk is labelled 'Affectives dominant' and it bears four branches 'Friendship dominant', 'Love dominant', 'Passion dominant' and 'Ambition dominant'.

Hardy was only twenty-three and learning architecture in Arthur Blomfield's office in London when he 'designed' this anthropometric and eclectic cipher and at first sight the drawings and inscriptions suggest a Casaubonian delusion, an eccentric Victorian systematising of humanity which may have been partly inspired by conversations with the likes of Horace Moule. We could patronizingly dismiss the drawings as adolescent doodles, searching for the great truths (a maturer Hardy prefers the word 'seemings'), were it not for the fact that Hardy's writing and his person as well as his cabbalistic trees are well-rooted. The diagrams in fact are based on Hardy's reading in translation of *The Passions of the Human Soul* by Francis Fourier (1772-1837),[2] and the sketches are, as W. F. Wright tells us, 'arbitrary and inconsistent'.[3] Arbitrariness and inconsistency are, however, signal constitutes in Hardy's writings and far more germane to a richer understanding of them than any youthful attraction to a 'French Utopian Socialist's' dialectic. In the composition of prose fiction and poetry Hardy's husbandry is scrupulous to the point of miserliness, and he does not waste much personal or vicarious experience or discard too many jottings. It is interesting, but not unexpected, to find that his concern with basic powers, which in his writings often mutate into terrible rages of will, passion and so on, existed at so youthful an age. Part of this concern is soon to be artistically expressed in his emotionally desiccated poem of 1867, 'Neutral Tones', and is then to continue through the prose fiction, *The Dynasts* and the remaining nine hundred or so poems.

While many critical books and articles have been written about Hardy's major novels and some of the more academically popular and anthologized poetry, there are broad areas of Hardy's *oeuvre* which are infrequently noticed, none more so than the short stories. They have not, obviously, the same lode of attraction as more familiar fiction but I propose, with due acknowledgement to Kristin Brady,[4] to lift for a time from the slough of uninterest a few of the short stories and to lay them alongside some of those roots and branches of Hardy's youthful diagrams to decide if there is any informative association between them of attitude or cast. In my appreciation of certain tales in *A Group of Noble Dames,* one of the four collections of the short stories, I shall be looking also for Hardyan sensitivities of passion, mind and character which lie beyond the perimeters of his sketches.

Hardy published his short stories over the period 1874 (**'Destiny and a Blue Cloak'** in *The New York Times*) to 1900 (**'Enter a Dragon'** in *Harper's Monthly Magazine*) and collected them in volume form over the period 1888 (*Wessex Tales*) to 1913 (*A Changed Man*). *A Group of Noble Dames* (the fourth collection is *Life's Little Ironies*) differs from the other three in that it was commissioned from the start as a collection, by the editor of the *Graphic,* for its Christmas number of 1890. In its final form, *Noble Dames* [*A Group of Noble Dames*] has ten stories and ten narrators, one tenth or one day of *The Decameron* with which it has, despite its Victorian social context, some surprising affinities. The most obvious of these lies in the fact that the Director of the *Graphic* caused the original six stories to be bowdlerized and three of them severely mutilated, as Edmond Willowes is in **'Barbara of the House of Grebe'**. On the altered manuscript of **'Squire Petrick's Lady'** Hardy has written 'the tyranny of Mrs. Grundy'.[5] The narrators of the *Noble Dame* stories comprise an entertainingly heterogeneous group in their own right and are members of the South-Wessex Field and Antiquarian Club, which, on a damp day, listens to the first story, **'The First Countess of Wessex'**. This tale set in a winter 'in days long ago' is 'made to do duty for the regulation papers on deformed butterflies, fossil ox-horns, prehistoric dung-mixens, and such like'.[6] The following nine stories are told because the Club becomes

storm-bound in 'The museum of the town whose buildings and environs were to be visited by the members' and the stories assimilate the haphazard antiquity of the museum and its dusty oddities, where scrutiny and participation afford both revulsion and affection, like the deformed butterflies, but sometimes, unlike the dung-mixens, a recalled pity. The substitute stories are, with slightly strained artifice, related to their narrators, about as much as the pilgrims are in *The Canterbury Tales*. The Old Surgeon tells of obscene disfigurement by fire; the Colonel, a story about the Civil War; and the Crimson Maltster, the 'fat member with a crimson face', bourgeois, retired, of comfortable means, recounts the only story in which the heroine has not a title. The club is 'of an inclusive and intersocial character; to a degree, indeed, remarkable for the part of England in which it had its being—dear delightful Wessex, whose statuesque dynasties are even now only just beginning to feel the shaking of the new and strange spirit without, like that which entered the lonely valley of Ezekiel's vision and made the dry bones move' (p. 49). Yet the stories, even from their historical distance, test the geniality of this nostalgic observation, shiver with a strange spirit and often, with casual synecdoche, bring about the movement of dry bones. But the interspersed passages, describing the appearance and relating the conversation of the 'inclusive and intersocial members', form only a cobbled unity, however diverting the narrative continuum may be. Hardy wrote the six stories of **Noble Dames** for the Christmas number of the *Graphic,* 1890, with what Purdy calls a 'frame',[7] which was necessarily recarpentered when four other, previously published, stories were added for book publication.[8]

Those impossible monsters of passions, intellect and will which comprise root and branch of Hardy's youthful sketches are characteristically obvious and unsubtle in **Noble Dames,** as they are, though more woundingly personal, in *Tess of the d'Urbervilles,* which Hardy had just finished writing when he turned to fulfilling his commission for the *Graphic,* and in much of his other fiction and in many a poem. Those other major forces, however, characteristically and fiercely Hardyan, of chance and local morality, which muster so ominously in the novels, which are often so crucial and tantalizing, and which for obvious reasons are not depicted in the sketches, work with different emphases and impacts in the short stories, although in their narrative consummation their effects can be just as caustically disheartening. Chance, which I use in its most commodious sense, is in many instances, for all practical and melodramatic purposes, the essential fulcrum on which the turning of the tales is totally dependent. Society's judgment—whatever would the village or the local gentry think—does not on the other hand weigh, in most cases, so much in the technical sum. It has, generally, an irritating presence but constitutes more a needling from the spectators rather than active implication. In **'The Lady Penelope'**, a Jacobean story set in the country between Dorchester and Yeovil. Penelope jestingly states that she will marry her three jealous and persistent suitors in turn. This is the way it works out and after the death of her second husband, Sir John Gale, rumour gets about in the village: '"Surely," they whispered, "there is something more than chance in this. . . . The death of the first was possibly natural; but what of the death of the second, who ill-used her, and whom, loving the third so desperately, she must have wished out of the way?"' (p. 185). Despite the fact that it is entirely a matter of chance, her third husband, Sir William Hervey, picks up the local scandal when he overhears 'a conversation among some basketmakers', which in its rustic malevolence echoes the chorus of idlers and topers in the taverns of *The Mayor of Casterbridge*. 'A cupboard close to his bed, and the key in her pocket', one of the speculators suggests as the pastoral insidiousness develops: 'And a blue phial therein—h'm!' says another; 'And spurge-laurel leaves among the hearth-ashes. Oh-oh!' says the third. 'From that hour a ghastly estrangement began' and Penelope's third husband leaves her and, as she wastes fatally away, the rumours are so thick in the atmosphere that 'they rustled in the air like night-birds of evil omen' (pp. 185-6). Henchard, Tess, Sue and Jude, all suffer grievously from an opprobrious form of social judgement which is registered as Mrs Grundyism, a concept for Hardy of particular distaste, a bourgeois morality which condemns with secret gratification, but which characterizes also other classes and institutions than bourgeois. It assumes many forms and intensities from High Church narrow-mindedness to the mindless passing of village gossip. This latter, curiously, has an intrinsic value of ironic entertainment and in the case of Penelope is apparent in Sir William's bizarre eavesdropping on the chat of the basketmakers. Village censure, however, is only sporadically introduced in this tale and, although the comic tattle makes a contribution of malice, the tragic substance lies elsewhere in the way both untoward events manipulate and are manipulated and wills and passions clash.

All the stories in **Noble Dames** are, with one exception, historical. The tenth story, **'The Honourable Laura'**, appeared as **'Benighted Travellers'** in the *Bolton Weekly Journal* ten years before the original six appeared in the *Graphic,* and is told by a member with the nickname of the Spark who 'preferred something . . . in which long separated lovers were ultimately united' and liked stories 'that were more modern in their date of action than those he had heard to-

day' (p. 206). Although it may be difficult to avoid a suspicion that this short melodramatic romance—it has a happy family ending which would have warmed Dickens' heart—was brought in to make up the ten mainly because of Laura's noble parentage, her father being Lord Quantock, the story sustains, nevertheless, the associations of menacing tone and of isolation of human spirit to be found in the others, set in earlier periods. The fictional dates of the other nine range from 'the early part of the reign of the first King James', the time of **'The Lady Penelope'**, to 'some fifty years ago', when **'The Duchess of Hamptonshire'** takes place—but we note that the latter was first published as **'The Impulsive Lady of Croome Castle'** in *Light* in 1878. Apart from **'Anna, Lady Baxby'**, in 'the time of the great Civil War' the remainder by definition or implication are set in the eighteenth century. The historical setting, however, is largely incidental, a common integrant re-enforcing the frame, and perhaps, if we insist, lending a distant plausibility to some of Hardy's wilder invention. But abnormalities of situation and behaviour occur no more frequently in **Noble Dames** than in some of the more contemporary fiction—the reddleman and Wildeve gambling by the light of fireflies in *The Return of the Native* or the murder of Sue's children by the grotesque Father Time in *Jude,* to mention just two. We receive no precise feeling of historical place, nor does it seem intended or necessary to the process of the story except in the sense of reinvigorating antiquity in contemporary idiom and metaphor, of the resurrection of ancient gossip and the rattling of dry bones. There is, undoubtedly, a certain superficial charm about the dating which hangs about the stories like motes over 'the varnished skulls, urns, penates, tesserae, costumes, coats of mail, weapons and missals' in the museum, but even the most modern of Hardy's writing is endowed with a particular and mannered historical connection.

Two stories, **'The Duchess of Hamptonshire'** and **'Barbara of the House of Grebe'**, markedly at variance in the application of their spiritual intensities yet ascertainably linked by the piteous innocence of their heroines, come immediately to mind as instances where historical light makes a refractive contribution to the general illusion of story-telling but has little to do with the inner and ultimate illumination of heart and station. This is more patently obvious in the disparity of their fictional dates: 'Hamptonshire', some 'fifty years ago', and 'Glebe' some 'twenty years before the end of the last century'. Mr Alwyn Hill is a poor curate, though with eyes so dreamy that 'to look long into them was like ascending and floating among summer clouds' (p. 192), assistant to the Rector, the Honourable and Reverend Mr Oldbourne, whose parish is dominated by 'the ten thousand acres of fat un-impeachable soil' of the Duke of Hamptonshire's estate. Alwyn is in love with Emmeline, Oldbourne's daughter, and she is forced, against her will, to marry the Duke, a fearsome man of 'bomb-like' oaths and a large mouth. Hill sails away disconsolate to America. Edmond Willowes, 'one of the handsomest men who ever set his lips on a maid's' (p. 63), is nevertheless a widow-woman's son (the phrase classifies him socially), whose 'father or grandfather was the last of the old glass-painters in that place' (p. 59), is in love with Barbara, daughter of Sir John and Lady Grebe, and elopes with her. The house of Grebe takes it fairly well, considering his position and theirs—the lower reaches of the upper classes—and after some knock-about dialogue when the penitent runaways return, they pack him off to Europe with a tutor for a year's improvement courses, 'till he became polished outwardly and inwardly to the degree required in the husband of such a lady as Barbara' (p. 60).

As well as chance and social disapprobation, another factor is missing from Hardy's Fourier-inspired diagrams of human passion, mind and character, a factor which is abundantly crucial in his fiction in both joyous and baneful forms, and that is humour, another word about which we must be linguistically commodious. Both these sad love stories open with a jaunty air, with the author setting a puckish distance between himself (and the reader) and any blatant narrative commitment; and even when the monsters of will and passion turn the screws of human distress and loneliness, a grim playfulness is to be discovered of the kind that suffuses the bleaker passages of Aphra Behn, say, or Graham Greene. Hamptonshire, ducally boorish, also falls at first sight in love with Emmeline, takes 'fire to a degree that was well nigh terrible' and goes home 'like a man who had seen a spirit. He ascended to the picture-gallery of his castle, and there passed some time in staring at the bygone beauties of his line as if he had never before considered what an important part those specimens of womankind played in the evolution of the Saxelbye race. He dined alone, drank rather freely, and declared to himself that Emmeline Oldbourne must be his' (p. 193). After Barbara's decampment with Willowes, her father and mother 'sat by the fireplace that was spanned by the four-centred arch bearing the family shields on its haunches, and groaned aloud—the lady more than Sir John. "To think that this should have come upon us in our old age!" said he. "Speak for yourself!" she snapped through her sobs, "I am only one-and-forty! . . . Why didn't ye ride faster and overtake 'em!"' (p. 61). The melodramatic jokes and the historical backcloth screen the monsters and the strange spirits without, as human distress gradually insinuates itself through the crevices of the quasi jocular narration, without there ever being any total tragic abandonment.

After Emmeline's peremptory and tearful translation to Duchess of Hamptonshire, Alwyn Hill makes, at her request, a final clandestine visit at which she pleads to sail with him on the *Western Glory*. She can live in England no longer as life is as death to her there. Her 'Antinous in orders' judges that to sneak off together would be sin but the new Duchess argues 'it *cannot* be sin, for I have never wanted to commit sin in my life; and it isn't likely I would begin now, when I pray every day to die and be sent to Heaven out of my misery!' Alwyn, however, is morally adamant and almost the last words we hear from Emmeline are 'Can it be that God holds me in derision?' (pp. 196-7).

The development of divine derision is slower paced in **'The House of Grebe'** [**"Barbara of the House of Grebe"**]. This tale's melodramatic equivalent to the Duke of Hamptonshire, whose uncomplicated assumption of droit de seigneur is more arrogant than villainous, is Lord Uplandtowers, who has not negligible affinities with George Eliot's Grandcourt or Henry James's Gilbert Osmond. Like Eliot and James, Hardy, in the case of Hamptonshire, only hints at sadistic practices in the bedroom: 'At first he would only taunt her for her folly in thinking of that milk-and-water parson; but as time went on his charges took a more positive shape. . . . This led to some strange scenes between them which need not be detailed' (p. 195). In contrast, Uplandtowers' sick perversity, his wife-battering of present day interest and idiom, to which he seems pathologically liable, is offered in unceremonious detail and had to be drastically censored for the *Graphic* publication. The first sentence of **'The House of Grebe'** suggests an unusual obsession: 'It was apparently an idea, rather than a passion, that inspired Lord Uplanders' resolve to win her.' From the age of nineteen, just when energy peaks in Hardy's diagram, he lies in wait, to borrow a Wessex simile, like a stoat, biding his sexual time with 'matured and cynical doggedness' until he is ready to seize and capture Barbara, not to devour her, but to torture her. Hardy's villainy in *Noble Dames* is more direct than in his more reputable novels but also, in some impressive ways, more overtly analysed. Uplandtowers' cynicism at nineteen, 'when impulse mostly rules calculation . . . might have owed its existence as much to his succession to the earldom . . . an elevation which jerked him into maturity . . . without his having known adolescence.' He is twelve when he assumes his title but family character has much to do with his sexual oddity: 'Determination was hereditary in his bearers of that escutcheon; sometimes for good, sometimes for evil' (p. 55). If determination is connotative with ambition, in Uplandtowers' case with sexual ambition, then it could be curiously linked to Hardy's diagrammatic tree when Ambition Dominant, a high branch, is shown springing from the trunk from which the Impossible monsters of Passion, Intellect and Will grow out as excrescences. But there speculation must end other than with a notion that ambition, which in the tree top is linked with Friendship, Love and Familism, is, in Uplandtowers' character, associated possibly with some obscenely fungoid means of gratification.

Both Uplandtowers and Hamptonshire are contemptuous of their handsomer rivals, much of the contempt having to do with Willowes' and Hill's inferior caste, to which, in the inflexible English tradition, they are condemned. For all his affection for agricultural workers, stone masons, furze-cutters, shepherds, foresters, thatchers and so on, Hardy, in his personal life, seemed often to be on the verge of touching his forelock as he waits outside the manorial gates, an impulse not always successfully resisted, and later to betray a naive pleasure in rubbing shoulders with the titled. In this respect he was no more and no less in behavioural accord with the majority of Victorian countrymen and women of all degrees of class. Despite the leftward leaning of his first and unpublished novel, *The Poor Man and the Lady,* whose attitudes a canny Meredith advised him to temper, he is not always unambiguous on the matter of class privilege in his fiction but in most writing he is, at least, more ironically observant and objective about these genetic barriers to human intercourse in English life. The handsome young curate, Alwyn Hill, does not really come out of his affair with Emmeline very well. He has no natural nobility, as opposed to the inherited kind, and there are in fact implications, in the after-taste of the tale, that the resolution he lacks may be attributed to his ignoble temperament in the former sense. He deserts Emmeline, much as Angel Clare does Tess,' when she most needs him, inadvertently buries her at sea, and during his nine-year sojourn in Boston, where he becomes a college professor of rhetoric and oratory and passes his winter evenings writing sonnets and elegies ('Lines to an Unfortunate Lady'), he is marked by an inadequacy and flaccidness of purpose which is far from being heroic or noble. This sickly romanticism, which also invests Clare, remains with him on his return to England on learning of the death of the Duke.

Hill's elation at the prospect of being re-united with Emmeline on an unimpeachable basis is bolstered by prissy assumptions as he winds up his professional affairs: 'If she has continued to love me nine years she will love me ten; she will think the more tenderly of me when her present hours of solitude have done their proper work' (p. 200). His tender anticipation, however, is followed by a series of disappointments during which his heroic stature shrinks: the dismal awareness on his return to the castle that the present Duchess is Hamptonshire's second wife: 'The wretched Alwyn murmured something about a stitch in his side from walking' (p. 202); the revelation of the villager at the ball: 'She ran away years and years ago with the young curate' (p. 202); the tracing of Captain Wheeler of the *Western Glory:* 'She took a common berth among the poorest emigrants . . . she died on the voyage out, at about five days' sail from Plymouth . . . she seemed a lady in manners and education' (p. 204); all these occasions do little, despite the intransigeant ironies, to exculpate his basic unworthiness. There is to be for Hill no ante mortem enjoyment of his deserted loved one as there is for Angel Clare. Alwyn's romance had ended before he reached America: 'On that unhappy evening when he left Emmeline in the shrubbery, forbidding her to follow him because it would be a sin, she must have disobeyed. She must have followed at his heels silently through the darkness, like a poor pet animal that will not be driven back. She could have accumulated nothing for the journey. . . . Her intention had doubtless been to make her presence on board known to him as soon as she could muster courage to do so' (pp. 205-6). That courage is never found but it has in the conscience of the story already been wryly displayed.

One of Hardy's stories, **'A Tragedy of Two Ambitions'**, collected in *Life's Little Ironies,* concerns two brothers who are determined to better themselves despite the social drag of their father, a drunken, dissipated millwright. It is a sad and persuasive tale. Hamptonshire and Hill are obviously fired by ambition of a discrepantly sexual kind but neither is really worthy of little Emmeline in any sort of moral or chivalrous or passionate context. In their contrary approaches of aggression and passivity, we witness yet one more promulgation of Hardy's dilemma of pairing where neither brutal machismo nor moral meekness serves love's final purpose as Troy and Oak, Fitzpiers and Winterborne well illustrate. The dames of the noble group are sometimes endowed with a nobility which is not inherited or married into, which is associated with concepts of behaviour and entailment of mediaeval noblesse, and which can belong, in any century, to a less restricted population, in the form of courageous decency—for all the contemporary debasement of this phrase. Within the limitations of her role in the story Emmeline is such a one. She is isolated and shy and 'whenever a strange visitor came to her father's house she slipped into the orchard and remained till he was gone, ridiculing her weakness in apostrophes but unable to overcome it' (p. 193); and she suffers for being beautiful at the hands of the only three men she really knows, her father, her husband and her lover. Betrayed by Oldbourne and maltreated by Hamptonshire, she looks for succour and romance to the young curate with whom she once has had 'some sweet and secret understanding', but, like so many would-be heroes in Hardy's fiction, Alwyn Hill just does not measure up. Emmeline 'had been bred in comparative solitude; a reencounter with men troubled and confused her' (p. 193); and during the course of her brief existence as the Duchess of Hamptonshire she is in the habit of 'turning to the wainscot and shedding stupid scalding tears at a time when a right-minded lady would have been overhauling her wardrobe' (p. 195). These tears are vain because the monsters of passion and will are, in Alwyn, mice, and his talents employed in Boston for rhetoric and oratory, sonnets and elegies, are not of the stuff to rescue Emmeline. Hardy concludes the story in his own elegiac phrase: 'Thus the ten years' chapter of Alwyn Hill's romance wound itself up under his eyes. That the poor young woman in the steerage had been the young Duchess of Hamptonshire was never publicly disclosed. Hill had no longer any reason for remaining in England and soon after left its shores with no intention to return (p. 206). Among the listening members of the Field and Antiquarian Club, Hardy informs us gratuitously, the Bookworm seems to be impressed by the quiet gentleman's tale.

'The House of Grebe' is told by the surgeon and on its completion evokes from the impressionable Bookworm sympathy for Barbara: 'a woman's natural instinct of fidelity would, indeed, send back her heart to a man after his death in a truly wonderful manner sometimes—if anything occurred to put before her forcibly the original affection between them, and his original aspect in her eyes—whatever his inferiority may have been, social or otherwise' (p. 92). The waiting game in this story is played not by the putative true lover, on the outskirts of privilege, in a badly matched rivalry with a duke of the realm, but by an earl, at the centre of power and wealth, patiently observing, with demonic amusement, the floundering around of the young married couple as the parents try to sculp an interloper into social acceptability. Memories are stirred of the sly voyeurism of William Dare, who seems to achieve gratification through watching the misfortune of others in *A Laodicean,* written some ten years previously. Lord Uplandtowers, 'though not yet thirty, had chuckled like a caustic fogey of threescore when he heard of Barbara's terror and flight at her husband's return' (pp. 77-8), and like Dare he seems to be satisfying some sexual need even at this period as he waits the achievement of 'the secret design of his heart' (p. 56). The physical romance between Barbara and Edmond Willowes, though sufficiently detailed with Hardy's tantalizing amalgam of

the eagerness, freshness and pain of love, is brief. They elope and 'the young married lovers, caring no more about their blood than about ditch-water, were intensely happy' (p. 61); they return to Barbara's family house of Grebe, 'not a word of chiding had been uttered to the pair' (p. 63); Willowes makes his cultural odyssey to the Continent where he is badly scarred by some fiery beams after heroically saving lives in a burning theatre in Venice; he returns with a face too horrible for his wife to tolerate—'a quick spasm of horror had passed through her' when the dreadful spectacle, 'this human remnant, this *écorché*' is revealed (pp. 73-4); he departs, and after a year or two is presumed dead. What Uplandtowers has to battle when he becomes Barbara's second husband is her post mortem infatuation, her falling in love again with Willowes after his death, especially, as the Bookworm suggests, when something occurs to remind her of his former beauty and her former passion.

If the first part of the **'House of Grebe'** raises the excitement of a swiftly unfolding romantic melodrama with glorious exploitation of foreign heroism, but with not too subtle intimations of a localized evil, then the second half is more static, graphically analysing the domestic torture to which Barbara is subject over a sustained period. It is nowadays more generally recognized that the social phenomenon of wife-battering is not limited to physical abuse only and that mental and emotional forms of marital assault can often be much more degrading and distressful. For all the curious levity which paradoxically lies about the grimness of this story, and for that matter all the stories in the volume, Hardy has from the time of the writing of *A Pair of Blue Eyes* been concerned with the psychological pain of women, inflicted on them, in a few cases unwittingly, by well-meaning, or resentful, or jealous or bumptiously malicious husbands and lovers, and, in the case of Miss Aldclyffe and Mrs Yeobright, sons. Hardy's women may well be erratically directed (with the splendid exception of Ethelberta) by what the Victorians called fickleness but, from the time of Elfride, who is so emotionally vulnerable to the preposterous Henry Knight, theirs is for undue periods an account of spiritual and mental suffering, for the most part undeservedly inflicted. The independent Bathsheba, inured to the pastoral heroics of Oak and the middle-aged anguish of Boldwood, is emotionally whipped by a nasty cavalry sergeant; Viviette, Lady Constantine, mature and well-connected, is cut to the heart-strings by the adolescent Swithin St Cleeve; in one of the most ambivalent relationships in Hardy's fiction, Elizabeth-Jane agonizes over the intemperate passions of her adoptive father, Henchard; Grace Melbury, together with two other women, is exploited by Fitzpiers; and finally, just before writing the **'House of Grebe'**, Hardy entitled Phase the Fifth of *Tess* 'The Woman Pays'.

In the story of Barbara there are less cautious occlusions of actual and suggestive detail than in all the previous cases with the exception of *Tess,* whose heroine's pain apparently still lingered with the author. After being fairly easily won by Uplandtowers—'hers was essentially one of these sweet-pea or with-wind natures which require a twig of stouter fibre than its own to hang upon and bloom' (p. 78)—Barbara, as she has previously warned, has not the ability to love the Earl passionately and 'now her lack of warmth seemed to irritate him, and he conducted himself towards her with a resentfulness which led to her passing many hours with him in painful silence' (p. 79). This unpropitious start to their marriage only substantiates some of Barbara's earlier misgivings which she had fairly easily dismissed, and an interesting feature of this phase is the presence of a 'normal' husbandly reaction in Uplandtowers' sexual surliness, whereas before this time, and later, his expectancy and gratification seem to be deployed in more unusual directions. They could no doubt be diagnosed psychologically as a slowly churning sadism, but this pseudo-scientific jargon does not penetrate the weird miasma of their doomed marriage. Uplandtowers behaves at times like any ordinary inconsiderate husband who, among other things, blames his wife for not presenting him with an heir ('he had set his mind upon a lineal successor'). This vulgar fallibility in such an arrogant and purposeful lord is an essential and surprisingly cogent part of Hardy's creation of a bizarre evil, which, already well germinated in the person of the Earl, is to invest his marriage and turn the once radiant and passionate Barbara into a sickly woman condemned to a cowed life of repeated and unsuccessful pregnancies: 'At length, completely worn out in mind and body, Lady Uplandtowers was taken abroad by her husband, to try the effect of a more genial climate upon her wasted frame. But nothing availed to strengthen her and she died at Florence . . .' (pp. 90-1). What I have designated as Uplandtowers' 'normal' behaviour—commonly recognizable spots of jealousy and churlishness—disagreeable as it is, nevertheless contributes, also, a pathological credibility to his sexual eccentricity. As, on the arrival of Willowes' statue from Pisa which immediately lightens her nuptial melancholy, Barbara moves off into a world of intensely experienced fantasies of a reborn romance, so the frustrated earl starts to tease and satisfy his own exceptional cravings; and it would appear that this creepy activity, solitarily and destructively indulged, is more pleasurable for him than any kind of real love from his wife. But this latter affection is, in any case, to be

denied him; and her lunatic dependency on him consequent to her permanent revulsion for Willowes ('How fright could have affected such a change of idiosyncrasy learned physicians alone can say'), and her 'obsequious amativeness' in their pursuit of a male heir, comprise a major strand of their marriage's web of perversion and irony. For all the degrees of contrast in their philosophic temperaments, Browning and Hardy have much in common in their sighting of human perspectives. The Duke of Ferrara, in 'My Last Duchess', suggests an appalling kinship of autocratic cruelty with the fifth Earl, Lord Uplandtowers. After witnessing the swiftly germinating fantasies and antics of his wife as, with a Pygmalion twist, she falls in love with a statue, Uplandtowers, to adapt the phrase of his Italian counterpart, determines that all smiles shall stop together.

Barbara's smiles are stopped by means of a fiendishly simple expedient, not so immediate in fatal effect as Ferrara's, but affording for Uplandtowers a more prolonged pleasure and ending in his wife's gradual physical wasting, increasing despondency and ultimate death. The melodrama of Uplandtowers' brutality, beside feeding the ordinary innocuous reader's fascination for horror, uncovers, as so many fictions of extreme cruelty do consistently from the time of the ancient Greek 'romances', human predispositions and potential, not more than a filament removed from so-called normal posture, and this may be part of the reason for Hardy's investing Uplandtowers' scheme of retribution and correction with a defiant jauntiness. Barbara undergoes a mystic transformation on the arrival of the statue, 'a full-length figure, in the purest Carrara marble, representing Edmond Willowes in all his original beauty' (p. 81). Having set up the statue in a 'tabernacle' in her boudoir, which, deserting her marital bed, she nightly visits, she experiences, with dishevelled hair and streaming tears, grief and a racking passion which exasperates Uplandtowers: 'My only love . . . I am ever faithful to you . . . during the long hours of the day, and in the night-watches. . . . I am always yours!' (p. 83). Uplandtowers rationalizes his motives for stopping this rot: 'This is where we evaporate—this is where my hopes of a successor in the title dissolve. . . . This must be seen to verily!' (p. 84). But jealousy and the desire for an heir, formidable though they may be, pale before the malign enjoyment of the means he uses to satisfy both. After consultation with the tutor on details of Willowes' disfigurement ('neither nose nor ears, nor lips scarcely!') he employs a sign-painter and has the handsome statue, Barbara's 'Phoebus-Apollo', converted into a sickeningly life-like burnt offering: 'A statue should represent a man as he appeared in life, and that's as he appeared. Ha! ha!' (p. 85). The trick is played 'to good purpose', he adds, presumably in exculpation of himself, to ensure an heir, but subconsciously it betrays the workings of arrogance and jealousy, and perhaps even further removed from his immediate awareness it provides the prospect for the pleasure he is about to take in his wife's humiliation and subjection.

Hardy's stagy villains frequent his fiction—Aeneas Manston, Baron von Xanten, Alec d'Urberville—often like comic fugitives from the Victorian theatre, but also bearing in their designated caricature, as Dickens' Quilps and Fagins do, uneasy intimations of humanity's common heritage of savagery. In his 'seeing to' Barbara's sexual obsession, Uplandtowers outdoes all the others in the battering of his demented wife into a cowed sanity. In the Earl's calculated plan of correction Hardy's elemental monsters of passion and will are manifest in knotted and twisted vagaries. Barbara is shocked into unconsciousness when, on a nightly visit to her tabernacle, she first sees the newly mutilated replica of Willowes and Uplandtowers carries her back to her room, 'endeavouring as he went to disperse her terrors by a laugh in her ear, oddly compounded of causticity, predilection and brutality' (p. 86). His weird chat to her, still unconscious in his arms, is persuasively maniacal with its condescending argot of fatherly comforting: 'Frightened, dear one, hey? What a baby 'tis! Only a joke, sure, Barbara—a splendid joke! But a baby should not go to closets at midnight to look for the ghost of the dear departed! If it do it must expect to be terrified at his aspect—ho—ho—ho!' (p. 86). When, however, she recovers consciousness, his Heathcliffian maladroitness is quite shaken off and he begins a stern inquisition, 'do you love him—eh?' which is to last until all feeling is hounded from her: 'Another dose or two and she will be cured' (p. 87).

The cure is more drastic than ever he could have visualized, and the consequences of it not at all what he intended. Having set up the monstrous statue in their own bedroom and forcing her to gaze upon it night after night, Uplandtowers realizes he has pushed the cure too far: 'when . . . she lay staring with immense wild eyes at the horrid fascination, on a sudden she gave an unnatural laugh; she laughed more and more, staring at the image, till she literally shrieked with laughter' (p. 88). Barbara collapses into an epileptic fit and on regaining consciousness her personality and obsessions change, and her dependency, her servile unhealthy affection for 'a perverse and cruel man' become a charge within the field of his evil. In a pathetic, enervated way she has become assimilated into his badness. She will not be out of his sight, will not have a separate sitting room, follows him around, is jealous of his attentions to other women 'till at length

her very fidelity became a burden to him, absorbing his time and curtailing his liberty, and causing him to curse and swear' (p. 90). And the evil sickness with which he infects their marriage practically wipes out the next generation: 'in brief she bore him no less than eleven children in the nine following years, but half of them came prematurely into the world, or died a few days old; only one, a girl, attained to maturity' (p. 90).

I have purposely treated **'The Duchess of Hamptonshire'** and **'Barbara of the House of Grebe'** at some length partly in order to question the generally received criticism that *A Group of Noble Dames* is not of much account in the Hardy canon—with the quite outstanding exception of Brady's chapter on the collection. She sees the stories as 'ambivalent exempla', which 'challenge the reader to think with a more enlightened point of view about the central moral issues which have led to such suffering and stifling of human affections'.[10] Indeed. There is much to be mined, not only through a critical connection of the fictional material and the theoretical notions of Hardy's early drawings, rather elemental but amusing as this may be, but also in discovering, and this does not exclude the primary clues of the drawings, the directions in which narrative suggestiveness leads; in cutting, too, the face of the morality, the ironic intimations, without in any way marring or interfering with the essential and supreme entertainment value of the tales, the simple human joy in story-telling. I have earlier referred to the apparently ambiguous jocularity which both tempers and underscores the cruelty and severity of these two stories; and this conjunction can be associated with their not being, or seeming, so personally felt or committed. One of the minor consequences of their historical isolation may be a greater diagnostic distance between author and character, between author and incident, as though Hardy is both shaking and vitalizing the dry bones of county legend and simultaneously labelling them with a somewhat unceremonious levity. His narrative postscript to **'The House of Grebe'** suggests, in its deceptive casualness, a disconcerting devaluation of the savagery and sadness of the main tale: 'Perhaps it may not be so generally known that, during the enlargement of the Hall for the sixth Earl, while digging in the grounds for the new foundation, the broken fragments of a marble statue were unearthed. They were submitted to various antiquaries who said that . . . the statue seemed to be that of a mutilated Roman satyr; or, if not, an allegorical figure of Death' (p. 91). It is as though any intimacy of sympathy, of revulsion or of understanding, for Uplandtowers, or for Barbara or Willowes for that matter, is authorially disallowed.

The noble dames (or for that matter the distinctive presence of the nobility as a species) in the collection do not form exclusively the major centres of interest. The Crimson Maltster's Tale—and how alien is he from the Ancient Maltster of Warren's who knew Shepherd Oak's grandparents at Norcombe—is a narrative jeu d'esprit at the expense of Squire Petrick rather than his lady and this is a story, incidentally, where the pathetic human joke relies on social misconception rather than on social conflict. Timothy is the unambitious grandson of an entrepreneurial lawyer, 'that trump of mortgagees', who outwitted the local nobility and acquired much of their lands, and is the personage in a limited cast who is presented for special but indulgent scrutiny in **'Squire Petrick's Lady'**. Maria Heymere, the dame of the story **'The Lady Icenway'**, a tale of casual marital deception, told unexpectedly by the 'chink-eyed churchwarden' after he is 'thoroughly primed' (p. 133), is an aberrant creature who rationalizes her passion and who in her wilful personality offers a forbidding extension of Hardy's concept of womanly fickleness. Yet the substantial tolerance and heart of the tale, the inevitable heartache which Hardy associates with the powerlessness of the good, belong to her bigamous first husband, Anderling, who consciously committed bigamy in marrying her—although, in a strictly legal sense, both Icenway and Maria are also guilty of the same crime. Besides shifting the emphasis from the eponymous dames, these two stories each adjust the perspective of nobility in *A Group of Noble Dames* as a whole.

Both the crimson maltster and Timothy Petrick are untainted by any blue blood, but one of the major proposals of **'Squire Petrick's Lady'** concerns the absurdity of popular belief in the aristocracy's vested grace, its genetic gifts, its inherited lineaments in facial feature and assumptions in political and military power and even in arts and letters. Not for the first time we are faced with Hardyan ambiguities. Whilst accepting the dilemma and perplexity of Petrick, as, despite a certain wicked archness and bold fantasy of a tale convincingly recorded, we question the narrative accessories, we have to consider to what extent 'the illustrious house ennobled as the Dukes of Southwesterland' is set up as a tease, and also what really eats at Timothy's heart. Similar questions arise in the case of the Guyanian expatriate, Anderling, in **'The Lady Icenway'**. After an initial disastrous marriage in Quebec to 'a woman whose reputation proved to be in every way bad and scandalous' (p. 139), Anderling falls in love with, and for the rest of his life remains devoted to, Maria Heymere, whom he marries with the pious hope that his first wife has died. Although she lives 'in "a faire maner-place"' . . . in one of the greenest bits of woodland between Bristol and

the city of Exonbury' (p. 137), Miss Heymere is of no great social account in Outer Wessex, but when she becomes Lady Icenway, her second husband being 'a worthy man of noble birth and title', Anderling, now penniless and destitute, is confronted with the imperiousness of her acquired nobility and is reduced to humiliating stratagems to catch a glimpse of his child. A primary matter to notice is that in the world of Hardy's noble dames her kind of aristocratic behaviour is not necessarily inherited. Long-standing Hardyan factors of will and ambition—passion here is either deluded or comparatively mute, and only its effect is monstrous—work their customary havoc in these two stories, chance occurrences as usual swing narrative directions, and some fear of scandal is sown here and there; but the influence and workings of the nobility, with its arching eminence and scandalous proportions, are proposed with a matter-of-factness which is deceptive. I have already noted Hardy's suspect awe of county aristocrats, themselves adhering punctiliously to an ordained pecking order; and although this collection is not only in a titular way very much about them, it could be, as we disassemble his machinery of nobility in these two stories, that, like the fact of their historical setting, Hardyan nobility is, to switch metaphors, more of a decorative harness, an overlay of brass and bells, to the final and humane meanings. Hardy's venial fallibility to that kind of patronage in his personal life is matched by both tolerance and cynicism in his writing, and he implies that Petrickian self-abasement and envy of the handsomer and the mightier is a universal characteristic not restricted to lords and lawyers, and to that extent the primacy of the peerage in the tales is diminished.

Although thanks to his grandfather he is wealthy enough, Squire Petrick—even his title bears an idiomatic derision—despises his present class and his past ancestry: 'He considered what ugly, idle, hard-drinking scamps many of his own relations had been; the miserable scriveners, usurers, and pawnbrokers that he had numbered among his forefathers' (pp. 158-9). Two of these forefathers have special relevance to his story, and at one (I think deliberately misleading) level of interpretation, they represent a demeaning bloodstock. His grandfather, also Timothy, who has become the owner of vast estates 'by granting sums of money on their title deeds' (p. 153), has been obviously a very astute business man, who, being also a lawyer, has successfully kept on the right side of the law. An unnamed uncle, with a particularly odious 'bull-lip', is transported for life for having forged a will, a crime of which, in ironically mitigating circumstances, Petrick is also guilty. The difference between this ancestry and, say, the Southwesterlands' may, for all Petrick's widower's hallucinations, be fundamentally very slight. Because of the jolt to his customary placidity shortly after the birth of his first and only son, the difference becomes monstrously exaggerated in Petrick's imagination and swells into so much of an obsession with him that he devoutly wishes to be convinced that the young Marquis of Christminster, son of the Duke of Southwesterland, has slept with Petrick's wife, Annetta, and fathered the child, Rupert. Four years after **'Squire Petrick's Lady'**, Hardy wrote **'An Imaginative Woman'** in which Ella Marchmill believes she has slept with a poet, Robert Trewe, and falsely confesses just before she dies in childbirth that Trewe is the father of her child; and it is noticeable in this later story, which shares a common theme of delusion in both husband and wife, that there is no factor of nobility. Ella's fantasy-lover is a poet, Annetta's a marquis; in other words the object of projected dream is a person removed by sleight of romanticism from what both wives regard as the dullness of their daily lives.

Petrick's vicarious delusions of grandeur have, although presented with a deviant humour, a sadder twist. His need to be associated with a noble presence, partly to counter his younger brother's smarter marriage, in the form of his wife's supposedly illegitimate son, is the consequence of his wife's prenatal fantasy. Before she relates to him 'an incident concerning the baby's parentage', Petrick seems perfectly content with his unaristocratic life. Though descended from a scheming family he is 'no great schemer himself'. Although he learns later that his wife's mother and grandmother have been subject 'to believing in certain dreams as realities' (p. 161), his early married life, conducted in the comfort of plebeian affluence, seems to be contentedly untoward. His heart has ever been 'greatly moved by sentiments which did not run in the groove of ambition; and on this account he had not married well, as the saying is; his wife having been the daughter of a family of no better beginnings than his own' (p. 154). He has married in 'a high tide of infatuation', and up to the time of the birth of his son has 'never found reason to regret his choice'. On Annetta's death, her confusion of dreams and realities is maritally transferred, and Petrick becomes the coxcomb of an intransigeant class system that over the centuries has become ingrained into the consciousness and patterns of behaviour of its victims.

In that he partly 'belongs' but is self-exiled in more than one sense, Anderling is paradoxically one of the victims; but in his story the jocularity is harsher and the presumptuousness of established class bears down on him to his death more indirectly. For all his being of Dutch extraction and a 'colonial', his wealth and the fact that her uncle is only too ready to marry off Maria gain him easy access to the lower slopes of the nobility where the Heymeres belong. In any Hardyan

fiction the familiar reader is liable to take for granted the incidence of fortuity—hap, hazard, accident, whatever—but it is as well occasionally to pause and take stock, and in this volume **'The Lady Icenway'** is as good a story as any in which to do this. Anderling's first meeting with Maria is fortuitous—she falls off her horse just as he appears; he learns that his first wife is still alive just after his marriage to Maria and just before sailing with her to Paramaribo; Maria receives Anderling's letter telling of his Quebecoise's death just after she has married Icenway and just before Anderling's return; at one time in his life Anderling happens to have become knowledgeable about tulip culture and thus is qualified for a job as under-gardener in the conservatories of Icenway's mansion; Maria, who so swiftly and inconveniently conceived with Anderling, cannot do the same with Icenway; when the possibly sterile peer complains about this to Maria—'All will go to that dolt of a cousin!' (p. 147)—she visits the under-gardener with the intention of becoming impregnated, but he is dying and the final chance is expressed in his infatuated irony: 'Too late, my darling, too late!' (p. 148) At any one of these improbable, or, depending on one's degree of narrative trust, plausible intersections, the fiction could have taken another direction. The Hardy familiar is accustomed to this, but occasionally the haphazard enormities need to be reaffirmed, although in **'The Lady Icenway'** they work no more or no less directly untoward than anywhere else in Hardy's fiction.

Chance aside, Anderling has access to Maria because he is a gentleman, in that advantaged sense, if not grandly entitled. His instinctual behaviour is acceptable and he subscribes to the eclectic codes of English—and European—gentry even when, totally blinded to his condition by his ineffable love for his wife and child, he accepts uncaringly the menial job in the nursery hot-houses. He suffers and dies because of the heritage system and because the one to whom he is passionately enslaved is sagaciously and unsentimentally slotted into it and has reached a higher level than she might have expected through a marriage which she is determined to protect. Anderling's effacement of self, in the face of such conceit and resolve, induces the same sort of anguish and exasperation as does Marty South's sustained disregard for self and happiness in *The Woodlanders*; but at least in that novel Giles, the object of Marty's all-consuming sacrifice, possesses, despite his critical insensitivity, many endearing and sterling qualities. It is hard to find any in Lady Icenway. Anderling may not altogether share Petrick's ignorance of and distorted veneration for the nobility; but from the moment of his first encounter with her, he finds himself at the mercy of a love for

Maria which persists to the moment of his death, a sardonic moment when he suddenly sees the grim joke of his wasted passion. She, physically attractive, of 'exceeding great beauty', riding in the woodland, has at first the semblance of a traditional romantic heroine, but the ancient qualities of romance, modesty, faithfulness, kindness and so on, stop there, after the first few lines, as though the chink-eyed churchwarden were leading us up the wrong aisle. Maria is narrow-minded but intelligent enough for her purposes, grossly insensitive in a nastier way than Giles, without pity and almost without fear and—a bullying presence to which Anderling always meekly bows—of an imperious manner and bad temper: 'the spirit of this proud and masterful lady showed itself in violent turmoil, like the raging of a nor'-west thunderstorm' (p. 139). It is before such a purposeful and shrewish lady that Anderling ignominiously abases himself. His extraordinary subjection to Maria's will, however, is not brought on by any undue obsequiousness of the English aristocrats; for, after all, he is a financially independent foreigner with both material assets and social graces and exhibits none of the grudging envy of, say, the crimson maltster. In certain deceptive lights—there are many in this very short story—Anderling with his 'amorous temperament' recalls occasionally the mysterious gentleman from South Carolina who courted so tempestuously Felice Charmond, and sometimes the sad and lonely figure of Farmer Boldwood, reduced to a nerveless disregard of his business affairs after receiving Bathsheba's valentine. It is to the compulsion of his unaccountable devotion, rather than to undue esteem for nobility, that Anderling is ingloriously subject.

Even though the narrative bias militates against the supposition, matters are not so different in the case of Squire Petrick. Petrick's disappointment in discovering that Rupert is his own son, that his wife has been faithful to him and that she has not foisted on him the illegitimate child of the Marquis of Christminster, apart from being a good Antiquarian Club joke, has a complexer source than mere envy and adulation of the nobility. At the conclusion of the master-malster's story, the surgeon, the Colonel, the historian and the Spark welcome 'such subtle and instructive psychological studies' and demand another story of 'curious mental delusion' (p. 163). In one way or another most of Hardy's fiction is strewn with mental delusions of greatly differing degrees of severity, generally without any aristocratic connection. With a rather pedagogic humour, characteristic of the late Victorian essay, Hardy once advised that no matter how preposterous his writings an 'author should be swallowed whole',[11] and this is obviously what can be done with uncritical

enjoyment in the reading of **'Squire Petrick's Lady'**. But there is finally more than preposterousness in the situation and monsters lurk behind the jest, good as it is.

Petrick's susceptibility, in the bewildered aftermath of a happy marriage and his wife's sudden death, to a delight in delegated paternity ennobled by adultery tugs, it is true, only gently at our sense of pathos. Feelings do not run very deeply and there is no great harm done except perhaps to Rupert, whose father's changing affections must seem unaccountable, but who does not appear to be very perturbed by their inconsistency. Petrick's ambition is perversely directed but not a matter of tremendous moment, and even the changing of the grandfather's will, in and out of the favour of Petrick's younger brother, is not charged with any particular unease about human injustice. The effect on Petrick of his wife's deception, both imagined and factual, only thickens the jocular canopy of the volume as a whole, and his hallucinations inspire some delightful lines which may well be swallowed whole. They are chiefly concerned with the imaginary and real genetic features of Rupert's face; but on his first noticing his son, and before the fun starts, there is, ambiguously in such a story, a passage of human thoughtfulness. Petrick comes upon his little boy playing with a snuff-box and sneezing: 'Then the man with the encrusted heart became interested in the little fellow's persistence in his play under such discomforts; he looked into the child's face, saw there his wife's countenance, though he did not see his own, and fell into thought on the piteousness of childhood—particularly of despised and rejected childhood, like this before him' (pp. 156-7).

The satire blowing across this little narrative drops at this point and the joke is momentarily deflated as the ubiquitous and ever imminent presence of Hardy's 'loving-kindness' intrudes. Yet as the tale gathers speed again, the little fellow appears not to be so badly damaged by his rejected childhood and in fact much of the irony depends on his father's developing affection for Rupert before the fashioning of any self-conscious motive. Over the years, however, Petrick's love for the child becomes linked to his pride in Rupert's illegitimacy and his wife's instinctual sagacity is highly praised. He is proud of her faithlessness: 'She was a woman of grand instincts after all. . . . To fix her choice upon the immediate successor in that ducal line—it was finely conceived! Had he been of low blood like myself or my relations she would scarce have deserved the harsh measure that I have dealt out to her and her offspring. How much less then, when grovelling tastes were furthest from her soul!' (p. 158). The pun in the word 'conceived' must be unintentional, and its authorial innocence affirms the basic simplicity of the unscheming Timothy's mind and delusions. Much of the joke lies in stretching such delusions to the limits of credulity allowed in a realistic story, but this kind of psychological study, as apprehended by the Club, can accommodate entertainment of a fiendish joviality with only a little room for loving-kindness. The contrast between aristocratic and plebeian potential, superbly characterized by the 'elegant knife-edged nose' of the Dukes of Southwesterland and 'the broad nostril and hollow bridge' of grandfather Timothy, constitutes part of the satiric superficiality of the story; but the motor of this psychological study generates a universal absurdity of which the traditional English grandee system is only one of a number of manifestations.

A remarkable variation in tragic pitch is evident in the progress of the substitute heroes of these two stories. In both there is 'so little cause for carolings', as Hardy protests to a singing thrush at the end of the nineteenth century, but the burden of lovelessness and the pain of unreturned affection are disproportionately large in **'The Lady Icenway'**. With the disconsolateness and unrewarded persistence of Anderling we touch the country of George Eliot's heart, who herself so dreaded not being loved, whilst the discomfiture of Petrick, basically decent though he is, arises almost accidentally in the cause of other narrative theses. 'The intolerable antilogy', Hardy also laments, this time in *The Dynasts*, 'of making figments feel', and it is the rawness of feelings, of both character and reader, which distinguishes **'The Lady Icenway'** and so markedly sets it off from most of the other stories in this collection. Of the primary human attributes which Hardy so jejunely delineated in 1863, the impossible monster of passion is, in the person of Anderling, tamed and dressed with dignity but at great emotional cost. The Dutchman's terminal infatuation constitutes a losing delusion which is brutally obvious even (and therein lies the simple poignancy) to himself. Timothy Petrick's, too, is a hopeless delusion, but we can entertain this 'instructive psychological study', like the Club members, with equanimity.

Any critical paper which attempts to follow the infinite suggestive contours of Hardy's fiction, even a small sampling of it, must accommodate its own induced ambiguities. The contrarieties are intrinsic and not only run deep but are cross-grained. To borrow once more a Wessex simile, the philosophic hints, the humane remoteness and the sardonic protests of bewilderment among other quiet directives are often modestly concealed like wild violets in a Dorset coppice, and so we must need set down our criticism in imitation, in a series of seemings and searchings. I started with drawings stuck on the fly leaf of Hardy's notebook and it is from these youthful confidences, be-

cause he always builds on basic simplicities, that Hardy draws initially his short stories in *Noble Dames*. At the foundation level 'passion dominant' controls, in strikingly dissimilar ways, Hill and Willowes as well as Hamptonshire and Uplandtowers. 'Ambition dominant' spurs many of the characters of dear, delightful Wessex of bygone days to varying achievements of success, but particularly Maria Heymere and Lord Uplandtowers, in the one case to gain a title, and in the other, in the final narrative phase, to preserve it. Emmeline, briefly Duchess of Hamptonshire, seeks a world where friendship is dominant and cannot find it; and in fact what is totally missing from the country of the noble dames is anything which substantiates the metaphor of the fruit of 'moral harmony'. Ironically, perhaps, there is a suggestion of it in the narrating chorus, the Antiquarian Club members themselves, who are sheltering from the rain in the peace of a deserted museum and are representative of that same Wessex 'where the honest squires, tradesmen, parsons, clerks, and people still praise the Lord with one voice for His best of all possible worlds' (p. 49). Comparisons between sketch and story are not difficult to make so long as we do not underestimate the insecurely leashed power of human primaries. Obvious and important as these are, however, what is comparably intriguing is what is added to them in the fictional process. The familiar increments are all present and fomenting in *A Group of Noble Dames*—cruel factors of extraneous chance, man-made morality, authorial disposition of humour, historical accessories and the charade of nobility—and they qualify and sustain these stories as much as they do the more august writings. Over-analysis, however, can poison appreciation, and it may be that finally we see lying about the stories a disarming simplicity and we too, again in imitation, may read them without pretensions, savouring only a tale, its fun, and its pity.

Notes

1. I examined this 'commonplace book' in the Dorset County Museum in 1970 thanks to the kindness of Mr R. Peers. See comments on the drawings in Walter F. Wright, *The Shaping of the Dynasts* (Lincoln: University of Nebraska Press, 1967) pp. 28-9 and Lennart A. Bjork (ed.), *The Literary Notes of Thomas Hardy, Vol. 1* (London: Macmillan, 1985) pp. 3-4, where there is a copy of the diagrams, and pp. 239-41.

2. Bjork, p. 200. The translator is John Reynell Morell. Bjork describes Fourier as a 'French Utopian Socialist'.

3. Wright, p. 29.

4. Kristin Brady, *The Short Stories of Thomas Hardy* (New York: St Martin's Press, 1982). Other commentaries on the short stories are to be found in:

Michael Millgate, *Thomas Hardy: A Biography* (New York: Randon House, 1982); and Norman Page, 'Hardy's Short Stories: a Reconsideration', in *Studies in Short Fiction*, XI, 1 (Winter, 1974) 75-84, and *Thomas Hardy* (London: Routledge & Kegan Paul, 1977).

5. Richard Little Purdy, *Thomas Hardy: A Bibliographical Study* (London: Oxford University Press, 1954) pp. 63-5.

6. Thomas Hardy, *A Group of Noble Dames, Library Edition* (London: Macmillan, 1952) pp. 48-9. Other page references are given in the text.

7. Purdy, p. 63. The original six stories with final titles are: 'Barbara of the House of Glebe', 'The Marchioness of Stonehenge', 'Anna, Lady Baxby', 'The Lady Icenway', 'Squire Petrick's Lady', and 'Lady Mottisfont'.

8. They are: 'The First Countess of Wessex', 'The Lady Penelope', 'The Duchess of Hamptonshire', and 'The Honourable Laura'.

9. Brady also makes the inevitable comparison with Angel Clare (p. 82), but it is worth making as Hardy obviously had him still very much in mind.

10. Brady, p. 94.

11. 'The Profitable Reading of Fiction', *The Forum*, March, 1888, collected in Harold Orel (ed.), *Hardy: Personal Writings* (London: Macmillan, 1967) p. 111.

Desmond Hawkins (essay date 1988)

SOURCE: Hawkins, Desmond. Introduction to *Collected Short Stories: The New Wessex Edition*, by Thomas Hardy, pp. xiii-xxiii. London: Macmillan London, 1988.

[*In the following essay, Hawkins investigates the thematic interplay between Hardy's short stories and his novels written during the same period, and provides an overview of the plots and source materials of his more notable tales.*]

Hardy the novelist, Hardy the poet, Hardy the begetter of that remarkable hybrid *The Dynasts*—these are the familiar and much celebrated aspects of Hardy's lifework. But Hardy the short-story writer? Is it perhaps going too far for one man to demand our attention in yet another field?

It is a poor spirit that complains of prodigality. Hardy's was a bountiful pen, in the hand of a man of industrious and unremitting application. That he exercised the full range of fiction, from its grand scale to its miniature, is a matter for rejoicing. Within the narrower compass of the short story he deployed themes and techniques that extend and enrich our appreciation of his novels, and indeed of his poetry also. The kinship that links some of his narrative poems with his short stories is particularly striking. 'The Dance at the Phœnix' and 'A Sunday Morning Tragedy' almost invite translation into prose to take their place in *Life's Little Ironies.*

The issue of sheer size remains. *Paradise Lost* must be regarded as a 'greater' poem than 'Il Penseroso'. By the same token *The Return of the Native* surpasses **'The Withered Arm'**, but it is a sterile criticism that presses the point home. The Himalayas acquire no added dignity by a belittling of the Malvern Hills. Both have their specific qualities and we need both, on their proper terms.

The main body of Hardy's short stories, contributed from 1874 onwards to a variety of periodicals, was brought together—after some revision—in three collected editions, **Wessex Tales, A Group of Noble Dames** and **Life's Little Ironies,** published within six years at the height of his creativity as a novelist. It was in that period, 1888-94, immediately following publication of *The Woodlanders,* that he was writing *Tess of the d'Urbervilles* and *Jude the Obscure.* The volumes of short stories added further weight and substance to his soaring reputation. It is perhaps indicative of his interest in the potential of the short story at that time that he first envisaged *Jude* in this form. In the spring of 1888 he noted as a future project 'A short story of a young man—"who could not go to Oxford"—His struggles and ultimate failure. Suicide'.

The remaining collection of short stories to be published in his lifetime was **A Changed Man,** which did not appear until 1913 and did so then only reluctantly. Hardy's determination to be seen in what he regarded as his true role, as a poet, obliged him increasingly to play down his career as a writer of prose, which he had terminated in the 1890s and did not wish to revive. In a prefatory note to **A Changed Man** he described the contents grudgingly as 'a dozen minor novels' reprinted 'for what they may be worth'. In private correspondence he was more ruthlessly candid. To Sir George Douglas he described the volume of stories as 'mostly bad—published in periodicals 20 years & more ago, which I am unhappily obliged to include in my set of books because pirated editions of some, vilely printed, are in circulation'. To emphasize his displeasure he added: 'I heartily wish I could snuff out several of them'. There were indeed potboilers of mediocre quality in the collection but Hardy's sweeping denigration reflects a mood of irritation in the circumstances of the time rather than a considered judgment. Four or five of the stories, notably **'The Waiting Supper'** and the title story **'A Changed Man'**, certainly merit a place beside his earlier publications.

It might be thought that this final collection, made long after he had ceased to write in the medium, would have gathered into a permanent form every remaining example—even the least—of Hardy's short fiction. There were, however, three further stories that remained uncollected during his lifetime and for many years afterwards. **'Old Mrs Chundle'**, rejected by Hardy, was published in America within a year of his death by his widow, in a women's magazine and in a separate limited edition for collectors, described as 'the only unpublished short story by the late Thomas Hardy'. **'Destiny and a Blue Cloak'** had appeared in the *New York Times* in 1874. **'The Doctor's Legend'** also appeared in America only, in the New York *Independent* in 1891. The three stories were brought together in volume form for the first time in 1977 in the New Wessex Edition of Hardy's complete works. Until then none of the three had been offered to British readers.

The date of **'Destiny and a Blue Cloak'** is particularly interesting. The year 1874 was a momentous one for Hardy, bringing both his first great success as a novelist, with the publication of *Far from the Madding Crowd*, and his marriage to Emma Gifford, thus providing the circumstances in which he finally committed himself to the profession of literature. A request from an American editor for a short story must have been a heartening surprise to a young author whose experience of editors had until recently been one of indifference or rejection. Hurriedly written and probably his first attempt in the *genre*, **'Destiny and a Blue Cloak'** is no masterpiece, but it drew Hardy's attention in a practical way to what could become a second string to his novelist's bow.

In *The Victorian Short Story* (Cambridge, 1986) Harold Orel has emphasized the newness of the short story as an art form and the intensity of its development in the latter part of the nineteenth century, due to a combination of powerful forces. The rapid extension of literacy following new educational initiatives created a widening readership for the magazines and periodicals that were made possible by advances in cheap, mass-circulation printing. In the arts it is often some new technology associated with a changing public demand which is the prime mover of what may appear to be a self-motivated artistic innovation. What distinguishes Hardy and Katherine Mansfield from Richardson and Jane Austen in their attitudes to the short story is not that the earlier writers saw no merit in it but that—to put it crudely—they had no call for it. For them the

only form of fiction that could command a more than ephemeral interest was the novel, elaborately worked out at full length.

So it was that, in writing his novels, Hardy could position himself in a recognizably grand procession led by Defoe and Fielding and Walter Scott and Dickens; but in the craft of the short story he had no such coherent and long-established tradition to draw on, or alternatively to rebel against. In some measure he had to put down his own markers as he ventured forward, testing the ground in various directions at different times. He might put his emphasis on a startling sequence of intricate twists in a plot, like an acrobat going through a series of traps to astonish us. He might turn instead to the lightly sketched humours of village life in Wessex. Yet again he might try to introduce the subtler, more introspective elements in the portrayal of individuals, and particularly women, that play so strong a part in his novels. It is also true that he would sometimes content himself with a proven formula that required little fresh effort and could be despatched in a hurried, impromptu way. Not all the geese here are swans; but a distinct pleasure in reading the best of Hardy's stories is the sense of being present at a strikingly fluid and creative stage in his development. In the 1880s and early 1890s he was reaching his peak of mastery as a novelist, to be superseded so swiftly by the new *persona* of Hardy the poet; and in these vibrant and fertile years he turned his hand also, on a prolific scale, to the additional medium of the short story. It helped him to maintain contact with his audience in the intervals between the publication of his novels; it augmented his reputation and his income; but it also, more positively, extended his talents in new ways and enriched his resourcefulness as a writer of prose fiction.

* * *

In a note made in February 1893 Hardy set down a clear definition of the ground rules on which his stories were based:

> A story must be exceptional enough to justify its telling. We tale-tellers are all Ancient Mariners, and none of us is warranted in stopping Wedding Guests (in other words, the hurrying public) unless he has something more unusual to relate than the ordinary experience of every average man & woman.
>
> The whole secret of fiction and the drama—in the constructional part—lies in the adjustment of things unusual to things eternal and universal. The writer who knows exactly how exceptional, and how non-exceptional, his events should be made, possesses the key to the art.

The 'Ancient Mariner' quality would be something Hardy had learnt from his experience of writing serials, which require in each episode the adrenalin of a fresh denouement and a further cliff-hanger. In the note just quoted his emphasis on 'events' is fully supported in his short stories by the plotting of a firm and sinewy story-line that generates a rhythm of interested excitement as it proceeds from event to event. Where the stories vary in quality one from another, the decisive factor is usually in the fine tuning of that crucial adjustment of the unusual pattern of events to the eternal and universal verities that they embody.

For his material Hardy drew from several distinct sources. He drew directly from the social settings of his early manhood—the respectable middle-classes of the towns of Wessex, the solidly established shopkeepers and the men of the professions who readily yielded his portraits of a solicitor, a wine-merchant, an army officer or a parson in their domestic lives and in their everyday appearances as he saw them going about their business in Dorchester or Bridport or Salisbury. Quite a different source was the legends and chronicles of local history in which Hardy was steeped almost from birth, but which he augmented by his own studies, in association with the antiquarian members of the Dorset Field Club and as an assiduous reader of John Hutchins's *History and Antiquities of the County of Dorset*. The assembled story-tellers who provide the framework for *A Group of Noble Dames* clearly represent this circle of Hardy's acquaintance.

The prestige of the great landowning dynasties of Wessex might be crumbling in Hardy's lifetime but it retained a potent atmosphere that fascinated him. He was perhaps mocking himself as well as Mr Melbury in *The Woodlanders* when the timber merchant glows with pride at the thought of his daughter's marriage to Dr Fitzpiers:

> You can't help being happy, Grace, in allying yourself with such a romantical family. Why, on the mother's side he's connected with the long line of the Lords Baxby of Sherton. You'll feel as if you've stepped into history.

Hardy did not share uncritically Mr Melbury's 'touching faith in members of long-established families as such, irrespective of their personal condition or character', but the names and titles of the great families had nevertheless a plangency for him that vibrated with rich memories of strange, compelling tales. *A Group of Noble Dames* stands apart as something unique in the history of the short story—as narrowly specific to a time and place and class as Kipling's *Plain Tales from the Hills*. The reader who pauses to wonder how reliably veracious the stories may be should recall Hardy's affectionate tribute to one of the old musicians of his native village—'a man who speaks neither truth nor lies, but a sort of Not Proven compound which is very relishable'.

The further source on which he drew was the folk culture of his family background, the seemingly inexhaustible fund of anecdote and country lore that came to him from his parents, his grandmother, his relatives and neighbours in the parishes of Stinsford and Puddletown, and out on Egdon Heath and down in the Valley of the Great Dairies. This was a darker world of superstition and violence, in which death might come by hanging or drowning, by a firing squad or some secret malevolent act of witchcraft, but where there was also a contrary ebullience of broad humour and conviviality. The world into which Hardy was born was one in which fear of French invasion was a lingering reality: the great fort on the Nothe at Weymouth was built during his boyhood to protect the harbour. Public hangings and whippings were common topics of conversation. The magic powers of conjurors were sought in times of difficulty: Hardy's notebooks record numerous acts of witchcraft that caught his attention and were to be embodied in his stories.

To this close native inheritance must be credited the tales that look across the English Channel to French Revolution and Napoleonic War for their provenance—**'The Melancholy Hussar of the German Legion'**, **'A Committee-Man of "the Terror"'** and **'A Tradition of Eighteen Hundred and Four'**—while the French connection appears in a different mode in the detailed account of smuggling that Hardy picked up from an old man in his father's employment and made the basis of **'The Distracted Preacher'**. The preface to *Wessex Tales* begins with an apology for the fact that, of the seven stories, two are about hangmen. It is a most inappropriate apology since they are two of Hardy's finest stories and well contrasted in mood. **'The Withered Arm'** stands as the classic epitome of witchcraft, with its intervention of an incubus, the conjuring up of human spirits in a tumbler of water and the magical power of the hangman's trade to produce the ultimate 'turning of the blood'. To find a comparable evocation of the black arts one might have to look to *Macbeth*. **'The Three Strangers'** is the best example of Hardy's skill in constructing an ingenious and tightly knit plot—so ingenious, indeed, that any Ancient Mariner must covet it. Here the hangman is lightly drawn as no more than the spring which operates the *coup de théâtre*. That it is truly and in the proper sense '*de théâtre*' was recognized by J. M. Barrie, who persuaded Hardy to dramatize the story for a London production.

In such a story as **'The Three Strangers'**, where the plot itself is the dominant feature, the characterization might excusably go no further than the circumstances require. For good measure, however, Hardy throws in a delightful cadenza on mead. It is typical of the gusty humour and expansive conviviality that so often transform the grimmer face of his prose. In the cottage on the heath that his great-grandfather had built at what in 1800 was New Bockhampton there were traditions of dancing and merry-making and the sweet scent of cider-pressing in the autumn days of Hardy's youth; and it is this pervasive good-fellowship and delight in the lighter side of rustic life that can warm Hardy's fiction with a genial humanity that is sometimes disregarded or undervalued. Among the 'crusted characters' in *Life's Little Ironies* the musicians of **'Absent-Mindedness in a Parish Choir'** and the sporting parson of **'Andrey Satchel and the Parson and Clerk'** are surely secure in popular esteem. No collection of country humour could justly omit them. As for that arch-deceiver, Tony Kytes, his Englishness—or more precisely his Wessex style—is so quintessential that it may illustrate the vastness of the chasm that separated Hardy from his French contemporaries if it is set beside a typically Gallic deceiver in Maupassant's 'Ce Cochon de Morin'. The English Channel was never wider.

It is not only in his deliberately comic stories that Hardy's indigenous bravura adds its distinctive quality. Just as the celebration of mead breaks into **'The Three Strangers'**, so in **'Interlopers at the Knap'** there comes this tribute to cider from the dairyman Mr Johns:

> Though I inherit the malt-liquor principle from my father, I am a cider-drinker on my mother's side. She came from these parts, you know. And there's this to be said for't—'tis a more peaceful liquor, and don't lie about a man like your hotter drinks. With care, one may live on it a twelve-month without knocking down a neighbour, or getting a black eye from an old acquaintance.

In his *Thomas Hardy: a biography* Michael Millgate states that the dairyman's journey with Farmer Darton to the Knap draws on episodes in the journey of Hardy's father to Melbury Osmond to marry his Jemima. It is certainly characteristic of Hardy that his inventiveness lay in the rearrangement of what he observed directly from life or was told by others. At times he even shows a curious anxiety to clutch at such literal truth as a necessary credential. He may hint darkly at 'an old woman still living' during his boyhood, whose recollected experiences add an authentic touch to **'The Withered Arm'**, just as he feels that his poem 'A Trampwoman's Tragedy' gains something from his disclosure that the trampwoman's name was Mary Ann Taylor and her tragedy occurred in 1827, so linking the poem with the traditional hanging ballads of earlier days. At the end of **'The Distracted Preacher'** he apologizes for the distortion made by the mandatory happy ending that editors required, and—as in *The Return of the Native*—invites his readers to make

their own realignment with the truth. Even more striking in its way, to the point of pedantry, is the footnote to the mention in **'Interlopers at the Knap'** of 'the "White Horse", the fine old Elizabethan inn at Chalk Newton', which we must needs be told 'is now pulled down, and its site occupied by a modern one in red brick (1912)'. Though we may know that 'Chalk Newton' is based on the Dorset village of Maiden Newton, it is nevertheless, within the strict compass of the story, a fictitious place not requiring—nor able to have—future correlations with a changing reality.

At the same time Hardy insists that 'the stories are but dreams, not records'. This tendency to operate on two levels of 'truth' quite overtly, and with evident tensions between them, is a marked feature of his writing. It is of course understood that writers draw in some degree from their direct experience, but the primary models are usually dissolved in the imaginative act of creation. Hardy liked to preserve his sources and exhibit an ability, even a readiness, to identify them if called upon to do so. When he made a complete fabrication, as in **'A Tradition of Eighteen Hundred and Four'**, he created a problem for himself. In his preface to *Wessex Tales* he was clearly eager to find this story subsumed within the body of 'real tradition' but he later conceded that 'there never had existed any such improbable tradition'; and to Sydney Cockerell he admitted privately that he had exercised 'the licence of a storyteller to tell lies . . . to give verisimilitude to *my* story'.

In the decade before 1888 Hardy published a dozen short stories, five of which he considered not worth preserving. Of the remainder, two were forerunners of what became his group of noble dames. **'The Distracted Preacher'**, despite the engaging novelty of its smuggling devices, relies on stereotyped characters; and the love story of the preacher and the lady smuggler is sadly anaemic. Three undoubted successes were **'The Three Strangers'**, **'Interlopers at the Knap'** and **'Fellow-Townsmen'**—the first a triumph of plot invention, the other two developing in quite a different direction. In particular the dark-toned subtlety of **'Fellow-Townsmen'**, in its finally revised form, points towards the searching examination of human relationships in and out of marriage that increasingly preoccupied Hardy in the 1880s and 1890s. In both stories a woman who, by conventional standards, should have been pleased to accept a proposal of marriage prefers to remain single, although with some ambiguity in the closing moments of **'Fellow-Townsmen'**.

In his preface to *The Woodlanders* Hardy spoke of 'the immortal puzzle—given the man and the woman, how to find a basis for their sexual relation'. This was a main theme in his novels during the 1890s and it became equally prominent in his short stories. His third collection, *Life's Little Ironies,* might well have been entitled 'Marriage's Little Ironies'. Edith Harnham in **'On the Western Circuit'** is presented as a victim of 'the belief of the British parent that a bad marriage with its aversions is better than free womanhood with its interests, dignity, and leisure'. Similarly, in **'An Imaginative Woman'** Ella Marchmill's ill-matched union springs from 'the necessity of getting life-leased at all costs, a cardinal virtue which all good mothers teach'.

Two stories in this group deliberately stand convention on its head. In **'For Conscience' Sake'** Mr Millborne does the honourable thing by returning after many years to marry the woman whom he had seduced and left to bear his child, but the easing of his conscience by this action brings disaster to what had been a stable and contented way of life. 'Why did you pester me with your conscience,' his wife demands, 'till I was driven to accept you to get rid of your importunity?'

The wife in **'The Fiddler of the Reels'** already has a daughter by the gypsy fiddler when she marries Ned Hipcroft. The abduction of the child by the gypsy some years later is of small concern to the mother: it is Ned, the stepfather, who grieves and searches for the little maid who, he says, 'is the whole world to me'. And when he is taunted for his folly in thinking of the child as his he replies, 'No, I don't think 'tis mine! But she *is* mine all the same! Ha'n't I nussed her? Ha'n't I fed her and teached her?'

That conviction that formal relationships must sometimes be subordinate to the deeper relationships that can arise emotionally and physically is most marked in *Tess of the d'Urbervilles* and *Jude the Obscure.* The short stories written in the same period are often variations on this theme. The culmination of **'On the Western Circuit'** is the cry of Charles Raye at his wedding to the 'wrong' bride: 'Legally I have married her—God help us both!—in soul and spirit I have married you, and no other woman in the world!' He has just learnt that the enchanting love-letters which tempted him to marry a simple servant-girl were in fact written for her by the girl's employer, Edith Harnham.

Ella Marchmill, in **'An Imaginative Woman'**, has much in common with Mrs Harnham. They both have dull husbands whose stolidity denies them any emotional fulfilment. They find relief in fantasy relationships—Ella with a poet whose lodgings she occupies temporarily but whom she never meets, Edith in writing her servant's love-letters to the barrister, Charles Raye, after having encountered him briefly only once, at the time when he first met and seduced the girl. On that occasion, in the darkness at the crowded fairground, he had mistakenly touched Edith's hand in a playfully amorous way, with far-reaching consequences. She wishes she had married a man who 'knew the subtleties of love-making' as he did. That he was able to seduce her servant in a couple of days was 'his crowning though unrecognized fascination for her as the she-animal'.

Ella Marchmill has no personal contact at all with the poet of her fantasy, but she reads his poems, studies his photograph and extends a vicarious intimacy by putting on his mackintosh, which she finds in a cupboard—'the mantle of Elijah!' In both women the effect of physical contact is powerful, even in these slight instances. Hardy's insistent probing of feminine nature in his later novels is echoed here in these stories which refine and subdue the exigencies of the plot to give more room and freedom to develop the intricacies of individual portraits. The emphasis on physical contact is particularly striking—the sudden donning of the mackintosh, the teasing finger in the palm of the hand—pointers, in their way, to D. H. Lawrence a generation later writing his short story 'You Touched Me'. More immediately, the two lonely women whose 'passionateness' has been rejected share a kinship with Tess in her conjecture that perhaps after all Alec d'Urberville is her *real* husband. Never far from Hardy's compassionate concern is the human muddling of the underlying truths of our nature with the formal patterns of law and convention that we endeavour to impose on them.

There are other themes, familiar to readers of the novels, which gain a fresh vitality from their treatment in the short stories. Hardy's movement away from the gentry in the choice of his leading characters gave added force to his criticism of 'Hodge'—that heartless burlesque of the peasant as a witless oaf, a mere figure of fun little better than a village idiot. When Angel Clare, in *Tess of the d'Urbervilles,* gets to know the dairyfolk at Talbothays as individuals he takes 'a real delight in their companionship. The conventional farmfolk of his imagination—personified in the newspaper-press by the pitiable dummy known as Hodge—were obliterated after a few days' residence. At close quarters no Hodge was to be seen.' The point is made even more forcefully in **'The Waiting Supper'** by the heroine, Christine, at a party when a sophisticated young man from London says to her, 'It does one's heart good to see these simple peasants enjoying themselves'; to which she replies, 'O Mr Bellston, don't be too sure about that word "simple"! You little think what they see and meditate! Their reasonings and emotions are as complicated as ours.'

The cruelties into which a rigid acceptance of 'class' values may lead are the subject of several stories, notably 'The Son's Veto' and 'A Tragedy of Two Ambitions'. The remarkable influence that dancing can have on human emotions is treated in 'The History of the Hardcomes' as well as in the better-known 'The Fiddler of the Reels'. All in all this later group of short stories is fully representative of Hardy's characteristic writing in prose. What he perfected was a tautly engineered plot culminating in a wry or sombre conclusion. Where there is irony it accompanies and precipitates an implicit depth of social comment.

* * *

The decision to terminate his career as a novelist implied that Hardy would go no further with short stories, beyond the honouring of outstanding commissions. The author of **Wessex Tales** gave way to the author of *Wessex Poems,* who was sometimes less than generous to his predecessor. In the struggle to win recognition as a poet Hardy came almost to resent the achievement of the years he had spent in the necessary task of earning a living by writing prose fiction. In his personal correspondence with friends and admirers he would make such comments as 'My old novels don't interest me enough to make me take much trouble about them' and 'The novels seem immature to me'.

Be that as it may, it can be argued with justice that his poetry gained immeasurably from that long proving of his command of narrative and dialogue and finely observed detail. It was Ezra Pound who first drew attention to this positive character in Hardy's progression from prose to verse. In his discursive, shrewd, wryly humorous book *Culture,* Pound gives his opinion that '20 novels form as good a gradus ad Parnassum as does metrical exercise: I daresay they form a better if the gods have granted light by that route'.

There is ample evidence of that light here, in the short stories. And if a reader wishes there were further and later instances of the little ironies of life that Hardy could sketch so inimitably, he or she need only turn to the versified anecdotes of *Satires of Circumstance* whose lineage is beyond doubt.

Simon Gatrell (essay date 1988)

SOURCE: Gatrell, Simon. "Hardy and the *Graphic*: 1883-1891." In *Hardy the Creator: A Textual Biography,* pp. 71-96. Oxford: Clarendon Press, 1988.

[*In the following excerpt, Gatrell surveys Hardy's contributions to the weekly journal the* Graphic *between 1883 to 1891, focusing on proofs and revisions of "The Romantic Adventures of a Milkmaid" and* A Group of Noble Dames. *Gatrell also describes the reaction of the journal's editorial staff to some of the risqué elements in Hardy's work.*]

'THE ROMANTIC ADVENTURES OF A MILKMAID'
AND THE MAYOR OF CASTERBRIDGE: A PAUSE
FOR REFLECTION

During the winter of 1882-3 Hardy was writing what he called a 'short novel', but what, since its inclusion in the volume **A Changed Man** in 1913, has usually been described as a long story. **'The Romantic Adventures of a Milkmaid'** was planned to appear in one of the special issues that the weekly journal the *Graphic* published twice a year, once in the summer to catch the holiday trade, and once at Christmas. These extra numbers of the magazine were more substantial than the normal weekly copies, and Hardy showed his professional versatility in meeting happily the demand for a tale of a length somewhere between the usual short story and the novel. The appearance of **'The Romantic Adventures'** ["The Romantic Adventures of a Milkmaid"] in the summer issue of 1883 marks the beginning of Hardy's nine-year connection with the *Graphic.* During that period only one of his important works, *The Woodlanders,* was not first published there.

Very little is known about the composition of **'The Romantic Adventures of a Milkmaid'**; *The Early Life* includes the single entry, for 25 February 1883: 'Sent a short hastily written novel to the *Graphic* for Summer Number'. The only relevant letter that survives is addressed to the editor of the magazine, Arthur Locker, and simply announces that the story is nearly ready.[1] We thus have no idea what Hardy's dealings with the editor were; but a note that he appended in 1927 to the story in his study-copy of **A Changed Man** (in the Wessex edition) gives a hint that Locker may have had some influence on its final shape: 'Note: The foregoing finish of the Milkmaid's adventures by a re-union with her husband was adopted to suit the requirements of the summer number of a periodical in which the story was first printed.' It is always possible that Hardy's professionalism extended by now to an awareness of what would be most acceptable in terms of narrative line to the average magazine editor (there was, the reader will recall, a similar note appended in 1912 to the ending of *The Return of the Native,* and another at the same time to the 1879 story **'The Distracted Preacher'**), but it is equally possible that he had continually to be reminded that serial readers liked a happy-ever-after ending.[2]

With **'The Romantic Adventures of a Milkmaid',** the only independent evidence of Hardy's attitude towards the ending, and indeed towards the fabric of the tale as a whole, is to be found in the history of the development of the text.

Hardy's sense of the **'Romantic Adventures'** as 'hastily written' is borne out to a degree by the changes of mind that the manuscript reveals; it is as if he had not allowed himself enough time for reflection before making the fair copy of the story. At the beginning, for instance, when Margery (the milkmaid in question) first encounters Baron von Xanten (the cause of her romantic adventures), in a deleted passage in the manuscript she witnesses his preparations for suicide, taking a revolver with its 'dull blue gleam' into his hand, and placing 'his finger on the trigger' (fo. 6). In the later version there is no more than a hint to the reader that he was thinking of killing himself; Margery herself only realizes that he is very unhappy: 'He started up with an air of bewilderment, and slipped something into the pocket of his dressing-gown' (fo. 7). It may be a further measure of Hardy's haste that there remained uncancelled on fo. 27 of the manuscript a reference to the occasion when Margery 'begged him to spare his own life', a remnant of the old plot that Hardy deleted in proof for the *Graphic*. Hardy half changed his mind again when he revised the text for the story's first English book edition, adding after 'dressing-gown' to the quotation from fo. 7 above: 'She was almost certain that it was a pistol.' Later, he also added that 'Margery had sufficient tact to say nothing about the pistol', thus avoiding the melodrama, but reintroducing the certainty.

Following this change of direction in the manuscript there are several cancelled details that show that Margery was originally to be less self-confident in her relations with the Baron—she did not imagine, for instance, that, in order to fulfil her wish to go to a Yeomanry Ball, the Baron might take her himself (fo. 15). There are hints, too, that the Baron was to be less scrupulous than he eventually is; a deleted passage of narratorial comment runs: 'It was noticeable that, either from recklessness or want of thought, he had said nothing to remind the unthinking Margery of any possible harm which might accrue to her fair fame by these proceedings' (fo. 16).

As far as the conclusion to the novel is concerned, the manuscript appears to refute almost as far as possible the claim in Hardy's 1927 note quoted above (that the changes were made to comply with the *Graphic*'s scrupulous morality), for the Baron is thoroughly virtuous in the earliest version of the plot that survives. The end of the story involves a series of carriage- and horse-rides: Margery thinks that Jim, her secretly married husband, has run off to London with a handsome widow, and the Baron insists on her getting into his carriage and pursuing him. Meanwhile, Jim (who has only been simulating love for the widow in order to make Margery jealous, and thereby force her to acknowledge their secret marriage) is told that the Baron

and Margery have eloped together, and so rides off after them. In the manuscript version, once Margery and the Baron discover by enquiry that Jim and the widow have not after all made for London, the Baron delivers Margery a lecture about her stubborn pride in not living with Jim, deposits her at Jim's house, and returns to try to find him. The two men meet at a village called Letscombe Cross, and all is made clear between them—the Baron's honour vindicated, Jim's ruse explained. Jim and Margery settle down together and raise a family; the Baron is seen no more. There was no question at this stage of the Baron whisking Margery away.

The first move in this direction came in proof-additions for the *Graphic,* when Hardy deleted the Baron's sermon to Margery, and in its place had the Baron drive her to the coast where a yacht was awaiting him, and ask her if she would come with him 'steaming away all the world over'. Margery has a sudden enlightenment as to her predicament, and exclaims: 'Oh sir! . . . I once saved your life—save me now, for pity's sake!' The Baron does as he is told, and the sequel is the same as in the manuscript.

In the version that we read now, the 1913 text, there are further differences in the ending. Some of these derive from the moving of the setting of the story from the Froom valley near Dorchester to the Exe valley near Exeter, a move first pointed out by Purdy (p. 49). Others focus on the detour to the shore; having expressed in the *Graphic* a more plausible response to the situation on the Baron's part, in the book edition he turned his attention to Margery. When the Baron asks if she thinks she ought to be at her husband's house, in the *Graphic* she replies 'Yes, sir.' In 1913 this is replaced by 'She did not answer'. After the Baron's reiterated 'Of course you ought', Hardy further added 'Still she did not speak', and it is then that the Baron decides to turn the carriage towards his yacht.

When they have pulled up facing the yacht, and he asks her directly 'Will you come?', instead of replying 'I cannot', as she did in the magazine, her response in 1913 is 'I cannot decide'. She looks 'bewildered' rather than 'agonized', and, instead of bending to the Baron, she leans on him. The onus for decision is firmly on the Baron in the later version, and ultimately his conscience wins. However, when they reach Jim's home the Baron asked in the *Graphic* 'can you forgive a bad impulse'; in 1913 'bad' becomes 'lover's'—the first time in the story that he openly acknowledges his feeling towards Margery. In the last pages of the text Jim and Margery hear a report that the Baron has succeeded in killing himself, and in 1913 Hardy added a comment by Margery: 'Now that he's dead I'll make a confession, Jim, that I have never made to a soul. If he had pressed me—which he did not—to go with him when I was in the carriage that night beside his yacht, I would have gone. And I was disappointed that he did not press me.' Another addition stresses the reason why the Baron would not now succeed in an attempt to persuade her to leave with him: 'It would be so unfair to baby.' But Jim is still content with a wife who cares much less for him than he does for her.

Thus, to return to Hardy's 1927 note on the end of the story, the surviving evidence suggests that the reunion with Jim was of the essence of the story at first, and that the hints of desire for the Baron and the approach towards the abandonment of Jim were gradually added to the story as Hardy's view of probabilities evolved. There would have been nothing to hinder Hardy from rewriting the end of the story in 1913 to include the disappearance over the horizon of Margery and the Baron, and yet he stopped short of doing so. Such was the power over him of an established plot. And yet all this does not remove the possibility that in 1882 he had had some form of communication with the editorial board of the *Graphic* that dictated the conventional ending.

The last time that Hardy handled the story was when he prepared a dramatic scenario from it, probably for the consideration of the Dorchester Hardy players. At first he provided alternative last scenes—one in which Margery absconds with the Baron, the other in which she settles down with Jim (to which he appended the note 'But this is not so good an ending'), and then later deleted the second version altogether. The scenario is undated.

Though Hardy published **'The Romantic Adventures of a Milkmaid'** and some other stories in 1883, as well as the essay 'The Dorsetshire Labourer', he did not commit himself to writing another novel until the spring of 1884, and it seems as if he were taking during that period a second 'sabbatical' from serious writing.

1883 was the year that Hardy moved back to Dorchester for the first time since his marriage, and most critics and biographers have sensed something symbolic about the move, as if Hardy were at last prepared to face his roots—a confrontation that would inevitably take some time to resolve. He began another concentrated bout of note-taking at about the same period, notes which were recorded in a commonplace-book with the self-explanatory title 'Facts, from Newspapers, Histories, Biographies, & other Chronicles—(mainly Local)'. He also set about purchasing the land for the house he planned that his father and brother

should build for him, and he began himself to design the house (his permanent commitment to Dorchester), Max Gate.

It is difficult to know whether Hardy's desire to write about his home town was a contributory factor to the move, or whether residence in the heart of Dorchester stimulated in him the need to embody the place in fiction. He would not, I think, have committed himself at this stage in his career to making Dorchester the centre of a novel as lightly as he committed himself to using Stinsford, the parish of his birth, in *Under the Greenwood Tree*—his conception of Wessex, and its implications, was by this time becoming clearer to him. When he did begin to write, he set the novel in approximately the same period as *Under the Greenwood Tree*; during the time of this childhood in the 1840s and 1850s. Just before he began writing *The Mayor of Casterbridge,* he also began a systematic reading through the early files (from 1826 onwards) of the local newspaper, the *Dorset County Chronicle.* Notes from this reading also found their way into the 'Facts' notebook and subsequently formed the basis for episodes in the novel.[3]

As is the case with **'The Romantic Adventures of a Milkmaid'**, there is very little external evidence in the form of letters or notes in Hardy's autobiography or publisher's records concerning either the early development of *The Mayor of Casterbridge* or arrangements with the *Graphic* for its publication.

It seems, though, that Hardy must have agreed terms with the *Graphic* well before the completion of the novel, since the manuscript shows that he designed the story at this stage to suit the requirements of a weekly magazine. In particular, he came to terms in the manuscript with the need for more and shorter episodes, and thus for a greater number of striking incidents in the plot, so that each episode would catch the reader's attention. Hardy wrote in old age, commenting on the novel's first book-publication, that he felt he had spoilt it more than any other by this superfluity of event,[4] but his comment is much less true of the novel as he had revised it for Smith, Elder's two volumes than it would have been of the serial of the manuscript. In fact, he removed many of the less well-integrated fragments of action in the *Graphic* version from the first-edition text, and it seems likely that he had intended from the first that they should be removed. The serial issue of his novels begins to have no relevance to anything but financial considerations in Hardy's mind.

The ascertainable timetable of events from conception to serialization of *The Mayor of Casterbridge* has a leisurely air about it: a note in *The Early Life* (p. 223) says that Hardy wrote the last page of the novel on 17 April 1885 and had taken more than a year over the composition. The serializations in England and America did not begin until January 1886, so there must have been almost two years between the preliminary work on the novel and its first appearance in print. We do not know for sure when Hardy sent the manuscript to Locker, the *Graphic*'s editor, but, as Purdy notes (p. 53), a letter from Locker to Hardy of 20 October (DCM) reports that proofs have already been despatched to America, so Hardy must have delivered copy well before then.

In fact, a little research shows that when writing for the *Graphic* Hardy worked to a timetable quite different from that he used in his writing for other journals. We know that his three other major contributions to the paper were submitted complete to Locker well in advance of publication: **'The Romantic Adventures of a Milkmaid'** four months ahead, *A Group of Noble Dames* six and a half months ahead, and *Tess of the d'Urbervilles* eight months ahead of their appearance in print.[5] These figures encourage the inference that Hardy sent off the manuscript of *The Mayor of Casterbridge* to the *Graphic* soon after finishing it, eight months or so before publication was scheduled.

We also know that Hardy received the first proofs of *Tess of the d'Urbervilles* about two months after sending the manuscript to the *Graphic,* and that he had not returned them six weeks later; it seems probable that it was similarly about two months before proofs of *A Group of Noble Dames* were ready.[6] It would therefore be reasonable to suggest that Hardy saw the galleys of *The Mayor of Casterbridge* also about two months after sending off the manuscript; some time, that is, in late June or early July 1885.

There is a striking contrast in tempo of composition and publication between these *Graphic* commitments and the only novel that intervened. Hardy probably began serious work on *The Woodlanders* in November 1885; publication began in *Macmillan's Magazine* in May 1886; he did not finish the manuscript until 4 February 1887 (see Purdy, pp. 55-7). This stressful pattern in which he was still at work on the last serial episodes well after the opening ones were in print is familiar from Hardy's earlier novels, and was also followed in *Jude the Obscure.*

It seems likely, then, that Locker or Thomas (the proprietor and publisher of the *Graphic*) made it a requirement of their serial contributors that their completed manuscript be submitted well in advance of the publication date. In part this may have been in order to give time for satisfactory illustration, an important feature of the *Graphic,* but it is also the case that a reading of the whole text long before it appeared in public would have given the editor and publisher more security about the nature of what they were purchasing, and a more relaxed opportunity to impose whatever censorship they felt was necessary.[7]

The story of their response to *A Group of Noble Dames* is told in the next section; Hardy's preparation of the manuscript of *Tess of the d'Urbervilles* for *Graphic* publication is well known, and is glanced at briefly in Chapter 6. It seems from evidence in the manuscript and the published serializations of *The Mayor of Casterbridge* that a certain amount of editorial interference may have been made in the development of the plot, similar to that which has been postulated earlier in this chapter for **'The Romantic Adventures of a Milkmaid'**.

Christine Winfield, in her essay 'The Manuscript of Hardy's *The Mayor of Casterbridge,*[8]' shows that Hardy's original conception of the Jersey relationship between Michael Henchard and Lucetta LeSueur was one of a six-year affair, euphemistically called by Lucetta an 'engagement'. This was replaced at a late stage, and in a certain amount of haste, in the manuscript by a story of her admiration of him, her rescue of him from drowning, and their marriage, the details of which were pencilled on the verso of a leaf and never inked over—something that occurs nowhere else in Hardy's manuscripts with substantial material that is ultimately intended for incorporation in the subsequent serialization. Winfield quite rightly feels that the change was probably made as a direct result of pressure from the *Graphic,* but she does not consider why the pressure should have resulted in changes to the manuscript itself rather than in proof-changes for the serial. Locker might have read the manuscript in April or May 1885 and sent it back to Hardy with a note of disapproval, but the editor would have been much more likely to wait for proofs before looking at the text, as he did with *A Group of Noble Dames.*

There are, however, two features of the manuscript that suggest a different scenario. Some leaves have a particularly faded appearance, as if they had at one time formed the opening or closing leaves of a separate batch of text (fos. 165, 249, 250, 283, 418, 419), and some have the notation 'The Mayor of Casterbridge' at the top in Hardy's hand (fos. 80, 165, 419). The fact that two leaves have both features makes it possible to suggest with some confidence that at some stage the manuscript was divided into sections. It would answer both questions if Hardy in fact sent off the manuscript to Locker in batches, for it then becomes rather more likely that the editor would have read and commented on manuscript rather than proof, and makes it easier to understand why Hardy might have responded to Grundian criticism in the manuscript rather than himself waiting for proof.

To set against this hypothesis there is the undoubted fact that twenty or so swear-words were bowdlerized in the *Graphic* proofs, probably by Hardy at editorial request—something, it will be remembered, that he had done quite happily for *The Trumpet-Major.* These, however, may have been made at the prompting of a different editorial authority.

Another interesting aspect of the early development of *The Mayor of Casterbridge* is that, for the first time in the history of Hardy's fictional texts, there are authorially motivated differences between the British and American serializations and first editions. Essentially, the texts of the *Graphic* and *Harper's Weekly* are the same, and thus the letter from Locker to Hardy of 20 October must mean that clean revises of the English serial were sent to America. However, the bowdlerizations of swear-words mentioned earlier do not appear in *Harper's Weekly,* and there is a handful of further alterations of the *Graphic* text that can hardly be attributable to editorial intervention in New York. It seems then that either the dilution of the profane language was made at a late stage to the English serial text, or else that it was made in the revises sent to America, and that Hardy, aware that American editors would tolerate more honest writing than English, included a restoration of the original words and phrases amongst a brief list, sent to the American editor, of other revisions that his restless creative mind felt necessary.[9] That these other changes were not made in the *Graphic* also, may have been because by this time the type had been plated, or else because Hardy's irritation with the small-mindedness of the English editor made him decide not to send the list for the English serial, but to keep it for the book-edition.

Hardy was anxious to make sure that the over-stuffed serial text should not get into book form in England or in America, but this caused a problem. From November 1885 Hardy was deeply involved in the writing and serialization of *The Woodlanders*; and had little time to spare for thought about revising *The Mayor of Casterbridge.* He must have delayed the work for as long as possible, since Henry Holt, who was to publish the first American edition (and was anxious, in order to forestall the pirates, to have it ready to go on to the stands before the serial finished on 15 May 1886), had only received revised copy of the first forty chapters by 11 May.[10] He either never got the last five chapters, or else received them too late to use; as it was, the American 'authorized' first edition only appeared towards the end of the month.

The copy Hardy sent to America would probably have been unrevised proofs for Smith, Elder's English edition, since though there were more than 500 revisions in the first forty chapters of Holt's edition, there were 250 further changes to these chapters in the English edition, changes presumably made on the proofs and incorporated in revises that were never sent to America. Additional differences are the radical alterations that Hardy made to the ending of the novel in Smith, Elder's edition, including the cancellation of Henchard's return to Casterbridge for Elizabeth-Jane's wedding to Farfrae—an episode that he restored in the first collected edition in response to the suggestions of friends.[11]

A GROUP OF NOBLE DAMES: THE DEAD HAND OF MRS GRUNDY

Hardy's next connection with the *Graphic* was considerably more painful. During 1889 Hardy corresponded with Locker about the possibility of providing a Christmas piece for his magazine the 'same length as the **"Romantic Adventures of a Milkmaid"**';[12] it seems that agreement for what was to be the short-story sequence *A Group of Noble Dames* was finally reached in November, for publication in the Christmas special number of 1890. At the same time Hardy was also arranging, after its rejection in three other places, to sell to the *Graphic* the novel that was to become *Tess of the d'Urbervilles,* and the reception by the periodical of the Christmas piece must directly have affected decisions that Hardy made about the shape of his greatest achievement in fiction.[13] In fact, *A Group of Noble Dames* may be taken to represent the third stage, after his experiences with Leslie Stephen and Donald Macleod, in the disintegration of Hardy's respect for the editors and readers of monthly and weekly serials, and well repays close attention.[14]

The serialization of the six stories that form the nucleus of *A Group of Noble Dames* is documented in letters that passed between Hardy and the Lockers, father and son, and in notebook entries that Hardy preserved for inclusion in *The Early Life.* There is some discrepancy between these documents that makes the establishment of the precise sequence of events difficult.

The first of these is on p. 295 of *The Early Life*: '*May 9.* MS. of *A Group of Noble Dames* sent to The *Graphic* as promised.' This was in the spring of 1890. There is then nothing surviving that relates to the next six weeks. One question that bears on the discussion of the serialization that follows, as it does on the serialization of *The Mayor of Casterbridge,* is whether the manuscript was sent straight to the printer for proofing before the editors and directors of the magazine read it, or whether it simply lay in a drawer untouched until the time came in the schedule of the *Graphic* for it to be considered. In this case the manuscript was destined for a Christmas supplement, so the end of June might have been time enough to look at the stories, even if illustration were a factor.

The next stage was apparently a letter of 20 June from William Locker, the editor's son and assistant, to Hardy, which has not survived (see Hardy's letter to Arthur Locker of 30 July below), and then there is a note in *The Early Life* (p. 297): '*June 23*. Called on Arthur Locker [editor] at the *Graphic* office in answer to his letter. He says he does not object to the stories [*A Group of Noble Dames*] but the Directors do. Here's a pretty job! Must smooth down these Directors somehow I suppose.'

This note may be a dramatization by Hardy, when writing *The Early Life,* of a diary entry, for something in it cannot be squared with the evidence of the two surviving letters that are quoted below. It must be mistaken in its date, in the name of the Locker he visited, or in the ascription of the letter, for William Locker wrote to Hardy on 25 June outlining exactly what was required of him in terms of revision, and why:

> I have now read *A Group of Noble Dames* and am sorry to say that in the main I agree with our Directors' opinion. In the matter of tone they seem to me to be too much in keeping with the supposed circumstances of their narration—in other words to be very suitable and entirely harmless to the robust minds of a Club smoking-room; but not at all suitable for the more delicate imaginations of young girls. Many fathers are accustomed to read or have read in their family circles the stories in the *Graphic*; and I cannot think that they would approve for this purpose a series of tales almost every one of which turns upon questions of childbirth, and those relations between the sexes over which conventionality is accustomed (wisely or unwisely) to draw a veil. To go through them *seriatim*—

> The Old Surgeon's story [**'Barbara'** (**"Barbara of the House of Grebe"**)] is, it is true, not the least what Mrs. Grundy would call "improper," but its main incident is very horrible—just the sort of story an old surgeon might be expected to tell, but none the less unpleasant for that.

> The Rural Dean is, as is natural, a good deal milder [**'The Lady Caroline'**]; but still insists rather more than is perhaps advisable upon the childbirth business.

> The Colonel's yarn is, of course, a mere anecdote; and would not suffer at all if some other ending were substituted for the discovery by Lady Baxby of her husband's vulgar amour.

> Similarly, all that wants cutting out in the Churchwarden's story is the suggestion at the end that Lady Icenway intended to raise up seed unto her second husband by means of her first.

> But the tales of the Crimson Maltster [**'Squire Petrick's Lady'**], and of the Sentimental Member [**'Lady Mottisfont'**] seem to me to be hopeless—Frankly, do you think it advisable to put into the hands of the Young Person stories, one of which turns upon the hysterical confession by a wife of an imaginary adultery, and the other upon the manner in which a husband foists upon his wife the offspring of a former illicit connection?

> I quite admit that if the stories were to be written they could not be better or more innocently done—But I still think it very unfortunate that they should have been written for a paper with the peculiar clientele of the *Graphic*; and I am sure we should not be justified in printing them as they stand.

> Now, what do you propose to do? Will you write us an entirely fresh story, or will you take the 'Noble Dames' and alter them to suit our taste; which means slightly chastening 1, 2, 3 & 4; and substituting others for 5 & 6? Please let me have an answer at your earliest convenience; or, if you can call, I shall be in every day except Saturday from 11 to 1 & 3 till 5.[15]

The first sentence of this letter may imply that Locker was reading the stories for the first time, in which case he would hardly have said that he did not object to them; on the other hand he may be indicating a rereading of the stories with the objections of his directors in mind. The last sentence seems to suggest that Hardy's note in *The Early Life* may have been misdated. Anyway, Hardy evidently set about the alterations to the stories that this section chronicles; the *Graphic* must have had Hardy's new version by the middle of July, for there is a letter Hardy wrote to his wife, probably on 24 July, which contains the following passage: 'I think it is all right with the *Graphic*—as they really don't themselves know what it is I have written, apparently: one of the directors having read the 1st proofs in mistake for the second.'

Arthur Locker wrote to Hardy on this matter, and Hardy's reply is dated 30 July:

> I am glad to say that on comparing the copy of the unrevised proof read by Mr Thomas (in mistake for the revised one) his marks thereon of passages for revision correspond almost exactly with changes I had already carried out in the revise which Mr Thomas has not seen, & which was the result of your son's original suggestions in his letter of June 20. So that there was nothing left for me to do beyond making a few additional changes in the wording—as shown on the revise herewith returned.

> When Mr Thomas, & your assistant editor, read this, they will both see that their wishes have been complied with to the letter—& more.[16]

But these letters do not tell the full story. It seems from an examination of the manuscript, and a comparison between it, the *Graphic,* and the American serialization in *Harper's Weekly,* that there were two or three different layers of bowdlerization, some made voluntarily, and others under pressure from the editorial staff of the English journal.

To take the manuscript first,[17] there are in three stories passages that have been cancelled in blue pencil in the way that is familiar to students of the manuscripts of *Tess* and *Jude*; the cancellations are subsequently marked for inclusion (presumably) in the book-edition. They are relatively minor in **'The Lady Icenway'** and in **'Lady Mottisfont'**, and seem to be early attempts by Hardy to avoid censure from the *Graphic*'s editors, a pre-empting of the kind of unpleasantness that in fact ensued. In **'Squire Petrick's Lady'**, though, the blue-pencil cancellations are at once more extensive and more problematic in origin; and, though some of the deletions are of the same sort as those in the other stories, there are features surrounding one or two that demand a rather different explanation. It is, thus, worth looking at the passages a little more closely.

There are, to begin with, a few cancellations in blue that are not marked for reinstatement; the first of these, after telling us that the infant born to Timothy Petrick and his wife was called Robert, originally read:

> and her husband had never thought of it as a name of any significance, till, now, he had learnt by accident that before her marriage Annetta had been desperately enamoured of the young Marquis of Chrisminster, son of the Duke of Hamptonshire. Robert was his name.

After the blue pencil has been at work it reads:

> and it was the name of the young Marquis of Chrisminster, son of the Duke of Hamptonshire.[18]

Though the *Graphic* omits even this, it is instructive to note that the more or less simultaneous American serialization in *Harper's Weekly* preserves the abbreviated manuscript version. In the first edition, despite its not being marked for retention (with stet marks under it), Hardy reintroduced the earlier reading, but with interesting variations:

> and her husband had never thought of it as a name of any significance, till, about this time, he learnt by accident that it was the name of the young Marquess of Christminster, son of the Duke of Southwesterland, for whom Annetta had cherished warm feelings before her marriage.

Thus the first-edition recasting of the earlier manuscript text was made with the *Harper's* version also in mind. This pattern of variation raises at once questions about what was copy for the American serial, and for the first edition, questions that need more data before they can be at all resolved.

As if to confirm that these blue cancellations were made before Hardy had any direct communication with the management of the *Graphic,* there is in be-

tween them in the manuscript a change that surely echoes the same impulse, though not this time made in blue: Robert is referred to by his father successively as 'the little bastard', 'the little wretch', and 'the little fellow'. In context, the first seems the most appropriate, as well as being accurate so far as he knows; and the final reading is really too weak for the situation in which it is made. But Hardy must have known that 'bastard' would not have gone down too well with any of the magazines in which he was likely to find a home for the stories. Why 'wretch' was turned into 'fellow' I cannot guess; it simply seems a misjudgement.

Such cancels unmarked for retention are the minority, and there follow in sequence several paragraphs which have blue-pencil cancels and black, dotted underlining marking them for retention. In addition three consecutive leaves (or rather one leaf and the versos of the next two) have an indignant notation, each a variant of: '[N. B. The above lines were deleted against the author's wish, by compulsion of Mrs Grundy, as were all other passages marked in blue.]'

One feature that these larger deletions have in common is that all the cancelled passages appear in the American serialization, though there are occasional small variations; this suggests that they are of a different kind from those earlier examined.

One of the cancelled passages has a detail that further suggests that they were made after the shorter unstetted cancellations. Squire Petrick is reflecting upon the implications of his perception that his son is illegitimate but of noble stock; in the heart of a paragraph that is all deleted in blue pencil there is:

> To choose as her lover the immediate successor in that ducal line

Harper's, however, does not reproduce this as it does the rest of the paragraph; instead it reads:

> To fix her choice upon the immediate successor in that ducal line

The first edition follows the *Harper's* reading. A clue to this deviation from the normal relationship between the blue deletions and the American serialization can be found in a close inspection of the manuscript, which reveals that the differing words have been much more heavily scored through, implying that the removal of 'as her lover' was made at an earlier stage than the rest of the cancellation, presumably at the same time as the first set of blue-pencil cancellations described above.

Upon consideration of these points it is right to conclude that the briefer cancellations in blue ink that have no dotted underlining were made some time shortly before Hardy submitted the manuscript to the *Graphic*. Hence the passages were omitted by the printers from the first proofs, and hence also their absence from the *Harper's* version which would have been set from these first *Graphic* proofs. The fact that there are small variants between the manuscript and *Harper's* makes it likely that Hardy had revised the set of proofs he sent to America.

The more lengthy deletions were then made by Hardy in the manuscript after getting it back from the printers with his proof, and after receiving first notice from the directors and editor of the English magazine that they were unhappy with the stories. He perhaps regarded the cancellations as a preliminary attempt to meet their unease. On the other hand, it seems at least possible that these deletions, with their accompanying anguished notes about the tyranny of Mrs Grundy, were made more as a physical reminder to himself, and anyone else who should see the manuscript, of the conditions under which the stories first saw print. In the introduction to the Clarendon edition of *Tess of the d'Urbervilles* I speculated that some of Hardy's dealings with editors over the serialization of the novel were deliberate attempts to provoke prudish or hostile responses that would provide further contemporary justification for the position he expressed in his essay 'Candour in English Fiction'; these cancellations and notes might be seen as directed to the same end.

Whatever Hardy may have expected in the way of trouble about the story, he cannot have imagined that the response would be so destructive; he cannot have conceived that he would have to ward off demands for a completely new narrative by altering the existing one out of all recognition. In the manuscript the story turns upon the claim of a wife dying in childbirth that her child was not fathered by her husband, with added hints that a young nobleman was the actual father. It explores the developing attitudes of the widower to the son thus left to him; at first he is outraged, then he is both attracted by the boy himself and seduced by the noble blood in him, and he becomes in time pleased by the child's irregular birth (until, that is, he learns first that his wife habitually suffered from delusions, and then that the nobleman in question was out of the country at the relevant time). Finally, the full development of the son's physiognomy as he grows into a man confirms that he is all too securely his own child, and Hardy observes with irony the father's dismay.

Extra-marital sex seems to have been the moral transgression that the editors of the *Graphic* would on no account accept; what Hardy did for the English serial was to make the deathbed confession one of substitution after the original child's death rather than of ille-

gitimacy. This meant that all the material dealing with the connection with the noble family was irrelevant, and was excluded, thus at a stroke reducing the story by half. Hardy deleted the passage:

> She thereupon related an incident concerning the baby's parentage, which was not as he supposed.

In its place the *Graphic* has:

> She thereupon declared to him that the baby was not theirs. Her infant had died when a few hours old, and, knowing his desire for an heir, she had with the assistance of the nurse exchanged her child for a poor woman's living one, born about the same day.

Hardy is forced to be more explicit; he cannot now risk leaving anything to the reader's imagination. If the enforced change has a virture, it is that in making the wife's motive her husband's great desire for an heir he brings the story even more in line with those around it, in which the inability to engender a male successor haunts most of the male protagonists. After this fundamental change of direction there are occasional adjustments to phrases to accommodate the different version, but mostly there is in the *Graphic* just the straightforward omission of paragraph after paragraph.

It seems probable that Hardy made these wholesale changes on the proofs, since, where it was possible, he showed skilful economy in adapting phrasing from one version to another, something seen to even greater effect in his revision of *The Well-Beloved*. In the light of this economy, it comes as a slight surprise to see that the ending of the story has been completely rewritten. Petrick's son in the new version tries to get money at school by fraud, and the father, instead of seeing ancestral features gradually fix themselves in his child's face, perceives 'in this deed of his son additional evidence of his being one of his own flesh and blood, but it was evidence of a terrifying kind.' So we have the dubious hypothesis advanced, that ability in forging documents is an inheritable faculty.

At its best, in the form in which it is now generally read, **'Squire Petrick's Lady'** is not one of Hardy's greatest stories, but it does have a satisfying ironic pattern to set against its deficiencies in characterization and plot. From the version in the *Graphic* nothing can be salvaged; and if we turn to another of the stories most heavily and awkwardly bowdlerized for the English serialization, **'Lady Mottisfont'**, the changes Hardy was forced to make (though smaller in volume than for **'Squire Petrick's Lady'**) are even more destructive of the original idea of the story. Indeed the alteration bears comparison, on a different scale, with what Hardy was constrained to do a year later to the central theme of *Tess of the d'Urbervilles* by the prospect of publishing in the same magazine.

At the heart of the story is another illegitimate child; this time Dorothy, the daughter of Sir Ashley Mottisfont and a Contessa of no other name. Sir Ashley is widowed, and when he marries again he successfully interests his wife in the infant whom he 'found one day in a patch of wild thyme'—the more easily since it seems that they can have no children of their own. The Contessa, however, is anxious to have the child, to 'adopt' her; the noble lady's wealth and the perfection of her mind and person make it difficult to deny her. As Lady Mottisfont works out the real relationship between the girl, her husband, and the Contessa—calling herself rather nicely 'a walking piece of simplicity' for not having recognized it earlier—she agrees, with some anguish, to let Dorothy go. She attempts suicide, but is prevented by her husband. The twist in the story is that the Contessa eventually wishes to remarry, and so offers Dorothy back to the Mottisfonts again, only to find that Lady Mottisfont is at last pregnant and has no longer room in her affections for her husband's illegitimate daughter. The victim of the story has to return to the house of the peasant countrywoman who had taken care of her as an infant, where the hardships of life cause her pain for a while; eventually she marries an engineer, a man who does something useful in the world.

The most convincingly created character in the story is Sir Ashley Mottisfont, whose low-key gentleness, patience, kindness, and concern for his wife and his child are well-established in a series of details, speeches, and actions; his failure to tell his wife the whole story of Dorothy's parentage stems more, we believe, from desire to save her pain than from intent to deceive her.

The crucial enforced change in the *Graphic* is the cancellation of this passage narrating Lady Mottisfont's response to Dorothy and her probable parentage:

> the baby whom her husband had so mysteriously lighted on during his ride home—concerning which remarkable discovery she had her own opinion; but being so extremely amiable and affectionate that she could have loved stocks and stones if there had been no living creatures to love, she uttered none of her thoughts.

It was replaced by a two-paragraph tale of secrecy, suicide, crime, and poltroonery:

> Lady Mottisfont did not at this time guess her husband's true relation to the child, the circumstances of which were rather remarkable. Before knowing Philippa, he had secretly married a young woman of the metropolis, of no position, daughter of a dealer in East India Stock; and a short time after the marriage this man was convicted and hung for forgery. The disgrace thereof made Sir Ashley reluctant to avow his marriage, since he had not yet done so: his wife's hopes in

her future were completely shattered; and soon after the birth of their child, in a moment of gloom at her husband's disgust with his alliance, she put an end to herself.

> She had an only sister, who, more fortunate, had wedded an Italian nobleman and left England before her father's crime was known. On this account she was not available as protector of the baby, who was thus thrown entirely upon Sir Ashley's hands. But still he would not own her by reason of the said events; and thus it fell out that the child was handed over to the tender care of a villager as though she were a child of shame.

There are other omissions and alterations to take account of the fact that the Contessa is now Dorothy's aunt; but this is the significant one. It represents an almost total reversal of Sir Ashley Mottisfont's character; he becomes so heartless that he drives his first wife to suicide, and abandons his quite legitimate child to the (ironically expressed) 'tender care' of a villager. It is pleasant amidst all this self-centred cruelty to see Hardy getting in at least a reference to the original situation in 'as though she were a child of shame'. But the rather delicate touches that earlier defined Sir Ashley, above all his affection and care for Dorothy once his wife has finally rejected her, all now run counter to the powerful impression created by the addition in the *Graphic,* making a nonsense of the story.

It is not hard to imagine the cynicism with which Hardy undertook this kind of destruction of his central themes, his minimal regard for the seriousness or intelligence of the readers of the *Graphic* (he must have been writing tongue in cheek when he added 'whom the shrewd reader may guess to be Dorothy's aunt' in the serial).

'Barbara of the House of Grebe' (**'Barbara'** as it was called in the *Graphic*) also received the hostile attentions of the magazine's editorial board. The first thing that was thrown out is much of the horror that Barbara felt at the revelation of the face of her husband Edmond on his return from Italy; Barbara's terror, Willowes's demand that she look a second time, her shudder at the sight, are all omitted. What remains is: 'when it was done she shut her eyes at the spectacle that was revealed.' Even the adjective 'hideous' is removed from before 'spectacle'. When Uplandtowers prepares to mutilate the statue of Willowes, a similar restraint was imposed by the *Graphic*'s editors.

Other enforced changes were connected with the desire for an heir and with childbirth. In a characteristic pattern, Hardy was allowed to retain this:

> he beheld the door of the private recess open, and Barbara within it, standing with her arms clasped tightly round the neck of her Edmond, and her mouth on his. The shawl which she had thrown round her nightclothes

had slipped from her shoulders, and her long white robe and pale face lent her the blanched appearance of a second statue embracing the first.

He was not, however, allowed to include Lord Up-landtowers's response to this sight, his feeling that what the statue of her first husband was getting, he was not. He had to omit:

> The heir presumptive to the title was a remote relative whom Lord Uplandtowers did not exclude from the dislike he entertained towards many things and persons besides; and he had set his mind upon a lineal successor. He blamed her much that there was no promise of this, and asked her what she was good for.

Without experiencing Barbara's extreme distress at the frightening aspect of her first husband, it becomes very difficult for the reader to accept the complete transformation in her attitude to her second husband after his 'treatment'. That Hardy also felt this, is implied by a final omission from the manuscript which may have been made as a corollary of the enforced changes rather than as part of the sequence of alterations demanded of him:

> How fright could have effected such a change of idiosyncracy learned physicians alone can say; but I believe such cases of reversional instinct are not unknown. The strange upshot was that the cure became so perfect as to be itself a new disease. She clung to him so slavishly that she would not willingly be out of his sight for a moment.

In **'The Lady Caroline (afterwards Marchioness of Stonehenge)'** it is again childbirth that is the most objectionable element, even though the woman is quite properly (though secretly) married. Lady Caroline is anxious to pass off her as yet unborn child as that of a cottager who had also loved her now-dead husband; this coy introduction of the topic:

> And Lady Caroline whispered a few words to the girl.
>
> "O my lady!" said the thunderstruck Milly,
>
> "What will you do?"

becomes in the *Graphic* the apparently inconsequential:

> My heart reproaches me so for having been ashamed of him that I get no rest night or day.

And, later, 'How can I, when he is the father of the poor child that's coming to me?' is altered to 'How can I, honestly?'

The conclusion of the debate between Milly and Lady Caroline is that both go away, and, in the words of the manuscript, 'Milly came home with an infant in her arms'. We may well wonder how the whole point of the story is to be saved in the *Graphic,* which has made not even an indirect allusion to pregnancy as a motive for Lady Caroline's behaviour. In fact, the editors bowed to the essential, and 'the child of the marriage of Lady Caroline' (not, it should be noted 'the child of Lady Caroline'; that would have been too direct) is added after 'arms'.

As noted earlier, the fact that the marriage in this story had taken place made no difference to the attitude of the editors of the *Graphic* towards pregnancy, and the same is true of their response to the details surrounding the secret visits that Lady Caroline's secretly wedded husband made to her: all the mechanism of his entry to the house of her parents is omitted, as is the idea of his staying there an hour, and the lateness of that particular hour ('the hour of one' is reduced to 'the hour'); it is no longer possible to imagine that they have been sleeping together. In fact, the *Graphic*'s 'hatchet men' seem to have disliked the whole concept of the story, and may have suggested to Hardy that he change the reaction of the just-married couple to their situation from 'both being supremely happy and content' to 'both being presumably happy and content' (though, the implication is, they should be utterly miserable if they had any right feeling). It is, on the other hand, just possible that the substitution of 'presumably' for 'supremely' was a compositorial error in the magazine; if so it was a pleasant piece of serendipity which Hardy saw no reason to change.

At least with **'Anna, Lady Baxby'** the meddling of the *Graphic* is straightforwardly concerned to remove a loose woman. In the manuscript Hardy introduces a girl from Sherton with whom Lord Baxby has made an assignation at the entrance to his castle. For the *Graphic* he replaces her with some characters who are plotting to remove Lord Baxby's wife Anna from the castle so that her brother, who is in charge of the parliamentary troops besieging the castle, will find himself able to storm it. This change alters the whole fabric of the climax of the story, but for once does not completely destroy the story's credibility, simply makes it something else. In both cases Anna discovers the outsiders, and the result is the same: instead of leaving the castle to join her brother as she had planned, she returns and remains faithful to her husband and the royalist cause. That in one version she is sent back by jealousy and an awakened sense of the sexual value of her husband, and in the other by patriotism and family feeling, might be seen to represent two facets inherent in Anna in any case. But it would have been sad to lose permanently the detail of Anna tying her husband's hair to the bed to make sure that he did not get up and go out after she managed to get back to sleep again; it was, naturally enough, omitted in the *Graphic* version.

The imposed changes made in **'The Lady Icenway'**, the last of the *Graphic*'s six stories to be looked at, resemble quite closely those made in **'Barbara'**. There are several substantial passages omitted from the *Graphic* or altered in it; the first is an omission which is very reminiscent of Lord Uplandtowers's attitude to his heir:

> It was a matter of great anxiety to him that there should be a lineal successor to the barony, yet no sign of that successor had as yet appeared. One day he complained to her quite roughly of his fate. "All will go to that dolt of a cousin!" he cried. "I'd sooner see my name and place at the bottom of the sea!"

The second is a passage cancelled in blue pencil in the manuscript, in which it is implied that Lady Icenway might have a son by her bigamous husband and pass it off as the child of Icenway. Without this possibility the story loses much of its point; and the ending has to be altered so that Lady Icenway simply regrets not waiting for her first love to be in a position to marry her, instead of wishing she had thought of her plan for getting Icenway an heir before that first love died.

The kinds of change forced upon Hardy, thus brought together for scrutiny, reveal the extent to which the stories in *A Group of Noble Dames* dramatize the dynastic sense of the ruling class, and rejoice in showing the twists by which the desire for an acceptable heir is thwarted or perverted. Examination of the alterations also highlights the thoughtful psychological understanding of relations between men and women over marriage and children which is for the most part destroyed in the *Graphic*'s versions of the stories. That Hardy felt that these interferences were more unwarranted than any in his fictional career to date is suggested by the fact that all bar one of the excised passages reappear in the first edition of the collection, sometimes in a revised form. This cannot be said of those equally mutilated serializations *Tess of the d'Urbervilles* and *Jude the Obscure*.

It has already been hinted that the magazine issue of the stories in America was substantially different from its appearance in the *Graphic*. And, in fact, while these violences were being done to the story sequence in England, the American serialization in *Harper's Weekly* remained more or less inviolate; the only bowdlerizations that it suffered were those marked in blue on the manuscript, already discussed. However, this is not the whole story of the *Harper's* text; there are other independent and unique differences. One example is in the first paragraph of **'Lady Mottisfont'**; in talking of the interior of Wintoncester Cathedral the phrase 'three hundred steps westward' occurs in the manuscript; in the *Graphic* 'amid those magnificent tombs' was added to it, and the first edition also has the addition, as does every subsequent text. There is, however, a further expanded version in *Harper's*: 'amid those magnificent ecclesiastical tombs and royal monuments', suggested by the subsequent reference in the story to the dust of kings and bishops. There are four similar instances of independent *Harper's* additions in the early part of the story.

These revisions are not of the kind that might have been made by the American editor, and so must have appeared on the copy that Hardy sent to *Harper's*; there is no reason to suspect that he saw proof of the American printing. It is virtually certain that copy for *Harper's* was a duplicate of the first set of proofs that he received from the *Graphic*. It is also probable that it would have been marked with approximately the same revisions that appeared on this first set of English proofs (though we have sufficient evidence, from the manuscript of *Two on a Tower* for instance, that Hardy found it very difficult to revise identically two copies of the same text). Thus the likelihood is that these unique readings in *Harper's* represent Hardy's earlier intentions for the magazine issue, which were lost sight of in the face of frantic messages about other aspects of the stories from prudish gentlemen.

A somewhat different pattern occurs in **'The Lady Caroline'** where in one sentence, for instance, the manuscript and the *Graphic* have 'walked' and 'a lake' and *Harper's* has the characteristically Hardyan 'trudged afoot' and 'fish-ponds'. The first edition in this case follows the American serial (though with what must be a compositorial error in 'trudged about'). The implication of this example and others like it is that Hardy must have retained a copy of the first *Graphic* proofs and consulted them as well as the manuscript and the published *Graphic* version when reconstituting the stories for the first book-edition.

It has already been suggested that Hardy was aware that some details in his stories might provoke an alarmed response from those in charge at the *Graphic*, and that as a result he blue-pencilled a few passages in the manuscript. Evidence from the American serial shows that Hardy still felt uneasy at the proof stage. In **'Barbara of the House of Grebe'** for instance, after her marriage to Lord Uplandtowers (in the manuscript and the first edition) Barbara seems to show no sign of producing an heir: 'He blamed her much that there was no promise of this, and asked her what she was good for.' The *Graphic* excludes the whole thing, as it does all those passages relating to childbirth; in *Harper's* the first part of the sentence stands, but the insult is omitted and it ends at 'this'. The American version seems to be another voluntary attempt by Hardy to pre-empt the foolish pruderies of the *Graphic* through self-bowdlerization, and as such the cancellation would also probably have been made in the early *Graphic* proofs. There are similar instances in this and other stories.

There are thus stranded in *Harper's* a number of authorial revisions, and an editor of **A Group of Noble Dames** would have to decide what to do with them. Though the self-censorship should be rejected, there is an adequate argument for retaining in an edited text other independent revisions in *Harper's*. Although Hardy almost certainly had a copy of the first *Graphic* proofs to refer to when making the first-edition text, it has also been pointed out that he may have made further revisions on the set he sent to America. Any decision about stranded variants will necessarily depend upon the priorities and principles of the individual editor.

The reader who is interested in considering in detail the effect that Hardy's experiences over the serialization of **A Group of Noble Dames** may have had upon the development of *Tess,* once he knew that it also was to appear in the *Graphic,* will find all the necessary material in the Clarendon edition of the novel. In general terms it may be said that the cynicism with which Hardy treated the readers of the periodical version of the short-story sequence was equalled in his handling of the novel. The substitution in the serial of a mock-marriage for Tess's violation in the Chase was made with no regard to probability and thematic integrity; what the readership of the *Graphic* thought of a story in which the whole of a girl's future happiness is made to depend upon her inability to tell a real registrar from a man dressed up as one is hard to say. At this moment in his career Hardy probably imagined that they were incapable of thinking about it at all.

It is of some interest that when the proof-sheets of *Tess* in the *Graphic* were sent to America for *Harper's Weekly,* Hardy felt sufficiently certain of the capacity of American audience to tolerate a greater degree of realism in sexual matters to omit the episode with the fake registrar, and replace it with the following:

> He said it must be private, even from you, on account of his mother, and by special licence. However it came to nothing, and then he pestered me and persecuted me—and I was in his power—and you may guess the rest . . . Since then I have been staying on at Trantridge. But at last I felt it was wrong, and would do so no longer, though he wished me to stay; and here I am.

Although he was unable to restore for Americans the episodes he had left out for the English, he contrived with his customary economy to ensure that for part of his serial audience at least he would tell the truth about Tess.[19]

Notes

1. *Early Life,* p. 205; *Letters,* i. 115.

2. Hardy's study-copy is in the Dorset County Museum. A few years later William Blackwood wrote to Hardy, concerning the story 'The Withered Arm' which Hardy was to publish in *Blackwood's Magazine*: 'On the margin of proof I have made a few suggestions for your consideration' (9 December 1887). Hardy's response is lost, but three weeks later Blackwood wrote: 'The little change you made of making the farmer die a natural death & as a chastened man was a decided improvement' (30 December 1887; letters in the Dorset County Museum). Perhaps this was one of Blackwood's hints to Hardy. But it is at least clear that the editor was involved to a degree in the creative process in this case, as has already been seen elsewhere.

3. See e.g. Christine Winfield, 'Factual Sources for Two Episodes in *The Mayor of Casterbridge*', *Nineteenth-Century Fiction,* 25 (1970), 224-31, and William Greenslade, 'Hardy's "Facts" Notebook: A Further Factual Source for *The Mayor of Casterbridge*', *The Thomas Hardy Journal,* 2.1 (Jan. 1986), 33-5.

4. *Early Life,* p. 235.

5. See Purdy, pp. 48, 63-5 and 68-73; *Letters,* i. 229.

6. *Letters,* i., 225-26, 229, 215.

7. It is certainly true that Arthur Hopkins had some trouble with his illustrations to *The Return of the Native* because he did not have the whole story before him when making drawings for the first few episodes. Hardy sent Hopkins a summary of the character-relationships in the story, and expressed at Hopkins's invitation some criticisms of the first portrait of Eustacia (*Letters,* i. 52-3). Leon Edel, in his biography of Henry James, points out that the publication of some of James's stories was delayed because of difficulties with the illustrations (*Henry James: A Life* (New York: Harper and Row, 1985), 346).

8. *PBSA* 67 (1973), 33-58.

9. One of the bowdlerizations is particularly crass. Riesner, in his essay on the development of the text of the novel, 'Kunstprosa in der Werkstatt', draws eloquent attention to it in a footnote (p. 272). This is my translation: 'One of the most delightful passages of the entire book is robbed of its punch-line: the constable, who in his reproduction of profane speech in front of the court abbreviates all curses, is impatiently interrupted by Henchard: "Come—we don't want to hear any more of them cust d's" (MS fo. 287, *Harper's Weekly,* p. 198). In the *Graphic* (p. 342) "cust" is missing.' It is also worth noting that the continuation of Henchard's speech was a proof-addition for the

serial: 'Say the word out like a man, and don't be so modest, Stubberd: or else leave it alone.' This might be taken as Hardy's comment on the previous enforced bowdlerization.

10. See Seth Weiner, 'Thomas Hardy and his First American Publisher', *Princeton University Library Chronicle,* 39 (1978), 134-57.

11. I am grateful to Professor Dale Kramer, who has shared with me the results of his work on the text of *The Mayor of Casterbridge,* some of which appear in the introduction to his World's Classics edition of the novel.

12. *Letters,* i., 189.

13. More details will be found in the introduction to the Clarendon edition of the novel.

14. The 1968 University of Notre Dame dissertation 'A Textual Study of Thomas Hardy's *A Group of Noble Dames*' by A. Macleod has aspects of interest, but is too often inaccurate and thus unreliable.

15. Letter in the Dorset County Museum.

16. *Letters,* i., 215-16.

17. The manuscript of the *Graphic* stories is in the Library of Congress, Washington.

18. Was Hardy's spelling here of the young nobleman's title an error, or his first version of what was to become a familiar name to his readers? That it was an interlined replacement in the manuscript for 'Trantridge' (from *Tess of the d'Urbervilles* to *Jude the Obscure* via *A Group of Noble Dames*!) is strong presumptive evidence that the spelling was deliberate. If it was, did Hardy then think of Christminster as being pronounced with a short 'i', as the manuscript version of the name must have been?

19. By the time Hardy came to serialize his last novel, *Jude the Obscure* (an eventually painful process well outlined by Patricia Ingham in her 'The Evolution of *Jude the Obscure*', *Review of English Studies,* NS 27 (1976)), he was clear about the nature of this version of his work. In a telling fragment from a letter of 16 February 1895 to Grant Allen he wrote: 'I wish I could send you the real copy of the story I have written for Harpers', as the form in which it is appearing there is a conventionalized one, in several points' (*Letters,* ii, 68-9). It is indeed the unreality of the serializations of *Tess* and *Jude* that most directly strikes a reader familiar with the first editions.

Pamela Dalziel (essay date December 1989)

SOURCE: Dalziel, Pamela. "Hardy as Collaborator: The Composition of 'The Spectre of the Real.'" *Papers of the Bibliographical Society of America* 83, no. 4 (December 1989): 473-501.

[*In the following essay, Dalziel documents the collaboration between Hardy and Florence Henniker on the development of "The Spectre of the Real," citing excerpts from their correspondence as well as from various drafts of the story.*]

Occupying a unique place in the Hardy canon as his only acknowledged collaborative work, **"The Spectre of the Real"** had its origins in the special nature of Thomas Hardy's relationship with his co-author, the novelist Florence Henniker, daughter of Richard Monckton Milnes, Lord Houghton, and wife of Arthur Henry Henniker-Major, a distinguished professional soldier. Hardy met Florence Henniker in Dublin on 19 May 1893 and was immediately attracted to her, describing her in his notebook entry for that date as "A charming, *intuitive* woman apparently."[1] The intensity of his subsequent feelings, glimpsed in the surviving letters and openly celebrated in some of his most moving poems,[2] led him to adopt any stratagems—from architectural lessons to literary discussions—which might help to establish an intimate friendship. For her part, as a successful but not particularly celebrated novelist, she was not reluctant to be on familiar terms with the author of *Tess of the d'Urbervilles*. It was, however, Hardy who was the suitor and he behaved as such, not scrupling to stoop to flattery. He read and praised her work, wrote a promotional paragraph about her,[3] described her as "a real woman of letters," and declared in his letter of 29 June: "If ever I were to consult any woman on a point in my own novels I should let that woman be yourself—my belief in your insight and your sympathies being strong, and increasing."[4]

Although it quickly became clear that Henniker had no intention of entering into a romantic liaison with Hardy, at the time when the possibility of their literary collaboration was first raised, he had not yet given up hope. It seems significant that in a letter of 20 July his promise to "think over the scheme of our collaborating in the talked of story" is immediately preceded by a reference to her conventional Christian views (and moral standards): "I cannot help wishing you were free from certain retrograde superstitions: and I believe you will be some day, and none the less happy for the emancipation."[5] Since Hardy said that he would "think over" the scheme, it was probably Henniker who had suggested it during his visit to her the previous day, perhaps desiring to direct his attentions into safe literary channels as much as to benefit professionally from an association with such a celebrated author. For him there was, of course, no possibility of gain except in personal terms, and there is some indication that he seriously took up the idea of their collaboration only as a kind of last resort following their trip to Winchester on 8 August, the occasion when Henniker made it clear that the relationship could not be as he wished.[6] A literary partnership would at least provide an excuse for meetings and correspondence, and Hardy may still have hoped that friendship might eventually lead to something more.

But collaborating with Henniker did not prove to be easy. Although she doubtless spoke truly when in subsequent years she insisted that Hardy's kindness in offering "hints & suggestions" for her work was both "an advantage" and "a great compliment,"[7] she was in fact quite sensitive to his criticisms. Unlike the novice author Evangeline Smith who in 1876 had sent Hardy a rejected story for comment—unlike, indeed, Agnes Grove and Florence Dugdale who succeeded Henniker as his literary protégées—Henniker had already published three quite successful novels,[8] and she to some extent approached Hardy more as a fellow author than as a pupil. That Hardy was aware of this is suggested by the conciliatory tone of his 6 September 1893 letter concerning the stories she had sent him:

> I was very glad to receive your letter, dear Mrs Henniker, & to hear about the stories, & that you received my scribblings for amendments on their pages without any of the umbrage you might have felt at the liberty I took in making them.
>
> If I may venture to say it, I think you have made a serious mistake in leaving "His Excellency" out of the collection. . . . The simple & sole fault of the tale was its conventional ending, as I said, which might easily have been remedied by rewriting a conclusion. I enclose for what it is worth a third suggestion on that point, which occurred to me just after dispatching my last letter.
>
> I should call the book "The Statesman's Love-Lapse, & other stories namely . . ." . . .
>
> [P.S.] (On second thoughts it is not worth while to enclose the note on the story.)[9]

Several weeks later, after recommending the collection to the literary agent A. P. Watt, Hardy expressed his hope that Henniker had carried out his suggestions, especially those concerning a story called "A Lost Illusion," and so made the volume more attractive to a potential publisher.[10] It is difficult to know just what her response was. She neither adopted his title (the volume was published as *Outlines*) nor included "His Excellency," but she perhaps did alter "A Lost Illusion": in the final scene of the story as published (it was retitled "A Sustained Illusion") the central figure, Purcell, after being given cause to question his granddaughter's respectability, believes her cover-up lie and dies before she breaks down and admits the truth.

Since Henniker's conclusions were often weak—prompting Hardy to suggest alternatives—the original version probably ended with the first revelation scene.

With **"The Spectre of the Real"** Hardy was of course much more actively involved in the compositional process—though not to the extent that has hitherto been assumed. Richard L. Purdy's theory—expanded by Michael Millgate and repeated by Simon Gatrell and Jeffrey S. Cramer—proposes that "the collaboration consisted in Hardy's discussing the outlines of his story with Mrs. Henniker and incorporating in the finished work some brief paragraphs she had written."[11] But, as will be demonstrated, the surviving correspondence, Henniker's fiction, and especially the two typescripts and the proofs of **"Spectre"** [**"The Spectre of the Real"**][12]—the first typescript revised by Henniker and then by Hardy, the second typescript (based on the corrected first typescript) and proofs revised by Hardy alone—suggest a considerably more complicated history. It can be summarized thus: after discussing the project, including potential plots, with Henniker, Hardy sent her two outlines; she selected one and wrote it up as a scenario which he altered slightly; she then wrote out the story in full and sent the manuscript to Hardy, who extensively revised it and completely rewrote the conclusion before dispatching it to be typed; after she had lightly corrected that first typescript, he altered it substantially, had a second typescript made, revised it, sent it to *To-Day,* and finally corrected the proofs when they arrived.

Work on the story—originally entitled **"Desire"**—must have begun by early September 1893, for on the 10th Hardy wrote to Henniker: "I send the **'Desire'** sketch, with the trifling modification. I think the insertion in red at the end improves it."[13] Evidently she did not immediately reply, for three days later he wrote again to say: "I hope you received the skeleton MS. If you don't like either of the two stories will you be frank, & tell me? I can send others, as I have several partly thought out: & it *must* be a good one."[14] Since Hardy asked for Henniker's frank opinion, the original idea for **"Desire"** had presumably been his, possibly influenced by earlier discussions they had had together, while the reference to "two stories" points to Hardy's having previously sent her outlines of some kind,[15] perhaps the "sketch-plots" she returned the following month.[16] As for "the skeleton MS" sent to Henniker, it has hitherto been assumed that this was Hardy's outline,[17] but his classification of it as a "sketch" suggests something more developed (such as a scenario), while his use of the placatory "trifling" clearly implies that it was her work he was modifying. Significantly, too, when he later suggested that they "put back the Desire for the present," he asked if she would "mind the trouble of writing . . . out" a "still better story" if he could think of one.[18]

Hardy's attempt to downplay his revision of the "skeleton MS" was apparently unsuccessful, since on 16 September he was obliged to reassure her: "As to my having 'contempt' as you suggest, for your rendering of the **'Desire'**, you know I *never* can have that for *anything* you do."[19] His protestations were, however, somewhat disingenuous: if he did not have "contempt" for her work, he would at least have preferred it to have been different. Earlier in the same letter he had written:

> Yes: I *do* sigh a little; over your position less than over your conventional views. I do not mind its results upon the present little story (which please alter as you like)— but upon your future literary career. If you mean to make the world listen to you, you must say now what they will all be thinking & saying five & twenty years hence: & if you do that you must offend your conventional friends.

It is true that Henniker's fiction suffers from her adherence to convention—the wicked and even the erring virtuous are killed off at an alarming rate—and doubtless Hardy did wish her to be successful, but his advice was scarcely disinterested. Having failed to convince her of the personal desirability of becoming the "enfranchised woman" he sought,[20] hence potentially more sympathetic to his romantic overtures, he somewhat unfairly invoked the possible literary consequences of her "conventional views." What becomes increasingly clear is that he remained more concerned with the possibilities of their relationship than with the quality of their story.

As a professional writer with an established reputation, he could hardly be indifferent to the latter, however, and after receiving the completed manuscript from her on 22 September,[21] he was apparently unable to refrain from suggesting alterations, although the letter in question has not survived. On 6 October, in any case, he again felt compelled to apologize: "I did not at all *mean* my last note to be unkind, & am sorry that it seemed so, & hurt you about the MS. . . . Never would I give *you* pain!"[22] A sense of frustration is apparent throughout this letter—in his reproach because she had not sent a specific address in Scotland, in his jealous comparison of himself, "a mere scribbler who would not kill a fly," to her "millionaire sportsmen" companions, and above all in his complaint about her absence:

> I have several things to ask you on our literary partnership, but I cannot enter into them till a distinct postal communication is re-established between us—or, still better, a meeting is feasible. . . . It is unfortunate that

just when this scheme rendered it necessary for us to communicate freely & easily you shd have rushed off to such outlandish latitudes: otherwise we should almost have been in print by this time.

Their collaboration had failed not only as a means of increasing intimacy but also, so it seemed, as a literary venture, for in spite of his assurances that he wished "as much as ever to carry out the joint story," Hardy was beginning to wonder whether their conflicting views could in fact be reconciled. He accordingly suggested putting back **"Desire"** for "the present" in favour of "a still better story."

This tactful attempt to withdraw from what was becoming an impossible situation was evidently not supported by Henniker, however, for on 22 October, after dispatching the stories for the *Life's Little Ironies* volume to Osgood, McIlvaine, Hardy again "turn[ed] to the 'Desire.'"[23] Discussion in the interim must have focused largely upon the question of alternative endings, for in explanation of the need for a new title he wrote:

> I have planned to carry out Ending II—since you like it so much better: I feel I ought not to force the other upon you—wh. is too uncompromising for one of the pretty sex to have a hand in. The question now is, what shall we call it?—'The ressurection [*sic*] of a Love"?

Hardy was obviously doing his utmost not to offend his collaborator, consulting her not only about the title of their joint project but also about the name for the heroine of his next novel (significantly, Sue Bridehead's second name is Florence). Moreover, he insisted that Henniker's "remarks on the various possibilities of the **'Desire'** [were] very thoughtful & good," and that he did not object to her criticisms ("please do any amount of them, dear fellow-scribbler").

But Hardy's artistic conscience again refused to be stifled altogether, and three days later he tentatively withdrew his previous concession: "A word as to our story: in working it out I find it may possibly be necessary to effect a compromise between the two endings: for on no account must it end weakly."[24] By 28 October he was able to report that the story was "finished virtually" and that the manuscript had been sent "early this morning" to a professional typist with instructions to send the resulting typescript directly to Henniker.[25] Hardy had come up with a new ending, one which, whether "good or bad," he saw as having "the merit of being in exact keeping with Lord P.'s character,"[26] and he broached the subject of this and other revisions cautiously, promising to defer to her wishes:

> Will you please read it from the beginning (*without glancing first at the end!*) so as to get the intended effect, & judge of its strength or weakness. It is, as you

wished, very tragic; a modified form of Ending II—which I think better than any we have thought of before. If anything in it is what you don't like please tell me quite freely,—& it shall be modified. As I said last time, all the wickedness (if it has any) will be laid on my unfortunate head, while all the tender & proper parts will be attributed to you. Without wishing to make you promise, I suggest that we keep it a secret to our two selves which is my work & which yours. We may be amusingly bothered by friends & others to confess.

To reconstruct the original version of Ending II preferred by Henniker is impossible, but what seems clear is that it, too, was "very tragic"—her own fiction, although conventional, very rarely ends happily—though without involving Parkhurst's suicide. More typical of Henniker would have been the accidental deaths of both Jim and Parkhurst, and perhaps Rosalys as well. As for the "uncompromising" Ending I referred to in the 22 October letter, it is tempting to think that it might have involved yet another reworking of the Elfride-Knight, Tess-Angel situation: confession followed by rejection. As it stands the conclusion is of course a variation on that theme, even though the "real" may on this occasion not have been voluntarily revealed, and it is therefore not surprising that Hardy thought it the best.

Having substantially—and independently—altered the plot of their story, Hardy attempted to reinstate Henniker as co-author by inviting her to revise the account of the wedding morning and to make the final choice of title:

> In reading it over, particularly the bride's doings in the morning from dawn till the wedding-hour, please insert in pencil any details that I have omitted, & that would only be known to a woman. I may not be quite correct in what I have hastily written, never having had the pleasure of being a bride-elect myself. . . .
>
> Our old title was in itself rather good, but as it does not quite apply, I have provisionally substituted **"The Spectre of the Real"**.—"The Looming of the Real" is perhaps almost better. I have also thought of "A passion & after"; "To-day's kiss & yesterday's."—"Husband's corpse & husband's kiss" "A shattering of Ideals". When you have read the modifications you will be able to choose; or suggest.

Henniker perhaps chose the title and she did make a few pencil alterations still visible on the typescript, but these were of a relatively minor kind, neither adding details to the wedding morning passages nor modifying the ending. What she evidently did insist upon, however, was the reinstatement of some descriptive passages of hers that Hardy had excised during his revision of the manuscript. He was clearly sensitive on this point and in the 28 October letter had attempted to forestall objections:

> I will send you back the pages of detail omitted, if you wd like to have them, as they may be useful. You will *quite* understand that they were not omitted because

they weren't good; but because the scale of the story was too small to admit them without injury to the proportion of the whole. I refer particularly to the description of the pool, & the bird tracks; which I *much* wished to retain.

Hardy also mentioned that he had asked the typist to return the manuscript "in case [he] should want to insert a little more detail from it," but he probably did not expect to have to restore quite as much as he did—not only the pool and bird-tracks passage but also shorter descriptions of butterflies playing hide-and-seek, Rosalys whistling to a robin, and birds sleeping in the park (1TS, ff. 24^v, 18, 31). All these passages were added to the typescript in Hardy's hand but are clearly restorations of Henniker's work. They were, however, rewritten—as Hardy's false starts and alterations demonstrate—and apparently moved on occasion from their original manuscript positions, for the typescript shows traces of two abandoned attempts to incorporate them: in the margin of folio 17, alongside the paragraph about the (lack of) view from the summer-house, a largely illegible erasure includes the words "copper-coloured butterfly" and "in the hedge with a little blue companion"; on the verso of folio 35, keyed for insertion after the sentence beginning "When the doctor had left," is the undeleted fragment of a version of the pool and bird-tracks passage, "The lake was before her, & from the mud at the edge."

That the descriptive passages were finally included is evidence not only of Henniker's strength of will but also of Hardy's willingness to accommodate her—and by extension the depth of his feelings—even at some cost to his professional integrity, for the details are essentially superfluous, contributing little or nothing to the story in terms of imagery, theme, mood, or even local colour. As such they are typical of Henniker's work: all her stories contain obtrusive description for its own sake,[27] usually involving birds, occasionally butterflies and small animals. The style, too, is essentially Henniker's, prosaic and thick with clichés. Compare, for example, the following lines from **"Spectre"**—even as improved by Hardy—with a passage from Henniker's *Bid Me Good-bye*:

> not a creature was conscious of the presence of these two but a little squirrel they had disturbed in a beech . . .
>
> (P 7)
>
> Suddenly the plovers rose into the air, uttering their customary wails, and dispersing like a group of stars from a rocket; and the herons drew up their flail-like legs, and flapped themselves away.
>
> (P 5)
>
> She was conscious that St. Aubyn was knocking off the head of a large-leaved plant at their feet; that a squirrel looked at them with his shy bright eyes, and sprang

into a hollow tree above their heads; that a pheasant, with a frightened whirr of wings, started up from the thicket and soared away into the sky.

(Bid Me Good-bye 126)

Henniker's written contributions to **"Spectre"** were not, however, limited to such descriptive passages, as has hitherto been believed. Millgate, developing Purdy's conclusions, assumes that "the pages of detail" to be returned to Henniker were all she wrote and that they were separate from the manuscript sent to the typist.[28] But since Hardy had asked for the manuscript back as a potential source of additional detail, it seems clear that the manuscript as returned to him contained both narrative and detail mixed together—otherwise the omitted descriptive passages could simply have been kept back in the first place. That Hardy should have mentioned "pages" of detail is not in itself problematic in light of Henniker's large hand and the length—up to 300 words—of some of her descriptive passages in other works; nor, of course, were all her descriptions necessarily reinstated. The phrase, too, could merely have been a concise designation for pages "predominantly of detail," "containing detail," and so forth. It is in any case improbable that Hardy, after reading page after page of stock description in Henniker's first three novels, would have asked her to supply similar passages for their story.

The manuscript sent to the typist on 28 October, then, was presumably the one Hardy had received from Henniker on 22 September. It had of course been extensively revised since then—as is suggested by Hardy's references to "tak[ing] the **'Desire'** in hand" on 22 October, "working it out" on 25 October, and having "finished [it] virtually" on 28 October[29]—but not to the extent of necessitating the production of a new manuscript, except perhaps of the rewritten ending. If it had been completely recopied, after all, it would not have contained the omitted detail that Hardy wanted to have available for possible reinsertion. Hardy's reworking of Henniker's material—and, indeed, of his own—was not, however, limited to the pre-typescript stage. Having asked her to forward the typewritten copy to him so that he could "go through it for final corrections, & send it off,"[30] Hardy found when he received it that his "corrections" in fact amounted to substantial revisions sufficient to justify a fresh typescript. Since he further revised that second typescript before sending it to *To-Day*—using the carbon copy, having presumably arranged for the ribbon copy to be sent to his collaborator—and in due course corrected the proofs, it is not surprising that Purdy, misled by the numerous Hardyan phrases and the characteristic plot, should have claimed that "The work was largely Hardy's."[31] But to a reader familiar with Henniker's fiction the style is for the most part unquestionably hers, as, indeed, a

perceptive contemporary American reviewer suggested: "The style seems Mrs. Henniker's, so possibly Mr. Hardy furnished the plot."[32]

Because Henniker's prose is distinctive primarily in its very banality, this claim is (given the absence of her manuscript) somewhat difficult to substantiate in detail: Hardy, too, was quite capable of succumbing to pedestrianism on occasion. Moreover, the very nature of the collaboration makes it difficult to identify with any confidence work that was *exclusively* hers: seemingly typical Henniker sentences were no doubt written by her but could well contain minor Hardy revisions. This degree of interaction renders useless any attempt to carry out a computerized stylistic analysis to determine their respective contributions, since a Hardyan prepositional sequence could easily turn up in a sentence otherwise wholly Henniker's. For the same reason it is impossible to distinguish examples of "masculine" and "feminine" prose in the story, and in any case Henniker firmly belongs, both ideologically and stylistically, to the group of female writers who imitated the prevailing modes of the dominant (patriarchal) tradition.[33]

In seeking internal evidence of Henniker's contribution to **"Spectre"** one must in fact turn to the content—not to the plot, since that is essentially Hardy's, but to the detailed working out of the events. For example, Henniker's characters tend, like Parkhurst, to answer questions with physical gestures[34] and to smile with their eyes;[35] during times of intense emotion they become oblivious, like Rosalys, of their surroundings[36] or feel as if they are living through a dream (a sensation experienced by at least thirteen other Henniker characters).[37] Significantly, Hardy attempted to improve upon that last trite idea by adding a reference to Jim's voice being heard "as the phantom of a dead sound." A few passages warrant comparison:

> He bade them a cool good-bye and left. She watched his retreating figure . . . He never turned his head.
>
> (1TS, ff. 19-20)[38]

> Then with rather a cold shake of the hand to Mary, . . . he started to walk home. And he never turned his head to look back, though Mary watched him until a bend in the avenue concealed him from sight.
>
> *(Bid Me Good-bye* 131)

> One last long kiss; and then from the shadow in which he stood he watched her skirting the lake and hurrying along in the shelter of the yew hedges . . .
>
> (1TS, fo. 5)

> One last pressure of the little hand, and she was through the gate, running down the lime avenue, . . . with her child-like smile shining on her lips and eyes.
>
> *(Bid Me Good-bye* 158-59)

the whole impression left by the church being one of singular harmony, loveliness, and above all, repose—which contrasted greatly with her experiences just then.

(1TS, fo. 10)

To both of them the contrast between its smiling tranquility and the restless ache of human life was so profound . . .

(*Sowing the Sand* 186)

If her mother had not been beside her she would have screamed out aloud in her pain.

(1TS, fo. 20)

She could almost have screamed for the very pain of keeping back her tears.

(*Outlines* 75)[39]

Other passages characteristic of Henniker include the evening at Colonel Lacy's with its banal dinner conversation and, especially, Rosalys' concern for the cab-horse and her comment about butchers not having hearts like other men.[40]

Henniker's prose is also marked by the repeated use of stock descriptive phrases: skies are velvet-like,[41] cheeks pink and eyes shining,[42] faces white and tired.[43] Images likewise recur, particularly allusions to the world of romance and fairy-tale or to favourite biblical passages:

the grand walk whose pebbles shone like precious stones. . . .

(1TS, fo. 1)

[a] princess emerging from her palace into a garden of roses and fountains to meet her lover-prince . . .

(1TS, fo. 6)

as she walked down the gravel paths where every pebble shone like a jewel in the strange light, it seemed to her that she was the heroine of a fairy story; a princess in an enchanted castle . . .

(*Bid Me Good-bye* 6)[44]

he might have been the direct descendant of a line of picked crusaders . . .

(1TS, fo. 3)

one who might have been a Viking, or knightly hero of romance . . .

(*Contrasts* 74)

From the crown of his head even to the sole of his foot there was no blemish in him.

(1TS, fo. 10)

From the crown of that exquisite *blonde cendré* head . . . down to her little *suède* shoe, there is no fault to be found . . .

(*Our Fatal Shadows* 60)[45]

Significantly, three of these four passages from **"Spectre"**—the exception being the biblical allusion—were substantially revised by Hardy.

Such evidence helps to confirm that the first six sections were predominantly Henniker's work—as, indeed, does the choice of setting. By 1893 the concept of Wessex had become one of the most dominant elements in Hardy's fiction,[46] and it seems unlikely that, even in a story which as a collaboration would in some sense be distinct from his other work, he would have created a location so topographically undefined and unsituated as Ambrose Towers. With its sixteenth-century "red tower," "shrouded mullions," and "old brick walls" surrounded by "broad paths and garden-lands" (P 5, 1), Ambrose Towers could be any number of English country estates. As such it is typical of Henniker's fiction, as is the use of actual London addresses: Eaton Place (later changed to Belgrave Road) and Porchester Terrace. If the inclusion of recognizable London locations—Kensington Gardens, the "great meat-market" (Smithfield), the "fashionable hotel on the Embankment" (the Savoy)—is typical of both Henniker and Hardy, the choice and description of the "East-London church," unmistakably Saint Bartholomew the Great, does suggest Henniker's authorship.[47] Writing to her in June 1893 about their arranged architectural lesson, Hardy had said: "Westminster Abbey, St. Saviour's Southwark, and St. Bartholemew's [*sic*] Smithfield, contain excellent features for study."[48] The inclusion of architectural details in **"Spectre"** can be seen as part of the dialogue between Hardy and Henniker, her attempt to demonstrate that she was, indeed, as Hardy had predicted, an "apt scholar." The Smithfield church is today still a

beautiful building, with its Norman apse and transverse arches of horse-shoe form, and the massive curves and cushion-capitals that [support] the tower-end; the whole impression left by the church being one of singular harmony, loveliness, and above all, repose . . .

(P 2)

And the sunlight continues to illuminate "the quaint tomb where the founder of the building [lies] in his dreamless sleep." There is, however, no "fine old Norman porch": the original porch was destroyed when Henry VIII dissolved the monasteries and the present ones (West and North) were in fact built in 1893,[49] the year **"Spectre"** was written. Perhaps Henniker was confused by the building work and assumed that in the late 1870s, the approximate date of these opening chapters,[50] the church entrance was indeed still Norman.

But even if Henniker is accepted as the primary author of the bulk of the story, it remains certain that Hardy introduced revisions and additions which are now difficult to identify with confidence, especially since Henniker's conventionality did not inhibit her from writing of life's little ironies and disillusionments. Even the authorship of a line as Hardyan as Rosalys' comment about the vicar being "too stupid to give anyone a pang" (P 4) is doubtful, for Henniker, devout Christian though she was, could allow a character to refer to a parson as "a well-meaning ass" (*In Scarlet and Grey* [hereafter *SG*] 156). Similarly, the remark about Parkhurst's chivalrous feelings towards women "originating perhaps in the fact that he knew very little about them" (P 5) could as easily have been written by the author of *Foiled*—in which the victimized hero exclaims, "It was the sort of infernal ingenuity of which no one but a woman could have been capable!" (iii.255)—as by the author of *Jude,* although the reviewer Coulson Kernahan, pretending to know but not to reveal who had written what, was probably correct in attributing it to Hardy.[51] That it was a manuscript addition is suggested by its pointing in the first typescript (fo. 22), where a dash marks its conclusion but no punctuation separates it from the preceding clause—an oversight more likely to occur in revision than in composition. Although Henniker made very few alterations when reading over the typescript, this particular error was sufficiently glaring even for her to notice and correct.

Textual evidence interpreted in the context of external evidence must primarily be relied upon in attempting to determine which passages are Hardy's. Henniker's bowdlerization of the story before collecting it in *In Scarlet and Grey* provides some clues: in the revised text Jim and Rosalys meet "at hotels or restaurants" instead of "in the private rooms of hotels" (*SG* 176, P 3); Rosalys' desire wanes because "the novelty of wifedom was past" not because "the sensuous part of her character was satisfied" (*SG* 177, P 3); their passion is "resistless" instead of "almost unholy" (*SG* 186, P 4); and Rosalys has supposedly "rejected all other men" rather than kept herself from them (*SG* 192, P 5). But it is difficult to know whether Hardy in fact wrote the entire passage in which the offending phrases occurred or merely the phrases themselves. It was apparently only Hardy's addition in the first typescript of "& sinful" (fo. 11) to Henniker's own prose which necessitated her alteration in *In Scarlet and Grey* of "Somehow I feel so dreadfully sad and sinful" to "Somehow I feel so depressed, so dreadfully sad" (P 2, *SG* 176). On the other hand, her most extensive bowdlerizations—deletions of Jim's unwanted embrace at the end of VI and the (not very) veiled allusions to his renewed sexual relations with Rosalys at the beginning of VII (P 7, *SG* 200-01)—suggest a much greater involvement on Hardy's part, and it was probably at this point that he departed radically from

Henniker's manuscript in order to rewrite the ending. For one of the sentences in this section ("When—did you part from her?") there is also textual evidence of Hardy's authorship, since in the first typescript Henniker, presumably not understanding his rhetorical punctuation, deleted the dash, which Hardy subsequently restored (1TS, fo. 33). There are clear similarities, too, between this passage and the scene in *Jude* in which Arabella confesses her bigamy after spending the night with Jude, notably his shock as he stands "pale and fixed," his "sense of degradation at his revived experiences with her," and her self-justification: "They don't think much of such as that over there! Lots of 'em do it."[52] Although such Hardyan echoes are of course frequent throughout **"Spectre"** and do not necessarily indicate the authorship of the passage in which they occur, in this instance the "objectionable" nature of the content provides a reasonably reliable indicator.

That Hardy also wrote the subsequent narration of the wedding-day events is implied by his invitation to Henniker to supply details of the "bride's doings" (cited above). If she appears not to have offered any suggestions about such essentially feminine preparations, she did delete the reference to Rosalys feeling that Parkhurst's title would be "a handy thing, a very handy thing, for a woman with a big house and park like hers" (1TS, fo. 36). The deletion is Henniker's only extensive revision to the typescript and it is perhaps also worth remarking that almost half of her alterations of wording (ten out of twenty-four) were made in the last three typescript pages of VI and in VII, as would be appropriate if these sections were predominantly Hardy's. Moreover, VII contains none of the characteristic Henniker phrases and incidents mentioned above.

The familiar features of the story first pointed out by Purdy—"the clandestine romance and marriage of a 'noble lady' and a poor officer, the return of the vanished husband on the eve of his wife's remarriage, the removal of a troublesome character by drowning in a water-meadow"[53]—as well as the post-nuptial disillusionment, the agreement to separate, and so forth, indicate little more than that the plot was Hardy's. Some similarities in detail and phrasing between **"Spectre"** and Hardy's earlier fiction are, however, sufficiently striking to suggest his authorship of specific passages. **"An Imaginative Woman,"** clearly inspired by his feelings for Henniker and written during the late summer of 1893[54] when they were beginning their collaborative work, parallels **"Spectre"** in its use of a newspaper paragraph to report the suicide of Trewe who, like Parkhurst, shoots himself through the head with a revolver. **"Spectre"** also offers an echo of **"A Trag-**

edy of Two Ambitions" when Rosalys regards the lake very much as the two brothers contemplate the meads where their father drowned:

> There was the lake from which the water had flowed down the river that had drowned Jim . . .
>
> (P 8)
>
> There were the hatches, there was the culvert; they could see the pebbly bed of the stream through the pellucid water.[55]

That there should be some resemblance between these stories is not surprising, since, as Hardy wrote to Henniker, it was the preparation of the *Life's Little Ironies* volume—involving not only collection but also revision,[56] hence rereading—which delayed his work on their project: "I could not take the '**Desire**' in hand till to-day, having been hunting up the tales I told you of ('**Two Ambitions**' ["**A Tragedy of Two Ambitions**"] being one of them). They are now fastened together to be dispatched to the publisher . . ."[57] "**A Mere Interlude**" was perhaps also reread at this time—in terms of content if not of quality it can be grouped with the *Life's Little Ironies* stories—for as Baptista allows "circumstances to pilot her along" and "things to drift,"[58] so Rosalys allows "things to take their course" (P 8), each remarrying within hours after the drowning of her first husband.

But the most striking similarities are to be found in "**The Waiting Supper**," which could equally well have been considered for inclusion in *Life's Little Ironies*. In addition to the familiar "poor man and the lady" situation (complete with nocturnal meetings and the discussion of a secret marriage), the unexpected return of the husband owing to the newspaper announcement of his wife's remarriage, and the death by drowning, there are several verbal parallels: when Christine arrives for the wedding ceremony, Nicholas kisses her "with a sort of surprise, as if he had expected that at the last moment her heart would fail her" (*CM* [*A Changed Man*] 37), while Jim greets Rosalys with "I was half afraid you might have failed me at the last moment" (P 2); Bellston defines his profession as "Travel and exploration" (*CM* 41), while Jim describes himself as a "traveller and explorer" (P 6); Christine sends Nicholas away saying, "I will tell you everything of my history then" (*CM* 64), while Jim leaves Rosalys promising, "and then I'll tell you all my history" (P 7). The accounts of the drownings are also similar:[59]

> It was supposed that . . . he had taken a short cut through the grounds, . . . and coming to the fall under the trees had expected to find there the plank which, during his occupancy of the premises with Christine and her father, he had placed there for crossing into the meads on the other side . . .
>
> (*CM* 81)

> it is supposed he took the old short cut across the moor where there used to be a path when he was a lad at home, crossing the big river by a plank.
>
> (P 8)

Significantly, all but one of these parallels with earlier stories either occur in VII or were added by Hardy to the first typescript, leaving little doubt of his authorship and thus exemplifying the extent to which he self-plagiarized, no doubt unconsciously, when his creative energies were not fully engaged.

The authorship of many phrases and sentences can of course be determined by the holograph revisions to the two typescripts and proofs, bearing in mind that apparent Hardy additions are not necessarily his, as the restoration of some of Henniker's descriptive passages has clearly shown. Whether Henniker saw the revised first typescript or took any action in respect of either the second typescript (assuming she did receive the ribbon copy) or the proofs is not clear. Her hand, in any case, appears only in the first typescript and not frequently there, her changes in wording being almost all stylistic: the addition of "that," the substitution of "lovely" for "handsome," "drive" for "trot," "Jove" for "Gad," and so forth (ff. 2, 12, 25, 32). Hardy accepted all but two of her corrections: he was doubtless willing to make some concessions after so radically altering her manuscript, and he had in any case promised to modify what she did not like. Her revision of "write" for "pen," however, he changed to "begin somehow," presumably because he was using "write" in the following sentence (ff. 28-29), and although he initially incorporated her alteration of "an officer" to "a soldier" he later restored the original reading (fo. 2).

The latter instance is one of the few where Henniker's revision is not essentially stylistic. The context is Mrs. Ambrose's not wanting her daughter to marry someone "who has nothing but the pay of an officer in the Line to live upon," and presumably Henniker, herself married to an officer, felt she should not belittle their salaries or status. It was, however, her persistent tendency to downgrade the social positions of both Jim and Rosalys: she changed Jim's London residence from an "hotel" to "rooms" (fo. 32), and when reprinting the story in her own collective volume, she moved Rosalys' house from Eaton Place to Belgrave Road, a "respectable" rather than "highly respectable"—itself a Hardy addition—"place of residences" (*SG* 170; 2TS, fo. 5; 1TS, fo. 6). The reason for these alterations is obscure: although the reference to Jim's hotel occurs in a passage almost certainly written by Hardy, it was presumably Henniker who originally named Eaton Place. Perhaps she simply wanted to distance these fictitious characters, whom Hardy's alterations were rendering increasingly unpleasant, from her own social circle. What is clear is that in Hardy's conception of the story Jim was somewhat more socially acceptable: Hardy altered the reference to Jim's father's "house and property" to "house and properties" (1TS, fo. 21) and added the description of Jim as a "'traveller & explorer' of the little known interiors of Asiatic countries" (1TS, fo. 26), an occupation which would have made him an interesting dinner guest, though not sufficiently so to prevent him from being the last to enter the Lacys' dining-room. In light of Hardy's various "poor man" suitors, all of whom are to some extent "superior" to others of their class, it is not surprising that Hardy should have insisted on Jim's being an officer rather than a soldier in the ranks, and it is of course more credible that Rosalys should be dazzled by an officer.

Hardy tended to emphasize Rosalys' sexual attraction to Jim, adding to the first typescript the details of her "ready mouth" and "quick breath" (ff. 2, 4) and perhaps to the manuscript the reference to her "full underlip" trembling: the typing of "full" over "face" (fo. 2) suggests that the typist was working from heavily revised copy. Possibly also a Hardy addition to the manuscript is the sentence fragment in the first typescript, "No premonitions that the entirely physical character of his affection for her, and perhaps of hers for him, was an almost certain proof of its transitoriness" (fo. 6).[60] Hardy certainly wrote "She had thoroughly abandoned herself to his good looks, his recklessness, his eagerness," added to the first typescript (fo. 12), and probably also the rest of the sentence, "and, now that the sensuous part of her character was satisfied, her fervour also began to burn itself down"—most of which was subsequently bowdlerized by Henniker (P 3, *SG* 177). In the final scenes Hardy not only reinvoked this sexual desire by inserting "Come—damn you, dear—put up your mouth as you used to!" (1TS, fo. 31) but also confirmed Rosalys' continuing inability to resist Jim's advances in those self-condemnatory lines later so carefully excised from Henniker's *In Scarlet and Grey*: "O—O—what have I done—what a fool—what a weak fool!" (1TS, fo. 33; *SG* 202); "O, how weak, how weak was I!" (1TS, fo. 33; *SG* 203). Henniker's deletion of the reference to Rosalys coveting Parkhurst's title (her only major alteration to the first typescript) no doubt reflects a reluctant acceptance of the accentuation of Rosalys' sexuality but at the same time a refusal to allow love of social position to be numbered among her heroine's failings. It does in fact seem out of character for a woman who, although "mentally matured under the touch of the gliding seasons" (P 5), originally wished to marry an army officer in the customary way and "get on as other people do" (P 1).

That after their marriage Jim and Rosalys did "get on as other people do"—though not in the sense Rosalys meant—is a common Hardy theme, and one which he brought out strongly in his revisions. In his addition to the opening paragraph of the story, he wrote of "that poetical drama of two which the world has beheld before; which leads up to a contract that causes a slight sinking in the poetry, and a certain lack of interest in the play" (1TS, fo. 1). Similarly, in the first typescript "this little romance" is altered to "this little excursion to purchase disillusion" (fo. 9). The length, pointing, style, and especially content of the following sentence—its central idea anticipatory of the Registrar's office scene in *Jude*—suggest that it, too, was originally a Hardy addition:

> Two or three other couples were also in the church on the same errand: a haggard woman in a tawdry white bonnet, hanging on to the arm of a short crimson-faced man, who had evidently been replenishing his inside with gin to nerve himself to the required pitch for the ordeal: a girl with a coarse, hard face, accompanied by a slender youth in shabby black: a tall man, of refined aspect, in very poor clothes, whose hollow cough shook his thin shoulders and chest, and told his bride that her happiness, such as it was, would probably last but a very short space.
>
> (1TS, ff. 9-10)

Many of Hardy's other revisions to the first typescript are attempts to flesh out Henniker's prose. His most frequent criticism of her stories over the years was that they were "too little": of "Lady Gilian" he wrote, "Like nearly all your stories, it makes one wish there were more of it."[61] It is true that while Henniker always included long descriptive passages, her narratives, especially in the stories, were often presented in little more than scenario form, invariably creating an impression of haste. "I fancy you write your MSS. a little too rapidly," wrote Hardy in one of his earliest letters to her, and in an interview with Raymond Blathwayt she herself admitted, "I write very quickly, and some of my short stories I have done in two or three days."[62] Some of Hardy's attempts to compensate for the frequently skeletal character of her prose involved only the addition of single adjectives: "harsh" stable-clock, "alert" birds, "gigantic" vans, "covered" carts, "quaint" tomb, "fashionable" hotel (ff. 1, 8, 10). Sometimes the revisions were more extensive, when, for example, he added descriptive phrases like "a fat and genial lady" or expanded "the walls" to "the old brick walls—red in the day-time, sable now" (ff. 26, 1). Hardy also attempted to make her descriptions more evocative: the "huge" shadow becomes "funereal," the "velvet-like sky" gives way to "reaching deeps of sky," and so forth (ff. 1, 5).

A similar process of revision can be traced in the second typescript. Another instance of Henniker's characteristic "velvet-like" sky is altered, this time to "a bottomless deep of blue" (fo. 12); so, too, the "last long" kiss becomes "clinging," the "handsome, boyish" face "healthy, virile"; the "hot" country "enervating" (ff. 4, 13, 15). Some of Hardy's familiar preoccupations also emerge from the revisions, as when, for example, Jim's comment, "Further back than my grandfather I am a little hazy as to my ancestors," is replaced by the description of his name in relation to Rosalys' as "merely the older one of the little freeholder turned out of this spot by your ancestor when he came" (fo. 2). And, unsurprisingly, Hardy still further emphasized the sexual suggestiveness of the story: Rosalys and Jim have luncheon "in a room all to themselves"; Parkhurst almost wishes that she were not so good and perfect "and innocent"; and Jim remarks of his relationship with Mélanie, "People do these things" (ff. 8, 20, 28).

Relatively few changes were made in proof. Most are stylistic, renewed attempts to rework Henniker's banal prose: "many yards" of turf becomes "a smooth plush," Jim's "handsome" countenance "now familiar," the "sad" arbour "queer" (1, 3, 4). Not that characterization or thematic concerns were ignored: by merely adding "to pay his debts" to the account of the disposal of Jim's father's property, for example, Hardy accentuated Jim's irresponsibility and extended his profligacy into areas beyond the sexual (8).

The proofs on which Hardy made these—his final—corrections were for Jerome K. Jerome's *To-Day,* a weekly periodical devoted primarily to short fiction, Jerome having purchased the story through the literary agent A. P. Watt. On 30 October 1893, two days after Hardy had dispatched the manuscript for typing, he informed Henniker that he would be "writing to Watt this evening about our story."[63] A copy of **"Spectre"** would not have been sent with that letter to Watt, but one must have followed soon after, since on 1 December Hardy was able to tell Henniker:

> I am glad to know that Watt sent you your dues—well-earned—on **"The Spectre"**. (£71:15:6 the sum shd be—i.e. half the total paid for the story, £159:10:0, less half his commission.) Considering the shortness of the tale—8000 to 9000 words—the price is a very fair one for serial use only—£18 per thousand words. As to your paying a share of the type-writing, certainly not; the charge was quite small.[64]

Hardy's revision of the first typescript, then, the typing and revision of the second typescript, and the actual sale of the story must all have taken place in November 1893.

"Spectre" did not, however, appear in *To-Day* until November 1894. That Hardy had seen and corrected the proofs some months earlier is indicated by his 26

August 1894 letter to Jerome: "By the way, is F.H.'s & my story to be illustrated? & when? I rather liked it when I read over the proofs."[65] This somewhat unusual delay—it was not common for a periodical story to be left standing in type for such an extended period[66]—can be explained by Jerome's decision to hold back **"Spectre"** for the special Christmas or Winter Number, published at sixpence (rather than the usual twopence) on 17 November 1894. Taking full advantage of Hardy's celebrity, the *To-Day* 3 November advertisement for the Winter Number promised "a COMPLETE STORY by THOMAS HARDY," and an announcement the following week included his name at the head of the list of contributors—in which Henniker's did not figure at all, though in the list of contents she is named as the story's co-author.[67]

The *To-Day* printing was not in fact the first. Sold to the American newspaperman and novelist Irving Bacheller, **"Spectre"** was distributed through his syndicate and appeared in the *Philadelphia Press,* 15-21 November 1894; the *Kansas City Star,* 17-22 November; the *Minneapolis Tribune,* 19-23 November; the New York *Press,* 19-23 November; the *Nebraska State Journal,* 20-24 November; and the San Francisco *Examiner,* 2 and 9 December.[68] The first two instalments of the *Philadelphia Press* serialization, then, anticipated the *To-Day* publication. These syndicated newspaper printings have no textual authority, however, and Hardy and Henniker were perhaps not even aware of their existence. Writing to Henniker on 28 October of the previous year, Hardy had asked:

> This question also arises: shall we print the story in America & c. simultaneously. It will cause a delay of a few weeks perhaps (not so long *possibly*). On the other hand if we sacrifice America for the sake of being sooner out here, we may lose, say, £20 or £25.[69]

They apparently decided to have the story published simultaneously, and Watt presumably sold the American as well as the English serial rights—Hardy refers broadly to the price being a fair one "for serial use."[70] Jerome, himself one of the Bacheller syndicate authors, may in fact have bought the rights for both countries and arranged the American sale, though Bacheller did purchase fiction through at least one London agent.[71] What is in any case clear from the wording and pointing of the six syndicate settings is that they all derive from uncorrected *To-Day* proofs. The large number of shared variants among the newspaper printings further reveals that there was an intervening text, probably proof sheets from Bacheller's type-setting of the story.[72] It can, however, be demonstrated on similar grounds that the *Nebraska State Journal* text was in fact set from that in the *Kansas City Star.*

To trace the nature and extent of editorial or compositorial interference in these syndicated printings is a fascinating exercise and one which is significant in terms of the story's publication history, but since none of the changes was in any sense authorial, it seems inappropriate, and would certainly be disproportionate, to offer a detailed analysis of them here. It is perhaps worth noting, however, that three of the syndicated printings were abridged. In the *Minneapolis Tribune* and the *Philadelphia Press* the cuts are relatively minor, amounting in the former to two short paragraphs relating to Mélanie (P 7; *Tribune,* 23 November, 4), probably omitted in error, and in the latter to two descriptive passages and the account of Rosalys' bitterness when Jim leaves for Burmah (P 4; *Press,* 17 November, 11), evidently deleted in order to limit the length of the instalment to two columns. Space restrictions also appear to have dictated most of the New York *Press* excisions, almost all of which occur in the third instalment (P 3-5; *Press,* 21 November, 7), again abridged to fit into two columns. Omissions in the fourth instalment involve only a couple of minor descriptive passages and the bowdlerization of "damn you" (P 7; *Press,* 22 November, 7), but in the fifth they are sufficiently radical to create a distinct story: all reference to Parkhurst's suicide has been removed, the narrative ending "happily ever after" with Rosalys and Parkhurst at the altar railings (P 8; *Press,* 23 November, 7). Presumably editorial, this revision was prepared for in advance by removing from the third instalment the comments about Parkhurst's rigid notions of honour. The resulting narrative is remarkably coherent, but it throws more strongly into relief the contrivance of Jim's convenient death and of course creates quite a different effect, the happy ending negating much of the preceding irony and cynicism. What one Bacheller syndicate advertisement described as "A pathetic love story"[73] becomes in the New York *Press* altogether more conventional and sentimental, as is, indeed, heralded by the tone of the summaries of the preceding action supplied at the beginning of the second and subsequent instalments: Jim, for instance, is described as "Impetuous Jim, an ambitious young soldier without fortune," while to the statement "Of course Rosalys agrees [to be married secretly]" is appended "What girl wouldn't?" (*Press,* 20 November, 7).

No mention of Henniker as co-author is made in any of the Bacheller printings, and in the *Minneapolis Tribune* no author at all is named. It was with its 1896 collection in Henniker's *In Scarlet and Grey,* published simultaneously by John Lane, London, and Roberts Brothers, Boston, that "Spectre" first appeared in America as a collaborative work. Both title-pages prominently display Hardy's name (though on the cover of the English edition only Henniker's appears), and if, as her bowdlerizations and comments suggest,

Henniker was less than pleased with Hardy's final version of the story, she was clearly prepared to exploit his reputation. The inclusion of a Hardy collaboration must have enhanced the potential interest in her volume, as was in fact acknowledged by a contemporary reviewer:

> One has learnt to look forward with very pleasant anticipations to each fresh work from the pen of Mrs. Henniker; and, in the case of her latest production, curiosity had been further stimulated by the announcement that the book would contain a contribution from Mr. Thomas Hardy.[74]

Writing to Henniker on 12 October 1896, Hardy congratulated her: "1000 copies' sale makes, I believe, what publishers consider a success; so you have achieved it."[75] The sales of *In Scarlet and Grey* were sufficient for it to be reprinted in three so-called "editions," as well as in John Lane's "Canvas-Back Library," but its success was perhaps attributable less to its own merits or to Hardy's reputation than to the fact that it was published in the popular Keynotes series, which included not only George Egerton's notorious *Keynotes* and *Discords* but also other best-sellers such as Grant Allen's *The Woman Who Did* and Arthur Machen's *The Great God Pan.*

Although the reviews of *In Scarlet and Grey* were on the whole positive, the assessments of **"Spectre"** radically differed. One of the earliest, in the 1 August 1896 *Speaker,* stated:

> We are paying no small compliment to Mrs. Henniker when we say that her unassisted work in this volume seems to us fully as effective, as artistic, and as pungent in its irony as that portion wherein the great master of modern English fiction has lent his aid.[76]

The 26 September *New Saturday* notice was also favourable, praising **"Spectre"** as a "powerful story,"[77] but on the same day the *Athenæum* review insisted that the characteristic morbidity of the Keynotes series was "unpleasantly emphasized" in **"Spectre,"** which "might well have been omitted," and advised Henniker not to allow "her humour and pathos to be overlaid by the advancing pessimism of a collaborator, however illustrious."[78] The 24 October *Academy* similarly described the story as "the most inferior in the book," regrettably "marred by those deflections from good taste which seem to have become characteristic of Mr. Hardy's later art," and the 31 October *Spectator* was only marginally less condemnatory: "[The story] is undoubtedly very effective and indeed gruesome, but also superfluously repulsive. . . . Mr. Thomas Hardy, in his later phases, is hardly a judicious literary counsellor."[79]

It was perhaps to these last two reviews that Hardy was alluding in his letter to Henniker of 8 November 1896:

The Jeunes are surprised at the unfounded attacks on me that the volume [*In Scarlet and Grey*] is made the vehicle of. She read **"The Spectre"** & Sir F. read it, & neither could discover the impropriety reiterated by the pure-minded reviewers—bless their prurient hearts! But you must keep better literary company in future than is

Your sincere friend

T.H.[80]

To some extent Henniker must have identified with the "pure-minded reviewers." Shortly after the volume was published she expressed her reservations about **"Spectre"** in a letter to Coulson Kernahan: "Though of course Mr H's share has great cleverness, it is not really a *sympathetic,* or pleasant story. For, before the tragedy of the close, *some* of it might have been more agreeable."[81] Her less than enthusiastic response—a not surprising one in view of the extent and nature of Hardy's revisions—reflects what appears to have been a mutual unwillingness to enter into further collaboration. Because of Henniker's sensitivity to criticism and Hardy's virtual inability to refrain from revision once a manuscript—his own or someone else's—was in front of him, their literary partnership, far from intensifying their intimacy as Hardy had hoped, had occasionally threatened to estrange them altogether. That the situation remained delicate even after the story's completion is evident from Hardy's 18 December 1893 letter concerning the placing of Henniker's "Bad and Worthless":

> I packed up the type-written story, & sent it on to Mr Shorter, *without altering a line.* One *letter* I had altered, & did not remember till it was sealed up: in the spelling of "Gawd"—which is Kipling's, & should decidedly be avoided. But you can restore it in proof if you care to.[82]

In a postscript Hardy was still more conciliatory: "You must overlook the liberty I took in suggesting alteration of the tale. I am vexed with myself for it."

But if Henniker did not want Hardy's criticism, she was perfectly willing—at least during these early years of their friendship—to accept his assistance in placing her stories or, indeed, to have his name linked publicly with hers. When in March 1895 Shorter accepted her "A Page from a Vicar's History"—originally recommended to him by Hardy[83]—Henniker suggested that Hardy be named as co-author. Hardy, however, adamantly refused. "I should be manifestly wrong to put my name as joint-author," he wrote to Shorter, "when it bears such clear internal evidence of the sex of the writer . . . that I could not possibly have had much to do with it—as was the case, my share having been editorial, my actual writing being limited to the rather commonplace incident of the last page or so. Possibly Mrs Henniker might be induced to reconsider her de-

cision, or to write a new ending: otherwise I see no course left but to withdraw the story from publication."[84] Hardy's contribution to the story may indeed have been minor, but it seems more likely that he now had no illusions about the nature of his friendship with Henniker and was not prepared to compromise his reputation for her sake. The incident evidently marked a turning point in their literary relationship. In August of the same year he reproached her for not continuing as his pupil, and in September he wrote: "I fear that after the Vicar I cannot be of much service in saying anything that would commend your stories to an editor or publisher."[85] Nearly three years later he did offer to recommend one of her stories to the New York *Independent,* but she, correctly anticipating that his response would be unfavourable, was reluctant to let him read it,[86] and seems thereafter to have sent him only published work.

Notes

1. *The Life and Work of Thomas Hardy,* ed. Michael Millgate (London: Macmillan, 1984), 270.

2. E.g., "At an Inn," "A Broken Appointment," "The Division," "In Death Divided," "The Month's Calendar," "A Thunderstorm in Town."

3. Hardy's "The Hon. Mrs. Henniker" was published anonymously in the *Illustrated London News,* 18 Aug. 1894.

4. *The Collected Letters of Thomas Hardy* (hereafter *CL*), ed. Richard Little Purdy and Michael Millgate, 7 vols. (Oxford: Clarendon Press, 1978-88), ii.20, 18.

5. *CL* ii.26.

6. See Michael Millgate, *Thomas Hardy: A Biography* (hereafter *Biography*), 1982 (Oxford: Oxford University Press, 1987), 339-40.

7. Letter to Coulson Kernahan, 23 July 1896 (New York Public Library, Berg Collection; quoted by Kernahan in "The 'Pessimism' of Thomas Hardy," *London Quarterly and Holborn Review,* 167 [July 1942], 280); Raymond Blathwayt, "The Hon. Mrs. Arthur Henniker," *Woman at Home,* 4 (July 1895), 55.

8. *Sir George* (London: Richard Bentley and Son, 1891), *Bid Me Good-bye* (London: Richard Bentley and Son, 1892), and *Foiled,* 3 vols. (London: Hurst and Blackett, 1893). References to these and Henniker's other books—*Outlines* (London: Hutchinson, 1894), *In Scarlet and Grey* (London: John Lane, 1896), *Sowing the Sand* (London: Harper & Brothers, 1898), *Contrasts* (London: John Lane, 1903), *Our Fatal Shadows* (London: Hurst and Blackett, 1907), and *Second Fiddle* (London: Eveleigh Nash, 1912)—are incorporated in the text.

9. *CL* ii.29.

10. 22 Oct. 1893 (*CL* ii.37).

11. Purdy, *Thomas Hardy: A Bibliographical Study* (hereafter Purdy), 1954 (Oxford: Clarendon Press, 1978), 347; *Biography* 343-44; Gatrell, "The Early Stages of Hardy's Fiction," in *Thomas Hardy Annual No. 2,* ed. Norman Page (London: Macmillan, 1984), 19-20; Cramer, "The Spectre of the Real," *The Thomas Hardy Year Book,* 13 (1986), 8.

12. I am most grateful to Mr. Frederick B. Adams for allowing me access to these (and other) items in his collection. Without his generosity and hospitality the writing of this article would not have been possible. References to the first typescript, second typescript, and proofs—preceded where necessary by "1TS," "2TS," and "P," respectively—appear in the text. Unless otherwise indicated quotations are from the corrected proof version of the story and references are to the slip numbers.

13. *CL* ii.30.

14. *CL* ii.31.

15. They were probably similar to the unused story plots now in the Dorset County Museum and transcribed (inaccurately) in Evelyn Hardy, "Plots for Five Unpublished Short Stories," *London Magazine* 5 (November 1958), 33-45, and in *Old Mrs Chundle and Other Stories,* ed. F. B. Pinion (London: Macmillan, 1977), 115-28.

16. *CL* ii.38.

17. Gatrell, "Early Stages," *op. cit.,* 19.

18. 6 Oct. 1893 (*CL* ii.36).

19. *CL* ii.33.

20. To Henniker, 16 July 1893 (*CL* ii.24).

21. *CL* ii.34.

22. *CL* ii.35.

23. *CL* ii.38.

24. *CL* ii.39.

25. *CL* ii.39; all quotations in the following paragraphs are from this letter unless otherwise identified.

26. Parkhurst commits suicide after marrying Rosalys in ignorance of the fact that she has been a widow for only a few hours, the accidental death of her long estranged husband, Jim, having occurred shortly after the latter's unexpected return and resumption of sexual relations the previous night.

27. On rare occasions the passages have a foreshadowing or mood-establishing function, as in the description in *Foiled* (iii.25) of Léo watching a sparrow-hawk seize "in his cruel talons" a "helpless small creature" (compare the much more powerful and better integrated account of the hawk and wild duck in *The Hand of Ethelberta*) shortly before she is herself victimized, or the final lines of "An Hour in October" reflecting the death of Hilary Chesney's happiness (note also the similarity to descriptions in "Spectre"): "The sky was red with the glow of an expiring fire, and would soon be uniform and sombre. The wailing cry of the water-fowl came towards her from a long distance. And all around her the leaves were falling. . . ." (*Contrasts* 269; Henniker's ellipsis).

28. *Biography* 343.

29. *CL* ii.38, 39.

30. 28 Oct. 1893 (*CL* ii.40).

31. Purdy 346.

32. Rev. of *In Scarlet and Grey, Literary World,* 14 Nov. 1896, 375.

33. See Toril Moi, "Feminist Literary Criticism," in *Modern Literary Theory: A Comparative Introduction,* ed. Ann Jefferson and David Robey, 2nd ed. (London: B. T. Batsford, 1986), 220, and Elaine Showalter, *A Literature of Their Own,* 1977, rev. ed. 1982 (London: Virago, 1988), 13.

34. P 5, as does Jim, P 1; the signalling phrase is always "For all answer": *Bid Me Good-bye* 149, *Foiled* iii.259, *Outlines* 137-38, *Second Fiddle* 196.

35. P 5, *Bid Me Good-bye* 149, 159, *Foiled* ii.36, *Outlines* 153, *Contrasts* 273, *Second Fiddle* 144.

36. P 2, *Bid Me Good-bye* 226, *Foiled* i.194, *Sowing the Sand* 33.

37. P 6, *Bid Me Good-bye* 126, 218, 239, 243, *Outlines* 58, 133, *In Scarlet and Grey* 27, 74, 157, *Sowing the Sand* 217, *Contrasts* 168, 188, 264, 290, *Our Fatal Shadows* 268.

38. In this paragraph and the following one quotations are from 1TS (before it was revised), the surviving witness closest to Henniker's MS.

39. Cf. *Contrasts* 209, 224. A similar phrase appears in *Jude* (Wessex Edition, 148)—"If he had been a woman he must have screamed under the nervous tension"—but the idea is certainly more characteristic of Henniker than Hardy and may in fact have been suggested by "Spectre."

40. 1TS, ff. 26-27, 7, 9; cf. *Bid Me Good-bye* 88-89, 50. Virtually all her stories contain some reference to animals, the treatment of them serving as a touchstone for character. Hardy's fiction—notably

Tess and *Jude*—also expresses his concern for animals, but much less obtrusively. Unlike Hardy, Henniker was unconsciously inconsistent (presumably because of her social position and military connections): her male animal-lovers are often keen, though "humane," sportsmen and/or soldiers. The irony of Rosalys remarking how revolting it must be to marry a butcher just as she is about to enter the church with a potential butcher of men is no doubt unintentional.

41. 1TS, ff. 5, 16 (both phrases were revised by Hardy); *In Scarlet and Grey* 11; *Contrasts* 130.

42. 1TS, fo. 6; *Outlines* 57; *In Scarlet and Grey* 16-17.

43. 1TS, fo. 27; *Bid Me Good-bye* 178.

44. See also *Bid Me Good-bye* 80, *Sowing the Sand* 81, 229, *Contrasts* 287, *Second Fiddle* 123.

45. That these two passages were written by the same author is suggested by the reversal of the II Samuel 14:25 sequence ("from the sole of his foot even to the crown of his head . . .").

46. See Simon Gatrell, *Hardy the Creator: A Textual Biography* (Oxford: Clarendon Press, 1988), 118 ff.

47. One wonders if Henniker was aware that St. Bartholomew's was (as it still is) the church of the Worshipful Company of Butchers: as such—at least for her—it would have been an appropriately morbid place for a marriage which would end in unhappiness and disillusion.

48. *CL* ii.11.

49. E. A. Webb, *The Records of St. Bartholomew's Priory and of the Church and Parish of St. Bartholomew the Great West Smithfield*, 2 vols. (Oxford: Oxford University Press, 1921), ii.109, 115.

50. Assuming that the discussion of the Home-Rule question seven years after Jim's departure is not anachronistic.

51. Kernahan, "A Woman Who Expected the Impossible," rev. of *Second Fiddle, Bookman,* 42 (March 1912), 299.

52. *Jude,* Wessex Edition, 222, 223.

53. Purdy 346.

54. *CL* ii.22, 32; *Biography* 342.

55. *Life's Little Ironies,* Wessex Edition, 105; the wording is identical in the 1888 serialization.

56. See Purdy 81-83.

57. 22 Oct. 1893 (*CL* ii.38).

58. *A Changed Man,* Wessex Edition, 276, 288; subsequent references appear in the text preceded by *CM.* Unless otherwise stated, all quotations from this volume are identical in the serial versions.

59. First remarked by Cramer ("Hardy, Henniker, and 'The Spectre of the Real,'" *Thomas Hardy Society Review* [1977], 90-91). The *CM* text resembles "Spectre" somewhat more closely than does the 1888 serial version: if Hardy did reread the story in 1893 with a view to its possible collection, he could have reworked it then.

60. Cf. the grammatically incorrect sentence which resulted from Hardy's extensive revision of a passage on fo. 26 of the first typescript.

61. *CL* ii.252, 245; see also ii.215, 264, iii.190, 214.

62. 10 June 1893 (*CL* ii.13); Blathwayt, *op. cit.,* 55.

63. *CL* ii.41.

64. *CL* ii.43.

65. *CL* ii.62.

66. This does appear to be what happened: the nature of the variants between the corrected proofs and the printed text—the addition or removal of quotation marks and hyphens, the alteration of colons to dashes when introducing speech, and so forth—suggests corrections (presumably editorial) to revises rather than a new type-setting.

67. *To-Day,* 3 Nov. 1894, 393; 10 Nov. 1894, 9.

68. The *Minneapolis Tribune* and *Nebraska State Journal* printings have not hitherto been identified; David Bonnell Green ("The First Publication of 'The Spectre of the Real,'" *Library,* 15 [1960], 60-61) found the *Philadelphia Press* printing, Cramer ("Spectre," *op. cit.,* 28) the other three.

69. *CL* ii.40.

70. 1 Dec. 1893 (*CL* ii.43).

71. Irving Bacheller, *Coming Up the Road: Memories of a North Country Boyhood* (Indianapolis: Bobbs-Merrill, 1928), 273.

72. According to Elmo Scott Watson, *A History of the Newspaper Syndicates in the United States 1865-1935* (Chicago: n.p., 1936), Bacheller's material was "supplied to newspapers in proof sheets or copy form" (43).

73. *Nebraska State Journal,* 19 Nov. 1894, 3.

74. *Speaker,* 1 Aug. 1896, 128.

75. *CL* ii.134.

76. *Speaker* 128.

77. *New Saturday* 99.

78. *Athenæum* 417.

79. *Academy* 305; *Spectator* 593. Cf. the New York *Critic*: "'No reason can be assigned for the rash act' is the concluding sentence of the book; and, if it may be taken to refer to Mr. Hardy's partnership in it, it will do very well for our own verdict" (23 Jan. 1897, 57).

80. *CL* ii.137.

81. 23 July 1896, *op. cit.*

82. *CL* ii.44.

83. *CL* vii.127.

84. *CL* ii.71-72.

85. *CL* ii.84, 87.

86. *CL* ii.197, 201, 205.

Norman D. Prentiss (essay date spring 1993)

SOURCE: Prentiss, Norman D. "The Poetics of Interruption in Hardy's Poetry and Short Stories." *Victorian Poetry* 31, no. 1 (spring 1993): 41-60.

[*In the following essay, Prentiss underscores the awkward construction and sudden shifts in tone endemic to Hardy's poetry and short fiction, characterizing this seeming lack of polish as a complex and purposeful technique that lends depth to the author's work.*]

Apologies, especially literary ones, are seldom entirely sincere. Thomas Hardy's authorial comments often lapse into apology, referring to flaws some critics wish he had revised rather than explained.[1] It is all too easy to find support for this depiction of Hardy as a careless editor of his own texts: even his mature works contain bad sentences or awkward lines of verse. Without denying the existence of such incidental passages,[2] I want to stress a structural awkwardness that, far from being the result of carelessness, is essential to Hardy's artistic achievement. Hardy's most characteristic effect depends on abrupt juxtaposition, most easily seen at the level of plot: gaps in a narrative's chronology, for example, bring conflicting situations into awkward proximity. Other significant juxtapositions result from sudden shifts in tone and in philosophy: a humorous poem can contrast with a more serious one, or a naive guess can contradict a more learned assertion. Such juxtapositions, when translated as carelessness, tend to undermine the reader's sense of Hardy's literary authority. The "Apology" to *Late Lyrics and*

Earlier addresses this problem, with specific reference to how a volume of poems is organized: the "juxtaposition of unrelated, even discordant, effusions" produces an unfortunate side-effect that some poems "have been read as misfires" (2:321).[3] Rather than achieving smooth transitions from poem to poem, Hardy allows discordance ("sudden change of key")—in his description of the arrangement, it is as if the poems interrupt each other. Through considering Hardy's poetry and short stories, I will suggest that what happens between poems recapitulates what occurs within any Hardy narrative. Hardy's texts demonstrate an uneasiness about the authority of an omniscient narrator: rejecting the idea of a pure and consistent authorial voice, his narratives invent a poetics of interruption.

In his later years Hardy advertised himself exclusively as a poet, distancing himself from the more famous prose narratives. But the generic distinction between poetry and prose—so evident in a chronological listing of his books, which declared him strictly a novelist until *The Well-Beloved* in 1897, strictly a poet thereafter—blurs with the recognition that Hardy started out as a poet, and continued to write verse during his years as a novelist. Unable to find a publisher for his early poems, Hardy confesses in the Preface to *Desperate Remedies* that he salvaged some of the verse by "dissolving it into prose."[4] Hardy's desire to accommodate publishers almost necessarily developed into a critical temperament that allowed genres to dissolve into each other. One of Hardy's speculations about poetry reinforces, almost despite itself, this idea of generic resemblance:

> Poetry. Perhaps I can express more fully in verse ideas and emotions which run counter to the inert crystallized opinion—hard as a rock—which the vast body of men have vested interests in supporting. To cry out in a passionate poem that (for instance) the Supreme Mover . . . must be either limited in power, unknowing, or cruel . . . will cause them merely a shake of the head; but to put it in argumentative prose will make them sneer, or foam, and set all of the literary contortionists jumping upon me.
>
> (*Life,* p. 302)

This is not so much an assertion of the difference between poetry and prose—you can say the same things in each, Hardy says—but an observation about how the different genres are received by readers. Admittedly this 1896 essay was written with the wounds still fresh from critics' moral objections to *Jude the Obscure,* but the comments are still suggestive in evaluating the direction of Hardy's literary career.[5] Hardy here suggests that he abandons novel writing in his later years because he cannot speak with the same freedom in prose that he might possess in verse. The author's experiences with the serialization of *Tess* and *Jude* especially reinforce this account: he had to make many damaging revisions to both novels in order to satisfy the editors of family-oriented magazines.[6] He turns to his first love, poetry, in order "to express [his views] more fully." But another scenario is equally plausible. I will argue for the structural coincidences between the verse and the prose: a comparison of the two genres demonstrates Hardy's continued interest in abrupt juxtapositions. But after years of writing novels with abrupt plotting and elaborate coincidences, and with his later novels, particularly *Jude* and *The Well-Beloved,* attempting more elaborate formal experiments, Hardy desired freedoms of expression that were structural as well as philosophical.[7] The shift to poetry in his later years allows him to explore further, without as much fear of "literary contortionists" jumping on him, the narrative principle that operates in all his prose: a poetics of interruption.

To clarify Hardy's position on abrupt juxtapositions, the relevant passage from the "Apology" to *Late Lyrics and Earlier* is worth quoting in full:

> I [refer to] the chance little shocks that may be caused over a book of various character like the present and its predecessors by the juxtaposition of unrelated, even discordant, effusions; poems perhaps years apart in the making, yet facing each other. An odd result of this has been that dramatic anecdotes of a satirical and humorous intention following verse in graver voice, have been read as misfires because they raise the smile that they were intended to raise, the journalist, deaf to the sudden change of key, being unconscious that he is laughing with the author and not at him. I admit that I did not foresee such contingencies as I ought to have done, and that people might not perceive when the tone altered. But the difficulties of arranging the themes in a gradated kinship of moods would have been so great that irrelation was almost unavoidable with efforts so diverse.
>
> (Hynes, 2:321-322)

In this passage Hardy outlines a quick and easy program for revising faulty texts: locate a problem not foreseen during composition, and then decide that fixing it would be too difficult. Hardy appears to avoid the literary dilemma here, rather than bothering to struggle with it. At the same time, however, Hardy seems proud of the "chance little shocks" produced by shifts in tone from poem to poem, and he implies that their arrangement meets with his approval. Although Hardy explicitly presents himself as unaware ("I admit that I did not foresee such contingencies"), most of the language of the passage suggests intention and choice. Of individual poems, Hardy observes that "anecdotes of a satirical and humorous *intention . . .* raise the smile that they were *intended* to raise" (my italics). Hardy stresses his conscious control when

writing, and when he discusses the apparently careless arrangement of the volume, he argues that each poem should produce the desired effect. His argument reacts against willful misreading by perverse journalists, rather than faulting the book's organization. While regretting the opportunities for misunderstanding ("misfires"), Hardy ultimately relies on his reader's sensitivity: "I must trust for right note-catching to those finely-touched spirits who can divine without half a whisper, whose intuitiveness is proof against all the accidents of inconsequence" (2:322).

For the sophisticated reader, the juxtaposition of dissimilar poems is not a problem. Underneath the "Apology," Hardy suggests that he could have avoided the inconsistencies had he really wanted to.[8] Hardy does present himself as a careless editor here, but it is significant that he describes the meticulously edited alternative in terms that are particularly unappealing— what could be more bland than a group of poems arranged to display "a gradated kinship of moods"? Throughout this essay I emphasize the physical nature of Hardy's juxtapositions: chronological gaps in a short story can allow dramatically different events to occur on the same page, or a volume can display "poems perhaps years apart in the making, *yet facing each other*" ("Apology," 2:321; emphasis mine). Hardy is not a master of smooth transitions; to understand his texts we must learn to appreciate abruptness.

STRUCTURE AND PLOT

The physical aspect of Hardy's juxtapositions is most obvious in his poetry. The "Apology" to *Late Lyrics and Earlier* discusses the shocks produced by placing contradictory poems in proximity, but similar shocks can occur within a single poem, especially when the poem is explicitly narrative. From the "Satires of Circumstance," where Hardy responds to the death of his first wife, the brief poem "The Walk" (2:49) offers the most compact version of a typical Hardy juxtaposition. The two-stanza poem divides neatly: the first stanza describes a stroll Hardy takes while his wife is still living; in the second stanza Hardy travels the same path after her death. There is no transition between the occasions—only a stanza break. Hardy asks "What difference, then?" between the two walks, and the answer appears in the arrangement of the poem. The second walk is important because it involves a poignant memory of the earlier walk, just as the second stanza of the poem gains significance through its proximity to the first stanza. A longer version of this technique appears in "At the Dinner Table" (2:432-433). I quote the poem in full:

> I sat at dinner in my prime,
> And glimpsed my face in the sideboard-glass,

And started as if I had seen a crime,
And prayed the ghastly show might pass.

Wrenched wrinkled features met my sight,
Grinning back to me as my own;
I well-nigh fainted with affright
At finding me a haggard crone,

My husband laughed. He had slily set
A warping mirror there, in whim
To startle me. My eyes grew wet;
I spoke not all the eve to him.

He was sorry, he said, for what he had done,
And took away the distorting glass,
Uncovering the accustomed one:
And so it ended? No, alas,

Fifty years later, when he died,
I sat me in the selfsame chair,
Thinking of him. Till, weary-eyed,
I saw the sideboard facing there;

And from its mirror looked the lean
Thing I'd become, each wrinkle and score
The image of me that I had seen
In jest there fifty years before.

The break between stanzas four and five corresponds to the obvious structural division of "The Walk." Here, Hardy gives two views of the female narrator's reflection, with the "jest" of the first four stanzas predicting the image of fifty years later. The passage of time is significant in the poem: time recreates, more gradually, the husband's cruel trick. But the dramatic effect of the poem to a large extent depends upon a chronological irregularity, allowing the reader to perceive the two reflections on the same page. The poem is itself a kind of warping mirror, with the first reflection in a disturbing proximity to the second.

But the technique translates into awkwardness: the chronological gap disrupts the expected forward movement of the narrative. Even when Hardy follows a more constant chronology, the forward movement of his narratives can still be awkward. The question-and-answer strategy common to the ballad form, which appears in much of Hardy's narrative poetry,[9] results in a poem that progresses in deliberate increments, rather than gradually. In "Ah, Are You Digging on My Grave?" (2:38-41), for example, Hardy allows a deceased woman to wonder who disturbs the soil. Each stanza begins by asking a question—is it "My loved one?" (l. 2) or "My dearest kin?" (l. 7)—and the voice above ground responds in the negative. Through process of elimination, each stanza brings us haltingly closer to the digger's true identity—the woman's dog, attempting merely to recover a bone. Hardy has assigned each section of the poem a particular function; thus, although the poem moves deliberately towards its mocking conclusion, the forward movement is not

smooth. The stanzas of "Heiress and Architect" (1:98-100), as Samuel Hynes notes, similarly follow a "series of steps"[10]: the poem alternates between an heiress' proposed designs and an architect's response. The architect rejects all her designs as impractical, and his reasons construct a narrative that predicts the heiress' future. In the final stanza the architect vetoes her plans for a narrow staircase by reminding the heiress of her death: "I must even fashion as the rule declares, / To wit: Give space (since life ends unawares) / To hale a coffined corpse adown the stairs" (ll. 57-59). The poem is an exercise in contrasts, with the architect's rules interrupting the heiress' wishes.

In his book on *The Pattern of Hardy's Poetry,* Hynes identifies an "antinomial pattern" in such contrasts:

> Briefly, Hardy's antinomial pattern works this way: thesis (usually a circumstance commonly accepted as good—marriage, youth, young love, the reunion of husband and wife) is set against antithesis (infidelity, age, death, separation) to form an ironic complex, which is left unresolved.
>
> (p. 44)

Hynes protests, however, that Hardy's structures can be "mechanical" or "clumsy" (p. 53): in the "simple before-and-after organization" of some poems, for example, Hardy's irony is "too easy" (p. 52). The criticism points to the author's effort: to earn the irony, Hynes implies, Hardy should work harder to create a smoother, more subtle narrative.[11] But the reader's perception of the irony depends upon its awkwardness: Hardy wants his structural contrasts to be obvious and disturbing, physically present on the same page. The shock that results when sections of a text interrupt each other is an achieved effect rather than a careless one. A moment in "A Wife and Another" (1:318-320) offers a good description of Hardy's technique. In the poem, a wife stalks her husband to discover his secret lover, only to be surprised by her husband's tender relationship with that other woman. The wife reacts:

> Then, as it were, within me
> Something snapped,
> As if my soul had largened:
> Conscience-capped,
> I saw myself the snarer—them the trapped.
>
> (ll. 46-50)

In an abrupt reversal ("Something snapped"), the characters exchange roles. This is the antinomial pattern Hynes describes, but it is a mistake to desire elegance from the narrative movement. Hardy's narratives, I suggest, intend to "snap" forward, with a poem advancing in deliberate stanzaic increments, or with a short story briskly shifting direction from one section to another.

But there is an important difference between the structures of poems and the structures of prose fiction. The forward movement within individual poems can be abrupt, but the abruptness seems less troublesome when linked to a structural principle. "At the Dinner Table," quoted above, produces a structural effect based on a "warping mirror" juxtaposition. Once readers discover the before-and-after design of the poem, they can explain the gap in chronology: by fulfilling its structural principle, the poem seems complete. Readers are more likely to object to a prose narrative's divergence from a regular chronology. Instead of referring to a structural principle, chronological distortions in a novel or short story often seem to be symptoms of clumsy plotting, or of missing character development. The underappreciated short stories serve as convenient specimens of the Hardy prose narrative: most of the stories were written in the 1880s and 90s, when Hardy was reaching maturity as a novelist; observations about the shorter fiction will thus have a corresponding relevance to Hardy's more famous novels. But my more important reason for emphasizing the short stories in this essay is that the genre's characteristic compression often reveals structural patterns in a more compact or exaggerated form.

More than any of Hardy's other narratives, the short stories are vulnerable to the charge that they lack a significant structure: composed in between work on the novels, the short stories do not appear to be written with the same attention as the lengthier projects.[12] Time passes rapidly in most of Hardy's stories, contributing to the illusion that they were written rapidly: in **"The Fiddler of the Reels"** he dismisses twelve months of the characters' lives by commenting that "the year glided away" (*LLI* [*Life's Little Ironies*], p. 177), and in **"An Indiscretion in the Life of an Heiress"** he remarks that "the reader must then imagine five years to have elapsed" (p. 85).[13] The same technique occurs in "At the Dinner Table" ("Fifty years later, when he died") and in the brief narrative poem, "A Practical Woman": "She went away. She disappeared, / Years, years. Then back she came" (3:219-220). In the short stories, however, the technique seems more like the result of carelessness; at the very least, it indicates a less formal, less structured writing style. In his "Introduction" to *The Selected Writings of Thomas Hardy*, Irving Howe assigns the looser attitude towards time to a particular category of short narrative: "Between tale and story there is a sharp difference in pacing, what might be called their respective versions of 'the time sense.' The tale stops, starts up again and wanders."[14] Classifying Hardy's short narratives as tales, then, involves accepting their more casual organization. But the short stories display freedoms with time not simply because Hardy follows a less literary storytelling tradition, but because he strives for a particular structural effect—the same effect he achieves in many of his poems.

The sentence from **"An Indiscretion"** [**"An Indiscretion in the Life of an Heiress"**] begins to explain this effect. Hardy quickly asks the reader to "imagine five years to have elapsed"—but what imaginative activity is Hardy soliciting here? The sentence is brief and not very suggestive, as if Hardy does not want his reader to reconstruct the years his narrative has neglected. Indeed, the specific request is not for readers to fill in what Hardy has omitted: rather than asking his readers to imagine the missing years, Hardy asks them only to imagine that the time has passed. He wants his readers to be aware that the characters have aged, their situations have changed—but on another level he wants the missing years to be ignored. The structural effect depends upon the reader being as careless with time as Hardy is. He mentions the passage of time, but readers should suspect that Hardy wants a juxtaposition of the before and after, as if the events separated by five years are simultaneous.

Exploring the chronological gaps found throughout Hardy's stories confirms this suspicion. Such gaps often occur between the numbered sections of a story. In **"The Son's Veto,"** for example, we learn from the opening sentence of section 2 that Mr. Twycott has died: "The next time we get a glimpse of [Sophy Twycott] is when she appears in the mournful attire of a widow" (*LLI*, p. 42). Hardy only informs us that "Mr. Twycott had never rallied, and now lay in a well-packed cemetery" (p. 42)—the body is barely cold before Hardy moves forward with the narrative. This seems a sloppy disposal of Mr. Twycott, but it serves the purpose of concentrating on Sophy's change in situation. By not allowing time for the funeral, Hardy creates an explicit contrast: the reader simultaneously sees Sophy as wife and Sophy as widow.[15]

A more striking chronological gap occurs between sections 5 and 6 of **"The Waiting Supper."** Section 6 opens "Some fifteen years after the date of the foregoing incidents" (*CM* [*A Changed Man*], p. 59). This story, like many of Hardy's, develops from a difference in two lovers' social status. At the beginning of the story, Christine Everard is the rich daughter of a squire, and is courted by the less affluent Nicholas Long. As Christine begins to reject him for social reasons, Nicholas protests:

> "If I had been a prince, and you a dairymaid, I'd have stood by you in the face of the world!"

> She shook her head. "Ah—you don't know what society is—you don't know."

> (p. 51)

Nicholas' speculation signals the change in plot: he will find out what society is. The fifteen-year gap between sections 5 and 6 realizes Nicholas' words in an instant: in this interval Nicholas makes his fortune as "one of the pioneers to the gold-fields" (p. 63), while Christine sinks into poverty. Hardy seems a particularly overexcited narrator: as soon as the story posits an alternate scenario, he rushes the plot in the new direction. But the fifteen-year gap in time is not necessarily a sign of sloppy storytelling. Even though the characters' transposed fortunes occur gradually in the fictional world, Hardy wants the change to be abrupt in his narrative; he does not bother with detailing the intervening time because he prefers to have the events of sections 5 and 6 in close proximity.

A moment in **"The Withered Arm"** suggests how proximity can affect the imagination. Rhoda Brook learns that her former lover has returned to town with his new bride and, after hearing a description of Gertrude, she meets a version of this rival in a dream. But in Rhoda's dream the new bride is a hideous and taunting specter; in revenge, Rhoda grabs the specter's arm and mangles it. Imagine Rhoda's surprise when she meets the real Gertrude the next morning:

> The impression remaining from the night's experience was still strong. Brook had almost expected to see the wrinkles, the scorn, and the cruelty on her visitor's face. . . .
>
> The figure and action were those of the phantom, but her voice was so indescribably sweet, her glance so winning, her smile so tender, so unlike that of Rhoda's midnight visitor, that the latter could hardly believe the evidence of her senses.
>
> (*WT* [*Wessex Tales*], p. 79)

Because the dream is recent, Rhoda has trouble separating the ghostly vision from the woman in front of her. There is, I believe, a pun on the word "impression" here. The dream leaves a mental impression on Rhoda, but it also leaves a physical impression on Gertrude. Gertrude's arm is injured like the specter's arm in the dream, and "Rhoda fancied that she discerned . . . the shape of her own fingers" in the discolored wounds (p. 80). Hardy's structural juxtapositions strive for the effect achieved by Rhoda's dream: the first part of a contrast hopes to leave a strong impression that complicates the reader's experience of the second. And Hardy's most effective means of producing the impression is through physical proximity. Through the warping mirror of narrative, events separated by time—even as much as fifteen or fifty years—can be physically present on the same page, keeping them both in the reader's memory.

But as the example from **"The Withered Arm"** suggests, Hardy's awkward juxtapositions result not just from chronological gaps, but also from sudden plot developments: Rhoda Brook's shock results from an unexpected meeting with the real-life subject of her recent dream. Hardy tends to fashion his plots around such sudden shifts in perspective. A typical scenario involves the reappearance of someone from the past who alters the main characters' plans: in **"A Tragedy of Two Ambitions"** a drunken father returns to interrupt the social aspirations of two brothers; in **"A Mere Interlude"** the heroine's plans to marry a rich older man are interrupted by a chance meeting with a former lover.[16] Even when a short story follows a regular chronology, Hardy favors plot devices that interrupt the gradual forward movement of the narrative. Just as the architect's confrontational statements force the heiress in Hardy's ballad poem to revise her designs, the significant moments in the prose narratives force characters into a reevaluation of their situation (what is Rhoda Brook's new opinion of her rival? which man will the heroine choose to marry?): like the movement across stanzas in Hardy's ballads, the short stories "snap" forward in abrupt increments. The forward movement of Hardy's narratives, then, is abrupt either because of a chronological distortion that skips large portions of the characters' lives (abrupt telling), or because of a rapid succession of incidents within the fictional world of a story or poem (abrupt plotting).[17] In either instance, the structural effect depends upon an awkward juxtaposition—a physical confrontation between differing perspectives.

In his study of the poetry, Dennis Taylor traces the development of such juxtapositions in Hardy's meditative lyrics. "Hardy dramatizes how impressions develop" (p. 40), Taylor argues; if the poems display abrupt juxtapositions, it is because moments of realization tend to occur "when a sudden shock expose[s] the sharp gap between present reality and the past image" (p. 24).[18] Taylor's analysis makes the connection between conventional plot and what he calls "the plot of the reverie" (p. xi), between events and the resultant changes in the narrator's mind. But whereas Taylor argues for a more consistent, chronological development in Hardy's poetry, I suggest that the poetic genre allows Hardy a greater freedom to explore the structural contrasts that interest him even in the earlier prose narratives. And an important element in both genres is the narrator's inconsistency: the tone or character of the narrator can change just as abruptly as the plot. Hardy's plot structures recreate the physical shock of a change in perspective; the narrator's inconsistency within such structures further demonstrates that all perspectives are subject to this kind of change. Even at the level of structure—perhaps especially at this level—Hardy's texts insist that philosophical consistency is impossible.

STRUCTURE AND PHILOSOPHY

When Hardy acknowledges that it is "almost impossible" to arrange a volume of poems "in a gradated kinship of moods," he is actually confessing to a disinclination rather than an inability. After speculating in the "Preface" to *Poems of the Past and the Present* that the poems in the volume "display little cohesion of thought," Hardy responds: "I do not greatly regret this. Unadjusted impressions have their value" (1:113). Hardy finds this value in explicit contrast, both in the arrangement of poems, and within the individual poems themselves. In the same preface Hardy observes that his poems were "written down in widely differing moods and circumstances, and at various dates." The observation explains that poems written at different times can display contradictory views, but the effect achieved is not simply an accident of compilation, occurring after the fact as Hardy groups his poems for publication. During the act of composition itself Hardy thinks in terms of contrast, and he tends to construct narratives that present abrupt juxtapositions of "widely differing moods." The relation of mood to narrative is particularly obvious in the poem Hardy significantly titles "A Thought in Two Moods" (2:228-229):

I saw it—pink and white—revealed
   Upon the white and green;
The white and green was a daisied field,
   The pink and white Ethleen.

And as I looked it seemed in kind
   That difference they had none;
The two fair bodiments combined
   As varied miens of one.

A sense that, in some mouldering year,
   As one they both would lie,
Made me move quickly on to her
   To pass the pale thought by.

                (ll. 1-12)

The title announces a poem of two distinct moods; what Hardy delivers is a narrative. The speaker of the poem begins by describing a neutral visual image of distinct colors blending into one picture. The narrative movement occurs in the third stanza when the speaker, completing the metaphor of a human figure blending with the earth, imagines Ethleen's death. The poem dramatizes an abrupt shift in perspective: the thought of death interrupts the calm, detached mood of the poem's opening. "A Thought in Two Moods," like any Hardy narrative, enacts the pattern of interruption Hardy describes in the "Apology" to *Late Lyrics and Earlier.*

Hardy's insistence on the dramatic character of his verse reinforces the idea that individual poems, and the volumes they comprise, should both be read as narratives. Hardy's "Preface" to *Wessex Poems,* his first collection of verse, points out that "the pieces are in a large degree dramatic or personative in conception; and this even where not obviously so" (1:5). He repeats the claim in other prefaces, but it is not a protest against readers interpreting his poems as autobiographical. Instead, as William W. Morgan rightly argues, Hardy uses the term "dramatic" to allow his poems to contradict each other: "He seems in fact to associate the dramatic persona with the entire issue of systematic consistency in mood, tone, and thought, and he is anxious that we should not expect consistency."[19] In the "Preface" to *Time's Laughingstocks* Hardy proposes that the poems "are to be regarded, in the main, as dramatic monologues by different characters" (1:235). There is no single authorial voice in his poetry.

Hardy establishes his narrative inconsistency by adopting a casual diction—one that critics have often identified with an oral storytelling tradition.[20] I have pointed to Hardy's tendency in his short stories to compress time with a linguistic flourish; the remark that "the year glided away" seems more appropriate to a spoken than to a written story. A similarly colloquial mannerism is common in the poetry. In his famous poem on the *Titanic,* Hardy signals the transition from the wreckage to the iceberg with a casual "Well":

VI

Well: while was fashioning
This creature of cleaving wing,
The Immanent Will that stirs and urges everything

VII

Prepared a sinister mate
For her—so gaily great—
A Shape of Ice.

        ("The Convergence of the Twain," 2:12)

The same casual transition appears elsewhere: in the poetic version of Hardy's unpublished first novel, "A Poor Man and a Lady" (3:111-113), the narrator resists the poem's shift toward tragedy ("Well: the woeful neared, you needn't be told," [l. 25]); in "Old Furniture" (2:227-228) the final stanza begins as a criticism of the attitude presented in the rest of the poem ("Well, well. It is best to be up and doing, / The world has no use for one to-day / Who eyes things thus," [ll. 31-33]). And in "Unkept Good Fridays" (3:175) the narrator signals an end to the poem's speculations with an abrupt "Let be." Through such language, Hardy recreates not only the spoken word, but the act of composition: the narrator muses about the poem—"Well, well"—as he writes it. The same mannerism appears in the prose, especially in the short stories.

The stories that make up **"A Few Crusted Characters"** and the volume entitled *A Group of Noble Dames* identify specific narrators who compose the stories as they tell them; and in **"The Romantic Adventures of a Milkmaid,"** the narrator gets so distracted by his own voice that he has to restart the story's opening sentence:

> It was half-past four o'clock (by the testimony of the land surveyor, my authority for the particulars of this story, a gentleman with the faintest curve of humour on his lips); it was half-past four o'clock on a May morning in the eighteen forties.

> (*CM,* p. 305)

In the poetry and the short stories, Hardy prefers an informal speaker, one who is always willing to interrupt the flow of the narrative.

The casual flavor of Hardy's language is a mannerism that reflects more significant freedoms Hardy allows himself with the structure of his texts. The colloquial voice induces a change in the narrative by omitting portions of a story, for example, or by questioning a poem's argument. The inconsistency of Hardy's narrative voice allows him to revisit the same subject in different poems, presenting them from an altered perspective. Hardy's poems thus begin to look like versions of each other. Even the subtitle of one of the poems identifies it as a repetition of one of Hardy's favorite themes: "So, Time (The same thought resumed)" (3:72). But rather than simply padding a volume with duplicates, Hardy presents variations on his themes to prevent any single opinion (no matter how forcefully voiced by the poem's "dramatic" narrator) from becoming the final word on the subject. Anyone wishing to characterize Hardy as a pessimist can easily find an example, such as the short poem "John and Jane" (1:256), which presents a family's misery as its final word:

I

> He sees the world as a boisterous place
> Where all things bear a laughing face,
> And humorous scenes go hourly on,
>   Does John.

II

> They find the world a pleasant place
> Where all is ecstasy and grace,
> Where a light has risen that cannot wane,
>   Do John and Jane.

III

> They see as a palace their cottage-place,
> Containing a pearl of the human race,
> A hero, maybe, hereafter styled,
>   Do John and Jane with a baby-child.

IV

> They rate the world as a gruesome place,
> Where fair looks fade to a skull's grimace—
> As a pilgrimage they would fain get done—
>   Do John and Jane with their worthless son.

The family gets larger with each stanza, and the final line gets longer, until the "pleasant" world of the first three stanzas becomes "gruesome" in stanza IV. As the poem progresses each increase in John's family leads to increased happiness, but the final impression of the poem is that this accumulation eventually results in tragedy. Other Hardy poems, however, can remedy this gloomy view. In the same volume, the narrator of "The Dark-Eyed Gentleman" (1:295-296) recovers from her affair with a man who abandons her (a man who once assisted the maiden with her garter) by profiting from an addition to her family:

> Yet now I've beside me a fine lissom lad,
> And my slip's nigh forgot, and my days are not sad;
> My own dearest joy is he, comrade, and friend,
> He it is who safe-guards me, on him I depend;
>   No sorrow brings he,
>   And thankful I be
> That his daddy once tied up my garter for me!

> (ll. 17-21)

Here the poem ends: Hardy allows the narrator to remain in the optimistic mood that stanza IV destroys for "John and Jane." Having both poems in the same volume produces an interesting uncertainty.[21] The reader, educated by "John and Jane," can imagine an unspoken conclusion to "The Dark-Eyed Gentleman." But the process can easily work in reverse: the pessimism is just as likely as the optimism to represent a transient mood. The two poems work like a discussion: Frederick W. Shilstone notes the "various voices" throughout all of Hardy's collections of poetry, commenting that, "As if in conversation, these voices modify each other."[22] Speculations about family happiness form just one of the many threads running through any volume of Hardy's poetry. When the reader follows such threads, the volume becomes a kind of narrative—one that dramatizes fluctuations in attitude toward particular themes.[23]

Through his different narrators, Hardy allows competing poems to enact a search for meaning. The speaker of one of Hardy's dramatic monologues, for example, explicitly presents his life as a desperate search for proof of existence beyond that life. "I have lain in dead men's beds," the speaker announces, "have walked / The tombs of those with whom I had talked" ("A Sign-Seeker," 1:65-67, ll. 42-43)—but the narrator ends with the admission that he is the only presence haunting the graveyards. He asks for a signal from beyond, "And panted for response. But none replies." Hardy describes this narrator in the poem's title, "A Sign-Seeker," but the description equally fits other Hardy narrators. An interesting companion to this poem is "The Last Signal" (2:212-213), Hardy's elegy in memory of William Barnes. Hardy describes walking up a hill and seeing a flash of light:

> Looking hard and harder I knew what it meant—
> The sudden shine sent from the livid east scene;
> It meant the west mirrored by the coffin of my friend
>   there,
>   Turning to the road from his green.
>
> (ll. 9-12)

In the poem, Hardy interprets the flash of light as a farewell signal from his dead friend, "As with a wave of his hand." This is a wholly original simile, but it is also an improbable one. The poem presents a striking image, but behind the image is, not the ghost of William Barnes, but the meaning imposed by the poem's narrator, who hopes for a signal from his dead friend. "Looking hard and harder I knew what it meant," the narrator says with conviction. The narrator's authority, however, is suspect: the harder people look, of course, the closer they come to the meaning they expect to find. The simile, I think, is meant to be a stretch of the imagination: the absurdity of the signal, by pointing to the narrator's struggle to interpret, is part of the poem's effect. Even this quiet elegy exhibits an underlying uncertainty about signals, about signs—especially when placed in dialogue with "sign-seekers" in other Hardy poems. The poems Hardy wrote after the death of his first wife achieve much of their poignancy from such an uncertainty. In the "Poems of 1912-13" Hardy reacts to Emma's death in different moods, revisiting key locations from their past with the hope that they retain some sign of her existence. In "The Haunter" (2:55-56) Hardy gives a voice to Emma's spirit, letting her express the comforting thought that she accompanies Hardy on his journey. But in the companion poem, "The Voice" (2:56-57), Hardy is not sure that he receives this comfort: "Can it be you that I hear?" he asks, "Or is it only the breeze . . . / You being ever dissolved to wan wistlessness. / Heard no more again far or near?" (ll. 9, 11-12). The narrator of "The Voice" begins to doubt what he hears, and cannot assign meaning to his experience with certainty. An earlier poem, "Nature's Questioning" (1:86-87), directs itself to the problem of explaining any phenomena. The poem does not end with a solution:

> Thus things around. No answerer I. . . .
>   Meanwhile the winds, and rains,
>   And Earth's old glooms and pains

> Are still the same, and Life and Death are neighbours
>   nigh.
>
> (ll. 25-28; Hardy's ellipsis)

Hardy is "no answerer": the world goes on, and resists his narrator's attempts to explain it. Sometimes Hardy's poems adopt the tone of an answer, an assertion. But a comparison with other poems exposes the assertion as an alternative: other interpretations are equally probable.[24]

Hardy's short stories can similarly enact a struggle to assign meaning. In **"The Withered Arm,"** for example, the different characters try to count for Gertrude Lodge's injury. Rhoda Brook sees her dream as the cause of Gertrude's injury, but Gertrude's husband interprets it as divine punishment: Farmer Lodge had abandoned a pregnant Rhoda in order to marry Gertrude, and he "feared [his wife's disfigurement] might be a judgment from heaven upon him" (*WT,* p. 91). And when Gertrude learns of a possible treatment, involving the corpse of a recently hanged man, she struggles with the language of the conjurer's prescription:

> Whenever her imagination pictured the act she shrank
> in terror from the possibility of it: then the words of
> the conjurer, "It will turn your blood," were seen to be
> capable of a scientific no less than a ghastly interpretation.
>
> (p. 95)

Hardy allows the characters to make different interpretations, just as the various narrators of Hardy's poetry, in different moods, offer different explanations of experience. The narrator of **"The Withered Arm"** seems as undecided as the characters. Romey T. Keys points to "the narrator's refusal to formulate final and absolute statements."[25] The traditionally objective third person narrator here seems a collection of different voices. Instead of establishing an omniscient narrator who specifies meaning, Hardy allows the characters' uncertainty to disturb how the tale is told.

Such a disturbed omniscience is equally operative in **"The Fiddler of the Reels,"** a story that seems collected by town gossips, none of them entirely certain about what happened. The narrator describes the fiddler Wat Ollamoor as he was perceived by the townspeople, rather than from an objective position:

> Many a worthy villager envied him his power over unsophisticated maidenhood—a power which seemed
> sometimes to have a touch of the weird and wizardly in
> it. Personally he was not ill-favoured. . . . On occasion he wore curls—a double row—running almost
> horizontally around his head. But as these were sometimes noticeably absent, it was concluded that they
> were not altogether of Nature's making.
>
> (*LLI,* p. 166)

Rather than stating outright that Wat's curls are fake, Hardy presents the detail as a jealous suspicion of the villagers. In the story, Ned Hipcroft hopes to make Car'line Aspent forget her passion for the mysterious fiddler, and when she decides to accept Ned's marriage proposal the narrative is only speculative about the young man's emotions: "A tide of warm feelings *must* have surged through Ned Hipcroft's frame on receipt of this news" (p. 172; emphasis mine). And the outcome of the story, after Wat disappears with his and Car'line's illegitimate child, is presented as a guess rather than a declaration: "That Carry and her father had emigrated to America was the general opinion" (p. 185). Rather than asserting facts, the narrator settles for "general opinion."

The passage of time in a Hardy text can further contribute to an uncertainty about reality. Hardy often upsets the conventional idea of time, I have argued, by allowing narrative gaps that bring distant events of a story into abrupt proximity. Any narrative, of course, leaves out unimportant details; Hardy's significant effect, however, depends on the reader experiencing the separated events as simultaneous. **"The Fiddler of the Reels"** opens with a description of how the Great Exhibition of 1851 interrupts the rural traditions of South Wessex:

> The year formed in many ways an extraordinary chronological frontier or transit-line, at which there occurred what one might call a precipice in Time. As in a geological "fault," we had presented to us a sudden bringing of ancient and modern into absolute contact.
>
> (*LLI,* p. 165)

Hardy's texts are filled with moments when "Time seemed fiction, Past and Present one" ("Rome: On the Palatine," [1:134]). Hardy's attitude toward time can make even his narratives without supernatural subject matter appear gothic, extraordinary.[26] In "The Two Rosalinds" (1:247-250) the poem's narrator sees a poster reminding him of a performance of *As You Like It* that he had attended forty years earlier, when he was charmed by the actress portraying Rosalind:

> So; all other plans discarding,
> I resolved on entrance, bent on seeing what I once had seen,
> And approached the gangway of my earlier knowledge, disregarding
> The tract of time between.
>
> (ll. 29-32)

But he experiences "chilling disappointment" upon seeing the lead actress of this performance: it is the same woman, forty years older. The narrator realizes time has passed—the woman has aged considerably!—but in his experience the two Rosalinds are simulta-

neous. The narrator's expectations produce a supernatural effect, a physical transformation: by "disregarding the tract of time between," it is as if the actress ages forty years in an instant.

There is no such thing as a "pure" moment in Hardy. He names one of his poetry collections *Moments of Vision,* suggesting that all vision is relative and temporary ("of the moment"). The most complete interpretation of the title, however, recognizes that the word "moment" is plural: any complete vision involves a multiplicity of perspectives. Present events gain significance through comparison with the past, just as a current mood gains significance through a dialogue with previous moods. Hardy's unwillingness to choose from among different philosophical explanations for the same phenomenon produces an uncertainty that often translates into abruptness, awkwardness. But this awkwardness is an achieved quality: he wants to complicate the reader's response by denying any definite answer (or by offering several definite answers that contradict each other). Any philosophy we see in Hardy is primarily a narrative philosophy: by offering a "series of seemings" Hardy avoids certainty and dramatizes philosophy in literary structures. Through awkward juxtapositions, relative viewpoints become a physical confrontation; the poetics of interruption that creates abrupt, sensational plots is the same strategy that makes his philosophy tangible.

I have called Hardy's narrative principle a poetics of interruption, and the idea of interruption is particularly appropriate to the extreme examples I have cited from the poems and short stories. But even where the contrasts are less abrupt, they still produce the unsettling effect of an interruption: any shift in tone, however subtle, contradicts the comforting certainty of an omniscient narrator, and makes the literary work seem less than perfect. Hardy, however, professed not to value perfection:

> He knew that in architecture cunning irregularity is of enormous worth, and it is obvious that he carried on into his verse, perhaps unconsciously, the Gothic art-principle in which he had been trained.
>
> (*Life,* p. 323)

The passage is from the biography once credited to Hardy's second wife, Florence, although now generally recognized as the work of Hardy himself. The observation applies equally to the "cunning irregularity" of Hardy's prose narratives, and his characteristic confession of naiveté—that he adopted this aesthetic "perhaps unconsciously"—follows the pattern of self-effacement common to many of Hardy's literary pronouncements. Like the short stories written late in Hardy's prose career, Hardy's mature novels demonstrate little inclination to improve upon what others perceive as the faults or irregularities of his earlier works. Willing to recognize that others might be disturbed by his narrative strategies, Hardy is unwilling to give up the benefits derived from these strategies. All of Hardy's self-criticisms thus echo the sentiment expressed in the "Apology" to *Late Lyrics and Earlier*: "I apologize, but cannot help it" (2:321).[27]

Notes

1. For example, Hardy apologizes for the complex plot in *The Mayor of Casterbridge* by referring to the demands of serial publication: "His aiming to get an incident into almost every week's part causing him in his own judgment to add events to the narrative somewhat too freely" (Thomas Hardy, *The Life and Work of Thomas Hardy*, ed. Michael Millgate [Athens, Georgia, 1985], p. 185). Hereafter referred to as *Life*.

2. For a partial listing, see Samuel Hynes, "On Hardy's Badnesses," *Essays on Aesthetics: Perspectives on the Work of Monroe C. Beardsley*, ed. John Fisher (Philadelphia, 1983). Hereafter cited as "Badnesses." I am less concerned with the possibility that such passages mar an individual work, than with the danger that these flaws be confused with similar appearances of carelessness that contribute to Hardy's strength.

3. All citations of Hardy's poetry and prefaces to volumes of poetry are taken from *The Complete Works of Thomas Hardy*, ed. Samuel Hynes, 3 vols. (Oxford, 1982-85).

4. Thomas Hardy, *Desperate Remedies* (London, 1903; rpt. 1971), p. vi.

5. Michael Millgate, in *Thomas Hardy: His Career as a Novelist* (London, 1971), points to Hardy's tendency to prefer his poetry, and suggests that "Hardy's dismissive comments upon [his fiction] were largely designed to challenge the reluctance of critics and readers to take him seriously as a poet" (p. 352). Millgate's delineation of Hardy's attitude toward revision on pp. 352-354 nicely complements the argument of this essay.

6. For an account of the bowdlerization of these two novels in serial see Mary Ellen Chase, *Thomas Hardy from Serial to Novel* (New York, 1964), pp. 69-112, 115-177.

7. My interpretation will seem less forced if we remember that Hardy himself consistently downplayed the significance of his philosophy. And as my argument below will suggest, Hardy's philosophy is itself a function of structure.

8. Another of Hardy's own defenses, from the *Life*: "The whole secret of a living style and the difference between it and a dead style, lies in not having too much style—being, in fact, a little careless, or rather seeming to be, here and there. It brings a wonderful life into the writing" (p. 108). The trouble with Hardy's logic here is that an assertion of intentional carelessness could be used after-the-fact to defend any flawed text. The issue of an author's intention while writing is, of course, difficult to prove—and, perhaps, not necessary. Whether Hardy was intentional when composing the "errors" is difficult to say; it is certain, however, that he did not revise many of these supposed flaws after they were frequently pointed out to him.

9. See Thom Gunn, "Hardy and the Ballads," *Agenda* 10 (1972): 23-24.

10. Samuel Hynes, *The Pattern of Hardy's Poetry* (Chapel Hill, 1961), p. 53.

11. When Hynes asserts that Hardy "was not good at short narrative, whether in prose or in verse" ("Badnesses," p. 249), the judgment stems from a limiting definition of narrative: elsewhere Hynes stresses that "narrative requires a regular unobtrusive metrical movement" (*Pattern*, p. 75).

12. J. I. M. Stewart indeed speaks of Hardy's short stories as "in the main sensational and perfunctory narratives, hastily and carelessly written" (*Thomas Hardy: A Critical Biography* [London, 1971], p. 150). For other negative reactions to Hardy as a short story writer, see Richard C. Carpenter, who complains that Hardy was "not scrupulous about the construction of the story" (*Thomas Hardy* [New York, 1964], p. 69). William R. Rutland, among others, objects particularly to the content of some of the stories: "it seems a misapplication of energy that so much ingenuity, and even power, should be directed merely to creating a nasty taste in the mouth" (*Thomas Hardy: A Study of His Writings and Their Background* [New York, 1962], p. 219). The most sustained sympathetic reading of the stories, however, appears in Kristin Brady, *The Short Stories of Thomas Hardy* (New York, 1982).

13. Unless otherwise indicated, passages from the prose are taken from *The Writings of Thomas Hardy* ("Anniversary Edition") (New York, 1920). The book titles are abbreviated as follows:

Wessex Tales = WT

Life's Little Ironies = LLI

A Changed Man = CM

The quotations from "An Indiscretion . . ." are from *Old Mrs. Chundle and Other Stories*, ed. F. B. Pinion (London, 1977).

14. Irving Howe, *The Selected Writings of Thomas Hardy* (New York, 1966), p. 16.

15. "The Walk" emphasizes the same contrast: the compressed design of the poem ensures that the reader's visions of the husband and the widow are nearly simultaneous.

16. For a more famous example (and one that nicely validates my use of the word "interruption") see the opening of "Part Second" of *Jude the Obscure*: "He was out of his apprenticeship, and with his tools at his back seemed to be in the way of making a new start—the start to which, barring the interruption involved in his intimacy and married experience with Arabella, he had been looking forward for about ten years." Dennis Taylor also uses the word "interruption" to describe Hardy's structural effects (*Hardy's Poetry, 1860-1928* [New York, 1981], pp. xi-xviii). I discuss Taylor's work below, and in note 18.

17. This distinction is, of course, a loose application of Gerard Genette's distinction between *récit* and *histoire* in *Narrative Discourse: An Essay in Method* (New York, 1980).

18. Taylor's book presents an excellent argument about the development of Hardy's idea of the mind, and of his ability to translate this idea into literary patterns. His comments on the meditative lyrics are especially good, locating a pattern of interruption similar to the one I suggest here. But although Taylor glances at the novels, his main emphasis is on locating a "mature Hardy" in the later poetry. I stress instead that there is no concluding/conclusive philosophy: what is important in Hardy is the structure of interruption, rather than any coherent interpretations that we can find in such structures.

19. William W. Morgan, "The Partial Vision: Hardy's Idea of Dramatic Poetry," in *Thomas Hardy: Poems: A Casebook,* ed. James Gibson and Trevor Johnson (London, 1979), pp. 244-252.

20. A. F. Cassis, in "A Note on the Structure of Hardy's Short Stories," *CLQ* 10 (1974), follows T. O. Beachcroft in distinguishing between "the tradition of the conscious, artistic literary short story, that of the *écrivain,* and the tradition of the *raconteur,* the narrator who simulates a spoken story in print" (p. 287). Cassis sees both traditions in Hardy's stories, although his article stresses the techniques of the *écrivain.*

21. The uncertainty I refer to here is entirely the reader's. The different narrators of the two poems offer their interpretations with certainty: to one, a "worthless" son is a curse; to the other a "fine lissom lad" is a blessing. Below I isolate examples of narrators who display an uncertainty similar to what Hardy produces in his reader, but this example emphasizes the important physical aspect of Hardy's juxtapositions: by not abandoning the language of certainty, Hardy makes the conflict between competing views more dramatic—even violent.

22. Frederick W. Shilstone, "Conversing Stances in Hardy's Shorter Poems," *CLQ* 12 (1976): 139-148.

23. Here we can see another possible explanation for Hardy's abandonment of novel-writing after *Jude the Obscure*. The idea of a poetic volume, offering more complex opportunities for tonal variation, replaced his idea of a novel. Despite the large expanse of Hardy's novels they are all (as *Jude* makes most obvious) to a large degree claustrophobic: in a novel, the poet's interest in tonal variation cannot help but produce repetitions and improbable coincidences.

24. In *The Linguistic Moment: From Wordsworth to Stevens* (Princeton, 1985), J. Hillis Miller also explores the effect of competing poems within a single volume:

A book of poems by Hardy presents the "fierce unreason" of a heterogeneous collection of detached moments, scenes, and episodes all going on side by side, interfering with one another, inhibiting one another, contradicting one another, refusing to form a coherent series. (p. 306)

Miller ultimately suggests that the best skill for reading Hardy is "an ability to suspend the demand for consecutiveness of logical thought" (p. 272). I would qualify Miller's remark by saying that we may no longer demand logical consistency, but we still desire it: the activity of reading Hardy depends on the tension between expected unity (and the reader's tendency to construct/discern patterns) and Hardy's attempts to defy such consistency. The reader is not, as Miller argues, a "helpless recipient of the pattern" (p. 298); instead, the reader is always aware of the pieces that do not fit (especially when trying to make them fit). It is essential that readers perceive the abruptness of Hardy's interruptions.

25. Romey T. Keys, "Hardy's Uncanny Narrative: A Reading of 'The Withered Arm,'" *TSLL* 27 (1985): 106-123.

26. Taylor's definition of the "grotesque" in Hardy is particularly relevant to the present discussion: "the mental distortion of reality produced by the juxtaposition of two time zones—the one we think we are in, the one we are actually in" (p. 108).

27. I am grateful to Miriam Bailin, Naomi Lebowitz, and my director Richard Stang for overseeing this

essay as part of my Washington University dissertation, "Secret Passages: Forgotten Structures in
the Novels of Thomas Hardy."

Martin Ray (essay date 1997)

SOURCE: Ray, Martin. "'The Duchess of
Hamptonshire.'" In *Thomas Hardy: A Textual Study of
the Short Stories*, pp. 146-56. Aldershot, U.K.: Ashgate,
1997.

[*In the following excerpt, Ray explores the changes
made to "The Duchess of Hamptonshire" as it appeared
in various periodicals and editions of* A Group of Noble
Dames *throughout the years.*]

'The Duchess of Hamptonshire' was the second short
story which Hardy wrote (after the uncollected **'Destiny and a Blue Cloak'** of 1874), and the first one he
published in England. It is also one of his most textually complicated tales. He wrote **'The Impulsive Lady
of Croome Castle'**, as it was originally called, in
Sturminster Newton in early 1878, while he was completing work on *The Return of the Native*. Six years
later, he substantially altered it, although the outline of
the plot remained the same, and then published it in
America under the title **'Emmeline'**. The story was
first collected in *A Group of Noble Dames* in 1891,
and for the first time it was called **'The Duchess of
Hamptonshire'**: this edition of the story combines
different parts of the two earlier published forms.

The versions of the story which have textual significance are as follows:

Light   As 'The Impulsive Lady of Croome Castle',
             Light, 6 April (pp. 7-8) and 13 April (pp. 51-2)
             1878. The division occurred at the end of Part
             First, when Hill leaves Emmeline in the shrub-
             bery.

HW   As 'The Impulsive Lady of Croome Castle',
             Harper's Weekly (New York), 11 May (pp. 370-
             71) and 18 May (p. 394) 1878. The division is
             the same as above.

Independent As 'Emmeline; or, Passion versus Principle',
             Independent (New York), 7 February 1884, pp.
             26-8. Like the previous versions, this is divided
             into Part First and Part Second.

1891   'The Duchess of Hamptonshire', *A Group of
             Noble Dames* (London: Osgood, McIlvaine,
             1891), pp. 215-35. This was the first collected
             edition of the story in the expanded *A Group of
             Noble Dames* which now included ten stories,
             of which 'The Duchess of Hamptonshire' was
             'Dame the Ninth'. The story is not divided into
             sections in this or subsequent editions. Pub-
             lished at 6*s.* in an edition of 2000 copies on 30
             May 1891. It was the first volume of Hardy's
             work which Osgood, McIlvaine had published.

1891H   'The Duchess of Hamptonshire', *A Group of
             Noble Dames* (New York: Harper & Brothers,
             1891), pp. 234-55. Published early in June
             1891.

1896   'The Duchess of Hamptonshire', *A Group of
             Noble Dames* (London: Osgood, McIlvaine,
             1896), pp. 215-35. Volume XV in the Wessex
             Novels, the first uniform and complete edition
             of Hardy's works. Plates of the original edition
             were used, and 'The Duchess of Hamptonshire'
             is identical in every respect to *1891*.

1912   'The Duchess of Hamptonshire', *A Group of
             Noble Dames* (London: Macmillan, 1912), pp.
             191-206. Volume XIV of the Wessex edition.

A bound manuscript of **'Emmeline'** is currently located in the Pierpont Morgan Library, which acquired
it in 1909.

The origin of part of the story may lie in an incident
which Hardy's brother-in-law told him. Caddell
Holder, who was married to Emma Hardy's sister, was
once a curate in Bristol during an outbreak of cholera,
and, as Hardy recalls in the *Life*,

> He related that one day at a friend's house he met a
> charming young widow, who invited him to call on her.
> With pleasant anticipations he went at tea-time a day or
> two later, and duly inquired if she was at home. The
> servant said with a strange face: 'Why, Sir, you buried
> her this morning!' He found that amongst the many fu-
> nerals of cholera victims he had conducted that day, as
> on every day, hers had been one.
>
>   (p. 161)

The first surviving reference to the story is to the version that became **'Emmeline'**. On 16 October 1883,
Hardy replied to John Bowen, assistant editor of the
New York *Independent*: 'I have received your letter of
the 14th Sept., together with a copy of the Independent. I will take your offer into consideration, & let
you know as soon as possible if I can send you a story,
such as you describe, on the terms proposed' (*Letters*,
VII, 98). As we shall see later, it may be very significant that Bowen had sent Hardy a copy of the *Independent*, which would allow him to gauge the interests
and outlook of the audience which he was being invited to address.

The three different titles of the story indicate the three
distinct versions in which it existed, first in 1878 (the
English publication in *Light* is effectively identical to
the American *Harper's Weekly*), then in 1884 in the
Independent, and finally in 1891 in the first collected
edition. What is the relationship between these three
versions? Purdy notes that 'the version of 1884 is
much the longest (and may be the earliest), as the version of 1878 is the shortest' (pp. 63-4). Purdy is correct about the respective lengths of the three versions,
but his conjecture about the order in which they were

composed is mistaken. A close study of the manuscript of the 1884 publication shows that the sequence of publication is the same as the sequence of composition: the earliest version was the first to be published, and the *Independent* was an augmented and revised version which Hardy prepared in 1884. He then combined parts from these two earlier versions to produce the collected edition in 1891: the 1878 version was the basis for the first part of the story in the collected edition (up to the point when Hill leaves Emmeline in the shrubbery), while the 1884 version provides the bulk of the second part.

Why might Hardy have wished to alter and augment the story for the *Independent*? This New York title was a leading Congregational newspaper, and in his later dealings with it Hardy always showed himself to be very aware of its religious outlook. For instance, in November 1885 he offered to serialize *The Woodlanders* in it, and was careful to emphasize that its 'moral tone will be unexceptionable', repeating in a letter of February 1886 that 'the tone of the story' was 'of a kind which I think would suit your readers'. Five years later, he proposed to write the story that became **'The Doctor's Legend'**: 'as it would be specially written I would do my best to keep it in harmony with the general tone of The Independent (with which I am familiar)'. In 1900, he sent the newspaper one of Florence Henniker's stories and recommended it to the editor because it had 'a moral which was as sound as it was unobtrusive'.[1] It seems likely, then, that Hardy would have been especially careful not to give offence to the editor or readers of the *Independent* when submitting a story about a curate in love with a married woman, and many of the unique features of the 1884 version are, as we shall see later, examples of the kind of self-censorship which Hardy performed elsewhere. For instance, there is no physical contact between the two lovers in 1884, and generally Hardy seems to have striven to produce a story that has the earnest clarity of a moral allegory, and the new subtitle, 'Passion versus Principle', reassures its readers from the outset of its lofty tone.

LIGHT AND HARPER'S WEEKLY

The serial publications of **'The Impulsive Lady of Croome Castle'** in *Light* and *Harper's Weekly* are substantively identical.

R. L. Purdy gives an account of the English serial:

> *Light: A Journal of Criticism and Belles Lettres* (London) was a short-lived weekly founded by Robert Buchanan. Fiction was printed in an independent *feuilleton*, 'Belles Lettres', and these were collected and reissued monthly as *Light Magazine*. Hardy's story appeared in the first two numbers, simultaneously with the opening instalments of Trollope's 'The Lady of Launay'. The British Museum has the only file I know of.

(p. 63n)

These two versions of 1878 uniquely locate the story in the parish of Croome. In the *Independent* this becomes Stroome and in *1891* it is called Batton.[2]

This 1878 version is the shortest of the three, and therefore it is best defined by what it does not contain. The first part of the story here will be familiar to readers of the collected edition in *A Group of Noble Dames,* since Hardy largely restored the 1878 version. Sir Byng has 5000 acres (as he does in the *Independent*) which increases to 10,000 in 1891. We learn nothing of what her husband taunted Emmeline with (we learn most in the *Independent,* and *1891* retains some of those details). In general, we discover most about her suffering in the *Independent,* less in *1878* and least in the collected editions. For instance, *1878* has Emmeline telling Hill that 'two days ago he shut me up in an attic in the middle of the night, and there was nothing for me to sit upon, and I was chilled and wretched'. The *Independent* retains this but Hardy deleted it in *1891*. The entire paragraph which describes Sir Byng being smitten by the sight of Emmeline and declaring to himself that he wants to marry her is not in *1878,* and it first appeared in *1884*.

The second part of the story in the collected edition, beginning with Hill's voyage to America, is largely based on the *Independent,* so the 1878 version will be unfamiliar to most readers. It is similar to later versions in its plot, but is shorter and lacks several details which appear for the first time in the *Independent*. For instance, it does not mention Hill officiating at a funeral on board the ship at the time it happened, so the later versions have a much stronger sense of retrospective irony. In *1878,* Hill does not write 'Lines to an Unfortunate Lady', another ironic touch introduced later to stress the pathos of addressing poems to a woman who, we eventually learn, has long been dead. We do not see him talking to his acquaintances and omitting the episode involving Emmeline, which is not described as being 'of towering importance to himself'.

The chronology of the story is slightly different in *1878*: Hill learns of Sir Byng's death five months after it occurred, and he cannot get free of his engagements for a further six, whereas in later versions he learns the news seven months after and is detained for a further four. *1878* does not have his reflection that 'old times will revive with the cessation of her recent experience, and every day will favour my return'. It also omits the information that Lady Saxelbye likes the villagers to enjoy themselves and often has them at the castle, leading Hill to think that she is 'kind-hearted, as always!', an ironic note since he does not yet know that Emmeline is dead. In the final paragraph, the narrator states that Hill never returned to England after he left; later versions merely say that he departed with no intention to return.

INDEPENDENT: THE MANUSCRIPT

The surviving manuscript of the 1884 version of the story, entitled **'Emmeline; or Passion versus Principle'**, is written on 25 leaves of ruled paper. Purdy describes it thus:

> Though printers' MS., it is cleaner than was common with Hardy at this time and there are comparatively few alterations, suggesting it was largely copied from an earlier draft. The sub-title seems to have been an afterthought.
>
> (p. 65)

The evidence that the sub-title was a later addition is that **'Emmeline'** is centred at the top of the page and has its own double underline. The sub-title was then written to the right of this and separately double-underlined. The MS. does appear to be copied from an earlier draft (presumably written shortly before): not only, as Purdy notes, is it cleaner than normal, but there are also numbers in many of the left-hand margins, in an irregular sequence from 2 to 16, which might indicate the leaves on which the material being copied appeared in the earlier draft.

The MS. reveals that the 1884 version derives from the earlier one of 1878. There are five occasions when Hardy began to write out the 1878 reading but then deleted it and continued immediately to the right of the deletion with the reading that was to appear in *1884*. This indicates that he made these revisions while copying out the draft. As an example, the opening sentence of the third paragraph of the story in the MS. reads

> This ~~pleasant~~ |edifying| gentleman's ~~castle stood~~ |personal| appearance was somewhat impressive
>
> (fo. 2)

In the 1878 versions, the paragraph begins 'This gentleman's castle stood', but in the MS. Hardy deleted the last two words and followed the deletion with the reading which was to appear in *1884*. Elsewhere in the MS., there are twelve other instances which show him deleting an 1878 reading and substituting above it the 1884 one. There are also fifteen interlineations which add a new 1884 reading to a passage which is the same as in *1878*.

There are eight substantive differences between the MS. and the *Independent*. All appear to be either misprints or compositorial misreadings: for instance, the MS. 'shutter' and 'sprouted' (fo. 3) appear in print as 'shuttle' and 'spurted'. This would suggest that Hardy did not see proofs of the *Independent*. The second part of the story in the MS. is substantively identical to that which appeared in the *Independent*, with the exception of two words (and the obvious misprint of 'wrote him to' instead of 'wrote to him'): the MS. reads 'experiences' and 'statements' (fos. 19, 22) which both appear as singular nouns in *1884*. Since they also appear as singular in the collected edition of 1891, Hardy must have consulted a printed copy of the story when preparing it, rather than the MS.

Two additions to the MS. in another hand are both printed in the *Independent*. Below Hardy's name on the first leaf is inserted 'Author of "A Pair of Blue Eyes," "Two on a Tower," etc.', the latter being his most recent novel in 1882, and at the end is written 'Shire-Hall Place, Dorchester, England', Hardy's home from June 1883 till June 1885.

INDEPENDENT

The first part of the story in its collected form, with which readers are now familiar, is largely the same as in the 1878 versions. The expanded version of the first part in the 1884 *Independent* has a number of unique features: sympathy for Emmeline is increased and her conduct is both more blameless and more understandable, while her father and husband are painted more critically. The key scene in the story, the meeting between Emmeline and Hill before his emigration, is especially revised to make it a quite innocent affair. Finally, the church and religion are portrayed in a kinder light. All of these features are revisions which Hardy might have undertaken to make the story more acceptable to the *Independent*.

Emmeline is more saintly in *1884*. For instance, we learn that she has a 'shortcoming', but this is only her ignorance of her own beauty, so that her one failing seems perversely to be an absence of vanity. In all other versions we learn nothing of Hill's courtship of her, the narrator dismissing it with 'particulars of the courtship remained unknown then and always'. In the *Independent*, however, we learn details of it which are much to the credit of both lovers:

> Attracted at first by her reverential attitude at church, he silently observed her long before making any advances; where and when the advances were made, and how their distant acquaintanceship ripened into warmer relations, is not precisely known, so extremely reserved and shy were both the young people in their conduct through the affair.

The narrator proceeds to imagine the accidental 'encounters by dale and down' which Hill engineered to sustain his 'tender fancy'. Their courtship is a tale of pastoral piety and chivalric discretion, in even greater contrast here to the coarser baronet which the *Independent* has just introduced. (In the serial versions, incidentally, the Duke was called Sir Byng Saxelbye.)

In the 1878 versions, we do not learn any details of her husband's behaviour before she decides to meet Hill in the shrubbery, so that her actions at this stage seem to be prompted solely by love for him, but the *Independent* gives many details of her husband's cruelty to her (none of the following quotation is in either of the 1878 versions, and italics indicate those parts of it which Hardy retained in the first collected edition in 1891):

> But as he [Sir Byng] was a rough man, so he was a careless man. *At first he would taunt her* with *her folly,* threaten her with all kinds of severities for daring to think *of that milk-and-water parson,* as he knew she did think of him, and then, with some coarse allusion, leave the room and go to his dogs and horses. *But, as time went on,* the scenes between them *took a more positive* shape—not on her side, for she was quietness personified, but on the part of Sir Byng. *He would not believe her assurance that she had in no way communicated with her former lover,* or *he with her, since their parting in the presence of her father.* He told her flatly that he knew she was deceiving him, that no woman would speak the truth in such circumstances, and many other cruel things of the sort *which need not be detailed.* Then, for the first time, this gentle woman seemed to form a resolution of a different nature from the course she had hitherto preserved with religious scrupulousness.

The last two words, Hardy perhaps felt, would placate any offence to his pious readership in the *Independent*. She is here exonerated of any blame and Sir Byng is wholly responsible for forcing her to seek escape.

In all other versions, the lovers meet two months after the wedding, but in the *Independent* she suffers for 'a few months' before Sir Byng's cruelty makes her contact Hill, and they have both remained scrupulously principled during that period. When they do meet, they 'impulsively approached each other; but they restrained the impulse, as if with pain'. In all other editions, they 'leapt together like a pair of dewdrops on a leaf', so the *Independent* reading removes any indiscreet physical contact, as well as removing the most poetical touch in the story.

The *Independent* again gives unique details of her suffering to justify her need to escape. When they meet after her marriage, her first words to him are '"I scarcely dare say," she answered in broken tones. "But I have nerved myself to this, and I will speak. Oh! Al-wyn, it grieves me that I should wound and distract you by letting you know my misery. I would not have done so, had I perceived any other course possible."' In all other versions, her first words are 'You are going to emigrate', giving us the immediate impression that her wish to see him has been caused not by her misery but by the thought that she is losing a lover. A little later, she again stresses her suffering, uniquely talking of 'the unutterable extremity of sending for you. Listen, Alwyn. Yet I can hardly say what—what I want to say. But if you only knew what I have suffered before coming to this, you would understand me.' This sounds equally like a plea from Hardy to his devout American readers, and at least she has the good grace to recognize the enormity of her proposal to run away. Indeed, the future which she conceives for them is very respectable: 'I wish you merely to watch over me—to give me a little assistance and protection after my escape—no more'. She then invokes divine sanction for her plan: 'it might be honestly done. God knows it might, seeing how wretched I am.'

The curate's rejection of her plea is markedly more decisive and pious in the *Independent*. He tells her 'in a dry, firm voice' that she must not go with him because it would be 'a terrible sin', and his scrupulous rectitude is even more prominent than in other versions: 'Honor and virtue above all things', he declares, and he informs her that 'your good name, your purity' are more precious than her life or her happiness. He begins his final address to her by acknowledging her 'suffering' heart yet again as an extenuation of her proposal, but says that it would be contrary to God's law, 'which it is my life's duty to uphold'. Perhaps Hardy hoped that his model curate would provide a moral authority to his tale which would conquer any scruples at the *Independent* about Emmeline's impropriety.

Religion has a prominence in this version of the story which may have been especially geared to the *Independent*'s readership. For instance, our attitude to Hill and to Emmeline's father, Mr Oldbourne, may be shaped by their respective qualities as preachers: when Hill delivered a sermon, 'the people were less interested in the subject of his discourse than in his manner of delivering it', whereas Oldbourne's sermons were 'mathematically divided into the time-honored first, secondly, and thirdly; and it is said that, during the life of his wife, this angularity of character in him led to no small amount of unhappiness in her'. The religious failings of most of the Saxelbyes are stressed: they had knelt in their church for generations, 'with and without hypocrisy', and in the *Independent* Hardy specifies that it is the 'other Saxelbye dames' who in their time have counted their rings, fallen asleep or laughed at the congregation. The devout reader is being asked to sympathize with Emmeline, married against her will into this ungodly family.

Sir Byng is a much more prominent, and much more unpleasant, character in the *Independent* than he is elsewhere. We learn, for instance, how his family acquired his baronetcy:

> it is said that the title was originally won by his ancestor rendering timely assistance in a court intrigue during the reign of the first George. Religion and social morality were, as is well known, at a pretty low ebb at that date; and it is therefore quite probable that the services of the first baronet reflected less credit upon him as a worthy gentleman than as an adroit time-server.

This information in the opening paragraph, never repeated in any other version of the story, immediately introduces the theme of religion and the unprincipled nature of the Saxelbye family. It also establishes an ironic parallel between the time-serving Saxelbye, who is rewarded for his worldliness, and the religious Hill, who waits patiently so many years for Emmeline, only to learn that she has been dead all along. The unrighteous thrive in this version. Sir Byng himself is a coarse boor: 'his highest intellectual aim was to preside at agricultural dinners of the jovial kind, where the speeches turned on the wildest country sports, practical jokes, feats in steeplechasing, and the latest coursing events', and we learn why he defends the 'ancient amusements' of cock-fighting and bull-baiting: '"Beasts suffer that men may dine," he would say. "Why shouldn't they suffer that men may laugh and sport and disperse dull care?"' This more brutal portrayal of Sir Byng mitigates Emmeline's flight and perhaps motivates it better than in the other versions. In the *Independent*, Emmeline's charms had 'unfortunately' been noticed by Sir Byng; in other versions, this 'unfortunately' is transferred to describe the relationship which had arisen between Emmeline and Hill. The other versions, that is, take a more worldly and conventional stance, judging her love for Hill to be regrettable, while the *Independent* sees the attraction of the rich but reprobate baronet to be worse than the love of a respectable curate.

Alwyn Hill is presented in contrast to the baronet as a principled man. In the conversation between the bell-ringers, one of them defends Emmeline and Hill thus:

> I don't believe she knows where he is gone to any more than we. Mr. Hill was not a man to force his memory upon her in any underhand way, when he decided to leave her, that she might not be hated by her father. He's a quiet, modest young fellow; but mind you that underneath that there's a good deal of strict, fair and square dealing even with people that don't deal so with him.
>
> Well, she's the one that will suffer most, if suffering there be in the business. Think of him she will at first,

but 'tis to be hoped she won't do so long. For what's the odds, after all? Anything, says I, for a quiet life.

Hill's ability to stand up for himself was presented earlier in the *Independent*, which uniquely gives details of his quarrel with Emmeline's father:

> Mr. Oldbourne accused the young fellow of attempting to undermine his daughter's happiness treacherously and by stealth, instead of asking his approval at the first; and Alwyn Hill replied in words too hasty for prudence, and too cutting to be forgiven. The gentle Emmeline could do nothing between them; and Alwyn Hill went away, his indignation against her father almost supplanting, for the moment, his tenderness toward herself.

In the second part of the story as it appeared in the *Independent*, there are only two notable unique features. The first is that we learn a further reason why Hill felt unable to continue in America as a minister of religion: he was 'still guided by that vigorous conscientiousness which some would have called puritanical self-abasement'. This is a sentiment which seems specifically designed to appeal to the New England Congregationalists who would be reading the story in the *Independent*. The other variant concerns the final paragraph; in the *Independent*, Hill does not confide his story to anyone before he emigrates again, presumably back to America.

1891 OSGOOD, MCILVAINE

In preparing the collected edition of **'The Duchess of Hamptonshire'** in 1891, Hardy collated the two serial versions of 1878 and 1884. The first part of the story, up to Hill leaving Emmeline in the shrubbery, is based on the first section of the 1878 version, and the second part closely follows the expanded version of the 1884 *Independent*. However, Hardy in each part includes variant readings from the other version not being copied at that point. Perhaps Hardy wished to restore the original version of the first part of the story because he regarded the *Independent* version as having been voluntarily bowdlerized for a specific audience.

In *1891,* Sir Byng is elevated to the status of a Duke for the first time, and Emmeline's father becomes the Honourable Mr Oldbourne, in keeping with the rank of the other characters in the volume. Following his marriage to Emmeline, the Duke is described as the 'august' husband, rather than merely as the 'new' one, stressing again the increased social gap between him and Hill. In the second paragraph, Hardy deleted a striking simile describing the castle which had appeared in both previous versions: 'from the high road it appeared set against the tangled boughs of the trees and over the dark lawns like a camellia in a raven head of hair'. In 1891, the housemaids who stalk the corridors of the castle at the fire-lighting hour are called 'ghostly' for the first time.

The opening four sentences of the second paragraph, describing the Duke's personal appearance, derive from the *Independent,* as does the account in the following paragraph which explains how Oldbourne's 'white neckcloth, well-kept gray hair, and right-lined face betokened none of those sympathetic traits whereon depends so much of a parson's power to do good among his fellow-creatures'. Hardy continues the critical presentation of the curate by retaining the *Independent*'s statement that 'his procedure was cold, hard, and inexorable' in separating Hill and Emmeline.

In the second part of the story, a key sentence describes Hill's decision to become a teacher:

> Distracted and weakened in his beliefs by his recent experiences, he decided that he could not for a time worthily fill the office of a minister of religion, and applied for the mastership of a school.

While the second part of the story largely follows the *Independent,* this sentence derives from the 1878 version, with the exception that 'could not for a time' is the *Independent* reading (*1878* had said that he could 'no longer' be a curate). This small revision shows the detailed collation of the two earlier versions which Hardy undertook when he came to prepare the 1891 collected edition. The only other feature of the second part which derives from *1878* and not *1884* is the description of Hill confiding his story to an old friend before he left the town. In 1891, Hardy adds that the identity of the dead woman was never publicly disclosed and that the friend in whom Hill confided was 'grandfather of the person who now relates it to you'. Previously, the story had not had a narrator, but in *A Group of Noble Dames* the story is related by the Quiet Gentleman, and Hardy also adds the final two paragraphs describing his audience's response.

In *A Group of Noble Dames,* **'The Duchess of Hamptonshire'** is placed as the penultimate story, possibly because, like the final one (**'The Honourable Laura'**), it had first been published a decade before the other stories in the volume.

1891 Harper

The American edition has some forty differences in accidentals from the Osgood, McIlvaine edition of 1891, ignoring variations in US spelling, and there are three substantive variants which would appear to be editorial or compositorial. For instance, the 'gentler sex' becomes the 'gentle sex', and news of Emmeline's illness on board the ship causes alarm among

'the passengers', instead of 'all the passengers' in the British edition. There is no indication that Hardy read proofs for the Harper edition.

1912 Macmillan Wessex edition

The only substantive variation between the Wessex edition and the 1891 Osgood, McIlvaine occurs in the following sentence, which reads thus in *1891*: 'Who shall wonder that his mind luxuriated in dreams of a sweet possibility now laid open for the first time these many years? for Emmeline was to him now as ever the one dear thing in all the world.' In the Wessex edition, Hardy changes the first 'now' to 'just' (p. 200), no doubt to avoid repetition.[3]

Notes

1. *Letters,* I, 138, 141, 220, and II, 205.

2. F. B. Pinion notes that '"Batton Castle" appeared on Wessex maps before 1912 (and it is still shown on the smaller map) at a point which suggests Tottenham House, southeast of Marlborough. The fictional name resembles that of the historic neighbouring borough of Bedwyn' (New Wessex edition, p. 379). Denys Kay-Robinson, however, suggests that '"Batton" is very like a Hardy substitution for Badminton, and Badminton is very near Castle Combe' (p. 256). See also *Letters,* IV, 175.

3. There are seven differences in punctuation and styling between the two editions: in the following list, the Wessex edition reading is given first and the pagination is that of *1912*: 'ago/ago,' (p. 191); 'incontestably/incontestibly' (p. 191); 'parish church/parish-church' (p. 191); 'O/Oh' (p. 197, twice); 'further end/farther end' (p. 202; 1912 however reads 'farther' later on the same page); 'majority,/majority' (p. 206).

Bibliography

PRIMARY WORKS BY THOMAS HARDY

Pinion, F. B. ed. (1977), *Wessex Tales [and] A Group of Noble Dames,* New Wessex edition, Macmillan, London.

SECONDARY WORKS

Hardy, Evelyn and Pinion, F. B., ed. (1972), *One Rare Fair Woman: Thomas Hardy's Letters to Florence Henniker, 1893-1922,* Macmillan, London.

Kay-Robinson, Denys (1972), *Hardy's Wessex Reappraised,* David & Charles, Newton Abbot.

Pinion, F. B. (1989), *A Thomas Hardy Dictionary,* Macmillan, London.

Carol L. Beran (essay date summer 1999)

SOURCE: Beran, Carol L. "Thomas Hardy, Alice Munro, and the Question of Influence." *American Review of Canadian Studies* 29, no. 2 (summer 1999): 237-58.

[*In the following essay, Beran compares the similar plots of "An Imaginative Woman" with Alice Munro's "Carried Away," noting the attention given to chance occurrences, rural communities, and narrative self-awareness in both stories.*]

Near the beginning of Alice Munro's "Carried Away," from her 1994 collection, *Open Secrets,* a soldier writes a letter to the town librarian, Louisa, asking her to write and send a photograph. In her reply Louisa writes: *"I had a great deal of time to read and my favorite authors are Thomas Hardy, who is accused of being gloomy but I think is very true to life—and Willa Cather"* (6). Ildikó de Papp Carrington picks up on the idea of Victorian writer Thomas Hardy's gloom and how it relates to Munro's story in "What's in a Title?", writing that Munro "suggests the nature of her plot by a self-reflexive allusion to Thomas Hardy"; accidents are a major source of gloominess in Hardy's writing (556). Carrington finds a second connection between the two writers by identifying the Tolpuddle Martyrs, mentioned near the end of Munro's story, as a group who were transported from Hardy's part of England to Munro's part of Canada for their role in labor unrest (559). Carrington, however, overlooks the implication of the phrase *"very true to life"*: Munro's Louisa considers Hardy's writing *"very true to life"* because her life is a variation on the life of Ella Marchmill, a character created by Thomas Hardy. Munro's allusion to Hardy evokes not only Hardy's use of accidents and the Dorset connections with the Tolpuddle Martyrs that Carrington notes, but also points to a particular story by Hardy: the story Munro tells in "Carried Away" is remarkably like the one Hardy tells in **"An Imaginative Woman,"** published in April 1894 in the *Pall Mall Magazine.*[1] Studying specific borrowings from **"An Imaginative Woman"** in "Carried Away" reveals Munro's conversation with Hardy in one story. Looking at the more general kinship of vision between Munro and her British predecessor helps place her work in the British literary tradition while clarifying some of the distinctively contemporary and Canadian aspects of her art.

Hardy's **"An Imaginative Woman"** introduces the reader to Ella Marchmill, wife of a thriving industrialist and mother of three children, vacationing with her family at Solentsea in Upper Wessex. She finds that her room has just been vacated by a poet she has admired, and with whom she feels a coincidental connection: one of her poems appeared in conjunction with one of his in a magazine. Left much alone (the children are cared for by servants and her husband pursues an active vacation style that does not include her), she imagines more and more connection between herself and the elusive poet she longs to know personally; however, through various accidents, Ella misses meeting him each time their paths nearly cross. In a muted Victorian bedroom scene, Ella and her husband procreate their fourth child, with the photo of the object of her fantasies under the pillow. She begins a correspondence with the poet under her pen name, John Ivy. The poet, despondent over harsh critical reviews and the lack of a woman to love him (ironically, since he believes Ella to be a man), commits suicide; Ella dies after childbirth. Her husband comes to believe the fourth child to be the poet's, which the narrator explains in terms which impart a sense of folk superstition or perhaps the supernatural to the reader: "By a known but inexplicable trick of Nature there were undoubtedly strong traces of resemblance to the man Ella had never seen; the dreamy and peculiar expression of the poet's face sat, as the transmitted idea, upon the child's, and the hair was of the same hue" (330).[2]

Munro's story builds on Hardy's story. Some of the changes Munro introduces reflect the more recent timeframe of her story. For example, whereas Hardy's nineteenth century heroine depends on her husband economically, Munro's more contemporary heroine has a job that makes her financially independent. Yet the two stories share the tale of a love affair carried on in the mind of a sensitive woman contrasted with the woman's actual marriage to a manufacturer. Both stories privilege writing and imaginative closeness over physical contact. In both an accident ends the possibility of the correspondents meeting. Each story has an ending that depends on a "trick."

In **"An Imaginative Woman,"** the poet's name, Trewe, hints that readers should regard this story as true (perhaps about Hardy himself, who was also a poet) and Ella's emotions for him as directed towards something true, both in the sense of "real" and in the sense of "faithful."[3] Louisa's comment that Hardy's writing is *"very true to life"* (6) echoes Hardy's use of Trewe for the poet's name; Louisa's belief in the unusual relationships found in Hardy's stories provides a psychological basis for her romance that helps Munro insist that this is true to life. Readers of either story are aware that the romances imagined by the heroines, like the stories imagined by Hardy and Munro, are constructs. However, because Munro grounds her story in Hardy's and in a sense Louisa bases her story in Ella's, the labyrinthine effect is multiplied in "Carried Away." For Hardy, Ella's story provides a forum for animadversions against marriage:

the necessity of getting life-leased at all cost, a cardinal virtue which all good mothers teach, kept her from thinking of it [his occupation as a gunmaker] at all till she had closed with William, had passed the honeymoon, and reached the reflecting stage. Then, like a person who has stumbled upon some object in the dark, she wondered what she had got; mentally walked round it, estimated it; whether it were rare or common; contained gold, silver, or lead; were a clog or a pedestal, everything to her or nothing.

(306)

In the natural way of passion under the too practical conditions which civilization has devised for its fruition, her husband's love for her had not survived, except in the form of fitful friendship, any more than, or even so much as, her own for him. . . .

(313)

The narrator refers to Ella's husband as "her proprietor" (306), reminding readers of the inequalities in marriage in Victorian England.[4]

Whereas Hardy unabashedly uses the omniscient narrator to assert theses about marriage and the human imagination, Munro states, "I never write about an idea" (Becker 36). Instead, in "Carried Away," Munro juxtaposes the romantic quality of the relationship between Louisa and Jack Agnew against the more sordid quality of her involvements with the married doctor at the sanitorium where she had been a tuberculosis patient or her evening with travelling salesman Jim Frarey, and her seemingly ordinary subsequent marriage to Arthur Doud, owner of the piano factory in which Jack was decapitated by a machine. Some contemporary writers might have played up the theme of the victimization of Louisa by three males. In some other writer's story, Arthur might have seemed like the chivalrous king whose name he bears as he rescues the librarian from her drab life and brings her into his relative wealth; however, in Munro's story, Arthur's surname—Doud—suggests how ordinary he is, the dowdiness of his life, and the humdrum quality of their marriage; his prosperity fails to lift Louisa Cinderella-like from rags to riches as the Depression affects even the piano factory in Carstairs. Instead of focusing on the aspects of the story that might seem most significant to contemporary feminists, Munro follows Hardy's lead and takes the story into another realm altogether. Like Hardy, Munro gives her heroine both a physical and a spiritual lover.[5] Hardy validates the spiritual affair and the mysterious workings of the human imagination with a child who resembles a man Ella has met only imaginatively. Munro literalizes the idea of spiritual contact through Louisa's ghostly or imagined or hallucinatory meeting with Jack long after his death.

Hardy uses the omniscient narrator's comments and the Shelleyan theme of two kindred spirits to make the tragic outcome seem a terrible loss of potential love

and art in the world. Editor Susan Hill's description of Marchmill as "prosaic and a philistine," yet "generous and affectionate in a limited way," and Ella as "a stupid woman," "someone with too many fancies and vague ambitions but no talent, and too much time on her hands" (32), overlooks the subtle shaping that engages the reader's sympathies for the wife, not the husband, in this story. By making the husband a "gunmaker" (305), Hardy ensures that readers sympathize with the wife: "An impressionable, palpitating creature was Ella, shrinking humanely from detailed knowledge of her husband's trade whenever she reflected that everything he manufactured had for its purpose the destruction of life" (306). Word choices such as "humanely" attached to Ella and "destruction of life" attached to Marchmill's enterprises direct readers' responses. "Palpitating creature" and "shrinking" evoke pity for Ella as a hunted animal likely to be destroyed by the guns her husband manufactures. When Marchmill concludes, incorrectly, that Ella's youngest child was fathered by the poet, his rejection of the toddler justifies dislike of the man: "Get away, you poor little brat! You are nothing to me!" (330). Ironically, "a story about an imaginative woman becomes a story about an imaginative man ready to believe his own fancies and reject his own son" (Ray 176). Martin Ray shows manuscript evidence to suggest that Hardy's revisions tended to enhance Marchmill's sympathetic qualities slightly (175) while making Ella seem more irresponsible (177) but less sexually interested in the poet (174). Nevertheless, given the program of sympathy that the omniscient narrator creates, we can state with certainty what could make a happy ending, at the same time we know with equal certainty that in Victorian England such an ending is unthinkable; indeed, if the characters were to attempt to create it by running off together, the tragedy would be equally great as it is in the story as we have it. The children Hill says Ella is "uninterested in" make any actual liaison with the poet unacceptable.

Although Munro refrains from using an omniscient narrator blatantly to control readers' responses to the characters and their actions, the final section raises questions about the happiness of the earlier seemingly happy ending. Because Arthur is presented as a decent human being (he manufactures pianos and diversifies to player pianos and outdoor bowling alleys, not munitions, although during World War Two the factory assists in the war effort by manufacturing radar cases for the Navy), concerned not only about his employees but also about the family of the man killed in his factory, we want to read this as a variant on Munro's earlier story, "How I Met My Husband," with its surprising but essentially happy ending (*Something* 53). Louisa has a good spouse, a family (a son plus a stepdaughter), and a comfortable lifestyle. If the story stopped here, its ending would seem happy. The actual ending is upsetting, since Jack's reappearance hints that something is missing. Although as Ajay Heble says, "Munro, in this story, continues to be fascinated by the way things might be or might have been" (186), what might have been is less attractive than it is in **"An Imaginative Woman."** We can not be certain of the nature of Louisa's feeling for the soldier from the statements Munro's narrator provides. After Louisa learns that Jack has married, she stops reading: "The covers of books looked like coffins to her, either shabby or ornate, and what was inside them might as well have been dust" (17). The death image attached to giving up a favorite pastime might signal depression, a sign of deep love being thwarted. However, we also learn that she wonders whether "it was all a joke on me" (18). Her question about whether "a man could be so diabolical" (18) suggests that Jack may be a folkloric demon lover, thus providing another explanation for his ghostly reappearance that does not make a connection with Jack seem desirable. When the hallucinated Jack says, "Love never dies," Louisa questions the concept: "Love dies all the time, or at any rate it becomes distracted, overlaid—it might as well be dead" (48). Munro further complicates this sequence by having Louisa say that she talks to her deceased husband in her head, feeling "very close to him still but it is hardly in a mystical way" (47), and having Jack metamorphose into Jim, the travelling salesman. Munro does not clarify whether the response to the transformation is the reaction of the third person narrator or of Louisa herself: "Oh, what kind of trick was being played on her, or what kind of trick was she playing on herself! She would not have it" (49). Whereas readers of Hardy's story know precisely what the narrator expects them to believe, readers of Munro's story realize that the narrator works to baffle rather than illuminate. The anticipated epiphany does not happen, in spite of the ghostly visitation. What are we to make of this loss of the love that might have been between Louisa and Jack?

Munro's use of the word "trick" recalls her earlier use of the word in "Material," when the first person narrator, evaluating a story written by her ex-husband, acknowledges being moved, ". . . and I am not moved by tricks. Or if I am, they have to be good tricks. Lovely tricks, honest tricks" (*Something* 35).[6] The ending of "Carried Away" seems not only a trick played on Louisa, but also one played on readers, who must judge for themselves if the trick is "good," "lovely," and "honest" as the word reappears a few paragraphs later: Louisa faces "Sudden holes and impromptu tricks and radiant vanishing consolations" (50). "Trick" is also the word that Hardy uses to ex-

plain why the inevitable tragedy of Ella and Trewe extends to her child; "a known but inexplicable trick of Nature" (330), a phrase that could apply equally well to Louisa's experiences, may seem as much a trick of an author as a trick of Nature. In the 1912 Prefatory Note to *Life's Little Ironies* Hardy clarifies that this "trick of Nature" is "a physical possibility that may attach to a wife of vivid imaginings, as is well known to medical practitioners and other observers of such manifestations" (v). Like Hardy's note on the trick, Munro's comment offering the kind of clarification and interpretation readers desire concerning Jack Agnew's reappearance occurs outside the narrative, in the notes to *Best American Stories 1992*, where she says that she was writing "a pretty realistic story," yet "all the time I felt a parallel story going in which the accident never happened and another reality developed" ("Contributors'" 371).[7] Whereas Hardy's comment insists on the realism of his story, Munro's points to the constructed nature of her story. In echoing Hardy's word, Munro points to the controlling hand of the writer in determining the ending of a story. For Hardy,

> Art is a disproportioning—that is, distorting, throwing out of proportion—of realities, to show more clearly the features that matter in those realities, which, if merely copied or reported inventorially, might possibly be observed, but would more probably be overlooked. Hence "realism" is not Art.
>
> (from Hardy's notebooks, qtd. in F. E. Hardy 229)

The writer's tricks, therefore, are what make a story art; the disproportioning in **"An Imaginative Woman"** directs readers to discover, among other things, that spiritual connections are strong enough to influence the physical world. Munro's readers are also aware of the artist's disproportioning. Julia O'Faolain notes that some of the stories in *Open Secrets* "pivot on reality's slipperiness—in the light of which, realism can only be a convention and a willed distortion," asserting that "it is by distorting that writers share their vision" (24). Josephine Humphreys attempts to explain the nature and effect of what Hardy would call disproportioning in "Carried Away" by saying that the story has horrible events such as Jack's decapitation and inexplicable ones such as Louisa's marriage and her supernatural vision, yet it also has "a solid realism that allows even the bizarre to appear normal" (36). The narrator of "Simon's Luck" from Munro's *Who Do You Think You Are?* states how the conventions of art used in a standard television series protect people in a way that real life does not: "People watching trusted that they would be protected from predictable disasters, also from those shifts of emphasis that throw the story line open to question, the disarrangements which demand new judgements and solutions, and throw the windows open on inappropriate unforgettable scenery"

(177). Jagged changes of course are characteristic of Munro's stories in *Open Secrets*: "Whenever a story is rolling along in one direction, or we think it is, it is apt to take a sharp turn and go someplace else" (Summers 39). By inserting Louisa's vision of long dead Jack near the end of "Carried Away," Munro has created a shift of the inappropriate sort described in the sentence from her earlier story which functions as the earlier narrator posits: to startle readers into complex reassessments. Munro's disarrangements, like Hardy's disproportioning, challenge readers' credulity about events within the story and demand that readers question assumptions about the relationship of art and reality.

The reference to Thomas Hardy in "Carried Away" not only points to the many connections between two specific stories, but also hints, when it labels Hardy's fiction *"very true to life"* (6)—a frequent focus of scholarly commentary regarding Munro's fiction—that interpreters of Munro's writings consider more general links to the Victorian writer. Earlier articles such as J. R. (Tim) Struthers's "Reality and Ordering" (connections to Joyce), W. R. Martin's "Alice Munro and James Joyce" or "The Strange and the Familiar in Alice Munro" (connections to Coleridge and Wordsworth), or Lorraine York's "The Rival Bards: Alice Munro's *Lives of Girls and Women* and Victorian Poetry" (connections to Tennyson and Browning) point up and discuss important interactions between Munro's texts and the British tradition. In fact, intertexts and allusions to works by many writers pepper Munro's stories. Although critics frequently explain the relevance of such allusions to the story in which they appear, the more general relevance of the art of these writers to Munro's art deserves study. Because an intertext places a work in a literary tradition, studying the general context is as important as studying the specific reference. Comments such as Martin's regarding one of Munro's uncollected tales as a "Hardyesque satire of circumstance" (*Paradox* 17), Carrington's regarding Munro's use of Hardyesque accidents (556; also noted by Miriam Marty Clark [60]) and of a specific incident of labor unrest that links Hardy's Dorset and Munro's Carstairs in "Carried Away" (559) begin the process of exploring Munro's debt to Thomas Hardy. This interaction goes beyond details to a shared artistic vision based on disproportioning and disarrangement.

Both Munro and Hardy create disproportioning in their stories by writing about a fictional world superimposed on a small portion of the real rural world, finding in that world stories that reflect major controversies of their times. Both disarrange assumptions of their contemporaries through an emphasis on fate, chance, accidents, and what might have been. Both

overtly acknowledge storytelling within their stories in ways that jar readers' expectations about realism in fiction. Studying the ties between Munro's writing and Hardy's makes visible some of the unique (and contemporary and Canadian) characteristics of Munro's fiction.

Hardy's Wessex is one of the most well-known fictional counties superimposed on a real map. Editions of Hardy's works generally provide readers with a map of Dorset with Hardy's fictional place names written in.[8] Similarly, Munro's repeated use of rural southwestern Ontario settings in which towns receive fictitious names allows readers to visit Huron County and identify Walley or Carstairs or Jubilee with actual towns. For both writers, large metropolises retain their actual names, but the rural world can be imaginatively reconstituted by the writer and reader alike. Both writers disproportion accepted visions by focusing on rural life in eras when urban life might seem to many observers more representative.

One of the specific ways Hardy's art disproportions accepted versions of reality is by insisting that the lives of rural people have plots akin to those found in Greek tragedy: although his stories are set in "sequestered spots outside the gates of the world," nevertheless, in such places "dramas of a grandeur and unity truly Sophoclean are enacted in the real, by virtue of the concentrated passions and closely-knit interdependence of the lives therein" (*Woodlanders* 10). For Hardy, identifying Sophoclean drama as a way of thinking about rural life includes a tragic vision; consequently, further disproportioning occurs in the way that the unhappy endings of the lives of so many of Hardy's characters deny the romantic stereotype of idyllic rural life. In Hardy's Wessex the old ways of life clash with the emerging way of life caused by progress in thought, which overturns traditional patterns of belief, and by industrialization and technological progress, which shatter the traditional communal life based on agriculture.[9] In **"An Imaginative Woman"** Ella and Trewe stand against the impersonalization of life, the lack of sensitivity to the human spirit that technology and industry, as represented by Marchmill, seem to bring. Ella's marriage to an industrialist suggests an allegory of the soul married to the physical industrialized world, drawn back into the emotionally and spiritually fulfilling world that preceded it as represented by the poet, but inevitably discovering that such a world cannot exist in the present.

Like Hardy, Munro shows us a microcosm that represents the macrocosm. In *Lives of Girls and Women* the narrator, a writer, asserts that "People's lives, in Jubilee as elsewhere, were dull, simple, amazing and unfathomable—deep caves paved with kitchen linoleum"

(210), a psychological restatement of Hardy's comment about dramas of Sophoclean grandeur that points to awe and mystery rather than tragedy as the core of the artist's vision. Munro is aware that her choice of setting presents a disproportioning that counters contemporary visions of reality. She told Graeme Gibson, "I think that the kind of writing I do is almost anachronistic, because it's so rooted in one place, and most people, even of my age, do not have a place like this any more" (248). However, Munro's rural fictional world offers plots that could easily come out of *Cosmopolitan* magazine (which Munro says she reads [Metcalf 57]), jarring because they contradict our romanticized concepts of the rural world and remind us that the mass media have invaded southwestern Ontario as well as Toronto. The opening scene of "Carried Away" invokes both the nostalgic ideal of an innocent rural existence and its antithesis when the narrator states that a widower dining in the hotel where Louisa resides "had told her he had never before seen a woman touch wine or spirits" (3). Similarly, the idealized stereotype of rural communities promises that everyone knows each other; therefore, when Louisa does not know who Jack Agnew is, and Arthur cannot describe him to her, our sense of how things should be gets disarranged.

In "Carried Away" industrialism dehumanizes and is one of the forces that divides people from each other in the rural community. Clark observes that Jack's father is "precapitalist," a fisherman and gardener "who lives by agricultural time and his own rhythms," whereas others "are governed by the posted rules (the story lists them) and the factory whistle" (56). Jack's decapitation "literalizes the fragmentation and alienation of life under a rationalized labor process, the mutilation of the laborer into a fragment of a man" (56). The evils of industrialization lead to the labor movement, but in Munro's rural Canada this movement is represented by the ceremony to honor the Tolpuddle Martyrs, a sign of the persistence of British history in rural Ontario: British men, transported to Canada after being convicted of "administering illegal oaths," are "considered now to be among the earliest founders of the Trade Union movement" (42). Soldier (in Britain's war) and rural factory worker Jack Agnew's reading encompasses British authors H. G. Wells, G. K. Chesterton, and Bertrand Russell (books about class struggle and revolution [Clark 56]) and American author Zane Grey as well as materials related to shared British and Canadian history (the Franklin Expedition and the search for the Northwest Passage), reflecting Ontario's Canadian, British, and American cultural mix. Louisa notices "oddly dressed folk," Mennonites, present "in this part of the country where they never used to be" (49). This awareness of

the confluence of cultures—economic, educational, historical, and ethnic—in southwestern Ontario is one particularly Canadian aspect of Munro's vision.

Munro follows Hardy's lead in localizing major conflicts of the era in the microcosm, disproportioning to highlight the controversies as they affect seemingly insignificant individual lives far from the perceived centers of the culture. Both writers take up not only the effects of industrialization on the traditional way of life, but also problems caused by vestiges of the social class system and changes in moral systems with respect to women. Not the greatest good for the greatest number, but individual pain and its meaning for the individual and the local community become the focus.

The rural worlds of both Hardy and Munro are marked by a social class system that is seen less in relation to its effect on society as a whole than with respect to the conflicts it causes in interpersonal relationships. Hardy's commentators note the persistence of the poor man and the lady theme, sometimes reversed, as in the businessman and the lady in **"An Imaginative Woman."**[10] Ella marries new money; she pities the "obtuseness and want of refinement" (306) of a husband educationally and culturally beneath her. The poet refuses to visit when he sees Marchmill's house: "it all looked so new and monied" (324), echoing typical class prejudice. Munro's Louisa moves from a room in the Commercial Hotel to the Doud's house (complete with housekeeper) with "wedding cake decoration" that has to be kept "fresh as Christmas snow" (32), details which mark her change in social status because of her marriage. The lists Munro gives of books Jack reads compared to the list of magazines Arthur peruses suggest the factory worker might have been more suited to Louisa because of his self-education (which Carrington links with the self-education of Hardy's hero in *Jude the Obscure* [561]) than the factory owner is. Although egalitarian New World ideas allow us to desire a connection for her with the lower class man who seems to have more in common with her intellectually, the British social class system colors our view of the contemporary Canadian characters enough that we feel Louisa does well in her marriage to Doud.

Mores concerning marriage often contribute to the unhappiness of characters in stories by both writers, bringing key social changes of each era into the rural microcosms.[11] If Ella were to have an affair with the poet, she would break Victorian social conventions regarding women; in addition, a physical consummation of a love that is portrayed as primarily spiritual would not be satisfactory in the terms of the story. Munro's characters have more flexibility regarding sexual morality and divorce than Hardy's do. Whereas Hardy's

Ella remains physically if not emotionally faithful to her husband, Munro's Louisa apparently has an affair with a married doctor; later she drunkenly goes to bed with a travelling salesman as if she were a character on an American soap opera or a woman who accepts the hedonistic outlook of *Cosmopolitan* magazine. In a recent interview, Munro says that she has always been interested in "the way women circumvented the rules" (Becker 36) as Louisa does here. Arthur, aware that Louisa has "not quite a spotless reputation," holds more liberal sexual attitudes than readers in the 1990s might expect in a rural community between the wars: "she was old enough to do as she liked" (35). In marrying Arthur to "get into a normal life" (48), Louisa opts for the ideals stated in the Canadian Constitution Act of 1867: peace, order, and good government. Ella has no choice because of the culture in which she lives; Louisa, in contrast, has a choice, which she makes in a specifically Canadian way.

The ultimate effects of Munro's stories differ from those of Hardy's stories in ways that are specific to their eras. Whereas Hardy shows us the strife between the traditional and industrialized worlds, the conflict between rich and poor, and the discord between old and new systems of morality in the lives of his characters, Munro goes beyond this to show us a clash in ourselves. We wish for an idyllic rural existence, but when Munro gives us one freed of the romantic overtones we attach to "idyllic" (the people of Carstairs suffer during the Depression) and "rural" (Carstairs has industry, and its machines can kill a man brutally), the disarrangement reveals a conflict between our emotional wishes and our intellectual understanding. If Hardy's tragic endings undercut our romanticism about his rural world, Munro's more open-ended conclusions deny us the satisfaction of closure as rural lives continue to change over time. Hardy's readers may feel unhappy about the gloomy outcome of the clashes of two modes of existence in a story like **"An Imaginative Woman,"** but Munro's readers may feel an even greater unease at the end of a story like "Carried Away" because of the frustration of what they recognize as their own irrational desire for endings. Hardy's stories may not satisfy desires for happy resolution of conflicts, but they do satisfy desires for endings. In contrast, Munro's stories fail to offer the consolation of a fixed world in the past while revealing to us how much we want that consolation.

Both writers personalize key philosophical questions of their times, letting the insignificant lives of their rural characters manifest significant intellectual patterns of thought. For Hardy, the ancient controversy regarding fate and free will, given a new twist by Darwinism, leads to a piling up of unhappy accidents and coincidences that disarrange plots, a disproportioning

that jars readers' sense of reality. Roy Morrell points out that Hardy's coincidences differ from those in most Victorian fiction in that Hardy's are "ironically unprovidential" (48). Readers of **"An Imaginative Woman"** can readily spot a sequence of chance events that build the story from its inciting incident to its denouement. However, in addition, Hardy repeatedly inserts words that emphasize the role of chance in creating the story: when Ella and Trewe had both written poems about the same tragic news incident, an editor publishes them simultaneously, "remarking in a note upon the coincidence" (309). Trewe's book of poems "was much or little praised according to chance" (310). "By an odd conjunction she [Ella] found herself in the rooms of Robert Trewe" (310). Ella's "living ardours . . . were beginning to feed on this chancing material, which was, indeed of a quality far better than chance usually offers" (313). Marchmill lacks Trewe's emotional qualities, "perhaps luckily for himself, considering that he had to provide for family expenses" (317). He believes the picture of the poet may have been "whisked off the mantelpiece by accident perhaps when they were making the bed" (319). "It seemed to be her doom not to meet the man" (320). Trewe sees a copy of the harsh review of his poetry "by accident" (323). In telling how Marchmill finds the lock of the poet's hair some years after Ella's death, the narrator says, "it chanced one day" (329). Set in the midst of so many evidences of the persistence of chance, Hardy's characters have little possibility of working out satisfactory destinies for themselves.

Munro's narrator also underlines accidents and coincidences, "disarrangements which demand new judgements and solutions" (*Who* 177), by reiterating words such as "chance," "fate," and "accident." A letter from Louisa to Jack near the beginning of the story speaks of "the man who had an accident at the factory" (8), foreshadowing Jack's accident. As a soldier, Jack was "not whining about his fate," but "expected to die" (16). He had "taken his chance" to leave a note on Louisa's desk (18). As Louisa and Jim Frarey spar verbally in the process of consenting to sex, they display "a fateful sort of kindness" (19). The third section of the story is titled "Accidents" (20), and records trivial ones (Jack's daughter wetting her pants, minor misspellings and omissions in the newspaper articles about Jack's death), major ones ("a particularly ghastly and tragic accident" at the factory [23] and a picture of the Franklin Expedition, "the boat trapped in the ice" [27]), and fortuitous ones (Arthur encountering Louisa again because he returns Jack's library books as a way to help his family); Arthur's proposal to Louisa seems almost another accident, coming unexpectedly at the end of this section. "The coincidence of the name was hardly even interesting" (43) when

Louisa learns that a Jack Agnew is to speak years after her Jack has died. The final episode of the story recounts the chance events that led to Louisa becoming the librarian in Carstairs: "it happened that Louisa was staying in the Commercial Hotel" (50); she "believed in the swift decision, the unforeseen intervention, the uniqueness of her fate" (51), reminiscent of what Hardy's narrator says of Elizabeth Jane in *The Mayor of Casterbridge*: "she did not cease to wonder at the persistence of the unforeseen" in her experiences (256). "Carried Away" ends with sleighs being pulled "beyond the streetlights, down the dark side roads. Somewhere out in the country they would lose the sound of each other's bells" (51). Munro chooses a typically Canadian image: sleighs suggest snow and cold, while going "beyond the streetlights" into the dark hints of the Canadian archetype of the great frozen north in which humans get lost seemingly forever (the Franklin Expedition image). The horses pulling the sleigh are "blinkered" (51), unable to see the full scene, even as any one story told leaves out other stories that might be told. Their "feathered hooves" (51) might be a simple metaphor, but might also suggest the mythological horses pulling Time's chariot. The uniqueness of Louisa's fate will disappear into the vastness of space and time; ironically, her unique fate becomes the common fate of all human beings.

The disproportionate emphasis on accidents and coincidences that disarrange characters' lives gains additional prominence by an emphasis on what might otherwise have been. Trevor Johnson writes of Hardy's heroine in *Tess of the D'Urbervilles* that because Hardy "constantly manages to show us vistas of possible delight opening out in front of Tess . . . her repeated failure to achieve the smallest measure of lasting happiness until the last phase of the book is so affecting" (143). Tess's "lasting happiness," however, is of short duration, which creates an even greater sense of loss of all that might have been. The narrator of **"An Imaginative Woman"** similarly emphasizes the way things might have been: "She might have asked him to call upon her, perhaps" (320). Trewe's suicide letter adds to the theme: "Perhaps had I been blessed with a mother, or a sister, or a female friend of another sort tenderly devoted to me, I might have thought it worth while to continue my present existence" (325). In describing Ella's reaction to the suicide, the narrator quotes Dante Gabriel Rossetti: "The hour which might have been, yet might not be" (326). Hardy might have declared his aim in this story to be the same as the one he stated in the preface to *Jude the Obscure*: "to point the tragedy of unfulfilled aims" (5). Our sense of what might have been functions to make the characters' unhappiness seem more poignantly tragic.

Words such as "might" and "perhaps" occur frequently in Munro's stories also. Munro's narrator, speaking of Louisa's inability to recall an incident that Jack describes in a letter, says, "He might as well have dreamed all that, and perhaps he had" (10). Anticipating Jack's return from the war, Louisa keeps the library open during the flu epidemic: "Whenever the door opened, she expected to look up into his face"; "she fancied that he might be across the street" (17). Her belief that "the one thing that could never happen was that he wouldn't approach her, wouldn't get in touch with her at all" (17) adds to the irony of her encounter with the dead Jack, who does get in touch with her, and whose statement that "Love never dies" (48) suggests what might have been. Heble sees a "discourse of absent and potential meanings" (187) as central to Munro's work: he argues that it "enables us, as it often enables Munro's characters, to imagine *possible* correlations between sets of phenomena and to consider how 'reality' might be different if something absent or potential were substituted for the way things are" (7).

Hardy's narrator describes Trewe as "a pessimist in so far as that character applies to a man who looks at the worst contingencies as well as the best in the human condition" (309). For Hardy, seeing what might have been is part of looking at the world seriously, acknowledging the frequent tragedy that comes in a universe where human beings feel pain because they can imagine for themselves happier fates than they have. Social Darwinism and agnosticism combine into a vision of fatedness, to which Hardy gives a romantic twist by longing for what might have been: "How arrives it joy lies slain, / And why unblooms the best hope ever sown?" ("Hap," *Poems* 9).

Whereas accidents and chance events in Hardy's stories emphasize that another, happier possibility might have been but is not, similar occurrences in Munro's stories suggest that the story we are told is only one of the stories that could be told, leaving the reader with a sense that multiple stories are inherent within any situation, parallel stories of the sort Munro felt going along with the "pretty realistic story" in "Carried Away" (Contributors' 371). In Munro's fiction, what might have been is sometimes part of a contrast between realism and romanticism. As the stories deconstruct romantic notions, readers, with the characters, note how beautiful or exciting or sensational the romanticized version would be, and how ordinary the realistic version is.[12] This multiple vision may be especially attractive to a Canadian author because the layering of the psyche mirrors a layering of cultures in Canada; characters and plots, like the nation, must be perceived from multiple standpoints. Because diverse and conflicting stories are told of what Canada is—

one nation, two founding peoples, a group of provinces and territories, a collection of ethnic groups—a Canadian writer's vision of many discontinuous stories within a story reflects significant national mythology.

In addition to disproportioning related to the importance of rural communities and the influence of chance occurrences, both Hardy and Munro persist to a startling degree in inventing narrators who overtly acknowledge that they are telling stories, jolting readers' expectations that realism in fiction requires maintaining a narrowly defined illusion of reality. Sometimes Hardy's narrators insist that they are telling true stories. These verifications are frequently accurate, since Hardy did often learn the stories he told from the people of Dorset. Yet his idea that "Art is a disproportioning . . . of realities" (from Hardy's notebooks, qtd. in F. E. Hardy 229) implies considerable potential for artistic reshaping as the story moves from oral to written form, from life to art. Any story he tells might have been changed: "Art consists in so depicting the common events of life as to bring out the features which illustrate the author's idiosyncratic mode of regard" (from Hardy's notebooks, qtd. in F. E. Hardy 225). Nevertheless, a story is "an impression, not an argument," he insists (Preface to *Tess* xi), for he does not intend his fiction to present a formal debate of the issues it represents in the lives of the characters.

Munro's overt acknowledgements of art within her stories often speak of a narrator's frustration at being unable to capture the whole story: Munro's disarrangements reveal that "the aesthetic pattern . . . does not provide an adequate rendering of the full truth of that experience" it records (Matthews 185). However, in "Carried Away" the disarrangements prompt questions about the nature of reality as well as about art's adequacy to capture reality. Nevertheless, as Katherine J. Mayberry notes, "storytelling is the central activity of the characters of Alice Munro's fiction"; they may realize that storytelling is an imperfect medium, but nevertheless they "all are impelled to manage their pain, ignorance, and occasional glimpses of knowledge by telling" (531). Heble carries this thought a step further: "The moment writing declares its own inadequacy in Munro's fiction, we are confronted with a kind of paradox whereby the everyday world of facts, details, and objects which we have been invited to accept as real and true is suddenly revealed to be a fictional construction of the narrator's" (9).

Louisa's letter names not only Hardy but also American writer Willa Cather, whose novel *My Ántonia* also tells the story of a woman with both physical and spiritual lovers whose life is affected by "those early accidents of fortune which predetermined for us all

that we can ever be" (372; see Stich, Thacker). There, when the narrator Jim Burden returns after twenty years, he finds Ántonia a happy wife, mother, and grandmother who says she never has the "sad spells I used to have" (343); however, when Jim tells one of the children, "I was very much in love with your mother once," the child replies, "she's always talked lots about you" (346). In the hallucination scene Munro's story follows Hardy's lead in breaking out of narrowly conceived realism and then leaps out of its repetition of Hardy's story to echo the ending of Cather's story; for Cather and Ántonia, as for Munro and Louisa (who uses "and" rather than "or" in speaking of her two favorite authors [6]), multiple and conflicting stories are part of human experience. In a nation where the construction of a national identity is an ongoing conscious process and where Canada's story is presented in terms of multiple stories, Munro's approach to storytelling as a way of managing life and a way of asserting individual vision in the context of alternative irreconcilable ones diverges from Hardy's "art of disproportioning" in a distinctively Canadian manner.

Margaret Atwood writes that "although in every culture many stories are told, only some are told and retold" (11). When Munro chooses to retell Hardy's **"An Imaginative Woman"** in "Carried Away," she indicates by that choice that the heritage of British storytelling still pertains to Canada today. When she adopts many of Hardy's techniques for telling stories, she places her art within an inherited tradition, a placement that points to both contrasts and continuities. American poet Robert Pinsky, discussing the responsibilities of the poet, defines two important roles: we must keep "an art that we did not invent, but were given, so that others who come after us can have it if they want it, as free to choose it and change it as we have been" and must use our own art "to behold the actual evidence before us. We must answer for what we see" (87). In revising Hardy's story, Munro both calls our attention to the relevance of the earlier writer and bears witness to the changes that have taken place in the rural world and way of life, the structure of society, the role of women, and the fabric of belief about life and about art. In letting Hardy's artistic vision resonate audibly in her stories, Munro affirms the British and European tradition within which Hardy writes and defines for her own art a Canadian tradition.

Notes

Research for this article has been supported by the Canadian Embassy Faculty Research Program and the Saint Mary's College Faculty Development Fund.

1. Carl J. Weber notes that Hardy published forty-seven short stories (299); Hardy collected "An Imaginative Woman" in the third edition of *Wessex Tales* (1896) but, in 1912, moved it to the col-

lection entitled *Life's Little Ironies* (Weber 304). In the Prefatory Note to that volume, Hardy writes that the story "was brought into this volume as being more nearly its place, turning as it does on a trick of Nature" (v). Hardy told Walter Pierce that it was his favorite story, "the best piece of prose fiction I ever wrote" (qtd. in Ray 171). The original title of the story was "A Woman of Imagination." Martin Ray sees the shift as giving "more prominence to Ella's imaginative faculty and less to her gender: it is to be a story more about imagination than a woman" (176).

2. Quotations from "An Imaginative Woman" are taken from *The Distracted Preacher and Other Tales,* ed. Susan Hill. Hill follows the Wessex Edition (1912). Ray notes that Hardy made approximately fifty substantive revisions of the magazine text of "An Imaginative Woman" for the 1896 collection (172), and additional alterations for the 1912 collection, including inserting the comment about "a trick of Nature" (179).

3. The poet's name in the manuscript is Crewe, changed to Trewe before magazine publication (Ray 171). This suggests the author's desire to include all the meanings of the revised name. Hill theorizes that young women Hardy met in London society may have "attached themselves to a famous artistic personality," enlarging "their scanty impressions by 'day-dreams and night-sighs' into all-consuming passions" (32). However, by 1894 Hardy was facing heavy critical attacks on *Tess of the D'Urbervilles* and his marriage to Emma Lavinia Hardy had long been painful; he himself would have been the true writer who needed a sensitive woman's compassion. James Gibson notes that the story is convincing "possibly because Hardy himself was at that time a frustrated poet longing for someone to love" (xviii).

Ray links Ella with Florence Henniker, a novelist and short story writer that Hardy met in 1893, whose husband was a military officer. Mrs. Henniker was interested in Shelley's poetry; her house may have been the model for the one Ella stays in at Solentsea (172-73). Ray concludes, on the basis of correspondence between Hardy and Mrs. Henniker, that some of Hardy's revisions of the story were intended to conceal details "which would have displayed all too clearly the elements of fantasy and role-reversal which contributed to the writing of 'An Imaginative Woman'" (174).

4. Written between July 13 and September 14, 1893 (Ray 172) and first published in 1894, the story comes between *Tess of the D'Urbervilles* (1891) and *Jude the Obscure* (1896), two of Hardy's novels which attack conventions surrounding sex and marriage.

5. Hardy's fiction frequently focuses on the opposition of spirit and flesh. In the Preface to the Wessex Edition (1912) of *Jude the Obscure,* Hardy writes that his aim was "to tell, without a mincing of words, a deadly war waged between flesh and spirit" (5). Jude has a physical lover (Arabella) and a soul mate (Sue). Similarly, in *Tess of the D'Urbervilles* the heroine has a physical lover (Alec) and a spiritual one (Angel). Shelley is often credited with influencing Hardy's Platonism (although Pauline doctrine from Hardy's religious upbringing might also have been an influence). Michael Millgate, in discussing Hardy's last novel, *The Well-Beloved,* which he notes was written in late 1891 and early 1892 (293), thus before "An Imaginative Woman," asserts that Hardy may have found "in the poems of Shelley and Swinburne . . . not only a diagnostic terminology but grounds for projecting the disease as a restless idealism endemic to the artistic temperament" (300). "An Imaginative Woman" contains a reference to Shelley: Robert Trewe's poetic graffiti are said to be "like Shelley's scraps" (317). In addition, there is one quotation from Shelley's *Prometheus Unbound* and one paraphrase of a line from it (Hill 360).

Ray discusses how "Hardy's general tendency in revising this tale over the years was to remove or tone down any words or scenes which might have indicated some kind of sexual or passionate basis to Ella's obsession with Trewe" (174). This preserves and enhances the contrast between the spiritual relationship with Trewe and the physical one with Marchmill.

6. In the essay "The Colonel's Hash Resettled" Munro uses the word "trick" to refer to her writing: "And even as I most feverishly, desperately practise it, I am a little afraid that the work with words may turn out to be a questionable trick, an evasion (and never more so than when it is most dazzling, apt, and striking), an unavoidable lie" (189). Martin notes two other important uses of the word "tricks" by Munro to refer to the artist's actions as artificer: the narrator of "Tell Me Yes or No" has "tricks and trap doors" (*Something* 101) and the narrator of "The Ottawa Valley" feels she can never "reach" her mother, but "could go on and on, applying what skills I have, using what tricks I know, and it would always be the same" (*Something* 197); for Martin this concept recalls James Joyce's *A Portrait of the Artist as a Young Man* (*Paradox* 50).

7. Similar concepts recur in Munro's stories. For example, the narrator in "The Moon in the Orange Street Skating Rink" asks, "Do such moments really mean, as they seem to, that we have a life of

happiness with which we only occasionally, knowingly, intersect?" (*Progress* 160).

The hallucination scene in "Carried Away" may have been suggested by Hardy's apparent resurgence of love for his wife Emma Lavinia Hardy after her death, expressed in poems in which he seems to hear her voice or see her ghost. For example, "The Voice" begins,

> Woman much missed, how you call to me, call to me,
> Saying that now you are not as you were
> When you had changed from the one who was all to me,
> But as at first, when our day was fair.

(Poems 346)

The poem ends with an image of the speaker "faltering forward," as he questions the reality of the vision. "After a Journey" presents a "voiceless ghost" of whom the speaker asks, "What have you now found to say of our past— / Scanned across the dark space wherein I have lacked you?" (*Poems* 349).

8. See, for example, Clive Holland's *Thomas Hardy's Wessex Scene* for a detailed discussion of the connections between Wessex and Dorset, or Hill's lists of actual and fictional place names (38-39).

9. Douglas Brown posits that memory of past rural life and dismay at the present animates Hardy's fiction, and that each novel plays out the theme of the disruption of the old agricultural order by forces coming from outside the community (131).

10. Hardy's first novel, rejected by publishers, was entitled "The Poor Man and the Lady." Weber attributes this theme to an experience of social inequality Hardy had as a child at a harvest-supper (5). Robert Gittings traces the theme to early childhood experiences of suffering because of poverty associated with Hardy's grandmother, and notes its presence even in Hardy's last novel, *Jude the Obscure* (217). Hardy reverses the theme in *Tess of the D'Urbervilles.* Similarly, class prejudices also affect Munro's characters such as Rose in *Who Do You Think You Are?* and Isabel in "White Dump" from *The Progress of Love,* who both marry upward uncomfortably.

11. Both Hardy and Munro use townspeople to suggest a societal norm from which the main characters diverge. The role of Hardy's rustic characters is "organic, not decorative. . . . They are, in fact, the basic pattern to which other characters conform or from which they differ," Donald Davidson writes (22). Minor characters serve as a chorus in Munro's stories as they do in Hardy's, creating a sense of the community and its beliefs. In "Carried Away" Jim Frarey is a commentator on Lou-

isa's aborted relationship with Jack. Arthur and newspaper clippings provide choral background on Jack's death and suggest a community norm from which Louisa differs. The chorus of villagers who comment on the actions of the main characters has been seen as a characteristic Hardy imported into his fiction from Greek and Shakespearean tragedy. For example, John Paterson links Thebes and Denmark with Hardy's Casterbridge, and compares "the brutalized populace" to "the pimps and whores" of *Measure for Measure* or the gravediggers of *Hamlet* (104-05). In "An Imaginative Woman" Mrs. Hooper, the landlady, plays the role of the chorus at the same time that she seems to be the matchmaking nurse of the type Shakespeare creates in *Romeo and Juliet* as she tries to arrange a meeting between Ella and Trewe. The townspeople also suggest continuity in the midst of change in the works of both writers: however, in "Carried Away" there is irony in the sense of "continuance" (50) Louisa gets from the Mennonites whose costume clarifies how much the world has changed.

12. See, for example, "How I Met My Husband," in which the narrator marries the ordinary postman instead of the romantic pilot (*Something* 53), or "Miles City, Montana," in which the narrator presents what she calls her "trashy" imagining of how the story of her trip would have gone if her daughter had drowned (*Progress* 102-03).

Works Cited

Atwood, Margaret. *Strange Things: The Malevolent North in Canadian Literature.* Oxford: Clarendon Press, 1995.

Becker, Alida. "Sex and Self Defense." *New York Times Book Review* (11 Sept. 1994): 36.

Brown, Douglas. *Thomas Hardy.* 1954. London: Longmans, 1961.

Carrington, Ildikó de Papp. "What's in a Title?: Alice Munro's 'Carried Away.'" *Studies in Short Fiction* 30 (1993): 555-64.

Cather, Willa. *My Ántonia.* 1918. Boston: Houghton Mifflin, 1977.

Clark, Miriam Marty. "Allegories of Reading in Alice Munro's 'Carried Away.'" *Contemporary Literature* 37 (1996): 49-61.

Davidson, Donald. "The Traditional Basis of Thomas Hardy's Fiction." *Still Rebels, Still Yankees, and Other Essays.* Baton Rouge: Louisiana State University Press, 1950. Rpt. in *Hardy: A Collection of Critical Essays.* Ed. Albert J. Guerard. Englewood Cliffs, NJ: Prentice Hall, 1963. 10-23.

Gibson, Graeme. "Alice Munro." *Eleven Canadian Novelists Interviewed by Graeme Gibson.* Toronto: Anansi, 1973. 237-64.

Gibson, James. Introduction. *Selected Short Stories and Poems.* By Thomas Hardy. Rutland, VT: Tuttle, 1992. ix-xxvi.

Gittings, Robert. *Young Thomas Hardy.* Boston: Little, Brown, 1975.

Hardy, Florence Emily. *The Life of Thomas Hardy.* Hamden, CT.: Archon Books, 1970. Contains *The Early Life of Thomas Hardy,* 1928, and *The Later Years of Thomas Hardy,* 1930.

Hardy, Thomas. *The Complete Poems.* Ed. James Gibson. New York: Macmillan, 1976.

——. *The Distracted Preacher and Other Tales.* Ed. Susan Hill. New York: Penguin, 1979.

——. *Jude the Obscure.* 1896. Ed. Norman Page. New York: W. W. Norton, 1978.

——. *Life's Little Ironies.* 1912. London: Macmillan, 1952.

——. *The Mayor of Casterbridge.* 1886. Ed. James K. Robinson. New York: W. W. Norton, 1977.

——. *Tess of the D'Urbervilles.* 1891. Ed. Scott Elledge. New York: W. W. Norton, 1991.

——. *The Woodlanders.* 1887. New York: St. Martin's, 1968.

Heble, Ajay. *The Tumble of Reason: Alice Munro's Discourse of Absence.* Toronto: University of Toronto Press, 1994.

Hill, Susan. Introduction. *The Distracted Preacher and Other Tales.* By Thomas Hardy. New York: Penguin, 1979. 11-39.

Holland, Clive. *Thomas Hardy's Wessex Scene.* Dorchester: Friary Press, 1948.

Humphreys, Josephine. "Mysteries Near at Hand." *New York Times Book Review* (11 Sept. 1994): 1+.

Johnson, Trevor. *Thomas Hardy.* New York: Arco, 1971.

Martin, W. R. "Alice Munro and James Joyce." *Journal of Canadian Fiction* 24 (1979): 120-26.

——. *Alice Munro: Paradox and Parallel.* Edmonton: University of Alberta Press, 1987.

——. "The Strange and the Familiar in Alice Munro." *Studies in Canadian Literature* 7 (1982): 214-26.

Matthews, Laurence. "*Who Do You Think You Are?*: Alice Munro's Art of Disarrangement." *Probable Fictions: Alice Munro's Narrative Acts.* Ed. Louis K. MacKendrick. Downsview, ON: ECW Press, 1983. 181-93.

Mayberry, Katherine J. "'Every last thing . . . everlasting': Alice Munro and the Limits of Narrative." *Studies in Short Fiction* 29 (1992): 531-41.

Metcalf, John. "A Conversation with Alice Munro." *Journal of Canadian Fiction* 1 (1972): 54-62.

Millgate, Michael. *Thomas Hardy: His Career as a Novelist.* New York: Random House, 1971.

Morrell, Roy. *Thomas Hardy: The Will and the Way.* 1965. Singapore: University of Malaya Press, 1968.

Munro, Alice. "The Colonel's Hash Resettled." *The Narrative Voice: Short Stories and Reflections by Canadian Authors.* Ed. John Metcalf. Toronto: McGraw-Hill Ryerson, 1972. Rpt. in *How Stories Mean.* Ed. John Metcalf and J. R. (Tim) Struthers. Don Mills, ON: Porcupine's Quill, 1973. 188-191.

——. "Contributors' Notes." *Best American Short Stories 1992.* Ed. Robert Stone and Katrina Kenison. New York: Houghton, 1992. 371.

——. *Lives of Girls and Women.* 1971. Scarborough, ON: NAL, 1974.

——. *Open Secrets.* New York: Knopf, 1994.

——. *The Progress of Love.* Toronto: McClelland and Stewart, 1986.

——. *Something I've Been Meaning to Tell You.* 1974. Scarborough, ON: NAL, 1975.

——. *Who Do You Think You Are?* 1978. Agincourt, ON: NAL, 1979.

O'Faolain, Julia. "In the territory of dreams." Rev. of Alice Munro's *Open Secrets. Times Literary Supplement* (14 Oct. 1994): 24.

Paterson, John. "*The Mayor of Casterbridge* as Tragedy." *Victorian Studies* 3 (1959): 151-72. Rpt. in *Hardy: A Collection of Critical Essays.* Ed. Albert J. Guerard. Englewood Cliffs, NJ: Prentice Hall, 1963. 91-112.

Pinsky, Robert. *Poetry and the World.* New York: Ecco, 1988.

Ray, Martin. *Thomas Hardy: A Textual Study of the Short Stories.* Brookfield, VT: Ashgate, 1997.

Stich, Klaus P. "The Cather Connection in Alice Munro's 'Dulse.'" *Modern Language Studies* 20 (1989): 102-11.

Struthers, J. R. (Tim). "Reality and Ordering: The Growth of a Young Artist in *Lives of Girls and Women.*" *Essays on Canadian Writing* 3 (1975): 32-46.

Summers, Myrna. "An Entertainer of the Spirit." *Canadian Forum* LXXII.836 (1995): 38-39.

Thacker, Robert. "Alice Munro's Willa Cather." *Canadian Literature* 134 (1992): 42-57.

Weber, Carl J. *Hardy of Wessex.* 1940. Rev. ed. New York: Columbia University Press, 1965.

York, Lorraine. "The Rival Bards: Alice Munro's *Lives of Girls and Women* and Victorian Poetry." *Canadian Literature* 112 (1987): 211-16.

Patrick Tolfree (essay date February 2000)

SOURCE: Tolfree, Patrick. "Hardy's Short Stories for Young People." *Thomas Hardy Journal* 16, no. 1 (February 2000): 53-62.

[*In the following essay, Tolfree lauds the insight into the adolescent mind exhibited by "The Thieves Who Couldn't Help Sneezing" and "Our Exploits at West Poley," underlining Hardy's sense of humor and lack of condescension in the stories.*]

It is measure of Hardy's versatility as a writer of prose fiction that his output of short stories should contain two for young people[1], **"The Thieves Who Couldn't Help Sneezing"** and **"Our Exploits at West Poley"**[2].

"The Thieves Who Couldn't Help Sneezing" was the third[3] of Hardy's stories to be published and very little is known of its publishing history. It appears to have been solicited for publication in July 1877 by Nancy Meugens on behalf of *The Illustrated London News,* who wanted it for the magazine's annual for children 'Father Christmas: Our Little One's Budget', where it appeared in early December 1877. There is no direct evidence of how it went down with the magazine's young readers but a letter from Hardy to Meugens at the end of January 1878 suggests that it had been well enough received for her to have asked him for another story for the 1878 Christmas annual. Hardy replied that he would consider it[4], but did not follow it up. Nothing much more was heard of it until it was reprinted in 1942, edited by Carl Weber[5]. It deserved better.

"The Thieves Who Couldn't Help Sneezing" is noteworthy for the economy of its writing and for its confident, fluent and polished style. It is also remarkable—in the context of Victorian fiction for children—for its lack of condescension and for the understanding it shows of what would appeal to boys of the age of its hero, the fourteen-year old Hubert. The first few sentences set the pace and the tone:

> Many years ago, when oak-trees now past their prime were about as large as elderly gentlemen's walking sticks, there lived in Wessex a yeoman's son, whose name was Hubert. He was about fourteen years of age, and was as remarkable for his candour and lightness of heart as for his physical courage, of which, indeed, he was a little vain.

One cold Christmas Eve his father, having no other help at hand, sent him on an important errand to a small town several miles from home. He travelled by horseback, and was detained by the business till a late hour of the evening.

That Hubert should be 'a little vain' of his courage provides a human touch which establishes him as a three-dimensional, flesh-and-blood character. Though only fourteen, Hubert is treated as an adult capable of undertaking adult's 'business', which would quickly engage the interest of young readers, and before the end of the first page there is excitement and action. Hubert is waylaid by robbers, tied up and thrown into a ditch and his horse, Jerry, is stolen.

One of the robbers has a deep voice, which is important for his identification not long after when Hubert bumps into the robbers again, in a mansion in which he seeks help and which the robbers are planning to rob—an example of Hardy's careful placing of pertinent detail in the build-up of a story. In the mansion Hubert discovers a sumptuous meal laid out at a deserted table. He cannot tuck in since after the attack he has been able to free his legs but not his arms. This means that—

> Even had Hubert been so inclined, he could not have eaten in his helpless state, unless by dipping into the dishes, like a pig or a cow—

a comment likely to appeal to the sense of humour of a young readership. Hiding from the robbers under the dining table Hubert overhears a snatch of their conversation, which reveals their ruse: they have lured the dinner guests outside so that they can find somewhere in the mansion to hide before robbing it.

The rest of the story is about how Hubert, with his quick wits and presence of mind, foils the robbers, and the essence of it is his control of events. The dinner is for Sir Simon, the owner of the mansion, and his family house party. When Hubert has made his presence known, some of the party suspect him of being a robber himself and he is understandably hurt. At first, to punish them for suspecting him, Hubert considers not telling them about the robbers, but Sir Simon gives orders for him to be untied and says "When you have had your fill we will listen to more particulars of your story." Hardy has stage-managed it well. The reader and Hubert know that the robbers are hiding in a cupboard waiting for the household to go to bed before robbing the house, but Sir Simon and his guests have no idea who Hubert is and what he was doing turning up the house with his hands tied. How will the story resolve itself? Hubert holds the cards. How will he play them?

Hubert's resentment at being suspected dissipates with good food and good cheer and towards the end of the meal one of Sir Simon's sons, a little drunk and sensing an opportunity for a bit of sport at Hubert's expense, offers him a pinch of snuff. Hubert rises to the occasion.

> "Thank you," said Hubert, accepting a pinch.
>
> "Tell the ladies who you are, what you are made of, and what you can do," the young man continued, slapping Hubert upon the shoulder.
>
> "Certainly," said our hero, drawing himself up, thinking it best to put a bold face on the matter. "I am a travelling magician."
>
> "Indeed!"
>
> "What shall we hear next?"
>
> "Can you conjure spirits up from the vasty deep, young wizard?"
>
> "I can conjure up a tempest in a cupboard," Hubert replied.
>
> "Ha-ha!" said the old Baronet, pleasantly rubbing his hands. "We must see this performance. Girls, don't go away: here's something to be seen."
>
> "Not dangerous, I hope?" said the old lady.

Everything in that piece of dialogue would appeal to a boy of Hubert's age: his unhesitating acceptance of the snuff, his ingenuity in presenting himself a travelling magician, and above all the audience of expectant women to whom he can now demonstrate his command of events. This he does by leading the house party to the cupboard where the robbers are hiding and by puffing in snuff to make them sneeze. Hubert is now in complete control:

> All the Christmas guests now perceived that this was no longer sport, but serious earnest. Guns and cudgels were procured; all the men-servants were called in, and arranged in position outside the closet. At a signal Hubert withdrew the bolt, and stood on the defensive. But the three robbers, far from attacking them, were found crouching in the corner, gasping for breath. They made no resistance; and, being pinioned, were placed in an out-house till the morning.

Hubert is the hero of the hour. He declines the offer to spend the night in a bed 'which had been occupied by Queen Elizabeth and King Charles successively when on their visits to this part of the country', recovers his faithful horse Jerry and canters off home.

Whereas **"The Thieves"** [**"The Thieves Who Couldn't Help Sneezing"**] has only around 2,500 words—similar in length to, say, **"A Tradition of Eighteen Hundred and Four"**—**"Our Exploits at West Poley"** is an altogether more substantial proposition, having 20,000 words or more. It has an intriguing publication history. Hardy was originally asked to write it in 1883 for *Youth's Companion,* a Boston-based American magazine. From a letter Hardy wrote to the publishers in April 1883 it would appear that they had impressed upon him the importance of writing a story with a clear moral message: "You may depend on my using my best efforts to please your numerous readers; and that the story shall have a healthy tone, suitable to intelligent youth of both sexes." he said[6]. Seven months later, when he sent the manuscript, in the same vein he wrote: "In constructing the story I have been careful to avoid making it a mere precept in narrative—a fatal defect, to my thinking, for the young, or for the old. That it carries with it, nevertheless, a sufficiently apparent moral, will I think be admitted."[7] It was then announced in the *Youth's Companion* of 22nd November 1883 that the story would appear some time in 1884. But it did not, even though the publishers asked him to make changes which were incorporated in a revised manuscript which he returned to them in March 1884[8]. One can only assume that the editors were still concerned about the suitability of the 'tone' and content of the story for their readership. Three years later, replying to a letter from one of the editors of the magazine, Hardy told him not to worry that the story had not yet been published and suggesting that it might come out later in an abridged form. "Our children here," he wrote, "are younger for their age than yours; and possibly the story is too juvenile for your side of the sea. I fancy you may be mistaken in that; but of course I do not know as well as yourselves."[9] Hardy had evidently ceased by then to care whether or not the story was published, though it did eventually come out in November 1892, in six monthly installments, in an obscure magazine called *The Household.* The magazine, which had some family connection with *Youth's Companion,* was described as 'Devoted to the Interests of the American Housewife'[10].

Hardy made no further reference to it. Indeed, R. L. Purdy suggests that he may not even have known that the story was eventually published.[11] It seems unlikely, however, that Hardy was neither informed of, nor paid for, its publication. A more likely explanation for Hardy drawing a veil over **"Our Exploits"** [**"Our Exploits at West Poley"**] is that he wanted the story to be forgotten. In the period between his first submission of **"Our Exploits"** in 1883 and its eventual publication nine years later Hardy's career surged forward and his literary output was prolific. In those nine years *The Mayor of Casterbridge, The Woodlanders* and *Tess of the D'Urbervilles* were published. In the same period he published no less than 24 short stories in magazines or periodicals and also brought out his first two collected volumes of short stories: *Wessex Tales* (1888) and *A Group of Noble Dames* (1891). As James Gibson has pointed out, the publication of *Tess* in

1891 Hardy went from being a well-known writer to a famous writer[12] He may well have regarded the publication of **"Our Exploits"** in 1892—the year after *Tess*—as an embarrassment. Because he felt it was of dubious value, he was quite happy for it to remain forgotten among the back numbers of *Youth's Companion* in Boston. In 1913 when he was reluctantly—largely for reasons to do with copyright—publishing his final collected volume of short stories, *A Changed Man and Other Tales,* he said it contained a number of stories he would willingly have 'snuffed out'[13]. **"Our Exploits"** was almost certainly a story he would have liked to snuff out in 1892. Fortunately for posterity it was rescued by Purdy from the archives of the *Youth's Companion* and published by Oxford University Press in 1952[14].

"Our Exploits" has one important feature in common with **"The Thieves"**. Just as Hubert controls events in **"The Thieves"**, so do Hardy's young characters control events in **"Our Exploits"**—Leonard, aged 13, Steve, his cousin, who is two or three years older, and Job the apprentice. In **"Our Exploits"** the story is told by Leonard looking back as an adult on his adventures at West Poley when he was a boy, but this narrative device is no more than a dressing; the story is written entirely from the perspective of the three youthful characters. To emphasise this, most of the adult characters—apart from Miller Griffin—are known only by their titles, for example, the shoemaker, the dairyman, the farmer, the baker, the hedger, the corn-factor, the blacksmith and the widow. There is even a curious character with the title 'the Man who has Failed'. Set in the Mendip Hills in Somerset, the story revolves around the discovery by Steve and Leonard in the labyrinth of caves behind West Poley of the source of the stream upon which the village, and in particular the mill, depends for its water. The source is in a secret cavern beyond a cave known as Nick's Pocket. By chance they learn that, from the cavern, they can divert the course of the stream through the neighbouring village of East Poley. Being able to determine which village the stream runs through gives the boys control over the prosperity of two villages, and so long as they keep secret the whereabouts of the source of the stream, they remain in control. Where **"Our Exploits"** differs fundamentally from the exclusively light-hearted **"Thieves"** is that it provides some serious lessons in citizenship—F. B. Pinion called **"Our Exploits"** 'a cautionary tale for boys'[15]. In **"The Thieves"** Hubert has an evening of swashbuckling glory and then rides back home. In **"Our Exploits"** the effects upon the boys of exercising power without responsibility become increasingly serious and disaster is only narrowly averted. In this respect **"Our Exploits"** bears some resemblance to William Golding's *Lord of the Flies*. While remaining at one level an action-packed adventure story, it also provides a case study in the behaviour of adolescent boys dealing with 'adult' issues and in the group dynamics of leadership.

Steve is the natural leader of the group, certainly by nature and probably by age—we do not learn the age of Job the apprentice but there is no doubting that he, with Leonard, is a team member. Steve has many of the qualities associated with leadership—for example, energy, enthusiasm, decisiveness, determination and courage—but it is also entirely due to his decisions and his manipulation of events that disaster comes upon them. Leonard, though 'robust and active', is small for his age and a little timorous. One can sense his awareness, as a sensitive 13-year old, of the age difference between himself and his confident, cocky, extrovert cousin. Being a visitor to Steve's house makes him even more vulnerable. In his bossy way Steve does not *ask* Leonard whether he would like to go to an expedition to the caves, he *tells* him: "I said I would show you inside the Mendips, and so I will". Steve occasionally taunts Leonard with being nervous or afraid, but to compensate for his lack of 'manly' characteristics Leonard is also sharp-eyed and quick-witted. It is he who spots how the stream can be diverted, the event upon which the whole of the rest of the story depends.

When they first realise that they have deprived West Poley of its stream Leonard's reaction is to own up and 'set it right'. Steve's initial reaction is to concede the latter but keep their secret: keeping control is what motivates him. When they discover that the diverted stream is running through East Poley, making it potentially very prosperous, Leonard articulates the central moral dilemma: re-directing the stream to West Poley would do as much harm to the people of East Poley as it would do good to the people of West Poley. Steve favours the people of East Poley on various specious grounds, including his shallow view that they are 'rather nicer'. But he defers taking immediate action. He is beginning to enjoy his power, and his mother's farm has a well, so he personally is not affected by West Poley's loss of water. Being able to champion Job in his dispute with his master, Miller Griffin, gives him further grounds to justify leaving East Poley with the stream. The miller is a cruel bully. Because there is no stream there is no work for the mill; because there is no work the miller cannot, within the rules of his indentures, force Job to remain in his employment. With the help of the Man who has Failed, Job is released. The people of East Poley are not only 'rather nicer', there are also more of them, and this too is added to Steve's argument. Leonard begins to try to grapple with the case Steve has so cleverly constructed, but solving 'the problem in utilitarian philosophy' is sidelined by Steve's plan that he and Leonard should use their ability to control the stream to play a game on the youths of East Poley. They dress up as wizards and, with Job's help at the source of the stream, successfully convince the boys of East Poley that they have magic power.

The introduction of this essentially childish prank is a frivolous diversion from their adult problem, which becomes even more complex when Steve and Leonard learn how, as a result of East Poley acquiring the stream, a poor widow has suffered grievously at the hands of a selfish corn-factor. Steve recognises that 'it is next to impossible, in this world, to do good to one set of folks without doing harm to another'. Leonard suggests that the corn-factor's exploitation of the widow is a reason for restoring the stream to West Poley, but Steve reminds him that would mean Job going back to persecution by the miller. Their discovery of 'equal persecution' (with its Orwellian undertones) co-incides with Job's discovery of a third channel down which the stream can be diverted. They are now saved from having to choose between West and East Poley and can settle for the totally negative solution of keeping both villages without water. Leonard learns that they are in danger of being discovered and urges that they consult an adult such as the Man who has Failed, but Steve is still unwilling to relinquish power. He is determined to keep the inner cavern a secret and to see through the plan of the third channel, 'so that we can consider which of the villages is most worthy to have the river, and act accordingly'. This decision nearly costs them their lives.

The remainder of the story falls broadly into two parts: the drama in the inner cavern, culminating in the boys' rescue; and the period in which Steve makes reparation for the trouble he has caused to West Poley.

A significant feature of the cavern drama is that all the hard physical work is undertaken by Steve and Job, leaving Leonard to make what contribution he can. 'Poor Lenny', as Steve calls him, is given the paltry job of managing the candles when, in an attempt to stop the water rising in the inner cavern, Steve and Job valiantly dive to try and find an outlet. In fact, ever sharp-eyed, it was he who first noticed that while the other two were blocking the channels to West and East Poley, the water had ceased to flow down the third channel because it had no outlet; the water was rising in the inner cavern to engulf them. The six installments in which the story originally appeared in *The Household* are retained as chapters in the unified version. The dramatic endings of the installments, designed to draw readers to the next installment, work well in the unified version, in particular here, where in an atmosphere of increasing desperation the chapter ends with Leonard asking about the level of the water—

> "I wonder if it rises still?" I said. "Perhaps not, after all."
>
> "Then we shall only exchange drowning for starving," said Steve. Job, instead of speaking, had endeavoured to answer my query by stooping down and stretching over the ledge with his arm. His face was very calm as he rose again. "It will be drowning," he said almost inaudibly, and held up his hand, which was wet.

In many ways the real star is Job. Though Steve is a better diver, Job can hold his breath under water longer and come back with more stones. It is he who cuts a step in the rock with his pickaxe which enables the three of them to climb clear of the water rising in the pool. It is he who devises the plan of sticking a candle in his straw hat and floating it round the pool on a current to enable them to see if there is a way out of the caves which has become their prison. When they think that they are doomed Job takes the blame, and it falls on him—the least 'educated' of the three—to spell out the truth: "It was hardly right to stop the grinding of flour that made bread for a whole parish, for my poor sake. We ought to ha' got the advice of someone wi' more experience than ourselves." When the miller falls through a hole in the roof of the cavern and plunges into the pool that is in danger of drowning them he takes pity on him. While the miller panics, Job remains calm and dignified. When help eventually comes it is he—not Steve—who supervises the process of them being hauled to safety.

The main source of humour in **"Our Exploits"** is Miller Griffin. From the start, when he sees himself ruined by the lack of river, he is a figure of fun, with declarations such as—

> "I don't drink hard; I don't stay away from church, and I only grind into Sabbath hours when there's no getting through the work otherwise, and I pay my way like a man!"
>
> "Yes—you do that," corroborated the others.
>
> "And yet, I be brought to ruinous despair, on this sixth day of September, Hannah Dominy; as if I were a villain! Oh, my mill, my mill-wheel—you'll never go round any more—never more!"

When he falls into the pool in the cavern and is obliged to join the three young heroes on the ledge his cowardice makes him an even greater figure of ridicule. He is terrified that the cobbler will not come back to rescue them—

> "He *must* mean to come back!" the miller murmured lugubriously, as we all stood in a row on the ledge, like sparrows on the moulding of a chimney.
>
> "I should think so," said Steve "if he's a man."

"Yes—he must!" the miller anxiously repeated. "I once said he was a two-penny sort of workman to his face—I wish I hadn't said it, oh—how I wish I hadn't; but 'twas years and years ago, and pray heaven he's forgot it! I once called him a stingy varmint—that I did! But we've made that up, and been friends ever since. And yet there's men who'll carry a snub in their buzzoms; and perhaps he's going to punish me now!"

The miller's jibbering outpourings contrast with the coolness and courage of the three youths, in a way which would have appealed to young readers.

In the aftermath of the rescue the miller at first wonders where the inner cavern with the source of the stream is, but once it is running through West Poley again, ceases to trouble himself further. But the secret weighs on Steve. He has caught a cold from getting wet in the pool which turns into a feverish illness. The burden of keeping his secret has begun to tell on him. He decides to reveal it to the people of West Poley and advises them to close off the entrance to the cavern. Having divested himself of the secret which gave him power and led to mischief, he is able to recover. The case study in how a group of adolescents coped with adult responsibilities ends there. But **'Our Exploits'** is also an adventure story with a moral. An act of heroism is required. Steve goes on to risk his life blowing up with dynamite the access to the inner cavern to secure the stream for West Poley forever.

In attempting to meet the requirements of the publishers of *Youth's Companion* Hardy almost certainly overdid the moral tone in **"Our Exploits"**. It is hard otherwise to understand, for example, why he included the Man who has Failed. Steve describes him thus at the beginning of the story: "He's a man who has been all over the world, and tried all sorts of lives, but he has never got rich, and now he has retired to this place for quietness. He calls himself the Man who has Failed." This description invests him with an element of mystery and raises expectations as to the part he will play in the story, but he never really lives up to his early promise. He always seems to be around, occasionally making an interjection or delivering a little homily, but the only really useful contribution he makes is in helping to interpret the terms of Job's indentures to Miller Griffin, which say that if there's no work for the apprentice he is released from his master. His final homily is a sententious put-down for the young heroes, which finishes:

> Exceptionally smart actions, such as you delight in, should be carefully weighed with a view to their utility before they are begun. Quiet perseverance in clearly defined courses is, as a rule, better than the erratic exploits that may do much harm.

Understandably irritated, Steve asks his mother afterwards: "He has failed in life, and how can his opinions be worth anything?" Defending him, his mother says, "He is one who has failed, not from want of sense, but from want of energy." Millgate takes the view that "there is more than a hint of the mature Hardy in the odd figure of the Man who has Failed." Hardy, says Millgate, often himself complained of a lack of energy, and he suggests that "As he contemplated his return to Dorchester [in the early 1880s], Hardy was perhaps already speculating whether it might not have been better if he had never left—and never embarked upon some, at least, of his erratic professional, emotional and geographical exploits of his past several years."[16] It is more likely that, as suggested by R. L. Purdy, Hardy put something of himself as a boy in Leonard[17].

Much of the language is stilted and academic. In using terms such as 'adipose tissues' and 'coign of vantage' Hardy might have had the American editors themselves reaching for their dictionaries. And one wonders what young readers would have made of Leonard saying—

> . . . the state of affairs was, in truth, one rather suited to the genius of Jeremy Bentham than to me. But the problem in utilitarian philosophy was shelved by Steve exclaiming, "I have it! I see how to get some real glory out of this."

It is unlikely that late 19th century American teenage readers would be familiar with Bentham's theory on 'the happiness of the greatest number'. And what would they have made of Leonard saying at the moment of greatest crisis: ". . . there came into my mind during this suspense the words I had remembered somewhere at school, as being of Flaminius, the consul, when he was penned up at Thrasymene: 'Friends, we must not hope to get out of this by vows and prayers alone. 'Tis by fortitude and strength we must escape.'"? Or of the East Poley men emerging from the caves and "walking between their vanquishers, like the Romans under the Caudine Forks, when they surrendered to the Samnites"? This was not what the readers of *The Adventures of Tom Sawyer* (1875) or *The Adventures of Huckleberry Finn* (1882) were used to.

Though **"Our Exploits"** now appears in selections of Hardy's short stories, it is unlikely that it would ever be published in an anthology of stories exclusively for teenagers, its original target audience. It would not, however, be surprising to find **"The Thieves Who Couldn't Help Sneezing"** in such an anthology. **"The Thieves"** is a story of charm and humour, capable of giving much pleasure to adult readers as to the adolescent boys for whom it was mainly intended. With **"Our Exploits"** Hardy misjudged his readership, and probably realised it. In that sense it is 'the Story that

Failed'. It remains, however, a substantial achievement, with its intricate plotting, strong story line and subtle characterisation as well as its insights into adolescent psychology.

Notes

Abbreviations used in these Notes:

CL: The Collected Letters of Thomas Hardy, edited by R. L. Purdy and Michael Millgate, OUP 1978

Purdy: Thomas Hardy: a Bibliographical Study, R. L. Purdy, OUP 1954.

1. In fact there can be little doubt that Hardy wrote both stories with boys in mind as his readers, though it seems always to have been customary to say they were for children or young people.

2. Both stories can be found in *An Indiscretion in the Life of an Heiress and Other Stories,* edited with an introduction and notes by Pamela Dalziel, OUP World's Classic Series 1994.

3. The first two were 'How I Built Myself a House' (1865) and 'Destiny and a Blue Cloak' (1874).

4. *CL* Vol (i) p. 50 and 52, letters to Nancy Meugens.

5. *Purdy*: p. 294.

6. *CL* Vol (i) p. 116, letter to Perry Mason & Co.

7. *CL* Vol (i) p. 123, letter to Perry Mason & Co.

8. *CL* Vol (i) p. 126, letter to Perry Mason & Co.

9. *CL* Vol (i) p. 158, letter to William H. Rideing.

10. *Purdy*: p. 303

11. *Purdy*: p. 303

12. *Thomas Hardy: Interviews and Recollections,* edited by James Gibson, Macmillan 1999, p. 28.

13. *CL* Vol (iv) p. 300, letter to Sir George Douglas.

14. *Purdy*: p. 303

15. *Purdy*: p. 303

16. *Thomas Hardy,* Michael Millgate, OUP 1982, pp. 238/239

17. *Purdy*: p. 303

Douglas Dunn (essay date 2000)

SOURCE: Dunn, Douglas. "Thomas Hardy's Narrative Art: The Poems and Short Stories." In *The Achievement of Thomas Hardy,* edited by Phillip Mallett, pp. 137-54. Basingstoke, U.K.: Macmillan, 2000.

[*In the following essay, Dunn explores the role of oral tradition and the thematic significance of time's passage in "The Withered Arm" and selections from Hardy's poetry.*]

Hardy was such a productive writer that I can hardly hope to do full and proper justice to my subject. *The Complete Stories,*[1] in Professor Page's edition, runs to some 839 pages of text, or about 50 tales, and I don't need to emphasise Hardy's plurality of poems. It's best summed up for me by Christopher Ricks in his essay 'A Note on Hardy's "A Spellbound Palace"', where he writes that, 'A friend of mine, when I recently presented him with "A Spellbound Palace", said, with simple truth, "There's *always* another Hardy poem"'.[2] There may even be a note of irritation in this constant discovery of '*another* Hardy poem'. However, for those of us who can't get enough of Hardy's poetry, the bottomlessness of *The Complete Poems* is a delight and fascination rather than an annoyance. It's when you find yourself having to write about them that the astonishing numerousness of his poems becomes—not irritating, but humbling, and perhaps even baffling.

Although not the first of his published stories, **'The Three Strangers'**[3] is especially interesting in that it contains a poem, or, rather, a song, '*As sung by* MR CHARLES CHARRINGTON *in the play of "The Three Wayfarers"'*, indicated beneath the title of 'The Stranger's Song' in *The Complete Poems.*[4] So, this is a work that appeared in three ways. First, it was published as a tale in *Longman's Magazine* in March 1883, and reprinted in **Wessex Tales** (1888). At the suggestion of J. M. Barrie it was made into a one-act play and performed for a brief period at the Terry Theatre in London in 1893. Then the lyric parts of an otherwise balladic prose narrative appeared in *Wessex Poems*. While the presence of the song is in itself effective as a narrative device—through it Hardy reveals the second stranger at the Fennels' christening party as a hangman—its impact and effectiveness are increased by the delays in its distribution of episodes and revelations. Hardy was too traditional a storyteller, too much in tune with the people about whom and for whom he was writing, to permit the song to be sung all at once. Instead, the narrative insists on purposeful postponements and surprises. Here, though, is the song.

The Stranger's Song

(As Sung by Mr Charles Charrington in the *Play of the Three Wayfarers*)

O my trade it is the rarest one,
　　　　　　　　　Simple shepherds all—
　My trade it is a sight to see;
For my customers I tie, and take 'em up on high,
　And waft 'em to a far countree!

My tools are but the common ones,
　　　　　　　　　Simple shepherds all—
　My tools are no sight to see:

A little hempen string, and a post whereon to swing
  Are implements enough for me!

Tomorrow is my working day,
            Simple shepherds all—
  Tomorrow is a working day for me:
For the farmer's sheep is slain, and the lad who did it
  ta'en,
  And on his soul may God ha' mer-cy!

It is artfully contrived as entirely appropriate for the mouth of who sings it in the story, and for the inhabitants of a remote and rural farm who listen to it; all the cleverness in the world would fail to achieve that naturalness without there being present in the writer a familiarity and loyalty to place and community so confirmed as to function at the level of instinct. And that's what I mean when I claim that Hardy was a traditional storyteller. In his essay 'The Storyteller', first published in 1936 as an introduction to a collection of the Russian writer, Leskov, Walter Benjamin found it possible to say: 'Familiar though his name may be to us, the storyteller in his living immediacy is by no means a present force. He has already become something remote from us and something that is getting even more distant.' A few pages later he becomes more pessimistic. 'The art of storytelling', he writes, 'is reaching its end because the epic side of truth, wisdom, is dying out.' And he continues:

> This, however, is a process that has been going on for a long time. And nothing would be more fatuous than to want to see in it merely a 'symptom of decay', let alone a 'modern' symptom. It is, rather, only a concomitant symptom of the secular productive forces of history, a concomitant that has quite gradually removed narrative from the realm of living speech and at the same time is making it possible to see a new beauty in what is vanishing.[5]

It seems to me that in his earlier stories Hardy is very aware of 'the realm of living speech', and of 'the epic side of truth, wisdom'. He asserts his authority as a storyteller of that place, although looking backwards in time, through the use of dialect, but especially through the kind of narrative he is writing. It has the symmetry and inevitability of ballad—three strangers, three knockings on the door, the discovery that the second arrival is the hangman, the false assumption that the third is an escaped prisoner, and the surprise that it is the first stranger who is the escaped prisoner awaiting execution in Casterbridge jail and that the third stranger is, in fact, the brother of the first. The crime was sheep-stealing, so the story also carries, although lightly, a burden of social comment. Much of that authority is conveyed by phrasemaking and descriptive touches in the writing. But while it is 'living speech' in the sense that it is closely in touch with the community it evokes, Hardy's prose outside of dia-

logue is more written than spoken, or to use terms coined apparently by critics of African-American writing, more writerly than speakerly. Consider this extract, for example, where the first stranger is introduced, but some time before he enters Higher Crowstairs, so that the reader sees him before the Fennels and their friends:

> It was nearly the time of the full moon, and on this account, though the sky was lined with a uniform sheet of dripping cloud, ordinary objects out of doors were readily visible. The sad wan light revealed the lonely pedestrian to be a man of supple frame; his gait suggested that he had somewhat passed the period of perfect and instinctive agility, though not so far as to be otherwise than rapid of motion when occasion required. At a rough guess he might have been about forty years of age. He appeared tall, but a recruiting sergeant, or other person accustomed to the judging of men's heights by the eye, would have discerned that this was chiefly owing to his gauntness, and that he was not more than five-feet-eight or nine.
>
> Notwithstanding the regularity of his tread there was caution in it, as in that of one who mentally feels his way; and despite the fact that it was not a black coat nor a dark garment of any sort that he wore, there was something about him which suggested that he naturally belonged to the black-coated tribes of men. His clothes were of fustian, and his boots hobnailed, yet in his progress he showed not the mud-accustomed bearing of hobnailed and fustian peasantry.[6]

Hardy's prose here is wonderfully measured, and although we haven't yet met the hangman, the one who turns out to be the escaped prisoner is described as if *he* were the executioner. At the same time Hardy comes close to giving the game away. If the reader remembers that passage I've just quoted, then, along with other clues—he's a pipe-smoker, but doesn't have a pipe or tobacco, for example—as soon as the mead-swilling hangman reveals who he is, a slightly confused or agitated atmosphere of suspicion surely arises.

But the skill of that passage, and the story's date (late 1870s, early 1880s) should remind us that Hardy had been a professional novelist for around ten years, even if *The Mayor of Casterbridge, Jude the Obscure* and *Tess of the d'Urbervilles* were still to come. My point is that for Hardy the short story was not the site of apprentice work as it has been for many more modern writers (or as it was for R. L. Stevenson, for example, in Hardy's younger lifetime). Indeed, unless you take seriously such antics as sound poetry, concrete poetry, cyberpoetry, and so on, then the literary short story is the newest of literary forms. Sir Walter Scott's 'The Two Drovers' is credited with being the first, but that forgets Pushkin, although Pushkin was much influenced by Scott's narrative poems and novels. The form had been in existence for only 60 or so years when Hardy wrote **'The Three Strangers'**. Its development in Europe and America was of course stimulated by the demands of a market in the form of the magazines from which writers like R. L. Stevenson and Hardy made much of their livelihood. Even more important, though, is that the short story in a sense had *always* existed except that it was expressed in verse, the chief medium of literature until the mid-to-late seventeenth century. I know of eighteenth-century chapbooks by Dugald Graham, the 'Skellit Bellman' of Glasgow—the Glasgow town-crier—and they are short prose tales, crudely written, but interesting enough for all that. There must be lots more from other parts of the island, waiting for a brass-bowelled scholar immune to book-dust to sift through and make a claim for the earlier, non-literary origins of the prose tale as a written form designed to be appropriated by the purchaser probably for spoken performance and adaptation.

Hardy came to the short story after considerable experience as a novelist and as a poet. This may not strike us as in any way remarkable, but there is at least one sense in which it is. 'What differentiates the novel from all other forms of prose literature', Walter Benjamin wrote in the essay from which I have already quoted,

> —the fairy tale, the legend, even the novella—is that it neither comes from oral tradition nor goes into it. This distinguishes it from storytelling in particular. The storyteller takes what he tells from experience—his own or that reported by others. And he in turn makes it the experience of those who are listening to his tale. The novelist has isolated himself. The birthplace of the novel is the solitary individual, who is no longer able to express himself by giving examples of his most important concerns, is himself uncounseled, and cannot counsel others.[7]

'Oral tradition' is quite clearly foregrounded in many of Hardy's stories. For example, the very last sentence of **'The Three Strangers'** reads: 'But the arrival of the three strangers at the shepherd's that night, and the details connected therewith, is a story as well known as ever in the country about Higher Crowstairs.' And I feel convinced that Hardy really enjoyed the resonance of that sentence. Above all, he enjoyed forging that link, whether through invention or re-telling, with 'a story as well known as ever'. Indeed, one of the most fascinating aspects of Hardy's writing as a whole is his status as a 'tradition-carrier', as they say of traditional singers and storytellers in Scotland and Ireland, especially in Gaelic culture and the balladists of the travellers. Written literature, the expression of High Culture, has much room for tradition-carriers too, for chroniclers of place and community. Similarly, at the end of **'The Melancholy Hussar of the German Legion'**,[8] Hardy concludes with a nod to 'the epic side of truth, wisdom', to the invaluableness of

communal epic, when he writes: 'The older villagers, however, who know of the episode from their parents, still recollect the place where the soldiers lie. Phyllis lies near.'[9] Also, it is Phyllis, cruelly thwarted in love, who has told the story to the narrator, presumably when she was very old and the narrator very young, a feature of Hardy's earlier tales shared by J. M. Barrie's of the 1880s which were founded on stories told to him by his mother. But the short story has always been much involved with memory. Part of its business has been the chronicles of the tribe, from Scott's 'The Two Drovers', James Hogg's and John Galt's stories, Hawthorne's, Turgenev's, Chekhov's, or Sherwood Anderson's *Winesburg, Ohio,* William Faulkner's stories, Dylan Thomas's early stories of the Jarvis Valley (and also *Portrait of the Artist as a Young Dog*), and through to some more recent writers.

John Bayley once described poems by Hardy—he mentions 'The Frozen Greenhouse'—as 'sung short stories'. (Incidentally, I've quoted his delightful phrase so often that it's high time I sent Professor Bayley an acknowledgement.) While it can apply to a great many of Hardy's poems, though far from all, it makes especial sense when thinking about such poems as 'A Trampwoman's Tragedy', which like his poems of Wessex traditions and memories from far back, stems from the same source as his stories and fiction in general.

As storytelling, 'A Trampwoman's Tragedy' is masterly in its unfolding of one of Hardy's habitual concerns—mistakes in love and their consequences. There would seem to be little more to be said. Reading Hardy's notes to the poem (dated April 1902) suggests that it could be an example of his archaeological imagination playing over recollections of local materials and family memories. Blue Jimmy in the tenth stanza is said to have stolen a horse belonging to a neighbour of Hardy's grandfather. Any memory at all can result in a poem, but this particular memory seems a bit unimportant, although perhaps not to a writer like Hardy with his fascination for memories and for hangings. It's a haunted poem, with a haunting in it. Strangely, too, it permits Hardy to use balladic speech to an extent that he could never quite get into the narrative parts of his stories. He had too much prose experience for that to be entirely possible in his tales where his best touches are literary and outside the linguistic scope of the oral tradition from which his stories emerged. In **'The Withered Arm'**,[10] for example, he writes of Mrs Lodge's face being as pale as Rhoda Brook's seen against 'the sad dun shades of the upland's garniture'. A little later we're told that 'a story was whispered about the many-dairied lowland that winter'. Diction and phrasings of that kind would have been inappropriate to the trampwoman. But Hardy's notes also add to the poem. In its final sentence, for example, the location of Ilchester jail is said to be 'now an innocent-looking green meadow'. It adds considerably to the poem's effect. For one thing, it returns the reader to the present. As a result 'A Trampwoman's Tragedy', as well as being spoken by an underdog, one of those marginalised beings which the short story especially seems drawn to represent, leaves the reader—or this reader—with the sense of a curiously farsighted glimpse of that rugged, wilder past which Hardy was determined should not be forgotten. Even in the movement of the verse he seems doggedly obedient to what was current long before and which he seems to be asserting as tuneful and authentic. But his meaning is a contemporary one—the power of jealousy, and the reckoning that will have to be paid when its passion overwhelms reason.

If 'A Trampwoman's Tragedy' is a bold and brave poem in its encounter with the past, then the same can be said of **'The Withered Arm'**. Unlike Stevenson, whose fondness for the supernatural was overdone, Hardy's tale hinges more on the impact of thoughts on another person, the intuitive transfer of hurt or disfigurement inflicted against the conscious wishes of the inflicter. It suggests dream as an active intermediary in human affairs. Rhoda Brook's vision of a withered arm materialises in Gertrude Lodge, who has just married the father of Rhoda's illegitimate son. There is something uncanny about Hardy's storytelling skill. 'Yes, mother,' said the boy. 'Is father married then?' In contemporary short fiction it is extremely difficult to get away with a sentence like this: 'Half a dozen years passed away, and Mr and Mrs Lodge's married experience sank into prosiness, and worse.' That is 'telling', not 'showing', and very unfashionable. However, the tale in Victorian times enjoyed a greater spaciousness of timescale than is nowadays preferred, just as a 'short' story then could be a great deal longer than is now the case, due to the generosity of page-space granted by magazines in response to what readers desired and expected. But even with such spaciousness at his command, there are some tricky moments in the narrative of **'The Withered Arm'**, where Hardy must have felt obliged to be both delicate and brief. After Rhoda and her son have left, due to the unbearable disclosure by Conjuror Trendle that Gertrude's withered arm has been inflicted by the power of an enemy, namely Rhoda, although it is not intentional, the childless Lodges are given this exchange followed by Hardy's necessary explanation. (And if there's one thing that story-writers detest, it's being obliged to explain.)

> 'Damned if you won't poison yourself with these apothecary messes and witch mixtures some time or other,' said her husband, when his eyes chanced to fall upon the multitudinous array.

She did not reply, but turned her sad, soft glance upon him in such heart-swollen reproach that he looked sorry for his words, and added, 'I only meant it for your good, you know, Gertrude.'

'I'll clear out the whole lot, and destroy them,' she said huskily, 'and try such remedies no more!'

'You want somebody to cheer you,' he observed. 'I once thought of adopting a boy; but he is too old now. And he is gone away I don't know where.'

And this is the moment which Hardy must have found obligatory, for although the reader knows, the reader also has to be told how Gertrude Lodge knows.

> She guessed to whom he alluded; for Rhoda Brook's story had in the course of years become known to her; though not a word had ever passed between her husband and herself on the subject. Neither had she ever spoken to him of her visit to Conjuror Trendle, and of what was revealed to her, or she thought was revealed to her, by that solitary heathman.[11]

Conjuror Trendle offers a cure. It is to touch the neck of a prisoner freshly cut down from the scaffold. 'It will turn the blood and change the constitution.' And you're dead right: it most certainly would. But during her conversation with the hangman the alert reader guesses who the unfortunate prisoner is—aged 18 and condemned to hang for burning a hayrick. It's Rhoda's son. Of course it is. High drama, of the kind in which Hardy revelled, is the result:

> Gertrude shrieked: 'the turn o' the blood', predicted by the conjuror, had taken place. But at that moment a second shriek rent the air of the enclosure: it was not Gertrude's, and its effect upon her was to make her start round.[12]

Quite probably, the reader won't be taken by surprise; but the reader will certainly be engrossed, with hair raised, by the sheer curiosity of the episode, the dead youth's neck already having been described as having on it 'a line the colour of an unripe blackberry', which Gertrude touches with her wasted arm.

> Immediately behind her stood Rhoda Brook, her face drawn, and her eyes red with weeping. Behind Rhoda stood Gertrude's own husband; his countenance lined, his eyes dim, but without a tear.
>
> 'D—n you! what are you doing here?' he said hoarsely.
>
> 'Hussy—to come between us and our child now!' cried Rhoda. 'This is the meaning of what Satan showed me in the vision! You are like her at last!' And clutching the bare arm of the younger woman, she pulled her unresistingly back against the wall. Immediately Brook had loosened her hold the fragile young Gertrude slid down against the feet of her husband. When he lifted her up she was unconscious.
>
> The mere sight of the twain had been enough to suggest to her that the dead young man was Rhoda's son.[13]

No, they don't write them like that any more. They don't even try to. But Hardy was right in engaging so much with stories set in the past, before he was born, but whose survivors lived on into his own earlier days. It enabled him to write freely about enormous and destructive passions. Gertrude dies three days later and Lodge sells his farms, dying after two years of lonely life in lodgings elsewhere, and leaving his money to a reformatory for boys 'subject to the payment of a small annuity to Rhoda Brook, if she could be found to claim it'. Most writers would end there, but Hardy adds a final paragraph which discreetly and perhaps for Hardy necessarily connects the story to the oral tradition and history from which it grew:

> For some time she could not be found; but eventually she reappeared in her old parish,—absolutely refusing, however, to have anything to do with the provision made for her. Her monotonous milking at the dairy was resumed, and followed for many long years, till her form became bent, and her once abundant dark hair white and worn away at the forehead—perhaps by long pressure against the cows. Here, sometimes, those who knew her experiences would stand and observe her, and wonder what sombre thoughts were beating inside that impassive, wrinkled brow, to the rhythm of the alternating milk-streams.[14]

'The Withered Arm' is a better title, but it could as easily have been called 'The Milkmaid's Tragedy'. Hardy's poem, 'The Milkmaid', from *Poems of the Past and Present*, while serious, is also more light-hearted.

> The maid breathes words—to vent,
> It seems, her sense of Nature's scenery,
> Of whose life, sentiment,
> And essence, very part itself is she.

We can take that as the serious aspect of the poem, that association of the milkmaid with the landscape of a remote place. However, the poem continues,

> She bends a glance of pain,
> And, at a moment, lets escape a tear;
> Is it that passing train,
> Whose alien whirr offends her country ear?—
>
> Nay! Phyllis does not dwell
> On visual and familiar things like these;
> What moves her is the spell
> Of inner themes and inner poetries: . . .

—which fairly sets up the reader's expectations, as if anticipating a Wordsworthian flourish. But it finishes with:

> Could but by Sunday morn
> Her gay new gown come, meads might dry to dun,
> Trains shriek till ears were torn,
> If Fred would not prefer that Other One.

The seeds of tragedy are there, perhaps, as in any love story; but Hardy chooses to observe with worldly amusement. But he must have his story, too.

Particularly successful as a short-story poem is 'At the Railway Station, Upway', from *Late Lyrics and Earlier.*

> 'There is not much that I can do,
>   For I've no money that's quite my own!'
>   Spoke up the pitying child—
> A little boy with a violin
> At the station before the train came in,—
>   'But I can play my fiddle to you,
> And a nice one 'tis, and good in tone!'
>
>   The man in the handcuffs smiled;
> The constable looked, and he smiled, too,
>   As the fiddle began to twang;
> And the man in the handcuffs suddenly sang
>   With grimful glee:
>   'This life so free
>   Is the thing for me!'
> And the constable smiled, and said no word,
> As if unconscious of what he heard;
> And so they went on till the train came in—
> The convict, and boy with the violin.

In telling the story of this encounter on a station platform, Hardy or his narrator is a perceiving presence (as in 'The Milkmaid'), and protected by an unannounced or absent first-person singular. Convict, boy and constable, are more than ciphers or unnamed strangers, though. They're untold stories. I agree with Tom Paulin, in his book *Thomas Hardy: the Poetry of Perception* (1975)[15] when he claims that when Hardy is at his most perceptive and observational the result is a quality of seeing that becomes what Paulin calls 'visionary'. What I would add to that is this: Hardy's observational/visionary dynamic is the direct result, not just of uncannily perceptive powers—and is there a finer poet at sheer *naming* than Hardy?—playing through 'inner themes and inner poetries', but of highly developed narrative, storytelling skills. A fine example is another railway poem, 'Midnight on the Great Western', from *Moments of Vision*—but where do you draw the line?—there's always another poem by Hardy. Note, though, the directness of the two titles—'At the Railway Station, Upway' and 'Midnight on the Great Western'. Each title asserts a fact of place and encounter. It is against the challenge of such a simplicity of statement that Hardy's tuneful skills are obliged to contest the real with the visionary. Note, too, the plainness of the opening lines of both poems. 'At the Railway Station, Upway', starts with the 'pitying child's' declaration of pennilessness, for which he compensates by playing his fiddle for the convict (and with innocent wisdom, for it leads the convict to break into ironic song: 'This life so free / Is the thing for me!'). 'Midnight on the Great Western' opens with plain statement: 'In the third class seat sat the journeying boy.' We could suppose that the phrase 'the journeying boy' (repeated four times in the poem) is poetic, but it could hardly be described as remarkable. What's peculiar about it is its timelessness: 'the journeying boy' could be from any place and age, and the fact that he's on a train is neither here nor there. Similarly, the descriptive purpose of the remaining lines of the first stanza seems to reach for a higher poetic level than the first line achieves (although I doubt if Hardy meant his first line to be in any way 'powerful'):

> And the roof-lamp's oily flame
> Played down on his listless form and face,
> Bewrapt past knowing to what he was going,
> Or whence he came.

So much of what is poetic in Hardy's poetry is a matter of narrative heightened by the vigour and delicacy of the tunes given to him by his venturesome, robust versification, flexible to the point of elasticity. The second stanza continues with a close-up, one of Hardy's best and most intuitive touches in his poetry. Readers at this point ought to be entranced by the commonplaceness of the objects evoked—the ticket, the key to the boy's box on a piece of string—and then the near-visionary leap of the play of light on the key. As a poem about vulnerable innocence then the key is surely significant, perhaps almost symbolic, but in too demotic, too real a manner for the concept of symbolism to be critically apt. (And this is a dimension of Hardy's poetry which I adore: the way he makes the commonplace proud of being what it is.)

> In the band of his hat the journeying boy
>   Had a ticket stuck; and a string
> Around his neck bore the key of his box,
> That twinkled gleams of the lamp's sad beams
>   Like a living thing.

Clearly, a poem by the author of 'Old Furniture'. But this, too, is a poem in which the story is that of an encounter. The story of 'the journeying boy' is untold, and if Hardy, poignantly, tries to guess, his speculation never gets beyond a question.

> What past can be yours, O journeying boy
>   Towards a world unknown,
> Who calmly, as if incurious quite
> On all at stake, can undertake
>   This plunge alone?

Strangely plain, and yet strangely soaring also, Hardy's question is primary to the narrative art of this poem. It invites the reader to make up the boy's story and yet because Hardy has himself refused to do so it also lays down the limits beyond which such guessing would be sentimental and condescending.

> Knows your soul a sphere, O journeying boy,
>   Our rude realms far above,

> Whence with spacious vision you mark and mete
> This region of sin that you find you in,
>   But are not of?

Presumably, 'region of sin' indicates that the train is approaching London, and for a reader of the present time the image evoked is of those runaway children of the North who somehow fetch up on the predatory concourses of King's Cross Station. 'But are not of' enforces the boy's innocence, perhaps with the rueful implication that it will not last for long in the Great Wen, or that his Dorsetshire origins (presumably) will help see him through. It could also suggest Hardy's conviction in the virtue of the district of the south-west of England from which the boy has come. But the boy has a box and round his neck on a piece of string the key to it. So someone has prepared him for his journey. Perhaps he's an orphan being sent to live with an aunt or other relative. Perhaps, perhaps. . . . Inevitably, the reader tries to make up a story, and Hardy encourages it while at the same time he forbids it. Indeed, it is not a story, but a lyrical anecdote that could become a story were more known by fact or provided by imagination. Or if it is a story then it is one of the poet's perception, the drama of compassion and speculation picked out on a verse melody from Hardy's immense and constantly plundered repertoire.

A poet's 'narrative art', especially that of a poet like Hardy, who excelled in the novel and shone in the short story, by itself introduces a constant possibility of fiction. Real persons and real events may well be changed to a lesser or greater extent by the poet's psychological momentum—'inner themes and inner poetries'—and by a need to re-experience the lived, which may be, according to the fact, imperfectly re-created (from the point of view of the prosaic), but which turns into perfect poetry. For example, was Hardy an habitual railway passenger in the third class? I doubt it. Who *was* the boy? Was it Hardy himself re-observed in adulthood? Is it a poem about ambition and cutting loose from the ties of livelihood and trade? Was the boy one whom Hardy sat opposite on the train? Was it an encounter he experienced or one that was told to him by another? Did he make it up? Does it matter?

There are clues in Hardy's poetry which can help us to define his 'psychological momentum' as I've called it. Essentially, it has to do with the status of time. In a sonnet either of April 1887 or written then, when he was in Italy, 'Rome: On the Palatine', he concludes:

> When lo, swift hands, on strings nigh overhead,
> Began to melodize a waltz by Strauss:
> It stirred me as I stood, in Cæsar's house,
> Raised the old routs Imperial lyres had led,

And blended pulsing life with lives long done,
Till Time seemed fiction, Past and Present one.

'Till Time seemed fiction, Past and Present one'—it is a remarkable declaration of principle, and, of course, Hardy did not need to visit Rome to find it. His work is pervaded by it. The past in the present, the present in the past, time as fact and history, and time as stuff and substance of fiction and of art and poetry—such themes are everywhere in his work as a kind of pulse, and inform his versification, his obstinately creative exercising of the possibilities of timeless song offered by the English language with a local or (in a good sense) provincial root. Hardy is the least deracinated and, next to Chaucer, Shakespeare, Wordsworth, Crabbe, and, more recently, Geoffrey Grigson, Ted Hughes and Philip Larkin, the most English of poets—and maybe it takes a disinterested Scot to see this exhilarating phenomenon.

When Hardy came to write his celebrated 'Poems of 1912-13', his poems recollecting Emma Hardy, and other poems after these dates on the same subject, he was already more than well-rehearsed in haunting and being haunted. This time, though, the haunting was even more real than those which had happened before. And the haunting was not fictitious, although the potency of fictitious hauntings is not one which I would care to dismiss. A poet's 'narrative art' is just as likely to be as powerful, and probably more so, when speaking *in persona propria* as in poems where the first-person singular is absent or observational merely. In Hardy's case, the result was a melismatic and elegiac complicatedness, for reasons which we all know about. It led to such a complex line as the last of 'Your Last Drive'—'You are past love, praise, indifference, blame', perhaps the best earned and truest of all his lines. The poem is full of minute give-aways, to such an extent that I would claim that a poet's 'narrative art' is not so very different from that of a novelist or a short-story writer (although, as has often been said, the short story is closer to the lyric poem than to the novel; and as a writer of both I find myself increasingly doubtful of this critical commonplace). Outside of his poems of first-person, haunted predicament, Hardy's work, it seems to me, is pretty well all of a piece; but it's his first-person poems, no matter their possible fictitiousness, that strike me as his masterpieces. 'Your Last Drive', though, is a risky poem to the extent that it introduces dialogue from his dead wife. In terms of fiction, an ethical hazard is undertaken in that it reports speech the actuality of which can only be asserted by the poet. Is it real? Did she say it? And then, once again, does it matter?

But more important, perhaps, is the question of how an accomplished versification can dulcify or change a real experience or set of emotions. Could the verse skills and narrative or storytelling skills of a writer like Hardy modify lived experience to a point where the result could be a kind of misrepresentation, or even mendacity? I think the answer is 'Of course, but does it matter, if the poet is also being honest to what we know of the biographical record?' And that's the case with these poems, especially when you consider the harshness of 'Without Ceremony', the last line of which is 'Good-bye is not worth while!', meaning what it did when Emma was alive and taking off without telling Hardy, and that her haunting of him would be permanent, and a reckoning which he would have to continue to meet until the day he died. Here, though, is 'Your Last Drive':

> Here by the moorway you returned,
> And saw the borough lights ahead
> That lit your face—all undiscerned
> To be in a week the face of the dead,
> And you told of the charm of that haloed view
> That never again would beam on you.
>
> And on your left you passed the spot
> Where eight days later you were to lie,
> And be spoken of as one who was not;
> Beholding it with a heedless eye
> As alien from you, though under its tree
> You soon would halt everlastingly.
>
> I drove not with you . . .

Already a reader's eyebrows may have risen in a tic of interior puzzlement or questioning at 'You told of the charm of that haloed view / That never again would beam on you' after a reading of 'The Going', which precedes 'Your Last Drive', and which expresses the surprise of Emma's death. Also, 'I drove not with you . . .', followed as it is by three dramatic dots . . . well, the three dots are themselves an expression of remorse—punctuation as gasp, as breath withheld. Hardy, however, doesn't persevere with his absence but, instead, imagines his presence:

> Yet had I sat
> At your side that eve I should not have seen
> That the countenance I was glancing at
> Had a last-time look in the flickering sheen,
> Nor have read the writing upon your face,
> 'I go hence soon to my resting-place;'
>
> 'You may miss me then.'

'You may miss me then'—is that not Hardy mounting a terrible indictment upon himself through speech directed at him from the wife whom he may have neglected and who could have been difficult and awkward towards him? From the biographical evidence, we think we know about this, but it's too easy to be prurient or decisive. Hardy's poem picks up the story—and it *is* a story, Hardy's own story, the story of his marriage, but as told by Hardy, even if part of it is told riskily and fictitiously through the words of his wife, Emma:

> But I shall not know
> How many times you visit me there,
> Or what your thoughts are, or if you go
> There never at all. And I shall not care.
> Should you censure me I shall take no heed,
> And even your praises no more shall need.

Clearly, there's something rueful there—'I shall not care. / Should you censure me' . . . and 'even your praises no more shall need.' Death, then, is a sort of release from the demands of her husband, Thomas Hardy. It's honest of Hardy not to say so, precisely, but to implicate himself in the truth of the matter. However, it's Hardy who, inevitably, has the last word:

> True, you'll never know. And you will not mind.
> But shall I then slight you because of such?
> Dear ghost, in the past did you ever find
> The thought 'What profit,' move me much?
> Yet abides the fact, indeed, the same,—
> You are past love, praise, indifference, blame.

To be perfectly blunt about the matter, a poet's narrative art is the dynamic of thought, disclosure, description, and so on, that leads up to the conclusion of a poem, especially the last line. Much the same design can be experienced in Hardy's short or shorter fiction, or in his novels—the distribution of time, or events, or of thoughts. But it is when we read a poem like 'During Wind and Rain' that we really find ourselves faced with Hardy's 'narrative art' in verse and poetry at its most powerful, when his passion, versification and tunefulness meet the invisible but communicative and moving story he has to tell. Never mind that it is one of Hardy's greatest poems, it is one of the great poems of the world.

> They sing their dearest songs—
> He, she, all of them—yea,
> Treble and tenor and bass,
>   And one to play;
> With the candles mooning each face . . .
>   Ah, no; the years O!
> How the sick leaves reel down in throngs!
>
> They clear the creeping moss—
> Elders and juniors—aye,
> Making the pathways neat
>   And the garden gay;
> And they build a shady seat . . .
>   Ah, no; the years, the years;
> See, the white storm-birds wing across!
>
> They are blithely breakfasting all—
> Men and maidens—yea,
> Under the summer tree,
>   With a glimpse of the bay,
> While pet fowl come to the knee . . .

Ah, no; the years O!
And the rotten rose is ript from the wall.

> They change to a high new house,
> He, she, all of them—aye,
> Clocks and carpets and chairs
>   On the lawn all day,
> And brightest things that are theirs. . . .
>   Ah, no; the years, the years;
> Down their carved names the rain-drop ploughs.

Notes

1. *Thomas Hardy: the Complete Stories,* ed. Norman Page (London, 1996).

2. Christopher Ricks, 'A Note on Hardy's "A Spellbound Palace"', in *Essays in Appreciation* (Oxford, 1998), p. 239.

3. *Complete Stories,* p. 7.

4. This is number 22 in *The Complete Poems.* Subsequent references are to this edition.

5. Walter Benjamin, *Illuminations,* ed. Hannah Arendt (London, 1970), pp. 83, 87.

6. *Complete Stories,* p. 10

7. Walter Benjamin, *Illuminations,* p. 87.

8. *Complete Stories,* pp. 32-47.

9. *Complete Stories,* p. 47.

10. *Complete Stories,* pp. 48-51.

11. *Complete Stories,* p. 61.

12. *Complete Stories,* p. 70.

13. *Complete Stories,* p. 70.

14. *Complete Stories,* p. 71.

15. Tom Paulin, *The Poetry of Perception* (London, 1975), p. 11 and passim.

Simon Gatrell (essay date autumn 2006)

SOURCE: Gatrell, Simon. "Dress, Body, and Psyche in 'The Romantic Adventures of a Milkmaid,' *Tess of the d'Urbervilles,* and *The Mayor of Casterbridge.*" *Thomas Hardy Journal* 22 (autumn 2006): 143-58.

[*In the following essay, Gatrell details the complicated relationship between clothing, physicality, and psychology in "The Romantic Adventures of a Milkmaid," Tess of the d'Urbervilles, and The Mayor of Casterbridge, paying particular attention to the protagonists of each narrative.*]

I want to begin with a sequence of events near the beginning of Hardy's version of Cinderella, **'The Romantic Adventures of a Milkmaid'**. The story will not perhaps be familiar to everyone, so I hope those who know it well will forgive me if I outline the early part of the plot. The milkmaid of the title, Margery Tucker, takes a short-cut across the grounds of a manor-house, and accidentally encounters the tenant, a darkly sinister foreign nobleman, Baron Xanten; he appears to be about to shoot himself. Her arrival prevents him, and the more or less simultaneous delivery of a letter containing good news, transforms his mood, and he decides to live. In an impulsive fit of gratitude, he offers Margery whatever she would like as a reward for saving his life. After some delay Margery tells him her heart's desire is to go to a proper ball in a proper ball dress. He tries to talk her out of it, suggesting more practical rewards, but eventually agrees to arrange matters. And now comes the interesting part, from my present point of view: in order, as he tells her, to be able to get her the right size in ball-dresses, he demands of Margery the 'tight little jacket' she is wearing (Hardy's fairy-godfather has to manage without a wand); she takes it off and gives it to him, still warm from her body (Chapter 3; as so many different editions of Hardy's texts are in current use, all quotations are identified by chapter only). He seizes it, rolls it up as small as a cricket ball and thrusts it into a pocket. Consider, for a moment, the insight Hardy offers here into the symbolic power of dress in human affairs; consider the intimacy and violence of the Baron's handling of the jacket that effectively stands in for the girl herself. In this one gesture Hardy reveals the degree to which the Baron controls Margery, and opens up sexual possibilities that had hitherto been latent in the brief relationship. The Baron has Margery in his pocket.

The Baron organises everything, and in the early evening before the ball Margery meets him, as instructed, in a wood, beside the remains of a once formidable tree: 'an elm, huge, hollow, distorted and headless, with a rift in its side.' Within the tree is a cavity four or five feet in diameter, just large enough to serve as a secret dressing-room for the milkmaid. She enters this womb-like chamber and finds therein a box and a mirror. Within the box there is—her ball-dress. In the evening light, filtered down through the trunk, the dress seems an apparition—the spirit of some self waiting to be filled by flesh. 'This marvel of art,' Hardy writes, 'was, briefly, a sort of heavenly cobweb. It was a gossamer texture of precious manufacture, artistically festooned in a dozen flounces or more.' (The whole of the dressing episode is in chapter 4.)

Margery is quite as amazed by the dress as if the Baron had waved a wand. She:

> lifted it, and could hardly refrain from kissing it. Had any one told her before this moment that such a dress

could exist she would have said "No; it's impossible." She drew back, went forward, flushed, laughed, raised her hands.

It is evident that she cares passionately about clothes, but still, in case we might think her reaction exaggerated, the narrator adds:

> To say that the maker of that dress had been an individual of talent was simply understatement: he was a genius; and she sunned herself in the rays of his creation.

This metaphor gives the dress the vivifying energy of the sun—simply looking at the dress stirs in Margery the self that can bring to life all the physical, emotional and social implications of the inert 'apparition'.

Margery is like a pianist contemplating the score of a new Beethoven sonata—she has the sensibility to understand its genius and the power of the imagination to see it come alive; but also, as the pianist has to have the skill, the technique, the passion for playing, she has to have the face, the body, the grace, and the profound commitment to clothes, to perform adequately the genius of the dress; otherwise, for all its genius, the art will fail. Without the fitting body and the informing mind the dress is just an apparition, however beautiful, as the sonata is just marks on a piece of paper.

The analogy works more fully in this instance, because Margery, like the pianist, has had no part in deciding the nature of the work of art, of the ball-gown she is to wear; she recognises its greatness when she sees it, and can transform her self to the performance of it, to the public display of the individual spirit of the genius in dressmaking. In this respect the situation is unusual, for most clothing is chosen by the wearer with some conscious end: to protect or keep warm the body, to expose or emphasise parts of it, or to represent some idea of the self to the world. The Baron has certainly made sure that Margery's costume will force Margery to represent a particular idea of herself to the world; it signifies wealth, class, taste, and it forces others (women as well as men), to look at the wearer of the dress with a kind of respect.

However, to perform the dress, Margery has first to get to the ball, and after she has put it on, she finds that she cannot get out of the 'rift' in the trunk by which she had entered the hollow tree because the skirt has much more volume than that of her daily clothes, and is also more fragile. In order to free her, the Baron first kicks away, and then, with a branch, levers away, rotten wood from the aperture, so that the new Margery can be born, fully formed—a birth that is hard on the tree, one might say.

It seems clear that Reinhart has entered into this idea of a new birth as fully as Hardy could have wished: I hope you will not think me fanciful if I suggest that, filled by Margery and part of her dress, the rift in the trunk is shaped after the female genitalia; we can imagine the sequel; as the Baron removes wood, the shape of the opening becomes more circular, and when Margery finally emerges, her head first, through the enlarged opening, it is not quite as a baby emerging from the birth canal into a new world, but as close as author and artist could get to it.

There are other interpretations possible of the Baron's actions, once the visual image of the rift in the trunk is taken in, but what is striking, given the possibilities foreshadowed by the fate of Margery's jacket, is how little of the sexual, or even of the romantic, enters into what follows. As soon as the girl is free of the tree the Baron ushers her into the interior of his carriage, and instead of stepping inside after her into the dark seclusion, he gets up outside with the coachman; the restrained note of the evening is sounded. Nor does Hardy do one of his sensual *tours de force* at the ball—such as Eustacia with Damon in *The Return of the Native*, or the dance at the hay-trusser's barn in *Tess of the d'Urbervilles*—there is no suggestion that the newborn Margery feels any sexual pull in dancing with the Baron, nor he for her.

On the other hand, after worrying about slipping and falling on the highly-polished dance floor she soon finds that it:

> was a positive assistance to one of her natural agility and litheness. Moreover her marvellous dress . . . inspired her as nothing else could have done. Externally a new creature she was prompted to new deeds.

> [The ball and the return to the wood are in chapter 5.]

The question is, though, whether in performing the ball-gown for an evening, in becoming to outward view a privileged member of the rural gentry, Margery herself is permanently altered by the performance?

When they leave, the Baron again eschews the opportunity for sexual engagement offered by the interior of the carriage; Margery falls asleep alone inside, to reawaken to the Baron's touch on her hand once they have reached the wood where her transformation was performed. Then the process within the decaying elm is reversed:

> She entered the trunk, dislodged the box containing her old clothing, pulled off the pretty slippers, and gloves, and dress, and in ten minutes emerged in the cotton gown and shawl of shepherd's plaid.

The Baron seizes the 'finery' and sets fire to it all. Margery pleads for something to be spared but the Baron is determined. The immolation pains Margery almost as much as if she is being burned herself—as indeed a part of her is:

> Margery was agonised. She ran forward: She implored, and intreated.

> 'Please sir—do spare it—do! My lovely dress—my dear, dear slippers—my fan—it is cruel! Don't burn them, please!'

> 'Nonsense. We shall have no further use for them if we live a hundred years.'

> 'But spare a bit of it—one little piece,—sir,—a scrap of the lace—one bow of the ribbon—the lovely fan—just something!'

But he is inexorable. The Baron hopes, by this after-midnight vanishing act, effectively to burn off the identity he brought into the world. But of course, the destruction of the dress, the material which has released the persona, only drives more deeply and vividly into Margery the change to her consciousness, to her spirit.

It is often suggested that Hardy chose not to publish **'The Romantic Adventures of a Milkmaid'** in book form for more than thirty years, because of the closeness of the narrative in some respects to that of *Tess of the d'Urbervilles*. And, indeed, Hardy does re-examine this experience of Margery Tucker through Tess Durbeyfield.

Tess also, sometime a milkmaid, has clothes in the current London or Paris fashion bought for her, both by Angel Clare and by Alec d'Urberville; but her response to such mind-altering dress is quite other.

It is not just a difference in nature, character, and temperament between the two girls. It is one of Hardy's fundamental arguments about Tess that her violation in the Chase by Alec, and its consequence, come so early in her life that her potential is warped, that circumstance and Alec fix aspects of her self at too early a point in her development towards womanhood. Dress is an important element in Hardy's demonstration of this idea. Throughout the novel, Tess herself chooses only dress that conforms to need and function. She has no incentive or opportunity to do otherwise.

Some might object to such a statement, thinking for instance of the much-discussed red ribbon that Tess wears to the Whitsun dance at the beginning of the novel, the ribbon that distinguishes her from all the other dancers. Does the ribbon not indicate clearly an attempt by Tess to define her personality through dress—how can such an adornment be for use or need?

Well, yes; but it is by no means certain that Tess chose the ribbon herself. It is just as likely that her mother did. Remember Tess preparing herself to go to work at Trantridge?

She . . . came down in her ordinary weekday clothes, her Sunday apparel being carefully folded in her box. Her mother expostulated: 'You will never set out to see your folks without dressing up more the dandy than that?'

'But I am going to work!' said Tess.

'Well, yes . . . at first there mid be a little pretence o't . . . But I think it will be wiser of 'ee to put your best side outward . . .'

'Very well; I suppose you know best,' replied Tess with calm abandonment. And to please her parent the girl put herself quite in Joan's hands, saying serenely, 'Do what you like with me, mother.'

Mrs Durbeyfield was only too delighted at this tractability. First she fetched a great basin, and washed Tess's hair with such thoroughness that when dried and brushed it looked twice as much as at other times. She tied it with a broader pink ribbon than usual. Then she put upon her the white frock that Tess had worn at the club-walking, the airy fulness of which, supplementing her enlarged coiffure, imparted to her developing figure an amplitude which belied her age, and might cause her to be estimated as a woman when she was not much more than a child.

(chapter 7)

This is an important small passage, not just because it shows Joan Durbeyfield selecting a ribbon for her daughter. It is one of the moments in which the narrator pauses to emphasise the disastrous discrepancy between Tess's appearance and her self, a discrepancy that is fixed by the dress and hairstyle and ribbon that mediate between her self, her body, and the rest of the world. Her dress is deceptive and is not her own choice, it is designed purely to advance the naïve plot of her mother. It is also, and perhaps even more importantly, one of those moments in which Tess displays a self-destructive passivity. Hardy has carefully placed and phrased the serene speech: 'Do what you like with me, mother.' And she does. Tess would have a similar response, we can imagine, to Alec's proposal to buy her a whole set of fashionable clothes before she goes to live with him at Sandbourne. And when she speaks with Angel in the doorway of the Herons, she says, 'These clothes are what he's put upon me: I didn't care what he did wi' me!' As a consequence Angel perceives, in what was a late but very significant addition to the text of the novel, that 'his original Tess had spiritually ceased to recognize the body before him as hers—allowing it to drift, like a corpse upon the current, in a direction dissociated from its living will' (chapter 55).

For Tess, her body has become a thing of use, for others to hang beautiful and fashionable clothes upon, and presumably again to be used by Alec at his will (and ultimately to be abandoned to the hangman with equal calm). Angel will have remembered that Tess

long ago had told the assembled breakfast table at Dairyman Crick's how 'our souls can be made to go outside our bodies when we are alive', by gazing at a bright star and fixing the mind upon it, whereupon, she said, 'you will soon find that you are hundreds and hundreds o' miles away from your body, which you don't seem to want at all' (chapter 18).

This ability, desire, the need to separate spirit and body, the certainty in Tess that her identity has nothing to do with her body, however else it may be constituted, makes it inevitable that she should only pay attention to dress in its functional aspect—with one exception: when the clothes embody her beloved.

Once Tess has agreed to marry Angel, he sees it as a necessity to provide her with a wardrobe that will be appropriate for her new life as a gentleman farmer's wife; Tess does not think beyond the wedding, wondering if her best white muslin frock will do for that or if she ought to buy a new one. But Angel has already sent an order to a tradeswoman in London, and a whole set of clothes arrives for her, from bonnets to shoes. Like Margery's dress, these clothes are not the result of any selection on Tess's part; she has not agonised over her future identity, as Lucetta Le Sueur does with her spring outfit in *The Mayor of Casterbridge*: '"settling upon new clothes is so trying"', she says. '"You are that person" (pointing to one [dress]), "or you are that totally different person" (pointing to the other) "for the whole of the coming spring".' (chapter 24)

Tess's self, unlike Margery's, is not altered by the clothes Angel buys her; what happens is that she invests Angel's gift with the personality of the donor—as, for instance when, at the extremity of her need, she decides to walk from Flintcomb Ash to Emminster, to make herself known to Angel's parents. It is characteristic of her that she lets Marian and Izz shape her appearance. They:

were much interested in her excursion, knowing that the journey concerned her husband. . . . they came and assisted Tess in her departure, and argued that she should dress up in her very prettiest guise to captivate the hearts of her parents-in-law . . .

And once they have persuaded her to dress in the last of Angel's clothes that remain to her, they continue to arrange her:

With a final tug and touch here, and a slight brush there, they let her go; and she was absorbed into the pearly air of the fore-dawn.

(chapter 44)

Of course they are expressing solidarity and friendship, but Tess is again content to resign her external identity to others.

When she turns back from the vicarage at Emminster without seeing her parents-in-law, and her stout walking boots are appropriated by Mercy Chant and Angel's brothers, the narrator says that her self-pity is channelled into sorrow that they could not know that the dress and pretty shoes she is wearing were loving presents from Angel. For Tess, the value of the prettiness of the shoes is not that they display her feet to the best advantage, nor that they shape or express a fragment of her personality, nor that they are intrinsically beautiful, but that they came from him; when she wears one of his dresses, it is as close as she can come to him—it is as if she is wearing him.

It is only one of a multitude of ironies in the novel that it is on the return journey, while wearing this last of Angel, that she comes across Alec again, in his surprising new guise as a preacher. As she hastily leaves the place where Alec is holding his meeting, it is the back of Angel's dress that 'seemed to be endowed with a sensitiveness to ocular beams . . . so alive was she to a fancied gaze which might be resting upon her from the outside of that barn' (chapter 45).

After all of Angel's clothes but this last one have worn out, Tess returns to what earlier Hardy had called 'the most appropriate dress of the fieldwoman':

> Thus Tess walks on; a figure which is part of the landscape; a fieldwoman pure and simple, in winter guise: a grey serge cape, a red woollen cravat, a stuff skirt covered by a whitey-brown rough wrapper, and buff leather gloves. Every thread of that old attire has become faded and thin under the stroke of rain-drops, the burn of sunbeams, and the stress of winds. There is no sign of young passion in her now . . . Inside this exterior, over which the eye might have roved as over a thing scarcely percipient, almost inorganic, there was the record of a pulsing life which had learnt too well, for its years, of the dust and ashes of things, of the cruelty of lust and the fragility of love.
>
> (chapter 42)

It is not just her harmony with the landscape, 'almost inorganic', indeed, as if she were a fragment of the primaeval rock that had somehow learned motion, to which Hardy wishes to draw our attention, but he wants us to note how her dress, the primary indicator of her self to the roving gaze of the rest of the world, conceals the truth of her self. The point is made the more forcibly in that, in dressing in this way, Tess's only concern is to conceal the beauty of her body, that troublesome other exterior. But Hardy is aware that dress is always a two-way series of signs—that the intention of the wearer may be countered by the perceptions of the observer. As a consequence of the clothes just described, and the snipping of her eyebrows, Tess fends off unwelcome attentions from those she meets

as she walks. But later, when the newly secular Alec talks to her beside the steam-threshing-machine at Flintcomb-Ash, it is the sexual allure of the same dress that he points out:

> Of course you have done nothing except retain your pretty face and shapely figure. I saw it on the rick before you saw me—that tight pinafore-thing sets it off, and that wing-bonnet—you field-girls should never wear those bonnets if you wish to keep out of danger.
>
> (chapter 47)

But then there is a third perception of the same costume, as worn by Tess and Marian, whose forms were:

> enshrouded in hessian 'wroppers'—sleeved brown pinafores, tied behind to the bottom, to keep their gowns from blowing about . . . The pensive character which the curtained hood lent to their bent heads would have reminded the observer of some early Italian conception of the two Marys.
>
> (chapter 43)

It is evident that the interpretation of the meaning of this working dress depends very much upon the particular observer—again making the point that dress is a series of two-way signs; there may or may not be a conscious intention shaping the nature of the clothing and adornment, but there is always also a response from those who see the ensemble, and there is always a varying proportion in the response between the intention of the wearer and the preconceptions of the observer. Though Alec's perception of Tess feeding the thresher and the narrator's interpretation of Marian and Tess as 'the two Marys' are quite different, yet in both the observer has imposed all meaning, and the wearers intended none.

One last example of Tess wearing working clothes comes as she digs in the twilight in her family allotment, after returning home from Flintcomb-Ash:

> She was oddly dressed to-night, and presented a somewhat staring aspect, her attire being a gown bleached by many washings, with a short black jacket over it, the effect of the whole being that of a wedding and funeral guest in one.
>
> (chapter 50)

As in the case of the red ribbon, the narrator determines the reader's response to the dress for his purposes—the weaving of wedding and funeral in Tess's life is evident. The further relevance of the odd description is at once made apparent, for, as she throws dead weeds onto the fire beside her plot, the flare-up reveals Alec d'Urberville to her:

> The unexpectedness of his presence, the grotesqueness of his appearance in a gathered smockfrock, such as was now worn only by the most old-fashioned of the labourers, had a ghastly comicality that chilled her as to its bearing.

The 'ghastly comicality' sorts well with Tess's wedding and funeral aspect, and both anticipate the ending of the novel, but what, we may ask, is the 'bearing' of Alec's wearing a smockfrock?

Like Margery Tucker, Alec has a strong interest in dress, and a clear conception of its significance. In appearing to Tess in what Hardy, in his nostalgic and utilitarian vein, would consider the appropriate costume for male agricultural workfolk, he implies to her that if she will not consent to rise through his protection, he is prepared to descend to hers in order to persuade her. It is only a gesture, of course, a way of continuing his pressure on her, and once he's made his point he removes the smockfrock and thrusts it into the flames (as Baron Xanten does with the finery he has bought for Margery).

Throughout the novel we are made aware that Alec is a snappy dresser. When he turns up with his gig to take Tess to Trantridge, he's 'wearing a dandy cap, drab jacket, breeches of the same hue, white neck-cloth, stick-up collar, and brown driving-gloves'. And the important word here is 'dandy'. I don't have enough time now to expatiate on the history of the dandy in the nineteenth century, and Hardy doesn't suggest that Alec might be a match for Oscar Wilde, but he does repeat the idea when describing another of Alec's guises, the evangelical preacher:

> now he wore neatly trimmed, old-fashioned whiskers, the sable moustache having disappeared; and his dress was half-clerical, a modification which had changed his expression sufficiently to abstract the dandyism from his features.
>
> (chapter 45)

And when he abandons the church and returns for Tess at Flintcomb-Ash, wearing 'a tweed suit of fashionable pattern', and twirling 'a gay walking-cane', Izz thinks he's after Tess, but Marian says: 'O no. 'Tis a ranter pa'son who's been sniffing after her lately—not a dandy like this.' (chapter 47) So dress becomes an element in the case Hardy builds up against Alec, exploiting the inherent hostility of his conventional readership towards Wilde and those men over the previous ten years who had emulated him.

Alec is the only character in the novel who has an aesthetic sense of dress; Angel by contrast has no interest in what he wears; when we first see him in company with his brothers at Marlott, his appearance 'would hardly have been sufficient to characterize him'; at Talbothays he wore 'the ordinary white pinner and leather leggings' and nowhere else does anything he wears merit attention (chapters 2 and 18).

The clothes that he buys for Tess are in muted colours, soft fabrics, of conservative cut, unexceptional dress that Tess can wear as an itinerant farm worker without

seeming out of place; the clothes that Alec buys for her are in the current metropolitan fashion, elegant, opulent, exotic in the rural environment. But the fact that Alec and Angel are opposed by Hardy in this respect, as in many others, should not blind us to the more important fact that both men feel free to dress her up like a doll—and we might add, to use her like one. Thus, they are united in relation to Tess as representatives of their class and gender, and it should not be surprising that at two of the moments of most intense crisis in Tess's life, the same pattern of identity between the two men underlying difference is shaped through clothing. When Alec deposits Tess on the ground in the Chase before trying to discover where exactly they are, he wraps his overcoat around her; Angel does the same when Tess lies down to sleep at Stonehenge.

You will remember that during the five days and nights immediately before Tess rests on the pagan stone, she and Angel consummate their marriage, with love and forgiveness, at Bramshurst Court. In her escape with Angel from Sandbourne after killing Alec, Tess is wearing Alec's clothes; but for neither, characteristically, is that a matter of concern. Hardy, however, understands the significance, and is careful to point out that as husband and wife make love, Alec's elegant gown, silk stockings and pretty parasol hang across a chair beside the bed, mute witnesses.

At first glance *The Mayor of Casterbridge* might not seem so fertile a field for enquiry. To be sure, as we have seen, Lucetta understands the potential of dress to shape the personality, and in a small way Elizabeth-Jane develops something of the same kind of awareness; but the rough impulsive bull of a man Michael Henchard, who is at the centre of the novel? It comes as something of a surprise perhaps to discover that he is much closer to Margery Tucker than to Tess Durbeyfield in his imaginative sensitivity where dress is concerned.

It is true that when the narrator introduces us to him as a young man at the beginning of the novel, there is nothing special about his clothing:

> He wore a short jacket of brown corduroy, newer than the remainder of his suit, which was a fustian waistcoat with white horn buttons, breeches of the same, tanned leggings, and a straw hat overlaid with black glazed canvas.
>
> (chapter 1)

But on the other hand a later description of this same youthful dress gives a different feeling:

> Then he had worn clean suitable clothes, light and cheerful in hue; leggings yellow as marigolds, corduroys immaculate as new flax, and a neckerchief like a flower-garden.
>
> (chapter 32)

The emphasis on gaiety and fertility is striking, and the tone in general, and the adjective 'immaculate' in particular, do suggest that young Michael Henchard was keenly alert to the nature and effect of his dress. The description of his evening dress as mayor is not particularly detailed, but it does show at least some interest in display: 'an expanse of frilled shirt showing on his broad breast; jewelled studs, and a heavy gold chain.' Though the heavy gold chain is official, certainly the frills and jewels are not (chapter 5).

In courting Elizabeth-Jane as his long-lost daughter, he gives her 'a box of delicately tinted gloves one spring day'. In itself a pair of gloves is not perhaps remarkable as a gift; it is the taste and thought that are implied in the words 'delicately tinted' that give a moment's pause. They force us to imagine Henchard standing in the shop, comparing and considering the gloves on offer, exercising his judgement and making a choice that satisfies at least the opinion of the narrator. And it adds a little to the significance the narrator invites us to place on the 'delicately tinted gloves' that they are the catalyst that stimulates Elizabeth-Jane finally to make use of some of the money to which she now has access to provide herself with fashionable clothes:

> She wanted to wear [the gloves], to show her appreciation of his kindness, but she had no bonnet that would harmonize. As an artistic indulgence she thought she would have such a bonnet. When she had a bonnet that would go with the gloves she had no dress that would go with the bonnet. It was now absolutely necessary to finish; she ordered the requisite article; and found that she had no sunshade to go with the dress. In for a penny in for a pound; she bought the sunshade; and the whole structure was at last complete.
>
> (chapter 15)

At once the new, carefully chosen display of clothing, what the narrator interestingly calls a 'structure', founded on Henchard's present, transforms her outward identity:

> Everybody was attracted, and some said that her bygone simplicity was the art that conceals art . . . she had produced an effect, a contrast; and it had been done on purpose. As a matter of fact this was not true, but it had its result; for as soon as Casterbridge thought her artful it thought her worth notice.

And the narrator notes the consequence of this single change of clothing for her inward sense of herself:

> altogether the time was an exciting one; sex had never before asserted itself in her so strongly, for in former days she had perhaps been too impersonally human to be distinctively feminine.

Although, characteristically, she weighs her lack of education against her new awareness of herself as a woman—'Better sell all this finery and buy myself grammar-books, and dictionaries, and a history of all the philosophies!'—she does not sell the finery.

After his competition with Farfrae has bankrupted him, Henchard accepts work with the Scotsman, but instead of dressing 'appropriately', he continues to wear his old corn-merchant suit. He understands that there is no more effective way of announcing his spiritual resistance to the change in his life and his resentment under it; the clothes, as they become more shabby and frayed, are also a reminder to Farfrae and Lucetta of the perpetual turning of the wheel of fortune.

It is in the same dress that he appears at a meeting of the town council, that is being held to formulate arrangements for the visit of a royal personage; he tells the council-members (remember he used to be Mayor), 'I have a particular reason for wishing to assist at the ceremony' (the royal visit and the conversation amongst the townsfolk are in chapter 37). Again the clothes are a reminder to his more successful fellow-townsmen of his former status, and of his present degradation. It is Farfrae as his replacement who voices the inevitable refusal.

When the Royal moment comes, Hardy again tells us of Henchard's dress; he 'had doggedly retained the fretted and weather-beaten garments of bygone years'. We also see him as Lucetta saw him: 'He was not only a journeyman, unable to appear as he formerly had appeared, but he disdained to appear as well as he might. Everybody else, from the mayor to the washer-woman, shone in new vesture according to means.' The narrator can't allow this version of Henchard to stand unchallenged, though: he comments that Henchard 'was far from attractive to a woman's eye, ruled as that is so largely by the superficies of things'. Behind the gender-stereotyping, his argument is that to an understanding more penetrating than Lucetta's (the narrator's own, that is) the clothes Henchard chooses to wear imply a nature and an intelligence worth more thoughtful consideration than Lucetta is able to give him.

As the Royal carriage draws up, and before anyone else can move, Henchard leaps to its side, and has to be hauled away by Farfrae, who tells him, roughly, to be off. Henchard gazes into Farfrae's eyes for a moment, and then leaves. After being so manhandled, he:

> had withdrawn behind the ladies' stand; and there he stood regarding with a stare of abstraction the spot on the lapel of his coat where Farfrae's hand had seized it. He put his own hand there, as if he could hardly realize such an outrage from one whom it had once been his wont to treat with ardent generosity.

The lapel of his coat is for minute or two as sensitive for Henchard as his skin, Farfrae's grasp might have been into his flesh, so intimately does Henchard feel it; under intense stress of emotion the boundary between self and the world constituted by clothes melts.

The narrator had said that Henchard's decision to retreat from the confrontation without provoking further conflict was unaccountable, but the gaze into the Scotsman's eye, the fingering of the fabric of his coat touched by Farfrae, even perhaps, unconsciously, the location of his withdrawal, behind the ladies' stand, are surely the fruit of thwarted and self-destructive love, and anticipate very clearly the wrestling match that Henchard precipitates the same evening.

The reaction of some of the working folk amongst the onlookers to the appearance in state of Farfrae and his wife is also of particular interest:

> In the crowd stood Coney, Buzzford, and Longways. 'Some difference between him now, and when he zung at the Dree Mariners,' said the first. ''Tis wonderful how he could get a lady of her quality to go snacks wi' en in such quick time.'
>
> 'True. Yet how folk do worship fine clothes. Now there's a better looking woman than she that nobody notices at all, because she's akin to that hontish fellow Henchard.'
>
> 'I could worship ye, Buzz, for saying that,' remarked Nance Mockridge. 'I do like to see the trimming pulled off such Christmas candles. I am quite unequal to the part of villain myself, or I'd give all my small silver to see that lady toppered. . . . And perhaps I shall soon,' she added significantly.

It is striking that Buzzford proposes 'fine clothes' as a synecdoche for Lucetta's wealth and 'Weltlust', for it is by their clothes, of course, that the figures at the centre of skimmity-ride that Nance anticipates will be recognised. And Nance's metaphor for Lucetta, a Christmas candle—one presumably decorated in bright red and green ribbon, or silver and gold tinsel, or some such festive wrapping—is at bottom also one of dress, dress that she would like to see stripped from Lucetta, leaving her a bare naked candle in the wind.

When the skimmity display that is carried around the town on the back of a donkey, comes near to the mayor's house, a maid in an attic gets the first view, and she tells her friend: 'The man has got on a blue coat and kerseymere leggings; he has black whiskers, and a reddish face.' (chapter 39) She offers no identification, but since we have recently seen Henchard in a worn-out suit of blue cloth, we might expect most onlookers to make the right connection; when it comes to the woman-figure though, the maid is able to be much more explicit:

> My—why—'tis dressed just as she was dressed when she sat in the front seat at the time the play-actors came to the Town-hall! . . . Her neck is uncovered, and her hair in bands, and her back-comb in place; she's got on a puce silk, and white stockings, and coloured shoes.

It is possible that the organisers of such a procession might have found some emblem, some object intimately associated with each target, by which to identify them; but Lucetta's style of dress in particular, so unusual in Casterbridge, made clothes the obvious choice. This has an interesting consequence, as Hardy narrates the sequel.

Lucetta hears the maids' conversation, and goes to a window to look, though she knows already what she will see. She cries: 'She's me—she's me—even to the parasol—my green parasol!', gives a hysterical laugh, and falls in a faint. Lucetta sees herself, makes the doppelgänger identification, and the uncanny strikes at her through what is perhaps her sharpest developed sense, that what she wears is intrinsic to her sense of her own identity. Thus, and unintentionally, by using Lucetta's own clothes, the skimmity organisers work a more directly fatal magic even than Susan Nunsuch's use of a red ribbon to distinguish the wax doll of Eustacia that she flung into the fire in *The Return of the Native*. And the effect does not end with Lucetta.

We don't know whether Henchard sees the ride itself, but we should not by now be surprised at the intensity of his response the following day to coming across the effigy dressed in his clothes. In the despair of self-disgust and loneliness, Michael approaches a weir-pool intending to drown himself, and he sees the figure turning in the current. He perceives the shape not as 'a man somewhat resembling him, but one in all respects his counterpart, his actual double', floating as if dead (chapter 41). Again it is the clothing that convinces the ex-mayor against all reason that what he sees is himself, that he is at once alive and dead. Henchard's response is to go home again, where he finds Elizabeth-Jane. He asks her to return with him to the pool, and when he stops short of it, he begs her to go and look in the weir and report what she sees there.

Hardy writes the traditional three-times sending; first Elizabeth Jane says she sees nothing; then that she sees a bundle of old clothes, and only on the third visit, with Henchard's urging in her ears, does she get her head close enough to the water to identify the skimmington effigy. Henchard's response is to wonder why only his is there, and not Lucetta's, to understand that the clothes on the effigies have saved him but killed her.

He feels that he has been preserved from death by a miracle, that (famously) 'Even I be in Somebody's hand', and of course the appearance of the effigy at the place and moment at which he intends to kill himself is either coincidence or agency, as you care to believe; but in order for it to have the intensely powerful effect that it does, Henchard has to recognise the clothes as his, as the appearance that he has presented to the world.

If you need more evidence of Henchard's awareness of the symbolic potential of dress, consider how he leaves Casterbridge in the face of Newson's imminent return. It is with a sense of the dramatic that he has:

> set himself up in fresh leggings, knee-naps and corduroys, and in other ways gone back to the working-clothes of his young-manhood, discarding for ever the shabby-genteel suit of cloth and rusty, silk hat that since his decline had characterized him in the Casterbridge streets as a man who had seen better days.

> (chapter 43)

And the narrator underlines the irony and self-pity inherent in the outfit—he:

> formed at this moment much the same picture as he had presented when entering Casterbridge for the first time, nearly a quarter of a century before; except, to be sure, that the serious addition to his years had considerably lessened the spring of his stride.

Later Henchard, in his aimless wandering, reviews the contents of his pack:

> Although everything he brought necessitated carriage at his own back he had secreted among his tools a few of Elizabeth-Jane's cast off belongings, in the shape of gloves, shoes, a scrap of her handwriting and the like; and in his pocket he carried a curl of her hair. Having looked at these things he closed them up again, and went onward.

> (chapter 44)

This fetishising of clothing as a representative of the passionately loved woman can well be compared with Boldwood's purchase of dress-lengths and jewellery in anticipation of his finally achieving Bathsheba. In *Far from the Madding Crowd* Hardy allows us (in something of an afterthought) to see this as evidence of Boldwood's insanity. Should we also think of Henchard as insane at the end? Well of course there is this difference, that Elizabeth-Jane has worn, indeed has outworn, these gloves and shoes, so they bear the impress of her hands and feet. Boldwood cannot experience the painful pleasure of touching the marks of the toes or the wear on a finger-tip (and if you doubt Hardy's own value for such evidences of human habitation, think, for instance of 'The Self-Unseeing').

I have tried here to glance at Hardy's understanding of the very wide range of significance that dress has in society; and more particularly to illuminate briefly his remarkable insight into the complex relationship amongst dress, body and psyche. But this is no more than a preliminary sketch for the much longer study the subject requires.

FURTHER READING

Criticism

Allingham, Philip V. "The Initial Publications of Thomas Hardy's Novella "The Romantic Adventures of a Milkmaid" in the *Graphic* and *Harper's* (Summer, 1883)." *Thomas Hardy Journal* 16, no. 3 (October 2000): 45-62.

Documents differences among the first printings of "The Romantic Adventures of a Milkmaid."

Cramer, Jeffrey S. "Introduction to 'The Spectre of the Real,' by Thomas Hardy and Florence Henniker." *Thomas Hardy Year Book,* no. 13 (1986): 6-12.

Recounts the professional relationship between Hardy and Florence Henniker during the composition and revisions of "The Spectre of the Real" and contrasts the writing style of the two authors.

Gatrell, Simon. "The Early Stages of Hardy's Fiction." In *Thomas Hardy Annual No. 2,* edited by Norman Page, pp. 3-29. Basingstoke, U.K.: Macmillan, 1984.

Discusses Hardy's journals as a source of insight into his writing process.

Johnstone, H. F. V. "Thomas Hardy and Old Poole." *Thomas Hardy Year Book,* no. 2 (1971): 84-7.

Examines references to the landmarks and general characteristics of the city of Poole in "To Please His Wife."

Potolsky, Matthew. "Hardy, Shaftesbury, and Aesthetic Education." *Studies in English Literature, 1500-1900* 46, no. 4 (autumn 2006): 863-78.

Contends that "Barbara of the House of Grebe" portrays aesthetic education as a vicious disciplinary action that results in social domination rather than in the ideal of moral improvement and personal harmony espoused by Victorian theorists.

Quinn, Maire A. "Thomas Hardy and the Short Story." In *Budmouth Essays on Thomas Hardy,* edited by F. B. Pinion, pp. 74-85. Dorchester, U.K.: The Thomas Hardy Society Ltd., 1976.

Illustrates the importance of folklore and local legend to the act of storytelling in Hardy's short fiction, and addresses Hardy's prevailing concern with irony.

Ray, Martin. "'A Tryst at an Ancient Earthwork.'" In *Thomas Hardy: A Textual Study of the Short Stories*, pp. 291-301. Aldershot, U.K.: Ashgate, 1997.

　　Focuses on the textual permutations of the various published versions of "A Tryst at an Ancient Earthwork."

Smith, J. B. "Dialect in Hardy's Short Stories." In *Thomas Hardy Annual No. 3*, edited by Norman Page, pp. 79-92. Basingstoke, U.K.: Macmillan, 1985.

　　Traces the regional sources of the dialects replicated in Hardy's stories.

Additional coverage of Hardy's life and career is contained in the following sources published by Gale: *Authors and Artists for Young Adults,* Vol. 69; *British Writers,* Vol. 6; *British Writers: The Classics,* Vols. 1, 2; *British Writers Retrospective Supplement,* Vol. 1; *Concise Dictionary of British Literary Biography,* 1890-1914; *Contemporary Authors,* Vols. 104, 123; *Dictionary of Literary Biography,* Vols. 18, 19, 135, 284; *DISCovering Authors*; *DISCovering Authors: British Edition*; *DISCovering Authors: Canadian Edition*; *DISCovering Authors Modules: Most-Studied Authors, Novelists,* and *Poets*; *DISCovering Authors 3.0*; *Encyclopedia of World Literature in the 20th Century,* Ed. 3; *Exploring Novels*; *Exploring Poetry*; *Literature and Its Times,* Vol. 2; *Literature Resource Center*; *Major 20th-Century Writers,* Eds. 1, 2; *Major 21st-Century Writers,* eBook 2005; *Modern British Literature,* Ed. 2; *Novels for Students,* Vols. 3, 11, 15, 19; *Poetry Criticism,* Vol. 8; *Poetry for Students,* Vols. 3, 4, 18; *Reference Guide to English Literature,* Ed. 2; *Reference Guide to Short Fiction,* Ed. 2; *Short Story Criticism,* Vols. 2, 60; *Twayne's English Authors*; *Twentieth-Century Literary Criticism,* Vols. 4, 10, 18, 32, 48, 53, 72, 143, 153; *World Literature and Its Times,* Ed. 4; and *World Literature Criticism,* Vol. 3.

Thomas Wolfe
1900-1938

(Full name Thomas Clayton Wolfe) American short fiction writer, novelist, poet, essayist, playwright, and author of nonfiction.

The following entry provides an overview of Wolfe's short fiction. For additional information on his short fiction career, see *SSC*, Volume 33.

INTRODUCTION

A highly autobiographical writer with a mixed critical reception, Wolfe is increasingly regaining his once-solid standing as one of the twentieth century's great authors. Although in his lifetime he achieved grand success with the novels *Look Homeward, Angel* (1929) and *Of Time and the River* (1935), his writing style was also the subject of harsh criticism just before he died and for many years thereafter. In recent decades, however, Wolfe's reputation has been reestablished as critics have begun to focus on his impressive body of short fiction.

BIOGRAPHICAL INFORMATION

The youngest child of seven, Wolfe was born to William Oliver and Julia Elizabeth Wolfe in Asheville, North Carolina, at the start of the twentieth century. Wolfe's father, a Pennsylvania native, was a lively, spirited stonecutter who enjoyed reciting Shakespeare. His mother began operating a boardinghouse near the family's home when her youngest son was six years old, and from that time on she resided there, along with all of the couple's children except one daughter. She later found success in real estate investment. Her personality and behavior influenced her children's development and years later they were portrayed in detail in Wolfe's fictionalized accounts of childhood. Wolfe's brother Grover was perhaps just as influential to Wolfe's youth and later career; the boy, who died when the future writer was only four years old, became the subject of much meditation in Wolfe's adulthood.

The young Wolfe started public school in Asheville, but after excelling and attracting the attention of a private school's administrators, he switched in 1912.

There he studied arts, classical literature, and writing until enrolling at the University of North Carolina at Chapel Hill at age fifteen to study drama. Many experiences from these years were later fictionalized in *Look Homeward, Angel,* including Wolfe's romance with one of his mother's boarders. Wolfe's first play, *The Return of Buck Gavin,* was performed at the university by the Carolina Playmakers in early 1919 and was received well, leading him to follow undergraduate study with graduate work at Harvard in 1920. There he was influenced by drama teacher George Pierce Baker, who led the famed 47 Workshop for playwrights, and by the theories of John Livingston Lowes. Wolfe completed his master's work in 1922 and, after New York producers failed to show interest in his plays, he took a position in 1924 at New York University's Washington Square College, where he taught composition off and on until 1930.

Also in 1924, Wolfe traveled to Europe for the first time—a trip that would prove pivotal. Not only did Wolfe meet and spend time with Sinclair Lewis and F. Scott Fitzgerald, but more significantly to both his personal life and his career, he also met successful New York set designer Aline Bernstein aboard ship on his return to the United States in 1925. Wolfe's five-year relationship with the much-older Bernstein turned out to be the most important romance of his life. Because of the writer's narrative, descriptive style, Bernstein encouraged Wolfe to shift his focus from drama to fiction and to draw from his own life for story lines. Beyond emotional and critical support, the wealthy Bernstein also provided Wolfe with financial assistance, supporting him while they lived together in Manhattan and he worked on his first novel. Wolfe initially struggled to find a publisher for the lengthy, somewhat disheveled, manuscript based on his own youth and family until Scribner editor Maxwell Perkins reviewed it and, seeing its potential, decided to work with Wolfe to make the book publishable—helping him to both reorganize it and substantially shorten it. *Look Homeward, Angel* was published in 1929 to wide acclaim.

Wolfe resigned from New York University the following year and just one month later received a Guggenheim fellowship, at which time he traveled to Europe to focus on his writing. His sequel to his first book, equally autobiographical and even more successful, appeared in 1935. *Of Time and the River* follows the Wolfe-like character Eugene Gant through the first half of the 1920s and documents, among other things, Wolfe's by-now-ended relationship with Bernstein through the characters of Gant and Esther Jack. The year 1935 was an important one for Wolfe; it also included publication of his first short-fiction collection, *From Death to Morning.* The following year, the writer embarked on his final trip to Europe, where he spent substantial time in Germany, his translated books being very popular there. This last trip left him disillusioned with a country he had once enjoyed, as he came to see and understand the changes taking place there under Adolf Hitler—a realization chronicled in his writings. While traveling in July 1938, shortly after delivering a large crate of disorganized writings to editor Edward Aswell, Wolfe fell ill. Treatment and operations were unsuccessful, and several months later, he died from related tuberculosis of the brain.

MAJOR WORKS OF SHORT FICTION

Wolfe's short fiction, which arguably proved to be a more suitable vehicle for the writer's talents than novels, is collected in several volumes, only one of which appeared before his early death. Published just eight months after Wolfe's second novel, *From Death to Morning* includes thirteen short stories and the novella *The Web of Earth,* in which a character based on Wolfe's mother narrates her life story. Like many of Wolfe's short works, the stories are connected to his novels in various ways; the same themes persist, and the stories often originated as episodes from larger works that were cut before publication. The volume is characterized by Wolfe's signature autobiographical tendencies and themes of isolation and death. Among the collection's stories are "No Door," "Only the Dead Know Brooklyn," and "Death the Proud Brother," all of which echo Wolfe's main themes. "No Door" is a prime example of the ways in which Wolfe's works interconnected and flowed in and out of one another. The story published in *From Death to Morning* as "No Door" was also the first part of a longer, four-part novella, also titled *No Door,* that appeared in *Scribner's Magazine* in 1933, with all four parts describing different periods of loneliness and the attempts to escape from it. Sections of the larger work were interspersed throughout *Of Time and the River.* In "Death the Proud Brother," the narrator is shaken upon witnessing several violent and untimely deaths, experiences which underscore in the character's mind the indifference to human life in a meaningless universe. Upon observing a man's natural death on a subway, Wolfe's narrator expresses hope, recognizing the dignity and pride in the fact that death can be shared by all. "Only the

Dead Know Brooklyn" is another example of Wolfe's representation of himself and the search for home—the character who wanders Brooklyn in this story even resembles Wolfe physically. A metaphor for an inner search, the man's journey through the borough, during which he ponders the city's geography and the notion of drowning, is simultaneously reminiscent of Wolfe's own late-night wanderings through Brooklyn. The development of Wolfe's social consciousness is apparent in such tales as "The Bums at Sunset," which features a group of transients awaiting the arrival of a train. Although he was known for his autobiographical style, he also increasingly tapped into the individual experiences, struggles, and loneliness that he witnessed in others.

The second collection of Wolfe's stories did not appear until after his death, with editor Aswell organizing manuscripts left behind by Wolfe into *The Hills Beyond* (1941), the most lauded stories of which are "The Lost Boy" and "Chickamauga." The first, in thinly fictionalized form, is the story of Wolfe's brother Grover and his death, an event which pre occupied Wolfe throughout his life. With four sections narrated from four points of view, the story features strong characterizations and is considered by critics to be one of Wolfe's best short works. "The Lost Boy" was published in several incarnations of varying lengths over the years, culminating in the 1992 publication of Wolfe's original, novella-length version. The latter is a tale narrated by an elderly Civil War veteran who tells of his friendship with a fellow soldier, a vibrant young man whose love for a woman drives his every thought and action until he is killed in the bloodiest battle of the war.

Other short works by Wolfe include the novella *The Party at Jack's,* originally published in *Scribner's Magazine* in 1939 just months after Wolfe's death, and "I Have a Thing to Tell You," which appeared in the *New Republic* in 1937. The former, set in Depression-era Manhattan, presents a gathering of socialites in an apartment building that is disturbed by episodes of underground tremors. The latter is an account of an incident that Wolfe witnessed on the Berlin-to-Paris train in 1936, when a frightened Jewish traveler was seized at the border by Nazi authorities. Both of these works, written in the last two years of Wolfe's life, demonstrate his shift to a more objective focus on social issues and their effects on people's lives, rather than on Wolfe's own personal history or an individual's private sorrows.

CRITICAL RECEPTION

The observations of Wolfe's critics have been, for the most part, uniform. Many have faulted him for depending too much on his own life for his plots and characters, and also for relying too heavily on his editors. Even in Wolfe's lifetime, some argued that his verbose books were as much the work of his editors as they were his own. They further claimed that Wolfe's habit of delivering to his editors manuscripts that were almost epic in length and without form or organization—and then allowing the editors to piece together the final product—reflected rather poorly on his skills as a writer. In recent years, however, other scholars have come to Wolfe's defense, contending that his style of writing was just that—an intentional style that was sometimes thwarted or mangled by his editors. Further, critics have increasingly argued that Wolfe's talents should not be judged on the basis of his novels and that his finest work can be seen in his more tightly structured short fiction. Recent years have featured efforts by Wolfe scholars to refocus on these short works and to rescue many of Wolfe's original and developing manuscripts, which, they have noted, offer insight into his complicated writing process and the intertwined nature of his works. Although criticism of his work was negative for a time, his writings are now being revisited and reexamined from different perspectives, with greater emphasis on his short fiction.

PRINCIPAL WORKS

Short Fiction

*From Death to Morning 1935
†"The Lost Boy" 1937; published in journal *Redbook Magazine*
‡"The Party at Jack's" 1939; published in journal *Scribner's Magazine*
§*The Hills Beyond* 1941
Stories by Thomas Wolfe 1944
The Short Novels of Thomas Wolfe (novellas) 1961
The Complete Short Stories of Thomas Wolfe 1987
The Good Child's River 1991

Other Major Works

The Return of Buck Gavin (play) 1919
Look Homeward, Angel: A Story of the Buried Life (novel) 1929
Of Time and the River: A Legend of Man's Hunger in His Youth (novel) 1935
The Story of a Novel (essay) 1936
The Face of a Nation: Poetical Passages from the Writings of Thomas Wolfe (poetry) 1939
The Web and the Rock (novel) 1939
You Can't Go Home Again (novel) 1940

Gentlemen of the Press: A Play (play) 1942
A Stone, A Leaf, A Door (poetry) 1945
Mannerhouse: A Play in a Prologue and Three Acts (play) 1948
A Western Journal: A Daily Log of the Great Parks Trip, June 20-July 2, 1938 (travel essay) 1951
The Letters of Thomas Wolfe (letters) 1956
The Letters of Thomas Wolfe to His Mother (letters) 1968
The Mountains: A Play in One Act (play) 1970
The Notebooks of Thomas Wolfe. 2 vols. (journal) 1970
‖*Beyond Love and Loyalty: The Letters of Thomas Wolfe and Elizabeth Nowell* (letters) 1983
My Other Loneliness: Letters of Thomas Wolfe and Aline Bernstein (letters) 1983
Welcome to Our City: A Play in Ten Scenes (play) 1983
The Starwick Episodes (novel fragment) 1994

*This volume contains the novella *The Web of Earth,* as well as the stories "No Door," "The Sun and the Rain," "Only the Dead Know Brooklyn," and "The Bums of Sunset," among others.

†A different version of this work was included in Wolfe's short story collection *The Hills Beyond* in 1941; it was published separately in 1965; and it was published in its complete novella form in 1992.

‡A novella-length version of this title was published in 1995.

§The stories "The Lost Boy" and "Chickamauga" are included in this collection.

‖Includes Wolfe's short story "No More Rivers."

CRITICISM

Sharon Doten (essay date 1974)

SOURCE: Doten, Sharon. "Thomas Wolfe's 'No Door': Some Textual Questions." *Papers of the Bibliographical Society of America* 68 (1974): 45-52.

[*In the following essay, Doten examines the connections between Wolfe's novels and his short fiction, focusing in particular on "No Door" and its various incarnations in and ties to* Of Time and the River.]

The recent rediscovery of a neglected portion of the work of Thomas Wolfe, the short stories and short novels that he published in periodicals during the 1930s, has led to a revaluation of the significance of these pieces for Wolfe's artistic reputation.[1] These recent studies, however, have failed to confront, or even to note, the textual problems that complicate critical assessment of the short fiction. The textual history of a short novel entitled **"No Door"** illustrates that the authority of existing texts has not yet been established. It is hoped that this example will lead to further examination of questions that should be answered before scholars attempt to determine the extent to which Wolfe's reputation as a writer depends on his short fiction.

The textual problems originate in the fact that Wolfe wrote and published most of these stories concurrently with work on his second novel, *Of Time and the River* (1935). Frequently he simply excerpted portions of the manuscript of the forthcoming novel and reworked them for periodical publication. With the exception of a change from a first to third person protagonist, the stories appear in the novel exactly as they did in the periodicals. Most of the stories appear as separate and distinct episodes in the novel, but a few are divided into parts that appear in various places throughout the novel interspersed with episodes not included in the short story version.

Manuscript and typescript evidence, as well as Wolfe's letters during this period, seem to indicate that many of the short pieces were originally parts of the novel in progress. Hence most of the stories published in periodicals appear in almost the same form in the subsequently published novel, *Of Time and the River.* Following the publication of that novel, Wolfe used his leftover material in *From Death to Morning* (1935), a collection composed entirely of short stories not included in *Of Time and the River.* The two books, published within eight months of each other in March and November of 1935, bear witness to Wolfe's need to use his material to his best financial advantage. The absence of any stories that had been included in *Of Time and the River* from the collection of stories also suggests the possibility that Wolfe may have felt that the stories which had become parts of his published novel should no longer be presented separately.

Wolfe seems not to have considered himself a short story writer. Biographical studies of this period in his life emphasize that Wolfe did not choose the form, but was driven to it by financial demands and a necessity to keep his name before his audience during the extended lapse between *Look Homeward Angel* (1929) and *Of Time and the River.*[2] His editors have testified to the difficulties that Wolfe encountered in his attempt to adapt his inclusive style to the short story.[3]

Much of the current interest in the short fiction has been generated by C. Hugh Holman's edition of *The Short Novels of Thomas Wolfe* (Scribner's, 1961), which has made readily available some of the periodical pieces not included in *From Death to Morning.* Because these pieces present the most complex problems, it is from them that I chose the example **"No Door"** although the specific problems encountered in

seeking a definitive text are not significantly different from the textual problems presented by the stories in general.

"No Door" first appeared as a short novel in four sections in *Scribner's Magazine,* July 1933. Each of the sections is designated by a date, and each deals with a period of wandering and loneliness. The four sections present a series of reflections on the theme of loneliness and the fruitless search for a home, symbolically represented by the search for "a door." Two years after publishing the magazine story, Wolfe scattered the sections of **"No Door"** throughout *Of Time and the River.* Parts of the story appear on pages 2, 90-93, 327-34, 601-08, and 611-13.[4]

Wolfe then took the first section of the magazine version of **"No Door,"** none of which was included in *Of Time and the River,* and used it as the first story in the collection **From Death to Morning.** To further confuse the issue, the single section is also entitled **"No Door."** This abbreviated version varies from the first section of the *Scribner's Magazine* text in accidentals and in the text of one paragraph.[5] A final fragment of **"No Door"** was incorporated into the posthumous *You Can't Go Home Again.*[6]

In his edition of the short novels, Holman resurrected the *Scribner's Magazine* version of **"No Door"** and added to it another story, **"The House of the Far and Lost,"** published by *Scribner's Magazine,* August 1934, to constitute the short novel that he also entitled **"No Door."** Holman used the text of the shorter version in **From Death to Morning** for the first section, the *Scribner's Magazine* text for the remaining sections of **"No Door,"** and the *Scribner's Magazine* text for **"The House of the Far and Lost."** He inserted the latter story into section three of the magazine version of **"No Door."** Like the **"No Door"** material, the material from **"The House of the Far and Lost"** also appears in *Of Time and the River.*[7] In his headnote Holman explains that he based the decision to combine the stories on a letter from Wolfe to Robert Raynolds. Feeling that the letter indicated Wolfe's intention for the stories to be one unit, Holman concluded that by combining the two he had restored the original story as written.[8]

The manuscript and typescript material relating to the story, now housed in the William C. Wisdom Collection in the Houghton Library at Harvard University,[9] reveals an original tentative plan for the short novel to include as many as nine sections. Two problems complicate study of the material. The first is the difficulty of verifying the order and arrangement of the various versions. Unlike *Look Homeward Angel,* which was written in bound ledgers, *Of Time and the River* was written in pencil on loose sheets of 8½ by 11 inch newsprint paper. Since most of the stories published in periodicals were written as part of the novel and eventually found their way into it, manuscripts and typescripts of the stories are themselves parts of the manuscript and typescript material of the novel as well. The loose sheets have been regrouped several times so that it is impossible to know what order, if any, Wolfe intended for them. The only clues to order and arrangement of the material are a series of page numbers in pencil in the lower left corner of the sheets. The numbering is done with a light and precise hand, however, and is thus very different from the heavy scrawl of Wolfe's handwritten text. The discrepancy in style creates uncertainty about the origin and authorship of the pagination.[10]

Secondly since the stories were envisioned by Wolfe as episodes in a long novel, many sections that relate to **"No Door"** material were not used in the periodical version. Thus no separate manuscript of the Scribner's text exists. The various manuscripts and typescripts each include several sections, some but not all of which were published in the various versions of **"No Door."**

The Wisdom Collection includes an incomplete manuscript of **"No Door,"** manuscript material for all of **"The House of the Far and Lost,"** a complete typescript of **"No Door"** identified by galley and typeface markings as that used by the printer to set up the *Scribner's Magazine* story, seven incomplete typescripts of **"No Door,"**[11] one incomplete typescript of material from **"The House of the Far and Lost,"** and two carbon copies of this last incomplete typescript. While it is both impractical and unnecessary to describe all of this material in detail, a brief summary of the evidence bears on the question of the text of **"No Door."**

The incomplete manuscript of **"No Door"** includes 65 penciled leaves of loose yellow sheets, usually written on one side only. The first two paginated leaves carry lists referring to numbered sections. On the first leaf the list names seven sections as follows:

1. Of wandering forever and the earth again

2. Brooklyn scene (September: 1931)

3. October had come again October: [1923] November the Seventh [Nov. 7, 1923]

4. The Hudson River Meets the Harbor [November: 19]

5. Time is a Fable and a Mystery, etc. June [1927]

6. The Station May 3, [1928]

7. The Man in the Window [June: 1928] April late April[12]

Below this list is a series of dates:

September: 1931

October: 1923

November 7, 1923

September: 1926

June: 1927

May 3, 1928

June: 1928

The entire leaf is canceled with three vertical lines, yet it shows Wolfe's early plans for the material. The evidence suggests that Wolfe originally intended to include seven sections, and indeed 1, 2, 3 and 7 of this list did become part of the published **"No Door."** The second leaf, also canceled, repeats the same list of sections. The third leaf, which also contains notes about the organization of the story, is uninformative and probably not in Wolfe's hand.

The text of the story begins on leaf four with material that was published as the first section of **"No Door."** The manuscript corresponds to the first section of the published story until leaf 47 where it ends with a row of asterisks. The forty-eighth leaf contains only one line, and does not follow logically from the preceding leaf. Leaves 49 through 51 appear to be other versions of first section material. Leaf 52 begins with a row of asterisks and then moves into section two. Then the material continues to correspond to the published versions until its abrupt end on leaf 65, one quarter of the way into the second section.[13]

The typescript used by the Scribner's printer provides the most complete information as to text, but also raises more questions. It is divided into two parts, both marked with typeface and galley numbers and revised in pencil on the copy. The first section is stamped in red "May 17 Rec'd" and the second "May 19 Rec'd." Since neither part corresponds exactly to the published story, the story must have been further revised on galley or page proofs, no longer extant.

The first part of the typescript used by the printer contains 44 leaves, paginated in sequence in pencil at the top of each page.[14] In this first part none of the variations from the published version affects the story line. Subsequent revision seems to have consisted of cutting down lengthy descriptions and explanations. The second part of the typescript includes 45 leaves, again paginated at the top of the page, but beginning on page 104. Beside this page number a note explains:

> Rush! Disregard fact that there is a gap in page numbers between part previously sent over and this part. ASD[15]

There are no clues as to what may have been on the pages deleted between sections two and three.

The second portion of the typescript contains a substantial amount of unpublished material, including a separate episode that never appeared in the magazine story. The episode describes an afternoon of drunken revelry spent by the protagonist with a group of Rhodes scholars at Oxford. It appears in this typescript on pages 127 to 132 or at about the point at which Holman later inserted **"The House of the Far and Lost"** in his edition of the story. This same episode appears on pages 652 to 655 of *Of Time and the River,* after the material published as **"The House of the Far and Lost."** It has never been included in any published version of **"No Door,"** and was evidently cut out of the *Scribner's Magazine* text at some time after the story had reached galley proofs. The final section of the magazine version follows, above which the number "9" has been deleted and "5" substituted. The typescript version of the section is longer and more detailed than the published text, in which the section is numbered "4."

The evidence of this typescript presents two problems concerning the text of the short novel. First, since the typescript provides no clues as to the material on pages 45 to 103 not sent to the printer, an attempt to substitute another story in this position must be regarded as an arbitrary editorial decision. Secondly, the numerical designation of sections in this typescript and the lists of sections among the manuscript material permit the conjecture that there may originally have been nine sections of the story, which were cut to five in this typescript, and then to four before publication. The number of sections may have been reduced because of limits on the amount of space available in the periodical. While the two problems remain unsolved, they contribute to the difficulty of determining the definitive length of **"No Door"** as a short novel.

The rest of the **"No Door"** material includes seven partial typescripts that provide little additional information. Four contain material from section one, and three material from section four. Each typescript varies slightly from the published version, but the variations are not significant for our purposes here.

There is no manuscript as such for **"The House of the Far and Lost."** Instead the material from which the story was taken is part of the manuscript of *Of Time and the River* and follows the order of the novel rather than that of the short story. The manuscript begins like section three of **"No Door"** and roughly corresponds to the short novel. Nevertheless the manuscript frequently includes material that did not become part of the short story. In most instances the unpublished material corresponds in text to sections of *Of Time and the River.*

The manuscript material provides evidence concerning Wolfe's method of composition and the development of this part of the novel from one version to the next, but it does not give information about the origin of the short story. The typescripts are equally unenlightening for the study of the periodical version. None of this material provides any information as to how or why the short story was assembled, in what form it originated, or its relation to the earlier *Scribner's Magazine* story **"No Door."**

The most difficult problem encountered in the study of the texts is that the evidence is ample to raise many questions but not sufficient to provide many answers. It does, however, suggest two major areas of concern that must be investigated before scholars can begin to make broad generalizations about the significance of the stories.

The first task is to determine a definitive text for each story. In the example of **"No Door,"** one might select one of the three published states, the *Scribner's Magazine* version, the version of *From Death to Morning,* or Holman's version, or create an eclectic text. At present the problem of an authoritative text remains unsolved, not only for **"No Door,"** but for many of the other stories as well.

Beyond the problem of specific texts, however, is a far more general and important concern. All of the evidence of manuscript and biographical material suggests that **"No Door,"** and possibly many of the other stories, cannot be disassociated from the novel *Of Time and the River.* The stories were written as episodes in the novel, and in manuscript they remain part of the novel. Biographical data reveals that Wolfe did not enjoy writing for periodicals and did it primarily for the financial reward. Can stories written under these conditions be considered on an equal basis with the novels to which Wolfe directed his full energy?

Recent studies have begun to adopt the position, first advanced by Holman, that in the short novels Wolfe displays a sense of form that is absent from his huge, rambling novels, and thus that the short novels show his true artistic potential. This assertion radically affects Wolfe's reputation as a writer. Before so important a claim is made, much more attention must be directed to such textual matters as are noted here.

Notes

1. Among these recent articles see especially: C. Hugh Holman, "Introduction," *The Short Novels of Thomas Wolfe* (New York: Charles Scribner's Sons, 1961); Walter A. Powell, "Thomas Wolfe's Short Novels as Related to his Long Fiction," Diss. University of South Carolina 1967; Clayton L. Eichelberger, "Wolfe's 'No Door' and the Brink of Discovery," *Georgia Review*, 21 (1967), 319-27; and Robert Spiller, "Thomas Wolfe is Still at the Door," *Sewanee Review*, 71 (Autumn 1963), 658-59.

2. Wolfe mentions his financial difficulties in letters to Stringfellow Barr, George McCoy, and to his sister Mabel Wolfe Wheaton. See *The Letters of Thomas Wolfe*, ed. Elizabeth Nowell (New York: Charles Scribner's Sons, 1956), pp. 325, 330, 359. He discusses the origin of the material in letters to Margaret Roberts, Maxwell Perkins, George Wallace, Robert Raynolds, and Henry Allen Moe. See *Letters*, pp. 169, 357, 365, 371, 385-86, 406, 413. Finally, in an unpublished letter to Mr. Moe he lists several stories (among them "No Door") and explains: "The relation of these various pieces to *Time and the River* is as follows: all of them, with the exception of *The Web of Earth*, were written as part of *Time and the River* and will be used in the book."

"You will understand, of course, that it was necessary to modify most of these pieces for magazine publication, and they will be used in the book, more or less, in their original form."

"In general, the chief modifications for the magazine were made by supplying beginnings and endings which would make them units for magazine publication, cutting and shortening to meet the magazine's space requirement, and occasionally deleting words and passages which did not seem to me in any way offensive, but which, apparently, can not be printed in a magazine."

"The other main change, I believe, is that the book throughout is written in the third person, but most of the magazine pieces make use of the first person. The chief reason for this being that in most of these magazine pieces the 'I' is not the central character but the narrator of events."

"With the above exceptions, most of the pieces will appear in the book more or less as printed in the magazine. The piece called 'No Door,' however, is composed of four episodes selected from various times and places in the book because of a unity of feeling and intention, and because their relation to one another in the magazine piece is, I think, apparent. The *No Door* piece, therefore, will go back into the book in the way it was originally written and not in the way it is here printed in the magazine." [T.l.s. 8 Feb. 1934, in Charles Scribner's Sons File, Princeton University Library, Princeton, N.J. I would like to thank William S. Dix and the Princeton University Library for permission to quote from this letter in their Scribner's Archive.]

3. See especially Charles Angoff, "Thomas Wolfe and the Opulent Manner," *Southwest Review*, 48 (Winter 1963), 81-84, and Maxwell Perkins, "Thomas Wolfe," *Harvard Library Bulletin* (Autumn 1947).

4. All page references are to the Charles Scribner's Sons edition (New York 1935).

5. The variant paragraph appears in *Scribner's Magazine*, July 1933, on page 11, column 1, lines 48-55 and column 2, lines 1-4. Cf. *From Death to Morning* (New York: Charles Scribner's Sons, 1935), p. 12, lines 1-3.

6. Thomas Wolfe, *You Can't Go Home Again* (New York: Harper and Brothers, 1940), pp. 27-44.

7. *Of Time and the River*, pp. 612-27, 637-52.

8. Holman quotes a portion of the following paragraph from a letter from Wolfe to Robert Raynolds, dated 2 Feb. 1934. *Letters*, p. 405: "I sold another story to *Scribner's*, and no longer have any confidence in my power of selection. Perkins has the most tender and paternal affection for the piece I ever saw in any editor, and swears he never saw it before, and why had I never shown it to him, which somewhat bewilders me since I wrote it seven or eight months ago as part of the manuscript that was printed as 'No Door,' and which we cut out of the magazine as being something which could go. Now, it appears, it is a gem of purest ray serene, with the same haunting strangeness as 'La Belle Dame Sans Merci,' but ye author goggles like an idiot now when he hears these words, grins stupidly and says, 'Yes sir. . . .'"

Wolfe goes on in the next paragraph to say: "The only surprising thing about this is that I swear I showed it to him two or three years ago when I wrote it, and he swears just as positively that he never saw it until a few weeks ago. It's pretty bewildering, but, then, isn't it beautiful to think of all the buried masterpieces which I will be able to unearth out of these manuscripts and give to the world after my seventieth year."

9. I would like to express my appreciation to Paul Gitlin, Wolfe's literary executor, for permission to examine the manuscripts, and to the Houghton Library staff for their kind assistance.

10. Pagination of this material is rather complex. All the material discussed herein is paginated in the lower left corner in this unknown hand. There are also three other instances of pagination on different manuscripts and typescripts. A typescript of section four is paginated in the lower right corner, in what appears to be Wolfe's hand with the numbers 74-88, 95-113, 115, and two unpaginated leaves. A version of section one is paginated in the upper right corner, again in a hand apparently Wolfe's, consecutively 1 to 14. A typescript of material from "The House of the Far and Lost" is paginated at the top of the page, in this same hand, 67 to 98 and 102 to 105, after which the leaves are unpaginated. A final pagination, on the typescript used by the Scribner's printer, will be discussed separately later in this paper.

11. Five of these typescripts appear to be carbons of the others (two of section one material and three of section four material), but since all have been to some extent revised in pencil by Wolfe, the result is different versions, which I have listed as separate typescripts.

12. I have inserted brackets to indicate material deleted with lines drawn through it in pencil on this holograph page.

13. The manuscript breaks off after ". . . or finally that I would write a book or play every year or so, which would be a great success, and yield me fifteen or twenty thousand dollars at a crack," which corresponds to page 173, line 20 of the Holman edition.

14. This pagination is in addition to that previously described, which is in the lower left corner of all this material.

15. The initials indicate that the note was written by Albert S. Dashiell, then editor of *Scribner's Magazine*.

James Boyer (essay date fall 1982)

SOURCE: Boyer, James. "The Metaphorical Level in Wolfe's 'The Sun and the Rain.'" *Studies in Short Fiction* 19, no. 4 (fall 1982): 384-87.

[*In the following essay, Boyer analyzes Wolfe's use of metaphor in "The Sun and the Rain," specifically his allusions to the earth, his extolment of simplicity, and his use of train imagery.*]

Thomas Wolfe wrote a significant body of fiction about events taking place on a train. Four different short stories—**"The Train and the City," "The Sun and the**

Rain," "Dark in the Forest, Strange as Time," and **"I Have a Thing to Tell You"**—as well as the long opening section for *Of Time and the River,* narrate events involving people accidentally thrown together there for a brief time. Some of this material came from the aborted *K-19,* an early novel framed by a train ride from New York to Lybia Hill (Asheville), a work which Max Perkins had persuaded Wolfe not to publish in 1932.[1] For Wolfe, the train remained a central metaphor of life: a few strangers sharing brief moments, the swift motion of the train always set against the vast, eternal earth.

During 1934 Wolfe and Perkins had been working together to get *Of Time and the River* ready for publication. Sprinkled throughout that manuscript were various short episodes, complete in themselves, with which Wolfe had intended to comment on or clarify the general direction of the novel. Some of these, like **"The Far and the Near,"** were finally cut because they were presented as visions and moved the novel away from Eugene Gant, on whom Perkins felt it should maintain focus. **"The Sun and the Rain,"** since it did present a small part of Eugene's trip south through France, stayed in the novel but was published first as a story in *Scribner's Magazine* in May, 1934. Though one of the shortest Wolfe published, it is a significant story, illustrating how skillful he had become at transforming experience into fiction and at using narrative as metaphor.

We find the raw material for the story in a brief account from the *Notebooks* of a trip Wolfe had taken through France in early 1925:

> I came here at evening, in a train mixed of freight and animals—I came with the animals—peasants from the North, a man and his two women. I smoked cigarettes at the time to kill the flat sharp rancid smell of their bodies—I gave them cigarettes. At Patay I had to change—the new compartment was lit by a smoky lamp. Peasants again, men and women, who shouted humorous, but not good humored, obscenities to the guards at each station—crying for more warmth.[2]

The dramatic transformation of this 1925 passage, with its feeling of strong repulsion for the peasants, into **"The Sun and the Rain"** reveals much about Wolfe's growth in technique and about his increasing identification with the common man during the 1930s.

The plot is simple enough. A young American enters a compartment on the train for Orleans and meets three peasants—a father, a mother and their daughter. He offers the father a cigarette, and the old man questions him about his destination and nationality. They have difficulty communicating in French, and the daughter—dark, sullen, ashamed of her parents—becomes exasperated with her father, calling him stupid for his inability to understand the young man's French. As the men continue to attempt conversation, she acts as translator, all the while heaping abuse on her father. But the peasant, undaunted, believing that the young man needs to learn French, proceeds to "teach" him three words—sun, rain, earth: "Le soleil . . . la pluie . . . la terre." And the youth indulgently plays along. When the time comes for him to change trains, he shakes hands with the peasants, and they help him find the train he is to take. As his train pulls out, he waves to the old man, who is still pointing toward the sun.

Wolfe's writing in this story exhibits unusual economy: no authorial comment is made on the action, and there are no lyric digressions. The language is more like Hemingway's. Of the young man's departure, Wolfe writes, "In the afternoon he went down to the station and took a train that was going to Orleans. He did not know where Orleans was. The train was a mixed train, made up of goods, cars, and passenger compartments. He bought a third-class ticket and got into one of the compartments. Then the shrill little whistle blew, and the train rattled out of Chartres into the countryside." In this manner throughout the story sentences are short, concrete, narrative; the reader is given only a spare account of what happens and what is said. And as the peasants depart at the story's close, Wolfe stays with this presentation of concrete fact: "Then they were lost from sight, the train swiftly left the little town behind, and now there was nothing but the fields, the earth, the smoky and mysterious distances. The rain fell steadily." There is no attempt to sum up the experience for the reader.

The characters, too, are sketched with economy, the focus maintained on the earthy qualities of the faces of the older peasants. The father has a "sprouting mustache" and a "weather-beaten face." The wife's face is "like an old brown bowl." Of the daughter we learn that she had a "dark, sullen face" and that she sat away from the peasants "as if she was ashamed of them."

We understand the girl's embarrassment, the feeling of the young who have had more education than their parents. The girl knows what is happening: her father doesn't understand that the American knows the words, has studied the language and speaks it. And on the surface level the girl is right. But Wolfe lets us recognize that in his innocence and friendliness the old peasant has not only the greater humanity, but the greater wisdom (the American really doesn't understand).

Like Delia in Wolfe's short novel, *The Web of Earth,* the older peasants have the strength of the earth in them. That strength grows not from learning, not even so much from experience, but from a closeness to and a harmony with the earth and natural processes. And, of course, the words the peasant teaches the youth— "Le soleil . . . la pluie . . . la terre"—say much more than the peasant knows: they direct the youth back to basic matters, to simplicity, to those things that are enduring and eternal. Wolfe later put the idea into a fine lyric passage used in *You Can't Go Home Again*: "All things belonging to the earth will never change—the leaf, the blade, the flower, the wind that cries and sleeps and wakes again, the tree whose stiff arms clash and tremble in the dark, and the dust of lovers long since buried in the earth—all things proceeding from the earth to seasons, all things that lapse and change and come again upon the earth—these things will always be the same, for they come up from the earth that never changes, they go back into the earth that lasts forever. Only the earth endures, but it endures forever."[3]

The needs of the young American are clearer, of course, in *Of Time and the River,* since we know what has come before. Eugene, an aspiring writer whose career has produced no tangible successes, has left America in a furious state of mind, has traveled first to England, then to France, trying to find some peace and a place to do his writing. In Paris he met Frank Starwick, a decadent college friend, and together with two women they traveled through the countryside, their trip one long drinking bout that ended in angry quarrels, separation, and for Eugene disappointment in love and in friendship. It is in a desperate state of mind growing out of these events that Eugene takes the train for Orleans and meets the peasants.

And this is a turning point for Eugene; though he still faces many trials, including the famous episode of the fight at the Octoberfest in Munich, he does begin here to find himself and the earth again.

Virtually everything in **"The Sun and the Rain"** functions on a metaphorical level: the land, "fat and well kept," introduces the story and assumes an almost life-like quality; the old peasant, with his "sprouting" mustache and his "seamed, weather-beaten face" and hands "with rock-like heaviness," seems an animate extension of the earth itself; the failure of communication between the old man and the youth represents the failure in general of the intellectual side of man to find answers—only the simple words point the way. When the old man "teaches" the youth "Le soleil . . . la pluie . . . la terre," the daughter insists that the youth already knows the words and the youth thinks so too and is merely humoring the old man. But the old man repeats that the youth will "learn them fast"; and he is right.

Thus the story is convincing on the literal and the symbolic level. The simplicity of character, of plot and of language all reinforce the theme: that one must find wisdom not in learning, not even in experience, but in the strength that comes from the earth.

Notes

1. Richard Kennedy, *The Window of Memory* (Chapel Hill: University of North Carolina Press, 1962), p. 248. See also John Hall Wheelock, *Editor To Author, The Letters of Maxwell E. Perkins* (New York: Charles Scribner's Sons, 1950), p. 123.

2. Richard Kennedy and Paschal Reeves, eds., *The Notebooks of Thomas Wolfe* (Chapel Hill: The University of North Carolina Press, 1970), p. 48.

3. (New York: Harper and Brothers, 1940), p. 44.

James Boyer (essay date 1983)

SOURCE: Boyer, James. "The Development of Form in Thomas Wolfe's Short Fiction." In *Thomas Wolfe: A Harvard Perspective,* edited by Richard S. Kennedy, pp. 31-42. Athens, Ohio: Croissant & Company, 1983.

[*In the following essay, Boyer argues that explicating Wolfe's novels can be problematic, but that studying his short stories offers a clearer view of the author's work and literary development.*]

John Halberstadt's *Yale Review* article on Thomas Wolfe revived a criticism of Wolfe's work that has persisted ever since Bernard DeVoto wrote his scorching critical review of Wolfe's *Story of a Novel* in 1936. Not surprisingly, Halberstadt quotes a later DeVoto statement to establish a frame for his current argument: "You are manifestly and, if you will excuse me, absurdly wrong," DeVoto wrote to Struthers Bert in 1950, "when you say that I created 'the legend of the Wolfe who couldn't write without Papa Perkins.' It is no legend but a fact so widely established that I wonder you have missed it that at any rate he did not produce novels without Perkins' and later Ed Aswell's symbiotic editing." The gist of Halberstadt's charge in this recent article is that Aswell did indeed overedit the posthumous Wolfe novels, that in fact he went so far beyond the ordinary role of editor in order to create a structure in those books that while "the words . . ., most of them anyway—were written by Wolfe . . ., the books were made by Aswell. He was the dominant contributor to the books that bore Wolfe's name . . ."[1]

It is not my purpose here to contend with Halberstadt; Richard Kennedy in *The Window of Memory* did a careful job of assessing what Aswell had done and why. Yet while Halberstadt's conclusions about Wolfe's work are overstated and extreme, it is true that those three posthumous novels contain an amalgam of Wolfe's early and late writing, making it difficult to assess his development as a writer through them. Thus even friendly critics tend to generalize about Wolfe and all of his work; Wolfe the eternal adolescent; Wolfe the giant of insatiable appetite; Wolfe the writer of formless autobiography.

It is possible to overcome some of this confusion on Wolfe's handling of formal matters, a confusion produced by the novels, if we turn to Wolfe's magazine stories, thirty-eight of which were published before his death in 1938. By examining this considerable body of work, we can see some important directions Wolfe's fiction was taking—specifically his increasing ability to control plot, character and conflict.

Objections, of course, can be raised here too. Elizabeth Nowell, Wolfe's agent for magazine publications, played a significant role in the production of Wolfe's short stories. She helped him to select episodes from the manuscripts and to gather information for new stories; she gave advice on plot and character; and she did patient cutting of words, phrases, even episodes to bring the stories down to size. I have written elsewhere on this relationship;[2] it is sufficient here to say that Nowell encouraged Wolfe's development in the form, but the significant changes in the products of the late period are clearly attributable to Wolfe himself.

One might also object, if we are making assertions about development, that while Wolfe revised stories before publication, he didn't write them in the order in which they were published. And this is true. But it is possible through information available in the Wisdom Collection at Harvard to date the writing of most stories, so that one can attribute particular characteristics in the writing to a particular time period in his career. It is these changing characteristics that I should like to consider in the following paper. What we shall find is that Wolfe was moving toward more conventional fiction, with plots more carefully organized, characters whose internal conflicts form the core of those plots, and imagery that supports and unifies.

In examining these magazine publications, it will be convenient to divide Wolfe's stories into three groups: those stories published between 1932-1934,[3] most of them before Elizabeth Nowell became his agent; those published in 1935, many of which were republished with some alteration in *From Death to Morning*; and those published between 1936 and his death in 1938. Significant formal distinctions divide these three groups of stories.

One feature of the early stories, which begin to appear in *Scribner's Magazine* in 1932, is their length. Of the five published before 1934, only **"The Train and the City"** runs under 20,000 words. (It is about 10,000.) Wolfe had given up on writing drama in part because of the demands of that genre for concision; he was at this point unwilling to shorten works to make them more attractive to magazines. Indeed, after the middle period where many of the stories are quite short, he returns to fuller development in his best stories of the final period.

Some of the length of these early stories results from the use of long lyric passages elaborating major Wolfe themes—spring in the city, death as a brother, loneliness as a friend, America as a land of promise. While these passages contain some vivid images and personifications and employ a rhythmic, verse-like prose, they interrupt the narrative element of the story. Wolfe was reluctant to reduce them, since they were a distinctive feature of his style that brought praise from some critics. Only by the very end of 1934 does he begin to use such passages as separate magazine pieces or as carefully limited and balanced components, a practice he continues thereafter.

This early emphasis on theme and lyric refrain often results in a casual handling of the narrative element in the story. **"The Four Lost Men"** begins with a father, a son, and boarders on the porch of a boarding house in a small Southern town, discussing the beginning of World War I and earlier wars; but the setting and event are forgotten as the story moves to a lyrical vision of four lost Presidents and never returns to the porch and the people on it. In **"The Train and the City,"** the narrator's trip out from and back to the city, including the well-known passage where the two trains race, is overbalanced by paragraph after paragraph of lyric tribute to spring and to the American people. The only carefully controlled plots of the early period are found in **"The Sun and the Rain,"** where a simple chronology provides sufficient structure, and *The Web of Earth,* which is carefully wrought like the late stories but exceptional because of the controlling voice of the old woman who narrates.

Characters in these early stories tend to be static rather than dynamic; often they represent something significant, but that something is a set idea little dependent on the action of the story. In the manner of Dickens, characters are identified by peculiar mannerisms rather than internal conflicts. What we remember about Bascom Hawke, in spite of a very long story that gives much of his life in summary, are his facial grimaces and "snuffling laugh;" his weakness and resignation, which in the end of the story are contrasted with the exuberance of the young narrator, come to the reader

as a surprise. The young and beautiful Edith Coulson, in **"The House of the Far and the Lost,"** always has a "hard bright look in her eyes" that separates her from others, but we never see behind the look, so that her romantic statements toward the narrator late in the story have an artificial ring to them, something unreal that the narrator perceived but the reader doesn't. And in **"Boomtown"** Delia Hawke, another fictional incarnation of Wolfe's mother, is so clearly identified by certain mannerisms that when she appears as Delia Flood in the final version of **"Boomtown"** used in *You Can't Go Home Again,* even though Wolfe has changed her relationship to the protagonist from mother (of Eugene) to friend of the family (of George Webber, whose mother is dead), the reader immediately recognizes her by her "pursed" lips and her characteristic expression "HAH? What say?"

Short, then, on conventional plot structure and characters in conflict, many of these early stories are structured with simple contrast—hopeful youth and resigned age, or "wandering" and "earth again" or violent death and quiet death—rather than conflict. Elaboration in such stories is often accomplished through multiple illustration: all three of the 1933 stories (**"Death the Proud Brother," "The Train and the City,"** and **"No Door"**), as well as **"The Face of the War,"** written then but published later, are composed of a series of unrelated events, each illustrating the same themes.

Finally, many of these early stories have passages that mean little to the stories themselves but relate in some significant way to Wolfe's big books. Delia Hawke's interest in the burial of her husband's first wife is simply perplexing in **"Boomtown,"** as are the references to Esther Jack in **"Death the Proud Brother."** If one has read the novels, he recognizes the loss suffered when these episodes are removed from the larger context. By contrast the later stories often lose some of their meaning and effect when they are forced into the framework of the larger novel. Clearly, at this stage in his career, Wolfe had much to learn about story writing.

By the latter half of 1934, however, Wolfe was publishing stories very different from those described above, and the changes become more striking in 1935. Much of the change at this time results not from the writing process but from the selection process. Elizabeth Nowell, who had begun to work with Wolfe's fiction while part of Max Lieber's Agency in 1934, now opened her own agency, with Wolfe as her best-known client. During this period she played an increasingly important role in selecting suitable materials from the manuscripts and in suggesting ways to shorten them and strengthen them for use as stories.

Some of her letters to Wolfe indicate her searches through the unused manuscripts and her specific suggestions, and an examination of the manuscripts and typescripts of the stories from 1935 on show her patient work at word counts and her suggested cuts of words, phrases and scenes to shorten episodes to the word limits of various publications. Through her efforts, nine different magazines published twelve of Wolfe's stories in 1935 alone.

Even more consistently than in the earlier period, these 1935-36 stories are episodes cut from the larger work. Richard Kennedy calls them "captured fugitives,"[4] as indeed they are, many of them having come from the *Of Time and the River* manuscript. But that fact is somewhat misleading, since it is specifically the discreteness of the episodes that caused them to be eliminated from that novel. Stories like **"Cottage by the Tracks"** or **"Bums at Sunset"** represent units complete in themselves which were to have functioned in the novel to illustrate various themes or facets of the national character. Obviously these episodes, once cut from the novel, were very easily adapted for use as separate magazine pieces, though they do not always have the elements we expect in a short story.

These stories of the second period are consistently short. Of the twelve 1935 stories, most of which reappear in *From Death to Morning,* ten have fewer than 6,000 words. More than half of them present a single event. Emphasis consistently remains on the narrative element. This shift toward a simpler structure undoubtedly reflects Nowell's involvement in the selection. The result is this sequence of stories that make us aware of the diversity in Wolfe's work.

Contrasting with the prevailing serious, lyrical tone of the early stories, we find in these stories a great variety in tone, from the humor of **"Only the Dead Know Brooklyn"** through the nostalgia of **"The Circus at Dawn"** to the folk-tale tone of **"Old Catawba."** Stories center on persons other than Eugene Gant—this is true, of course, of stories in the first period, too, but not so apparent in the novels. And we have some stories that demonstrate an increasing capacity in Wolfe, even when he is dealing with his Eugene-George protagonist, for getting outside himself; it is hard to imagine the humorous reconciliation of **"Gulliver"** or the ironic self-portrait of **"Only the Dead"** [**"Only the Dead Know Brooklyn"**] having been written in the earlier period. Especially the tone of such stories contrasts sharply with much of *Of Time and the River,* also published in 1935, where the central character is presented at an earlier state of development, almost completely absorbed with internal concern and consistently suspicious of others around him.

Along with varying tone, these stories present a great variety in dialogue. The *Notebooks* show the extent to which Wolfe recorded conversations he had heard in bars, on the street, or from the window of his room in Brooklyn. Not only does he use these voices in dialogue; he uses them as narrators of episodes. While in the novels, where the narrative focus remains on Eugene Gant-George Webber, we find only a few of these narrators—Esther Jack, for example, tells some short sections of *The Web and the Rock*—in the stories, especially these in the middle period, we see a fuller range of experimentation. Voices in the earlier period, in **"Bascom Hawke," "The Four Lost Men"** and other stories, had been prophetic, choric voices; here in the 1935 stories Wolfe uses the varied voices of specific people. **"One of the Girls in Our Party"** gives us the voice of a female midwestern school teacher, a type Wolfe no doubt encountered during his travels in Europe. **"In the Park"** features the voice of Esther Jack, mistress of George Webber in the later novels. **"Only the Dead Know Brooklyn"** uses the city voice as the teller of the tale. Both with narrative voice, male and female, and with dialogue, there is more variety in these stories.

Since the stories are short, character development is more limited than in the early period, but it is in some instances more interesting, too. **"Arnold Pentland,"** whose central character is the son of Uncle Bascom, gives us a man totally alienated from his family and society, a character whose conflict is concisely dramatized in a few scenes of the Bascom Pentland family—dramatized in a way Bascom's own struggle never is. The action is left to speak for itself, those passages of authorial comment having been carefully omitted. And the tall stranger in **"Only the Dead Know Brooklyn"** (the same figure who serves as protagonist in the novels), torn by an insatiable desire to experience all things, is presented to the reader through the narration of a typical Brooklyn tough guy, so that the reader has distance and recognizes the affliction as that of the character of the story, not the author, a confusion sometimes troubling in *Of Time and the River.*

Some plots in these stories, too, show Wolfe's developing concern with structure. **"Cottage by the Tracks"** has an ironic reversal for its structuring device: a railroad engineer passes on his daily route a home where a young woman always waves greeting as he goes by. She ages, has a child, and the ritual persists throughout a lifetime, giving the engineer an idea of her strength and warmth as a person. When he retires, however, and seeks her out at her home, she is hard and suspicious, and he recognized in an instant of meeting that all he had cherished over the years was but his own illusion. It is interesting to note that this simple insight—the recognition of life's illusions—is developed later into the structuring device for Wolfe's fourth novel, *You Can't Go Home Again.*

Other illustrations of conscious simple plotting in this second period can be found in **"In the Park"** (written in 1930 but later revised), **"The Bell Remembered,"** and a little known ironic blast at Aline Bernstein titled **"Fame and the Poet."** But the finest examples of both plot and character development come a little later.

During that final period, in 1936-38, Wolfe published eleven stories, including three which are generally considered his best—**"I Have a Thing to Tell You," "The Child by Tiger,"** and **"The Lost Boy."** From the standpoint of form, the stories of this period, especially the three mentioned, show dramatic development.

It was, of course, part of Wolfe's pattern to use magazine publication as a means of support as he worked to complete a major novel. But there were other reasons at this time for his focusing his efforts on short story publication. His relations with Max Perkins and Scribner's had badly deteriorated in 1936 because of some troubling lawsuits he felt Perkins had helped to precipitate, some troubling interference by Perkins in his selection of subject matter for his writing, and that very troubling critical attack by Bernard DeVoto, which pictured Wolfe and Perkins as a sort of team for turning out novels. While Wolfe vacillated over the question of changing publishers, he spent much of his time with Elizabeth Nowell working on the stories.

Wolfe had begun working on a new book, his *Vision of Spangler's Paul,* in March of 1936. **"The Bell Remembered"** was to be one episode in the first section of that book, which was to give a sense of the family history and the community that had shaped the central character, Paul (and later George) Spangler, a writer. From there, the novel was to move to the experience of Spangler's life, and he was to serve not as central focus but as a reflector for a wide variety of experiences involving other people. In a June 1936 letter to Heinz Ledig, his German editor, Wolfe explains his intentions: "The idea as I conceive it is the story of a good man abroad in the world—shall we say the naturally innocent man, the man who sets out in life with his own vision of what life is going to be like, what men and women are going to be like, what he is going to find, and then the story of what he really finds."[5] Wolfe went on to cite *Don Quixote, Candide* and *Gulliver* as models for what he was attempting.

One notes, of course, that this frame is very flexible, allowing Wolfe to use any of his experiences, with the focus remaining on other people and events, the narrator serving simply as story teller and interpreter. Thus,

though the 1937 stories are written as separate units and move in very different directions, Wolfe no doubt had a clear notion of how he would eventually incorporate all of them into the major work. Yet his impulse for writing them came from diverse sources rather than a single conception of the "big book," he spent considerable time with Elizabeth Nowell sharpening and shortening them, and they are often more effective as separate units than as parts of the book. And a careful look at them reveals significant changes from the earlier stories in formal matters.

They are longer than the stories of the middle period; two of the best, **"I Have a Thing to Tell You"** and **"The Lost Boy,"** approach the length of **"Bascom Hawke."** But their content remains almost exclusively narrative. Gone are the long lyric passages of the earliest period and the visions of both earlier periods; gone are the expository passages on youth and exuberance.

Wolfe has become more careful, too, in use of images. Description effectively foreshadows and reinforces action or theme. The contrast of the dark forests of Germany, with "their legendary sense of magic and of time," and the shiny German tram, "perfect in its function," gives the first indication in **"I Have a Thing to Tell You"** of the two sides of the German character, its great heritage of art but its preoccupation with a dehumanizing scientific precision. In **"The Child by Tiger"** the "stamp of the military" on Dick Prosser, illustrated in the beginning of the story by the faultlessly cut firewood and the spotless room, foreshadows his expert skill with the rifle and his cool, methodical manner on the killing spree that forms the climax of the story. Not only descriptive detail but characters themselves are used to represent or reinforce theme: Daisy Purvis in "E" is significant because in her willing subservience to the aristocracy she represents a European type, one of the little people of England, for whom America had no direct counterpart. It is not simply that Wolfe now sees persons, places or things as representational—he had always consciously done that—but he begins now to integrate them more carefully with action and theme to form a unified whole.

More important still, Wolfe is developing characters in conflict, characters who are trying to resolve something. All characters are functional, and the action of the stories brings both character and reader to a point of clarification. Prosser in **"The Child by Tiger"** is a complex figure, his orderly exterior undercut by a smoldering anger over his blackness that erupts against everyone, black and white alike. And the white mob, the antagonist of the story, reinforces the picture of that animal side of man that moves by primitive forces deep within it, forces that civilization has failed to control. The narrator in the first part of **"The Lost Boy,"** is trying to recapture his own past—to make time transpose past into living present. In the end he recognizes the impossibility of this quest. Perhaps the greatest character of all in the stories is "Fuss and Fidget," the little German lawyer in **"I Have a Thing to Tell You,"** who develops from an unpleasant little man into an image of mankind, one of a small family of people trying to survive in a fascist world. These characters, in their complexity and their reality, rank with the greatest of fictional creations.

The plots of these stories are generally simple, focusing on a few days in time, a crucial event, a single idea. **"I Have a Thing to Tell You"** takes place in one day, with only four important scenes, three of them on the train leaving Germany. **"The Child by Tiger"** covers more time but maintains its concentration on the shooting spree and the hunting down of Prosser. And while the structure of **"The Lost Boy"** is more complex, covering years and shifting from one narrator to another, the unrelenting purpose is to recapture the essence of the dead child.

What we are describing is certainly a more conventional story, with what Wallace Stegner, in his analysis of **"The Lost Boy"** refers to as "unmistakable form, which arises immediately and inevitably out of intention . . . and is inseparable from it." But contrary to Stegner's implication that one finds such unity only in **"The Lost Boy,"** organic unity becomes a common characteristic of the stories of this final period.

Wolfe's reputation as a writer from whom a stream of undigested experience simply poured is undeserved. As the stories illustrate, his later writing shows genuine improvement in his craft—in dramatizing rather than telling, in careful plotting, in building characters with significant internal conflicts, and in using imagery to reinforce theme.

Notes

1. "The Making of Thomas Wolfe's Posthumous Novels," *Yale Review,* 70 (Fall, 1980), 93.

2. "Nowell and Wolfe: The Working Relationship," *Thomas Wolfe Review,* 5 (Spring, 1981), 18-21.

3. It is true, of course, that Wolfe had published his first story back in 1929. An episode from *Look Homeward, Angel* had been selected by Perkins, given an introduction by Wolfe, and published by *Scribner's Magazine* as "An Angel on the Porch." Though obviously not written as a separate work—many of the short stories were taken from the bigger works, though in a variety of ways, so

that one must exercise care in generalizing about them—this one is, as Perkins had assured Wolfe, a fine short story. It is, however, uncharacteristic of the early stories of 1932-34.

4. *The Window of Memory* (Chapel Hill: U. of North Carolina Press, 1962), p. 279.

5. *The Letters of Thomas Wolfe,* ed. Elizabeth Nowell (New York: Charles Scribner's Sons, 1956), p. 526.

Webb Salmon (essay date 1985)

SOURCE: Salmon, Webb. "Thomas Wolfe's Search to Know Brooklyn." In *Critical Essays on Thomas Wolfe,* edited by John S. Phillipson, pp. 174-82. Boston: G. K. Hall & Co., 1985.

[*In the following essay, Salmon laments the lack of critical attention given to the short story "Only the Dead Know Brooklyn," which, Salmon notes, sheds light on Wolfe's other works and reflects the author's personal experiences.*]

Thomas Wolfe's **"Only the Dead Know Brooklyn,"**[1] though often anthologized, has received little critical attention.[2] The two best biographies of Wolfe, Nowell's and Turnbull's, do not acknowledge the story. There is no mention of **"Only the Dead Know Brooklyn"** in Wolfe's published letters and only two references by Wolfe in his notebooks—one that merely lists it under his stories written about New York and one, with the word *Exile* written after the title, that classifies the story as one of his works about "The Jungle Years."[3] Yet I should like to suggest that this brief story, only about 2000 words long, has an important role to play in our understanding of a basic theme in much of Wolfe's work—man's loneliness and lostness, and his search to find some relief from the resulting grief.

As we consider this basic idea, I shall try to show that both Thomas Wolfe and his fictional counterparts experienced the search to know Brooklyn; that the search was closely related in Wolfe's mind with his attempts to solve the artistic problems that plagued and almost destroyed him; and that the search, in addition to being viewed literally as an actual, physical search, should be interpreted figuratively to represent a search for calmness of spirit, for peace of mind.

"Only the Dead Know Brooklyn" is narrated by a Brooklyn native who tries to help a stranger—a very large man, who has been drinking but "talks good and is walkin' straight enough"—find his way by subway to a particular section of Brooklyn. En route, the guide becomes upset when he learns that the stranger, determined to learn all of Brooklyn with the help of a map, has wandered at night through an exceptionally dangerous section of the city. The narrator's concern becomes alarm when the big fellow persists in asking strange questions: how long would it take to learn all of Brooklyn, and what happens to people after they have drowned in Brooklyn? Fearing that the man is "some kind of nut," the guide leaves the train at the next stop as the stranger looks at his map and repeats "Drownin'," "Drownin'." Some time later the narrator still wonders about the "poor guy"—whether "someone knocked him on duh head" during his nighttime wandering and whether "he's found out by now dat he'll neveh live long enough to know deh whole of Brooklyn."

From March 1931 till March 1935, Wolfe lived and wrote in Brooklyn. These were the years when, after the generally favorable reception of *Look Homeward, Angel,* he struggled to find for his next novel the artistic pattern through which he could organize the hundreds of thousands of words that flowed from his creative and tortured mind.

He tells us in *The Story of a Novel,* a long essay about these four years of writing in Brooklyn, that he knew the central idea he wanted to express: "The deepest search in life, . . . the thing that in one way or another was central to all living was man's search to find a father, . . . not merely the lost father of his youth, but the image of a strength and wisdom . . . to which the belief and power of his own life could be united."[4] Of necessity, to keep from being destroyed by a thwarted obsession to write, he committed himself irrevocably to his work.

But, Wolfe says, ". . . a terrible doubt began to creep into my mind that I might not live long enough to get it out of me, that I had created a labor so large and so impossible that the energy of a dozen lifetimes would not suffice for its accomplishment."[5] Wolfe is certainly speaking of himself when he has George Webber, a Brooklyn resident for a time and the protagonist in *You Can't Go Home Again,* say, "I was more involved than I had ever been before with my inner struggle. Those were the years of the greatest doubt and desperation I had ever known."[6] Frustrated, Wolfe was tempted to change his residence, but he decided that leaving was no solution; he wrote his uncle, who had urged the move, that, though his "tendency [had] been to wander and roam in search of . . . peace and security, he must find these inside himself."[7] And so he stayed to search in Brooklyn and through his writing.

Wolfe could have said, as did Webber, "For four years . . . I lived and explored the jungle depths of Brooklyn—jungle depths coincident with those of my own soul. . . ."[8]

This concept of the coincidence of an area and a search and one's soul takes us back to the closing of Wolfe's first novel, back to the imagined exchange between Eugene Gant and his dead brother Ben. Gene, believing in "harbors at the end," says he wants to find himself, "an end to hunger, and the happy land"; but Ben replies: "There is no happy land. There is no end to hunger." Gene insists on an answer with his question "Where, Ben? Where is the world?" "Nowhere. . . . *You* are your world."[9]

Thomas Wolfe and some of his characters learned that the outward search was truly representative of an inner search; and this search was for Wolfe related to his struggles to be a good writer, to find the map that would help him master his own Brooklyn, to avoid drowning in the flood of problems associated with his own creativity. Andrew Turnbull writes: "He knew that he would never again sleep the sweet sleep of childhood. . . . At last he knew the cost of being a writer; he saw what happens to a man who makes the writer's life his own."[10]

We do not have to wonder whether the nocturnal wanderings of Wolfe's characters are based on his own. In a letter written in late 1933 he says that he has lived in recent years in Brooklyn, in Manhattan, and in foreign countries—"and that the largest and most unknown continent of all is Brooklyn. . . . I have gone out into the wilderness five hundred times," he continues, "armed with a trusty map, now worn to tatters, and have prowled about, exploring the place in the dark hours of the night. . . ." In the same letter he says, "The Brooklyn people boast that you can live here a lifetime and never get to know their town, and they are right about it. . . ."[11] The evidence could hardly be more conclusive that in **"Only the Dead Know Brooklyn,"** "duh big guy" (Wolfe was about 6' 7" tall and weighed 240 pounds), "wanderin' aroun' in duh subway in duh middle of duh night wit his little map" and concerned about what happens to people after they have drowned in Brooklyn, is based on Wolfe himself.

Prowling through the city streets was habitual with Wolfe. Maxwell Perkins, his loyal friend and editor, tells the now well-known story about Wolfe's walking through the rain in the early morning hours chanting "I wrote ten thousand words today—I wrote ten thousand words today."[12] Sometimes Wolfe would walk home with Perkins in Manhattan after an evening editorial session and a drink, and occasionally he would become so engrossed in talk that he would not leave until Perkins went out to get an early morning edition of the newspaper.[13] Then he might walk across the bridge and through the streets of Brooklyn. He particularly liked to walk along the waterfront and to go to the wholesale markets to watch the fresh produce unloaded at dawn. His friend and agent and biographer, Elizabeth Nowell, says that sometimes he would "roam around in the toughest sections" of Brooklyn. Like the large fellow in **"Only the Dead Know Brooklyn,"** "he would stop in a bar and drink, or roam from bar to bar. . . ." Miss Nowell writes, "It was a wonder he never got held up or sandbagged: evidently his tremendous size and wild appearance intimidated even the Brooklyn thugs."[14] By dawn he would be so exhausted that he could finally fall asleep—though, according to his own account, the sleep was likely to be "an unceasing nightmare of blazing visions that swept across my fevered and unresting mind," a "nightmare pageantry to which my consciousness lay chained a spectator."[15]

But it would be erroneous to assume that Wolfe's night wandering served only to exhaust him and so make sleep possible. Turnbull explains that his ears were "tuned to the shouts of the drivers and grocery boys" and that he was sensitive to the language he heard on the docks and in the bars.[16] Conversations he heard were likely to appear in Wolfe's stories of the city at night. Robert Raynolds, a novelist and friend who occasionally walked in the city with Wolfe, explains that these walks were part of Wolfe's creative process. Raynolds writes, "Wolfe walked along the street as if his business were right there; his business was to hear, see, feel, taste and touch and smell the life on the street; he was working as he walked."[17]

We should remember that the years Wolfe lived in Brooklyn were years of the Depression. What he saw in his night wanderings contributed to the development of the social consciousness that is so obvious in his writings of this period. In *The Story of a Novel* Wolfe relates his own experience:

> I saw a man whose life had subsided into a mass of shapeless and filthy rags, devoured by vermin; wretches huddled together for a little warmth in freezing cold squatting in doorless closets upon the foul seat of a public latrine within the very shadow, the cold shelter of palatial and stupendous monuments of wealth. I saw acts of sickening violence and cruelty, the menace of brute privilege, a cruel and corrupt authority trampling ruthlessly below its feet the lives of the poor, the weak, the wretched, and defenseless of the earth.
>
> And the staggering impact of this black picture of man's inhumanity to his fellow man . . . left a scar upon my life, a conviction in my soul which I shall never lose.[18]

George Webber, the protagonist in Wolfe's two posthumous novels, experienced, of course, the same New York that Thomas Wolfe explored. And Webber, like Wolfe, is a novelist. In *You Can't Go Home Again* Webber writes to his editor, Foxhall Edwards, of "the memory of my exploration of the jungle trails of night" and of unemployed boys and men who "had been cast loose by a society that had no need for them and left to shift in any way they could—to find their food in garbage cans, to seek for warmth and fellowship in foul latrines like the one near New York's City Hall, to sleep wrapped up in old newspapers on the concrete floors of subway corridors."[19] Like Wolfe, Webber was horrified by the "blind injustice" of the situation: "all around him in the cold moonlight, only a few blocks away from the abyss of human wretchedness and misery, blazed the pinnacles of power where a large portion of the entire world's wealth was locked in mighty vaults."[20] The similarity between Wolfe's and Webber's observations and reactions is, of course, inescapable.

Like Wolfe, Webber was cursed with sleeplessness. He would work "for hours at a stretch at his novel. Finally, he would stagger forth into the nightless streets, reeling like a drunkard with his weariness . . . because his mind was feverish and he knew he could not sleep, [Webber] would walk to the Brooklyn Bridge and cross it to Manhattan, and ferret out the secret heart of darkness in all the city's ways, and then at dawn come back across the Bridge once more, and so to bed in Brooklyn."[21]

In the earlier Webber novel, *The Web and the Rock,* we read of his prowling "a hundred streets" in the "darkness that stretched from light to light"; "he would come back in the morning, come back from death to morning, walking on the bridge."[22] And this restlessness plagued Webber (and Wolfe) whether he was writing in Brooklyn or agonizing abroad over the reception his first book would receive. In London after "prowling feverishly through the . . . streets until three or four in the morning, Webber would go to bed and fall into a diseased coma. . . ."[23] In Munich it was the same: "At night he walked the streets"; he "could find no end and seek no rest."[24]

George Webber began to understand that being lonely and being lost are inseparable and that loneliness is at the center of the "experience of every man."[25] He felt that men are lost; but he, like other Wolfe characters, was comforted by the thought of ships calling from the harbor. (The big fellow in **"Only the Dead Know Brooklyn"** was fascinated by the "ships oveh deh all lighted up.")

Other Wolfe characters in the Brooklyn period know about loneliness. The narrator of the short novel, *No*

Door, who lives in "the huge and rusty jungle of the earth that is known as Brooklyn,"[26] says that he has been alone more than anyone he knows. He feels that he is a ghost walking among the city people; and he, like the big fellow trying to learn Brooklyn, has "the sensation of drowning in a sea of horror."[27] (He would have deplored the narrator of **"Only the Dead Know Brooklyn,"** who does not even know that people can drown in the city.) The narrator in *No Door* is allowed to express only implicitly what the speaker in a second Brooklyn story, **"Death the Proud Brother,"** says explicitly. The second narrator is relieved to come out into the open air from the presence of a man who has died alone—and for some time unnoticed—in a subway tunnel; the narrator says, "I knew I should not die and strangle like a mad dog in the tunnel's dark. I knew I should see light once more and know new coasts and come into strange harbors, and see again, as I had once, new lands and morning."[28]

As we move backwards into the earlier years of Wolfe's counterpart—this time Eugene Gant in *Of Time and the River*—we see another young man who, like Webber, believes in "harbors at the end."[29] He knows that men "walk the streets of life alone,"[30] unsuccessful in their search for the word or the stone or the door that will open the way to the knowledge they seek; but he cannot agree when an older youth, Francis Starwick, tries to tell him that his hunger will exhaust him, will break his heart, will drive him mad.[31] Starwick does not know of the compulsion that governs Eugene's search: he did not see him several years earlier in that memorable scene with the ghost of Ben on the porch of their father's marble shop. In that predawn scene Eugene vows that he will hunt "the ghost and haunter of [him]self," even though the search will lead to strange coasts and to "seas stranger than those haunted by the Albatross." A determined Eugene continues:

> . . . no leaf hangs for me in the forest; I shall lift no stone upon the hills; I shall find no door in any city. But in the city of myself, upon the continent of my soul, I shall find the forgotten language, the lost world, a door where I may enter . . . ; I shall haunt you, ghost, along the labyrinthine ways until—until? O Ben, my ghost, an answer?[32]

Ben, not so optimistic as Eugene, has no answer. Ben may understand, but cannot express, the cryptic thought that an older Eugene become the writer Thomas Wolfe can articulate:

> Naked and alone we came into exile. In her dark womb we did not know our mother's face; from the prison of her flesh have we come into the unspeakable and incommunicable prison of this earth.

> . . . Which of us is not forever a stranger and alone?

> . . . Remembering speechlessly we seek the great forgotten language, the lost lane-end into heaven, a stone, a leaf, an unfound door.[33]

The young Eugene is a kindred spirit to the big fellow who is convinced he can learn all of Brooklyn. "Lost? . . . No, I wouldn't get lost. I got a map." An older Eugene become George Webber become Thomas Wolfe might agree with the Brooklyn narrator when he says of the big stranger, "Maybe he's found out by now dat he'll neveh live long enough to know duh whole of Brooklyn. It'd take a guy a lifetime to know Brooklyn t'roo and t'roo. An' even den yuh wouldn't know it all."

* * *

Thomas Wolfe never learned in his lifetime the whole of Brooklyn, and he never was convinced that in his writing he had found the language that would release him from the "incommunicable prison." But, as Faulkner said, he failed more gloriously than other writers because he put more of himself into the attempt to develop his marvelous talent.[34]

For Wolfe the search was over a few days before his thirty-eighth birthday. His death came, ironically, at a time when he was optimistic about his work. In May of 1938 he wrote Miss Nowell that he thought he had "come through a kind of transition period in [his] life . . . and [had] now found a kind of belief and hope and faith [he] never had before."[35] Four months later he was dead.

When Maxwell Perkins heard that his friend would die, he kept thinking over and over of Kent's lines about the dying King Lear:

> He hates him
> That would upon the rack of this tough world
> Stretch him out longer.

"For," Perkins would write later, "he was on the rack almost always, and almost always would have been. . . ."[36]

Thomas Wolfe was dead. Perhaps, at last, he could know Brooklyn.

Notes

1. In Thomas Wolfe, *From Death to Morning* (New York: Charles Scribner's Sons, 1935), pp. 91-97.

2. The merit of the story was recognized early. It was included in Edward J. O'Brien's collection, *The Best Short Stories, 1936.*

   Bruce R. McElderberry [*Thomas Wolfe* (New York: Twayne Publishers, 1964), pp. 116-17] thinks the story is "much more successful" and "less pretentious" than "Death the Proud Brother." He believes "the ugly idiom and monotonous rhythm of the dialect" are appropriate for expressing a "callousness of feeling." Herbert Muller [*Thomas Wolfe* (Norfolk: New Directions Books, 1947), p. 77], on the other hand, says the dialect is "a tiresome exercise in Brooklynese." Muller thinks the story is merely one of several "exercises from a writer's notebook" that appear in *From Death to Morning*. Richard Walser [*Thomas Wolfe: An Introduction and Interpretation* (New York: Holt, Rinehart, & Winston, 1961), p. 124] speaks of the theme of loneliness in the Brooklyn stories and says that "the vast area [of Brooklyn] is undiscovered even by the 'pavement ciphers' who people it." None of these three critics devotes as much as a paragraph to "Only the Dead Know Brooklyn."

The most extensive discussion of the story that I know is Edward A. Bloom's [*The Order of Fiction: An Introduction* (New York: Odyssey Press, 1964), pp. 143-46; reprinted as "Critical Commentary on 'Only the Dead Know Brooklyn,'" ed. Leslie Field, *Three Decades of Criticism* (New York: New York Univ. Press, 1968), pp. 269-72]. Bloom thinks the story is an allegorical portrayal of the conflict between "the restless individual search for the bluebird and the passivity of acceptance," a struggle "between a broad idea of absorptive materialism and threatened ideals."

3. Thomas Wolfe, *The Notebooks of Thomas Wolfe*, ed. Richard S. Kennedy and Paschal Reeves (Chapel Hill: Univ. of North Carolina Press, 1970), Vol. II, pp. 879, 956.

4. Thomas Wolfe, *The Story of a Novel* (New York: Charles Scribner's Sons, 1936), p. 39.

5. *The Story of a Novel*, p. 55.

6. Thomas Wolfe, *You Can't Go Home Again* (New York: Harper & Bros, 1940), p. 725.

7. Thomas Wolfe, *The Letters of Thomas Wolfe*, ed. Elizabeth Nowell (New York: Charles Scribner's Sons, 1956), pp. 316-17.

8. *You Can't Go Home Again*, p. 739.

9. Thomas Wolfe, *Look Homeward, Angel* (New York: Charles Scribner's Sons, 1929), p. 624.

10. Andrew Turnbull, *Thomas Wolfe* (New York: Charles Scribner's Sons, 1967), p. 177.

11. *The Letters of Thomas Wolfe*, p. 390.

12. Maxwell Perkins, Introduction to *Look Homeward, Angel* (New York: Charles Scribner's Sons, 1957), p. xiv. [Reprinted from the *Harvard Library Bulletin*, I, No. 3 (Autumn 1947.)] Perkins attributes this story to Nancy Hale, who lived near the Perkinses at the time.

13. Turnbull, p. 192.

14. Elizabeth Nowell, *Thomas Wolfe: A Biography* (Garden City, N.Y.: Doubleday & Co., 1960), p. 200.

15. *The Story of a Novel*, pp. 61-62.

16. Turnbull, p. 175.

17. Robert Raynolds, *Thomas Wolfe: Memoir of a Friendship* (Austin: Univ. of Texas Press, 1965), p. 23.

18. *The Story of a Novel*, pp. 59-60.

19. *You Can't Go Home Again*, p. 729.

20. *You Can't Go Home Again*, p. 414.

21. *You Can't Go Home Again*, p. 398.

22. Thomas Wolfe, *The Web and the Rock* (New York: Harper & Bros, 1939), p. 555.

23. *The Web and the Rock*, p. 623.

24. *The Web and the Rock*, p. 661.

25. *You Can't Go Home Again*, p. 499.

26. Thomas Wolfe, "No Door," in *From Death to Morning*, p. 12.

27. "No Door," p. 4.

28. Thomas Wolfe, "Death the Proud Brother," in *From Death to Morning*, p. 67.

29. *The Web and the Rock*, p. 299.

30. Thomas Wolfe, *Of Time and the River* (New York: Charles Scribner's Sons, 1935), p. 74.

31. *Of Time and the River*, pp. 708-09.

32. *Look Homeward, Angel*, p. 625.

33. *Look Homeward, Angel*, p. 2.

34. Frederick L. Gwynn and Joseph L. Blotner, *Faulkner in the University* (Charlottesville: Univ. of Virginia Press, 1939), pp. 144, 206.

35. Nowell, p. 16. Also, *The Letters of Thomas Wolfe*, p. 763.

36. Nowell, p. 16.

Suzanne Stutman (essay date summer 1987)

SOURCE: Stutman, Suzanne. "Reconsideration: Mediation, Aline Bernstein, and Thomas Wolfe's 'The Good Child's River.'" *MELUS* 14, no. 2 (summer 1987): 95-101.

[*In the following essay, Stutman discusses Wolfe's complicated romantic relationship with Aline Bernstein, a Jewish woman almost twenty years his senior, and re-*

marks on Wolfe's varying attitude toward her in the context of his story "The Good Child's River," a fictionalized account of Bernstein's youth.]

The writing of Thomas Wolfe teems with the confusion and contradiction inherent in the tensions which exist between the poles of ethnicity and melting pot, consent and descent, as he struggled throughout his literary career to move beyond the bonds of prejudice which consumed and at times overshadowed his work.

Thomas Wolfe was born in 1900, literally at the turn of the century. A great American romantic, he sought, like Whitman, to embrace all diversity in his writings, to bridge the gap between past and present, North and South. Throughout his writings, beginning with his masterwork *Look Homeward, Angel,* Wolfe translated into epic form this quest of a young American hero who would flee the chains that bound him and would some day emerge not only ruler of himself, the new American Adam, but, as a writer, prophet for his people, a Moses leading all Americans into the brave new world, the American promised land.

Yet although Thomas Wolfe sought exodus throughout his lifetime, he was never really able to leave his consciousness of descent behind. Thomas Wolfe considered himself a "true" American. Both sets of ancestors came to America during the Colonial period. His father's family, which settled in York, Pa., had come from Germany around 1727. His Scottish maternal ancestors were known in Asheville, North Carolina as one of its most prominent families from pre-Revolutionary times. Like his forbearers, Wolfe was always seeking the journey outward. First he fled the small town of Asheville for the University of North Carolina at Chapel Hill. After graduation, he continued his exodus, leaving the South for Harvard and then, finally, for a teaching job at New York University which brought him to the legendary big city. Totally different from his provincial, homogeneous hometown, New York was teeming with diversity of culture and background. For the rest of his life, Wolfe was to remain simultaneously attracted to and repelled by this "otherness," as was Henry James in *The American Scene,* and as much as he sought to embrace diversity, he was never fully able to do so. From New York he wrote to his mother:

> As I walk through the crowded and noisy streets of this immense city, and look at the dark swarthy faces of Jews, Italians, Greeks, and all the people of the New America that is roaring up around us here, I realize more keenly than ever that I come from the Old Americans—the people who settled the country, who fought its wars, who pushed westward.

(*Letters* 162)

Wolfe was trapped between hating America's diversity and loving it—between repulsion and acceptance and therefore left with a guilty ambiguity which was to plague him throughout his writing. As Matthews notes in his essay "The Revolt Against Americanism,"

> for American intellectuals, folk romanticism tended to lead not to hatred of 'outsiders' . . . but rather to a sense of guilt about their own society's exploitation of the strangers. . . . In the American context, alienated romanticism created not xenophobia but xenophilia.[1]

From Europe, to which Wolfe would often flee in order to find the peace and freedom from reality which he needed in order to write, Wolfe wrote this revealing passage to his mistress Aline Bernstein in 1928, one year before the publication of *Look Homeward, Angel*:

> All I see now is the magical towers of New York, made by money and power. I even have a sense of power and pride because my country is so young and strong. I want to become part of it, to make use of it in my life,—I wonder if we do see things better when we are away from them—from here I see only the glorious elements in America, the great towers, the wealth, the hope, the opportunity, the possibility of everything happening. But deeper in my Soul is the remembrance of other things, the horrible, fatal things that sicken me when I'm there—the bigotry, the hypocrisy, the intolerance, the Kluxers, the politicians—the cruelty and evil cynicism of the men in power.

(284)

Throughout his lifetime, Thomas Wolfe was haunted by the fires of love and hate which simultaneously consumed him, and this haunting ambiguity often finds its way into his writing. Although he is not often thought of as a writer who explores race relationships, Wolfe wrote one of twentieth century America's finest short stories, **"Child by Tiger,"** about the evil which prejudice elicits in both black and white alike, and of mankind's guilty union. It is interesting to note as well that the story is full of biblical imagery, and that Dick Prosser, the black man who kills indiscriminately and is then mutilated by the avenging mob, becomes a Christ figure at the end of the tale, and by his very dignity in the face of death, restores a sense of hope and promise to all who have been initiated into evil.

In no part of Wolfe's life was his desire to embrace "the other" as apparent as in his relationship with his mistress, Aline Bernstein. The two met aboard ship en route from Europe in 1925. At the time of their meeting, Wolfe was 25 and Aline Bernstein was 44—old enough to be his mother. In fact, Mrs. Bernstein, married and the mother of two grown children at the time she began her tempestuous relationship with Wolfe, took over the role of mother figure from Julia Wolfe. It was Aline Bernstein who was to provide Wolfe with both financial and emotional support until their dramatic breakup in 1932, at which time he almost literally returned to his mother's lap.

Wolfe's ambivalent relationship with these two most important women in his life can be easily viewed through Werner Sollors' terminology: By embracing this new mother, he was turning from descent to consent, from past to future, from the concept of arranged marriage to the freedom of romantic love. Wolfe is infamous for remaining adolescent until the age of thirty—interestingly the time during which his relationship with Mrs. Bernstein began to deteriorate dramatically. By breaking away from his mother, he was reenacting the classic American theme of coming of age. As Sollors notes: "Many motifs of American culture stem from the stresses of adolescence and ethnogenesis (the individual and the collective 'coming of age' after separating from a parent/country), of urbanization, of immigration, and of social mobility" (211). With his Jewish lover, Thomas Wolfe was indeed "melting into," becoming one with his mysterious other, much as the characters in Zangwill's *The Melting Pot*. As Sollors notes, "In Vera, David loves his true shadow, his absolute other" (72). Thomas Wolfe wrote to Aline Bernstein in 1928: "My tender and golden love, you were my other loneliness, the only clasp of hand and heart that I had. I was a stranger, alone and lost in the wilderness, and I found you" (194).

Aline Bernstein became for Thomas Wolfe a symbol of "American earth mother goddess" into which Wolfe indeed melted in order to be reborn into a new identity. From England in November 1926 Wolfe wrote:

> It seems to me that this great pageant of my life beginning in cheap legendry, in which all was victory, faultless perfection, has led my dark soul across perilous seas, scarring me here, taking a tooth or an ear, putting its splendid blemish on until now I come to my autumn home, the streaked hairs, the rich wide-hipped body, the brief repose which lasts forever for it is founded on sorrow and the skirts of winter—beyond youth, beyond life, beyond death. You live timelessly like Helen, like deep-breasted Demeter, like Holvig . . . my grey-haired wide-hipped timeless mother.
>
> (119-20)

Thomas Wolfe was unable to maintain a realistic perception of Aline Bernstein for several reasons. His need to idealize and romanticize her beyond time reflects an inability to come to terms with her age and often with her as a real flesh and blood woman. He had throughout his lifetime an ambivalent attitude toward women and a basic distrust of all females. In addition, Wolfe reacted irrationally to Mrs. Bernstein's Jewish heritage. In the early correspondence, Wolfe

referred to Mrs. Bernstein as "My Jew," or "My Dear Jew." As the relationship progressed, however, he became increasingly ambivalent in his feelings, often becoming openly hostile about Mrs. Bernstein's background. Wolfe was wont to tiptoe into paranoia, as he did in some early passages from his letters to her in which he reflected bitterly against those trying to destroy him and his art, ranging from "Them," to the *Dial* subscribers, to Phi Beta Kappa Jews (52, 87). He seemed to be constantly aware of Mrs. Bernstein's Jewishness. Indeed, he referred in his notebooks to all Jewish girls as "Rebeccas" and to Mrs. Bernstein as "Grey Rebecca." The earliest name for his fictional representation of Aline Bernstein was Rebecca Feitlebaum, who was subsequently renamed Esther Jack.

From 1930 until 1933, just five years before his death, Thomas Wolfe worked on a manuscript entitled **"The Good Child's River,"** his fictional recreation of the early life of Aline Bernstein and of her family. Wolfe wrote this novel primarily into three huge ledgers which are part of the William Wisdom Collection of Wolfe papers housed at Harvard's Houghton Library, and which I am currently transcribing and editing, with the kind permission of the executor of the Wolfe estate, Paul Gitlin.[2] He intended this material to be part of his huge work-in-progress, and as he was often to do, he dipped into this resource later to develop portions of manuscript for his novels *The Web and the Rock* and *You Can't Go Home Again.* In addition, a short story, published in 1936 and now out of print, entitled **"In the Park,"** was taken from this manuscript.

Of all of the characters of Thomas Wolfe's later writing, Esther Jack, based upon his real life mistress Aline Bernstein, is the greatest fictional creation. In **"The Good Child's River,"** Wolfe imaginatively recreates the larger-than-life characters from her early life: her actor father, her gentle mother, her exotic and sensuous Aunt Nana, and finally, the "good child" herself, Aline Bernstein.

Throughout the years of their relationship, Aline Bernstein served as a visionary for Thomas Wolfe, infusing into him her sense of humanity, love of people and the beauty of all life around her. "This is what I think," she had once written to Wolfe, "there is nothing that cannot be made beautiful" (334). They spent long hours together recreating for one another the wonder of their early lives. As the relationship began to deteriorate, Wolfe asked Mrs. Bernstein to record the events of her early life for him. In her May 23, 1930 letter, she wrote to Wolfe prophetically: "I have been writing the events of my life for you, but find it very hard to make it simple. I keep putting down all kinds of extraneous things, first thing you know it will turn into a novel and then I'll have to use it myself" (304). True to her word, Mrs. Bernstein did produce a body of works, among them *An Actor's Daughter,* published in 1941. Richard Kennedy reports that Aline Bernstein once asked him in an interview, "Have you read *An Actor's Daughter?* . . . That was Tom's book. He was going to write my life, you know" (228).

In his introduction to *Beyond Ethnicity,* Sollors has written:

> Works of ethnic literature—written by, about or for persons who perceived themselves, or were perceived by others as members of ethnic groups—may thus be read not only as expressions of mediation between cultures but also as handbooks of socialization into the codes of Americanness.
>
> (7)

Think of this: **"The Good Child's River"** is a story of the early life of a young Jewish girl written by none other than Thomas Wolfe! The title itself is significant. The adult Aline Bernstein, sexual, seductive, presented both threat and promise to the young Christian hero, and as such served as a symbol of duplicity. Throughout Wolfe's fiction, references are made to the split between the trueness and falsity of his Jewish mistress. By removing the sexuality, she becomes simply "the good child," and the threat is removed. The river is a unifying symbol used throughout Wolfe's fiction. Certainly here it serves not only as an image of the flow of memory, but also as a transcending symbol unifying the poles of past and future, of generations themselves. In the story, Wolfe has made Aline's father a Christian, thereby altering the line of descent and somewhat "neutralizing" the otherness of this young Jewish child. What is fascinating to reflect upon is that Wolfe in this novel is actually merging with the other: he becomes imaginatively not only the Jewish child, but all of her relatives as well! It is also interesting to note, in the light of Sollors' chapter entitled "Romantic Love, Arranged Marriage, and Indian Melancholy," that the complete title of his novel is **"The Good Child's River: The Story of a True Woman."**

The writing of **"The Good Child's River"** is somewhat uneven, as Wolfe struggles to maintain the persona of his heroine, who narrates the story of her early life. Aline Bernstein was born on December 22, 1880, and her autobiography *An Actor's Daughter* begins on the night of her birth—as does Wolfe's novel. It is Wolfe's account, however, that is decidedly self-conscious about the family's Jewish background. As the drama of the impending birth unfolds, Wolfe captures the sense of excitement and expectancy that fills the home of Aunt Bella, the heroine's favorite relative

besides her father. Several pages deal with the experiences of Robert, Esther's twelve year old cousin, who "had the plump freckled skin, the blue eyes and the curly hair of flaming red that one sees in Jewish children."[3] Robert loves the Christmas holiday, for Aunt Bella, though Jewish, always has a Christmas tree with presents for everyone. He has had no cause to question this practice until he is challenged by a young tough named Rags Cassidy—similar to many of the youthful characters who populate Wolfe's novels. When Robert is told that "Jews don't have Christmas," he runs home crying. It is Esther's kind and humorous father, who, although a "goy," instructs Robert in how to answer Rags' taunt that Christ was not a Jew: "He wasn't nothing. . . . He was the Loid."

> 'There are a lot of Loids,' my father said. 'First of all there is the North German Loid. Then there are all the Loids in the insurance business. Then there is Loids and Taylors. Then there are all the English Loids: There is Loid Tennyson and Loid Cornwallis and Loid Burguyne and Loid Halpus. . . . Ask him if he doesn't mean Loid Halpus.'

When Robert relays these arguments back to Rags, Rags gets very angry and swears to "someday . . . kill himself a Jew . . .," much as the young Eugene Gant swears with his friends to "Drown a Jew and hit a nigger" in the early pages of *Look Homeward, Angel.* What becomes apparent is that Wolfe is playing both sides of the fence, as he moves from the perceptions of his Jewish heroine to his own memories of past encounters with these outsiders.

It is when Wolfe enters into the mind and shares the vision of his heroine that he is truly at his best, as in this passage from **"The Good Child's River"** in which Esther recalls her first awareness of the world around her:

> Now, also, I was aware of the living presence of the seasons: I saw the first sharp green of city trees with all their lively piercing ecstasy and I knew for the first time the immense youth and sweetness of the back yards of New York. The vital living air fell with such shining purity upon all things and, imperial, unperplexed, the bird song rose with its proud liquid clarity. At this moment I heard a sudden shout of children playing, the cry struck strong and hard upon the air with the certitude of gravel, and a feeling of the most unspeakable joy and triumph swept across my spirit. The entire earth came to life before my eyes like music, and everything about me lived, and I saw Bella there before me, and I knew where ever she was, there, too was glory.

In *Beyond Ethnicity,* Werner Sollors has noted that "imperceptibly and sometimes involuntarily, writers begin to function as translators of ethnicity to ignorant, and sometimes hostile, outsiders and, at the same time as mediators between 'America' and Greenhorns" (7). There was in Wolfe a pronounced provincialism which exhibited itself in a fear and distrust of outsiders of any kind: Jews, blacks, even intellectuals, whom he classified in a similar manner. Yet beyond this "blindness" or shortsightedness Wolfe possessed a determination to grapple with his own shortcomings, and to depict his characters as complex, believable human beings. In so doing, Thomas Wolfe was able, if only haltingly, to transcend his limitations and to become as a writer both translator and mediator.

Notes

1. Fred H. Matthews, "The Revolt against Americanism: Cultural Pluralism and Cultural Relativism as an Ideology of Liberation." *Canadian Review of American Studies* 1.1 (Spring 1970): 9, quoted in Werner Sollors, *Beyond Ethnicity: Consent and Descent in American Culture* (New York: Oxford U P, 1986), 29.

2. Thomas Wolfe, "The Good Child's River," The William B. Wisdom Collection of Thomas Wolfe Manuscripts, Houghton Library, Harvard University.

3. "The Good Child's River," Wisdom Collection Ledger 1, p. 7. All quotations from "The Good Child's River" are from the first of the three ledgers in the William B. Wisdom Collection at Harvard.

Works Cited

Bernstein, Aline. *An Actor's Daughter.* New York: Alfred A. Knopf, 1941.

Kennedy, Richard S. *The Window of Memory: The Literary Career of Thomas Wolfe.* Chapel Hill: U of North Carolina P, 1962.

Klein, Carole. *Aline.* New York: Harper & Row, 1979.

Reeves, Paschal. *Thomas Wolfe's Albatross: Race and Nationality in America.* Athens: U of Georgia P, 1968.

Sollors, Werner. *Beyond Ethnicity: Consent and Descent in American Culture.* New York: Oxford U P, 1986.

Wolfe, Thomas. "The Good Child's River." The William B. Wisdom Collection of Thomas Wolfe Manuscripts. Houghton Library, Harvard U.

————. *My Other Loneliness: Letters of Thomas Wolfe and Aline Bernstein.* Edited by Suzanne Stutman. Chapel Hill: U of North Carolina P, 1983.

————. *Thomas Wolfe's Letters to His Mother.* Edited by C. Hugh Holman and Sue Fields Ross. Chapel Hill: U of North Carolina P, 1968.

Edward Gillin (essay date spring 1989)

SOURCE: Gillin, Edward. "'Julia' and Julia's Son." *Modern Language Studies* 19, no. 2 (spring 1989): 3-11.

[*In this essay, Gillin compares Wolfe's "I Have a Thing to Tell You" with the episode titled "Julia" from Lillian Hellman's memoir* Pentimento, *discussing the possibility that Hellman borrowed the idea for "Julia" from Wolfe's short story about his experiences in Nazi Germany.*]

Fifty years after his death, Thomas Wolfe's memory is still darkened by his threefold reputation for anti-Semitism, drunkenness, and an inartistic disregard for the boundary between fiction and confessional autobiography. A less tarnished angel is Lillian Hellman, who died a few years ago a cherished crusader for liberal causes, a dramatist and celebrated memoirist with a reputation for integrity. We might well consider these figures unfairly matched in a matter involving their respective moral confrontations with Adolf Hitler's Germany in the mid-1930s. Yet a surprisingly telling contrast exists between one incident that really happened and a more famous one that probably never occurred.

Novelist Thomas Wolfe grew up amid anti-Semitic attitudes. These were as endemic in Asheville, North Carolina, during the early years of the twentieth century as bigotry against blacks and Catholics, the other "outsiders" in the post-Reconstruction triad of indigenous social enemies. But by the time Wolfe made his first series of comet-swings away from his North Carolina home—to Harvard University for graduate study and to New York as an English professor and then as a published author—Jews became an unalterable part of his daily life. Notwithstanding his lingering prejudices, it is generally considered that he treated his numerous Jewish students fairly, and he numbered Jews among close friends. Most noteworthy, of course, was Wolfe's turbulent, years-long affair with Broadway stage designer Aline Bernstein. Given such indications of growing open-mindedness, therefore, it is easy to share the dismay of the author's most recent biographer, David Donald, who recounts that even at age 30 Wolfe invited his mother, Julia, up North to his New York City apartment partly because she might help him sever the relationship with Bernstein. Knowing full well Julia Wolfe's ethnic prejudices, Wolfe understood that his mistress's married status hardly counted against her as much as the fact that Aline was always "the *Jew* woman" in his mother's eyes. And after Julia's sharp antagonism helped effect the break, Donald reports, the novelist was not above appreciating Julia Wolfe's jejune final solution to the Bernstein problem. Just toss a coin off the Brooklyn Bridge in sight of her, she urged her son: "I've never known one yet that if you drop a nickel but what they'd jump over and scramble for it" (264-266).

If such a strain of anti-Semitism formed a long stream in Thomas Wolfe, stretching from his youthful upbringing right up to the beak-nosed stereotypes of his later fiction, the current was also a shallow one. In fact his fictional examinations of Jews portray equal stereotypes of good and bad qualities. Thus if acquisitive and manipulative, the Jew in Wolfe's fiction typically places a high value on family, cultural achievement, and education. Negative financial greed is balanced by an intellectual ravening which the writer viewed quite favorably.

However insidious such simple-minded attitudes may be, playwright Lillian Hellman was more or less insulated from their serious consequences. Though a Southern Jew herself, she was born into a relatively privileged family in sophisticated New Orleans, a city which prided itself on a singular tolerance for diversity. Her ethnic heritage proved no serious handicap, either, to her career as dramatist during a period when much of Broadway's great theatrical talent was Jewish. What Hellman did bring to New York was a certain high-minded devotion to liberal and leftist causes, an inclination that led her to join the pro-Communist drift so evident in American intelligentsia by the thirties. She held all the proper attitudes of this intellectual milieu, including fervid pro-unionism, anti-Fascism, and a defense of Stalinist Russia so steadfast that as late as 1938 she co-signed a *New Masses* advertisement which endorsed the legitimacy of the Moscow show trials of the Great Purge (Wright 139).

When it came time for Lillian Hellman to compile her memoirs—actually three books, *An Unfinished Woman* (1969), *Pentimento* (1973), and *Scoundrel Time* (1976)—perhaps one incident crystallized in the public mind her position during those radical years better than any other. This was the episode involving Hellman and her heroic friend "Julia," whose name entitled a major section of *Pentimento* as well as a highly successful film of 1977. According to the scenario (and Hellman's memoir reads here like a movie screenplay, opening at the height of action, with flashbacks and jump cuts to present the situation most dramatically), Julia was a girlhood friend, a young woman who graduated Oxford and proceeded to study psychiatric medicine under Freud. While in Austria the always socially-conscious Julia becomes attached to the anti-Nazi underground movement which developed during the thirties, providing aid to refugees and funding to resistance elements within Germany. When Hellman decides to attend the Moscow Theatre Festival in 1937, she wishes to pay a visit to this courageous friend, only to find herself drawn into a dangerous smuggling operation. The now-famous dramatist is asked to accept a large sum of money in Paris and carry it into Germany en route to Moscow; Julia will meet Hellman's train in Berlin and receive the cash transfer there. Over the course of these events, which feature an extraordinary number of breathless cloak-and-dagger encounters with unknown operatives and various complicated exchanges involving a candy box and fur hat, Hellman's character moves from jittery nervousness to cool courage at the moment of crisis: "I laughed at that side of me that so often panics at a moment of no consequence, so often grows listless and sleepy near danger," she blithely recalls (136). By the time she encounters Julia in a Berlin restaurant—the medical student having been crippled during student riots in Vienna—there is little to choose between the two women in terms of heroism.

Certainly the release of the 1977 film based on this *Pentimento* incident climaxed a decade-long rise in celebrity for the playwright, and public appearances, effusive Hollywood salutes and literary tributes continued up to her death in 1984.

Almost, but not quite, drowned out by this thunderous acclaim were the voices of a few skeptical writers and critics who claimed that Hellman often prevaricated in her self-serving memoirs—that the whole "Julia" episode was a fiction, for instance—and they had discomfiting facts to support these allegations. Thus in a 1981 *Paris Review* article Martha Gellhorn, reacting primarily to misstatements about her late ex-husband Ernest Hemingway in Hellman's memoirs, pointed out serious discrepancies in the dates of the "Julia" train episode. According to Gellhorn's analysis, it was chronologically impossible for Hellman to have done all that she claimed to in the late summer and early fall of 1937. Gellhorn concluded that the memoir accounts dangerously partook of "fiction passed off as fact" (301).

Perhaps more damning, if engagingly nonassertive, was the publication of Dr. Muriel Gardiner's *Code Name Mary* in 1983. In the modest autobiographical volume Gardiner remarks that many of her friends told her after the appearance of *Pentimento* that *she* must be "Julia." Reading Hellman's volume, Gardiner too was struck by the undeniable resemblance between Julia and herself—another Oxford graduate medical student who studied with Freud in Vienna between the wars and actively participated in the anti-Fascist underground. Assured by administrators of the Documentation Archives of the Austrian Resistance that no other American woman had been significantly involved with the resistance movement, Gardiner notes in her unassuming introduction, "I have never met Lillian Hellman but had often heard about her from a friend" (xv).

In a 1984 *Commentary* article Samuel McCracken points out that Gardiner's friend, an attorney named Wolf Schwabacher, was also friendly with Hellman for many years and represented her as a client. Schwabacher, who died in 1951, told many of his acquaintances about Gardiner's remarkable pre-war adventures. Furthermore, McCracken's scrutiny of well-documented European train schedules of 1937 also indicate the impossibility of Hellman's "early morning" train arriving in Berlin on the afternoon of the same day it left Paris, as *Pentimento* recounts; and where Julia urges Hellman to depart for Moscow on the train from Berlin's smaller Zoo Station, McCracken points out that no train service ran from that facility to the Russian capital during those years (38). Beyond such problems, McCracken complains that Hellman's "account of the trip rings false wherever it is struck." He notes that money could be brought into Nazi Germany quite openly during this period (as Gardiner's experience also testifies)—thus negating the need for *Pentimento*'s showy, overstaffed operation involving perhaps a dozen agents. "Almost every detail is either improbable to a degree that would disgrace a third-rate thriller, or plainly contradicted by the historical record," he concludes (39).

Hellman's 1986 biographer, William Wright, is all but convinced by such analyses and by the documented evidence Mary McCarthy's lawyers had amassed to counter the famous defamation suit Hellman had filed in 1980.[1] Wright's entire biographical portrait develops a premise that Hellman altered the truth in part to enhance her public image—"to leave with posterity a portrait of the woman she would have liked to have been, a life she would have liked to have led" (414). Acknowledging that the character of "Julia" is perhaps nothing more than a fleshed-out plagiarism from Gardiner's resume, Wright nonetheless argues on behalf of the "creative achievement" exemplified in works such as *Pentimento*. However, if "Julia" is, indeed, a figure inspired by a real source, we might well ask whether the famous money-smuggling incident itself could have its origin in exterior fact. This question brings us back to Thomas Wolfe.

The mid thirties marked a crucial turning point in the novelist's literary career. The autobiographical story of Eugene Gant which had begun in *Look Homeward, Angel* (1929) reached its climax in a sprawling second novel, *Of Time and the River* (1935). When this book was criticized for symptoms of gross overwriting and careless construction, Wolfe took the criticisms to heart. Believing himself unfairly condemned by thirties leftwingers and rightwingers because his own political philosophy seemed unclear, and victimized by the women who entered his life in the wake of Aline Bernstein, the author decided to escape these frustrations by taking a vacation trip to Germany—what was to be his fifth visit to that country in ten years. His novels had been translated there and very well received. Along with critical praise came celebrity: the Germans lionized Wolfe, whose towering figure provoked delighted smiles of recognition from the Tiergarten to the Bavarian Alps.

Drunk with such adulation, the American had been slow to comprehend how the Nazi nation of his brief 1935 sojourn had been a place spiritually different from the Weimer Republic of his first three visits. And his continued appreciation for the cleanliness and efficiency of things German added a significant bonus to the 1936 tour. "This is the cheapest trip I have ever made," he wrote his brother Fred before setting out from New York: the North German Lloyd steamship line had agreed to reimburse the bulk of his fare on the prospect of his writing one or two articles for their travel magazine (23 July 1936, *Letters* 538).

Certainly there were no financial hindrances to another enjoyable vacation. The translations of Wolfe's novels had earned him royalties, but due to German currency restrictions these sums had to be spent within the country. To a person with Wolfe's appetite for life in general and food in particular this posed little difficulty. Along with other tourists he attended the Berlin Olympics every day, cheering on fellow American Jesse Owens boisterously enough to draw a wrathful stare from Adolf Hitler at those propagandized games. If the author was personally unaware of the Fuhrer's displeasure, though, on this trip he could not help becoming aware of the atmosphere of tension, fear and paranoia which had pervaded all levels of German society. Added to the ever more open persecution of the Jews, there were now countless people he was not to associate with, invitations he should not accept, and (most difficult of all) opinions he was not to express. Germany was as lovely as ever that summer, but as Wolfe prepared to depart the country the dulling of the summer green and the browning of a few leaves struck him as symbolic.

Wolfe left Berlin from the Zoo Station on an early morning train bound for Paris. In **"I Have a Thing to Tell You"** he would later write that he shared a compartment with four other passengers, including a naturalized American and "a drab, stuffy, irascible-looking little fellow" Wolfe mentally dubbed "old Fuss-and-Fidget" (II, 161). Remembering the law which permitted travelers to take only ten marks (about thirty dollars) out of the Third Reich, the two Americans spent their remaining cash in the train's dining car. When they returned to the compartment Wolfe and his acquaintance found their German traveling companions unexpectedly convivial; even the unpleasant stranger joined in the new spirit of genial intimacy. "In the most extraordinary way, and in the space of fifteen minutes' time, we seemed to have entered into the lives of all these people and they in ours," Wolfe wrote of the experience. "Now we were not only immensely interested in the information they had given about themselves: we were as warmly, eagerly concerned with the problems that confronted them as if their troubles were our own. . . ." Now he even had a word of praise for Fuss-and-Fidget: "After we had cracked his crusty shell the old codger was not bad. He really was quite friendly underneath" (III, 202).

One of their common complaints, it develops, is the hardship imposed by the currency restrictions. A blonde German woman particularly mentions how difficult it is to conduct her business in Paris with such limited funds, and her companions nod sympathetically. Because the Americans' pockets are now emptied, each offers to carry the ten-mark limit across the Belgian border on behalf of the Germans in the compartment. Fuss-and-Fidget nervously entrusts Wolfe with his portion of excess currency.

But at the border crossing this light-hearted conspiracy turns suddenly grim. The novelist has strolled down the platform after a customs check; he glances favorably at the big German locomotive being uncoupled from the train now, a "magnificent machine" which seems to typify the "powerful, solid and indomitable race" that fashioned it (III, 203). Returning toward his compartment, he discovers that various police and military officials have surrounded the area. Wolfe's first reaction compares the circumstance to various accident scenes he has witnessed before: "You know that someone has just died or is dying, and in the terrible eloquence of backs and shoulders, the *feeding* silence of the watching men, you sense a tragedy that is even deeper. It is the tragedy of man's cruelty and his lust for pain, the tragic weakness that corrupts him, that he loathes but that he cannot cure" (III, 204).

Yet the truth is even more ominous. It appears that all these border-crossing officials have descended on one man, old Fuss-and-Fidget, who is still very alive. The little man sits huddled, his face white and pasty, forehead greased with sweat, making a trembling attempt to explain himself to the sinister crowd of uniformed men. "In the very posture of the men as they bent over him there was something revolting and unclean," Wolfe remarks (III, 204).

The blonde woman quickly explains the scene on the platform. Their traveling companion is Jewish, she says, "doing what so many of the others have done—he was trying to get out with his money." His life savings

had been found in his baggage. Now Wolfe is sickeningly conscious of the "accursed ten marks" he is holding. When he impulsively decides to return the small amount, the woman seizes his arm. It would make things much worse for the arrested man, she argues. Besides: "God knows . . . what he has said already. If he has told that we have transferred money to one another—we may all be in for it!" This unforeseen consequence leaves each of the travelers dazed and silent as the officials prepare to remove their criminal.

> They marched him right along the platform, white as a sheet, greasy looking, protesting volubly, in a voice that had a kind of anguished lilt. He came right by us. I made a movement with my arms. The greasy money sweated in my hand and I did not know what to do. I started to speak to him. And at the same time I was praying that he would not speak. I tried to look away from him, but I could not look away.

(III, 205)

Boarded on the train once more, the solemn passengers gaze out their windows at the arresting officers and their former companion.

> They had him. They just stood and watched him, each with the faint suggestion of that intolerable slow smile upon his face. They raised their eyes, unspeaking, looked at us as we rolled past, with the obscene communication of their glance and of their smile.

> And he—he too paused once more from his voluble and feverish discourse as we passed him. He lifted his eyes to us, his pasty face, and he was silent for a moment. And we looked at him for the last time, and he at us—this time, more direct and steadfastly. And in that glance there was all the silence of man's mortal anguish. And we were all somehow naked and ashamed, and somehow guilty. We all felt somehow that we were saying farewell, not to a man but to humanity. . . .

(III, 205-6)

In the shamed silence of the railroad car, Wolfe remarks that he feels as if he is holding blood money in his hands. "*Nein. Nicht* Blut*geld*—Jud*geld*!" ("Not *blood*-money—*Jew*-money!") the blonde woman responds. She explains apologetically that thousands of Jews had been escaping her country, taking millions of marks with them: "Germany has had to protect herself," she says (III, 206).

But the man with the coins in his pocket can accept no such defense, nor avoid the fact that Germany—"the other half of my heart's home"—has spawned the evil which, once glimpsed so nakedly, could never be forgotten. In relating this discovery, through a work confessionally entitled **"I Have a Thing to Tell You,"** Wolfe painfully acknowledges that he is this awakened traveler, come home to tell a true story which would abrogate his welcome in "that old German land with all the measure of its truth, its glory, beauty, magic and its ruin" (III, 207). The thing Wolfe felt he had to tell, the story which in fact did cause his books to be banned in the Third Reich, was both an epitaph for one lost man and a statement of belief that he had also found himself:

> Something has spoken to me in the night, burning the tapers of the waning year; something has spoken in the night and told me I shall die, I know not where. Losing the earth we know for greater knowing, losing the life we have for greater life, and leaving the friends we loved for greater loving, men find a land more kind than home, more large than earth.
>
> Whereon the pillars of this earth are founded, toward which the spirits of the nations draw, toward which the conscience of the world is tending—a wind is rising, and the rivers flow.

> (III, 207)

Wolfe's story was, like so much of his published "fiction," based almost entirely on his actual experience. In fact he originally thought to use as title "I Have Them Yet," a phrase referring to the scattered coins which the author kept on his table while writing the piece (Nowell 337). The money was greasy with evil, he believed, but also the token of a moral exchange.

Could this story of one writer's awakened social conscience have somehow inspired the daring action of Lillian Hellman's *Pentimento* episode? **"I Have a Thing to Tell You"** was first published in three issues of *The New Republic,* a magazine with wide circulation in liberal New York circles of 1937. It also formed the penultimate section of Wolfe's posthumous bestseller *You Can't Go Home Again* (1940). Both appearances are significant, since Hellman submitted her own short fiction to *The New Republic* in 1938, and did voluminous research on the history and background of events in Europe before drafting her 1941 play, *Watch on the Rhine* (Harriman 104). Given Hellman's probable familiarity with Muriel Gardiner's exploits through the agency of a mutual acquaintance, furthermore, it is interesting to consider another set of facts. Aline Bernstein helped herself recover from a suicidal depression after her break-up with Thomas Wolfe by taking on the costuming duties for Hellman's *The Children's Hour* in 1934; the designer was subsequently hired to work on Hellman's *Days to Come* (1936) and *The Little Foxes* (1939) as well. Though by no means intimate, the two professional women did socialize on occasion (Rollyson, 133, 136).

At any rate there is a general resemblance between the two stories of American writers undergoing ethical crises aboard trains in pre-war Nazi Germany (granting that Wolfe's fear-stricken silence in the face of danger is far more believable than Hellman's self-described

yawns). Moreover, Wolfe's story suspiciously jibes with Hellman's memoir in just those areas where Gellhorn and McCracken discovered flat impossibilities. The known events of Hellman's life can't be reconciled with a late summer/early fall 1937 trip through Germany, for example—but this is the time of the year when Wolfe sets his story of 1936, the tree leaves "already touched here and there by the yellowing tinge of autumn" (I, 132). Hellman's late afternoon arrival at the German border following a morning departure from Paris matches no known train schedule of the period, while Wolfe's journey from Berlin to the Belgian border is properly placed within such a time span. And though no trains left from Berlin's Zoo Station for Moscow, as Hellman's itinerary demands, it *was* possible to travel west from that branch terminal, as Wolfe's version has it. Above all, whereas no rationale explains "Julia"'s plot requisite for carrying funds into Nazi Germany secretly, the smuggling situation Wolfe depicts is historically verified by the provisions of Nazi law specifically designed to bankrupt refugees—especially Jews—fleeing the Third Reich.

Thus we are faced with the prospect of one author's memoirs—"reality" which seems untrue—possibly having made use of another author's writing—which is paradoxically a "fiction" based on autobiographical experience. To the end of her life Hellman maintained that, while she had changed the proper names in "Julia" (for reasons which do not stand up well under scrutiny),[2] all other facts are accurate. "I trust absolutely what I remember about Julia," she states in *Pentimento* (112).

But a variety of inaccuracies bring us back to the opening words of that volume:

> Old paint on canvas as it ages, sometimes becomes transparent. When that happens it is possible, in some pictures, to see the original lines: a tree will show through a woman's dress, a child makes way for a dog, a large boat is no longer on an open sea. That is called pentimento because the painter "repented," changed his mind. Perhaps it would be as well to say that the old conception, replaced by a later choice, is a way of seeing and then seeing again.

> (3)

This statement about revision, while appropriate to creative art, is indeed curious as foreword to a volume of memoirs. It unconsciously invites us to view the writer as a reviser of history, too, and in that light we cannot read *Pentimento* or the other Hellman autobiographies without noting how consistently the author places herself on the side of the angels, cementing in the public mind her reputation for principled action and honesty. And how odd to think that the "original lines" beneath her stirring account of anti-Nazism, in particular, may have been written by an author who, fifty years after his death, still retains, like a scarlet letter, the stigma of his anti-Semitism.

For Thomas Wolfe died in 1938—the same year to which Hellman ascribes Julia's tragically early death. The 37-year-old Wolfe hardly had the chance to revise his life in a practical sense, much less a literary one. What he did leave, in **"I Have a Thing to Tell You,"** is merely an implication that, before his passing he may, indeed, have learned *some*thing when an unpleasant, undesirable fellow-passenger, a Jew, had turned out to be "really quite friendly underneath." Out of his own fearful silence in the face of that man's agony he had conceived, somewhat sooner than most Americans, a conviction that Hitler's Germany demanded a response from the world's conscience. Accordingly he returned the travel-fare money advanced by the North German Lloyd, explaining that now "certain deep and earnest convictions of my own" would prevent him from composing suitable travel articles for the line's magazine, though the summer's trip provided material "not only for three articles, but for thirty" ("To Elsa C. Sperling" 12 Oct. 1936, *Letters* 544).

Whether Hellman modeled the "Julia" episode on **"I Have a Thing to Tell You"** is perhaps ultimately unfathomable. But I believe it is nonetheless time to put the two accounts side by side: if only to suggest that Wolfe's thirty dollars represented more real change than Hellman's fifty thousand.

Notes

1. McCarthy had declared in a television interview that Hellman was an overrated, dishonest writer and that "every word she writes is a lie, including 'and' and 'the.'" For one account of the subsequent lawsuit, see Wright 386-396.

2. Hellman claimed that, writing *Pentimento* in the Willy Brandt era of 1973, she still felt compelled to protect the identity of Germany's "premature anti-Nazis" (101); added to the strangeness of this claim is the strangeness of making any name changes at all, since no last names are provided in the "Julia" account.

Works Cited

Donald, David Herbert. *Look Homeward: A Life of Thomas Wolfe*. Boston: Little, Brown, 1987.

Gardiner, Muriel. *Code Name "Mary": Memoirs of an American Woman in the Austrian Underground*. New Haven: Yale UP, 1983.

Gellhorn, Martha. "On Apocryphism." *Paris Review* 23.79 (spring 1981): 280-304.

Harriman, Margaret. *Take Them Up Tenderly*. New York: Knopf, 1945.

Hellman, Lillian. *Pentimento: A Book of Portraits*. Boston: Little, Brown, 1973.

McCracken, Samuel. "'Julia' and Other Fictions by Lillian Hellman." *Commentary* June 1984: 35-43.

Nowell, Elizabeth, ed. *The Letters of Thomas Wolfe.* New York: Scribner's, 1956. Cited in the text of this article as *Letters*.

———. *Thomas Wolfe: A Biography*. Garden City, N.Y.: Doubleday, 1960.

Rollyson, Carl. *Lillian Hellman: Her Legend and Her Legacy*. New York: St. Martin's, 1988.

Wolfe, Thomas. "I Have a Thing to Tell You (*Nun Will Ich Ihnen Was Sagen*)," *New Republic,* published in three consecutive numbers. Part I, 10 March 1937: 132-136; II, 17 March 1937: 159-164; III, 24 March 1937: 202-207.

Wright, William. *Lillian Hellman: The Image, the Woman*. New York: Simon and Schuster, 1986.

James W. Clark Jr. (essay date 1992)

SOURCE: Clark, James W. Jr. Introduction to *The Lost Boy: A Novella,* by Thomas Wolfe, edited by James W. Clark Jr., pp. ix-xiv. Chapel Hill: The University of North Carolina Press, 1992.

[*In the following essay, Clark chronicles* The Lost Boy's *various incarnations—both as novella and as short story—and the role Wolfe's brother Grover played in life as well as in death.*]

In 1929 Thomas Wolfe made himself famous by portraying his voluble Asheville family as the memorable Gants of Altamont in *Look Homeward, Angel*. His proud and prescient mother always insisted, nonetheless, that an older son named Grover, not her youngest child Tom, was the brightest and best of her offspring. Born in 1900, Wolfe could barely remember this remarkable brother their mother continued to long for and memorialize; but he, too, craved information about Grover, as letters, notebook entries, an autobiographical outline, and two chapters of his first novel illustrate. In early March 1937 Wolfe completed a hauntingly beautiful and mysterious account of his own search for Grover. This belated addition to the Gant cycle of his fiction is the four-part novella entitled **The Lost Boy.**

In each part of this work Wolfe presents Grover from the perspective of a different family member. Part I is a third-person prose poem that relates Grover's own impressions and comprehensions of his afternoon experiences on the hometown square in April 1904. The father defends Grover in an episode that leaves the quiet boy changed forever. Part II presents Grover through his mother's adoring eyes; she focuses especially on a long-ago train trip that same April to St. Louis and the World's Fair. An older sister gives her acutely personal retrospection from the 1930s in Part III. In Part IV the youngest brother relates his own unsuccessful attempt to find Grover in the hot darkness of a late summer evening as he returns to the house in St. Louis where the family had spent seven months more than thirty years earlier.

Wolfe wrote *The Lost Boy* during a very demanding period, a time when he was realizing and expressing an expansion of his already abundant curiosities and human sympathies. Assisted by his splendid agent Elizabeth Nowell, he produced short novels like this one. He was also setting his giant compass on his southern mountain home for the first time since he had become famous. Moreover, Wolfe was anxious about his health and finances. As soon as the novella about Grover Gant was finished, Nowell helped Wolfe edit a short story out of it, and *Redbook Magazine* soon paid him $1,500 for this version—the largest sum he had ever received for a story. With some of this income he paid his passage from New York to Asheville later in the spring of 1937 when he went to visit his mother at home for the first time since the publication of *Look Homeward, Angel*. During the summer he returned for a longer, working vacation. That November **"The Lost Boy"** appeared in *Redbook* with the title character renamed Robert.

In September 1938 Elizabeth Nowell was in Baltimore with Julia Wolfe and her daughter Mabel when Wolfe lay dying of tuberculosis of the brain at Johns Hopkins Hospital. According to Nowell's biography of the author, when Mrs. Wolfe was told by Dr. Walter Dandy that her famous son was doomed, she instantly reverted to her memories of Grover and expressed them almost exactly as Wolfe had in Part II of **The Lost Boy**: "Child, child, it was so long ago, but when I hear the name again, it all comes back, as if it happened yesterday. And the old raw sore is open. I can see him just the way he was, the way he looked. . . ."

Edward Aswell of Harper and Brothers, the last editor to work personally with Wolfe, included a short version of **The Lost Boy**—different from the *Redbook* text—in the 1941 posthumous collection called **The Hills Beyond**. It is this rendition of the story based on Grover Wolfe that has become critically acclaimed, while the 1937 story that Wolfe and Nowell cut out of the novella and sold remains less well known. It is true that Francis E. Skipp selected the *Redbook* version for his 1987 edition of **The Complete Short Stories of Thomas Wolfe**. Yet by doing so he effectively moved the work out of the Gant cycle in which the novella is written, for he retained *Robert* as the name for Grover Gant.

By the time Wolfe wrote **The Lost Boy**, he had, in fact, largely moved from his Gant cycle to his Webber cycle, with George Webber succeeding Eugene Gant as the semi-autobiographical protagonist of his fictional world. In the 1939 posthumous novel *The Web and the Rock*, George Webber comments on the changes in the life of a boy between his twelfth and thirteenth years by entitling his own inaugural story "The End of the Golden Weather." This title is especially instructive for readers of Part I of **The Lost Boy**. Grover's father powerfully defends his son, but Mr. Gant cannot restore the boy's lively dream of life, his shimmering lights of boyhood. In the words of chapter 15 of *The Web and the Rock*, "For the first time, some of the troubling weathers of a man's soul are revealed to him . . . for the first time, he becomes aware of the thousand changing visages of time; and how his clear and radiant legend of the earth is, for the first time, touched with confusion and bewilderment, menaced by terrible depths and enigmas of experience he has never known before." George Webber's story opens with a twelve-year-old boy in his uncle's front yard at three o'clock in the afternoon. **The Lost Boy** opens as Grover, about that age, comes into the three o'clock radiance of the square, that haggis of images of abundance and loss, of fixity and change.

From Wolfe family photographs we know that Julia Wolfe and her son Grover looked remarkably alike. He is more than her physical tally, however. The mother's account of her lost boy in the second part of the novella presents him as an ace trader like herself, complete with her coloring, her hair. He also has her strong racial prejudices and pride. In the father's absence on the trip to St. Louis, young Grover is the man of the Gant family. It is he who tells their black retainer Simpson Featherstone to leave their train car and return to his accustomed place—although the Jim Crow laws in force back home are not the code of Indiana. Confronted by Grover, the black man obeys; years later the boy's proud mother still exults.

In bringing this particular family episode to light in **The Lost Boy**, Wolfe's fiction shows the extent to which his brother Grover had been, would always be, the best and brightest Wolfe child in their mother's judgment. Grover is her double, body and soul. That this illustrative Jim Crow episode is among the numerous cuts made in the narrative as Wolfe and Nowell shaped it for a magazine audience is especially regrettable. The honest passage, however troubling to modern readers, is one more indication of what the famous son believed his mother's immense pride in Grover amounted to. Elizabeth Nowell, for her part, understood what Wolfe intended by the full novella portrait he had originally provided of this mother-son team. In a March 5, 1937 letter, included by Richard S. Kennedy in *Beyond Love and Loyalty,* the agent wrote to the author that she had cut his edited typescript down to magazine size and popular taste in desperation. She knew, she said, that some of her suggested excisions would probably make Wolfe's heart bleed.

Grover's inventory of Garrett's grocery store on the square in Part I is another example of significant material left out of the *Redbook* version. So is the description in Part IV of Eugene's dark evening of hot despair in St. Louis. The one balances the other by contrasting kinds and tones of perceived abundance or excess. Neither these instances at the opening and closing of this short novel nor Grover's bold confrontation of Simpson Featherstone on the train in Part II has been known or even expected by readers of Wolfe until now.

Wolfe's artistic power in the short novel form is neither unknown nor unexpected, however. Both C. Hugh Holman and David Herbert Donald have stressed the effective demonstration of Wolfe's literary genius in the novella. Donald comments in *Look Homeward: A Life of Thomas Wolfe* that even if Wolfe himself had demurred, "little books would have been good for Wolfe's reputation. They would have demonstrated that, whatever Wolfe's limitations in crafting a long novel, he displayed a splendid sense of artistry in the short novel of 15,000 to 40,000 words. . . . Years later C. Hugh Holman edited five of *The Short Novels of Thomas Wolfe,* which reminded readers that this was the form in which Wolfe worked best."

The Lost Boy is not included in Holman's 1961 collection, nor is it incorporated into one of the novels that Wolfe considered real writing. But this novella is a finely crafted realization of the author's genius for little books, especially this one he had contemplated so long and so actively. If Wolfe could not find Grover—even by visiting the house in St. Louis in 1935—his concentrated sense of artistry has found in this four-part tribute a most memorable way to express the spacious presence of his, and our, abundant sense of loss. Here is more of Wolfe's magic in a dusty world.

Readers inspired to look further for information about what happened to Grover Wolfe will be rewarded by examining chapters 17 and 18 of *Thomas Wolfe and His Family* (1961) by Mabel Wolfe Wheaton and

LeGette Blythe. Julia Wolfe left us no independent account of her favorite child. The final chapter of *The Marble Man's Wife* by Hayden Norwood is the closest nonfictional approximation of her views.

Suzanne Stutman and John L. Idol Jr. (essay date 1995)

SOURCE: Stutman, Suzanne, and John L. Idol Jr. Introduction to *The Party at Jack's,* by Thomas Wolfe, edited by Suzanne Stutman and John L. Idol Jr., pp. ix-xxv. Chapel Hill: The University of North Carolina Press, 1995.

[*In the following essay, Stutman and Idol consider some of Wolfe's manuscript outlines of* The Party at Jack's *and provide a detailed analysis of the novella, which they term "a social fable of universal proportions."*]

BACKGROUND

At Oteen in the North Carolina mountains during the summer of 1937, where he was busily revising a piece for which he had made notebook entries in 1930, Thomas Wolfe started adding fresh material. Pleased with his efforts, despite numerous interruptions from kinfolk and literary lion hunters, Wolfe wrote to his literary agent, Elizabeth Nowell, to report how his work was going:

> I have completely rewritten it and rewoven it. It is a very difficult piece of work, but I think it is now a single thing, as much a single thing as anything I've ever written. I am not through with it yet. There is a great deal more revision to be done, but I am sending it to you anyway to let you see what I have done, and I think you will be able to see what it may be like when I'm finished with it.
>
> (Nowell, ed., *The Letters of Thomas Wolfe* [New York: Scribner's, 1956], 651)

The piece was *The Party at Jack's,* portions of which have seen print through the efforts of Elizabeth Nowell and Edward Aswell, Wolfe's editor at Harper's, who included portions of it in *You Can't Go Home Again.*

Just when he first wrote the parts he was now rewriting cannot be fixed precisely. Besides bits of dialogue done as early as 1930, the earliest definite outline of a chronological sequence for the events occurring on the day of the party appeared on a manila envelope dating to the fall of 1932. Here Wolfe scrawled

MORNING: THREE IN A CITY

I Jacobs—German background—Schoolboy scene
II Jacobs Awake

III Esther and the Maid
IV Jacobs and Esther.

Since Wolfe used such outlines both to show what he wanted to write and to list those pieces already done for some project he had in mind, it is impossible to claim that the present outline launched what he would in time call *The Party at Jack's.*

Whatever came first, manuscript drafts of the story as he conceived it or the outline recounting what he had done, papers in the Wisdom Collection in the Houghton Library reveal that he set to work to create accounts of Frederick and Esther Jacobs and one of Esther's maids, Katy Fogarty. Frederick (Fritz), a German Jew, dreams about his schoolboy days and his return to the Rhineland after becoming fabulously rich in America. He awakens to luxuriate in his princely Park Avenue apartment (bMS Am 1883 [932]). Esther awakens in the tastefully furnished Jacobs household to enjoy her awareness of her body and to chastise Katy for becoming a victim of strong drink. This episode ends with Esther musing further on what she's made of her life and the wonder she feels about her lot as a beautiful, talented, admired woman (bMS Am 1883 [933]). Following their separate awakenings, Fritz and Esther come together. He proudly reads reviews of her stage designs for an otherwise undistinguished play. Together, they revel in her success. On his way to his office, he thinks about the lies, thefts, and chicanery of his driver, dismissing his behavior as typical of servants. Upon reaching his office, he meets a fellow broker, Rosenthal, who is a bona fide crackpot. Tales of Rosenthal's crazy behavior are told by his Irish secretary (bMS Am 1883 [934]).

As arranged in the Wisdom Collection, the next manuscript indicates further development of the story.

Synopsis
1. Before sunrise
2. Morning [Jacob's Dream]
    [Character of Jacobs The Day]
    [Jacobs getting up]
    Mrs. Esther Jacobs
    Esther with Jacobs
    Esther's morning—canceled
    Esther with Alma, Edith, Freddy
    Esther's morning
3. Noon
4. Afternoon
5. Evening

The chronological scheme set down here would hold throughout Wolfe's many revisions and provide a classic touch to his use of time, less than twenty-four hours from the awakening scenes to George Webber's farewell words to Esther Jack. In outline form as Wolfe

looked forward to embodying this material in his chronicle of his new protagonist's (George Webber's) life, that scheme appears in the William Wisdom Collection of Wolfe manuscripts at the Houghton Library under the index bMS Am 1883 (1336).

Part IV

You Can't Go Home Again

(1930-1938)

Book

The Party at Jack's (1930)

Chapters:
    Morning
    Morning: Jack Asleep
    Morning: Jack Erect
    Morning: Jack Afloat
    Morning: Mrs. Jack Awake
    Morning: Mrs. Jack And The Maid
    Morning: Jack And His Wife
    Morning: The World That Jack Built
    The Great Building (April, 1930)
    The Elevator Men
    Before The Party (Mrs. Jack And The Maids)
    Piggy Logan
    The Family (Mrs. Jack, Alma, etc.)
    The Party Beginning
    The Guests Arriving
    The Lover
    Mr. Hirsch Was Wounded Sorrowfully
    Piggy Logan's Circus
    The Guests Departing: The Fire
    The Fire: The Outpouring of the Honeycomb
    The Fire: The Tunneled Rock
    After The Fire: These Two Together

This outline probably reflects the story as Wolfe had shaped it before leaving New York for a speaking engagement at Purdue University in 1938. (It is the basis of our reconstruction of *The Party at Jack's.*)

Exactly how Wolfe arrived at this scheme cannot be precisely traced in surviving versions of the story. The central event, a party and fire at the Park Avenue apartment of Aline Bernstein, his mistress and patron, occurred on 3 January 1930 and was to be included as part of Eugene Gant's story. But over a period of years, Wolfe added actions and characters, finally reshaping the story to show shifts in characterization, symbolic import, and values (more about these later). Although he had settled on a time scheme, he remained uncertain about whether his fictional surrogate would attend the party and witness the fire. One draft (bMS Am 1883 [985]) follows the storyline from preparation for the party through Piggy Logan's circus on to the fire and its aftermath. In this version, Esther telephones her lover to report on the party and to tell him about the unexpected fire. With George Webber not on the scene, Stephen Hook figures more prominently here than in the version where Esther's lover makes a belated appearance at the party. As he filled out the action, Wolfe faced decisions about what his surrogate would do once Wolfe had decided to have him appear. How would he show his resentment that Esther had insisted that he be there? With whom would he converse? How much would he eat and drink? How would he respond to Piggy Logan and his wire circus act? What would he do during the fire and its aftermath? How would he reveal his decision to break with Esther? In one episode involving Esther's lover—not called George or Eugene—Esther, seeing her lover and Lily Mandell talking together, comes to them, calls them her best friends, and wishes they could know each other better. She senses the raw sexual attraction between Lily and her lover and leads them off to a bedroom, where they become the two-backed animal. This episode (bMS Am 1883 [938]) complicates Esther's character considerably. Interpreted charitably, it reveals her as someone capable of rising above sexual possessiveness in order to foster friendship. Read uncharitably, it reduces her to a panderer, a wily spider spinning a web of iniquity, showing her to be no better morally than the decadent, privileged crowd she has invited to her party.

Having opted to include Esther's lover at the party, Wolfe makes him largely a guest among many, many guests until the outbreak of the fire and the hurried departure of most of the other partygoers. Those partygoers and their interactions would come to constitute the central portions of his novel. Their numbers could swell or shrink as Wolfe's needs and purposes changed. (They could also dwindle—and did—when Elizabeth Nowell and Edward Aswell shaped the material for its appearance in *Scribner's Magazine* and *You Can't Go Home Again*.) Prominent among those added is Roy Farley, a homosexual, whose mincing ways create laughter and applause. Like Saul Levinson and his wife and a sculptor named Krock, Farley would not survive as a partygoer when Nowell and Aswell edited Wolfe's various drafts for publication. Cut from the guest list, with some of his traits then assigned to his father, was Freddie Jack, his removal being made with Wolfe's consent as Nowell began to condense the story for periodical publication. (She later suggested to Aswell that Freddie be restored in order to correct some inconsistencies in Fritz Jack's character, a suggestion Aswell chose to ignore.)

Wolfe's potential list of partygoers originated in the guests gathered at Aline Bernstein's home to enjoy a performance of Alexander Calder's celebrated wire circus. Excepting such respected persons as Thomas Beer and his sister, Wolfe cast a satiric eye at most of Bernstein's guests, largely an assemblage of New York's financial and artistic elite. True to his longtime practice, he sometimes used real names in early drafts, a factor that forced Aswell later to check with Bernstein to learn who could possibly bring a libel suit against Harper's. Aswell's concern probably stemmed from conversations with Nowell. She had earlier told Maxwell Perkins that the longer version of the story "may be libelous since it tells the dirt on the private lives of practically every person at the party" (personal letter from Nowell to Perkins, Dec. 1938). However long or short the final list, Wolfe obviously meant to present Esther Jack's guests, in the main, as privileged, corrupt, decadent, hypocritical, and hostile to the true artist.

A further stage of development, the introduction of working-class characters, first involved two elevator men, one young, the other elderly. The older man, John Enborg (the surname finally chosen), grateful to have a job, defends his privileged employers. His reasons to speak for them are challenged by a third representative of the working class, Hank, who apparently emerged as the voice of organized labor when Wolfe reworked his material at Oteen. In the handwritten pages dating from Oteen and in typed pages done in New York after Wolfe's return to the city, these working-class men are both individualized and, except for Hank, made more sympathetic. If Wolfe were to have his surrogate cast his lot with the working class, proletarian traits and ideas needed to be understood. To make the proletarian pill less easy to swallow, Wolfe coated Hank with more than a little sourness. If he were to show that old loyalties to the upper classes were no longer fitting in a greedy, corrupt age, he needed someone to provide tough arguments against John Enborg's nostalgic attachment to such wealthy people as the Jacks.

Wolfe came to see, as Richard S. Kennedy convincingly argued, that the building in which the workers served the wealthy could be presented as a symbol of the American economic system. Efficient, strong, durable, and secure as it seemed to be, the building was honeycombed with shafts and situated on tunnels connecting it, by rail, to the rest of the nation. Problems in the shafts or tunnels could weaken or undermine it. Without the workers, the building could not operate effectively. The more he became socially and economically aware, the more Wolfe believed he must fashion a story capable of addressing some of the nation's ills. Thus as *The Party at Jack's* evolved from its first drafts through those portions written at Oteen and later in New York, Wolfe was not content to have his surrogate reject Esther's world because it was artistically decadent and, at bottom, hostile to the creative spirit: Now he would warn his fellow citizens about the callousness, greed, and hypocrisy of the privileged.

His story now had the three unities: a single setting at the Jacks' Park Avenue apartment, a party interrupted by a fire and its aftermath, and time running from the Jacks' awakening until their retiring to bed. Until the material could take its place in some work in progress, the narrative of Eugene Gant's and George Webber's discoveries and deeds, Wolfe frequently listed episodes and tallied his word count, giving variously 18,000, 35,000, and 60,000, the last a reckoning taken as he recorded pieces completed after 1935 and 1936. The variations perhaps resulted from additions made to the story over the years or possibly, for the lowest number, the maximum that Nowell considered marketable to a periodical. In her effort to help him place the story before he went to Oteen, Nowell trimmed it to 25,000 words. (She later submitted a 26,000-word version to *Redbook* and after its rejection there slashed more than 10,000 more words to make it acceptable to *Scribner's,* where it appeared in May 1939.)

Although Wolfe had participated in trimming the version sent to *Redbook,* he was by no means ready to put the story aside. Settled in at Oteen, he turned to it once more, restoring text that he and Nowell had sliced for *Redbook* and adding to it, thinking as he did so that it would be "very long, difficult and closely woven." He went on to tell Hamilton Basso,

> I don't know how it's going to turn out, but if I succeed with it, it ought to be good. It is one of the most curious and difficult problems I have been faced with in a long time and maybe I shall learn something from it. It is a story that in its essence and without trying or intending to be, has got to be somewhat Proustian— that is to say its life depends upon the most thorough and comprehensive investigation of character—or characters, for there are more than thirty characters in it. In addition, however, there is a tremendous amount of submerged action which involves the lives of all these people and which includes not only the life of a great apartment house but also a fire and the death of two people. I suppose really a whole book could be made out of it but I am trying to do it in a story.

> (*Letters of Thomas Wolfe,* 631)

A few days later (29 July 1937) he told Nowell much the same thing and then, sometime in late August, that he was sending the story to her, adding that he now considered it "a single thing" but still in need of revision. Back in New York, he resumed work on it, eventually producing a typescript from which Aswell shaped the portion of *You Can't Go Home Again* that he called "The World That Jack Built." From the various drafts in the Wisdom Collection, we have at-

tempted to restore to Wolfe and American literature the "single thing" that Wolfe named **The Party at Jack's.**

THEMES AND CHARACTERS

Many filaments in Wolfe's complex web of themes— those that he spins out time after time—coalesce to make this work one of his richest. Here he spreads before readers a table so groaning with food that both Bacchus and Brueghel would surely rush to pay compliments to Esther and her cook and maids. Here he gives such meticulous attention to clothing, furnishings, and wall hangings that the swankiness of the Jacks' Park Avenue apartment becomes palpably real, the fullness of Wolfe's description rivaling his detailing of the Pierces' luxurious Hudson River mansion. This attention to how well, how sumptuously, and how far above the struggles and worries of the working class the Jacks live affords Wolfe another chance to chronicle life among the privileged class. His account stretches from the dream of wealth, power, and fame of Frederick Jack in Germany through Frederick's and Esther's awakening voluptuously in quarters where his dream has become a proud reality. In relation to Wolfe's thematic interests in the present work and elsewhere in his canon, Frederick's rise from the status of an immigrant German Jew to his position as a lord of wealth and sophistication invites contrastive and comparative looks at the yearnings of another provincial, George Webber. Comfortable and secure though the Jacks appear in their Park Avenue surroundings, Wolfe provides hints of coming trouble by having trains send tremors through their building. Unlike trains in other passages in his canon, where Wolfe tends to be lyrical about their size and might, trains in this work are associated with the potential collapse of structures that could be taken as symbolic of the nation's capitalistic economy. More than that, the tracks carrying them beneath the proud towers of Manhattan come to represent here the ties existing between the rich, the poor, and those in between. In a sense, the tracks parallel Herman Melville's monkeyrope as a symbol of men's interconnections.

Wolfe's emphasis on wealth and the power, corruption, and decadence it affords the Jacks and their circle enables him to trace the ignoble use of money and position among the privileged class. While they show themselves to be the apes of fashion—by wanting to see Piggy Logan perform—and tolerant of crimes both petty and major among their servants, they have little genuine interest in promoting art that has stood the test of time and fail to dismiss or prosecute their thieving and conniving servants. All the wrongs and decadence laid bare here add proof that Libya Hill, the microcosm of corrupt economic and cultural life presented early in the Webber cycle, has its sordid counterpart in bustling and greed-driven Manhattan. As an artist, Wolfe wanted to show that he was just as obliged to expose and revile corruption in the nation's greatest city as he was to set forth the dark deeds of Judge Rumford Bland and others living or working on the square of Libya Hill. His protagonist must assume the role of Hercules, attempting to lead the nation to join him in cleansing this American version of the Aegean stables. To perform that labor meant that his protagonist would arouse the ire of Libya Hillians and New Yorkers. To find the strength, time, and, more important, freedom to combat the forces threatening to undermine the nation, Wolfe asked George Webber to cast aside his hope for fame and love. Speaking the truth carried a heavy price, Webber had learned upon publishing his first novel, and another sacrifice he must make if he is to continue to expose the hypocrisy of the Jacks' circle is Esther's love and support. Here, then, is how the episodes making up this work fulfill Wolfe's plan (expressed in Statement of Purpose for the Webber cycle) of illustrating "essential elements of any man's progress and discovery of life and as they illustrate the world itself, not in the terms of personal and self-centered conflict with the world, but in terms of ever-increasing discovery of life and the world, with a consequent diminution of the more personal and self-centered vision of the world which a young man has."

Here Wolfe tries hard—but not always successfully—to cast off self-centeredness, the Eugene Gant-i-ness of his first two novels. (Something of Eugene Gant remains because portions of the present work come, with little or no revision, from "The October Fair," that portion of his grand plan for a series of novels treating his love affair with Aline Bernstein, the model for Esther Jack.) An early draft of the farewell scene with Esther Jack has the young hero speaking like some Faustian aesthete—the Jacks and their peers are represented as deadly enemies from whom the artist must escape if he is to render the world at large, the privileged and the wretched of the world, "with a young man's mind, with that wonderful, active, hungry, flaming, seething mind of a young man." A later draft portrays a socially conscious artist, one capable of seeing the dross behind the glitter, the self-serving motive underlying a show of compassion, and the moral and intellectual emptiness masked by a push to be up-to-date in everything. To do the job awaiting him as a champion of the working class, he swallowed a bitter pill, a farewell to love, and departed knowing that "there were new lands; dark windings, strange and subtle webs there in the deep delved earth, a tide was running in the hearts of men—and he must go." As *George,* he would choose sides with men of the

earth and help them reveal the fact that the privileged class merely occupied a structure supported by the sweat, agony, and deprivation of the common men; as *Webber* he would be the artist helping the common man understand the value of his work, thought, and talents. Ultimately, the party he chose was not one of jack—money and the power and the privileges it brings—but one of honest toil.

In effect, the opening dream sequence prefigures the many themes that Wolfe presented throughout his entire book-length manuscript. Indeed, it seems as if humanity itself takes a haunted ride down the river of time and memory into its deepest soul to examine the profoundest truths of mankind with Frederick in his moments before awakening. Frederick Jack, and the life he has created, seems to rest like some enfabled city, with which he is so much in tune, on solid ground. Yet in his dream, Frederick is trapped in time suspended. In this nether world of his mind's creation he has neither power nor control, as past and present surrealistically form their own strange reality. The classmates who taunt him about his Jewishness and who pursue him with a violent anti-Semitism are prophetic of Germany's hate-filled future, a future that George Webber encounters in the latter portion of *You Can't Go Home Again.*

In his dream, Frederick finds that his family treats him as if he were a child, not the adult he has become, and their smothering attention suffocates him, much like the adult Wolfe found himself to be when he returned to Asheville. To assert his power and "manliness," Frederick recounts his wealth and ownership, much like King Midas counting his gold. Yet the ancient cobbled streets and his connection with the past fill him with exquisite happiness. When he encounters his old schoolmates, whom he feels somehow destined to meet, they are old and battered, and he knows that they have all suffered blows from life. He feels a sense of unity with his enemies and, indeed, with all mankind. He longs to tell them of his life in America after he left Germany, of his loneliness and poverty in his early years, and of his empty success. He yearns to tell them how he gained power yet somehow lost the dream, how like smoke and sand the boy's dream has vanished.

Like the characters who come and go at the Jacks' party that very evening, Frederick has become one of the hollow men, possessing a "suave and kindly cynicism" and "the varnish of complaisance." Like J. Alfred Prufrock, who lived in the world between the real and the unreal, between imagination and reality—who lived a life stunted and dulled and full of emptiness in that great city London—Frederick Jack stood, in the final moments of his dream, looking toward the water, rocking in time's harbor and listening to the mermaids sing.

In the next four chapters, Wolfe sets about establishing his themes and further developing his characterization of Frederick and Esther Jack. Frederick (Fritz) believes that he is in total control of his world. Like a Roman emperor, he sensuously luxuriates in his sumptuous surroundings, narcissistically adoring his own health and vigor. He possesses not only the luxury of wealth but that of time as well, time enough to reflect from his height and distance upon the antlike populace who "swarm" to and fro, both literally and figuratively beneath him. Yet, from the beginning, the almost imperceptible tremor coming from deep within the rock below causes him a vague sense of foreboding and apprehension. The natural world seems overshadowed by the cruel, piercing dominance of these lifeless, monstrous buildings. Indeed, his connection with nature is an artificial one, experienced through the "expensive" sport of golf. He walks upon the "rich velvet of the greens" and "luxuriates" upon the "cool veranda of the club." Even nature has been tamed for his rich men's pursuits. The artificiality of the buildings mock the golden light of the day, an imitation of gold and silver: "silver-burnished steel and cliffs of harsh white-yellow brick, haggard in young light," imagery of false idols, craven images. Indeed, "the immense and vertical shapes of the great buildings . . . dwindled to glittering needles of cold silver [as] light cut sharply the crystal weather of a blue shell-fragile sky." Nature seems to bleed, indeed, to face destruction from these needlelike buildings. The creatures of the city seem to be miniature representations of this lifeless creation. Their cabs are like "hard-shelled prehistoric beasts emerging from Grand Central projectile-like in solid beetle-bullet flight." Mr. Jack has paid for this sense of order and power out of chaos "with the ransom of an emperor." He has indeed paid dearly, with his very soul. The window of his apartment building is paralleled by the window of his eye from which the narrowness of his vision is reflected. He worships illusion—the illusion of power, the illusion of youth, the illusion of eternal potency—and "in that insolent boast of steel and stone [he sees] . . . a permanence surviving every danger, an answer, crushing and convulsive in its silence, to every doubt."

Frederick is characterized as a hollow man, fragmented and full of self-delusion. In contrast, Esther is characterized as a woman possessing a sense of oneness, a connectedness with life, past and present, rich and poor, old and young. Through Esther is "always the clear design, the line of life, running like a thread of gold" from childhood to the present. Her beauty is real, not artificial. Her face reveals complex emotions; it is not smooth and controlled as is Frederick's. Esther is capable of genuine sorrow and depth of feeling. She does not merely take from others, as does Fritz and others like him, for her own gain. She is an artist, a creator. She possesses the ability to create real gold, to transform people and to give them hope. In fact, Esther is like nature herself: "that one deathless flower of a face that bloomed among so many millions of the dead." Like a fertility goddess, she offers hope in the wasteland of modern society.

In these chapters, Wolfe satirizes capitalistic waste and greed, tellingly representative of both the privileged class and their poorer counterparts. Both patron and servant are alike, the only difference being the degree of wealth and power each possesses. Above all else, the goal is to win, and corruption trickles down through the hive, the honeycomb. This corruption is represented, respectively, by the relationship between Esther and her maid and between Frederick and his chauffeur. In words reminiscent of a song of the period and used in *The Great Gatsby,* "the rich get rich and the poor get children." Within the Jacks' household, privilege and dishonesty are paralleled within the city at large.

Wolfe develops a universal theme of blindness and despair in which the false values and self-interest of society at large preshadow, much like the tremor below the earth, the coming apocalypse that Frederick and his united family will experience. The narrator foresees that when financial calamity strikes, Frederick's "gaudy bubble" will explode "overnight before his eye." For all his plumpness, ruddiness, and assurance, he will "shrink and wither visibly in three days' time into withered and palsied senility."

Yet another representative of the falsehood and sterility worshiped in this hollow and anchorless society is Piggy Logan. He is contrasted to Esther, Wolfe's symbol of the "true" artist. His attire and demeanor are artificial, and he is described as being almost inhuman. His round and heavy face smudged darkly with the shaven grain of a thick beard, he seems like the brutal, ignorant characters in the earlier dream sequence. His forehead is "corrugated" and his close-cropped hair is composed of "stiff black bristles, mounting to a little brush-like pompadour" like the lifeless wire dolls he creates. In this upside-down world the real is perceived as artificial and the trivial superb, so that great writers, like Dickens and Balzac, have been found to be "largely composed of straw wadding" by both critics and readers at large. The partygoers, like the people of the wasteland, are indeed people living in a damned world, bored with all of the elements of life. They are bored with love and hate and life and death, but not with Piggy Logan and his wire dolls, at least not so long as his wire circus remains fashionable.

Like Virginia Woolf's Mrs. Dalloway, Esther has within her an ability to bring people together into a magical confluence, a "wonderful harmony." Indeed, the party seems to take on its own separate life, creating a world of enchantment in which all assembled seem like creatures from a land where only wealth, joy, and beauty reside. Esther's heart and soul infuse her world with splendor: "the warm heart and the wise, the subtle childlike spirit that was Mrs. Jack." She is able to do what few others in her world—or any—are able to do: to create unity out of chaos. The characters in this dramatic sequence—for the party scene is dramatic in form—are introduced almost as through a receiving line, like the characters in a play. It is her very humanity that saves Esther from the death-in-life surrounding her in this Wolfean version of wasteland. She possesses "the common heart of life" and thus can associate easily with the wealthy and celebrated as well as with her servants and co-workers. She escapes the sterile and limited lives of her family and guests by unifying all classes, all time. She remembers the sorrow of her youth, and her recollections enrich her. Yet, she is still part of this world and is corrupted by it, so that she is unable to reject the hollowness at its core.

It remains for her lover, George Webber, to view the party and the behavior of her guests from the perspective of an observer. He can see what she will not, or cannot, see. George moves in and out of the activities of the party, but ultimately he is more clearly a Proustian onlooker than a participant. He penetrates the surface glitter of this wealthy, sophisticated gathering and sees Esther's guests as they really are. His growing awareness of the guests' corruption—and of his own potential for being swept down into their moral cesspool—enables him, finally, to leave this illusory world, even though he must sacrifice his love for Esther in going his own way. He now perceives that he faces the disillusionment of youth and the aching knocks of experience: "To see the starred face of the night with a high soul of exaltation and of noble aspiration, to dream great dreams, to think great thoughts. And in that instant have the selfless grandeur turn to dust, and to see great night itself, a reptile coiled and waiting in the nocturnal blood of life." In lifting the veil and seeing the ugliness and inherent danger of this world, George catches more than a glimpse of the serpent in Esther's paradise of love and chooses to cast himself out while he still has the will to do so.

George's keen vision helps readers see each character with penetrating awareness: The beautiful and seductive Lily Mandell is "corrupt and immodest." Stephen

Hook, damned and tormented, assumes a mask of disdain and boredom and is too self-conscious to allow himself to respond honestly to Esther's delight and gratitude at his generous gift of a book of Brueghel's drawings. Roberta Heilprinn is cool and manipulative, acting not spontaneously but out of some planned strategy to exert her control over others. Even Esther, George notes, like her friend and counterpart, Roberta, manipulates others with her deceptive innocence. It is Amy Van Leer who symbolizes the tragic waste and corruption of this decadent age, her broken and fragmented speech and consequent inability to communicate except by frenzied, half-articulated phrases personifying a corruption and impending decay almost as old as civilization itself: "her life seemed to go back through aeons of iniquity, through centuries of vice and dissipation . . . [like] the dread Medusa . . . some ageless creature, some enchantress of Circean cunning whose life was older than the ages and whose heart was old as Hell." Wolfe leaves no doubt that the serpent has wholly claimed this wastelandish flapper.

He worked tirelessly on the chapter entitled "Mr. Hirsch Was Wounded Sorrowfully," creating several variants until he was satisfied with his cutting counterpoint depicting the tired lust and bored ennui of the partygoers. The social chatter of the rich whose indiscriminate lust for wealth and power creates the misery of the poor rings with "political correctness." Only Mr. Robert Ahrens is depicted as a genuine human being. He does not engage in empty conversation and refuses to be baited by Lily Mandell when she asks him about the writer Beddoes. Ahrens's knowledge is real, not a contrived pastiche like that of Lawrence Hirsch. Amidst the glitter and meaningless chatter, he moves quietly, not engaging in conversation but actually browsing through books in Esther's library, in contrast to Piggy Logan, who pulls volumes from the shelves and hurls them to the floor.

Young and old, man and woman, they were an ark of lost humanity drifting, doomed, toward some eventual disaster:

> Well, here they were then, three dozen of the highest and the best, with shimmer of silk, and ripple of laughter, with the tumultuous babel of fine voices, with tinkle of ice in shell-thin glasses, and with silvern clatter, in thronging webs of beauty, wit and loveliness—as much passion, joy, and hope, and fear, as much triumph and defeat, as much anguish and despair and victory, as much sin, viciousness, cruelty and pride, as much base intrigue and ignoble striving, as much unnoble aspiration as flesh and blood can know, or as a room can hold—enough, God knows, to people hell, inhabit heaven, or fill out the universe—were all here, now, miraculously composed, in magic interweft—at Jack's.

As Piggy Logan prepares his wire circus, his admiring claque of socialites rudely enters the Jacks' apartment. Amy, offended by their slight of her beloved Esther, utters her only complete sentences of the evening: "Six little vaginas standing in a row and not a grain of difference between them. Chapin's School last year. Harvard and their first—this! All these little Junior League bitches." Piggy Logan's circus is a grotesque parody of art. His "celebrated sword swallowing act" is a brutal display of ignorance, obscene in its banality. Indeed, the guests themselves seem to be little more than hollow dummies: the young society girl speaking through motionless lips; Krock, the depraved sculptor, making crudely aggressive sexual advances; and even Esther herself forcing George and her closest friend upon each other and enticing them to engage in sexual promiscuity. Finally, the depravity of the party-goers becomes too much for George to endure. He understands that if he remains in this jaded world of illusion and glitter, he too will be destroyed.

After the party, the noises of the great city once again enter the Jacks' apartment; the cause is the outbreak of a fire in the building. Almost immediately the intimate little group remaining with Esther undergoes some frenzy when it hears the sirens and smells smoke, but eventually everyone joins the "ghostly" procession and leaves the building. The honeycomb of the apartment building takes on an atmosphere of unreality as the dim lights and thick, acrid smoke cast a haze over this world. Wolfe makes this frightening ordeal of escape a kind of hell. From this strange world, a "tide of refugees . . . marched steadily" out of the building. It seems as if, the old order destroyed as in Frederick's dream, all humanity comes together in "an extraordinary and bizarre conglomeration—a parade of such fantastic quality as had never been witnessed in the world before." The lover is moved by this "enormous honeycomb of life," young and old, rich and poor, speaking together a babel of languages representative of all the languages of mankind. Indeed, the apartment building itself seems a little world representative of the larger world of the city, "with a whole universe of flesh, and blood, a world incarnate with all the ecstasy, anguish, hatred, joy, and vexed intrigue that life could know." Only a great writer or painter like Shakespeare or Brueghel (or Wolfe perhaps) can present the enormity of such a spectacle. George realizes that this great event unraveling before him, this symphonic sweep of brotherhood and humanity, seems to take on the majesty of a vision, and he notes as well a sense of prophetic doom. For this mass of humanity gathered before him seems like victims of some great shipwreck, like the *Titanic,* "all the huge honeycomb of life . . . assembled now, at this last hour of peril, in a living fellowship—the whole family of earth, and all

its classes, at length united on these slanting decks." Man is indeed united in the vast honeycomb of life, and every action is ineluctably interwoven.

Eventually the fire is brought under control and the crowd is dispersed, but there is a sense of foreboding within the small group taking refuge in a little drugstore nearby. These "lords and masters of the earth" have for a moment relinquished the illusion of control to which they have become accustomed. They are like "shipwrecked voyagers . . . caught up and borne onwards, as unwitting of the power that ruled them as blind flies fastened to the revolutions of a wheel." Like Hemingway's ants upon a burning log, Wolfe's inhabitants are little more than insects blinded to the larger world beyond their small realities and propelled from life to death by forces greater than their own.

The various cells in which concurrent action is taking place are exposed for us to see. For example, in the vast hive of the tunnels beneath the apartment building decisions are being made that will affect the lives of 500 train passengers traveling outward to their individual destinies, and some design begins to formulate itself: "lights changed and flashed . . . poignant as remembered grief, burned there upon the checkerboard of the eternal dark." As the men in the train tunnel work to restore "order," firemen free the bodies of two trapped elevator operators whose deaths will be noted by a hardened reporter in the few lines he files with his newspaper.

Faced with a common danger, these Park Avenue apartment dwellers and their high-society guests had mingled with maids, butlers, cooks, and other workers and had briefly felt a common bond of humanity. With the all-clear signal, the privileged class returns to the building with the assorted retainers. The old order is quickly reestablished. Nothing has really changed; the sense of brotherhood, indeed, the prophetic hope for the future, has vanished like smoke from the extinguished fire, as the old "ordered formality" and "cold restraint" once more prevail. Class animosity boils up again when Esther feels bruised by Henry's cold and unyielding lack of response. She longs for what she will probably never again have, the cordial and familiar humanity of someone like John Enborg and Herbert Anderson.

Like her lover, Esther is aware that something great and perilous has happened, something that somehow threatens their very lives: "When you think of how sort of *big*—things have got—. . . And how a fire can break out in the same building where you live and you won't even know about it—I mean, there's something sort of *terrible* about it, isn't there?" She is aware as well of the greatness of the spectacle in which both she and George have been participants and observers. But when she attempts to return the world to just the two of them, to the fantasy of the "good child's" dream, George realizes that he has already left her behind.

George now knows that his allegiances lie elsewhere. George must search for that vaster world, the world of fellowship, deprivation, and social injustice awaiting an articulate voice. Esther is indeed noble and worthy of his love if viewed in isolation from her class, but she is doomed like the others; and if George stays, he too will perish. Two good men have already perished, their deaths the direct result of their eagerness to serve the class that the Jacks represent. "The dark green wagon . . . with a softly throbbing motor" that removes the bodies of the dead is reminiscent of the earlier imagery of automobiles, vehicles associated with the frenzied life of a money-grubbing city. As Mr. Jack prepares for sleep, he feels that peace has been restored. "It was so solid, splendid, everlasting and so good. And it was all as if it had always been—all so magically itself as it must be saved for its magical increasements, forever." Yet the reader, remembering the tremors that Frederick has felt before and now senses again, understands that all is not the same. The world that Jack has built, the world of moneyed luxury and power, is an endangered world, precipitously resting on a foundation now cracking apart.

In *The Party at Jack's,* Thomas Wolfe conceived and wrought to a virtually complete state a social fable of universal proportions, a work prefiguring other socially conscious themes and images in the Webber cycle, a work offering powerful and prophetic testimony of the writer he was striving to become.

James D. Boyer (essay date fall 1998)

SOURCE: Boyer, James D. "Revisions of Thomas Wolfe's *The Lost Boy*." *Studies in Short Fiction* 35, no. 1 (fall 1998): 1-11.

[*In the following essay, Boyer outlines the development of* The Lost Boy *in its many versions, documenting Wolfe's concurrent maturation as a writer.*]

> Since [Thomas] Wolfe's success in achieving the larger unity for which he strove in the last three long novels is considerably less than total, the materials which he had organized into short novels have an integrity and a consummate craftsmanship which they seem to lack in the long books. . . . In the short novel form Wolfe was a master of his craft.
>
> —C. Hugh Holman, *The Short Novels of Thomas Wolfe*

It is the care that went into the planes and surfaces of Wolfe's work—the tactile areas—that makes it an inhabitable literary world, just as it was the continuous rehearsal of his experience in his own mind—and the slow discovery of the underlying substratum of meaning—that made it, finally, a durable world.

> —Maxwell Geismar, *The Portable Thomas Wolfe*

James Clark's recent edition of **"The Lost Boy,"** differing in significant ways from earlier published versions of that story, has renewed critical interest in what many feel is Wolfe's finest, most complex and carefully crafted piece of short fiction. I want in this essay to trace that careful crafting of the story as we find it in the typescripts preserved in the William Wisdom Collection of the Houghton Library and to discuss the significance of the story's theme as it relates to a major portion of Wolfe's late work—that is, **"The Lost Boy"** as a gateway into *You Can't Go Home Again.* Such an examination helps to define the dramatic redirection of Wolfe's late writing—that work written or reworked in 1936-1937 and later incorporated into the posthumous novels. Through the typescripts of this story we can trace the complex process of composition through which Wolfe himself came to understand what he wanted to say with the material— the "slow discovery," as Geismar calls it, of "the underlying substratum of meaning." No other Wolfe story illustrates so well both his experimentation with narrative technique and his sustained effort at revision and restructuring to get the final effect of a story just right.

From the beginning of Wolfe's fiction writing in the late 1920s, his work gives evidence of the ferment of American fiction during those years and of his drawing on the experiments of other writers. *Look Homeward, Angel* and *Of Time and the River* both show Wolfe's considerable debt to James Joyce in his experiments with stream of consciousness and with juxtaposing myth and plot. Wolfe learned from Sherwood Anderson to anchor episodes with imagery and to center them on aspects other than plot; Joseph Bentz in a recent essay discusses similarities in the way the two writers structured stories around what he calls "climactic lyrical insights" (151). Most important of all for **"The Lost Boy,"** Wolfe had as a model Faulkner's use of the shifting narrator to tell a story—both *As I Lay Dying* and *The Sound and the Fury* had been published before Wolfe began work on this four-part story with its three first-person narrators and four perspectives.

Wolfe himself had already tried, in his stories from 1932-1935, a variety of experiments—the joining of discrete episodes related only by setting and theme in **"Death, the Proud Brother"** and **"The Face of the War,"** the use of choric voices in **"The Four Lost**

Men," the use of visions in **"Bascom Hawke,"** the use of allegory in **"Fame and the Poet,"** the use of various first-person voices, from the wonderful rambling voice of Eliza Gant in *The Web of Earth,* (a voice that he returns to in a more restrained form in the second part of **"The Lost Boy"**) to the voice of the Brooklyn tough guy in the often-anthologized **"Only the Dead Know Brooklyn."** He was, when we look back at particulars, a surprisingly experimental writer. Only in **"The Lost Boy,"** however, does he experiment with the shifting narrative voice, which gives this particular story its distinctive depth and force.

It is difficult to say exactly when Wolfe began the writing of this story, which was first published in *Redbook* in 1937. It has generally been assumed that the story was written in 1936 and that the inspiration for the story had grown out of his trip to St. Louis in 1935, when he revisited the home where the Wolfe family had lived during the 1904 World's Fair. But Wolfe had, of course, already included a brief account of Grover's death at the Fair in the *Autobiographical Outline* (1920s) and a brief fictional account in *Look Homeward, Angel* (1929), long before he mentioned in his notebooks this story on the subject in the fall of 1935 (*Notebooks* 779). It is likely that the first three parts of the four-part story were drafted earlier than 1935—especially Part 2, with an Eliza who sounds very much like the narrator of *The Web of Earth,* written in 1932, and Part 3, narrated by the sister, a caricatured Helen similar to the character of Luke in **"Boomtown,"** published in 1934. Both of these sections may have been written initially for a 1930-1932 manuscript called **"Antaeus,"** wherein Wolfe went back to the family characters developed in *Look Homeward, Angel* and gave an extended account of some conversations among the family, or more specifically among Eugene, Luke, Helen and Eliza (Wisdom Collection, bMS Am 1883 [409]). It is clear that Wolfe and his magazine agent, Elizabeth Nowell, came back to the material in 1936 and produced the story published in *Redbook* Magazine in 1937.[1]

The dramatic changes in **"The Lost Boy,"** as we follow it through a few fragments of manuscript and the various typescript revisions in the Wisdom Collection, certainly suggest that it was composed over an extended period of time. There are alterations in the names of characters and places,[2] in the selection of incident and detail, in tone, characterization, central metaphors, even a reversal of the theme itself. Establishing the passage of years between the original composition of each part and the final revisions is important, since the earliest draft of the story in the Houghton Library exhibits many features from the list above that are not characteristic of Wolfe's late writing as we see it in stories like **"The Child by Tiger,"**

"I Have a Thing to Tell You" and **"The Party at Jack's,"** those other significant works he completed in 1937.

"The Lost Boy"[3] is the story of a Southern family that suffers a terrible loss—Grover, the 12-year-old son, dies of typhoid fever during an extended family visit to the World's Fair in St. Louis in 1904. The story is composed of four parts. Part 1, written in third person, takes the reader back to 1904 and presents Grover's perception of a childhood epiphany experienced months before the family move from North Carolina to St. Louis. Cheated and accused of stealing by a candy-store owner, the boy seeks out his father, who returns with him to the store and extracts retribution, leaving the boy with a restored sense of self but a deeper understanding of life's darker side. In Part 2, some 30 years after the boy's death, the still-grieving mother reflects on her "best" son and recounts the high excitement of the train trip to the Fair and the son's amazing maturity. Throughout her narrative, the mother exemplifies life's irreparable wounding. In Part 3, also 30 years later, the older sister tells of an adventure at the Fair when she and the boy, youngsters in a strange place, sneak into downtown St. Louis and eat in a cheap restaurant. Upon their return home, the boy becomes ill with the onset of typhoid fever. In the sister's story we confront not only her long-sustained grief and guilt, but her vision of the incomprehensibility of life: "How is it," she asks, "that nothing turns out the way we thought it would be." In Part 4, Eugene, the younger brother who has in the 30 intervening years become a famous writer, narrates his return to the house in St. Louis where the family had lived and the boy had died. Eugene hopes to recapture and recreate in fiction the essence of the boy, a hope not fulfilled, as the title of the story suggests. Instead, the writer-brother comes to see the limits of time and memory in recapturing the past, which marks a significant epiphany for him and a redirection of his work as writer.

As we trace the story through the typescripts at the Houghton, in each of these four parts we find significant revision. The earliest of these typescripts [bMS Am 1883 (1030)][4] presents a story very different from the first published version summarized above, the one that appeared in *Redbook* in November, 1937, the only one that Wolfe lived to see in print. Each part of this earliest typescript exhibits a variety of problems that Wolfe needed to work through—problems of focus, tone, and theme—to create the work as it now stands.

Part 1 of File 1030 is almost three times as long as the first part of the *Redbook* version. It opens with an extensive tour of the town square of Altamont as Grover, the "lost boy" of the title, walks along examining store windows with Singer sewing machines, pianos, saws, rakes, a tool box full of brand new tools, and groceries of all kinds. Along the way he greets a music store clerk, a grocery store clerk who is describing his wares over the telephone, and other named characters. He also experiences a sudden summer rainstorm in which a poor old horse gets soaked, and he reflects on the various things that remind him of either the North, a kind of mythic version of his father's country, or the South of his mother's people, where he himself had grown up. While this descriptive material is wonderfully evocative of the sights and moods of a small Southern town at the turn of the century, providing the kind of detail and texture of American life that Wolfe wanted his long books to present, it delays and dilutes the focus of this story, which needs in Part One to remain centered on the boy and his first experience with evil, or at least complexity. This longer version of the episode seems to have been written originally for a more comprehensive work than **"The Lost Boy."**

In Part 2 of 1030, this earliest typed version, the mother gives her account of the family's trip to St. Louis. She makes the reader aware of the great adventure of this trip to the Fair for her and the children and of the great promise of Grover at age 12. And we sense, though it remains unspoken, the tragedy that will be recounted in Part Three. But one problem in this earliest version is that Eliza presents more reflections on Eugene, the younger brother who lives on to become a famous writer, than on Grover, the boy who is lost. Recognizing this, Wolfe at one point adds to Eliza's remembrance of Grover, "He had the judgment of one twice his years—he had more sense, more judgment, more understanding, than any child I ever saw. . . ." Another problem is that in her narration Eliza comes across as a kind of folksy caricature whose mannerisms—"Lord, Lord . . ." or "I reckon . . ." she keeps repeating—tend to undercut the restrained grief of the section, which rests on her unspoken but powerful loss.

Part 3 of this first version is the most unsuitable episode of all. Through the sister's monologue to Eugene, the youngest brother, we are to learn of Grover's illness and death. But the sister, with her peculiar nervous laugh and her occasional poking of the brother's ribs, constantly distracts from the poignant story she is telling. Her characterization here strongly resembles in the emphasis on peculiar mannerisms the Luke of the earliest versions of the 1933 story **"Boomtown,"** with his persistent stuttering that Wolfe initially defended but eventually cut from that story. Eugene, who is audience for Helen in this section, also interrupts the sister's narrative with such exclamations as "I wish you'd quit pulling at your chin" or "Helen, if you don't keep those damned hands of yours out of my ribs. . . ."

The result is a kind of cartoon-like humor overlaying this nostalgic look at the two young children's adventure just before the onset of the fatal illness of the boy.

And in File 1030 there is no Part 4, at least as the typescript is contained at the Houghton, leaving one to speculate that to produce this story either Wolfe had gathered two or three earlier fragments out of his famous packing cases to start from, or he had, when he started the composing of **"The Lost Boy,"** only a vague notion of where the story was going or what ideas he wanted to explore with it. The unity of action, tone and theme in the published story comes only after extensive revision.

In tracing changes in the three succeeding typescripts at the Houghton—bMS AM 1883 (1029, 1031, 1028)—it becomes difficult to discuss the next complete revision of the story, since in the Collection a few parts of the various succeeding versions are incorrectly placed together. Part One of File 1031, for example, is an earlier version than the other parts placed with it and probably belongs to File 1029. So it will be simple for our purpose here to take each section of the story and trace the changes as they occur in all three files in the movement toward the final revision before publication. The proper sequence of each part of the story as it goes through such revisions is readily traceable through specific manuscript changes of words, phrases and sentences, both additions and deletions. These changes are substantial and consistently improve the story by tightening structure, by clarifying focus, by improving tone, by selecting appropriate illustrative detail, and by deepening theme.

In the succeeding versions of Part One (1031, 1029, 1028) Wolfe tightens the focus on Grover's encounter with evil in the person of these two candy-store owners, his rescue by the father, and his epiphany on life, time, and change. The long descriptions of the shops and merchants on the square are reduced to introductory proportions, the summer storm is eliminated, and the ruminations about North and South as the father-mother polarities for the boy are cut, since neither the epiphany for Grover in Part 1 nor for Eugene in Part 4 relates to them. This version, with its much quicker movement to the candy store, the boy's encounter with these two accusing old people, the father's rescue, and the return of light to the square, retains the powerful opening images of time in the Square—the bell and the fountain and the father's stone-carving shop—which give thematic substance and direction for the remaining parts; and the transition to part two—a streetcar carrying an advertisement for the St. Louis World's Fair comes into the square—remains.

Even more interesting transformations take place in Part 2 (1029, 1031, 1028), the mother's recollection of the train ride to St. Louis. The discussions of Eugene, now a famous writer, and of the questions reporters ask about him are gradually reduced. In one sentence cut, for example, Eliza says of a reporter's question about Eugene's being different from the others,

> "Why no," I says, real slow-like, after I studied it over, "he had two good eyes and a nose and a mouth, two arms and legs and a good head of hair, and the regular number of fingers and toes just like all the rest of them—now I think if he'd been different from any of the rest of them in those respects I'd have noticed right off."

> (1031)

Such cute, folksy observations had worked well for Wolfe in his crafting of a narrative voice for Eliza in *The Web of Earth,* published in 1933, where she was the only narrator of her story and her narrative's indirection is one remarkable tactic of Wolfe's composition. But the cutting of such stuff here works to maintain not only an appropriate balance between Eugene and Grover, but also an appropriate tone for the long-grieving mother whose lifetime dream came crashing down in the loss of this 12-year-old. Wolfe balanced the cuts of Eugene material with a new story about Grover (1029, Folder 1): The Gant family serving man Simon Featherstone intrudes into the white car after the train crosses into free-state Indiana; and Grover, with notable composure, maturity and authority for a 12-year-old, convinces Simpson to return to the car for blacks. While this anecdote provides insight into Grover's sense of self and ability to assume responsibility, it also suggests approval of Jim Crow laws and customs that Wolfe was by the mid-1930s seriously questioning; significantly, in the next version (1029, Folders 7-9), Wolfe crosses out the Featherstone incident and replaces it—the *manuscript* revision is there—with a very different passage depicting Grover as a better trader among the many merchants of the town than Eliza herself, a very high tribute indeed, and an anecdote that involves a bargain Grover makes in buying tomatoes. Other mentions of "niggers" tending horses and "Niggertown" itself are also cut from the story. It is especially important to note that Wolfe himself made such changes to improve and not to shorten the story, since the new material is approximately as long as the old.

In Part 3 (1029, 1031, 1028) the intrusive comments of Eugene as he listens to Helen's story ("Helen, if you don't keep those damned hands of yours out of my ribs . . ." etc.) are removed; and the erratic behavior of Helen is reduced, allowing the reader's attention to remain focused where it belongs, on the sister's remembrance of the adventure in downtown St. Louis and of Grover's illness and eventual death.

Helen's snickers—signified by k k k k k's in the text—are also removed, first a few, then many, then all. And the reference to Grover's death as taking "all those weeks that followed" as "he wasted away to a little bundle of skin and bones," is removed, compressing the time dimension and, consequently, the impact of the tragic death.

Part 4 of the story, which first appears in File 1029, would probably have to have been written after 1935. At any rate, it gives much concrete detail about the streets and people of St. Louis as Eugene experiences them on his return (especially the King's Highway), and the feelings of Eugene as he returns after 30 years to the home where Grover died. He finds the house, discusses the past with Mrs. Bell, the current owner, and sees the death room. In the several revisions of this part of the story (1031, 1028) we see Wolfe reversing the theme of the story and searching for an appropriate ending. Initially he hasn't yet found the wonderful naming routine that eventually becomes the climactic moment of the whole story. (He has, in fact, used the anecdote as a passing remembrance of Helen's in Part 2 of 1029, but he didn't at that time see its potential as climax.) The change in concluding statement comes first. In this earliest version Part 4 ends rather inconclusively, ". . . and through the thicket of man's memory, from the enchanted wood, the ancient and swarm-haunted mind of man, the dark eye and the quiet face, the voice of the lost boy calling yet" (1029), with its implication that the connection with the past is still open, that the writer can still go back, can recapture the past, can give an eternal present to that past through its recreation in art. But this understanding reverses by the final version, where Wolfe concludes:

> But I knew that it could not come back—the cry of absence in the afternoon, the house that waited and the boy that dreamed; and through the thicket of man's memory, from the enchanted wood, the dark eye and the quiet face,—poor child, life's stranger and life's exile, lost, like all of us, a cipher in blind mazes, long ago—my parent, friend and brother, the lost boy, was gone forever and would not return.

In still-later revisions of Part 4, Wolfe supplies the naming climax that embodies this revised theme in the published story. In 1031, Folder 5, Wolfe inserts that short section of text in which Mrs. Bell, the current owner of the St. Louis home, suggests to Eugene that since he had been only four years old when he had experienced Grover's death, he probably didn't remember much about Grover. Originally in 1029, as I noted above, the conversation had ended there, they had parted, and Eugene had gone on to his concluding statements about "the voice of the lost boy calling yet." But here in 1031, the comment by Mrs. Bell sends Eugene back in memory to his four-year-old re-membrance of his brother, and to a bargain Grover had made: Grover would take him for a treat on the King's Highway if he would say the name Grover correctly. Eugene tries and tries, but always it comes out "Gova."

> No—not Gova: Grover. . . . Say it!
>
> Gova.
>
> Ah-h—you didn't say it. . . . You said Gova: Grover . . . now say it.
>
> Gova.
>
> Look, I'll tell you what I'll do if you say it right. . . . Would you like to go down to the King's Highway? Would you like Grover to set you up? All right then . . . if you say Grover and say it right, I'll take you to King's Highway and set you up to ice cream. . . . Now say it right: Grover.
>
> Gova.

In this simple action the two levels of the story coalesce. While the infant Eugene is trying to speak the name, the grown writer Eugene is trying to say the incantation and create the magic. The anecdote mirrors the important truth Eugene (and Wolfe) has uncovered in his attempt to record in fiction this epiphany: He as writer can't bring back the boy, can't recapture the past and make it coexist with the present, can't give eternity to anything. In a wonderful analysis of the story's ending, Wallace Stegner explains,

> Among the ancient Irish it was a capital crime to put a man by name into a poem, for both poem and name were potent with magic and power could be got over anyone so be-spelled. It is the name that reveals Grover briefly and brings him up from the dark cellar of Time. It is as if, if only the child Eugene could say the name right, Grover might now literally appear. . . . Wolfe's magic, like Eugene's, invokes the ghost briefly and holds him a moment before he fades. The ghost that troubled Eugene, the rival that he loved and half envied, is laid and quieted. The man sick with Time is healed, the voodoo spell is finished, the spirit has spoken its cryptic word and departed.

> (258)

That cryptic message had to do with Time. And it had to do with the writer's work. The lost boy was gone and would not return. Eugene now saw, and Wolfe saw, that one couldn't go home again, "which means back home to one's family, back home to one's childhood, . . . to one's youthful idea of the 'artist,' and the all-sufficiency of art and beauty and love, . . . back home to the escapes of time and memory" (*Notebooks* 939). One couldn't establish fixed truth through time and memory. History, as Wolfe and other modernists came to see, was never truth but only perspective. One had to live in the present, had to con-

front the world of change. As George Webber writes in that wonderful passage at the end of *You Can't Go Home Again,* to explain his differences with his editor and friend Foxhall Edwards: "The essence of faith is the knowledge that all flows and everything must change. The growing man is Man-Alive . . ." (731-33). And then later . . .

> Mankind was fashioned for eternity, but Man-Alive was fashioned for a day.

> New evils will come after him, but it is with the present evils that he is now concerned. And the essence of all faith, it seems to me, for such a man as I, the essence of religion for people of my belief, is that man's life can be, and will be, better; that man's greatest enemies, in the forms in which they now exist—the forms we see on every hand of fear, hatred, slavery, cruelty, poverty, and need—can be conquered and destroyed.

> (737-38)

This changed conviction leads directly to that final productive period in 1936-1937 when Wolfe produced not only this story but **"I Have a Thing to Tell You,"** **"The Child by Tiger,"** and **"The Party at Jack's,"** each one a powerful examination of a social problem facing America.

My purpose in tracing this story through its many revisions is three-fold. I have wanted first to demonstrate that Wolfe in his later writing had become a much more careful and controlled writer, one who purposefully shaped and revised not only this story but the other major late stories listed above, and more. I also wanted to challenge the assumption, sometimes made even by Wolfe scholars, that Wolfe saw magazine publishing primarily as a money-making operation, that he always preferred the longer versions of things and would have restored material that had been cut from the published stories had he lived long enough to do so. No one, obviously, can know what he might have done, so it seems sensible to me to give preference to the versions of his short works that he saw through publication, especially if such versions are better. I find the longer versions of **"The Lost Boy"** extremely interesting for the Wolfe aficionado but less impressive than the *Redbook* version as fiction. Finally I have tried to give continued support to the notion that Wolfe did mature as a writer and that we can see this maturity plainly if we keep clear the sequence of his works, a sequence clouded both by the posthumous publications and by statements made by his final editor Ed Aswell. The record of his growth is not news; evidence can be found in Richard Kennedy, John Phillipson, Leslie Field and John Idol, and, most especially, in the work of Hugh Holman. But it needs to be repeated until it is recognized in the broader literary community.

Notes

1. Elizabeth Nowell began working with Wolfe as an agent for magazine publication in 1933 and continued in that role until his death in 1938. Richard Kennedy's *Beyond Love and Loyalty* and Mary Aswell Doll's and Clara Stites's *In the Shadow of the Giant: Thomas Wolfe* give extensive information on that working relationship. Various typescripts of this story which show Nowell's suggestions for cuts of words, sentences, and incidents confirm the positive effect of Nowell's work. Wolfe accepted most of her suggestions for cutting.

2. To simplify discussion of the various drafts of the story, I have stayed with the Gant family names, familiar to many from their appearance in the first two novels. Wolfe, in writing the story, used those names initially. But in revisions he moved to different names as he changed his plan for his larger works, into which he expected to incorporate "The Lost Boy." Those name changes in the typescripts help to establish the sequence for the various versions. When the story was finally completed and first published in *Redbook* in 1937, the alternative names were used (Grover becomes Robert, etc.).

3. There are three different published versions of the story: the version that Elizabeth Nowell, Wolfe's magazine agent and editor, sold to *Redbook* Magazine (which was later republished in Skipp's collection of Wolfe stories in 1987); the version that Edward Aswell revised and published in *The Hills Beyond* in 1941, which switches back to the Gant names but changes the last part of the story into third-person narrative (thereby weakening the plan of shifting narration) and uses headings to name the narrator rather than letting the reader discover them; and James Clark's recent edition, which draws on earlier typescripts of some sections of the story.

4. The Wisdom Collection [bMS Am 1883] contains six files on "The Lost Boy." File 1027 contains fragments of manuscript, some early, some later. File 1030 contains typescripts of the first three parts of the story. Files 1028, 1029, and 1031 contain the various typescripts of all four parts, many of them with extensive manuscript revisions. File 1032 contains four sheets of typescript revision. Since these materials are not in sequence, I have tried above to make clear the sequence of revision for the individual parts of the story.

References Consulted

Aswell, Edward. *The Hills Beyond*. New York: Harpers, 1941.

Bentz, Joseph. "Modernist Structure in the Short Fiction of Thomas Wolfe." *Studies in Short Fiction* 31 (1993): 150-61.

Clark, James W., Jr., ed. *The Lost Boy: A Novella by Thomas Wolfe*. Chapel Hill: U of North Carolina P, 1995.

Doll, Mary Aswell, and Clara Stites, eds. *In the Shadow of the Giant: Thomas Wolfe*. Athens, Ohio: U of Ohio P, 1988.

Geismar, Maxwell. *American Moderns: From Rebellion to Conformity*. New York: Hill and Wang, 1958.

Holman, C. Hugh. *The Short Novels of Thomas Wolfe*. New York: Scribner's, 1961.

Kennedy, Richard S. *The Window of Memory: The Literary Career of Thomas Wolfe*. Chapel Hill: U of North Carolina P, 1962.

———, ed. *Beyond Love and Loyalty: The Letters of Thomas Wolfe and Elizabeth Nowell*. Chapel Hill: The U of North Carolina P, 1983.

Skipp, Francis, ed. *The Complete Short Stories of Thomas Wolfe*. New York: Macmillan, 1987.

Stegner, Wallace. "Analysis of 'The Lost Boy.'" *Thomas Wolfe: Three Decades of Criticism*. Leslie Field, ed. New York: New York UP, 1968.

Wolfe, Thomas. "The Lost Boy." William Wisdom Collection, Houghton Library, Harvard University (bMS AM 1883 [1027-32]).

———. "The Lost Boy." *Redbook,* 70 (Nov. 1937): 25-28, 80-90. Republished in Aswell, Skipp, and Clark.

———. *The Notebooks of Thomas Wolfe*. Ed. Richard S. Kennedy and Paschal Reeves. Chapel Hill: U of North Carolina P, 1970.

———. *The Story of a Novel*. New York: Scribner's, 1936.

Terry Roberts (essay date fall 2000)

SOURCE: Roberts, Terry. "Resurrecting Thomas Wolfe." *Southern Literary Journal* 33, no. 1 (fall 2000): 27-41.

[*In the following essay, Roberts defends Wolfe's somewhat tarnished reputation as a literary figure, detailing the maturation, complexity, and skill evident in the author's best works.*]

When Thomas Wolfe died of tubercular meningitis on September 15, 1938, his literary reputation was equal in the United States to that of Faulkner, Hemingway, and Fitzgerald. In the sixty plus years since, his artistic reputation has been all but destroyed. With the exception of his first novel, *Look Homeward, Angel,* he is read less and less often, and the academics who design anthologies and teach influential college courses routinely dismiss his work. So on the 100th anniversary of his birth, we are compelled to ask, Who killed Thomas Wolfe?

By far the most common image of Wolfe is that of a bloated, self-obsessed Romantic, whose emotions are so intense and whose rhetoric is so inflated that critics assume he must have had almost no artistic or self-control. And indeed, from his earliest success with *Look Homeward, Angel* (published in October 1929), Wolfe was an easy figure to satirize. First, there is the writing itself. As David Donald wrote in introducing his Pulitzer Prize-winning biography, "Thomas Wolfe wrote more bad prose than any other major writer I can think of" (xiii).[1] Further, there was the man's life, certainly no more dramatic than that of Hemingway but somehow tainted in the public eye by the "autobiographical controversy" that haunted Wolfe. Wolfe's height (and in later years his girth); his family, straight out of Dickens; his truly gargantuan love for alcohol and food as well as books and art; his tendency toward manic depressive behavior—all worked their way into the novels and contributed to the myth of raw, unpolished genius run amok.

So who, then, murdered his literary reputation? Let us first round up the usual suspects. As early as April 25, 1936, Bernard DeVoto used the excuse of reviewing Wolfe's *The Story of a Novel* to blast Wolfe in a cutting essay entitled "Genius Is Not Enough." DeVoto paid a passing compliment to *The Story of a Novel* (written by Wolfe as an exploration of how *Of Time and the River* was created) and then went on to write that Wolfe "has mastered neither the psychic material out of which a novel is made nor the technique of writing fiction" (4). DeVoto attributed the success of *Look Homeward, Angel* to cditor Max Perkins and the Scribner's' "assembly line" (14). DeVoto's essay wounded Wolfe more deeply than he would at first admit and may have contributed to his eventual break with Perkins. Even more significantly, however, it set the tone for critics ever since who wished to establish their own intellectual superiority by attacking Wolfe in print. More recent comments in the same vein include those by no less a cultural heavyweight than Harold Bloom, who wrote in reviewing Donald's biography that "there is no possibility for critical dispute about Wolfe's literary merits; he has none whatsoever. Open him at any page, and that will suffice" (13). Most all of these attacks flow out of the original notion that Wolfe was forever what Wright Morris described as a

"raw young giant" who produced literally crates of prose but who had no notion of how to produce a "well-made" book from those crates.

I believe, however, that Wolfe's critics, no matter how strident, could never have so reduced his reputation had not the author himself contributed to the undoing. In fact, the true culprit may well be a creature of Wolfe's own making. Consider for a moment Thomas Wolfe in his late twenties as like another young, ambitious genius in love with his own generative power—Victor Frankenstein. And just as Frankenstein produced his monster, so Wolfe did as well: the autobiographical monster Eugene Gant, the protagonist of *Look Homeward, Angel* and *Of Time and the River,* the only two novels published during Wolfe's lifetime. In short, Wolfe's reputation was murdered by his own brainchild. Wolfe's readers often fall in love with Eugene when they first encounter him, but he grew into something Wolfe could never have foreseen: not just the prototypical Wolfe character but the only Wolfe character. This confusion has become true to the extent that even now, over seventy years after the publication of *Look Homeward, Angel,* Eugene Gant has all but become the author. In Victor Frankenstein's case, the obsessive, young genius made the creature that destroyed the creator. In Thomas Wolfe's case, literary history has very nearly repeated itself.

So powerful was this creation—the character that became the author—that as late as September 1935, when Wolfe wrote to Perkins about his plans for "The Book of Night" (later *The Hound of Darkness*), he admitted he was locked in combat with the autobiographical monster. In this new book, Wolfe wrote, America would not be seen by a

> definite personality, but haunted throughout by a consciousness of personality. In other words, I want to assert my divine right once and for all to be the God Almighty of a book—to be at once the spirit to move it, the spirit behind it, never to appear, to blast forever the charge of autobiography while being triumphantly and impersonally autobiographical.
>
> *(Letters* 489)

Perhaps in the naked fury of that letter, we can sense both the mortal nature of the struggle and, perhaps, why it is so tempting to say that he lost it. Why it is so tempting to say that Wolfe never wrote successfully about any subject other than himself.

If this is true, if Thomas Wolfe and Eugene Gant have become so conflated in the literary consciousness, the consequences are several. First of all, because Eugene is such an unabashed and often unselfconscious Romantic, he and his creator are increasingly vulnerable to the sharp wits and even sharper pens of contemporary intellectuals. Second, because Eugene Gant was a creature of large appetites and even larger emotions, he is often associated with Wolfe's own intense desires, desires too often expressed in an ungovernable flow of words. Thus, Wolfe's books (or do they belong to Eugene?) are stereotypically assumed to be the least "well-made" of the great modernist classics. For this reason, as we come to the end of Wolfe's century, we have to ask whether he will be read at all in the next.

What I have come to believe is that in the years between 1930 and 1938, Wolfe held his own against the autobiographical monster, and it is high time that we as readers finish the job of resurrecting his reputation. When we read the mature Wolfe, we discover that: 1) his best work is most often his short work; 2) his best work tends to be dominated by points of view distant from his own; 3) his short fiction, when it is autobiographical, is rigorously controlled; and 4) his best work often features multiple, even choral, points of view. In other words, in the short fiction he wrote during the nine brief years between the publication of *Look Homeward, Angel* and his death, Wolfe managed to turn almost all of the critical stereotypes about his work inside-out.

As proof, we should examine eight separate pieces of evidence: eight works by Thomas Wolfe that should remain in print, that should be anthologized, that should be taught, that should be read through this century and into the next. First, however, we should examine the argument that Wolfe's short fiction is in many instances his best fiction. In a typically thoughtful essay, C. Hugh Holman introduced the 1961 **Short Novels of Thomas Wolfe** by arguing that "the intrinsic qualities of the short novel [15,000-40,000 words] were remarkably well adapted to Wolfe's special talents and creative methods" (xvii).[2] This volume contains five novellas (three of which are discussed here), and in justifying their collection and publication Holman says:

> Upon these . . . short novels Wolfe had expended great effort, and in them he had given the clearest demonstrations he ever made of his craftsmanship and his artistic control. Each of these . . . novellas is marked in its unique way by a sharp focus and a controlling unity, and each represents a serious experiment with form. Yet they have been virtually lost from the corpus of Wolfe's work, lost even to most of those who know that work well.
>
> (xvi-xvii)

Holman admits that one of the reasons even the short novels are not known is "the nature of Wolfe's work and his attitude toward it" (xvii): in other words, the long, often autobiographical fiction that Wolfe contin-

ued to attempt during the 1930s. Even after 1935, when Wolfe was less concerned with his own life and more with the interconnected lives of others, his reputation for artistic excess ruled the public discourse about his work. In 1935, when *Of Time and the River* appeared, *The Saturday Review of Literature* published a wonderful cartoon showing New York's book reviewers picketing the front door of Scribner's, protesting the sheer length of Wolfe's books. And as David Donald notes, Scribner's Book Store on Fifth Avenue turned the tables by enlarging the cartoon to poster size and displaying it over a small mountain of the novels in its storefront window. Thus, Wolfe the man, even Wolfe the artist, was being replaced by Wolfe the myth.

My antidote to this case of cultural mythmaking is to cite those works of Wolfe's that capture his mature craft, especially his sense of authorial distance and editorial control. Even as early as 1929, in *Look Homeward, Angel,* there is evidence that Wolfe was willing and able to look beyond his own experience for the raw material of his work and to express that material in a voice other than his own. In Chapter Seven, "Gant the Far Wanderer," W. O. Gant, Eugene's father, returns home from a cross-country trip. During a trolley ride from the train station into town, the narrative shifts suddenly from third-person omniscient into a Gantian interior monologue:

> There was a warm electric smell and one of hot burnt steel.
>
> But two months dead! But two months dead! Ah, Lord! So it's come to this. Merciful God, this fearful, awful, and damnable climate. Death, death! Is it too late? A land of life, a flower land. How clear the green clear sea was. And all the fishes swimming there. Santa Catalina. Those in the East should always go West. How came I here? Down, down—always down. . . .
>
> (71)

And Gant is off into a rambling spiel of modified interior monologue that Wolfe wove into the next two pages of dialogue and description. This passage is both a funny and fascinating study of Gant's personality and is so well integrated into the movement of the chapter that most of us never notice that Wolfe has adopted an entirely different voice for an extended period. *Look Homeward, Angel* is neither short nor rigorously controlled, but this one interesting passage does suggest that even in his early work Wolfe has the capacity for adopting points of view removed from his own and for capturing those points of view in dramatic narrative voices.[3] Published in October 2000, *O Lost: A Story of the Buried Life,* the original typescript for *Look Homeward, Angel,* makes it even more apparent that Wolfe was interested in multiple points of view, even in his first novel.

The second piece of evidence is the short novel that first appeared in *Scribner's Magazine* in July 1932 and was later included in *From Death to Morning.* This novella, evocatively titled *The Web of Earth,* is narrated by a garrulous old woman who is visiting her son in New York. It captures in the narrative voice of Eliza Gant—Eugene Gant's mother in *Look Homeward, Angel*—all the complex and mysterious interweavings of Wolfe's best work, and yet achieves this complexity in a fundamentally spare narrative. Wolfe's letters from the period repeatedly cite Perkins' praise of the story and in one instance describe his method:

> It is different from anything I have ever done; it's about an old woman, who sits down to tell a little story, but then her octopal memory weaves back and forth across the whole fabric of her life until everything has gone into it. It's all told in her own language. . . . That story about the old woman has got everything in it, murder and cruelty, and hate and love, and greed and enormous unconscious courage, yet the whole thing is told with the stark innocence of a child.

> (*Letters* 339)

The Web of Earth is significant here because it represents Wolfe's growing ability to capture a point of view decidedly not his own. Interestingly, this long story contains a listener as well as a teller. Eliza Gant's long, earthy meditation is delivered in a dramatic context, with her son as audience. And yet, even though Eugene Gant is present during the delivery of his mother's dramatic monologue, Wolfe does not allow Eugene's presence to intrude on the telling of the story. *The Web of Earth* belongs entirely to the voice that tell it. And, as Monica Melloni has pointed out, that is the source of its greatness. The plot, the setting, the characters of Eliza's reminiscence are all an organic part of the web spun by her voice. Compare it to Gant's interior monologue from Chapter Seven of *Look Homeward, Angel,* and immediately one sees how much more complex and compelling is Eliza's voice in *The Web of Earth.* This complexity alone suggests that the voice telling the story is significantly different from that of Wolfe's mother and represents all the more significant an artistic achievement.

No less an authority on the narrative arts than Wallace Stegner noticed Wolfe's growing ability to create a compelling voice not his own. In his introduction to several of Wolfe's stories in the 1965 anthology, *American Literary Masters,* Stegner wrote:

> Fiction is a combination of the objective world and the eye that sees it. Though Thomas Wolfe was more powerful and more passionate, as a general rule, when he wrote through a Eugene Gant or a George Webber [a later protagonist], both essentially himself, he did in a handful of stories invent sensibilities not his own, and tell stories through them. *Web of Earth* . . . [and]

"Only the Dead Know Brooklyn" demonstrate that on occasion he was capable of the objectivity that his critics said he did not possess.

> (1075)

It may well be, however, that Stegner understated the case and that Wolfe was "more powerful and more passionate" when he did adopt "sensibilities not his own," or at least more successful in creating a similar passion in his reader.

Perhaps none of Wolfe's narrative adoptions was more unlike his native voice than the voice that narrates his 1935 story "Only the Dead Know Brooklyn":

> Dere's no guy livin' dat knows Brooklyn t'roo an' t'roo, (only the dead know Brooklyn t'roo and t'roo) because it'd take a guy a lifetime just to find his way aroun' duh goddam town. . . .

> So like I say, I'm waitin' for my train t' come when I sees dis big guy standin' deh—dis is duh foist I eveh see of him. Well, he's lookin' wild, y'know, an' I can see dat he's had plenty, but still he's holdin' it; he talks good an' is walkin' straight enough. So den, dis big guy steps up to a little guy dat's standin' deh, an' says, "How d'yuh get t' Eighteent' Avenoo an' Sixty-sevent' Street?" he says.

> "Jesus! Yuh got me chief," duh little guy says to him.

> (260)

What follows is one of the most fascinating stories in the entire Wolfe canon: in part because of the ambiguity around just who is narrating the story and just what part of Wolfe's own half-drunk, map-obsessed personality is represented by "duh big guy." As in *The Web of Earth,* Wolfe's own persona is present in the story, and yet the story finally is not about Eugene Gant or "duh big guy"; rather, it is about the voice that is struggling to make sense out of reality by giving faithful directions—in other words, by telling the tale itself. One idea at the core of Wolfe's work from this period is that all storytelling is in a sense about the desire to "give good directions"—whether to Red Hook (the destination in the story) or to some other destination as profound as understanding itself.

One of the unfortunate characteristics of Wolfe's early work—notably the more autobiographical work associated with Eugene Gant—is that it is tainted by racial stereotype and, on occasion, by outright racial prejudice. This element has precipitated several important essays and one significant book-length study, Paschal Reeves' *Thomas Wolfe's Albatross: Race and Nationality in America.* Those commentators who have read Wolfe most carefully, however, agree that his attitude toward his black and Jewish characters shifted considerably during the 1930s. I would argue that as Wolfe became less interested in his own history during the early 1930s and more interested in the history of others, he naturally grew more sympathetic to the social and cultural plight of others. As his writing became less autobiographical, and so less self-centered, so did his social and cultural point of view. The most remarkable evidence of this change is a story Wolfe wrote after visiting Germany in 1936. The narrative concerned a young Jew who is traveling by train with the narrator but who is removed forcefully at the German border by Nazi guards. Wolfe had long regarded Germany as his spiritual home, and the incident upset him terribly. On the back of a postcard he sent to Elizabeth Nowell from Paris in September, he wrote:

> I've written a wonderful piece—after it gets published I won't be able to go back to the place where I'm liked best and have more friends than anywhere in the world—but I'm going to publish it (or what's a heaven for?)—I'm going to call it (for various reasons) "**I Have A Thing To Tell You**"—which may not be so foolish as it sounds. W.
>
> (*Beyond Love and Loyalty* 46)

Wolfe's growing sympathy for the oppressed did exact a personal cost in this instance. When, after vigorous advocacy and equally vigorous editing by Nowell, the story appeared in *The New Republic* (March 10, 17, and 24, 1937), Wolfe's books were banned in Germany, and he was never able to return there. Wolfe did not himself consider "**I Have a Thing to Tell You**" a political statement but a human one. He later wrote to Nowell that "its greatest value, it seems to me, lies in the fact—that I wrote it as I write all my other stories about a human situation and living characters" (65). It may well be that Wolfe's narrative skills had to mature in order to encompass his growing sensitivity to the emotional and spiritual lives of others. This symbiotic evolution of his sensibility and his craft would soon be seen in other work from the period.

Wolfe finally went back to Asheville in the spring and summer of 1937, having been banned from his hometown for eight years by the public outcry against *Look Homeward, Angel*. Much biographical speculation has resulted from the long summer visit—Wolfe's apparent ability to go home again—but the fact remains that he found it very difficult to work there, even in the isolated Oteen cabin where he stayed, because of the constant interruptions from local fans. Furthermore, Wolfe himself was a changed man, having in some sense outgrown his thirty-year love-hate relationship with the town. This growth can be seen in the material he was working on during his visit home—the complex manuscript he called "**Party at Jack's**."[4] Esther Jack was the fictional name Wolfe had assigned the character he based on Aline Bernstein, his mistress of

some years; the story is about a young author who attends an elegant party at the Park Avenue apartment of the Jacks, Esther and her husband. The autobiographical monster looms. But, in fact, Wolfe again places Eugene (by now renamed Monk Webber) firmly in the background, and as the story unfolds, even Esther Jack becomes only a single figure in a rich social fabric.

Wolfe's stated purpose in writing "**The Party at Jack's**" was not to revisit through his art a complex time in his life when he was in love with Aline Bernstein. Rather, he used the historical setting of an actual party he attended at the Bernsteins' as an artistic jumping-off place for pointed social commentary. During the period he was in Asheville, he corresponded with his agent, Elizabeth Nowell, about the difficulties he faced in weaving together all the story's elements:

> My plan when I get thru is to have a complete section of the social order, a kind of dense, closely interwoven tapestry made up of the lives and thoughts and destinies of thirty or forty people and all embodied in the structure of the story. It is an elaborate design, it has to be . . .
>
> (*Beyond Love and Loyalty* 71)

Thus the Bernsteins' apartment building becomes a symbol of America's stratified society, with the rich and sophisticated partygoers at the top, supported by the working class cooks, maids, and elevator operators working to make the rich tapestry of the party possible. The whole structure is literally hollow at the core, with the subway tunnels deep under the building causing the building to be fundamentally unsound:

> Therefore, it happened sometimes, that dwellers in this imperial tenement would feel a tremor at their feet as something faint and instant passed below them, and perhaps remember that there were trains, far, far below them in these tunneled depths. Then all would fade away into the riddled distances of the tormented rock. The great building would grow solidly to stone again, and people would smile faintly, knowing that it was enduring and unshaken, now and forever, as it had always been.
>
> (282-283)

But the structure is, of course, not entirely unshaken. It is no accident that when a fire starts in the building, the subway tunnels far beneath the ground have to be flooded and two elevator operators die from smoke inhalation. And even though the partygoers must evacuate their "imperial tenement" for a time, they treat it as an interesting holiday and remain oblivious to the deaths involved. American society may be spiritually hollow at the core and built on the bodies of the working class, but it remains, or so Wolfe seems to say, defiantly strong, barely shaken by the socialism propounded in the story's early pages by one of the elevator operators who would later die.

This is the mature Wolfe, much less artistically concerned with his autobiographical hero, or even the character based on his beloved Aline, than he is with the entire sweep of American society in all its splendor and injustice. Wolfe's own growing socialism during the period is reflected in his growing impatience with the artistic community in New York. The older author who befriends Eugene at the party is emotionally sterile even when sensitive and sympathetic. And in one brilliant set piece, Wolfe satirized the precious world of the New York art scene with his portrayal of "Piggy" Hartwell and his circus constructed entirely out of wire:[5]

> People were not always able to identify each act, but when they were, they applauded vigorously. There was now an act by the trapeze performers. This occupied a long time, largely because Mr. Hartwell was not able to make it work. . . . Again and again the little wire figure soared through the air, caught at the outstretched hands of the other doll—and missed ingloriously. It became painful: people craned their necks and looked embarrassed—all, indeed, except Mr. Hartwell, who giggled happily with each new failure and tried again. . . . And the gathering, after a brief and puzzled pause, broke into applause.
>
> (307)

Wolfe's satire isn't limited to the creator of this "circus"; however, he also found ridiculous the rich and famous partygoers who accepted this bizarre performance as "art" even though it had apparently nothing whatsoever to do with the human drama he saw all around him. The Eugene Gant of *Look Homeward, Angel* and *Of Time and the River* had been fascinated with the power and glory of the New York arts scene, a world he ached to join. By 1937, however, when **"The Party at Jack's"** was being constructed, Wolfe had outgrown both Eugene and his lust for fame.

This use of his own past (but in an entirely different and more mature way) is also reflected in the next piece of evidence: the 1937 story **"The Child by Tiger."** In part because of the story's length and because it concerns a hideous mid-winter night shooting spree that happened in Asheville in November 1906, the story has become one of Wolfe's most commonly anthologized pieces. There are two aspects of the story that are especially important to our discussion, however. First, the story suggests immediately the mature Wolfe's changing attitude toward his black characters. The mysterious protagonist of the story, Dick Prosser, is a strong and sympathetic character who, under the social pressure of the Jim Crow South, metamorpho-

ses into a monster. Both the young boy who is present at the events in the story and the older narrator who recounts them (two aspects of the same authorial presence) struggle to reconcile Dick Prosser's fundamental humanity with the inhuman society that mauls him. Even though Wolfe was a six-year old boy only a few months removed to his mother's boarding house in November 1906, the story is not about Eugene Gant's memories of these events (indeed, internal evidence suggests Wolfe had to consult the Asheville newspapers from the time to even partially recreate what happened). Rather, it is about the struggle of the narrator to construct a meaningful sense of his society through the process of storytelling. It is a story about race, about society, about the fundamental question of what it means to be human. And it is a story about storytelling.

It is precisely because of this element—Wolfe's growing concern with the purpose of storytelling as well as its craft—that we should here recognize one of the most important figures in his life. For decades, critics and scholars alike have written about the personal and professional significance of Max Perkins in Wolfe's history, but a figure who was at least as important as an editor (and perhaps as a friend) was the woman who entered his life in late 1933. Elizabeth Nowell was a clerk at Scribner's who later joined the Maxim Lieber Literary Agency and began to represent Wolfe's work in 1933, replacing Madeline Boyd as his agent. Nowell left Lieber and became an independent in 1934, writing Wolfe a touching letter asking him to remain as her client. From that moment until his death, she became and remained Wolfe's agent, confidant, friend, and significantly, his editor. Not in a formal sense the editor of his novels in progress: that lot fell to Edward Aswell at Harper and Brothers after Wolfe left Scribner's in 1937. Elizabeth Nowell become the editor not of Wolfe's long work but of his best work. Witness this letter she wrote to Wolfe in April 1936 describing the process she had gone through with *The Story of a Novel*:

> I know you think cutting like that is easy, but it really is the hardest thing in the world and the one which take[s] most patience, going over and over and taking out just a few words at a time and putting back half of them in an effort to be sure not to slaughter your meaning, and then counting up the whole estimate and finding it STILL much too long and reading the whole thing over in a search for more words to come out and then estimating etc. etc. and with it always too long until at the end of a good week's work you're sure that it's as tight as it can be without butchering. Oh Jesus, I'm not complaining because it's worth it in your case.
>
> (*Beyond Love and Loyalty* 37)

By this point in Wolfe's career, he was typically dictating his narrative material in long, often rambling fabrics of words that a secretary then typed into rough drafts. The original draft of **"The Child by Tiger,"** for example, Nowell cut almost by half for *The Saturday Evening Post,* where it appeared on September 11, 1937. It was Elizabeth Nowell's "nasty little brackets" (her description of the penciled marks she used to suggest cuts) that Wolfe came to respect as the most practical editorial guidance he ever had.

It is important to admit that Nowell's original mission was to keep Wolfe financially afloat during the long dry spells between novel publication by carving publishable stories out of his manuscript and then selling them. But this mission immediately went to the very core of Wolfe's life, involving Nowell in his artistic production, his finances, his relations to Perkins (and later Aswell), and even his relations to Aline Bernstein and his family. Of profound significance to Wolfe, however, was that of all of his contemporaries, she came to understand what he was trying to accomplish as a writer and consistently helped him see his dreams into print. Of the seven pieces other than *Look Homeward, Angel* that are here discussed, Elizabeth Nowell had an intimate hand in at least five, including all those written after 1935. It was she who could see most clearly the artistic patterns in Wolfe's fiction and unearth them for readers. And it was she who, in September 1938 when Wolfe lay dying in a Baltimore hospital room, was present to comfort his wildly grieving mother and sister. If Wolfe is read for another 100 years, it is Elizabeth Nowell whom we have to thank.[6]

During 1937 Nowell struggled to place the seventh piece of evidence in Wolfe's favor, his Civil War short story **"Chickamauga."** On July 13, 1937, Wolfe wrote friend and novelist Hamilton Basso from Oteen (this the same summer he was working on **"The Party at Jack's"**) that he had written:

> a story called **"Chickamauga"** and if I do say so, it is one of the best stories I ever wrote. I got the idea for it from an old, old man, my great-uncle, John Westall, who lives over in Yancy [sic] County and who is ninety-five years old. When I saw him this spring, he began to tell me about the Civil War and about the battle of Chickamauga, which was, as he said, the bloodiest, most savage battle he was ever in. *He told me about it so wonderfully and in such pungent and poetic language, such as so many of the old country people around here use, that I couldn't wait to . . . begin on it.* My idea was simply to tell the story of a great battle in the language of a common soldier—the kind of country mountain boy who did so much of the fighting in the war.
>
> (*Letters* 625; emphasis added)

Wolfe the mature artist was captured and motivated not by the plot of the story or (as Eugene Gant would have been) by the fact that his blood relative had experienced the events, but by the voice in which he heard the story told. Once again, the mature Wolfe takes on a narrative stance quite alien from his own autobiographical persona to tell a compelling story.

As Wolfe's narrative craft outgrew the autobiographical, he became fascinated not only with other voices but also with multiple, even choral, points of view.[7] The complete version of **"The Lost Boy"** that Wolfe scholar James Clark discovered and edited for publication several years ago consists of four sections, all of which focus on Grover, the boy who is lost in death. The first is narrated in third-person omniscience by a wistful and poetic, but carefully controlled, voice; the second in first person by Grover's mother reminiscing about her lost son (and as in *The Web of Earth,* she is speaking to her son, Grover's brother); the third section in first person by Grover's sister retelling the events leading to Grover's death; the fourth in first person by Grover's brother as an adult, who only barely remembers the dead boy but who is looking for the house in St. Louis where he died. All four sections are in and of themselves complete. And all four sections are united in various ways. Significantly, the narrator of the last section is probably also the implied audience of the second part (the mother's story) and the third part (the sister's). He is probably also the omniscient "spirit behind" the telling of the first section. Thus the four sections are a chorus of voices and the whole a choral symphony. Even though the sections must, by necessity, be read one at a time (so you can only "hear" one voice at a time), the four voices are, to the very limit of Wolfe's mature craft, intertwined. And, finally, even though Part One is the first section, it begins with an ellipsis, suggesting that it follows after something else. What it follows is Part Four, because the whole novella is circular in design. The troubled, searching narrator of the last section would not have been capable of imagining or telling the first section if he had not found that haunted house in St. Louis where his brother died.

Many of the eight fictions cited here are, in some sense or other, "autobiographical." The protagonists, and often the first-person narrators, are based on people that Wolfe knew, often family members. What is important to our understanding of his growth as an artist is that he triumphed over the autobiographical nature of his materials to create what Holman called clear "demonstrations . . . of his craftsmanship and . . . artistic control." In other words, as he turned away from himself as a subject, Wolfe learned how to paint beautifully on a smaller canvas.

There is also a further reason to believe that these eight works not only should but will be read in the twenty-first century. As his artistic control grew, he remained interested in the power of storytelling to create meaning in an otherwise chaotic world. **The Web of Earth, "Only the Dead Know Brooklyn," "The Child by Tiger,"** and **"The Lost Boy"** are all "about" the individual voice busily, even desperately, striving to construct meaning out of a complex world. For this reason, post-modernist critics like Igina Tattoni are seeing in Wolfe a type of metafiction: literature that examines its own power and structure even as the story unfolds. But before large numbers of readers can appreciate this new aspect of Wolfe, they will have to return to his mature work: the short stories and short novels written after 1930. If, indeed, that autobiographical monster Eugene Gant has almost undone Thomas Wolfe, then it is time to declare a moratorium on *Look Homeward, Angel* and take up the more mature fiction that came later. Therein we may find Wolfe's true artistic angels.

Notes

1. Countless critics have discussed Wolfe's intense desire to create large, all-encompassing "books," part of the reason for so much "bad prose" being driven into publication. Fewer have investigated the artistic vision and creative habits that produced such overwrought first drafts.

2. Holman's argument was echoed both by Donald in the closing reflections of his biography and by James Clark in introducing his edition of "The Lost Boy."

3. This passage is one of several in the novel that clearly reflect Wolfe's reading of Joyce during the years he worked on *Look Homeward, Angel*.

4. I refer throughout to the version of the story edited by Elizabeth Nowell and published in *Scribner's Magazine* in 1939. My page references are to that same version as it appeared in the 1961 *Short Novels of Thomas Wolfe*. I use this version rather than the complete manuscript edited for the University of North Carolina Press in 1995 by Suzanne Stutman and John L. Idol because the earlier version is much tighter and more obviously focused on the social issues that fascinated Wolfe. It is also the version edited for publication by Nowell.

5. Piggy Hartwell was based on the young artist Alexander "Sandy" Calder, who actually "performed" his tiny circus at the Bernsteins' party on January 3, 1930.

6. After Wolfe's death, Nowell edited his letters for publication and wrote the first valuable biography of Wolfe, typically downplaying her own importance in his life. Her own modesty in this and other memoirs may well have led later commentators to underestimate both her personal as well as professional significance in Wolfe's life.

7. For a discussion of the democratic implications of Wolfe's multiple voices, see Anne Zahlan, "'The Song of the Whole Land': Thomas Wolfe's Multi-Voiced Discourse in Narratives of *The Web and the Rock*." *Thomas Wolfe Review* 23:2 (1999): 4-12.

Works Cited

Bloom, Harold. "Passionate Beholder of America in Trouble." Rev. of *Look Homeward: A Life of Thomas Wolfe*. By David Herbert Donald. *New York Times Book Review* 8 Feb. 1987: 13-14.

Clark, James W., Jr. "Introduction." *The Lost Boy*. Ed. James W. Clark, Jr. Chapel Hill: U of North Carolina P, 1992. ix-xiv.

DeVoto, Bernard. "Genius Is Not Enough." Rev. of *The Story of a Novel*. By Thomas Wolfe. *Saturday Review of Literature* 25 April 1936: 3-4, 14-15.

Donald, David Herbert. *Look Homeward: A Life of Thomas Wolfe*. Boston: Little, Brown, 1987.

Holman, C. Hugh. "Introduction." *The Short Novels of Thomas Wolfe*. Ed. C. Hugh Holman. New York: Scribner's, 1961. vii-xx.

Kennedy, Richard S., ed. *Beyond Love and Loyalty: The Letters of Thomas Wolfe and Elizabeth Nowell*. Chapel Hill: U of North Carolina P, 1983.

Melloni, Monica. "'The Web of Earth': Wolfe's Art in a Nutshell." *Thomas Wolfe Review* 23.1 (1999): 3-10.

Reeves, Paschal. *Thomas Wolfe's Albatross: Race and Nationality in America*. Athens: U of Georgia P, 1968.

Stegner, Wallace. "Introduction to Thomas Wolfe." *American Literary Masters*. Ed. Charles R. Anderson. Vol. 2. New York: Holt, Rinehart, and Winston, 1965. 1071-1081.

Tattoni, Igina. *The Unfound Door: Innovative Trends in Thomas Wolfe's Fiction*. Rome: Bulzoni, 1992.

Wolfe, Thomas. "Chickamauga." *The Complete Short Stories of Thomas Wolfe*. Ed. Francis E. Skipp. New York: Scribner's, 1987. 381-396.

———. *Look Homeward, Angel*. New York: Scribner's, 1929.

———. *O Lost: A Story of the Buried Life*. Text established by Arlyn and Matthew J. Bruccoli. Columbia: U of South Carolina P, 2000.

———. "Only the Dead Know Brooklyn." *The Complete Short Stories of Thomas Wolfe*. Ed. Francis E. Skipp. New York: Scribner's, 1987. 260-264.

———. *The Party at Jack's*. Ed. Suzanne Stutman and John L. Idol, Jr. Chapel Hill: U of North Carolina P, 1995.

————. "The Party at Jack's." *The Short Novels of Thomas Wolfe.* Ed. C. Hugh Holman. New York: Scribner's, 1961. 282-323.

————. "The Child by Tiger." *The Complete Short Stories of Thomas Wolfe.* Ed. Francis E. Skipp. New York: Scribner's, 1987. 332-348.

————. *The Letters of Thomas Wolfe.* Ed. Elizabeth Nowell. New York: Scribner's, 1956.

————. *The Lost Boy.* Ed. James W. Clark, Jr. Chapel Hill: U of North Carolina P, 1992.

————. "Web of Earth." *From Death to Morning.* New York: Scribner's, 1935. 212-304.

Jerry Leath Mills (essay date 2003)

SOURCE: Mills, Jerry Leath. "The Dark Side of the Tracks in Thomas Wolfe's 'The Bums at Sunset.'" *Thomas Wolfe Review* 27, nos. 1 & 2 (2003): 14-21.

[*In the following essay, Mills assesses the thematic role of musical allusion in Wolfe's "The Bums at Sunset."*]

I'll show you the bees,
And the cigarette trees,
And the soda-water fountains,
And the lemonade springs
Where the bluebird sings
In the Big Rock Candy Mountains.

In reply to a query by University of North Carolina folklorist Arthur Palmer Hudson in 1933, Thomas Wolfe described the use of music in his writing as essentially atmospheric and evocative in purpose, a sensory aid to the recapture of memory (*Letters* 377). While Wolfe's works at large bear out this strategy of allusion (see Blackwelder passim), a notable exception lies in the brief short story—or, more accurately, vignette—**"The Bums at Sunset,"** first published in the October 1935 issue of *Vanity Fair* and collected the same year in ***From Death to Morning.*** In this work, musical allusion is specifically thematic and leads us to a core of meaning either missed or glossed over by the few critics who have mentioned the story at all.

The five-page segment that constitutes **"The Bums at Sunset"** was conceived as part of an expansive work that Wolfe thought of under a number of possible titles, including *Antaeus* or *The Immortal Earth.* In June 1930 Wolfe established in a letter to Maxwell Perkins that the central intelligence of these materials, the observer of the hoboes gathered at the water tower, was his persona David Hawke (*Letters* 242-43). To Elizabeth Nowell four years later he wrote "I also have a piece called **'The Bums at Sunset'** which we cut out

of the book the other day, and which is about some hoboes waiting beside the track to pick up the train, but I don't know if this is any good or could be used" (*Letters* 403).

Interestingly, Wolfe's first mention of the mise-en-scène of a gathering at the water tower corresponds with the appearance of a book that introduced to the public a large collection of hobo songs and the lore behind them, George Milburn's annotated compilation *The Hobo's Hornbook: A Repertory for a Gutter Jongleur* (1930). The water tower setting is a structural convention employed in many of these songs and ballads—for example, "The Dying Hobo" (67), "The Hobo's Last Lament" (74), "The Whistle in the Night" (203), "The Bum at the Stem" (125), and "The Railroad Bum" (231). In addition, the tower and its tank serve as a log for recording in graffiti the nicknames or "monikas" of the various itinerants—"Monikas Seen on the Water Tank" (Milburn 33-36)—a subject in which Wolfe shows interest in a passage written for *Antaeus* (55) in 1930 and later incorporated into *Of Time and the River* (867). I will argue, moreover, that another of the songs in Milburn's anthology provides us with direct entry into both the structure and the fundamental issue of the story.

"The Bums at Sunset" has only the barest of plots. Five men emerge from a hobo jungle and convene at a water tower, where three of them engage in a drama of which one, the youngest, is naively unaware. This young man, "a fresh-skinned country lad with bright wondering eyes . . . perhaps not more than sixteen years old" (150), is new to hobo life and about to acquire a mentor in the person of Bull, a vagrant in his mid-fifties who has "the powerful shambling figure, the seamed face of the professional vagabond" (151), and is obviously the leader of the group. Bull is possessed of "a curious brutal nobility" (151) that inspires trust in this young man unsure of direction in his new milieu (152). A third figure, a man of about thirty "with a ferret face and very few upper teeth" (150) is, on the surface, the most sinister of the group—"everything about him suggested unclean secrecy" (151). He protests the inclusion of the boy in their company but is overruled and intimidated by Bull.

As mentioned above, the very sparse commentary on this story has tended toward the perfunctory, or disingenuous, or both. Elizabeth Evans approaches it as "slice-of-life" narrative, linking it with **"Only the Dead Know Brooklyn"** as explorations of a problem of loneliness "for which no solution is reached," and observes that "the appearance of the young, uninitiated bum threatens those who know the ropes and are suspicious of his lack of experience" (103). Richard Walser also sees a theme of loneliness, and remarks that Wolfe "communicates the friendliness existing among those who wander the 'lonely distances of America'" (124).

The true nature of the "friendliness" offered the boy, however, is invoked through allusion to "The Big Rock Candy Mountain," a song first recorded in 1928 and printed in two versions in *The Hobo's Hornbook* two years later. Its alleged author, Harry ("Haywire Mac") McClintock, claimed to have written it from traditional materials sometime around 1895 (Rammel 10). The song now exists in a number of "sanitized" versions, including a popular children's version by Burl Ives; but McClintock made no bones about his original theme. Describing experiences in his own hobo youth, McClintock told how in hobo life "a kid who could not only beg handouts but could also bring in money for alcohol, was a valuable piece of property for the jocker who could snare him" (Lomax 410). A *jocker*, according to the *Dictionary of American Slang,* is "A homosexual hobo who lives off the begging of his boy companion." The term is common in hobo literature, such as Jack London's *The Road* (1907), and is certainly clarified by McClintock as he goes on to relate how "there were times when I fought like a wildcat or ran like a deer to preserve my independence and my virginity" (Lomax 410). In McClintock's "original" version, the lines printed above as the epigraph for this article are introduced with these stanzas:

> One sunny day in the month of May,
> A jocker he come hiking;
> He come to a tree and ["]Ah!["] says he
> ["]This is just to my liking!["]
>
> In the very same month on the very same day
> A hoosier's son came hiking;
> Said the bum to the son, ["]O, will you come
> To the Big Rock Candy Mountains.["]

> (Milburn 61-62)

That the song, which belongs to a tradition of "folk utopias" harking back to the medieval Land of Cockaigne (Morton 15-45; Rammel passim), constitutes a grotesquely cynical *suasio*, a perverse "Come Live with Me and Be My Love," has long been understood by folklorists and social historians. James R. Chiles, in a recent article on hoboes in America, writes:

> Young people who traveled alone were in real danger from sexual predators. . . . "Jockers," or male homosexuals, took on boys. Sometimes the relationship required the boys to beg in towns for food or money. Usually it would begin with the older man assisting the boy with advice or food and then turn into slavery that could last months or years. Some hobo versions of "The Big Rock Candy Mountains" song describe this predator-prey relationship.

> (74)

Surely, then, it is to such a relationship that the ferret-faced man refers in Wolfe's story when he applies his voice of cynical experience to the boy's obvious innocence:

> "Yeah. You stick to Bull, kid. He'll see yuh t'roo. He'll show yuh de—woild, I ain't kiddin' yuh! He'll take yuh up to Lemonade Lake an' all t'roo Breadloaf Valley—won't yuh, Bull? He'll show yuh where de ham trees are and where de toikeys grow on bushes—won't yuh, Bull?" he said with ugly yet fawning insinuations. "You stick to Bull, kid, an' you'll be wearin' poils. . . . A-a-a-ah! yuh punk kid!"

> (153, ellipsis in original)

The images of lemonade lakes, ham- and turkey-bearing trees, and so forth occur in various versions of "The Big Rock Candy Mountain" and related songs in the tradition, such as a version subtitled "the hoboes paradise," in which the ham is joined by eggs in the trees, and chickens jump into skillets while bread grows in the fields and cows churn their own butter. Sometimes the lakes contain gin, an added convenience ("Big Rock Candy Mountain"). Clearly, Wolfe is familiar enough with the tradition to have in mind a composite version, and the context of images, as we will see, makes it equally clear that he understood the sexual implications in his characterization of the lives of the men in his story as "a legend of pounding wheel and thrumming rod, of bloody brawl and brutal shambles" (151). Wolfe understood, further, that "The Big Rock Candy Mountain" is a song of ultimate disillusionment. As Haywire Mac concluded one version of his song:

> The punk rolled up his big blue eyes
> And said to the jocker, ["]Sandy,
> I've hiked and hiked and wandered, too
> But I ain't seen any candy.
> I've hiked and hiked till my feet are sore,
> I'll be God-damned if I hike any more
> To be——
> In the Big Rock Candy Mountains.["]

> (Lomax 411)

We have no record of the omitted phrase, but the necessity for a rhyme on *more* and *sore* makes speculation relatively easy.

"The Bums at Sunset," then, presents a liminal scene, poised, as the image of sunset implies, just before the boy's descent into a darkness of experience not commonly acknowledged in older accounts of the adventures of vagabondage and the open road, although it exists by strong implication in Jack London's *The Road* (232-85 passim) and has been treated in detail in such recent scholarly studies as George Chauncy's *Gay New York* (1994) and Jonathan Auerbach's *Male Call: Becoming Jack London* (1996). Wolfe strikes an anticipatory note in his opening paragraph, with its play on literal implications of the word *jungle* and its images of predatory beasts coming forth into the welcome twilight to begin their hunt around the watering place:

> Slowly, singly, with the ambling gait of men who have just fed, and who are faced with no pressure of time and business, the hoboes came from the jungle, descended the few feet of clay embankment that sloped to the road bed, and in an unhurried manner walked down the tracks toward the water tower. The time was the exact moment of sunset, the sun indeed had disappeared from sight, but its last shafts fell remotely, without violence or heat, upon the treetops of the already darkening woods and on the top of the water tower.
>
> (150)

The ferret-faced man's objections notwithstanding, Bull rather quickly achieves his goals of seduction and dominance, which he symbolizes consciously and triumphantly by confiscating the boy's cigarettes as he directs him to sit down on the handcar beside him:

> Bull took a cigarette from the package, lighted it with a single movement, between his tough seamed face and his cupped paw, and then dropped the package of cigarettes in his pocket, with the same spacious and powerful gesture.
>
> (154)

Evans seems generally correct in asserting that the characters in Wolfe's little story are "flat, distinguished only by age and basic reactions" (103). After all, we might reply, they derive directly from a tradition of songs and ballads. Our observation of the underlying theme, however, perhaps allows us to see an exception in the characterization of the ferret-faced man, whose surface hostility toward the boy may be taken as a circuitous way of trying to save the youth from a fate he may himself have suffered at a similar stage of life. There is a fallen quality about him that suggests some previous corruption of his youth. Though not over thirty, he has lost a number of teeth, and he moves "gingerly on tender feet that were obviously unaccustomed to the work he was now putting them to: he was a triumph of dirty elegance . . ." (150). In resisting the boy's inclusion he seems, like the lady in the play, to protest too much:

> "Wat t'hell am I supposed to be—a noice-maid or sump'n? . . . G'wan, yuh little punk," he snarled once more, and lifted his fist in a sudden backhand movement, as if to strike the boy. "Scram! We got no use fer yuh! . . . G'wan, now. . . . Get t'hell away from here before I smash yuh one."
>
> (153, ellipses in original)

Is his hostility authentic, or are we presented with a failed attempt at decency in an otherwise thoroughly deceitful world?

It remains to speculate about why this theme of coercion and betrayal of innocence at the outset of potential adventure appealed to Wolfe at the time when **"The Bums at Sunset"** found its form. Quite likely the form itself was suggested by materials appearing in *The Hobo's Hornbook* in 1930, but there are reasons more germane.

First, it is difficult not to see in the story a connection with issues developed with considerable intensity in the Starwick episodes of *Of Time and the River*—and with even greater intensity in the deleted sections made available much later by Richard S. Kennedy. As most of Wolfe's biographers have recounted, Wolfe's relationship at Harvard with Kenneth Raisbeck, the model for the fictional Starwick, became a focal point for his disillusionment with the artistic and intellectual life as he came to believe he found it there—frequently a sham system of posturing, pretense, and mutual congratulation among people long on current notions of taste and sophistication but short on genuine talent and the ability to recognize it in others. Though close to Wolfe in age, Raisbeck supplied, through his connection as assistant to Professor George Pierce Baker, as well as through his own well-developed aesthetic façade, a mentoring role for the young Southerner. In the fictional account, the relationship ends with the revelations of Starwick's homosexuality that Wolfe allows to Eugene Gant (*Starwick Episodes* 78-108).

With the impression of an "unclean secrecy" (151) in the ferret-faced man in **"The Bums at Sunset,"** it is interesting to compare Wolfe's remarks about Starwick in one of the deleted sections, where he observes that "even among his friends he maintained a secrecy that was unreasonable and somewhat arrogant in its indifference" (*Starwick Episodes* 11), and, further:

> even a friend was likely to feel that a secrecy so strenuously maintained over a period of years was unnatural and that the friend to whom he had revealed his own life without concealment had, on his part, yielded only occasional and guarded glimpses.
>
> (12)

As Kennedy notes, it is likely that Wolfe shared current opinions that Baker himself was bisexual. If, as Kennedy finds "entirely possible," Baker had "initiated Raisbeck into homosexual activity during the time they were traveling together in England" (*Starwick Episodes* 3), Wolfe's tendency to regard homosexuality as a metaphor for betrayal of innocence and trust takes on additional force in the triad of Bull, the ferret-faced man, and the naive youth of **"The Bums at Sunset."**

A second context for the short story may be Wolfe's fascination with the Antaeus myth during the same period and in the same general body of material. David

Hawke, the unnamed observer of **"The Bums at Sunset,"** was to be assigned a personal history based on that of the mythical Libyan giant, whose quest was a search for his father, Poseidon, whom he had never seen. Because he drew his strength from his mother, the Earth, his travels became for Wolfe an expression of the dual American desires for wandering and eternal motion on the one hand and fixity, permanence, and repose on the other (Donald 239). One product of this fascination was the collection of lyrical vignettes constituting *Antaeus, or A Memory of Earth,* edited by Ted Mitchell for the Thomas Wolfe Society. Another, much darker variation, with its own place in Wolfe's panoramic view, was **"The Bums at Sunset,"** with an Antaeus figure, the boy, seeking—and unfortunately about to find—a surrogate father on his perilous journey into the regions of American night.

Works Cited

Auerbach, Jonathan. *Male Call: Becoming Jack London.* Durham, NC: Duke University Press, 1996.

"The Big Rock Candy Mountain." *"A-No.1 At Rest At Last": Life and Adventures of America's Most Celebrated Tramp!* 2001. Grahamqckr. 3 Oct. 2003 <http://www.angelfire.com/folk/famoustramp/song.html>

Blackwelder, James Ray. "Literary Allusions in *Look Homeward, Angel*: The Narrator's Perspective." *Thomas Wolfe Review* 8.2 (1984): 14-25.

Chauncy, George. *Gay New York.* New York: Basic Books, 1994.

Chiles, James R. "Hallelujah, I'm a Bum." *Smithsonian* Aug. 1998: 64-76.

Donald, David Herbert. *Look Homeward: A Life of Thomas Wolfe.* Boston: Little, Brown, 1987.

Evans, Elizabeth. *Thomas Wolfe.* New York: Frederick Ungar, 1984.

Lomax, Alan. *The Folk Songs of North America in the English Language.* Garden City, NY: Doubleday, 1960.

London, Jack. *The Road. Social Writings.* Ed. David Pizer. New York: Library of America, 1982. 185-314.

Milburn, George, comp. *The Hobo's Hornbook: A Repertory for a Gutter Jongleur.* New York: Ives Washburn, 1930.

Morton, A. L. *The English Utopia.* London: Lawrence and Wishart, 1969.

Rammel, Hal. *Nowhere in America: The Big Rock Candy Mountain and Other Comic Utopias.* Urbana: University of Illinois Press, 1990.

Walser, Richard. *Thomas Wolfe: An Introduction and Interpretation.* New York: Barnes and Noble, 1961.

Wentworth, Harold, and Stuart Berg Flexner, comps. *Dictionary of American Slang.* New York: Thomas Y. Crowell, 1960.

Wolfe, Thomas. *Antaeus, or A Memory of Earth.* Ed. Ted Mitchell. N.p.: The Thomas Wolfe Society, 1996.

———. "The Bums at Sunset." *From Death to Morning.* New York: Scribner's, 1935. 150-54.

———. *The Letters of Thomas Wolfe.* Ed. Elizabeth Nowell. New York: Scribner's, 1956.

———. *Of Time and the River.* New York: Scribner's, 1935.

———. *The Starwick Episodes.* Ed. Richard S. Kennedy. Baton Rouge: Louisiana State University Press, 1994.

Carlton N. Morse (essay date 2003)

SOURCE: Morse, Carlton N. "Thomas Wolfe's *The Lost Boy*: A Bildungsroman for the Modern Reader." *Thomas Wolfe Review* 27, nos. 1 & 2 (2003): 43-52.

[*In the following essay, Morse highlighs the modernist qualities of* The Lost Boy *and asserts that Wolfe's talents as an author should be judged on the basis of his short works.*]

Since the nascent days of Wolfe criticism, critics have challenged the prolixity that characterizes his fiction, especially his novels. Some contemporary scholars have addressed this unfortunate stigma and breathed new life into the reading of Wolfe by illuminating the more neglected elements of his canon, the short fiction. Wolfe scholar Joseph Bentz argues that Wolfe's greatest accomplishments as an author are found in his short stories, a genre wherein his literary techniques become most effective:

> The overemphasis on Wolfe's seemingly loosely structured novels has obscured his experimentation in the short story. While the structure of his novels owes a greater debt to nineteenth-century fiction than to the modernist fiction of the 1920s and '30s, the structure of many of Wolfe's short stories was heavily influenced by modernism.
>
> . . . [and] measuring some of them against modernist rather than traditional criteria may reveal Wolfe's real artistic achievement.
>
> (149, 154)

One of the finest of Wolfe's short works is **"The Lost Boy."** The story first appeared in *Redbook* magazine in 1937, and a different short version was published in the 1941 collection ***The Hills Beyond*** to much acclaim (Clark xi). In 1992 James W. Clark Jr., using

Wolfe's original manuscript, edited the first version of "**The Lost Boy**" to appear as a book. Unlike many of Wolfe's novels, *The Lost Boy* exhibits established modernist qualities, including an innovative lyrical form and emphasis on a single moment of significance (Bentz 153, 156). And the preoccupation with youth is a characteristic of modernity (Minden 122). With these insights in mind, I believe that an interpretation of the work is further enhanced by recognizing not only *The Lost Boy*'s modernist qualities but also its distinctly modern message—a critical personification of the larger concerns of modernism. *The Lost Boy* is a *unique* coming of age story, a bildungsroman for a modern audience living in a dynamic and insecure world. A traditional bildungsroman follows the maturation of one character, culminating in a confidence and ability to face the adult world. Wolfe, however, bridges the lives of two separate characters, beginning in young Grover what he finishes thirty years later in the adult Eugene, and, uncharacteristically, portrays the achievement of adulthood as an empty and unfulfilling milestone.

The journey represents not only Wolfe's own efforts to unite his present with his past but also the "growing pains" of modern America. Two characters, Grover and Eugene, on opposite sides of life and of time, emerge from the magical, finite world of the child into the vast, nebulous, commercialized universe of adulthood—America in 1938. Eugene's quest for his brother is indeed a search for himself; he, like the narrative, moves invariably forward but is also grounded in the past. Unlike most "coming of age" stories, the protagonist does not reach maturity by establishing autonomy in the adult world but rather by uniting himself with his past—not that he dwells there, but he prefers the past because the adult world is a vast, lonely place where one "is drowned in desolation and in no belief" (66). It is a realm devoid of the security and control one enjoys as a child. Eugene's peace is found "in the union of forever and of now" (2), a condition that allows him to unite past, present, and future to achieve a momentary escape from the modern world's endemic disillusionment and loneliness. In this sense, the tip of Wolfe's literary iceberg is a bildungsroman wherein the lonely protagonist longs for a reconnection with childhood. Submerged beneath its symbolism, however, is the story of an emerging nation, chaotic and lonely, whose jaded people long for a similar return to a more romantic era of history before the callous advent of modernity.

The establishment of *The Lost Boy* as a bildungsroman in the modernist vein demands special attention to the story's structure and veiled plot. The bildungsroman has several defining features. The typical bildungsroman includes a protagonist who experiences a

significant change of knowledge about the world leading to the development of self or self-revelation (Minden 122). The plot typically participates in the picaresque and confessional modes of literature by portraying the formative experiences and epiphanic revelations that define a young person's character in adulthood (Griesinger).

In the first chapter, Grover's unsavory experience at the candy store when "Old stingy Crocker" unjustly accuses him of theft leads to an epiphany about the cruelty of mankind. This is Grover's first exposure to the world beyond the childish boundaries of his town square, the arena of adult conflict and painful isolation. His uncorrupted, childish conscience permits him no other defense than to demand of Crocker what *must* happen; Grover's desperation is evident in his pleas as they progress from "Will you give me the three ones, please?" (22) to "You've got to give me those three ones" (24), as if he cannot appreciate the human capacity for deceit. The episode scars him. Upon surveying all that is familiar, Grover perceives a marked difference in his own self:

> He felt the overwhelming, the soul-sickening guilt that all the children, all the good men of the earth have felt since time began. . . . "This the square"—thought Grover as before—"This is Now. There is my father's shop. And all of it is as it has always been—save I."
>
> (24-25)

Lois Hartley states that, at this moment, Grover "is now the lost boy" (262). She points out that "Through time and experience Grover has changed. . . . He has learned something about separateness, about isolation, about inhumanity . . ." (262). Grover has certainly caught a glimpse of the darker side of human nature; however, I maintain that Grover is not yet fully "lost." He is essentially rescued by his father and as "Light came again into the day" (31), Grover reaffirms his place in his universe but is forever changed. Quite symbolically, he then sees a "car [curving] out into the square, [and] upon the bill-board of the car-end was a poster and it said St. Louis and Excursion and The Fair" (32). The car intrudes upon the scene and directs the narrative, and Grover, toward the 1904 St. Louis World's Fair where he will encounter the modern adult world and, both physically and in memory, become "lost" in it.

In a typical bildungsroman, the first steps toward autonomy are similarly painful, and in Grover's case the magnitude of this incipient event makes his trajectory irreversible. The rest of Grover's life is related by his mother and sister in parts 2 and 3 of *The Lost Boy,* where the reader observes Grover eating at a restaurant with his sister (a step toward independence that is still tempered by childish anxiety over his mother's disapproval), and understands that he has acquired a job at the World's Fair. Wolfe biographer Elizabeth Nowell exposes the importance of the latter detail to the story: Wolfe's own brother, Grover, died of typhoid contracted from the fairgrounds where he worked, an ironic coincidence that underscores the perilous nature of a youth's transition to adulthood (26).

By this point, the events of Grover's life fit well into the bildungsroman archetype, because he has gained a degree of independence and some autonomy. Wolfe's narrative, of course, is not traditional; it has a distinctly modernist composition. The use of Grover's "epiphanic revelation" at Crocker's as a turning point after the candy shop incident is one such product of the modernist influence that owes its prominence to the work of James Joyce. Joyce defines the literary epiphany as "a sudden spiritual manifestation, whether in the vulgarity of speech or of gesture or in a memorable phrase of the mind itself" (qtd. in Kershner 18).[1] Historian of the novel Richard Kostelanetz states that often "the [modern short-] story's end comes as an anticlimax after the earlier epiphany" (qtd. in Bentz 150). This effect is at work in Grover's story, as his climactic revelation (a "memorable phrase of the mind") is soon followed not by further maturation but, instead, his sudden death—an anticlimax. His ascension into adulthood is not fully realized as in a typical bildungsroman from previous literary periods. Something new is at work in Wolfe's fiction.

Wolfe's creative genius is evident in the fourth section, as the deceased Grover's aborted growth is instead realized in Eugene, who appears thirty years later. Wolfe's break from convention is committed here, as the narrative jumps ahead thirty years, omitting the conventional life lessons that one would expect to find in a typical bildungsroman. His new protagonist is mature in the traditional sense and, rather than looking forward, looks longingly to the past, in a sort of reversed bildungsroman that does not end with the attainment of maturity in adulthood. Rather, he longs to resurrect the past, to bring it alive by finding the memory of Grover, who died during the perilous transition into adulthood.

Thus, in Wolfe's bildungsroman, Eugene achieves a type of maturity when he unites past with present in his own meaningful epiphany. The epiphany is complex, and it is difficult to grasp its significance outside of the context of Wolfe's medium—time—and the work's overall theme—loneliness.

I call time as used by Wolfe a "medium" in the sense that Eugene achieves maturity by effectively molding time—as if time were material—in much the same way that the author crafts it in creating his story. Many modernist writers employ this technique but, as evident in *The Lost Boy,* Wolfe is a master. The basic characteristic of the novel, as outlined by Ian Watt, is the narrative procedure that abandons "traditional plots and 'purple patches' of rhetoric and the stress on developing individual characters and situations *so that time, place, person, and even causation are given a new particularity*" (emphasis added) (cited in Kershner 21). In modernist novels, R. B. Kershner explains:

> the idea is that an image or action, rooted in physical sensation, has the capability of encapsulating a larger experience, meaning, or emotion, or some amalgam of all these, that has enormous artistic significance. The artist's role is to capture, create, or re-create such moments, in which a special, nondiscursive kind of knowledge is imparted.
>
> (59)

Such knowledge, communicated through Eugene's emotional journey to reclaim the memory of his brother, embodies the modernist message of *The Lost Boy*—a portrayal of the loneliness, disillusionment, and emptiness of modern existence, a condition distinctly different than that experienced in the safe and defined world of a child.

This is most fully explored in Eugene, but the reader can find hints of this truth in the revealing accounts of Grover's mother and sister. His mother recalls when a "good substantial sort of person" (36) came from New Jersey inquiring about her now-famous son, Eugene. Her response is not that of a proud mother—"I don't believe in bragging on my own kind" (37)—but of an impartial, disinterested observer who downplays his accomplishments as an adult:

> . . . he had two good eyes and a nose and a mouth, two arms and legs and a good head of hair . . . he was a good, ordinary, normal sort of boy, just like all the others—. . . I never heard of the teacher putting a dunce cap on him. . . .
>
> . . . Of course, he went off to college and read a lot of books, and I reckon that's where he got this flow of language they say he has . . . [ellipsis in original]. But as I said to him the last time that I saw him 'Now look a-here' I said 'If you can earn your living doing a light easy class of work like this you do,' I says, 'you're mighty lucky, because none of the rest of your people,' I says, 'had any such luck as that. . . .'
>
> (37-38)

Eugene's mother speaks as if she does not value her elder son's achievements; they pale in comparison to the boyish qualities of Grover and the praise bestowed upon him as a child.

> [Grover] is for her, paradoxically, the symbol of all that has changed, of all who have either died or gone away, and yet of the changeless, because he is fixed forever

in memory as he was "that morning when we went down through Indiana, by the river, to the Fair." The mother has known change and loss, and even in the words of her refrain there is a loneliness.

(Hartley 263-64)

For her, the past, personified in Grover, is to be praised while the present, personified in Eugene, is unfamiliar, and all of its achievements tempered with confusion and a longing for the past.

Grover's older sister is similarly disillusioned; her reminiscence over her lost brother is intertwined with lamentations of the grown-up present: "all of us have grown up, and I am forty-six years old. And nothing has turned out the way I thought it would. . . . And all my hopes and dreams and big ambitions have all come to nothing" (55, ellipsis in original). She continues:

> It's all so long ago, as if it happened in another world. And then it all comes back, as if it happened yesterday . . . [ellipsis in original]. And sometimes I will lie awake at night and think of all the people who have come and gone and all the things that happened. And how everything is different from the way we thought that it would be. . . .
>
> . . . And then it goes away and seems farther off and stranger than if it happened in a dream.
>
> (55, 57)

Her lonesome state is no fault of her own. One gets the sense from her account that life invariably ends in disappointment. As if by design, life works to foil the hopes and ambitions of one's childhood.

The novella's episodes expose the incompatibility between the world of the child and the realm of the modern adult, an antithetical relationship that culminates in Eugene's pilgrimage back to the family's one-time home in St. Louis, near the fairgrounds. This journey to resurrect the memory of his lost brother is the epiphany toward which his bildungsroman is regressing (rather than progressing, in this case); the house on the corner is not simply where he thinks intently on the memory of his brother, but rather where he rolls back time to unite the past and present.

His journey is both a physical search for the house and a spiritual reflection, in which he navigates between the conflicting images codified by his childhood impressions and the current landscape. Symbolically, he first encounters the King's Highway, a rather fancifully named street that "had not been a street in those days but a kind of road that wound from magic out of some dim and haunted land . . ." (61). This is his childhood memory, which differs remarkably from its present, nearly unrecognizable appearance: "I looked

about me, and I saw what King's Highway was. King's Highway was a street, a broad and busy street with new hotels and hard bright lights, and endless flocks of motors swarming up and down" (61). Eugene's memory, an abstraction that captured the newness, magic, and excitement of this new environment as a child, senses that it is consumed and devoured by this realistic perspective in the present.

This experience is similar to Grover's stroll through the square before his "conversion" at Crockers' with one striking difference: the conflicting perspectives and appraisals of the adult and the child. Grover surveys all that inhabits his town square, from Mr. Thrash's Singer sewing machine shop to Mr. Markham's music and piano store, Garrett's grocery store, and J. Wilson's Printer Shop. Each of these is lively, friendly, personal, full of things to explore, and contributes to the splendor of the square (much as Eugene remembers the King's Highway). Interestingly, there are also elements that Grover disapproves of:

> He didn't like the look of banks, of real estate or fire insurance offices. . . . He did not like windows full of patent medicines and hot water bags, for somehow they depressed him. . . . He did not like the roll-top desk nor the diploma that hung over it, nor the potted plant, nor the drooping fern. He did not like the dark look of the place behind it. He didn't like an undertaker's shop and therefore he would never stop before it.
>
> (7)

Had Grover returned to the square as an adult, his perspective would probably be as Eugene's—realistic—with little selectivity in taste; however, the difference between that which Grover dismisses and that in which he revels is that the things he dislikes are exclusively for the adult world, and nearly all of them modern necessities. Banks, real estate firms, and insurance offices represent commercialism and the deity of money. Roll-top desks and diplomas symbolize the urban professions, the demands of work and education, things unrelated to the blissful world Grover enjoys. He is able to ignore these intrusions and is wholly unshaken by their presence. In Eugene's case, the magic of King's Highway died with his youth and is replaced by jaded disinterest that sees only the impersonal modern constructions, "hard bright lights" and the "endless flocks of motors swarming [invading] up and down." If modernity is America's "coming of age," the juxtaposition of Grover's youthful perception and Eugene's jaded outlook parallels the character of America before the advent of modernity and then well after it. Wolfe, like Eugene, stands undeniably in the present but looks longingly backward and, from that position, uses his narrative to address modernity's influence upon the American landscape and the American psyche.

There are many transitions children experience as they mature, but this new, stale awareness of, and disillusion with, the world is specifically a product of the loneliness that accompanies modern existence. Lois Hartley notes that **The Lost Boy** "says something tentatively about time and change, it says something more about isolation, about loneliness" (262). She quotes Wolfe describing the prevalence of loneliness:

> The whole conviction of my life now rests upon the belief that loneliness, far from being a rare and curious phenomenon, peculiar to myself and to a few other solitary men, is the central and inevitable fact of human existence. When we examine the moments, acts, and statements of all kinds of people—not only the grief and ecstasy of the greatest poets, but also the huge unhappiness of the average soul, as evidenced by the innumerable strident words of abuse, hatred, contempt, mistrust, and scorn that forever grate upon our ears as the manswarm passes us in the streets—we find, I think, that they are all suffering from the same thing. The final cause of their complaint is loneliness.

> **("God's Lonely Man"** 186)

This loneliness inherent in all men is evident in Eugene:

> He knows that it [America] is endless, he is drowned, that he cannot escape. He knows that he is lost and sunken in America, that it is too big for him, and that he has no home. . . . He knows now that he is only a nameless atom lost in vacancy, a brief and dusty cipher, whirled homelessly in unnumbered time, and that all the dreams, the strength, the passion, the belief of youth have gone amort.

> (**The Lost Boy** 65)

Thus, the modern landscape has altered mankind, making all of us homeless and small, extracting us from the finite, comparatively halcyon realm of youth and tossing us into a vulgar "manswarm" of humanity. A traditional bildungsroman would celebrate youth's ascension into this world; however, the world is changed with the advent of modernity, and Wolfe's bildungsroman reflects this change, culminating not in a step forward, but in a look backward to reclaim what was lost.

Eugene's highly symbolic return to the house on Edgemont Street momentarily frees him from these "blind mazes" of existence. His conversation with Mrs. Bell, the current owner, is the spark that brings the memory of Grover, of youth, of a better life up from the abyss of time. He remembers the instance when his brother coaxed him to pronounce his name, "Grover," a difficult task, as he is so young. Wallace Stegner notes the significance of this "name magic":

> The closest we get to Grover's quiet ghost is his little brother's lisping "Gova."

But this is enough. Wolfe's magic, like Eugene's, invokes the ghost briefly and holds him a moment before he fades.

(259)

In Eugene's epiphany, he momentarily transcends the present and reverts to the formative years of childhood when Grover, himself a child, acted as teacher. In the narrative, as the lost boy, Grover is also a teacher in the sense that his idealized memory transcends the desolate present and compels both Eugene and the reader to discover the buried memories of more secure times. This is the destination of Wolfe's bildungsroman—a maturity of the mind and spirit that fills the void of loneliness with the memory of past fulfillment. Eugene connects, if briefly, with the precious memory of childhood and escapes from the desolation and loneliness that tarnishes one man's life after childhood just as it does the landscape of America after the advent of modernity. In **The Lost Boy,** Wolfe translates into accessible prose the complex phenomena of memory, remembrance, inescapable loneliness, and the search for lost harmony between what was and what is. It is a modern story of growth and the loss that accompanies maturity and is meaningful for all who ever regret rushing to grow up, and who long for even a momentary return to a time when life was more simple, more familiar, and more fulfilling.

Note

1. Wolfe admits the influence of Joyce's fiction upon his own in his *Purdue Speech: 'Writing and Living.'* There, he specifically cites the influence of Joyce's *A Portrait of the Artist as a Young Man* (50), a well-established kunstlerroman, a specific type of bildungsroman that follows the maturation of the artist.

Works Cited

Bentz, Joseph. "The Influence of Modernist Structure in the Short Fiction of Thomas Wolfe." *Studies in Short Fiction* 31.2 (1994): 149-61.

Clark, James W., Jr. Introduction. *The Lost Boy.* By Thomas Wolfe. Ed. James W. Clark Jr. Chapel Hill: University of North Carolina Press, 1992. ix-xiv.

Griesinger, Emily. Lecture. Azusa Pacific University, Azusa, CA. 10 Nov. 2001.

Hartley, Lois. "Theme in Thomas Wolfe's 'The Lost Boy' and 'God's Lonely Man.'" *Georgia Review* 15.2 (1961): 230-35. Rpt. in *Thomas Wolfe: Three Decades of Criticism.* Ed. Leslie A. Field. New York: New York University Press, 1968. 261-67.

Kershner, R. B. *The Twentieth-Century Novel: An Introduction.* Boston: Bedford Books, 1997.

Minden, Michael. "Bildungsroman." *Encyclopedia of the Novel*. Ed. Paul Schellinger. Vol. 1. Chicago: Fitzroy Dearborn, 1998. 118-22.

Nowell, Elizabeth. *Thomas Wolfe: A Biography*. Garden City, NY: Doubleday, 1960.

Stegner, Wallace. "Analysis of 'The Lost Boy.'" *The Writer's Art: A Collection of Short Stories*. Ed. Wallace Stegner, Richard Scowcraft, and Boris Ilyin. Boston: Heath (1950). 178-83. Rpt. in *Thomas Wolfe: Three Decades of Criticism*. Ed. Leslie A. Field. New York: New York University Press, 1968. 255-60.

Wolfe, Thomas. "God's Lonely Man." *The Hills Beyond*. New York: Harper, 1941. 186-97.

————. *The Lost Boy*. Ed. James W. Clark Jr. Chapel Hill: University of North Carolina Press, 1992.

————. *Thomas Wolfe's Purdue Speech: "Writing and Living."* Ed. William Braswell and Leslie A. Field. Lafayette, IN: Purdue University Studies, 1964.

Ruth Winchester Ware (essay date 2004)

SOURCE: Ware, Ruth Winchester. "Thomas Wolfe's Grover-Story: Journey through Grief to Resolution." *Thomas Wolfe Review* 28, nos. 1 & 2 (2004): 51-62.

[*In the following essay, Ware explores what she terms Wolfe's "Grover-story"—the various writings in which Wolfe dealt with the childhood death of his brother—and how the author worked through his grief creatively over the course of years.*]

> But I knew that it could not come back—the cry of absence in the afternoon, the house that waited and the child that dreamed; and through the thicket of man's memory, from the enchanted wood, the dark eye and the quiet face,—poor child, life's stranger and life's exile, lost, like all of us, a cipher in blind mazes, long ago—my parent, friend, and brother, the lost boy, was gone forever and would not return.
>
> —*The Lost Boy* (77)

With words like these Wolfe joined the company of others who survived the death of someone they loved and wrote about it. "Across the centuries, from the raw emotions of private journals to the distillations of poetry, writers speak of the pain of grief and describe their process through the spiral of mourning" (Moffat xxiii). During his childhood Wolfe was faced with the death of his brother Grover and later wrote about his loss. His writings about Grover are found in several sources, but for the purposes of this paper are grouped together as his Grover-story. The Grover-story is significant both as a major concern in a number of Wolfe's works, but also as it relates to the many nar-

ratives by other writers that deal with personal loss and grief. These works are important because coping with death is a universal human experience. Both quantitative and qualitative research methods are used to learn how people cope with death, and qualitative research often uses narratives about loss and grief to posit theories about the grief process (Gilbert 223). Reading Wolfe's Grover-story from this perspective helps readers understand how he perceived the loss of Grover and how he resolved it.

Wolfe's most complete narrative about the death of Grover is contained in the novella *The Lost Boy,* which he completed years after his brother died. During the intervening years Wolfe resolved his grief not in a pathological way, but creatively. His acceptance that Grover would not return and that the past was gone was not a sudden epiphany but grew out of a long process of thinking about and writing about the unexpected death of twelve-year-old Grover.

Wolfe wrote extensively about his memories of the family's stay in St. Louis during the 1904 World's Fair, a visit that ended with Grover's death. Out of the raw material of these memories and family stories, he transformed Grover's death into literature. According to Richard Kennedy, a basic question in Wolfe scholarship is that of "why Wolfe wrote the kind of books that he did" (2). Why, for instance, did Wolfe spend years writing and rewriting his Grover-story? The death of Grover may have been one of his first memories, and his continued preoccupation with it suggests the tragic impact it had on Wolfe and his family. Writing about Grover's death helped Wolfe absorb what happened and allowed him to keep the family memories of Grover alive. Leo Gurko suggests that in writing and rewriting the Grover-story, Wolfe was trying to find meaning in the tragedy (163-67). And Stephen Souris writes that Wolfe had a "brother's need to come to terms with the meaning of Grover's death" (23). Consciously or unconsciously, Wolfe probably strove to reach these goals.

Wolfe's method of working on the Grover-story over an extended time is analogous to the grief process. Grief involves shock, disbelief, searching, despair, and eventually healing and rebuilding (Huntley 51). The grief process doesn't occur in a linear direction, but is similar to the way a tree forms concentric patterns. Wolfe wrote and rewrote his material in a circular and overlapping pattern. He seems to have felt that his earlier versions of the Grover-story had not been fully developed. *The Lost Boy* allowed him to "*create* as well as re-create" Grover's story (Louis Rubin 164). The essence of this loss included not only what happened, but also how Wolfe and his family were affected.

In addition to his personal need to tell the Grover-story, Wolfe was aware that autobiographical remembrance offered him possibilities as a writer. Although autobiography seldom attains the level of art, Wolfe used his imagination to move beyond a transcription of the facts. The novella *The Lost Boy,* edited by James W. Clark (1992), is a creatively modified rendering of Grover's death. Considered the version that is closest to Wolfe's intent, it is rich in detail and meaning. Here, the Grover-story is told from the viewpoints of several family members whose memories are both unique and redundant. The characters are not static, but gradually reveal themselves as changing in a psychological sense as a result of Grover's death.

This analysis of Wolfe's creative engagement with the story of Grover draws on three approaches. Embedded examples of psychological time are shown to reveal Wolfe's depiction of the changes in perception, thought, and feeling that he and other members of his family undergo as they grieve the loss of Grover. Second, current theories about how preschool children grieve and how best to manage their grief offer possible explanations for Wolfe's need to work so long on his Grover-story. Finally, the customs and rituals surrounding death in early-twentieth-century America serve as standards by which to determine whether or not Wolfe received the support he needed to resolve his feelings about Grover's death.

Time is a recurring motif that weaves throughout Wolfe's Grover-story, and it is a motif that has engaged scholars and critics. Most recently, Erin Sullivan has expounded on the multiple symbols and motifs used to explore time in *The Lost Boy.* Although time as we experience it ranges from eternal or unchanging time to clock time (past-present-future), it is psychological time that primarily engages Wolfe. In the words of Larry Rubin, "For Wolfe, the nature of time at any given moment is determined by the state of his own consciousness at that moment. It is in this sense that his view of the passage of time may be termed a psychological one—as contrasted to the conventional one" (189). The title itself of *The Lost Boy* suggests a concern with a time that is experienced psychologically: The word *Lost* connotes something possessed in the past but missing in the present. Searching for the lost object involves expectation and yearning for it to be regained in the future. The need to search for the deceased person appears to be a strongly ingrained behavior. There is often "a compelling urge to recover the lost loved one" (Jarratt 37).

Psychological time is explored in all four sections of *The Lost Boy.* In part 1, Grover, following the intervention of his father with the Crockers over the stamp incident, becomes aware that something in his mind

has shifted irretrievably and that this shift involves not only how he sees the external world, but how he sees himself. Part 1 ends with another shift in psychological time after Grover sees his stonecutter father confront the Crockers. "And light came and went into the Square, and Grover stood there thinking quietly: 'Here the square, and here is Grover, here is my father's shop, and here am I'" (32).

Part 2 depicts the change in the mother's emotional state between the excitement of the springtime journey to the St. Louis World's Fair and the return home to North Carolina in bleak November to bury Grover. She has happy memories of the train ride down through Indiana. She retains pictures in her head of how Grover looked and behaved during the journey. But years later as she reminisces, just hearing or thinking about St. Louis opens up her "old raw sore" (43). Her insistence that among all her children Grover had the most potential may have set Eugene on a path of trying to learn what was so special about his brother and rival.

Part 3 depicts the sister grieving not only about Grover's death, but also about time passing for all of them. She is characterized as having some of the same traits as the mother: good recall of the past and a tendency to engage in lengthy monologues. She asks her brother several times if he remembers Grover and his berry birthmark, black eyes, and olive skin. She refers to family photos and laments the ravages of time on appearance and expectations. She is aware that life has a dream-like quality: ". . . It all comes back as if it happened yesterday. And then it goes away and seems farther off and stranger than if it happened in a dream. . . ." (57). She plants a seed in Eugene's mind that would culminate years later in his search for their brother.

Part 4 depicts Wolfe's alter ego returning to St. Louis thirty years after the death of Grover. One may conjecture that the writer has returned to the scene of the family tragedy to engage in research as both brother and observer. And finally:

> . . . The years dropped off like fallen leaves: the face came back again—the soft dark oval, the dark eyes, the soft brown berry on the neck, the raven hair, all bending down, approaching—the whole ghost-wise, intent and instant, like faces from a haunted wood.
>
> (75)

Wolfe's own return to St. Louis and to the house where Grover died allowed him to reach some degree of closure. He came seeking to learn where time had gone and left knowing, ". . . the lost boy, was gone forever and would not return" (77). This psychological shift meant that it was time to say good-bye and that he would not need to come again to the scene of Grover's death.

It is not unusual that Wolfe, thirty years after Grover's death, was still trying to resolve his feelings about his family's tragedy. Obsession with thoughts of the deceased is a normal component of grief. After a major loss, everything else is "viewed through the lens of that event" (Akner 8). The death of a loved one is the most severe of life's stresses. If this loss is not expressed and resolved, "the risk of mental and physical illness in the survivors can be increased" (Cider 114). Thomas Wolfe, marked by death during childhood, turned to the trauma of Grover's death in his creative work. Resolving his grief was a lengthy internal process. Because he was a writer, Wolfe used writing as his mode of expression.

Members of the Wolfe family coped with Grover's death the best way they knew how. In 1904 they would have relied on family, community, and religious resources. At the beginning of the twenty-first century, American families facing the death of a loved one have an array of additional resources available to them. Grief therapists of diverse educational and religious backgrounds, as well as both print and nonprint materials, are readily available. Research has identified the special needs of children facing the death of a loved one, and circumstances that predict a complicated grief have been identified. Applying current knowledge about grief to Wolfe's situation is one way to enhance an interpretation of the Grover-story.

Current knowledge suggests that the circumstances of Grover's death could well have resulted in Wolfe's experiencing a complicated and prolonged grief process. These circumstances included the following: (1) Wolfe was a young child when faced with Grover's death; (2) Grover's death was unexpected, following a brief illness; (3) Initially Wolfe's mother was unable to care for the family because of her own grief; and (4) Shortly after Grover's death Wolfe was faced with other major changes.

The age of the person facing the death of a family member is an important consideration, and Wolfe was barely four when Grover died. While adults are cognitively able to accept death as inevitable and final, children between the ages of three and six are not. They understand temporary separations, but not finality. Years after Grover's death, Wolfe was still hungry to learn more about this remarkable brother he could remember only dimly. His curiosity about Grover sparked an internal and external journey that turned Wolfe back toward St. Louis.[1] His journey eventually came to fruition in his Grover-story.

Between ages three and five, children engage in magical thinking. They may feel responsible for the death of a loved one and have fantasies that the deceased will return. Adults also cope with death through magical thinking. Wolfe's belief that if he returned to the place where Grover briefly lived and died, he would then remember his brother suggests a degree of magical thinking. But magical thinking or not, "It all came back and faded and was lost again" (76).

The circumstances surrounding a death are also an important consideration: Whether or not a death is seen as part of the normal life cycle has ramifications. Whereas an expected death allows the child to begin the process of grieving gradually, an unexpected death results in an immediately unstable environment. Grover died from an infectious, not a chronic, illness, and his death was unexpected and untimely. The family had only a few weeks to accept the seriousness of Grover's condition, and those weeks were spent in a strange environment, not at their Woodfin Street home.

Grover became ill in October 1904 (Wheaton 106) and over several weeks, according to Wolfe's fictionalized version in *The Lost Boy,* he "wasted away to a little bundle of skin and bones" (54). During those weeks the children were isolated from the sickroom out of necessity, as typhoid is an acute infectious disease for which in 1904 there was no antibiotic. Shortly after Grover died, Tom was awakened by his sister Mabel and told that Grover was on a cooling board (a hard flat surface used to keep the body flat and straight prior to embalming). It was a positive that Mabel, who was close to Tom and often acted as a mother substitute, was the one to break the news that Grover had died.[2] Nevertheless, in the fictionalized account of this episode in *O Lost,* Eugene Gant immediately senses that "the house was full of menace" (83). In the room where Grover lay, he at first sees only the "little wasted shell" his brother has become, but then "he remembered that forgotten face he had not seen in weeks, that strange bright loneliness that would not return" (83).

To allay the anxiety of children who have been close to a death from illness, Theresa M. Huntley suggests that someone explain to the child that the fatal illness was more serious than common childhood conditions (28). Preschoolers, in particular, need to be reassured that while we all get sick, we usually get well soon. Wolfe, who as a child had seen two of his siblings die, grew up into an adult who both neglected his health and obsessed about it. As James Clark notes in his introduction to *The Lost Boy,* Wolfe wrote this novella during a demanding period of his life when, among other concerns, he was worried about his own health (x).

When faced with death, each family member must grieve, regardless of age. Children, even those too young to "verbalize thoughts or feelings at the time," are traumatized by a death and retain memories of it (Schuurman 64). Not only is there a tendency for adults to be given more support during this time than children, but also adults caught up in their own grief may not have the emotional resources to attend to the needs of the young. When such is the case, the absence of the physical and emotional presence of the parent is a "secondary loss" for the child (Goldman 25). There is reason to believe that Wolfe suffered such secondary loss in the aftermath of Grover's death.

Wolfe's sister Mable Wheaton discussed the effect of Grover's death on the family: "Mamma was disconsolate. She blamed herself for having brought us out to St. Louis. We were all dreadfully torn up, all of us. It was the first experience we children had had with death in the family . . ." (108). Wheaton also recalled that her father was terribly upset, and Wolfe evokes a father's pain in *O Lost*: "his heart shrivelled as he saw the boy" (82).

One component of grieving for a deceased child is grieving for the child's lost potential, and when an idealized child dies there is a tendency for the child's image to become frozen in time. Wolfe's mother saw Grover as "the brightest and best of her offspring" and continued "to long for and memorialize" him (Clark ix). Wolfe's father also idealized Grover. In *O Lost,* after the undertakers have taken Grover away in a basket, the bereaved W. O. Gant mutters, "By God, he was the best of the lot" (83). As the train returns home with Grover's body, both parents make "restless expeditions to the baggage car" (84). Although *The Lost Boy* suggests that Grover's lost potential is eventually realized in the youngest child (Morse 46), Wolfe's mother admitted that following the death of Grover, she had to make an effort to be interested in Tom (Norwood 185). Part 2 of *The Lost Boy* addresses this aspect of grieving on the part of the mother.

After the loss of Grover, Julia Wolfe grieved during the rest of the winter. She had experienced the death of members of her birth family, as well as the death of her first-born, Leslie, and she took the loss of loved ones heavily: "I thought the end of the world had come when Leslie died" (qtd. in Norwood 44). Grover's death was another deep wound. But surviving one death is no inoculation against the pain of other losses. When a loved one's life is lost or in jeopardy, a typical reaction is to recall the death of other family members. Years after the loss of Grover, when Wolfe's mother was told that Tom was not expected to recover, she reverted to her memories of Grover (Clark x). Grover's death had broken the family unit, as Wolfe's death would once again. Learning to live with "the broken circle" is difficult.[3]

Of Julia Gant, Wolfe writes in *O Lost*: "With desperate sadness she encysted herself within her house . . ." and "During the grim winter the shadows lifted slowly" (85). After she recovered from her initial grief reaction, or what was probably a clinical depression, "the powerful germinal instinct for property and freedom began to re-awaken" (89). Similarly, Julia Wolfe found that the advice given to her by a minister not to brood about Grover's death, but to keep busy and work, was helpful. She later acknowledged, "He was right" (qtd. in Norwood 186). When she turned her immense energy to the boardinghouse venture, she acted contrary to today's beliefs that following a death other changes in the environment should be postponed. Too many changes or losses around the same time may result in what Donna Schuurman terms "bereavement overload" (46).

Julia Wolfe's recovery prompted her to make changes in the family's living conditions that proved stressful for her husband and children, and particularly for her youngest son. She was aware of the impact Grover's death had on him: "It was a sad time for Tom. It might have affected him for the worse, too" (qtd. in Norwood 185). Prior to Grover's death the Wolfe family already was dissolving (Donald 10-11), and the loss of a child accelerated the process of dissolution. Tom in particular was subjected to stressful changes and dislocations in addition to the loss of his brother. He was taken to live with his mother at 48 Spruce Street, where she operated the Old Kentucky Home, while the others remained at the home their father had built at 92 Woodfin Street. Never again would Wolfe live with his entire family under one roof. As he was later to write of his fictional alter ego, "Thus, before he was eight, Eugene gained another roof and lost forever the tumultuous, unhappy, warm centre of his home" (*O Lost* 140). During childhood Tom, like Eugene, faced more than one life-changing event within a brief period of time, and the impact of these accumulated changes was great.

It is important for everyone in the family, including children, to participate in the rituals of death. After a death in a family, there is instability and chaos, but rituals facilitate the return of some degree of control. Experts on grieving agree that children should be included in such death rituals as spending time with the dying, viewing the body of the deceased, attending the wake or funeral, and being present at the burial. "The funeral," for example, "provides a structure for the child to see how people comfort each other openly, mourn a loved one, and honor his or her life" (Goldman 31).

On November 17, 1904, the *Asheville Gazette-News* noted that a telegram had been received from St. Louis announcing the death of Grover Wolfe following several weeks of illness. The notice stated that his remains, accompanied by his parents, were being returned to Asheville. Grover was described as

> a bright and manly little fellow, with a sunny and cheerful disposition and withal an industrious temperament that would have done credit to one twice his age. He was deservedly popular and his lisping, cheery voice and pleasant smile will be sadly missed by those who knew him best.
>
> ("Death of Grover Wolfe")

In the nineteenth and early twentieth centuries, cemeteries were filled with graves of children; in 1904 it was still not uncommon for families to lose children during epidemics. This passage from *O Lost* puts Julia Gant's grief into the context of the times: "As Julia came slowly down the hill, Mrs. Parkinson rushed from her house sobbing. Her eldest daughter had died a month before. The two women gave loud cries as they saw each other and rushed together" (84-85). According to the burial customs and rituals of the day, neighbors and friends would have offered the Wolfe family food, drink, and comfort. It was the norm for the coffin to be placed next to the parlor wall and for flowers to be placed on tables at each end. Family and friends likely took turns sitting up all night with Grover's body (Crissman 28-31). In 1904 children were included in the rituals. Years later Wolfe wrote, "In Gant's parlor, the coffin had already been placed on trestles; the neighbors, funeral-faced and whispering, were assembled to greet them. That was all" (*O Lost* 85).

Grover's Wolfe's funeral was conducted at the family home on Woodfin Street at ten o'clock on Saturday, November 19. Rev. Dr. Lunsford officiated at the home and Rev. Dr. Campbell at the gravesite. Interment was at Newton Academy Graveyard ("Funeral of Grover Wolfe"), where W. O. Wolfe had purchased lots following the death of his second wife, Cynthia. On September 1, 1921, Grover was reinterred at Riverside Cemetery. While Wolfe didn't write specifically about Grover's burial, it is likely he was present and that later he returned to his brother's grave with other family members.

While there were difficult circumstances surrounding Grover's death that resulted in Wolfe's experiencing a complicated grief process, there were positives as well. In 1904 death was an integral part of family life. Families were not as isolated as many are now, but rather were connected to extended families. People were nursed at home and usually died at home. Adults and children experienced death together, mourned together, and comforted each other. They received support from their community and church. The Wolfe family also provided support for each other. Later, Julia Wolfe was to acknowledge that her husband, in spite of their differences, "was a good family man" (qtd. in Norwood 175), and for a brief time the parents consoled each other over their mutual loss. In *O Lost*, when Julia Gant offers apologies for having taken Grover to St. Louis, her husband tries to comfort her: "'Never mind,' he said, and he stroked her awkwardly" (84). A persistent sense of guilt complicates Julia's recovery. During his wife's extended grief, the fictional husband and father helps the shadows of the grim winter depart: "Gant brought back the roaring fires, the groaning succulent table, the lavish and explosive ritual of the daily life. The old gusto surged back in their lives" (85). Tom turned his energies to boyhood tasks and pleasures, but never forgot his brother with the berry birthmark, black eyes, olive complexion, and keen observation of life.

Thomas Wolfe can be assumed to have achieved several goals through transforming the raw material of Grover's death into creative work. He explored and expressed his grief through words, and doing so probably facilitated healing from his loss and allowed him to reach some degree of closure. Current theories about grief-work suggest that this type of expression promotes healing and rebuilding. Expressing grief results in what Theresa M. Huntley describes as "relocating the deceased emotionally" (51-52). As Wolfe's Grover-story illustrates, death does not end a relationship. Rather we carry memories of the deceased with us into the future and incorporate aspects of the other into our own lives. Commemorating the dead is an important aspect of the grief process, and storytelling, journaling, and writing are some of the ways to commemorate. Writing clarifies one's thoughts and feelings, assists in absorbing what happened, documents the progress one is making, and keeps memories alive (Brooke 62). That grief-stories are passed from generation to generation illustrates an important aspect of being human. Wolfe found meaning in Grover's death by writing about it. As T. J. Wray has noted: "Acceptance usually happens once we have attached meaning to our loss" (225). In its essence Wolfe's Grover-story is a memorial to Grover built one word at a time.

Was Wolfe able to find meaning in Grover's death? For many the meaning of death is sought and found in religion. Wolfe was not conventional in his religious beliefs, but his family used religious rituals. The Wolfe family attended First Presbyterian Church in Asheville, and Christmas was celebrated lavishly in their home. Two ministers were asked to conduct Grover's funeral and burial services. But Wolfe makes no references to someday seeing Grover again in heaven, and a thread of fatalism is dominant in meditations on death in *O Lost*:

O waste of loss, in the hot mazes, lost, among bright stars on this most weary unbright cinder, lost! Remembering speechlessly we seek the great forgotten language, the lost land-end into heaven, a stone, a leaf, an unfound door. Where? When?

O lost, and by the wind grieved, ghost, come back again.

(5)

While Wolfe did not find meaning in a fundamental religious sense, his Grover-story did provide him a structure that allowed him safely to explore and express his feelings about his lost brother. Wolfe's experiences of grief and his observations of those of his family bear out current theories about circumstances that complicate the grief process and those that make it easier. His Grover-story is intensely personal, but in a broader sense it belongs to the universe of narratives that contribute to our knowledge and understanding of grief.

Notes

1. See Clark ix.

2. See Jarratt 2.

3. See Wray 5.

Works Cited

Akner, Lois. *How to Survive the Loss of a Parent.* New York: Quill, 1993.

Brooke, Jill. *Don't Let Death Ruin Your Life.* New York: Penguin Putnam, 2002.

Cider, Tom. *Give Sorrow Words: A Father's Passage through Grief.* Chapel Hill, NC: Algonquin, 1996.

Clark, James W., Jr. Introduction. *The Lost Boy.* By Thomas Wolfe. Ed. Clark. Chapel Hill: University of North Carolina Press, 1992. ix-xiv.

Crissman, James K. *From Death and Dying in Central Appalachia.* Urbana: University of Illinois Press, 1994.

"Death of Grover Wolfe in St. Louis Yesterday." *Asheville Gazette-News* 17 Nov. 1904.

Donald, David Herbert. *Look Homeward: A Life of Thomas Wolfe.* Boston: Little, Brown, 1987.

"Funeral of Grover Wolfe." *Asheville Gazette-News* 19 Nov. 1904.

Gilbert, Kathleen R. "Taking a Narrative Approach to Grief Research: Finding Meaning in Stories." *Death Studies* 26 (2002): 223-39.

Goldman, Linda. *Life and Loss: A Guide to Help Grieving Children.* Bristol, PA: Accelerated Development, 1994.

Gurko, Leo. *Thomas Wolfe: Beyond the Romantic Ego.* New York: Crowell, 1975.

Huntley, Theresa M. *Helping Children Grieve: When Someone They Love Dies.* Rev. ed. Minneapolis: Augsburg Fortress, 2002.

Jarratt, Claudia Jewett. *Helping Children Cope with Separation and Loss.* Cambridge, MA: Harvard Common Press, 1982.

Kennedy, Richard S. *The Window of Memory: The Literary Career of Thomas Wolfe.* Chapel Hill: University of North Carolina Press, 1962.

Moffat, Mary Jane. Introduction. *In the Midst of Winter: Selections from the Literature of Mourning.* Ed. Moffat. 1982. New York: Vintage, 1992. xxiii-xxviii.

Morse, Carlton N. "Thomas Wolfe's *The Lost Boy*: A Bildungsroman for the Modern Reader." *Thomas Wolfe Review* 27.1-2 (2003): 43-52.

Norwood, Hayden. *The Marble Man's Wife: Thomas Wolfe's Mother.* New York: Scribner's, 1947.

Rubin, Larry. "Thomas Wolfe: Halting the Flow of Time." *Americana-Austriaca* 4 (1978): 105-18. Rpt. in *Critical Essays on Thomas Wolfe.* Ed. John S. Phillipson. Boston: G. K. Hall, 1985. 188-98.

Rubin, Louis D., Jr. *Thomas Wolfe: The Weather of His Youth.* Baton Rouge: Louisiana State University Press, 1955.

Schuurman, Donna. *Never the Same: Coming to Terms with the Death of a Parent.* New York: St. Martin's, 2003.

Souris, Stephen. "Dialogic Agreement: Thomas Wolfe's *The Lost Boy* and the Multiple Narrator Novel." *Thomas Wolfe Review* 22.2 (1998) 17-27.

Sullivan, Erin. "Recovering the Past: Models of Time in Thomas Wolfe's *The Lost Boy.*" *Thomas Wolfe Review* 26.1-2 (2002): 68-75.

Wheaton, Mabel Wolfe, with LeGette Blythe. *Thomas Wolfe and His Family.* Garden City, NY: Doubleday, 1961.

Wolfe, Thomas. *The Lost Boy.* Ed. James W. Clark Jr. Chapel Hill: University of North Carolina Press, 1992.

———. *O Lost: A Story of the Buried Life.* ed. Arlyn and Matthew J. Bruccoli. Columbia: University of South Carolina Press, 2000.

Wray, T. J. *Surviving the Death of a Sibling.* New York: Three River Press, 2003.

Shawn Holliday (essay date spring 2004)

SOURCE: Holliday, Shawn. "Thomas Wolfe's *Web of Earth* and Modernist Orality." *South Carolina Review* 36, no. 2 (spring 2004): 97-103.

[*In the following essay, Holliday evaluates the role of oral narrative in modernist texts, specifically in Wolfe's*

The Web of Earth, *and demonstrates how Wolfe's use of this technique places him among the figures of high-modernist literature.*]

In her book *Ezra Pound and The Cantos: A Record of Struggle,* Wendy Flory notes that Pound first intended his poetic sequence, *The Cantos,* to be a record of "intellectual struggle" (2), a work that explored the modern poet's place within three thousand years of literary tradition, world history, and ideological conflict. To express this aim, Pound opens Canto I by invoking Book XI of Homer's *Odyssey,* which parallels the poet's journey through personal and world memory with Odysseus's dark voyage to the underworld. While Pound's nod to Homer in the opening canto acknowledges a debt to preliterate poetic tradition, it is ironic in that his translation is at least three steps away from its original oral source. To compose this canto, Pound relied heavily on Andreas Divus's Latin version (Flory 102), a translation from the original Greek, which, in turn, had been transcribed onto parchment or papyrus in the 8th century B.C. from the singing of one or many oral poets (Havelock 83). Pound's journey in the ensuing 116 cantos is actually a voyage through literate consciousness. A work of such allusive breadth and world scope, with references to such varied figures as Confucius, Dante, the French Troubadours, and Martin Van Buren, could not have been achieved without the aid of literacy and books, which allows for extreme intertextuality and the modern poet's play with typographic space. Because of this slavery to texts, Pound begins *The Cantos* in media res.[1] The absence of words before the first poetic line represents the oral world of Homer that no longer exists; a world of silence Pound cannot access. "Then went down to the ship" presents a version of Homer's words that is forever textually bound (Pound 3). In his poem, Pound is unable to tap the completely oral consciousness of Homer and his forerunners, a world absent of phonetic writing and chirography.

Pound's concern with orality in the opening sections of *The Cantos* is not a modernist anomaly, for one of the implicit concerns of high modernism is the writer's awareness of textual limitation, reflexivity, and the exploration of differences between oral and written communication. Those poets and writers living in the first half of the twentieth century were privy to a pivotal cultural moment, the onslaught of "the electronic age" that consequently began the "age of secondary orality, the orality of telephones, [phonographs], radio, and television, which depends on print for its existence" but of which the listener is only vaguely aware (Ong 3). Thus, Pound's concern with Homeric epics and the Anglo-Saxon "Seafarer" in the opening cantos occurs in the same atmosphere where James Joyce attempts to subvert the very sound of the English language in *Ulysses*; T. S. Eliot alludes to an Australian folk song in *The Waste Land*; Ernest Hemingway emulates the syncopated rhythms of jazz in his short fiction (Appel 15-16); and Langston Hughes soaks his poetry in the beats, rhythms, and themes of the blues.

This backward glance at orality was also due, in part, to the dehumanizing effects of World War I caused by increased industrialization and mechanization. Pound's and Joyce's use of Odysseus and Eliot's use of Tiresias show a return to orality's "'heavy' characters, persons whose deeds are monumental, memorable, or commonly public," which allow authors to "organize experience in some sort of memorable form" (Ong 70). Indeed, Eliot documents this oral impulse in his essay "*Ulysses,* Order, and Myth" where he argues that using ancient epics and mythic heroes provides "a way of controlling, of ordering, of giving a shape and a significance to the immense panorama of futility and anarchy which is contemporary history" (Kermode 177). Gone are the banal middle-class characters and linear plot structures of realist fiction, replaced by colorful, odd, enigmatic figures in mosaic, stream-of-consciousness, and bricolage narrative forms, types that had existed in oral cultures before "the deadening hand of print" (Havelock 27). Paradoxically, this continual borrowing from Greek and Roman myth kept high-modernist writers tied to texts more than ever. Just as James Joyce intended "to echo everybody on purpose" in *Ulysses* and *Finnegans Wake* (Ong 131), so did Pound in *The Cantos* and Eliot, to a lesser extent, in *The Waste Land*. Although all three writers used their works to establish a stable Western tradition into which they could place themselves, their fetish for texts denied them access to the completely oral world they wished to penetrate but could not.

Thomas Wolfe's **The Web of Earth** is an experimental novella that provides particular insight into modernism's oral/textual dynamic. Still under the influence of *Ulysses* during the novella's composition in early 1932, Wolfe emulates Joyce's "Penelope" section but opts to present the innermost thoughts of his female narrator in a completely oral monologue instead of an interior one. He also denies himself Joyce's intertextual jouissance, which had played such an important role in *Look Homeward, Angel*. Three pages into the novella, Wolfe immediately sets orality and literacy in opposition, having the story's narrator, Eliza Gant,[2] minimize the significance of books and recorded history to the importance of personal encounters. Even though Eliza had sold books for the Larkin Publishing Company earlier in life, as Wolfe depicts in the first chapter of *Look Homeward, Angel* (9), as an old woman, she puts more stock in life experiences, which exist for her as a different kind of recorded remembrance:

Lord, God! I reckon I remember things you never read about—the way it was, the things they never wrote about in books. I reckon that they tried to put it down in books, all of the wars and battles, child, I guess they got that part of it all right, but Lord!—how could these fellers know the way it was when they weren't born, when they weren't there to see it. [. . .]

(Wolfe, *The Web* [*The Web of Earth*] 214-15)

Here, Wolfe echoes Plato, a writer stuck on the cusp between orality and literacy, whose fictional Socrates argues that writing is not superior to orality since it distorts history and weakens the mind (Ong 79). While Wolfe follows Socrates' edict and makes almost no direct allusions to written texts in *The Web of Earth,* he does connote Eliza as an "earth mother" (Kennedy 242), which the reader immediately associates with the goddess Demeter and ancient fertility rites from mythological tales that come to us through writing but are derived from oral sources. It also immediately reminds us of Joyce's Molly Bloom, who represents both Homer's Penelope and "the Earth herself, Gaea-Tellus" (Gilbert 398). Wolfe's emulation of Molly Bloom's subconscious musings is one of only two direct textual allusions that occur in the novella, the other being Eliza's mention of *The Holy Bible,* an instructive text where additive sentence structures, non-verbatim duplication of ritual utterances, and the continual use of genealogical lists speak to the book's oral composition and derivation from oral tradition (Ong 36, 65, 99). In her beliefs and methods of storytelling, Eliza Gant is the closest thing to an oral poet that exists in high-modernist literature, a body of writing obsessed with its own relation to print culture and secondary orality.

In preliterate societies, oral poets preserved the history and traditions of their culture within their verse (Havelock 79). During Greek antiquity, poets served as both instructors, informing their listeners of society's moral codes (8), and as entertainers, performing their verse through songs and chants during communal holidays and festivals (79). In *The Web of Earth,* Eliza Gant fulfills both roles. As a Southern storyteller, she relays the post-bellum history of Altamont to her son who now lives among strangers in New York, fulfilling her obligation as cultural harbinger. Although she sets out to tell him about a strange premonition she had before the birth of her twin sons, Grover and Ben, she ends up recounting, among other things, the time Yankee stragglers from Sherman's army came through Catawba during the Civil War; Clarissy Stevens' illegitimate pregnancy; Dock Hensley's unusual bloodlust; William Jennings Bryan's real-estate speculations; and Ed Mears' near escape from a lynch mob and eventual reappearance in Mexico. In all, over 30 townspeople appear in her story, creating a thrilling

account of Altamont and its environs that chronicle, in her words, "things you never heard of . . . with all your reading out of books" (Wolfe, *The Web* 223).

While Ezra Pound intended *The Cantos* as a "tribal encyclopedia" to stand as the ultimate epic of literate knowledge (Alexander 142), Wolfe's novella achieves its unique aim as community archive, albeit on a much smaller scale, by remaining strictly oral, relying on a plethora of oral characteristics and techniques that exist independently of literacy and books. Wolfe's ability to keep textual allusions out of *The Web of Earth* also makes the novella his most innovative high-modernist text. Not only does it allow the author to keep "himself out of the story," avoiding the "over-emotionalism of Eugene Gant" (Kennedy 243), but it also provides a template for his most innovative plot pattern, a non-linear "web" that weaves through Eliza Gant's central consciousness, much like the intricate tapestry Penelope weaves and unweaves throughout Homer's *Odyssey.*[3] Wolfe is able to avoid the usual pitfalls of textual narrative by basing the novella heavily on the oral tales of his mother, Julia Wolfe; his own personal memory of local folklore; the oral plot structures of *The Iliad* and *The Odyssey,* which he claims to have read as early as age ten (Kennedy and Reeves 79); and on the overheard conversations he jotted down regularly in his notebooks. All of these sources affected Wolfe's ability to emulate successfully the rhythms, repetitions, spontaneity, and improvisation of orality needed for a completely verbal style.

In *The Web of Earth,* Wolfe employs the rhythmic talk of oral poets who relied on regular cadences and parataxis to aid their memory and to convey their thoughts (Havelock 71). Eliza's account, when written on the page, appears as a series of exclamations and run-on sentences joined by dashes, ellipses, and colons that give her voice a halting yet predictable rhythm set in reliable crescendo and diminuendo through which Wolfe relays its lyrical quality:

Lord God! I never saw a man like that for wanderin.' I'll vow! a rollin' stone, a wanderer—that's all he'd a-been, oh! California, China, anywheres—forever wantin' to be up and gone, who'd never have accumulated a stick of property if I hadn't married him. Here Truman wrote to him that time from California, this same Perfesser Truman, why, yes! the father-in-law of these two murderers I'm telling you about (and how that night I got the warning, boy: "Two . . . Two—and Twenty . . . Twenty"), Ed Mears and Lawrence Wayne, who married sisters, Truman's daughters, why, yes!—but oh! the scholar and the gentleman, you know, no murderer to *him,* I can assure you—oh too *fine,* too *fine,* oh! too *honorable,* you know: he wouldn't soil his hands with blood, always the finest broadcloth and the

patent-leather shoes, wrote to him of course, to come
on out there. Says, "The Lord has rained his blessings
on this country with a prodigal hand." [. . .]

(Wolfe, *The Web* 250-51)

The additive nature of Eliza's narrative, continually
interrupted with new remembrances, qualifications,
and repeated phrases, reflects the cumulative structure
of oral narratives and the process of composition
whereby thoughts are not subordinated but are given
equal weight in a continuous river of sound (Havelock
76). Like Molly Bloom's mental soliloquy, Eliza's
lengthy monologue shows her "moving, growing, expanding" until she becomes the very voice of the Earth
itself by story's end (Gilbert 403). All of the vocifera-
tions, exhortations, and maxims that occur throughout
her tale reveal her emotional ties to her material and
her working knowledge of life, oral characteristics
traced back to Hesiod and Homer, both of whom revealed their personal stakes in the tales they relayed
and served as inspiration to their respective audiences
(89).

Ultimately, the novella's web-like pattern derives from
the fact that oral poets "stitched together prefabricated
parts" not in linear progression but in a collage of
scenes weaved around accumulating sets of epithets,
clichés, phrases, formulas, and proverbs that were balanced through repetition (Ong 22, 143; Havelock 76).
Since oral stories are performance pieces, they take on
an air of impermanence with little time for reflection.
These few techniques are the only glue that holds the
various episodes together in any type of recurring, recognizable form for the oral storyteller.

Epithets were one of the most important oral devices
that Wolfe echoes in *The Web of Earth* since they
also tie Eliza to the tradition of Appalachian folktales.
In oral storytelling, epithets serve as phrases that sur-
round proper names by which poets remind listeners
of their characters' different personalities and narrative
functions. Homer continually relies on this device in
The Odyssey to set Odysseus into different heroic contexts for each adventurous episode: "Great Odysseus /
who excels all men in wisdom" (79); "Odysseus, the
great teller of tales" (211); "Odysseus, / raider of cities" (227); "odysseus, man of twists and turns" (240).
In Appalachian tall tales, epithets aid the overall exaggeration of a story by attaching a character's feat with
his name, hence John Henry, "the steel drivin' man"
and Davy Crockett, "King of the Wild Frontier." When
Eliza speaks of "that miserable old rip, Rufe Porter"
and "that rotten old Gus Tolly" (Wolfe, *The Web* 227,
261), she invokes a similar oral tradition, one that reveals her negative attitudes toward the townspeople
she despises, predetermining their characterization in a
narrative full of colorful stories that reveal her own

suspicions and prejudices. Wolfe's ability to link
mountain folklore with ancient storytelling in a complex, high-modernist narrative is a unique achievement
in itself.

Another important oral technique that Wolfe employs
is the cliché. While trite expressions and phrases are
frowned upon in literate cultures, in oral cultures they
serve as important formulas that set characters and
themes into familiar contexts. When Eliza repeats the
phrase "and that's the way it was," she attempts to
force some sort of inherent truth onto her oral account, even though she continually relies on rumors,
innuendo, and hearsay throughout. Her use of such
biblical maxims as "those who live by the sword will
perish by the sword" (274) and "judge not lest ye be
judged" (276) further her morally superior voice, especially when she gives "the devil his due" when denying Dock Hensley's rumored love affairs and confirming Ambrose Radiker's supposed honesty (277,
282). To privilege her version of events even more,
she repeats the phrase "that story just won't wash," a
cliché that denies the hegemonic power of other versions by dismissing their accuracy, lending her account an immediate air of familiarity due to the clichés communal overuse.

In oral societies, repetition is also key in advancing
the speaker's narrative. Recurring words and phrases
emphasize important elements of the plot and keep silence at bay until the poet formulates his next thought.
Such repetition continually recurs in *The Web of
Earth*. Eliza's early use of the phrase "the year the lo-
custs came" lends her story a mythic quality by echoing the vague time frame used by ancient bards who
had no knowledge of calendars by which to measure
the continual flow of time.[4] The "two . . . two [. . .]
twenty . . . twenty" that once echoed as a premonition in Eliza's ears now begin her story and reappear
as signposts as to her intended direction in her circular
plot. She eventually weaves her way back to this narrative strand some 25,000 words later, having gone
through at least thirty different episodes in town history in the process of relaying her tale.

Getting lost in a narrative was a usual occurrence in a
completely oral culture. Since oral poets had no written list of characters, settings, or episodes ready at
their command, they had no way of organizing their
plot into a coherent chronological order. Since human
memory is both limited and imperfect, working from
verbatim memorization was impossible. This often
caused the poet "to leave out one or another episode
. . . where it should fit chronologically," having to fit
it in later (Ong 143-44). This oral technique allowed
Wolfe to present the dynamics of Eliza's mind in a as-
sociative pattern similar to the narrative structure employed by Pound in *The Cantos* or Joyce in *Ulysses*,

albeit in a less artificial way. The techniques Wolfe employs derive from centuries of language development more than natural to humans who still feel the urge to relay appropriate cultural codes through the rituals of oral storytelling.

Throughout Wolfe's novella, Eliza gets lost and follows different narrative threads only to reorient herself by stating "as I was going to say"—only to get lost yet again. In the novella's first ten pages alone, she begins by recounting her premonition, gets interrupted by the sound of ships in the harbor, imparts some Gant family genealogy, and relates the story of Bill Pentland's foretold death hour. That Wolfe was conscious of this complex narrative plan is obvious in his letter to his mother dated May 29, 1932:

> the story is told completely in the words of one person, a woman, who starts out to tell her son about a single incident and in the course of telling it brings in memories, stories, and recollections that cover a period of seventy years. In the telling, the story weaves back and forth like a web . . . the story is about everything that goes to make up life—the happiness, the sorrow, the joy, the pain, the triumph, and the suffering—it tells about everything. [. . .]

(Holman and Ross 181)

While "everything" is best used to describe Wolfe's overall scheme for *Look Homeward, Angel* and his *October Fair* manuscript, which he was hard at work on at the time, *The Web of Earth* ups Wolfe's ante on modernist experimentation and "everything" in a way few expected. The novella stands as Wolfe's greatest literary achievement for helping to reintroduce oral techniques to high-modernist literature and for depicting an oral world that Pound, Joyce, and Eliot, with all of their reliance on books, found impossible to access completely. That Wolfe was aware of his achievement appears in a letter he wrote to Helen Jenkins Meade in the spring of 1932. He boasts that he knows his unnamed female character "[. . .] better than Joyce knew that woman at the end of *Ulysses*," and he claims that his "old woman is a grander, richer and more tremendous figure than she was" (Nowell 339). Oddly enough, Wolfe's modernist bravado here also dates back to the ancient days of oral storytelling where verbal ingenuity determined a poet's status among his peers.

The oral tradition Wolfe evokes in *The Web of Earth* is one where "bragging about one's own prowess" and "tongue-lashing" one's rivals is as important as the story one relates (Ong 44). While flyting, the ability to duel verbally, may have its origins in oral societies, it stands at a premium in modernist literature, where experimentation was as much a display of linguistic adeptness as it was an attempt to stretch the bound-

aries of language and imagination through innovative narrative techniques, ingenious plot patterns, and new ways of delimiting genre. To be taken seriously as an artist, Wolfe possibly felt compelled to join this stylized fighting. With *The Web of Earth* he more than answered the challenge set by his peers, composing the novella in the same era in which Sinclair Lewis parodied bourgeois discourses in *Babbit,* William Faulkner played with point of view in *The Sound and the Fury,* Henry Miller mixed philosophy, scatology, and biography in *Tropic of Cancer,* and James Joyce created a whole new language from all existing languages in *Finnegans Wake.* The strength of *The Web of Earth* lies in Wolfe's ability to employ oral narrative methods that stay true to modernist invention, relaying folkloric and cultural information in an intricate collage-like pattern that seems yet ordinarily conversant. This groundbreaking mode of composition, which relies so heavily on the power of personal memory, would become a necessity a decade later during the societal ruptures of World War II, when Ezra Pound composed *The Pisan Cantos* bereft of all but two books;[5] Erich Auerbach wrote *Mimesis* without the aid of an adequate library in Istanbul; and The United States Armed Forces relied on the Navajo language, which had no system of writing, to create an unbreakable secret radio code to help win the war.

In a now ironic move, Maxwell Perkins realized that *The Web of Earth* was Thomas Wolfe's best piece of writing and advised him to publish it in the collection *From Death to Morning* in order for it to "survive the impermanence of magazine publication" (Kennedy 282), an impermanence similar to the evanescence of oral narratives that pass forever into forgetfulness and silence once the last word is uttered (Ong 32).[6] Only through Wolfe's act of writing a completely oral account can we analyze the elements that make it an important but oft-ignored text in the high-modernist canon, a body of literature that looks back at primary orality for continual inspiration but which relies on typography to convey the skill of the storyteller for future generations, achieving an influential permanence within society that ancient poets did not have.[7] In this way, *The Web of Earth* is more important to the modernist movement than most have realized and must be considered in any discussion of narrative innovations that developed in high-modernist literature throughout the first half of the twentieth century.

Notes

1. Most oral narratives begin in media res. Since such narratives are improvised according to the context of their performance, sung in episodic

fashion to meet the demands of their audience, oral poets begin a story a different way almost every time. Often, these poets have difficulty beginning their narratives since their string of memorized episodes are not linked in a linear pattern and do not follow one another in a cause-effect relationship (Havelock 70; Ong 106, 143). Although he is a literate poet, Pound mirrors this oral phenomenon by showing the difficulty of choosing an ancient episode to tap that presents the oral threshold he is unable to cross.

2. In the novella's original version, published in the July 1932 edition of *Scribner's Magazine,* the narrator is Delia Hawke, who is speaking to her son, John Crockett Hawke.

3. Wolfe employed this "weaving" metaphor more explicitly in *The Web and the Rock*'s chapter 26, "Penelope's Web," where Esther Jack tells Monk Webber of her girlhood in New York.

4. Eliza finally mentions a specific date and time for her premonition some sixty-nine pages into Wolfe's novella with still no reference to a definite year: "it was on the twenty-seventh day of September [. . .] at twenty minutes to ten o'clock in the evening" (282-83).

5. The books Pound took with him to the Disciplinary Training Center at Pisa after his arrest by Italian partisans were Confucius's *Four Books* and a simple dictionary, both of which fit easily into his pockets (Flory 185).

6. Unfortunately, *The Web of Earth* still faces the danger of falling into forgetfulness and silence. The two book collections in which it appears, *From Death to Morning* and *The Short Novels of Thomas Wolfe,* are both currently out of print, unavailable to a wide reading audience.

7. In a final ironic twist, one reason for Wolfe's continued canonical decline may be caused by the growing pervasiveness of secondary orality in American society. The length of Wolfe's novels probably overwhelms an MTV generation used to quick camera cuts, channel surfing, and a barrage of Internet links. Because of its short, episodic, collage-like pattern, *The Web of Earth* may speak to future generations better than the author's more widely known "fat" novels did fifty years ago.

Works Cited

Alexander, Michael. *The Poetic Achievement of Ezra Pound.* Berkeley: University of California Press, 1981.

Appel, Jr., Alfred. *Jazz Modernism.* New York: Knopf, 2002.

Eliot, T. S. *Collected Poems, 1909-1962.* San Diego: Harcourt, 1963.

Flory, Wendy Stallard. *Ezra Pound and The Cantos: A Record of Struggle.* New Haven: Yale University Press, 1980.

Gilbert, Stuart. *James Joyce's Ulysses: A Study.* New York: Vintage, 1955.

Havelock, Eric A. *The Muse Learns to Write: Reflections on Orality and Literacy from Antiquity to the Present.* New Haven: Yale UP, 1986.

Holman, C. Hugh, and Sue Fields Ross. *The Letters of Thomas Wolfe to His Mother.* Chapel Hill: University of North Carolina Press, 1968.

Homer. *The Odyssey.* Trans. Robert Fagles. New York: Viking, 1996.

Kennedy, Richard S. *The Window of Memory: The Career of Thomas Wolfe.* Chapel Hill: University of North Carolina Press, 1962.

Kennedy, Richard S. and Paschal Reeves, eds. *The Notebooks of Thomas Wolfe.* Chapel Hill: University of North Carolina Press, 1970.

Kermode, Frank, ed. *Selected Prose of T. S. Eliot.* 1975. San Diego: Harcourt, 1988.

Nowell, Elizabeth. *The Letters of Thomas Wolfe.* New York: Scribner's, 1956.

Ong, Walter J. *Orality and Literacy: The Technologizing of the Word.* New York: Routledge, 1982.

Pound, Ezra. *The Cantos.* New York: New Directions, 1970.

Wolfe, Thomas. *Look Homeward, Angel.* New York: Scribner's, 1929.

————. *The Web and the Rock.* 1939. Baton Rouge: Louisiana State UP, 1999.

————. *The Web of Earth. From Death to Morning.* New York: Scribner's, 1935. 212-304.

FURTHER READING

Criticism

Anderson, Donald R. "Thomas Wolfe, 'Chickamauga,' and the Truth about Knowin'." *Thomas Wolfe Review* 27, nos. 1 & 2 (2003): 22-36.

Examines the nature of perspective and awareness in the short story "Chickamauga."

Flora, Joseph M. "Finding the Lost Boy." *Thomas Wolfe*

Review 27, nos. 1 & 2 (2003): 37-42.

Explores thematic notions of loss in Wolfe's work and life.

Additional coverage of Wolfe's life and career is contained in the following sources published by Gale: *American Writers*; *Beacham's Encyclopedia of Popular Fiction: Biography & Resources,* Vol. 3; *Concise Dictionary of American Literary Biography,* 1929-1941; *Contemporary Authors,* Vols. 104, 132; *Contemporary Authors New Revision Series,* Vol. 102; *Dictionary of Literary Biography,* Vols. 9, 102, 229; *Dictionary of Literary Biography Documentary Series,* Vols. 2, 16; *Dictionary of Literary Biography Yearbook,* 1985, 1997; *DISCovering Authors*; *DISCovering Authors: British Edition*; *DISCovering Authors: Canadian Edition*; *DISCovering Authors Modules: Most-Studied Authors* and *Novelists*; *DISCovering Authors 3.0*; *Encyclopedia of World Literature in the 20th Century,* Ed. 3; *Literature Resource Center*; *Major 20th Century Writers,* Eds. 1, 2; *Modern American Literature,* Ed. 5; *Novels for Students,* Vol. 18; *Reference Guide to American Literature,* Ed. 4; *Short Stories for Students,* Vol. 18; *Short Story Criticism,* Vol. 33; *Twayne's United States Authors*; *Twentieth-Century Literary Criticism,* Vols. 4, 13, 29, 61; and *World Literature Criticism,* Vol. 6.

How to Use This Index

The main references

Calvino, Italo
1923-1985 .... **CLC 5, 8, 11, 22, 33, 39,**
73; SSC 3, 48

---

list all author entries in the following Gale Literary Criticism series:

AAL = *Asian American Literature*
BG = *The Beat Generation: A Gale Critical Companion*
BLC = *Black Literature Criticism*
BLCS = *Black Literature Criticism Supplement*
CLC = *Contemporary Literary Criticism*
CLR = *Children's Literature Review*
CMLC = *Classical and Medieval Literature Criticism*
DC = *Drama Criticism*
FL = *Feminism in Literature: A Gale Critical Companion*
GL = *Gothic Literature: A Gale Critical Companion*
HLC = *Hispanic Literature Criticism*
HLCS = *Hispanic Literature Criticism Supplement*
HR = *Harlem Renaissance: A Gale Critical Companion*
LC = *Literature Criticism from 1400 to 1800*
NCLC = *Nineteenth-Century Literature Criticism*
NNAL = *Native North American Literature*
PC = *Poetry Criticism*
SSC = *Short Story Criticism*
TCLC = *Twentieth-Century Literary Criticism*
WLC = *World Literature Criticism, 1500 to the Present*
WLCS = *World Literature Criticism Supplement*

The cross-references

See also CA 85-88, 116; CANR 23, 61;
DAM NOV; DLB 196; EW 13; MTCW 1, 2;
RGSF 2; RGWL 2; SFW 4; SSFS 12

---

list all author entries in the following Gale biographical and literary sources:

AAYA = *Authors & Artists for Young Adults*
AFAW = *African American Writers*
AFW = *African Writers*
AITN = *Authors in the News*
AMW = *American Writers*
AMWR = *American Writers Retrospective Supplement*
AMWS = *American Writers Supplement*
ANW = *American Nature Writers*
AW = *Ancient Writers*
BEST = *Bestsellers*
BPFB = *Beacham's Encyclopedia of Popular Fiction: Biography and Resources*
BRW = *British Writers*
BRWS = *British Writers Supplement*
BW = *Black Writers*
BYA = *Beacham's Guide to Literature for Young Adults*
CA = *Contemporary Authors*
CAAS = *Contemporary Authors Autobiography Series*
CABS = *Contemporary Authors Bibliographical Series*
CAD = *Contemporary American Dramatists*
CANR = *Contemporary Authors New Revision Series*
CAP = *Contemporary Authors Permanent Series*
CBD = *Contemporary British Dramatists*
CCA = *Contemporary Canadian Authors*
CD = *Contemporary Dramatists*
CDALB = *Concise Dictionary of American Literary Biography*

CDALBS = *Concise Dictionary of American Literary Biography Supplement*
CDBLB = *Concise Dictionary of British Literary Biography*
CMW = *St. James Guide to Crime & Mystery Writers*
CN = *Contemporary Novelists*
CP = *Contemporary Poets*
CPW = *Contemporary Popular Writers*
CSW = *Contemporary Southern Writers*
CWD = *Contemporary Women Dramatists*
CWP = *Contemporary Women Poets*
CWRI = *St. James Guide to Children's Writers*
CWW = *Contemporary World Writers*
DA = *DISCovering Authors*
DA3 = *DISCovering Authors 3.0*
DAB = *DISCovering Authors: British Edition*
DAC = *DISCovering Authors: Canadian Edition*
DAM = *DISCovering Authors: Modules*
   DRAM: *Dramatists Module;* **MST:** *Most-studied Authors Module;*
   MULT: *Multicultural Authors Module;* **NOV:** *Novelists Module;*
   POET: *Poets Module;* **POP:** *Popular Fiction and Genre Authors Module*
DFS = *Drama for Students*
DLB = *Dictionary of Literary Biography*
DLBD = *Dictionary of Literary Biography Documentary Series*
DLBY = *Dictionary of Literary Biography Yearbook*
DNFS = *Literature of Developing Nations for Students*
EFS = *Epics for Students*
EXPN = *Exploring Novels*
EXPP = *Exploring Poetry*
EXPS = *Exploring Short Stories*
EW = *European Writers*
FANT = *St. James Guide to Fantasy Writers*
FW = *Feminist Writers*
GFL = *Guide to French Literature,* Beginnings to 1789, 1798 to the Present
GLL = *Gay and Lesbian Literature*
HGG = *St. James Guide to Horror, Ghost & Gothic Writers*
HW = *Hispanic Writers*
IDFW = *International Dictionary of Films and Filmmakers: Writers and Production Artists*
IDTP = *International Dictionary of Theatre: Playwrights*
LAIT = *Literature and Its Times*
LAW = *Latin American Writers*
JRDA = *Junior DISCovering Authors*
MAICYA = *Major Authors and Illustrators for Children and Young Adults*
MAICYAS = *Major Authors and Illustrators for Children and Young Adults Supplement*
MAWW = *Modern American Women Writers*
MJW = *Modern Japanese Writers*
MTCW = *Major 20th-Century Writers*
NCFS = *Nonfiction Classics for Students*
NFS = *Novels for Students*
PAB = *Poets: American and British*
PFS = *Poetry for Students*
RGAL = *Reference Guide to American Literature*
RGEL = *Reference Guide to English Literature*
RGSF = *Reference Guide to Short Fiction*
RGWL = *Reference Guide to World Literature*
RHW = *Twentieth-Century Romance and Historical Writers*
SAAS = *Something about the Author Autobiography Series*
SATA = *Something about the Author*
SFW = *St. James Guide to Science Fiction Writers*
SSFS = *Short Stories for Students*
TCWW = *Twentieth-Century Western Writers*
WLIT = *World Literature and Its Times*
WP = *World Poets*
YABC = *Yesterday's Authors of Books for Children*
YAW = *St. James Guide to Young Adult Writers*

Literary Criticism Series
Cumulative Author Index

Aeschylus 525(?)B.C.-456(?)B.C. .. **CMLC 11, 51, 94; DC 8; WLCS**
See also AW 1; CDWLB 1; DA; DAB; DAC; DAM DRAM, MST; DFS 5, 10; DLB 176; LMFS 1; RGWL 2, 3; TWA; WLIT 8

Aesop 620(?)B.C.-560(?)B.C. .... **CMLC 24**
See also CLR 14; MAICYA 1, 2; SATA 64

Affable Hawk
See MacCarthy, Sir (Charles Otto) Desmond

Africa, Ben
See Bosman, Herman Charles

Afton, Effie
See Harper, Frances Ellen Watkins

Agapida, Fray Antonio
See Irving, Washington

Agee, James (Rufus) 1909-1955 ...... **TCLC 1, 19, 180**
See also AAYA 44; AITN 1; AMW; CA 108; 148; CANR 131; CDALB 1941-1968; DAM NOV; DLB 2, 26, 152; DLBY 1989; EWL 3; LAIT 3; LATS 1:2; MAL 5; MTCW 2; MTFW 2005; NFS 22; RGAL 4; TUS

A Gentlewoman in New England
See Bradstreet, Anne

A Gentlewoman in Those Parts
See Bradstreet, Anne

Aghill, Gordon
See Silverberg, Robert

Agnon, S(hmuel) Y(osef Halevi) 1888-1970 **CLC 4, 8, 14; SSC 30; TCLC 151**
See also CA 17-18; 25-28R; CANR 60, 102; CAP 2; DLB 329; EWL 3; MTCW 1, 2; RGHL; RGSF 2; RGWL 2, 3; WLIT 6

Agrippa von Nettesheim, Henry Cornelius 1486-1535 .... **LC 27**

Aguilera Malta, Demetrio 1909-1981 .... **HLCS 1**
See also CA 111; 124; CANR 87; DAM MULT, NOV; DLB 145; EWL 3; HW 1; RGWL 3

Agustini, Delmira 1886-1914 .... **HLCS 1**
See also CA 166; DLB 290; HW 1, 2; LAW

Aherne, Owen
See Cassill, R(onald) V(erlin)

Ai 1947- .... **CLC 4, 14, 69; PC 72**
See also CA 85-88; CAAS 13; CANR 70; CP 6, 7; DLB 120; PFS 16

Aickman, Robert (Fordyce) 1914-1981 .... **CLC 57**
See also CA 5-8R; CANR 3, 72, 100; DLB 261; HGG; SUFW 1, 2

Aidoo, (Christina) Ama Ata 1942- .... **BLCS; CLC 177**
See also AFW; BW 1; CA 101; CANR 62, 144; CD 5, 6; CDWLB 3; CN 6, 7; CWD; CWP; DLB 117; DNFS 1, 2; EWL 3; FW; WLIT 2

Aiken, Conrad (Potter) 1889-1973 .... **CLC 1, 3, 5, 10, 52; PC 26; SSC 9**
See also AMW; CA 5-8R; 45-48; CANR 4, 60; CDALB 1929-1941; CN 1; CP 1; DAM NOV, POET; DLB 9, 45, 102; EWL 3; EXPS; HGG; MAL 5; MTCW 1, 2; MTFW 2005; PFS 24; RGAL 4; RGSF 2; SATA 3, 30; SSFS 8; TUS

Aiken, Joan (Delano) 1924-2004 ...... **CLC 35**
See also AAYA 1, 25; CA 9-12R; 182; 223; CAAE 182; CANR 4, 23, 34, 64, 121; CLR 1, 19, 90; DLB 161; FANT; HGG; JRDA; MAICYA 1, 2; MTCW 1; RHW; SAAS 1; SATA 2, 30, 73; SATA-Essay 109; SATA-Obit 152; SUFW 2; WYA; YAW

Ainsworth, William Harrison 1805-1882 **NCLC 13**
See also DLB 21; HGG; RGEL 2; SATA 24; SUFW 1

Aitmatov, Chingiz (Torekulovich) 1928- .... **CLC 71**
See Aytmatov, Chingiz
See also CA 103; CANR 38; CWW 2; DLB 302; MTCW 1; RGSF 2; SATA 56

Akers, Floyd
See Baum, L(yman) Frank

Akhmadulina, Bella Akhatovna 1937- .... **CLC 53; PC 43**
See also CA 65-68; CWP; CWW 2; DAM POET; EWL 3

Akhmatova, Anna 1888-1966 ..... **CLC 11, 25, 64, 126; PC 2, 55**
See also CA 19-20; 25-28R; CANR 35; CAP 1; DA3; DAM POET; DLB 295; EW 10; EWL 3; FL 1:5; MTCW 1, 2; PFS 18, 27; RGWL 2, 3

Aksakov, Sergei Timofeevich 1791-1859 **NCLC 2, 181**
See also DLB 198

Aksenov, Vasilii (Pavlovich)
See Aksyonov, Vassily (Pavlovich)
See also CWW 2

Aksenov, Vassily
See Aksyonov, Vassily (Pavlovich)

Akst, Daniel 1956- .... **CLC 109**
See also CA 161; CANR 110

Aksyonov, Vassily (Pavlovich) 1932- .... **CLC 22, 37, 101**
See Aksenov, Vasilii (Pavlovich)
See also CA 53-56; CANR 12, 48, 77; DLB 302; EWL 3

Akutagawa Ryunosuke 1892-1927 ... **SSC 44; TCLC 16**
See also CA 117; 154; DLB 180; EWL 3; MJW; RGSF 2; RGWL 2, 3

Alabaster, William 1568-1640 .... **LC 90**
See also DLB 132; RGEL 2

Alain 1868-1951 .... **TCLC 41**
See also CA 163; EWL 3; GFL 1789 to the Present

Alain de Lille c. 1116-c. 1203 .... **CMLC 53**
See also DLB 208

Alain-Fournier .... **TCLC 6**
See Fournier, Henri-Alban
See also DLB 65; EWL 3; GFL 1789 to the Present; RGWL 2, 3

Al-Amin, Jamil Abdullah 1943- ...... **BLC 1:1**
See also BW 1, 3; CA 112; 125; CANR 82; DAM MULT

Alanus de Insluis
See Alain de Lille

Alarcon, Pedro Antonio de 1833-1891 .... **NCLC 1; SSC 64**

Alas (y Urena), Leopoldo (Enrique Garcia) 1852-1901 .... **TCLC 29**
See also CA 113; 131; HW 1; RGSF 2

Albee, Edward (III) 1928- ..... **CLC 1, 2, 3, 5, 9, 11, 13, 25, 53, 86, 113; DC 11; WLC 1**
See also AAYA 51; AITN 1; AMW; CA 5-8R; CABS 3; CAD; CANR 8, 54, 74, 124; CD 5, 6; CDALB 1941-1968; DA; DA3; DAB; DAC; DAM DRAM, MST; DFS 25; DLB 7, 266; EWL 3; INT CANR-8; LAIT 4; LMFS 2; MAL 5; MTCW 1, 2; MTFW 2005; RGAL 4; TUS

Alberti (Merello), Rafael
See Alberti, Rafael
See also CWW 2

Alberti, Rafael 1902-1999 .... **CLC 7**
See Alberti (Merello), Rafael
See also CA 85-88; 185; CANR 81; DLB 108; EWL 3; HW 2; RGWL 2, 3

Albert the Great 1193(?)-1280 ...... **CMLC 16**
See also DLB 115

Alcaeus c. 620B.C.- .... **CMLC 65**
See also DLB 176

Alcala-Galiano, Juan Valera y
See Valera y Alcala-Galiano, Juan

Alcayaga, Lucila Godoy
See Godoy Alcayaga, Lucila

Alciato, Andrea 1492-1550 .... **LC 116**

Alcott, Amos Bronson 1799-1888 ... **NCLC 1, 167**
See also DLB 1, 223

Alcott, Louisa May 1832-1888 . **NCLC 6, 58, 83; SSC 27, 98; WLC 1**
See also AAYA 20; AMWS 1; BPFB 1; BYA 2; CDALB 1865-1917; CLR 1, 38, 109; DA; DA3; DAB; DAC; DAM MST, NOV; DLB 1, 42, 79, 223, 239, 242; DLBD 14; FL 1:2; FW; JRDA; LAIT 2; MAICYA 1, 2; NFS 12; RGAL 4; SATA 100; TUS; WCH; WYA; YABC 1; YAW

Alcuin c. 730-804 .... **CMLC 69**
See also DLB 148

Aldanov, M. A.
See Aldanov, Mark (Alexandrovich)

Aldanov, Mark (Alexandrovich) 1886-1957 **TCLC 23**
See also CA 118; 181; DLB 317

Aldhelm c. 639-709 .... **CMLC 90**

Aldington, Richard 1892-1962 .... **CLC 49**
See also CA 85-88; CANR 45; DLB 20, 36, 100, 149; LMFS 2; RGEL 2

Aldiss, Brian W. 1925- .. **CLC 5, 14, 40; SSC 36**
See also AAYA 42; CA 5-8R, 190; CAAE 190; CAAS 2; CANR 5, 28, 64, 121, 168; CN 1, 2, 3, 4, 5, 6, 7; DAM NOV; DLB 14, 261, 271; MTCW 1, 2; MTFW 2005; SATA 34; SCFW 1, 2; SFW 4

Aldiss, Brian Wilson
See Aldiss, Brian W.

Aldrich, Bess Streeter 1881-1954 .... **TCLC 125**
See also CLR 70; TCWW 2

Alegria, Claribel
See Alegria, Claribel
See also CWW 2; DLB 145, 283

Alegria, Claribel 1924- .... **CLC 75; HLCS 1; PC 26**
See Alegria, Claribel
See also CA 131; CAAS 15; CANR 66, 94, 134; DAM MULT; EWL 3; HW 1; MTCW 2; MTFW 2005; PFS 21

Alegria, Fernando 1918-2005 .... **CLC 57**
See also CA 9-12R; CANR 5, 32, 72; EWL 3; HW 1, 2

Aleixandre, Vicente 1898-1984 .... **HLCS 1; TCLC 113**
See also CANR 81; DLB 108, 329; EWL 3; HW 2; MTCW 1, 2; RGWL 2, 3

Alekseev, Konstantin Sergeivich
See Stanislavsky, Constantin

Alekseyer, Konstantin Sergeyevich
See Stanislavsky, Constantin

Aleman, Mateo 1547-1615(?) .... **LC 81**

Alencar, Jose de 1829-1877 .... **NCLC 157**
See also DLB 307; LAW; WLIT 1

Alencon, Marguerite d'
See de Navarre, Marguerite

Alepoudelis, Odysseus
See Elytis, Odysseus
See also CWW 2

Aleshkovsky, Joseph 1929-
See Aleshkovsky, Yuz
See also CA 121; 128

Aleshkovsky, Yuz .... **CLC 44**
See Aleshkovsky, Joseph
See also DLB 317

Alexander, Barbara
See Ehrenreich, Barbara

Ammons, A.R. 1926-2001 .. **CLC 2, 3, 5, 8, 9, 25, 57, 108; PC 16**
See also AITN 1; AMWS 7; CA 9-12R; 193; CANR 6, 36, 51, 73, 107, 156; CP 1, 2, 3, 4, 5, 6, 7; CSW; DAM POET; DLB 5, 165; EWL 3; MAL 5; MTCW 1, 2; PFS 19; RGAL 4; TCLE 1:1

Ammons, Archie Randolph
See Ammons, A.R.

Amo, Tauraatua i
See Adams, Henry (Brooks)

Amory, Thomas 1691(?)-1788 .... **LC 48**
See also DLB 39

Anand, Mulk Raj 1905-2004 ..... **CLC 23, 93, 237**
See also CA 65-68; 231; CANR 32, 64; CN 1, 2, 3, 4, 5, 6, 7; DAM NOV; DLB 323; EWL 3; MTCW 1, 2; MTFW 2005; RGSF 2

Anatol
See Schnitzler, Arthur

Anaximander c. 611B.C.-c. 546B.C. .... **CMLC 22**

Anaya, Rudolfo A. 1937- . **CLC 23, 148, 255; HLC 1**
See also AAYA 20; BYA 13; CA 45-48; CAAS 4; CANR 1, 32, 51, 124, 169; CLR 129; CN 4, 5, 6, 7; DAM MULT, NOV; DLB 82, 206, 278; HW 1; LAIT 4; LLW; MAL 5; MTCW 1, 2; MTFW 2005; NFS 12; RGAL 4; RGSF 2; TCWW 2; WLIT 1

Anaya, Rudolpho Alfonso
See Anaya, Rudolfo A.

Andersen, Hans Christian 1805-1875 .... **NCLC 7, 79; SSC 6, 56; WLC 1**
See also AAYA 57; CLR 6, 113; DA; DA3; DAB; DAC; DAM MST, POP; EW 6; MAICYA 1, 2; RGSF 2; RGWL 2, 3; SATA 100; TWA; WCH; YABC 1

Anderson, C. Farley
See Mencken, H(enry) L(ouis); Nathan, George Jean

Anderson, Jessica (Margaret) Queale 1916- **CLC 37**
See also CA 9-12R; CANR 4, 62; CN 4, 5, 6, 7; DLB 325

Anderson, Jon (Victor) 1940- .... **CLC 9**
See also CA 25-28R; CANR 20; CP 1, 3, 4, 5; DAM POET

Anderson, Lindsay (Gordon) 1923-1994 .... **CLC 20**
See also CA 125; 128; 146; CANR 77

Anderson, Maxwell 1888-1959 .... **TCLC 2, 144**
See also CA 105; 152; DAM DRAM; DFS 16, 20; DLB 7, 228; MAL 5; MTCW 2; MTFW 2005; RGAL 4

Anderson, Poul 1926-2001 .... **CLC 15**
See also AAYA 5, 34; BPFB 1; BYA 6, 8, 9; CA 1-4R, 181; 199; CAAE 181; CAAS 2; CANR 2, 15, 34, 64, 110; CLR 58; DLB 8; FANT; INT CANR-15; MTCW 1, 2; MTFW 2005; SATA 90; SATA-Brief 39; SATA-Essay 106; SCFW 1, 2; SFW 4; SUFW 1, 2

Anderson, Robert (Woodruff) 1917- .... **CLC 23**
See also AITN 1; CA 21-24R; CANR 32; CD 6; DAM DRAM; DLB 7; LAIT 5

Anderson, Roberta Joan
See Mitchell, Joni

Anderson, Sherwood 1876-1941 ... **SSC 1, 46, 91; TCLC 1, 10, 24, 123; WLC 1**
See also AAYA 30; AMW; AMWC 2; BPFB 1; CA 104; 121; CANR 61; CDALB 1917-1929; DA; DA3; DAB; DAC; DAM MST, NOV; DLB 4, 9, 86; DLBD 1; EWL

3; EXPS; GLL 2; MAL 5; MTCW 1, 2; MTFW 2005; NFS 4; RGAL 4; RGSF 2; SSFS 4, 10, 11; TUS

Anderson, Wes 1969- .... **CLC 227**
See also CA 214

Andier, Pierre
See Desnos, Robert

Andouard
See Giraudoux, Jean(-Hippolyte)

Andrade, Carlos Drummond de ...... **CLC 18**
See Drummond de Andrade, Carlos
See also EWL 3; RGWL 2, 3

Andrade, Mario de .... **TCLC 43**
See de Andrade, Mario
See also DLB 307; EWL 3; LAW; RGWL 2, 3; WLIT 1

Andreae, Johann V(alentin) 1586-1654 .... **LC 32**
See also DLB 164

Andreas Capellanus fl. c. 1185- .... **CMLC 45**
See also DLB 208

Andreas-Salome, Lou 1861-1937 ... **TCLC 56**
See also CA 178; DLB 66

Andreev, Leonid
See Andreyev, Leonid (Nikolaevich)
See also DLB 295; EWL 3

Andress, Lesley
See Sanders, Lawrence

Andrewes, Lancelot 1555-1626 .... **LC 5**
See also DLB 151, 172

Andrews, Cicily Fairfield
See West, Rebecca

Andrews, Elton V.
See Pohl, Frederik

Andrews, Peter
See Soderbergh, Steven

Andrews, Raymond 1934-1991 .... **BLC 2:1**
See also BW 2; CA 81-84; 136; CANR 15, 42

Andreyev, Leonid (Nikolaevich) 1871-1919 **TCLC 3**
See Andreev, Leonid
See also CA 104; 185

Andric, Ivo 1892-1975 .... **CLC 8; SSC 36; TCLC 135**
See also CA 81-84; 57-60; CANR 43, 60; CDWLB 4; DLB 147, 329; EW 11; EWL 3; MTCW 1; RGSF 2; RGWL 2, 3

Androvar
See Prado (Calvo), Pedro

Angela of Foligno 1248(?)-1309 .... **CMLC 76**

Angelique, Pierre
See Bataille, Georges

Angell, Roger 1920- .... **CLC 26**
See also CA 57-60; CANR 13, 44, 70, 144; DLB 171, 185

Angelou, Maya 1928- ...... **BLC 1:1; CLC 12, 35, 64, 77, 155; PC 32; WLCS**
See also AAYA 7, 20; AMWS 4; BPFB 1; BW 2, 3; BYA 2; CA 65-68; CANR 19, 42, 65, 111, 133; CDALBS; CLR 53; CP 4, 5, 6, 7; CPW; CSW; CWP; DA; DA3; DAB; DAC; DAM MST, MULT, POET, POP; DLB 38; EWL 3; EXPN; EXPP; FL 1:5; LAIT 4; MAICYA 2; MAICYAS 1; MAL 5; MBL; MTCW 1, 2; MTFW 2005; NCFS 2; NFS 2; PFS 2, 3; RGAL 4; SATA 49, 136; TCLE 1:1; WYA; YAW

Angouleme, Marguerite d'
See de Navarre, Marguerite

Anna Comnena 1083-1153 .... **CMLC 25**

Annensky, Innokentii Fedorovich
See Annensky, Innokenty (Fyodorovich)
See also DLB 295

Annensky, Innokenty (Fyodorovich) 1856-1909 .... **TCLC 14**
See also CA 110; 155; EWL 3

Annunzio, Gabriele d'
See D'Annunzio, Gabriele

Anodos
See Coleridge, Mary E(lizabeth)

Anon, Charles Robert
See Pessoa, Fernando (Antonio Nogueira)

Anouilh, Jean 1910-1987 ..... **CLC 1, 3, 8, 13, 40, 50; DC 8, 21; TCLC 195**
See also AAYA 67; CA 17-20R; 123; CANR 32; DAM DRAM; DFS 9, 10, 19; DLB 321; EW 13; EWL 3; GFL 1789 to the Present; MTCW 1, 2; MTFW 2005; RGWL 2, 3; TWA

Ansa, Tina McElroy 1949- .... **BLC 2:1**
See also BW 2; CA 142; CANR 143; CSW

Anselm of Canterbury 1033(?)-1109 .... **CMLC 67**
See also DLB 115

Anthony, Florence
See Ai

Anthony, John
See Ciardi, John (Anthony)

Anthony, Peter
See Shaffer, Anthony; Shaffer, Peter

Anthony, Piers 1934- .... **CLC 35**
See also AAYA 11, 48; BYA 7; CA 200; CAAE 200; CANR 28, 56, 73, 102, 133; CLR 118; CPW; DAM POP; DLB 8; FANT; MAICYA 2; MAICYAS 1; MTCW 1, 2; MTFW 2005; SAAS 22; SATA 84, 129; SATA-Essay 129; SFW 4; SUFW 1, 2; YAW

Anthony, Susan B(rownell) 1820-1906 .... **TCLC 84**
See also CA 211; FW

Antiphon c. 480B.C.-c. 411B.C. .... **CMLC 55**

Antoine, Marc
See Proust, (Valentin-Louis-George-Eugene) Marcel

Antoninus, Brother
See Everson, William (Oliver)
See also CP 1

Antonioni, Michelangelo 1912-2007 .... **CLC 20, 144**
See also CA 73-76; 262; CANR 45, 77

Antschel, Paul 1920-1970
See Celan, Paul
See also CA 85-88; CANR 33, 61; MTCW 1; PFS 21

Anwar, Chairil 1922-1949 .... **TCLC 22**
See Chairil Anwar
See also CA 121; 219; RGWL 3

Anyidoho, Kofi 1947- .... **BLC 2:1**
See also BW 3; CA 178; CP 5, 6, 7; DLB 157; EWL 3

Anzaldua, Gloria (Evanjelina) 1942-2004 **CLC 200; HLCS 1**
See also CA 175; 227; CSW; CWP; DLB 122; FW; LLW; RGAL 4; SATA-Obit 154

Apess, William 1798-1839(?) .... **NCLC 73; NNAL**
See also DAM MULT; DLB 175, 243

Apollinaire, Guillaume 1880-1918 .... **PC 7; TCLC 3, 8, 51**
See Kostrowitzki, Wilhelm Apollinaris de
See also CA 152; DAM POET; DLB 258, 321; EW 9; EWL 3; GFL 1789 to the Present; MTCW 2; PFS 24; RGWL 2, 3; TWA; WP

Apollonius of Rhodes
See Apollonius Rhodius
See also AW 1; RGWL 2, 3

Apollonius Rhodius c. 300B.C.-c. 220B.C. **CMLC 28**
See Apollonius of Rhodes
See also DLB 176

Appelfeld, Aharon 1932- ... **CLC 23, 47; SSC 42**
See also CA 112; 133; CANR 86, 160; CWW 2; DLB 299; EWL 3; RGHL; RGSF 2; WLIT 6

Appelfeld, Aron
See Appelfeld, Aharon

Apple, Max (Isaac) 1941- .... **CLC 9, 33; SSC 50**
See also AMWS 17; CA 81-84; CANR 19, 54; DLB 130

Appleman, Philip (Dean) 1926- .... **CLC 51**
See also CA 13-16R; CAAS 18; CANR 6, 29, 56

Appleton, Lawrence
See Lovecraft, H. P.

Apteryx
See Eliot, T(homas) S(tearns)

Apuleius, (Lucius Madaurensis) c. 125-c. 164 .... **CMLC 1, 84**
See also AW 2; CDWLB 1; DLB 211; RGWL 2, 3; SUFW; WLIT 8

Aquin, Hubert 1929-1977 .... **CLC 15**
See also CA 105; DLB 53; EWL 3

Aquinas, Thomas 1224(?)-1274 ..... **CMLC 33**
See also DLB 115; EW 1; TWA

Aragon, Louis 1897-1982 .... **CLC 3, 22; TCLC 123**
See also CA 69-72; 108; CANR 28, 71; DAM NOV, POET; DLB 72, 258; EW 11; EWL 3; GFL 1789 to the Present; GLL 2; LMFS 2; MTCW 1, 2; RGWL 2, 3

Arany, Janos 1817-1882 .... **NCLC 34**

Aranyos, Kakay 1847-1910
See Mikszath, Kalman

Aratus of Soli c. 315B.C.-c. 240B.C. .... **CMLC 64**
See also DLB 176

Arbuthnot, John 1667-1735 .... **LC 1**
See also DLB 101

Archer, Herbert Winslow
See Mencken, H(enry) L(ouis)

Archer, Jeffrey 1940- .... **CLC 28**
See also AAYA 16; BEST 89:3; BPFB 1; CA 77-80; CANR 22, 52, 95, 136; CPW; DA3; DAM POP; INT CANR-22; MTFW 2005

Archer, Jeffrey Howard
See Archer, Jeffrey

Archer, Jules 1915- .... **CLC 12**
See also CA 9-12R; CANR 6, 69; SAAS 5; SATA 4, 85

Archer, Lee
See Ellison, Harlan

Archilochus c. 7th cent. B.C.- .... **CMLC 44**
See also DLB 176

Ard, William
See Jakes, John

Arden, John 1930- .... **CLC 6, 13, 15**
See also BRWS 2; CA 13-16R; CAAS 4; CANR 31, 65, 67, 124; CBD; CD 5, 6; DAM DRAM; DFS 9; DLB 13, 245; EWL 3; MTCW 1

Arenas, Reinaldo 1943-1990 .. **CLC 41; HLC 1; TCLC 191**
See also CA 124; 128; 133; CANR 73, 106; DAM MULT; DLB 145; EWL 3; GLL 2; HW 1; LAW; LAWS 1; MTCW 2; MTFW 2005; RGSF 2; RGWL 3; WLIT 1

Arendt, Hannah 1906-1975 .... **CLC 66, 98; TCLC 193**
See also CA 17-20R; 61-64; CANR 26, 60, 172; DLB 242; MTCW 1, 2

Aretino, Pietro 1492-1556 .... **LC 12**
See also RGWL 2, 3

Arghezi, Tudor .... **CLC 80**
See Theodorescu, Ion N.
See also CA 167; CDWLB 4; DLB 220; EWL 3

Arguedas, Jose Maria 1911-1969 .... **CLC 10, 18; HLCS 1; TCLC 147**
See also CA 89-92; CANR 73; DLB 113; EWL 3; HW 1; LAW; RGWL 2, 3; WLIT 1

Argueta, Manlio 1936- .... **CLC 31**
See also CA 131; CANR 73; CWW 2; DLB 145; EWL 3; HW 1; RGWL 3

Arias, Ron 1941- .... **HLC 1**
See also CA 131; CANR 81, 136; DAM MULT; DLB 82; HW 1, 2; MTCW 2; MTFW 2005

Ariosto, Lodovico
See Ariosto, Ludovico
See also WLIT 7

Ariosto, Ludovico 1474-1533 ... **LC 6, 87; PC 42**
See Ariosto, Lodovico
See also EW 2; RGWL 2, 3

Aristides
See Epstein, Joseph

Aristophanes 450B.C.-385B.C. .... **CMLC 4, 51; DC 2; WLCS**
See also AW 1; CDWLB 1; DA; DA3; DAB; DAC; DAM DRAM, MST; DFS 10; DLB 176; LMFS 1; RGWL 2, 3; TWA; WLIT 8

Aristotle 384B.C.-322B.C. .... **CMLC 31; WLCS**
See also AW 1; CDWLB 1; DA; DA3; DAB; DAC; DAM MST; DLB 176; RGWL 2, 3; TWA; WLIT 8

Arlt, Roberto (Godofredo Christophersen) 1900-1942 .... **HLC 1; TCLC 29**
See also CA 123; 131; CANR 67; DAM MULT; DLB 305; EWL 3; HW 1, 2; IDTP; LAW

Armah, Ayi Kwei 1939- . **BLC 1:1, 2:1; CLC 5, 33, 136**
See also AFW; BRWS 10; BW 1; CA 61-64; CANR 21, 64; CDWLB 3; CN 1, 2, 3, 4, 5, 6, 7; DAM MULT, POET; DLB 117; EWL 3; MTCW 1; WLIT 2

Armatrading, Joan 1950- .... **CLC 17**
See also CA 114; 186

Armin, Robert 1568(?)-1615(?) .... **LC 120**

Armitage, Frank
See Carpenter, John (Howard)

Armstrong, Jeannette (C.) 1948- .... **NNAL**
See also CA 149; CCA 1; CN 6, 7; DAC; DLB 334; SATA 102

Arnette, Robert
See Silverberg, Robert

Arnim, Achim von (Ludwig Joachim von Arnim) 1781-1831 .. **NCLC 5, 159; SSC 29**
See also DLB 90

Arnim, Bettina von 1785-1859 ...... **NCLC 38, 123**
See also DLB 90; RGWL 2, 3

Arnold, Matthew 1822-1888 ..... **NCLC 6, 29, 89, 126; PC 5; WLC 1**
See also BRW 5; CDBLB 1832-1890; DA; DAB; DAC; DAM MST, POET; DLB 32, 57; EXPP; PAB; PFS 2; TEA; WP

Arnold, Thomas 1795-1842 .... **NCLC 18**
See also DLB 55

Arnow, Harriette (Louisa) Simpson 1908-1986 ...... **CLC 2, 7, 18; TCLC 196**
See also BPFB 1; CA 9-12R; 118; CANR 14; CN 2, 3, 4; DLB 6; FW; MTCW 1, 2; RHW; SATA 42; SATA-Obit 47

Arouet, Francois-Marie
See Voltaire

Arp, Hans
See Arp, Jean

Arp, Jean 1887-1966 .... **CLC 5; TCLC 115**
See also CA 81-84; 25-28R; CANR 42, 77; EW 10

Arrabal
See Arrabal, Fernando

Arrabal (Teran), Fernando
See Arrabal, Fernando
See also CWW 2

Arrabal, Fernando 1932- ... **CLC 2, 9, 18, 58**
See Arrabal (Teran), Fernando
See also CA 9-12R; CANR 15; DLB 321; EWL 3; LMFS 2

Arreola, Juan Jose 1918-2001 .... **CLC 147; HLC 1; SSC 38**
See also CA 113; 131; 200; CANR 81; CWW 2; DAM MULT; DLB 113; DNFS 2; EWL 3; HW 1, 2; LAW; RGSF 2

Arrian c. 89(?)-c. 155(?) .... **CMLC 43**
See also DLB 176

Arrick, Fran .... **CLC 30**
See Gaberman, Judie Angell
See also BYA 6

Arrley, Richmond
See Delany, Samuel R., Jr.

Artaud, Antonin (Marie Joseph) 1896-1948 **DC 14; TCLC 3, 36**
See also CA 104; 149; DA3; DAM DRAM; DFS 22; DLB 258, 321; EW 11; EWL 3; GFL 1789 to the Present; MTCW 2; MTFW 2005; RGWL 2, 3

Arthur, Ruth M(abel) 1905-1979 ..... **CLC 12**
See also CA 9-12R; 85-88; CANR 4; CWRI 5; SATA 7, 26

Artsybashev, Mikhail (Petrovich) 1878-1927 **TCLC 31**
See also CA 170; DLB 295

Arundel, Honor (Morfydd) 1919-1973 .... **CLC 17**
See also CA 21-22; 41-44R; CAP 2; CLR 35; CWRI 5; SATA 4; SATA-Obit 24

Arzner, Dorothy 1900-1979 .... **CLC 98**

Asch, Sholem 1880-1957 .... **TCLC 3**
See also CA 105; DLB 333; EWL 3; GLL 2; RGHL

Ascham, Roger 1516(?)-1568 .... **LC 101**
See also DLB 236

Ash, Shalom
See Asch, Sholem

Ashbery, John 1927- ... **CLC 2, 3, 4, 6, 9, 13, 15, 25, 41, 77, 125, 221; PC 26**
See also AMWS 3; CA 5-8R; CANR 9, 37, 66, 102, 132, 170; CP 1, 2, 3, 4, 5, 6, 7; DA3; DAM POET; DLB 5, 165; DLBY 1981; EWL 3; GLL 1; INT CANR-9; MAL 5; MTCW 1, 2; MTFW 2005; PAB; PFS 11, 28; RGAL 4; TCLE 1:1; WP

Ashbery, John Lawrence
See Ashbery, John

Ashbridge, Elizabeth 1713-1755 .... **LC 147**
See also DLB 200

Ashdown, Clifford
See Freeman, R(ichard) Austin

Ashe, Gordon
See Creasey, John

Ashton-Warner, Sylvia (Constance) 1908-1984 .... **CLC 19**
See also CA 69-72; 112; CANR 29; CN 1, 2, 3; MTCW 1, 2

Asimov, Isaac 1920-1992 ..... **CLC 1, 3, 9, 19, 26, 76, 92**
See also AAYA 13; BEST 90:2; BPFB 1; BYA 4, 6, 7, 9; CA 1-4R; 137; CANR 2, 19, 36, 60, 125; CLR 12, 79; CMW 4; CN 1, 2, 3, 4, 5; CPW; DA3; DAM POP; DLB 8; DLBY 1992; INT CANR-19; JRDA; LAIT 5; LMFS 2; MAICYA 1, 2; MAL 5; MTCW 1, 2; MTFW 2005; RGAL 4; SATA 1, 26, 74; SCFW 1, 2; SFW 4; SSFS 17; TUS; YAW

Askew, Anne 1521(?)-1546 .... **LC 81**
See also DLB 136

Assis, Joaquim Maria Machado de
See Machado de Assis, Joaquim Maria

Astell, Mary 1666-1731 .... **LC 68**
See also DLB 252, 336; FW

Badanes, Jerome 1937-1995 .... CLC 59
  See also CA 234
Bage, Robert 1728-1801 .... NCLC 182
  See also DLB 39; RGEL 2
Bagehot, Walter 1826-1877 .... NCLC 10
  See also DLB 55
Bagnold, Enid 1889-1981 .... CLC 25
  See also AAYA 75; BYA 2; CA 5-8R; 103;
  CANR 5, 40; CBD; CN 2; CWD; CWRI
  5; DAM DRAM; DLB 13, 160, 191, 245;
  FW; MAICYA 1, 2; RGEL 2; SATA 1, 25
Bagritsky, Eduard .... TCLC 60
  See Dzyubin, Eduard Georgievich
Bagrjana, Elisaveta
  See Belcheva, Elisaveta Lyubomirova
Bagryana, Elisaveta .... CLC 10
  See Belcheva, Elisaveta Lyubomirova
  See also CA 178; CDWLB 4; DLB 147;
  EWL 3
Bailey, Paul 1937- .... CLC 45
  See also CA 21-24R; CANR 16, 62, 124;
  CN 1, 2, 3, 4, 5, 6, 7; DLB 14, 271; GLL
  2
Baillie, Joanna 1762-1851 ...... NCLC 71, 151
  See also DLB 93; GL 2; RGEL 2
Bainbridge, Beryl 1934- ...... CLC 4, 5, 8, 10,
  14, 18, 22, 62, 130
  See also BRWS 6; CA 21-24R; CANR 24,
  55, 75, 88, 128; CN 2, 3, 4, 5, 6, 7; DAM
  NOV; DLB 14, 231; EWL 3; MTCW 1,
  2; MTFW 2005
Baker, Carlos (Heard)
  1909-1987 .... TCLC 119
  See also CA 5-8R; 122; CANR 3, 63; DLB
  103
Baker, Elliott 1922-2007 .... CLC 8
  See also CA 45-48; 257; CANR 2, 63; CN
  1, 2, 3, 4, 5, 6, 7
Baker, Elliott Joseph
  See Baker, Elliott
Baker, Jean H. .... TCLC 3, 10
  See Russell, George William
Baker, Nicholson 1957- .... CLC 61, 165
  See also AMWS 13; CA 135; CANR 63,
  120, 138; CN 6; CPW; DA3; DAM POP;
  DLB 227; MTFW 2005
Baker, Ray Stannard 1870-1946 .... TCLC 47
  See also CA 118
Baker, Russell 1925- .... CLC 31
  See also BEST 89:4; CA 57-60; CANR 11,
  41, 59, 137; MTCW 1, 2; MTFW 2005
Bakhtin, M.
  See Bakhtin, Mikhail Mikhailovich
Bakhtin, M. M.
  See Bakhtin, Mikhail Mikhailovich
Bakhtin, Mikhail
  See Bakhtin, Mikhail Mikhailovich
Bakhtin, Mikhail Mikhailovich 1895-1975
  CLC 83; TCLC 160
  See also CA 128; 113; DLB 242; EWL 3
Bakshi, Ralph 1938(?)- .... CLC 26
  See also CA 112; 138; IDFW 3
Bakunin, Mikhail (Alexandrovich)
  1814-1876 .... NCLC 25, 58
  See also DLB 277
Bal, Mieke (Maria Gertrudis)
  1946- .... CLC 252
  See also CA 156; CANR 99
Baldwin, James 1924-1987 ...... BLC 1:1, 2:1;
  **CLC 1, 2, 3, 4, 5, 8, 13, 15, 17, 42, 50,
  67, 90, 127; DC 1; SSC 10, 33, 98;
  WLC 1**
  See also AAYA 4, 34; AFAW 1, 2; AMWR
  2; AMWS 1; BPFB 1; BW 1; CA 1-4R;
  124; CABS 1; CAD; CANR 3, 24;
  CDALB 1941-1968; CN 1, 2, 3, 4; CPW;
  DA; DA3; DAB; DAC; DAM MST,
  MULT, NOV, POP; DFS 11, 15; DLB 2,
  7, 33, 249, 278; DLBY 1987; EWL 3;

EXPS; LAIT 5; MAL 5; MTCW 1, 2;
  MTFW 2005; NCFS 4; NFS 4; RGAL 4;
  RGSF 2; SATA 9; SATA-Obit 54; SSFS
  2, 18; TUS
Baldwin, William c. 1515-1563 .... LC 113
  See also DLB 132
Bale, John 1495-1563 .... LC 62
  See also DLB 132; RGEL 2; TEA
Ball, Hugo 1886-1927 .... TCLC 104
Ballard, J.G. 1930- .... CLC 3, 6, 14, 36, 137;
  SSC 1, 53
  See also AAYA 3, 52; BRWS 5; CA 5-8R;
  CANR 15, 39, 65, 107, 133; CN 1, 2, 3,
  4, 5, 6, 7; DA3; DAM NOV, POP; DLB
  14, 207, 261, 319; EWL 3; HGG; MTCW
  1, 2; MTFW 2005; NFS 8; RGEL 2;
  RGSF 2; SATA 93; SCFW 1, 2; SFW 4
Balmont, Konstantin (Dmitriyevich)
  1867-1943 .... TCLC 11
  See also CA 109; 155; DLB 295; EWL 3
Baltausis, Vincas 1847-1910
  See Mikszath, Kalman
Balzac, Honore de 1799-1850 ... NCLC 5, 35,
  53, 153; SSC 5, 59, 102; WLC 1
  See also DA; DA3; DAB; DAC; DAM
  MST, NOV; DLB 119; EW 5; GFL 1789
  to the Present; LMFS 1; RGSF 2; RGWL
  2, 3; SSFS 10; SUFW; TWA
Bambara, Toni Cade 1939-1995 ..... BLC 1:1,
  **2:1; CLC 19, 88; SSC 35, 107; TCLC
  116; WLCS**
  See also AAYA 5, 49; AFAW 2; AMWS 11;
  BW 2, 3; BYA 12, 14; CA 29-32R; 150;
  CANR 24, 49, 81; CDALBS; DA; DA3;
  DAC; DAM MST, MULT; DLB 38, 218;
  EXPS; MAL 5; MTCW 1, 2; MTFW
  2005; RGAL 4; RGSF 2; SATA 112; SSFS
  4, 7, 12, 21
Bamdad, A.
  See Shamlu, Ahmad
Bamdad, Alef
  See Shamlu, Ahmad
Banat, D. R.
  See Bradbury, Ray
Bancroft, Laura
  See Baum, L(yman) Frank
Banim, John 1798-1842 .... NCLC 13
  See also DLB 116, 158, 159; RGEL 2
Banim, Michael 1796-1874 .... NCLC 13
  See also DLB 158, 159
Banjo, The
  See Paterson, A(ndrew) B(arton)
Banks, Iain 1954- .... CLC 34
  See Banks, Iain M.
  See also CA 123; 128; CANR 61, 106; DLB
  194, 261; EWL 3; HGG; INT CA-128;
  MTFW 2005; SFW 4
Banks, Iain M.
  See Banks, Iain
  See also BRWS 11
Banks, Iain Menzies
  See Banks, Iain
Banks, Lynne Reid .... CLC 23
  See Reid Banks, Lynne
  See also AAYA 6; BYA 7; CN 4, 5, 6
Banks, Russell 1940- . CLC 37, 72, 187; SSC
  42
  See also AAYA 45; AMWS 5; CA 65-68;
  CAAS 15; CANR 19, 52, 73, 118; CN 4,
  5, 6, 7; DLB 130, 278; EWL 3; MAL 5;
  MTCW 2; MTFW 2005; NFS 13
Banks, Russell Earl
  See Banks, Russell
Banville, John 1945- .... CLC 46, 118, 224
  See also CA 117; 128; CANR 104, 150,
  176; CN 4, 5, 6, 7; DLB 14, 271, 326;
  INT CA-128

Banville, Theodore (Faullain) de 1832-1891
  NCLC 9
  See also DLB 217; GFL 1789 to the Present
Baraka, Amiri 1934- .. BLC 1:1, 2:1; CLC 1,
  **2, 3, 5, 10, 14, 33, 115, 213; DC 6; PC
  4; WLCS**
  See Jones, LeRoi
  See also AAYA 63; AFAW 1, 2; AMWS 2;
  BW 2, 3; CA 21-24R; CABS 3; CAD;
  CANR 27, 38, 61, 133, 172; CD 3, 5, 6;
  CDALB 1941-1968; CP 4, 5, 6, 7; CPW;
  DA; DA3; DAC; DAM MST, MULT,
  POET, POP; DFS 3, 11, 16; DLB 5, 7,
  16, 38; DLBD 8; EWL 3; MAL 5; MTCW
  1, 2; MTFW 2005; PFS 9; RGAL 4;
  TCLE 1:1; TUS; WP
Baratynsky, Evgenii Abramovich 1800-1844
  NCLC 103
  See also DLB 205
Barbauld, Anna Laetitia
  1743-1825 .... NCLC 50, 185
  See also DLB 107, 109, 142, 158, 336;
  RGEL 2
Barbellion, W. N. P. .... TCLC 24
  See Cummings, Bruce F(rederick)
Barber, Benjamin R. 1939- .... CLC 141
  See also CA 29-32R; CANR 12, 32, 64, 119
Barbera, Jack (Vincent) 1945- .... CLC 44
  See also CA 110; CANR 45
Barbey d'Aurevilly, Jules-Amedee 1808-1889
  NCLC 1; SSC 17
  See also DLB 119; GFL 1789 to the Present
Barbour, John c. 1316-1395 .... CMLC 33
  See also DLB 146
Barbusse, Henri 1873-1935 .... TCLC 5
  See also CA 105; 154; DLB 65; EWL 3;
  RGWL 2, 3
Barclay, Alexander c. 1475-1552 .... LC 109
  See also DLB 132
Barclay, Bill
  See Moorcock, Michael
Barclay, William Ewert
  See Moorcock, Michael
Barea, Arturo 1897-1957 .... TCLC 14
  See also CA 111; 201
Barfoot, Joan 1946- .... CLC 18
  See also CA 105; CANR 141
Barham, Richard Harris
  1788-1845 .... NCLC 77
  See also DLB 159
Baring, Maurice 1874-1945 .... TCLC 8
  See also CA 105; 168; DLB 34; HGG
Baring-Gould, Sabine 1834-1924 ... TCLC 88
  See also CA 156; 190
Barker, Clive 1952- .... CLC 52, 205; SSC 53
  See also AAYA 10, 54; BEST 90:3; BPFB
  1; CA 121; 129; CANR 71, 111, 133;
  CPW; DA3; DAM POP; DLB 261; HGG;
  INT CA-129; MTCW 1, 2; MTFW 2005;
  SUFW 2
Barker, George Granville
  1913-1991 .... CLC 8, 48; PC 77
  See also CA 9-12R; 135; CANR 7, 38; CP
  1, 2, 3, 4, 5; DAM POET; DLB 20; EWL
  3; MTCW 1
Barker, Harley Granville
  See Granville-Barker, Harley
  See also DLB 10
Barker, Howard 1946- .... CLC 37
  See also CA 102; CBD; CD 5, 6; DLB 13,
  233
Barker, Jane 1652-1732 .... LC 42, 82
  See also DLB 39, 131
Barker, Pat 1943- .... CLC 32, 94, 146
  See also BRWS 4; CA 117; 122; CANR 50,
  101, 148; CN 6, 7; DLB 271, 326; INT
  CA-122
Barker, Patricia
  See Barker, Pat

Beaumarchais, Pierre-Augustin Caron de
1732-1799 .... **DC 4; LC 61**
See also DAM DRAM; DFS 14, 16; DLB
313; EW 4; GFL Beginnings to 1789;
RGWL 2, 3

Beaumont, Francis 1584(?)-1616 .. **DC 6; LC
33**
See also BRW 2; CDBLB Before 1660;
DLB 58; TEA

Beauvoir, Simone de 1908-1986 .... **CLC 1, 2,
4, 8, 14, 31, 44, 50, 71, 124; SSC 35;
WLC 1**
See also BPFB 1; CA 9-12R; 118; CANR
28, 61; DA; DA3; DAB; DAC; DAM
MST, NOV; DLB 72; DLBY 1986; EW
12; EWL 3; FL 1:5; FW; GFL 1789 to the
Present; LMFS 2; MTCW 1, 2; MTFW
2005; RGSF 2; RGWL 2, 3; TWA

**Beauvoir, Simone Lucie Ernestine Marie
Bertrand de**
See Beauvoir, Simone de

Becker, Carl (Lotus) 1873-1945 ..... **TCLC 63**
See also CA 157; DLB 17

Becker, Jurek 1937-1997 .... **CLC 7, 19**
See also CA 85-88; 157; CANR 60, 117;
CWW 2; DLB 75, 299; EWL 3; RGHL

Becker, Walter 1950- .... **CLC 26**

Becket, Thomas a 1118(?)-1170 .... **CMLC 83**

Beckett, Samuel 1906-1989 ... **CLC 1, 2, 3, 4,
6, 9, 10, 11, 14, 18, 29, 57, 59, 83; DC
22; SSC 16, 74; TCLC 145; WLC 1**
See also BRWC 2; BRWR 1; BRWS 1; CA
5-8R; 130; CANR 33, 61; CBD; CDBLB
1945-1960; CN 1, 2, 3, 4; CP 1, 2, 3, 4;
DA; DA3; DAB; DAC; DAM DRAM,
MST, NOV; DFS 2, 7, 18; DLB 13, 15,
233, 319, 321, 329; DLBY 1990; EWL 3;
GFL 1789 to the Present; LATS 1:2;
LMFS 2; MTCW 1, 2; MTFW 2005;
RGSF 2; RGWL 2, 3; SSFS 15; TEA;
WLIT 4

Beckford, William 1760-1844 .... **NCLC 16**
See also BRW 3; DLB 39, 213; GL 2; HGG;
LMFS 1; SUFW

Beckham, Barry (Earl) 1944- .... **BLC 1:1**
See also BW 1; CA 29-32R; CANR 26, 62;
CN 1, 2, 3; DAM MULT; DLB 33

Beckman, Gunnel 1910- .... **CLC 26**
See also CA 33-36R; CANR 15, 114; CLR
25; MAICYA 1, 2; SAAS 9; SATA 6

Becque, Henri 1837-1899 .... **DC 21; NCLC 3**
See also DLB 192; GFL 1789 to the Present

Becquer, Gustavo Adolfo
1836 1870 .... **HLCS 1; NCLC 106**
See also DAM MULT

Beddoes, Thomas Lovell 1803-1849 .. **DC 15;
NCLC 3, 154**
See also BRWS 11; DLB 96

Bede c. 673-735 .... **CMLC 20**
See also DLB 146; TEA

Bedford, Denton R. 1907-(?) .... **NNAL**

Bedford, Donald F.
See Fearing, Kenneth (Flexner)

Beecher, Catharine Esther
1800-1878 .... **NCLC 30**
See also DLB 1, 243

Beecher, John 1904-1980 .... **CLC 6**
See also AITN 1; CA 5-8R; 105; CANR 8;
CP 1, 2, 3

Beer, Johann 1655-1700 .... **LC 5**
See also DLB 168

Beer, Patricia 1924- .... **CLC 58**
See also CA 61-64; 183; CANR 13, 46; CP
1, 2, 3, 4, 5, 6; CWP; DLB 40; FW

Beerbohm, Max
See Beerbohm, (Henry) Max(imilian)

Beerbohm, (Henry) Max(imilian) 1872-1956
TCLC 1, 24
See also BRWS 2; CA 104; 154; CANR 79;
DLB 34, 100; FANT; MTCW 2

Beer-Hofmann, Richard
1866-1945 .... **TCLC 60**
See also CA 160; DLB 81

Beg, Shemus
See Stephens, James

Begiebing, Robert J(ohn) 1946- .... **CLC 70**
See also CA 122; CANR 40, 88

Begley, Louis 1933- .... **CLC 197**
See also CA 140; CANR 98, 176; DLB 299;
RGHL; TCLE 1:1

Behan, Brendan (Francis)
1923-1964 .... **CLC 1, 8, 11, 15, 79**
See also BRWS 2; CA 73-76; CANR 33,
121; CBD; CDBLB 1945-1960; DAM
DRAM; DFS 7; DLB 13, 233; EWL 3;
MTCW 1, 2

Behn, Aphra 1640(?)-1689 .. **DC 4; LC 1, 30,
42, 135; PC 13, 88; WLC 1**
See also BRWS 3; DA; DA3; DAB; DAC;
DAM DRAM, MST, NOV, POET; DFS
16, 24; DLB 39, 80, 131; FW; TEA;
WLIT 3

Behrman, S(amuel) N(athaniel) 1893-1973
CLC 40
See also CA 13-16; 45-48; CAD; CAP 1;
DLB 7, 44; IDFW 3; MAL 5; RGAL 4

Bekederemo, J. P. Clark
See Clark Bekederemo, J.P.
See also CD 6

Belasco, David 1853-1931 .... **TCLC 3**
See also CA 104; 168; DLB 7; MAL 5;
RGAL 4

Belcheva, Elisaveta Lyubomirova 1893-1991
CLC 10
See Bagryana, Elisaveta

Beldone, Phil "Cheech"
See Ellison, Harlan

Beleno
See Azuela, Mariano

Belinski, Vissarion Grigoryevich 1811-1848
NCLC 5
See also DLB 198

Belitt, Ben 1911- .... **CLC 22**
See also CA 13-16R; CAAS 4; CANR 7,
77; CP 1, 2, 3, 4, 5, 6; DLB 5

Belknap, Jeremy 1744-1798 .... **LC 115**
See also DLB 30, 37

Bell, Gertrude (Margaret Lowthian)
1868-1926 .... **TCLC 67**
See also CA 167; CANR 110; DLB 174

Bell, J. Freeman
See Zangwill, Israel

Bell, James Madison 1826-1902 ..... **BLC 1:1;
TCLC 43**
See also BW 1; CA 122; 124; DAM MULT;
DLB 50

Bell, Madison Smartt 1957- ..... **CLC 41, 102,
223**
See also AMWS 10; BPFB 1; CA 111, 183;
CAAE 183; CANR 28, 54, 73, 134, 176;
CN 5, 6, 7; CSW; DLB 218, 278; MTCW
2; MTFW 2005

Bell, Marvin (Hartley) 1937- ...... **CLC 8, 31;
PC 79**
See also CA 21-24R; CAAS 14; CANR 59,
102; CP 1, 2, 3, 4, 5, 6, 7; DAM POET;
DLB 5; MAL 5; MTCW 1; PFS 25

Bell, W. L. D.
See Mencken, H(enry) L(ouis)

Bellamy, Atwood C.
See Mencken, H(enry) L(ouis)

Bellamy, Edward 1850-1898 ..... **NCLC 4, 86,
147**
See also DLB 12; NFS 15; RGAL 4; SFW
4

Belli, Gioconda 1948- .... **HLCS 1**
See also CA 152; CANR 143; CWW 2;
DLB 290; EWL 3; RGWL 3

Bellin, Edward J.
See Kuttner, Henry

Bello, Andres 1781-1865 .... **NCLC 131**
See also LAW

**Belloc, (Joseph) Hilaire (Pierre Sebastien
Rene Swanton)** 1870-1953 .... **PC 24;
TCLC 7, 18**
See also CA 106; 152; CLR 102; CWRI 5;
DAM POET; DLB 19, 100, 141, 174;
EWL 3; MTCW 2; MTFW 2005; SATA
112; WCH; YABC 1

Belloc, Joseph Peter Rene Hilaire
See Belloc, (Joseph) Hilaire (Pierre Sebastien Rene Swanton)

Belloc, Joseph Pierre Hilaire
See Belloc, (Joseph) Hilaire (Pierre Sebastien Rene Swanton)

Belloc, M. A.
See Lowndes, Marie Adelaide (Belloc)

Belloc-Lowndes, Mrs.
See Lowndes, Marie Adelaide (Belloc)

Bellow, Saul 1915-2005 ...... **CLC 1, 2, 3, 6, 8,
10, 13, 15, 25, 33, 34, 63, 79, 190, 200;
SSC 14, 101; WLC 1**
See also AITN 2; AMW; AMWC 2; AMWR
2; BEST 89:3; BPFB 1; CA 5-8R; 238;
CABS 1; CANR 29, 53, 95, 132; CDALB
1941-1968; CN 1, 2, 3, 4, 5, 6, 7; DA;
DA3; DAB; DAC; DAM MST, NOV,
POP; DLB 2, 28, 299, 329; DLBD 3;
DLBY 1982; EWL 3; MAL 5; MTCW 1,
2; MTFW 2005; NFS 4, 14, 26; RGAL 4;
RGHL; RGSF 2; SSFS 12, 22; TUS

Belser, Reimond Karel Maria de 1929-
See Ruyslinck, Ward
See also CA 152

Bely, Andrey .... **PC 11; TCLC 7**
See Bugayev, Boris Nikolayevich
See also DLB 295; EW 9; EWL 3

Belyi, Andrei
See Bugayev, Boris Nikolayevich
See also RGWL 2, 3

Bembo, Pietro 1470-1547 .... **LC 79**
See also RGWL 2, 3

Benary, Margot
See Benary-Isbert, Margot

Benary-Isbert, Margot 1889-1979 .... **CLC 12**
See also CA 5-8R; 89-92; CANR 4, 72;
CLR 12; MAICYA 1, 2; SATA 2; SATA-
Obit 21

Benavente (y Martinez), Jacinto 1866-1954
DC 26; HLCS 1; TCLC 3
See also CA 106; 131; CANR 81; DAM
DRAM, MULT; DLB 329; EWL 3; GLL
2; HW 1, 2; MTCW 1, 2

Benchley, Peter 1940-2006 .... **CLC 4, 8**
See also AAYA 14; AITN 2; BPFB 1; CA
17-20R; 248; CANR 12, 35, 66, 115;
CPW; DAM NOV, POP; HGG; MTCW 1,
2; MTFW 2005; SATA 3, 89, 164

Benchley, Peter Bradford
See Benchley, Peter

Benchley, Robert (Charles)
1889-1945 .... **TCLC 1, 55**
See also CA 105; 153; DLB 11; MAL 5;
RGAL 4

Benda, Julien 1867-1956 .... **TCLC 60**
See also CA 120; 154; GFL 1789 to the
Present

Benedict, Ruth 1887-1948 .... **TCLC 60**
See also CA 158; CANR 146; DLB 246

Benedict, Ruth Fulton
See Benedict, Ruth

Benedikt, Michael 1935- .... **CLC 4, 14**
See also CA 13-16R; CANR 7; CP 1, 2, 3,
4, 5, 6, 7; DLB 5

Benet, Juan 1927-1993 .... CLC 28
See also CA 143; EWL 3

Benet, Stephen Vincent 1898-1943 ..... PC 64;
SSC 10, 86; TCLC 7
See also AMWS 11; CA 104; 152; DA3;
DAM POET; DLB 4, 48, 102, 249, 284;
DLBY 1997; EWL 3; HGG; MAL 5;
MTCW 2; MTFW 2005; RGAL 4; RGSF
2; SSFS 22; SUFW; WP; YABC 1

Benet, William Rose 1886-1950 ..... TCLC 28
See also CA 118; 152; DAM POET; DLB
45; RGAL 4

Benford, Gregory 1941- .... CLC 52
See also BPFB 1; CA 69-72, 175, 268;
CAAE 175, 268; CAAS 27; CANR 12,
24, 49, 95, 134; CN 7; CSW; DLBY 1982;
MTFW 2005; SCFW 2; SFW 4

Benford, Gregory Albert
See Benford, Gregory

Bengtsson, Frans (Gunnar)
1894-1954 .... TCLC 48
See also CA 170; EWL 3

Benjamin, David
See Slavitt, David R.

Benjamin, Lois
See Gould, Lois

Benjamin, Walter 1892-1940 .... TCLC 39
See also CA 164; DLB 242; EW 11; EWL
3

Ben Jelloun, Tahar 1944- .... CLC 180
See also CA 135, 162; CANR 100, 166;
CWW 2; EWL 3; RGWL 3; WLIT 2

Benn, Gottfried 1886-1956 .. PC 35; TCLC 3
See also CA 106; 153; DLB 56; EWL 3;
RGWL 2, 3

Bennett, Alan 1934- .... CLC 45, 77
See also BRWS 8; CA 103; CANR 35, 55,
106, 157; CBD; CD 5, 6; DAB; DAM
MST; DLB 310; MTCW 1, 2; MTFW
2005

Bennett, (Enoch) Arnold
1867-1931 .... TCLC 5, 20, 197
See also BRW 6; CA 106; 155; CDBLB
1890-1914; DLB 10, 34, 98, 135; EWL 3;
MTCW 2

Bennett, Elizabeth
See Mitchell, Margaret (Munnerlyn)

Bennett, George Harold 1930-
See Bennett, Hal
See also BW 1; CA 97-100; CANR 87

Bennett, Gwendolyn B. 1902-1981 .... HR 1:2
See also BW 1; CA 125; DLB 51; WP

Bennett, Hal .... CLC 5
See Bennett, George Harold
See also CAAS 13; DLB 33

Bennett, Jay 1912- .... CLC 35
See also AAYA 10, 73; CA 69-72; CANR
11, 42, 79; JRDA; SAAS 4; SATA 41, 87;
SATA-Brief 27; WYA; YAW

Bennett, Louise 1919-2006 .... BLC 1:1; CLC
28
See also BW 2, 3; CA 151; 252; CDWLB
3; CP 1, 2, 3, 4, 5, 6, 7; DAM MULT;
DLB 117; EWL 3

Bennett, Louise Simone
See Bennett, Louise

Bennett-Coverley, Louise
See Bennett, Louise

Benoit de Sainte-Maure fl. 12th cent.
- .... CMLC 90

Benson, A. C. 1862-1925 .... TCLC 123
See also DLB 98

Benson, E(dward) F(rederic) 1867-1940
TCLC 27
See also CA 114; 157; DLB 135, 153;
HGG; SUFW 1

Benson, Jackson J. 1930- .... CLC 34
See also CA 25-28R; DLB 111

Benson, Sally 1900-1972 .... CLC 17
See also CA 19-20; 37-40R; CAP 1; SATA
1, 35; SATA-Obit 27

Benson, Stella 1892-1933 .... TCLC 17
See also CA 117; 154, 155; DLB 36, 162;
FANT; TEA

Bentham, Jeremy 1748-1832 .... NCLC 38
See also DLB 107, 158, 252

Bentley, E(dmund) C(lerihew) 1875-1956
TCLC 12
See also CA 108; 232; DLB 70; MSW

Bentley, Eric 1916- .... CLC 24
See also CA 5-8R; CAD; CANR 6, 67;
CBD; CD 5, 6; INT CANR-6

Bentley, Eric Russell
See Bentley, Eric

ben Uzair, Salem
See Horne, Richard Henry Hengist

Beolco, Angelo 1496-1542 .... LC 139

Beranger, Pierre Jean de
1780-1857 .... NCLC 34

Berdyaev, Nicolas
See Berdyaev, Nikolai (Aleksandrovich)

Berdyaev, Nikolai (Aleksandrovich)
1874-1948 .... TCLC 67
See also CA 120; 157

Berdyayev, Nikolai (Aleksandrovich)
See Berdyaev, Nikolai (Aleksandrovich)

Berendt, John 1939- .... CLC 86
See also CA 146; CANR 75, 83, 151

Berendt, John Lawrence
See Berendt, John

Beresford, J(ohn) D(avys)
1873-1947 .... TCLC 81
See also CA 112; 155; DLB 162, 178, 197;
SFW 4; SUFW 1

Bergelson, David (Rafailovich) 1884-1952
TCLC 81
See Bergelson, Dovid
See also CA 220; DLB 333

Bergelson, Dovid
See Bergelson, David (Rafailovich)
See also EWL 3

Berger, Colonel
See Malraux, (Georges-)Andre

Berger, John 1926- .... CLC 2, 19
See also BRWS 4; CA 81-84; CANR 51,
78, 117, 163; CN 1, 2, 3, 4, 5, 6, 7; DLB
14, 207, 319, 326

Berger, John Peter
See Berger, John

Berger, Melvin H. 1927- .... CLC 12
See also CA 5-8R; CANR 4, 142; CLR 32;
SAAS 2; SATA 5, 88, 158; SATA-Essay
124

Berger, Thomas 1924- .... CLC 3, 5, 8, 11, 18,
38
See also BPFB 1; CA 1-4R; CANR 5, 28,
51, 128; CN 1, 2, 3, 4, 5, 6, 7; DAM
NOV; DLB 2; DLBY 1980; EWL 3;
FANT; INT CANR-28; MAL 5; MTCW
1, 2; MTFW 2005; RHW; TCLE 1:1;
TCWW 1, 2

Bergman, Ernst Ingmar
See Bergman, Ingmar

Bergman, Ingmar 1918-2007 ..... CLC 16, 72,
210
See also AAYA 61; CA 81-84; 262; CANR
33, 70; CWW 2; DLB 257; MTCW 2;
MTFW 2005

Bergson, Henri(-Louis) 1859-1941 . TCLC 32
See also CA 164; DLB 329; EW 8; EWL 3;
GFL 1789 to the Present

Bergstein, Eleanor 1938- .... CLC 4
See also CA 53-56; CANR 5

Berkeley, George 1685-1753 .... LC 65
See also DLB 31, 101, 252

Berkoff, Steven 1937- .... CLC 56
See also CA 104; CANR 72; CBD; CD 5, 6

Berlin, Isaiah 1909-1997 .... TCLC 105
See also CA 85-88; 162

Bermant, Chaim (Icyk) 1929-1998 ... CLC 40
See also CA 57-60; CANR 6, 31, 57, 105;
CN 2, 3, 4, 5, 6

Bern, Victoria
See Fisher, M(ary) F(rances) K(ennedy)

Bernanos, (Paul Louis) Georges 1888-1948
TCLC 3
See also CA 104; 130; CANR 94; DLB 72;
EWL 3; GFL 1789 to the Present; RGWL
2, 3

Bernard, April 1956- .... CLC 59
See also CA 131; CANR 144

Bernard, Mary Ann
See Soderbergh, Steven

Bernard of Clairvaux 1090-1153 .. CMLC 71
See also DLB 208

Bernard Silvestris fl. c. 1130-fl. c. 1160
CMLC 87
See also DLB 208

Bernart de Ventadorn c. 1130-c.
1190 .... CMLC 98

Berne, Victoria
See Fisher, M(ary) F(rances) K(ennedy)

Bernhard, Thomas 1931-1989 ..... CLC 3, 32,
61; DC 14; TCLC 165
See also CA 85-88; 127; CANR 32, 57; CD-
WLB 2; DLB 85, 124; EWL 3; MTCW 1;
RGHL; RGWL 2, 3

Bernhardt, Sarah (Henriette Rosine)
1844-1923 .... TCLC 75
See also CA 157

Bernstein, Charles 1950- .... CLC 142,
See also CA 129; CAAS 24; CANR 90; CP
4, 5, 6, 7; DLB 169

Bernstein, Ingrid
See Kirsch, Sarah

Beroul fl. c. 12th cent. - .... CMLC 75

Berriault, Gina 1926-1999 .... CLC 54, 109;
SSC 30
See also CA 116; 129; 185; CANR 66; DLB
130; SSFS 7,11

Berrigan, Daniel 1921- .... CLC 4
See also CA 33-36R, 187; CAAE 187;
CAAS 1; CANR 11, 43, 78; CP 1, 2, 3, 4,
5, 6, 7; DLB 5

Berrigan, Edmund Joseph Michael, Jr.
1934-1983
See Berrigan, Ted
See also CA 61-64; 110; CANR 14, 102

Berrigan, Ted .... CLC 37
See Berrigan, Edmund Joseph Michael, Jr.
See also CP 1, 2, 3; DLB 5, 169; WP

Berry, Charles Edward Anderson 1931-
See Berry, Chuck
See also CA 115

Berry, Chuck .... CLC 17
See Berry, Charles Edward Anderson

Berry, Jonas
See Ashbery, John

Berry, Wendell 1934- .... CLC 4, 6, 8, 27, 46;
PC 28
See also AITN 1; AMWS 10; ANW; CA
73-76; CANR 50, 73, 101, 132, 174; CP
1, 2, 3, 4, 5, 6, 7; CSW; DAM POET;
DLB 5, 6, 234, 275; MTCW 2; MTFW
2005; TCLE 1:1

Berryman, John 1914-1972 ... CLC 1, 2, 3, 4,
6, 8, 10, 13, 25, 62; PC 64
See also AMW; CA 13-16; 33-36R; CABS
2; CANR 35; CAP 1; CDALB 1941-1968;
CP 1; DAM POET; DLB 48; EWL 3;
MAL 5; MTCW 1, 2; MTFW 2005; PAB;
PFS 27; RGAL 4; WP

Bertolucci, Bernardo 1940- ...... CLC 16, 157
See also CA 106; CANR 125

Berton, Pierre (Francis de Marigny)
1920-2004 .... **CLC 104**
   See also CA 1-4R; 233; CANR 2, 56, 144;
   CPW; DLB 68; SATA 99; SATA-Obit 158

Bertrand, Aloysius 1807-1841 .... **NCLC 31**
   See Bertrand, Louis oAloysiusc

Bertrand, Louis oAloysiusc
   See Bertrand, Aloysius
   See also DLB 217

Bertran de Born c. 1140-1215 .... **CMLC 5**

Besant, Annie (Wood) 1847-1933 ..... **TCLC 9**
   See also CA 105; 185

Bessie, Alvah 1904-1985 .... **CLC 23**
   See also CA 5-8R; 116; CANR 2, 80; DLB
   26

Bestuzhev, Aleksandr Aleksandrovich
1797-1837 .... **NCLC 131**
   See also DLB 198

Bethlen, T.D.
   See Silverberg, Robert

Beti, Mongo .... **BLC 1:1; CLC 27**
   See Biyidi, Alexandre
   See also AFW; CANR 79; DAM MULT;
   EWL 3; WLIT 2

Betjeman, John 1906-1984 ...... **CLC 2, 6, 10,
34, 43; PC 75**
   See also BRW 7; CA 9-12R; 112; CANR
   33, 56; CDBLB 1945-1960; CP 1, 2, 3;
   DA3; DAB; DAM MST, POET; DLB 20;
   DLBY 1984; EWL 3; MTCW 1, 2

Bettelheim, Bruno 1903-1990 .... **CLC 79;
TCLC 143**
   See also CA 81-84; 131; CANR 23, 61;
   DA3; MTCW 1, 2; RGHL

Betti, Ugo 1892-1953 .... **TCLC 5**
   See also CA 104; 155; EWL 3; RGWL 2, 3

Betts, Doris (Waugh) 1932- ..... **CLC 3, 6, 28;
SSC 45**
   See also CA 13-16R; CANR 9, 66, 77; CN
   6, 7; CSW; DLB 218; DLBY 1982; INT
   CANR-9; RGAL 4

Bevan, Alistair
   See Roberts, Keith (John Kingston)

Bey, Pilaff
   See Douglas, (George) Norman

Beyala, Calixthe 1961- .... **BLC 2:1**
   See also EWL 3

Bialik, Chaim Nachman
1873-1934 .... **TCLC 25, 201**
   See Bialik, Hayyim Nahman
   See also CA 170; EWL 3

Bialik, Hayyim Nahman
   See Bialik, Chaim Nachman
   See also WLIT 6

Bickerstaff, Isaac
   See Swift, Jonathan

Bidart, Frank 1939- .... **CLC 33**
   See also AMWS 15; CA 140; CANR 106;
   CP 5, 6, 7; PFS 26

Bienek, Horst 1930- .... **CLC 7, 11**
   See also CA 73-76; DLB 75

Bierce, Ambrose (Gwinett)
1842-1914(?) ..... **SSC 9, 72; TCLC 1, 7,
44; WLC 1**
   See also AAYA 55; AMW; BYA 11; CA
   104; 139; CANR 78; CDALB 1865-1917;
   DA; DA3; DAC; DAM MST; DLB 11,
   12, 23, 71, 74, 186; EWL 3; EXPS; HGG;
   LAIT 2; MAL 5; RGAL 4; RGSF 2; SSFS
   9; SUFW 1

Biggers, Earl Derr 1884-1933 .... **TCLC 65**
   See also CA 108; 153; DLB 306

Billiken, Bud
   See Motley, Willard (Francis)

Billings, Josh
   See Shaw, Henry Wheeler

Billington, (Lady) Rachel (Mary)
1942- .... **CLC 43**
   See also AITN 2; CA 33-36R; CANR 44;
   CN 4, 5, 6, 7

Binchy, Maeve 1940- .... **CLC 153**
   See also BEST 90:1; BPFB 1; CA 127; 134;
   CANR 50, 96, 134; CN 5, 6, 7; CPW;
   DA3; DAM POP; DLB 319; INT CA-134;
   MTCW 2; MTFW 2005; RHW

Binyon, T(imothy) J(ohn)
1936-2004 .... **CLC 34**
   See also CA 111; 232; CANR 28, 140

Bion 335B.C.-245B.C. .... **CMLC 39**

Bioy Casares, Adolfo 1914-1999 ... **CLC 4, 8,
13, 88; HLC 1; SSC 17, 102**
   See Casares, Adolfo Bioy; Miranda, Javier;
   Sacastru, Martin
   See also CA 29-32R; 177; CANR 19, 43,
   66; CWW 2; DAM MULT; DLB 113;
   EWL 3; HW 1, 2; LAW; MTCW 1, 2;
   MTFW 2005

Birch, Allison .... **CLC 65**

Bird, Cordwainer
   See Ellison, Harlan

Bird, Robert Montgomery
1806-1854 .... **NCLC 1, 197**
   See also DLB 202; RGAL 4

Birdwell, Cleo
   See DeLillo, Don

Birkerts, Sven 1951- .... **CLC 116**
   See also CA 128; 133, 176; CAAE 176;
   CAAS 29; CANR 151; INT CA-133

Birney, (Alfred) Earle 1904-1995 .. **CLC 1, 4,
6, 11; PC 52**
   See also CA 1-4R; CANR 5, 20; CN 1, 2,
   3, 4; CP 1, 2, 3, 4, 5, 6; DAC; DAM MST,
   POET; DLB 88; MTCW 1; PFS 8; RGEL
   2

Biruni, al 973-1048(?) .... **CMLC 28**

Bishop, Elizabeth 1911-1979 ..... **CLC 1, 4, 9,
13, 15, 32; PC 3, 34; TCLC 121**
   See also AMWR 2; AMWS 1; CA 5-8R;
   89-92; CABS 2; CANR 26, 61, 108;
   CDALB 1968-1988; CP 1, 2, 3; DA;
   DA3; DAC; DAM MST, POET; DLB 5,
   169; EWL 3; GLL 2; MAL 5; MBL;
   MTCW 1, 2; PAB; PFS 6, 12, 27; RGAL
   4; SATA-Obit 24; TUS; WP

Bishop, John 1935- .... **CLC 10**
   See also CA 105

Bishop, John Peale 1892-1944 ..... **TCLC 103**
   See also CA 107; 155; DLB 4, 9, 45; MAL
   5; RGAL 4

Bissett, Bill 1939- .... **CLC 18; PC 14**
   See also CA 69-72; CAAS 19; CANR 15;
   CCA 1; CP 1, 2, 3, 4, 5, 6, 7; DLB 53;
   MTCW 1

Bissoondath, Neil 1955- .... **CLC 120**
   See also CA 136; CANR 123, 165; CN 6,
   7; DAC

Bissoondath, Neil Devindra
   See Bissoondath, Neil

Bitov, Andrei (Georgievich) 1937- ... **CLC 57**
   See also CA 142; DLB 302

Biyidi, Alexandre 1932-
   See Beti, Mongo
   See also BW 1, 3; CA 114; 124; CANR 81;
   DA3; MTCW 1, 2

Bjarme, Brynjolf
   See Ibsen, Henrik (Johan)

Bjoernson, Bjoernstjerne (Martinius)
1832-1910 .... **TCLC 7, 37**
   See also CA 104

Black, Benjamin
   See Banville, John

Black, Robert
   See Holdstock, Robert

Blackburn, Paul 1926-1971 .... **CLC 9, 43**
   See also BG 1:2; CA 81-84; 33-36R; CANR
   34; CP 1; DLB 16; DLBY 1981

Black Elk 1863-1950 .... **NNAL; TCLC 33**
   See also CA 144; DAM MULT; MTCW 2;
   MTFW 2005; WP

Black Hawk 1767-1838 .... **NNAL**

Black Hobart
   See Sanders, (James) Ed(ward)

Blacklin, Malcolm
   See Chambers, Aidan

Blackmore, R(ichard) D(oddridge)
1825-1900 .... **TCLC 27**
   See also CA 120; DLB 18; RGEL 2

Blackmur, R(ichard) P(almer) 1904-1965
CLC 2, 24
   See also AMWS 2; CA 11-12; 25-28R;
   CANR 71; CAP 1; DLB 63; EWL 3;
   MAL 5

Black Tarantula
   See Acker, Kathy

Blackwood, Algernon 1869-1951 .... **SSC 107;
TCLC 5**
   See also CA 105; 150; CANR 169; DLB
   153, 156, 178; HGG; SUFW 1

Blackwood, Algernon Henry
   See Blackwood, Algernon

Blackwood, Caroline (Maureen) 1931-1996
CLC 6, 9, 100
   See also BRWS 9; CA 85-88; 151; CANR
   32, 61, 65; CN 3, 4, 5, 6; DLB 14, 207;
   HGG; MTCW 1

Blade, Alexander
   See Hamilton, Edmond; Silverberg, Robert

Blaga, Lucian 1895-1961 .... **CLC 75**
   See also CA 157; DLB 220; EWL 3

Blair, Eric (Arthur) 1903-1950 .... **TCLC 123**
   See Orwell, George
   See also CA 104; 132; DA; DA3; DAB;
   DAC; DAM MST, NOV; MTCW 1, 2;
   MTFW 2005; SATA 29

Blair, Hugh 1718-1800 .... **NCLC 75**

Blais, Marie-Claire 1939- .... **CLC 2, 4, 6, 13,
22**
   See also CA 21-24R; CAAS 4; CANR 38,
   75, 93; CWW 2; DAC; DAM MST; DLB
   53; EWL 3; FW; MTCW 1, 2; MTFW
   2005; TWA

Blaise, Clark 1940- .... **CLC 29**
   See also AITN 2; CA 53-56, 231; CAAE
   231; CAAS 3; CANR 5, 66, 106; CN 4,
   5, 6, 7; DLB 53; RGSF 2

Blake, Fairley
   See De Voto, Bernard (Augustine)

Blake, Nicholas
   See Day Lewis, C(ecil)
   See also DLB 77; MSW

Blake, Sterling
   See Benford, Gregory

Blake, William 1757-1827 . **NCLC 13, 37, 57,
127, 173, 190; PC 12, 63; WLC 1**
   See also AAYA 47; BRW 3; BRWR 1; CD-
   BLB 1789-1832; CLR 52; DA; DA3;
   DAB; DAC; DAM MST, POET; DLB 93,
   163; EXPP; LATS 1:1; LMFS 1; MAI-
   CYA 1, 2; PAB; PFS 2, 12, 24; SATA 30;
   TEA; WCH; WLIT 3; WP

Blanchot, Maurice 1907-2003 .... **CLC 135**
   See also CA 117; 144; 213; CANR 138;
   DLB 72, 296; EWL 3

Blasco Ibanez, Vicente 1867-1928 . **TCLC 12**
   See Ibanez, Vicente Blasco
   See also BPFB 1; CA 110; 131; CANR 81;
   DA3; DAM NOV; EW 8; EWL 3; HW 1,
   2; MTCW 1

Blatty, William Peter 1928- .... **CLC 2**
   See also CA 5-8R; CANR 9, 124; DAM
   POP; HGG

Borowski, Tadeusz 1922-1951 .... **SSC 48;
    TCLC 9**
    See also CA 106; 154; CDWLB 4; DLB
    215; EWL 3; RGHL; RGSF 2; RGWL 3;
    SSFS 13
Borrow, George (Henry)
    1803-1881 .... **NCLC 9**
    See also BRWS 12; DLB 21, 55, 166
Bosch (Gavino), Juan 1909-2001 ..... **HLCS 1**
    See also CA 151; 204; DAM MST, MULT;
    DLB 145; HW 1, 2
Bosman, Herman Charles
    1905-1951 .... **TCLC 49**
    See Malan, Herman
    See also CA 160; DLB 225; RGSF 2
Bosschere, Jean de 1878(?)-1953 ... **TCLC 19**
    See also CA 115; 186
Boswell, James 1740-1795 ... **LC 4, 50; WLC
    1**
    See also BRW 3; CDBLB 1660-1789; DA;
    DAB; DAC; DAM MST; DLB 104, 142;
    TEA; WLIT 3
Bottomley, Gordon 1874-1948 ..... **TCLC 107**
    See also CA 120; 192; DLB 10
Bottoms, David 1949- .... **CLC 53**
    See also CA 105; CANR 22; CSW; DLB
    120; DLBY 1983
Boucicault, Dion 1820-1890 .... **NCLC 41**
Boucolon, Maryse
    See Conde, Maryse
Bourdieu, Pierre 1930-2002 .... **CLC 198**
    See also CA 130; 204
Bourget, Paul (Charles Joseph) 1852-1935
    TCLC 12
    See also CA 107; 196; DLB 123; GFL 1789
    to the Present
Bourjaily, Vance (Nye) 1922- .... **CLC 8, 62**
    See also CA 1-4R; CAAS 1; CANR 2, 72;
    CN 1, 2, 3, 4, 5, 6, 7; DLB 2, 143; MAL
    5
Bourne, Randolph S(illiman) 1886-1918
    TCLC 16
    See also AMW; CA 117; 155; DLB 63;
    MAL 5
Bova, Ben 1932- .... **CLC 45**
    See also AAYA 16; CA 5-8R; CAAS 18;
    CANR 11, 56, 94, 111, 157; CLR 3, 96;
    DLBY 1981; INT CANR-11; MAICYA 1,
    2; MTCW 1; SATA 6, 68, 133; SFW 4
Bova, Benjamin William
    See Bova, Ben
Bowen, Elizabeth (Dorothea Cole) 1899-1973
    **CLC 1, 3, 6, 11, 15, 22, 118; SSC 3, 28,
    66; TCLC 148**
    See also BRWS 2; CA 17-18; 41-44R;
    CANR 35, 105; CAP 2; CDBLB 1945-
    1960; CN 1; DA3; DAM NOV; DLB 15,
    162; EWL 3; EXPS; FW; HGG; MTCW
    1, 2; MTFW 2005; NFS 13; RGSF 2;
    SSFS 5, 22; SUFW 1; TEA; WLIT 4
Bowering, George 1935- .... **CLC 15, 47**
    See also CA 21-24R; CAAS 16; CANR 10;
    CN 7; CP 1, 2, 3, 4, 5, 6, 7; DLB 53
Bowering, Marilyn R(uthe) 1949- .... **CLC 32**
    See also CA 101; CANR 49; CP 4, 5, 6, 7;
    CWP; DLB 334
Bowers, Edgar 1924-2000 .... **CLC 9**
    See also CA 5-8R; 188; CANR 24; CP 1, 2,
    3, 4, 5, 6, 7; CSW; DLB 5
Bowers, Mrs. J. Milton 1842-1914
    See Bierce, Ambrose (Gwinett)
Bowie, David .... **CLC 17**
    See Jones, David Robert
Bowles, Jane (Sydney) 1917-1973 ..... **CLC 3,
    68**
    See Bowles, Jane Auer
    See also CA 19-20; 41-44R; CAP 2; CN 1;
    MAL 5

Bowles, Jane Auer
    See Bowles, Jane (Sydney)
    See also EWL 3
Bowles, Paul 1910-1999 ..... **CLC 1, 2, 19, 53;
    SSC 3, 98**
    See also AMWS 4; CA 1-4R; 186; CAAS
    1; CANR 1, 19, 50, 75; CN 1, 2, 3, 4, 5,
    6; DA3; DLB 5, 6, 218; EWL 3; MAL 5;
    MTCW 1, 2; MTFW 2005; RGAL 4;
    SSFS 17
Bowles, William Lisle 1762-1850 . **NCLC 103**
    See also DLB 93
Box, Edgar
    See Vidal, Gore
Boyd, James 1888-1944 .... **TCLC 115**
    See also CA 186; DLB 9; DLBD 16; RGAL
    4; RHW
Boyd, Nancy
    See Millay, Edna St. Vincent
    See also GLL 1
Boyd, Thomas (Alexander)
    1898-1935 .... **TCLC 111**
    See also CA 111; 183; DLB 9; DLBD 16,
    316
Boyd, William 1952- .... **CLC 28, 53, 70**
    See also CA 114; 120; CANR 51, 71, 131,
    174; CN 4, 5, 6, 7; DLB 231
Boyesen, Hjalmar Hjorth
    1848-1895 .... **NCLC 135**
    See also DLB 12, 71; DLBD 13; RGAL 4
Boyle, Kay 1902-1992 .... **CLC 1, 5, 19, 58,
    121; SSC 5, 102**
    See also CA 13-16R; 140; CAAS 1; CANR
    29, 61, 110; CN 1, 2, 3, 4, 5; CP 1, 2, 3,
    4, 5; DLB 4, 9, 48, 86; DLBY 1993; EWL
    3; MAL 5; MTCW 1, 2; MTFW 2005;
    RGAL 4; RGSF 2; SSFS 10, 13, 14
Boyle, Mark
    See Kienzle, William X.
Boyle, Patrick 1905-1982 .... **CLC 19**
    See also CA 127
Boyle, T. C.
    See Boyle, T. Coraghessan
    See also AMWS 8
Boyle, T. Coraghessan 1948- ..... **CLC 36, 55,
    90; SSC 16**
    See Boyle, T. C.
    See also AAYA 47; BEST 90:4; BPFB 1;
    CA 120; CANR 44, 76, 89, 132; CN 6, 7;
    CPW; DA3; DAM POP; DLB 218, 278;
    DLBY 1986; EWL 3; MAL 5; MTCW 2;
    MTFW 2005; SSFS 13, 19
Boz
    See Dickens, Charles (John Huffam)
Brackenridge, Hugh Henry
    1748-1816 .... **NCLC 7**
    See also DLB 11, 37; RGAL 4
Bradbury, Edward P.
    See Moorcock, Michael
    See also MTCW 2
Bradbury, Malcolm (Stanley)
    1932-2000 .... **CLC 32, 61**
    See also CA 1-4R; CANR 1, 33, 91, 98,
    137; CN 1, 2, 3, 4, 5, 6, 7; CP 1; DA3;
    DAM NOV; DLB 14, 207; EWL 3;
    MTCW 1, 2; MTFW 2005
Bradbury, Ray 1920- ... **CLC 1, 3, 10, 15, 42,
    98, 235; SSC 29, 53; WLC 1**
    See also AAYA 15; AITN 1, 2; AMWS 4;
    BPFB 1; BYA 4, 5, 11; CA 1-4R; CANR
    2, 30, 75, 125; CDALB 1968-1988; CN
    1, 2, 3, 4, 5, 6, 7; CPW; DA; DA3; DAB;
    DAC; DAM MST, NOV, POP; DLB 2, 8;
    EXPN; EXPS; HGG; LAIT 3, 5; LATS
    1:2; LMFS 2; MAL 5; MTCW 1, 2;
    MTFW 2005; NFS 1, 22; RGAL 4; RGSF
    2; SATA 11, 64, 123; SCFW 1, 2; SFW 4;
    SSFS 1, 20; SUFW 1, 2; TUS; YAW

Braddon, Mary Elizabeth
    1837-1915 .... **TCLC 111**
    See also BRWS 8; CA 108; 179; CMW 4;
    DLB 18, 70, 156; HGG
Bradfield, Scott 1955- .... **SSC 65**
    See also CA 147; CANR 90; HGG; SUFW
    2
Bradfield, Scott Michael
    See Bradfield, Scott
Bradford, Gamaliel 1863-1932 .... **TCLC 36**
    See also CA 160; DLB 17
Bradford, William 1590-1657 .... **LC 64**
    See also DLB 24, 30; RGAL 4
Bradley, David, Jr. 1950- ...... **BLC 1:1; CLC
    23, 118**
    See also BW 1, 3; CA 104; CANR 26, 81;
    CN 4, 5, 6, 7; DAM MULT; DLB 33
Bradley, David Henry, Jr.
    See Bradley, David, Jr.
Bradley, John Ed 1958- .... **CLC 55**
    See also CA 139; CANR 99; CN 6, 7; CSW
Bradley, John Edmund, Jr.
    See Bradley, John Ed
Bradley, Marion Zimmer
    1930-1999 .... **CLC 30**
    See Chapman, Lee; Dexter, John; Gardner,
    Miriam; Ives, Morgan; Rivers, Elfrida
    See also AAYA 40; BPFB 1; CA 57-60; 185;
    CAAS 10; CANR 7, 31, 51, 75, 107;
    CPW; DA3; DAM POP; DLB 8; FANT;
    FW; MTCW 1, 2; MTFW 2005; SATA 90,
    139; SATA-Obit 116; SFW 4; SUFW 2;
    YAW
Bradshaw, John 1933- .... **CLC 70**
    See also CA 138; CANR 61
Bradstreet, Anne 1612(?)-1672 .... **LC 4, 30,
    130; PC 10**
    See also AMWS 1; CDALB 1640-1865;
    DA; DA3; DAC; DAM MST, POET; DLB
    24; EXPP; FW; PFS 6; RGAL 4; TUS;
    WP
Brady, Joan 1939- .... **CLC 86**
    See also CA 141
Bragg, Melvyn 1939- .... **CLC 10**
    See also BEST 89:3; CA 57-60; CANR 10,
    48, 89, 158; CN 1, 2, 3, 4, 5, 6, 7; DLB
    14, 271; RHW
Brahe, Tycho 1546-1601 .... **LC 45**
    See also DLB 300
Braine, John (Gerard) 1922-1986 . **CLC 1, 3,
    41**
    See also CA 1-4R; 120; CANR 1, 33; CD-
    BLB 1945-1960; CN 1, 2, 3, 4; DLB 15;
    DLBY 1986; EWL 3; MTCW 1
Braithwaite, William Stanley (Beaumont)
    1878-1962 ...... **BLC 1:1; HR 1:2; PC 52**
    See also BW 1; CA 125; DAM MULT; DLB
    50, 54; MAL 5
Bramah, Ernest 1868-1942 .... **TCLC 72**
    See also CA 156; CMW 4; DLB 70; FANT
Brammer, Billy Lee
    See Brammer, William
Brammer, William 1929-1978 .... **CLC 31**
    See also CA 235; 77-80
Brancati, Vitaliano 1907-1954 .... **TCLC 12**
    See also CA 109; DLB 264; EWL 3
Brancato, Robin F(idler) 1936- .... **CLC 35**
    See also AAYA 9, 68; BYA 6; CA 69-72;
    CANR 11, 45; CLR 32; JRDA; MAICYA
    2; MAICYAS 1; SAAS 9; SATA 97;
    WYA; YAW
Brand, Dionne 1953- .... **CLC 192**
    See also BW 2; CA 143; CANR 143; CWP;
    DLB 334
Brand, Max
    See Faust, Frederick (Schiller)
    See also BPFB 1; TCWW 1, 2
Brand, Millen 1906-1980 .... **CLC 7**
    See also CA 21-24R; 97-100; CANR 72

Branden, Barbara 1929- .... **CLC 44**
See also CA 148

Brandes, Georg (Morris Cohen) 1842-1927
TCLC 10
See also CA 105; 189; DLB 300

Brandys, Kazimierz 1916-2000 .... **CLC 62**
See also CA 239; EWL 3

Branley, Franklyn M(ansfield) 1915-2002
CLC 21
See also CA 33-36R; 207; CANR 14, 39;
CLR 13; MAICYA 1, 2; SAAS 16; SATA
4, 68, 136

Brant, Beth (E.) 1941- .... **NNAL**
See also CA 144; FW

Brant, Sebastian 1457-1521 .... **LC 112**
See also DLB 179; RGWL 2, 3

Brathwaite, Edward Kamau
1930- ..... **BLC 2:1; BLCS; CLC 11; PC
56**
See also BRWS 12; BW 2, 3; CA 25-28R;
CANR 11, 26, 47, 107; CDWLB 3; CP 1,
2, 3, 4, 5, 6, 7; DAM POET; DLB 125;
EWL 3

Brathwaite, Kamau
See Brathwaite, Edward Kamau

Brautigan, Richard (Gary)
1935-1984 .... **CLC 1, 3, 5, 9, 12, 34, 42;
TCLC 133**
See also BPFB 1; CA 53-56; 113; CANR
34; CN 1, 2, 3; CP 1, 2, 3, 4; DA3; DAM
NOV; DLB 2, 5, 206; DLBY 1980, 1984;
FANT; MAL 5; MTCW 1; RGAL 4;
SATA 56

Brave Bird, Mary
See Crow Dog, Mary

Braverman, Kate 1950- .... **CLC 67**
See also CA 89-92; CANR 141; DLB 335

Brecht, (Eugen) Bertolt (Friedrich)
1898-1956 ..... **DC 3; TCLC 1, 6, 13, 35,
169; WLC 1**
See also CA 104; 133; CANR 62; CDWLB
2; DA; DA3; DAB; DAC; DAM DRAM,
MST; DFS 4, 5, 9; DLB 56, 124; EW 11;
EWL 3; IDTP; MTCW 1, 2; MTFW 2005;
RGHL; RGWL 2, 3; TWA

Brecht, Eugen Berthold Friedrich
See Brecht, (Eugen) Bertolt (Friedrich)

Bremer, Fredrika 1801-1865 .... **NCLC 11**
See also DLB 254

Brennan, Christopher John
1870-1932 .... **TCLC 17**
See also CA 117; 188; DLB 230; EWL 3

Brennan, Maeve 1917-1993 ... **CLC 5; TCLC
124**
See also CA 81-84; CANR 72, 100

Brenner, Jozef 1887-1919
See Csath, Geza
See also CA 240

Brent, Linda
See Jacobs, Harriet A(nn)

Brentano, Clemens (Maria)
1778-1842 .... **NCLC 1, 191**
See also DLB 90; RGWL 2, 3

Brent of Bin Bin
See Franklin, (Stella Maria Sarah) Miles
(Lampe)

Brenton, Howard 1942- .... **CLC 31**
See also CA 69-72; CANR 33, 67; CBD;
CD 5, 6; DLB 13; MTCW 1

Breslin, James 1930-
See Breslin, Jimmy
See also CA 73-76; CANR 31, 75, 139;
DAM NOV; MTCW 1, 2; MTFW 2005

Breslin, Jimmy .... **CLC 4, 43**
See Breslin, James
See also AITN 1; DLB 185; MTCW 2

Bresson, Robert 1901(?)-1999 .... **CLC 16**
See also CA 110; 187; CANR 49

Breton, Andre 1896-1966 .. **CLC 2, 9, 15, 54;
PC 15**
See also CA 19-20; 25-28R; CANR 40, 60;
CAP 2; DLB 65, 258; EW 11; EWL 3;
GFL 1789 to the Present; LMFS 2;
MTCW 1, 2; MTFW 2005; RGWL 2, 3;
TWA; WP

Breton, Nicholas c. 1554-c. 1626 .... **LC 133**
See also DLB 136

Breytenbach, Breyten 1939(?)- .. **CLC 23, 37,
126**
See also CA 113; 129; CANR 61, 122;
CWW 2; DAM POET; DLB 225; EWL 3

Bridgers, Sue Ellen 1942- .... **CLC 26**
See also AAYA 8, 49; BYA 7, 8; CA 65-68;
CANR 11, 36; CLR 18; DLB 52; JRDA;
MAICYA 1, 2; SAAS 1; SATA 22, 90;
SATA-Essay 109; WYA; YAW

Bridges, Robert (Seymour)
1844-1930 .... **PC 28; TCLC 1**
See also BRW 6; CA 104; 152; CDBLB
1890-1914; DAM POET; DLB 19, 98

Bridie, James .... **TCLC 3**
See Mavor, Osborne Henry
See also DLB 10; EWL 3

Brin, David 1950- .... **CLC 34**
See also AAYA 21; CA 102; CANR 24, 70,
125, 127; INT CANR-24; SATA 65;
SCFW 2; SFW 4

Brink, Andre 1935- .... **CLC 18, 36, 106**
See also AFW; BRWS 6; CA 104; CANR
39, 62, 109, 133; CN 4, 5, 6, 7; DLB 225;
EWL 3; INT CA-103; LATS 1:2; MTCW
1, 2; MTFW 2005; WLIT 2

Brinsmead, H. F.
See Brinsmead, H(esba) F(ay)

Brinsmead, H. F(ay)
See Brinsmead, H(esba) F(ay)

Brinsmead, H(esba) F(ay) 1922- ...... **CLC 21**
See also CA 21-24R; CANR 10; CLR 47;
CWRI 5; MAICYA 1, 2; SAAS 5; SATA
18, 78

Brittain, Vera (Mary) 1893(?)-1970 . **CLC 23**
See also BRWS 10; CA 13-16; 25-28R;
CANR 58; CAP 1; DLB 191; FW; MTCW
1, 2

Broch, Hermann 1886-1951 ... **TCLC 20, 204**
See also CA 117; 211; CDWLB 2; DLB 85,
124; EW 10; EWL 3; RGWL 2, 3

Brock, Rose
See Hansen, Joseph
See also GLL 1

Brod, Max 1884-1968 .... **TCLC 115**
See also CA 5-8R; 25-28R; CANR 7; DLB
81; EWL 3

Brodkey, Harold (Roy) 1930-1996 .. **CLC 56;
TCLC 123**
See also CA 111; 151; CANR 71; CN 4, 5,
6; DLB 130

Brodsky, Iosif Alexandrovich 1940-1996
See Brodsky, Joseph
See also AITN 1; CA 41-44R; 151; CANR
37, 106; DA3; DAM POET; MTCW 1, 2;
MTFW 2005; RGWL 2, 3

Brodsky, Joseph .. **CLC 4, 6, 13, 36, 100; PC
9**
See Brodsky, Iosif Alexandrovich
See also AAYA 71; AMWS 8; CWW 2;
DLB 285, 329; EWL 3; MTCW 1

Brodsky, Michael 1948- .... **CLC 19**
See also CA 102; CANR 18, 41, 58, 147;
DLB 244

Brodsky, Michael Mark
See Brodsky, Michael

Brodzki, Bella .... **CLC 65**

Brome, Richard 1590(?)-1652 .... **LC 61**
See also BRWS 10; DLB 58

Bromell, Henry 1947- .... **CLC 5**
See also CA 53-56; CANR 9, 115, 116

Bromfield, Louis (Brucker)
1896-1956 .... **TCLC 11**
See also CA 107; 155; DLB 4, 9, 86; RGAL
4; RHW

Broner, E(sther) M(asserman)
1930- .... **CLC 19**
See also CA 17-20R; CANR 8, 25, 72; CN
4, 5, 6; DLB 28

Bronk, William (M.) 1918-1999 .... **CLC 10**
See also CA 89-92; 177; CANR 23; CP 3,
4, 5, 6, 7; DLB 165

Bronstein, Lev Davidovich
See Trotsky, Leon

Bronte, Anne
See Bronte, Anne

Bronte, Anne 1820-1849 ..... **NCLC 4, 71, 102**
See also BRW 5; BRWR 1; DA3; DLB 21,
199, 340; NFS 26; TEA

Bronte, (Patrick) Branwell
1817-1848 .... **NCLC 109**
See also DLB 340

Bronte, Charlotte
See Bronte, Charlotte

Bronte, Charlotte 1816-1855 ...... **NCLC 3, 8,
33, 58, 105, 155; WLC 1**
See also AAYA 17; BRW 5; BRWC 2;
BRWR 1; BYA 2; CDBLB 1832-1890;
DA; DA3; DAB; DAC; DAM MST, NOV;
DLB 21, 159, 199, 340; EXPN; FL 1:2;
GL 2; LAIT 2; NFS 4; TEA; WLIT 4

Bronte, Emily
See Bronte, Emily (Jane)

Bronte, Emily (Jane) 1818-1848 ... **NCLC 16,
35, 165; PC 8; WLC 1**
See also AAYA 17; BPFB 1; BRW 5;
BRWC 1; BRWR 1; BYA 3; CDBLB
1832-1890; DA; DA3; DAB; DAC; DAM
MST, NOV, POET; DLB 21, 32, 199, 340;
EXPN; FL 1:2; GL 2; LAIT 1; TEA;
WLIT 3

Brontes
See Bronte, Anne; Bronte, (Patrick) Bran-
well; Bronte, Charlotte; Bronte, Emily
(Jane)

Brooke, Frances 1724-1789 .... **LC 6, 48**
See also DLB 39, 99

Brooke, Henry 1703(?)-1783 .... **LC 1**
See also DLB 39

Brooke, Rupert (Chawner)
1887-1915 .. **PC 24; TCLC 2, 7; WLC 1**
See also BRWS 3; CA 104; 132; CANR 61;
CDBLB 1914-1945; DA; DAB; DAC;
DAM MST, POET; DLB 19, 216; EXPP;
GLL 2; MTCW 1, 2; MTFW 2005; PFS
7; TEA

Brooke-Haven, P.
See Wodehouse, P(elham) G(renville)

Brooke-Rose, Christine 1926(?)- .... **CLC 40,
184**
See also BRWS 4; CA 13-16R; CANR 58,
118; CN 1, 2, 3, 4, 5, 6, 7; DLB 14, 231;
EWL 3; SFW 4

Brookner, Anita 1928- . **CLC 32, 34, 51, 136,
237**
See also BRWS 4; CA 114; 120; CANR 37,
56, 87, 130; CN 4, 5, 6, 7; CPW; DA3;
DAB; DAM POP; DLB 194, 326; DLBY
1987; EWL 3; MTCW 1, 2; MTFW 2005;
NFS 23; TEA

Brooks, Cleanth 1906-1994 . **CLC 24, 86, 110**
See also AMWS 14; CA 17-20R; 145;
CANR 33, 35; CSW; DLB 63; DLBY
1994; EWL 3; INT CANR-35; MAL 5;
MTCW 1, 2; MTFW 2005

Brooks, George
See Baum, L(yman) Frank

Byars, Betsy 1928- .... **CLC 35**
　　See also AAYA 19; BYA 3; CA 33-36R,
　　183; CAAE 183; CANR 18, 36, 57, 102,
　　148; CLR 1, 16, 72; DLB 52; INT CANR-
　　18; JRDA; MAICYA 1, 2; MAICYAS 1;
　　MTCW 1; SAAS 1; SATA 4, 46, 80, 163;
　　SATA-Essay 108; WYA; YAW

Byars, Betsy Cromer
　　See Byars, Betsy

Byatt, Antonia Susan Drabble
　　See Byatt, A.S.

Byatt, A.S. 1936- .... **CLC 19, 65, 136, 223;**
　　SSC 91
　　See also BPFB 1; BRWC 2; BRWS 4; CA
　　13-16R; CANR 13, 33, 50, 75, 96, 133;
　　CN 1, 2, 3, 4, 5, 6; DA3; DAM NOV,
　　POP; DLB 14, 194, 319, 326; EWL 3;
　　MTCW 1, 2; MTFW 2005; RGSF 2;
　　RHW; TEA

Byrd, William II 1674-1744 .... **LC 112**
　　See also DLB 24, 140; RGAL 4

Byrne, David 1952- .... **CLC 26**
　　See also CA 127

Byrne, John Keyes 1926-
　　See Leonard, Hugh
　　See also CA 102; CANR 78, 140; INT CA-
　　102

Byron, George Gordon (Noel)
　　1788-1824 ..... **DC 24; NCLC 2, 12, 109,**
　　149; PC 16; WLC 1
　　See also AAYA 64; BRW 4; BRWC 2; CD-
　　BLB 1789-1832; DA; DA3; DAB; DAC;
　　DAM MST, POET; DLB 96, 110; EXPP;
　　LMFS 1; PAB; PFS 1, 14; RGEL 2; TEA;
　　WLIT 3; WP

Byron, Robert 1905-1941 .... **TCLC 67**
　　See also CA 160; DLB 195

C. 3. 3.
　　See Wilde, Oscar

Caballero, Fernan 1796-1877 .... **NCLC 10**

Cabell, Branch
　　See Cabell, James Branch

Cabell, James Branch 1879-1958 .... **TCLC 6**
　　See also CA 105; 152; DLB 9, 78; FANT;
　　MAL 5; MTCW 2; RGAL 4; SUFW 1

Cabeza de Vaca, Alvar Nunez 1490-1557(?)
　　LC 61

Cable, George Washington
　　1844-1925 .... **SSC 4; TCLC 4**
　　See also CA 104; 155; DLB 12, 74; DLBD
　　13; RGAL 4; TUS

Cabral de Melo Neto, Joao
　　1920-1999 .... **CLC 76**
　　See Melo Neto, Joao Cabral de
　　See also CA 151; DAM MULT; DLB 307;
　　LAW; LAWS 1

Cabrera Infante, G. 1929-2005 ... **CLC 5, 25,**
　　45, 120; HLC 1; SSC 39
　　See also CA 85-88; 236; CANR 29, 65, 110;
　　CDWLB 3; CWW 2; DA3; DAM MULT;
　　DLB 113; EWL 3; HW 1, 2; LAW; LAWS
　　1; MTCW 1, 2; MTFW 2005; RGSF 2;
　　WLIT 1

Cabrera Infante, Guillermo
　　See Cabrera Infante, G.

Cade, Toni
　　See Bambara, Toni Cade

Cadmus and Harmonia
　　See Buchan, John

Caedmon fl. 658-680 .... **CMLC 7**
　　See also DLB 146

Caeiro, Alberto
　　See Pessoa, Fernando (Antonio Nogueira)

Caesar, Julius .... **CMLC 47**
　　See Julius Caesar
　　See also AW 1; RGWL 2, 3; WLIT 8

Cage, John (Milton), (Jr.)
　　1912-1992 .... **CLC 41; PC 58**
　　See also CA 13-16R; 169; CANR 9, 78;
　　DLB 193; INT CANR-9; TCLE 1:1

Cahan, Abraham 1860-1951 .... **TCLC 71**
　　See also CA 108; 154; DLB 9, 25, 28; MAL
　　5; RGAL 4

Cain, G.
　　See Cabrera Infante, G.

Cain, Guillermo
　　See Cabrera Infante, G.

Cain, James M(allahan) 1892-1977 .. **CLC 3,**
　　11, 28
　　See also AITN 1; BPFB 1; CA 17-20R; 73-
　　76; CANR 8, 34, 61; CMW 4; CN 1, 2;
　　DLB 226; EWL 3; MAL 5; MSW; MTCW
　　1; RGAL 4

Caine, Hall 1853-1931 .... **TCLC 97**
　　See also RHW

Caine, Mark
　　See Raphael, Frederic (Michael)

Calasso, Roberto 1941- .... **CLC 81**
　　See also CA 143; CANR 89

Calderon de la Barca, Pedro
　　1600-1681 . **DC 3; HLCS 1; LC 23, 136**
　　See also DFS 23; EW 2; RGWL 2, 3; TWA

Caldwell, Erskine 1903-1987 ... **CLC 1, 8, 14,**
　　50, 60; SSC 19; TCLC 117
　　See also AITN 1; AMW; BPFB 1; CA 1-4R;
　　121; CAAS 1; CANR 2, 33; CN 1, 2, 3,
　　4; DA3; DAM NOV; DLB 9, 86; EWL 3;
　　MAL 5; MTCW 1, 2; MTFW 2005;
　　RGAL 4; RGSF 2; TUS

Caldwell, (Janet Miriam) Taylor (Holland)
　　1900-1985 .... **CLC 2, 28, 39**
　　See also BPFB 1; CA 5-8R; 116; CANR 5;
　　DA3; DAM NOV, POP; DLBD 17;
　　MTCW 2; RHW

Calhoun, John Caldwell
　　1782-1850 .... **NCLC 15**
　　See also DLB 3, 248

Calisher, Hortense 1911- ..... **CLC 2, 4, 8, 38,**
　　134; SSC 15
　　See also CA 1-4R; CANR 1, 22, 117; CN
　　1, 2, 3, 4, 5, 6, 7; DA3; DAM NOV; DLB
　　2, 218; INT CANR-22; MAL 5; MTCW
　　1, 2; MTFW 2005; RGAL 4; RGSF 2

Callaghan, Morley Edward
　　1903-1990 ..... **CLC 3, 14, 41, 65; TCLC**
　　145
　　See also CA 9-12R; 132; CANR 33, 73;
　　CN 1, 2, 3, 4; DAC; DAM MST; DLB
　　68; EWL 3; MTCW 1, 2; MTFW 2005;
　　RGEL 2; RGSF 2; SSFS 19

Callimachus c. 305B.C.-c.
　　240B.C. .... **CMLC 18**
　　See also AW 1; DLB 176; RGWL 2, 3

Calvin, Jean
　　See Calvin, John
　　See also DLB 327; GFL Beginnings to 1789

Calvin, John 1509-1564 .... **LC 37**
　　See Calvin, Jean

Calvino, Italo 1923-1985 .... **CLC 5, 8, 11, 22,**
　　33, 39, 73; SSC 3, 48; TCLC 183
　　See also AAYA 58; CA 85-88; 116; CANR
　　23, 61, 132; DAM NOV; DLB 196; EW
　　13; EWL 3; MTCW 1, 2; MTFW 2005;
　　RGHL; RGSF 2; RGWL 2, 3; SFW 4;
　　SSFS 12; WLIT 7

Camara Laye
　　See Laye, Camara
　　See also EWL 3

Camden, William 1551-1623 .... **LC 77**
　　See also DLB 172

Cameron, Carey 1952- .... **CLC 59**
　　See also CA 135

Cameron, Peter 1959- .... **CLC 44**
　　See also AMWS 12; CA 125; CANR 50,
　　117; DLB 234; GLL 2

Camoens, Luis Vaz de 1524(?)-1580
　　See Camoes, Luis de
　　See also EW 2

Camoes, Luis de 1524(?)-1580 . **HLCS 1; LC**
　　62; PC 31
　　See Camoens, Luis Vaz de
　　See also DLB 287; RGWL 2, 3

Camp, Madeleine L'Engle
　　See L'Engle, Madeleine

Campana, Dino 1885-1932 .... **TCLC 20**
　　See also CA 117; 246; DLB 114; EWL 3

Campanella, Tommaso 1568-1639 .... **LC 32**
　　See also RGWL 2, 3

Campbell, Bebe Moore 1950-2006 . **BLC 2:1;**
　　CLC 246
　　See also AAYA 26; BW 2, 3; CA 139; 254;
　　CANR 81, 134; DLB 227; MTCW 2;
　　MTFW 2005

Campbell, John Ramsey
　　See Campbell, Ramsey

Campbell, John W(ood, Jr.)
　　1910-1971 .... **CLC 32**
　　See also CA 21-22; 29-32R; CANR 34;
　　CAP 2; DLB 8; MTCW 1; SCFW 1, 2;
　　SFW 4

Campbell, Joseph 1904-1987 .... **CLC 69;**
　　TCLC 140
　　See also AAYA 3, 66; BEST 89:2; CA 1-4R;
　　124; CANR 3, 28, 61, 107; DA3; MTCW
　　1, 2

Campbell, Maria 1940- .... **CLC 85; NNAL**
　　See also CA 102; CANR 54; CCA 1; DAC

Campbell, Ramsey 1946- ... **CLC 42; SSC 19**
　　See also AAYA 51; CA 57-60, 228; CAAE
　　228; CANR 7, 102, 171; DLB 261; HGG;
　　INT CANR-7; SUFW 1, 2

Campbell, (Ignatius) Roy (Dunnachie)
　　1901-1957 .... **TCLC 5**
　　See also AFW; CA 104; 155; DLB 20, 225;
　　EWL 3; MTCW 2; RGEL 2

Campbell, Thomas 1777-1844 .... **NCLC 19**
　　See also DLB 93, 144; RGEL 2

Campbell, Wilfred .... **TCLC 9**
　　See Campbell, William

Campbell, William 1858(?)-1918
　　See Campbell, Wilfred
　　See also CA 106; DLB 92

Campbell, William Edward March
　　1893-1954
　　See March, William
　　See also CA 108

Campion, Jane 1954- .... **CLC 95, 229**
　　See also AAYA 33; CA 138; CANR 87

Campion, Thomas 1567-1620 . **LC 78; PC 87**
　　See also CDBLB Before 1660; DAM POET;
　　DLB 58, 172; RGEL 2

Camus, Albert 1913-1960 ...... **CLC 1, 2, 4, 9,**
　　11, 14, 32, 63, 69, 124; DC 2; SSC 9,
　　76; WLC 1
　　See also AAYA 36; AFW; BPFB 1; CA 89-
　　92; CANR 131; DA; DA3; DAB; DAC;
　　DAM DRAM, MST, NOV; DLB 72, 321,
　　329; EW 13; EWL 3; EXPN; EXPS; GFL
　　1789 to the Present; LATS 1:2; LMFS 2;
　　MTCW 1, 2; MTFW 2005; NFS 6, 16;
　　RGHL; RGSF 2; RGWL 2, 3; SSFS 4;
　　TWA

Canby, Vincent 1924-2000 .... **CLC 13**
　　See also CA 81-84; 191

Cancale
　　See Desnos, Robert

Canetti, Elias 1905-1994 .. **CLC 3, 14, 25, 75,**
　　86; TCLC 157
　　See also CA 21-24R; 146; CANR 23, 61,
　　79; CDWLB 2; CWW 2; DA3; DLB 85,
　　124, 329; EW 12; EWL 3; MTCW 1, 2;
　　MTFW 2005; RGWL 2, 3; TWA

Canfield, Dorothea F.
　　See Fisher, Dorothy (Frances) Canfield

Chin, Frank (Chew, Jr.) 1940- .... **AAL; CLC 135; DC 7**
See also CA 33-36R; CAD; CANR 71; CD 5, 6; DAM MULT; DLB 206, 312; LAIT 5; RGAL 4

Chin, Marilyn (Mei Ling) 1955- .... **PC 40**
See also CA 129; CANR 70, 113; CWP; DLB 312; PFS 28

Chislett, (Margaret) Anne 1943- ...... **CLC 34**
See also CA 151

Chitty, Thomas Willes 1926- .... **CLC 11**
See Hinde, Thomas
See also CA 5-8R; CN 7

Chivers, Thomas Holley
1809-1858 .... **NCLC 49**
See also DLB 3, 248; RGAL 4

Choi, Susan 1969- .... **CLC 119**
See also CA 223

Chomette, Rene Lucien 1898-1981
See Clair, Rene
See also CA 103

Chomsky, Avram Noam
See Chomsky, Noam

Chomsky, Noam 1928- .... **CLC 132**
See also CA 17-20R; CANR 28, 62, 110, 132; DA3; DLB 246; MTCW 1, 2; MTFW 2005

Chona, Maria 1845(?)-1936 .... **NNAL**
See also CA 144

Chopin, Kate ..... **SSC 8, 68, 110; TCLC 127; WLCS**
See Chopin, Katherine
See also AAYA 33; AMWR 2; AMWS 1; BYA 11, 15; CDALB 1865-1917; DA; DAB; DLB 12, 78; EXPN; EXPS; FL 1:3; FW; LAIT 3; MAL 5; MBL; NFS 3; RGAL 4; RGSF 2; SSFS 2, 13, 17; TUS

Chopin, Katherine 1851-1904
See Chopin, Kate
See also CA 104; 122; DA3; DAC; DAM MST, NOV

Chretien de Troyes c. 12th cent. - . **CMLC 10**
See also DLB 208; EW 1; RGWL 2, 3; TWA

Christie
See Ichikawa, Kon

Christie, Agatha (Mary Clarissa) 1890-1976
CLC 1, 6, 8, 12, 39, 48, 110
See also AAYA 9; AITN 1, 2; BPFB 1; BRWS 2; CA 17-20R; 61-64; CANR 10, 37, 108; CBD; CDBLB 1914-1945; CMW 4; CN 1, 2; CPW; CWD; DA3; DAB; DAC; DAM NOV; DFS 2; DLB 13, 77, 245; MSW; MTCW 1, 2; MTFW 2005; NFS 8; RGEL 2; RHW; SATA 36; TEA; YAW

Christie, Philippa .... **CLC 21**
See Pearce, Philippa
See also BYA 5; CANR 109; CLR 9; DLB 161; MAICYA 1; SATA 1, 67, 129

Christine de Pisan
See Christine de Pizan
See also FW

Christine de Pizan 1365(?)-1431(?) ...... **LC 9, 130; PC 68**
See Christine de Pisan; de Pizan, Christine
See also DLB 208; FL 1:1; RGWL 2, 3

Chuang-Tzu c. 369B.C.-c.
286B.C. .... **CMLC 57**

Chubb, Elmer
See Masters, Edgar Lee

Chulkov, Mikhail Dmitrievich
1743-1792 .... **LC 2**
See also DLB 150

Churchill, Caryl 1938- .... **CLC 31, 55, 157; DC 5**
See Churchill, Chick
See also BRWS 4; CA 102; CANR 22, 46, 108; CBD; CD 6; CWD; DFS 25; DLB 13, 310; EWL 3; FW; MTCW 1; RGEL 2

Churchill, Charles 1731-1764 .... **LC 3**
See also DLB 109; RGEL 2

Churchill, Chick
See Churchill, Caryl
See also CD 5

Churchill, Sir Winston (Leonard Spencer)
1874-1965 .... **TCLC 113**
See also BRW 6; CA 97-100; CDBLB 1890-1914; DA3; DLB 100, 329; DLBD 16; LAIT 4; MTCW 1, 2

Chute, Carolyn 1947- .... **CLC 39**
See also CA 123; CANR 135; CN 7

Ciardi, John (Anthony) 1916-1986 . **CLC 10, 40, 44, 129; PC 69**
See also CA 5-8R; 118; CAAS 2; CANR 5, 33; CLR 19; CP 1, 2, 3, 4; CWRI 5; DAM POET; DLB 5; DLBY 1986; INT CANR-5; MAICYA 1, 2; MAL 5; MTCW 1, 2; MTFW 2005; RGAL 4; SAAS 26; SATA 1, 65; SATA-Obit 46

Cibber, Colley 1671-1757 .... **LC 66**
See also DLB 84; RGEL 2

Cicero, Marcus Tullius 106B.C.-43B.C.
CMLC 3, 81
See also AW 1; CDWLB 1; DLB 211; RGWL 2, 3; WLIT 8

Cimino, Michael 1943- .... **CLC 16**
See also CA 105

Cioran, E(mil) M. 1911-1995 .... **CLC 64**
See also CA 25-28R; 149; CANR 91; DLB 220; EWL 3

Cisneros, Sandra 1954- .... **CLC 69, 118, 193; HLC 1; PC 52; SSC 32, 72**
See also AAYA 9, 53; AMWS 7; CA 131; CANR 64, 118; CLR 123; CN 7; CWP; DA3; DAM MULT; DLB 122, 152; EWL 3; EXPN; FL 1:5; FW; HW 1, 2; LAIT 5; LATS 1:2; LLW; MAICYA 2; MAL 5; MTCW 2; MTFW 2005; NFS 2; PFS 19; RGAL 4; RGSF 2; SSFS 3, 13; WLIT 1; YAW

Cixous, Helene 1937- .... **CLC 92, 253**
See also CA 126; CANR 55, 123; CWW 2; DLB 83, 242; EWL 3; FL 1:5; FW; GLL 2; MTCW 1, 2; MTFW 2005; TWA

Clair, Rene .... **CLC 20**
See Chomette, Rene Lucien

Clampitt, Amy 1920-1994 .... **CLC 32; PC 19**
See also AMWS 9; CA 110; 146; CANR 29, 79; CP 4, 5; DLB 105; MAL 5; PFS 27

Clancy, Thomas L., Jr. 1947-
See Clancy, Tom
See also CA 125; 131; CANR 62, 105; DA3; INT CA-131; MTCW 1, 2; MTFW 2005

Clancy, Tom .... **CLC 45, 112**
See Clancy, Thomas L., Jr.
See also AAYA 9, 51; BEST 89:1, 90:1; BPFB 1; BYA 10, 11; CANR 132; CMW 4; CPW; DAM NOV, POP; DLB 227

Clare, John 1793-1864 .. **NCLC 9, 86; PC 23**
See also BRWS 11; DAB; DAM POET; DLB 55, 96; RGEL 2

Clarin
See Alas (y Urena), Leopoldo (Enrique Garcia)

Clark, Al C.
See Goines, Donald

Clark, Brian (Robert)
See Clark, (Robert) Brian
See also CD 6

Clark, (Robert) Brian 1932- .... **CLC 29**
See Clark, Brian (Robert)
See also CA 41-44R; CANR 67; CBD; CD 5

Clark, Curt
See Westlake, Donald E.

Clark, Eleanor 1913-1996 .... **CLC 5, 19**
See also CA 9-12R; 151; CANR 41; CN 1, 2, 3, 4, 5, 6; DLB 6

Clark, J. P.
See Clark Bekederemo, J.P.
See also CDWLB 3; DLB 117

Clark, John Pepper
See Clark Bekederemo, J.P.
See also AFW; CD 5; CP 1, 2, 3, 4, 5, 6, 7; RGEL 2

Clark, Kenneth (Mackenzie) 1903-1983
TCLC 147
See also CA 93-96; 109; CANR 36; MTCW 1, 2; MTFW 2005

Clark, M. R.
See Clark, Mavis Thorpe

Clark, Mavis Thorpe 1909-1999 ...... **CLC 12**
See also CA 57-60; CANR 8, 37, 107; CLR 30; CWRI 5; MAICYA 1, 2; SAAS 5; SATA 8, 74

Clark, Walter Van Tilburg
1909-1971 .... **CLC 28**
See also CA 9-12R; 33-36R; CANR 63, 113; CN 1; DLB 9, 206; LAIT 2; MAL 5; RGAL 4; SATA 8; TCWW 1, 2

Clark Bekederemo, J.P. 1935- .... **BLC 1:1; CLC 38; DC 5**
See Bekederemo, J. P. Clark; Clark, J. P.; Clark, John Pepper
See also BW 1; CA 65-68; CANR 16, 72; DAM DRAM, MULT; DFS 13; EWL 3; MTCW 2; MTFW 2005

Clarke, Arthur C. 1917-2008 .. **CLC 1, 4, 13, 18, 35, 136; SSC 3**
See also AAYA 4, 33; BPFB 1; BYA 13; CA 1-4R; CANR 2, 28, 55, 74, 130; CLR 119; CN 1, 2, 3, 4, 5, 6, 7; CPW; DA3; DAM POP; DLB 261; JRDA; LAIT 5; MAICYA 1, 2; MTCW 1, 2; MTFW 2005; SATA 13, 70, 115; SCFW 1, 2; SFW 4; SSFS 4, 18; TCLE 1:1; YAW

Clarke, Arthur Charles
See Clarke, Arthur C.

Clarke, Austin 1896-1974 .... **CLC 6, 9**
See also CA 29-32; 49-52; CAP 2; CP 1, 2; DAM POET; DLB 10, 20; EWL 3; RGEL 2

Clarke, Austin C. 1934- .... **BLC 1:1; CLC 8, 53; SSC 45**
See also BW 1; CA 25-28R; CAAS 16; CANR 14, 32, 68, 140; CN 1, 2, 3, 4, 5, 6, 7; DAC; DAM MULT; DLB 53, 125; DNFS 2; MTCW 2; MTFW 2005; RGSF 2

Clarke, Gillian 1937- .... **CLC 61**
See also CA 106; CP 3, 4, 5, 6, 7; CWP; DLB 40

Clarke, Marcus (Andrew Hislop) 1846-1881
NCLC 19; SSC 94
See also DLB 230; RGEL 2; RGSF 2

Clarke, Shirley 1925-1997 .... **CLC 16**
See also CA 189

Clash, The
See Headon, (Nicky) Topper; Jones, Mick; Simonon, Paul; Strummer, Joe

Claudel, Paul (Louis Charles Marie)
1868-1955 .... **TCLC 2, 10**
See also CA 104; 165; DLB 192, 258, 321; EW 8; EWL 3; GFL 1789 to the Present; RGWL 2, 3; TWA

Claudian 370(?)-404(?) .... **CMLC 46**
See also RGWL 2, 3

Claudius, Matthias 1740-1815 .... **NCLC 75**
See also DLB 97

Clavell, James 1925-1994 .... **CLC 6, 25, 87**
See also BPFB 1; CA 25-28R; 146; CANR 26, 48; CN 5; CPW; DA3; DAM NOV, POP; MTCW 1, 2; MTFW 2005; NFS 10; RHW

Croves, Hal
    See Traven, B.
Crow Dog, Mary (?)- .... **CLC 93; NNAL**
    See also CA 154
Crowfield, Christopher
    See Stowe, Harriet (Elizabeth) Beecher
Crowley, Aleister .... **TCLC 7**
    See Crowley, Edward Alexander
    See also GLL 1
Crowley, Edward Alexander 1875-1947
    See Crowley, Aleister
    See also CA 104; HGG
Crowley, John 1942- .... **CLC 57**
    See also AAYA 57; BPFB 1; CA 61-64;
    CANR 43, 98, 138; DLBY 1982; FANT;
    MTFW 2005; SATA 65, 140; SFW 4;
    SUFW 2
Crowne, John 1641-1712 .... **LC 104**
    See also DLB 80; RGEL 2
Crud
    See Crumb, R.
Crumarums
    See Crumb, R.
Crumb, R. 1943- .... **CLC 17**
    See also CA 106; CANR 107, 150
Crumb, Robert
    See Crumb, R.
Crumbum
    See Crumb, R.
Crumski
    See Crumb, R.
Crum the Bum
    See Crumb, R.
Crunk
    See Crumb, R.
Crustt
    See Crumb, R.
Crutchfield, Les
    See Trumbo, Dalton
Cruz, Victor Hernandez 1949- ... **HLC 1; PC 37**
    See also BW 2; CA 65-68; CAAS 17;
    CANR 14, 32, 74, 132; CP 1, 2, 3, 4, 5,
    6, 7; DAM MULT, POET; DLB 41; DNFS
    1; EXPP; HW 1, 2; LLW; MTCW 2;
    MTFW 2005; PFS 16; WP
Cryer, Gretchen (Kiger) 1935- .... **CLC 21**
    See also CA 114; 123
Csath, Geza .... **TCLC 13**
    See Brenner, Jozef
    See also CA 111
Cudlip, David R(ockwell) 1933- .... **CLC 34**
    See also CA 177
Cullen, Countee 1903-1946 ..... **BLC 1:1; HR 1:2; PC 20; TCLC 4, 37; WLCS**
    See also AFAW 2; AMWS 4; BW 1; CA
    108; 124; CDALB 1917-1929; DA; DA3;
    DAC; DAM MST, MULT, POET; DLB 4,
    48, 51; EWL 3; EXPP; LMFS 2; MAL 5;
    MTCW 1, 2; MTFW 2005; PFS 3; RGAL
    4; SATA 18; WP
Culleton, Beatrice 1949- .... **NNAL**
    See also CA 120; CANR 83; DAC
Cum, R.
    See Crumb, R.
Cumberland, Richard
    1732-1811 .... **NCLC 167**
    See also DLB 89; RGEL 2
Cummings, Bruce F(rederick) 1889-1919
    See Barbellion, W. N. P.
    See also CA 123
Cummings, E(dward) E(stlin) 1894-1962
    CLC 1, 3, 8, 12, 15, 68; PC 5; TCLC 137; WLC 2
    See also AAYA 41; AMW; CA 73-76;
    CANR 31; CDALB 1929-1941; DA;
    DA3; DAB; DAC; DAM MST, POET;

DLB 4, 48; EWL 3; EXPP; MAL 5;
MTCW 1, 2; MTFW 2005; PAB; PFS 1,
3, 12, 13, 19; RGAL 4; TUS; WP
Cummins, Maria Susanna
    1827-1866 .... **NCLC 139**
    See also DLB 42; YABC 1
Cunha, Euclides (Rodrigues Pimenta) da
    1866-1909 .... **TCLC 24**
    See also CA 123; 219; DLB 307; LAW;
    WLIT 1
Cunningham, E. V.
    See Fast, Howard
Cunningham, J(ames) V(incent) 1911-1985
    CLC 3, 31
    See also CA 1-4R; 115; CANR 1, 72; CP 1,
    2, 3, 4; DLB 5
Cunningham, Julia (Woolfolk)
    1916- .... **CLC 12**
    See also CA 9-12R; CANR 4, 19, 36; CWRI
    5; JRDA; MAICYA 1, 2; SAAS 2; SATA
    1, 26, 132
Cunningham, Michael 1952- .... **CLC 34, 243**
    See also AMWS 15; CA 136; CANR 96,
    160; CN 7; DLB 292; GLL 2; MTFW
    2005; NFS 23
Cunninghame Graham, R. B.
    See Cunninghame Graham, Robert
    (Gallnigad) Bontine
Cunninghame Graham, Robert (Gallnigad)
    Bontine 1852-1936 .... **TCLC 19**
    See Graham, R(obert) B(ontine) Cunning-
    hame
    See also CA 119; 184
Curnow, (Thomas) Allen (Monro) 1911-2001
    PC 48
    See also CA 69-72; 202; CANR 48, 99; CP
    1, 2, 3, 4, 5, 6, 7; EWL 3; RGEL 2
Currie, Ellen 19(?)- .... **CLC 44**
Curtin, Philip
    See Lowndes, Marie Adelaide (Belloc)
Curtin, Phillip
    See Lowndes, Marie Adelaide (Belloc)
Curtis, Price
    See Ellison, Harlan
Cusanus, Nicolaus 1401-1464 .... **LC 80**
    See Nicholas of Cusa
Cutrate, Joe
    See Spiegelman, Art
Cynewulf c. 770- .... **CMLC 23**
    See also DLB 146; RGEL 2
Cyrano de Bergerac, Savinien de 1619-1655
    LC 65
    See also DLB 268; GFL Beginnings to
    1789; RGWL 2, 3
Cyril of Alexandria c. 375-c. 430 . **CMLC 59**
Czaczkes, Shmuel Yosef Halevi
    See Agnon, S(hmuel) Y(osef Halevi)
Dabrowska, Maria (Szumska) 1889-1965
    CLC 15
    See also CA 106; CDWLB 4; DLB 215;
    EWL 3
Dabydeen, David 1955- .... **CLC 34**
    See also BW 1; CA 125; CANR 56, 92; CN
    6, 7; CP 5, 6, 7
Dacey, Philip 1939- .... **CLC 51**
    See also CA 37-40R, 231; CAAE 231;
    CAAS 17; CANR 14, 32, 64; CP 4, 5, 6,
    7; DLB 105
Dacre, Charlotte c. 1772-1825(?) . **NCLC 151**
Dafydd ap Gwilym c. 1320-c. 1380 ..... **PC 56**
Dagerman, Stig (Halvard)
    1923-1954 .... **TCLC 17**
    See also CA 117; 155; DLB 259; EWL 3
D'Aguiar, Fred 1960- ..... **BLC 2:1; CLC 145**
    See also CA 148; CANR 83, 101; CN 7;
    CP 5, 6, 7; DLB 157; EWL 3

Dahl, Roald 1916-1990 ...... **CLC 1, 6, 18, 79;**
    TCLC 173
    See also AAYA 15; BPFB 1; BRWS 4; BYA
    5; CA 1-4R; 133; CANR 6, 32, 37, 62;
    CLR 1, 7, 41, 111; CN 1, 2, 3, 4; CPW;
    DA3; DAB; DAC; DAM MST, NOV,
    POP; DLB 139, 255; HGG; JRDA; MAI-
    CYA 1, 2; MTCW 1, 2; MTFW 2005;
    RGSF 2; SATA 1, 26, 73; SATA-Obit 65;
    SSFS 4; TEA; YAW
Dahlberg, Edward 1900-1977 .. **CLC 1, 7, 14**
    See also CA 9-12R; 69-72; CANR 31, 62;
    CN 1, 2; DLB 48; MAL 5; MTCW 1;
    RGAL 4
Daitch, Susan 1954- .... **CLC 103**
    See also CA 161
Dale, Colin .... **TCLC 18**
    See Lawrence, T(homas) E(dward)
Dale, George E.
    See Asimov, Isaac
d'Alembert, Jean Le Rond
    1717-1783 .... **LC 126**
Dalton, Roque 1935-1975(?) ..... **HLCS 1; PC 36**
    See also CA 176; DLB 283; HW 2
Daly, Elizabeth 1878-1967 .... **CLC 52**
    See also CA 23-24; 25-28R; CANR 60;
    CAP 2; CMW 4
Daly, Mary 1928- .... **CLC 173**
    See also CA 25-28R; CANR 30, 62, 166;
    FW; GLL 1; MTCW 1
Daly, Maureen 1921-2006 .... **CLC 17**
    See also AAYA 5, 58; BYA 6; CA 253;
    CANR 37, 83, 108; CLR 96; JRDA; MAI-
    CYA 1, 2; SAAS 1; SATA 2, 129; SATA-
    Obit 176; WYA; YAW
Damas, Leon-Gontran 1912-1978 ... **CLC 84;**
    TCLC 204
    See also BW 1; CA 125; 73-76; EWL 3
Dana, Richard Henry Sr.
    1787-1879 .... **NCLC 53**
Dangarembga, Tsitsi 1959- .... **BLC 2:1**
    See also BW 3; CA 163; WLIT 2
Daniel, Samuel 1562(?)-1619 .... **LC 24**
    See also DLB 62; RGEL 2
Daniels, Brett
    See Adler, Renata
Dannay, Frederic 1905-1982 .... **CLC 11**
    See Queen, Ellery
    See also CA 1-4R; 107; CANR 1, 39; CMW
    4; DAM POP; DLB 137; MTCW 1
D'Annunzio, Gabriele 1863-1938 ... **TCLC 6,**
    40
    See also CA 104; 155; EW 8; EWL 3;
    RGWL 2, 3; TWA; WLIT 7
Danois, N. le
    See Gourmont, Remy(-Marie-Charles) de
Dante 1265-1321 .... **CMLC 3, 18, 39, 70; PC**
    21; WLCS
    See Alighieri, Dante
    See also DA; DA3; DAB; DAC; DAM
    MST, POET; EFS 1; EW 1; LAIT 1;
    RGWL 2, 3; TWA; WP
d'Antibes, Germain
    See Simenon, Georges (Jacques Christian)
Danticat, Edwidge 1969- . **BLC 2:1; CLC 94,**
    139, 228; SSC 100
    See also AAYA 29; CA 152, 192; CAAE
    192; CANR 73, 129; CN 7; DNFS 1;
    EXPS; LATS 1:2; MTCW 2; MTFW
    2005; SSFS 1, 25; YAW
Danvers, Dennis 1947- .... **CLC 70**
Danziger, Paula 1944-2004 .... **CLC 21**
    See also AAYA 4, 36; BYA 6, 7, 14; CA
    112; 115; 229; CANR 37, 132; CLR 20;
    JRDA; MAICYA 1, 2; MTFW 2005;
    SATA 36, 63, 102, 149; SATA-Brief 30;
    SATA-Obit 155; WYA; YAW

Da Ponte, Lorenzo 1749-1838 .... **NCLC 50**

d'Aragona, Tullia 1510(?)-1556 .... **LC 121**

Dario, Ruben 1867-1916 .... **HLC 1; PC 15;
TCLC 4**
See also CA 131; CANR 81; DAM MULT;
DLB 290; EWL 3; HW 1, 2; LAW;
MTCW 1, 2; MTFW 2005; RGWL 2, 3

Darko, Amma 1956- .... **BLC 2:1**

Darley, George 1795-1846 .... **NCLC 2**
See also DLB 96; RGEL 2

Darrow, Clarence (Seward)
1857-1938 .... **TCLC 81**
See also CA 164; DLB 303

Darwin, Charles 1809-1882 .... **NCLC 57**
See also BRWS 7; DLB 57, 166; LATS 1:1;
RGEL 2; TEA; WLIT 4

Darwin, Erasmus 1731-1802 .... **NCLC 106**
See also DLB 93; RGEL 2

Darwish, Mahmoud 1942- .... **PC 86**
See Darwish, Mahmud
See also CA 164; CANR 133; MTCW 2;
MTFW 2005

Darwish, Mahmud
See Darwish, Mahmoud
See also CWW 2; EWL 3

Daryush, Elizabeth 1887-1977 ...... **CLC 6, 19**
See also CA 49-52; CANR 3, 81; DLB 20

Das, Kamala 1934- .... **CLC 191; PC 43**
See also CA 101; CANR 27, 59; CP 1, 2, 3,
4, 5, 6, 7; CWP; DLB 323; FW

Dasgupta, Surendranath
1887-1952 .... **TCLC 81**
See also CA 157

Dashwood, Edmee Elizabeth Monica de la
Pasture 1890-1943
See Delafield, E. M.
See also CA 119; 154

da Silva, Antonio Jose
1705-1739 .... **NCLC 114**

Daudet, (Louis Marie) Alphonse 1840-1897
NCLC 1
See also DLB 123; GFL 1789 to the Present;
RGSF 2

Daudet, Alphonse Marie Leon
1867-1942 .... **SSC 94**
See also CA 217

d'Aulnoy, Marie-Catherine c.
1650-1705 .... **LC 100**

Daumal, Rene 1908-1944 .... **TCLC 14**
See also CA 114; 247; EWL 3

Davenant, William 1606-1668 .... **LC 13**
See also DLB 58, 126; RGEL 2

Davenport, Guy (Mattison, Jr.) 1927-2005
CLC 6, 14, 38, 241; SSC 16
See also CA 33-36R; 235; CANR 23, 73;
CN 3, 4, 5, 6; CSW; DLB 130

David, Robert
See Nezval, Vitezslav

Davidson, Avram (James) 1923-1993
See Queen, Ellery
See also CA 101; 171; CANR 26; DLB 8;
FANT; SFW 4; SUFW 1, 2

Davidson, Donald (Grady)
1893-1968 .... **CLC 2, 13, 19**
See also CA 5-8R; 25-28R; CANR 4, 84;
DLB 45

Davidson, Hugh
See Hamilton, Edmond

Davidson, John 1857-1909 .... **TCLC 24**
See also CA 118; 217; DLB 19; RGEL 2

Davidson, Sara 1943- .... **CLC 9**
See also CA 81-84; CANR 44, 68; DLB
185

Davie, Donald (Alfred) 1922-1995 .... **CLC 5,
8, 10, 31; PC 29**
See also BRWS 6; CA 1-4R; 149; CAAS 3;
CANR 1, 44; CP 1, 2, 3, 4, 5, 6; DLB 27;
MTCW 1; RGEL 2

Davie, Elspeth 1918-1995 .... **SSC 52**
See also CA 120; 126; 150; CANR 141;
DLB 139

Davies, Ray(mond Douglas) 1944- ... **CLC 21**
See also CA 116; 146; CANR 92

Davies, Rhys 1901-1978 .... **CLC 23**
See also CA 9-12R; 81-84; CANR 4; CN 1,
2; DLB 139, 191

Davies, Robertson 1913-1995 .. **CLC 2, 7, 13,
25, 42, 75, 91; WLC 2**
See Marchbanks, Samuel
See also BEST 89:2; BPFB 1; CA 33-36R;
150; CANR 17, 42, 103; CN 1, 2, 3, 4, 5,
6; CPW; DA; DA3; DAB; DAC; DAM
MST, NOV, POP; DLB 68; EWL 3; HGG;
INT CANR-17; MTCW 1, 2; MTFW
2005; RGEL 2; TWA

Davies, Sir John 1569-1626 .... **LC 85**
See also DLB 172

Davies, Walter C.
See Kornbluth, C(yril) M.

Davies, William Henry 1871-1940 ... **TCLC 5**
See also BRWS 11; CA 104; 179; DLB 19,
174; EWL 3; RGEL 2

Davies, William Robertson
See Davies, Robertson

Da Vinci, Leonardo 1452-1519 ..... **LC 12, 57,
60**
See also AAYA 40

Davis, Angela (Yvonne) 1944- .... **CLC 77**
See also BW 2, 3; CA 57-60; CANR 10,
81; CSW; DA3; DAM MULT; FW

Davis, B. Lynch
See Bioy Casares, Adolfo; Borges, Jorge
Luis

Davis, Frank Marshall 1905-1987 ... **BLC 1:1**
See also BW 2, 3; CA 125; 123; CANR 42,
80; DAM MULT; DLB 51

Davis, Gordon
See Hunt, E. Howard

Davis, H(arold) L(enoir) 1896-1960 . **CLC 49**
See also ANW; CA 178; 89-92; DLB 9,
206; SATA 114; TCWW 1, 2

Davis, Hart
See Poniatowska, Elena

Davis, Natalie Zemon 1928- .... **CLC 204**
See also CA 53-56; CANR 58, 100, 174

Davis, Rebecca (Blaine) Harding 1831-1910
SSC 38, 109; TCLC 6
See also AMWS 16; CA 104; 179; DLB 74,
239; FW; NFS 14; RGAL 4; TUS

Davis, Richard Harding
1864-1916 .... **TCLC 24**
See also CA 114; 179; DLB 12, 23, 78, 79,
189; DLBD 13; RGAL 4

Davison, Frank Dalby 1893-1970 ..... **CLC 15**
See also CA 217; 116; DLB 260

Davison, Lawrence H.
See Lawrence, D(avid) H(erbert Richards)

Davison, Peter (Hubert) 1928-2004 . **CLC 28**
See also CA 9-12R; 234; CAAS 4; CANR
3, 43, 84; CP 1, 2, 3, 4, 5, 6, 7; DLB 5

Davys, Mary 1674-1732 .... **LC 1, 46**
See also DLB 39

Dawson, (Guy) Fielding (Lewis) 1930-2002
CLC 6
See also CA 85-88; 202; CANR 108; DLB
130; DLBY 2002

Dawson, Peter
See Faust, Frederick (Schiller)
See also TCWW 1, 2

Day, Clarence (Shepard, Jr.) 1874-1935
TCLC 25
See also CA 108; 199; DLB 11

Day, John 1574(?)-1640(?) .... **LC 70**
See also DLB 62, 170; RGEL 2

Day, Thomas 1748-1789 .... **LC 1**
See also DLB 39; YABC 1

Day Lewis, C(ecil) 1904-1972 . **CLC 1, 6, 10;
PC 11**
See Blake, Nicholas; Lewis, C. Day
See also BRWS 3; CA 13-16; 33-36R;
CANR 34; CAP 1; CP 1; CWRI 5; DAM
POET; DLB 15, 20; EWL 3; MTCW 1, 2;
RGEL 2

Dazai Osamu .... **SSC 41; TCLC 11**
See Tsushima, Shuji
See also CA 164; DLB 182; EWL 3; MJW;
RGSF 2; RGWL 2, 3; TWA

de Andrade, Carlos Drummond
See Drummond de Andrade, Carlos

de Andrade, Mario 1892(?)-1945
See Andrade, Mario de
See also CA 178; HW 2

Deane, Norman
See Creasey, John

Deane, Seamus (Francis) 1940- ...... **CLC 122**
See also CA 118; CANR 42

de Beauvoir, Simone
See Beauvoir, Simone de

de Beer, P.
See Bosman, Herman Charles

De Botton, Alain 1969- .... **CLC 203**
See also CA 159; CANR 96

de Brissac, Malcolm
See Dickinson, Peter (Malcolm de Brissac)

de Campos, Alvaro
See Pessoa, Fernando (Antonio Nogueira)

de Chardin, Pierre Teilhard
See Teilhard de Chardin, (Marie Joseph)
Pierre

de Crenne, Helisenne c. 1510-c.
1560 .... **LC 113**

Dee, John 1527-1608 .... **LC 20**
See also DLB 136, 213

Deer, Sandra 1940- .... **CLC 45**
See also CA 186

De Ferrari, Gabriella 1941- .... **CLC 65**
See also CA 146

de Filippo, Eduardo 1900-1984 ... **TCLC 127**
See also CA 132; 114; EWL 3; MTCW 1;
RGWL 2, 3

Defoe, Daniel 1660(?)-1731 .... **LC 1, 42, 108;
WLC 2**
See also AAYA 27; BRW 3; BRWR 1; BYA
4; CDBLB 1660-1789; CLR 61; DA;
DA3; DAB; DAC; DAM MST, NOV;
DLB 39, 95, 101, 336; JRDA; LAIT 1;
LMFS 1; MAICYA 1, 2; NFS 9, 13;
RGEL 2; SATA 22; TEA; WCH; WLIT 3

de Gouges, Olympe
See de Gouges, Olympe

de Gouges, Olympe 1748-1793 .... **LC 127**
See also DLB 313

de Gourmont, Remy(-Marie-Charles)
See Gourmont, Remy(-Marie-Charles) de

de Gournay, Marie le Jars
1566-1645 .... **LC 98**
See also DLB 327; FW

de Hartog, Jan 1914-2002 .... **CLC 19**
See also CA 1-4R; 210; CANR 1; DFS 12

de Hostos, E. M.
See Hostos (y Bonilla), Eugenio Maria de

de Hostos, Eugenio M.
See Hostos (y Bonilla), Eugenio Maria de

Deighton, Len .... **CLC 4, 7, 22, 46**
See Deighton, Leonard Cyril
See also AAYA 6; BEST 89:2; BPFB 1; CD-
BLB 1960 to Present; CMW 4; CN 1, 2,
3, 4, 5, 6, 7; CPW; DLB 87

Deighton, Leonard Cyril 1929-
See Deighton, Len
See also AAYA 57; CA 9-12R; CANR 19,
33, 68; DA3; DAM NOV, POP; MTCW
1, 2; MTFW 2005

Domecq, H(onorio) Bustos
See Bioy Casares, Adolfo; Borges, Jorge Luis

Domini, Rey
See Lorde, Audre
See also GLL 1

Dominique
See Proust, (Valentin-Louis-George-Eugene) Marcel

Don, A
See Stephen, Sir Leslie

Donaldson, Stephen R. 1947- ... **CLC 46, 138**
See also AAYA 36; BPFB 1; CA 89-92; CANR 13, 55, 99; CPW; DAM POP; FANT; INT CANR-13; SATA 121; SFW 4; SUFW 1, 2

Donleavy, J(ames) P(atrick) 1926- .... **CLC 1, 4, 6, 10, 45**
See also AITN 2; BPFB 1; CA 9-12R; CANR 24, 49, 62, 80, 124; CBD; CD 5, 6; CN 1, 2, 3, 4, 5, 6, 7; DLB 6, 173; INT CANR-24; MAL 5; MTCW 1, 2; MTFW 2005; RGAL 4

Donnadieu, Marguerite
See Duras, Marguerite

Donne, John 1572-1631 ... **LC 10, 24, 91; PC 1, 43; WLC 2**
See also AAYA 67; BRW 1; BRWC 1; BRWR 2; CDBLB Before 1660; DA; DAB; DAC; DAM MST, POET; DLB 121, 151; EXPP; PAB; PFS 2, 11; RGEL 3; TEA; WLIT 3; WP

Donnell, David 1939(?)- .... **CLC 34**
See also CA 197

Donoghue, Denis 1928- .... **CLC 209**
See also CA 17-20R; CANR 16, 102

Donoghue, Emma 1969- .... **CLC 239**
See also CA 155; CANR 103, 152; DLB 267; GLL 2; SATA 101

Donoghue, P.S.
See Hunt, E. Howard

Donoso (Yanez), Jose 1924-1996 ... **CLC 4, 8, 11, 32, 99; HLC 1; SSC 34; TCLC 133**
See also CA 81-84; 155; CANR 32, 73; CD-WLB 3; CWW 2; DAM MULT; DLB 113; EWL 3; HW 1, 2; LAW; LAWS 1; MTCW 1, 2; MTFW 2005; RGSF 2; WLIT 1

Donovan, John 1928-1992 .... **CLC 35**
See also AAYA 20; CA 97-100; 137; CLR 3; MAICYA 1, 2; SATA 72; SATA-Brief 29; YAW

Don Roberto
See Cunninghame Graham, Robert (Gallnigad) Bontine

Doolittle, Hilda 1886-1961 . **CLC 3, 8, 14, 31, 34, 73; PC 5; WLC 3**
See H. D.
See also AAYA 66; AMWS 1; CA 97-100; CANR 35, 131; DA; DAC; DAM MST, POET; DLB 4, 45; EWL 3; FW; GLL 1; LMFS 2; MAL 5; MBL; MTCW 1, 2; MTFW 2005; PFS 6, 28; RGAL 4

Doppo, Kunikida .... **TCLC 99**
See Kunikida Doppo

Dorfman, Ariel 1942- .... **CLC 48, 77, 189; HLC 1**
See also CA 124; 130; CANR 67, 70, 135; CWW 2; DAM MULT; DFS 4; EWL 3; HW 1, 2; INT CA-130; WLIT 1

Dorn, Edward (Merton)
1929-1999 .... **CLC 10, 18**
See also CA 93-96; 187; CANR 42, 79; CP 1, 2, 3, 4, 5, 6, 7; DLB 5; INT CA-93-96; WP

Dor-Ner, Zvi .... **CLC 70**

Dorris, Michael 1945-1997 .... **CLC 109; NNAL**
See also AAYA 20; BEST 90:1; BYA 12; CA 102; 157; CANR 19, 46, 75; CLR 58; DA3; DAM MULT, NOV; DLB 175;

LAIT 5; MTCW 2; MTFW 2005; NFS 3; RGAL 4; SATA 75; SATA-Obit 94; TCWW 2; YAW

Dorris, Michael A.
See Dorris, Michael

Dorsan, Luc
See Simenon, Georges (Jacques Christian)

Dorsange, Jean
See Simenon, Georges (Jacques Christian)

Dorset
See Sackville, Thomas

Dos Passos, John (Roderigo)
1896-1970 ... **CLC 1, 4, 8, 11, 15, 25, 34, 82; WLC 2**
See also AMW; BPFB 1; CA 1-4R; 29-32R; CANR 3; CDALB 1929-1941; DA; DA3; DAB; DAC; DAM MST, NOV; DLB 4, 9, 274, 316; DLBD 1, 15; DLBY 1996; EWL 3; MAL 5; MTCW 1, 2; MTFW 2005; NFS 14; RGAL 4; TUS

Dossage, Jean
See Simenon, Georges (Jacques Christian)

Dostoevsky, Fedor Mikhailovich 1821-1881
NCLC 2, 7, 21, 33, 43, 119, 167; SSC 2, 33, 44; WLC 2
See Dostoevsky, Fyodor
See also AAYA 40; DA; DA3; DAB; DAC; DAM MST, NOV; EW 7; EXPN; NFS 3, 8; RGSF 2; RGWL 2, 3; SSFS 8; TWA

Dostoevsky, Fyodor
See Dostoevsky, Fedor Mikhailovich
See also DLB 238; LATS 1:1; LMFS 1, 2

Doty, Mark 1953(?)- .... **CLC 176; PC 53**
See also AMWS 11; CA 161; 183; CAAE 183; CANR 110, 173; CP 7; PFS 28

Doty, Mark A.
See Doty, Mark

Doty, Mark Alan
See Doty, Mark

Doty, M.R.
See Doty, Mark

Doughty, Charles M(ontagu) 1843-1926
TCLC 27
See also CA 115; 178; DLB 19, 57, 174

Douglas, Ellen .... **CLC 73**
See Haxton, Josephine Ayres; Williamson, Ellen Douglas
See also CN 5, 6, 7; CSW; DLB 292

Douglas, Gavin 1475(?)-1522 .... **LC 20**
See also DLB 132; RGEL 2

Douglas, George
See Brown, George Douglas
See also RGEL 2

Douglas, Keith (Castellain)
1920-1944 .... **TCLC 40**
See also BRW 7; CA 160; DLB 27; EWL 3; PAB; RGEL 2

Douglas, Leonard
See Bradbury, Ray

Douglas, Michael
See Crichton, Michael

Douglas, (George) Norman
1868-1952 .... **TCLC 68**
See also BRW 6; CA 119; 157; DLB 34, 195; RGEL 2

Douglas, William
See Brown, George Douglas

Douglass, Frederick 1817(?)-1895 .. **BLC 1:1; NCLC 7, 55, 141; WLC 2**
See also AAYA 48; AFAW 1, 2; AMWC 1; AMWS 3; CDALB 1640-1865; DA; DA3; DAC; DAM MST, MULT; DLB 1, 43, 50, 79, 243; FW; LAIT 2; NCFS 2; RGAL 4; SATA 29

Dourado, (Waldomiro Freitas) Autran 1926-
CLC 23, 60
See also CA 25-28R; 179; CANR 34, 81; DLB 145, 307; HW 2

Dourado, Waldomiro Freitas Autran
See Dourado, (Waldomiro Freitas) Autran

Dove, Rita 1952- . **BLC 2:1; BLCS; CLC 50, 81; PC 6**
See also AAYA 46; AMWS 4; BW 2; CA 109; CAAS 19; CANR 27, 42, 68, 76, 97, 132; CDALBS; CP 5, 6, 7; CSW; CWP; DA3; DAM MULT, POET; DLB 120; EWL 3; EXPP; MAL 5; MTCW 2; MTFW 2005; PFS 1, 15; RGAL 4

Dove, Rita Frances
See Dove, Rita

Doveglion
See Villa, Jose Garcia

Dowell, Coleman 1925-1985 .... **CLC 60**
See also CA 25-28R; 117; CANR 10; DLB 130; GLL 2

Downing, Major Jack
See Smith, Seba

Dowson, Ernest (Christopher) 1867-1900
TCLC 4
See also CA 105; 150; DLB 19, 135; RGEL 2

Doyle, A. Conan
See Doyle, Sir Arthur Conan

Doyle, Sir Arthur Conan
1859-1930 ..... **SSC 12, 83, 95; TCLC 7; WLC 2**
See Conan Doyle, Arthur
See also AAYA 14; BRWS 2; CA 104; 122; CANR 131; CDBLB 1890-1914; CLR 106; CMW 4; DA; DA3; DAB; DAC; DAM MST, NOV; DLB 18, 70, 156, 178; EXPS; HGG; LAIT 2; MSW; MTCW 1, 2; MTFW 2005; RGEL 2; RGSF 2; RHW; SATA 24; SCFW 1, 2; SFW 4; SSFS 2; TEA; WCH; WLIT 4; WYA; YAW

Doyle, Conan
See Doyle, Sir Arthur Conan

Doyle, John
See Graves, Robert

Doyle, Roddy 1958- .... **CLC 81, 178**
See also AAYA 14; BRWS 5; CA 143; CANR 73, 128, 168; CN 6, 7; DA3; DLB 194, 326; MTCW 2; MTFW 2005

Doyle, Sir A. Conan
See Doyle, Sir Arthur Conan

Dr. A
See Asimov, Isaac; Silverstein, Alvin; Silverstein, Virginia B(arbara Opshelor)

Drabble, Margaret 1939- ...... **CLC 2, 3, 5, 8, 10, 22, 53, 129**
See also BRWS 4; CA 13-16R; CANR 18, 35, 63, 112, 131, 174; CDBLB 1960 to Present; CN 1, 2, 3, 4, 5, 6, 7; CPW; DA3; DAB; DAC; DAM MST, NOV, POP; DLB 14, 155, 231; EWL 3; FW; MTCW 1, 2; MTFW 2005; RGEL 2; SATA 48; TEA

Drakulic, Slavenka 1949- .... **CLC 173**
See also CA 144; CANR 92

Drakulic-Ilic, Slavenka
See Drakulic, Slavenka

Drapier, M. B.
See Swift, Jonathan

Drayham, James
See Mencken, H(enry) L(ouis)

Drayton, Michael 1563-1631 .... **LC 8**
See also DAM POET; DLB 121; RGEL 2

Dreadstone, Carl
See Campbell, Ramsey

Dreiser, Theodore 1871-1945 .... **SSC 30; TCLC 10, 18, 35, 83; WLC 2**
See also AMW; AMWC 2; AMWR 2; BYA 15, 16; CA 106; 132; CDALB 1865-1917; DA; DA3; DAC; DAM MST, NOV; DLB 9, 12, 102, 137; DLBD 1; EWL 3; LAIT 2; LMFS 2; MAL 5; MTCW 1, 2; MTFW 2005; NFS 8, 17; RGAL 4; TUS

Dreiser, Theodore Herman Albert
See Dreiser, Theodore
Drexler, Rosalyn 1926- .... **CLC 2, 6**
See also CA 81-84; CAD; CANR 68, 124;
CD 5, 6; CWD; MAL 5
Dreyer, Carl Theodor 1889-1968 ...... **CLC 16**
See also CA 116
Drieu la Rochelle, Pierre
1893-1945 .... **TCLC 21**
See also CA 117; 250; DLB 72; EWL 3;
GFL 1789 to the Present
Drieu la Rochelle, Pierre-Eugene 1893-1945
See Drieu la Rochelle, Pierre
Drinkwater, John 1882-1937 .... **TCLC 57**
See also CA 109; 149; DLB 10, 19, 149;
RGEL 2
Drop Shot
See Cable, George Washington
Droste-Hulshoff, Annette Freiin von
1797-1848 .... **NCLC 3, 133**
See also CDWLB 2; DLB 133; RGSF 2;
RGWL 2, 3
Drummond, Walter
See Silverberg, Robert
Drummond, William Henry
1854-1907 .... **TCLC 25**
See also CA 160; DLB 92
Drummond de Andrade, Carlos 1902-1987
CLC 18; TCLC 139
See Andrade, Carlos Drummond de
See also CA 132; 123; DLB 307; LAW
Drummond of Hawthornden, William
1585-1649 .... **LC 83**
See also DLB 121, 213; RGEL 2
Drury, Allen (Stuart) 1918-1998 .... **CLC 37**
See also CA 57-60; 170; CANR 18, 52; CN
1, 2, 3, 4, 5, 6; INT CANR-18
Druse, Eleanor
See King, Stephen
Dryden, John 1631-1700 ..... **DC 3; LC 3, 21,**
115; PC 25; WLC 2
See also BRW 2; CDBLB 1660-1789; DA;
DAB; DAC; DAM DRAM, MST, POET;
DLB 80, 101, 131; EXPP; IDTP; LMFS
1; RGEL 2; TEA; WLIT 3
du Bellay, Joachim 1524-1560 .... **LC 92**
See also DLB 327; GFL Beginnings to
1789; RGWL 2, 3
Duberman, Martin 1930- .... **CLC 8**
See also CA 1-4R; CAD; CANR 2, 63, 137,
174; CD 5, 6
Dubie, Norman (Evans) 1945- .... **CLC 36**
See also CA 69-72; CANR 12, 115; CP 3,
4, 5, 6, 7; DLB 120; PFS 12
Du Bois, W(illiam) E(dward) B(urghardt)
1868-1963 .. **BLC 1:1; CLC 1, 2, 13, 64,**
96; HR 1:2; TCLC 169; WLC 2
See also AAYA 40; AFAW 1, 2; AMWC 1;
AMWS 2; BW 1, 3; CA 85-88; CANR
34, 82, 132; CDALB 1865-1917; DA;
DA3; DAC; DAM MST, MULT, NOV;
DLB 47, 50, 91, 246, 284; EWL 3; EXPP;
LAIT 2; LMFS 2; MAL 5; MTCW 1, 2;
MTFW 2005; NCFS 1; PFS 13; RGAL 4;
SATA 42
Dubus, Andre 1936-1999 ..... **CLC 13, 36, 97;**
SSC 15
See also AMWS 7; CA 21-24R; 177; CANR
17; CN 5, 6; CSW; DLB 130; INT CANR-
17; RGAL 4; SSFS 10; TCLE 1:1
Duca Minimo
See D'Annunzio, Gabriele
Ducharme, Rejean 1941- .... **CLC 74**
See also CA 165; DLB 60
du Chatelet, Emilie 1706-1749 .... **LC 96**
See Chatelet, Gabrielle-Emilie Du
Duchen, Claire .... **CLC 65**
Duck, Stephen 1705(?)-1756 .... **PC 89**
See also DLB 95; RGEL 2

Duclos, Charles Pinot- 1704-1772 .... **LC 1**
See also GFL Beginnings to 1789
Ducornet, Erica 1943-
See Ducornet, Rikki
See also CA 37-40R; CANR 14, 34, 54, 82;
SATA 7
Ducornet, Rikki .... **CLC 232**
See Ducornet, Erica
Dudek, Louis 1918-2001 .... **CLC 11, 19**
See also CA 45-48; 215; CAAS 14; CANR
1; CP 1, 2, 3, 4, 5, 6, 7; DLB 88
Duerrenmatt, Friedrich 1921-1990 ... **CLC 1,**
4, 8, 11, 15, 43, 102
See Durrenmatt, Friedrich
See also CA 17-20R; CANR 33; CMW 4;
DAM DRAM; DLB 69, 124; MTCW 1, 2
Duffy, Bruce 1953(?)- .... **CLC 50**
See also CA 172
Duffy, Maureen (Patricia) 1933- ...... **CLC 37**
See also CA 25-28R; CANR 33, 68; CBD;
CN 1, 2, 3, 4, 5, 6, 7; CP 5, 6, 7; CWD;
CWP; DFS 15; DLB 14, 310; FW; MTCW
1
Du Fu
See Tu Fu
See also RGWL 2, 3
Dugan, Alan 1923-2003 .... **CLC 2, 6**
See also CA 81-84; 220; CANR 119; CP 1,
2, 3, 4, 5, 6, 7; DLB 5; MAL 5; PFS 10
du Gard, Roger Martin
See Martin du Gard, Roger
Duhamel, Georges 1884-1966 .... **CLC 8**
See also CA 81-84; 25-28R; CANR 35;
DLB 65; EWL 3; GFL 1789 to the
Present; MTCW 1
du Hault, Jean
See Grindel, Eugene
Dujardin, Edouard (Emile Louis) 1861-1949
TCLC 13
See also CA 109; DLB 123
Duke, Raoul
See Thompson, Hunter S.
Dulles, John Foster 1888-1959 .... **TCLC 72**
See also CA 115; 149
Dumas, Alexandre (pere)
1802-1870 .... **NCLC 11, 71; WLC 2**
See also AAYA 22; BYA 3; CLR 134; DA;
DA3; DAB; DAC; DAM MST, NOV;
DLB 119, 192; EW 6; GFL 1789 to the
Present; LAIT 1, 2; NFS 14, 19; RGWL
2, 3; SATA 18; TWA; WCH
Dumas, Alexandre (fils) 1824-1895 .... **DC 1;**
NCLC 9
See also DLB 192; GFL 1789 to the Present;
RGWL 2, 3
Dumas, Claudine
See Malzberg, Barry N(athaniel)
Dumas, Henry L. 1934-1968 . **BLC 2:1; CLC**
6, 62; SSC 107
See also BW 1; CA 85-88; DLB 41; RGAL
4
du Maurier, Daphne 1907-1989 .. **CLC 6, 11,**
59; SSC 18
See also AAYA 37; BPFB 1; BRWS 3; CA
5-8R; 128; CANR 6, 55; CMW 4; CN 1,
2, 3, 4; CPW; DA3; DAB; DAC; DAM
MST, POP; DLB 191; GL 2; HGG; LAIT
3; MSW; MTCW 1, 2; NFS 12; RGEL 2;
RGSF 2; RHW; SATA 27; SATA-Obit 60;
SSFS 14, 16; TEA
Du Maurier, George 1834-1896 ..... **NCLC 86**
See also DLB 153, 178; RGEL 2
Dunbar, Paul Laurence
1872-1906 .... **BLC 1:1; PC 5; SSC 8;**
TCLC 2, 12; WLC 2
See also AAYA 75; AFAW 1, 2; AMWS 2;
BW 1, 3; CA 104; 124; CANR 79;
CDALB 1865-1917; DA; DA3; DAC;
DAM MST, MULT, POET; DLB 50, 54,
78; EXPP; MAL 5; RGAL 4; SATA 34

Dunbar, William 1460(?)-1520(?) .... **LC 20;**
PC 67
See also BRWS 8; DLB 132, 146; RGEL 2
Dunbar-Nelson, Alice .... **HR 1:2**
See Nelson, Alice Ruth Moore Dunbar
Duncan, Dora Angela
See Duncan, Isadora
Duncan, Isadora 1877(?)-1927 .... **TCLC 68**
See also CA 118; 149
Duncan, Lois 1934- .... **CLC 26**
See also AAYA 4, 34; BYA 6, 8; CA 1-4R;
CANR 2, 23, 36, 111; CLR 29, 129;
JRDA; MAICYA 1, 2; MAICYAS 1;
MTFW 2005; SAAS 2; SATA 1, 36, 75,
133, 141; SATA-Essay 141; WYA; YAW
Duncan, Robert 1919-1988 ... **CLC 1, 2, 4, 7,**
15, 41, 55; PC 2, 75
See also BG 1:2; CA 9-12R; 124; CANR
28, 62; CP 1, 2, 3, 4; DAM POET; DLB
5, 16, 193; EWL 3; MAL 5; MTCW 1, 2;
MTFW 2005; PFS 13; RGAL 4; WP
Duncan, Sara Jeannette
1861-1922 .... **TCLC 60**
See also CA 157; DLB 92
Dunlap, William 1766-1839 .... **NCLC 2**
See also DLB 30, 37, 59; RGAL 4
Dunn, Douglas (Eaglesham) 1942- .... **CLC 6,**
40
See also BRWS 10; CA 45-48; CANR 2,
33, 126; CP 1, 2, 3, 4, 5, 6, 7; DLB 40;
MTCW 1
Dunn, Katherine 1945- .... **CLC 71**
See also CA 33-36R; CANR 72; HGG;
MTCW 2; MTFW 2005
Dunn, Stephen 1939- .... **CLC 36, 206**
See also AMWS 11; CA 33-36R; CANR
12, 48, 53, 105; CP 3, 4, 5, 6, 7; DLB
105; PFS 21
Dunn, Stephen Elliott
See Dunn, Stephen
Dunne, Finley Peter 1867-1936 ...... **TCLC 28**
See also CA 108; 178; DLB 11, 23; RGAL
4
Dunne, John Gregory 1932-2003 ..... **CLC 28**
See also CA 25-28R; 222; CANR 14, 50;
CN 5, 6, 7; DLBY 1980
Dunsany, Lord .... **TCLC 2, 59**
See Dunsany, Edward John Moreton Drax
Plunkett
See also DLB 77, 153, 156, 255; FANT;
IDTP; RGEL 2; SFW 4; SUFW 1
Dunsany, Edward John Moreton Drax
Plunkett 1878-1957
See Dunsany, Lord
See also CA 104; 148; DLB 10; MTCW 2
Duns Scotus, John 1266(?)-1308 ... **CMLC 59**
See also DLB 115
du Perry, Jean
See Simenon, Georges (Jacques Christian)
Durang, Christopher 1949- .... **CLC 27, 38**
See also CA 105; CAD; CANR 50, 76, 130;
CD 5, 6; MTCW 2; MTFW 2005
Durang, Christopher Ferdinand
See Durang, Christopher
Duras, Claire de 1777-1832 .... **NCLC 154**
Duras, Marguerite 1914-1996 . **CLC 3, 6, 11,**
20, 34, 40, 68, 100; SSC 40
See also BPFB 1; CA 25-28R; 151; CANR
50; CWW 2; DFS 21; DLB 83, 321; EWL
3; FL 1:5; GFL 1789 to the Present; IDFW
4; MTCW 1, 2; RGWL 2, 3; TWA
Durban, (Rosa) Pam 1947- .... **CLC 39**
See also CA 123; CANR 98; CSW
Durcan, Paul 1944- .... **CLC 43, 70**
See also CA 134; CANR 123; CP 1, 5, 6, 7;
DAM POET; EWL 3
d'Urfe, Honore
See Urfe, Honore d'

Durfey, Thomas 1653-1723 .... **LC 94**
See also DLB 80; RGEL 2

Durkheim, Emile 1858-1917 .... **TCLC 55**
See also CA 249

Durrell, Lawrence (George)
1912-1990 ..... **CLC 1, 4, 6, 8, 13, 27, 41**
See also BPFB 1; BRWS 1; CA 9-12R; 132;
CANR 40, 77; CDBLB 1945-1960; CN 1,
2, 3, 4; CP 1, 2, 3, 4, 5; DAM NOV; DLB
15, 27, 204; DLBY 1990; EWL 3; MTCW
1, 2; RGEL 2; SFW 4; TEA

Durrenmatt, Friedrich
See Duerrenmatt, Friedrich
See also CDWLB 2; EW 13; EWL 3;
RGHL; RGWL 2, 3

Dutt, Michael Madhusudan
1824-1873 .... **NCLC 118**

Dutt, Toru 1856-1877 .... **NCLC 29**
See also DLB 240

Dwight, Timothy 1752-1817 .... **NCLC 13**
See also DLB 37; RGAL 4

Dworkin, Andrea 1946-2005 ..... **CLC 43, 123**
See also CA 77-80; 238; CAAS 21; CANR
16, 39, 76, 96; FL 1:5; FW; GLL 1; INT
CANR-16; MTCW 1, 2; MTFW 2005

Dwyer, Deanna
See Koontz, Dean

Dwyer, K.R.
See Koontz, Dean

Dybek, Stuart 1942- .... **CLC 114; SSC 55**
See also CA 97-100; CANR 39; DLB 130;
SSFS 23

Dye, Richard
See De Voto, Bernard (Augustine)

Dyer, Geoff 1958- .... **CLC 149**
See also CA 125; CANR 88

Dyer, George 1755-1841 .... **NCLC 129**
See also DLB 93

Dylan, Bob 1941- .... **CLC 3, 4, 6, 12, 77; PC
37**
See also CA 41-44R; CANR 108; CP 1, 2,
3, 4, 5, 6, 7; DLB 16

Dyson, John 1943- .... **CLC 70**
See also CA 144

Dzyubin, Eduard Georgievich 1895-1934
See Bagritsky, Eduard
See also CA 170

E. V. L.
See Lucas, E(dward) V(errall)

Eagleton, Terence (Francis) 1943- .. **CLC 63,
132**
See also CA 57-60; CANR 7, 23, 68, 115;
DLB 242; LMFS 2; MTCW 1, 2; MTFW
2005

Eagleton, Terry
See Eagleton, Terence (Francis)

Early, Jack
See Scoppettone, Sandra
See also GLL 1

East, Michael
See West, Morris L(anglo)

Eastaway, Edward
See Thomas, (Philip) Edward

Eastlake, William (Derry)
1917-1997 .... **CLC 8**
See also CA 5-8R; 158; CAAS 1; CANR 5,
63; CN 1, 2, 3, 4, 5, 6; DLB 6, 206; INT
CANR-5; MAL 5; TCWW 1, 2

Eastman, Charles A(lexander) 1858-1939
NNAL; TCLC 55
See also CA 179; CANR 91; DAM MULT;
DLB 175; YABC 1

Eaton, Edith Maude 1865-1914 .... **AAL**
See Far, Sui Sin
See also CA 154; DLB 221, 312; FW

Eaton, (Lillie) Winnifred 1875-1954 .... **AAL**
See also CA 217; DLB 221, 312; RGAL 4

Eberhart, Richard 1904-2005 ...... **CLC 3, 11,
19, 56; PC 76**
See also AMW; CA 1-4R; 240; CANR 2,
125; CDALB 1941-1968; CP 1, 2, 3, 4, 5,
6, 7; DAM POET; DLB 48; MAL 5;
MTCW 1; RGAL 4

Eberhart, Richard Ghormley
See Eberhart, Richard

Eberstadt, Fernanda 1960- .... **CLC 39**
See also CA 136; CANR 69, 128

Ebner, Margaret c. 1291-1351 ...... **CMLC 98**

**Echegaray (y Eizaguirre), Jose (Maria
Waldo)** 1832-1916 .... **HLCS 1; TCLC 4**
See also CA 104; CANR 32; DLB 329;
EWL 3; HW 1; MTCW 1

Echeverria, (Jose) Esteban (Antonino)
1805-1851 .... **NCLC 18**
See also LAW

Echo
See Proust, (Valentin-Louis-George-Eugene)
Marcel

Eckert, Allan W. 1931- .... **CLC 17**
See also AAYA 18; BYA 2; CA 13-16R;
CANR 14, 45; INT CANR-14; MAICYA
2; MAICYAS 1; SAAS 21; SATA 29, 91;
SATA-Brief 27

Eckhart, Meister 1260(?)-1327(?) .. **CMLC 9,
80**
See also DLB 115; LMFS 1

Eckmar, F. R.
See de Hartog, Jan

Eco, Umberto 1932- .... **CLC 28, 60, 142, 248**
See also BEST 90:1; BPFB 1; CA 77-80;
CANR 12, 33, 55, 110, 131; CPW; CWW
2; DA3; DAM NOV, POP; DLB 196, 242;
EWL 3; MSW; MTCW 1, 2; MTFW
2005; NFS 22; RGWL 3; WLIT 7

Eddison, E(ric) R(ucker)
1882-1945 .... **TCLC 15**
See also CA 109; 156; DLB 255; FANT;
SFW 4; SUFW 1

Eddy, Mary (Ann Morse) Baker 1821-1910
TCLC 71
See also CA 113; 174

Edel, (Joseph) Leon 1907-1997 .. **CLC 29, 34**
See also CA 1-4R; 161; CANR 1, 22, 112;
DLB 103; INT CANR-22

Eden, Emily 1797-1869 .... **NCLC 10**

Edgar, David 1948- .... **CLC 42**
See also CA 57-60; CANR 12, 61, 112;
CBD; CD 5, 6; DAM DRAM; DFS 15;
DLB 13, 233; MTCW 1

Edgerton, Clyde (Carlyle) 1944- ...... **CLC 39**
See also AAYA 17; CA 118; 134; CANR
64, 125; CN 7; CSW; DLB 278; INT CA-
134; TCLE 1:1; YAW

Edgeworth, Maria 1768-1849 ... **NCLC 1, 51,
158; SSC 86**
See also BRWS 3; DLB 116, 159, 163; FL
1:3; FW; RGEL 2; SATA 21; TEA; WLIT
3

Edmonds, Paul
See Kuttner, Henry

Edmonds, Walter D(umaux)
1903-1998 .... **CLC 35**
See also BYA 2; CA 5-8R; CANR 2; CWRI
5; DLB 9; LAIT 1; MAICYA 1, 2; MAL
5; RHW; SAAS 4; SATA 1, 27; SATA-
Obit 99

Edmondson, Wallace
See Ellison, Harlan

Edson, Margaret 1961- ...... **CLC 199; DC 24**
See also CA 190; DFS 13; DLB 266

Edson, Russell 1935- .... **CLC 13**
See also CA 33-36R; CANR 115; CP 2, 3,
4, 5, 6, 7; DLB 244; WP

Edwards, Bronwen Elizabeth
See Rose, Wendy

Edwards, G(erald) B(asil)
1899-1976 .... **CLC 25**
See also CA 201; 110

Edwards, Gus 1939- .... **CLC 43**
See also CA 108; INT CA-108

Edwards, Jonathan 1703-1758 .... **LC 7, 54**
See also AMW; DA; DAC; DAM MST;
DLB 24, 270; RGAL 4; TUS

Edwards, Sarah Pierpont 1710-1758 .. **LC 87**
See also DLB 200

Efron, Marina Ivanovna Tsvetaeva
See Tsvetaeva (Efron), Marina (Ivanovna)

Egeria fl. 4th cent. - .... **CMLC 70**

Eggers, Dave 1970- .... **CLC 241**
See also AAYA 56; CA 198; CANR 138;
MTFW 2005

Egoyan, Atom 1960- .... **CLC 151**
See also AAYA 63; CA 157; CANR 151

Ehle, John (Marsden, Jr.) 1925- ...... **CLC 27**
See also CA 9-12R; CSW

Ehrenbourg, Ilya (Grigoryevich)
See Ehrenburg, Ilya (Grigoryevich)

Ehrenburg, Ilya (Grigoryevich) 1891-1967
CLC 18, 34, 62
See Erenburg, Il'ia Grigor'evich
See also CA 102; 25-28R; EWL 3

Ehrenburg, Ilyo (Grigoryevich)
See Ehrenburg, Ilya (Grigoryevich)

Ehrenreich, Barbara 1941- .... **CLC 110**
See also BEST 90:4; CA 73-76; CANR 16,
37, 62, 117, 167; DLB 246; FW; MTCW
1, 2; MTFW 2005

Ehrlich, Gretel 1946- .... **CLC 249**
See also ANW; CA 140; CANR 74, 146;
DLB 212, 275; TCWW 2

Eich, Gunter
See Eich, Gunter
See also RGWL 2, 3

Eich, Gunter 1907-1972 .... **CLC 15**
See Eich, Gunter
See also CA 111; 93-96; DLB 69, 124;
EWL 3

Eichendorff, Joseph 1788-1857 .... **NCLC 8**
See also DLB 90; RGWL 2, 3

Eigner, Larry .... **CLC 9**
See Eigner, Laurence (Joel)
See also CAAS 23; CP 1, 2, 3, 4, 5, 6; DLB
5; WP

Eigner, Laurence (Joel) 1927-1996
See Eigner, Larry
See also CA 9-12R; 151; CANR 6, 84; CP
7; DLB 193

Eilhart von Oberge c. 1140-c.
1195 .... **CMLC 67**
See also DLB 148

Einhard c. 770-840 .... **CMLC 50**
See also DLB 148

Einstein, Albert 1879-1955 .... **TCLC 65**
See also CA 121; 133; MTCW 1, 2

Eiseley, Loren
See Eiseley, Loren Corey
See also DLB 275

Eiseley, Loren Corey 1907-1977 .... **CLC 7**
See Eiseley, Loren
See also AAYA 5; ANW; CA 1-4R; 73-76;
CANR 6; DLBD 17

Eisenstadt, Jill 1963- .... **CLC 50**
See also CA 140

Eisenstein, Sergei (Mikhailovich) 1898-1948
TCLC 57
See also CA 114; 149

Eisner, Simon
See Kornbluth, C(yril) M.

Eisner, Will 1917-2005 .... **CLC 237**
See also AAYA 52; CA 108; 235; CANR
114, 140; MTFW 2005; SATA 31, 165

Eisner, William Erwin
See Eisner, Will

Ephron, Nora 1941- .... **CLC 17, 31**
    See also AAYA 35; AITN 2; CA 65-68;
    CANR 12, 39, 83, 161; DFS 22
Epicurus 341B.C.-270B.C. .... **CMLC 21**
    See also DLB 176
Epinay, Louise d' 1726-1783 .... **LC 138**
    See also DLB 313
Epsilon
    See Betjeman, John
Epstein, Daniel Mark 1948- .... **CLC 7**
    See also CA 49-52; CANR 2, 53, 90
Epstein, Jacob 1956- .... **CLC 19**
    See also CA 114
Epstein, Jean 1897-1953 .... **TCLC 92**
Epstein, Joseph 1937- .... **CLC 39, 204**
    See also AMWS 14; CA 112; 119; CANR
    50, 65, 117, 164
Epstein, Leslie 1938- .... **CLC 27**
    See also AMWS 12; CA 73-76, 215; CAAE
    215; CAAS 12; CANR 23, 69, 162; DLB
    299; RGHL
Equiano, Olaudah 1745(?)-1797 ..... **BLC 1:2;
    LC 16, 143**
    See also AFAW 1, 2; CDWLB 3; DAM
    MULT; DLB 37, 50; WLIT 2
Erasmus, Desiderius 1469(?)-1536 ..... **LC 16,
    93**
    See also DLB 136; EW 2; LMFS 1; RGWL
    2, 3; TWA
Erdman, Paul E. 1932-2007 .... **CLC 25**
    See also AITN 1; CA 61-64; 259; CANR
    13, 43, 84
Erdman, Paul Emil
    See Erdman, Paul E.
Erdrich, Karen Louise
    See Erdrich, Louise
Erdrich, Louise 1954- .... **CLC 39, 54, 120,
    176; NNAL; PC 52**
    See also AAYA 10, 47; AMWS 4; BEST
    89:1; BPFB 1; CA 114; CANR 41, 62,
    118, 138; CDALBS; CN 5, 6, 7; CP 6, 7;
    CPW; CWP; DA3; DAM MULT, NOV,
    POP; DLB 152, 175, 206; EWL 3; EXPP;
    FL 1:5; LAIT 5; LATS 1:2; MAL 5;
    MTCW 1, 2; MTFW 2005; NFS 5; PFS
    14; RGAL 4; SATA 94, 141; SSFS 14,
    22; TCWW 2
Erenburg, Ilya (Grigoryevich)
    See Ehrenburg, Ilya (Grigoryevich)
Erickson, Stephen Michael
    See Erickson, Steve
Erickson, Steve 1950- .... **CLC 64**
    See also CA 129; CANR 60, 68, 136;
    MTFW 2005; SFW 4; SUFW 2
Erickson, Walter
    See Fast, Howard
Ericson, Walter
    See Fast, Howard
Eriksson, Buntel
    See Bergman, Ingmar
Eriugena, John Scottus c.
    810-877 .... **CMLC 65**
    See also DLB 115
Ernaux, Annie 1940- .... **CLC 88, 184**
    See also CA 147; CANR 93; MTFW 2005;
    NCFS 3, 5
Erskine, John 1879-1951 .... **TCLC 84**
    See also CA 112; 159; DLB 9, 102; FANT
Erwin, Will
    See Eisner, Will
Eschenbach, Wolfram von
    See von Eschenbach, Wolfram
    See also RGWL 3
Eseki, Bruno
    See Mphahlele, Ezekiel
Esenin, S.A.
    See Esenin, Sergei
    See also EWL 3

Esenin, Sergei 1895-1925 .... **TCLC 4**
    See Esenin, S.A.
    See also CA 104; RGWL 2, 3
Esenin, Sergei Aleksandrovich
    See Esenin, Sergei
Eshleman, Clayton 1935- .... **CLC 7**
    See also CA 33-36R, 212; CAAE 212;
    CAAS 6; CANR 93; CP 1, 2, 3, 4, 5, 6,
    7; DLB 5
Espada, Martin 1957- .... **PC 74**
    See also CA 159; CANR 80; CP 7; EXPP;
    LLW; MAL 5; PFS 13, 16
Espriella, Don Manuel Alvarez
    See Southey, Robert
Espriu, Salvador 1913-1985 .... **CLC 9**
    See also CA 154; 115; DLB 134; EWL 3
Espronceda, Jose de 1808-1842 ..... **NCLC 39**
Esquivel, Laura 1950(?)- ... **CLC 141; HLCS
    1**
    See also AAYA 29; CA 143; CANR 68, 113,
    161; DA3; DNFS 2; LAIT 3; LMFS 2;
    MTCW 2; MTFW 2005; NFS 5; WLIT 1
Esse, James
    See Stephens, James
Esterbrook, Tom
    See Hubbard, L. Ron
Esterhazy, Peter 1950- .... **CLC 251**
    See also CA 140; CANR 137; CDWLB 4;
    CWW 2; DLB 232; EWL 3; RGWL 3
Estleman, Loren D. 1952- .... **CLC 48**
    See also AAYA 27; CA 85-88; CANR 27,
    74, 139; CMW 4; CPW; DA3; DAM
    NOV, POP; DLB 226; INT CANR-27;
    MTCW 1, 2; MTFW 2005; TCWW 1, 2
Etherege, Sir George 1636-1692 . **DC 23; LC
    78**
    See also BRW 2; DAM DRAM; DLB 80;
    PAB; RGEL 2
Euclid 306B.C.-283B.C. .... **CMLC 25**
Eugenides, Jeffrey 1960(?)- .... **CLC 81, 212**
    See also AAYA 51; CA 144; CANR 120;
    MTFW 2005; NFS 24
Euripides c. 484B.C.-406B.C. .... **CMLC 23,
    51; DC 4; WLCS**
    See also AW 1; CDWLB 1; DA; DA3;
    DAB; DAC; DAM DRAM, MST; DFS 1,
    4, 6, 25; DLB 176; LAIT 1; LMFS 1;
    RGWL 2, 3; WLIT 8
Evan, Evin
    See Faust, Frederick (Schiller)
Evans, Caradoc 1878-1945 ... **SSC 43; TCLC
    85**
    See also DLB 162
Evans, Evan
    See Faust, Frederick (Schiller)
Evans, Marian
    See Eliot, George
Evans, Mary Ann
    See Eliot, George
    See also NFS 20
Evarts, Esther
    See Benson, Sally
Evelyn, John 1620-1706 .... **LC 144**
    See also BRW 2; RGEL 2
Everett, Percival
    See Everett, Percival L.
    See also CSW
Everett, Percival L. 1956- .... **CLC 57**
    See Everett, Percival
    See also BW 2; CA 129; CANR 94, 134;
    CN 7; MTFW 2005
Everson, R(onald) G(ilmour)
    1903-1992 .... **CLC 27**
    See also CA 17-20R; CP 1, 2, 3, 4; DLB 88

Everson, William (Oliver)
    1912-1994 .... **CLC 1, 5, 14**
    See Antoninus, Brother
    See also BG 1:2; CA 9-12R; 145; CANR
    20; CP 2, 3, 4, 5; DLB 5, 16, 212; MTCW
    1
Evtushenko, Evgenii Aleksandrovich
    See Yevtushenko, Yevgeny (Alexandrovich)
    See also CWW 2; RGWL 2, 3
Ewart, Gavin (Buchanan)
    1916-1995 .... **CLC 13, 46**
    See also BRWS 7; CA 89-92; 150; CANR
    17, 46; CP 1, 2, 3, 4, 5, 6; DLB 40;
    MTCW 1
Ewers, Hanns Heinz 1871-1943 ..... **TCLC 12**
    See also CA 109; 149
Ewing, Frederick R.
    See Sturgeon, Theodore (Hamilton)
Exley, Frederick (Earl) 1929-1992 .... **CLC 6,
    11**
    See also AITN 2; BPFB 1; CA 81-84; 138;
    CANR 117; DLB 143; DLBY 1981
Eynhardt, Guillermo
    See Quiroga, Horacio (Sylvestre)
Ezekiel, Nissim (Moses) 1924-2004 .. **CLC 61**
    See also CA 61-64; 223; CP 1, 2, 3, 4, 5, 6,
    7; DLB 323; EWL 3
Ezekiel, Tish O'Dowd 1943- .... **CLC 34**
    See also CA 129
Fadeev, Aleksandr Aleksandrovich
    See Bulgya, Alexander Alexandrovich
    See also DLB 272
Fadeev, Alexandr Alexandrovich
    See Bulgya, Alexander Alexandrovich
    See also EWL 3
Fadeyev, A.
    See Bulgya, Alexander Alexandrovich
Fadeyev, Alexander .... **TCLC 53**
    See Bulgya, Alexander Alexandrovich
Fagen, Donald 1948- .... **CLC 26**
Fainzil'berg, Il'ia Arnol'dovich
    See Fainzilberg, Ilya Arnoldovich
Fainzilberg, Ilya Arnoldovich 1897-1937
    TCLC 21
    See Il'f, Il'ia
    See also CA 120; 165; EWL 3
Fair, Ronald L. 1932- .... **CLC 18**
    See also BW 1; CA 69-72; CANR 25; DLB
    33
Fairbairn, Roger
    See Carr, John Dickson
Fairbairns, Zoe (Ann) 1948- .... **CLC 32**
    See also CA 103; CANR 21, 85; CN 4, 5,
    6, 7
Fairfield, Flora
    See Alcott, Louisa May
Fairman, Paul W. 1916-1977
    See Queen, Ellery
    See also CA 114; SFW 4
Falco, Gian
    See Papini, Giovanni
Falconer, James
    See Kirkup, James
Falconer, Kenneth
    See Kornbluth, C(yril) M.
Falkland, Samuel
    See Heijermans, Herman
Fallaci, Oriana 1930-2006 .... **CLC 11, 110**
    See also CA 77-80; 253; CANR 15, 58, 134;
    FW; MTCW 1
Faludi, Susan 1959- .... **CLC 140**
    See also CA 138; CANR 126; FW; MTCW
    2; MTFW 2005; NCFS 3
Faludy, George 1913- .... **CLC 42**
    See also CA 21-24R
Faludy, Gyoergy
    See Faludy, George

Fiedler, Leslie A(aron) 1917-2003 ..... **CLC 4, 13, 24**
See also AMWS 13; CA 9-12R; 212; CANR 7, 63; CN 1, 2, 3, 4, 5, 6; DLB 28, 67; EWL 3; MAL 5; MTCW 1, 2; RGAL 4; TUS

Field, Andrew 1938- .... **CLC 44**
See also CA 97-100; CANR 25

Field, Eugene 1850-1895 .... **NCLC 3**
See also DLB 23, 42, 140; DLBD 13; MAICYA 1, 2; RGAL 4; SATA 16

Field, Gans T.
See Wellman, Manly Wade

Field, Michael 1915-1971 .... **TCLC 43**
See also CA 29-32R

Fielding, Helen 1958- .... **CLC 146, 217**
See also AAYA 65; CA 172; CANR 127; DLB 231; MTFW 2005

Fielding, Henry 1707-1754 .... **LC 1, 46, 85, 151; WLC 2**
See also BRW 3; BRWR 1; CDBLB 1660-1789; DA; DA3; DAB; DAC; DAM DRAM, MST, NOV; DLB 39, 84, 101; NFS 18; RGEL 2; TEA; WLIT 3

Fielding, Sarah 1710-1768 .... **LC 1, 44**
See also DLB 39; RGEL 2; TEA

Fields, W. C. 1880-1946 .... **TCLC 80**
See also DLB 44

Fierstein, Harvey (Forbes) 1954- ..... **CLC 33**
See also CA 123; 129; CAD; CD 5, 6; CPW; DA3; DAM DRAM, POP; DFS 6; DLB 266; GLL; MAL 5

Figes, Eva 1932- .... **CLC 31**
See also CA 53-56; CANR 4, 44, 83; CN 2, 3, 4, 5, 6, 7; DLB 14, 271; FW; RGHL

Filippo, Eduardo de
See de Filippo, Eduardo

Finch, Anne 1661-1720 ..... **LC 3, 137; PC 21**
See also BRWS 9; DLB 95

Finch, Robert (Duer Claydon) 1900-1995 **CLC 18**
See also CA 57-60; CANR 9, 24, 49; CP 1, 2, 3, 4, 5, 6; DLB 88

Findley, Timothy (Irving Frederick) 1930-2002 .... **CLC 27, 102**
See also CA 25-28R; 206; CANR 12, 42, 69, 109; CCA 1; CN 4, 5, 6, 7; DAC; DAM MST; DLB 53; FANT; RHW

Fink, William
See Mencken, H(enry) L(ouis)

Firbank, Louis 1942-
See Reed, Lou
See also CA 117

Firbank, (Arthur Annesley) Ronald 1886-1926 .... **TCLC 1**
See also BRWS 2; CA 104; 177; DLB 36; EWL 3; RGEL 2

Firdawsi, Abu al-Qasim
See Ferdowsi, Abu'l Qasem
See also WLIT 6

Fish, Stanley
See Fish, Stanley Eugene

Fish, Stanley E.
See Fish, Stanley Eugene

Fish, Stanley Eugene 1938- .... **CLC 142**
See also CA 112; 132; CANR 90; DLB 67

Fisher, Dorothy (Frances) Canfield 1879-1958 .... **TCLC 87**
See also CA 114; 136; CANR 80; CLR 71; CWRI 5; DLB 9, 102, 284; MAICYA 1, 2; MAL 5; YABC 1

Fisher, M(ary) F(rances) K(ennedy) 1908-1992 .... **CLC 76, 87**
See also AMWS 17; CA 77-80; 138; CANR 44; MTCW 2

Fisher, Roy 1930- .... **CLC 25**
See also CA 81-84; CAAS 10; CANR 16; CP 1, 2, 3, 4, 5, 6, 7; DLB 40

Fisher, Rudolph 1897-1934 ...... **BLC 1:2; HR 1:2; SSC 25; TCLC 11**
See also BW 1, 3; CA 107; 124; CANR 80; DAM MULT; DLB 51, 102

Fisher, Vardis (Alvero) 1895-1968 .... **CLC 7; TCLC 140**
See also CA 5-8R; 25-28R; CANR 68; DLB 9, 206; MAL 5; RGAL 4; TCWW 1, 2

Fiske, Tarleton
See Bloch, Robert (Albert)

Fitch, Clarke
See Sinclair, Upton

Fitch, John IV
See Cormier, Robert

Fitzgerald, Captain Hugh
See Baum, L(yman) Frank

FitzGerald, Edward 1809-1883 ...... **NCLC 9, 153; PC 79**
See also BRW 4; DLB 32; RGEL 2

Fitzgerald, F(rancis) Scott (Key) 1896-1940 **SSC 6, 31, 75; TCLC 1, 6, 14, 28, 55, 157; WLC 2**
See also AAYA 24; AITN 1; AMW; AMWC 2; AMWR 1; BPFB 1; CA 110; 123; CDALB 1917-1929; DA; DA3; DAB; DAC; DAM MST, NOV; DLB 4, 9, 86, 219, 273; DLBD 1, 15, 16; DLBY 1981, 1996; EWL 3; EXPN; EXPS; LAIT 3; MAL 5; MTCW 1, 2; MTFW 2005; NFS 2, 19, 20; RGAL 4; RGSF 2; SSFS 4, 15, 21, 25; TUS

Fitzgerald, Penelope 1916-2000 . **CLC 19, 51, 61, 143**
See also BRWS 5; CA 85-88; 190; CAAS 10; CANR 56, 86, 131; CN 3, 4, 5, 6, 7; DLB 14, 194, 326; EWL 3; MTCW 2; MTFW 2005

Fitzgerald, Robert (Stuart) 1910-1985 .... **CLC 39**
See also CA 1-4R; 114; CANR 1; CP 1, 2, 3, 4; DLBY 1980; MAL 5

FitzGerald, Robert D(avid) 1902-1987 .... **CLC 19**
See also CA 17-20R; CP 1, 2, 3, 4; DLB 260; RGEL 2

Fitzgerald, Zelda (Sayre) 1900-1948 .... **TCLC 52**
See also AMWS 9; CA 117; 126; DLBY 1984

Flanagan, Thomas (James Bonner) 1923-2002 .... **CLC 25, 52**
See also CA 108; 206; CANR 55; CN 3, 4, 5, 6, 7; DLBY 1980; INT CA-108; MTCW 1; RHW; TCLE 1:1

Flaubert, Gustave 1821-1880 .... **NCLC 2, 10, 19, 62, 66, 135, 179, 185; SSC 11, 60; WLC 2**
See also DA; DA3; DAB; DAC; DAM MST, NOV; DLB 119, 301; EW 7; EXPS; GFL 1789 to the Present; LAIT 2; LMFS 1; NFS 14; RGSF 2; RGWL 2, 3; SSFS 6; TWA

Flavius Josephus
See Josephus, Flavius

Flecker, Herman Elroy
See Flecker, (Herman) James Elroy

Flecker, (Herman) James Elroy 1884-1915 **TCLC 43**
See also CA 109; 150; DLB 10, 19; RGEL 2

Fleming, Ian 1908-1964 ... **CLC 3, 30; TCLC 193**
See also AAYA 26; BPFB 1; CA 5-8R; CANR 59; CDBLB 1945-1960; CMW 4; CPW; DA3; DAM POP; DLB 87, 201; MSW; MTCW 1, 2; MTFW 2005; RGEL 2; SATA 9; TEA; YAW

Fleming, Ian Lancaster
See Fleming, Ian

Fleming, Thomas 1927- .... **CLC 37**
See also CA 5-8R; CANR 10, 102, 155; INT CANR-10; SATA 8

Fleming, Thomas James
See Fleming, Thomas

Fletcher, John 1579-1625 . **DC 6; LC 33, 151**
See also BRW 2; CDBLB Before 1660; DLB 58; RGEL 2; TEA

Fletcher, John Gould 1886-1950 .... **TCLC 35**
See also CA 107; 167; DLB 4, 45; LMFS 2; MAL 5; RGAL 4

Fleur, Paul
See Pohl, Frederik

Flieg, Helmut
See Heym, Stefan

Flooglebuckle, Al
See Spiegelman, Art

Flora, Fletcher 1914-1969
See Queen, Ellery
See also CA 1-4R; CANR 3, 85

Flying Officer X
See Bates, H(erbert) E(rnest)

Fo, Dario 1926- .... **CLC 32, 109, 227; DC 10**
See also CA 116; 128; CANR 68, 114, 134, 164; CWW 2; DA3; DAM DRAM; DFS 23; DLB 330; DLBY 1997; EWL 3; MTCW 1, 2; MTFW 2005; WLIT 7

Foden, Giles 1967- .... **CLC 231**
See also CA 240; DLB 267; NFS 15

Fogarty, Jonathan Titulescu Esq.
See Farrell, James T(homas)

Follett, Ken 1949- .... **CLC 18**
See also AAYA 6, 50; BEST 89:4; BPFB 1; CA 81-84; CANR 13, 33, 54, 102, 156; CMW 4; CPW; DA3; DAM NOV, POP; DLB 87; DLBY 1981; INT CANR-33; MTCW 1

Follett, Kenneth Martin
See Follett, Ken

Fondane, Benjamin 1898-1944 ..... **TCLC 159**

Fontane, Theodor 1819-1898 . **NCLC 26, 163**
See also CDWLB 2; DLB 129; EW 6; RGWL 2, 3; TWA

Fonte, Moderata 1555-1592 .... **LC 118**

Fontenelle, Bernard Le Bovier de 1657-1757 **LC 140**
See also DLB 268, 313; GFL Beginnings to 1789

Fontenot, Chester .... **CLC 65**

Fonvizin, Denis Ivanovich 1744(?)-1792 .... **LC 81**
See also DLB 150; RGWL 2, 3

Foote, Horton 1916- .... **CLC 51, 91**
See also CA 73-76; CAD; CANR 34, 51, 110; CD 5, 6; CSW; DA3; DAM DRAM; DFS 20; DLB 26, 266; EWL 3; INT CANR-34; MTFW 2005

Foote, Mary Hallock 1847-1938 .. **TCLC 108**
See also DLB 186, 188, 202, 221; TCWW 1

Foote, Samuel 1721-1777 .... **LC 106**
See also DLB 89; RGEL 2

Foote, Shelby 1916-2005 .... **CLC 75, 224**
See also AAYA 40; CA 5-8R; 240; CANR 3, 45, 74, 131; CN 1, 2, 3, 4, 5, 6, 7; CPW; CSW; DA3; DAM NOV, POP; DLB 2, 17; MAL 5; MTCW 2; MTFW 2005; RHW

Forbes, Cosmo
See Lewton, Val

Forbes, Esther 1891-1967 .... **CLC 12**
See also AAYA 17; BYA 2; CA 13-14; 25-28R; CAP 1; CLR 27; DLB 22; JRDA; MAICYA 1, 2; RHW; SATA 2, 100; YAW

Forche, Carolyn 1950- .. **CLC 25, 83, 86; PC 10**
See also CA 109; 117; CANR 50, 74, 138; CP 4, 5, 6, 7; CWP; DA3; DAM POET; DLB 5, 193; INT CA-117; MAL 5; MTCW 2; MTFW 2005; PFS 18; RGAL 4

Forche, Carolyn Louise
See Forche, Carolyn

Ford, Elbur
See Hibbert, Eleanor Alice Burford

Ford, Ford Madox 1873-1939 ... **TCLC 1, 15, 39, 57, 172**
See Chaucer, Daniel
See also BRW 6; CA 104; 132; CANR 74; CDBLB 1914-1945; DA3; DAM NOV; DLB 34, 98, 162; EWL 3; MTCW 1, 2; RGEL 2; TEA

Ford, Henry 1863-1947 .... **TCLC 73**
See also CA 115; 148

Ford, Jack
See Ford, John

Ford, John 1586-1639 .... **DC 8; LC 68**
See also BRW 2; CDBLB Before 1660; DA3; DAM DRAM; DFS 7; DLB 58; IDTP; RGEL 2

Ford, John 1895-1973 .... **CLC 16**
See also AAYA 75; CA 187; 45-48

Ford, Richard 1944- .... **CLC 46, 99, 205**
See also AMWS 5; CA 69-72; CANR 11, 47, 86, 128, 164; CN 5, 6, 7; CSW; DLB 227; EWL 3; MAL 5; MTCW 2; MTFW 2005; NFS 25; RGAL 4; RGSF 2

Ford, Webster
See Masters, Edgar Lee

Foreman, Richard 1937- .... **CLC 50**
See also CA 65-68; CAD; CANR 32, 63, 143; CD 5, 6

Forester, C(ecil) S(cott) 1899-1966 . **CLC 35; TCLC 152**
See also CA 73-76; 25-28R; CANR 83; DLB 191; RGEL 2; RHW; SATA 13

Forez
See Mauriac, Francois (Charles)

Forman, James
See Forman, James D.

Forman, James D. 1932- .... **CLC 21**
See also AAYA 17; CA 9-12R; CANR 4, 19, 42; JRDA; MAICYA 1, 2; SATA 8, 70; YAW

Forman, James Douglas
See Forman, James D.

Forman, Milos 1932- .... **CLC 164**
See also AAYA 63; CA 109

Fornes, Maria Irene 1930- .... **CLC 39, 61, 187; DC 10; HLCS 1**
See also CA 25-28R; CAD; CANR 28, 81; CD 5, 6; CWD; DFS 25; DLB 7, 341; HW 1, 2; INT CANR-28; LLW; MAL 5; MTCW 1; RGAL 4

Forrest, Leon (Richard) 1937-1997 .... **BLCS; CLC 4**
See also AFAW 2; BW 2; CA 89-92; 162; CAAS 7; CANR 25, 52, 87; CN 4, 5, 6; DLB 33

Forster, E(dward) M(organ) 1879-1970 ...... **CLC 1, 2, 3, 4, 9, 10, 13, 15, 22, 45, 77; SSC 27, 96; TCLC 125; WLC 2**
See also AAYA 2, 37; BRW 6; BRWR 2; BYA 12; CA 13-14; 25-28R; CANR 45; CAP 1; CDBLB 1914-1945; DA; DA3; DAB; DAC; DAM MST, NOV; DLB 34, 98, 162, 178, 195; DLBD 10; EWL 3; EXPN; LAIT 3; LMFS 1; MTCW 1, 2; MTFW 2005; NCFS 1; NFS 3, 10, 11; RGEL 2; RGSF 2; SATA 57; SUFW 1; TEA; WLIT 4

Forster, John 1812-1876 .... **NCLC 11**
See also DLB 144, 184

Forster, Margaret 1938- .... **CLC 149**
See also CA 133; CANR 62, 115, 175; CN 4, 5, 6, 7; DLB 155, 271

Forsyth, Frederick 1938- .... **CLC 2, 5, 36**
See also BEST 89:4; CA 85-88; CANR 38, 62, 115, 137; CMW 4; CN 3, 4, 5, 6, 7; CPW; DAM NOV, POP; DLB 87; MTCW 1, 2; MTFW 2005

Forten, Charlotte L. 1837-1914 ..... **BLC 1:2; TCLC 16**
See Grimke, Charlotte L(ottie) Forten
See also DLB 50, 239

Fortinbras
See Grieg, (Johan) Nordahl (Brun)

Foscolo, Ugo 1778-1827 .... **NCLC 8, 97**
See also EW 5; WLIT 7

Fosse, Bob 1927-1987
See Fosse, Robert L.
See also CA 110; 123

Fosse, Robert L. .... **CLC 20**
See Fosse, Bob

Foster, Hannah Webster 1758-1840 .... **NCLC 99**
See also DLB 37, 200; RGAL 4

Foster, Stephen Collins 1826-1864 .... **NCLC 26**
See also RGAL 4

Foucault, Michel 1926-1984 . **CLC 31, 34, 69**
See also CA 105; 113; CANR 34; DLB 242; EW 13; EWL 3; GFL 1789 to the Present; GLL 1; LMFS 2; MTCW 1, 2; TWA

Fouque, Friedrich (Heinrich Karl) de la Motte 1777-1843 .... **NCLC 2**
See also DLB 90; RGWL 2, 3; SUFW 1

Fourier, Charles 1772-1837 .... **NCLC 51**

Fournier, Henri-Alban 1886-1914
See Alain-Fournier
See also CA 104; 179

Fournier, Pierre 1916-1997 .... **CLC 11**
See Gascar, Pierre
See also CA 89-92; CANR 16, 40

Fowles, John 1926-2005 .... **CLC 1, 2, 3, 4, 6, 9, 10, 15, 33, 87; SSC 33**
See also BPFB 1; BRWS 1; CA 5-8R; 245; CANR 25, 71, 103; CDBLB 1960 to Present; CN 1, 2, 3, 4, 5, 6, 7; DA3; DAB; DAC; DAM MST; DLB 14, 139, 207; EWL 3; HGG; MTCW 1, 2; MTFW 2005; NFS 21; RGEL 2; RHW; SATA 22; SATA-Obit 171; TEA; WLIT 4

Fowles, John Robert
See Fowles, John

Fox, Paula 1923- .... **CLC 2, 8, 121**
See also AAYA 3, 37; BYA 3, 8; CA 73-76; CANR 20, 36, 62, 105; CLR 1, 44, 96; DLB 52; JRDA; MAICYA 1, 2; MTCW 1; NFS 12; SATA 17, 60, 120, 167; WYA; YAW

Fox, William Price (Jr.) 1926- .... **CLC 22**
See also CA 17-20R; CAAS 19; CANR 11, 142; CSW; DLB 2; DLBY 1981

Foxe, John 1517(?)-1587 .... **LC 14**
See also DLB 132

Frame, Janet 1924-2004 ...... **CLC 2, 3, 6, 22, 66, 96, 237; SSC 29**
See also CA 1-4R; 224; CANR 2, 36, 76, 135; CN 1, 2, 3, 4, 5, 6, 7; CP 2, 3, 4; CWP; EWL 3; MTCW 1,2; RGEL 2; RGSF 2; SATA 119; TWA

France, Anatole .... **TCLC 9**
See Thibault, Jacques Anatole Francois
See also DLB 123, 330; EWL 3; GFL 1789 to the Present; RGWL 2, 3; SUFW 1

Francis, Claude .... **CLC 50**
See also CA 192

Francis, Dick
See Francis, Richard Stanley
See also CN 2, 3, 4, 5, 6

Francis, Richard Stanley 1920- ... **CLC 2, 22, 42, 102**
See Francis, Dick
See also AAYA 5, 21; BEST 89:3; BPFB 1; CA 5-8R; CANR 9, 42, 68, 100, 141; CD-BLB 1960 to Present; CMW 4; CN 7; DA3; DAM POP; DLB 87; INT CANR-9; MSW; MTCW 1, 2; MTFW 2005

Francis, Robert (Churchill) 1901-1987 .... **CLC 15; PC 34**
See also AMWS 9; CA 1-4R; 123; CANR 1; CP 1, 2, 3, 4; EXPP; PFS 12; TCLE 1:1

Francis, Lord Jeffrey
See Jeffrey, Francis
See also DLB 107

Frank, Anne(lies Marie) 1929-1945 .... **TCLC 17; WLC 2**
See also AAYA 12; BYA 1; CA 113; 133; CANR 68; CLR 101; DA; DA3; DAB; DAC; DAM MST; LAIT 4; MAICYA 2; MAICYAS 1; MTCW 1, 2; MTFW 2005; NCFS 2; RGHL; SATA 87; SATA-Brief 42; WYA; YAW

Frank, Bruno 1887-1945 .... **TCLC 81**
See also CA 189; DLB 118; EWL 3

Frank, Elizabeth 1945- .... **CLC 39**
See also CA 121; 126; CANR 78, 150; INT CA-126

Frankl, Viktor E(mil) 1905-1997 ...... **CLC 93**
See also CA 65-68; 161; RGHL

Franklin, Benjamin
See Hasek, Jaroslav (Matej Frantisek)

Franklin, Benjamin 1706-1790 .. **LC 25, 134; WLCS**
See also AMW; CDALB 1640-1865; DA; DA3; DAB; DAC; DAM MST; DLB 24, 43, 73, 183; LAIT 1; RGAL 4; TUS

Franklin, Madeleine
See L'Engle, Madeleine

Franklin, Madeleine L'Engle
See L'Engle, Madeleine

Franklin, Madeleine L'Engle Camp
See L'Engle, Madeleine

Franklin, (Stella Maria Sarah) Miles (Lampe) 1879-1954 .... **TCLC 7**
See also CA 104; 164; DLB 230; FW; MTCW 2; RGEL 2; TWA

Franzen, Jonathan 1959- .... **CLC 202**
See also AAYA 65; CA 129; CANR 105, 166

Fraser, Antonia 1932- .... **CLC 32, 107**
See also AAYA 57; CA 85-88; CANR 44, 65, 119, 164; CMW; DLB 276; MTCW 1, 2; MTFW 2005; SATA-Brief 32

Fraser, George MacDonald 1925-2008 .... **CLC 7**
See also AAYA 48; CA 45-48, 180; 268; CAAE 180; CANR 2, 48, 74; MTCW 2; RHW

Fraser, Sylvia 1935- .... **CLC 64**
See also CA 45-48; CANR 1, 16, 60; CCA 1

Frayn, Michael 1933- .... **CLC 3, 7, 31, 47, 176; DC 27**
See also AAYA 69; BRWC 2; BRWS 7; CA 5-8R; CANR 30, 69, 114, 133, 166; CBD; CD 5, 6; CN 1, 2, 3, 4, 5, 6, 7; DAM DRAM, NOV; DFS 22; DLB 13, 14, 194, 245; FANT; MTCW 1, 2; MTFW 2005; SFW 3

Fraze, Candida (Merrill) 1945- .... **CLC 50**
See also CA 126

Frazer, Andrew
See Marlowe, Stephen

Frazer, J(ames) G(eorge) 1854-1941 .... **TCLC 32**
See also BRWS 3; CA 118; NCFS 5

Frazer, Robert Caine
    See Creasey, John
Frazer, Sir James George
    See Frazer, J(ames) G(eorge)
Frazier, Charles 1950- .... **CLC 109, 224**
    See also AAYA 34; CA 161; CANR 126, 170; CSW; DLB 292; MTFW 2005; NFS 25
Frazier, Charles R.
    See Frazier, Charles
Frazier, Charles Robinson
    See Frazier, Charles
Frazier, Ian 1951- .... **CLC 46**
    See also CA 130; CANR 54, 93
Frederic, Harold 1856-1898 ... **NCLC 10, 175**
    See also AMW; DLB 12, 23; DLBD 13; MAL 5; NFS 22; RGAL 4
Frederick, John
    See Faust, Frederick (Schiller)
    See also TCWW 2
Frederick the Great 1712-1786 .... **LC 14**
Fredro, Aleksander 1793-1876 .... **NCLC 8**
Freeling, Nicolas 1927-2003 .... **CLC 38**
    See also CA 49-52; 218; CAAS 12; CANR 1, 17, 50, 84; CMW 4; CN 1, 2, 3, 4, 5, 6; DLB 87
Freeman, Douglas Southall
    1886-1953 .... **TCLC 11**
    See also CA 109; 195; DLB 17; DLBD 17
Freeman, Judith 1946- .... **CLC 55**
    See also CA 148; CANR 120; DLB 256
Freeman, Mary E(leanor) Wilkins 1852-1930
    SSC 1, 47, 113; TCLC 9
    See also CA 106; 177; DLB 12, 78, 221; EXPS; FW; HGG; MBL; RGAL 4; RGSF 2; SSFS 4, 8; SUFW 1; TUS
Freeman, R(ichard) Austin
    1862-1943 .... **TCLC 21**
    See also CA 113; CANR 84; CMW 4; DLB 70
French, Albert 1943- .... **CLC 86**
    See also BW 3; CA 167
French, Antonia
    See Kureishi, Hanif
French, Marilyn 1929- .. **CLC 10, 18, 60, 177**
    See also BPFB 1; CA 69-72; CANR 3, 31, 134, 163; CN 5, 6, 7; CPW; DAM DRAM, NOV, POP; FL 1:5; FW; INT CANR-31; MTCW 1, 2; MTFW 2005
French, Paul
    See Asimov, Isaac
Freneau, Philip Morin 1752-1832 .. **NCLC 1, 111**
    See also AMWS 2; DLB 37, 43; RGAL 4
Freud, Sigmund 1856-1939 .... **TCLC 52**
    See also CA 115; 133; CANR 69; DLB 296; EW 8; EWL 3; LATS 1:1; MTCW 1, 2; MTFW 2005; NCFS 3; TWA
Freytag, Gustav 1816-1895 .... **NCLC 109**
    See also DLB 129
Friedan, Betty 1921-2006 .... **CLC 74**
    See also CA 65-68; 248; CANR 18, 45, 74; DLB 246; FW; MTCW 1, 2; MTFW 2005; NCFS 5
Friedan, Betty Naomi
    See Friedan, Betty
Friedlander, Saul 1932- .... **CLC 90**
    See also CA 117; 130; CANR 72; RGHL
Friedman, B(ernard) H(arper)
    1926- .... **CLC 7**
    See also CA 1-4R; CANR 3, 48
Friedman, Bruce Jay 1930- ...... **CLC 3, 5, 56**
    See also CA 9-12R; CAD; CANR 25, 52, 101; CD 5, 6; CN 1, 2, 3, 4, 5, 6, 7; DLB 2, 28, 244; INT CANR-25; MAL 5; SSFS 18

Friel, Brian 1929- .. **CLC 5, 42, 59, 115, 253; DC 8; SSC 76**
    See also BRWS 5; CA 21-24R; CANR 33, 69, 131; CBD; CD 5, 6; DFS 11; DLB 13, 319; EWL 3; MTCW 1; RGEL 2; TEA
Friis-Baastad, Babbis Ellinor
    1921-1970 .... **CLC 12**
    See also CA 17-20R; 134; SATA 7
Frisch, Max 1911-1991 ...... **CLC 3, 9, 14, 18, 32, 44; TCLC 121**
    See also CA 85-88; 134; CANR 32, 74; CD-WLB 2; DAM DRAM, NOV; DFS 25; DLB 69, 124; EW 13; EWL 3; MTCW 1, 2; MTFW 2005; RGHL; RGWL 2, 3
Fromentin, Eugene (Samuel Auguste)
    1820-1876 .... **NCLC 10, 125**
    See also DLB 123; GFL 1789 to the Present
Frost, Frederick
    See Faust, Frederick (Schiller)
Frost, Robert 1874-1963 . **CLC 1, 3, 4, 9, 10, 13, 15, 26, 34, 44; PC 1, 39, 71; WLC 2**
    See also AAYA 21; AMW; AMWR 1; CA 89-92; CANR 33; CDALB 1917-1929; CLR 67; DA; DA3; DAB; DAC; DAM MST, POET; DLB 54, 284; DLBD 7; EWL 3; EXPP; MAL 5; MTCW 1, 2; MTFW 2005; PAB; PFS 1, 2, 3, 4, 5, 6, 7, 10, 13; RGAL 4; SATA 14; TUS; WP; WYA
Frost, Robert Lee
    See Frost, Robert
Froude, James Anthony
    1818-1894 .... **NCLC 43**
    See also DLB 18, 57, 144
Froy, Herald
    See Waterhouse, Keith (Spencer)
Fry, Christopher 1907-2005 ... **CLC 2, 10, 14**
    See also BRWS 3; CA 17-20R; 240; CAAS 23; CANR 9, 30, 74, 132; CBD; CD 5, 6; CP 1, 2, 3, 4, 5, 6, 7; DAM DRAM; DLB 13; EWL 3; MTCW 1, 2; MTFW 2005; RGEL 2; SATA 66; TEA
Frye, (Herman) Northrop
    1912-1991 .... **CLC 24, 70; TCLC 165**
    See also CA 5-8R; 133; CANR 8, 37; DLB 67, 68, 246; EWL 3; MTCW 1, 2; MTFW 2005; RGAL 4; TWA
Fuchs, Daniel 1909-1993 .... **CLC 8, 22**
    See also CA 81-84; 142; CAAS 5; CANR 40; CN 1, 2, 3, 4, 5; DLB 9, 26, 28; DLBY 1993; MAL 5
Fuchs, Daniel 1934- .... **CLC 34**
    See also CA 37-40R; CANR 14, 48
Fuentes, Carlos 1928- .. **CLC 3, 8, 10, 13, 22, 41, 60, 113; HLC 1; SSC 24; WLC 2**
    See also AAYA 4, 45; AITN 2; BPFB 1; CA 69-72; CANR 10, 32, 68, 104, 138; CDWLB 3; CWW 2; DA; DA3; DAB; DAC; DAM MST, MULT, NOV; DLB 113; DNFS 2; EWL 3; HW 1, 2; LAIT 3; LATS 1:2; LAW; LAWS 1; LMFS 2; MTCW 1, 2; MTFW 2005; NFS 8; RGSF 2; RGWL 2, 3; TWA; WLIT 1
Fuentes, Gregorio Lopez y
    See Lopez y Fuentes, Gregorio
Fuertes, Gloria 1918-1998 .... **PC 27**
    See also CA 178, 180; DLB 108; HW 2; SATA 115
Fugard, (Harold) Athol 1932- . **CLC 5, 9, 14, 25, 40, 80, 211; DC 3**
    See also AAYA 17; AFW; CA 85-88; CANR 32, 54, 118; CD 5, 6; DAM DRAM; DFS 3, 6, 10, 24; DLB 225; DNFS 1, 2; EWL 3; LATS 1:2; MTCW 1; MTFW 2005; RGEL 2; WLIT 2
Fugard, Sheila 1932- .... **CLC 48**
    See also CA 125
Fujiwara no Teika 1162-1241 .... **CMLC 73**
    See also DLB 203

Fukuyama, Francis 1952- .... **CLC 131**
    See also CA 140; CANR 72, 125, 170
Fuller, Charles (H.), (Jr.) 1939- .. **BLC 1:2; CLC 25; DC 1**
    See also BW 2; CA 108; 112; CAD; CANR 87; CD 5, 6; DAM DRAM, MULT; DFS 8; DLB 38, 266; EWL 3; INT CA-112; MAL 5; MTCW 1
Fuller, Henry Blake 1857-1929 .... **TCLC 103**
    See also CA 108; 177; DLB 12; RGAL 4
Fuller, John (Leopold) 1937- .... **CLC 62**
    See also CA 21-24R; CANR 9, 44; CP 1, 2, 3, 4, 5, 6, 7; DLB 40
Fuller, Margaret
    See Ossoli, Sarah Margaret (Fuller)
    See also AMWS 2; DLB 183, 223, 239; FL 1:3
Fuller, Roy (Broadbent) 1912-1991 ... **CLC 4, 28**
    See also BRWS 7; CA 5-8R; 135; CAAS 10; CANR 53, 83; CN 1, 2, 3, 4, 5; CP 1, 2, 3, 4, 5; CWRI 5; DLB 15, 20; EWL 3; RGEL 2; SATA 87
Fuller, Sarah Margaret
    See Ossoli, Sarah Margaret (Fuller)
Fuller, Sarah Margaret
    See Ossoli, Sarah Margaret (Fuller)
Fuller, Thomas 1608-1661 .... **LC 111**
    See also DLB 151
Fulton, Alice 1952- .... **CLC 52**
    See also CA 116; CANR 57, 88; CP 5, 6, 7; CWP; DLB 193; PFS 25
Furphy, Joseph 1843-1912 .... **TCLC 25**
    See Collins, Tom
    See also CA 163; DLB 230; EWL 3; RGEL 2
Furst, Alan 1941- .... **CLC 255**
    See also CA 69-72; CANR 12, 34, 59, 102, 159; DLBY 01
Fuson, Robert H(enderson) 1927- .... **CLC 70**
    See also CA 89-92; CANR 103
Fussell, Paul 1924- .... **CLC 74**
    See also BEST 90:1; CA 17-20R; CANR 8, 21, 35, 69, 135; INT CANR-21; MTCW 1, 2; MTFW 2005
Futabatei, Shimei 1864-1909 .... **TCLC 44**
    See Futabatei Shimei
    See also CA 162; MJW
Futabatei Shimei
    See Futabatei, Shimei
    See also DLB 180; EWL 3
Futrelle, Jacques 1875-1912 .... **TCLC 19**
    See also CA 113; 155; CMW 4
Gaboriau, Emile 1835-1873 .... **NCLC 14**
    See also CMW 4; MSW
Gadda, Carlo Emilio 1893-1973 ...... **CLC 11; TCLC 144**
    See also CA 89-92; DLB 177; EWL 3; WLIT 7
Gaddis, William 1922-1998 ... **CLC 1, 3, 6, 8, 10, 19, 43, 86**
    See also AMWS 4; BPFB 1; CA 17-20R; 172; CANR 21, 48, 148; CN 1, 2, 3, 4, 5, 6; DLB 2, 278; EWL 3; MAL 5; MTCW 1, 2; MTFW 2005; RGAL 4
Gage, Walter
    See Inge, William (Motter)
Gaiman, Neil 1960- .... **CLC 195**
    See also AAYA 19, 42; CA 133; CANR 81, 129; CLR 109; DLB 261; HGG; MTFW 2005; SATA 85, 146; SFW 4; SUFW 2
Gaiman, Neil Richard
    See Gaiman, Neil
Gaines, Ernest J. 1933- ..... **BLC 1:2; CLC 3, 11, 18, 86, 181; SSC 68**
    See also AAYA 18; AFAW 1, 2; AITN 1; BPFB 2; BW 2, 3; BYA 6; CA 9-12R; CANR 6, 24, 42, 75, 126; CDALB 1968-1988; CLR 62; CN 1, 2, 3, 4, 5, 6, 7;

Gassendi, Pierre 1592-1655 .... **LC 54**
See also GFL Beginnings to 1789

Gasset, Jose Ortega y
See Ortega y Gasset, Jose

Gates, Henry Louis, Jr. 1950- ... **BLCS; CLC 65**
See also BW 2, 3; CA 109; CANR 25, 53, 75, 125; CSW; DA3; DAM MULT; DLB 67; EWL 3; MAL 5; MTCW 2; MTFW 2005; RGAL 4

Gatos, Stephanie
See Katz, Steve

Gautier, Theophile 1811-1872 .. **NCLC 1, 59; PC 18; SSC 20**
See also DAM POET; DLB 119; EW 6; GFL 1789 to the Present; RGWL 2, 3; SUFW; TWA

Gay, John 1685-1732 .... **LC 49**
See also BRW 3; DAM DRAM; DLB 84, 95; RGEL 2; WLIT 3

Gay, Oliver
See Gogarty, Oliver St. John

Gay, Peter 1923- .... **CLC 158**
See also CA 13-16R; CANR 18, 41, 77, 147; INT CANR-18; RGHL

Gay, Peter Jack
See Gay, Peter

Gaye, Marvin (Pentz, Jr.) 1939-1984 .... **CLC 26**
See also CA 195; 112

Gebler, Carlo 1954- .... **CLC 39**
See also CA 119; 133; CANR 96; DLB 271

Gee, Maggie 1948- .... **CLC 57**
See also CA 130; CANR 125; CN 4, 5, 6, 7; DLB 207; MTFW 2005

Gee, Maurice 1931- .... **CLC 29**
See also AAYA 42; CA 97-100; CANR 67, 123; CLR 56; CN 2, 3, 4, 5, 6, 7; CWRI 5; EWL 3; MAICYA 2; RGSF 2; SATA 46, 101

Gee, Maurice Gough
See Gee, Maurice

Geiogamah, Hanay 1945- .... **NNAL**
See also CA 153; DAM MULT; DLB 175

Gelbart, Larry
See Gelbart, Larry (Simon)
See also CAD; CD 5, 6

Gelbart, Larry (Simon) 1928- .... **CLC 21, 61**
See Gelbart, Larry
See also CA 73-76; CANR 45, 94

Gelber, Jack 1932-2003 ...... **CLC 1, 6, 14, 79**
See also CA 1-4R; 216; CAD; CANR 2; DLB 7, 228; MAL 5

Gellhorn, Martha (Ellis) 1908-1998 .... **CLC 14, 60**
See also CA 77-80; 164; CANR 44; CN 1, 2, 3, 4, 5, 6 7; DLBY 1982, 1998

Genet, Jean 1910-1986 .. **CLC 1, 2, 5, 10, 14, 44, 46; DC 25; TCLC 128**
See also CA 13-16R; CANR 18; DA3; DAM DRAM; DFS 10; DLB 72, 321; DLBY 1986; EW 13; EWL 3; GFL 1789 to the Present; GLL 1; LMFS 2; MTCW 1, 2; MTFW 2005; RGWL 2, 3; TWA

Genlis, Stephanie-Felicite Ducrest 1746-1830 **NCLC 166**
See also DLB 313

Gent, Peter 1942- .... **CLC 29**
See also AITN 1; CA 89-92; DLBY 1982

Gentile, Giovanni 1875-1944 .... **TCLC 96**
See also CA 119

Geoffrey of Monmouth c. 1100-1155 .... **CMLC 44**
See also DLB 146; TEA

George, Jean
See George, Jean Craighead

George, Jean Craighead 1919- .... **CLC 35**
See also AAYA 8, 69; BYA 2, 4; CA 5-8R; CANR 25; CLR 1; 80; DLB 52; JRDA; MAICYA 1, 2; SATA 2, 68, 124, 170; WYA; YAW

George, Stefan (Anton) 1868-1933 . **TCLC 2, 14**
See also CA 104; 193; EW 8; EWL 3

Georges, Georges Martin
See Simenon, Georges (Jacques Christian)

Gerald of Wales c. 1146-c. 1223 ... **CMLC 60**

Gerhardi, William Alexander
See Gerhardie, William Alexander

Gerhardie, William Alexander 1895-1977 **CLC 5**
See also CA 25-28R; 73-76; CANR 18; CN 1, 2; DLB 36; RGEL 2

Gerson, Jean 1363-1429 .... **LC 77**
See also DLB 208

Gersonides 1288-1344 .... **CMLC 49**
See also DLB 115

Gerstler, Amy 1956- .... **CLC 70**
See also CA 146; CANR 99

Gertler, T. .... **CLC 34**
See also CA 116; 121

Gertsen, Aleksandr Ivanovich
See Herzen, Aleksandr Ivanovich

Ghalib .... **NCLC 39, 78**
See Ghalib, Asadullah Khan

Ghalib, Asadullah Khan 1797-1869
See Ghalib
See also DAM POET; RGWL 2, 3

Ghelderode, Michel de 1898-1962 ..... **CLC 6, 11; DC 15; TCLC 187**
See also CA 85-88; CANR 40, 77; DAM DRAM; DLB 321; EW 11; EWL 3; TWA

Ghiselin, Brewster 1903-2001 .... **CLC 23**
See also CA 13-16R; CAAS 10; CANR 13; CP 1, 2, 3, 4, 5, 6, 7

Ghose, Aurabinda 1872-1950 .... **TCLC 63**
See Ghose, Aurobindo
See also CA 163

Ghose, Aurobindo
See Ghose, Aurabinda
See also EWL 3

Ghose, Zulfikar 1935- .... **CLC 42, 200**
See also CA 65-68; CANR 67; CN 1, 2, 3, 4, 5, 6, 7; CP 1, 2, 3, 4, 5, 6, 7; DLB 323; EWL 3

Ghosh, Amitav 1956- .... **CLC 44, 153**
See also CA 147; CANR 80, 158; CN 6, 7; DLB 323; WWE 1

Giacosa, Giuseppe 1847-1906 .... **TCLC 7**
See also CA 104

Gibb, Lee
See Waterhouse, Keith (Spencer)

Gibbon, Edward 1737-1794 .... **LC 97**
See also BRW 3; DLB 104, 336; RGEL 2

Gibbon, Lewis Grassic .... **TCLC 4**
See Mitchell, James Leslie
See also RGEL 2

Gibbons, Kaye 1960- .... **CLC 50, 88, 145**
See also AAYA 34; AMWS 10; CA 151; CANR 75, 127; CN 7; CSW; DA3; DAM POP; DLB 292; MTCW 2; MTFW 2005; NFS 3; RGAL 4; SATA 117

Gibran, Kahlil 1883-1931 ..... **PC 9; TCLC 1, 9, 205**
See also CA 104; 150; DA3; DAM POET, POP; EWL 3; MTCW 2; WLIT 6

Gibran, Khalil
See Gibran, Kahlil

Gibson, Mel 1956- .... **CLC 215**

Gibson, William 1914- .... **CLC 23**
See also CA 9-12R; CAD; CANR 9, 42, 75, 125; CD 5, 6; DA; DAB; DAC; DAM DRAM, MST; DFS 2; DLB 7; LAIT 2; MAL 5; MTCW 2; MTFW 2005; SATA 66; YAW

Gibson, William 1948- .... **CLC 39, 63, 186, 192; SSC 52**
See also AAYA 12, 59; AMWS 16; BPFB 2; CA 126; 133; CANR 52, 90, 106, 172; CN 6, 7; CPW; DA3; DAM POP; DLB 251; MTCW 2; MTFW 2005; SCFW 2; SFW 4

Gibson, William Ford
See Gibson, William

Gide, Andre (Paul Guillaume) 1869-1951 ...... **SSC 13; TCLC 5, 12, 36, 177; WLC 3**
See also CA 104; 124; DA; DA3; DAB; DAC; DAM MST, NOV; DLB 65, 321, 330; EW 8; EWL 3; GFL 1789 to the Present; MTCW 1, 2; MTFW 2005; NFS 21; RGSF 2; RGWL 2, 3; TWA

Gifford, Barry (Colby) 1946- .... **CLC 34**
See also CA 65-68; CANR 9, 30, 40, 90

Gilbert, Frank
See De Voto, Bernard (Augustine)

Gilbert, W(illiam) S(chwenck) 1836-1911 **TCLC 3**
See also CA 104; 173; DAM DRAM, POET; RGEL 2; SATA 36

Gilbert of Poitiers c. 1085-1154 .... **CMLC 85**

Gilbreth, Frank B(unker), Jr. 1911-2001 .... **CLC 17**
See also CA 9-12R; SATA 2

Gilchrist, Ellen (Louise) 1935- .. **CLC 34, 48, 143; SSC 14, 63**
See also BPFB 2; CA 113; 116; CANR 41, 61, 104; CN 4, 5, 6, 7; CPW; CSW; DAM POP; DLB 130; EWL 3; EXPS; MTCW 1, 2; MTFW 2005; RGAL 4; RGSF 2; SSFS 9

Gildas fl. 6th cent. - .... **CMLC 99**

Giles, Molly 1942- .... **CLC 39**
See also CA 126; CANR 98

Gill, Eric .... **TCLC 85**
See Gill, (Arthur) Eric (Rowton Peter Joseph)

Gill, (Arthur) Eric (Rowton Peter Joseph) 1882-1940
See Gill, Eric
See also CA 120; DLB 98

Gill, Patrick
See Creasey, John

Gillette, Douglas .... **CLC 70**

Gilliam, Terry 1940- .... **CLC 21, 141**
See Monty Python
See also AAYA 19, 59; CA 108; 113; CANR 35; INT CA-113

Gilliam, Terry Vance
See Gilliam, Terry

Gillian, Jerry
See Gilliam, Terry

Gilliatt, Penelope (Ann Douglass) 1932-1993 **CLC 2, 10, 13, 53**
See also AITN 2; CA 13-16R; 141; CANR 49; CN 1, 2, 3, 4, 5; DLB 14

Gilligan, Carol 1936- .... **CLC 208**
See also CA 142; CANR 121; FW

Gilman, Charlotte (Anna) Perkins (Stetson) 1860-1935 ...... **SSC 13, 62; TCLC 9, 37, 117, 201**
See also AAYA 75; AMWS 11; BYA 11; CA 106; 150; DLB 221; EXPS; FL 1:5; FW; HGG; LAIT 2; MBL; MTCW 2; MTFW 2005; RGAL 4; RGSF 2; SFW 4; SSFS 1, 18

Gilmore, Mary (Jean Cameron) 1865-1962 **PC 87**
See also CA 114; DLB 260; RGEL 2; SATA 49

Gilmour, David 1946- .... **CLC 35**

Gilpin, William 1724-1804 .... **NCLC 30**

Gilray, J. D.
See Mencken, H(enry) L(ouis)

Grimble, Reverend Charles James
See Eliot, T(homas) S(tearns)
Grimke, Angelina (Emily) Weld 1880-1958 **HR 1:2**
See Weld, Angelina (Emily) Grimke
See also BW 1; CA 124; DAM POET; DLB 50, 54
Grimke, Charlotte L(ottie) Forten 1837(?)-1914
See Forten, Charlotte L.
See also BW 1; CA 117; 124; DAM MULT, POET
Grimm, Jacob Ludwig Karl 1785-1863 **NCLC 3, 77; SSC 36**
See Grimm Brothers
See also CLR 112; DLB 90; MAICYA 1, 2; RGSF 2; RGWL 2, 3; SATA 22; WCH
Grimm, Wilhelm Karl 1786-1859 .. **NCLC 3, 77; SSC 36**
See Grimm Brothers
See also CDWLB 2; CLR 112; DLB 90; MAICYA 1, 2; RGSF 2; RGWL 2, 3; SATA 22; WCH
Grimm and Grim
See Grimm, Jacob Ludwig Karl; Grimm, Wilhelm Karl
Grimm Brothers .... **SSC 88**
See Grimm, Jacob Ludwig Karl; Grimm, Wilhelm Karl
See also CLR 112
Grimmelshausen, Hans Jakob Christoffel von
See Grimmelshausen, Johann Jakob Christoffel von
See also RGWL 2, 3
Grimmelshausen, Johann Jakob Christoffel von 1621-1676 .... **LC 6**
See Grimmelshausen, Hans Jakob Christoffel von
See also CDWLB 2; DLB 168
Grindel, Eugene 1895-1952 .... **PC 38; TCLC 7, 41**
See also CA 104; 193; EWL 3; GFL 1789 to the Present; LMFS 2; RGWL 2, 3
Grisham, John 1955- .... **CLC 84**
See also AAYA 14, 47; BPFB 3; CA 138; CANR 47, 69, 114, 133; CMW 4; CN 6, 7; CPW; CSW; DA3; DAM POP; MSW; MTCW 2; MTFW 2005
Grosseteste, Robert 1175(?)-1253 . **CMLC 62**
See also DLB 115
Grossman, David 1954- .... **CLC 67, 231**
See also CA 138; CANR 114, 175; CWW 2; DLB 299; EWL 3; RGHL; WLIT 6
Grossman, Vasilii Semenovich
See Grossman, Vasily (Semenovich)
See also DLB 272
Grossman, Vasily (Semenovich) 1905-1964 **CLC 41**
See Grossman, Vasilii Semenovich
See also CA 124; 130; MTCW 1; RGHL
Grove, Frederick Philip .... **TCLC 4**
See Greve, Felix Paul (Berthold Friedrich)
See also DLB 92; RGEL 2; TCWW 1, 2
Grubb
See Crumb, R.
Grumbach, Doris 1918- .... **CLC 13, 22, 64**
See also CA 5-8R; CAAS 2; CANR 9, 42, 70, 127; CN 6, 7; INT CANR-9; MTCW 2; MTFW 2005
Grundtvig, Nikolai Frederik Severin 1783-1872 .... **NCLC 1, 158**
See also DLB 300
Grunge
See Crumb, R.
Grunwald, Lisa 1959- .... **CLC 44**
See also CA 120; CANR 148
Gryphius, Andreas 1616-1664 .... **LC 89**
See also CDWLB 2; DLB 164; RGWL 2, 3

Guare, John 1938- .... **CLC 8, 14, 29, 67; DC 20**
See also CA 73-76; CAD; CANR 21, 69, 118; CD 5, 6; DAM DRAM; DFS 8, 13; DLB 7, 249; EWL 3; MAL 5; MTCW 1, 2; RGAL 4
Guarini, Battista 1538-1612 .... **LC 102**
See also DLB 339
Gubar, Susan 1944- .... **CLC 145**
See also CA 108; CANR 45, 70, 139; FW; MTCW 1; RGAL 4
Gubar, Susan David
See Gubar, Susan
Gudjonsson, Halldor Kiljan 1902-1998
See Halldor Laxness
See also CA 103; 164
Guenter, Erich
See Eich, Gunter
Guest, Barbara 1920-2006 ... **CLC 34; PC 55**
See also BG 1:2; CA 25-28R; 248; CANR 11, 44, 84; CP 1, 2, 3, 4, 5, 6, 7; CWP; DLB 5, 193
Guest, Edgar A(lbert) 1881-1959 ... **TCLC 95**
See also CA 112; 168
Guest, Judith 1936- .... **CLC 8, 30**
See also AAYA 7, 66; CA 77-80; CANR 15, 75, 138; DA3; DAM NOV, POP; EXPN; INT CANR-15; LAIT 5; MTCW 1, 2; MTFW 2005; NFS 1
Guevara, Che .... **CLC 87; HLC 1**
See Guevara (Serna), Ernesto
Guevara (Serna), Ernesto 1928-1967 .... **CLC 87; HLC 1**
See Guevara, Che
See also CA 127; 111; CANR 56; DAM MULT; HW 1
Guicciardini, Francesco 1483-1540 ..... **LC 49**
Guido delle Colonne c. 1215-c. 1290 .... **CMLC 90**
Guild, Nicholas M. 1944- .... **CLC 33**
See also CA 93-96
Guillemin, Jacques
See Sartre, Jean-Paul
Guillen, Jorge 1893-1984 . **CLC 11; HLCS 1; PC 35**
See also CA 89-92; 112; DAM MULT, POET; DLB 108; EWL 3; HW 1; RGWL 2, 3
Guillen, Nicolas (Cristobal) 1902-1989 .... **BLC 1:2; CLC 48, 79; HLC 1; PC 23**
See also BW 2; CA 116; 125; 129; CANR 84; DAM MST, MULT, POET; DLB 283; EWL 3; HW 1; LAW; RGWL 2, 3; WP
Guillen y Alvarez, Jorge
See Guillen, Jorge
Guillevic, (Eugene) 1907-1997 .... **CLC 33**
See also CA 93-96; CWW 2
Guillois
See Desnos, Robert
Guillois, Valentin
See Desnos, Robert
Guimaraes Rosa, Joao 1908-1967 .... **HLCS 2**
See Rosa, Joao Guimaraes
See also CA 175; LAW; RGSF 2; RGWL 2, 3
Guiney, Louise Imogen 1861-1920 .... **TCLC 41**
See also CA 160; DLB 54; RGAL 4
Guinizelli, Guido c. 1230-1276 ...... **CMLC 49**
See Guinizzelli, Guido
Guinizzelli, Guido
See Guinizelli, Guido
See also WLIT 7
Guiraldes, Ricardo (Guillermo) 1886-1927 **TCLC 39**
See also CA 131; EWL 3; HW 1; LAW; MTCW 1

Gumilev, Nikolai (Stepanovich) 1886-1921 **TCLC 60**
See Gumilyov, Nikolay Stepanovich
See also CA 165; DLB 295
Gumilyov, Nikolay Stepanovich
See Gumilev, Nikolai (Stepanovich)
See also EWL 3
Gump, P. Q.
See Card, Orson Scott
Gunesekera, Romesh 1954- .... **CLC 91**
See also BRWS 10; CA 159; CANR 140, 172; CN 6, 7; DLB 267, 323
Gunn, Bill .... **CLC 5**
See Gunn, William Harrison
See also DLB 38
Gunn, Thom(son William) 1929-2004 . **CLC 3, 6, 18, 32, 81; PC 26**
See also BRWS 4; CA 17-20R; 227; CANR 9, 33, 116; CDBLB 1960 to Present; CP 1, 2, 3, 4, 5, 6, 7; DAM POET; DLB 27; INT CANR-33; MTCW 1; PFS 9; RGEL 2
Gunn, William Harrison 1934(?)-1989
See Gunn, Bill
See also AITN 1; BW 1, 3; CA 13-16R; 128; CANR 12, 25, 76
Gunn Allen, Paula
See Allen, Paula Gunn
Gunnars, Kristjana 1948- .... **CLC 69**
See also CA 113; CCA 1; CP 6, 7; CWP; DLB 60
Gunter, Erich
See Eich, Gunter
Gurdjieff, G(eorgei) I(vanovich) 1877(?)-1949 .... **TCLC 71**
See also CA 157
Gurganus, Allan 1947- .... **CLC 70**
See also BEST 90:1; CA 135; CANR 114; CN 6, 7; CPW; CSW; DAM POP; GLL 1
Gurney, A. R.
See Gurney, A(lbert) R(amsdell), Jr.
See also DLB 266
Gurney, A(lbert) R(amsdell), Jr. 1930- .... **CLC 32, 50, 54**
See Gurney, A. R.
See also AMWS 5; CA 77-80; CAD; CANR 32, 64, 121; CD 5, 6; DAM DRAM; EWL 3
Gurney, Ivor (Bertie) 1890-1937 ... **TCLC 33**
See also BRW 6; CA 167; DLBY 2002; PAB; RGEL 2
Gurney, Peter
See Gurney, A(lbert) R(amsdell), Jr.
Guro, Elena (Genrikhovna) 1877-1913 .... **TCLC 56**
See also DLB 295
Gustafson, James M(oody) 1925- ... **CLC 100**
See also CA 25-28R; CANR 37
Gustafson, Ralph (Barker) 1909-1995 .... **CLC 36**
See also CA 21-24R; CANR 8, 45, 84; CP 1, 2, 3, 4, 5, 6; DLB 88; RGEL 2
Gut, Gom
See Simenon, Georges (Jacques Christian)
Guterson, David 1956- .... **CLC 91**
See also CA 132; CANR 73, 126; CN 7; DLB 292; MTCW 2; MTFW 2005; NFS 13
Guthrie, A(lfred) B(ertram), Jr. 1901-1991 **CLC 23**
See also CA 57-60; 134; CANR 24; CN 1, 2, 3; DLB 6, 212; MAL 5; SATA 62; SATA-Obit 67; TCWW 1, 2
Guthrie, Isobel
See Grieve, C(hristopher) M(urray)
Guthrie, Woodrow Wilson 1912-1967
See Guthrie, Woody
See also CA 113; 93-96

Handy, W(illiam) C(hristopher) 1873-1958
TCLC 97
See also BW 3; CA 121; 167
Hanley, James 1901-1985 ..... **CLC 3, 5, 8, 13**
See also CA 73-76; 117; CANR 36; CBD;
CN 1, 2, 3; DLB 191; EWL 3; MTCW 1;
RGEL 2
Hannah, Barry 1942- .. **CLC 23, 38, 90; SSC
94**
See also BPFB 2; CA 108; 110; CANR 43,
68, 113; CN 4, 5, 6, 7; CSW; DLB 6, 234;
INT CA-110; MTCW 1; RGSF 2
Hannon, Ezra
See Hunter, Evan
Hansberry, Lorraine (Vivian)
1930-1965 ... **BLC 1:2, 2:2; CLC 17, 62;
DC 2; TCLC 192**
See also AAYA 25; AFAW 1, 2; AMWS 4;
BW 1, 3; CA 109; 25-28R; CABS 3;
CAD; CANR 58; CDALB 1941-1968;
CWD; DA; DA3; DAB; DAC; DAM
DRAM, MST, MULT; DFS 2; DLB 7, 38;
EWL 3; FL 1:6; FW; LAIT 4; MAL 5;
MTCW 1, 2; MTFW 2005; RGAL 4; TUS
Hansen, Joseph 1923-2004 .... **CLC 38**
See Brock, Rose; Colton, James
See also BPFB 2; CA 29-32R; 233; CAAS
17; CANR 16, 44, 66, 125; CMW 4; DLB
226; GLL 1; INT CANR-16
Hansen, Karen V. 1955- .... **CLC 65**
See also CA 149; CANR 102
Hansen, Martin A(lfred)
1909-1955 .... **TCLC 32**
See also CA 167; DLB 214; EWL 3
Hanson, Kenneth O(stlin) 1922- .... **CLC 13**
See also CA 53-56; CANR 7; CP 1, 2, 3, 4,
5
Hardwick, Elizabeth 1916-2007 .... **CLC 13**
See also AMWS 3; CA 5-8R; 267; CANR
3, 32, 70, 100, 139; CN 4, 5, 6; CSW;
DA3; DAM NOV; DLB 6; MBL; MTCW
1, 2; MTFW 2005; TCLE 1:1
Hardwick, Elizabeth Bruce
See Hardwick, Elizabeth
Hardwick, Elizabeth Bruce
See Hardwick, Elizabeth
Hardy, Thomas 1840-1928 . **PC 8; SSC 2, 60,
113; TCLC 4, 10, 18, 32, 48, 53, 72,
143, 153; WLC 3**
See also AAYA 69; BRW 6; BRWC 1, 2;
BRWR 1; CA 104; 123; CDBLB 1890-
1914; DA; DA3; DAB; DAC; DAM MST,
NOV, POET; DLB 18, 19, 135, 284; EWL
3; EXPN; EXPP; LAIT 2; MTCW 1, 2;
MTFW 2005; NFS 3, 11, 15, 19; PFS 3,
4, 18; RGEL 2; RGSF 2; TEA; WLIT 4
Hare, David 1947- . **CLC 29, 58, 136; DC 26**
See also BRWS 4; CA 97-100; CANR 39,
91; CBD; CD 5, 6; DFS 4, 7, 16; DLB
13, 310; MTCW 1; TEA
Harewood, John
See Van Druten, John (William)
Harford, Henry
See Hudson, W(illiam) H(enry)
Hargrave, Leonie
See Disch, Thomas M.
**Hariri, Al- al-Qasim ibn 'Ali Abu
Muhammad al-Basri**
See al-Hariri, al-Qasim ibn 'Ali Abu Mu-
hammad al-Basri
Harjo, Joy 1951- ..... **CLC 83; NNAL; PC 27**
See also AMWS 12; CA 114; CANR 35,
67, 91, 129; CP 6, 7; CWP; DAM MULT;
DLB 120, 175; EWL 3; MTCW 1; MTFW
2005; PFS 15; RGAL 4
Harlan, Louis R(udolph) 1922- .... **CLC 34**
See also CA 21-24R; CANR 25, 55, 80
Harling, Robert 1951(?)- .... **CLC 53**
See also CA 147

Harmon, William (Ruth) 1938- .... **CLC 38**
See also CA 33-36R; CANR 14, 32, 35;
SATA 65
Harper, F. E. W.
See Harper, Frances Ellen Watkins
Harper, Frances E. W.
See Harper, Frances Ellen Watkins
Harper, Frances E. Watkins
See Harper, Frances Ellen Watkins
Harper, Frances Ellen
See Harper, Frances Ellen Watkins
Harper, Frances Ellen Watkins 1825-1911
BLC 1:2; PC 21; TCLC 14
See also AFAW 1, 2; BW 1, 3; CA 111; 125;
CANR 79; DAM MULT, POET; DLB 50,
221; MBL; RGAL 4
Harper, Michael S(teven) 1938- ..... **BLC 2:2;
CLC 7, 22**
See also AFAW 2; BW 1; CA 33-36R; 224;
CAAE 224; CANR 24, 108; CP 2, 3, 4, 5,
6, 7; DLB 41; RGAL 4; TCLE 1:1
Harper, Mrs. F. E. W.
See Harper, Frances Ellen Watkins
Harpur, Charles 1813-1868 .... **NCLC 114**
See also DLB 230; RGEL 2
Harris, Christie
See Harris, Christie (Lucy) Irwin
Harris, Christie (Lucy) Irwin
1907-2002 .... **CLC 12**
See also CA 5-8R; CANR 6, 83; CLR 47;
DLB 88; JRDA; MAICYA 1, 2; SAAS 10;
SATA 6, 74; SATA-Essay 116
Harris, Frank 1856-1931 .... **TCLC 24**
See also CA 109; 150; CANR 80; DLB 156,
197; RGEL 2
Harris, George Washington
1814-1869 .... **NCLC 23, 165**
See also DLB 3, 11, 248; RGAL 4
Harris, Joel Chandler 1848-1908 ..... **SSC 19,
103; TCLC 2**
See also CA 104; 137; CANR 80; CLR 49,
128; DLB 11, 23, 42, 78, 91; LAIT 2;
MAICYA 1, 2; RGSF 2; SATA 100; WCH;
YABC 1
**Harris, John (Wyndham Parkes Lucas)
Beynon** 1903-1969
See Wyndham, John
See also CA 102; 89-92; CANR 84; SATA
118; SFW 4
Harris, MacDonald .... **CLC 9**
See Heiney, Donald (William)
Harris, Mark 1922-2007 .... **CLC 19**
See also CA 5-8R; 260; CAAS 3; CANR 2,
55, 83; CN 1, 2, 3, 4, 5, 6, 7; DLB 2;
DLBY 1980
Harris, Norman .... **CLC 65**
Harris, (Theodore) Wilson 1921- ... **BLC 2:2;
CLC 25, 159**
See also BRWS 5; BW 2, 3; CA 65-68;
CAAS 16; CANR 11, 27, 69, 114; CD-
WLB 3; CN 1, 2, 3, 4, 5, 6, 7; CP 1, 2, 3,
4, 5, 6, 7; DLB 117; EWL 3; MTCW 1;
RGEL 2
Harrison, Barbara Grizzuti
1934-2002 .... **CLC 144**
See also CA 77-80; 205; CANR 15, 48; INT
CANR-15
Harrison, Elizabeth (Allen) Cavanna
1909-2001
See Cavanna, Betty
See also CA 9-12R; 200; CANR 6, 27, 85,
104, 121; MAICYA 2; SATA 142; YAW
Harrison, Harry (Max) 1925- .... **CLC 42**
See also CA 1-4R; CANR 5, 21, 84; DLB
8; SATA 4; SCFW 2; SFW 4
Harrison, James
See Harrison, Jim
Harrison, James Thomas
See Harrison, Jim

Harrison, Jim 1937- .... **CLC 6, 14, 33, 66,
143; SSC 19**
See also AMWS 8; CA 13-16R; CANR 8,
51, 79, 142; CN 5, 6; CP 1, 2, 3, 4, 5, 6;
DLBY 1982; INT CANR-8; RGAL 4;
TCWW 2; TUS
Harrison, Kathryn 1961- .... **CLC 70, 151**
See also CA 144; CANR 68, 122
Harrison, Tony 1937- .... **CLC 43, 129**
See also BRWS 5; CA 65-68; CANR 44,
98; CBD; CD 5, 6; CP 2, 3, 4, 5, 6, 7;
DLB 40, 245; MTCW 1; RGEL 2
Harriss, Will(ard Irvin) 1922- .... **CLC 34**
See also CA 111
Hart, Ellis
See Ellison, Harlan
Hart, Josephine 1942(?)- .... **CLC 70**
See also CA 138; CANR 70, 149; CPW;
DAM POP
Hart, Moss 1904-1961 .... **CLC 66**
See also CA 109; 89-92; CANR 84; DAM
DRAM; DFS 1; DLB 7, 266; RGAL 4
Harte, (Francis) Bret(t)
1836(?)-1902 ... **SSC 8, 59; TCLC 1, 25;
WLC 3**
See also AMWS 2; CA 104; 140; CANR
80; CDALB 1865-1917; DA; DA3; DAC;
DAM MST; DLB 12, 64, 74, 79, 186;
EXPS; LAIT 2; RGAL 4; RGSF 2; SATA
26; SSFS 3; TUS
Hartley, L(eslie) P(oles) 1895-1972 ... **CLC 2,
22**
See also BRWS 7; CA 45-48; 37-40R;
CANR 33; CN 1; DLB 15, 139; EWL 3;
HGG; MTCW 1, 2; MTFW 2005; RGEL
2; RGSF 2; SUFW 1
Hartman, Geoffrey H. 1929- .... **CLC 27**
See also CA 117; 125; CANR 79; DLB 67
Hartmann, Sadakichi 1869-1944 ... **TCLC 73**
See also CA 157; DLB 54
Hartmann von Aue c. 1170-c.
1210 .... **CMLC 15**
See also CDWLB 2; DLB 138; RGWL 2, 3
Hartog, Jan de
See de Hartog, Jan
Haruf, Kent 1943- .... **CLC 34**
See also AAYA 44; CA 149; CANR 91, 131
Harvey, Caroline
See Trollope, Joanna
Harvey, Gabriel 1550(?)-1631 .... **LC 88**
See also DLB 167, 213, 281
Harvey, Jack
See Rankin, Ian
Harwood, Ronald 1934- .... **CLC 32**
See also CA 1-4R; CANR 4, 55, 150; CBD;
CD 5, 6; DAM DRAM, MST; DLB 13
Hasegawa Tatsunosuke
See Futabatei, Shimei
Hasek, Jaroslav (Matej Frantisek)
1883-1923 .... **SSC 69; TCLC 4**
See also CA 104; 129; CDWLB 4; DLB
215; EW 9; EWL 3; MTCW 1, 2; RGSF
2; RGWL 2, 3
Hass, Robert 1941- ... **CLC 18, 39, 99; PC 16**
See also AMWS 6; CA 111; CANR 30, 50,
71; CP 3, 4, 5, 6, 7; DLB 105, 206; EWL
3; MAL 5; MTFW 2005; RGAL 4; SATA
94; TCLE 1:1
Hastings, Hudson
See Kuttner, Henry
Hastings, Selina .... **CLC 44**
See also CA 257
Hastings, Selina Shirley
See Hastings, Selina
Hathorne, John 1641-1717 .... **LC 38**
Hatteras, Amelia
See Mencken, H(enry) L(ouis)

Hemans, Felicia 1793-1835 ...... **NCLC 29, 71**
  See also DLB 96; RGEL 2
Hemingway, Ernest (Miller)
    1899-1961 .... **CLC 1, 3, 6, 8, 10, 13, 19,
    30, 34, 39, 41, 44, 50, 61, 80; SSC 1, 25,
    36, 40, 63; TCLC 115, 203; WLC 3**
    See also AAYA 19; AMW; AMWC 1;
    AMWR 1; BPFB 2; BYA 2, 3, 13, 15; CA
    77-80; CANR 34; CDALB 1917-1929;
    DA; DA3; DAB; DAC; DAM MST, NOV;
    DLB 4, 9, 102, 210, 308, 316, 330; DLBD
    1, 15, 16; DLBY 1981, 1987, 1996, 1998;
    EWL 3; EXPN; EXPS; LAIT 3, 4; LATS
    1:1; MAL 5; MTCW 1, 2; MTFW 2005;
    NFS 1, 5, 6, 14; RGAL 4; RGSF 2; SSFS
    17; TUS; WYA
Hempel, Amy 1951- .... **CLC 39**
    See also CA 118; 137; CANR 70, 166;
    DA3; DLB 218; EXPS; MTCW 2; MTFW
    2005; SSFS 2
Henderson, F. C.
    See Mencken, H(enry) L(ouis)
Henderson, Sylvia
    See Ashton-Warner, Sylvia (Constance)
Henderson, Zenna (Chlarson)
    1917-1983 .... **SSC 29**
    See also CA 1-4R; 133; CANR 1, 84; DLB
    8; SATA 5; SFW 4
Henkin, Joshua 1964- .... **CLC 119**
    See also CA 161
Henley, Beth .... **CLC 23, 255; DC 6, 14**
    See Henley, Elizabeth Becker
    See also AAYA 70; CABS 3; CAD; CD 5,
    6; CSW; CWD; DFS 2, 21; DLBY 1986;
    FW
Henley, Elizabeth Becker 1952-
    See Henley, Beth
    See also CA 107; CANR 32, 73, 140; DA3;
    DAM DRAM, MST; MTCW 1, 2; MTFW
    2005
Henley, William Ernest 1849-1903 .. **TCLC 8**
    See also CA 105; 234; DLB 19; RGEL 2
Hennissart, Martha 1929-
    See Lathen, Emma
    See also CA 85-88; CANR 64
Henry VIII 1491-1547 .... **LC 10**
    See also DLB 132
Henry, O. ... **SSC 5, 49; TCLC 1, 19; WLC 3**
    See Porter, William Sydney
    See also AAYA 41; AMWS 2; EXPS; MAL
    5; RGAL 4; RGSF 2; SSFS 2, 18; TCWW
    1, 2
Henry, Patrick 1736-1799 .... **LC 25**
    See also LAIT 1
Henryson, Robert 1430(?)-1506(?) ..... **LC 20,
    110; PC 65**
    See also BRWS 7; DLB 146; RGEL 2
Henschke, Alfred
    See Klabund
Henson, Lance 1944- .... **NNAL**
    See also CA 146; DLB 175
Hentoff, Nat(han Irving) 1925- .... **CLC 26**
    See also AAYA 4, 42; BYA 6; CA 1-4R;
    CAAS 6; CANR 5, 25, 77, 114; CLR 1,
    52; INT CANR-25; JRDA; MAICYA 1,
    2; SATA 42, 69, 133; SATA-Brief 27;
    WYA; YAW
Heppenstall, (John) Rayner
    1911-1981 .... **CLC 10**
    See also CA 1-4R; 103; CANR 29; CN 1,
    2; CP 1, 2, 3; EWL 3
Heraclitus c. 540B.C.-c. 450B.C. ... **CMLC 22**
    See also DLB 176
Herbert, Frank 1920-1986 ... **CLC 12, 23, 35,
    44, 85**
    See also AAYA 21; BPFB 2; BYA 4, 14;
    CA 53-56; 118; CANR 5, 43; CDALBS;
    CPW; DAM POP; DLB 8; INT CANR-5;
    LAIT 5; MTCW 1, 2; MTFW 2005; NFS
    17; SATA 9, 37; SATA-Obit 47; SCFW 1,
    2; SFW 4; YAW

Herbert, George 1593-1633 . **LC 24, 121; PC
    4**
    See also BRW 2; BRWR 2; CDBLB Before
    1660; DAB; DAM POET; DLB 126;
    EXPP; PFS 25; RGEL 2; TEA; WP
Herbert, Zbigniew 1924-1998 ..... **CLC 9, 43;
    PC 50; TCLC 168**
    See also CA 89-92; 169; CANR 36, 74; CD-
    WLB 4; CWW 2; DAM POET; DLB 232;
    EWL 3; MTCW 1; PFS 22
Herbst, Josephine (Frey)
    1897-1969 .... **CLC 34**
    See also CA 5-8R; 25-28R; DLB 9
Herder, Johann Gottfried von 1744-1803
    NCLC 8, 186
    See also DLB 97; EW 4; TWA
Heredia, Jose Maria 1803-1839 .... **HLCS 2**
    See also LAW
Hergesheimer, Joseph 1880-1954 ... **TCLC 11**
    See also CA 109; 194; DLB 102, 9; RGAL
    4
Herlihy, James Leo 1927-1993 .... **CLC 6**
    See also CA 1-4R; 143; CAD; CANR 2;
    CN 1, 2, 3, 4, 5
Herman, William
    See Bierce, Ambrose (Gwinett)
Hermogenes fl. c. 175- .... **CMLC 6**
Hernandez, Jose 1834-1886 .... **NCLC 17**
    See also LAW; RGWL 2, 3; WLIT 1
Herodotus c. 484B.C.-c. 420B.C. .. **CMLC 17**
    See also AW 1; CDWLB 1; DLB 176;
    RGWL 2, 3; TWA; WLIT 8
Herr, Michael 1940(?)- .... **CLC 231**
    See also CA 89-92; CANR 68, 142; DLB
    185; MTCW 1
Herrick, Robert 1591-1674 .. **LC 13, 145; PC
    9**
    See also BRW 2; BRWC 2; DA; DAB;
    DAC; DAM MST, POP; DLB 126; EXPP;
    PFS 13; RGAL 4; RGEL 2; TEA; WP
Herring, Guilles
    See Somerville, Edith Oenone
Herriot, James 1916-1995 .... **CLC 12**
    See Wight, James Alfred
    See also AAYA 1, 54; BPFB 2; CA 148;
    CANR 40; CLR 80; CPW; DAM POP;
    LAIT 3; MAICYA 2; MAICYAS 1;
    MTCW 2; SATA 86, 135; TEA; YAW
Herris, Violet
    See Hunt, Violet
Herrmann, Dorothy 1941- .... **CLC 44**
    See also CA 107
Herrmann, Taffy
    See Herrmann, Dorothy
Hersey, John 1914-1993 .. **CLC 1, 2, 7, 9, 40,
    81, 97**
    See also AAYA 29; BPFB 2; CA 17-20R;
    140; CANR 33; CDALBS; CN 1, 2, 3, 4,
    5; CPW; DAM POP; DLB 6, 185, 278,
    299; MAL 5; MTCW 1, 2; MTFW 2005;
    RGHL; SATA 25; SATA-Obit 76; TUS
Hervent, Maurice
    See Grindel, Eugene
Herzen, Aleksandr Ivanovich 1812-1870
    NCLC 10, 61
    See Herzen, Alexander
Herzen, Alexander
    See Herzen, Aleksandr Ivanovich
    See also DLB 277
Herzl, Theodor 1860-1904 .... **TCLC 36**
    See also CA 168
Herzog, Werner 1942- .... **CLC 16, 236**
    See also CA 89-92
Hesiod fl. 8th cent. B.C.- .... **CMLC 5, 102**
    See also AW 1; DLB 176; RGWL 2, 3;
    WLIT 8

Hesse, Hermann 1877-1962 ... **CLC 1, 2, 3, 6,
    11, 17, 25, 69; SSC 9, 49; TCLC 148,
    196; WLC 3**
    See also AAYA 43; BPFB 2; CA 17-18;
    CAP 2; CDWLB 2; DA; DA3; DAB;
    DAC; DAM MST, NOV; DLB 66, 330;
    EW 9; EWL 3; EXPN; LAIT 1; MTCW
    1, 2; MTFW 2005; NFS 6, 15, 24; RGWL
    2, 3; SATA 50; TWA
Hewes, Cady
    See De Voto, Bernard (Augustine)
Heyen, William 1940- .... **CLC 13, 18**
    See also CA 33-36R, 220; CAAE 220;
    CAAS 9; CANR 98; CP 3, 4, 5, 6, 7; DLB
    5; RGHL
Heyerdahl, Thor 1914-2002 .... **CLC 26**
    See also CA 5-8R; 207; CANR 5, 22, 66,
    73; LAIT 4; MTCW 1, 2; MTFW 2005;
    SATA 2, 52
Heym, Georg (Theodor Franz Arthur)
    1887-1912 .... **TCLC 9**
    See also CA 106; 181
Heym, Stefan 1913-2001 .... **CLC 41**
    See also CA 9-12R; 203; CANR 4; CWW
    2; DLB 69; EWL 3
Heyse, Paul (Johann Ludwig von) 1830-1914
    TCLC 8
    See also CA 104; 209; DLB 129, 330
Heyward, (Edwin) DuBose
    1885-1940 .... **HR 1:2; TCLC 59**
    See also CA 108; 157; DLB 7, 9, 45, 249;
    MAL 5; SATA 21
Heywood, John 1497(?)-1580(?) .... **LC 65**
    See also DLB 136; RGEL 2
Heywood, Thomas 1573(?)-1641 . **DC 29; LC
    111**
    See also DAM DRAM; DLB 62; LMFS 1;
    RGEL 2; TEA
Hiaasen, Carl 1953- .... **CLC 238**
    See also CA 105; CANR 22, 45, 65, 113,
    133, 168; CMW 4; CPW; CSW; DA3;
    DLB 292; MTCW 2; MTFW 2005
Hibbert, Eleanor Alice Burford 1906-1993
    CLC 7
    See Holt, Victoria
    See also BEST 90:4; CA 17-20R; 140;
    CANR 9, 28, 59; CMW 4; CPW; DAM
    POP; MTCW 2; MTFW 2005; RHW;
    SATA 2; SATA-Obit 74
Hichens, Robert (Smythe)
    1864-1950 .... **TCLC 64**
    See also CA 162; DLB 153; HGG; RHW;
    SUFW
Higgins, Aidan 1927- .... **SSC 68**
    See also CA 9-12R; CANR 70, 115, 148;
    CN 1, 2, 3, 4, 5, 6, 7; DLB 14
Higgins, George V(incent)
    1939-1999 .... **CLC 4, 7, 10, 18**
    See also BPFB 2; CA 77-80; 186; CAAS 5;
    CANR 17, 51, 89, 96; CMW 4; CN 2, 3,
    4, 5, 6; DLB 2; DLBY 1981, 1998; INT
    CANR-17; MSW; MTCW 1
Higginson, Thomas Wentworth 1823-1911
    TCLC 36
    See also CA 162; DLB 1, 64, 243
Higgonet, Margaret .... **CLC 65**
Highet, Helen
    See MacInnes, Helen (Clark)
Highsmith, Patricia 1921-1995 ...... **CLC 2, 4,
    14, 42, 102**
    See Morgan, Claire
    See also AAYA 48; BRWS 5; CA 1-4R; 147;
    CANR 1, 20, 48, 62, 108; CMW 4; CN 1,
    2, 3, 4, 5; CPW; DA3; DAM NOV, POP;
    DLB 306; MSW; MTCW 1, 2; MTFW
    2005; NFS 27; SSFS 25

Highwater, Jamake (Mamake) 1942(?)-2001
    CLC 12
    See also AAYA 7, 69; BPFB 2; BYA 4; CA
      65-68; 199; CAAS 7; CANR 10, 34, 84;
      CLR 17; CWRI 5; DLB 52; DLBY 1985;
      JRDA; MAICYA 1, 2; SATA 32, 69;
      SATA-Brief 30

Highway, Tomson 1951- ...... **CLC 92; NNAL**
    See also CA 151; CANR 75; CCA 1; CD 5,
      6; CN 7; DAC; DAM MULT; DFS 2;
      DLB 334; MTCW 2

Hijuelos, Oscar 1951- .... **CLC 65; HLC 1**
    See also AAYA 25; AMWS 8; BEST 90:1;
      CA 123; CANR 50, 75, 125; CPW; DA3;
      DAM MULT, POP; DLB 145; HW 1, 2;
      LLW; MAL 5; MTCW 2; MTFW 2005;
      NFS 17; RGAL 4; WLIT 1

Hikmet, Nazim 1902-1963 .... **CLC 40**
    See Nizami of Ganja
    See also CA 141; 93-96; EWL 3; WLIT 6

Hildegard von Bingen 1098-1179 . **CMLC 20**
    See also DLB 148

Hildesheimer, Wolfgang 1916-1991 .. **CLC 49**
    See also CA 101; 135; DLB 69, 124; EWL
      3; RGHL

Hill, Aaron 1685-1750 .... **LC 148**
    See also DLB 84; RGEL 2

Hill, Geoffrey (William) 1932- ...... **CLC 5, 8,**
      18, 45, 251
    See also BRWS 5; CA 81-84; CANR 21,
      89; CDBLB 1960 to Present; CP 1, 2, 3,
      4, 5, 6, 7; DAM POET; DLB 40; EWL 3;
      MTCW 1; RGEL 2; RGHL

Hill, George Roy 1921-2002 .... **CLC 26**
    See also CA 110; 122; 213

Hill, John
    See Koontz, Dean

Hill, Susan 1942- .... **CLC 4, 113**
    See also CA 33-36R; CANR 29, 69, 129,
      172; CN 2, 3, 4, 5, 6, 7; DAB; DAM
      MST, NOV; DLB 14, 139; HGG; MTCW
      1; RHW; SATA 183

Hill, Susan Elizabeth
    See Hill, Susan

Hillard, Asa G. III .... **CLC 70**

Hillerman, Tony 1925- .... **CLC 62, 170**
    See also AAYA 40; BEST 89:1; BPFB 2;
      CA 29-32R; CANR 21, 42, 65, 97, 134;
      CMW 4; CPW; DA3; DAM POP; DLB
      206, 306; MAL 5; MSW; MTCW 2;
      MTFW 2005; RGAL 4; SATA 6; TCWW
      2; YAW

Hillesum, Etty 1914-1943 .... **TCLC 49**
    See also CA 137; RGHL

Hilliard, Noel (Harvey) 1929-1996 ... **CLC 15**
    See also CA 9-12R; CANR 7, 69; CN 1, 2,
      3, 4, 5, 6

Hillis, Rick 1956- .... **CLC 66**
    See also CA 134

Hilton, James 1900-1954 .... **TCLC 21**
    See also AAYA 76; CA 108; 169; DLB 34,
      77; FANT; SATA 34

Hilton, Walter (?)-1396 .... **CMLC 58**
    See also DLB 146; RGEL 2

Himes, Chester (Bomar)
      1909-1984 .... **BLC 1:2; CLC 2, 4, 7, 18,**
      58, 108; TCLC 139
    See also AFAW 2; AMWS 16; BPFB 2; BW
      2; CA 25-28R; 114; CANR 22, 89; CMW
      4; CN 1, 2, 3; DAM MULT; DLB 2, 76,
      143, 226; EWL 3; MAL 5; MSW; MTCW
      1, 2; MTFW 2005; RGAL 4

Himmelfarb, Gertrude 1922- .... **CLC 202**
    See also CA 49-52; CANR 28, 66, 102, 166

Hinde, Thomas .... **CLC 6, 11**
    See Chitty, Thomas Willes
    See also CN 1, 2, 3, 4, 5, 6; EWL 3

Hine, (William) Daryl 1936- .... **CLC 15**
    See also CA 1-4R; CAAS 15; CANR 1, 20;
      CP 1, 2, 3, 4, 5, 6, 7; DLB 60

Hinkson, Katharine Tynan
    See Tynan, Katharine

Hinojosa, Rolando 1929- .... **HLC 1**
    See Hinojosa-Smith, Rolando
    See also CA 131; CAAS 16; CANR 62;
      DAM MULT; DLB 82; HW 1, 2; LLW;
      MTCW 2; MTFW 2005; RGAL 4

Hinton, S.E. 1950- .... **CLC 30, 111**
    See also AAYA 2, 33; BPFB 2; BYA 2, 3;
      CA 81-84; CANR 32, 62, 92, 133;
      CDALBS; CLR 3, 23; CPW; DA; DA3;
      DAB; DAC; DAM MST, NOV; JRDA;
      LAIT 5; MAICYA 1, 2; MTCW 1, 2;
      MTFW 2005; NFS 5, 9, 15, 16; SATA 19,
      58, 115, 160; WYA; YAW

Hippius, Zinaida (Nikolaevna) .... **TCLC 9**
    See Gippius, Zinaida (Nikolaevna)
    See also DLB 295; EWL 3

Hiraoka, Kimitake 1925-1970
    See Mishima, Yukio
    See also CA 97-100; 29-32R; DA3; DAM
      DRAM; GLL 1; MTCW 1, 2

Hirsch, E.D., Jr. 1928- .... **CLC 79**
    See also CA 25-28R; CANR 27, 51, 146;
      DLB 67; INT CANR-27; MTCW 1

Hirsch, Edward 1950- .... **CLC 31, 50**
    See also CA 104; CANR 20, 42, 102, 167;
      CP 6, 7; DLB 120; PFS 22

Hirsch, Eric Donald, Jr.
    See Hirsch, E.D., Jr.

Hitchcock, Alfred (Joseph)
      1899-1980 .... **CLC 16**
    See also AAYA 22; CA 159; 97-100; SATA
      27; SATA-Obit 24

Hitchens, Christopher 1949- .... **CLC 157**
    See also CA 152; CANR 89, 155

Hitchens, Christopher Eric
    See Hitchens, Christopher

Hitler, Adolf 1889-1945 .... **TCLC 53**
    See also CA 117; 147

Hoagland, Edward (Morley) 1932- .. **CLC 28**
    See also ANW; CA 1-4R; CANR 2, 31, 57,
      107; CN 1, 2, 3, 4, 5, 6, 7; DLB 6; SATA
      51; TCWW 2

Hoban, Russell 1925- .... **CLC 7, 25**
    See also BPFB 2; CA 5-8R; CANR 23, 37,
      66, 114, 138; CLR 3, 69; CN 4, 5, 6, 7;
      CWRI 5; DAM NOV; DLB 52; FANT;
      MAICYA 1, 2; MTCW 1, 2; MTFW 2005;
      SATA 1, 40, 78, 136; SFW 4; SUFW 2;
      TCLE 1:1

Hobbes, Thomas 1588-1679 .... **LC 36, 142**
    See also DLB 151, 252, 281; RGEL 2

Hobbs, Perry
    See Blackmur, R(ichard) P(almer)

Hobson, Laura Z(ametkin)
      1900-1986 .... **CLC 7, 25**
    See also BPFB 2; CA 17-20R; 118; CANR
      55; CN 1, 2, 3, 4; DLB 28; SATA 52

Hoccleve, Thomas c. 1368-c. 1437 ...... **LC 75**
    See also DLB 146; RGEL 2

Hoch, Edward D. 1930-2008
    See Queen, Ellery
    See also CA 29-32R; CANR 11, 27, 51, 97;
      CMW 4; DLB 306; SFW 4

Hochhuth, Rolf 1931- .... **CLC 4, 11, 18**
    See also CA 5-8R; CANR 33, 75, 136;
      CWW 2; DAM DRAM; DLB 124; EWL
      3; MTCW 1, 2; MTFW 2005; RGHL

Hochman, Sandra 1936- .... **CLC 3, 8**
    See also CA 5-8R; CP 1, 2, 3, 4, 5; DLB 5

Hochwaelder, Fritz 1911-1986 .... **CLC 36**
    See Hochwalder, Fritz
    See also CA 29-32R; 120; CANR 42; DAM
      DRAM; MTCW 1; RGWL 3

Hochwalder, Fritz
    See Hochwaelder, Fritz
    See also EWL 3; RGWL 2

Hocking, Mary (Eunice) 1921- .... **CLC 13**
    See also CA 101; CANR 18, 40

Hodge, Merle 1944- .... **BLC 2:2**
    See also EWL 3

Hodgins, Jack 1938- .... **CLC 23**
    See also CA 93-96; CN 4, 5, 6, 7; DLB 60

Hodgson, William Hope
      1877(?)-1918 .... **TCLC 13**
    See also CA 111; 164; CMW 4; DLB 70,
      153, 156, 178; HGG; MTCW 2; SFW 4;
      SUFW 1

Hoeg, Peter 1957- .... **CLC 95, 156**
    See also CA 151; CANR 75; CMW 4; DA3;
      DLB 214; EWL 3; MTCW 2; MTFW
      2005; NFS 17; RGWL 3; SSFS 18

Hoffman, Alice 1952- .... **CLC 51**
    See also AAYA 37; AMWS 10; CA 77-80;
      CANR 34, 66, 100, 138, 170; CN 4, 5, 6,
      7; CPW; DAM NOV; DLB 292; MAL 5;
      MTCW 1, 2; MTFW 2005; TCLE 1:1

Hoffman, Daniel (Gerard) 1923- . **CLC 6, 13,**
      23
    See also CA 1-4R; CANR 4, 142; CP 1, 2,
      3, 4, 5, 6, 7; DLB 5; TCLE 1:1

Hoffman, Eva 1945- .... **CLC 182**
    See also AMWS 16; CA 132; CANR 146

Hoffman, Stanley 1944- .... **CLC 5**
    See also CA 77-80

Hoffman, William 1925- .... **CLC 141**
    See also CA 21-24R; CANR 9, 103; CSW;
      DLB 234; TCLE 1:1

Hoffman, William M.
    See Hoffman, William M(oses)
    See also CAD; CD 5, 6

Hoffman, William M(oses) 1939- ..... **CLC 40**
    See Hoffman, William M.
    See also CA 57-60; CANR 11, 71

Hoffmann, E(rnst) T(heodor) A(madeus)
      1776-1822 ..... **NCLC 2, 183; SSC 13, 92**
    See also CDWLB 2; CLR 133; DLB 90;
      EW 5; GL 2; RGSF 2; RGWL 2, 3; SATA
      27; SUFW 1; WCH

Hofmann, Gert 1931-1993 .... **CLC 54**
    See also CA 128; CANR 145; EWL 3;
      RGHL

Hofmannsthal, Hugo von 1874-1929 ... **DC 4;**
      TCLC 11
    See also CA 106; 153; CDWLB 2; DAM
      DRAM; DFS 17; DLB 81, 118; EW 9;
      EWL 3; RGWL 2, 3

Hogan, Linda 1947- ..... **CLC 73; NNAL; PC**
      35
    See also AMWS 4; ANW; BYA 12; CA 120,
      226; CAAE 226; CANR 45, 73, 129;
      CWP; DAM MULT; DLB 175; SATA
      132; TCWW 2

Hogarth, Charles
    See Creasey, John

Hogarth, Emmett
    See Polonsky, Abraham (Lincoln)

Hogarth, William 1697-1764 .... **LC 112**
    See also AAYA 56

Hogg, James 1770-1835 .... **NCLC 4, 109**
    See also BRWS 10; DLB 93, 116, 159; GL
      2; HGG; RGEL 2; SUFW 1

Holbach, Paul-Henri Thiry
      1723-1789 .... **LC 14**
    See also DLB 313

Holberg, Ludvig 1684-1754 .... **LC 6**
    See also DLB 300; RGWL 2, 3

Holcroft, Thomas 1745-1809 .... **NCLC 85**
    See also DLB 39, 89, 158; RGEL 2

Holden, Ursula 1921- .... **CLC 18**
    See also CA 101; CAAS 8; CANR 22

Holderlin, (Johann Christian) Friedrich
1770-1843 .... **NCLC 16, 187; PC 4**
See also CDWLB 2; DLB 90; EW 5; RGWL
2, 3

Holding, James (Clark Carlisle, Jr.)
1907-1997
See Queen, Ellery
See also CA 25-28R; SATA 3

Holdstock, Robert 1948- .... **CLC 39**
See also CA 131; CANR 81; DLB 261;
FANT; HGG; SFW 4; SUFW 2

Holdstock, Robert P.
See Holdstock, Robert

Holinshed, Raphael fl. 1580- .... **LC 69**
See also DLB 167; RGEL 2

Holland, Isabelle (Christian)
1920-2002 .... **CLC 21**
See also AAYA 11, 64; CA 21-24R; 205;
CAAE 181; CANR 10, 25, 47; CLR 57;
CWRI 5; JRDA; LAIT 4; MAICYA 1, 2;
SATA 8, 70; SATA-Essay 103; SATA-Obit
132; WYA

Holland, Marcus
See Caldwell, (Janet Miriam) Taylor
(Holland)

Hollander, John 1929- .... **CLC 2, 5, 8, 14**
See also CA 1-4R; CANR 1, 52, 136; CP 1,
2, 3, 4, 5, 6, 7; DLB 5; MAL 5; SATA 13

Hollander, Paul
See Silverberg, Robert

Holleran, Andrew .... **CLC 38**
See Garber, Eric
See also CA 144; GLL 1

Holley, Marietta 1836(?)-1926 .... **TCLC 99**
See also CA 118; DLB 11; FL 1:3

Hollinghurst, Alan 1954- .... **CLC 55, 91**
See also BRWS 10; CA 114; CN 5, 6, 7;
DLB 207, 326; GLL 1

Hollis, Jim
See Summers, Hollis (Spurgeon, Jr.)

Holly, Buddy 1936-1959 .... **TCLC 65**
See also CA 213

Holmes, Gordon
See Shiel, M(atthew) P(hipps)

Holmes, John
See Souster, (Holmes) Raymond

Holmes, John Clellon 1926-1988 ...... **CLC 56**
See also BG 1:2; CA 9-12R; 125; CANR 4;
CN 1, 2, 3, 4; DLB 16, 237

Holmes, Oliver Wendell, Jr.
1841-1935 .... **TCLC 77**
See also CA 114; 186

Holmes, Oliver Wendell
1809-1894 .... **NCLC 14, 81; PC 71**
See also AMWS 1; CDALB 1640-1865;
DLB 1, 189, 235; EXPP; PFS 24; RGAL
4; SATA 34

Holmes, Raymond
See Souster, (Holmes) Raymond

Holt, Victoria
See Hibbert, Eleanor Alice Burford
See also BPFB 2

Holub, Miroslav 1923-1998 .... **CLC 4**
See also CA 21-24R; 169; CANR 10; CD-
WLB 4; CWW 2; DLB 232; EWL 3;
RGWL 3

Holz, Detlev
See Benjamin, Walter

Homer c. 8th cent. B.C.- .... **CMLC 1, 16, 61;
PC 23; WLCS**
See also AW 1; CDWLB 1; DA; DA3;
DAB; DAC; DAM MST, POET; DLB
176; EFS 1; LAIT 1; LMFS 1; RGWL 2,
3; TWA; WLIT 8; WP

Hongo, Garrett Kaoru 1951- .... **PC 23**
See also CA 133; CAAS 22; CP 5, 6, 7;
DLB 120, 312; EWL 3; EXPP; PFS 25;
RGAL 4

Honig, Edwin 1919- .... **CLC 33**
See also CA 5-8R; CAAS 8; CANR 4, 45,
144; CP 1, 2, 3, 4, 5, 6, 7; DLB 5

Hood, Hugh (John Blagdon) 1928- . **CLC 15,
28; SSC 42**
See also CA 49-52; CAAS 17; CANR 1,
33, 87; CN 1, 2, 3, 4, 5, 6, 7; DLB 53;
RGSF 2

Hood, Thomas 1799-1845 .... **NCLC 16**
See also BRW 4; DLB 96; RGEL 2

Hooker, (Peter) Jeremy 1941- .... **CLC 43**
See also CA 77-80; CANR 22; CP 2, 3, 4,
5, 6, 7; DLB 40

Hooker, Richard 1554-1600 .... **LC 95**
See also BRW 1; DLB 132; RGEL 2

Hooker, Thomas 1586-1647 .... **LC 137**
See also DLB 24

hooks, bell 1952(?)- .... **BLCS; CLC 94**
See also BW 2; CA 143; CANR 87, 126;
DLB 246; MTCW 2; MTFW 2005; SATA
115, 170

Hooper, Johnson Jones
1815-1862 .... **NCLC 177**
See also DLB 3, 11, 248; RGAL 4

Hope, A(lec) D(erwent) 1907-2000 .... **CLC 3,
51; PC 56**
See also BRWS 7; CA 21-24R; 188; CANR
33, 74; CP 1, 2, 3, 4, 5; DLB 289; EWL
3; MTCW 1, 2; MTFW 2005; PFS 8;
RGEL 2

Hope, Anthony 1863-1933 .... **TCLC 83**
See also CA 157; DLB 153, 156; RGEL 2;
RHW

Hope, Brian
See Creasey, John

Hope, Christopher (David Tully)
1944- .... **CLC 52**
See also AFW; CA 106; CANR 47, 101;
CN 4, 5, 6, 7; DLB 225; SATA 62

Hopkins, Gerard Manley
1844-1889 .... **NCLC 17, 189; PC 15;
WLC 3**
See also BRW 5; BRWR 2; CDBLB 1890-
1914; DA; DA3; DAB; DAC; DAM MST,
POET; DLB 35, 57; EXPP; PAB; PFS 26;
RGEL 2; TEA; WP

Hopkins, John (Richard) 1931-1998 .. **CLC 4**
See also CA 85-88; 169; CBD; CD 5, 6

Hopkins, Pauline Elizabeth
1859-1930 .... **BLC 1:2; TCLC 28**
See also AFAW 2; BW 2, 3; CA 141; CANR
82; DAM MULT; DLB 50

Hopkinson, Francis 1737-1791 .... **LC 25**
See also DLB 31; RGAL 4

Hopley-Woolrich, Cornell George 1903-1968
See Woolrich, Cornell
See also CA 13-14; CANR 58, 156; CAP 1;
CMW 4; DLB 226; MTCW 2

Horace 65B.C.-8B.C. .... **CMLC 39; PC 46**
See also AW 2; CDWLB 1; DLB 211;
RGWL 2, 3; WLIT 8

Horatio
See Proust, (Valentin-Louis-George-Eugene)
Marcel

Horgan, Paul (George Vincent
O'Shaughnessy) 1903-1995 .. **CLC 9, 53**
See also BPFB 2; CA 13-16R; 147; CANR
9, 35; CN 1, 2, 3, 4, 5; DAM NOV; DLB
102, 212; DLBY 1985; INT CANR-9;
MTCW 1, 2; MTFW 2005; SATA 13;
SATA-Obit 84; TCWW 1, 2

Horkheimer, Max 1895-1973 .... **TCLC 132**
See also CA 216; 41-44R; DLB 296

Horn, Peter
See Kuttner, Henry

Hornby, Nick 1957(?)- .... **CLC 243**
See also AAYA 74; CA 151; CANR 104,
151; CN 7; DLB 207

Horne, Frank (Smith) 1899-1974 ...... **HR 1:2**
See also BW 1; CA 125; 53-56; DLB 51;
WP

Horne, Richard Henry Hengist 1802(?)-1884
NCLC 127
See also DLB 32; SATA 29

Hornem, Horace Esq.
See Byron, George Gordon (Noel)

Horne Tooke, John 1736-1812 ..... **NCLC 195**

Horney, Karen (Clementine Theodore
Danielsen) 1885-1952 .... **TCLC 71**
See also CA 114; 165; DLB 246; FW

Hornung, E(rnest) W(illiam) 1866-1921
TCLC 59
See also CA 108; 160; CMW 4; DLB 70

Horovitz, Israel 1939- .... **CLC 56**
See also CA 33-36R; CAD; CANR 46, 59;
CD 5, 6; DAM DRAM; DLB 7, 341;
MAL 5

Horton, George Moses 1797(?)-1883(?)
NCLC 87
See also DLB 50

Horvath, odon von 1901-1938
See von Horvath, Odon
See also EWL 3

Horvath, Oedoen von -1938
See von Horvath, Odon

Horwitz, Julius 1920-1986 .... **CLC 14**
See also CA 9-12R; 119; CANR 12

Horwitz, Ronald
See Harwood, Ronald

Hospital, Janette Turner 1942- .... **CLC 42,
145**
See also CA 108; CANR 48, 166; CN 5, 6,
7; DLB 325; DLBY 2002; RGSF 2

Hosseini, Khaled 1965- .... **CLC 254**
See also CA 225; SATA 156

Hostos, E. M. de
See Hostos (y Bonilla), Eugenio Maria de

Hostos, Eugenio M. de
See Hostos (y Bonilla), Eugenio Maria de

Hostos, Eugenio Maria
See Hostos (y Bonilla), Eugenio Maria de

Hostos (y Bonilla), Eugenio Maria de
1839-1903 .... **TCLC 24**
See also CA 123; 131; HW 1

Houdini
See Lovecraft, H. P.

Houellebecq, Michel 1958- .... **CLC 179**
See also CA 185; CANR 140; MTFW 2005

Hougan, Carolyn 1943-2007 .... **CLC 34**
See also CA 139; 257

Household, Geoffrey (Edward West)
1900-1988 .... **CLC 11**
See also CA 77-80; 126; CANR 58; CMW
4; CN 1, 2, 3, 4; DLB 87; SATA 14;
SATA-Obit 59

Housman, A(lfred) E(dward)
1859-1936 .... **PC 2, 43; TCLC 1, 10;
WLCS**
See also AAYA 66; BRW 6; CA 104; 125;
DA; DA3; DAB; DAC; DAM MST,
POET; DLB 19, 284; EWL 3; EXPP;
MTCW 1, 2; MTFW 2005; PAB; PFS 4,
7; RGEL 2; TEA; WP

Housman, Laurence 1865-1959 .... **TCLC 7**
See also CA 106; 155; DLB 10; FANT;
RGEL 2; SATA 25

Houston, Jeanne Wakatsuki 1934- .... **AAL**
See also AAYA 49; CA 103, 232; CAAE
232; CAAS 16; CANR 29, 123, 167;
LAIT 4; SATA 78, 168; SATA-Essay 168

Hove, Chenjerai 1956- .... **BLC 2:2**
See also CP 7

Howard, Elizabeth Jane 1923- ..... **CLC 7, 29**
See also BRWS 11; CA 5-8R; CANR 8, 62,
146; CN 1, 2, 3, 4, 5, 6, 7

Howard, Maureen 1930- .... **CLC 5, 14, 46, 151**
See also CA 53-56; CANR 31, 75, 140; CN 4, 5, 6, 7; DLBY 1983; INT CANR-31; MTCW 1, 2; MTFW 2005

Howard, Richard 1929- .... **CLC 7, 10, 47**
See also AITN 1; CA 85-88; CANR 25, 80, 154; CP 1, 2, 3, 4, 5, 6, 7; DLB 5; INT CANR-25; MAL 5

Howard, Robert E 1906-1936 .... **TCLC 8**
See also BPFB 2; BYA 5; CA 105; 157; CANR 155; FANT; SUFW 1; TCWW 1, 2

Howard, Robert Ervin
See Howard, Robert E

Howard, Warren F.
See Pohl, Frederik

Howe, Fanny (Quincy) 1940- .... **CLC 47**
See also CA 117, 187; CAAE 187; CAAS 27; CANR 70, 116; CP 6, 7; CWP; SATA-Brief 52

Howe, Irving 1920-1993 .... **CLC 85**
See also AMWS 6; CA 9-12R; 141; CANR 21, 50; DLB 67; EWL 3; MAL 5; MTCW 1, 2; MTFW 2005

Howe, Julia Ward 1819-1910 . **PC 81; TCLC 21**
See also CA 117; 191; DLB 1, 189, 235; FW

Howe, Susan 1937- .... **CLC 72, 152; PC 54**
See also AMWS 4; CA 160; CP 5, 6, 7; CWP; DLB 120; FW; RGAL 4

Howe, Tina 1937- .... **CLC 48**
See also CA 109; CAD; CANR 125; CD 5, 6; CWD; DLB 341

Howell, James 1594(?)-1666 .... **LC 13**
See also DLB 151

Howells, W. D.
See Howells, William Dean

Howells, William D.
See Howells, William Dean

Howells, William Dean 1837-1920 ... **SSC 36; TCLC 7, 17, 41**
See also AMW; CA 104; 134; CDALB 1865-1917; DLB 12, 64, 74, 79, 189; LMFS 1; MAL 5; MTCW 2; RGAL 4; TUS

Howes, Barbara 1914-1996 .... **CLC 15**
See also CA 9-12R; 151; CAAS 3; CANR 53; CP 1, 2, 3, 4, 5, 6; SATA 5; TCLE 1:1

Hrabal, Bohumil 1914-1997 ...... **CLC 13, 67; TCLC 155**
See also CA 106; 156; CAAS 12; CANR 57; CWW 2; DLB 232; EWL 3; RGSF 2

Hrabanus Maurus 776(?)-856 .... **CMLC 78**
See also DLB 148

Hrotsvit of Gandersheim c. 935-c. 1000 **CMLC 29**
See also DLB 148

Hsi, Chu 1130-1200 .... **CMLC 42**

Hsun, Lu
See Lu Hsun

Hubbard, L. Ron 1911-1986 .... **CLC 43**
See also AAYA 64; CA 77-80; 118; CANR 52; CPW; DA3; DAM POP; FANT; MTCW 2; MTFW 2005; SFW 4

Hubbard, Lafayette Ronald
See Hubbard, L. Ron

Huch, Ricarda (Octavia)
1864-1947 .... **TCLC 13**
See also CA 111; 189; DLB 66; EWL 3

Huddle, David 1942- .... **CLC 49**
See also CA 57-60, 261; CAAS 20; CANR 89; DLB 130

Hudson, Jeffrey
See Crichton, Michael

Hudson, W(illiam) H(enry)
1841-1922 .... **TCLC 29**
See also CA 115; 190; DLB 98, 153, 174; RGEL 2; SATA 35

Hueffer, Ford Madox
See Ford, Ford Madox

Hughart, Barry 1934- .... **CLC 39**
See also CA 137; FANT; SFW 4; SUFW 2

Hughes, Colin
See Creasey, John

Hughes, David (John) 1930-2005 ..... **CLC 48**
See also CA 116; 129; 238; CN 4, 5, 6, 7; DLB 14

Hughes, Edward James
See Hughes, Ted
See also DA3; DAM MST, POET

Hughes, (James Mercer) Langston
1902-1967 .. **BLC 1:2; CLC 1, 5, 10, 15, 35, 44, 108; DC 3; HR 1:2; PC 1, 53; SSC 6, 90; WLC 3**
See also AAYA 12; AFAW 1, 2; AMWR 1; AMWS 1; BW 1, 3; CA 1-4R; 25-28R; CANR 1, 34, 82; CDALB 1929-1941; CLR 17; DA; DA3; DAB; DAC; DAM DRAM, MST, MULT, POET; DFS 6, 18; DLB 4, 7, 48, 51, 86, 228, 315; EWL 3; EXPP; EXPS; JRDA; LAIT 3; LMFS 2; MAICYA 1, 2; MAL 5; MTCW 1, 2; MTFW 2005; NFS 21; PAB; PFS 1, 3, 6, 10, 15; RGSF 2; RGAL 4; SATA 4, 33; SSFS 4, 7; TUS; WCH; WP; YAW

Hughes, Richard (Arthur Warren)
1900-1976 .... **CLC 1, 11; TCLC 204**
See also CA 5-8R; 65-68; CANR 4; CN 1, 2; DAM NOV; DLB 15, 161; EWL 3; MTCW 1; RGEL 2; SATA 8; SATA-Obit 25

Hughes, Ted 1930-1998 . **CLC 2, 4, 9, 14, 37, 119; PC 7, 89**
See Hughes, Edward James
See also BRWC 2; BRWR 2; BRWS 1; CA 1-4R; 171; CANR 1, 33, 66, 108; CLR 3, 131; CP 1, 2, 3, 4, 5, 6; DAB; DAC; DLB 40, 161; EWL 3; EXPP; MAICYA 1, 2; MTCW 1, 2; MTFW 2005; PAB; PFS 4, 19; RGEL 2; SATA 49; SATA-Brief 27; SATA-Obit 107; TEA; YAW

Hugo, Richard
See Huch, Ricarda (Octavia)

Hugo, Richard F(ranklin)
1923-1982 .... **CLC 6, 18, 32; PC 68**
See also AMWS 6; CA 49-52; 108; CANR 3; CP 1, 2, 3; DAM POET; DLB 5, 206; EWL 3; MAL 5; PFS 17; RGAL 4

Hugo, Victor (Marie) 1802-1885 .... **NCLC 3, 10, 21, 161, 189; PC 17; WLC 3**
See also AAYA 28; DA; DA3; DAB; DAC; DAM DRAM, MST, NOV, POET; DLB 119, 192, 217; EFS 2; EW 6; EXPN; GFL 1789 to the Present; LAIT 1, 2; NFS 5, 20; RGWL 2, 3; SATA 47; TWA

Huidobro, Vicente
See Huidobro Fernandez, Vicente Garcia
See also DLB 283; EWL 3; LAW

Huidobro Fernandez, Vicente Garcia
1893-1948 ..... **TCLC 31**
See Huidobro, Vicente
See also CA 131; HW 1

Hulme, Keri 1947- .... **CLC 39, 130**
See also CA 125; CANR 69; CN 4, 5, 6, 7; CP 6, 7; CWP; DLB 326; EWL 3; FW; INT CA-125; NFS 24

Hulme, T(homas) E(rnest)
1883-1917 .... **TCLC 21**
See also BRWS 6; CA 117; 203; DLB 19

Humboldt, Alexander von
1769-1859 .... **NCLC 170**
See also DLB 90

Humboldt, Wilhelm von
1767-1835 .... **NCLC 134**
See also DLB 90

Hume, David 1711-1776 .... **LC 7, 56**
See also BRWS 3; DLB 104, 252, 336; LMFS 1; TEA

Humphrey, William 1924-1997 .... **CLC 45**
See also AMWS 9; CA 77-80; 160; CANR 68; CN 1, 2, 3, 4, 5, 6; CSW; DLB 6, 212, 234, 278; TCWW 1, 2

Humphreys, Emyr Owen 1919- .... **CLC 47**
See also CA 5-8R; CANR 3, 24; CN 1, 2, 3, 4, 5, 6, 7; DLB 15

Humphreys, Josephine 1945- ..... **CLC 34, 57**
See also CA 121; 127; CANR 97; CSW; DLB 292; INT CA-127

Huneker, James Gibbons
1860-1921 .... **TCLC 65**
See also CA 193; DLB 71; RGAL 4

Hungerford, Hesba Fay
See Brinsmead, H(esba) F(ay)

Hungerford, Pixie
See Brinsmead, H(esba) F(ay)

Hunt, E. Howard 1918-2007 .... **CLC 3**
See also AITN 1; CA 45-48; 256; CANR 2, 47, 103, 160; CMW 4

Hunt, Everette Howard, Jr.
See Hunt, E. Howard

Hunt, Francesca
See Holland, Isabelle (Christian)

Hunt, Howard
See Hunt, E. Howard

Hunt, Kyle
See Creasey, John

Hunt, (James Henry) Leigh
1784-1859 .... **NCLC 1, 70; PC 73**
See also DAM POET; DLB 96, 110, 144; RGEL 2; TEA

Hunt, Marsha 1946- .... **CLC 70**
See also BW 2, 3; CA 143; CANR 79

Hunt, Violet 1866(?)-1942 .... **TCLC 53**
See also CA 184; DLB 162, 197

Hunter, E. Waldo
See Sturgeon, Theodore (Hamilton)

Hunter, Evan 1926-2005 .... **CLC 11, 31**
See McBain, Ed
See also AAYA 39; BPFB 2; CA 5-8R; 241; CANR 5, 38, 62, 97, 149; CMW 4; CN 1, 2, 3, 4, 5, 6, 7; CPW; DAM POP; DLB 306; DLBY 1982; INT CANR-5; MSW; MTCW 1; SATA 25; SATA-Obit 167; SFW 4

Hunter, Kristin
See Lattany, Kristin (Elaine Eggleston) Hunter
See also CN 1, 2, 3, 4, 5, 6

Hunter, Mary
See Austin, Mary (Hunter)

Hunter, Mollie 1922- .... **CLC 21**
See McIlwraith, Maureen Mollie Hunter
See also AAYA 13, 71; BYA 6; CANR 37, 78; CLR 25; DLB 161; JRDA; MAICYA 1, 2; SAAS 7; SATA 54, 106, 139; SATA-Essay 139; WYA; YAW

Hunter, Robert (?)-1734 .... **LC 7**

Hurston, Zora Neale 1891-1960 ..... **BLC 1:2; CLC 7, 30, 61; DC 12; HR 1:2; SSC 4, 80; TCLC 121, 131; WLCS**
See also AAYA 15, 71; AFAW 1, 2; AMWS 6; BW 1, 3; BYA 12; CA 85-88; CANR 61; CDALBS; DA; DA3; DAC; DAM MST, MULT, NOV; DFS 6; DLB 51, 86; EWL 3; EXPN; EXPS; FL 1:6; FW; LAIT 3; LATS 1:1; LMFS 2; MAL 5; MBL; MTCW 1, 2; MTFW 2005; NFS 3; RGAL 4; RGSF 2; SSFS 1, 6, 11, 19, 21; TUS; YAW

Husserl, E. G.
See Husserl, Edmund (Gustav Albrecht)

Jensen, Laura (Linnea) 1948- .... **CLC 37**
See also CA 103

Jerome, Saint 345-420 .... **CMLC 30**
See also RGWL 3

Jerome, Jerome K(lapka)
1859-1927 .... **TCLC 23**
See also CA 119; 177; DLB 10, 34, 135;
RGEL 2

Jerrold, Douglas William
1803-1857 .... **NCLC 2**
See also DLB 158, 159; RGEL 2

Jewett, (Theodora) Sarah Orne 1849-1909
SSC 6, 44, 110; TCLC 1, 22
See also AAYA 76; AMW; AMWC 2;
AMWR 2; CA 108; 127; CANR 71; DLB
12, 74, 221; EXPS; FL 1:3; FW; MAL 5;
MBL; NFS 15; RGAL 4; RGSF 2; SATA
15; SSFS 4

Jewsbury, Geraldine (Endsor) 1812-1880
NCLC 22
See also DLB 21

Jhabvala, Ruth Prawer 1927- . **CLC 4, 8, 29,
94, 138; SSC 91**
See also BRWS 5; CA 1-4R; CANR 2, 29,
51, 74, 91, 128; CN 1, 2, 3, 4, 5, 6, 7;
DAB; DAM NOV; DLB 139, 194, 323,
326; EWL 3; IDFW 3, 4; INT CANR-29;
MTCW 1, 2; MTFW 2005; RGSF 2;
RGWL 2; RHW; TEA

Jibran, Kahlil
See Gibran, Kahlil

Jibran, Khalil
See Gibran, Kahlil

Jiles, Paulette 1943- .... **CLC 13, 58**
See also CA 101; CANR 70, 124, 170; CP
5; CWP

Jimenez (Mantecon), Juan Ramon
1881-1958 .... **HLC 1; PC 7; TCLC 4,
183**
See also CA 104; 131; CANR 74; DAM
MULT, POET; DLB 134, 330; EW 9;
EWL 3; HW 1; MTCW 1, 2; MTFW
2005; RGWL 2, 3

Jimenez, Ramon
See Jimenez (Mantecon), Juan Ramon

Jimenez Mantecon, Juan
See Jimenez (Mantecon), Juan Ramon

Jin, Ba 1904-2005
See Pa Chin
See also CA 244; CWW 2; DLB 328

Jin, Xuefei
See Ha Jin

Jodelle, Etienne 1532-1573 .... **LC 119**
See also DLB 327; GFL Beginnings to 1789

Joel, Billy .... **CLC 26**
See Joel, William Martin

Joel, William Martin 1949-
See Joel, Billy
See also CA 108

John, St.
See John of Damascus, St.

John of Damascus, St. c.
675-749 .... **CMLC 27, 95**

John of Salisbury c. 1115-1180 ..... **CMLC 63**

John of the Cross, St. 1542-1591 .... **LC 18,
146**
See also RGWL 2, 3

John Paul II, Pope 1920-2005 .... **CLC 128**
See also CA 106; 133; 238

Johnson, B(ryan) S(tanley William)
1933-1973 .... **CLC 6, 9**
See also CA 9-12R; 53-56; CANR 9; CN 1;
CP 1, 2; DLB 14, 40; EWL 3; RGEL 2

Johnson, Benjamin F., of Boone
See Riley, James Whitcomb

Johnson, Charles (Richard) 1948- . **BLC 1:2,
2:2; CLC 7, 51, 65, 163**
See also AFAW 2; AMWS 6; BW 2, 3; CA
116; CAAS 18; CANR 42, 66, 82, 129;
CN 5, 6, 7; DAM MULT; DLB 33, 278;
MAL 5; MTCW 2; MTFW 2005; RGAL
4; SSFS 16

Johnson, Charles S(purgeon)
1893-1956 .... **HR 1:3**
See also BW 1, 3; CA 125; CANR 82; DLB
51, 91

Johnson, Denis 1949- . **CLC 52, 160; SSC 56**
See also CA 117; 121; CANR 71, 99; CN
4, 5, 6, 7; DLB 120

Johnson, Diane 1934- ...... **CLC 5, 13, 48, 244**
See also BPFB 2; CA 41-44R; CANR 17,
40, 62, 95, 155; CN 4, 5, 6, 7; DLBY
1980; INT CANR-17; MTCW 1

Johnson, E(mily) Pauline 1861-1913 . **NNAL**
See also CA 150; CCA 1; DAC; DAM
MULT; DLB 92, 175; TCWW 2

Johnson, Eyvind (Olof Verner) 1900-1976
CLC 14
See also CA 73-76; 69-72; CANR 34, 101;
DLB 259, 330; EW 12; EWL 3

Johnson, Fenton 1888-1958 .... **BLC 1:2**
See also BW 1; CA 118; 124; DAM MULT;
DLB 45, 50

Johnson, Georgia Douglas (Camp)
1880-1966 .... **HR 1:3**
See also BW 1; CA 125; DLB 51, 249; WP

Johnson, Helene 1907-1995 .... **HR 1:3**
See also CA 181; DLB 51; WP

Johnson, J. R.
See James, C(yril) L(ionel) R(obert)

Johnson, James Weldon
1871-1938 .... **BLC 1:2; HR 1:3; PC 24;
TCLC 3, 19, 175**
See also AAYA 73; AFAW 1, 2; BW 1, 3;
CA 104; 125; CANR 82; CDALB 1917-
1929; CLR 32; DA3; DAM MULT, POET;
DLB 51; EWL 3; EXPP; LMFS 2; MAL
5; MTCW 1, 2; MTFW 2005; NFS 22;
PFS 1; RGAL 4; SATA 31; TUS

Johnson, Joyce 1935- .... **CLC 58**
See also BG 1:3; CA 125; 129; CANR 102

Johnson, Judith (Emlyn) 1936- .... **CLC 7, 15**
See Sherwin, Judith Johnson
See also CA 25-28R; 153; CANR 34; CP 6,
7

Johnson, Lionel (Pigot)
1867-1902 .... **TCLC 19**
See also CA 117; 209; DLB 19; RGEL 2

Johnson, Marguerite Annie
See Angelou, Maya

Johnson, Mel
See Malzberg, Barry N(athaniel)

Johnson, Pamela Hansford
1912-1981 .... **CLC 1, 7, 27**
See also CA 1-4R; 104; CANR 2, 28; CN
1, 2, 3; DLB 15; MTCW 1, 2; MTFW
2005; RGEL 2

Johnson, Paul 1928- .... **CLC 147**
See also BEST 89:4; CA 17-20R; CANR
34, 62, 100, 155

Johnson, Paul Bede
See Johnson, Paul

Johnson, Robert .... **CLC 70**

Johnson, Robert 1911(?)-1938 .... **TCLC 69**
See also BW 3; CA 174

Johnson, Samuel 1709-1784 . **LC 15, 52, 128;
PC 81; WLC 3**
See also BRW 3; BRWR 1; CDBLB 1660-
1789; DA; DAB; DAC; DAM MST; DLB
39, 95, 104, 142, 213; LMFS 1; RGEL 2;
TEA

Johnson, Uwe 1934-1984 .. **CLC 5, 10, 15, 40**
See also CA 1-4R; 112; CANR 1, 39; CD-
WLB 2; DLB 75; EWL 3; MTCW 1;
RGWL 2, 3

Johnston, Basil H. 1929- .... **NNAL**
See also CA 69-72; CANR 11, 28, 66;
DAC; DAM MULT; DLB 60

Johnston, George (Benson) 1913- .... **CLC 51**
See also CA 1-4R; CANR 5, 20; CP 1, 2, 3,
4, 5, 6, 7; DLB 88

Johnston, Jennifer (Prudence)
1930- .... **CLC 7, 150, 228**
See also CA 85-88; CANR 92; CN 4, 5, 6,
7; DLB 14

Joinville, Jean de 1224(?)-1317 ..... **CMLC 38**

Jolley, Elizabeth 1923-2007 ..... **CLC 46, 256;
SSC 19**
See also CA 127; 257; CAAS 13; CANR
59; CN 4, 5, 6, 7; DLB 325; EWL 3;
RGSF 2

Jolley, Monica Elizabeth
See Jolley, Elizabeth

Jones, Arthur Llewellyn 1863-1947
See Machen, Arthur
See also CA 104; 179; HGG

Jones, D(ouglas) G(ordon) 1929- ..... **CLC 10**
See also CA 29-32R; CANR 13, 90; CP 1,
2, 3, 4, 5, 6, 7; DLB 53

Jones, David (Michael) 1895-1974 .... **CLC 2,
4, 7, 13, 42**
See also BRW 6; BRWS 7; CA 9-12R; 53-
56; CANR 28; CDBLB 1945-1960; CP 1,
2; DLB 20, 100; EWL 3; MTCW 1; PAB;
RGEL 2

Jones, David Robert 1947-
See Bowie, David
See also CA 103; CANR 104

Jones, Diana Wynne 1934- .... **CLC 26**
See also AAYA 12; BYA 6, 7, 9, 11, 13, 16;
CA 49-52; CANR 4, 26, 56, 120, 167;
CLR 23, 120; DLB 161; FANT; JRDA;
MAICYA 1, 2; MTFW 2005; SAAS 7;
SATA 9, 70, 108, 160; SFW 4; SUFW 2;
YAW

Jones, Edward P. 1950- .. **BLC 2:2; CLC 76,
223**
See also AAYA 71; BW 2, 3; CA 142;
CANR 79, 134; CSW; MTFW 2005; NFS
26

Jones, Everett LeRoi
See Baraka, Amiri

Jones, Gayl 1949- ... **BLC 1:2; CLC 6, 9, 131**
See also AFAW 1, 2; BW 2, 3; CA 77-80;
CANR 27, 66, 122; CN 4, 5, 6, 7; CSW;
DA3; DAM MULT; DLB 33, 278; MAL
5; MTCW 1, 2; MTFW 2005; RGAL 4

Jones, James 1921-1977 ...... **CLC 1, 3, 10, 39**
See also AITN 1, 2; AMWS 11; BPFB 2;
CA 1-4R; 69-72; CANR 6; CN 1, 2; DLB
2, 143; DLBD 17; DLBY 1998; EWL 3;
MAL 5; MTCW 1; RGAL 4

Jones, John J.
See Lovecraft, H. P.

Jones, LeRoi .... **CLC 1, 2, 3, 5, 10, 14**
See Baraka, Amiri
See also CN 1, 2; CP 1, 2, 3; MTCW 2

Jones, Louis B. 1953- .... **CLC 65**
See also CA 141; CANR 73

Jones, Madison 1925- .... **CLC 4**
See also CA 13-16R; CAAS 11; CANR 7,
54, 83, 158; CN 1, 2, 3, 4, 5, 6, 7; CSW;
DLB 152

Jones, Madison Percy, Jr.
See Jones, Madison

Jones, Mervyn 1922- .... **CLC 10, 52**
See also CA 45-48; CAAS 5; CANR 1, 91;
CN 1, 2, 3, 4, 5, 6, 7; MTCW 1

Jones, Mick 1956(?)- .... **CLC 30**

Jones, Nettie (Pearl) 1941- .... **CLC 34**
   See also BW 2; CA 137; CAAS 20; CANR
   88

Jones, Peter 1802-1856 .... **NNAL**

Jones, Preston 1936-1979 .... **CLC 10**
   See also CA 73-76; 89-92; DLB 7

Jones, Robert F(rancis) 1934-2003 .... **CLC 7**
   See also CA 49-52; CANR 2, 61, 118

Jones, Rod 1953- .... **CLC 50**
   See also CA 128

Jones, Terence Graham Parry
   1942- .... **CLC 21**
   See Jones, Terry; Monty Python
   See also CA 112; 116; CANR 35, 93, 173;
   INT CA-116; SATA 127

Jones, Terry
   See Jones, Terence Graham Parry
   See also SATA 67; SATA-Brief 51

Jones, Thom (Douglas) 1945(?)- ..... **CLC 81;**
   SSC 56
   See also CA 157; CANR 88; DLB 244;
   SSFS 23

Jong, Erica 1942- .... **CLC 4, 6, 8, 18, 83**
   See also AITN 1; AMWS 5; BEST 90:2;
   BPFB 2; CA 73-76; CANR 26, 52, 75,
   132, 166; CN 3, 4, 5, 6, 7; CP 2, 3, 4, 5,
   6, 7; CPW; DA3; DAM NOV, POP; DLB
   2, 5, 28, 152; FW; INT CANR-26; MAL
   5; MTCW 1, 2; MTFW 2005

Jonson, Ben(jamin) 1572(?)-1637 . **DC 4; LC**
   6, 33, 110; PC 17; WLC 3
   See also BRW 1; BRWC 1; BRWR 1; CD-
   BLB Before 1660; DA; DAB; DAC;
   DAM DRAM, MST, POET; DFS 4, 10;
   DLB 62, 121; LMFS 1; PFS 23; RGEL 2;
   TEA; WLIT 3

Jordan, June 1936-2002 .. **BLCS; CLC 5, 11,**
   23, 114, 230; PC 38
   See also AAYA 2, 66; AFAW 1, 2; BW 2,
   3; CA 33-36R; 206; CANR 25, 70, 114,
   154; CLR 10; CP 3, 4, 5, 6, 7; CWP;
   DAM MULT, POET; DLB 38; GLL 2;
   LAIT 5; MAICYA 1, 2; MTCW 1; SATA
   4, 136; YAW

Jordan, June Meyer
   See Jordan, June

Jordan, Neil 1950- .... **CLC 110**
   See also CA 124; 130; CANR 54, 154; CN
   4, 5, 6, 7; GLL 2; INT CA-130

Jordan, Neil Patrick
   See Jordan, Neil

Jordan, Pat(rick M.) 1941- .... **CLC 37**
   See also CA 33-36R; CANR 121

Jorgensen, Ivar
   See Ellison, Harlan

Jorgenson, Ivar
   See Silverberg, Robert

Joseph, George Ghevarughese .... **CLC 70**

Josephson, Mary
   See O'Doherty, Brian

Josephus, Flavius c. 37-100 ..... **CMLC 13, 93**
   See also AW 2; DLB 176; WLIT 8

Josiah Allen's Wife
   See Holley, Marietta

Josipovici, Gabriel 1940- ...... **CLC 6, 43, 153**
   See also CA 37-40R, 224; CAAE 224;
   CAAS 8; CANR 47, 84; CN 3, 4, 5, 6, 7;
   DLB 14, 319

Josipovici, Gabriel David
   See Josipovici, Gabriel

Joubert, Joseph 1754-1824 .... **NCLC 9**

Jouve, Pierre Jean 1887-1976 .... **CLC 47**
   See also CA 252; 65-68; DLB 258; EWL 3

Jovine, Francesco 1902-1950 .... **TCLC 79**
   See also DLB 264; EWL 3

Joyaux, Julia
   See Kristeva, Julia

Joyce, James (Augustine Aloysius)
   1882-1941 .... **DC 16; PC 22; SSC 3, 26,**
   44, 64; TCLC 3, 8, 16, 35, 52, 159;
   WLC 3
   See also AAYA 42; BRW 7; BRWC 1;
   BRWR 1; BYA 11, 13; CA 104; 126; CD-
   BLB 1914-1945; DA; DA3; DAB; DAC;
   DAM MST, NOV, POET; DLB 10, 19,
   36, 162, 247; EWL 3; EXPN; EXPS;
   LAIT 3; LMFS 1, 2; MTCW 1, 2; MTFW
   2005; NFS 7, 26; RGSF 2; SSFS 1, 19;
   TEA; WLIT 4

Jozsef, Attila 1905-1937 .... **TCLC 22**
   See also CA 116; 230; CDWLB 4; DLB
   215; EWL 3

Juana Ines de la Cruz, Sor 1651(?)-1695
   HLCS 1; LC 5, 136; PC 24
   See also DLB 305; FW; LAW; RGWL 2, 3;
   WLIT 1

Juana Inez de La Cruz, Sor
   See Juana Ines de la Cruz, Sor

Juan Manuel, Don 1282-1348 .... **CMLC 88**

Judd, Cyril
   See Kornbluth, C(yril) M.; Pohl, Frederik

Juenger, Ernst 1895-1998 .... **CLC 125**
   See Junger, Ernst
   See also CA 101; 167; CANR 21, 47, 106;
   DLB 56

Julian of Norwich 1342(?)-1416(?) . **LC 6, 52**
   See also BRWS 12; DLB 146; LMFS 1

Julius Caesar 100B.C.-44B.C.
   See Caesar, Julius
   See also CDWLB 1; DLB 211

Junger, Ernst
   See Juenger, Ernst
   See also CDWLB 2; EWL 3; RGWL 2, 3

Junger, Sebastian 1962- .... **CLC 109**
   See also AAYA 28; CA 165; CANR 130,
   171; MTFW 2005

Juniper, Alex
   See Hospital, Janette Turner

Junius
   See Luxemburg, Rosa

Junzaburo, Nishiwaki
   See Nishiwaki, Junzaburo
   See also EWL 3

Just, Ward 1935- .... **CLC 4, 27**
   See also CA 25-28R; CANR 32, 87; CN 6,
   7; DLB 335; INT CANR-32

Just, Ward Swift
   See Just, Ward

Justice, Donald 1925-2004 ... **CLC 6, 19, 102;**
   PC 64
   See also AMWS 7; CA 5-8R; 230; CANR
   26, 54, 74, 121, 122, 169; CP 1, 2, 3, 4,
   5, 6, 7; CSW; DAM POET; DLBY 1983;
   EWL 3; INT CANR-26; MAL 5; MTCW
   2; PFS 14; TCLE 1:1

Justice, Donald Rodney
   See Justice, Donald

Juvenal c. 60-c. 130 .... **CMLC 8**
   See also AW 2; CDWLB 1; DLB 211;
   RGWL 2, 3; WLIT 8

Juvenis
   See Bourne, Randolph S(illiman)

K., Alice
   See Knapp, Caroline

Kabakov, Sasha .... **CLC 59**

Kabir 1398(?)-1448(?) .... **LC 109; PC 56**
   See also RGWL 2, 3

Kacew, Romain 1914-1980
   See Gary, Romain
   See also CA 108; 102

Kadare, Ismail 1936- .... **CLC 52, 190**
   See also CA 161; CANR 165; EWL 3;
   RGWL 3

Kadohata, Cynthia 1956(?)- ..... **CLC 59, 122**
   See also AAYA 71; CA 140; CANR 124;
   CLR 121; SATA 155, 180

Kafka, Franz 1883-1924 ... **SSC 5, 29, 35, 60;**
   TCLC 2, 6, 13, 29, 47, 53, 112, 179;
   WLC 3
   See also AAYA 31; BPFB 2; CA 105; 126;
   CDWLB 2; DA; DA3; DAB; DAC; DAM
   MST, NOV; DLB 81; EW 9; EWL 3;
   EXPS; LATS 1:1; LMFS 2; MTCW 1, 2;
   MTFW 2005; NFS 7; RGSF 2; RGWL 2,
   3; SFW 4; SSFS 3, 7, 12; TWA

Kafu
   See Nagai, Sokichi
   See also MJW

Kahanovitch, Pinchas
   See Der Nister

Kahanovitsch, Pinkhes
   See Der Nister

Kahanovitsh, Pinkhes
   See Der Nister

Kahn, Roger 1927- .... **CLC 30**
   See also CA 25-28R; CANR 44, 69, 152;
   DLB 171; SATA 37

Kain, Saul
   See Sassoon, Siegfried (Lorraine)

Kaiser, Georg 1878-1945 .... **TCLC 9**
   See also CA 106; 190; CDWLB 2; DLB
   124; EWL 3; LMFS 2; RGWL 2, 3

Kaledin, Sergei .... **CLC 59**

Kaletski, Alexander 1946- .... **CLC 39**
   See also CA 118; 143

Kalidasa fl. c. 400-455 .... **CMLC 9; PC 22**
   See also RGWL 2, 3

Kallman, Chester (Simon)
   1921-1975 .... **CLC 2**
   See also CA 45-48; 53-56; CANR 3; CP 1,
   2

Kaminsky, Melvin .... **CLC 12, 217**
   See Brooks, Mel
   See also AAYA 13, 48; DLB 26

Kaminsky, Stuart M. 1934- .... **CLC 59**
   See also CA 73-76; CANR 29, 53, 89, 161;
   CMW 4

Kaminsky, Stuart Melvin
   See Kaminsky, Stuart M.

Kamo no Chomei 1153(?)-1216 .... **CMLC 66**
   See also DLB 203

Kamo no Nagaakira
   See Kamo no Chomei

Kandinsky, Wassily 1866-1944 .... **TCLC 92**
   See also AAYA 64; CA 118; 155

Kane, Francis
   See Robbins, Harold

Kane, Henry 1918-
   See Queen, Ellery
   See also CA 156; CMW 4

Kane, Paul
   See Simon, Paul

Kane, Sarah 1971-1999 .... **DC 31**
   See also BRWS 8; CA 190; CD 5, 6; DLB
   310

Kanin, Garson 1912-1999 .... **CLC 22**
   See also AITN 1; CA 5-8R; 177; CAD;
   CANR 7, 78; DLB 7; IDFW 3, 4

Kaniuk, Yoram 1930- .... **CLC 19**
   See also CA 134; DLB 299; RGHL

Kant, Immanuel 1724-1804 ..... **NCLC 27, 67**
   See also DLB 94

Kantor, MacKinlay 1904-1977 .... **CLC 7**
   See also CA 61-64; 73-76; CANR 60, 63;
   CN 1, 2; DLB 9, 102; MAL 5; MTCW 2;
   RHW; TCWW 1, 2

Kanze Motokiyo
   See Zeami

Kaplan, David Michael 1946- .... **CLC 50**
   See also CA 187

Kaplan, James 1951- .... **CLC 59**
   See also CA 135; CANR 121

Karadzic, Vuk Stefanovic
1787-1864 .... **NCLC 115**
See also CDWLB 4; DLB 147

Karageorge, Michael
See Anderson, Poul

Karamzin, Nikolai Mikhailovich 1766-1826
NCLC 3, 173
See also DLB 150; RGSF 2

Karapanou, Margarita 1946- .... **CLC 13**
See also CA 101

Karinthy, Frigyes 1887-1938 .... **TCLC 47**
See also CA 170; DLB 215; EWL 3

Karl, Frederick R(obert)
1927-2004 .... **CLC 34**
See also CA 5-8R; 226; CANR 3, 44, 143

Karr, Mary 1955- .... **CLC 188**
See also AMWS 11; CA 151; CANR 100;
MTFW 2005; NCFS 5

Kastel, Warren
See Silverberg, Robert

Kataev, Evgeny Petrovich 1903-1942
See Petrov, Evgeny
See also CA 120

Kataphusin
See Ruskin, John

Katz, Steve 1935- .... **CLC 47**
See also CA 25-28R; CAAS 14, 64; CANR
12; CN 4, 5, 6, 7; DLBY 1983

Kauffman, Janet 1945- .... **CLC 42**
See also CA 117; CANR 43, 84; DLB 218;
DLBY 1986

Kaufman, Bob (Garnell)
1925-1986 .... **CLC 49; PC 74**
See also BG 1:3; BW 1; CA 41-44R; 118;
CANR 22; CP 1; DLB 16, 41

Kaufman, George S. 1889-1961 ...... **CLC 38;
DC 17**
See also CA 108; 93-96; DAM DRAM;
DFS 1, 10; DLB 7; INT CA-108; MTCW
2; MTFW 2005; RGAL 4; TUS

Kaufman, Moises 1964- .... **DC 26**
See also CA 211; DFS 22; MTFW 2005

Kaufman, Sue .... **CLC 3, 8**
See Barondess, Sue K(aufman)

Kavafis, Konstantinos Petrou 1863-1933
See Cavafy, C(onstantine) P(eter)
See also CA 104

Kavan, Anna 1901-1968 .... **CLC 5, 13, 82**
See also BRWS 7; CA 5-8R; CANR 6, 57;
DLB 255; MTCW 1; RGEL 2; SFW 4

Kavanagh, Dan
See Barnes, Julian

Kavanagh, Julie 1952- .... **CLC 119**
See also CA 163

Kavanagh, Patrick (Joseph)
1904-1967 .... **CLC 22; PC 33**
See also BRWS 7; CA 123; 25-28R; DLB
15, 20; EWL 3; MTCW 1; RGEL 2

Kawabata, Yasunari 1899-1972 ..... **CLC 2, 5,
9, 18, 107; SSC 17**
See Kawabata Yasunari
See also CA 93-96; 33-36R; CANR 88;
DAM MULT; DLB 330; MJW; MTCW 2;
MTFW 2005; RGSF 2; RGWL 2, 3

Kawabata Yasunari
See Kawabata, Yasunari
See also DLB 180; EWL 3

Kaye, Mary Margaret
See Kaye, M.M.

Kaye, M.M. 1908-2004 .... **CLC 28**
See also CA 89-92; 223; CANR 24, 60, 102,
142; MTCW 1, 2; MTFW 2005; RHW;
SATA 62; SATA-Obit 152

Kaye, Mollie
See Kaye, M.M.

Kaye-Smith, Sheila 1887-1956 .... **TCLC 20**
See also CA 118; 203; DLB 36

Kaymor, Patrice Maguilene
See Senghor, Leopold Sedar

Kazakov, Iurii Pavlovich
See Kazakov, Yuri Pavlovich
See also DLB 302

Kazakov, Yuri Pavlovich 1927-1982 . **SSC 43**
See Kazakov, Iurii Pavlovich; Kazakov,
Yury
See also CA 5-8R; CANR 36; MTCW 1;
RGSF 2

Kazakov, Yury
See Kazakov, Yuri Pavlovich
See also EWL 3

Kazan, Elia 1909-2003 .... **CLC 6, 16, 63**
See also CA 21-24R; 220; CANR 32, 78

Kazantzakis, Nikos 1883(?)-1957 .... **TCLC 2,
5, 33, 181**
See also BPFB 2; CA 105; 132; DA3; EW
9; EWL 3; MTCW 1, 2; MTFW 2005;
RGWL 2, 3

Kazin, Alfred 1915-1998 ..... **CLC 34, 38, 119**
See also AMWS 8; CA 1-4R; CAAS 7;
CANR 1, 45, 79; DLB 67; EWL 3

Keane, Mary Nesta (Skrine) 1904-1996
See Keane, Molly
See also CA 108; 114; 151; RHW

Keane, Molly .... **CLC 31**
See Keane, Mary Nesta (Skrine)
See also CN 5, 6; INT CA-114; TCLE 1:1

Keates, Jonathan 1946(?)- .... **CLC 34**
See also CA 163; CANR 126

Keaton, Buster 1895-1966 .... **CLC 20**
See also CA 194

Keats, John 1795-1821 ...... **NCLC 8, 73, 121;
PC 1; WLC 3**
See also AAYA 58; BRW 4; BRWR 1; CD-
BLB 1789-1832; DA; DA3; DAB; DAC;
DAM MST, POET; DLB 96, 110; EXPP;
LMFS 1; PAB; PFS 1, 2, 3, 9, 17; RGEL
2; TEA; WLIT 3; WP

Keble, John 1792-1866 .... **NCLC 87**
See also DLB 32, 55; RGEL 2

Keene, Donald 1922- .... **CLC 34**
See also CA 1-4R; CANR 5, 119

Keillor, Garrison 1942- ..... **CLC 40, 115, 222**
See also AAYA 2, 62; AMWS 16; BEST
89:3; BPFB 2; CA 111; 117; CANR 36,
59, 124; CPW; DA3; DAM POP; DLBY
1987; EWL 3; MTCW 1, 2; MTFW 2005;
SATA 58; TUS

Keith, Carlos
See Lewton, Val

Keith, Michael
See Hubbard, L. Ron

Keller, Gottfried 1819-1890 .... **NCLC 2; SSC
26, 107**
See also CDWLB 2; DLB 129; EW; RGSF
2; RGWL 2, 3

Keller, Nora Okja 1965- .... **CLC 109**
See also CA 187

Kellerman, Jonathan 1949- .... **CLC 44**
See also AAYA 35; BEST 90:1; CA 106;
CANR 29, 51, 150; CMW 4; CPW; DA3;
DAM POP; INT CANR-29

Kelley, William Melvin 1937- .... **BLC 2:2;
CLC 22**
See also BW 1; CA 77-80; CANR 27, 83;
CN 1, 2, 3, 4, 5, 6, 7; DLB 33; EWL 3

Kellogg, Marjorie 1922-2005 .... **CLC 2**
See also CA 81-84; 246

Kellow, Kathleen
See Hibbert, Eleanor Alice Burford

Kelly, Lauren
See Oates, Joyce Carol

Kelly, M(ilton) T(errence) 1947- ...... **CLC 55**
See also CA 97-100; CAAS 22; CANR 19,
43, 84; CN 6

Kelly, Robert 1935- .... **SSC 50**
See also CA 17-20R; CAAS 19; CANR 47;
CP 1, 2, 3, 4, 5, 6, 7; DLB 5, 130, 165

Kelman, James 1946- .... **CLC 58, 86**
See also BRWS 5; CA 148; CANR 85, 130;
CN 5, 6, 7; DLB 194, 319, 326; RGSF 2;
WLIT 4

Kemal, Yasar
See Kemal, Yashar
See also CWW 2; EWL 3; WLIT 6

Kemal, Yashar 1923(?)- .... **CLC 14, 29**
See also CA 89-92; CANR 44

Kemble, Fanny 1809-1893 .... **NCLC 18**
See also DLB 32

Kemelman, Harry 1908-1996 .... **CLC 2**
See also AITN 1; BPFB 2; CA 9-12R; 155;
CANR 6, 71; CMW 4; DLB 28

Kempe, Margery 1373(?)-1440(?) ... **LC 6, 56**
See also BRWS 12; DLB 146; FL 1:1;
RGEL 2

Kempis, Thomas a 1380-1471 .... **LC 11**

Kenan, Randall (G.) 1963- .... **BLC 2:2**
See also BW 2, 3; CA 142; CANR 86; CN
7; CSW; DLB 292; GLL 1

Kendall, Henry 1839-1882 .... **NCLC 12**
See also DLB 230

Keneally, Thomas 1935- .... **CLC 5, 8, 10, 14,
19, 27, 43, 117**
See also BRWS 4; CA 85-88; CANR 10,
50, 74, 130, 165; CN 1, 2, 3, 4, 5, 6, 7;
CPW; DA3; DAM NOV, 299,
326; EWL 3; MTCW 1, 2; MTFW 2005;
NFS 17; RGEL 2; RGHL; RHW

Keneally, Thomas Michael
See Keneally, Thomas

Kennedy, A. L. 1965- .... **CLC 188**
See also CA 168, 213; CAAE 213; CANR
108; CD 5, 6; CN 6, 7; DLB 271; RGSF
2

Kennedy, Adrienne (Lita) 1931- .... **BLC 1:2;
CLC 66; DC 5**
See also AFAW 2; BW 2, 3; CA 103; CAAS
20; CABS 3; CAD; CANR 26, 53, 82;
CD 5, 6; DAM MULT; DFS 9; DLB 38,
341; FW; MAL 5

Kennedy, Alison Louise
See Kennedy, A. L.

Kennedy, John Pendleton
1795-1870 .... **NCLC 2**
See also DLB 3, 248, 254; RGAL 4

Kennedy, Joseph Charles 1929-
See Kennedy, X. J.
See also CA 1-4R, 201; CAAE 201; CANR
4, 30, 40; CWRI 5; MAICYA 2; MAIC-
YAS 1; SATA 14, 86, 130; SATA-Essay
130

Kennedy, William 1928- .. **CLC 6, 28, 34, 53,
239**
See also AAYA 1, 73; AMWS 7; BPFB 2;
CA 85-88; CANR 14, 31, 76, 134; CN 4,
5, 6, 7; DA3; DAM NOV; DLB 143;
DLBY 1985; EWL 3; INT CANR-31;
MAL 5; MTCW 1, 2; MTFW 2005; SATA
57

Kennedy, X. J. .... **CLC 8, 42**
See Kennedy, Joseph Charles
See also AMWS 15; CAAS 9; CLR 27; CP
1, 2, 3, 4, 5, 6, 7; DLB 5; SAAS 22

Kenny, Maurice (Francis) 1929- ..... **CLC 87;
NNAL**
See also CA 144; CAAS 22; CANR 143;
DAM MULT; DLB 175

Kent, Kelvin
See Kuttner, Henry

Kenton, Maxwell
See Southern, Terry

Kenyon, Jane 1947-1995 .... **PC 57**
See also AAYA 63; AMWS 7; CA 118; 148;
CANR 44, 69, 172; CP 6, 7; CWP; DLB
120; PFS 9, 17; RGAL 4

Kenyon, Robert O.
See Kuttner, Henry

Kirkham, Dinah
  See Card, Orson Scott
Kirkland, Caroline M. 1801-1864 . **NCLC 85**
  See also DLB 3, 73, 74, 250, 254; DLBD
  13
Kirkup, James 1918- .... **CLC 1**
  See also CA 1-4R; CAAS 4; CANR 2; CP
  1, 2, 3, 4, 5, 6, 7; DLB 27; SATA 12
Kirkwood, James 1930(?)-1989 .... **CLC 9**
  See also AITN 2; CA 1-4R; 128; CANR 6,
  40; GLL 2
Kirsch, Sarah 1935- .... **CLC 176**
  See also CA 178; CWW 2; DLB 75; EWL
  3
Kirshner, Sidney
  See Kingsley, Sidney
Kis, Danilo 1935-1989 .... **CLC 57**
  See also CA 109; 118; 129; CANR 61; CD-
  WLB 4; DLB 181; EWL 3; MTCW 1;
  RGSF 2; RGWL 2, 3
Kissinger, Henry A(lfred) 1923- ..... **CLC 137**
  See also CA 1-4R; CANR 2, 33, 66, 109;
  MTCW 1
Kittel, Frederick August
  See Wilson, August
Kivi, Aleksis 1834-1872 .... **NCLC 30**
Kizer, Carolyn 1925- ..... **CLC 15, 39, 80; PC
  66**
  See also CA 65-68; CAAS 5; CANR 24,
  70, 134; CP 1, 2, 3, 4, 5, 6, 7; CWP; DAM
  POET; DLB 5, 169; EWL 3; MAL 5;
  MTCW 2; MTFW 2005; PFS 18; TCLE
  1:1
Klabund 1890-1928 .... **TCLC 44**
  See also CA 162; DLB 66
Klappert, Peter 1942- .... **CLC 57**
  See also CA 33-36R; CSW; DLB 5
Klausner, Amos
  See Oz, Amos
Klein, A(braham) M(oses)
  1909-1972 .... **CLC 19**
  See also CA 101; 37-40R; CP 1; DAB;
  DAC; DAM MST; DLB 68; EWL 3;
  RGEL 2; RGHL
Klein, Joe
  See Klein, Joseph
Klein, Joseph 1946- .... **CLC 154**
  See also CA 85-88; CANR 55, 164
Klein, Norma 1938-1989 .... **CLC 30**
  See also AAYA 2, 35; BPFB 2; BYA 6, 7,
  8; CA 41-44R; 128; CANR 15, 37; CLR
  2, 19; INT CANR-15; JRDA; MAICYA
  1, 2; SAAS 1; SATA 7, 57; WYA; YAW
Klein, T.E.D. 1947- .... **CLC 34**
  See also CA 119; CANR 44, 75, 167; HGG
Klein, Theodore Eibon Donald
  See Klein, T.E.D.
Kleist, Heinrich von 1777-1811 .... **DC 29;
  NCLC 2, 37; SSC 22**
  See also CDWLB 2; DAM DRAM; DLB
  90; EW 5; RGSF 2; RGWL 2, 3
Klima, Ivan 1931- .... **CLC 56, 172**
  See also CA 25-28R; CANR 17, 50, 91;
  CDWLB 4; CWW 2; DAM NOV; DLB
  232; EWL 3; RGWL 3
Klimentev, Andrei Platonovich
  See Klimentov, Andrei Platonovich
Klimentov, Andrei Platonovich 1899-1951
  SSC 42; TCLC 14
  See Platonov, Andrei Platonovich; Platonov,
  Andrey Platonovich
  See also CA 108; 232
Klinger, Friedrich Maximilian von
  1752-1831 .... **NCLC 1**
  See also DLB 94
Klingsor the Magician
  See Hartmann, Sadakichi

Klopstock, Friedrich Gottlieb 1724-1803
  NCLC 11
  See also DLB 97; EW 4; RGWL 2, 3
Kluge, Alexander 1932- .... **SSC 61**
  See also CA 81-84; CANR 163; DLB 75
Knapp, Caroline 1959-2002 .... **CLC 99**
  See also CA 154; 207
Knebel, Fletcher 1911-1993 .... **CLC 14**
  See also AITN 1; CA 1-4R; 140; CAAS 3;
  CANR 1, 36; CN 1, 2, 3, 4, 5; SATA 36;
  SATA-Obit 75
Knickerbocker, Diedrich
  See Irving, Washington
Knight, Etheridge 1931-1991 .... **BLC 1:2;
  CLC 40; PC 14**
  See also BW 1, 3; CA 21-24R; 133; CANR
  23, 82; CP 1, 2, 3, 4, 5; DAM POET; DLB
  41; MTCW 2; MTFW 2005; RGAL 4;
  TCLE 1:1
Knight, Sarah Kemble 1666-1727 .... **LC 7**
  See also DLB 24, 200
Knister, Raymond 1899-1932 .... **TCLC 56**
  See also CA 186; DLB 68; RGEL 2
Knowles, John 1926-2001 ... **CLC 1, 4, 10, 26**
  See also AAYA 10, 72; AMWS 12; BPFB
  2; BYA 3; CA 17-20R; 203; CANR 40,
  74, 76, 132; CDALB 1968-1988; CLR 98;
  CN 1, 2, 3, 4, 5, 6, 7; DA; DAC; DAM
  MST, NOV; DLB 6; EXPN; MTCW 1, 2;
  MTFW 2005; NFS 2; RGAL 4; SATA 8,
  89; SATA-Obit 134; YAW
Knox, Calvin M.
  See Silverberg, Robert
Knox, John c. 1505-1572 .... **LC 37**
  See also DLB 132
Knye, Cassandra
  See Disch, Thomas M.
Koch, C(hristopher) J(ohn) 1932- .... **CLC 42**
  See also CA 127; CANR 84; CN 3, 4, 5, 6,
  7; DLB 289
Koch, Christopher
  See Koch, C(hristopher) J(ohn)
Koch, Kenneth 1925-2002 .... **CLC 5, 8, 44;
  PC 80**
  See also AMWS 15; CA 1-4R; 207; CAD;
  CANR 6, 36, 57, 97, 131; CD 5, 6; CP 1,
  2, 3, 4, 5, 6, 7; DAM POET; DLB 5; INT
  CANR-36; MAL 5; MTCW 2; MTFW
  2005; PFS 20; SATA 65; WP
Kochanowski, Jan 1530-1584 .... **LC 10**
  See also RGWL 2, 3
Kock, Charles Paul de 1794-1871 . **NCLC 16**
Koda Rohan
  See Koda Shigeyuki
Koda Rohan
  See Koda Shigeyuki
Koda Shigeyuki 1867-1947 .... **TCLC 22**
  See also CA 121; 183; DLB 180
Koestler, Arthur 1905-1983 ... **CLC 1, 3, 6, 8,
  15, 33**
  See also BRWS 1; CA 1-4R; 109; CANR 1,
  33; CDBLB 1945-1960; CN 1, 2, 3;
  DLBY 1983; EWL 3; MTCW 1, 2; MTFW
  2005; NFS 19; RGEL 2
Kogawa, Joy Nozomi 1935- ...... **CLC 78, 129**
  See also AAYA 47; CA 101; CANR 19, 62,
  126; CN 6, 7; CP 1; CWP; DAC; DAM
  MST, MULT; DLB 334; FW; MTCW 2;
  MTFW 2005; NFS 3; SATA 99
Kohout, Pavel 1928- .... **CLC 13**
  See also CA 45-48; CANR 3
Koizumi, Yakumo
  See Hearn, (Patricio) Lafcadio (Tessima
  Carlos)
Kolmar, Gertrud 1894-1943 .... **TCLC 40**
  See also CA 167; EWL 3; RGHL

Komunyakaa, Yusef 1947- . **BLC 2:2; BLCS;
  CLC 86, 94, 207; PC 51**
  See also AFAW 2; AMWS 13; CA 147;
  CANR 83, 164; CP 6, 7; CSW; DLB 120;
  EWL 3; PFS 5, 20; RGAL 4
Konigsberg, Alan Stewart
  See Allen, Woody
Konrad, George
  See Konrad, Gyorgy
Konrad, George
  See Konrad, Gyorgy
Konrad, Gyorgy 1933- .... **CLC 4, 10, 73**
  See also CA 85-88; CANR 97, 171; CD-
  WLB 4; CWW 2; DLB 232; EWL 3
Konwicki, Tadeusz 1926- .... **CLC 8, 28, 54,
  117**
  See also CA 101; CAAS 9; CANR 39, 59;
  CWW 2; DLB 232; EWL 3; IDFW 3;
  MTCW 1
Koontz, Dean 1945- .... **CLC 78, 206**
  See also AAYA 9, 31; BEST 89:3, 90:2; CA
  108; CANR 19, 36, 52, 95, 138, 176;
  CMW 4; CPW; DA3; DAM NOV, POP;
  DLB 292; HGG; MTCW 1; MTFW 2005;
  SATA 92, 165; SFW 4; SUFW 2; YAW
Koontz, Dean Ray
  See Koontz, Dean
Kopernik, Mikolaj
  See Copernicus, Nicolaus
Kopit, Arthur (Lee) 1937- ...... **CLC 1, 18, 33**
  See also AITN 1; CA 81-84; CABS 3;
  CAD; CD 5, 6; DAM DRAM; DFS 7, 14,
  24; DLB 7; MAL 5; MTCW 1; RGAL 4
Kopitar, Jernej (Bartholomaus) 1780-1844
  NCLC 117
Kops, Bernard 1926- .... **CLC 4**
  See also CA 5-8R; CANR 84, 159; CBD;
  CN 1, 2, 3, 4, 5, 6, 7; CP 1, 2, 3, 4, 5, 6,
  7; DLB 13; RGHL
Kornbluth, C(yril) M. 1923-1958 .... **TCLC 8**
  See also CA 105; 160; DLB 8; SCFW 1, 2;
  SFW 4
Korolenko, V.G.
  See Korolenko, Vladimir G.
Korolenko, Vladimir
  See Korolenko, Vladimir G.
Korolenko, Vladimir G.
  1853-1921 .... **TCLC 22**
  See also CA 121; DLB 277
Korolenko, Vladimir Galaktionovich
  See Korolenko, Vladimir G.
Korzybski, Alfred (Habdank Skarbek)
  1879-1950 .... **TCLC 61**
  See also CA 123; 160
Kosinski, Jerzy 1933-1991 ..... **CLC 1, 2, 3, 6,
  10, 15, 53, 70**
  See also AMWS 7; BPFB 2; CA 17-20R;
  134; CANR 9, 46; CN 1, 2, 3, 4; DA3;
  DAM NOV; DLB 2, 299; DLBY 1982;
  EWL 3; HGG; MAL 5; MTCW 1, 2;
  MTFW 2005; NFS 12; RGAL 4; RGHL;
  TUS
Kostelanetz, Richard (Cory) 1940- .. **CLC 28**
  See also CA 13-16R; CAAS 8; CANR 38,
  77; CN 4, 5, 6; CP 2, 3, 4, 5, 6, 7
Kostrowitzki, Wilhelm Apollinaris de
  1880-1918
  See Apollinaire, Guillaume
  See also CA 104
Kotlowitz, Robert 1924- .... **CLC 4**
  See also CA 33-36R; CANR 36
Kotzebue, August (Friedrich Ferdinand) von
  1761-1819 .... **NCLC 25**
  See also DLB 94
Kotzwinkle, William 1938- ..... **CLC 5, 14, 35**
  See also BPFB 2; CA 45-48; CANR 3, 44,
  84, 129; CLR 6; CN 7; DLB 173; FANT;
  MAICYA 1, 2; SATA 24, 70, 146; SFW
  4; SUFW 2; YAW

La Guma, Alex 1925-1985 .. **BLCS; CLC 19; TCLC 140**
See also AFW; BW 1, 3; CA 49-52; 118; CANR 25, 81; CDWLB 3; CN 1, 2, 3; CP 1; DAM NOV; DLB 117, 225; EWL 3; MTCW 1, 2; MTFW 2005; WLIT 2; WWE 1

Lahiri, Jhumpa 1967- .... **SSC 96**
See also AAYA 56; CA 193; CANR 134; DLB 323; MTFW 2005; SSFS 19

Laidlaw, A. K.
See Grieve, C(hristopher) M(urray)

Lainez, Manuel Mujica
See Mujica Lainez, Manuel
See also HW 1

Laing, R(onald) D(avid) 1927-1989 . **CLC 95**
See also CA 107; 129; CANR 34; MTCW 1

Laishley, Alex
See Booth, Martin

Lamartine, Alphonse (Marie Louis Prat) de 1790-1869 .... **NCLC 11, 190; PC 16**
See also DAM POET; DLB 217; GFL 1789 to the Present; RGWL 2, 3

Lamb, Charles 1775-1834 ..... **NCLC 10, 113; SSC 112; WLC 3**
See also BRW 4; CDBLB 1789-1832; DA; DAB; DAC; DAM MST; DLB 93, 107, 163; RGEL 2; SATA 17; TEA

Lamb, Lady Caroline 1785-1828 ... **NCLC 38**
See also DLB 116

Lamb, Mary Ann 1764-1847 ...... **NCLC 125; SSC 112**
See also DLB 163; SATA 17

Lame Deer 1903(?)-1976 .... **NNAL**
See also CA 69-72

Lamming, George (William) 1927- . **BLC 1:2, 2:2; CLC 2, 4, 66, 144**
See also BW 2, 3; CA 85-88; CANR 26, 76; CDWLB 3; CN 1, 2, 3, 4, 5, 6, 7; CP 1; DAM MULT; DLB 125; EWL 3; MTCW 1, 2; MTFW 2005; NFS 15; RGEL 2

L'Amour, Louis 1908-1988 .... **CLC 25, 55**
See also AAYA 16; AITN 2; BEST 89:2; BPFB 2; CA 1-4R; 125; CANR 3, 25, 40; CPW; DA3; DAM NOV, POP; DLB 206; DLBY 1980; MTCW 1, 2; MTFW 2005; RGAL 4; TCWW 1, 2

Lampedusa, Giuseppe (Tomasi) di .... **TCLC 13**
See Tomasi di Lampedusa, Giuseppe
See also CA 164; EW 11; MTCW 2; MTFW 2005; RGWL 2, 3

Lampman, Archibald 1861-1899 .. **NCLC 25, 194**
See also DLB 92; RGEL 2; TWA

Lancaster, Bruce 1896-1963 .... **CLC 36**
See also CA 9-10; CANR 70; CAP 1; SATA 9

Lanchester, John 1962- .... **CLC 99**
See also CA 194; DLB 267

Landau, Mark Alexandrovich
See Aldanov, Mark (Alexandrovich)

Landau-Aldanov, Mark Alexandrovich
See Aldanov, Mark (Alexandrovich)

Landis, Jerry
See Simon, Paul

Landis, John 1950- .... **CLC 26**
See also CA 112; 122; CANR 128

Landolfi, Tommaso 1908-1979 .... **CLC 11, 49**
See also CA 127; 117; DLB 177; EWL 3

Landon, Letitia Elizabeth 1802-1838 .... **NCLC 15**
See also DLB 96

Landor, Walter Savage 1775-1864 .... **NCLC 14**
See also BRW 4; DLB 93, 107; RGEL 2

Landwirth, Heinz
See Lind, Jakov

Lane, Patrick 1939- .... **CLC 25**
See also CA 97-100; CANR 54; CP 3, 4, 5, 6, 7; DAM POET; DLB 53; INT CA-97-100

Lane, Rose Wilder 1887-1968 ...... **TCLC 177**
See also CA 102; CANR 63; SATA 29; SATA-Brief 28; TCWW 2

Lang, Andrew 1844-1912 .... **TCLC 16**
See also CA 114; 137; CANR 85; CLR 101; DLB 98, 141, 184; FANT; MAICYA 1, 2; RGEL 2; SATA 16; WCH

Lang, Fritz 1890-1976 .... **CLC 20, 103**
See also AAYA 65; CA 77-80; 69-72; CANR 30

Lange, John
See Crichton, Michael

Langer, Elinor 1939- .... **CLC 34**
See also CA 121

Langland, William 1332(?)-1400(?) .... **LC 19, 120**
See also BRW 1; DA; DAB; DAC; DAM MST, POET; DLB 146; RGEL 2; TEA; WLIT 3

Langstaff, Launcelot
See Irving, Washington

Lanier, Sidney 1842-1881 . **NCLC 6, 118; PC 50**
See also AMWS 1; DAM POET; DLB 64; DLBD 13; EXPP; MAICYA 1; PFS 14; RGAL 4; SATA 18

Lanyer, Aemilia 1569-1645 .... **LC 10, 30, 83; PC 60**
See also DLB 121

Lao-Tzu
See Lao Tzu

Lao Tzu c. 6th cent. B.C.-3rd cent. B.C. **CMLC 7**

Lapine, James (Elliot) 1949- .... **CLC 39**
See also CA 123; 130; CANR 54, 128; DFS 25; DLB 341; INT CA-130

Larbaud, Valery (Nicolas) 1881-1957 .... **TCLC 9**
See also CA 106; 152; EWL 3; GFL 1789 to the Present

Larcom, Lucy 1824-1893 .... **NCLC 179**
See also AMWS 13; DLB 221, 243

Lardner, Ring
See Lardner, Ring(gold) W(ilmer)
See also BPFB 2; CDALB 1917-1929; DLB 11, 25, 86, 171; DLBD 16; MAL 5; RGAL 4; RGSF 2

Lardner, Ring W., Jr.
See Lardner, Ring(gold) W(ilmer)

Lardner, Ring(gold) W(ilmer) 1885-1933 .... **SSC 32; TCLC 2, 14**
See Lardner, Ring
See also AMW; CA 104; 131; MTCW 1, 2; MTFW 2005; TUS

Laredo, Betty
See Codrescu, Andrei

Larkin, Maia
See Wojciechowska, Maia (Teresa)

Larkin, Philip (Arthur) 1922-1985 ... **CLC 3, 5, 8, 9, 13, 18, 33, 39, 64; PC 21**
See also BRWS 1; CA 5-8R; 117; CANR 24, 62; CDBLB 1960 to Present; CP 1, 2, 3, 4; DA3; DAB; DAM MST, POET; DLB 27; EWL 3; MTCW 1, 2; MTFW 2005; PFS 3, 4, 12; RGEL 2

La Roche, Sophie von 1730-1807 .... **NCLC 121**
See also DLB 94

La Rochefoucauld, Francois 1613-1680 .... **LC 108**
See also DLB 268; EW 3; GFL Beginnings to 1789; RGWL 2, 3

Larra (y Sanchez de Castro), Mariano Jose de 1809-1837 .... **NCLC 17, 130**

Larsen, Eric 1941- .... **CLC 55**
See also CA 132

Larsen, Nella 1893(?)-1963 ... **BLC 1:2; CLC 37; HR 1:3; TCLC 200**
See also AFAW 1, 2; BW 1; CA 125; CANR 83; DAM MULT; DLB 51; FW; LATS 1:1; LMFS 2

Larson, Charles R(aymond) 1938- ... **CLC 31**
See also CA 53-56; CANR 4, 121

Larson, Jonathan 1960-1996 .... **CLC 99**
See also AAYA 28; CA 156; DFS 23; MTFW 2005

La Sale, Antoine de c. 1386-1460(?) . **LC 104**
See also DLB 208

Las Casas, Bartolome de 1474-1566 .... **HLCS; LC 31**
See Casas, Bartolome de las
See also DLB 318; LAW

Lasch, Christopher 1932-1994 .... **CLC 102**
See also CA 73-76; 144; CANR 25, 118; DLB 246; MTCW 1, 2; MTFW 2005

Lasker-Schueler, Else 1869-1945 ... **TCLC 57**
See Lasker-Schuler, Else
See also CA 183; DLB 66, 124

Lasker-Schuler, Else
See Lasker-Schueler, Else
See also EWL 3

Laski, Harold J(oseph) 1893-1950 . **TCLC 79**
See also CA 188

Latham, Jean Lee 1902-1995 .... **CLC 12**
See also AITN 1; BYA 1; CA 5-8R; CANR 7, 84; CLR 50; MAICYA 1, 2; SATA 2, 68; YAW

Latham, Mavis
See Clark, Mavis Thorpe

Lathen, Emma .... **CLC 2**
See Hennissart, Martha; Latsis, Mary J(ane)
See also BPFB 2; CMW 4; DLB 306

Lathrop, Francis
See Leiber, Fritz (Reuter, Jr.)

Latsis, Mary J(ane) 1927-1997
See Lathen, Emma
See also CA 85-88; 162; CMW 4

Lattany, Kristin
See Lattany, Kristin (Elaine Eggleston) Hunter

Lattany, Kristin (Elaine Eggleston) Hunter 1931- .... **CLC 35**
See Hunter, Kristin
See also AITN 1; BW 1; BYA 3; CA 13-16R; CANR 13, 108; CLR 3; CN 7; DLB 33; INT CANR-13; MAICYA 1, 2; SAAS 10; SATA 12, 132; YAW

Lattimore, Richmond (Alexander) 1906-1984 **CLC 3**
See also CA 1-4R; 112; CANR 1; CP 1, 2, 3; MAL 5

Laughlin, James 1914-1997 .... **CLC 49**
See also CA 21-24R; 162; CAAS 22; CANR 9, 47; CP 1, 2, 3, 4, 5, 6; DLB 48; DLBY 1996, 1997

Laurence, Margaret 1926-1987 ..... **CLC 3, 6, 13, 50, 62; SSC 7**
See also BYA 13; CA 5-8R; 121; CANR 33; CN 1, 2, 3, 4; DAC; DAM MST; DLB 53; EWL 3; FW; MTCW 1, 2; MTFW 2005; NFS 11; RGEL 2; RGSF 2; SATA-Obit 50; TCWW 2

Laurent, Antoine 1952- .... **CLC 50**

Lauscher, Hermann
See Hesse, Hermann

Lautreamont 1846-1870 .... **NCLC 12, 194; SSC 14**
See Lautreamont, Isidore Lucien Ducasse
See also GFL 1789 to the Present; RGWL 2, 3

Mackenzie, Henry 1745-1831 .... **NCLC 41**
　　See also DLB 39; RGEL 2
Mackey, Nathaniel 1947- .... **BLC 2:3; PC 49**
　　See also CA 153; CANR 114; CP 6, 7; DLB 169
Mackey, Nathaniel Ernest
　　See Mackey, Nathaniel
MacKinnon, Catharine A. 1946- .... **CLC 181**
　　See also CA 128; 132; CANR 73, 140; FW; MTCW 2; MTFW 2005
Mackintosh, Elizabeth 1896(?)-1952
　　See Tey, Josephine
　　See also CA 110; CMW 4
Macklin, Charles 1699-1797 .... **LC 132**
　　See also DLB 89; RGEL 2
MacLaren, James
　　See Grieve, C(hristopher) M(urray)
MacLaverty, Bernard 1942- ..... **CLC 31, 243**
　　See also CA 116; 118; CANR 43, 88, 168; CN 5, 6, 7; DLB 267; INT CA-118; RGSF 2
MacLean, Alistair (Stuart)
　　1922(?)-1987 .... **CLC 3, 13, 50, 63**
　　See also CA 57-60; 121; CANR 28, 61; CMW 4; CP 2, 3, 4, 5, 6, 7; CPW; DAM POP; DLB 276; MTCW 1; SATA 23; SATA-Obit 50; TCWW 2
Maclean, Norman (Fitzroy)
　　1902-1990 .... **CLC 78; SSC 13**
　　See also AMWS 14; CA 102; 132; CANR 49; CPW; DAM POP; DLB 206; TCWW 2
MacLeish, Archibald 1892-1982 ... **CLC 3, 8, 14, 68; PC 47**
　　See also AMW; CA 9-12R; 106; CAD; CANR 33, 63; CDALBS; CP 1, 2; DAM POET; DFS 15; DLB 4, 7, 45; DLBY 1982; EWL 3; EXPP; MAL 5; MTCW 1, 2; MTFW 2005; PAB; PFS 5; RGAL 4; TUS
MacLennan, (John) Hugh
　　1907-1990 .... **CLC 2, 14, 92**
　　See also CA 5-8R; 142; CANR 33; CN 1, 2, 3, 4; DAC; DAM MST; DLB 68; EWL 3; MTCW 1, 2; MTFW 2005; RGEL 2; TWA
MacLeod, Alistair 1936- .. **CLC 56, 165; SSC 90**
　　See also CA 123; CCA 1; DAC; DAM MST; DLB 60; MTCW 2; MTFW 2005; RGSF 2; TCLE 1:2
Macleod, Fiona
　　See Sharp, William
　　See also RGEL 2; SUFW
MacNeice, (Frederick) Louis
　　1907-1963 .... **CLC 1, 4, 10, 53; PC 61**
　　See also BRW 7; CA 85-88; CANR 61; DAB; DAM POET; DLB 10, 20; EWL 3; MTCW 1, 2; MTFW 2005; RGEL 2
MacNeill, Dand
　　See Fraser, George MacDonald
Macpherson, James 1736-1796 .... **LC 29**
　　See Ossian
　　See also BRWS 8; DLB 109, 336; RGEL 2
Macpherson, (Jean) Jay 1931- .... **CLC 14**
　　See also CA 5-8R; CANR 90; CP 1, 2, 3, 4, 6, 7; CWP; DLB 53
Macrobius fl. 430- .... **CMLC 48**
MacShane, Frank 1927-1999 .... **CLC 39**
　　See also CA 9-12R; 186; CANR 3, 33; DLB 111
Macumber, Mari
　　See Sandoz, Mari(e Susette)
Madach, Imre 1823-1864 .... **NCLC 19**
Madden, (Jerry) David 1933- .... **CLC 5, 15**
　　See also CA 1-4R; CAAS 3; CANR 4, 45; CN 3, 4, 5, 6, 7; CSW; DLB 6; MTCW 1
Maddern, Al(an)
　　See Ellison, Harlan

Madhubuti, Haki R. 1942- .... **BLC 1:2; CLC 6, 73; PC 5**
　　See Lee, Don L.
　　See also BW 2, 3; CA 73-76; CANR 24, 51, 73, 139; CP 6, 7; CSW; DAM MULT, POET; DLB 5, 41; DLBD 8; EWL 3; MAL 5; MTCW 2; MTFW 2005; RGAL 4
Madison, James 1751-1836 .... **NCLC 126**
　　See also DLB 37
Maepenn, Hugh
　　See Kuttner, Henry
Maepenn, K. H.
　　See Kuttner, Henry
Maeterlinck, Maurice 1862-1949 ..... **TCLC 3**
　　See also CA 104; 136; CANR 80; DAM DRAM; DLB 192, 331; EW 8; EWL 3; GFL 1789 to the Present; LMFS 2; RGWL 2, 3; SATA 66; TWA
Maginn, William 1794-1842 .... **NCLC 8**
　　See also DLB 110, 159
Mahapatra, Jayanta 1928- .... **CLC 33**
　　See also CA 73-76; CAAS 9; CANR 15, 33, 66, 87; CP 4, 5, 6, 7; DAM MULT; DLB 323
Mahfouz, Nagib
　　See Mahfouz, Naguib
Mahfouz, Naguib 1911(?)-2006 ..... **CLC 153; SSC 66**
　　See Mahfuz, Najib
　　See also AAYA 49; BEST 89:2; CA 128; 253; CANR 55, 101; DA3; DAM NOV; MTCW 1, 2; MTFW 2005; RGWL 2, 3; SSFS 9
Mahfouz, Naguib Abdel Aziz Al-Sabilgi
　　See Mahfouz, Naguib
Mahfouz, Najib
　　See Mahfouz, Naguib
Mahfuz, Najib .... **CLC 52, 55**
　　See Mahfouz, Naguib
　　See also AFW; CWW 2; DLB 331; DLBY 1988; EWL 3; RGSF 2; WLIT 6
Mahon, Derek 1941- .... **CLC 27; PC 60**
　　See also BRWS 6; CA 113; 128; CANR 88; CP 1, 2, 3, 4, 5, 6, 7; DLB 40; EWL 3
Maiakovskii, Vladimir
　　See Mayakovski, Vladimir (Vladimirovich)
　　See also IDTP; RGWL 2, 3
Mailer, Norman 1923-2007 ... **CLC 1, 2, 3, 4, 5, 8, 11, 14, 28, 39, 74, 111, 234**
　　See also AAYA 31; AITN 2; AMW; AMWC 2; AMWR 2; BPFB 2; CA 9-12R; 266; CABS 1; CANR 28, 74, 77, 130; CDALB 1968-1988; CN 1, 2, 3, 4, 5, 6, 7; CPW; DA; DA3; DAB; DAC; DAM MST, NOV, POP; DLB 2, 16, 28, 185, 278; DLBD 3; DLBY 1980, 1983; EWL 3; MAL 5; MTCW 1, 2; MTFW 2005; NFS 10; RGAL 4; TUS
Mailer, Norman Kingsley
　　See Mailer, Norman
Maillet, Antonine 1929- .... **CLC 54, 118**
　　See also CA 115; 120; CANR 46, 74, 77, 134; CCA 1; CWW 2; DAC; DLB 60; INT CA-120; MTCW 2; MTFW 2005
Maimonides, Moses 1135-1204 ..... **CMLC 76**
　　See also DLB 115
Mais, Roger 1905-1955 .... **TCLC 8**
　　See also BW 1, 3; CA 105; 124; CANR 82; CDWLB 3; DLB 125; EWL 3; MTCW 1; RGEL 2
Maistre, Joseph 1753-1821 .... **NCLC 37**
　　See also GFL 1789 to the Present
Maitland, Frederic William
　　1850-1906 .... **TCLC 65**
Maitland, Sara (Louise) 1950- .... **CLC 49**
　　See also BRWS 11; CA 69-72; CANR 13, 59; DLB 271; FW

Major, Clarence 1936- ...... **BLC 1:2; CLC 3, 19, 48**
　　See also AFAW 2; BW 2, 3; CA 21-24R; CAAS 6; CANR 13, 25, 53, 82; CN 3, 4, 5, 6, 7; CP 2, 3, 4, 5, 6, 7; CSW; DAM MULT; DLB 33; EWL 3; MAL 5; MSW
Major, Kevin (Gerald) 1949- .... **CLC 26**
　　See also AAYA 16; CA 97-100; CANR 21, 38, 112; CLR 11; DAC; DLB 60; INT CANR-21; JRDA; MAICYA 1, 2; MAIC-YAS 1; SATA 32, 82, 134; WYA; YAW
Maki, James
　　See Ozu, Yasujiro
Makin, Bathsua 1600-1675(?) .... **LC 137**
Makine, Andrei 1957-
　　See Makine, Andrei
Makine, Andrei 1957- .... **CLC 198**
　　See also CA 176; CANR 103, 162; MTFW 2005
Malabaila, Damiano
　　See Levi, Primo
Malamud, Bernard 1914-1986 .. **CLC 1, 2, 3, 5, 8, 9, 11, 18, 27, 44, 78, 85; SSC 15; TCLC 129, 184; WLC 4**
　　See also AAYA 16; AMWS 1; BPFB 2; BYA 15; CA 5-8R; 118; CABS 1; CANR 28, 62, 114; CDALB 1941-1968; CN 1, 2, 3, 4; CPW; DA; DA3; DAB; DAC; DAM MST, NOV, POP; DLB 2, 28, 152; DLBY 1980, 1986; EWL 3; EXPS; LAIT 4; LATS 1:1; MAL 5; MTCW 1, 2; MTFW 2005; NFS 27; RGAL 4; RGHL; RGSF 2; SSFS 8, 13, 16; TUS
Malan, Herman
　　See Bosman, Herman Charles; Bosman, Herman Charles
Malaparte, Curzio 1898-1957 .... **TCLC 52**
　　See also DLB 264
Malcolm, Dan
　　See Silverberg, Robert
Malcolm, Janet 1934- .... **CLC 201**
　　See also CA 123; CANR 89; NCFS 1
Malcolm X .. **BLC 1:2; CLC 82, 117; WLCS**
　　See Little, Malcolm
　　See also LAIT 5; NCFS 3
Malebranche, Nicolas 1638-1715 .... **LC 133**
　　See also GFL Beginnings to 1789
Malherbe, Francois de 1555-1628 .... **LC 5**
　　See also DLB 327; GFL Beginnings to 1789
Mallarme, Stephane 1842-1898 ...... **NCLC 4, 41; PC 4**
　　See also DAM POET; DLB 217; EW 7; GFL 1789 to the Present; LMFS 2; RGWL 2, 3; TWA
Mallet-Joris, Francoise 1930- .... **CLC 11**
　　See also CA 65-68; CANR 17; CWW 2; DLB 83; EWL 3; GFL 1789 to the Present
Malley, Ern
　　See McAuley, James Phillip
Mallon, Thomas 1951- .... **CLC 172**
　　See also CA 110; CANR 29, 57, 92
Mallowan, Agatha Christie
　　See Christie, Agatha (Mary Clarissa)
Maloff, Saul 1922- .... **CLC 5**
　　See also CA 33-36R
Malone, Louis
　　See MacNeice, (Frederick) Louis
Malone, Michael (Christopher)
　　1942- .... **CLC 43**
　　See also CA 77-80; CANR 14, 32, 57, 114
Malory, Sir Thomas 1410(?)-1471(?) . **LC 11, 88; WLCS**
　　See also BRW 1; BRWR 2; CDBLB Before 1660; DA; DAB; DAC; DAM MST; DLB 146; EFS 2; RGEL 2; SATA 59; SATA-Brief 33; TEA; WLIT 3

Malouf, David 1934- .... **CLC 28, 86, 245**
See also BRWS 12; CA 124; CANR 50, 76;
CN 3, 4, 5, 6, 7; CP 1, 3, 4, 5, 6, 7; DLB
289; EWL 3; MTCW 2; MTFW 2005;
SSFS 24

Malouf, George Joseph David
See Malouf, David

Malraux, (Georges-)Andre
1901-1976 .... **CLC 1, 4, 9, 13, 15, 57**
See also BPFB 2; CA 21-22; 69-72; CANR
34, 58; CAP 2; DA3; DAM NOV; DLB
72; EW 12; EWL 3; GFL 1789 to the
Present; MTCW 1, 2; MTFW 2005;
RGWL 2, 3; TWA

Malthus, Thomas Robert
1766-1834 .... **NCLC 145**
See also DLB 107, 158; RGEL 2

Malzberg, Barry N(athaniel) 1939- ... **CLC 7**
See also CA 61-64; CAAS 4; CANR 16;
CMW 4; DLB 8; SFW 4

Mamet, David 1947- .. **CLC 9, 15, 34, 46, 91,
166; DC 4, 24**
See also AAYA 3, 60; AMWS 14; CA 81-
84; CABS 3; CAD; CANR 15, 41, 67, 72,
129, 172; CD 5, 6; DA3; DAM DRAM;
DFS 2, 3, 6, 12, 15; DLB 7; EWL 3;
IDFW 4; MAL 5; MTCW 1, 2; MTFW
2005; RGAL 4

Mamet, David Alan
See Mamet, David

Mamoulian, Rouben (Zachary) 1897-1987
CLC 16
See also CA 25-28R; 124; CANR 85

Mandelshtam, Osip
See Mandelstam, Osip (Emilievich)
See also EW 10; EWL 3; RGWL 2, 3

Mandelstam, Osip (Emilievich)
1891(?)-1943(?) .... **PC 14; TCLC 2, 6**
See Mandelshtam, Osip
See also CA 104; 150; MTCW 2; TWA

Mander, (Mary) Jane 1877-1949 ... **TCLC 31**
See also CA 162; RGEL 2

Mandeville, Bernard 1670-1733 .... **LC 82**
See also DLB 101

Mandeville, Sir John fl. 1350- ...... **CMLC 19**
See also DLB 146

Mandiargues, Andre Pieyre de .... **CLC 41**
See Pieyre de Mandiargues, Andre
See also DLB 83

Mandrake, Ethel Belle
See Thurman, Wallace (Henry)

Mangan, James Clarence
1803-1849 .... **NCLC 27**
See also BRWS 13; RGEL 2

Maniere, J.-E.
See Giraudoux, Jean(-Hippolyte)

Mankiewicz, Herman (Jacob) 1897-1953
TCLC 85
See also CA 120; 169; DLB 26; IDFW 3, 4

Manley, (Mary) Delariviere
1672(?)-1724 .... **LC 1, 42**
See also DLB 39, 80; RGEL 2

Mann, Abel
See Creasey, John

Mann, Emily 1952- .... **DC 7**
See also CA 130; CAD; CANR 55; CD 5,
6; CWD; DLB 266

Mann, (Luiz) Heinrich 1871-1950 ... **TCLC 9**
See also CA 106; 164, 181; DLB 66, 118;
EW 8; EWL 3; RGWL 2, 3

Mann, (Paul) Thomas 1875-1955 . **SSC 5, 80,
82; TCLC 2, 8, 14, 21, 35, 44, 60, 168;
WLC 4**
See also BPFB 2; CA 104; 128; CANR 133;
CDWLB 2; DA; DA3; DAB; DAC; DAM
MST, NOV; DLB 66, 331; EW 9; EWL 3;
GLL 1; LATS 1:1; LMFS 1; MTCW 1, 2;
MTFW 2005; NFS 17; RGSF 2; RGWL
2, 3; SSFS 4, 9; TWA

Mannheim, Karl 1893-1947 .... **TCLC 65**
See also CA 204

Manning, David
See Faust, Frederick (Schiller)

Manning, Frederic 1882-1935 .... **TCLC 25**
See also CA 124; 216; DLB 260

Manning, Olivia 1915-1980 .... **CLC 5, 19**
See also CA 5-8R; 101; CANR 29; CN 1,
2; EWL 3; FW; MTCW 1; RGEL 2

Mannyng, Robert c. 1264-c.
1340 .... **CMLC 83**
See also DLB 146

Mano, D. Keith 1942- .... **CLC 2, 10**
See also CA 25-28R; CAAS 6; CANR 26,
57; DLB 6

Mansfield, Katherine .... **SSC 9, 23, 38, 81;
TCLC 2, 8, 39, 164; WLC 4**
See Beauchamp, Kathleen Mansfield
See also BPFB 2; BRW 7; DAB; DLB 162;
EWL 3; EXPS; FW; GLL 1; RGEL 2;
RGSF 2; SSFS 2, 8, 10, 11; WWE 1

Manso, Peter 1940- .... **CLC 39**
See also CA 29-32R; CANR 44, 156

Mantecon, Juan Jimenez
See Jimenez (Mantecon), Juan Ramon

Mantel, Hilary 1952- .... **CLC 144**
See also CA 125; CANR 54, 101, 161; CN
5, 6, 7; DLB 271; RHW

Mantel, Hilary Mary
See Mantel, Hilary

Manton, Peter
See Creasey, John

Man Without a Spleen, A
See Chekhov, Anton (Pavlovich)

Manzano, Juan Franciso
1797(?)-1854 .... **NCLC 155**

Manzoni, Alessandro 1785-1873 ... **NCLC 29,
98**
See also EW 5; RGWL 2, 3; TWA; WLIT 7

Map, Walter 1140-1209 .... **CMLC 32**

Mapu, Abraham (ben Jekutiel) 1808-1867
NCLC 18

Mara, Sally
See Queneau, Raymond

Maracle, Lee 1950- .... **NNAL**
See also CA 149

Marat, Jean Paul 1743-1793 .... **LC 10**

Marcel, Gabriel Honore 1889-1973 . **CLC 15**
See also CA 102; 45-48; EWL 3; MTCW 1,
2

March, William .... **TCLC 96**
See Campbell, William Edward March
See also CA 216; DLB 9, 86, 316; MAL 5

Marchbanks, Samuel
See Davies, Robertson
See also CCA 1

Marchi, Giacomo
See Bassani, Giorgio

Marcus Aurelius
See Aurelius, Marcus
See also AW 2

Marcuse, Herbert 1898-1979 .... **TCLC 207**
See also CA 188; 89-92; DLB 242

Marguerite
See de Navarre, Marguerite

Marguerite d'Angouleme
See de Navarre, Marguerite
See also GFL Beginnings to 1789

Marguerite de Navarre
See de Navarre, Marguerite
See also RGWL 2, 3

Margulies, Donald 1954- .... **CLC 76**
See also AAYA 57; CA 200; CD 6; DFS 13;
DLB 228

Marias, Javier 1951- .... **CLC 239**
See also CA 167; CANR 109, 139; DLB
322; HW 2; MTFW 2005

Marie de France c. 12th cent. - ..... **CMLC 8;
PC 22**
See also DLB 208; FW; RGWL 2, 3

Marie de l'Incarnation 1599-1672 ...... **LC 10**

Marier, Captain Victor
See Griffith, D(avid Lewelyn) W(ark)

Mariner, Scott
See Pohl, Frederik

Marinetti, Filippo Tommaso 1876-1944
TCLC 10
See also CA 107; DLB 114, 264; EW 9;
EWL 3; WLIT 7

Marivaux, Pierre Carlet de Chamblain de
1688-1763 .... **DC 7; LC 4, 123**
See also DLB 314; GFL Beginnings to
1789; RGWL 2, 3; TWA

Markandaya, Kamala .... **CLC 8, 38**
See Taylor, Kamala
See also BYA 13; CN 1, 2, 3, 4, 5, 6, 7;
DLB 323; EWL 3

Markfield, Wallace (Arthur)
1926-2002 .... **CLC 8**
See also CA 69-72; 208; CAAS 3; CN 1, 2,
3, 4, 5, 6, 7; DLB 2, 28; DLBY 2002

Markham, Edwin 1852-1940 .... **TCLC 47**
See also CA 160; DLB 54, 186; MAL 5;
RGAL 4

Markham, Robert
See Amis, Kingsley

Marks, J.
See Highwater, Jamake (Mamake)

Marks-Highwater, J.
See Highwater, Jamake (Mamake)

Markson, David M. 1927- .... **CLC 67**
See also AMWS 17; CA 49-52; CANR 1,
91, 158; CN 5, 6

Markson, David Merrill
See Markson, David M.

Marlatt, Daphne (Buckle) 1942- .... **CLC 168**
See also CA 25-28R; CANR 17, 39; CN 6,
7; CP 4, 5, 6, 7; CWP; DLB 60; FW

Marley, Bob .... **CLC 17**
See Marley, Robert Nesta

Marley, Robert Nesta 1945-1981
See Marley, Bob
See also CA 107; 103

Marlowe, Christopher 1564-1593 . **DC 1; LC
22, 47, 117; PC 57; WLC 4**
See also BRW 1; BRWR 1; CDBLB Before
1660; DA; DA3; DAB; DAC; DAM
DRAM, MST; DFS 1, 5, 13, 21; DLB 62;
EXPP; LMFS 1; PFS 22; RGEL 2; TEA;
WLIT 3

Marlowe, Stephen 1928-2008 .... **CLC 70**
See Queen, Ellery
See also CA 13-16R; 269; CANR 6, 55;
CMW 4; SFW 4

Marmion, Shakerley 1603-1639 .... **LC 89**
See also DLB 58; RGEL 2

Marmontel, Jean-Francois 1723-1799 .. **LC 2**
See also DLB 314

Maron, Monika 1941- .... **CLC 165**
See also CA 201

Marot, Clement c. 1496-1544 .... **LC 133**
See also DLB 327; GFL Beginnings to 1789

Marquand, John P(hillips)
1893-1960 .... **CLC 2, 10**
See also AMW; BPFB 2; CA 85-88; CANR
73; CMW 4; DLB 9, 102; EWL 3; MAL
5; MTCW 2; RGAL 4

Marques, Rene 1919-1979 .. **CLC 96; HLC 2**
See also CA 97-100; 85-88; CANR 78;
DAM MULT; DLB 305; EWL 3; HW 1,
2; LAW; RGSF 2

Marquez, Gabriel Garcia
See Garcia Marquez, Gabriel

Marquis, Don(ald Robert Perry) 1878-1937 .... **TCLC 7**
  See also CA 104; 166; DLB 11, 25; MAL 5; RGAL 4

Marquis de Sade
  See Sade, Donatien Alphonse Francois

Marric, J. J.
  See Creasey, John
  See also MSW

Marryat, Frederick 1792-1848 .... **NCLC 3**
  See also DLB 21, 163; RGEL 2; WCH

Marsden, James
  See Creasey, John

Marsh, Edward 1872-1953 .... **TCLC 99**

Marsh, (Edith) Ngaio 1895-1982 .. **CLC 7, 53**
  See also CA 9-12R; CANR 6, 58; CMW 4; CN 1, 2, 3; CPW; DAM POP; DLB 77; MSW; MTCW 1, 2; RGEL 2; TEA

Marshall, Allen
  See Westlake, Donald E.

Marshall, Garry 1934- .... **CLC 17**
  See also AAYA 3; CA 111; SATA 60

Marshall, Paule 1929- .... **BLC 1:3, 2:3; CLC 27, 72, 253; SSC 3**
  See also AFAW 1, 2; AMWS 11; BPFB 2; BW 2, 3; CA 77-80; CANR 25, 73, 129; CN 1, 2, 3, 4, 5, 6, 7; DA3; DAM MULT; DLB 33, 157, 227; EWL 3; LATS 1:2; MAL 5; MTCW 1, 2; MTFW 2005; RGAL 4; SSFS 15

Marshallik
  See Zangwill, Israel

Marsten, Richard
  See Hunter, Evan

Marston, John 1576-1634 .... **LC 33**
  See also BRW 2; DAM DRAM; DLB 58, 172; RGEL 2

Martel, Yann 1963- .... **CLC 192**
  See also AAYA 67; CA 146; CANR 114; DLB 326, 334; MTFW 2005; NFS 27

Martens, Adolphe-Adhemar
  See Ghelderode, Michel de

Martha, Henry
  See Harris, Mark

Marti, Jose .... **PC 76**
  See Marti (y Perez), Jose (Julian)
  See also DLB 290

Marti (y Perez), Jose (Julian) 1853-1895 .... **HLC 2; NCLC 63**
  See Marti, Jose
  See also DAM MULT; HW 2; LAW; RGWL 2, 3; WLIT 1

Martial c. 40-c. 104 .... **CMLC 35; PC 10**
  See also AW 2; CDWLB 1; DLB 211; RGWL 2, 3

Martin, Ken
  See Hubbard, L. Ron

Martin, Richard
  See Creasey, John

Martin, Steve 1945- .... **CLC 30, 217**
  See also AAYA 53; CA 97-100; CANR 30, 100, 140; DFS 19; MTCW 1; MTFW 2005

Martin, Valerie 1948- .... **CLC 89**
  See also BEST 90:2; CA 85-88; CANR 49, 89, 165

Martin, Violet Florence 1862-1915 .. **SSC 56; TCLC 51**

Martin, Webber
  See Silverberg, Robert

Martindale, Patrick Victor
  See White, Patrick (Victor Martindale)

Martin du Gard, Roger 1881-1958 .... **TCLC 24**
  See also CA 118; CANR 94; DLB 65, 331; EWL 3; GFL 1789 to the Present; RGWL 2, 3

Martineau, Harriet 1802-1876 ...... **NCLC 26, 137**
  See also DLB 21, 55, 159, 163, 166, 190; FW; RGEL 2; YABC 2

Martines, Julia
  See O'Faolain, Julia

Martinez, Enrique Gonzalez
  See Gonzalez Martinez, Enrique

Martinez, Jacinto Benavente y
  See Benavente (y Martinez), Jacinto

Martinez de la Rosa, Francisco de Paula 1787-1862 .... **NCLC 102**
  See also TWA

Martinez Ruiz, Jose 1873-1967
  See Azorin; Ruiz, Jose Martinez
  See also CA 93-96; HW 1

Martinez Sierra, Gregorio
  See Martinez Sierra, Maria

Martinez Sierra, Gregorio 1881-1947 .... **TCLC 6**
  See also CA 115; EWL 3

Martinez Sierra, Maria 1874-1974 .. **TCLC 6**
  See also CA 250; 115; EWL 3

Martinsen, Martin
  See Follett, Ken

Martinson, Harry (Edmund) 1904-1978 .... **CLC 14**
  See also CA 77-80; CANR 34, 130; DLB 259, 331; EWL 3

Martyn, Edward 1859-1923 .... **TCLC 131**
  See also CA 179; DLB 10; RGEL 2

Marut, Ret
  See Traven, B.

Marut, Robert
  See Traven, B.

Marvell, Andrew 1621-1678 .... **LC 4, 43; PC 10, 86; WLC 4**
  See also BRW 2; BRWR 2; CDBLB 1660-1789; DA; DAB; DAC; DAM MST; POET; DLB 131; EXPP; PFS 5; RGEL 2; TEA; WP

Marx, Karl (Heinrich) 1818-1883 .... **NCLC 17, 114**
  See also DLB 129; LATS 1:1; TWA

Masaoka, Shiki -1902 .... **TCLC 18**
  See Masaoka, Tsunenori
  See also RGWL 3

Masaoka, Tsunenori 1867-1902
  See Masaoka, Shiki
  See also CA 117; 191; TWA

Masefield, John (Edward) 1878-1967 .... **CLC 11, 47; PC 78**
  See also CA 19-20; 25-28R; CANR 33; CAP 2; CDBLB 1890-1914; DAM POET; DLB 10, 19, 153, 160; EWL 3; EXPP; FANT; MTCW 1, 2; PFS 5; RGEL 2; SATA 19

Maso, Carole 1955(?)- .... **CLC 44**
  See also CA 170; CANR 148; CN 7; GLL 2; RGAL 4

Mason, Bobbie Ann 1940- ... **CLC 28, 43, 82, 154; SSC 4, 101**
  See also AAYA 5, 42; AMWS 8; BPFB 2; CA 53-56; CANR 11, 31, 58, 83, 125, 169; CDALBS; CN 5, 6, 7; CSW; DA3; DLB 173; DLBY 1987; EWL 3; EXPS; INT CANR-31; MAL 5; MTCW 1, 2; MTFW 2005; NFS 4; RGAL 4; RGSF 2; SSFS 3, 8, 20; TCLE 1:2; YAW

Mason, Ernst
  See Pohl, Frederik

Mason, Hunni B.
  See Sternheim, (William Adolf) Carl

Mason, Lee W.
  See Malzberg, Barry N(athaniel)

Mason, Nick 1945- .... **CLC 35**

Mason, Tally
  See Derleth, August (William)

Mass, Anna .... **CLC 59**

Mass, William
  See Gibson, William

Massinger, Philip 1583-1640 .... **LC 70**
  See also BRWS 11; DLB 58; RGEL 2

Master Lao
  See Lao Tzu

Masters, Edgar Lee 1868-1950 ...... **PC 1, 36; TCLC 2, 25; WLCS**
  See also AMWS 1; CA 104; 133; CDALB 1865-1917; DA; DAC; DAM MST; POET; DLB 54; EWL 3; EXPP; MAL 5; MTCW 1, 2; MTFW 2005; RGAL 4; TUS; WP

Masters, Hilary 1928- .... **CLC 48**
  See also CA 25-28R; 217; CAAE 217; CANR 13, 47, 97, 171; CN 6, 7; DLB 244

Masters, Hilary Thomas
  See Masters, Hilary

Mastrosimone, William 1947- .... **CLC 36**
  See also CA 186; CAD; CD 5, 6

Mathe, Albert
  See Camus, Albert

Mather, Cotton 1663-1728 .... **LC 38**
  See also AMWS 2; CDALB 1640-1865; DLB 24, 30, 140; RGAL 4; TUS

Mather, Increase 1639-1723 .... **LC 38**
  See also DLB 24

Mathers, Marshall
  See Eminem

Mathers, Marshall Bruce
  See Eminem

Matheson, Richard 1926- .... **CLC 37**
  See also AAYA 31; CA 97-100; CANR 88, 99; DLB 8, 44; HGG; INT CA-97-100; SCFW 1, 2; SFW 4; SUFW 2

Matheson, Richard Burton
  See Matheson, Richard

Mathews, Harry 1930- .... **CLC 6, 52**
  See also CA 21-24R; CAAS 6; CANR 18, 40, 98, 160; CN 5, 6, 7

Mathews, John Joseph 1894-1979 .. **CLC 84; NNAL**
  See also CA 19-20; 142; CANR 45; CAP 2; DAM MULT; DLB 175; TCWW 1, 2

Mathias, Roland 1915-2007 .... **CLC 45**
  See also CA 97-100; 263; CANR 19, 41; CP 1, 2, 3, 4, 5, 6, 7; DLB 27

Mathias, Roland Glyn
  See Mathias, Roland

Matsuo Basho 1644(?)-1694 ...... **LC 62; PC 3**
  See Basho, Matsuo
  See also DAM POET; PFS 2, 7, 18

Mattheson, Rodney
  See Creasey, John

Matthew of Vendome c. 1130-c. 1200 .... **CMLC 99**
  See also DLB 208

Matthews, (James) Brander 1852-1929 .... **TCLC 95**
  See also CA 181; DLB 71, 78; DLBD 13

Matthews, Greg 1949- .... **CLC 45**
  See also CA 135

Matthews, William (Procter III) 1942-1997 **CLC 40**
  See also AMWS 9; CA 29-32R; 162; CAAS 18; CANR 12, 57; CP 2, 3, 4, 5, 6; DLB 5

Matthias, John (Edward) 1941- .... **CLC 9**
  See also CA 33-36R; CANR 56; CP 4, 5, 6, 7

Matthiessen, F(rancis) O(tto) 1902-1950 **TCLC 100**
  See also CA 185; DLB 63; MAL 5

Matthiessen, Peter 1927- ... **CLC 5, 7, 11, 32, 64, 245**
See also AAYA 6, 40; AMWS 5; ANW; BEST 90:4; BPFB 2; CA 9-12R; CANR 21, 50, 73, 100, 138; CN 1, 2, 3, 4, 5, 6, 7; DA3; DAM NOV; DLB 6, 173, 275; MAL 5; MTCW 1, 2; MTFW 2005; SATA 27

Maturin, Charles Robert
1780(?)-1824 .... **NCLC 6, 169**
See also BRWS 8; DLB 178; GL 3; HGG; LMFS 1; RGEL 2; SUFW

Matute (Ausejo), Ana Maria 1925- .. **CLC 11**
See also CA 89-92; CANR 129; CWW 2; DLB 322; EWL 3; MTCW 1; RGSF 2

Maugham, W. S.
See Maugham, W(illiam) Somerset

Maugham, W(illiam) Somerset 1874-1965
CLC 1, 11, 15, 67, 93; SSC 8, 94; WLC 4
See also AAYA 55; BPFB 2; BRW 6; CA 5-8R; 25-28R; CANR 40, 127; CDBLB 1914-1945; CMW 4; DA; DA3; DAB; DAC; DAM DRAM, MST, NOV; DFS 22; DLB 10, 36, 77, 100, 162, 195; EWL 3; LAIT 3; MTCW 1, 2; MTFW 2005; NFS 23; RGEL 2; RGSF 2; SATA 54; SSFS 17

Maugham, William Somerset
See Maugham, W(illiam) Somerset

Maupassant, (Henri Rene Albert) Guy de 1850-1893 . **NCLC 1, 42, 83; SSC 1, 64; WLC 4**
See also BYA 14; DA; DA3; DAB; DAC; DAM MST; DLB 123; EW 7; EXPS; GFL 1789 to the Present; LAIT 2; LMFS 1; RGSF 2; RGWL 2, 3; SSFS 4, 21; SUFW; TWA

Maupin, Armistead 1944- .... **CLC 95**
See also CA 125; 130; CANR 58, 101; CPW; DA3; DAM POP; DLB 278; GLL 1; INT CA-130; MTCW 2; MTFW 2005

Maupin, Armistead Jones, Jr.
See Maupin, Armistead

Maurhut, Richard
See Traven, B.

Mauriac, Claude 1914-1996 .... **CLC 9**
See also CA 89-92; 152; CWW 2; DLB 83; EWL 3; GFL 1789 to the Present

Mauriac, Francois (Charles)
1885-1970 .... **CLC 4, 9, 56; SSC 24**
See also CA 25-28; CAP 2; DLB 65, 331; EW 10; EWL 3; GFL 1789 to the Present; MTCW 1, 2; MTFW 2005; RGWL 2, 3; TWA

Mavor, Osborne Henry 1888-1951
See Bridie, James
See also CA 104

Maxwell, Glyn 1962- .... **CLC 238**
See also CA 154; CANR 88; CP 6, 7; PFS 23

Maxwell, William (Keepers, Jr.) 1908-2000
CLC 19
See also AMWS 8; CA 93-96; 189; CANR 54, 95; CN 1, 2, 3, 4, 5, 6, 7; DLB 218, 278; DLBY 1980; INT CA-93-96; MAL 5; SATA-Obit 128

May, Elaine 1932- .... **CLC 16**
See also CA 124; 142; CAD; CWD; DLB 44

Mayakovski, Vladimir (Vladimirovich)
1893-1930 .... **TCLC 4, 18**
See Maiakovskii, Vladimir; Mayakovsky, Vladimir
See also CA 104; 158; EWL 3; MTCW 2; MTFW 2005; SFW 4; TWA

Mayakovsky, Vladimir
See Mayakovski, Vladimir (Vladimirovich)
See also EW 11; WP

Mayhew, Henry 1812-1887 .... **NCLC 31**
See also DLB 18, 55, 190

Mayle, Peter 1939(?)- .... **CLC 89**
See also CA 139; CANR 64, 109, 168

Maynard, Joyce 1953- .... **CLC 23**
See also CA 111; 129; CANR 64, 169

Mayne, William (James Carter)
1928- .... **CLC 12**
See also AAYA 20; CA 9-12R; CANR 37, 80, 100; CLR 25, 123; FANT; JRDA; MAICYA 1, 2; MAICYAS 1; SAAS 11; SATA 6, 68, 122; SUFW 2; YAW

Mayo, Jim
See L'Amour, Louis

Maysles, Albert 1926- .... **CLC 16**
See also CA 29-32R

Maysles, David 1932-1987 .... **CLC 16**
See also CA 191

Mazer, Norma Fox 1931- .... **CLC 26**
See also AAYA 5, 36; BYA 1, 8; CA 69-72; CANR 12, 32, 66, 129; CLR 23; JRDA; MAICYA 1, 2; SAAS 1; SATA 24, 67, 105, 168; WYA; YAW

Mazzini, Guiseppe 1805-1872 .... **NCLC 34**

McAlmon, Robert (Menzies) 1895-1956
TCLC 97
See also CA 107; 168; DLB 4, 45; DLBD 15; GLL 1

McAuley, James Phillip 1917-1976 .. **CLC 45**
See also CA 97-100; CP 1, 2; DLB 260; RGEL 2

McBain, Ed
See Hunter, Evan
See also MSW

McBrien, William (Augustine)
1930- .... **CLC 44**
See also CA 107; CANR 90

McCabe, Patrick 1955- .... **CLC 133**
See also BRWS 9; CA 130; CANR 50, 90, 168; CN 6, 7; DLB 194

McCaffrey, Anne 1926- .... **CLC 17**
See also AAYA 6, 34; AITN 2; BEST 89:2; BPFB 2; BYA 5; CA 25-28R, 227; CAAE 227; CANR 15, 35, 55, 96, 169; CLR 49, 130; CPW; DA3; DAM NOV, POP; DLB 8; JRDA; MAICYA 1, 2; MTCW 1, 2; MTFW 2005; SAAS 11; SATA 8, 70, 116, 152; SATA-Essay 152; SFW 4; SUFW 2; WYA; YAW

McCaffrey, Anne Inez
See McCaffrey, Anne

McCall, Nathan 1955(?)- .... **CLC 86**
See also AAYA 59; BW 3; CA 146; CANR 88

McCann, Arthur
See Campbell, John W(ood, Jr.)

McCann, Edson
See Pohl, Frederik

McCarthy, Charles
See McCarthy, Cormac

McCarthy, Charles, Jr.
See McCarthy, Cormac

McCarthy, Cormac 1933- .... **CLC 4, 57, 101, 204**
See also AAYA 41; AMWS 8; BPFB 2; CA 13-16R; CANR 10, 42, 69, 101, 161, 171; CN 6, 7; CPW; CSW; DA3; DAM POP; DLB 6, 143, 256; EWL 3; LATS 1:2; MAL 5; MTCW 2; MTFW 2005; TCLE 1:2; TCWW 2

McCarthy, Mary (Therese)
1912-1989 .. **CLC 1, 3, 5, 14, 24, 39, 59; SSC 24**
See also AMW; BPFB 2; CA 5-8R; 129; CANR 16, 50, 64; CN 1, 2, 3, 4; DA3; DLB 2; DLBY 1981; EWL 3; FW; INT CANR-16; MAL 5; MBL; MTCW 1, 2; MTFW 2005; RGAL 4; TUS

McCartney, James Paul
See McCartney, Paul

McCartney, Paul 1942- .... **CLC 12, 35**
See also CA 146; CANR 111

McCauley, Stephen (D.) 1955- .... **CLC 50**
See also CA 141

McClaren, Peter .... **CLC 70**

McClure, Michael (Thomas) 1932- ... **CLC 6, 10**
See also BG 1:3; CA 21-24R; CAD; CANR 17, 46, 77, 131; CD 5, 6; CP 1, 2, 3, 4, 5, 6, 7; DLB 16; WP

McCorkle, Jill (Collins) 1958- .... **CLC 51**
See also CA 121; CANR 113; CSW; DLB 234; DLBY 1987; SSFS 24

McCourt, Frank 1930- .... **CLC 109**
See also AAYA 61; AMWS 12; CA 157; CANR 97, 138; MTFW 2005; NCFS 1

McCourt, James 1941- .... **CLC 5**
See also CA 57-60; CANR 98, 152

McCourt, Malachy 1931- .... **CLC 119**
See also SATA 126

McCoy, Horace (Stanley)
1897-1955 .... **TCLC 28**
See also AMWS 13; CA 108; 155; CMW 4; DLB 9

McCrae, John 1872-1918 .... **TCLC 12**
See also CA 109; DLB 92; PFS 5

McCreigh, James
See Pohl, Frederik

McCullers, (Lula) Carson (Smith) 1917-1967
CLC 1, 4, 10, 12, 48, 100; SSC 9, 24, 99; TCLC 155; WLC 4
See also AAYA 21; AMW; AMWC 2; BPFB 2; CA 5-8R; 25-28R; CABS 1, 3; CANR 18, 132; CDALB 1941-1968; DA; DA3; DAB; DAC; DAM MST, NOV; DFS 5, 18; DLB 2, 7, 173, 228; EWL 3; EXPS; FW; GLL 1; LAIT 3, 4; MAL 5; MBL; MTCW 1, 2; MTFW 2005; NFS 6, 13; RGAL 4; RGSF 2; SATA 27; SSFS 5; TUS; YAW

McCulloch, John Tyler
See Burroughs, Edgar Rice

McCullough, Colleen 1937- ...... **CLC 27, 107**
See also AAYA 36; BPFB 2; CA 81-84; CANR 17, 46, 67, 98, 139; CPW; DA3; DAM NOV, POP; MTCW 1, 2; MTFW 2005; RHW

McCunn, Ruthanne Lum 1946- .... **AAL**
See also CA 119; CANR 43, 96; DLB 312; LAIT 2; SATA 63

McDermott, Alice 1953- .... **CLC 90**
See also CA 109; CANR 40, 90, 126; CN 7; DLB 292; MTFW 2005; NFS 23

McElroy, Joseph 1930- .... **CLC 5, 47**
See also CA 17-20R; CANR 149; CN 3, 4, 5, 6, 7

McElroy, Joseph Prince
See McElroy, Joseph

McEwan, Ian 1948- ... **CLC 13, 66, 169; SSC 106**
See also BEST 90:4; BRWS 4; CA 61-64; CANR 14, 41, 69, 87, 132; CN 3, 4, 5, 6, 7; DAM NOV; DLB 14, 194, 319, 326; HGG; MTCW 1, 2; MTFW 2005; RGSF 2; SUFW 2; TEA

McFadden, David 1940- .... **CLC 48**
See also CA 104; CP 1, 2, 3, 4, 5, 6, 7; DLB 60; INT CA-104

McFarland, Dennis 1950- .... **CLC 65**
See also CA 165; CANR 110

McGahern, John 1934-2006 .... **CLC 5, 9, 48, 156; SSC 17**
See also CA 17-20R; 249; CANR 29, 68, 113; CN 1, 2, 3, 4, 5, 6, 7; DLB 14, 231, 319; MTCW 1

McGinley, Patrick (Anthony) 1937- . **CLC 41**
See also CA 120; 127; CANR 56; INT CA-127

McGinley, Phyllis 1905-1978 .... **CLC 14**
See also CA 9-12R; 77-80; CANR 19; CP 1, 2; CWRI 5; DLB 11, 48; MAL 5; PFS 9, 13; SATA 2, 44; SATA-Obit 24

McGinniss, Joe 1942- .... **CLC 32**
See also AITN 2; BEST 89:2; CA 25-28R; CANR 26, 70, 152; CPW; DLB 185; INT CANR-26

McGivern, Maureen Daly
See Daly, Maureen

McGivern, Maureen Patricia Daly
See Daly, Maureen

McGrath, Patrick 1950- .... **CLC 55**
See also CA 136; CANR 65, 148; CN 5, 6, 7; DLB 231; HGG; SUFW 2

McGrath, Thomas (Matthew) 1916-1990
CLC 28, 59
See also AMWS 10; CA 9-12R; 132; CANR 6, 33, 95; CP 1, 2, 3, 4, 5; DAM POET; MAL 5; MTCW 1; SATA 41; SATA-Obit 66

McGuane, Thomas 1939- .. **CLC 3, 7, 18, 45, 127**
See also AITN 2; BPFB 2; CA 49-52; CANR 5, 24, 49, 94, 164; CN 2, 3, 4, 5, 6, 7; DLB 2, 212; DLBY 1980; EWL 3; INT CANR-24; MAL 5; MTCW 1; MTFW 2005; TCWW 1, 2

McGuane, Thomas Francis III
See McGuane, Thomas

McGuckian, Medbh 1950- .... **CLC 48, 174; PC 27**
See also BRWS 5; CA 143; CP 4, 5, 6, 7; CWP; DAM POET; DLB 40

McHale, Tom 1942(?)-1982 .... **CLC 3, 5**
See also AITN 1; CA 77-80; 106; CN 1, 2, 3

McHugh, Heather 1948- .... **PC 61**
See also CA 69-72; CANR 11, 28, 55, 92; CP 4, 5, 6, 7; CWP; PFS 24

McIlvanney, William 1936- .... **CLC 42**
See also CA 25-28R; CANR 61; CMW 4; DLB 14, 207

McIlwraith, Maureen Mollie Hunter
See Hunter, Mollie
See also SATA 2

McInerney, Jay 1955- .... **CLC 34, 112**
See also AAYA 18; BPFB 2; CA 116; 123; CANR 45, 68, 116, 176; CN 5, 6, 7; CPW; DA3; DAM POP; DLB 292; INT CA-123; MAL 5; MTCW 2; MTFW 2005

McIntyre, Vonda N. 1948- .... **CLC 18**
See also CA 81-84; CANR 17, 34, 69; MTCW 1; SFW 4; YAW

McIntyre, Vonda Neel
See McIntyre, Vonda N.

McKay, Claude ...... **BLC 1:3; HR 1:3; PC 2; TCLC 7, 41; WLC 4**
See McKay, Festus Claudius
See also AFAW 1, 2; AMWS 10; DAB; DLB 4, 45, 51, 117; EWL 3; EXPP; GLL 2; LAIT 3; LMFS 2; MAL 5; PAB; PFS 4; RGAL 4; WP

McKay, Festus Claudius 1889-1948
See McKay, Claude
See also BW 1, 3; CA 104; 124; CANR 73; DA; DAC; DAM MST, MULT, NOV, POET; MTCW 1, 2; MTFW 2005; TUS

McKuen, Rod 1933- .... **CLC 1, 3**
See also AITN 1; CA 41-44R; CANR 40; CP 1

McLoughlin, R. B.
See Mencken, H(enry) L(ouis)

McLuhan, (Herbert) Marshall 1911-1980
CLC 37, 83
See also CA 9-12R; 102; CANR 12, 34, 61; DLB 88; INT CANR-12; MTCW 1, 2; MTFW 2005

McManus, Declan Patrick Aloysius
See Costello, Elvis

McMillan, Terry 1951- .. **BLCS; CLC 50, 61, 112**
See also AAYA 21; AMWS 13; BPFB 2; BW 2, 3; CA 140; CANR 60, 104, 131; CN 7; CPW; DA3; DAM MULT, NOV, POP; MAL 5; MTCW 2; MTFW 2005; RGAL 4; YAW

McMurtry, Larry 1936- .... **CLC 2, 3, 7, 11, 27, 44, 127, 250**
See also AAYA 15; AITN 2; AMWS 5; BEST 89:2; BPFB 2; CA 5-8R; CANR 19, 43, 64, 103, 170; CDALB 1968-1988; CN 2, 3, 4, 5, 6, 7; CPW; CSW; DA3; DAM NOV, POP; DLB 2, 143, 256; DLBY 1980, 1987; EWL 3; MAL 5; MTCW 1, 2; MTFW 2005; RGAL 4; TCWW 1, 2

McMurtry, Larry Jeff
See McMurtry, Larry

McNally, Terrence 1939- ... **CLC 4, 7, 41, 91, 252; DC 27**
See also AAYA 62; AMWS 13; CA 45-48; CAD; CANR 2, 56, 116; CD 5, 6; DA3; DAM DRAM; DFS 16, 19; DLB 7, 249; EWL 3; GLL 1; MTCW 2; MTFW 2005

McNally, Thomas Michael
See McNally, T.M.

McNally, T.M. 1961- .... **CLC 82**
See also CA 246

McNamer, Deirdre 1950- .... **CLC 70**
See also CA 188; CANR 163

McNeal, Tom .... **CLC 119**
See also CA 252

McNeile, Herman Cyril 1888-1937
See Sapper
See also CA 184; CMW 4; DLB 77

McNickle, (William) D'Arcy
1904-1977 .... **CLC 89; NNAL**
See also CA 9-12R; 85-88; CANR 5, 45; DAM MULT; DLB 175, 212; RGAL 4; SATA-Obit 22; TCWW 1, 2

McPhee, John 1931- .... **CLC 36**
See also AAYA 61; AMWS 3; ANW; BEST 90:1; CA 65-68; CANR 20, 46, 64, 69, 121, 165; CPW; DLB 185, 275; MTCW 1, 2; MTFW 2005; TUS

McPhee, John Angus
See McPhee, John

McPherson, James Alan 1943- . **BLCS; CLC 19, 77; SSC 95**
See also BW 1, 3; CA 25-28R; CAAS 17; CANR 24, 74, 140; CN 3, 4, 5, 6; CSW; DLB 38, 244; EWL 3; MTCW 1, 2; MTFW 2005; RGAL 4; RGSF 2; SSFS 23

McPherson, William (Alexander)
1933- ....**CLC 34**
See also CA 69-72; CANR 28; INT CANR-28

McTaggart, J. McT. Ellis
See McTaggart, John McTaggart Ellis

McTaggart, John McTaggart Ellis 1866-1925
TCLC 105
See also CA 120; DLB 262

Mda, Zakes 1948- .... **BLC 2:3**
See also CA 205; CANR 151; CD 5, 6; DLB 225

Mead, George Herbert 1863-1931 . **TCLC 89**
See also CA 212; DLB 270

Mead, Margaret 1901-1978 .... **CLC 37**
See also AITN 1; CA 1-4R; 81-84; CANR 4; DA3; FW; MTCW 1, 2; SATA-Obit 20

Meaker, Marijane 1927-
See Kerr, M. E.
See also CA 107; CANR 37, 63, 145; INT CA-107; JRDA; MAICYA 1, 2; MAIC-YAS 1; MTCW 1; SATA 20, 61, 99, 160; SATA-Essay 111; YAW

Mechthild von Magdeburg c. 1207-c. 1282
CMLC 91
See also DLB 138

Medoff, Mark (Howard) 1940- .... **CLC 6, 23**
See also AITN 1; CA 53-56; CAD; CANR 5; CD 5, 6; DAM DRAM; DFS 4; DLB 7; INT CANR-5

Medvedev, P. N.
See Bakhtin, Mikhail Mikhailovich

Meged, Aharon
See Megged, Aharon

Meged, Aron
See Megged, Aharon

Megged, Aharon 1920- .... **CLC 9**
See also CA 49-52; CAAS 13; CANR 1, 140; EWL 3; RGHL

Mehta, Deepa 1950- .... **CLC 208**

Mehta, Gita 1943- .... **CLC 179**
See also CA 225; CN 7; DNFS 2

Mehta, Ved 1934- .... **CLC 37**
See also CA 1-4R, 212; CAAE 212; CANR 2, 23, 69; DLB 323; MTCW 1; MTFW 2005

Melanchthon, Philipp 1497-1560 .... **LC 90**
See also DLB 179

Melanter
See Blackmore, R(ichard) D(oddridge)

Meleager c. 140B.C.-c. 70B.C. ...... **CMLC 53**

Melies, Georges 1861-1938 .... **TCLC 81**

Melikow, Loris
See Hofmannsthal, Hugo von

Melmoth, Sebastian
See Wilde, Oscar

Melo Neto, Joao Cabral de
See Cabral de Melo Neto, Joao
See also CWW 2; EWL 3

Meltzer, Milton 1915- .... **CLC 26**
See also AAYA 8, 45; BYA 2, 6; CA 13-16R; CANR 38, 92, 107; CLR 13; DLB 61; JRDA; MAICYA 1, 2; SAAS 1; SATA 1, 50, 80, 128; SATA-Essay 124; WYA; YAW

Melville, Herman 1819-1891 ..... **NCLC 3, 12, 29, 45, 49, 91, 93, 123, 157, 181, 193; PC 82; SSC 1, 17, 46, 95; WLC 4**
See also AAYA 25; AMW; AMWR 1; CDALB 1640-1865; DA; DA3; DAB; DAC; DAM MST, NOV; DLB 3, 74, 250, 254; EXPN; EXPS; GL 3; LAIT 1, 2; NFS 7, 9; RGAL 4; RGSF 2; SATA 59; SSFS 3; TUS

Members, Mark
See Powell, Anthony

Membreno, Alejandro .... **CLC 59**

Menand, Louis 1952- .... **CLC 208**
See also CA 200

Menander c. 342B.C.-c. 293B.C. .... **CMLC 9, 51, 101; DC 3**
See also AW 1; CDWLB 1; DAM DRAM; DLB 176; LMFS 1; RGWL 2, 3

Menchu, Rigoberta 1959- .. **CLC 160; HLCS 2**
See also CA 175; CANR 135; DNFS 1; WLIT 1

Mencken, H(enry) L(ouis)
1880-1956 .... **TCLC 13**
See also AMW; CA 105; 125; CDALB 1917-1929; DLB 11, 29, 63, 137, 222; EWL 3; MAL 5; MTCW 1, 2; MTFW 2005; NCFS 4; RGAL 4; TUS

Mendelsohn, Jane 1965- .... **CLC 99**
See also CA 154; CANR 94

Mendelssohn, Moses 1729-1786 .... **LC 142**
See also DLB 97

Mendoza, Inigo Lopez de
See Santillana, Inigo Lopez de Mendoza,
Marques de

Menton, Francisco de
See Chin, Frank (Chew, Jr.)

Mercer, David 1928-1980 .... **CLC 5**
See also CA 9-12R; 102; CANR 23; CBD;
DAM DRAM; DLB 13, 310; MTCW 1;
RGEL 2

Merchant, Paul
See Ellison, Harlan

Meredith, George 1828-1909 .. **PC 60; TCLC 17, 43**
See also CA 117; 153; CANR 80; CDBLB
1832-1890; DAM POET; DLB 18, 35, 57,
159; RGEL 2; TEA

Meredith, William 1919-2007 ...... **CLC 4, 13, 22, 55; PC 28**
See also CA 9-12R; 260; CAAS 14; CANR
6, 40, 129; CP 1, 2, 3, 4, 5, 6, 7; DAM
POET; DLB 5; MAL 5

Meredith, William Morris
See Meredith, William

Merezhkovsky, Dmitrii Sergeevich
See Merezhkovsky, Dmitry Sergeyevich
See also DLB 295

Merezhkovsky, Dmitry Sergeyevich
See Merezhkovsky, Dmitry Sergeyevich
See also EWL 3

Merezhkovsky, Dmitry Sergeyevich
1865-1941 .... **TCLC 29**
See Merezhkovsky, Dmitrii Sergeevich;
Merezhkovsky, Dmitry Sergeyevich
See also CA 169

Merimee, Prosper 1803-1870 ... **NCLC 6, 65; SSC 7, 77**
See also DLB 119, 192; EW 6; EXPS; GFL
1789 to the Present; RGSF 2; RGWL 2,
3; SSFS 8; SUFW

Merkin, Daphne 1954- .... **CLC 44**
See also CA 123

Merleau-Ponty, Maurice
1908-1961 .... **TCLC 156**
See also CA 114; 89-92; DLB 296; GFL
1789 to the Present

Merlin, Arthur
See Blish, James (Benjamin)

Mernissi, Fatima 1940- .... **CLC 171**
See also CA 152; FW

Merrill, James 1926-1995 ...... **CLC 2, 3, 6, 8, 13, 18, 34, 91; PC 28; TCLC 173**
See also AMWS 3; CA 13-16R; 147; CANR
10, 49, 63, 108; CP 1, 2, 3, 4; DA3; DAM
POET; DLB 5, 165; DLBY 1985; EWL 3;
INT CANR-10; MAL 5; MTCW 1, 2;
MTFW 2005; PAB; PFS 23; RGAL 4

Merrill, James Ingram
See Merrill, James

Merriman, Alex
See Silverberg, Robert

Merriman, Brian 1747-1805 .... **NCLC 70**

Merritt, E. B.
See Waddington, Miriam

Merton, Thomas (James)
1915-1968 . **CLC 1, 3, 11, 34, 83; PC 10**
See also AAYA 61; AMWS 8; CA 5-8R;
25-28R; CANR 22, 53, 111, 131; DA3;
DLB 48; DLBY 1981; MAL 5; MTCW 1,
2; MTFW 2005

Merwin, W.S. 1927- ..... **CLC 1, 2, 3, 5, 8, 13, 18, 45, 88; PC 45**
See also AMWS 3; CA 13-16R; CANR 15,
51, 112, 140; CP 1, 2, 3, 4, 5, 6, 7; DA3;
DAM POET; DLB 5, 169; EWL 3; INT
CANR-15; MAL 5; MTCW 1, 2; MTFW
2005; PAB; PFS 5, 15; RGAL 4

Metastasio, Pietro 1698-1782 .... **LC 115**
See also RGWL 2, 3

Metcalf, John 1938- .... **CLC 37; SSC 43**
See also CA 113; CN 4, 5, 6, 7; DLB 60;
RGSF 2; TWA

Metcalf, Suzanne
See Baum, L(yman) Frank

Mew, Charlotte (Mary) 1870-1928 .. **TCLC 8**
See also CA 105; 189; DLB 19, 135; RGEL
2

Mewshaw, Michael 1943- .... **CLC 9**
See also CA 53-56; CANR 7, 47, 147;
DLBY 1980

Meyer, Conrad Ferdinand
1825-1898 .... **NCLC 81; SSC 30**
See also DLB 129; EW; RGWL 2, 3

Meyer, Gustav 1868-1932
See Meyrink, Gustav
See also CA 117; 190

Meyer, June
See Jordan, June

Meyer, Lynn
See Slavitt, David R.

Meyers, Jeffrey 1939- .... **CLC 39**
See also CA 73-76, 186; CAAE 186; CANR
54, 102, 159; DLB 111

**Meynell, Alice (Christina Gertrude
Thompson)** 1847-1922 .... **TCLC 6**
See also CA 104; 177; DLB 19, 98; RGEL
2

Meyrink, Gustav .... **TCLC 21**
See Meyer, Gustav
See also DLB 81; EWL 3

Mhlophe, Gcina 1960- .... **BLC 2:3**

Michaels, Leonard 1933-2003 ..... **CLC 6, 25; SSC 16**
See also AMWS 16; CA 61-64; 216; CANR
21, 62, 119; CN 3, 45, 6, 7; DLB 130;
MTCW 1; TCLE 1:2

Michaux, Henri 1899-1984 .... **CLC 8, 19**
See also CA 85-88; 114; DLB 258; EWL 3;
GFL 1789 to the Present; RGWL 2, 3

Micheaux, Oscar (Devereaux) 1884-1951
TCLC 76
See also BW 3; CA 174; DLB 50; TCWW
2

Michelangelo 1475-1564 .... **LC 12**
See also AAYA 43

Michelet, Jules 1798-1874 .... **NCLC 31**
See also EW 5; GFL 1789 to the Present

Michels, Robert 1876-1936 .... **TCLC 88**
See also CA 212

Michener, James A. 1907(?)-1997 . **CLC 1, 5, 11, 29, 60, 109**
See also AAYA 27; AITN 1; BEST 90:1;
BPFB 2; CA 5-8R; 161; CANR 21, 45,
68; CN 1, 2, 3, 4, 5, 6; CPW; DA3; DAM
NOV, POP; DLB 6; MAL 5; MTCW 1, 2;
MTFW 2005; RHW; TCWW 1, 2

Mickiewicz, Adam 1798-1855 . **NCLC 3, 101; PC 38**
See also EW 5; RGWL 2, 3

Middleton, (John) Christopher
1926- .... **CLC 13**
See also CA 13-16R; CANR 29, 54, 117;
CP 1, 2, 3, 4, 5, 6, 7; DLB 40

Middleton, Richard (Barham) 1882-1911
TCLC 56
See also CA 187; DLB 156; HGG

Middleton, Stanley 1919- .... **CLC 7, 38**
See also CA 25-28R; CAAS 23; CANR 21,
46, 81, 157; CN 1, 2, 3, 4, 5, 6, 7; DLB
14, 326

Middleton, Thomas 1580-1627 ...... **DC 5; LC 33, 123**
BRW 2; DAM DRAM, MST; DFS
18, 22; DLB 58; RGEL 2

Mieville, China 1972(?)- .... **CLC 235**
See also AAYA 52; CA 196; CANR 138;
MTFW 2005

Migueis, Jose Rodrigues 1901-1980 . **CLC 10**
See also DLB 287

Mikszath, Kalman 1847-1910 .... **TCLC 31**
See also CA 170

Miles, Jack .... **CLC 100**
See also CA 200

Miles, John Russiano
See Miles, Jack

Miles, Josephine (Louise)
1911-1985 .... **CLC 1, 2, 14, 34, 39**
See also CA 1-4R; 116; CANR 2, 55; CP 1,
2, 3, 4; DAM POET; DLB 48; MAL 5;
TCLE 1:2

Militant
See Sandburg, Carl (August)

Mill, Harriet (Hardy) Taylor 1807-1858
NCLC 102
See also FW

Mill, John Stuart 1806-1873 ... **NCLC 11, 58, 179**
See also CDBLB 1832-1890; DLB 55, 190,
262; FW 1; RGEL 2; TEA

Millar, Kenneth 1915-1983 .... **CLC 14**
See Macdonald, Ross
See also CA 9-12R; 110; CANR 16, 63,
107; CMW 4; CPW; DA3; DAM POP;
DLB 2, 226; DLBD 6; DLBY 1983;
MTCW 1, 2; MTFW 2005

Millay, E. Vincent
See Millay, Edna St. Vincent

Millay, Edna St. Vincent 1892-1950 ..... **PC 6, 61; TCLC 4, 49, 169; WLCS**
See Boyd, Nancy
See also AMW; CA 104; 130; CDALB
1917-1929; DA; DA3; DAB; DAC; DAM
MST, POET; DLB 45, 249; EWL 3;
EXPP; FL 1:6; MAL 5; MBL; MTCW 1,
2; MTFW 2005; PAB; PFS 3, 17; RGAL
4; TUS; WP

Miller, Arthur 1915-2005 ..... **CLC 1, 2, 6, 10, 15, 26, 47, 78, 179; DC 1, 31; WLC 4**
See also AAYA 15; AITN 1; AMW; AMWC
1; CA 1-4R; 236; CABS 3; CAD; CANR
2, 30, 54, 76, 132; CD 5, 6; CDALB
1941-1968; DA; DA3; DAB; DAC; DAM
DRAM, MST; DFS 1, 3, 8; DLB 7, 266;
EWL 3; LAIT 1, 4; LATS 1:2; MAL 5;
MTCW 1, 2; MTFW 2005; RGAL 4;
RGHL; TUS; WYAS 1

Miller, Henry (Valentine)
1891-1980 .... **CLC 1, 2, 4, 9, 14, 43, 84; WLC 4**
See also AMW; BPFB 2; CA 9-12R; 97-
100; CANR 33, 64; CDALB 1929-1941;
CN 1, 2; DA; DA3; DAB; DAC; DAM
MST, NOV; DLB 4, 9; DLBY 1980; EWL
3; MAL 5; MTCW 1, 2; MTFW 2005;
RGAL 4; TUS

Miller, Hugh 1802-1856 .... **NCLC 143**
See also DLB 190

Miller, Jason 1939(?)-2001 .... **CLC 2**
See also AITN 1; CA 73-76; 197; CAD;
CANR 130; DFS 12; DLB 7

Miller, Sue 1943- .... **CLC 44**
See also AMWS 12; BEST 90:3; CA 139;
CANR 59, 91, 128; DA3; DAM POP;
DLB 143

Miller, Walter M(ichael, Jr.)
1923-1996 .... **CLC 4, 30**
See also BPFB 2; CA 85-88; CANR 108;
DLB 8; SCFW 1, 2; SFW 4

Millett, Kate 1934- .... **CLC 67**
See also AITN 1; CA 73-76; CANR 32, 53,
76, 110; DA3; DLB 246; FW; GLL 1;
MTCW 1, 2; MTFW 2005

Millhauser, Steven 1943- ... **CLC 21, 54, 109; SSC 57**
See also AAYA 76; CA 110; 111; CANR 63, 114, 133; CN 6, 7; DA3; DLB 2; FANT; INT CA-111; MAL 5; MTCW 2; MTFW 2005

Millhauser, Steven Lewis
See Millhauser, Steven

Millin, Sarah Gertrude 1889-1968 ... **CLC 49**
See also CA 102; 93-96; DLB 225; EWL 3

Milne, A. A. 1882-1956 .... **TCLC 6, 88**
See also BRWS 5; CA 104; 133; CLR 1, 26, 108; CMW 4; CWRI 5; DA3; DAB; DAC; DAM MST; DLB 10, 77, 100, 160; FANT; MAICYA 1, 2; MTCW 1, 2; MTFW 2005; RGEL 2; SATA 100; WCH; YABC 1

Milne, Alan Alexander
See Milne, A. A.

Milner, Ron(ald) 1938-2004 .. **BLC 1:3; CLC 56**
See also AITN 1; BW 1; CA 73-76; 230; CAD; CANR 24, 81; CD 5, 6; DAM MULT; DLB 38; MAL 5; MTCW 1

Milnes, Richard Monckton
1809-1885 .... **NCLC 61**
See also DLB 32, 184

Milosz, Czeslaw 1911-2004 .... **CLC 5, 11, 22, 31, 56, 82, 253; PC 8; WLCS**
See also AAYA 62; CA 81-84; 230; CANR 23, 51, 91, 126; CDWLB 4; CWW 2; DA3; DAM MST, POET; DLB 215, 331; EW 13; EWL 3; MTCW 1, 2; MTFW 2005; PFS 16; RGHL; RGWL 2, 3

Milton, John 1608-1674 ..... **LC 9, 43, 92; PC 19, 29; WLC 4**
See also AAYA 65; BRW 2; BRWR 2; CD-BLB 1660-1789; DA; DA3; DAB; DAC; DAM MST, POET; DLB 131, 151, 281; EFS 1; EXPP; LAIT 1; PAB; PFS 3, 17; RGEL 2; TEA; WLIT 3; WP

Min, Anchee 1957- .... **CLC 86**
See also CA 146; CANR 94, 137; MTFW 2005

Minehaha, Cornelius
See Wedekind, Frank

Miner, Valerie 1947- .... **CLC 40**
See also CA 97-100; CANR 59; FW; GLL 2

Minimo, Duca
See D'Annunzio, Gabriele

Minot, Susan (Anderson) 1956- ...... **CLC 44, 159**
See also AMWS 6; CA 134; CANR 118; CN 6, 7

Minus, Ed 1938- .... **CLC 39**
Scc also CA 185

Mirabai 1498(?)-1550(?) .... **LC 143; PC 48**
See also PFS 24

Miranda, Javier
See Bioy Casares, Adolfo
See also CWW 2

Mirbeau, Octave 1848-1917 .... **TCLC 55**
See also CA 216; DLB 123, 192; GFL 1789 to the Present

Mirikitani, Janice 1942- .... **AAL**
See also CA 211; DLB 312; RGAL 4

Mirk, John (?)-c. 1414 .... **LC 105**
See also DLB 146

Miro (Ferrer), Gabriel (Francisco Victor)
1879-1930 .... **TCLC 5**
See also CA 104; 185; DLB 322; EWL 3

Misharin, Alexandr .... **CLC 59**

Mishima, Yukio .... **CLC 2, 4, 6, 9, 27; DC 1; SSC 4; TCLC 161; WLC 4**
See Hiraoka, Kimitake
See also AAYA 50; BPFB 2; DLB 182; EWL 3; GLL 1; MJW; RGSF 2; RGWL 2, 3; SSFS 5, 12

Mistral, Frederic 1830-1914 .... **TCLC 51**
See also CA 122; 213; DLB 331; GFL 1789 to the Present

Mistral, Gabriela
See Godoy Alcayaga, Lucila
See also DLB 283, 331; DNFS 1; EWL 3; LAW; RGWL 2, 3; WP

Mistry, Rohinton 1952- ... **CLC 71, 196; SSC 73**
See also BRWS 10; CA 141; CANR 86, 114; CCA 1; CN 6, 7; DAC; DLB 334; SSFS 6

Mitchell, Clyde
See Ellison, Harlan; Silverberg, Robert

Mitchell, Emerson Blackhorse Barney 1945- **NNAL**
See also CA 45-48

Mitchell, James Leslie 1901-1935
See Gibbon, Lewis Grassic
See also CA 104; 188; DLB 15

Mitchell, Joni 1943- .... **CLC 12**
See also CA 112; CCA 1

Mitchell, Joseph (Quincy)
1908-1996 .... **CLC 98**
See also CA 77-80; 152; CANR 69; CN 1, 2, 3, 4, 5, 6; CSW; DLB 185; DLBY 1996

Mitchell, Margaret (Munnerlyn) 1900-1949
TCLC 11, 170
See also AAYA 23; BPFB 2; BYA 1; CA 109; 125; CANR 55, 94; CDALBS; DA3; DAM NOV, POP; DLB 9; LAIT 2; MAL 5; MTCW 1, 2; MTFW 2005; NFS 9; RGAL 4; RHW; TUS; WYAS 1; YAW

Mitchell, Peggy
See Mitchell, Margaret (Munnerlyn)

Mitchell, S(ilas) Weir 1829-1914 .... **TCLC 36**
See also CA 165; DLB 202; RGAL 4

Mitchell, W(illiam) O(rmond) 1914-1998
CLC 25
See also CA 77-80; 165; CANR 15, 43; CN 1, 2, 3, 4, 5, 6; DAC; DAM MST; DLB 88; TCLE 1:2

Mitchell, William (Lendrum) 1879-1936
TCLC 81
See also CA 213

Mitford, Mary Russell 1787-1855 ... **NCLC 4**
See also DLB 110, 116; RGEL 2

Mitford, Nancy 1904-1973 .... **CLC 44**
See also BRWS 10; CA 9-12R; CN 1; DLB 191; RGEL 2

Miyamoto, (Chujo) Yuriko
1899-1951 .... **TCLC 37**
See Miyamoto Yuriko
See also CA 170, 174

Miyamoto Yuriko
See Miyamoto, (Chujo) Yuriko
See also DLB 180

Miyazawa, Kenji 1896-1933 .... **TCLC 76**
See Miyazawa Kenji
See also CA 157; RGWL 3

Miyazawa Kenji
See Miyazawa, Kenji
See also EWL 3

Mizoguchi, Kenji 1898-1956 .... **TCLC 72**
See also CA 167

Mo, Timothy (Peter) 1950- .... **CLC 46, 134**
See also CA 117; CANR 128; CN 5, 6, 7; DLB 194; MTCW 1; WLIT 4; WWE 1

Modarressi, Taghi (M.) 1931-1997 .... **CLC 44**
See also CA 121; 134; INT CA-134

Modiano, Patrick (Jean) 1945- .... **CLC 18, 218**
See also CA 85-88; CANR 17, 40, 115; CWW 2; DLB 83, 299; EWL 3; RGHL

Mofolo, Thomas (Mokopu) 1875(?)-1948
BLC 1:3; TCLC 22
See also AFW; CA 121; 153; CANR 83; DAM MULT; DLB 225; EWL 3; MTCW 2; MTFW 2005; WLIT 2

Mohr, Nicholasa 1938- .... **CLC 12; HLC 2**
See also AAYA 8, 46; CA 49-52; CANR 1, 32, 64; CLR 22; DAM MULT; DLB 145; HW 1, 2; JRDA; LAIT 5; LLW; MAICYA 2; MAICYAS 1; RGAL 4; SAAS 8; SATA 8, 97; SATA-Essay 113; WYA; YAW

Moi, Toril 1953- .... **CLC 172**
See also CA 154; CANR 102; FW

Mojtabai, A(nn) G(race) 1938- ..... **CLC 5, 9, 15, 29**
See also CA 85-88; CANR 88

Moliere 1622-1673 ..... **DC 13; LC 10, 28, 64, 125, 127; WLC 4**
See also DA; DA3; DAB; DAC; DAM DRAM, MST; DFS 13, 18, 20; DLB 268; EW 3; GFL Beginnings to 1789; LATS 1:1; RGWL 2, 3; TWA

Molin, Charles
See Mayne, William (James Carter)

Molnar, Ferenc 1878-1952 .... **TCLC 20**
See also CA 109; 153; CANR 83; CDWLB 4; DAM DRAM; DLB 215; EWL 3; RGWL 2, 3

Momaday, N. Scott 1934- ...... **CLC 2, 19, 85, 95, 160; NNAL; PC 25; WLCS**
See also AAYA 11, 64; AMWS 4; ANW; BPFB 2; BYA 12; CA 25-28R; CANR 14, 34, 68, 134; CDALBS; CN 2, 3, 4, 5, 6, 7; CPW; DA; DA3; DAB; DAC; DAM MST, MULT, NOV, POP; DLB 143, 175, 256; EWL 3; EXPP; INT CANR-14; LAIT 4; LATS 1:2; MAL 5; MTCW 1, 2; MTFW 2005; NFS 10; PFS 2, 11; RGAL 4; SATA 48; SATA-Brief 30; TCWW 1, 2; WP; YAW

Monette, Paul 1945-1995 .... **CLC 82**
See also AMWS 10; CA 139; 147; CN 6; GLL 1

Monroe, Harriet 1860-1936 .... **TCLC 12**
See also CA 109; 204; DLB 54, 91

Monroe, Lyle
See Heinlein, Robert A.

Montagu, Elizabeth 1720-1800 .... **NCLC 7, 117**
See also FW

Montagu, Mary (Pierrepont) Wortley
1689-1762 .... **LC 9, 57; PC 16**
See also DLB 95, 101; FL 1:1; RGEL 2

Montagu, W. H.
See Coleridge, Samuel Taylor

Montague, John (Patrick) 1929- ..... **CLC 13, 46**
See also CA 9-12R; CANR 9, 69, 121; CP 1, 2, 3, 4, 5, 6, 7; DLB 40; EWL 3; MTCW 1; PFS 12; RGEL 2; TCLE 1:2

Montaigne, Michel (Eyquem) de 1533-1592
LC 8, 105; WLC 4
See also DA; DAB; DAC; DAM MST; DLB 327; EW 2; GFL Beginnings to 1789; LMFS 1; RGWL 2, 3; TWA

Montale, Eugenio 1896-1981 ... **CLC 7, 9, 18; PC 13**
See also CA 17-20R; 104; CANR 30; DLB 114, 331; EW 11; EWL 3; MTCW 1; PFS 22; RGWL 2, 3; TWA; WLIT 7

Montesquieu, Charles-Louis de Secondat
1689-1755 .... **LC 7, 69**
See also DLB 314; EW 3; GFL Beginnings to 1789; TWA

Montessori, Maria 1870-1952 ...... **TCLC 103**
See also CA 115; 147

Montgomery, (Robert) Bruce 1921(?)-1978
See Crispin, Edmund
See also CA 179; 104; CMW 4

Montgomery, L(ucy) M(aud) 1874-1942
TCLC 51, 140
See also AAYA 12; BYA 1; CA 108; 137; CLR 8, 91; DA3; DAC; DAM MST; DLB 92; DLBD 14; JRDA; MAICYA 1, 2; MTCW 2; MTFW 2005; RGEL 2; SATA 100; TWA; WCH; WYA; YABC 1

Mortimer, John 1923- .... **CLC 28, 43**
See also CA 13-16R; CANR 21, 69, 109, 172; CBD; CD 5, 6; CDBLB 1960 to Present; CMW 4; CN 5, 6, 7; CPW; DA3; DAM DRAM, POP; DLB 13, 245, 271; INT CANR-21; MSW; MTCW 1, 2; MTFW 2005; RGEL 2

Mortimer, John Clifford
See Mortimer, John

Mortimer, Penelope (Ruth)
1918-1999 .... **CLC 5**
See also CA 57-60; 187; CANR 45, 88; CN 1, 2, 3, 4, 5, 6

Mortimer, Sir John
See Mortimer, John

Morton, Anthony
See Creasey, John

Morton, Thomas 1579(?)-1647(?) .... **LC 72**
See also DLB 24; RGEL 2

Mosca, Gaetano 1858-1941 .... **TCLC 75**

Moses, Daniel David 1952- .... **NNAL**
See also CA 186; CANR 160; DLB 334

Mosher, Howard Frank 1943- .... **CLC 62**
See also CA 139; CANR 65, 115

Mosley, Nicholas 1923- .... **CLC 43, 70**
See also CA 69-72; CANR 41, 60, 108, 158; CN 1, 2, 3, 4, 5, 6, 7; DLB 14, 207

Mosley, Walter 1952- .... **BLCS; CLC 97, 184**
See also AAYA 57; AMWS 13; BPFB 2; BW 2; CA 142; CANR 57, 92, 136, 172; CMW 4; CN 7; CPW; DA3; DAM MULT, POP; DLB 306; MSW; MTCW 2; MTFW 2005

Moss, Howard 1922-1987 . **CLC 7, 14, 45, 50**
See also CA 1-4R; 123; CANR 1, 44; CP 1, 2, 3, 4; DAM POET; DLB 5

Mossgiel, Rab
See Burns, Robert

Motion, Andrew 1952- .... **CLC 47**
See also BRWS 7; CA 146; CANR 90, 142; CP 4, 5, 6, 7; DLB 40; MTFW 2005

Motion, Andrew Peter
See Motion, Andrew

Motley, Willard (Francis)
1909-1965 .... **CLC 18**
See also AMWS 17; BW 1; CA 117; 106; CANR 88; DLB 76, 143

Motoori, Norinaga 1730-1801 .... **NCLC 45**

Mott, Michael (Charles Alston)
1930- .... **CLC 15, 34**
See also CA 5-8R; CAAS 7; CANR 7, 29

Mountain Wolf Woman 1884-1960 . **CLC 92; NNAL**
See also CA 144; CANR 90

Moure, Erin 1955- .... **CLC 88**
See also CA 113; CP 5, 6, 7; CWP; DLB 60

Mourning Dove 1885(?)-1936 .... **NNAL**
See also CA 144; CANR 90; DAM MULT; DLB 175, 221

Mowat, Farley 1921- .... **CLC 26**
See also AAYA 1, 50; BYA 2; CA 1-4R; CANR 4, 24, 42, 68, 108; CLR 20; CPW; DAC; DAM MST; DLB 68; INT CANR-24; JRDA; MAICYA 1, 2; MTCW 1, 2; MTFW 2005; SATA 3, 55; YAW

Mowat, Farley McGill
See Mowat, Farley

Mowatt, Anna Cora 1819-1870 ..... **NCLC 74**
See also RGAL 4

Mo Yan .... **CLC 257**
See Moye, Guan

Moye, Guan 1956(?)-
See Mo Yan
See also CA 201

Moyers, Bill 1934- .... **CLC 74**
See also AITN 2; CA 61-64; CANR 31, 52, 148

Mphahlele, Es'kia
See Mphahlele, Ezekiel
See also AFW; CDWLB 3; CN 4, 5, 6; DLB 125, 225; RGSF 2; SSFS 11

Mphahlele, Ezekiel 1919- ...... **BLC 1:3; CLC 25, 133**
See Mphahlele, Es'kia
See also BW 2, 3; CA 81-84; CANR 26, 76; CN 1, 2, 3; DA3; DAM MULT; EWL 3; MTCW 2; MTFW 2005; SATA 119

Mqhayi, S(amuel) E(dward) K(rune Loliwe)
1875-1945 .... **BLC 1:3; TCLC 25**
See also CA 153; CANR 87; DAM MULT

Mrozek, Slawomir 1930- .... **CLC 3, 13**
See also CA 13-16R; CAAS 10; CANR 29; CDWLB 4; CWW 2; DLB 232; EWL 3; MTCW 1

Mrs. Belloc-Lowndes
See Lowndes, Marie Adelaide (Belloc)

Mrs. Fairstar
See Horne, Richard Henry Hengist

M'Taggart, John M'Taggart Ellis
See McTaggart, John McTaggart Ellis

Mtwa, Percy (?)- .... **CLC 47**
See also CD 6

Mueller, Lisel 1924- .... **CLC 13, 51; PC 33**
See also CA 93-96; CP 6, 7; DLB 105; PFS 9, 13

Muggeridge, Malcolm (Thomas) 1903-1990 **TCLC 120**
See also AITN 1; CA 101; CANR 33, 63; MTCW 1, 2

Muhammad 570-632 .... **WLCS**
See also DA; DAB; DAC; DAM MST; DLB 311

Muir, Edwin 1887-1959 . **PC 49; TCLC 2, 87**
See Moore, Edward
See also BRWS 6; CA 104; 193; DLB 20, 100, 191; EWL 3; RGEL 2

Muir, John 1838-1914 .... **TCLC 28**
See also AMWS 9; ANW; CA 165; DLB 186, 275

Mujica Lainez, Manuel 1910-1984 ... **CLC 31**
See Lainez, Manuel Mujica
See also CA 81-84; 112; CANR 32; EWL 3; HW 1

Mukherjee, Bharati 1940- ..... **AAL; CLC 53, 115, 235; SSC 38**
See also AAYA 46; BEST 89:2; CA 107, 232; CAAE 232; CANR 45, 72, 128; CN 5, 6, 7; DAM NOV; DLB 60, 218, 323; DNFS 1, 2; EWL 3; FW; MAL 5; MTCW 1, 2; MTFW 2005; RGAL 4; RGSF 2; SSFS 7, 24; TUS; WWE 1

Muldoon, Paul 1951- .... **CLC 32, 72, 166**
See also BRWS 4; CA 113; 129; CANR 52, 91, 176; CP 2, 3, 4, 5, 6, 7; DAM POET; DLB 40; INT CA-129; PFS 7, 22; TCLE 1:2

Mulisch, Harry (Kurt Victor)
1927- .... **CLC 42**
See also CA 9-12R; CANR 6, 26, 56, 110; CWW 2; DLB 299; EWL 3

Mull, Martin 1943- .... **CLC 17**
See also CA 105

Muller, Wilhelm .... **NCLC 73**

Mulock, Dinah Maria
See Craik, Dinah Maria (Mulock)
See also RGEL 2

Multatuli 1820-1881 .... **NCLC 165**
See also RGWL 2, 3

Munday, Anthony 1560-1633 .... **LC 87**
See also DLB 62, 172; RGEL 2

Munford, Robert 1737(?)-1783 .... **LC 5**
See also DLB 31

Mungo, Raymond 1946- .... **CLC 72**
See also CA 49-52; CANR 2

Munro, Alice 1931- .... **CLC 6, 10, 19, 50, 95, 222; SSC 3, 95; WLCS**
See also AITN 2; BPFB 2; CA 33-36R; CANR 33, 53, 75, 114; CCA 1; CN 1, 2, 3, 4, 5, 6, 7; DA3; DAC; DAM MST, NOV; DLB 53; EWL 3; MTCW 1, 2; MTFW 2005; NFS 27; RGEL 2; RGSF 2; SATA 29; SSFS 5, 13, 19; TCLE 1:2; WWE 1

Munro, H(ector) H(ugh) 1870-1916
See Saki
See also AAYA 56; CA 104; 130; CANR 104; CDBLB 1890-1914; DA; DA3; DAB; DAC; DAM MST, NOV; DLB 34, 162; EXPS; MTCW 1, 2; MTFW 2005; RGEL 2; SSFS 15

Murakami, Haruki 1949- .... **CLC 150**
See Murakami Haruki
See also CA 165; CANR 102, 146; MJW; RGWL 3; SFW 4; SSFS 23

Murakami Haruki
See Murakami, Haruki
See also CWW 2; DLB 182; EWL 3

Murasaki, Lady
See Murasaki Shikibu

Murasaki Shikibu 978(?)-1026(?) .. **CMLC 1, 79**
See also EFS 2; LATS 1:1; RGWL 2, 3

Murdoch, Iris 1919-1999 .. **CLC 1, 2, 3, 4, 6, 8, 11, 15, 22, 31, 51; TCLC 171**
See also BRWS 1; CA 13-16R; 179; CANR 8, 43, 68, 103, 142; CBD; CDBLB 1960 to Present; CN 1, 2, 3, 4, 5, 6; CWD; DA3; DAB; DAC; DAM MST, NOV; DLB 14, 194, 233, 326; EWL 3; INT CANR-8; MTCW 1, 2; MTFW 2005; NFS 18; RGEL 2; TCLE 1:2; TEA; WLIT 4

Murfree, Mary Noailles 1850-1922 .. **SSC 22; TCLC 135**
See also CA 122; 176; DLB 12, 74; RGAL 4

Murglie
See Murnau, F.W.

Murnau, Friedrich Wilhelm
See Murnau, F.W.

Murnau, F.W. 1888-1931 .... **TCLC 53**
See also CA 112

Murphy, Richard 1927- .... **CLC 41**
See also BRWS 5; CA 29-32R; CP 1, 2, 3, 4, 5, 6, 7; DLB 40; EWL 3

Murphy, Sylvia 1937- .... **CLC 34**
See also CA 121

Murphy, Thomas (Bernard) 1935- ... **CLC 51**
See Murphy, Tom
See also CA 101

Murphy, Tom
See Murphy, Thomas (Bernard)
See also DLB 310

Murray, Albert 1916- .... **BLC 2:3; CLC 73**
See also BW 2; CA 49-52; CANR 26, 52, 78, 160; CN 7; CSW; DLB 38; MTFW 2005

Murray, Albert L.
See Murray, Albert

Murray, James Augustus Henry 1837-1915 **TCLC 117**

Murray, Judith Sargent
1751-1820 .... **NCLC 63**
See also DLB 37, 200

Murray, Les(lie Allan) 1938- .... **CLC 40**
See also BRWS 7; CA 21-24R; CANR 11, 27, 56, 103; CP 1, 2, 3, 4, 5, 6, 7; DAM POET; DLB 289; DLBY 2001; EWL 3; RGEL 2

Murry, J. Middleton
See Murry, John Middleton

Murry, John Middleton
1889-1957 .... **TCLC 16**
See also CA 118; 217; DLB 149

GL 3; HGG; INT CANR-25; LAIT 4; MAL 5; MBL; MTCW 1, 2; MTFW 2005; NFS 8, 24; RGAL 4; RGSF 2; SATA 159; SSFS 1, 8, 17; SUFW 2; TUS

O'Brian, E. G.
See Clarke, Arthur C.

O'Brian, Patrick 1914-2000 .... **CLC 152**
See also AAYA 55; BRWS 12; CA 144; 187; CANR 74; CPW; MTCW 2; MTFW 2005; RHW

O'Brien, Darcy 1939-1998 .... **CLC 11**
See also CA 21-24R; 167; CANR 8, 59

O'Brien, Edna 1932- ..... **CLC 3, 5, 8, 13, 36, 65, 116, 237; SSC 10, 77**
See also BRWS 5; CA 1-4R; CANR 6, 41, 65, 102, 169; CDBLB 1960 to Present; CN 1, 2, 3, 4, 5, 6, 7; DA3; DAM NOV; DLB 14, 231, 319; EWL 3; FW; MTCW 1, 2; MTFW 2005; RGSF 2; WLIT 4

O'Brien, Fitz-James 1828-1862 ..... **NCLC 21**
See also DLB 74; RGAL 4; SUFW

O'Brien, Flann .... **CLC 1, 4, 5, 7, 10, 47**
See O Nuallain, Brian
See also BRWS 2; DLB 231; EWL 3; RGEL 2

O'Brien, Richard 1942- .... **CLC 17**
See also CA 124

O'Brien, Tim 1946- .... **CLC 7, 19, 40, 103, 211; SSC 74**
See also AAYA 16; AMWS 5; CA 85-88; CANR 40, 58, 133; CDALBS; CN 5, 6, 7; CPW; DA3; DAM POP; DLB 152; DLBY 1980; LATS 1:2; MAL 5; MTCW 2; MTFW 2005; RGAL 4; SSFS 5, 15; TCLE 1:2

Obstfelder, Sigbjoern 1866-1900 .... **TCLC 23**
See also CA 123

O'Casey, Sean 1880-1964 .... **CLC 1, 5, 9, 11, 15, 88; DC 12; WLCS**
See also BRW 7; CA 89-92; CANR 62; CBD; CDBLB 1914-1945; DA3; DAB; DAC; DAM DRAM; MST; DFS 19; DLB 10; EWL 3; MTCW 1, 2; MTFW 2005; RGEL 2; TEA; WLIT 4

O'Cathasaigh, Sean
See O'Casey, Sean

Occom, Samson 1723-1792 .... **LC 60; NNAL**
See also DLB 175

Occomy, Marita (Odette) Bonner
1899(?)-1971
See Bonner, Marita
See also BW 2; CA 142; DFS 13; DLB 51, 228

Ochs, Phil(ip David) 1940-1976 .... **CLC 17**
See also CA 185; 65-68

O'Connor, Edwin (Greene)
1918-1968 .... **CLC 14**
See also CA 93-96; 25-28R; MAL 5

O'Connor, (Mary) Flannery
1925-1964 .... **CLC 1, 2, 3, 6, 10, 13, 15, 21, 66, 104; SSC 1, 23, 61, 82, 111; TCLC 132; WLC 4**
See also AAYA 7; AMW; AMWR 2; BPFB 3; BYA 16; CA 1-4R; CANR 3, 41; CDALB 1941-1968; DA; DA3; DAB; DAC; DAM MST, NOV; DLB 2, 152; DLBD 12; DLBY 1980; EWL 3; EXPS; LAIT 5; MAL 5; MBL; MTCW 1, 2; MTFW 2005; NFS 3, 21; RGAL 4; RGSF 2; SSFS 2, 7, 10, 19; TUS

O'Connor, Frank 1903-1966 ... **CLC 23; SSC 5, 109**
See O'Donovan, Michael Francis
See also DLB 162; EWL 3; RGSF 2; SSFS 5

O'Dell, Scott 1898-1989 .... **CLC 30**
See also AAYA 3, 44; BPFB 3; BYA 1, 2, 3, 5; CA 61-64; 129; CANR 12, 30, 112; CLR 1, 16, 126; DLB 52; JRDA; MAICYA 1, 2; SATA 12, 60, 134; WYA; YAW

Odets, Clifford 1906-1963 ..... **CLC 2, 28, 98; DC 6**
See also AMWS 2; CA 85-88; CAD; CANR 62; DAM DRAM; DFS 3, 17, 20; DLB 7, 26, 341; EWL 3; MAL 5; MTCW 1, 2; MTFW 2005; RGAL 4; TUS

O'Doherty, Brian 1928- .... **CLC 76**
See also CA 105; CANR 108

O'Donnell, K. M.
See Malzberg, Barry N(athaniel)

O'Donnell, Lawrence
See Kuttner, Henry

O'Donovan, Michael Francis
1903-1966 .... **CLC 14**
See O'Connor, Frank
See also CA 93-96; CANR 84

Oe, Kenzaburo 1935- .. **CLC 10, 36, 86, 187; SSC 20**
See Oe Kenzaburo
See also CA 97-100; CANR 36, 50, 74, 126; DA3; DAM NOV; DLB 182, 331; DLBY 1994; LATS 1:2; MJW; MTCW 1, 2; MTFW 2005; RGSF 2; RGWL 2, 3

Oe Kenzaburo
See Oe, Kenzaburo
See also CWW 2; EWL 3

O'Faolain, Julia 1932- .... **CLC 6, 19, 47, 108**
See also CA 81-84; CAAS 2; CANR 12, 61; CN 2, 3, 4, 5, 6, 7; DLB 14, 231, 319; FW; MTCW 1; RHW

O'Faolain, Sean 1900-1991 ...... **CLC 1, 7, 14, 32, 70; SSC 13; TCLC 143**
See also CA 61-64; 134; CANR 12, 66; CN 1, 2, 3, 4; DLB 15, 162; MTCW 1, 2; MTFW 2005; RGEL 2; RGSF 2

O'Flaherty, Liam 1896-1984 .... **CLC 5, 34; SSC 6**
See also CA 101; 113; CANR 35; CN 1, 2, 3; DLB 36, 162; DLBY 1984; MTCW 1, 2; MTFW 2005; RGEL 2; RGSF 2; SSFS 5, 20

Ogai
See Mori Ogai
See also MJW

Ogilvy, Gavin
See Barrie, J(ames) M(atthew)

O'Grady, Standish (James)
1846-1928 .... **TCLC 5**
See also CA 104; 157

O'Grady, Timothy 1951- .... **CLC 59**
See also CA 138

O'Hara, Frank 1926-1966 .... **CLC 2, 5, 13, 78; PC 45**
See also CA 9-12R; 25-28R; CANR 33; DA3; DAM POET; DLB 5, 16, 193; EWL 3; MAL 5; MTCW 1, 2; MTFW 2005; PFS 8, 12; RGAL 4; WP

O'Hara, John (Henry) 1905-1970 . **CLC 1, 2, 3, 6, 11, 42; SSC 15**
See also AMW; BPFB 3; CA 5-8R; 25-28R; CANR 31, 60; CDALB 1929-1941; DAM NOV; DLB 9, 86, 324; DLBD 2; EWL 3; MAL 5; MTCW 1, 2; MTFW 2005; NFS 11; RGAL 4; RGSF 2

O'Hehir, Diana 1929- .... **CLC 41**
See also CA 245

Ohiyesa
See Eastman, Charles A(lexander)

Okada, John 1923-1971 .... **AAL**
See also BYA 14; CA 212; DLB 312; NFS 25

Okigbo, Christopher 1930-1967 ..... **BLC 1:3; CLC 25, 84; PC 7; TCLC 171**
See also AFW; BW 1, 3; CA 77-80; CANR 74; CDWLB 3; DAM MULT, POET; DLB 125; EWL 3; MTCW 1, 2; MTFW 2005; RGEL 2

Okigbo, Christopher Ifenayichukwu
See Okigbo, Christopher

Okri, Ben 1959- .... **BLC 2:3; CLC 87, 223**
See also AFW; BRWS 5; BW 2, 3; CA 130; 138; CANR 65, 128; CN 5, 6, 7; DLB 157, 231, 319, 326; EWL 3; INT CA-138; MTCW 2; MTFW 2005; RGSF 2; SSFS 20; WLIT 2; WWE 1

Olds, Sharon 1942- .. **CLC 32, 39, 85; PC 22**
See also AMWS 10; CA 101; CANR 18, 41, 66, 98, 135; CP 5, 6, 7; CPW; CWP; DAM POET; DLB 120; MAL 5; MTCW 2; MTFW 2005; PFS 17

Oldstyle, Jonathan
See Irving, Washington

Olesha, Iurii
See Olesha, Yuri (Karlovich)
See also RGWL 2

Olesha, Iurii Karlovich
See Olesha, Yuri (Karlovich)
See also DLB 272

Olesha, Yuri (Karlovich) 1899-1960 . **CLC 8; SSC 69; TCLC 136**
See Olesha, Iurii; Olesha, Iurii Karlovich; Olesha, Yury Karlovich
See also CA 85-88; EW 11; RGWL 3

Olesha, Yury Karlovich
See Olesha, Yuri (Karlovich)
See also EWL 3

Oliphant, Mrs.
See Oliphant, Margaret (Oliphant Wilson)
See also SUFW

Oliphant, Laurence 1829(?)-1888 .. **NCLC 47**
See also DLB 18, 166

Oliphant, Margaret (Oliphant Wilson)
1828-1897 .... **NCLC 11, 61; SSC 25**
See Oliphant, Mrs.
See also BRWS 10; DLB 18, 159, 190; HGG; RGEL 2; RGSF 2

Oliver, Mary 1935- ... **CLC 19, 34, 98; PC 75**
See also AMWS 7; CA 21-24R; CANR 9, 43, 84, 92, 138; CP 4, 5, 6, 7; CWP; DLB 5, 193; EWL 3; MTFW 2005; PFS 15

Olivier, Laurence (Kerr) 1907-1989 . **CLC 20**
See also CA 111; 150; 129

Olsen, Tillie 1912-2007 .... **CLC 4, 13, 114; SSC 11, 103**
See also AAYA 51; AMWS 13; BYA 11; CA 1-4R; 256; CANR 1, 43, 74, 132; CDALBS; CN 2, 3, 4, 5, 6, 7; DA; DA3; DAB; DAC; DAM MST; DLB 28, 206; DLBY 1980; EWL 3; EXPS; FW; MAL 5; MTCW 1, 2; MTFW 2005; RGAL 4; RGSF 2; SSFS 1; TCLE 1:2; TCWW 2; TUS

Olson, Charles (John) 1910-1970 .. **CLC 1, 2, 5, 6, 9, 11, 29; PC 19**
See also AMWS 2; CA 13-16; 25-28R; CABS 2; CANR 35, 61; CAP 1; CP 1; DAM POET; DLB 5, 16, 193; EWL 3; MAL 5; MTCW 1, 2; RGAL 4; WP

Olson, Merle Theodore
See Olson, Toby

Olson, Toby 1937- .... **CLC 28**
See also CA 65-68; CAAS 11; CANR 9, 31, 84, 175; CP 3, 4, 5, 6, 7

Olyesha, Yuri
See Olesha, Yuri (Karlovich)

Olympiodorus of Thebes c. 375-c. 430 .... **CMLC 59**

Omar Khayyam
See Khayyam, Omar
See also RGWL 2, 3

Ondaatje, Michael 1943- ..... **CLC 14, 29, 51, 76, 180; PC 28**
See also AAYA 66; CA 77-80; CANR 42, 74, 109, 133, 172; CN 5, 6, 7; CP 1, 2, 3, 4, 5, 6, 7; DA3; DAB; DAC; DAM MST; DLB 60, 323, 326; EWL 3; LATS 1:2; LMFS 2; MTCW 2; MTFW 2005; NFS 23; PFS 8, 19; TCLE 1:2; TWA; WWE 1

Ondaatje, Philip Michael
See Ondaatje, Michael
Oneal, Elizabeth 1934-
See Oneal, Zibby
See also CA 106; CANR 28, 84; MAICYA 1, 2; SATA 30, 82; YAW
Oneal, Zibby .... **CLC 30**
See Oneal, Elizabeth
See also AAYA 5, 41; BYA 13; CLR 13; JRDA; WYA
O'Neill, Eugene (Gladstone) 1888-1953 ... **DC 20; TCLC 1, 6, 27, 49; WLC 4**
See also AAYA 54; AITN 1; AMW; AMWC 1; CA 110; 132; CAD; CANR 131; CDALB 1929-1941; DA; DA3; DAB; DAC; DAM DRAM, MST; DFS 2, 4, 5, 6, 9, 11, 12, 16, 20; DLB 7, 331; EWL 3; LAIT 3; LMFS 2; MAL 5; MTCW 1, 2; MTFW 2005; RGAL 4; TUS
Onetti, Juan Carlos 1909-1994 ... **CLC 7, 10; HLCS 2; SSC 23; TCLC 131**
See also CA 85-88; 145; CANR 32, 63; CD-WLB 3; CWW 2; DAM MULT, NOV; DLB 113; EWL 3; HW 1, 2; LAW; MTCW 1, 2; MTFW 2005; RGSF 2
O Nuallain, Brian 1911-1966
See O'Brien, Flann
See also CA 21-22; 25-28R; CAP 2; DLB 231; FANT; TEA
Ophuls, Max
See Ophuls, Max
Ophuls, Max 1902-1957 .... **TCLC 79**
See also CA 113
Opie, Amelia 1769-1853 .... **NCLC 65**
See also DLB 116, 159; RGEL 2
Oppen, George 1908-1984 ..... **CLC 7, 13, 34; PC 35; TCLC 107**
See also CA 13-16R; 113; CANR 8, 82; CP 1, 2, 3; DLB 5, 165
Oppenheim, E(dward) Phillips 1866-1946 **TCLC 45**
See also CA 111; 202; CMW 4; DLB 70
Oppenheimer, Max
See Ophuls, Max
Opuls, Max
See Ophuls, Max
Orage, A(lfred) R(ichard) 1873-1934 .... **TCLC 157**
See also CA 122
Origen c. 185-c. 254 .... **CMLC 19**
Orlovitz, Gil 1918-1973 .... **CLC 22**
See also CA 77-80; 45-48; CN 1; CP 1, 2; DLB 2, 5
Orosius c. 385-c. 420 .... **CMLC 100**
O'Rourke, Patrick Jake
See O'Rourke, P.J.
O'Rourke, P.J. 1947- .... **CLC 209**
See also CA 77-80; CANR 13, 41, 67, 111, 155; CPW; DAM POP; DLB 185
Orris
See Ingelow, Jean
Ortega y Gasset, Jose 1883-1955 ...... **HLC 2; TCLC 9**
See also CA 106; 130; DAM MULT; EW 9; EWL 3; HW 1, 2; MTCW 1, 2; MTFW 2005
Ortese, Anna Maria 1914-1998 .... **CLC 89**
See also DLB 177; EWL 3
Ortiz, Simon
See Ortiz, Simon J.
Ortiz, Simon J. 1941- . **CLC 45, 208; NNAL; PC 17**
See also AMWS 4; CA 134; CANR 69, 118, 164; CP 3, 4, 5, 6, 7; DAM MULT, POET; DLB 120, 175, 256; EXPP; MAL 5; PFS 4, 16; RGAL 4; SSFS 22; TCWW 2
Ortiz, Simon Joseph
See Ortiz, Simon J.

Orton, Joe .... **CLC 4, 13, 43; DC 3; TCLC 157**
See Orton, John Kingsley
See also BRWS 5; CBD; CDBLB 1960 to Present; DFS 3, 6; DLB 13, 310; GLL 1; RGEL 2; TEA; WLIT 4
Orton, John Kingsley 1933-1967
See Orton, Joe
See also CA 85-88; CANR 35, 66; DAM DRAM; MTCW 1, 2; MTFW 2005
Orwell, George . **SSC 68; TCLC 2, 6, 15, 31, 51, 128, 129; WLC 4**
See Blair, Eric (Arthur)
See also BPFB 3; BRW 7; BYA 5; CDBLB 1945-1960; CLR 68; DAB; DLB 15, 98, 195, 255; EWL 3; EXPN; LAIT 4, 5; LATS 1:1; NFS 3, 7; RGEL 2; SCFW 1, 2; SFW 4; SSFS 4; TEA; WLIT 4; YAW
Osborne, David
See Silverberg, Robert
Osborne, Dorothy 1627-1695 .... **LC 141**
Osborne, George
See Silverberg, Robert
Osborne, John 1929-1994 .... **CLC 1, 2, 5, 11, 45; TCLC 153; WLC 4**
See also BRWS 1; CA 13-16R; 147; CANR 21, 56; CBD; CDBLB 1945-1960; DA; DAB; DAC; DAM DRAM, MST; DFS 4, 19, 24; DLB 13; EWL 3; MTCW 1, 2; MTFW 2005; RGEL 2
Osborne, Lawrence 1958- .... **CLC 50**
See also CA 189; CANR 152
Osbourne, Lloyd 1868-1947 .... **TCLC 93**
Osgood, Frances Sargent 1811-1850 .... **NCLC 141**
See also DLB 250
Oshima, Nagisa 1932- .... **CLC 20**
See also CA 116; 121; CANR 78
Oskison, John Milton 1874-1947 .... **NNAL; TCLC 35**
See also CA 144; CANR 84; DAM MULT; DLB 175
Ossian c. 3rd cent. - .... **CMLC 28**
See Macpherson, James
Ossoli, Sarah Margaret (Fuller) 1810-1850 **NCLC 5, 50**
See Fuller, Margaret
See also CDALB 1640-1865; DLB 1, 59, 73; FW; LMFS 1; SATA 25
Ostriker, Alicia 1937- .... **CLC 132**
See also CA 25-28R; CAAS 24; CANR 10, 30, 62, 99, 167; CWP; DLB 120; EXPP; PFS 19, 26
Ostriker, Alicia Suskin
See Ostriker, Alicia
Ostrovsky, Aleksandr Nikolaevich
See Ostrovsky, Alexander
See also DLB 277
Ostrovsky, Alexander 1823-1886 .. **NCLC 30, 57**
See Ostrovsky, Aleksandr Nikolaevich
Osundare, Niyi 1947- .... **BLC 2:3**
See also AFW; BW 3; CA 176; CDWLB 3; CP 7; DLB 157
Otero, Blas de 1916-1979 .... **CLC 11**
See also CA 89-92; DLB 134; EWL 3
O'Trigger, Sir Lucius
See Horne, Richard Henry Hengist
Otto, Rudolf 1869-1937 .... **TCLC 85**
Otto, Whitney 1955- .... **CLC 70**
See also CA 140; CANR 120
Otway, Thomas 1652-1685 ... **DC 24; LC 106**
See also DAM DRAM; DLB 80; RGEL 2
Ouida .... **TCLC 43**
See De La Ramee, Marie Louise
See also DLB 18, 156; RGEL 2
Ouologuem, Yambo 1940- .... **CLC 146**
See also CA 111; 176

Ousmane, Sembene 1923-2007 .... **BLC 1:3, 2:3; CLC 66**
See also AFW; BW 1, 3; CA 117; 125; 261; CANR 81; CWW 2; EWL 3; MTCW 1; WLIT 2
Ovid 43B.C.-17 .... **CMLC 7; PC 2**
See also AW 2; CDWLB 1; DA3; DAM POET; DLB 211; PFS 22; RGWL 2, 3; WLIT 8; WP
Owen, Hugh
See Faust, Frederick (Schiller)
Owen, Wilfred (Edward Salter) 1893-1918 **PC 19; TCLC 5, 27; WLC 4**
See also BRW 6; CA 104; 141; CDBLB 1914-1945; DA; DAB; DAC; DAM MST, POET; DLB 20; EWL 3; EXPP; MTCW 2; MTFW 2005; PFS 10; RGEL 2; WLIT 4
Owens, Louis (Dean) 1948-2002 .... **NNAL**
See also CA 137, 179; 207; CAAE 179; CAAS 24; CANR 71
Owens, Rochelle 1936- .... **CLC 8**
See also CA 17-20R; CAAS 2; CAD; CANR 39; CD 5, 6; CP 1, 2, 3, 4, 5, 6, 7; CWD; CWP
Oz, Amos 1939- ...... **CLC 5, 8, 11, 27, 33, 54; SSC 66**
See also CA 53-56; CANR 27, 47, 65, 113, 138, 175; CWW 2; DAM NOV; EWL 3; MTCW 1, 2; MTFW 2005; RGHL; RGSF 2; RGWL 3; WLIT 6
Ozick, Cynthia 1928- .... **CLC 3, 7, 28, 62, 155; SSC 15, 60**
See also AMWS 5; BEST 90:1; CA 17-20R; CANR 23, 58, 116, 160; CN 3, 4, 5, 6, 7; CPW; DA3; DAM NOV, POP; DLB 28, 152, 299; DLBY 1982; EWL 3; EXPS; INT CANR-23; MAL 5; MTCW 1, 2; MTFW 2005; RGAL 4; RGHL; RGSF 2; SSFS 3, 12, 22
Ozu, Yasujiro 1903-1963 .... **CLC 16**
See also CA 112
Pabst, G. W. 1885-1967 .... **TCLC 127**
Pacheco, C.
See Pessoa, Fernando (Antonio Nogueira)
Pacheco, Jose Emilio 1939- .... **HLC 2**
See also CA 111; 131; CANR 65; CWW 2; DAM MULT; DLB 290; EWL 3; HW 1, 2; RGSF 2
Pa Chin .... **CLC 18**
See Jin, Ba
See also EWL 3
Pack, Robert 1929- .... **CLC 13**
See also CA 1-4R; CANR 3, 44, 82; CP 1, 2, 3, 4, 5, 6, 7; DLB 5; SATA 118
Padgett, Lewis
See Kuttner, Henry
Padilla (Lorenzo), Heberto 1932-2000 .... **CLC 38**
See also AITN 1; CA 123; 131; 189; CWW 2; EWL 3; HW 1
Page, James Patrick 1944-
See Page, Jimmy
See also CA 204
Page, Jimmy 1944- .... **CLC 12**
See Page, James Patrick
Page, Louise 1955- .... **CLC 40**
See also CA 140; CANR 76; CBD; CD 5, 6; CWD; DLB 233
Page, P(atricia) K(athleen) 1916- ...... **CLC 7, 18; PC 12**
See Cape, Judith
See also CA 53-56; CANR 4, 22, 65; CP 1, 2, 3, 4, 5, 6, 7; DAC; DAM MST; DLB 68; MTCW 1; RGEL 2
Page, Stanton
See Fuller, Henry Blake

DLBD 17; EWL 3; EXPN; LAIT 4; MTCW 1, 2; MTFW 2005; NFS 3, 12; RGEL 2; SATA 11; SATA-Obit 56; TWA; WLIT 2; WWE 1

Paton Walsh, Gillian
See Paton Walsh, Jill
See also AAYA 47; BYA 1, 8

Paton Walsh, Jill 1937- .... **CLC 35**
See Paton Walsh, Gillian; Walsh, Jill Paton
See also AAYA 11; CA 262; CAAE 262; CANR 38, 83, 158; CLR 2, 65; DLB 161; JRDA; MAICYA 1, 2; SAAS 3; SATA 4, 72, 109; YAW

Patsauq, Markoosie 1942- .... **NNAL**
See also CA 101; CLR 23; CWRI 5; DAM MULT

Patterson, (Horace) Orlando (Lloyd) 1940- **BLCS**
See also BW 1; CA 65-68; CANR 27, 84; CN 1, 2, 3, 4, 5, 6

Patton, George S(mith), Jr.
1885-1945 .... **TCLC 79**
See also CA 189

Paulding, James Kirke 1778-1860 ... **NCLC 2**
See also DLB 3, 59, 74, 250; RGAL 4

Paulin, Thomas Neilson
See Paulin, Tom

Paulin, Tom 1949- .... **CLC 37, 177**
See also CA 123; 128; CANR 98; CP 3, 4, 5, 6, 7; DLB 40

Pausanias c. 1st cent. - .... **CMLC 36**

Paustovsky, Konstantin (Georgievich)
1892-1968 .... **CLC 40**
See also CA 93-96; 25-28R; DLB 272; EWL 3

Pavese, Cesare 1908-1950 .... **PC 13; SSC 19; TCLC 3**
See also CA 104; 169; DLB 128, 177; EW 12; EWL 3; PFS 20; RGSF 2; RGWL 2, 3; TWA; WLIT 7

Pavic, Milorad 1929- .... **CLC 60**
See also CA 136; CDWLB 4; CWW 2; DLB 181; EWL 3; RGWL 3

Pavlov, Ivan Petrovich 1849-1936 . **TCLC 91**
See also CA 118; 180

Pavlova, Karolina Karlovna 1807-1893
NCLC 138
See also DLB 205

Payne, Alan
See Jakes, John

Payne, Rachel Ann
See Jakes, John

Paz, Gil
See Lugones, Leopoldo

Paz, Octavio 1914-1998 . **CLC 3, 4, 6, 10, 19, 51, 65, 119; HLC 2; PC 1, 48; WLC 4**
See also AAYA 50; CA 73-76; 165; CANR 32, 65, 104; CWW 2; DA; DA3; DAB; DAC; DAM MST, MULT, POET; DLB 290, 331; DLBY 1990, 1998; DNFS 1; EWL 3; HW 1, 2; LAW; LAWS 1; MTCW 1, 2; MTFW 2005; PFS 18; RGWL 2, 3; SSFS 13; TWA; WLIT 1

p'Bitek, Okot 1931-1982 . **BLC 1:3; CLC 96; TCLC 149**
See also AFW; BW 2, 3; CA 124; 107; CANR 82; CP 1, 2, 3; DAM MULT; DLB 125; EWL 3; MTCW 1, 2; MTFW 2005; RGEL 2; WLIT 2

Peabody, Elizabeth Palmer
1804-1894 .... **NCLC 169**
See also DLB 1, 223

Peacham, Henry 1578-1644(?) .... **LC 119**
See also DLB 151

Peacock, Molly 1947- .... **CLC 60**
See also CA 103, 262; CAAE 262; CAAS 21; CANR 52, 84; CP 5, 6, 7; CWP; DLB 120, 282

Peacock, Thomas Love
1785-1866 .... **NCLC 22; PC 87**
See also BRW 4; DLB 96, 116; RGEL 2; RGSF 2

Peake, Mervyn 1911-1968 .... **CLC 7, 54**
See also CA 5-8R; 25-28R; CANR 3; DLB 15, 160, 255; FANT; MTCW 1; RGEL 2; SATA 23; SFW 4

Pearce, Philippa 1920-2006
See Christie, Philippa
See also CA 5-8R; 255; CANR 4, 109; CWRI 5; FANT; MAICYA 2; SATA-Obit 179

Pearl, Eric
See Elman, Richard (Martin)

Pearson, Jean Mary
See Gardam, Jane

Pearson, T. R. 1956- .... **CLC 39**
See also CA 120; 130; CANR 97, 147; CSW; INT CA-130

Pearson, Thomas Reid
See Pearson, T. R.

Peck, Dale 1967- .... **CLC 81**
See also CA 146; CANR 72, 127; GLL 2

Peck, John (Frederick) 1941- .... **CLC 3**
See also CA 49-52; CANR 3, 100; CP 4, 5, 6, 7

Peck, Richard 1934- .... **CLC 21**
See also AAYA 1, 24; BYA 1, 6, 8, 11; CA 85-88; CANR 19, 38, 129; CLR 15; INT CANR-19; JRDA; MAICYA 1, 2; SAAS 2; SATA 18, 55, 97, 110, 158; SATA-Essay 110; WYA; YAW

Peck, Richard Wayne
See Peck, Richard

Peck, Robert Newton 1928- .... **CLC 17**
See also AAYA 3, 43; BYA 1, 6; CA 81-84, 182; CAAE 182; CANR 31, 63, 127; CLR 45; DA; DAC; DAM MST; JRDA; LAIT 3; MAICYA 1, 2; SAAS 1; SATA 21, 62, 111, 156; SATA-Essay 108; WYA; YAW

Peckinpah, David Samuel
See Peckinpah, Sam

Peckinpah, Sam 1925-1984 .... **CLC 20**
See also CA 109; 114; CANR 82

Pedersen, Knut 1859-1952
See Hamsun, Knut
See also CA 104; 119; CANR 63; MTCW 1, 2

Peele, George 1556-1596 .... **DC 27; LC 115**
See also BRW 1; DLB 62, 167; RGEL 2

Peeslake, Gaffer
See Durrell, Lawrence (George)

Peguy, Charles (Pierre)
1873-1914 .... **TCLC 10**
See also CA 107; 193; DLB 258; EWL 3; GFL 1789 to the Present

Peirce, Charles Sanders
1839-1914 .... **TCLC 81**
See also CA 194; DLB 270

Pelecanos, George P. 1957- .... **CLC 236**
See also CA 138; CANR 122, 165; DLB 306

Pelevin, Victor 1962- .... **CLC 238**
See Pelevin, Viktor Olegovich
See also CA 154; CANR 88, 159

Pelevin, Viktor Olegovich
See Pelevin, Victor
See also DLB 285

Pellicer, Carlos 1897(?)-1977 .... **HLCS 2**
See also CA 153; 69-72; DLB 290; EWL 3; HW 1

Pena, Ramon del Valle y
See Valle-Inclan, Ramon (Maria) del

Pendennis, Arthur Esquir
See Thackeray, William Makepeace

Penn, Arthur
See Matthews, (James) Brander

Penn, William 1644-1718 .... **LC 25**
See also DLB 24

PEPECE
See Prado (Calvo), Pedro

Pepys, Samuel 1633-1703 ... **LC 11, 58; WLC 4**
See also BRW 2; CDBLB 1660-1789; DA; DA3; DAB; DAC; DAM MST; DLB 101, 213; NCFS 4; RGEL 2; TEA; WLIT 3

Percy, Thomas 1729-1811 .... **NCLC 95**
See also DLB 104

Percy, Walker 1916-1990 .... **CLC 2, 3, 6, 8, 14, 18, 47, 65**
See also AMWS 3; BPFB 3; CA 1-4R; 131; CANR 1, 23, 64; CN 1, 2, 3, 4; CPW; CSW; DA3; DAM NOV, POP; DLB 2; DLBY 1980, 1990; EWL 3; MAL 5; MTCW 1, 2; MTFW 2005; RGAL 4; TUS

Percy, William Alexander
1885-1942 .... **TCLC 84**
See also CA 163; MTCW 2

Perec, Georges 1936-1982 .... **CLC 56, 116**
See also CA 141; DLB 83, 299; EWL 3; GFL 1789 to the Present; RGHL; RGWL 3

Pereda (y Sanchez de Porrua), Jose Maria de 1833-1906 .... **TCLC 16**
See also CA 117

Pereda y Porrua, Jose Maria de
See Pereda (y Sanchez de Porrua), Jose Maria de

Peregoy, George Weems
See Mencken, H(enry) L(ouis)

Perelman, S(idney) J(oseph)
1904-1979 .. **CLC 3, 5, 9, 15, 23, 44, 49; SSC 32**
See also AITN 1, 2; BPFB 3; CA 73-76; 89-92; CANR 18; DAM DRAM; DLB 11, 44; MTCW 1, 2; MTFW 2005; RGAL 4

Peret, Benjamin 1899-1959 .... **PC 33; TCLC 20**
See also CA 117; 186; GFL 1789 to the Present

Peretz, Isaac Leib
See Peretz, Isaac Loeb
See also CA 201; DLB 333

Peretz, Isaac Loeb 1851(?)-1915 ...... **SSC 26; TCLC 16**
See Peretz, Isaac Leib
See also CA 109

Peretz, Yitzkhok Leibush
See Peretz, Isaac Loeb

Perez Galdos, Benito 1843-1920 ..... **HLCS 2; TCLC 27**
See Galdos, Benito Perez
See also CA 125; 153; EWL 3; HW 1; RGWL 2, 3

Peri Rossi, Cristina 1941- .. **CLC 156; HLCS 2**
See also CA 131; CANR 59, 81; CWW 2; DLB 145, 290; EWL 3; HW 1, 2

Perlata
See Peret, Benjamin

Perloff, Marjorie G(abrielle)
1931- .... **CLC 137**
See also CA 57-60; CANR 7, 22, 49, 104

Perrault, Charles 1628-1703 .... **LC 2, 56**
See also BYA 4; CLR 79, 134; DLB 268; GFL Beginnings to 1789; MAICYA 1, 2; RGWL 2, 3; SATA 25; WCH

Perry, Anne 1938- .... **CLC 126**
See also CA 101; CANR 22, 50, 84, 150; CMW 4; CN 6, 7; CPW; DLB 276

Perry, Brighton
See Sherwood, Robert E(mmet)

Perse, St.-John
See Leger, (Marie-Rene Auguste) Alexis Saint-Leger

4; MAL 5; MBL; MTCW 1, 2; MTFW 2005; NFS 1; PAB; PFS 1, 15, 28; RGAL 4; SATA 96; TUS; WP; YAW

Plato c. 428B.C.-347B.C. .... **CMLC 8, 75, 98; WLCS**
See also AW 1; CDWLB 1; DA; DA3; DAB; DAC; DAM MST; DLB 176; LAIT 1; LATS 1:1; RGWL 2, 3; WLIT 8

Platonov, Andrei
See Klimentov, Andrei Platonovich

Platonov, Andrei Platonovich
See Klimentov, Andrei Platonovich
See also DLB 272

Platonov, Andrey Platonovich
See Klimentov, Andrei Platonovich
See also EWL 3

Platt, Kin 1911- .... **CLC 26**
See also AAYA 11; CA 17-20R; CANR 11; JRDA; SAAS 17; SATA 21, 86; WYA

Plautus c. 254B.C.-c. 184B.C. .... **CMLC 24, 92; DC 6**
See also AW 1; CDWLB 1; DLB 211; RGWL 2, 3; WLIT 8

Plick et Plock
See Simenon, Georges (Jacques Christian)

Plieksans, Janis
See Rainis, Janis

Plimpton, George 1927-2003 .... **CLC 36**
See also AITN 1; AMWS 16; CA 21-24R; 224; CANR 32, 70, 103, 133; DLB 185, 241; MTCW 1, 2; MTFW 2005; SATA 10; SATA-Obit 150

Pliny the Elder c. 23-79 .... **CMLC 23**
See also DLB 211

Pliny the Younger c. 61-c. 112 ...... **CMLC 62**
See also AW 2; DLB 211

Plomer, William Charles Franklin 1903-1973 **CLC 4, 8**
See also AFW; BRWS 11; CA 21-22; CANR 34; CAP 2; CN 1; CP 1, 2; DLB 20, 162, 191, 225; EWL 3; MTCW 1; RGEL 2; RGSF 2; SATA 24

Plotinus 204-270 .... **CMLC 46**
See also CDWLB 1; DLB 176

Plowman, Piers
See Kavanagh, Patrick (Joseph)

Plum, J.
See Wodehouse, P(elham) G(renville)

Plumly, Stanley (Ross) 1939- .... **CLC 33**
See also CA 108; 110; CANR 97; CP 3, 4, 5, 6, 7; DLB 5, 193; INT CA-110

Plumpe, Friedrich Wilhelm
See Murnau, F.W.

Plutarch c. 46-c. 120 .... **CMLC 60**
See also AW 2; CDWLB 1; DLB 176; RGWL 2, 3; TWA; WLIT 8

Po Chu-i 772-846 .... **CMLC 24**

Podhoretz, Norman 1930- .... **CLC 189**
See also AMWS 8; CA 9-12R; CANR 7, 78, 135

Poe, Edgar Allan 1809-1849 ..... **NCLC 1, 16, 55, 78, 94, 97, 117; PC 1, 54; SSC 1, 22, 34, 35, 54, 88, 111; WLC 4**
See also AAYA 14; AMW; AMWC 1; AMWR 1; BPFB 3; BYA 5, 11; CDALB 1640-1865; CMW 4; DA; DA3; DAB; DAC; DAM MST, POET; DLB 3, 59, 73, 74, 248, 254; EXPP; EXPS; GL 3; HGG; LAIT 2; LATS 1:1; LMFS 1; MSW; PAB; PFS 1, 3, 9; RGAL 4; RGSF 2; SATA 23; SCFW 1, 2; SFW 4; SSFS 2, 4, 7, 8, 16; SUFW; TUS; WP; WYA

Poet of Titchfield Street, The
See Pound, Ezra (Weston Loomis)

Poggio Bracciolini, Gian Francesco 1380-1459 .... **LC 125**

Pohl, Frederik 1919- .... **CLC 18; SSC 25**
See also AAYA 24; CA 61-64, 188; CAAE 188; CAAS 1; CANR 11, 37, 81, 140; CN

1, 2, 3, 4, 5, 6; DLB 8; INT CANR-11; MTCW 1, 2; MTFW 2005; SATA 24; SCFW 1, 2; SFW 4

Poirier, Louis
See Gracq, Julien

Poitier, Sidney 1927- .... **CLC 26**
See also AAYA 60; BW 1; CA 117; CANR 94

Pokagon, Simon 1830-1899 .... **NNAL**
See also DAM MULT

Polanski, Roman 1933- .... **CLC 16, 178**
See also CA 77-80

Poliakoff, Stephen 1952- .... **CLC 38**
See also CA 106; CANR 116; CBD; CD 5, 6; DLB 13

Police, The
See Copeland, Stewart (Armstrong); Summers, Andy

Polidori, John William 1795-1821 .... **NCLC 51; SSC 97**
See also DLB 116; HGG

Poliziano, Angelo 1454-1494 .... **LC 120**
See also WLIT 7

Pollitt, Katha 1949- .... **CLC 28, 122**
See also CA 120; 122; CANR 66, 108, 164; MTCW 1, 2; MTFW 2005

Pollock, (Mary) Sharon 1936- .... **CLC 50**
See also CA 141; CANR 132; CD 5; CWD; DAC; DAM DRAM, MST; DFS 3; DLB 60; FW

Pollock, Sharon 1936- .... **DC 20**
See also CD 6

Polo, Marco 1254-1324 .... **CMLC 15**
See also WLIT 7

Polonsky, Abraham (Lincoln) 1910-1999 **CLC 92**
See also CA 104; 187; DLB 26; INT CA-104

Polybius c. 200B.C.-c. 118B.C. ...... **CMLC 17**
See also AW 1; DLB 176; RGWL 2, 3

Pomerance, Bernard 1940- .... **CLC 13**
See also CA 101; CAD; CANR 49, 134; CD 5, 6; DAM DRAM; DFS 9; LAIT 2

Ponge, Francis 1899-1988 .... **CLC 6, 18**
See also CA 85-88; 126; CANR 40, 86; DAM POET; DLBY 2002; EWL 3; GFL 1789 to the Present; RGWL 2, 3

Poniatowska, Elena 1932- . **CLC 140; HLC 2**
See also CA 101; CANR 32, 66, 107, 156; CDWLB 3; CWW 2; DAM MULT; DLB 113; EWL 3; HW 1, 2; LAWS 1; WLIT 1

Pontoppidan, Henrik 1857-1943 .... **TCLC 29**
See also CA 170; DLB 300, 331

Ponty, Maurice Merleau
See Merleau-Ponty, Maurice

Poole, Josephine .... **CLC 17**
See Helyar, Jane Penelope Josephine
See also SAAS 2; SATA 5

Popa, Vasko 1922-1991 . **CLC 19; TCLC 167**
See also CA 112; 148; CDWLB 4; DLB 181; EWL 3; RGWL 2, 3

Pope, Alexander 1688-1744 ...... **LC 3, 58, 60, 64; PC 26; WLC 5**
See also BRW 3; BRWC 1; BRWR 1; CDBLB 1660-1789; DA; DA3; DAB; DAC; DAM MST, POET; DLB 95, 101, 213; EXPP; PAB; PFS 12; RGEL 2; WLIT 3; WP

Popov, Evgenii Anatol'evich
See Popov, Yevgeny
See also DLB 285

Popov, Yevgeny .... **CLC 59**
See Popov, Evgenii Anatol'evich

Poquelin, Jean-Baptiste
See Moliere

Porete, Marguerite (?)-1310 .... **CMLC 73**
See also DLB 208

Porphyry c. 233-c. 305 .... **CMLC 71**

Porter, Connie (Rose) 1959(?)- .... **CLC 70**
See also AAYA 65; BW 2, 3; CA 142; CANR 90, 109; SATA 81, 129

Porter, Gene(va Grace) Stratton ... **TCLC 21**
See Stratton-Porter, Gene(va Grace)
See also BPFB 3; CA 112; CWRI 5; RHW

Porter, Katherine Anne 1890-1980 ... **CLC 1, 3, 7, 10, 13, 15, 27, 101; SSC 4, 31, 43, 108**
See also AAYA 42; AITN 2; AMW; BPFB 3; CA 1-4R; 101; CANR 1, 65; CDALBS; CN 1, 2; DA; DA3; DAB; DAC; DAM MST, NOV; DLB 4, 9, 102; DLBD 12; DLBY 1980; EWL 3; EXPS; LAIT 3; MAL 5; MBL; MTCW 1, 2; MTFW 2005; NFS 14; RGAL 4; RGSF 2; SATA 39; SATA-Obit 23; SSFS 1, 8, 11, 16, 23; TCWW 2; TUS

Porter, Peter (Neville Frederick) 1929- .... **CLC 5, 13, 33**
See also CA 85-88; CP 1, 2, 3, 4, 5, 6, 7; DLB 40, 289; WWE 1

Porter, William Sydney 1862-1910
See Henry, O.
See also CA 104; 131; CDALB 1865-1917; DA; DA3; DAB; DAC; DAM MST; DLB 12, 78, 79; MTCW 1, 2; MTFW 2005; TUS; YABC 2

Portillo (y Pacheco), Jose Lopez
See Lopez Portillo (y Pacheco), Jose

Portillo Trambley, Estela 1927-1998 .. **HLC 2**
See Trambley, Estela Portillo
See also CANR 32; DAM MULT; DLB 209; HW 1

Posey, Alexander (Lawrence) 1873-1908 **NNAL**
See also CA 144; CANR 80; DAM MULT; DLB 175

Posse, Abel .... **CLC 70**
See also CA 252

Post, Melville Davisson 1869-1930 .... **TCLC 39**
See also CA 110; 202; CMW 4

Postman, Neil 1931(?)-2003 .... **CLC 244**
See also CA 102; 221

Potok, Chaim 1929-2002 ... **CLC 2, 7, 14, 26, 112**
See also AAYA 15, 50; AITN 1, 2; BPFB 3; BYA 1; CA 17-20R; 208; CANR 19, 35, 64, 98; CLR 92; CN 4, 5, 6; DA3; DAM NOV; DLB 28, 152; EXPN; INT CANR-19; LAIT 4; MTCW 1, 2; MTFW 2005; NFS 4; RGHL; SATA 33, 106; SATA-Obit 134; TUS; YAW

Potok, Herbert Harold -2002
See Potok, Chaim

Potok, Herman Harold
See Potok, Chaim

Potter, Dennis (Christopher George) 1935-1994 .... **CLC 58, 86, 123**
See also BRWS 10; CA 107; 145; CANR 33, 61; CBD; DLB 233; MTCW 1

Pound, Ezra (Weston Loomis) 1885-1972 **CLC 1, 2, 3, 4, 5, 7, 10, 13, 18, 34, 48, 50, 112; PC 4; WLC 5**
See also AAYA 47; AMW; AMWR 1; CA 5-8R; 37-40R; CANR 40; CDALB 1917-1929; CP 1; DA; DA3; DAB; DAC; DAM MST, POET; DLB 4, 45, 63; DLBD 15; EFS 2; EWL 3; EXPP; LMFS 2; MAL 5; MTCW 1, 2; MTFW 2005; PAB; PFS 2, 8, 16; RGAL 4; TUS; WP

Povod, Reinaldo 1959-1994 .... **CLC 44**
See also CA 136; 146; CANR 83

Powell, Adam Clayton, Jr. 1908-1972 .... **BLC 1:3; CLC 89**
See also BW 1, 3; CA 102; 33-36R; CANR 86; DAM MULT

Powell, Anthony 1905-2000 ... **CLC 1, 3, 7, 9, 10, 31**
See also BRW 7; CA 1-4R; 189; CANR 1, 32, 62, 107; CDBLB 1945-1960; CN 1, 2, 3, 4, 5, 6; DLB 15; EWL 3; MTCW 1, 2; MTFW 2005; RGEL 2; TEA

Powell, Dawn 1896(?)-1965 .... **CLC 66**
See also CA 5-8R; CANR 121; DLBY 1997

Powell, Padgett 1952- .... **CLC 34**
See also CA 126; CANR 63, 101; CSW; DLB 234; DLBY 01; SSFS 25

Powell, (Oval) Talmage 1920-2000
See Queen, Ellery
See also CA 5-8R; CANR 2, 80

Power, Susan 1961- .... **CLC 91**
See also BYA 14; CA 160; CANR 135; NFS 11

Powers, J(ames) F(arl) 1917-1999 ..... **CLC 1, 4, 8, 57; SSC 4**
See also CA 1-4R; 181; CANR 2, 61; CN 1, 2, 3, 4, 5, 6; DLB 130; MTCW 1; RGAL 4; RGSF 2

Powers, John J(ames) 1945-
See Powers, John R.
See also CA 69-72

Powers, John R. .... **CLC 66**
See Powers, John J(ames)

Powers, Richard 1957- .... **CLC 93**
See also AMWS 9; BPFB 3; CA 148; CANR 80; CN 6, 7; MTFW 2005; TCLE 1:2

Powers, Richard S.
See Powers, Richard

Pownall, David 1938- .... **CLC 10**
See also CA 89-92, 180; CAAS 18; CANR 49, 101; CBD; CD 5, 6; CN 4, 5, 6, 7; DLB 14

Powys, John Cowper 1872-1963 ... **CLC 7, 9, 15, 46, 125**
See also CA 85-88; CANR 106; DLB 15, 255; EWL 3; FANT; MTCW 1, 2; MTFW 2005; RGEL 2; SUFW

Powys, T(heodore) F(rancis) 1875-1953
TCLC 9
See also BRWS 8; CA 106; 189; DLB 36, 162; EWL 3; FANT; RGEL 2; SUFW

Pozzo, Modesta
See Fonte, Moderata

Prado (Calvo), Pedro 1886-1952 ... **TCLC 75**
See also CA 131; DLB 283; HW 1; LAW

Prager, Emily 1952- .... **CLC 56**
See also CA 204

Pratchett, Terence David John
See Pratchett, Terry

Pratchett, Terry 1948- .... **CLC 197**
See also AAYA 19, 54; BPFB 3; CA 143; CANR 87, 126, 170; CLR 64; CN 6, 7; CPW; CWRI 5; FANT; MTFW 2005; SATA 82, 139, 185; SFW 4; SUFW 2

Pratolini, Vasco 1913-1991 .... **TCLC 124**
See also CA 211; DLB 177; EWL 3; RGWL 2, 3

Pratt, E(dwin) J(ohn) 1883(?)-1964 . **CLC 19**
See also CA 141; 93-96; CANR 77; DAC; DAM POET; DLB 92; EWL 3; RGEL 2; TWA

Premchand .... **TCLC 21**
See Srivastava, Dhanpat Rai
See also EWL 3

Prescott, William Hickling
1796-1859 .... **NCLC 163**
See also DLB 1, 30, 59, 235

Preseren, France 1800-1849 .... **NCLC 127**
See also CDWLB 4; DLB 147

Preussler, Otfried 1923- .... **CLC 17**
See also CA 77-80; SATA 24

Prevert, Jacques (Henri Marie) 1900-1977
CLC 15
See also CA 77-80; 69-72; CANR 29, 61; DLB 258; EWL 3; GFL 1789 to the Present; IDFW 3, 4; MTCW 1; RGWL 2, 3; SATA-Obit 30

Prevost, (Antoine Francois)
1697-1763 .... **LC 1**
See also DLB 314; EW 4; GFL Beginnings to 1789; RGWL 2, 3

Price, Reynolds 1933- .. **CLC 3, 6, 13, 43, 50, 63, 212; SSC 22**
See also AMWS 6; CA 1-4R; CANR 1, 37, 57, 87, 128; CN 1, 2, 3, 4, 5, 6, 7; CSW; DAM NOV; DLB 2, 218, 278; EWL 3; INT CANR-37; MAL 5; MTFW 2005; NFS 18

Price, Richard 1949- .... **CLC 6, 12**
See also CA 49-52; CANR 3, 147; CN 7; DLBY 1981

Prichard, Katharine Susannah 1883-1969
CLC 46
See also CA 11-12; CANR 33; CAP 1; DLB 260; MTCW 1; RGEL 2; RGSF 2; SATA 66

Priestley, J(ohn) B(oynton)
1894-1984 .... **CLC 2, 5, 9, 34**
See also BRW 7; CA 9-12R; 113; CANR 33; CDBLB 1914-1945; CN 1, 2, 3; DA3; DAM DRAM, NOV; DLB 10, 34, 77, 100, 139; DLBY 1984; EWL 3; MTCW 1, 2; MTFW 2005; RGEL 2; SFW 4

Prince 1958- .... **CLC 35**
See also CA 213

Prince, F(rank) T(empleton)
1912-2003 .... **CLC 22**
See also CA 101; 219; CANR 43, 79; CP 1, 2, 3, 4, 5, 6, 7; DLB 20

Prince Kropotkin
See Kropotkin, Peter (Aleksieevich)

Prior, Matthew 1664-1721 .... **LC 4**
See also DLB 95; RGEL 2

Prishvin, Mikhail 1873-1954 .... **TCLC 75**
See Prishvin, Mikhail Mikhailovich

Prishvin, Mikhail Mikhailovich
See Prishvin, Mikhail
See also DLB 272; EWL 3

Pritchard, William H(arrison)
1932- .... **CLC 34**
See also CA 65-68; CANR 23, 95; DLB 111

Pritchett, V(ictor) S(awdon)
1900-1997 ... **CLC 5, 13, 15, 41; SSC 14**
See also BPFB 3; BRWS 3; CA 61-64; 157; CANR 31, 63; CN 1, 2, 3, 4, 5, 6; DA3; DAM NOV; DLB 15, 139; EWL 3; MTCW 1, 2; MTFW 2005; RGEL 2; RGSF 2; TEA

Private 19022
See Manning, Frederic

Probst, Mark 1925- .... **CLC 59**
See also CA 130

Procaccino, Michael
See Cristofer, Michael

Proclus c. 412-c. 485 .... **CMLC 81**

Prokosch, Frederic 1908-1989 ...... **CLC 4, 48**
See also CA 73-76; 128; CANR 82; CN 1, 2, 3, 4; CP 1, 2, 3, 4; DLB 48; MTCW 2

Propertius, Sextus c. 50B.C.-c.
16B.C. .... **CMLC 32**
See also AW 2; CDWLB 1; DLB 211; RGWL 2, 3; WLIT 8

Prophet, The
See Dreiser, Theodore

Prose, Francine 1947- .... **CLC 45, 231**
See also AMWS 16; CA 109; 112; CANR 46, 95, 132, 175; DLB 234; MTFW 2005; SATA 101, 149

Protagoras c. 490B.C.-420B.C. ...... **CMLC 85**
See also DLB 176

Proudhon
See Cunha, Euclides (Rodrigues Pimenta) da

Proulx, Annie
See Proulx, E. Annie

Proulx, E. Annie 1935- ...... **CLC 81, 158, 250**
See also AMWS 7; BPFB 3; CA 145; CANR 65, 110; CN 6, 7; CPW 1; DA3; DAM POP; DLB 335; MAL 5; MTCW 2; MTFW 2005; SSFS 18, 23

Proulx, Edna Annie
See Proulx, E. Annie

**Proust, (Valentin-Louis-George-Eugene)
Marcel** 1871-1922 ..... **SSC 75; TCLC 7, 13, 33; WLC 5**
See also AAYA 58; BPFB 3; CA 104; 120; CANR 110; DA; DA3; DAB; DAC; DAM MST, NOV; DLB 65; EW 8; EWL 3; GFL 1789 to the Present; MTCW 1, 2; MTFW 2005; RGWL 2, 3; TWA

Prowler, Harley
See Masters, Edgar Lee

Prudentius, Aurelius Clemens 348-c. 405
CMLC 78
See also EW 1; RGWL 2, 3

Prudhomme, Rene Francois Armand
1839-1907
See Sully Prudhomme, Rene-Francois-Armand
See also CA 170

Prus, Boleslaw 1845-1912 .... **TCLC 48**
See also RGWL 2, 3

Prynne, William 1600-1669 .... **LC 148**

Prynne, Xavier
See Hardwick, Elizabeth

Pryor, Aaron Richard
See Pryor, Richard

Pryor, Richard 1940-2005 .... **CLC 26**
See also CA 122; 152; 246

Pryor, Richard Franklin Lenox Thomas
See Pryor, Richard

Przybyszewski, Stanislaw
1868-1927 .... **TCLC 36**
See also CA 160; DLB 66; EWL 3

Pseudo-Dionysius the Areopagite fl. c. 5th
cent. - .... **CMLC 89**
See also DLB 115

Pteleon
See Grieve, C(hristopher) M(urray)
See also DAM POET

Puckett, Lute
See Masters, Edgar Lee

Puig, Manuel 1932-1990 .... **CLC 3, 5, 10, 28, 65, 133; HLC 2**
See also BPFB 3; CA 45-48; CANR 2, 32, 63; CDWLB 3; DA3; DAM MULT; DLB 113; DNFS 1; EWL 3; GLL 1; HW 1, 2; LAW; MTCW 1, 2; MTFW 2005; RGWL 2, 3; TWA; WLIT 1

Pulitzer, Joseph 1847-1911 .... **TCLC 76**
See also CA 114; DLB 23

Pullman, Philip 1946- .... **CLC 245**
See also AAYA 15, 41; BRWS 13; BYA 8, 13; CA 127; CANR 50, 77, 105, 134; CLR 20, 62, 84; JRDA; MAICYA 1, 2; MAICYAS 1; MTFW 2005; SAAS 17; SATA 65, 103, 150; SUFW 2; WYAS 1; YAW

Purchas, Samuel 1577(?)-1626 .... **LC 70**
See also DLB 151

Purdy, A(lfred) W(ellington)
1918-2000 .... **CLC 3, 6, 14, 50**
See also CA 81-84; 189; CAAS 17; CANR 42, 66; CP 1, 2, 3, 4, 5, 6, 7; DAC; DAM MST, POET; DLB 88; PFS 5; RGEL 2

Purdy, James (Amos) 1923- .... **CLC 2, 4, 10, 28, 52**
See also AMWS 7; CA 33-36R; CAAS 1; CANR 19, 51, 132; CN 1, 2, 3, 4, 5, 6, 7; DLB 2, 218; EWL 3; INT CANR-19; MAL 5; MTCW 1; RGAL 4

Pure, Simon
See Swinnerton, Frank Arthur

Pushkin, Aleksandr Sergeevich
See Pushkin, Alexander (Sergeyevich)
See also DLB 205

Pushkin, Alexander (Sergeyevich) 1799-1837 **NCLC 3, 27, 83; PC 10; SSC 27, 55, 99; WLC 5**
See Pushkin, Aleksandr Sergeevich
See also DA; DA3; DAB; DAC; DAM DRAM, MST, POET; EW 5; EXPS; PFS 28; RGSF 2; RGWL 2, 3; SATA 61; SSFS 9; TWA

P'u Sung-ling 1640-1715 .... **LC 49; SSC 31**

Putnam, Arthur Lee
See Alger, Horatio, Jr.

Puttenham, George 1529(?)-1590 ...... **LC 116**
See also DLB 281

Puzo, Mario 1920-1999 .... **CLC 1, 2, 6, 36, 107**
See also BPFB 3; CA 65-68; 185; CANR 4, 42, 65, 99, 131; CN 1, 2, 3, 4, 5, 6; CPW; DA3; DAM NOV, POP; DLB 6; MTCW 1, 2; MTFW 2005; NFS 16; RGAL 4

Pygge, Edward
See Barnes, Julian

Pyle, Ernest Taylor 1900-1945
See Pyle, Ernie
See also CA 115; 160

Pyle, Ernie .... **TCLC 75**
See Pyle, Ernest Taylor
See also DLB 29; MTCW 2

Pyle, Howard 1853-1911 .... **TCLC 81**
See also AAYA 57; BYA 2, 4; CA 109; 137; CLR 22, 117; DLB 42, 188; DLBD 13; LAIT 1; MAICYA 1, 2; SATA 16, 100; WCH; YAW

Pym, Barbara (Mary Crampton) 1913-1980 **CLC 13, 19, 37, 111**
See also BPFB 3; BRWS 2; CA 13-14; 97-100; CANR 13, 34; CAP 1; DLB 14, 207; DLBY 1987; EWL 3; MTCW 1, 2; MTFW 2005; RGEL 2; TEA

Pynchon, Thomas 1937- .. **CLC 2, 3, 6, 9, 11, 18, 33, 62, 72, 123, 192, 213; SSC 14, 84; WLC 5**
See also AMWS 2; BEST 90:2; BPFB 3; CA 17-20R; CANR 22, 46, 73, 142; CN 1, 2, 3, 4, 5, 6, 7; CPW 1; DA; DA3; DAB; DAC; DAM MST, NOV, POP; DLB 2, 173; EWL 3; MAL 5; MTCW 1, 2; MTFW 2005; NFS 23; RGAL 4; SFW 4; TCLE 1:2; TUS

Pythagoras c. 582B.C.-c. 507B.C. . **CMLC 22**
See also DLB 176

Q
See Quiller-Couch, Sir Arthur (Thomas)

Qian, Chongzhu
See Ch'ien, Chung-shu

Qian, Sima 145B.C.-c. 89B.C. .... **CMLC 72**

Qian Zhongshu
See Ch'ien, Chung-shu
See also CWW 2; DLB 328

Qroll
See Dagerman, Stig (Halvard)

Quarles, Francis 1592-1644 .... **LC 117**
See also DLB 126; RGEL 2

Quarrington, Paul 1953- .... **CLC 65**
See also CA 129; CANR 62, 95

Quarrington, Paul Lewis
See Quarrington, Paul

Quasimodo, Salvatore 1901-1968 .... **CLC 10; PC 47**
See also CA 13-16; 25-28R; CAP 1; DLB 114, 332; EW 12; EWL 3; MTCW 1; RGWL 2, 3

Quatermass, Martin
See Carpenter, John (Howard)

Quay, Stephen 1947- .... **CLC 95**
See also CA 189

Quay, Timothy 1947- .... **CLC 95**
See also CA 189

Queen, Ellery .... **CLC 3, 11**
See Dannay, Frederic; Davidson, Avram (James); Deming, Richard; Fairman, Paul W.; Flora, Fletcher; Hoch, Edward D.; Holding, James (Clark Carlisle, Jr.); Kane, Henry; Lee, Manfred B.; Marlowe, Stephen; Powell, (Oval) Talmage; Sheldon, Walter J(ames); Sturgeon, Theodore (Hamilton); Tracy, Don(ald Fiske); Vance, Jack
See also BPFB 3; CMW 4; MSW; RGAL 4

Queneau, Raymond 1903-1976 ..... **CLC 2, 5, 10, 42**
See also CA 77-80; 69-72; CANR 32; DLB 72, 258; EW 12; EWL 3; GFL 1789 to the Present; MTCW 1, 2; RGWL 2, 3

Quevedo, Francisco de 1580-1645 .... **LC 23**

Quiller-Couch, Sir Arthur (Thomas) 1863-1944 .... **TCLC 53**
See also CA 118; 166; DLB 135, 153, 190; HGG; RGEL 2; SUFW 1

Quin, Ann 1936-1973 .... **CLC 6**
See also CA 9-12R; 45-48; CANR 148; CN 1; DLB 14, 231

Quin, Ann Marie
See Quin, Ann

Quincey, Thomas de
See De Quincey, Thomas

Quindlen, Anna 1953- .... **CLC 191**
See also AAYA 35; AMWS 17; CA 138; CANR 73, 126; DA3; DLB 292; MTCW 2; MTFW 2005

Quinn, Martin
See Smith, Martin Cruz

Quinn, Peter 1947- .... **CLC 91**
See also CA 197; CANR 147

Quinn, Peter A.
See Quinn, Peter

Quinn, Simon
See Smith, Martin Cruz

Quintana, Leroy V. 1944- ...... **HLC 2; PC 36**
See also CA 131; CANR 65, 139; DAM MULT; DLB 82; HW 1, 2

Quintilian c. 40-c. 100 .... **CMLC 77**
See also AW 2; DLB 211; RGWL 2, 3

Quintillian 0035-0100 .... **CMLC 77**

Quiroga, Horacio (Sylvestre) 1878-1937 ... **HLC 2; SSC 89; TCLC 20**
See also CA 117; 131; DAM MULT; EWL 3; HW 1; LAW; MTCW 1; RGSF 2; WLIT 1

Quoirez, Francoise 1935-2004 .... **CLC 9**
See Sagan, Francoise
See also CA 49-52; 231; CANR 6, 39, 73; MTCW 1, 2; MTFW 2005; TWA

Raabe, Wilhelm (Karl) 1831-1910 . **TCLC 45**
See also CA 167; DLB 129

Rabe, David (William) 1940- .. **CLC 4, 8, 33, 200; DC 16**
See also CA 85-88; CABS 3; CAD; CANR 59, 129; CD 5, 6; DAM DRAM; DFS 3, 8, 13; DLB 7, 228; EWL 3; MAL 5

Rabelais, Francois 1494-1553 .... **LC 5, 60; WLC 5**
See also DA; DAB; DAC; DAM MST; DLB 327; EW 2; GFL Beginnings to 1789; LMFS 1; RGWL 2, 3; TWA

Rabi'a al-'Adawiyya c. 717-c. 801 .... **CMLC 83**
See also DLB 311

Rabinovitch, Sholem 1859-1916
See Sholom Aleichem
See also CA 104

Rabinyan, Dorit 1972- .... **CLC 119**
See also CA 170; CANR 147

Rachilde
See Vallette, Marguerite Eymery; Vallette, Marguerite Eymery
See also EWL 3

Racine, Jean 1639-1699 .... **LC 28, 113**
See also DA3; DAB; DAM MST; DLB 268; EW 3; GFL Beginnings to 1789; LMFS 1; RGWL 2, 3; TWA

Radcliffe, Ann (Ward) 1764-1823 ... **NCLC 6, 55, 106**
See also DLB 39, 178; GL 3; HGG; LMFS 1; RGEL 2; SUFW; WLIT 3

Radclyffe-Hall, Marguerite
See Hall, Radclyffe

Radiguet, Raymond 1903-1923 ...... **TCLC 29**
See also CA 162; DLB 65; EWL 3; GFL 1789 to the Present; RGWL 2, 3

Radishchev, Aleksandr Nikolaevich 1749-1802 .... **NCLC 190**
See also DLB 150

Radishchev, Alexander
See Radishchev, Aleksandr Nikolaevich

Radnoti, Miklos 1909-1944 .... **TCLC 16**
See also CA 118; 212; CDWLB 4; DLB 215; EWL 3; RGHL; RGWL 2, 3

Rado, James 1939- .... **CLC 17**
See also CA 105

Radvanyi, Netty 1900-1983
See Seghers, Anna
See also CA 85-88; 110; CANR 82

Rae, Ben
See Griffiths, Trevor

Raeburn, John (Hay) 1941- .... **CLC 34**
See also CA 57-60

Ragni, Gerome 1942-1991 .... **CLC 17**
See also CA 105; 134

Rahv, Philip .... **CLC 24**
See Greenberg, Ivan
See also DLB 137; MAL 5

Raimund, Ferdinand Jakob 1790-1836 **NCLC 69**
See also DLB 90

Raine, Craig 1944- .... **CLC 32, 103**
See also BRWS 13; CA 108; CANR 29, 51, 103, 171; CP 3, 4, 5, 6, 7; DLB 40; PFS 7

Raine, Craig Anthony
See Raine, Craig

Raine, Kathleen (Jessie) 1908-2003 .. **CLC 7, 45**
See also CA 85-88; 218; CANR 46, 109; CP 1, 2, 3, 4, 5, 6, 7; DLB 20; EWL 3; MTCW 1; RGEL 2

Rainis, Janis 1865-1929 .... **TCLC 29**
See also CA 170; CDWLB 4; DLB 220; EWL 3

Rakosi, Carl .... **CLC 47**
See Rawley, Callman
See also CA 228; CAAS 5; CP 1, 2, 3, 4, 5, 6, 7; DLB 193

Ralegh, Sir Walter
See Raleigh, Sir Walter
See also BRW 1; RGEL 2; WP

Raleigh, Richard
See Lovecraft, H. P.

Raleigh, Sir Walter 1554(?)-1618 .... **LC 31, 39; PC 31**
See Ralegh, Sir Walter
See also CDBLB Before 1660; DLB 172; EXPP; PFS 14; TEA

Rallentando, H. P.
See Sayers, Dorothy L(eigh)

Roa Bastos, Augusto 1917-2005 ...... **CLC 45;**
  HLC 2
  See also CA 131; 238; CWW 2; DAM
  MULT; DLB 113; EWL 3; HW 1; LAW;
  RGSF 2; WLIT 1
Roa Bastos, Augusto Jose Antonio
  See Roa Bastos, Augusto
Robbe-Grillet, Alain 1922-2008 ..... **CLC 1, 2,**
  4, 6, 8, 10, 14, 43, 128
  See also BPFB 3; CA 9-12R; 269; CANR
  33, 65, 115; CWW 2; DLB 83; EW 13;
  EWL 3; GFL 1789 to the Present; IDFW
  3, 4; MTCW 1, 2; MTFW 2005; RGWL
  2, 3; SSFS 15
Robbins, Harold 1916-1997 .... **CLC 5**
  See also BPFB 3; CA 73-76; 162; CANR
  26, 54, 112, 156; DA3; DAM NOV;
  MTCW 1, 2
Robbins, Thomas Eugene 1936-
  See Robbins, Tom
  See also CA 81-84; CANR 29, 59, 95, 139;
  CN 7; CPW; CSW; DA3; DAM NOV,
  POP; MTCW 1, 2; MTFW 2005
Robbins, Tom .... **CLC 9, 32, 64**
  See Robbins, Thomas Eugene
  See also AAYA 32; AMWS 10; BEST 90:3;
  BPFB 3; CN 3, 4, 5, 6, 7; DLBY 1980
Robbins, Trina 1938- .... **CLC 21**
  See also AAYA 61; CA 128; CANR 152
Robert de Boron fl. 12th cent. - .... **CMLC 94**
Roberts, Charles G(eorge) D(ouglas)
  1860-1943 .... **SSC 91; TCLC 8**
  See also CA 105; 188; CLR 33; CWRI 5;
  DLB 92; RGEL 2; RGSF 2; SATA 88;
  SATA-Brief 29
Roberts, Elizabeth Madox
  1886-1941 .... **TCLC 68**
  See also CA 111; 166; CLR 100; CWRI 5;
  DLB 9, 54, 102; RGAL 4; RHW; SATA
  33; SATA-Brief 27; TCWW 2; WCH
Roberts, Kate 1891-1985 .... **CLC 15**
  See also CA 107; 116; DLB 319
Roberts, Keith (John Kingston) 1935-2000
  CLC 14
  See also BRWS 10; CA 25-28R; CANR 46;
  DLB 261; SFW 4
Roberts, Kenneth (Lewis)
  1885-1957 .... **TCLC 23**
  See also CA 109; 199; DLB 9; MAL 5;
  RGAL 4; RHW
Roberts, Michele 1949- .... **CLC 48, 178**
  See also CA 115; CANR 58, 120, 164; CN
  6, 7; DLB 231; FW
Roberts, Michele Brigitte
  See Roberts, Michele
Robertson, Ellis
  See Ellison, Harlan; Silverberg, Robert
Robertson, Thomas William 1829-1871
  NCLC 35
  See Robertson, Tom
  See also DAM DRAM
Robertson, Tom
  See Robertson, Thomas William
  See also RGEL 2
Robeson, Kenneth
  See Dent, Lester
Robinson, Edwin Arlington
  1869-1935 .... **PC 1, 35; TCLC 5, 101**
  See also AAYA 72; AMW; CA 104; 133;
  CDALB 1865-1917; DA; DAC; DAM
  MST, POET; DLB 54; EWL 3; EXPP;
  MAL 5; MTCW 1, 2; MTFW 2005; PAB;
  PFS 4; RGAL 4; WP
Robinson, Henry Crabb
  1775-1867 .... **NCLC 15**
  See also DLB 107
Robinson, Jill 1936- .... **CLC 10**
  See also CA 102; CANR 120; INT CA-102

Robinson, Kim Stanley 1952- ... **CLC 34, 248**
  See also AAYA 26; CA 126; CANR 113,
  139, 173; CN 6, 7; MTFW 2005; SATA
  109; SCFW 2; SFW 4
Robinson, Lloyd
  See Silverberg, Robert
Robinson, Marilynne 1944- ...... **CLC 25, 180**
  See also AAYA 69; CA 116; CANR 80, 140;
  CN 4, 5, 6, 7; DLB 206; MTFW 2005;
  NFS 24
Robinson, Mary 1758-1800 .... **NCLC 142**
  See also BRWS 13; DLB 158; FW
Robinson, Smokey .... **CLC 21**
  See Robinson, William, Jr.
Robinson, William, Jr. 1940-
  See Robinson, Smokey
  See also CA 116
Robison, Mary 1949- .... **CLC 42, 98**
  See also CA 113; 116; CANR 87; CN 4, 5,
  6, 7; DLB 130; INT CA-116; RGSF 2
Roches, Catherine des 1542-1587 ...... **LC 117**
  See also DLB 327
Rochester
  See Wilmot, John
  See also RGEL 2
Rod, Edouard 1857-1910 .... **TCLC 52**
Roddenberry, Eugene Wesley 1921-1991
  See Roddenberry, Gene
  See also CA 110; 135; CANR 37; SATA 45;
  SATA-Obit 69
Roddenberry, Gene .... **CLC 17**
  See Roddenberry, Eugene Wesley
  See also AAYA 5; SATA-Obit 69
Rodgers, Mary 1931- .... **CLC 12**
  See also BYA 5; CA 49-52; CANR 8, 55,
  90; CLR 20; CWRI 5; INT CANR-8;
  JRDA; MAICYA 1, 2; SATA 8, 130
Rodgers, W(illiam) R(obert)
  1909-1969 .... **CLC 7**
  See also CA 85-88; DLB 20; RGEL 2
Rodman, Eric
  See Silverberg, Robert
Rodman, Howard 1920(?)-1985 .... **CLC 65**
  See also CA 118
Rodman, Maia
  See Wojciechowska, Maia (Teresa)
Rodo, Jose Enrique 1871(?)-1917 .... **HLCS 2**
  See also CA 178; EWL 3; HW 2; LAW
Rodolph, Utto
  See Ouologuem, Yambo
Rodriguez, Claudio 1934-1999 .... **CLC 10**
  See also CA 188; DLB 134
Rodriguez, Richard 1944- .... **CLC 155; HLC**
  2
  See also AMWS 14; CA 110; CANR 66,
  116; DAM MULT; DLB 82, 256; HW 1,
  2; LAIT 5; LLW; MTFW 2005; NCFS 3;
  WLIT 1
Roethke, Theodore 1908-1963 ... **CLC 1, 3, 8,**
  11, 19, 46, 101; PC 15
  See also AMW; CA 81-84; CABS 2;
  CDALB 1941-1968; DA3; DAM POET;
  DLB 5, 206; EWL 3; EXPP; MAL 5;
  MTCW 1, 2; PAB; PFS 3; RGAL 4; WP
Roethke, Theodore Huebner
  See Roethke, Theodore
Rogers, Carl R(ansom)
  1902-1987 .... **TCLC 125**
  See also CA 1-4R; 121; CANR 1, 18;
  MTCW 1
Rogers, Samuel 1763-1855 .... **NCLC 69**
  See also DLB 93; RGEL 2
Rogers, Thomas 1927-2007 .... **CLC 57**
  See also CA 89-92; 259; CANR 163; INT
  CA-89-92
Rogers, Thomas Hunton
  See Rogers, Thomas

Rogers, Will(iam Penn Adair) 1879-1935
  NNAL; TCLC 8, 71
  See also CA 105; 144; DA3; DAM MULT;
  DLB 11; MTCW 2
Rogin, Gilbert 1929- .... **CLC 18**
  See also CA 65-68; CANR 15
Rohan, Koda
  See Koda Shigeyuki
Rohlfs, Anna Katharine Green
  See Green, Anna Katharine
Rohmer, Eric .... **CLC 16**
  See Scherer, Jean-Marie Maurice
Rohmer, Sax .... **TCLC 28**
  See Ward, Arthur Henry Sarsfield
  See also DLB 70; MSW; SUFW
Roiphe, Anne 1935- .... **CLC 3, 9**
  See also CA 89-92; CANR 45, 73, 138, 170;
  DLBY 1980; INT CA-89-92
Roiphe, Anne Richardson
  See Roiphe, Anne
Rojas, Fernando de 1475-1541 ... **HLCS 1, 2;**
  LC 23
  See also DLB 286; RGWL 2, 3
Rojas, Gonzalo 1917- .... **HLCS 2**
  See also CA 178; HW 2; LAWS 1
Roland (de la Platiere), Marie-Jeanne
  1754-1793 .... **LC 98**
  See also DLB 314
Rolfe, Frederick (William Serafino Austin
  Lewis Mary) 1860-1913 .... **TCLC 12**
  See Al Siddik
  See also CA 107; 210; DLB 34, 156; RGEL
  2
Rolland, Romain 1866-1944 .... **TCLC 23**
  See also CA 118; 197; DLB 65, 284, 332;
  EWL 3; GFL 1789 to the Present; RGWL
  2, 3
Rolle, Richard c. 1300-c. 1349 ...... **CMLC 21**
  See also DLB 146; LMFS 1; RGEL 2
Rolvaag, O.E.
  See Rolvaag, O.E.
Rolvaag, O.E. 1876-1931 .... **TCLC 17, 207**
  See also AAYA 75; CA 117; 171; DLB 9,
  212; MAL 5; NFS 5; RGAL 4; TCWW
  1,2
Romain Arnaud, Saint
  See Aragon, Louis
Romains, Jules 1885-1972 .... **CLC 7**
  See also CA 85-88; CANR 34; DLB 65,
  321; EWL 3; GFL 1789 to the Present;
  MTCW 1
Romero, Jose Ruben 1890-1952 .... **TCLC 14**
  See also CA 114; 131; EWL 3; HW 1; LAW
Ronsard, Pierre de 1524-1585 . **LC 6, 54; PC**
  11
  See also DLB 327; EW 2; GFL Beginnings
  to 1789; RGWL 2, 3; TWA
Rooke, Leon 1934- .... **CLC 25, 34**
  See also CA 25-28R; CANR 23, 53; CCA
  1; CPW; DAM POP
Roosevelt, Franklin Delano
  1882-1945 .... **TCLC 93**
  See also CA 116; 173; LAIT 3
Roosevelt, Theodore 1858-1919 ..... **TCLC 69**
  See also CA 115; 170; DLB 47, 186, 275
Roper, Margaret c. 1505-1544 .... **LC 147**
Roper, William 1498-1578 .... **LC 10**
Roquelaure, A. N.
  See Rice, Anne
Rosa, Joao Guimaraes 1908-1967 ... **CLC 23;**
  HLCS 1
  See Guimaraes Rosa, Joao
  See also CA 89-92; DLB 113, 307; EWL 3;
  WLIT 1
Rose, Wendy 1948- . **CLC 85; NNAL; PC 13**
  See also CA 53-56; CANR 5, 51; CWP;
  DAM MULT; DLB 175; PFS 13; RGAL
  4; SATA 12

Saltykov, Mikhail Evgrafovich 1826-1889
NCLC 16
See also DLB 238:

Saltykov-Shchedrin, N.
See Saltykov, Mikhail Evgrafovich

Samarakis, Andonis
See Samarakis, Antonis
See also EWL 3

Samarakis, Antonis 1919-2003 .... **CLC 5**
See Samarakis, Andonis
See also CA 25-28R; 224; CAAS 16; CANR
36

Sanchez, Florencio 1875-1910 .... **TCLC 37**
See also CA 153; DLB 305; EWL 3; HW 1;
LAW

Sanchez, Luis Rafael 1936- .... **CLC 23**
See also CA 128; DLB 305; EWL 3; HW 1;
WLIT 1

Sanchez, Sonia 1934- . **BLC 1:3, 2:3; CLC 5,
116, 215; PC 9**
See also BW 2, 3; CA 33-36R; CANR 24,
49, 74, 115; CLR 18; CP 2, 3, 4, 5, 6, 7;
CSW; CWP; DA3; DAM MULT; DLB 41;
DLBD 8; EWL 3; MAICYA 1, 2; MAL 5;
MTCW 1, 2; MTFW 2005; PFS 26; SATA
22, 136; WP

Sancho, Ignatius 1729-1780 .... **LC 84**

Sand, George 1804-1876 .... **DC 29; NCLC 2,
42, 57, 174; WLC 5**
See also DA; DA3; DAB; DAC; DAM
MST, NOV; DLB 119, 192; EW 6; FL 1:3;
FW; GFL 1789 to the Present; RGWL 2,
3; TWA

Sandburg, Carl (August) 1878-1967 . **CLC 1,
4, 10, 15, 35; PC 2, 41; WLC 5**
See also AAYA 24; AMW; BYA 1, 3; CA
5-8R; 25-28R; CANR 35; CDALB 1865-
1917; CLR 67; DA; DA3; DAB; DAC;
DAM MST, POET; DLB 17, 54, 284;
EWL 3; EXPP; LAIT 2; MAICYA 1, 2;
MAL 5; MTCW 1, 2; MTFW 2005; PAB;
PFS 3, 6, 12; RGAL 4; SATA 8; TUS;
WCH; WP; WYA

Sandburg, Charles
See Sandburg, Carl (August)

Sandburg, Charles A.
See Sandburg, Carl (August)

Sanders, (James) Ed(ward) 1939- .... **CLC 53**
See Sanders, Edward
See also BG 1:3; CA 13-16R; CAAS 21;
CANR 13, 44, 78; CP 1, 2, 3, 4, 5, 6, 7;
DAM POET; DLB 16, 244

Sanders, Edward
See Sanders, (James) Ed(ward)
See also DLB 244

Sanders, Lawrence 1920-1998 .... **CLC 41**
See also BEST 89:4; BPFB 3; CA 81-84;
165; CANR 33, 62; CMW 4; CPW; DA3;
DAM POP; MTCW 1

Sanders, Noah
See Blount, Roy, Jr.

Sanders, Winston P.
See Anderson, Poul

Sandoz, Mari(e Susette) 1900-1966 .. **CLC 28**
See also CA 1-4R; 25-28R; CANR 17, 64;
DLB 9, 212; LAIT 2; MTCW 1, 2; SATA
5; TCWW 1, 2

Sandys, George 1578-1644 .... **LC 80**
See also DLB 24, 121

Saner, Reg(inald Anthony) 1931- .... **CLC 9**
See also CA 65-68; CP 3, 4, 5, 6, 7

Sankara 788-820 .... **CMLC 32**

Sannazaro, Jacopo 1456(?)-1530 .... **LC 8**
See also RGWL 2, 3; WLIT 7

Sansom, William 1912-1976 . **CLC 2, 6; SSC
21**
See also CA 5-8R; 65-68; CANR 42; CN 1,
2; DAM NOV; DLB 139; EWL 3; MTCW
1; RGEL 2; RGSF 2

Santayana, George 1863-1952 .... **TCLC 40**
See also AMW; CA 115; 194; DLB 54, 71,
246, 270; DLBD 13; EWL 3; MAL 5;
RGAL 4; TUS

Santiago, Danny .... **CLC 33**
See James, Daniel (Lewis)
See also DLB 122

**Santillana, Inigo Lopez de Mendoza,
Marques de** 1398-1458 .... **LC 111**
See also DLB 286

Santmyer, Helen Hooven
1895-1986 .... **CLC 33; TCLC 133**
See also CA 1-4R; 118; CANR 15, 33;
DLBY 1984; MTCW 1; RHW

Santoka, Taneda 1882-1940 .... **TCLC 72**

Santos, Bienvenido N(uqui)
1911-1996 ... **AAL; CLC 22; TCLC 156**
See also CA 101; 151; CANR 19, 46; CP 1;
DAM MULT; DLB 312; EWL; RGAL 4;
SSFS 19

Sapir, Edward 1884-1939 .... **TCLC 108**
See also CA 211; DLB 92

Sapper .... **TCLC 44**
See McNeile, Herman Cyril

Sapphire 1950- .... **CLC 99**
See also CA 262

Sapphire, Brenda
See Sapphire

Sappho fl. 6th cent. B.C.- ... **CMLC 3, 67; PC
5**
See also CDWLB 1; DA3; DAM POET;
DLB 176; FL 1:1; PFS 20; RGWL 2, 3;
WLIT 8; WP

Saramago, Jose 1922- ..... **CLC 119; HLCS 1**
See also CA 153; CANR 96, 164; CWW 2;
DLB 287, 332; EWL 3; LATS 1:2; NFS
27; SSFS 23

Sarduy, Severo 1937-1993 .... **CLC 6, 97;
HLCS 2; TCLC 167**
See also CA 89-92; 142; CANR 58, 81;
CWW 2; DLB 113; EWL 3; HW 1, 2;
LAW

Sargeson, Frank 1903-1982 ..... **CLC 31; SSC
99**
See also CA 25-28R; 106; CANR 38, 79;
CN 1, 2, 3; EWL 3; GLL 2; RGEL 2;
RGSF 2; SSFS 20

Sarmiento, Domingo Faustino 1811-1888
HLCS 2; NCLC 123
See also LAW; WLIT 1

Sarmiento, Felix Ruben Garcia
See Dario, Ruben

Saro-Wiwa, Ken(ule Beeson)
1941-1995 .... **CLC 114; TCLC 200**
See also BW 2; CA 142; 150; CANR 60;
DLB 157

Saroyan, William 1908-1981 ... **CLC 1, 8, 10,
29, 34, 56; DC 28; SSC 21; TCLC 137;
WLC 5**
See also AAYA 66; CA 5-8R; 103; CAD;
CANR 30; CDALBS; CN 1, 2; DA; DA3;
DAB; DAC; DAM DRAM, MST, NOV;
DFS 17; DLB 7, 9, 86; DLBY 1981; EWL
3; LAIT 4; MAL 5; MTCW 1, 2; MTFW
2005; RGAL 4; RGSF 2; SATA 23; SATA-
Obit 24; SSFS 14; TUS

Sarraute, Nathalie 1900-1999 .... **CLC 1, 2, 4,
8, 10, 31, 80; TCLC 145**
See also BPFB 3; CA 9-12R; 187; CANR
23, 66, 134; CWW 2; DLB 83, 321; EW
12; EWL 3; GFL 1789 to the Present;
MTCW 1, 2; MTFW 2005; RGWL 2, 3

Sarton, May 1912-1995 ... **CLC 4, 14, 49, 91;
PC 39; TCLC 120**
See also AMWS 8; CA 1-4R; 149; CANR
1, 34, 55, 116; CN 1, 2, 3, 4, 5, 6; CP 1,
2, 3, 4, 5, 6; DAM POET; DLB 48; DLBY
1981; EWL 3; FW; INT CANR-34; MAL
5; MTCW 1, 2; MTFW 2005; RGAL 4;
SATA 36; SATA-Obit 86; TUS

Sartre, Jean-Paul 1905-1980 . **CLC 1, 4, 7, 9,
13, 18, 24, 44, 50, 52; DC 3; SSC 32;
WLC 5**
See also AAYA 62; CA 9-12R; 97-100;
CANR 21; DA; DA3; DAB; DAC; DAM
DRAM, MST, NOV; DFS 5; DLB 72,
296, 321, 332; EW 12; EWL 3; GFL 1789
to the Present; LMFS 2; MTCW 1, 2;
MTFW 2005; NFS 21; RGHL; RGSF 2;
RGWL 2, 3; SSFS 9; TWA

Sassoon, Siegfried (Lorraine)
1886-1967 .... **CLC 36, 130; PC 12**
See also BRW 6; CA 104; 25-28R; CANR
36; DAB; DAM MST, NOV, POET; DLB
20, 191; DLBD 18; EWL 3; MTCW 1, 2;
MTFW 2005; PAB; PFS 28; RGEL 2;
TEA

Satterfield, Charles
See Pohl, Frederik

Satyremont
See Peret, Benjamin

Saul, John (W. III) 1942- .... **CLC 46**
See also AAYA 10, 62; BEST 90:4; CA 81-
84; CANR 16, 40, 81; CPW; DAM NOV,
POP; HGG; SATA 98

Saunders, Caleb
See Heinlein, Robert A.

Saura (Atares), Carlos 1932-1998 .... **CLC 20**
See also CA 114; 131; CANR 79; HW 1

Sauser, Frederic Louis
See Sauser-Hall, Frederic

Sauser-Hall, Frederic 1887-1961 ...... **CLC 18**
See Cendrars, Blaise
See also CA 102; 93-96; CANR 36, 62;
MTCW 1

Saussure, Ferdinand de
1857-1913 .... **TCLC 49**
See also DLB 242

Savage, Catharine
See Brosman, Catharine Savage

Savage, Richard 1697(?)-1743 .... **LC 96**
See also DLB 95; RGEL 2

Savage, Thomas 1915-2003 .... **CLC 40**
See also CA 126; 132; 218; CAAS 15; CN
6, 7; INT CA-132; SATA-Obit 147;
TCWW 2

Savan, Glenn 1953-2003 .... **CLC 50**
See also CA 225

Sax, Robert
See Johnson, Robert

Saxo Grammaticus c. 1150-c.
1222 .... **CMLC 58**

Saxton, Robert
See Johnson, Robert

Sayers, Dorothy L(eigh) 1893-1957 . **SSC 71;
TCLC 2, 15**
See also BPFB 3; BRWS 3; CA 104; 119;
CANR 60; CDBLB 1914-1945; CMW 4;
DAM POP; DLB 10, 36, 77, 100; MSW;
MTCW 1, 2; MTFW 2005; RGEL 2;
SSFS 12; TEA

Sayers, Valerie 1952- .... **CLC 50, 122**
See also CA 134; CANR 61; CSW

Sayles, John (Thomas) 1950- .... **CLC 7, 10,
14, 198**
See also CA 57-60; CANR 41, 84; DLB 44

Scamander, Newt
See Rowling, J.K.

Scammell, Michael 1935- .... **CLC 34**
See also CA 156

Scannel, John Vernon
See Scannell, Vernon

Scannell, Vernon 1922-2007 .... **CLC 49**
See also CA 5-8R; 266; CANR 8, 24, 57,
143; CN 1, 2; CP 1, 2, 3, 4, 5, 6, 7; CWRI
5; DLB 27; SATA 59; SATA-Obit 188

Scarlett, Susan
See Streatfeild, (Mary) Noel

Scarron 1847-1910
See Mikszath, Kalman
Scarron, Paul 1610-1660 .... **LC 116**
See also GFL Beginnings to 1789; RGWL
2, 3
Schaeffer, Susan Fromberg 1941- ..... **CLC 6,
11, 22**
See also CA 49-52; CANR 18, 65, 160; CN
4, 5, 6, 7; DLB 28, 299; MTCW 1, 2;
MTFW 2005; SATA 22
Schama, Simon 1945- .... **CLC 150**
See also BEST 89:4; CA 105; CANR 39,
91, 168
Schama, Simon Michael
See Schama, Simon
Schary, Jill
See Robinson, Jill
Schell, Jonathan 1943- .... **CLC 35**
See also CA 73-76; CANR 12, 117
Schelling, Friedrich Wilhelm Joseph von
1775-1854 .... **NCLC 30**
See also DLB 90
Scherer, Jean-Marie Maurice 1920-
See Rohmer, Eric
See also CA 110
Schevill, James (Erwin) 1920- .... **CLC 7**
See also CA 5-8R; CAAS 12; CAD; CD 5,
6; CP 1, 2, 3, 4, 5
Schiller, Friedrich von 1759-1805 ...... **DC 12;
NCLC 39, 69, 166**
See also CDWLB 2; DAM DRAM; DLB
94; EW 5; RGWL 2, 3; TWA
Schisgal, Murray (Joseph) 1926- .... **CLC 6**
See also CA 21-24R; CAD; CANR 48, 86;
CD 5, 6; MAL 5
Schlee, Ann 1934- .... **CLC 35**
See also CA 101; CANR 29, 88; SATA 44;
SATA-Brief 36
Schlegel, August Wilhelm von 1767-1845
NCLC 15, 142
See also DLB 94; RGWL 2, 3
Schlegel, Friedrich 1772-1829 .... **NCLC 45**
See also DLB 90; EW 5; RGWL 2, 3; TWA
Schlegel, Johann Elias (von) 1719(?)-1749
LC 5
Schleiermacher, Friedrich
1768-1834 .... **NCLC 107**
See also DLB 90
Schlesinger, Arthur M., Jr.
1917-2007 .... **CLC 84**
See Schlesinger, Arthur Meier
See also AITN 1; CA 1-4R; 257; CANR 1,
28, 58, 105; DLB 17; INT CANR-28;
MTCW 1, 2; SATA 61; SATA-Obit 181
Schlink, Bernhard 1944- .... **CLC 174**
See also CA 163; CANR 116, 175; RGHL
Schmidt, Arno (Otto) 1914-1979 ...... **CLC 56**
See also CA 128; 109; DLB 69; EWL 3
Schmitz, Aron Hector 1861-1928
See Svevo, Italo
See also CA 104; 122; MTCW 1
Schnackenberg, Gjertrud 1953- ...... **CLC 40;
PC 45**
See also AMWS 15; CA 116; CANR 100;
CP 5, 6, 7; CWP; DLB 120, 282; PFS 13,
25
Schnackenberg, Gjertrud Cecelia
See Schnackenberg, Gjertrud
Schneider, Leonard Alfred 1925-1966
See Bruce, Lenny
See also CA 89-92
Schnitzler, Arthur 1862-1931 ..... **DC 17; SSC
15, 61; TCLC 4**
See also CA 104; CDWLB 2; DLB 81, 118;
EW 8; EWL 3; RGSF 2; RGWL 2, 3
Schoenberg, Arnold Franz Walter 1874-1951
TCLC 75
See also CA 109; 188

Schonberg, Arnold
See Schoenberg, Arnold Franz Walter
Schopenhauer, Arthur 1788-1860 . **NCLC 51,
157**
See also DLB 90; EW 5
Schor, Sandra (M.) 1932(?)-1990 ..... **CLC 65**
See also CA 132
Schorer, Mark 1908-1977 .... **CLC 9**
See also CA 5-8R; 73-76; CANR 7; CN 1,
2; DLB 103
Schrader, Paul (Joseph) 1946- . **CLC 26, 212**
See also CA 37-40R; CANR 41; DLB 44
Schreber, Daniel 1842-1911 .... **TCLC 123**
Schreiner, Olive (Emilie Albertina)
1855-1920 .... **TCLC 9**
See also AFW; BRWS 2; CA 105; 154;
DLB 18, 156, 190, 225; EWL 3; FW;
RGEL 2; TWA; WLIT 2; WWE 1
Schulberg, Budd (Wilson) 1914- .. **CLC 7, 48**
See also BPFB 3; CA 25-28R; CANR 19,
87; CN 1, 2, 3, 4, 5, 6, 7; DLB 6, 26, 28;
DLBY 1981, 2001; MAL 5
Schulman, Arnold
See Trumbo, Dalton
Schulz, Bruno 1892-1942 .. **SSC 13; TCLC 5,
51**
See also CA 115; 123; CANR 86; CDWLB
4; DLB 215; EWL 3; MTCW 2; MTFW
2005; RGSF 2; RGWL 2, 3
Schulz, Charles M. 1922-2000 .... **CLC 12**
See also AAYA 39; CA 9-12R; 187; CANR
6, 132; INT CANR-6; MTFW 2005;
SATA 10; SATA-Obit 118
Schulz, Charles Monroe
See Schulz, Charles M.
Schumacher, E(rnst) F(riedrich) 1911-1977
CLC 80
See also CA 81-84; 73-76; CANR 34, 85
Schumann, Robert 1810-1856 ...... **NCLC 143**
Schuyler, George Samuel 1895-1977 . **HR 1:3**
See also BW 2; CA 81-84; 73-76; CANR
42; DLB 29, 51
Schuyler, James Marcus 1923-1991 .. **CLC 5,
23; PC 88**
See also CA 101; 134; CP 1, 2, 3, 4, 5;
DAM POET; DLB 5, 169; EWL 3; INT
CA-101; MAL 5; WP
Schwartz, Delmore (David)
1913-1966 . **CLC 2, 4, 10, 45, 87; PC 8;
SSC 105**
See also AMWS 2; CA 17-18; 25-28R;
CANR 35; CAP 2; DLB 28, 48; EWL 3;
MAL 5; MTCW 1, 2; MTFW 2005; PAB;
RGAL 4; TUS
Schwartz, Ernst
See Ozu, Yasujiro
Schwartz, John Burnham 1965- .... **CLC 59**
See also CA 132; CANR 116
Schwartz, Lynne Sharon 1939- .... **CLC 31**
See also CA 103; CANR 44, 89, 160; DLB
218; MTCW 2; MTFW 2005
Schwartz, Muriel A.
See Eliot, T(homas) S(tearns)
Schwarz-Bart, Andre 1928-2006 .... **CLC 2, 4**
See also CA 89-92; 253; CANR 109; DLB
299; RGHL
Schwarz-Bart, Simone 1938- . **BLCS; CLC 7**
See also BW 2; CA 97-100; CANR 117;
EWL 3
Schwerner, Armand 1927-1999 .... **PC 42**
See also CA 9-12R; 179; CANR 50, 85; CP
2, 3, 4, 5, 6; DLB 165
**Schwitters, Kurt (Hermann Edward Karl
Julius)** 1887-1948 .... **TCLC 95**
See also CA 158
Schwob, Marcel (Mayer Andre) 1867-1905
TCLC 20
See also CA 117; 168; DLB 123; GFL 1789
to the Present

Sciascia, Leonardo 1921-1989 .. **CLC 8, 9, 41**
See also CA 85-88; 130; CANR 35; DLB
177; EWL 3; MTCW 1; RGWL 2, 3
Scoppettone, Sandra 1936- .... **CLC 26**
See Early, Jack
See also AAYA 11, 65; BYA 8; CA 5-8R;
CANR 41, 73, 157; GLL 1; MAICYA 2;
MAICYAS 1; SATA 9, 92; WYA; YAW
Scorsese, Martin 1942- .... **CLC 20, 89, 207**
See also AAYA 38; CA 110; 114; CANR
46, 85
Scotland, Jay
See Jakes, John
Scott, Duncan Campbell
1862-1947 .... **TCLC 6**
See also CA 104; 153; DAC; DLB 92;
RGEL 2
Scott, Evelyn 1893-1963 .... **CLC 43**
See also CA 104; 112; CANR 64; DLB 9,
48; RHW
Scott, F(rancis) R(eginald)
1899-1985 .... **CLC 22**
See also CA 101; 114; CANR 87; CP 1, 2,
3, 4; DLB 88; INT CA-101; RGEL 2
Scott, Frank
See Scott, F(rancis) R(eginald)
Scott, Joan .... **CLC 65**
Scott, Joanna 1960- .... **CLC 50**
See also AMWS 17; CA 126; CANR 53,
92, 168
Scott, Joanna Jeanne
See Scott, Joanna
Scott, Paul (Mark) 1920-1978 ...... **CLC 9, 60**
See also BRWS 1; CA 81-84; 77-80; CANR
33; CN 1, 2; DLB 14, 207, 326; EWL 3;
MTCW 1; RGEL 2; RHW; WWE 1
Scott, Ridley 1937- .... **CLC 183**
See also AAYA 13, 43
Scott, Sarah 1723-1795 .... **LC 44**
See also DLB 39
Scott, Sir Walter 1771-1832 .... **NCLC 15, 69,
110; PC 13; SSC 32; WLC 5**
See also AAYA 22; BRW 4; BYA 2; CD-
BLB 1789-1832; DA; DAB; DAC; DAM
MST, NOV, POET; DLB 93, 107, 116,
144, 159; GL 3; HGG; LAIT 1; RGEL 2;
RGSF 2; SSFS 10; SUFW 1; TEA; WLIT
3; YABC 2
Scribe, (Augustin) Eugene 1791-1861 . **DC 5;
NCLC 16**
See also DAM DRAM; DLB 192; GFL
1789 to the Present; RGWL 2, 3
Scrum, R.
See Crumb, R.
Scudery, Georges de 1601-1667 .... **LC 75**
See also GFL Beginnings to 1789
Scudery, Madeleine de 1607-1701 .. **LC 2, 58**
See also DLB 268; GFL Beginnings to 1789
Scum
See Crumb, R.
Scumbag, Little Bobby
See Crumb, R.
Seabrook, John
See Hubbard, L. Ron
Seacole, Mary Jane Grant
1805-1881 .... **NCLC 147**
See also DLB 166
Sealy, I(rwin) Allan 1951- .... **CLC 55**
See also CA 136; CN 6, 7
Search, Alexander
See Pessoa, Fernando (Antonio Nogueira)
Sebald, W(infried) G(eorg)
1944-2001 .... **CLC 194**
See also BRWS 8; CA 159; 202; CANR 98;
MTFW 2005; RGHL
Sebastian, Lee
See Silverberg, Robert
Sebastian Owl
See Thompson, Hunter S.

Sebestyen, Igen
  See Sebestyen, Ouida
Sebestyen, Ouida 1924- .... **CLC 30**
  See also AAYA 8; BYA 7; CA 107; CANR
  40, 114; CLR 17; JRDA; MAICYA 1, 2;
  SAAS 10; SATA 39, 140; WYA; YAW
Sebold, Alice 1963(?)- .... **CLC 193**
  See also AAYA 56; CA 203; MTFW 2005
Second Duke of Buckingham
  See Villiers, George
Secundus, H. Scriblerus
  See Fielding, Henry
Sedges, John
  See Buck, Pearl S(ydenstricker)
Sedgwick, Catharine Maria
  1789-1867 .... **NCLC 19, 98**
  See also DLB 1, 74, 183, 239, 243, 254; FL
  1:3; RGAL 4
Sedulius Scottus 9th cent. -c. 874 .. **CMLC 86**
Seebohm, Victoria
  See Glendinning, Victoria
Seelye, John (Douglas) 1931- .... **CLC 7**
  See also CA 97-100; CANR 70; INT CA-
  97-100; TCWW 1, 2
Seferiades, Giorgos Stylianou 1900-1971
  See Seferis, George
  See also CA 5-8R; 33-36R; CANR 5, 36;
  MTCW 1
Seferis, George .... **CLC 5, 11; PC 66**
  See Seferiades, Giorgos Stylianou
  See also DLB 332; EW 12; EWL 3; RGWL
  2, 3
Segal, Erich (Wolf) 1937- .... **CLC 3, 10**
  See also BEST 89:1; BPFB 3; CA 25-28R;
  CANR 20, 36, 65, 113; CPW; DAM POP;
  DLBY 1986; INT CANR-20; MTCW 1
Seger, Bob 1945- .... **CLC 35**
Seghers, Anna .... **CLC 7**
  See Radvanyi, Netty
  See also CDWLB 2; DLB 69, EWL 3
Seidel, Frederick (Lewis) 1936- .... **CLC 18**
  See also CA 13-16R; CANR 8, 99; CP 1, 2,
  3, 4, 5, 6, 7; DLBY 1984
Seifert, Jaroslav 1901-1986 . **CLC 34, 44, 93;**
    PC 47
  See also CA 127; CDWLB 4; DLB 215,
  332; EWL 3; MTCW 1, 2
Sei Shonagon c. 966-1017(?) ..... **CMLC 6, 89**
Sejour, Victor 1817-1874 .... **DC 10**
  See also DLB 50
Sejour Marcou et Ferrand, Juan Victor
  See Sejour, Victor
Selby, Hubert, Jr. 1928-2004 ..... **CLC 1, 2, 4,**
    8; SSC 20
  See also CA 13-16R; 226; CANR 33, 85;
  CN 1, 2, 3, 4, 5, 6, 7; DLB 2, 227; MAL
  5
Selzer, Richard 1928- .... **CLC 74**
  See also CA 65-68; CANR 14, 106
Sembene, Ousmane
  See Ousmane, Sembene
Senancour, Etienne Pivert de 1770-1846
    NCLC 16
  See also DLB 119; GFL 1789 to the Present
Sender, Ramon (Jose) 1902-1982 ...... **CLC 8;**
    HLC 2; TCLC 136
  See also CA 5-8R; 105; CANR 8; DAM
  MULT; DLB 322; EWL 3; HW 1; MTCW
  1; RGWL 2, 3
Seneca, Lucius Annaeus c. 4B.C.-c.
  65 .... **CMLC 6; DC 5**
  See also AW 2; CDWLB 1; DAM DRAM;
  DLB 211; RGWL 2, 3; TWA; WLIT 8
Senghor, Leopold Sedar
  1906-2001 .. **BLC 1:3; CLC 54, 130; PC
    25**
  See also AFW; BW 2; CA 116; 125; 203;
  CANR 47, 74, 134; CWW 2; DAM
  MULT, POET; DNFS 2; EWL 3; GFL
  1789 to the Present; MTCW 1, 2; MTFW
  2005; TWA

Senior, Olive (Marjorie) 1941- .... **SSC 78**
  See also BW 3; CA 154; CANR 86, 126;
  CN 6; CP 6, 7; CWP; DLB 157; EWL 3;
  RGSF 2
Senna, Danzy 1970- .... **CLC 119**
  See also CA 169; CANR 130
Serling, (Edward) Rod(man)
  1924-1975 .... **CLC 30**
  See also AAYA 14; AITN 1; CA 162; 57-
  60; DLB 26; SFW 4
Serna, Ramon Gomez de la
  See Gomez de la Serna, Ramon
Serpieres
  See Guillevic, (Eugene)
Service, Robert
  See Service, Robert W(illiam)
  See also BYA 4; DAB; DLB 92
Service, Robert W(illiam)
  1874(?)-1958 ... **PC 70; TCLC 15; WLC
    5**
  See Service, Robert
  See also CA 115; 140; CANR 84; DA;
  DAC; DAM MST, POET; PFS 10; RGEL
  2; SATA 20
Seth, Vikram 1952- .... **CLC 43, 90**
  See also BRWS 10; CA 121; 127; CANR
  50, 74, 131; CN 6, 7; CP 5, 6, 7; DA3;
  DAM MULT; DLB 120, 271, 282, 323;
  EWL 3; INT CA-127; MTCW 2; MTFW
  2005; WWE 1
Seton, Cynthia Propper 1926-1982 .. **CLC 27**
  See also CA 5-8R; 108; CANR 7
Seton, Ernest (Evan) Thompson 1860-1946
    TCLC 31
  See also ANW; BYA 3; CA 109; 204; CLR
  59; DLB 92; DLBD 13; JRDA; SATA 18
Seton-Thompson, Ernest
  See Seton, Ernest (Evan) Thompson
Settle, Mary Lee 1918-2005 .... **CLC 19, 61**
  See also BPFB 3; CA 89-92; 243; CAAS 1;
  CANR 44, 87, 126; CN 6, 7; CSW; DLB
  6; INT CA-89-92
Seuphor, Michel
  See Arp, Jean
Sevigne, Marie (de Rabutin-Chantal)
  1626-1696 .... **LC 11, 144**
  See Sevigne, Marie de Rabutin Chantal
  See also GFL Beginnings to 1789; TWA
Sevigne, Marie de Rabutin Chantal
  See Sevigne, Marie (de Rabutin-Chantal)
  See also DLB 268
Sewall, Samuel 1652-1730 .... **LC 38**
  See also DLB 24; RGAL 4
Sexton, Anne (Harvey) 1928-1974 ..... **CLC 2,
    4, 6, 8, 10, 15, 53, 123; PC 2, 79; WLC
    5**
  See also AMWS 2; CA 1-4R; 53-56; CABS
  2; CANR 3, 36; CDALB 1941-1968; CP
  1, 2; DA; DA3; DAB; DAC; DAM MST,
  POET; DLB 5, 169; EWL 3; EXPP; FL
  1:6; FW; MAL 5; MBL; MTCW 1, 2;
  MTFW 2005; PAB; PFS 4, 14; RGAL 4;
  RGHL; SATA 10; TUS
Shaara, Jeff 1952- .... **CLC 119**
  See also AAYA 70; CA 163; CANR 109,
  172; CN 7; MTFW 2005
Shaara, Michael 1929-1988 .... **CLC 15**
  See also AAYA 71; AITN 1; BPFB 3; CA
  102; 125; CANR 52, 85; DAM POP;
  DLBY 1983; MTFW 2005; NFS 26
Shackleton, C.C.
  See Aldiss, Brian W.
Shacochis, Bob .... **CLC 39**
  See Shacochis, Robert G.
Shacochis, Robert G. 1951-
  See Shacochis, Bob
  See also CA 119; 124; CANR 100; INT CA-
  124

Shadwell, Thomas 1641(?)-1692 .... **LC 114**
  See also DLB 80; IDTP; RGEL 2
Shaffer, Anthony 1926-2001 .... **CLC 19**
  See also CA 110; 116; 200; CBD; CD 5, 6;
  DAM DRAM; DFS 13; DLB 13
Shaffer, Anthony Joshua
  See Shaffer, Anthony
Shaffer, Peter 1926- ... **CLC 5, 14, 18, 37, 60;
    DC 7**
  See also BRWS 1; CA 25-28R; CANR 25,
  47, 74, 118; CBD; CD 5, 6; CDBLB 1960
  to Present; DA3; DAB; DAM DRAM,
  MST; DFS 5, 13; DLB 13, 233; EWL 3;
  MTCW 1, 2; MTFW 2005; RGEL 2; TEA
Shakespeare, William 1564-1616 . **PC 84, 89;
    WLC 5**
  See also AAYA 35; BRW 1; CDBLB Be-
  fore 1660; DA; DA3; DAB; DAC; DAM
  DRAM, MST, POET; DFS 20, 21; DLB
  62, 172, 263; EXPP; LAIT 1; LATS 1:1;
  LMFS 1; PAB; PFS 1, 2, 3, 4, 5, 8, 9;
  RGEL 2; TEA; WLIT 3; WP; WS; WYA
Shakey, Bernard
  See Young, Neil
Shalamov, Varlam (Tikhonovich) 1907-1982
    CLC 18
  See also CA 129; 105; DLB 302; RGSF 2
Shamloo, Ahmad
  See Shamlu, Ahmad
Shamlou, Ahmad
  See Shamlu, Ahmad
Shamlu, Ahmad 1925-2000 .... **CLC 10**
  See also CA 216; CWW 2
Shammas, Anton 1951- .... **CLC 55**
  See also CA 199
Shandling, Arline
  See Berriault, Gina
Shange, Ntozake 1948- .. **BLC 1:3, 2:3; CLC
    8, 25, 38, 74, 126; DC 3**
  See also AAYA 9, 66; AFAW 1, 2; BW 2;
  CA 85-88; CABS 3; CAD; CANR 27, 48,
  74, 131; CD 5, 6; CP 5, 6, 7; CWD; CWP;
  DA3; DAM DRAM, MULT; DFS 2, 11;
  DLB 38, 249; FW; LAIT 4, 5; MAL 5;
  MTCW 1, 2; MTFW 2005; NFS 11;
  RGAL 4; SATA 157; YAW
Shanley, John Patrick 1950- .... **CLC 75**
  See also AAYA 74; AMWS 14; CA 128;
  133; CAD; CANR 83, 154; CD 5, 6; DFS
  23
Shapcott, Thomas W(illiam) 1935- .. **CLC 38**
  See also CA 69-72; CANR 49, 83, 103; CP
  1, 2, 3, 4, 5, 6, 7; DLB 289
Shapiro, Jane 1942- .... **CLC 76**
  See also CA 196
Shapiro, Karl 1913-2000 ... **CLC 4, 8, 15, 53;
    PC 25**
  See also AMWS 2; CA 1-4R; 188; CAAS
  6; CANR 1, 36, 66; CP 1, 2, 3, 4, 5, 6;
  DLB 48; EWL 3; EXPP; MAL 5; MTCW
  1, 2; MTFW 2005; PFS 3; RGAL 4
Sharp, William 1855-1905 .... **TCLC 39**
  See Macleod, Fiona
  See also CA 160; DLB 156; RGEL 2
Sharpe, Thomas Ridley 1928-
  See Sharpe, Tom
  See also CA 114; 122; CANR 85; INT CA-
  122
Sharpe, Tom .... **CLC 36**
  See Sharpe, Thomas Ridley
  See also CN 4, 5, 6, 7; DLB 14, 231
Shatrov, Mikhail .... **CLC 59**
Shaw, Bernard
  See Shaw, George Bernard
  See also DLB 10, 57, 190
Shaw, G. Bernard
  See Shaw, George Bernard

Sigourney, Lydia H.
See Sigourney, Lydia Howard (Huntley)
See also DLB 73, 183

Sigourney, Lydia Howard (Huntley)
1791-1865 .... **NCLC 21, 87**
See Sigourney, Lydia H.; Sigourney, Lydia
Huntley
See also DLB 1

Sigourney, Lydia Huntley
See Sigourney, Lydia Howard (Huntley)
See also DLB 42, 239, 243

Siguenza y Gongora, Carlos de 1645-1700
HLCS 2; LC 8
See also LAW

Sigurjonsson, Johann
See Sigurjonsson, Johann

Sigurjonsson, Johann 1880-1919 ... TCLC 27
See also CA 170; DLB 293; EWL 3

Sikelianos, Angelos 1884-1951 .... PC 29;
TCLC 39
See also EWL 3; RGWL 2, 3

Silkin, Jon 1930-1997 .... CLC 2, 6, 43
See also CA 5-8R; CAAS 5; CANR 89; CP
1, 2, 3, 4, 5, 6; DLB 27

Silko, Leslie 1948- ...... CLC 23, 74, 114, 211;
NNAL; SSC 37, 66; WLCS
See also AAYA 14; AMWS 4; ANW; BYA
12; CA 115; 122; CANR 45, 65, 118; CN
4, 5, 6, 7; CP 4, 5, 6, 7; CPW 1; CWP;
DA; DA3; DAC; DAM MST, MULT,
POP; DLB 143, 175, 256, 275; EWL 3;
EXPP; EXPS; LAIT 4; MAL 5; MTCW
2; MTFW 2005; NFS 4; PFS 9, 16; RGAL
4; RGSF 2; SSFS 4, 8, 10, 11; TCWW 1,
2

Sillanpaa, Frans Eemil 1888-1964 ... CLC 19
See also CA 129; 93-96; DLB 332; EWL 3;
MTCW 1

Sillitoe, Alan 1928- .. CLC 1, 3, 6, 10, 19, 57,
148
See also AITN 1; BRWS 5; CA 9-12R, 191;
CAAE 191; CAAS 2; CANR 8, 26, 55,
139; CDBLB 1960 to Present; CN 1, 2, 3,
4, 5, 6; CP 1, 2, 3, 4, 5; DLB 14, 139;
EWL 3; MTCW 1, 2; MTFW 2005; RGEL
2; RGSF 2; SATA 61

Silone, Ignazio 1900-1978 .... CLC 4
See also CA 25-28; 81-84; CANR 34; CAP
2; DLB 264; EW 12; EWL 3; MTCW 1;
RGSF 2; RGWL 2, 3

Silone, Ignazione
See Silone, Ignazio

Silver, Joan Micklin 1935- .... CLC 20
See also CA 114; 121; INT CA-121

Silver, Nicholas
See Faust, Frederick (Schiller)

Silverberg, Robert 1935- .... CLC 7, 140
See also AAYA 24; BPFB 3; BYA 7, 9; CA
1-4R, 186; CAAE 186; CAAS 3; CANR
1, 20, 36, 85, 140, 175; CLR 59; CN 6, 7;
CPW; DAM POP; DLB 8; INT CANR-
20; MAICYA 1, 2; MTCW 1, 2; MTFW
2005; SATA 13, 91; SATA-Essay 104;
SCFW 1, 2; SFW 4; SUFW 2

Silverstein, Alvin 1933- .... CLC 17
See also CA 49-52; CANR 2; CLR 25;
JRDA; MAICYA 1, 2; SATA 8, 69, 124

Silverstein, Shel 1932-1999 .... PC 49
See also AAYA 40; BW 3; CA 107; 179;
CANR 47, 74, 81; CLR 5, 96; CWRI 5;
JRDA; MAICYA 1, 2; MTCW 2; MTFW
2005; SATA 33, 92; SATA-Brief 27;
SATA-Obit 116

Silverstein, Virginia B(arbara Opshelor)
1937- .... **CLC 17**
See also CA 49-52; CANR 2; CLR 25;
JRDA; MAICYA 1, 2; SATA 8, 69, 124

Sim, Georges
See Simenon, Georges (Jacques Christian)

Simak, Clifford D(onald) 1904-1988 . CLC 1,
55
See also CA 1-4R; 125; CANR 1, 35; DLB
8; MTCW 1; SATA-Obit 56; SCFW 1, 2;
SFW 4

Simenon, Georges (Jacques Christian)
1903-1989 .... **CLC 1, 2, 3, 8, 18, 47**
See also BPFB 3; CA 85-88; CANR
35; CMW 4; DA3; DAM POP; DLB 72;
DLBY 1989; EW 12; EWL 3; GFL 1789
to the Present; MSW; MTCW 1, 2; MTFW
2005; RGWL 2, 3

Simic, Charles 1938- .... CLC 6, 9, 22, 49, 68,
130, 256; PC 69
See also AMWS 8; CA 29-32R; CAAS 4;
CANR 12, 33, 52, 61, 96, 140; CP 2, 3, 4,
5, 6, 7; DA3; DAM POET; DLB 105;
MAL 5; MTCW 2; MTFW 2005; PFS 7;
RGAL 4; WP

Simmel, Georg 1858-1918 .... TCLC 64
See also CA 157; DLB 296

Simmons, Charles (Paul) 1924- .... CLC 57
See also CA 89-92; INT CA-89-92

Simmons, Dan 1948- .... CLC 44
See also AAYA 16, 54; CA 138; CANR 53,
81, 126, 174; CPW; DAM POP; HGG;
SUFW 2

Simmons, James (Stewart Alexander) 1933-
CLC 43
See also CA 105; CAAS 21; CP 1, 2, 3, 4,
5, 6, 7; DLB 40

Simmons, Richard
See Simmons, Dan

Simms, William Gilmore
1806-1870 .... **NCLC 3**
See also DLB 3, 30, 59, 73, 248, 254;
RGAL 4

Simon, Carly 1945- .... CLC 26
See also CA 105

Simon, Claude 1913-2005 ... CLC 4, 9, 15, 39
See also CA 89-92; 241; CANR 33, 117;
CWW 2; DAM NOV; DLB 83, 332; EW
13; EWL 3; GFL 1789 to the Present;
MTCW 1

Simon, Claude Eugene Henri
See Simon, Claude

Simon, Claude Henri Eugene
See Simon, Claude

Simon, Marvin Neil
See Simon, Neil

Simon, Myles
See Follett, Ken

Simon, Neil 1927- .... CLC 6, 11, 31, 39, 70,
233; DC 14
See also AAYA 32; AITN 1; AMWS 4; CA
21-24R; CAD; CANR 26, 54, 87, 126;
CD 5, 6; DA3; DAM DRAM; DFS 2, 6,
12, 18,, 24; DLB 7, 266; LAIT 4; MAL 5;
MTCW 1, 2; MTFW 2005; RGAL 4; TUS

Simon, Paul 1941(?)- .... CLC 17
See also CA 116; 153; CANR 152

Simon, Paul Frederick
See Simon, Paul

Simonon, Paul 1956(?)- .... CLC 30

Simonson, Rick .... CLC 70

Simpson, Harriette
See Arnow, Harriette (Louisa) Simpson

Simpson, Louis 1923- ... CLC 4, 7, 9, 32, 149
See also AMWS 9; CA 1-4R; CAAS 4;
CANR 1, 61, 140; CP 1, 2, 3, 4, 5, 6, 7;
DAM POET; DLB 5; MAL 5; MTCW 1,
2; MTFW 2005; PFS 7, 11, 14; RGAL 4

Simpson, Mona 1957- .... CLC 44, 146
See also CA 122; 135; CANR 68, 103; CN
6, 7; EWL 3

Simpson, Mona Elizabeth
See Simpson, Mona

Simpson, N(orman) F(rederick)
1919- .... **CLC 29**
See also CA 13-16R; CBD; DLB 13; RGEL
2

Sinclair, Andrew (Annandale) 1935- . CLC 2,
14
See also CA 9-12R; CAAS 5; CANR 14,
38, 91; CN 1, 2, 3, 4, 5, 6, 7; DLB 14;
FANT; MTCW 1

Sinclair, Emil
See Hesse, Hermann

Sinclair, Iain 1943- .... CLC 76
See also CA 132; CANR 81, 157; CP 5, 6,
7; HGG

Sinclair, Iain MacGregor
See Sinclair, Iain

Sinclair, Irene
See Griffith, D(avid Lewelyn) W(ark)

Sinclair, Julian
See Sinclair, May

Sinclair, Mary Amelia St. Clair (?)-
See Sinclair, May

Sinclair, May 1865-1946 .... TCLC 3, 11
See also CA 104; 166; DLB 36, 135; EWL
3; HGG; RGEL 2; RHW; SUFW

Sinclair, Roy
See Griffith, D(avid Lewelyn) W(ark)

Sinclair, Upton 1878-1968 ...... CLC 1, 11, 15,
63; TCLC 160; WLC 5
See also AAYA 63; AMWS 5; BPFB 3;
BYA 2; CA 5-8R; 25-28R; CANR 7;
CDALB 1929-1941; DA; DA3; DAB;
DAC; DAM MST, NOV; DLB 9; EWL 3;
INT CANR-7; LAIT 3; MAL 5; MTCW
1, 2; MTFW 2005; NFS 6; RGAL 4;
SATA 9; TUS; YAW

Sinclair, Upton Beall
See Sinclair, Upton

Singe, (Edmund) J(ohn) M(illington)
1871-1909 .... **WLC**

Singer, Isaac
See Singer, Isaac Bashevis

Singer, Isaac Bashevis 1904-1991 .. CLC 1, 3,
6, 9, 11, 15, 23, 38, 69, 111; SSC 3, 53,
80; WLC 5
See also AAYA 32; AITN 1, 2; AMW;
AMWR 2; BPFB 3; BYA 1, 4; CA 1-4R;
134; CANR 1, 39, 106; CDALB 1941-
1968; CLR 1; CN 1, 2, 3, 4; CWRI 5;
DA; DA3; DAB; DAC; DAM MST, NOV;
DLB 6, 28, 52, 278, 332, 333; DLBY
1991; EWL 3; EXPS; HGG; JRDA; LAIT
3; MAICYA 1, 2; MAL 5; MTCW 1, 2;
MTFW 2005; RGAL 4; RGHL; RGSF 2;
SATA 3, 27; SATA-Obit 68; SSFS 2, 12,
16; TUS; TWA

Singer, Israel Joshua 1893-1944 .... TCLC 33
See also CA 169; DLB 333; EWL 3

Singh, Khushwant 1915- .... CLC 11
See also CA 9-12R; CAAS 9; CANR 6, 84;
CN 1, 2, 3, 4, 5, 6, 7; DLB 323; EWL 3;
RGEL 2

Singleton, Ann
See Benedict, Ruth

Singleton, John 1968(?)- .... CLC 156
See also AAYA 50; BW 2, 3; CA 138;
CANR 67, 82; DAM MULT

Siniavskii, Andrei
See Sinyavsky, Andrei (Donatevich)
See also CWW 2

Sinjohn, John
See Galsworthy, John

Sinyavsky, Andrei (Donatevich) 1925-1997
CLC 8
See Siniavskii, Andrei; Sinyavsky, Andrey
Donatovich; Tertz, Abram
See also CA 85-88; 159

Sokolov, Raymond 1941- .... **CLC 7**
See also CA 85-88
Sokolov, Sasha .... **CLC 59**
See Sokolov, Alexander V(sevolodovich)
See also CWW 2; DLB 285; EWL 3; RGWL 2, 3
Solo, Jay
See Ellison, Harlan
Sologub, Fyodor .... **TCLC 9**
See Teternikov, Fyodor Kuzmich
See also EWL 3
Solomons, Ikey Esquir
See Thackeray, William Makepeace
Solomos, Dionysios 1798-1857 .... **NCLC 15**
Solwoska, Mara
See French, Marilyn
Solzhenitsyn, Aleksandr I. 1918- .. **CLC 1, 2, 4, 7, 9, 10, 18, 26, 34, 78, 134, 235; SSC 32, 105; WLC 5**
See Solzhenitsyn, Aleksandr Isayevich
See also AAYA 49; AITN 1; BPFB 3; CA 69-72; CANR 40, 65, 116; DA; DA3; DAB; DAC; DAM MST, NOV; DLB 302, 332; EW 13; EXPS; LAIT 4; MTCW 1, 2; MTFW 2005; NFS 6; RGSF 2; RGWL 2, 3; SSFS 9; TWA
Solzhenitsyn, Aleksandr Isayevich
See Solzhenitsyn, Aleksandr I.
See also CWW 2; EWL 3
Somers, Jane
See Lessing, Doris
Somerville, Edith Oenone
1858-1949 .... **SSC 56; TCLC 51**
See also CA 196; DLB 135; RGEL 2; RGSF 2
Somerville & Ross
See Martin, Violet Florence; Somerville, Edith Oenone
Sommer, Scott 1951- .... **CLC 25**
See also CA 106
Sommers, Christina Hoff 1950- ...... **CLC 197**
See also CA 153; CANR 95
Sondheim, Stephen 1930- .. **CLC 30, 39, 147; DC 22**
See also AAYA 11, 66; CA 103; CANR 47, 67, 125; DAM DRAM; DFS 25; LAIT 4
Sondheim, Stephen Joshua
See Sondheim, Stephen
Sone, Monica 1919- .... **AAL**
See also DLB 312
Song, Cathy 1955- .... **AAL; PC 21**
See also CA 154; CANR 118; CWP; DLB 169, 312; EXPP; FW; PFS 5
Sontag, Susan 1933-2004 ... **CLC 1, 2, 10, 13, 31, 105, 195**
See also AMWS 3; CA 17-20R; 234; CANR 25, 51, 74, 97; CN 1, 2, 3, 4, 5, 6, 7; CPW; DA3; DAM POP; DLB 2, 67; EWL 3; MAL 5; MBL; MTCW 1, 2; MTFW 2005; RGAL 4; RHW; SSFS 10
Sophocles 496(?)B.C.-406(?)B.C. .... **CMLC 2, 47, 51, 86; DC 1; WLCS**
See also AW 1; CDWLB 1; DA; DA3; DAB; DAC; DAM DRAM, MST; DFS 1, 4, 8, 24; DLB 176; LAIT 1; LATS 1:1; LMFS 1; RGWL 2, 3; TWA; WLIT 8
Sordello 1189-1269 .... **CMLC 15**
Sorel, Georges 1847-1922 .... **TCLC 91**
See also CA 118; 188
Sorel, Julia
See Drexler, Rosalyn
Sorokin, Vladimir .... **CLC 59**
See Sorokin, Vladimir Georgievich
See also CA 258
Sorokin, Vladimir Georgievich
See Sorokin, Vladimir
See also DLB 285

Sorrentino, Gilbert 1929-2006 .... **CLC 3, 7, 14, 22, 40, 247**
See also CA 77-80; 250; CANR 14, 33, 115, 157; CN 3, 4, 5, 6, 7; CP 1, 2, 3, 4, 5, 6, 7; DLB 5, 173; DLBY 1980; INT CANR-14
Soseki
See Natsume, Soseki
See also MJW
Soto, Gary 1952- ... **CLC 32, 80; HLC 2; PC 28**
See also AAYA 10, 37; BYA 11; CA 119; 125; CANR 50, 74, 107, 157; CLR 38; CP 4, 5, 6, 7; DAM MULT; DLB 82; EWL 3; EXPP; HW 1, 2; INT CA-125; JRDA; LLW; MAICYA 2; MAICYAS 1; MAL 5; MTCW 2; MTFW 2005; PFS 7; RGAL 4; SATA 80, 120, 174; WYA; YAW
Soupault, Philippe 1897-1990 .... **CLC 68**
See also CA 116; 147; 131; EWL 3; GFL 1789 to the Present; LMFS 2
Souster, (Holmes) Raymond 1921- .... **CLC 5, 14**
See also CA 13-16R; CAAS 14; CANR 13, 29, 53; CP 1, 2, 3, 4, 5, 6, 7; DA3; DAC; DAM POET; DLB 88; RGEL 2; SATA 63
Southern, Terry 1924(?)-1995 .... **CLC 7**
See also AMWS 11; BPFB 3; CA 1-4R; 150; CANR 1, 55, 107; CN 1, 2, 3, 4, 5, 6; DLB 2; IDFW 3, 4
Southerne, Thomas 1660-1746 .... **LC 99**
See also DLB 80; RGEL 2
Southey, Robert 1774-1843 .... **NCLC 8, 97**
See also BRW 4; DLB 93, 107, 142; RGEL 2; SATA 54
Southwell, Robert 1561(?)-1595 .... **LC 108**
See also DLB 167; RGEL 2; TEA
Southworth, Emma Dorothy Eliza Nevitte
1819-1899 .... **NCLC 26**
See also DLB 239
Souza, Ernest
See Scott, Evelyn
Soyinka, Wole 1934- .. **BLC 1:3, 2:3; CLC 3, 5, 14, 36, 44, 179; DC 2; WLC 5**
See also AFW; BW 2, 3; CA 13-16R; CANR 27, 39, 82, 136; CD 5, 6; CDWLB 3; CN 6, 7; CP 1, 2, 3, 4, 5, 6, 7; DA; DA3; DAB; DAC; DAM DRAM, MST, MULT; DFS 10; DLB 125, 332; EWL 3; MTCW 1, 2; MTFW 2005; PFS 27; RGEL 2; TWA; WLIT 2; WWE 1
Spackman, W(illiam) M(ode)
1905-1990 .... **CLC 46**
See also CA 81-84; 132
Spacks, Barry (Bernard) 1931- .... **CLC 14**
See also CA 154; CANR 33, 109; CP 3, 4, 5, 6, 7; DLB 105
Spanidou, Irini 1946- .... **CLC 44**
See also CA 185
Spark, Muriel 1918-2006 .... **CLC 2, 3, 5, 8, 13, 18, 40, 94, 242; PC 72; SSC 10**
See also BRWS 1; CA 5-8R; 251; CANR 12, 36, 76, 89, 131; CDBLB 1945-1960; CN 1, 2, 3, 4, 5, 6, 7; CP 1, 2, 3, 4, 5, 6, 7; DA3; DAB; DAC; DAM MST, NOV; DLB 15, 139; EWL 3; FW; INT CANR-12; LAIT 4; MTCW 1, 2; MTFW 2005; NFS 22; RGEL 2; TEA; WLIT 4; YAW
Spark, Muriel Sarah
See Spark, Muriel
Spaulding, Douglas
See Bradbury, Ray
Spaulding, Leonard
See Bradbury, Ray
Speght, Rachel 1597-c. 1630 .... **LC 97**
See also DLB 126
Spence, J. A. D.
See Eliot, T(homas) S(tearns)

Spencer, Anne 1882-1975 ...... **HR 1:3; PC 77**
See also BW 2; CA 161; DLB 51, 54
Spencer, Elizabeth 1921- .... **CLC 22; SSC 57**
See also CA 13-16R; CANR 32, 65, 87; CN 1, 2, 3, 4, 5, 6, 7; CSW; DLB 6, 218; EWL 3; MTCW 1; RGAL 4; SATA 14
Spencer, Leonard G.
See Silverberg, Robert
Spencer, Scott 1945- .... **CLC 30**
See also CA 113; CANR 51, 148; DLBY 1986
Spender, Stephen 1909-1995 ..... **CLC 1, 2, 5, 10, 41, 91; PC 71**
See also BRWS 2; CA 9-12R; 149; CANR 31, 54; CDBLB 1945-1960; CP 1, 2, 3, 4, 5, 6; DA3; DAM POET; DLB 20; EWL 3; MTCW 1, 2; MTFW 2005; PAB; PFS 23; RGEL 2; TEA
Spengler, Oswald (Arnold Gottfried)
1880-1936 .... **TCLC 25**
See also CA 118; 189
Spenser, Edmund 1552(?)-1599 ...... **LC 5, 39, 117; PC 8, 42; WLC 5**
See also AAYA 60; BRW 1; CDBLB Before 1660; DA; DA3; DAB; DAC; DAM MST, POET; DLB 167; EFS 2; EXPP; PAB; RGEL 2; TEA; WLIT 3; WP
Spicer, Jack 1925-1965 .... **CLC 8, 18, 72**
See also BG 1:3; CA 85-88; DAM POET; DLB 5, 16, 193; GLL 1; WP
Spiegelman, Art 1948- .... **CLC 76, 178**
See also AAYA 10, 46; CA 125; CANR 41, 55, 74, 124; DLB 299; MTCW 2; MTFW 2005; RGHL; SATA 109, 158; YAW
Spielberg, Peter 1929- .... **CLC 6**
See also CA 5-8R; CANR 4, 48; DLBY 1981
Spielberg, Steven 1947- .... **CLC 20, 188**
See also AAYA 8, 24; CA 77-80; CANR 32; SATA 32
Spillane, Frank Morrison
See Spillane, Mickey
See also BPFB 3; CMW 4; DLB 226; MSW
Spillane, Mickey 1918-2006 .. **CLC 3, 13, 241**
See Spillane, Frank Morrison
See also CA 25-28R; 252; CANR 28, 63, 125; DA3; MTCW 1, 2; MTFW 2005; SATA 66; SATA-Obit 176
Spinoza, Benedictus de 1632-1677 .. **LC 9, 58**
Spinrad, Norman (Richard) 1940- ... **CLC 46**
See also BPFB 3; CA 37-40R, 233; CAAE 233; CAAS 19; CANR 20, 91; DLB 8; INT CANR-20; SFW 4
Spitteler, Carl 1845-1924 .... **TCLC 12**
See also CA 109; DLB 129, 332; EWL 3
Spitteler, Karl Friedrich Georg
See Spitteler, Carl
Spivack, Kathleen (Romola Drucker) 1938-
CLC 6
See also CA 49-52
Spivak, Gayatri Chakravorty
1942- .... **CLC 233**
See also CA 110; 154; CANR 91; FW; LMFS 2
Spofford, Harriet (Elizabeth) Prescott
1835-1921 .... **SSC 87**
See also CA 201; DLB 74, 221
Spoto, Donald 1941- .... **CLC 39**
See also CA 65-68; CANR 11, 57, 93, 173
Springsteen, Bruce 1949- .... **CLC 17**
See also CA 111
Springsteen, Bruce F.
See Springsteen, Bruce
Spurling, Hilary 1940- .... **CLC 34**
See also CA 104; CANR 25, 52, 94, 157
Spurling, Susan Hilary
See Spurling, Hilary
Spyker, John Howland
See Elman, Richard (Martin)

Tamayo y Baus, Manuel
1829-1898 .... **NCLC 1**

Tammsaare, A(nton) H(ansen) 1878-1940
TCLC 27
See also CA 164; CDWLB 4; DLB 220;
EWL 3

Tam'si, Tchicaya U
See Tchicaya, Gerald Felix

Tan, Amy 1952- ..... **AAL; CLC 59, 120, 151,
257**
See also AAYA 9, 48; AMWS 10; BEST
89:3; BPFB 3; CA 136; CANR 54, 105,
132; CDALBS; CN 6, 7; CPW 1; DA3;
DAM MULT, NOV, POP; DLB 173, 312;
EXPN; FL 1:6; FW; LAIT 3, 5; MAL 5;
MTCW 2; MTFW 2005; NFS 1, 13, 16;
RGAL 4; SATA 75; SSFS 9; YAW

Tandem, Carl Felix
See Spitteler, Carl

Tandem, Felix
See Spitteler, Carl

Tanizaki, Jun'ichiro 1886-1965 ... **CLC 8, 14,
28; SSC 21**
See Tanizaki Jun'ichiro
See also CA 93-96; 25-28R; MJW; MTCW
2; MTFW 2005; RGSF 2; RGWL 2

Tanizaki Jun'ichiro
See Tanizaki, Jun'ichiro
See also DLB 180; EWL 3

Tannen, Deborah 1945- .... **CLC 206**
See also CA 118; CANR 95

Tannen, Deborah Frances
See Tannen, Deborah

Tanner, William
See Amis, Kingsley

Tante, Dilly
See Kunitz, Stanley

Tao Lao
See Storni, Alfonsina

Tapahonso, Luci 1953- .... **NNAL; PC 65**
See also CA 145, CANR 72, 127; DLB 175

Tarantino, Quentin (Jerome)
1963- .... **CLC 125, 230**
See also AAYA 58; CA 171; CANR 125

Tarassoff, Lev
See Troyat, Henri

Tarbell, Ida M(inerva) 1857-1944 . **TCLC 40**
See also CA 122; 181; DLB 47

Tardieu d'Esclavelles,
Louise-Florence-Petronille
See Epinay, Louise d'

Tarkington, (Newton) Booth 1869-1946
TCLC 9
See also BPFB 3; BYA 3; CA 110; 143;
CWRI 5; DLB 9, 102; MAL 5; MTCW 2;
RGAL 4; SATA 17

Tarkovskii, Andrei Arsen'evich
See Tarkovsky, Andrei (Arsenyevich)

Tarkovsky, Andrei (Arsenyevich) 1932-1986
CLC 75
See also CA 127

Tartt, Donna 1964(?)- .... **CLC 76**
See also AAYA 56; CA 142; CANR 135;
MTFW 2005

Tasso, Torquato 1544-1595 .... **LC 5, 94**
See also EFS 2; EW 2; RGWL 2, 3; WLIT
7

Tate, (John Orley) Allen 1899-1979 .. **CLC 2,
4, 6, 9, 11, 14, 24; PC 50**
See also AMW; CA 5-8R; 85-88; CANR
32, 108; CN 1, 2; CP 1, 2; DLB 4, 45, 63;
DLBD 17; EWL 3; MAL 5; MTCW 1, 2;
MTFW 2005; RGAL 4; RHW

Tate, Ellalice
See Hibbert, Eleanor Alice Burford

Tate, James (Vincent) 1943- ..... **CLC 2, 6, 25**
See also CA 21-24R; CANR 29, 57, 114;
CP 1, 2, 3, 4, 5, 6, 7; DLB 5, 169; EWL
3; PFS 10, 15; RGAL 4; WP

Tate, Nahum 1652(?)-1715 .... **LC 109**
See also DLB 80; RGEL 2

Tauler, Johannes c. 1300-1361 ...... **CMLC 37**
See also DLB 179; LMFS 1

Tavel, Ronald 1940- .... **CLC 6**
See also CA 21-24R; CAD; CANR 33; CD
5, 6

Taviani, Paolo 1931- .... **CLC 70**
See also CA 153

Taylor, Bayard 1825-1878 .... **NCLC 89**
See also DLB 3, 189, 250, 254; RGAL 4

Taylor, C(ecil) P(hilip) 1929-1981 .... **CLC 27**
See also CA 25-28R; 105; CANR 47; CBD

Taylor, Edward 1642(?)-1729 . **LC 11; PC 63**
See also AMW; DA; DAB; DAC; DAM
MST, POET; DLB 24; EXPP; RGAL 4;
TUS

Taylor, Eleanor Ross 1920- .... **CLC 5**
See also CA 81-84; CANR 70

Taylor, Elizabeth 1912-1975 .... **CLC 2, 4, 29;
SSC 100**
See also CA 13-16R; CANR 9, 70; CN 1,
2; DLB 139; MTCW 1; RGEL 2; SATA
13

Taylor, Frederick Winslow
1856-1915 .... **TCLC 76**
See also CA 188

Taylor, Henry (Splawn) 1942- .... **CLC 44**
See also CA 33-36R; CAAS 7; CANR 31;
CP 6, 7; DLB 5; PFS 10

Taylor, Kamala 1924-2004
See Markandaya, Kamala
See also CA 77-80; 227; MTFW 2005; NFS
13

Taylor, Mildred D. 1943- .... **CLC 21**
See also AAYA 10, 47; BW 1; BYA 3, 8;
CA 85-88; CANR 25, 115, 136; CLR 9,
59, 90; CSW; DLB 52; JRDA; LAIT 3;
MAICYA 1, 2; MTCW 2; MTFW 2005; SAAS 5;
SATA 135; WYA; YAW

Taylor, Peter (Hillsman) 1917-1994 .. **CLC 1,
4, 18, 37, 44, 50, 71; SSC 10, 84**
See also AMWS 5; BPFB 3; CA 13-16R;
147; CANR 9, 50; CN 1, 2, 3, 4, 5; CSW;
DLB 218, 278; DLBY 1981, 1994; EWL
3; EXPS; INT CANR-9; MAL 5; MTCW
1, 2; MTFW 2005; RGSF 2; SSFS 9; TUS

Taylor, Robert Lewis 1912-1998 .... **CLC 14**
See also CA 1-4R; 170; CANR 3, 64; CN
1, 2; SATA 10; TCWW 1, 2

Tchekhov, Anton
See Chekhov, Anton (Pavlovich)

Tchicaya, Gerald Felix 1931-1988 .. **CLC 101**
See Tchicaya U Tam'si
See also CA 129; 125; CANR 81

Tchicaya U Tam'si
See Tchicaya, Gerald Felix
See also EWL 3

Teasdale, Sara 1884-1933 .... **PC 31; TCLC 4**
See also CA 104; 163; DLB 45; GLL 1;
PFS 14; RGAL 4; SATA 32; TUS

Tecumseh 1768-1813 .... **NNAL**
See also DAM MULT

Tegner, Esaias 1782-1846 .... **NCLC 2**

Teilhard de Chardin, (Marie Joseph) Pierre
1881-1955 .... **TCLC 9**
See also CA 105; 210; GFL 1789 to the
Present

Temple, Ann
See Mortimer, Penelope (Ruth)

Tennant, Emma 1937- .... **CLC 13, 52**
See also BRWS 9; CA 65-68; CAAS 9;
CANR 10, 38, 59, 88; CN 3, 4, 5, 6, 7;
DLB 14; EWL 3; SFW 4

Tenneshaw, S.M.
See Silverberg, Robert

Tenney, Tabitha Gilman
1762-1837 .... **NCLC 122**
See also DLB 37, 200

Tennyson, Alfred 1809-1892 ... **NCLC 30, 65,
115; PC 6; WLC 6**
See also AAYA 50; BRW 4; CDBLB 1832-
1890; DA; DA3; DAB; DAC; DAM MST,
POET; DLB 32; EXPP; PAB; PFS 1, 2, 4,
11, 15, 19; RGEL 2; TEA; WLIT 4; WP

Teran, Lisa St. Aubin de .... **CLC 36**
See St. Aubin de Teran, Lisa

Terence c. 184B.C.-c. 159B.C. ...... **CMLC 14;
DC 7**
See also AW 1; CDWLB 1; DLB 211;
RGWL 2, 3; TWA; WLIT 8

Teresa de Jesus, St. 1515-1582 .... **LC 18, 149**

Teresa of Avila, St.
See Teresa de Jesus, St.

Terkel, Louis .... **CLC 38**
See Terkel, Studs
See also AAYA 32; AITN 1; MTCW 2; TUS

Terkel, Studs 1912-
See Terkel, Louis
See also CA 57-60; CANR 18, 45, 67, 132;
DA3; MTCW 1, 2; MTFW 2005

Terry, C. V.
See Slaughter, Frank G(ill)

Terry, Megan 1932- .... **CLC 19; DC 13**
See also CA 77-80; CABS 3; CAD; CANR
43; CD 5, 6; CWD; DFS 18; DLB 7, 249;
GLL 2

Tertullian c. 155-c. 245 .... **CMLC 29**

Tertz, Abram
See Sinyavsky, Andrei (Donatevich)
See also RGSF 2

Tesich, Steve 1943(?)-1996 .... **CLC 40, 69**
See also CA 105; 152; CAD; DLBY 1983

Tesla, Nikola 1856-1943 .... **TCLC 88**

Teternikov, Fyodor Kuzmich 1863-1927
See Sologub, Fyodor
See also CA 104

Tevis, Walter 1928-1984 .... **CLC 42**
See also CA 113; SFW 4

Tey, Josephine .... **TCLC 14**
See Mackintosh, Elizabeth
See also DLB 77; MSW

Thackeray, William Makepeace 1811-1863
NCLC 5, 14, 22, 43, 169; WLC 6
See also BRW 5; BRWC 2; CDBLB 1832-
1890; DA; DA3; DAB; DAC; DAM MST,
NOV; DLB 21, 55, 159, 163; NFS 13;
RGEL 2; SATA 23; TEA; WLIT 3

Thakura, Ravindranatha
See Tagore, Rabindranath

Thames, C. H.
See Marlowe, Stephen

Tharoor, Shashi 1956- .... **CLC 70**
See also CA 141; CANR 91; CN 6, 7

Thelwall, John 1764-1834 .... **NCLC 162**
See also DLB 93, 158

Thelwell, Michael Miles 1939- .... **CLC 22**
See also BW 2; CA 101

Theobald, Lewis, Jr.
See Lovecraft, H. P.

Theocritus c. 310B.C.- .... **CMLC 45**
See also AW 1; DLB 176; RGWL 2, 3

Theodorescu, Ion N. 1880-1967
See Arghezi, Tudor
See also CA 116

Theriault, Yves 1915-1983 .... **CLC 79**
See also CA 102; CANR 150; CCA 1;
DAC; DAM MST; DLB 88; EWL 3

Theroux, Alexander 1939- .... **CLC 2, 25**
See also CA 85-88; CANR 20, 63; CN 4, 5,
6, 7

Theroux, Alexander Louis
See Theroux, Alexander

Theroux, Paul 1941- .... **CLC 5, 8, 11, 15, 28,
46, 159**
See also AAYA 28; AMWS 8; BEST 89:4;
BPFB 3; CA 33-36R; CANR 20, 45, 74,
133; CDALBS; CN 1, 2, 3, 4, 5, 6, 7; CP

1; CPW 1; DA3; DAM POP; DLB 2, 218; EWL 3; HGG; MAL 5; MTCW 1, 2; MTFW 2005; RGAL 4; SATA 44, 109; TUS

Thesen, Sharon 1946- .... **CLC 56**
See also CA 163; CANR 125; CP 5, 6, 7; CWP

Thespis fl. 6th cent. B.C.- .... **CMLC 51**
See also LMFS 1

Thevenin, Denis
See Duhamel, Georges

Thibault, Jacques Anatole Francois
1844-1924
See France, Anatole
See also CA 106; 127; DA3; DAM NOV; MTCW 1, 2; TWA

Thiele, Colin 1920-2006 .... **CLC 17**
See also CA 29-32R; CANR 12, 28, 53, 105; CLR 27; CP 1, 2; DLB 289; MAI-CYA 1, 2; SAAS 2; SATA 14, 72, 125; YAW

Thiong'o, Ngugi Wa
See Ngugi wa Thiong'o

Thistlethwaite, Bel
See Wetherald, Agnes Ethelwyn

Thomas, Audrey (Callahan) 1935- .... **CLC 7,
13, 37, 107; SSC 20**
See also AITN 2; CA 21-24R; 237; CAAE 237; CAAS 19; CANR 36, 58; CN 2, 3, 4, 5, 6, 7; DLB 60; MTCW 1; RGSF 2

Thomas, Augustus 1857-1934 .... **TCLC 97**
See also MAL 5

Thomas, D.M. 1935- ..... **CLC 13, 22, 31, 132**
See also BPFB 3; BRWS 4; CA 61-64; CAAS 11; CANR 17, 45, 75; CDBLB 1960 to Present; CN 4, 5, 6, 7; CP 1, 2, 3, 4, 5, 6, 7; DA3; DLB 40, 207, 299; HGG; INT CANR-17; MTCW 1, 2; MTFW 2005; RGHL; SFW 4

Thomas, Dylan (Marlais) 1914-1953 .... **PC 2,
52; SSC 3, 44; TCLC 1, 8, 45, 105;
WLC 6**
See also AAYA 45; BRWS 1; CA 104; 120; CANR 65; CDBLB 1945-1960; DA; DA3; DAB; DAC; DAM DRAM, MST, POET; DLB 13, 20, 139; EWL 3; EXPP; LAIT 3; MTCW 1, 2; MTFW 2005; PAB; PFS 1, 3, 8; RGEL 2; RGSF 2; SATA 60; TEA; WLIT 4; WP

Thomas, (Philip) Edward 1878-1917 . **PC 53;
TCLC 10**
See also BRW 6; BRWS 3; CA 106; 153; DAM POET; DLB 19, 98, 156, 216; EWL 3; PAB; RGEL 2

Thomas, Joyce Carol 1938- .... **CLC 35**
See also AAYA 12, 54; BW 2, 3; CA 113; 116; CANR 48, 114, 135; CLR 19; DLB 33; INT CA-116; JRDA; MAICYA 1, 2; MTCW 1, 2; MTFW 2005; SAAS 7; SATA 40, 78, 123, 137; SATA-Essay 137; WYA; YAW

Thomas, Lewis 1913-1993 .... **CLC 35**
See also ANW; CA 85-88; 143; CANR 38, 60; DLB 275; MTCW 1, 2

Thomas, M. Carey 1857-1935 .... **TCLC 89**
See also FW

Thomas, Paul
See Mann, (Paul) Thomas

Thomas, Piri 1928- .... **CLC 17; HLCS 2**
See also CA 73-76; HW 1; LLW

Thomas, R(onald) S(tuart)
1913-2000 .... **CLC 6, 13, 48**
See also BRWS 12; CA 89-92; 189; CAAS 4; CANR 30; CDBLB 1960 to Present; CP 1, 2, 3, 4, 5, 6, 7; DAB; DAM POET; DLB 27; EWL 3; MTCW 1; RGEL 2

Thomas, Ross (Elmore) 1926-1995 .. **CLC 39**
See also CA 33-36R; 150; CANR 22, 63; CMW 4

Thompson, Francis (Joseph) 1859-1907
TCLC 4
See also BRW 5; CA 104; 189; CDBLB 1890-1914; DLB 19; RGEL 2; TEA

Thompson, Francis Clegg
See Mencken, H(enry) L(ouis)

Thompson, Hunter S. 1937(?)-2005 .. **CLC 9,
17, 40, 104, 229**
See also AAYA 45; BEST 89:1; BPFB 3; CA 17-20R; 236; CANR 23, 46, 74, 77, 111, 133; CPW; CSW; DA3; DAM POP; DLB 185; MTCW 1, 2; MTFW 2005; TUS

Thompson, James Myers
See Thompson, Jim (Myers)

Thompson, Jim (Myers)
1906-1977(?) .... **CLC 69**
See also BPFB 3; CA 140; CMW 4; CPW; DLB 226; MSW

Thompson, Judith (Clare Francesca) 1954-
CLC 39
See also CA 143; CD 5, 6; CWD; DFS 22; DLB 334

Thomson, James 1700-1748 .... **LC 16, 29, 40**
See also BRWS 3; DAM POET; DLB 95; RGEL 2

Thomson, James 1834-1882 .... **NCLC 18**
See also DAM POET; DLB 35; RGEL 2

Thoreau, Henry David 1817-1862 .. **NCLC 7,
21, 61, 138; PC 30; WLC 6**
See also AAYA 42; AMW; ANW; BYA 3; CDALB 1640-1865; DA; DA3; DAB; DAC; DAM MST; DLB 1, 183, 223, 270, 298; LAIT 2; LMFS 1; NCFS 3; RGAL 4; TUS

Thorndike, E. L.
See Thorndike, Edward L(ee)

Thorndike, Edward L(ee)
1874-1949 .... **TCLC 107**
See also CA 121

Thornton, Hall
See Silverberg, Robert

Thorpe, Adam 1956- .... **CLC 176**
See also CA 129; CANR 92, 160; DLB 231

Thorpe, Thomas Bangs
1815-1878 .... **NCLC 183**
See also DLB 3, 11, 248; RGAL 4

Thubron, Colin 1939- .... **CLC 163**
See also CA 25-28R; CANR 12, 29, 59, 95, 171; CN 5, 6, 7; DLB 204, 231

Thubron, Colin Gerald Dryden
See Thubron, Colin

Thucydides c. 455B.C.-c. 395B.C. . **CMLC 17**
See also AW 1; DLB 176; RGWL 2, 3; WLIT 8

Thumboo, Edwin Nadason 1933- .... **PC 30**
See also CA 194; CP 1

Thurber, James (Grover)
1894-1961 .. **CLC 5, 11, 25, 125; SSC 1,
47**
See also AAYA 56; AMWS 1; BPFB 3; BYA 5; CA 73-76; CANR 17, 39; CDALB 1929-1941; CWRI 5; DA; DA3; DAB; DAC; DAM DRAM, MST, NOV; DLB 4, 11, 22, 102; EWL 3; EXPS; FANT; LAIT 3; MAICYA 1, 2; MAL 5; MTCW 1, 2; MTFW 2005; RGAL 4; RGSF 2; SATA 13; SSFS 1, 10, 19; SUFW; TUS

Thurman, Wallace (Henry)
1902-1934 .. **BLC 1:3; HR 1:3; TCLC 6**
See also BW 1, 3; CA 104; 124; CANR 81; DAM MULT; DLB 51

Tibullus c. 54B.C.-c. 18B.C. .... **CMLC 36**
See also AW 2; DLB 211; RGWL 2, 3; WLIT 8

Ticheburn, Cheviot
See Ainsworth, William Harrison

Tieck, (Johann) Ludwig
1773-1853 ..... **NCLC 5, 46; SSC 31, 100**
See also CDWLB 2; DLB 90; EW 5; IDTP; RGSF 2; RGWL 2, 3; SUFW

Tiger, Derry
See Ellison, Harlan

Tilghman, Christopher 1946- .... **CLC 65**
See also CA 159; CANR 135, 151; CSW; DLB 244

Tillich, Paul (Johannes)
1886-1965 .... **CLC 131**
See also CA 5-8R; 25-28R; CANR 33; MTCW 1, 2

Tillinghast, Richard (Williford)
1940- .... **CLC 29**
See also CA 29-32R; CAAS 23; CANR 26, 51, 96; CP 2, 3, 4, 5, 6, 7; CSW

Tillman, Lynne (?)- .... **CLC 231**
See also CA 173; CANR 144, 172

Timrod, Henry 1828-1867 .... **NCLC 25**
See also DLB 3, 248; RGAL 4

Tindall, Gillian (Elizabeth) 1938- ...... **CLC 7**
See also CA 21-24R; CANR 11, 65, 107; CN 1, 2, 3, 4, 5, 6, 7

Tiptree, James, Jr. .... **CLC 48, 50**
See Sheldon, Alice Hastings Bradley
See also DLB 8; SCFW 1, 2; SFW 4

Tirone Smith, Mary-Ann 1944- .... **CLC 39**
See also CA 118; 136; CANR 113; SATA 143

Tirso de Molina 1580(?)-1648 .... **DC 13;
HLCS 2; LC 73**
See also RGWL 2, 3

Titmarsh, Michael Angelo
See Thackeray, William Makepeace

**Tocqueville, Alexis (Charles Henri Maurice
Clerel Comte) de** 1805-1859 .. **NCLC 7,
63**
See also EW 6; GFL 1789 to the Present; TWA

Toer, Pramoedya Ananta
1925-2006 .... **CLC 186**
See also CA 197; 251; CANR 170; RGWL 3

Toffler, Alvin 1928- .... **CLC 168**
See also CA 13-16R; CANR 15, 46, 67; CPW; DAM POP; MTCW 1, 2

Toibin, Colm 1955- .... **CLC 162**
See also CA 142; CANR 81, 149; CN 7; DLB 271

Tolkien, John Ronald Reuel
See Tolkien, J.R.R

Tolkien, J.R.R 1892-1973 ...... **CLC 1, 2, 3, 8,
12, 38; TCLC 137; WLC 6**
See also AAYA 10; AITN 1; BPFB 3; BRWC 2; BRWS 2; CA 17-18; 45-48; CANR 36, 134; CAP 2; CDBLB 1914-1945; CLR 56; CN 1; CPW 1; CWRI 5; DA; DA3; DAB; DAC; DAM MST, NOV, POP; DLB 15, 160, 255; EFS 2; EWL 3; FANT; JRDA; LAIT 1; LATS 1:2; LMFS 2; MAICYA 1, 2; MTCW 1, 2; MTFW 2005; NFS 8, 26; RGEL 2; SATA 2, 32, 100; SATA-Obit 24; SFW 4; SUFW; TEA; WCH; WYA; YAW

Toller, Ernst 1893-1939 .... **TCLC 10**
See also CA 107; 186; DLB 124; EWL 3; RGWL 2, 3

Tolson, M. B.
See Tolson, Melvin B(eaunorus)

Tolson, Melvin B(eaunorus) 1898(?)-1966
BLC 1:3; CLC 36, 105; PC 88
See also AFAW 1, 2; BW 1, 3; CA 124; 89-92; CANR 80; DAM MULT, POET; DLB 48, 76; MAL 5; RGAL 4

Tolstoi, Aleksei Nikolaevich
See Tolstoy, Alexey Nikolaevich

Tolstoi, Lev
See Tolstoy, Leo (Nikolaevich)
See also RGSF 2; RGWL 2, 3

Tolstoy, Aleksei Nikolaevich
See Tolstoy, Alexey Nikolaevich
See also DLB 272

Tolstoy, Alexey Nikolaevich
1882-1945 .... **TCLC 18**
See Tolstoy, Aleksei Nikolaevich
See also CA 107; 158; EWL 3; SFW 4

Tolstoy, Leo (Nikolaevich)
1828-1910 . **SSC 9, 30, 45, 54; TCLC 4, 11, 17, 28, 44, 79, 173; WLC 6**
See Tolstoi, Lev
See also AAYA 56; CA 104; 123; DA; DA3; DAB; DAC; DAM MST, NOV; DLB 238; EFS 2; EW 7; EXPS; IDTP; LAIT 2; LATS 1:1; LMFS 1; NFS 10; SATA 26; SSFS 5; TWA

Tolstoy, Count Leo
See Tolstoy, Leo (Nikolaevich)

Tomalin, Claire 1933- .... **CLC 166**
See also CA 89-92; CANR 52, 88, 165; DLB 155

Tomasi di Lampedusa, Giuseppe 1896-1957
See Lampedusa, Giuseppe (Tomasi) di
See also CA 111; DLB 177; EWL 3; WLIT 7

Tomlin, Lily 1939(?)-
See Tomlin, Mary Jean
See also CA 117

Tomlin, Mary Jean .... **CLC 17**
See Tomlin, Lily

Tomline, F. Latour
See Gilbert, W(illiam) S(chwenck)

Tomlinson, (Alfred) Charles 1927- .... **CLC 2, 4, 6, 13, 45; PC 17**
See also CA 5-8R; CANR 33; CP 1, 2, 3, 4, 5, 6, 7; DAM POET; DLB 40; TCLE 1:2

Tomlinson, H(enry) M(ajor) 1873-1958
TCLC 71
See also CA 118; 161; DLB 36, 100, 195

Tonna, Charlotte Elizabeth
1790-1846 .... **NCLC 135**
See also DLB 163

Tonson, Jacob fl. 1655(?)-1736 .... **LC 86**
See also DLB 170

Toole, John Kennedy 1937-1969 ..... **CLC 19, 64**
See also BPFB 3; CA 104; DLBY 1981; MTCW 2; MTFW 2005

Toomer, Eugene
See Toomer, Jean

Toomer, Eugene Pinchback
See Toomer, Jean

Toomer, Jean 1894-1967 ... **BLC 1:3; CLC 1, 4, 13, 22; HR 1:3; PC 7; SSC 1, 45; TCLC 172; WLCS**
See also AFAW 1, 2; AMWS 3, 9; BW 1; CA 85-88; CDALB 1917-1929; DA3; DAM MULT; DLB 45, 51; EWL 3; EXPP; EXPS; LMFS 2; MAL 5; MTCW 1, 2; MTFW 2005; NFS 11; RGAL 4; RGSF 2; SSFS 5

Toomer, Nathan Jean
See Toomer, Jean

Toomer, Nathan Pinchback
See Toomer, Jean

Torley, Luke
See Blish, James (Benjamin)

Tornimparte, Alessandra
See Ginzburg, Natalia

Torre, Raoul della
See Mencken, H(enry) L(ouis)

Torrence, Ridgely 1874-1950 .... **TCLC 97**
See also DLB 54, 249; MAL 5

Torrey, E. Fuller 1937- .... **CLC 34**
See also CA 119; CANR 71, 158

Torrey, Edwin Fuller
See Torrey, E. Fuller

Torsvan, Ben Traven
See Traven, B.

Torsvan, Benno Traven
See Traven, B.

Torsvan, Berick Traven
See Traven, B.

Torsvan, Berwick Traven
See Traven, B.

Torsvan, Bruno Traven
See Traven, B.

Torsvan, Traven
See Traven, B.

Tourneur, Cyril 1575(?)-1626 .... **LC 66**
See also BRW 2; DAM DRAM; DLB 58; RGEL 2

Tournier, Michel 1924- .... **CLC 6, 23, 36, 95, 249; SSC 88**
See also CA 49-52; CANR 3, 36, 74, 149; CWW 2; DLB 83; EWL 3; GFL 1789 to the Present; MTCW 1, 2; SATA 23

Tournier, Michel Edouard
See Tournier, Michel

Tournimparte, Alessandra
See Ginzburg, Natalia

Towers, Ivar
See Kornbluth, C(yril) M.

Towne, Robert (Burton) 1936(?)- ..... **CLC 87**
See also CA 108; DLB 44; IDFW 3, 4

Townsend, Sue .... **CLC 61**
See Townsend, Susan Lilian
See also AAYA 28; CA 119; 127; CANR 65, 107; CBD; CD 5, 6; CPW; CWD; DAB; DAC; DAM MST; DLB 271; INT CA-127; SATA 55, 93; SATA-Brief 48; YAW

Townsend, Susan Lilian 1946-
See Townsend, Sue

Townshend, Pete
See Townshend, Peter (Dennis Blandford)

Townshend, Peter (Dennis Blandford) 1945-
CLC 17, 42
See also CA 107

Tozzi, Federigo 1883-1920 .... **TCLC 31**
See also CA 160; CANR 110; DLB 264; EWL 3; WLIT 7

Tracy, Don(ald Fiske) 1905-1970(?)
See Queen, Ellery
See also CA 1-4R; 176; CANR 2

Trafford, F. G.
See Riddell, Charlotte

Traherne, Thomas 1637(?)-1674 .. **LC 99; PC 70**
See also BRW 2; BRWS 11; DLB 131; PAB; RGEL 2

Traill, Catharine Parr 1802-1899 .. **NCLC 31**
See also DLB 99

Trakl, Georg 1887-1914 .... **PC 20; TCLC 5**
See also CA 104; 165; EW 10; EWL 3; LMFS 2; MTCW 2; RGWL 2, 3

Trambley, Estela Portillo .... **TCLC 163**
See Portillo Trambley, Estela
See also CA 77-80; RGAL 4

Tranquilli, Secondino
See Silone, Ignazio

Transtroemer, Tomas Gosta
See Transtromer, Tomas

Transtromer, Tomas (Gosta)
See Transtromer, Tomas
See also CWW 2

Transtromer, Tomas 1931- .... **CLC 52, 65**
See also CA 117; 129; CAAS 17; CANR 115, 172; DAM POET; DLB 257; EWL 3; PFS 21

Transtromer, Tomas Goesta
See Transtromer, Tomas

Transtromer, Tomas Gosta
See Transtromer, Tomas

Transtromer, Tomas Gosta
See Transtromer, Tomas

Traven, B. 1882(?)-1969 .... **CLC 8, 11**
See also CA 19-20; 25-28R; CAP 2; DLB 9, 56; EWL 3; MTCW 1; RGAL 4

Trediakovsky, Vasilii Kirillovich 1703-1769
LC 68
See also DLB 150

Treitel, Jonathan 1959- .... **CLC 70**
See also CA 210; DLB 267

Trelawny, Edward John
1792-1881 .... **NCLC 85**
See also DLB 110, 116, 144

Tremain, Rose 1943- .... **CLC 42**
See also CA 97-100; CANR 44, 95; CN 4, 5, 6, 7; DLB 14, 271; RGSF 2; RHW

Tremblay, Michel 1942- .... **CLC 29, 102, 225**
See also CA 116; 128; CCA 1; CWW 2; DAC; DAM MST; DLB 60; EWL 3; GLL 1; MTCW 1, 2; MTFW 2005

Trevanian .... **CLC 29**
See Whitaker, Rod

Trevisa, John c. 1342-c. 1402 .... **LC 139**
See also BRWS 9; DLB 146

Trevor, Glen
See Hilton, James

Trevor, William .... **CLC 7, 9, 14, 25, 71, 116; SSC 21, 58**
See Cox, William Trevor
See also BRWS 4; CBD; CD 5, 6; CN 1, 2, 3, 4, 5, 6, 7; DLB 14, 139; EWL 3; LATS 1:2; RGEL 2; RGSF 2; SSFS 10; TCLE 1:2

Trifonov, Iurii (Valentinovich)
See Trifonov, Yuri (Valentinovich)
See also DLB 302; RGWL 2, 3

Trifonov, Yuri (Valentinovich) 1925-1981
CLC 45
See Trifonov, Iurii (Valentinovich); Trifonov, Yury Valentinovich
See also CA 126; 103; MTCW 1

Trifonov, Yury Valentinovich
See Trifonov, Yuri (Valentinovich)
See also EWL 3

Trilling, Diana (Rubin) 1905-1996 . **CLC 129**
See also CA 5-8R; 154; CANR 10, 46; INT CANR-10; MTCW 1, 2

Trilling, Lionel 1905-1975 ..... **CLC 9, 11, 24; SSC 75**
See also AMWS 3; CA 9-12R; 61-64; CANR 10, 105; CN 1, 2; DLB 28, 63; EWL 3; INT CANR-10; MAL 5; MTCW 1, 2; RGAL 4; TUS

Trimball, W. H.
See Mencken, H(enry) L(ouis)

Tristan
See Gomez de la Serna, Ramon

Tristram
See Housman, A(lfred) E(dward)

Trogdon, William (Lewis) 1939-
See Heat-Moon, William Least
See also AAYA 66; CA 115; 119; CANR 47, 89; CPW; INT CA-119

Trollope, Anthony 1815-1882 .... **NCLC 6, 33, 101; SSC 28; WLC 6**
See also BRW 5; CDBLB 1832-1890; DA; DA3; DAB; DAC; DAM MST, NOV; DLB 21, 57, 159; RGEL 2; RGSF 2; SATA 22

Trollope, Frances 1779-1863 .... **NCLC 30**
See also DLB 21, 166

Trollope, Joanna 1943- .... **CLC 186**
See also CA 101; CANR 58, 95, 149; CN 7; CPW; DLB 207; RHW

Trotsky, Leon 1879-1940 .... **TCLC 22**
See also CA 118; 167

Wagner, Richard 1813-1883 ..... NCLC 9, 119
See also DLB 129; EW 6

Wagner-Martin, Linda (C.) 1936- .... CLC 50
See also CA 159; CANR 135

Wagoner, David (Russell) 1926- .... CLC 3, 5, 15; PC 33
See also AMWS 9; CA 1-4R; CAAS 3; CANR 2, 71; CN 1, 2, 3, 4, 5, 6, 7; CP 1, 2, 3, 4, 5, 6, 7; DLB 5, 256; SATA 14; TCWW 1, 2

Wah, Fred(erick James) 1939- .... CLC 44
See also CA 107; 141; CP 1, 6, 7; DLB 60

Wahloo, Per 1926-1975 .... CLC 7
See also BPFB 3; CA 61-64; CANR 73; CMW 4; MSW

Wahloo, Peter
See Wahloo, Per

Wain, John (Barrington) 1925-1994 . CLC 2, 11, 15, 46
See also CA 5-8R; 145; CAAS 4; CANR 23, 54; CDBLB 1960 to Present; CN 1, 2, 3, 4, 5; CP 1, 2, 3, 4, 5; DLB 15, 27, 139, 155; EWL 3; MTCW 1, 2; MTFW 2005

Wajda, Andrzej 1926- .... CLC 16, 219
See also CA 102

Wakefield, Dan 1932- .... CLC 7
See also CA 21-24R, 211; CAAE 211; CAAS 7; CN 4, 5, 6, 7

Wakefield, Herbert Russell
1888-1965 .... TCLC 120
See also CA 5-8R; CANR 77; HGG; SUFW

Wakoski, Diane 1937- ...... CLC 2, 4, 7, 9, 11, 40; PC 15
See also CA 13-16R, 216; CAAE 216; CAAS 1; CANR 9, 60, 106; CP 1, 2, 3, 4, 5, 6, 7; CWP; DAM POET; DLB 5; INT CANR-9; MAL 5; MTCW 2; MTFW 2005

Wakoski-Sherbell, Diane
See Wakoski, Diane

Walcott, Derek 1930- . BLC 1:3, 2:3; CLC 2, 4, 9, 14, 25, 42, 67, 76, 160; DC 7; PC 46
See also BW 2; CA 89-92; CANR 26, 47, 75, 80, 130; CBD; CD 5, 6; CDWLB 3; CP 1, 2, 3, 4, 5, 6, 7; DA3; DAB; DAC; DAM MST, MULT, POET; DLB 117, 332; DLBY 1981; DNFS 1; EFS 1; EWL 3; LMFS 2; MTCW 1, 2; MTFW 2005; PFS 6; RGEL 2; TWA; WWE 1

Waldman, Anne (Lesley) 1945- .... CLC 7
See also BG 1:3; CA 37-40R; CAAS 17; CANR 34, 69, 116; CP 1, 2, 3, 4, 5, 6, 7; CWP; DLB 16

Waldo, E. Hunter
See Sturgeon, Theodore (Hamilton)

Waldo, Edward Hamilton
See Sturgeon, Theodore (Hamilton)

Walker, Alice 1944- .... BLC 1:3, 2:3; CLC 5, 6, 9, 19, 27, 46, 58, 103, 167; PC 30; SSC 5; WLCS
See also AAYA 3, 33; AFAW 1, 2; AMWS 3; BEST 89:4; BPFB 3; BW 2, 3; CA 37-40R; CANR 9, 27, 49, 66, 82, 131; CDALB 1968-1988; CN 4, 5, 6, 7; CPW; CSW; DA; DA3; DAB; DAC; DAM MST, MULT, NOV, POET, POP; DLB 6, 33, 143; EWL 3; EXPN; EXPS; FL 1:6; FW; INT CANR-27; LAIT 3; MAL 5; MBL; MTCW 1, 2; MTFW 2005; NFS 5; RGAL 4; RGSF 2; SATA 31; SSFS 2, 11; TUS; YAW

Walker, Alice Malsenior
See Walker, Alice

Walker, David Harry 1911-1992 ...... CLC 14
See also CA 1-4R; 137; CANR 1; CN 1, 2; CWRI 5; SATA 8; SATA-Obit 71

Walker, Edward Joseph 1934-2004
See Walker, Ted
See also CA 21-24R; 226; CANR 12, 28, 53

Walker, George F(rederick) 1947- .. CLC 44, 61
See also CA 103; CANR 21, 43, 59; CD 5, 6; DAB; DAC; DAM MST; DLB 60

Walker, Joseph A. 1935-2003 .... CLC 19
See also BW 1, 3; CA 89-92; CAD; CANR 26, 143; CD 5, 6; DAM DRAM, MST; DFS 12; DLB 38

Walker, Margaret 1915-1998 .... BLC 1:3; CLC 1, 6; PC 20; TCLC 129
See also AFAW 1, 2; BW 2, 3; CA 73-76; 172; CANR 26, 54, 76, 136; CN 1, 2, 3, 4, 5, 6; CP 1, 2, 3, 4, 5, 6; CSW; DAM MULT; DLB 76, 152; EXPP; FW; MAL 5; MTCW 1, 2; MTFW 2005; RGAL 4; RHW

Walker, Ted .... CLC 13
See Walker, Edward Joseph
See also CP 1, 2, 3, 4, 5, 6, 7; DLB 40

Wallace, David Foster 1962- ... CLC 50, 114; SSC 68
See also AAYA 50; AMWS 10; CA 132; CANR 59, 133; CN 7; DA3; MTCW 2; MTFW 2005

Wallace, Dexter
See Masters, Edgar Lee

Wallace, (Richard Horatio) Edgar 1875-1932 TCLC 57
See also CA 115; 218; CMW 4; DLB 70; MSW; RGEL 2

Wallace, Irving 1916-1990 .... CLC 7, 13
See also AITN 1; BPFB 3; CA 1-4R; 132; CAAS 1; CANR 1, 27; CPW; DAM NOV, POP; INT CANR-27; MTCW 1, 2

Wallant, Edward Lewis 1926-1962 ... CLC 5, 10
See also CA 1-4R; CANR 22; DLB 2, 28, 143, 299; EWL 3; MAL 5; MTCW 1, 2; RGAL 4; RGHL

Wallas, Graham 1858-1932 .... TCLC 91

Waller, Edmund 1606-1687 .... LC 86; PC 72
See also BRW 2; DAM POET; DLB 126; PAB; RGEL 2

Walley, Byron
See Card, Orson Scott

Walpole, Horace 1717-1797 .... LC 2, 49
See also BRW 3; DLB 39, 104, 213; GL 3; HGG; LMFS 1; RGEL 2; SUFW 1; TEA

Walpole, Hugh (Seymour)
1884-1941 .... TCLC 5
See also CA 104; 165; DLB 34; HGG; MTCW 2; RGEL 2; RHW

Walrond, Eric (Derwent) 1898-1966 . HR 1:3
See also BW 1; CA 125; DLB 51

Walser, Martin 1927- .... CLC 27, 183
See also CA 57-60; CANR 8, 46, 145; CWW 2; DLB 75, 124; EWL 3

Walser, Robert 1878-1956 ..... SSC 20; TCLC 18
See also CA 118; 165; CANR 100; DLB 66; EWL 3

Walsh, Gillian Paton
See Paton Walsh, Jill

Walsh, Jill Paton .... CLC 35
See Paton Walsh, Jill
See also CLR 2, 65, 128; WYA

Walter, Villiam Christian
See Andersen, Hans Christian

Walters, Anna L(ee) 1946- .... NNAL
See also CA 73-76

Walther von der Vogelweide c. 1170-1228 CMLC 56

Walton, Izaak 1593-1683 .... LC 72
See also BRW 2; CDBLB Before 1660; DLB 151, 213; RGEL 2

Walzer, Michael (Laban) 1935- ...... CLC 238
See also CA 37-40R; CANR 15, 48, 127

Wambaugh, Joseph, Jr. 1937- ...... CLC 3, 18
See also AITN 1; BEST 89:3; BPFB 3; CA 33-36R; CANR 42, 65, 115, 167; CMW 4; CPW 1; DA3; DAM NOV, POP; DLB 6; DLBY 1983; MSW; MTCW 1, 2

Wambaugh, Joseph Aloysius
See Wambaugh, Joseph, Jr.

Wang Wei 699(?)-761(?) . CMLC 100; PC 18
See also TWA

Warburton, William 1698-1779 .... LC 97
See also DLB 104

Ward, Arthur Henry Sarsfield 1883-1959
See Rohmer, Sax
See also CA 108; 173; CMW 4; HGG

Ward, Douglas Turner 1930- .... CLC 19
See also BW 1; CA 81-84; CAD; CANR 27; CD 5, 6; DLB 7, 38

Ward, E. D.
See Lucas, E(dward) V(errall)

Ward, Mrs. Humphry 1851-1920
See Ward, Mary Augusta
See also RGEL 2

Ward, Mary Augusta 1851-1920 ... TCLC 55
See Ward, Mrs. Humphry
See also DLB 18

Ward, Nathaniel 1578(?)-1652 .... LC 114
See also DLB 24

Ward, Peter
See Faust, Frederick (Schiller)

Warhol, Andy 1928(?)-1987 .... CLC 20
See also AAYA 12; BEST 89:4; CA 89-92; 121; CANR 34

Warner, Francis (Robert Le Plastrier) 1937-
CLC 14
See also CA 53-56; CANR 11; CP 1, 2, 3, 4

Warner, Marina 1946- .... CLC 59, 231
See also CA 65-68; CANR 21, 55, 118; CN 5, 6, 7; DLB 194; MTFW 2005

Warner, Rex (Ernest) 1905-1986 ...... CLC 45
See also CA 89-92; 119; CN 1, 2, 3, 4; CP 1, 2, 3, 4; DLB 15; RGEL 2; RHW

Warner, Susan (Bogert)
1819-1885 .... NCLC 31, 146
See also DLB 3, 42, 239, 250, 254

Warner, Sylvia (Constance) Ashton
See Ashton-Warner, Sylvia (Constance)

Warner, Sylvia Townsend
1893-1978 .. CLC 7, 19; SSC 23; TCLC 131
See also BRWS 7; CA 61-64; 77-80; CANR 16, 60, 104; CN 1, 2; DLB 34, 139; EWL 3; FANT; FW; MTCW 1, 2; RGEL 2; RGSF 2; RHW

Warren, Mercy Otis 1728-1814 ..... NCLC 13
See also DLB 31, 200; RGAL 4; TUS

Warren, Robert Penn 1905-1989 .. CLC 1, 4, 6, 8, 10, 13, 18, 39, 53, 59; PC 37; SSC 4, 58; WLC 6
See also AITN 1; AMW; AMWC 2; BPFB 3; BYA 1; CA 13-16R; 129; CANR 10, 47; CDALB 1968-1988; CN 1, 2, 3, 4; CP 1, 2, 3, 4; DA; DA3; DAB; DAC; DAM MST, NOV, POET; DLB 2, 48, 152, 320; DLBY 1980, 1989; EWL 3; INT CANR-10; MAL 5; MTCW 1, 2; MTFW 2005; NFS 13; RGAL 4; RGSF 2; RHW; SATA 46; SATA-Obit 63; SSFS 8; TUS

Warrigal, Jack
See Furphy, Joseph

Warshofsky, Isaac
See Singer, Isaac Bashevis

Warton, Joseph 1722-1800 ... LC 128; NCLC 118
See also DLB 104, 109; RGEL 2

Warton, Thomas 1728-1790 .... LC 15, 82
See also DAM POET; DLB 104, 109, 336; RGEL 2

Waruk, Kona
See Harris, (Theodore) Wilson

Warung, Price .... **TCLC 45**
See Astley, William
See also DLB 230; RGEL 2

Warwick, Jarvis
See Garner, Hugh
See also CCA 1

Washington, Alex
See Harris, Mark

Washington, Booker T(aliaferro) 1856-1915
BLC 1:3; TCLC 10
See also BW 1; CA 114; 125; DA3; DAM
MULT; LAIT 2; RGAL 4; SATA 28

Washington, George 1732-1799 .... **LC 25**
See also DLB 31

Wassermann, (Karl) Jakob
1873-1934 .... **TCLC 6**
See also CA 104; 163; DLB 66; EWL 3

Wasserstein, Wendy 1950-2006 . **CLC 32, 59,
90, 183; DC 4**
See also AAYA 73; AMWS 15; CA 121;
129; 247; CABS 3; CAD; CANR 53, 75,
128; CD 5, 6; CWD; DA3; DAM DRAM;
DFS 5, 17; DLB 228; EWL 3; FW; INT
CA-129; MAL 5; MTCW 2; MTFW 2005;
SATA 94; SATA-Obit 174

Waterhouse, Keith (Spencer) 1929- . **CLC 47**
See also BRWS 13; CA 5-8R; CANR 38,
67, 109; CBD; CD 6; CN 1, 2, 3, 4, 5, 6,
7; DLB 13, 15; MTCW 1, 2; MTFW 2005

Waters, Frank (Joseph) 1902-1995 .. **CLC 88**
See also CA 5-8R; 149; CAAS 13; CANR
3, 18, 63, 121; DLB 212; DLBY 1986;
RGAL 4; TCWW 1, 2

Waters, Mary C. .... **CLC 70**

Waters, Roger 1944- .... **CLC 35**

Watkins, Frances Ellen
See Harper, Frances Ellen Watkins

Watkins, Gerrold
See Malzberg, Barry N(athaniel)

Watkins, Gloria Jean
See hooks, bell

Watkins, Paul 1964- .... **CLC 55**
See also CA 132; CANR 62, 98

Watkins, Vernon Phillips
1906-1967 .... **CLC 43**
See also CA 9-10; 25-28R; CAP 1; DLB
20; EWL 3; RGEL 2

Watson, Irving S.
See Mencken, H(enry) L(ouis)

Watson, John H.
See Farmer, Philip Jose

Watson, Richard F.
See Silverberg, Robert

Watts, Ephraim
See Horne, Richard Henry Hengist

Watts, Isaac 1674-1748 .... **LC 98**
See also DLB 95; RGEL 2; SATA 52

Waugh, Auberon (Alexander) 1939-2001
CLC 7
See also CA 45-48; 192; CANR 6, 22, 92;
CN 1, 2, 3; DLB 14, 194

Waugh, Evelyn (Arthur St. John) 1903-1966
**CLC 1, 3, 8, 13, 19, 27, 44, 107; SSC
41; WLC 6**
See also BPFB 3; BRW 7; CA 85-88; 25-
28R; CANR 22; CDBLB 1914-1945; DA;
DA3; DAB; DAC; DAM MST, NOV,
POP; DLB 15, 162, 195; EWL 3; MTCW
1, 2; MTFW 2005; NFS 13, 17; RGEL 2;
RGSF 2; TEA; WLIT 4

Waugh, Harriet 1944- .... **CLC 6**
See also CA 85-88; CANR 22

Ways, C.R.
See Blount, Roy, Jr.

Waystaff, Simon
See Swift, Jonathan

Webb, Beatrice (Martha Potter) 1858-1943
TCLC 22
See also CA 117; 162; DLB 190; FW

Webb, Charles (Richard) 1939- .... **CLC 7**
See also CA 25-28R; CANR 114

Webb, Frank J. .... **NCLC 143**
See also DLB 50

Webb, James, Jr.
See Webb, James

Webb, James 1946- .... **CLC 22**
See also CA 81-84; CANR 156

Webb, James H.
See Webb, James

Webb, James Henry
See Webb, James

Webb, Mary Gladys (Meredith) 1881-1927
TCLC 24
See also CA 182; 123; DLB 34; FW; RGEL
2

Webb, Mrs. Sidney
See Webb, Beatrice (Martha Potter)

Webb, Phyllis 1927- .... **CLC 18**
See also CA 104; CANR 23; CCA 1; CP 1,
2, 3, 4, 5, 6, 7; CWP; DLB 53

Webb, Sidney (James) 1859-1947 .. **TCLC 22**
See also CA 117; 163; DLB 190

Webber, Andrew Lloyd .... **CLC 21**
See Lloyd Webber, Andrew
See also DFS 7

Weber, Lenora Mattingly
1895-1971 .... **CLC 12**
See also CA 19-20; 29-32R; CAP 1; SATA
2; SATA-Obit 26

Weber, Max 1864-1920 .... **TCLC 69**
See also CA 109; 189; DLB 296

Webster, John 1580(?)-1634(?) ...... **DC 2; LC
33, 84, 124; WLC 6**
See also BRW 2; CDBLB Before 1660; DA;
DAB; DAC; DAM DRAM, MST; DFS
17, 19; DLB 58; IDTP; RGEL 2; WLIT 3

Webster, Noah 1758-1843 .... **NCLC 30**
See also DLB 1, 37, 42, 43, 73, 243

Wedekind, Benjamin Franklin
See Wedekind, Frank

Wedekind, Frank 1864-1918 .... **TCLC 7**
See also CA 104; 153; CANR 121, 122;
CDWLB 2; DAM DRAM; DLB 118; EW
8; EWL 3; LMFS 2; RGWL 2, 3

Wehr, Demaris .... **CLC 65**

Weidman, Jerome 1913-1998 .... **CLC 7**
See also AITN 2; CA 1-4R; 171; CAD;
CANR 1; CD 1, 2, 3, 4, 5; DLB 28

Weil, Simone (Adolphine)
1909-1943 .... **TCLC 23**
See also CA 117; 159; DLB 72; EW 12; FW;
GFL 1789 to the Present; MTCW 2

Weininger, Otto 1880-1903 .... **TCLC 84**

Weinstein, Nathan
See West, Nathanael

Weinstein, Nathan von Wallenstein
See West, Nathanael

Weir, Peter (Lindsay) 1944- .... **CLC 20**
See also CA 113; 123

Weiss, Peter (Ulrich) 1916-1982 .. **CLC 3, 15,
51; TCLC 152**
See also CA 45-48; 106; CANR 3; DAM
DRAM; DFS 3; DLB 69, 124; EWL 3;
RGHL; RGWL 2, 3

Weiss, Theodore (Russell)
1916-2003 .... **CLC 3, 8, 14**
See also CA 9-12R, 189; 216; CAAE 189;
CAAS 2; CANR 46, 94; CP 1, 2, 3, 4, 5,
6, 7; DLB 5; TCLE 1:2

Welch, (Maurice) Denton
1915-1948 .... **TCLC 22**
See also BRWS 8, 9; CA 121; 148; RGEL
2

Welch, James (Phillip) 1940-2003 ..... **CLC 6,
14, 52, 249; NNAL; PC 62**
See also CA 85-88; 219; CANR 42, 66, 107;
CN 5, 6, 7; CP 2, 3, 4, 5, 6, 7; CPW;
DAM MULT, POP; DLB 175, 256; LATS
1:1; NFS 23; RGAL 4; TCWW 1, 2

Weldon, Fay 1931- . **CLC 6, 9, 11, 19, 36, 59,
122**
See also BRWS 4; CA 21-24R; CANR 16,
46, 63, 97, 137; CDBLB 1960 to Present;
CN 3, 4, 5, 6, 7; CPW; DAM POP; DLB
14, 194, 319; EWL 3; FW; HGG; INT
CANR-16; MTCW 1, 2; MTFW 2005;
RGEL 2; RGSF 2

Wellek, Rene 1903-1995 .... **CLC 28**
See also CA 5-8R; 150; CAAS 7; CANR 8;
DLB 63; EWL 3; INT CANR-8

Weller, Michael 1942- .... **CLC 10, 53**
See also CA 85-88; CAD; CD 5, 6

Weller, Paul 1958- .... **CLC 26**

Wellershoff, Dieter 1925- .... **CLC 46**
See also CA 89-92; CANR 16, 37

Welles, (George) Orson 1915-1985 .. **CLC 20,
80**
See also AAYA 40; CA 93-96; 117

Wellman, John McDowell 1945-
See Wellman, Mac
See also CA 166; CD 5

Wellman, Mac .... **CLC 65**
See Wellman, John McDowell; Wellman,
John McDowell
See also CAD; CD 6; RGAL 4

Wellman, Manly Wade 1903-1986 ... **CLC 49**
See also CA 1-4R; CANR 6, 16, 44;
FANT; SATA 6; SATA-Obit 47; SFW 4;
SUFW

Wells, Carolyn 1869(?)-1942 .... **TCLC 35**
See also CA 113; 185; CMW 4; DLB 11

Wells, H(erbert) G(eorge) 1866-1946 . **SSC 6,
70; TCLC 6, 12, 19, 133; WLC 6**
See also AAYA 18; BPFB 3; BRW 6; CA
110; 121; CDBLB 1914-1945; CLR 64,
133; DA; DA3; DAB; DAC; DAM MST,
NOV; DLB 34, 70, 156, 178; EWL 3;
EXPS; HGG; LAIT 3; LMFS 2; MTCW
1, 2; MTFW 2005; NFS 17, 20; RGEL 2;
RGSF 2; SATA 20; SCFW 1, 2; SFW 4;
SSFS 3; SUFW; TEA; WCH; WLIT 4;
YAW

Wells, Rosemary 1943- .... **CLC 12**
See also AAYA 13; BYA 7, 8; CA 85-88;
CANR 48, 120; CLR 16, 69; CWRI 5;
MAICYA 1, 2; SAAS 1; SATA 18, 69,
114, 156; YAW

Wells-Barnett, Ida B(ell)
1862-1931 .... **TCLC 125**
See also CA 182; DLB 23, 221

Welsh, Irvine 1958- .... **CLC 144**
See also CA 173; CANR 146; CN 7; DLB
271

Welty, Eudora 1909-2001 .... **CLC 1, 2, 5, 14,
22, 33, 105, 220; SSC 1, 27, 51, 111;
WLC 6**
See also AAYA 48; AMW; AMWR 1; BPFB
3; CA 9-12R; 199; CABS 1; CANR 32,
65, 128; CDALB 1941-1968; CN 1, 2, 3,
4, 5, 6, 7; CSW; DA; DA3; DAB; DAC;
DAM MST, NOV; DLB 2, 102, 143;
DLBD 12; DLBY 1987, 2001; EWL 3;
EXPS; HGG; LAIT 3; MAL 5; MBL;
MTCW 1, 2; MTFW 2005; NFS 13, 15;
RGAL 4; RGSF 2; RHW; SSFS 2, 10;
TUS

Welty, Eudora Alice
See Welty, Eudora

Wen I-to 1899-1946 .... **TCLC 28**
See also EWL 3

Wentworth, Robert
See Hamilton, Edmond

Werfel, Franz (Viktor) 1890-1945 ... **TCLC 8**
See also CA 104; 161; DLB 81, 124; EWL
3; RGWL 2, 3

Wergeland, Henrik Arnold
1808-1845 .... **NCLC 5**

Werner, Friedrich Ludwig Zacharias
1768-1823 .... **NCLC 189**
See also DLB 94

Werner, Zacharias
See Werner, Friedrich Ludwig Zacharias

Wersba, Barbara 1932- .... **CLC 30**
See also AAYA 2, 30; BYA 6, 12, 13; CA
29-32R, 182; CAAE 182; CANR 16, 38;
CLR 3, 78; DLB 52; JRDA; MAICYA 1,
2; SAAS 2; SATA 1, 58; SATA-Essay 103;
WYA; YAW

Wertmueller, Lina 1928- .... **CLC 16**
See also CA 97-100; CANR 39, 78

Wescott, Glenway 1901-1987 .. **CLC 13; SSC
35**
See also CA 13-16R; 121; CANR 23, 70;
CN 1, 2, 3, 4; DLB 4, 9, 102; MAL 5;
RGAL 4

Wesker, Arnold 1932- .... **CLC 3, 5, 42**
See also CA 1-4R; CAAS 7; CANR 1, 33;
CBD; CD 5, 6; CDBLB 1960 to Present;
DAB; DAM DRAM; DLB 13, 310, 319;
EWL 3; MTCW 1; RGEL 2; TEA

Wesley, Charles 1707-1788 .... **LC 128**
See also DLB 95; RGEL 2

Wesley, John 1703-1791 .... **LC 88**
See also DLB 104

Wesley, Richard (Errol) 1945- .... **CLC 7**
See also BW 1; CA 57-60; CAD; CANR
27; CD 5, 6; DLB 38

Wessel, Johan Herman 1742-1785 .... **LC 7**
See also DLB 300

West, Anthony (Panther)
1914-1987 .... **CLC 50**
See also CA 45-48; 124; CANR 3, 19; CN
1, 2, 3, 4; DLB 15

West, C. P.
See Wodehouse, P(elham) G(renville)

West, Cornel 1953- .... **BLCS; CLC 134**
See also CA 144; CANR 91, 159; DLB 246

West, Cornel Ronald
See West, Cornel

West, Delno C(loyde), Jr. 1936- .... **CLC 70**
See also CA 57-60

West, Dorothy 1907-1998 ...... **HR 1:3; TCLC
108**
See also BW 2; CA 143; 169; DLB 76

West, (Mary) Jessamyn 1902-1984 ... **CLC 7,
17**
See also CA 9-12R; 112; CANR 27; CN 1,
2, 3; DLB 6; DLBY 1984; MTCW 1, 2;
RGAL 4; RHW; SATA-Obit 37; TCWW
2; TUS; YAW

West, Morris L(anglo) 1916-1999 ..... **CLC 6,
33**
See also BPFB 3; CA 5-8R; 187; CANR
24, 49, 64; CN 1, 2, 3, 4, 5, 6; CPW; DLB
289; MTCW 1, 2; MTFW 2005

West, Nathanael 1903-1940 .. **SSC 16; TCLC
1, 14, 44**
See also AAYA 77; AMW; AMWR 2; BPFB
3; CA 104; 125; CDALB 1929-1941;
DA3; DLB 4, 9, 28; EWL 3; MAL 5;
MTCW 1, 2; MTFW 2005; NFS 16;
RGAL 4; TUS

West, Owen
See Koontz, Dean

West, Paul 1930- .... **CLC 7, 14, 96, 226**
See also CA 13-16R; CAAS 7; CANR 22,
53, 76, 89, 136; CN 1, 2, 3, 4, 5, 6, 7;
DLB 14; INT CANR-22; MTCW 2;
MTFW 2005

West, Rebecca 1892-1983 ... **CLC 7, 9, 31, 50**
See also BPFB 3; BRWS 3; CA 5-8R; 109;
CANR 19; CN 1, 2, 3; DLB 36; DLBY
1983; EWL 3; FW; MTCW 1, 2; MTFW
2005; NCFS 4; RGEL 2; TEA

Westall, Robert (Atkinson)
1929-1993 .... **CLC 17**
See also AAYA 12; BYA 2, 6, 7, 8, 9, 15;
CA 69-72; 141; CANR 18, 68; CLR 13;
FANT; JRDA; MAICYA 1, 2; MAICYAS
1; SAAS 2; SATA 23, 69; SATA-Obit 75;
WYA; YAW

Westermarck, Edward 1862-1939 . **TCLC 87**

Westlake, Donald E. 1933- .... **CLC 7, 33**
See also BPFB 3; CA 17-20R; CAAS 13;
CANR 16, 44, 65, 94, 137; CMW 4;
CPW; DAM POP; INT CANR-16; MSW;
MTCW 2; MTFW 2005

Westlake, Donald Edwin
See Westlake, Donald E.

Westmacott, Mary
See Christie, Agatha (Mary Clarissa)

Weston, Allen
See Norton, Andre

Wetcheek, J. L.
See Feuchtwanger, Lion

Wetering, Janwillem van de
See van de Wetering, Janwillem

Wetherald, Agnes Ethelwyn
1857-1940 .... **TCLC 81**
See also CA 202; DLB 99

Wetherell, Elizabeth
See Warner, Susan (Bogert)

Whale, James 1889-1957 .... **TCLC 63**
See also AAYA 75

Whalen, Philip (Glenn) 1923-2002 .... **CLC 6,
29**
See also BG 1:3; CA 9-12R; 209; CANR 5,
39; CP 1, 2, 3, 4, 5, 6, 7; DLB 16; WP

Wharton, Edith (Newbold Jones) 1862-1937
**SSC 6, 84; TCLC 3, 9, 27, 53, 129, 149;
WLC 6**
See also AAYA 25; AMW; AMWC 2;
AMWR 1; BPFB 3; CA 104; 132; CDALB
1865-1917; DA; DA3; DAB; DAC; DAM
MST, NOV; DLB 4, 9, 12, 78, 189; DLBD
13; EWL 3; EXPS; FL 1:6; GL 3; HGG;
LAIT 2, 3; LATS 1:1; MAL 5; MBL;
MTCW 1, 2; MTFW 2005; NFS 5, 11,
15, 20; RGAL 4; RGSF 2; RHW; SSFS 6,
7; SUFW; TUS

Wharton, James
See Mencken, H(enry) L(ouis)

Wharton, William (a pseudonym)
1925- .... **CLC 18, 37**
See also CA 93-96; CN 4, 5, 6, 7; DLBY
1980; INT CA-93-96

Wheatley (Peters), Phillis
1753(?)-1784 .... **BLC 1:3; LC 3, 50; PC
3; WLC 6**
See also AFAW 1, 2; CDALB 1640-1865;
DA; DA3; DAC; DAM MST, MULT,
POET; DLB 31, 50; EXPP; FL 1:1; PFS
13; RGAL 4

Wheelock, John Hall 1886-1978 .... **CLC 14**
See also CA 13-16R; 77-80; CANR 14; CP
1, 2; DLB 45; MAL 5

Whim-Wham
See Curnow, (Thomas) Allen (Monro)

Whisp, Kennilworthy
See Rowling, J.K.

Whitaker, Rod 1931-2005
See Trevanian
See also CA 29-32R; 246; CANR 45, 153;
CMW 4

White, Babington
See Braddon, Mary Elizabeth

White, E. B. 1899-1985 .... **CLC 10, 34, 39**
See also AAYA 62; AITN 2; AMWS 1; CA
13-16R; 116; CANR 16, 37; CDALBS;
CLR 1, 21, 107; CPW; DA3; DAM POP;
DLB 11, 22; EWL 3; FANT; MAICYA 1,
2; MAL 5; MTCW 1, 2; MTFW 2005;
NCFS 5; RGAL 4; SATA 2, 29, 100;
SATA-Obit 44; TUS

White, Edmund 1940- .... **CLC 27, 110**
See also AAYA 7; CA 45-48; CANR 3, 19,
36, 62, 107, 133, 172; CN 5, 6, 7; DA3;
DAM POP; DLB 227; MTCW 1, 2;
MTFW 2005

White, Edmund Valentine III
See White, Edmund

White, Elwyn Brooks
See White, E. B.

White, Hayden V. 1928- .... **CLC 148**
See also CA 128; CANR 135; DLB 246

White, Patrick (Victor Martindale)
1912-1990 ...... **CLC 3, 4, 5, 7, 9, 18, 65,
69; SSC 39; TCLC 176**
See also BRWS 1; CA 81-84; 132; CANR
43; CN 1, 2, 3, 4; DLB 260, 332; EWL 3;
MTCW 1; RGEL 2; RGSF 2; RHW;
TWA; WWE 1

White, Phyllis Dorothy James 1920-
See James, P. D.
See also CA 21-24R; CANR 17, 43, 65,
112; CMW 4; CN 7; CPW; DA3; DAM
POP; MTCW 1, 2; MTFW 2005; TEA

White, T(erence) H(anbury)
1906-1964 .... **CLC 30**
See also AAYA 22; BPFB 3; BYA 4, 5; CA
73-76; CANR 37; DLB 160; FANT;
JRDA; LAIT 1; MAICYA 1, 2; RGEL 2;
SATA 12; SUFW 1; YAW

White, Terence de Vere 1912-1994 ... **CLC 49**
See also CA 49-52; 145; CANR 3

White, Walter
See White, Walter F(rancis)

White, Walter F(rancis)
1893-1955 ..... **BLC 1:3; HR 1:3; TCLC
15**
See also BW 1; CA 115; 124; DAM MULT;
DLB 51

White, William Hale 1831-1913
See Rutherford, Mark
See also CA 121; 189

Whitehead, Alfred North
1861-1947 .... **TCLC 97**
See also CA 117; 165; DLB 100, 262

Whitehead, Colson 1969- ...... **BLC 2:3; CLC
232**
See also CA 202; CANR 162

Whitehead, E(dward) A(nthony)
1933- .... **CLC 5**
See Whitehead, Ted
See also CA 65-68; CANR 58, 118; CBD;
CD 5; DLB 310

Whitehead, Ted
See Whitehead, E(dward) A(nthony)
See also CD 6

Whiteman, Roberta J. Hill 1947- ...... **NNAL**
See also CA 146

Whitemore, Hugh (John) 1936- .... **CLC 37**
See also CA 132; CANR 77; CBD; CD 5,
6; INT CA-132

Whitman, Sarah Helen (Power) 1803-1878
NCLC 19
See also DLB 1, 243

Whitman, Walt(er) 1819-1892 .. **NCLC 4, 31,
81; PC 3; WLC 6**
See also AAYA 42; AMW; AMWR 1;
CDALB 1640-1865; DA; DA3; DAB;
DAC; DAM MST, POET; DLB 3, 64,
224, 250; EXPP; LAIT 2; LMFS 1; PAB;
PFS 2, 3, 13, 22; RGAL 4; SATA 20;
TUS; WP; WYAS 1

Williamson, Ellen Douglas 1905-1984
See Douglas, Ellen
See also CA 17-20R; 114; CANR 39

Williamson, Jack .... **CLC 29**
See Williamson, John Stewart
See also CAAS 8; DLB 8; SCFW 1, 2

Williamson, John Stewart 1908-2006
See Williamson, Jack
See also AAYA 76; CA 17-20R; 255; CANR 23, 70, 153; SFW 4

Willie, Frederick
See Lovecraft, H. P.

Willingham, Calder (Baynard, Jr.) 1922-1995 .... **CLC 5, 51**
See also CA 5-8R; 147; CANR 3; CN 1, 2, 3, 4, 5; CSW; DLB 2, 44; IDFW 3, 4; MTCW 1

Willis, Charles
See Clarke, Arthur C.

Willis, Nathaniel Parker 1806-1867 .... **NCLC 194**
See also DLB 3, 59, 73, 74, 183, 250; DLBD 13; RGAL 4

Willy
See Colette, (Sidonie-Gabrielle)

Willy, Colette
See Colette, (Sidonie-Gabrielle)
See also GLL 1

Wilmot, John 1647-1680 .... **LC 75; PC 66**
See Rochester
See also BRW 2; DLB 131; PAB

Wilson, A.N. 1950- .... **CLC 33**
See also BRWS 6; CA 112; 122; CANR 156; CN 4, 5, 6, 7; DLB 14, 155, 194; MTCW 2

Wilson, Andrew Norman
See Wilson, A.N.

Wilson, Angus (Frank Johnstone) 1913-1991 **CLC 2, 3, 5, 25, 34; SSC 21**
See also BRWS 1; CA 5-8R; 134; CANR 21; CN 1, 2, 3, 4; DLB 15, 139, 155; EWL 3; MTCW 1, 2; MTFW 2005; RGEL 2; RGSF 2

Wilson, August 1945-2005 .... **BLC 1:3, 2:3; CLC 39, 50, 63, 118, 222; DC 2, 31; WLCS**
See also AAYA 16; AFAW 2; AMWS 8; BW 2, 3; CA 115; 122; 244; CAD; CANR 42, 54, 76, 128; CD 5, 6; DA; DA3; DAB; DAC; DAM DRAM, MST, MULT; DFS 3, 7, 15, 17, 24; DLB 228; EWL 3; LAIT 4; LATS 1:2; MAL 5; MTCW 1, 2; MTFW 2005; RGAL 4

Wilson, Brian 1942- .... **CLC 12**

Wilson, Colin (Henry) 1931- .... **CLC 3, 14**
See also CA 1-4R; CAAS 5; CANR 1, 22, 33, 77; CMW 4; CN 1, 2, 3, 4, 5, 6; DLB 14, 194; HGG; MTCW 1; SFW 4

Wilson, Dirk
See Pohl, Frederik

Wilson, Edmund 1895-1972 .. **CLC 1, 2, 3, 8, 24**
See also AMW; CA 1-4R; 37-40R; CANR 1, 46, 110; CN 1; DLB 63; EWL 3; MAL 5; MTCW 1, 2; MTFW 2005; RGAL 4; TUS

Wilson, Ethel Davis (Bryant) 1888(?)-1980 **CLC 13**
See also CA 102; CN 1, 2; DAC; DAM POET; DLB 68; MTCW 1; RGEL 2

Wilson, Harriet
See Wilson, Harriet E. Adams
See also DLB 239

Wilson, Harriet E.
See Wilson, Harriet E. Adams
See also DLB 243

Wilson, Harriet E. Adams 1827(?)-1863(?) **BLC 1:3; NCLC 78**
See Wilson, Harriet; Wilson, Harriet E.
See also DAM MULT; DLB 50

Wilson, John 1785-1854 .... **NCLC 5**
See also DLB 110

Wilson, John (Anthony) Burgess 1917-1993
See Burgess, Anthony
See also CA 1-4R; 143; CANR 2, 46; DA3; DAC; DAM NOV; MTCW 1, 2; MTFW 2005; NFS 15; TEA

Wilson, Katharina .... **CLC 65**

Wilson, Lanford 1937- .. **CLC 7, 14, 36, 197; DC 19**
See also CA 17-20R; CABS 3; CAD; CANR 45, 96; CD 5, 6; DAM DRAM; DFS 4, 9, 12, 16, 20; DLB 7, 341; EWL 3; MAL 5; TUS

Wilson, Robert M. 1941- .... **CLC 7, 9**
See also CA 49-52; CAD; CANR 2, 41; CD 5, 6; MTCW 1

Wilson, Robert McLiam 1964- .... **CLC 59**
See also CA 132; DLB 267

Wilson, Sloan 1920-2003 .... **CLC 32**
See also CA 1-4R; 216; CANR 1, 44; CN 1, 2, 3, 4, 5, 6

Wilson, Snoo 1948- .... **CLC 33**
See also CA 69-72; CBD; CD 5, 6

Wilson, William S(mith) 1932- .... **CLC 49**
See also CA 81-84

Wilson, (Thomas) Woodrow 1856-1924 **TCLC 79**
See also CA 166; DLB 47

Winchester, Simon 1944- .... **CLC 257**
See also AAYA 66; CA 107; CANR 90, 130

Winchilsea, Anne (Kingsmill) Finch 1661-1720
See Finch, Anne
See also RGEL 2

Winckelmann, Johann Joachim 1717-1768 **LC 129**
See also DLB 97

Windham, Basil
See Wodehouse, P(elham) G(renville)

Wingrove, David 1954- .... **CLC 68**
See also CA 133; SFW 4

Winnemucca, Sarah 1844-1891 .... **NCLC 79; NNAL**
See also DAM MULT; DLB 175; RGAL 4

Winstanley, Gerrard 1609-1676 .... **LC 52**

Wintergreen, Jane
See Duncan, Sara Jeannette

Winters, Arthur Yvor
See Winters, Yvor

Winters, Janet Lewis .... **CLC 41**
See Lewis, Janet
See also DLBY 1987

Winters, Yvor 1900-1968 .. **CLC 4, 8, 32; PC 82**
See also AMWS 2; CA 11-12; 25-28R; CAP 1; DLB 48; EWL 3; MAL 5; MTCW 1; RGAL 4

Winterson, Jeanette 1959- .... **CLC 64, 158**
See also BRWS 4; CA 136; CANR 58, 116; CN 5, 6, 7; CPW; DA3; DAM POP; DLB 207, 261; FANT; FW; GLL 1; MTCW 2; MTFW 2005; RHW

Winthrop, John 1588-1649 .... **LC 31, 107**
See also DLB 24, 30

Winton, Tim 1960- .... **CLC 251**
See also AAYA 34; CA 152; CANR 118; CN 6, 7; DLB 325; SATA 98

Wirth, Louis 1897-1952 .... **TCLC 92**
See also CA 210

Wiseman, Frederick 1930- .... **CLC 20**
See also CA 159

Wister, Owen 1860-1938 ..... **SSC 100; TCLC 21**
See also BPFB 3; CA 108; 162; DLB 9, 78, 186; RGAL 4; SATA 62; TCWW 1, 2

Wither, George 1588-1667 .... **LC 96**
See also DLB 121; RGEL 2

Witkacy
See Witkiewicz, Stanislaw Ignacy

Witkiewicz, Stanislaw Ignacy 1885-1939 **TCLC 8**
See also CA 105; 162; CDWLB 4; DLB 215; EW 10; EWL 3; RGWL 2, 3; SFW 4

Wittgenstein, Ludwig (Josef Johann) 1889-1951 .... **TCLC 59**
See also CA 113; 164; DLB 262; MTCW 2

Wittig, Monique 1935-2003 .... **CLC 22**
See also CA 116; 135; 212; CANR 143; CWW 2; DLB 83; EWL 3; FW; GLL 1

Wittlin, Jozef 1896-1976 .... **CLC 25**
See also CA 49-52; 65-68; CANR 3; EWL 3

Wodehouse, P(elham) G(renville) 1881-1975 **CLC 1, 2, 5, 10, 22; SSC 2; TCLC 108**
See also AAYA 65; AITN 2; BRWS 3; CA 45-48; 57-60; CANR 3, 33; CDBLB 1914-1945; CN 1, 2; CPW 1; DA3; DAB; DAC; DAM NOV; DLB 34, 162; EWL 3; MTCW 1, 2; MTFW 2005; RGEL 2; RGSF 2; SATA 22; SSFS 10

Woiwode, L.
See Woiwode, Larry (Alfred)

Woiwode, Larry (Alfred) 1941- ... **CLC 6, 10**
See also CA 73-76; CANR 16, 94; CN 3, 4, 5, 6, 7; DLB 6; INT CANR-16

Wojciechowska, Maia (Teresa) 1927-2002 **CLC 26**
See also AAYA 8, 46; BYA 3; CA 9-12R; 183; 209; CAAE 183; CANR 4, 41; CLR 1; JRDA; MAICYA 1, 2; SAAS 1; SATA 1, 28, 83; SATA-Essay 104; SATA-Obit 134; YAW

Wojtyla, Karol (Josef)
See John Paul II, Pope

Wojtyla, Karol (Jozef)
See John Paul II, Pope

Wolf, Christa 1929- .... **CLC 14, 29, 58, 150**
See also CA 85-88; CANR 45, 123; CD-WLB 2; CWW 2; DLB 75; EWL 3; FW; MTCW 1; RGWL 2, 3; SSFS 14

Wolf, Naomi 1962- .... **CLC 157**
See also CA 141; CANR 110; FW; MTFW 2005

Wolfe, Gene 1931- .... **CLC 25**
See also AAYA 35; CA 57-60; CAAS 9; CANR 6, 32, 60, 152; CPW; DAM POP; DLB 8; FANT; MTCW 2; MTFW 2005; SATA 118, 165; SCFW 2; SFW 4; SUFW 2

Wolfe, Gene Rodman
See Wolfe, Gene

Wolfe, George C. 1954- .... **BLCS; CLC 49**
See also CA 149; CAD; CD 5, 6

Wolfe, Thomas (Clayton) 1900-1938 .... **SSC 33, 113; TCLC 4, 13, 29, 61; WLC 6**
See also AMW; BPFB 3; CA 104; 132; CANR 102; CDALB 1929-1941; DA; DA3; DAB; DAC; DAM MST, NOV; DLB 9, 102, 229; DLBD 2, 16; DLBY 1985, 1997; EWL 3; MAL 5; MTCW 1, 2; NFS 18; RGAL 4; SSFS 18; TUS

Wolfe, Thomas Kennerly, Jr. 1931- .... **CLC 147**
See Wolfe, Tom
See also CA 13-16R; CANR 9, 33, 70, 104; DA3; DAM POP; DLB 185; EWL 3; INT CANR-9; MTCW 1, 2; MTFW 2005; TUS

Author Index

Zuk, Georges
  See Skelton, Robin
  See also CCA 1
Zukofsky, Louis 1904-1978 ... **CLC 1, 2, 4, 7,**
    11, 18; PC 11
  See also AMWS 3; CA 9-12R; 77-80;

CANR 39; CP 1, 2; DAM POET; DLB 5,
    165; EWL 3; MAL 5; MTCW 1; RGAL 4
Zweig, Arnold 1887-1968 .... **TCLC 199**
  See also CA 189; 115; DLB 66; EWL 3
Zweig, Paul 1935-1984 .... **CLC 34, 42**
  See also CA 85-88; 113

Zweig, Stefan 1881-1942 .... **TCLC 17**
  See also CA 112; 170; DLB 81, 118; EWL
    3; RGHL
Zwingli, Huldreich 1484-1531 .... **LC 37**
  See also DLB 179

Literary Criticism Series
Cumulative Topic Index

This index lists all topic entries in Gale's *Children's Literature Review* (CLR), *Classical and Medieval Literature Criticism* (CMLC), *Contemporary Literary Criticism* (CLC), *Drama Criticism* (DC), *Literature Criticism from 1400 to 1800* (LC), *Nineteenth-Century Literature Criticism* (NCLC), *Short Story Criticism* (SSC), and *Twentieth-Century Literary Criticism* (TCLC). The index also lists topic entries in the Gale Critical Companion Collection, which includes the following publications: *The Beat Generation* (BG), *Feminism in Literature* (FL), *Gothic Literature* (GL), and *Harlem Renaissance* (HR).

Topic Index

Topic Index

Topic Index

SSC Cumulative Nationality Index

O'Faolain, Sean **13**
O'Flaherty, Liam **6**
Ross, Martin **56**
Somerville, Edith **56**
Stephens, James **50**
Stoker, Abraham **55, 62**
Trevor, William **21, 58**
Wilde, Oscar (Fingal O'Flahertie Wills) **11, 77**

ISRAELI

Agnon, S(hmuel) Y(osef Halevi) **30**
Appelfeld, Aharon **42**
Oz, Amos **66**

ITALIAN

Boccaccio, Giovanni **10, 87**
Calvino, Italo **3, 48**
Ginzburg, Natalia **65**
Levi, Primo **12**
Moravia, Alberto **26**
Pavese, Cesare **19**
Pirandello, Luigi **22**
Svevo, Italo (Schmitz, Aron Hector) **25**
Verga, Giovanni (Carmelo) **21, 87**

JAMAICAN

Senior, Olive (Marjorie) **78**

JAPANESE

Abe, Kobo **61**
Akutagawa, Ryunosuke **44**
Dazai Osamu **41**
Endo, Shūsaku **48**
Kawabata, Yasunari **17**
Oe, Kenzaburo **20**
Shiga, Naoya **23**
Tanizaki, Junichirō **21**

MEXICAN

Arreola, Juan José **38**
Castellanos, Rosario **39, 68**
Fuentes, Carlos **24**
Rulfo, Juan **25**

NEW ZEALANDER

Frame, Janet **29**
Mansfield, Katherine **9, 23, 38, 81**
Sargeson, Frank **99**

NIGERIAN

Achebe, Chinua **105**

POLISH

Agnon, S(hmuel) Y(osef Halevi) **30**
Borowski, Tadeusz **48**
Conrad, Joseph **9, 71**
Peretz, Isaac Loeb **26**
Schulz, Bruno **13**
Singer, Isaac Bashevis **3, 53, 80**

PUERTO RICAN

Ferré, Rosario **36, 106**

RUSSIAN

Babel, Isaak (Emmanuilovich) **16, 78**
Bulgakov, Mikhail (Afanas'evich) **18**
Bunin, Ivan Alexeyevich **5**
Chekhov, Anton (Pavlovich) **2, 28, 41, 51, 85, 102**
Dostoevsky, Fedor Mikhailovich **2, 33, 44**
Gogol, Nikolai (Vasilyevich) **4, 29, 52**
Gorky, Maxim **28**
Kazakov, Yuri Pavlovich **43**
Leskov, Nikolai (Semyonovich) **34, 96**
Nabokov, Vladimir (Vladimirovich) **11, 86**
Olesha, Yuri **69**
Pasternak, Boris (Leonidovich) **31**
Pilnyak, Boris **48**
Platonov, Andrei (Klimentov, Andrei Platonovich) **42**
Pushkin, Alexander (Sergeyevich) **27, 55, 99**
Solzhenitsyn, Aleksandr I(sayevich) **32, 105**
Tolstoy, Leo (Nikolaevich) **9, 30, 45, 54**
Turgenev, Ivan (Sergeevich) **7, 57**
Zamyatin, Yevgeny **89**
Zoshchenko, Mikhail (Mikhailovich) **15**

SCOTTISH

Davie, Elspeth **52**
Doyle, Arthur Conan **12, 83, 95**
Oliphant, Margaret (Oliphant Wilson) **25**

Scott, Walter **32**
Spark, Muriel (Sarah) **10**
Stevenson, Robert Louis (Balfour) **11, 51**

SOUTH AFRICAN

Gordimer, Nadine **17, 80**
Head, Bessie **52**

SPANISH

Alarcón, Pedro Antonio de **64**
Baroja, Pío **112**
Cela, Camilo José **71**
Cervantes (Saavedra), Miguel de **12, 108**
Pardo Bazán, Emilia **30**
Unamuno (y Jugo), Miguel de **11, 69**
de Zayas y Sotomayor, María **94**

SWEDISH

Lagervist, Par **12**

SWISS

Hesse, Hermann **9, 49**
Keller, Gottfried **26, 107**
Meyer, Conrad Ferdinand **30**
Walser, Robert **20**

TRINIDADIAN

Naipaul, V(idiadhar) S(urajprasad) **38**

UKRAINIAN

Aleichem, Sholom **33**

URUGUAYAN

Onetti, Juan Carlos **23**
Quiroga, Horacio **89**

WELSH

Evans, Caradoc **43**
Lewis, Alun **40**
Machen, Arthur **20**
Thomas, Dylan (Marlais) **3, 44**

YUGOSLAVIAN

Andrić, Ivo **36**

Nationality Index

SSC-113 Title Index